Evolving Financial Markets and International Capital Flows

This study examines the impact of British capital flows on the evolution of capital markets in four countries – Argentina, Australia, Canada, and the United States – over the years 1865 to 1914. In substantive chapters on each of the five countries it offers parallel histories of the evolution of their financial infrastructures – commercial banks, non-bank intermediaries, primary security markets, formal secondary security markets – and the institutions that provide the international financial links connecting the frontier country with the British capital market. It then explains the differences in the experiences of the frontier countries and provides historical insights into current economic problems in Asia and Latin America. At one level the work constitutes a quantitative history of the development of the capital markets of five countries in the late nineteenth century. At a second level it provides the basis for a usable taxonomy for the study of institutional invention and innovation. At a third it suggests some lessons from the past about modern policy issues.

Lance E. Davis has taught at the California Institute of Technology since 1968 and has served as Mary Stillman Harkness Professor of Social Science since 1980. He also taught at the University of Washington and Purdue and Johns Hopkins Universities and held visiting fellowships at Nuffield College, Oxford, and the Australian National University. The author or editor of more than ten works, including *Institutional Change and American Economic Growth* (1971, with Douglass North), *Mammon and the Pursuit of Empire: The Political Economy of British Imperialism* (1986, with Robert Huttenback, revised and abridged edition, 1988), and *International Capital Markets and American Economic Growth, 1820–1914* (1994, with Robert Cull), all published by Cambridge University Press, Professor Davis has also contributed chapters to the *Cambridge Economic History of the United States*. He received the Alice Hanson Jones Prize in 1998, was named a Fellow of the American Academy of Arts and Sciences in 1991, served as a Fellow at the Center for Advanced Study in the Behavioral Sciences in 1985–86, and served as President of the Economic History Association in 1978–79. Professor Davis has been a member of several editorial boards, including *THESIS, Explorations in Economic History*, and the *Journal of Economic History*.

Robert E. Gallman was Kenan Professor of Economics and History at the University of North Carolina, Chapel Hill, at the time of his death in November 1998. He had been a member of the faculty since 1962. Previously Professor Gallman taught at the University of Pennsylvania and Ohio State University and held visiting professorships at Johns Hopkins and Stanford Universities and Nuffield College, Oxford. The author or editor of eight books, including the first volume of the *Cambridge Economic History of the United States* (1996, with Stanley Engerman), he also served on the editorial board of the Cambridge University Press Studies in Economic History and Policy series. Professor Gallman was managing editor of the *Southern Economic Journal* and a member of the editorial boards of the *Journal of Economic History, THESIS, Social Science History*, and *Explorations in Economic History*. He served as President of the Economic History Association in 1975–76 and as President of the Southern Economic Association in 1977–78. Professor Gallman was a Guggenheim Fellow in 1972–73 and the honoree of the Festschrift *Economic Development in Historical Perspective*, published by Stanford University Press in 1994.

Evolving Financial Markets and International Capital Flows

Britain, the Americas, and Australia, 1865–1914

LANCE E. DAVIS
California Institute of Technology

ROBERT E. GALLMAN

CAMBRIDGE
UNIVERSITY PRESS

PUBLISHED BY THE PRESS SYNDICATE OF THE UNIVERSITY OF CAMBRIDGE
The Pitt Building, Trumpington Street, Cambridge, United Kingdom

CAMBRIDGE UNIVERSITY PRESS
The Edinburgh Building, Cambridge CB2 2RU, UK
40 West 20th Street, New York, NY 10011-4211, USA
10 Stamford Road, Oakleigh, VIC 3166, Australia
Ruiz de Alarcón 13, 28014 Madrid, Spain
Dock House, The Waterfront, Cape Town 8001, South Africa

http://www.cambridge.org

First published 2001

Printed in the United States of America

Typeface Times 10/12 pt.   *System* QuarkXPress [BTS]

A catalog record for this book is available from the British Library.

Library of Congress Cataloging in Publication Data

Davis, Lance Edwin.
Evolving financial markets and international capital flows: Britain, the Americas,
and Australia, 1865–1914 / Lance E. Davis, Robert E. Gallman.
p. cm.
Includes bibliographical references.
ISBN 0-521-55352-0
1. Investments, British – History. 2. Capital movements – History. I. Title.
II. Gallman, Robert E.
HG4538 .D32 2000
332'.042 21 – dc21   99-042142

ISBN 0 521 55352 0 hardback

CONTENTS

1 Institutional invention and innovation: Foreign capital
  transfers and the evolution of the domestic capital markets
  in four frontier countries: Argentina, Australia, Canada,
  and the United States, 1865–1914   *page* 1
  Appendix: The role of financial intermediaries in
  decisions to save and invest   42

2 The United Kingdom   50

3 International capital movements, domestic capital markets,
  and American economic growth, 1865–1914   234
  Appendix: U.S. estimates of national product   342

4 Domestic savings, international capital flows, and the
  evolution of domestic capital markets: The Canadian
  experience   345

5 Domestic saving, international capital flows, and the
  evolution of domestic capital markets: The Australian
  experience   471

6 Argentine savings, investment, and economic growth
  before World War I   644
  Appendix: Estimating investment and savings series   723

7 Lessons from the past: International financial flows
  and the evolution of capital markets, Britain and
  Argentina, Australia, Canada, and the United States
  before World War I   753

8 Skipping ahead: The evolution of the world's finance
  markets 1914–1990 – A brief sketch   839

9 Lessons from the past   875

Bibliography   926
Index   964

CHAPTER 1

Institutional invention and innovation: foreign capital transfers and the evolution of the domestic capital markets in four frontier countries: Argentina, Australia, Canada, and the United States, 1865–1914

1-1. Introduction

1-1a. History and current events

No one believes that history repeats itself exactly, but many economic historians must have nodded knowingly when they opened their morning newspapers on February 27, 1995. On that day newspapers throughout the world reported that the House of Baring – one of the world's oldest private banks – had gone into bankruptcy. Over one hundred years earlier, in 1890, Barings had also teetered on the verge of bankruptcy.[1] The cases are remarkably similar. Not only did the two crises involve the same institution, but in both cases Barings was involved in financial operations in the less-developed world. In 1890 it was Latin America, particularly Argentina and Uruguay. One hundred and five years later the newspapers reported that Barings was a "strong niche player in the emerging markets of Asia, Latin America, Africa and Eastern Europe." Moreover, despite the passage of time and the growth in the size of the British economy, the magnitudes of the potential losses, then and now, are not dissimilar. In 1890, £17.25 million was sufficient to cover Barings potential liabilities; in today's dollars that figure amounts to just over $850 million. In 1995, if the press is to be believed, the funds required to save "the world's oldest private bank" fell in the $950 million to $1.27 billion range.[2]

---

[1] In 1890 the Bank of England was also one of the world's oldest private banks. It was nationalized at the end of World War II.

[2] The *Wall Street Journal* of February 27, 1995, reported initial losses of $950 million. It also reported that private banks had pledged $477 million, leaving between $473 million and $794 million for the Bank of England to cover.

1

What was different was the reaction of the managers of the Bank of England to the potential crisis. In 1890 the Bank had only recently assumed the mantle of a true lender of last resort; its Governor, William Lidderdale, reacted quickly to "invoke the aid and support of the financial community."[3] Support was immediately forthcoming: £6 million was pledged on the first day, and the total eventually reached £17.25 million. The action of the Bank of England, operating in concert with the London and provincial joint-stock banks, was entirely successful: "Before the difficulties of Barings were known to the general public, the severest potential dangers had been averted, and the resulting disturbance was confined strictly to London, while the eminent position of the famous firm was shortly restored."[4]

In 1995 the story begins in the same way. On the night of Thursday February 23, word leaked out that the House of Baring was in trouble. Eddie George, the Governor of the Bank of England, immediately flew back to London from a skiing vacation in Switzerland. An attempt, similar to the one executed a century before, was made to organize a bank-backed bailout. The endeavor met with initial success: Fourteen international banks pledged $477 million. Despite this response, on Sunday February 26, "the Bank of England threw in the towel . . . after crisis talks to finance a rescue plan failed over uncertainty about the extent of the losses."[5]

What explains the difference between the behavior of the Governors of the Bank of England in 1890 and 1995? In 1890 the Bank had just begun to act as a true central bank. Its management felt that, to achieve a commercial environment free of bank suspensions and failures, it was necessary that the Bank establish a reputation as a *reliable* lender of last resort. The action was successful, and for almost four decades there were no bank failures in the United Kingdom.

In 1995 circumstances were different. The Bank was *the* recognized lender of last resort – its reputation did not have to be reaffirmed – but a new problem had emerged. Although there had always been some speculative activity in the financial markets, the Governors of the Bank

---

[3] Speech of the Governor, William Lidderdale, at the Bank of England meeting, March 11, 1891. "The subsequent liquidation of Baring Brothers – including the personal fortunes of the Baring family – covered the firm's liabilities and freed the outsiders from having to pay. Barings was quickly reconstituted as a limited liability company." Richard S. Grossman, *The Journal of Commerce*, March 27, 1995.

[4] W.F. Crick and J.E. Wadsworth, *A Hundred Years of Joint Stock Banking*, 4th ed. (London: Hodder & Stoughton, 1964), p. 314.

[5] *Wall Street Journal*, February 27, 1995.

feared that a new and rapidly escalating speculative craze in derivatives would lead to worldwide financial instability. The cases of the International Bank of Credit and Commerce, Orange County, California, Proctor and Gamble, and Metallgesellschaft A.G. were all well known on Threadneedle Street. The Governors may have decided to discourage these lines of activity, rather than simply attempting to counter their effects.[6] If a message were to be sent to the financial community, Barings was the ideal candidate for the role of messenger. Unlike some other institutions, Barings was not too big to fail. In the words of one major U.S. banking executive, "If I were a central banker that's what I'd do. The central bankers need to put more discipline into the banking system. They are taking an opportunity here."[7] History does not repeat itself exactly, but a knowledge of history can illuminate the problems of the modern world.

1-1b. *The formation of capital markets*

As the recent experience of the Eastern Bloc countries has underscored, a modern market structure, unlike Athena, does not automatically spring full blown from the head of Zeus. Instead, it is almost always the result of an evolutionary process that often involves the invention and innovation of new institutional technologies. Capital markets are no exceptions. Furthermore, the process of invention and innovation in the financial sector may take longer and prove more difficult than in other, less complicated *product and factor markets.*

The principal problems that must be overcome in the creation of effective capital markets were ably enumerated by Frederick Lavington in 1921. Lavington did not use modern finance terms such as "reputational signals" and "asymmetric information," but he had a firm grip on the relevant ideas:

> It can hardly be doubted that the dominating characteristic of the market for negotiable securities – that which covers most of their incidents – lies in the fact that the value of the security, the commodity in which they deal, depends upon a set of present and future circumstances so complex that an adequate description can be made only in the light of expert knowledge. If, as in the wholesale market for sugar and coffee, buyers and sellers were usually equally expert, the pecu-

---

[6] "Noting that the bailout with financing from other institutions was nearly worked out, some bankers suggested that the Bank of England might have let Barings go under as a warning to other financial institutions around the world about the risk of derivatives and poor risk management." *Wall Street Journal,* February 27, 1995.

[7] *Wall Street Journal,* February 27, 1995.

liarity would perhaps have no special significance; but in fact this is not so, for those whose business it is to buy and sell securities are often in contact with an unskilled and speculating public. Sellers have a more intimate knowledge of the commodity with which they deal than buyers, and this superior bargaining knowledge gives wide scope for deception. In the market for new securities this enables the company promoter to sell worthless securities to the public; in that for old securities, the Stock Exchange, it enables the speculator with inside knowledge to draw abnormal profits by dealing with investors less well informed than himself. When the new issue consists of the stocks and bonds of a reputable State or well secured bonds of a sound American railway, public knowledge of the reputation of the borrower, or of the prospects of the undertaking, may be sufficient to yield a fair estimate of their true value; bargaining knowledge is fairly equal, and the marketing agency cannot obtain excessive profits at the expense of the public. It happens too that the natural safeguard accompanying the sale of these securities is supplemented by a further safeguard arising from the circumstances that their sale is frequently effected by first-class firms whose reputations and profit are dependent on fair dealing. In the multitude of securities of more dubious value where the safeguard of public knowledge does not exist, protection of such middlemen is in general also lacking, so that the principal limitation to deceptions lies in the advisory organization of the market – the investment broker and financial press – and the legal enactments devised to secure the publication of essential particulars necessary to form a sound judgment of the securities in question.[8]

Although capital markets developed over hundreds of years, the period between the end of the American Civil War and the outbreak of World War I was particularly important to the evolution of international finance. Those decades saw a tendency toward convergence of interest rates based on the spread of the international gold standard and the evolution of the international capital market to a near-modern level. The institutional structures of domestic capital markets, however, ranged from primitive to modern.

The economic environment (governmental, private, or some mix of the two) and the particular set of financial institutions that evolved in each country were certainly influenced by economic and political considerations. Those considerations ranged from the policies of governments (both past and present) to the experiences of local businessmen to the preferences of consumers. Environments and institutions were, however, also influenced by the availability of foreign finance. To the extent that

---

[8] Frederick Lavington, *The English Capital Market* (London: Methuen, 1921), pp. 191–2 [Hereafter cited as Lavington, *The English Capital Market*].

there are differences in relative prices, or if the preferences and incomes of foreign suppliers are not identical to those of domestic savers, substantial gains can be realized from international capital movements. The extent of the capital flow and its effects will be influenced by the character of the economic environment and of the set of existing institutions, but the flows themselves will affect both the environment and the timing, the trajectory, and the final structure of the emerging capital market institutions.

Although scholars still debate the extent of foreign involvement, in the eighteenth century Britain certainly drew some of the capital required to finance its industrial revolution from the Continent, particularly from Holland.[9] By the middle decades of the next century, the investments in commercialization and industrialization had paid off. Britain had become the most highly developed economy in the world, and British domestic savings had begun to flow abroad in increasing volume. Over the years 1870–1914 about one-third of all British savings was directed overseas, and Britain dominated international finance. Thus, the preferences of British savers and the relative prices prevailing in the British capital markets had major consequences for developing economies.

About one-half of British overseas finance found its way to four developing countries: Argentina, Australia, Canada, and the United States. Although they were at different stages of development in the late nineteenth century, all four were frontier countries whose economic future, in large part, depended on their ability to bring new lands and resources within the scope of the market. To accomplish that end it was necessary to invest in transport, mining, land development, agriculture, agricultural and mineral processing, and a myriad of services and products that were designed to support frontier development.

In all four countries, much of the required investment was destined for activities located well away from the existing centers of domestic economic activity: Buenos Aires in Argentina, Melbourne and Sydney in Australia, Toronto and Montreal in Canada, and the New England, Middle Atlantic, South Atlantic, and East North Central regions in the United States. In each case, although government and railroads absorbed

---

[9] See, for example, Elise S. Brezis, "Foreign Capital Flows in the Century of Britain's Industrial Revolution: New Estimates, Controlled Conjunctures," *The Economic History Review*, Vol. 48, No. 1 (February 1995), pp. 46–67. J.F. Wright, "The Contribution of Overseas Savings to the Funded National Debt of Great Britain, 1750–1815," *The Economic History Review*, Vol. 50, No. 4 (November 1997), pp. 657–71.

the largest volumes of capital, a significant proportion of the demand for finance originated in new industries. The variety of the industries that were supported by British finance suggests something of the development of the international capital market. For example, in the United States the new demands ranged from mining the porphyry copper ores in the West to milling winter wheat in the upper Midwest to producing open hearth steel in Pittsburgh. In Canada they included the finance required to innovate new processes designed to turn the forests into newsprint as well as the resources needed to build manufacturing plants to operate behind the newly erected tariff barriers. In Argentina there were opportunities to exploit the new refrigeration technology that made it possible to export chilled and frozen beef. In Australia entrepreneurs even discovered that the weather and temperature were ideal for producing wine.

During the half century leading up to World War I, all four of the countries appear to have been successful in exploiting their frontier positions, if success is measured by the usual economic indicators. In each country real gross output rose, and although a part of that increase was absorbed by increases in population – a requirement for growth in any frontier economy – real output per capita rose as well (see Table 1:1-1). For Argentina, Canada, and the United States, despite rates of population growth that ranged from 1.7 to 3.7 percent a year, the increase in real income per capita averaged about 2 percent. Those figures stand in marked contrast to the 1.4 percent that Angus Maddison found for the average of fourteen industrialized countries over the same period of time.[10] Even Australia, a country with very high income at the beginning of the period, probably enjoyed an increase of real per capita GDP in excess of 0.5 percent a year.[11]

Such rates of increase of output per capita, when coupled with rates of population growth of 3.4 percent for Argentina, 2.5 percent for Australia, 2.1 percent for the United States, and 1.8 percent for Canada, suggest that there must have been a very rapid increase in the rate of new capital formation. If, for example, the capital/output ratio was stable

---

[10] Angus Maddison, *Phases of Capitalist Development* (Oxford: Oxford University Press, 1982), pp. 44–5 [Hereafter cited as Maddison, *Capitalist Development*].

[11] Throughout this book Australia is often called a country, despite the fact that the six colonies did not join to become the Commonwealth until 1901. Similarly, although the six colonies did not become states until after Federation, they will often be referred to as states. Through most of the period, although all had responsible government for at least some part of the time, the six states – Victoria, New South Wales, South Australia, Queensland, Western Australia, and Tasmania – operated largely independently.

Table 1:1-1. *Rates of growth 1870–1914 (percent per year)*

	Real Gross Output		Population		Real Output per capita	
	(1)	(2)	(1)	(2)	(1)	(2)
Argentina[a]	5.75%	n.d.	3.41%	3.81%	2.27%	3.40%
Australia	3.19	3.24%	2.48	2.55	0.69	0.48
Canada	3.71	4.64	1.78	1.67	1.90	2.59
United States[b]	3.70	4.61	2.09	2.17	1.58	1.90

Notes: (1) Rates are calculated between actual beginning and end points.
(2) Rates are calculated from beginning and end points estimated from a linear regression.
[a] Argentina 1875–1914.
[b] United States 1909–1914 by extrapolation.

Sources: Argentina: Roberto Cortes Conde, "Estimaciones del PBI en la Argentina, 1875–1935," Universidad de San Andres, Ciclo de Seminarios, 1994, Departamento de Economia. Australia: Noel G. Butlin, *Australian Domestic Product, Investment, and Foreign Borrowing, 1861–1938/39* (Cambridge: Cambridge University Press, 1962), table 1, pp. 6–7, table 269, pp. 460–1. Canada: M.C. Urquhart, *Gross National Product, Canada, 1870–1926: The Derivation of the Estimates* (Montreal: McGill-Queens University Press, 1993), table 1.6, pp. 24–25. United States: Robert Gallman, private communication, March 25, 1994.

at 3.0 – and given heavy investment in housing, railroads, and other structures, it may have been higher – an investment rate of between 5.4 and 10.2 percent was needed just to prevent per capita income from declining.[12]

Initially, all four of the frontier countries depended on Europe – particularly on Great Britain – for some fraction of their capital requirements. For the United States, domestic savings rates were high as early as the 1870s. As a result, although in some periods and some industries the import of foreign capital was both substantial and important, the overall fraction was not great, but for the other three countries, it was very large. Gradually, in two of the remaining three cases, as in the United States, domestic savings assumed a larger share of the task of

---

[12] These conditions were not met in all four cases. The Argentine capital/output ratio seems to have fallen. See Chapter 6 for a description of the record and a discussion of its significance.

underwriting domestic investment. The interaction between the inflow of foreign savings and the gradual evolution of domestic financial institutions, however, played out quite differently in each of the four. As a result, the final equilibriums were very different. A comparison of the four histories provides some insights into the questions of institutional change and of financial innovation, and it offers some clues about current issues of public and private policy.

1-2. Capital accumulation and mobilization

Investment requires that someone save, and if the full benefits of savings are to be realized, that those savings be invested in activities yielding the highest returns. In settler countries such activities are often located at the frontier, and they frequently involve new firms in new industries. The savings can be either domestic or foreign, but they tend to be generated by well-settled regions and well-established industries. Thus, according to M.M. Postan, there are two distinct problems: capital accumulation and capital mobilization.[13]

The savings decision can be voluntary or involuntary – the former the product of the voluntary decisions of consumers or firms, and the latter the result of government taxes or inflation engendered either by the government or by the commercial banks. The mobilization process can be based on either direct government fiat or on private individuals interacting through a structure of financial intermediaries and formal securities markets. The composition and nature of those intermediaries depends in turn on the state of institutional technology and the nature of the public, private, or public–private decisions that led to their innovation.

If government fiat is the model of choice, economically efficient mobilization requires not only that the new institutional arrangement be put in place, but also that economic growth must carry a very large weight in the politicians' utility functions. If either the private or the public–private partnership route is chosen, the appropriate institutional structure may have to be invented, and it has to be innovated. In addition, whether the structure is the product of public, private, or public–private decisions, its operation will very likely be constrained by governmental rules and regulations. Those rules and regulations may well reflect non-economic political goals. Moreover, even if there is no legal coercion and participation is voluntary, the savers must

---

[13] M.M. Postan, "Some Recent Problems in the Accumulation of Capital," *Economic History Review*, Vol. 6, No. 1 (October 1935), pp. 1–12 [Hereafter cited as Postan, "Some Recent Problems"].

still be educated to use the facilities offered by the new structure. The new institutions, although in part the product of the domestic environment, are also in part the product of the type and availability of foreign finance. There are numerous examples of the impact of British finance on the structures of the domestic capital markets in the four countries, but at this point, for purposes of illustration, let us touch on only four.

First, the demand of Canadian cities for capital to underwrite local infrastructure coupled with the bias of British savers in favor of investment in railroads and federal and provincial debt placed a premium on a domestic institutional structure that could channel savings into the issues of local governments. The result was the innovation, growth, and ultimate dominance of the bond house, an institution initially designed to direct domestic savings toward municipal finance, but that later became a channel to direct those savings into commercial and industrial enterprise. The bond house had no exact institutional counterpart in any of the other three countries.

Second, in the case of the United States, initially each of seven great London international banking houses recruited a junior American partner to help it funnel British savings into U.S. railroad construction.[14] At the time they were organized, those American firms, although also operating in the domestic capital market, devoted the majority of their efforts to providing local intelligence to help their London partners overcome the substantial informational asymmetries that existed and to handling a few administrative details. Gradually, capitalizing on their evolving reputations, the American firms began to operate independently. By the 1880s their attention had largely turned to the mobilization of domestic capital. The role those funds played in U.S. railroad finance had become at least as important as that of their European parents, and the role they later played in commercial and industrial finance was much greater.

Third, in Australia the local environment produced a different result. British investors had long shown a preference for Australian government issues, and when debentures were replaced by inscribed stock, a flood of

---

[14] There was also one major German connection. The seven London firms and their American junior partners were J.S. Morgan (Drexel Morgan), Brown Shipley (Brown Brothers), Morton, Rose (Morton Bliss), Baring Brothers (first T.W. Ward, then his two sons, and finally two firms: Baring Mougon in New York and Kidder Peabody in Boston), N.M. Rothschild (August Belmont & Company), Seligman Brothers (J&W Seligman), and Speyer Brothers (Phillip Speyer and Co.).

British capital flowed into Australia.[15] Since the colonial governments could raise funds cheaply, it was the public sector that benefited. State governments undertook the construction and operation of a myriad of economic activities – activities that ranged from railroads to agricultural finance and activities that in other countries were often carried out by private enterprise. As a result, there were few economic incentives for innovation in the private financial sector (either domestic or international). Institutional innovation is almost always slow and incremental, and in the absence of an efficient private institutional structure the range of government enterprise continued to expand. Thus, in part as a result of the preferences of British savers in the nineteenth century, as late as the 1940s the structure of Australian private domestic financial institutions remained relatively undeveloped.

Finally, in Argentina British investors mistrusted the private sector, and a very large fraction of British investment took the form of direct transfers to firms owned and managed by the British themselves. That ownership structure, coupled with the relatively low rate of Argentine domestic savings, meant that there were few profits to be earned from domestic financial innovation. By 1914 the financial infrastructure was far more primitive than the level of economic development alone would have indicated.

Although it is theoretically possible for a country to grow and develop with foreign capital alone, there is no evidence that any country has actually done so. The nations that successfully underwent commercialization or industrialization in the nineteenth and twentieth centuries have been marked by an increase in the domestic savings rate. The histories of three of the four frontier countries conform to that generalization. Although there is evidence that in some developing countries the increase in the savings rate during the late nineteenth century was based on involuntary decisions – through taxation in Russia and bank-engendered inflation in Germany, to cite two often-used examples – there is little evidence that such involuntary coercive policies played an important role in any of the frontier four.[16]

---

[15] Between 1874 and 1893 the four colonies of New South Wales, Victoria, South Australia, and Queensland raised (net) £136,350,000 ($664,024,500) on the British market.

[16] There may be some evidence for Argentina in the years before 1899. Carlos F. Diaz Alejandro, *Essays on the Economic History of the Argentine Republic*, Economic Growth Center, Yale University (New Haven, Conn.: Yale University Press, 1970), pp. 295–6 (especially fn. 31) [Hereafter cited as Diaz Alejandro, *Essays*].

The economics profession's inability to provide a fully adequate explanation for the collapse of the American savings rate in the early 1980s proves that we still have a great deal to learn about the reasons why individuals, corporations, and governments save. There is, however, a substantial economic literature on the motives for saving, as well as a not-insignificant body of work on the causes of the observed increases in the domestic savings rates in developing countries.[17] Raymond Goldsmith, in his classic *Study of Savings*, concludes that individuals save to enter business, purchase major assets, and provide for their retirement.[18] Others, including Nobel Prize winners Milton Friedman and Franco Modigliani, have pointed to the importance of demographic variables.[19] The life-cycle hypothesis suggests that people tend to save when they are between the ages of twenty and sixty and to *dissave* when they are younger and older. Frank Lewis, for example, attributes between one-fifth and one-quarter of the rise in the American savings rate to the fall in the dependency rate.[20] Similarly, work by Taylor and Williamson in the 1990s indicates that in Australia and Canada in the late nineteenth and twentieth centuries and in Argentina in the twentieth, nations with high dependency rates saved significantly less than those with lower ones.[21]

In his work on overseas investment in the nineteenth century, Michael Edelstein has estimated savings ratios in the United States, United Kingdom, and Canada and has pointed to the underlying forces that pushed those rates upward.[22] Of more direct relevance to this book, Davis and Gallman have stressed the importance of the development of

---

[17] For a more detailed discussion of the literature on the savings/investment questions see the appendix to this chapter.

[18] Raymond W. Goldsmith, *A Study in Savings*, 3 Vols. (Princeton: Princeton University Press, 1955).

[19] See, for example, F. Modigliani and R. Brumberg, "Utility Analysis and the Consumption Function: An Interpretation of Cross-Section Data," in K.K. Kurihara (ed.), *Post-Keynesian Economics* (New Brunswick, N.J.: Rutgers University Press, 1954); M. Friedman, *A Theory of the Consumption Function* (Princeton: Princeton University Press, 1957).

[20] Frank Lewis, "Fertility and Savings in the United States: 1830–1900," *Journal of Political Economy*, Vol. 91, No. 5 (October 1983), pp. 825–40.

[21] Alan M. Taylor and Jeffrey G. Williamson, "Capital Flows to the New World as an Intergenerational Transfer," *Journal of Political Economy*, Vol. 102, No. 2 (1994), pp. 348–71 [Hereafter cited as Taylor and Williamson, "Capital Flows to the New World"].

[22] Michael Edelstein, *Overseas Investment in the Age of High Imperialism* (New York: Columbia University, 1982) [Hereafter cited as Edelstein, *Overseas Investment*]. For a more detailed discussion of his arguments, see the appendix to this chapter.

financial institutions and markets designed to intermediate between savers and investors. They argue that commercial banks, other financial intermediaries, and formal securities markets make savings more attractive relative to consumption. First, the innovation of these institutions permits potential savers to benefit from substantial economies of scale in transaction and search costs, resulting in higher net returns to savings. Second, because most financial intermediaries – savings banks, life insurance companies and investment trusts, for example – hold portfolios of assets and sell claims against these portfolios rather than the assets themselves, and because the formal markets sell paper claims on assets, the existence of functioning markets and intermediaries makes it possible for savers to diversify their investment portfolios and thus reduce the risk discount on the returns on assets. Third, the imprimatur of a recognized intermediary or a formal listing on an established securities market can lead to a reduction in the uncertainty discount that a saver attaches to unfamiliar investment alternatives.[23]

The Davis-Gallman conclusions have found support in the work of Raymond Goldsmith. Goldsmith's evidence indicates that the fraction of financial assets in the total of all national assets in the United States and

---

[23] See, for example, L. Davis and R. Gallman, "The Share of Savings and Investment in Gross National Product During the Nineteenth Century in the U.S.A.," in F.C. Lane (ed.), *Fourth International Conference of Economic History* (Paris: Mouton, 1973) [Hereafter cited as Davis and Gallman, "The Share of Savings"]; L. Davis and R. Gallman, "Capital Formation in the United States during the Nineteenth Century," in P. Mathias and M.M. Postan (eds.), *The Cambridge Economic History of Europe*, Vol. 7, *the Industrial Economies: Capital, Labour, and Enterprise, Part 2, The United States, Japan, and Russia* (Cambridge: Cambridge University Press, 1978), pp. 1–69 [Hereafter cited as Davis and Gallman, "Capital Formation"]; L. Davis and R. Gallman, "Savings, Investment, and Economic Growth: The United States in the Nineteenth Century," in J. James and M. Thomas (eds.), *Capitalism in Context: Essays in Honor of Max Hartwell* (Chicago: University of Chicago Press, 1994) [Hereafter cited as Davis and Gallman, "Savings, Investment, and Economic Growth"]; J. James and Jonathan Skinner, "Sources of Savings in the Nineteenth Century United States," in P. Kilby (ed.), *Quantity and Quiddity: Essays in U.S. Economic History* (Middletown, Conn.: Wesleyan University Press, 1987), pp. 255–85 [Hereafter cited as James and Skinner, "Sources of Savings"]; Taylor and Williamson, "Capital Flows to the New World."

The word "uncertainty" is used in this work in the "Knightian" sense, that is, a discount applied to an uncertain situation, one in which the decision maker has no knowledge of the distribution of outcomes. In contrast, a "risk" discount refers to a situation in which the decision maker knows the distribution of outcomes (but not *the* outcome) and can, therefore, insure himself out from under the risk. In the case of uncertainty, insurance is not possible. Frank H. Knight, *Risk, Uncertainty, and Profit* (Boston: Houghton Mifflin, 1921).

Europe almost doubled during the period of rising savings rates and that there has been little change in that proportion since that time. Moreover, the increase was effected despite almost no change in the fraction of assets represented by currency and demand deposits and in the face of substantial declines in the share of government debt and trade credit in total assets. The increase was concentrated in the assets of non-bank intermediaries – other deposits, insurance and pension funds, and mortgages – and in the stocks and bonds of private corporations.[24] The Davis-Gallman hypothesis is also indirectly supported by the findings of John James and James Skinner, who find a close relationship between the increase in the savings rate and the change in the occupational structure. As the fraction of educated workers rises, so does the savings rate. These educated savers are more sophisticated and are therefore better able to overcome informational asymmetries and take advantage of the newly emerging institutional structure.[25]

Because the concept of mobilization is less tractable to precise measurement, much less work has been done on capital mobilization than on capital accumulation. Only recently has a satisfactory theory of capital mobility been developed. Contemporaries spoke only of "a disinclination of capital to migrate," and Postan's argument is not couched in terms readily translated into economics. The mobilization problem can, however, be cast in a transaction-cost framework. Investment alternatives that are far removed from the savers' immediate knowledge are subject to substantial uncertainty discounts. Such discounts are one type of transaction cost, and those costs can be reduced by innovation in the financial sector. The pooling of assets in a financial intermediary not only permits savers to benefit from the insurance provided by investment in claims on a portfolio of assets, but also permits them to benefit from the economies of scale inherent in gathering the data needed to overcome informational asymmetries. In addition, the signal of quality provided by the endorsement of a formal intermediary, a trusted individual, or a listing on a securities market with a reputation for trading in quality issues can reduce the level of the savers' uncertainty discounts.

The issue of capital mobility is probably of less direct policy relevance for the already developed countries, although the crucial role still played by venture capitalists in the financing of high-tech firms suggests that even in the United States, with its formidable institutional endowment, capital is still not perfectly mobile. Moreover, in recent years the saliency

---

[24] Raymond W. Goldsmith, *Comparative National Balance Sheets: A Study of Twenty Countries, 1688–1978* (Chicago: University of Chicago Press, 1985).

[25] James and Skinner, "Sources of Savings," pp. 255–85.

of the issue has increased for nations attempting major regime changes, the governments in Eastern Europe that are attempting to privatize their economies, for example. As Barry Eichengreen has shown, the problem remains important not only in Eastern Europe but in the developing economies of Africa, Asia, and Latin America as well.[26] Despite the generally recognized importance of capital-market imperfections, there are still a few economists who interpret history as though all markets are, and always were, perfect.[27]

Since the early 1960s there has been a steadily increasing body of research that underscores the process of institutional evolution in the capital markets of developing economies. Alexander Gershenkron has explored the cases of Germany, Russia, and Italy. Richard Tilly has worked on the problem of Germany. In the case of the United States, Lance Davis has studied the evolution of a national capital market,

[26] Barry Eichengreen, "Financing Infrastructure in Developing Countries: An Historical Perspective from the 19th Century," paper prepared for the World Bank's *World Development Report*, September 1993 [Hereafter cited as Eichengreen, "Financing Infrastructure in Developing Countries"].

[27] For example, Howard Bodenhorn and Hugh Rockoff have argued that there were no interregional interest rate differentials in the United States in the 1850s; Barry Eichengreen has concluded that there was no regional capital immobility during the populist period, once proper adjustment for local usury laws have been made; and, more recently, Howard Bodenhorn has reached a similar finding using yet another estimate of risk adjustment. H. Bodenhorn and H. Rockoff, "Regional Interest Rates in Antebellum America," in C. G. and H. Rockoff (eds.), *Strategic Factors in Nineteenth Century American Economic History: A Volume to Honor Robert W. Fogel*, A National Bureau of Economic Research Conference Report (Chicago: University of Chicago Press, 1992); Barry Eichengreen, "Mortgage Rates in the Populist Era," *American Economic Review*, Vol. 74, No. 5 (December 1984), pp. 995–1015; Howard Bodenhorn, "A More Perfect Union: Regional Interest Rates in the United States, 1880–1960," in Michael D. Bordo and Richard Sylla (eds.), *Anglo-American Financial Systems: Institutions and Markets in the Twentieth Century* (Burr Ridge, Ill.: Irwin Professional Publishing and Stern School of Business, New York University, 1995), pp. 415–54. These views have been strongly challenged, but their adherents continue to deny that the mobilization problem exists or that, if it does exist, it is important. Responses to: (1) Bodenhorn and Rockoff can be found in Davis and Gallman, "Savings, Investment, and Economic Growth"; (2) Eichengreen in Kenneth A. Snowden, "Mortgage Rates and American Capital Market Development in the Late Nineteenth Century," *Journal of Economic History*, Vol. 47, No. 3 (September 1987), and in Snowden, "Mortgage Lending and American Urbanization," *Journal of Economic History*, Vol. 48, No. 2 (June 1988); and (3) Bodenhorn in Lance Davis, "Discussion: Financial Integration Within and Between Countries," in Michael D. Bordo and Richard Sylla (eds.), *Anglo-American Financial Systems: Institutions and Markets in the Twentieth Century*, pp. 455–68.

Richard Sylla the role of banking legislation, Naomi Lamoreaux the contributions of the commercial banks, and Bradford DeLong the role of the investment bankers.[28] This literature demonstrates that if capital markets are primitive or nonexistent or if savers are uneducated, savings and capital accumulation alone are insufficient to guarantee productive investment. If savings are to be used efficiently, they must be directed into the most productive investments, even if those investments are far removed – geographically and industrially – from the savers themselves.

Postan argued that in Great Britain at the time of the Industrial Revolution, merchants saved, but they did not make savings available to the new textile, iron, and pottery industries. Instead, although very substantial returns were available in the new manufacturing activities, they directed their accumulations into agriculture, where returns, if Postan is correct, were close to zero, or perhaps even negative. Investment in the new manufacturing industries was highly uncertain, while investments in modern farming, although financially unrewarding, could at least purchase social position.[29] In Britain capital remained highly personal until, during the more than half a century of wars with the French, savers

[28] Alexander Gershenkron, *Economic Backwardness in Historical Perspective* (Cambridge, Mass.: Harvard University Press, 1962); Richard Tilly, *Financial Institutions and Industrialization in the Rhineland, 1815–1870* (Madison, Wisc.: University of Wisconsin Press, 1966), and "Capital Formation in Germany in the Nineteenth Century," in P. Mathias and M.M. Postan (eds.), *The Cambridge Economic History of Europe*, Vol. 7. *The Industrial Economies: Capital, Labour, and Enterprise, Part 1* (Cambridge: Cambridge University Press, 1978); Lance Davis, "Capital Immobilities and Finance Capitalism: A Study of Economic Evolution in the United States, 1820–1920," *Explorations in Entrepreneurial History*, Second Series, Vol. 1, No. 1 (fall 1963), and "The Investment Market, 1870–1914: The Evolution of a National Market," *The Journal of Economic History*, Vol. 25, No. 3 (September 1965); Richard Sylla, "Federal Policy, Banking Market Structure, and Capital Mobilization in the United States, 1863–1913," *The Journal of Economic History*, Vol. 26, No. 4 (December 1969); Naomi Lamoreaux, "Banks, Kinship, and Economic Development: The New England Case," *The Journal of Economic History*, Vol. 47, No. 3 (September 1986), and *Insider Lending: Banks, Personal Connections, and Economic Development in Industrial New England*, NBER Series on Long-Term Factors in Economic Development (Cambridge: Cambridge University Press, 1994); Bradford DeLong, "Did Morgan's Men Add Great Value?" in P. Temin (ed.), *Inside the Business Enterprise: Historical Perspectives on the Use of Information* (Chicago: University of Chicago Press, 1991).

[29] Modern farming implied investments in draining, fencing, and buildings that made the estate look modern, even if, by any economic criteria, those investments may well have been unprofitable. See Postan, "Some Recent Problems." It should, however, be noted that the British, like their Continental peers, also directed a portion of their savings toward church construction.

discovered that investment in government bonds was not only patriotic, but also profitable. That lesson was reinforced by their experience with railroad securities during the Hudson boom of the 1840s. At that time, despite the short-term paper losses they incurred when the boom collapsed, savers found that in the medium and long term, investments in pieces of paper were very profitable.

Similarly, in Canada, Australia, Argentina, and the United States, farmers saved but invested in their farms, merchants saved but invested in commercial buildings and inventories, and manufacturers saved but invested in larger plants and new machines. Even when they raised their horizons beyond their immediate environment, they tended to restrict their financial commitments to activities well within their personal knowledge. For example, much of the finance raised in support of the early New England short-haul railroads was channeled through family, friends, and personal contacts.[30] In the case of the Massachusetts-type textile mills, the nation's first venture into large-scale manufacturing, although the firms were organized as corporations and their shares listed on the Boston Stock Exchange, there is little evidence of the existence of mobile depersonalized capital. To a large extent, the initial capital was raised from a small group of Boston capitalists – the so-called Associates – who made their fortunes in commerce and, to a lesser extent, in shipping and whaling. Such merchants and their firms were responsible for more than one-half of the industry's initial capitalization. As late as 1839, they still owned more than half of the industry's equity, and they appear to have contributed almost one-quarter of all the long-term loans raised by the textile firms between 1840 and 1860. The Associates held stock in the mills, but those holdings cannot be taken as evidence that the investors had begun to let their savings take the form of depersonalized paper assets. When commenting on movements in the share prices of these firms, the chronicler of the Boston Stock Exchange notes, "This class of securities may be termed an 'exclusive' one; for it is almost exclusively in the hands of certain capitalists, who have no desire to sell, when it is up, and can afford to hold it when down. It seldom finds its way to market, except in stray shares or in case of executors' sales, is the most variable stock on the list, and exceedingly difficult to obtain reliable quotations of."[31] In the words of Johnson and Supple, "investors and busi-

---

[30] Eichengreen, "Financing Infrastructure in Developing Countries," p. 10. Naomi Lamoreaux, "Banks, Kinship, and Economic Development: The New England Case," *Journal of Economic History*, Vol. 46, No. 3 (September 1986).

[31] Lance E. Davis, "Stock Ownership in the Early New England Textile Industry," *Business History Review*, Vol. 32, No. 2 (summer 1958), pp. 204–22; Lance E. Davis, "The New England Textile Mills and the Capital Markets," *The Journal*

nessmen derived their outlook and personal potentialities, as well as their wealth and command over others' wealth, from a close-knit and quite distinctive community. Boston capitalists, operating through a series of closely interlocking groups, owed their economic strength, and in some measure their behavioral characteristics, to the social background and cohesiveness of Boston's mercantile inheritance"; thus, "investment tended to be a cumulative social process in an environment lacking an impersonal, national money market."[32] Even in Boston, the home of some of the nation's most sophisticated investors, capital remained highly personalized in the years before the 1870s.

In short, before the British, Argentine, Australian, Canadian, or American saver was willing to risk his accumulations in regions and industries far removed from his own experience, he had to be educated about the safety and potential profitability of depersonalized capital, pieces of paper that represented claims on assets far removed from his experience, and therefore assets that were initially subject to very high uncertainty discounts.

The problem, then, was one of an informational asymmetry that could lead to problems of moral hazard and adverse selection. The owners or promoters of firms in distant places or in new and unfamiliar industries were in a position to evaluate the relative merits of their enterprises, but the unsophisticated saver – a saver living and working spatially or industrially far from the firms that were seeking finance – was not. Nor could the potential investor necessarily trust those owners or promoters to act in good faith. There were potentially substantial moral hazard problems in those relationships. Faced with a myriad of uncertain choices, the saver often turned away from distant alternatives, even when those alternatives were in fact relatively the most profitable of his potential choices. He chose instead to invest in activities whose potential profitability he

of Economic History, Vol. 20, No. 1 (March 1960), pp. 1–30; Joseph G. Martin, *Seventy-Three Year History of the Boston Stock Market, From January 1, 1798, to January 1, 1878; with the Semi-Annual Dividends Paid from the Commencement of the Boston Banks, Insurance, Railroad, Manufacturing, and Miscellaneous Companies. Also the Prices of American Gold, Government Securities, State, City, and Railroad Bonds, Bank, Insurance, Manufacturing, Railroad, Mining, Gas-Light, and Miscellaneous Stocks; with Quotations of Exchange on London the Past Seventy-Three Years; &c. With Full Explanatory Notes* (Boston: Published by the Author, 1871), p. 64 [Hereafter cited as Martin, *Seventy-Three Year History of the Boston Stock Market*].

[32] Arthur M. Johnson and Barry E. Supple, *Boston Capitalists and Western Railroads: A Study in the Nineteenth-Century Railroad Investment Process*, Harvard Studies in Business History, Vol. XXIII (Cambridge, Mass.: Harvard University Press, 1967), p. 338.

was in a position to evaluate: his farm, his store, his factory or, perhaps, the offerings of a local individual financier with a reputation for honesty whose past enterprises and willingness to risk his own funds signaled his reliability.[33] Before the saver was willing to risk his savings in distant alternatives, it was necessary that he achieve at least some minimum level of education; that is, before he was willing to invest in claims on deper-sonalized paper assets, he had to learn to interpret and trust some set of signals about the quality of those unfamiliar choices – the uncertainty discounts had to be reduced. If the reputation of a known financial inter-mediary or of a J.P. Morgan could be attached to the distant investment alternative, the choice often appeared less uncertain.

Not only was it true that a saver could not fully participate in the capital mobilization process until he had learned enough to overcome informational asymmetrys, but, equally important, the borrowing firm also found it necessary to operate within the existing informational struc-ture. To put the argument from the point of view of the borrowing firm in the jargon of the economists: "Higher quality parties are usually adversely affected by the presence of lower quality parties; either the higher quality parties are pooled with the lower quality parties, to their detriment, or they must invest in signals beyond the point that they would if there were no informational asymmetry to distinguish them-selves from their low-quality peers." In this context, for "parties" read firms seeking capital.[34] The weaker the financial infrastructure, the more serious the problem for both parties.

Financial institutions play an important role in the educational process. For example, in the United States, savings banks were initially established by the business elites of Eastern cities as semi-philanthropic organizations designed to show the working poor that thrift was both moral and profitable. The businessmen used their reputations to signal potential depositors that these institutions were safe. The beneficiaries were the working poor who earned interest, business firms that were able to attract needed capital, and, perhaps not surprisingly, the business elites themselves. The elites were, after all, the lowest-risk borrowers and there-fore entitled to the lowest interest rates on any money they borrowed or, if usury laws were binding, to a preferred position in the queue of

---

[33] See Eichengreen, "Financing Infrastructure in Developing Countries," p. 10.

[34] David M. Kreps, *A Course in Microeconomic Theory*, chapter 17, "Adverse Selection and Market Signaling" (Princeton: Princeton University Press, 1990), p. 651. The term "lower quality" appears pejorative, but in this case it should be taken as a synonym for *either* unable or unwilling (that is, the firm could find alternative sources of capital and, therefore, it did not need to purchase the signal).

potential borrowers.[35] Decades later, when the educational process was farther along, the imprimatur of a respected investment banker – J.P. Morgan or Kuhn Loeb, to cite two examples – or an official listing on the New York Stock Exchange provided a similar signal of quality to American savers who were beginning to consider adding the debt and equity issues of private firms to their portfolios.

In Australia, on the other hand, it was the state governments, rather than the business elites, that established safe savings banks; not surprisingly, those banks invested almost entirely in government issues. Later, when private land banks and building and loan associations collapsed during the economic depression of the 1890s, those same state governments established "safe" mortgage banks.

The Canadian experience falls somewhere between the American and the Australian. Quebec aside, savings banks bore the imprimatur of the government and invested the vast bulk of their assets in government issues. The bond houses, however, each bearing the quality signal of one of the well-known and respected domestic capitalist groups, taught savers that investment in selected private commercial and industrial firms was much less uncertain than they, the savers, had previously assumed.

1-3. **Britain and the four frontier countries: an overview**

By 1865, the savings rate in Britain had reached double digits. A not insignificant number of savers were relatively well educated in the vagaries of both domestic and international finance; that is, he, or increasingly she, had become a fairly sophisticated investor willing to hold the securities of a variety of public and private enterprises.[36] In addition, a near-modern structure of financial institutions was in place. That structure included commercial banks, savings banks, discount houses,

---

[35] See, for example, Lance E. Davis and Peter L. Payne, "From Benevolence to Business: The Story of Two Savings Banks," *Business History Review*, Vol. 32, No. 2 (winter 1958); Peter L. Payne and Lance E. Davis, *The Savings Bank of Baltimore, 1818–1866: A Historical and Analytical Study*, The Johns Hopkins University Studies in Historical and Political Science, Series LXXII, No. 2, 1954 (Baltimore: Johns Hopkins University Press, 1956), pp. 204–22. Emerson W. Keyes, *A History of Savings Banks in the United States* (New York: Bradford Rhodes, 1876); Charles E. Knowles, *History of the Bank for Savings in the City of New York, 1819–1929* (New York: Bank for Savings, 1929); Alan L. Olmstead, *New York City, Mutual Savings Banks, 1819–1961* (Chapel Hill: University of North Carolina Press, 1976).

[36] R.C.O. Matthews, C.H. Feinstein, and J.C. Odling-Smee, *British Economic Growth, 1856–1973* (Stanford, Calif.: Stanford University Press, 1982), pp. 131–51.

insurance companies, and a set of formal securities markets that was dominated by the London Stock Exchange. The four frontier countries were institutionally much less well endowed, savers were substantially less well educated, and the institutional structure was far more primitive. But the excess demand for capital was almost certainly higher.

As a result, foreign – largely British – capital played an important role in the development of those four countries. Foreign capital served some combination of three functions. It supported a level of investment needed to finance commercialization and industrialization when domestic savings rates were insufficient. It funded sudden surges in investment demand even when domestic rates were in the long run sufficient to supply the required resources. It supplied capital to economic activities that were, from the point of view of domestic savers, located in "distant" regions or industrial sectors at a time when savers were still relatively uneducated and the institutional structure was not sufficiently developed to support transfers from domestic savers to those "distant" firms.

As the rates reported in Table 1:1-1 indicate, each of the four frontier countries was experiencing rapid growth; however, the developmental paths of the four were quite different. At one end of the spectrum, the domestic savings rate in the United States had reached double digits by midcentury, and it exceeded 20 percent by the 1870s.[37] For the United States, to the extent that there was an accumulation problem, it was largely one of timing. For some periods even the high rate of domestic savings was insufficient to meet short-term surges in the demand for capital: The need to refinance the Civil War debt in the 1870s, the rapid industrial transformation of the 1880s, and the railway construction booms of the post–Civil War decades are three cases in point. In the United States, however, it was the need to mobilize savings that raised the most serious problems.

At the other extreme, in Argentina the domestic savings rate before 1914 seldom reached 10 percent. It was 5.6 percent in the period 1910–14 and it averaged 6.7 percent between 1881 and 1914. Given the observed rates of population growth, foreign capital was needed to finance *any* significant long-term growth. In Argentina, capital had to be accumulated, *and* it had to be mobilized.

In Canada savings rates similar to those in Britain in the early decades were superseded by very high levels of accumulation in the twentieth century. Domestic savings averaged about 12 percent of income between 1870 and 1899, but they reached 25 percent in the years 1900–14. In the

---

[37] Davis and Gallman, "The Share of Savings;" Davis and Gallman, "Capital Formation."

years from 1870 to the mid-1880s, at a time when domestic savings alone were inadequate to meet the increase in investment demand inherent in the government's attempt to implement Macdonald's National Plan, foreign capital supported the development of the transport network. Later, in the fifteen years before World War I, although the level of domestic savings was high, international transfers were still required to fund and mobilize the investments that supported the very rapid growth that was, temporally at least, associated with the wheat boom. Early and late, Canada faced both accumulation and mobilization problems; in the middle period the issue was largely one of mobilization.

In Australia, although domestic savings rates in the 1870s were in the mid-teens, they fell to just more than 10 percent over the next two decades, and then only gradually edged upward to about 18 percent in the last pre–World War I decade. Marked by what was probably the highest per capita income in the world in 1870, income increased only slowly between the mid-1870s and 1889, and it fell by almost 40 percent over the next five years.[38] Although foreign capital played an important role in the nation's development, it was frequently the government that assumed the task of directing those flows, and those decisions were often based on a political rather than an economic calculus. From the early 1890s onward, however, the importation of private foreign capital almost ceased; it was not that there were no profitable investment opportunities nor that domestic savings were sufficient and adequately effectively mobilized to meet these demands. The private sector of the Australian economy had simply become too uncertain for the British investor.

In all four countries there is evidence of institutional invention and innovation in the financial sector, but the pace and timing of those changes were very different. The United States had the most developed structure at both the beginning and the end of the period, but with the growth of the life insurance industry, the rise of the national banking system, and the maturation of the formal securities markets, the structure was much different in 1914 than it had been a half century earlier. Legal limits on interstate branching limited the commercial banks' role

---

[38] N.G. Butlin, *Australian Domestic Product, Investment and Foreign Borrowing, 1861–1938/39* (Cambridge: Cambridge University Press, 1962), table 1, pp. 6–7; table 4, pp. 16–17; table 250, p. 422; table 265, p. 444. N.G. Butlin, *Investment in Australian Economic Development, 1861–1900* (Cambridge: Cambridge University Press, 1964), table 1, p. 11; appendix table II, p. 454. A. Barnard and N.G. Butlin, "Australian Public and Private Capital Formation, 1901–75," *The Economic Record*, Vol. 57, No. 159 (December 1981), appendix table, p. 366. Note: Data for 1901 through 1914 were estimated by averaging fiscal years, e.g., 1901 = (1900/01 + 1901/02)/2.

in solving the mobilization problem, and governmental regulations that tended to preclude long-term investments magnified the importance of the non-bank intermediaries, particularly savings banks in the early decades of the nineteenth century and life insurance companies in the years after 1872. The process of investor education had begun, but even as late as 1914 it still took the guarantee provided by a known investment banker or an official listing on a securities exchange with a reputation for carefully vetting its listings – the New York Stock Exchange, for example – to assure the would-be-investor about the viability of depersonalized paper assets.

The Canadian financial structure was initially somewhat more primitive than its American counterpart, and the pattern of institutional innovation that emerged was somewhat different, but its development was almost equally rapid. No legal restrictions prevented the commercial banks from developing nationwide branch networks, although large-scale nationwide branch banking largely awaited the twentieth century. The laws strictly precluded making long-term mortgage commitments, and the law, coupled with the conservatism of Canadian bankers, led to the real-bills doctrine remaining in force longer in Canada than it did in the United States. The relative role of commercial banks within the financial infrastructure was similar in the two countries. Canadian building and loan and mortgage companies played a significantly larger role than their American counterparts did, and life insurance firms a somewhat greater one. Savings banks, however, represented a much smaller fraction of the financial structure. Although the formal securities markets remained thin, bond houses after the mid-1880s, emerged to directly distribute the debt and preferred equity issues of private companies. Like the stamp of quality attached to the names of American investment banks (J.P. Morgan or Goldman, Sachs, for example) on an American issue, the reputation of the Canadian financial groups associated with the bond house signaled the quality of the issues distributed in Canada. With the widespread innovation of nationwide branch banking, and the emergence of the bond houses as significant players in the formal securities markets, the Canadian financial structure was, by 1914, almost as well developed as the American.

In Australia the private markets were more primitive than in Canada, and they were relatively slower to develop. The trading banks were quick to capitalize on their ability to branch, and by the 1870s they were prepared to make long-term loan commitments. These banks played a relatively larger role in the domestic financial structure than the commercial banks in either the United States or Canada. The securities markets, however, were very thin – even thinner than the Canadian – and no ade-

quate equivalent of the Canadian bond house or the American investment banker emerged to reduce uncertainty discounts on paper assets.
There were some private placements, and precious metal mines were
easily financed. Otherwise, there was a dearth of private bond and equity
issues. The question remains: Why was innovation so slow, and how did
the pace of development affect economic growth? Clearly the depression of the 1890s had a far more drastic impact on the evolution of
private financial institutions in Australia than it did in any of the other
three countries. In addition, it has been argued that the very low ratio of
private to public issues reflected not a shortage in the supply of domestic savings directed toward the private sector but the dominant role
played by state enterprise in the Australian economy and the concentration of the most capital intensive activities – railroads and public
utilities – in state hands.[39] Government savings banks largely limited
their portfolios to government bonds, and after 1900 state mortgage
banks came to play a major role in mortgage lending. The states' quality
guarantees, however, came at the cost of defining viable investment
alternatives very narrowly.

The Argentine financial structure was the least developed of the four.
The banking system had followed a rocky road from the early 1880s to
the Barings Crisis, and that crisis produced widespread banking failures.
Thereafter the system was reconstructed on a much sounder basis, but
the government's Banco de la Naciòn Argentina (reconstituted in 1891)
accounted for about 45 percent of commercial bank assets at the end of
the period, and foreign banks accounted for an additional 25 percent. In
1914 commercial bank assets per capita amounted to only 240 paper
pesos, or about U.S. $101. In contrast, the figure for Australia was $245,
for the United States it was $234, and for Canada $172. Mortgage institutions were important (mortgage debt had risen from 1 billion to almost
3 billion paper pesos – $422 million to $1.255 billion in U.S. dollars –
between 1905 and 1915). Private mortgage banks and associations were
the primary suppliers, but the government's National Mortgage Bank
(established in 1886) contributed about one-fifth of the total. In the other
sectors of the capital market, commercial and industrial companies relied
on the commercial banks for short-term credit and on retained earnings
and ad hoc arrangements for long-term financing. Even as late as 1926–9,
transactions on the Buenos Aires Bourse averaged only 640 million
paper pesos a year (U.S.$272 million); of that total, mortgage paper

[39] See, for example, Ian M. Drummond, *Capital Markets in Australia and Canada,*
1895–1914, Ph.D. diss. Yale University, May 1959 [Hereafter cited as Drummond,
Capital Markets].

represented almost two-thirds, the issues of national and local governments accounted for about one-quarter, and the stocks and bonds of
private corporations a mere 11 percent.[40]

When faced with a choice of institutions potentially capable of
overcoming accumulation and mobilization problems, the Americans
depended the least on the government. In that array they were followed
by the Argentines and the Canadians. At the other extreme were the residents of the oft-termed "socialist colonies" of Australia. Finally, although
there are chicken-egg problems, in terms of the level of investor education, the process had advanced furthest in the United States. After the
turn of the century, however, there is ample evidence to indicate that
the American–Canadian gap was rapidly closing. Both of the Southern
hemisphere nations lagged far behind their Northern counterparts;
however, given the government's role in the Australian economy, there
may have been relatively less pressure for private education.

One caveat: Neither public nor private institutional structures were
completely free of problems. In Australia, in the face of political pressure,
the government devoted far too many resources to railroads and to the
agricultural sector. In Canada, in an attempt to place its national development plan in effect, the government drastically overbuilt its railway
network, and then, since its reputation was at stake, it incurred substantial additional costs in bailing out the system's bondholders. In Argentina
neither government nor private institutional innovation was sufficient
to bring domestic savings rates to levels that would sustain long-run economic growth; continued foreign capital infusions were required, but
World War I caused those sources to dry up. Nor was the relatively free-
market environment of the United States without its problems, although
those problems flowed less from the political arguments in the decision
makers' utility functions than those in Australia and Canada.[41] The high
levels of uncertainty discounts applied by the relatively unsophisticated
domestic savers made it difficult for firms in the West and South and those
in the newly emerging industrial sector to obtain domestic capital, and the
underlying informational asymmetries were only gradually overcome.
Both the Canadian and Australian economies encountered a similar

---

[40] Diaz Alejandro, *Essays*, pp. 33–5. The issues of the National Mortgage Bank
alone accounted for 57 percent of the total. The exchange rate conversions from
paper pesos to U.S. $ are made on the basis of the estimates in table 71, p. 484.

[41] In the 1830s and 1840s, state and federal governments had been involved in canal
construction; in the 1850s some states had provided funds for railway construction, and the federal government had provided some land grants and engineering support. New land grants were discontinued in the early 1870s, but old grants
continued to be exploited, and some states provided financial support. There
were, however, no government-owned railroads.

problem, but at least for short-term capital the problem was alleviated by the developing branch networks. Moreover, since their private sectors – particularly the Australian – were somewhat smaller, the costs, at least in the short term, may have been less. In all four countries, in the years before 1914, although the relative magnitudes differed, the availability of foreign – particularly British – capital helped solve both the accumulation and the mobilization problems.

1-4. **British long-term capital transfers**

Ideally, for any given year and for any pair of countries – Britain and Canada, for example – it would be desirable to be able to estimate each of the four components of the international capital flows that moved from one country to the other. In the case of Britain and Canada, for example, a scholar would like to have data on new British investments in Canada, British repatriations of previous investments in Canada, new Canadian investments in Britain, and Canadian repatriations of previous investments in Britain. In addition, he or she would like to be able to decompose each of the four into its spatial and industrial elements. Unfortunately, such data do not exist for the late twentieth century, let alone for the nineteenth. The international flow data that are most often employed – data calculated from the balance of payment accounts, i.e. the balance on goods and service adjusted for unilateral transfers and change in the monetary goldstock – are both aggregate (that is, they provide no clue as to identity of the suppliers or the recipients) and net (that is, there is no way of separately identifying the magnitudes of the inflows and outflows). Not surprisingly, the flow data – data reported as the net value of capital exports and imports – although available for three of the four frontier countries, are not disaggregated by country of origin or destination, and they cannot be disaggregated by industry or region.

The data problem can be at least partially overcome. Since Britain was the chief supplier of foreign capital to the four, and since the London Stock Exchange was the major channel for British portfolio investment, an examination of the capital "created and called" on the Exchange can provide a rough idea of the gross flows from Britain as well as some important clues about the spatial and industrial distribution of those funds.[42] Some feeling for the magnitudes and the timing of gross transfers can be found in the data reported in Tables 1:4-1 through 1:4-7.

---

[42] The data are drawn from *The Investor's Monthly Manual*, a supplement to the *Economist*. The monthly periodical began publication in February 1865, and it regularly included a list of publicly floated issues. Included in those lists was not only the name of the issuer, but also the amount of capital that had been "created" or "called." The term "capital creation" was used to denote a new

As Table 1:4-1 indicates, the United States drew the largest share of the four countries' total; given the relative sizes of the four, the share is surprisingly small. Over the years 1865–1914, the combined population of Argentina, Australia, and Canada never exceeded one-fifth of the U.S. population. As a result, on a per capita basis the level of transfers to the

capital issue that was subscribed to at the "market price" at the time of issue. Unlike current practice, in the nineteenth century issues were sometimes sold on time; that is, £1,000 equity might be sold to an investor for an initial payment of £100 and his promise to pay the remainder as the issuing firm demanded. At times there was an agreed schedule of payments; at times the requests were periodic demands at unscheduled intervals. Moreover, in a significant number of cases, the total amount was never demanded. The term "call" was used to describe the announcements of the "periodic installments that were to be paid by the subscribers of the new issue." For purposes of simplicity we use the term "capital called" to describe both the capital that was created and called at the same time and the capital that was later called after it was created. For a more complete discussion of the issue, see Harvey H. Segal and Matthew Simon, "British Foreign Capital Issues, 1865–1914," *The Journal of Economic History*, Vol. 21, No. 4 (December 1961).

The reader should bear in mind that the series represent an enumeration of new issues, and that it does not include securities that British investors may have purchased privately or on some other exchange.

A few additional words of caution. First, although it is sometimes possible to unambiguously classify a firm into the appropriate industry – a railroad is usually (but not always) a railroad – there are sometimes questions. When there was any doubt, the classification adopted by the *Stock Exchange Annual Yearbook* has been employed.

Second, as Segal and Simon noted more than three decades ago, "one can never be sure that a foreign capital issue floated in the British market actually resulted in a foreign capital transfer." Since many of the foreign issues were made by British-owned firms, the issuing firm very likely carried on at least a small fraction of its business in the United Kingdom; and it might have had a portion of its business located in yet a third country. There is no way of estimating the fraction of funds "called" that remained in Britain or that were directed to a third country; however, a sampling of firms for which other records exist suggests that the proportion, in most cases, was not large. In a few cases, however, it was very significant. Certainly only a small part of the $21.4 million of new issues that the British-American Tobacco Company floated between 1909 and 1914 were ever actually invested in its American operations.

Third, since the London market was open to any investors, there is no guarantee that all of the securities were purchased by British citizens, so the term "British capital" does not imply that all the capital came initially from Britain. External evidence, however, indicates that the London market was principally used by British investors. We are not dealing with ultimate ownership, but with the funds that passed through the London market, the first foreign parent. Thus, the "capital called" data primarily reflect capital flows from Britain to firms and governments in the four frontier countries; it does not appear to overly distort reality to term the capital calls in London "British" flows.

Table 1:4-1. *Four frontier countries: total capital called: British capital markets (thousands of dollars)*

Years	Argentina	Australia	Canada	United States	Four-Country Total
1865–1879	94,393	192,408	245,533	2,038,344	2,570,678
1880–1899	580,312	945,620	359,813	1,230,988	3,116,733
1900–1914	1,221,966	554,825	1,492,865	1,953,256	5,222,912
1865–1914	1,896,671	1,692,854	2,098,211	5,222,588	10,910,324

Percentage of four-country total: total capital called:
British capital markets

Years	Argentina	Australia	Canada	United States	Four-Country Total
1865–1879	3.67	7.48	9.55	79.29	100.00
1880–1899	18.62	30.34	11.54	39.50	100.00
1900–1914	23.40	10.62	28.58	37.40	100.00
1865–1914	17.38	15.52	19.23	47.87	100.00

Four frontier countries total capital called per capita: British capital markets (U.S. dollars)

Years	Argentina	Australia	Canada	United States	Four-Country Average
1865–1879	3.35	7.12	4.16	3.06	4.42
1880–1899	8.79	16.49	3.85	1.01	7.54
1900–1914	12.81	8.67	14.54	1.48	9.38
1865–1914	8.36	11.33	7.15	1.77	7.15

Note: In the tables in this book, dollars are U.S. dollars unless specified otherwise.

Source: Davis–Gallman, *Investor's Monthly* manual tape.

three smaller countries was much greater than the British capital infusions to the American economy.[43] Although the timing of the capital imports differed from country to country, over the fifty-year span, the

[43] Over the fifty-year period, the relative population of Argentina rose from 4.4 to 8.0 percent of the U.S. population; that of Australia increased from 3.8 to 4.8 percent; but that of Canada declined from 9.5 to 7.0 percent. Overall, then, the three countries' total rose from 17.8 to 20.0 percent of the U.S. total.

Table 1:4-2. *Manufacturing and commercial capital called: British capital markets (thousands of U.S. dollars)*

Years	Argentina	Australia	Canada	United States
1865–1879	0	1,730	1,062	16,692
1880–1899	10,486	12,674	7,917	138,192
1900–1914	17,243	4,130	89,929	78,751
1865–1914	27,729	18,535	98,908	233,635

Percentage distribution, manufacturing and commercial capital called: British capital markets

Years	Argentina	Australia	Canada	United States
1865–1879	0.00	0.90	0.43	0.82
1880–1899	1.81	1.34	2.20	11.23
1900–1914	1.41	0.74	6.02	4.03
1865–1914	1.46	1.09	4.71	4.47

Manufacturing and commercial capital called per capita: British capital markets (U.S. dollars)

Years	Argentina	Australia	Canada	United States
1865–1879	0.00	0.07	0.04	0.03
1880–1899	0.16	0.19	0.08	0.11
1900–1914	0.16	0.07	0.84	0.06
1865–1914	0.11	0.12	0.29	0.07

Source: Davis–Gallman, *Investor's Monthly* manual tape.

Australian economy received, on average, $11.33 per person per year, the Argentine economy $8.36, and the Canadian economy $7.15. At $1.77 per capita, the U.S. average was less than one-quarter the Canadian, only slightly more than one-fifth that of the Argentine, and only about 15 percent of the Australian. Moreover, if the focus is shifted from the entire half century to the last thirty-five years – 1880–1914 – the ratio is 1:7 for Canada, 1:9 for Argentina, and 1:11 for Australia.

Moreover, although the U.S. accounted for 48 percent of the four-country total over the fifty-year span, if the 1870s – a decade that saw a massive refunding of the American Civil War debt – are excluded, the U.S. fraction of the forty-year total was only 38 percent.

Table 1:4-3. *Finance capital called: British capital markets (thousands of U.S. dollars)*

Years	Argentina	Australia	Canada	United States
1865–1879	3,555	6,635	0	9,047
1880–1899	3,226	51,069	5,531	48,387
1900–1914	11,809	34,518	12,142	21,782
1865–1914	18,591	92,222	17,674	79,217

Percentage distribution, finance capital called: British capital markets

Years	Argentina	Australia	Canada	United States
1865–1879	3.77	3.45	0.00	0.44
1880–1899	0.56	5.40	1.54	3.93
1900–1914	0.97	6.22	0.81	1.12
1865–1914	0.98	5.45	0.84	1.52

Finance capital called per capita: British capital markets (U.S. dollars)

Years	Argentina	Australia	Canada	United States
1865–1879	0.14	0.22	0.00	0.02
1880–1899	0.05	0.83	0.06	0.04
1900–1914	0.11	0.51	0.11	0.02
1865–1914	0.09	0.55	0.06	0.03

Source: Davis–Gallman, *Investor's Monthly* manual tape.

The four countries differed not only in the size and relative importance of the infusions of foreign capital but also in the timing of those transfers (see Table 1:4-1). In the case of Argentina, capital imports surged to more than two and a half times the fifty-year average in the period 1885–99, fell to a low of barely one-fifth of that average in 1895–9, and then rose again to a level more than 70 percent above the norm during the decade 1900–9. In Australia it was the decade of the 1880s – the end of the long boom – that witnessed the greatest flow of new British portfolio finance. Gross capital imports were more than 70 percent above the fifty-year average in the first half of the decade and more than twice that benchmark in the second. In Canada, although imports reached the fifty-year average in the late 1870s and again a decade later, the massive flows (reaching three times the standard) came during the wheat boom that spanned most of the decade and a half before World War I. Finally,

Table 1:4-4. *Government capital called: British capital markets (thousands of U.S. dollars)*

Years	Argentina-1	Argentina-2	Australia-1	Australia-2	Australia-3	Canada-1	Canada-2	United States-1
1865–1879	56,640	56,640	160,737	130,875	58,573	153,517	43,947	1,532,538
1880–1899	199,762	194,963	684,219	652,015	261,130	129,081	50,334	68,975
1900–1914	98,224	98,224	414,824	413,972	186,870	460,421	230,595	2,280
1865–1914	354,626	349,827	1,259,780	1,196,862	506,574	743,019	324,876	1,603,793

Percentage distribution, government capital called: British capital markets

Years	Argentina-1	Argentina-2	Australia-1	Australia-2	Australia-3	Canada-1	Canada-2	United States-1
1865–1879	60.00	60.00	82.07	68.02	30.44	62.52	17.90	75.19
1880–1899	34.47	33.60	72.32	68.95	27.61	35.97	13.99	5.60
1900–1914	8.30	8.04	74.86	74.61	33.68	30.79	15.45	0.12
1865–1914	19.09	18.44	74.28	70.70	29.92	35.39	15.48	30.71

Government capital called per capita: British capital markets (U.S. dollars)

Years	Argentina-1	Argentina-2	Australia-1	Australia-2	Australia-3	Canada-1	Canada-2	United States-1
1865–1879	1.95	1.98	5.88	4.78	2.16	2.57	0.74	2.26
1880–1899	3.31	3.09	12.26	11.59	4.58	1.37	0.54	0.05
1900–1914	1.05	0.99	6.42	6.44	2.92	4.27	2.15	0.00
1865–1914	2.22	2.13	8.59	7.61	3.36	2.60	1.09	0.70

Notes: (1) In columns designated 1, all government bonds are assigned to the Government sector.
(2) In columns designated 2, government bonds issued in support of railroads are assigned to the Transport sector.
(3) In columns designated 3, government bonds issued in support of the railroads are assigned to the Transport sector as is an estimate of the share of other government expenditures that were directed toward the railroads.

Source: Davis–Gallman, *Investor's Monthly* manual tape.

Table 1:4-5. *Agricultural and extractive capital called: British capital markets (thousands of U.S. dollars)*

Years	Argentina	Australia	Canada	United States
1865–79	913	10,967	6,165	32,532
1880–99	10,269	187,757	33,323	123,917
1900–14	50,473	91,097	112,818	100,339
1865–1914	61,654	289,821	152,306	256,787

Percentage distribution, agricultural and extractive capital called: British capital markets

Years	Argentina	Australia	Canada	United States
1865–79	0.97	5.70	2.51	1.60
1880–99	1.77	19.86	9.26	10.07
1900–14	4.13	16.42	7.56	5.14
1865–1914	3.25	17.12	7.26	4.92

Agricultural and extractive capital called per capita: British capital markets (U.S. dollars)

Years	Argentina	Australia	Canada	United States
1865–79	0.03	0.44	0.11	0.05
1880–99	0.17	3.01	0.36	0.10
1900–14	0.47	1.47	1.05	0.07
1865–1914	0.22	1.78	0.49	0.08

Source: Davis–Gallman, *Investor's Monthly* manual tape.

in the case of the United States, the average level of imports was significantly breached only during the 1870s: 2.3 times the average in the first half and 2.7 times in the second half of the decade. The peak reflected the federal government's successful attempts to refinance its Civil War debt.

In every country, if adjustments are made for funds channeled through the government, transport drew the largest share of British portfolio finance – 74 percent in Argentina, 70 percent in Canada, 54 percent in the United States, and 46 percent in Australia (see Table 1:4-6). Obviously, even in the case of the transport sector, there were intercountry differences. There were, however, even more marked differences

Table 1:4-6. *Transport capital called: British capital markets (thousands of U.S. dollars)*

Years	Argentina-1	Argentina-2	Australia-1	Australia-2	Australia-3	Canada-1	Canada-2	United States-1
1865–1879	32,573	32,573	7,226	38,566	110,868	84,788	194,358	418,919
1880–1899	331,172	336,701	3,962	37,952	428,836	179,211	258,904	838,748
1900–1914	987,699	1,025,705	3,299	4,995	232,096	771,034	1,010,580	1,584,072
1865–1914	1,351,444	1,394,979	14,487	81,513	771,800	1,035,033	1,463,842	2,841,739

Percentage distribution of coutry's total transport capital called: British capital markets

Years	Argentina-1	Argentina-2	Australia-1	Australia-2	Australia-3	Canada-1	Canada-2	United States-1
1865–1879	34.51	34.51	4.50	20.04	57.62	34.53	79.16	20.55
1880–1899	57.14	58.02	0.58	4.01	45.35	49.94	71.96	68.14
1900–1914	83.43	83.94	0.80	0.90	41.83	51.57	67.69	81.10
1865–1914	72.74	73.55	1.15	4.82	45.59	49.30	69.77	54.41

Transport capital called per capita: British capital markets (U.S. dollars)

Years	Argentina-1	Argentina-2	Australia-1	Australia-2	Australia-3	Canada-1	Canada-2	United States-1
1865–1879	1.17	1.17	0.27	1.47	4.09	1.49	3.29	0.66
1880–1899	5.13	4.97	0.06	0.78	7.80	1.93	2.77	0.70
1900–1914	11.4	10.9	0.05	0.08	3.60	7.63	10.03	1.21
1865–1914	5.82	5.61	0.12	0.78	5.43	3.51	5.10	0.84

Notes: (1) In columns designated 1, all government bonds are assigned to the Government sector.
(2) In columns designated 2, government bonds in support of railroads are assigned to the Transport sector.
(3) In columns designated 3, government bonds issued in support of the railroads are assigned to the Transport sector as is an estimate of the share of other government expenditures that were directed to the railroads.

Source: Davis–Gallman tape.

Table 1:4-7. *Public utility capital called: British capital markets (thousands of U.S. dollars)*

Years	Argentina	Australia	Canada	United States
1865–1879	712	3,635	0	28,615
1880–1899	24,668	4,153	3,803	12,769
1900–1914	18,512	6,113	48,800	166,033
1865–1914	43,892	13,902	52,603	207,417

Percentage distribution, public utility capital called: British capital markets

Years	Argentina	Australia	Canada	United States
1865–1879	0.75	1.89	0.00	1.40
1880–1899	4.25	0.44	1.06	1.04
1900–1914	1.51	1.10	3.27	8.50
1865–1914	2.31	0.82	2.51	3.97

Public utility capital called per capita: British capital markets (U.S. dollars)

Years	Argentina	Australia	Canada	United States
1865–1879	0.03	0.13	0.00	0.05
1880–1899	0.36	0.08	0.04	0.01
1900–1914	0.18	0.10	0.46	0.12
1865–1914	0.20	0.10	0.15	0.05

Source: Davis–Gallman, *Investor's Monthly* manual tape.

among the four countries in terms of the industrial distribution of the remainder of the transfers.

In every country the government sector was the second largest beneficiary, but there were substantial country-to-country differences (see Table 1:4-4). In Argentina and Canada the public sector's share averaged between 15 and 20 percent. The average figures for Australia and the United States over the half-century were about three-quarters again as large, but the similarity ends there. In Australia the numbers seldom deviated far from the three in ten average. In the American case, however, the government drew three-quarters of the total over the first three quinquennia, but only twelve *cents* of every one hundred *dollars* over the last six.

In both the United States and Canada, manufacturing and commerce drew about 5 percent of the total, but in Argentina and Australia the proportion was between 1 and 2 percent (see Table 1:4-2). Finance drew only about 1 percent of the total in Argentina, Canada, and the United States, but more than 5 percent in Australia (see Table 1:4-3). The agricultural and extractive industries absorbed less than 5 percent of all British finance in Argentina and the United States, about half that amount again in Canada, but more than three times that 5 percent benchmark in Australia (see Table 1:4-5). Finally, Australian public utilities drew less than 1 percent of the total, a reflection of the all-encompassing role of government (see Table 1:4-7).

Given the differences in the level, timing, and composition of the British capital flows, it is not surprising that the domestic capital markets evolved quite differently in the four countries. It is the relationship between the flows and the development of the local markets that is the subject of most of the remainder of this book.

Finally, returning to the question of why British savers chose to channel their resources into overseas investments, the evidence strongly suggests that the London-based transfers were driven by demand in the frontier countries rather than by an excess supply of capital in the home country. Since there is no reason to believe that investment opportunities in one frontier country were temporally associated with those in another, if the transfers were demand driven, one would not expect a high level of correlation between the flotations of one country and those of another. If, on the other hand, they were supply driven, one would expect a fairly high degree of temporal correlation. Table 1:4-8 displays the coefficients of determination between the annual total capital calls of each pair of countries. Overall, there is little evidence of any significant degree of association between them. The coefficients – the fraction of the variation in the flow to one country that can be explained by the flow to the other – range from a high of 0.10 in the Canada–Argentine pair to a low of 0.04 for the Australia-U.S. regression, and none are statistically different from zero. Nor does disaggregation do much to improve the apparent level of temporal association. For the six industries in the four countries, there are thirty-six pairs of series of annual capital calls. For ten of those comparisons, the coefficients are less than 0.01; for eight the coefficients are between 0.01 and 0.05; for another six they are between 0.05 and 0.10; and for seven between 0.10 and 0.20. In only five of the thirty-six pairs does the explanatory power of the calls from one country account for more than one-fifth of the variation of the flow to the other. Of the five that are marked by coefficients greater than 0.20, the largest are for the Argentina-Canada Manufacturing & Com-

Table 1:4-8. *R2 matrix: capital created and called on the British capital markets, four frontier countries, 1865–1914, all capital*

Country	Argentina	Australia	Canada	United States
Argentina	1.000			
Australia	0.027	1.000		
Canada	0.104	0.049	1.000	
United States	0.001	0.004	0.026	1.000

Source: Davis–Gallman, *Investors' Monthly* manual tape.

merce and the Agriculture & Extractive comparisons – a product, no doubt, of the worldwide wheat boom. In those two cases the explanatory power reaches almost one-half. For the other three pairs in the over 0.20 set, the coefficients suggest that about one-quarter of the variance can be explained. Taken together, the evidence from both the total and the disaggregated calls strongly suggests that for the four frontier countries at least, the size and composition of the capital flotations reflected conditions of domestic demand rather than either the conditions prevailing in the British economy or the political decisions of Her Majesty's government that might have affected supply.

1-5. Conclusions

History can provide lessons that may be useful to present-day policy makers. It may have been coincidental, but the policy ultimately adopted by the Mexican government to solve the debt crisis of the 1980s was essentially the same policy that was used by Alexander Hamilton to solve the Revolutionary War debt crisis of two centuries earlier.[44] In 1782 the federal government defaulted on its domestic debts and its debts to France. In 1790 Alexander Hamilton, then Secretary of the Treasury, launched a plan to convert outstanding federal and state debt into long-term bonds and created mechanisms to both service and amortize the debt.[45] An analysis of Hamilton's plan probably did not contribute to the

[44] Peter M. Gerber, "Alexander Hamilton's Market-Based Debt Reduction Plan," *Carnegie-Rochester Conference Series on Public Policy*, Vol. 35 (1991), pp. 79–104.

[45] Michael D. Bordo and Carlos A. Vegh, "If Only Alexander Hamilton Had Been Argentinean: A Comparison of the Early Monetary Experiences of Argentina and the United States," paper delivered to NBER Monetary Group, summer 1995, pp. 24–5. Edwin J. Perkins, *American Public Finance and Financial Services* (Columbus: Ohio State University Press, 1994), pp. 108–9, 218.

solution of the Mexican debt crisis, but one of the functions of economic history is to provide a perspective on current economic problems. Take, for example, the experience of American commercial banks in the 1980s – banks that were responsible for a growing fraction of the total U.S. foreign commitment – and compare the problems that those banks faced with their loans to Mexican banks with the experience of British savers with Australian banks during the 1890s. In the earlier case, by placing their funds in time deposits, British investors thought they were making intermediate-term (six months to two years) investments in the activities (self-extinguishing commercial credit and bills of exchange) that were normally supported by commercial banks. The Australian banks, however, quickly recycled those deposits into long-term loans to companies engaged in pastoral finance and in urban real-estate development. When the deposits matured in 1893, the banks found themselves unable to repay the principal. Savers suffered very substantial losses; however, a significant share of the medium-term deposits were converted into either long-term certificates of deposit or into preferred shares. The final adjustment was an institutional innovation: the development of a secondary market for those certificates and shares in both Australia and London.

Almost a century later the supposedly more sophisticated New York banks were led to take on Mexican loans that they were ill-equipped to either handle or monitor. The banks assumed that they were making short-term loans, but the Mexican banks quickly converted them into long-term commitments. Again, as in 1893, the loans went into default. Some losses were suffered, but the primary solution was again, as in 1893, a financial innovation. This time the New York banks found themselves obliged to invent a secondary market, a market where the so-called short-term debt instruments could be marketed and traded as equities.

A second use of history is to assemble the data needed to test the perceptions of historical development that underlie economists' current efforts to understand the real world. A third is to describe how countries, empires, trading blocs, or the entire world have moved from one regime to another – that is, from a system dominated by one set of institutions to one governed by a quite different set. Although recent events in Eastern Europe and in China have tended to underscore the importance of the third, over the long-term all three have proved to be important. Economic historians are concerned with the implications of economic history for understanding current problems. Both the comparative analysis of the different paths followed by the four frontier countries as their savings and investment patterns shifted and as their financial sectors evolved and the understanding of the role played by foreign capital in shaping those evolutionary paths that an examination of their histories provide have implications for our understanding of current economic problems.

Recently economists have become preoccupied with the relations among deficit finance (public and private, but chiefly the former), trade deficits, and capital flows. This book casts some light on those questions. The histories of the four frontier countries all provide examples of these connected phenomena. In contrast to current circumstances, however, the deficits in three of the frontier countries were chiefly private, not public. Their relative scales were very different, running from quite modest ones for the United States – deficits that turned to frequent surpluses before the close of the period – to very substantial ones indeed in the case of Canada. There were clear macro-consequences that parallel modern developments, cases where foreign capital was an effective engine of growth. There is also, among the four, one example – Argentina – of a country that after achieving substantial success in the pre–World War I decades ended with ultimate failure – again a case that has modern parallels.

There are also modern lessons of another type. For example, in the case of the United States, British capital markets played an important role in promoting development, even though the volume of British capital entering the country was relatively small. British investors were much more experienced and sophisticated than were their American counterparts. In order to assure less sophisticated and skittish American investors of the quality of a new issue or paper security offered, trusted investment bankers – bankers like J.P. Morgan – successfully offered potential investors their imprimaturs as a quality signal. They, of course, earned monopoly profits in the process. In the secondary market, stringent rules were imposed on firms seeking to list their securities on the New York Stock Exchange (NYSE). Firms that could not, or would not, meet these rules were not accommodated. Those firms, however, had alternatives. On the one hand, they could enter the British markets, markets populated with far better educated savers. And indeed many an American promoter boarded a ship bound for England with a satchel full of securities to sell in London, the provinces, or on the less stringently constrained London Stock Exchange. On the other hand, the NYSE was not the only domestic secondary market, and the representatives of the "excluded" firms could choose to list their securities on one of the less-regulated domestic markets – the Consolidated or the Curb in New York or local markets in such cities as Boston, Philadelphia, Chicago, or San Francisco – although, if they chose that route, they were forced to recognize that the potential market was limited to savers with local information and to the still relatively small number of educated American savers. Taken together, the J.P. Morgans, the NYSE, the British alternative, and even the local domestic exchanges promoted American growth at a time when most American savers were still not willing to support the activities in question. British savers were well rewarded; but at the same time, in the protected American credit markets, investors were being educated in the potential profitability of paper assets. Again, in the case of Canada, bond dealers devised methods of successfully distributing securities – methods that did not depend on the thin Canadian securities markets. The institutional innovations in the two countries can be thought of as species of Romer-type externalities, and those institutions helped endogenize growth. It was this kind of transition that Argentina failed to make.

There are also parallels in the modern world for developing nations of the Canadian, U.S., and Argentine molds. Between World War II and the early 1980s, the United States played the British role. Between 1946 and 1980, American private long-term overseas investment exceeded foreign long-term investment in the United States by more than $125 billion. Of that total, perhaps one-third was directed toward the underdeveloped world. In the 1980s a new leader emerged, and for a decade and a half the Japanese supplied the greatest volume of foreign investment. Between 1965 and 1980 the volume of that country's private long-term direct investment rose steadily, and much of it was directed toward the developing world. Although the Asian "tigers" were the major beneficiaries, between 1951 and 1980 the countries of Latin America drew about one-quarter of the direct less developed country (LDC) total.[46] Since 1980 the largest portion of Japanese savings has been directed toward the United States and Western Europe, but a not insignificant fraction of total direct investment – some $40 billion over the 1980s – was channeled to the Asian and Latin American less developed countries (LDCs). Over the three decades from 1965 to 1995, Japan, in its relationship with the Asian Newly Industrializing Countries (NICS) and the developing countries of Latin America, appears to have played a smaller, but somewhat similar, role to the one Britain assumed in the late nineteenth and early twentieth centuries. Despite recent setbacks, the majority of the "tigers" and one or two – but not all – of the Latin

---

[46] Kwang W. Jun, Frank Sader, Haruo Horaguchi, and Hyuntai Kwak, "Japanese Foreign Direct Investment: Recent Trends, Determinants and Prospects," The World Bank, International Economics Department, Debt and International Finance Divisions, Policy Research Working Paper No. 1213, November 1993. The region's total could have been higher, since they may have received some part of the $31 billion that went to the Caribbean Six.

American countries appear all but assured of a long-run successful transition, and institutional innovation – innovation partly shaped by the availability of Japanese capital – will almost certainly have contributed to that transition. Policy makers, however, might ask if the impact of the innovation of a "Japanese type" financial structure may also have contributed to the present-day troubles in the two regions.

The future evolutionary path of the financial structure in the former Soviet republics provides an even more striking example of the potential impact of foreign capital. In a region where the problems of both accumulation and mobilization have historically been solved by government fiat, existing financial markets are, to say the least, thin. If capital is imported from the United States, Japan, and Western Europe, and if foreign capital encourages capital deepening in the former republics, the lessons drawn from the histories of the four frontier countries could help policy makers design efficient innovations in their financial infrastructures, while at the same time avoiding disastrous mistakes: Not all foreign-capital-induced innovations are necessarily efficient or stable. Policy makers should remember the case of Australia.

The study of the four also clearly demonstrates that some financial innovations were better managed in the pre–World War I period than they have been in recent years, and that there is still room for financial innovation. In terms of the historical scenario, for "the United States" write "Mexico" and for "the sophisticated British investors" substitute "New York banks." In reflecting on the contrast between past and present in a similar context, Albert Fishlow notes:

> The present institutional structure has much to do with the difference. Unlike in the past, commercial banks are not merely intermediaries but also the final holder of loans. Investment banks were [in the earlier period] immune from financial loss from a declining value of foreign securities. That market verdict affected the wealth of others; the banks' task was to make the best of it, which depended on some sharing of the burden between debtor and creditor to facilitate recovery. The dispersion of bondholders concentrated decision authority in the hands of the merchant banks. One of the objectives of present policy is to preserve bank solvency and to prevent systemic distress. The means of doing so is forcing the real burden on the debtor countries. When Baring Brothers was caught with Argentine securities in 1890, moreover, the Bank was bailed out (at some expense to the partners) rather than letting it fail; Argentina was not held responsible.[47]

---

[47] Albert Fishlow, "Lessons from the Past: Capital Markets During the Nineteenth Century and the Interwar Period," *Industrial Organization*, Vol. 39, No. 3 (summer 1985), p. 437 [Hereafter cited as Fishlow, "Lessons from the Past"].

In the case of the Mexican loans of the 1980s, as in the earlier period, the problem was finally solved by innovation in the financial sector.

There are two respects in which an exploration of the differences between the earlier and the modern world are instructive. First, in the earlier period, overseas – largely British – investors were chiefly interested in equities and long-term debt. Certainly there was substantial trade credit, but the financial world was not troubled then, as it is now, by large, changing, destabilizing, short-term capital movements. Consequently, in the past capital inflows – inflows that were in large part generated at the initiative of the borrowers and of the issuers of equities – were not surrounded by ambiguity. Those flows were, from the point of view of the recipients, on the whole clearly desirable. While those who found themselves in competition with foreign capital raised some doubts about the usefulness of those infusions, there were no doubts of the order of magnitude of those held by debtors today.

Second, in the modern world, large capital inflows tend to put the exchange rate under pressure; if the rate is held fixed, they tend to generate inflation. In the frontier countries in the earlier period, exchange rates were typically fixed, and most often the production response to investment came so quickly and on such a scale that inflationary forces were moderated. Even while they were still under construction, canals and railroads often tended to open agricultural regions along the right of way; as a result, investment in transport was frequently able to trigger a productivity response within one or two growing seasons. The opening of the prairie provinces in Canada involved an enormous investment, much of it obtained from overseas. Canadian prices, however, followed the pattern of world prices, drifting upward gently after the mid-1890s, without generating significant domestic problems.

At a somewhat higher level of generality, and focusing on the issue of historical relevance from a slightly different angle, this book also provides the basis for coming to terms with two quite different sets of issues. On one level, can our understanding of the past make it possible to theorize about – and perhaps predict – the future? Albert Fishlow, in his seminal article "Lessons from the Past," has suggested that a reading of Latin American history should have raised warning signals about American-held debt before the crisis of the 1980s.[48] Nor was the debt crisis a unique event. There are a number of twentieth-

---

[48] Fishlow, "Lessons from the Past."

century policy issues that appear to have had a nineteenth-century parallel, and this old-new study offers the possibility of exploring the similarities or differences of the observed outcomes. For example, the American experience in the earlier era suggests that portfolio investment in American-controlled industries such as railroads appear to have produced far less adverse political response than direct investment in agriculture. Do we still find that there has been less adverse response to American or Japanese portfolio investment than to direct financial intrusion?

On a much more general level, the study permits us to explore just how far it is possible to explain or predict the relationship between foreign finance and the evolving structure of capital markets in the receiving countries. Did similar patterns of foreign investment produce similar patterns of institutional innovation? For example, the decisions of Canadian national and provincial governments and of the nation's railroads to focus their financial attention on London meant that first cities and then private companies were able to exploit the domestic market. In the absence of investment bankers with recognized status, or a national stock exchange with a reputation for a high level of selectivity, the informational asymmetries led in the short run to firms bypassing the formal markets and in the long run to the dominance of the bond houses in industrial finance. In the United States, on the other hand, governments and railroads preempted the formal securities markets, and that preemption initially induced firms in new industries and in developing regions to turn abroad for a significant fraction of their external financial demands. The institutional counterparts of the bond house were the second-generation Anglo-American and the third-generation American investment banks. Over time, informational asymmetries were overcome both by the emergence of those intermediaries and by the evolving micro-structure of rules adopted by formal securities markets.

In the recent past American financial institutions have absorbed large quantities of the bonds of developing nations. Given the explicit encouragement of the federal government, it was initially assumed that those issues carried an implicit U.S. government guarantee; but time proved that assumption false. How, then, has this policy affected the domestic capital markets and what institutions have emerged to overcome the informational asymmetries; that is, has some counterpart of the Canadian bond house or the American investment bank begun to evolve in these developing countries? Comparative historical studies in general, and we, in this study in particular, provide a basis for exploring these types of issues.

Appendix: The role of financial intermediaries in decisions to save and invest

Given the recent transformation of the United States from a nation of high gross and net savers to one whose aggregate savings rates pale even in comparison with the very low rates observed in the underdeveloped world, questions about the determinants of savings must remain high on the agenda of any economist concerned with issues of long-term growth and development.[49] Despite the importance of the issue, it is not the purpose of this book to explain the aggregate savings rate, nor to assess the relative contribution of such factors as personal income, demography, and occupational structure to the savings/consumption decision. It is, however, partly its purpose to suggest that improvements in the financial infrastructure, in addition to mobilizing capital more efficiently, can, by reducing transaction and search costs, increase net returns to savers and reduce the net cost of capital to firms. Although the evidence suggests that savings are at least somewhat interest-elastic, more importantly, the evidence also indicates that innovations in intermediation cause an outward shift in the savings supply schedule and thus produce higher aggregate savings.

Theory suggests that improvements in intermediation can affect the savings-investment process in any of three ways. First, they may reduce transaction costs and therefore increase net returns to savers, and they may reduce the gross costs that firms must bear to realize any required net level of finance. The question of the relative gains to the two parties will depend on the elasticities of supply and demand. Second, the interposition of an intermediary can reduce the level of asymmetrical information between the saver and the receiving firm and, as a result, diminish the uncertainty discounts attached to the particular investment and increase the expected net (after discount) return to savers. Third, such improvements may increase the liquidity of any asset, and, to the extent that the saver is risk-averse, make the asset appear "safer" and therefore more "profitable" at any given rate of return. All of these effects will tend to shift the savings supply schedule to the right.

Transaction costs can be divided into two categories: search costs and negotiation costs. The former include the costs incurred by the firm seeking finance and those borne by the saver as he searches for a profitable outlet for his accumulation. The latter include both the costs of bargaining between saver and investor and the purely administrative costs involved in effecting the transaction. Since an innovation in inter-

---

[49] The Bureau of Commerce reported that the private savings rate was negative in October 1998.

mediation can reduce both search and negotiation costs, it will usually yield a higher net return to the saver, and to the extent that savings are responsive to changes in relative prices, it will produce an increase in the savings rate. Where the institutional structure is primitive and financial markets not well developed, search costs are high – and particularly high when there is a marked geographical or occupational distance between saver and investor. Moreover, since information once generated about those distant alternatives can frequently be used by many savers and investors at little extra cost, there are usually substantial economies of scale inherent in any institutionalization of the search procedure. Similarly, the administrative costs of negotiating a number of small loans may be prohibitive to a potential demander, and a supplier may respond in a similar fashion to the requirement that he devote time and energy to administering one of a large number of small loans. An intermediary, however, can pool the resources of a number of savers and make a single large loan, and, given the new structure, the burden on the saver may be no more than the time or energy it takes to deposit his accumulation in a bank or similar institution.

Not only are transaction costs reduced by financial innovation, but those same innovations often make potential investments appear "safer" from the saver's point of view. Since hoards can be stolen, one might argue that they have negative returns; but, under any conditions, unless the saver can utilize the savings himself, if savings are to earn a positive return, they must be surrendered to someone. In the absence of intermediation, to the extent that they are indivisible, such transfers are often subject to substantial variance in returns, and regardless of whether or not they were indivisible, they were almost always illiquid. Savers tend to be risk-averse, and those who are tend to heavily discount both assets with a high variance in returns and those that are illiquid. Once again, to the extent that savings decisions are responsive to such "outside forces," those discounts, by making consumption relatively more attractive, hold savings rates down. Financial intermediaries can pool the accumulations of many individual savers and invest that pool in a wide variety of assets, thus insuring the savers against fluctuations in any particular asset. Similarly, liquidity can be furnished by the innovation of formal securities markets – markets that provide a place where public and private paper securities can be easily turned into cash, a direct benefit for the saver and a benefit generated indirectly by the additional flexibility it provides the financial intermediaries. Finally, the uncertainty discounts placed by the saver on little-known investments can be reduced by innovations that lower the price of information and by new intermediaries (a known alternative) that are interposed between the saver and the investor (frequently an unknown quantity).[50]

Although most scholars agree that innovations in intermediation can increase savings rates, there are questions about the effect of inter-mediation on the supply schedule.[51] Much of the work, like the original Davis-Gallman studies cited earlier, is drawn from an analysis of the American experience. In that country the domestic savings rose from about 15 percent of GNP in 1850 to about 25 percent in 1880, and that increase was particularly pronounced over the course of the Civil War. Paul David (writing by himself and with a number of co-authors), for example, argues that the savings schedule was very elastic at the going rates of return on money, and that it is best to think of the chief devel-opments in this market as consisting of rightward movements of both the supply and demand schedules. Although he acknowledges that there was a shift in the supply schedule, and that the shift was partly due to improvements in intermediation, David believes that the movement of the demand schedule was more important in terms of the observed nineteenth-century increase in the savings rate.[52] The elasticity of supply is important to David because he must square his notion of a rapidly growing demand for capital with the generally acknowledged fact that the real return on savings was falling. Were savings highly interest-elastic? David sets out to adduce some evidence to that effect. To that end he describes changes in the economy that might have freed uncon-ventional forms of savings for conventional purposes. For example, since family size was declining, the typical family at midcentury faced more claims against it for child rearing (investment in human capital) than did the typical family at the beginning of the next century. Therefore, *ceteris paribus*, it had a greater ability to save. But presumably in 1900 each child

---

[50] For a more detailed discussion of these points see Davis and Gallman, "The Share of Savings"; Davis and Gallman, "Capital Formation" (particularly pp. 49–50 and 59–65).

[51] The following discussion draws very heavily on Davis and Gallman, "Savings, Investment, and Economic Growth."

[52] Paul A. David, "Invention and Accumulation in America's Economic Growth: A Nineteenth Century Parable," in K. Brunner and A. Meltzer (eds.), *International Organization, Public Policies and Economic Development* (Amsterdam: North Holland Press, 1977). See also Moses Abromowitz and Paul A. David, "Economic Growth in America: Historical Parallels and Realities," *The Economist*, Vol. 121 (1973), pp. 251–72, and "Reinterpreting Economic Growth: Parallels and Realities of the American Experience," *American Economic Review, Papers and Proceedings*, Vol. 63 (May 1973), pp. 428–39. See also Paul A. David and John L. Scadding, "Private Savings: Ultrarationality, Aggregation, and 'Denison's Law,'" *Journal of Political Economy*, Vol. 82 (1973), pp. 225–49.

cost more because it was given more schooling. Overall, David's evidence appears less compelling than that supporting the alternative story that the major effect of innovations in intermediation was a shift in the supply schedule. Thus, unless better reasons for the assumed highly elastic savings schedule can be adduced, it is difficult to conclude that demand was *the* primary active agent (as David argues); instead, it appears that changes in attitudes toward "thrift" played a more important role than he recognized.

Michael Edelstein made an important contribution to the argument in his work on overseas investment in the late nineteenth century.[53] While placing the main emphasis of his explanation of the increase in the savings rate on the changes in the age structure of the population and on the functional distribution of income, he also argues that the remaining part of the 1854–71 rise was associated with an increase in the real interest rate, and that improvements in intermediation were a response to the considerable investment demand pressures that produced the high interest rates. Edelstein concludes that this interpretation is at odds with the belief that savings rates increased because of institutional innovation, but it almost certainly is not. Although it is generally recognized that institutional innovations normally arise in response to economic needs – that is, that invention and innovation are demand-driven – the ability to invent and innovate is, at least in part, independent of demand conditions. Thus, while improvements in technology (including the financial infrastructure) may only rarely be regarded as an initiating factor in growth, such innovations can still be major permissive factors. In the U.S. case, it appears that they triggered an increase in the returns from savings relative to those from consumption and thus induced consumers to substitute savings for consumption.

John James and Jonathan Skinner approach the problem from a different direction. Instead of examining savings or investment or the capital/output ratio, they focus their attention on the wealth/income ratio. They find that the ratio rose from 1850 to 1890, and they believe that the increase reflects the same forces that underlay the contemporary shifts in the savings/income and capital/output ratios. They conclude that about 23 percent of the increase in the wealth/income ratio was due to demographic factors, 61 percent to the structure of occupations, and a minimum of 16 percent to improved intermediation. The role they assign to occupational shifts seems rather too large, but the authors themselves point out that their occupational variable may be picking up other factors: ". . . to the extent that high-savings occupations had better

[53] Edelstein, *Overseas Investment.*

access to financial markets and institutions, at least part of the influence of the changing occupational mix on asset accumulation may be attributed to financial intermediation."[54]

More recently Jeffrey Williamson has argued that the major impetus for the upward movement in the savings ratios came, not from innovations in intermediation, but from increasing investment demand and the decline in capital goods prices.[55] Williamson makes use of a general equilibrium model to decompose the change in the savings rate into its constituent parts and to estimate the contribution of each part to the total change. He acknowledges that his conclusions depend crucially on his estimate of the interest elasticity of savings; however, he feels that the most plausible estimate of the elasticity is unity, and that figure is the basis for his "most likely" case. To the extent that his model captures reality and his estimate of interest elasticity is correct, 53 percent of the observed change can be attributed to the impact of investment demand, 21 percent to the redistribution of income, and 29 percent to the decline in the price of capital goods. Obviously, this leaves a negligible share (−3 percent) to be attributed to "exogenous savings mobilization."

Williamson recognizes that this last conclusion is at variance not only with the standard interpretation of U.S. growth but also with the recent development literature, and he attributes his "trivial and negative" findings to two factors, one historical and one rooted in his estimation procedures. First, he argues that there was the historical tendency for the United States to substitute domestic for foreign financing. In reality, however, this tendency was very slight – the lion's share of American financing was domestic throughout – and, therefore, substitution could hardly be a major element in any explanation of the savings/investment process. Second, since he estimated the impact of mobilization as a residual, he admits that his estimate of that residual would be biased downward if the impact of any of his other three variables was exaggerated; and the evidence suggests that such exaggeration is very likely to be the case.

In addition, Williamson does not fully treat two other sources of difficulty in his analysis. First, improvements in intermediation and the capital markets may have permitted potential investment demand to be translated into effective demand; the introduction of new technology and the resulting increase in the demand for capital may have, at least in part,

---

[54] James and Skinner, "Sources of Savings."

[55] Jeffrey G. Williamson, *Inequality, Poverty, and History: The Kuznets Memorial Lectures of the Economic Growth Center, Yale University* (Oxford: Basil Blackwell, 1991).

been a response to changes in the financial infrastructure that made capital less expensive. Second, the evidence supporting Williamson's choice of the interest elasticity of savings (1.0) is very weak. Michael Boskin, for example, has argued that the elasticity might have been as high as 0.3, but, both before and since, most economists have concluded that it is more likely 0.1 or less. A recalculation of Williamson's results using more plausible elasticities changes his conclusions markedly. If the elasticity were as high as Boskin concludes "it might have been," the "exogenous savings contribution" would have been 9 percent; if the elasticity were the more likely 0.1, the contribution would have been 21 percent; and if, in the extreme and unlikely case, the elasticity were 0.0, the contribution of the innovations in the financial system would have been almost 33 percent.

The work of Raymond Goldsmith provides indirect support for the financial innovation hypothesis, although certainly more research could provide better evidence of the magnitude of the observed shift.[56] Goldsmith found that the fraction of financial assets in all U.S. national assets rose from 23 to 54 percent between early in the nineteenth century and 1929, and that there is little evidence of further change thereafter. Moreover, of the 31 percent increase, currency and demand deposits accounted for only slightly more than one percentage point; the share of government debt actually declined slightly, and the share of trade credit fell even further. The increase was concentrated in non-bank intermediaries – other deposits, insurance and pension funds, and mortgages (together nine percentage points) – and in the stocks and bonds of private corporations (twenty percentage points).

Goldsmith also found that the American secular pattern was repeated in the balance sheets of other developed nations but not in those of the underdeveloped world. For example, the rise in the proportion of financial to all assets in Europe closely paralleled the American movements, but the figures for underdeveloped countries (India, for example) showed no similar pattern, while those for developing countries (Mexico and Yugoslavia) followed paths intermediate between those of the developed and those of the less-developed world. Goldsmith concluded that "national balance sheets by themselves cannot answer the crucial question of the role of the financial superstructure in economic growth. They indicate, however, that modern economic growth has been accompanied in all market economies in the early and intermediate stages of their development by a substantially more than proportionate expansion of

---

[56] Raymond W. Goldsmith, *Comparative National Balance Sheets: A Study of Twenty Countries, 1688–1978* (Chicago: University of Chicago Press, 1985).

their financial structure. This suggests that the expansion is a necessary concomitant of economic development in countries of this type until they reach maturity."

Qualitative evidence also suggests that the response of savings to improvements in the financial system may have been even greater in early stages of economic development when a relatively sophisticated financial system suddenly replaces a much more primitive one. Contemporary records are replete with statements concerning the impact of new financial institutions on personal savings decisions. For example, in the words of one of the Directors of the Savings Bank of Baltimore:

> There are on the books of the Institution some pleasing instances of the rapid increase in small sums regularly deposited by persons who, persevering in economy and sobriety, are enabled weekly to save a part of their earnings and thus secure for themselves and families a resource in sickness and old age. How different must be the hopes and future prospects of the poor wretches who spend a like proportion of their earnings in grog shops to the utter ruin of themselves, and the misery of their families; besides forfeiting all claims to the mercy of the offended Deity.[57]

Or again, "the Institution recommends itself to the rich who can, by their influence, do much to preserve the poor from becoming burdens on the community and to the poor by its tendency to foster the habits which will avert the evils of dependence on the cold and uncertain charities of the world."[58] Nor were the observations limited to the United States. Across the Atlantic at about the same time, the Reverend Mr. Gillan made the following remarks concerning a man given to smoking a pipe:

> "If he had saved the money spent on this debauchery between the ages of twenty and fifty, he would have had in the Savings Bank £72:18:11, hard heavy glittering gold" instead of "a nasty, offensively smelling, muddefying narcotic weed – for which, in the shape of return, he gets smoke and fumes, as if his body was on fire and the flames twisting out at the garret, and ashes, and blackened burned pipes, with an unnatural precocity of parts, ending in premature decay."[59]

Moreover, those early-nineteenth-century contemporaries were well aware of the basis for their conclusions about the impact of finan-

---

[57] "Minutes and Proceedings of the Board of Directors," the Savings Bank of Baltimore, January 14, 1819.

[58] "Minutes and Proceedings," January 5, 1832, Report of the Audit Committee.

[59] Cited in H.O. Thorne, *A History of Savings Banks* (London: Oxford University Press, 1947), pp. 138–9.

cial innovation on consumer choice. At that time a majority of the population was in the unhappy position of having neither a secure place to keep their savings nor the means of investing them with any safety. In the words of one English author:

> The laboring man can make no profit on money retained. He also lies under many chances of being able to preserve it. The coarse and imperfect means of shutting his house or any receptacle which it may contain exposes his little treasures to the hand even of a clumsy depredator. Accordingly we find that persons in the lower situation of life who acquire a reputation for the possession of hoards are almost always robbed. If they are disposed to lend the fruit of their industry and frugality, their limited experience of mankind makes them yield to the man who takes the most pains to persuade them; and that is often the man who never means to pay them again, and who has therefore the strongest resolve to take the measures necessary for gaining their confidence.[60]

Taking all of the evidence together, it seems reasonable to conclude that a number of forces affected savings, and among those forces were financial innovation and the growth of intermediation – two changes that reduced net charges for capital while increasing net returns to savers. Moreover, those changes almost certainly shifted the supply schedule of savings to the right.

---

[60] Quoted in ibid., p. 21.

CHAPTER 2

The United Kingdom

2-1. Introduction

It was not that British savers were born with a lesser degree of aversion to uncertainty than their counterparts in the four frontier countries, it was simply that Britain had begun to develop earlier, and by the middle of the nineteenth century the process of educating savers had proceeded much further than it had in the outlands. Although a double-digit savings rate was not achieved until the early decades of that century, capital had been accumulating in trade and commerce for at least 300 years. It may well have been true, as Postan has noted, that at least two fifteenth-century families could have provided all the finance required to fund the entire Industrial Revolution. However, those (and other elite) families chose not to redirect their existing portfolios, to meet either the relatively small demands of the manufacturing sector – demands that were met largely out of retained earnings – or, much more importantly, the demands for supporting investment in infrastructure, particularly canal construction.

Although her findings have been subject to criticism, Elise S. Brezis has concluded that from 1740 to the end of the century the national savings rate, although rising, rose by substantially less than the investment rate. As a result, for the century as a whole, given the level of military expenditures, domestic savings were insufficient to finance the observed level of investment, and there was a need for foreign capital imports. She concludes that "foreign capital flows, in great majority Dutch, financed budget deficits, investments, and investments in the colonies."[61] R.C. Nash disputes Brezis's estimates of the deficits in the balance of payment and concludes that the capital inflows were substantially smaller. He estimates that the accumulated net foreign indebtedness was probably nearer £18 million in the 1780s and £31 million a

---

[61] Elise S. Brezis, "Foreign Capital Flows in the Century of Britain's Industrial Revolution: New Estimates, Controlled Conjectures," *Economic History Review*, Vol. XLVIII, No. 1 (February 1995), pp. 55–56 and table 2, p. 51.

decade later.[62] More recently J.F. Wright has put foreign holdings of British government "registered bonds and trading stock" at £9.85 million in 1750 and at more than £23 million in 1781. He concludes that over the three decades those holdings averaged something more than 15 percent of the total issues of the British government.[63] Thus, it appears that although Brezis's estimates may well be too high, foreign savers made it possible for Britain to continue to industrialize and fight a series of major wars at the same time.

Moreover, not only was the domestic saving rate insufficient to finance domestic investment, but mobilization problems also persisted throughout the eighteenth century. A promising experiment in investor education had collapsed with the South Sea Bubble in 1720. As a result, although economic returns to investments in agriculture may have been close to zero, and investments in the new industries were earning between 25 and 30 percent, domestic savings continued to flow into agriculture, but not into industry.[64]

Similarly, until the 1840s the capital needed to finance the transport network was for the most part raised locally from merchants and gentlemen farmers who saw the immediate benefits of a transport system that would integrate their businesses into the national market. Among the few exceptions were Lancashire businessmen, who, because of profits they had earned on their investments in the Liverpool and Manchester Railway, were prepared to commit their savings to some relatively distant railroad ventures.[65] The local investors "were employing their funds in a tangible venture that could be closely watched. In contrast to manufacturing concerns using exotic technologies, where more amorphous forms of capital mattered (receivables, for example), neither local railroads nor canals required extreme levels of investor sophistication." Similarly, in Scotland savers did not display the same levels of sophisti-

---

[62] R.C. Nash, "The Balance of Payments and Foreign Capital Flows in Eighteenth-Century England: A Comment," *Economic History Review*, Vol. 50, No. 1 (February 1997), pp. 110–28. Brezis responds that Nash's adjustments, if done correctly, would only slightly reduce her overall figures. Elise S. Brezis, "Did Foreign Capital Flows Finance the Industrial Revolution? A Reply," *Economic History Review*, Vol. 50, No. 1 (February 1997), pp. 129–32.

[63] J.F. Wright, "The Contribution of Overseas Savings to the Funded National Debt of Great Britain, 1750–1815," *Economic History Review*, Vol. 50, No. 6 (November 1997), table 1, p. 658.

[64] See Chapter 1, pp. 15–16.

[65] The original equity issues of the canals were very largely sold locally; however, there is some evidence that the later issues of mortgage bonds had a more geographically diverse clientele.

cation and enterprise that were to be their hallmark later in the century.[66] Michie, for example, writes, "What is immediately obvious concerning the nature of Scottish investment is the early influence of the investor's own locality in determining what he invested in. Much investment was in securities of companies that had been formed to operate not just in Scotland but in the investor's own part of the country." In this respect, then, except for the question of timing, the experience of British firms in raising capital was similar to that of early railroads in both the United States and France.[67]

Even outside of Lancashire the process of investor education had begun, and the first lessons were transmitted through the medium of the national debt. The debt had amounted to £133 million at the end of the Seven Years War. It had risen to £232 million by 1783. And reflecting the cost of the Napoleonic Wars, it had exploded to £844 million by 1819. That figure amounted to more than £40 for every man, woman, and child in the British Isles. In 1817, for example, the annual interest alone (£23 million) was about 75 percent more than the entire prewar government budget.[68]

[66] Jonathan Barron Baskin, "The Development of Corporate Financial Markets in Britain and the United States, 1600–1914: Overcoming Asymmetric Information," *Business History Review*, Vol. 42, No. 2 (summer 1988), pp. 211–12. [Hereafter cited as Baskin, "Financial Markets."] More recently, Larry Neal, citing the same source as Baskin – M.C. Reed, *Investment in Railways in Britain, 1820–1844: A Study in the Development of Capital Markets* (London: Oxford University Press, 1975) – concludes that early railways drew from a much wider geographical range of investors. Perhaps he is referring to the Manchester and Liverpool stockholders to whom Baskin refers. Baskin explains the apparent anomaly in terms of the education effect of the "first highly profitable railroad . . . completed in 1830, linking the port of Liverpool with Manchester, then the largest inland manufacturing center in the world" (p. 212). Larry Neal, "The Response of the London Stock Market to New Issues: Canals, Railways and Empire in the 19th Century," paper prepared for the Allied Social Science Association meetings, Washington, D.C., January 9, 1995, p. 20.

[67] Ranald C. Michie, *Money, Mania and Markets: Investment, Company Promotion and the Stock Exchange in Nineteenth-Century Scotland* (Edinburgh: John Donald, 1981), p. 245. [Hereafter cited as Michie, *Money, Mania and Markets*.] Arthur Stone Dewing, *The Financial Policy of Corporations*, 2 vols. in one, 4th ed. (New York: 1941), p. 64. Charles Elton Freedeman, *Joint Stock Enterprise in France, 1807–1867: From Privileged Company to Modern Corporation* (Chapel Hill: University of North Carolina Press, 1979), p. 30.

[68] This discussion is drawn from M.M. Postan, "Some Recent Problems in Capital Accumulation," *Economic History Review*, 1935 [Hereafter cited as Postan, "Some Recent Problems"], and from a series of lectures delivered at The Johns Hopkins University during the academic year 1954–55 [Hereafter cited as Postan, "Hopkins Lectures"]. Data on the size of the debt and the amount of

By the summer of 1815, Napoleon was defeated, and British savers discovered that their purchases of transferable pieces of paper had proved not to be only a patriotic gesture, but a profitable investment as well.[69] Thus, when the government acted to reduce its war-inflated debt and the supply of bonds began to dry up (in 1844 the yield on government Consols fell to 3 percent for the first time since the Seven Years War), the now more sophisticated savers were prepared to explore other paper alternatives.[70] At first, their choice was the securities of foreign governments, but their financial experience with those issues soon led them to turn inward and focus their attention on domestic securities.[71]

interest payments are from Sydney Homer and Richard Sylla, *A History of Interest Rates*, new 3d ed. (New Brunswick, N.J.: Rutgers University Press, 1991), pp. 188 and 195 [hereafter cited as Homer and Sylla, *Interest Rates*] and from B.R. Mitchell, with the collaboration of Phyllis Dean, *Abstract of British Historical Statistics* (Cambridge: Cambridge University Press, 1962), table 3, p. 8, and table 5, pp. 401–3. [Hereafter cited as Mitchell, *Historical Statistics.*]

[69] Over the years 1800–1815 the yield on Consols averaged 4.79 percent.

[70] In 1853 British government securities (both national and local) accounted for 70 percent of the paid-up capital of the securities quoted on the London Stock Exchange, and a decade later it was still 56 percent; however, by 1913 the figure had declined to less than 14 percent. Morgan and Thomas write, "By 1914 the quoted debt of the central government amounted to only 5% of the value of all quoted securities, and the inclusion of guaranteed and corporation stock would have raised the figure to barely 10%." Ranald C. Michie, *The London and New York Stock Exchanges, 1850–1914* (London: Allen and Unwin, 1987), table 2.3, p. 52. [Hereafter cited as Michie, *London and New York.*] E. Victor Morgan and W.A. Thomas, *The Stock Exchange: Its History and Functions* (London: Elek Books, 1962), p. 113. [Hereafter cited as Morgan and Thomas, *The Stock Exchange.*] By decade, beginning in 1800 and running through 1899, the nominal return on 3% Consols averaged 4.80, 4.57, 3.72, 3.40, 3.26, 3.16, 3.27, 3.19, 2.81, and 2.47 percent. Homer and Sylla, *Interest Rates*, table 19, pp. 193–97.

[71] Between March 1822 and June 1825 Brazil, Argentina, Chile, Colombia, Mexico, and Peru had floated issues on the London Stock Exchange. Until the latter date, those issues, like the French rentes, had been issued and traded at about 80% of par. Beginning in June 1825, however, the prices of the Latin American bonds had plummeted; by the end of the year they were trading at 30–60% of par. Larry Neal, "The First Latin-American Debt Crisis and the Stock Market Crash of 1825," paper delivered at economics workshop, California Institute of Technology, June 6, 1996, figures 2 and 3. [Hereafter cited as Neal, "The First Latin-American Debt Crisis."] Nor did the British savers' experience in the next decade with the issues of American state bonds do much to change their view of foreign issues. In 1841 and 1842 nine states stopped payment of interest on their debt. Two (Michigan and Mississippi) repudiated them outright, Florida "pleaded minority, she was only a territory, a ward of the federal government, when her debt was incurred," but the legislatures of Indiana, Illinois, Louisiana, Arkansas, Pennsylvania, and Maryland merely shrugged their collective

At the same time the largely locally financed railroads were proving to be profitable. Following the seductive advice of Robert Stephenson and George Hudson, British savers turned their attention to the nation's transport network and to a lesser extent toward private gas and water companies.

Through the early 1840s Parliament had authorized only 2,285 miles of domestic railroads, but over the years 1844–47 it approved 9,397 miles of additional construction.[72] Nor did the results of the Hudson Crisis of October 1845 (a crisis in the railway share market) stifle the railroad mania or mirror the effects of the South Sea Bubble on the level of investor education.[73] Although investors who had bought at the top of the market lost money, those who had purchased shares before the mania became hysteria found their long-run returns more than satisfactory. They continued to support railroad construction. In fact, the average rate of growth of the railway network was almost two-thirds again more rapid in the six years after 1845 than it had been in the five years from 1840 through 1845.[74]

Once railroad securities had proved themselves to be safe, the British saver found that he had graduated from grade school. He was now prepared to search out other depersonalized investment alternatives. In a

shoulders and announced that they were unable to pay. Leland H. Jerks, *The Migration of British Capital to 1875* (London: Thomas Nelson and Sons, 1963), p. 103. Reginald C. McGrane, *Foreign Bondholders and American State Debts* (New York: Macmillan, 1935), pp. 265–66.

[72] J.H. Clapham, *An Economic History of Modern Britain: The Early Railway Age, 1820–1850* (Cambridge: Cambridge University Press, 1964), p. 391.

[73] In 1845 the editors of the *Economist* wrote, "Everybody is in the stocks now. Needy clerks, poor tradesmen's apprentices, discarded serving men and bank-rupts – all have entered the ranks of the great moneyed interests." Morgan and Thomas note, "Contemporary writings abound with similar lurid, and doubtless exaggerated, descriptions." Morgan and Thomas, *The Stock Exchange*, p. 108.

See also Asa Briggs, *The Making of Modern England: 1783–1867: The Age of Improvement* (New York: Harper and Row, 1959), p. 296. "As early as 1848 the Court of the Bank of England agreed to the purchase of £2 ½ million of railway debentures and, after 1850, these stocks were finding their way increasingly into the portfolios of commercial banks. Eventually, in 1889, they achieved Trustee status. In the forty years before the First World War, railway stocks were regarded as among the safest of the securities and, after the consol market, that in home rails was among the widest in the House. In 1913, they still accounted for more than 12 percent of the value of the paid-up capital of the securities traded on the London Stock Exchange." Morgan and Thomas, *The Stock Exchange*, p. 110. Michie, *London and New York*, table 2.3, p. 52.

[74] Brian R. Mitchell, *European Historical Statistics, 1750–1970*, abridged edition (New York: Columbia University Press, 1978), table F1, pp. 315–20. [Hereafter cited as Mitchell, *European Statistics*.]

very short period other pieces of paper were deemed acceptable by large numbers of the investing public. For example, investment in all phases of ocean shipping had always been regarded as highly speculative, and that term had been used to refer to the organization of the Cunard and Royal Mail fleets following the passage of the 1837 Letters of Patent Act.[75] By the mid-1850s ownership in both firms was widely held, and their stockholder registers contained the names of many widows and orphans. In short, these firms' stocks and debentures had almost obtained de facto, if not de jure, trusteeship status.[76] Much of the capital required by domestic industry and commerce continued to be raised locally. Profits were high, and most of the growth was concentrated in already established industries. Thus, retained earnings supplemented by additional contributions from existing investors met most of the new demands for finance. London was emerging as the most important formal capital market, and savings were channeled into investment not only through the London and provincial stock exchanges, but also through an increasingly sophisticated set of financial intermediaries.

At the same time British investors seeking paper securities yielding more than the 2 or 3 percent on government Consols began to look abroad. Total British overseas investment at the end of the Napoleonic Wars has been estimated at only about £10 million. Thereafter it grew rapidly: The total reached £208 million by 1850, £1.065 billion by 1875, £2.397 billion by 1900, and £3.990 billion by 1913 (see Tables 2:2-5 and 2:2-6).[77] Over the ninety-five year 1815–1910, the annual transfer from British savers to overseas investments averaged more than £35 million ($172 million). The rate of increase of the investment flow slowed somewhat between 1890 and 1910, but across the earlier period (1820–90) it was more than 5 percent a year.[78] Given the growing sophistication of the British investor, it is only a little surprising to find that when Edward Weatherley, meat merchant and poulterer and master of the London Fishmongers and Poulters Company, died in 1892, his estate – valued at

---

[75] I Victoria C73 allowed the Crown to give to companies by Letters Patent certain of the privileges that hitherto had been attainable only by Charter of Incorporation or Act of Parliament. J.H. Clapham, *An Economic History of Modern Britain. Vol. II: Free Trade and Steel* (Cambridge: Cambridge University Press, 1963), p. 134.

[76] Postan, "Hopkins Lectures."

[77] Albert H. Imlah, *Economic Elements in the Pax Britannica: Studies in British Foreign Trade in the Nineteenth Century* (Cambridge, Mass.: Harvard University Press, 1958), table 4, pp. 70–75. [Hereafter cited as Imlah, *Pax Britannica*.]

[78] The overall 1815–1910 figure (6.1%) is biased upward by the very rapid rate of growth (77% a year) in the first quinquennia. For the entire 95-year period the average annual rate of growth of the flow was 4.8%.

£156,000 – included, in addition to the usual real and personal property and £98,000 in British Consols, bonds of Argentina, Brazil, Chile, China, Egypt, Greece, Hungary, New Zealand, the Ottoman Empire, Russia, Spain, and Uruguay. The inventory also listed, in addition to the issues of a number of British local authorities (Billingsborough, Hounslow, Chingford, and Birchington), the bonds of Quebec City and Ottawa in Canada, of Wellington and New Plymouth in New Zealand, and of Santa Fé in Argentina. Also included were the railroad securities of the Cordoba Central, the Great Indian Peninsula, the Quebec and Latre de John, the Royal Trans Africa, the Russian Consolidated, the Scinde, Punjab and Delhi, and the Temiscanta. Moreover, while British non-government nonrailroad securities (Brentford Gas, London General Omnibus, the London Provincial and the London Joint Stock Banks, as well as the Scottish Widows' Fund) appeared on the list, it also included the issues of a set of miscellaneous foreign enterprises: the Daira Sanieh Corporation, the Oceana and the Transvaal Land Companies, and the East India Tramways.[79] Samuel Crompton's textile mill near Bolton may have appeared "foreign" to the middle-class merchants and the gentlemen farmers of the eighteenth century, but nothing seems to have appeared "foreign" to their nineteenth-century counterparts.

2-2. Income, savings, and investment

Between 1870 and 1914 British Gross National Product increased from £1.155 to £2.743 billion, a rate of growth of just less than 2 percent per year. Although a part of the increase was absorbed by population growth, GNP per capita rose from £37 to £60 – something more than 1 percent a year (see Tables 2:2-1 and 2:2-2). The growth rate of per capita GNP was below the levels experienced by the four frontier countries, but it was only slightly less than the average of Angus Maddison's industrialized countries, and it was much better than many critics have charged – it reached almost 2 percent in the 1890s and more than 2.5 percent during the last quinquennium before World War I.[80]

In 1910 British domestic savings rates were not as high as those in Australia, Canada, or the United States, but this has more to do with the high savings rates in the frontier countries than with low rates in Britain. British savings rates had reached double digits by the 1820s, and they

---

[79] Lance Davis and Robert Huttenback, *Mammon and the Pursuit of Empire: The Political Economy of British Imperialism, 1860–1912* (Cambridge: Cambridge University Press, 1986), p. 312. [Hereafter cited as Davis and Huttenback, *Mammon.*]

[80] Maddison, *Phases of Capitalist Development*, pp. 44–45.

Table 2:2-1. *United Kingdom: Gross National Product*

Year	Gross National Product (millions of pounds)	Population (thousands)	Gross National Product per capita (pounds)
1870	1,155	31,257	36.95
1871	1,259	31,556	39.90
1872	1,322	31,874	41.48
1873	1,365	32,177	42.42
1874	1,405	32,501	43.23
1875	1,371	32,839	41.75
1876	1,357	33,200	40.87
1877	1,335	33,576	39.76
1878	1,323	33,932	38.99
1879	1,243	34,304	36.23
1880	1,388	34,623	40.09
1881	1,362	34,935	38.99
1882	1,405	35,206	39.91
1883	1,450	35,450	40.90
1884	1,403	35,724	39.27
1885	1,364	36,015	37.87
1886	1,359	36,313	37.42
1887	1,428	36,598	39.02
1888	1,451	36,881	39.34
1889	1,501	37,178	40.37
1890	1,550	37,485	41.35
1891	1,594	37,802	42.17
1892	1,567	38,134	41.09
1893	1,550	38,490	40.27
1894	1,606	38,859	41.33
1895	1,637	39,221	41.74
1896	1,707	39,599	43.11
1897	1,730	39,987	43.26
1898	1,835	40,381	45.44
1899	1,963	40,773	48.14
1900	2,054	41,155	49.91
1901	2,125	41,538	51.16
1902	2,110	41,893	50.37
1903	2,109	42,246	49.92
1904	2,128	42,611	49.94
1905	2,182	42,981	50.77
1906	2,248	43,361	51.84
1907	2,300	43,737	52.59
1908	2,230	44,124	50.54
1909	2,301	44,520	51.68
1910	2,403	44,916	53.50
1911	2,493	45,268	55.07
1912	2,565	45,436	56.45
1913	2,717	45,649	59.52
1914	2,743	46,049	59.57

Source: Charles H. Feinstein, *National Income, Expenditure and Output of the United Kingdom, 1855–1965* (Cambridge, U.K.: Cambridge University Press, 1972), Table 3, p. T 10 and Table 55, p. T 120.

Table 2:2-2. *United Kingdom: annual rates of growth (percent per year)*

Years	Gross National Product	Gross National Population	Product per capita
1870–1880	1.84	1.02	0.82
1880–1890	1.10	0.79	0.31
1890–1900	2.82	0.93	1.89
1900–1910	1.57	0.87	0.70
1910–1914	3.30	0.62	2.68
1870–1914	1.97	0.88	1.09

Source: Table 2.2-1.

remained at those levels until the outbreak of World War I. Over the period from 1870 through 1914, the annual gross savings rate fluctuated between 7 and 17 percent, and it averaged more than 13 percent (see Table 2:2-3a). Between 1870 and 1914 net national wealth grew from £4.110 to £11.750 billion pounds and net wealth per capita from £151 to £257. These figures imply annual growth rates of 1.7 and 0.85 percent per year (see Table 2:2-4).

In the four frontier countries capital imports augmented domestic savings; in Britain, a country that was rapidly becoming the world's banker, overseas opportunities drew more than one-third of the total of domestic savings. Although falling to less than 2 percent of GNP in the late 1870s and again at the turn of the century, foreign and colonial transfers exceeded 6 percent in the early 1870s, the late 1880s, and in every year from 1907 through 1913. In 1850 overseas assets accounted for less than 7 percent of net national wealth. By 1890 the fraction was more than one-quarter, and by 1913, 35 percent (see Tables 2:2-3 and 2:2-4).

Imlah's research has provided the accepted estimates of the net capital flows, but there are no equally well-grounded estimates of the gross figures, nor has anyone yet produced a generally accepted description of the spatial and/or industrial profile of transfers (see Tables 2:2-5 and 2:2-6). Government/private and spatial profiles of the flows of portfolio capital raised on the British market were estimated by Davis and Huttenback. To the extent that their percentage distribution can be used as a proxy for the distributions of the actual net transfers, a rough idea of the relevant values can be obtained by using those estimates to distribute the net totals from the Imlah series.[81] Tables 2:2-7 through 2:2-11 display the results of that exercise.

Taking all years together, the Empire received just less than two-fifths of the British overseas total. The only important exceptions occurred in the first half of the 1870s, when the Empire's share fell to just more than one-fourth, over the next quinquennium, when it rose to more than 60 percent, and finally the years 1900–4, when it stood at 45 percent. Taking the foreign and Empire sectors together, private enterprise probably exceeded government borrowing by a ratio of at least 3:2.

In terms of spatial distribution, North America received about one-third of British capital exports and South America about one-fifth. Asia was the recipient of about one-seventh and Australasia, Europe, and Africa about 10 percent each. Those long-run averages, with few exceptions, capture fairly closely the short-run behavior of the series as well. There were, however, a few notable outliers. The North American share of the total exceeded 40 percent during the second half of the 1870s and over the years 1905–14; however, it represented less than one-quarter in 1895–99. South American receipts amounted to more than one-third of the total in the quinquennium 1885–89, but they were less than one-half the fifty-year average in 1875–79 and almost that low in the first five years of the twentieth century. The Asian total accounted for almost one-quarter of all overseas investment in 1865–69 and again in 1895–99, but it fell to less than 10 percent during the 1880s. Australasia received an average of more than 20 percent in the fifteen years from 1875 to 1889, while Europe was the recipient of nearly one-quarter in 1880–84 and nearly one-fifth in both 1865–69 and 1895–99. Finally, Africa received more than one-quarter of the total in the first quinquennium of the twentieth century.

South America drew more than one-third of the overseas total in the second half of the 1880s. In terms of the volume of finance, the surge can be traced to the funds directed to the railroad and government sectors (much of the latter was in turn also ultimately channeled into railroad construction). In those years the two sectors drew more than twice their fifty-year average. Relatively, however, the largest increases were in funds directed to the private agriculture, extractive, and public utility industries; all received about three times their average infusions. The

---

[81] The Davis and Huttenback data exclude both direct investment and short-term transfers; to the extent that repayments offset new investment, they overstate the level of net transfers. Davis and Huttenback, *Mammon*, tables 2.4, pp. 48–49, and 2.9, pp. 64–67.

Table 2:2-3(a). *United Kingdom: Gross National Product and domestic and foreign investment (current prices)*

| | Millions of Pounds | | | | Percents | | |
| | (1) Gross National Product | (2) Total domestic investment | (3) Net investment abroad | (4) Total domestic & foreign investment | (5) Domestic investment rate (2)/(1) | (6) Foreign investment rate (3)/(1) | (7) Total domestic & foreign investment rate (4)/(1) |
Year							
1870	1,155	127	52	179	11.0	4.5	15.5
1871	1,259	105	82	187	8.3	6.5	14.9
1872	1,322	96	98	194	7.3	7.4	14.7
1873	1,365	134	82	216	9.8	6.0	15.8
1874	1,405	197	71	268	14.0	5.1	19.1
1875	1,371	143	54	197	10.4	3.9	14.4
1876	1,357	129	25	154	9.5	1.8	11.3
1877	1,335	93	8	101	7.0	0.6	7.6
1878	1,323	168	14	182	12.7	1.1	13.8
1879	1,243	49	41	90	3.9	3.3	7.2
1880	1,388	192	29	221	13.8	2.1	15.9
1881	1,362	107	63	170	7.9	4.6	12.5
1882	1,405	103	60	163	7.3	4.3	11.6
1883	1,450	152	48	200	10.5	3.3	13.8
1884	1,403	133	71	204	9.5	5.1	14.5
1885	1,364	102	62	164	7.5	4.5	12.0
1886	1,359	105	78	183	7.7	5.7	13.5
1887	1,428	104	85	189	7.3	6.0	13.2
1888	1,451	88	94	182	6.1	6.5	12.5
1889	1,501	122	83	205	8.1	5.5	13.7
1890	1,550	121	103	224	7.8	6.6	14.5

	(1)	(2)	(3)	(4)			
1891	1,594	115	72	187	7.2	4.5	11.7
1892	1,567	119	64	183	7.6	4.1	11.7
1893	1,550	97	54	151	6.3	3.5	9.7
1894	1,606	157	45	202	9.8	2.8	12.6
1895	1,637	134	54	188	8.2	3.3	11.5
1896	1,707	168	51	219	9.8	3.0	12.8
1897	1,730	134	41	175	7.7	2.4	10.1
1898	1,835	197	23	220	10.7	1.3	12.0
1899	1,963	229	48	277	11.7	2.4	14.1
1900	2,054	181	26	207	8.8	1.3	10.1
1901	2,125	257	19	276	12.1	0.9	13.0
1902	2,110	217	16	233	10.3	0.8	11.0
1903	2,109	191	41	232	9.1	1.9	11.0
1904	2,128	205	53	258	9.6	2.5	12.1
1905	2,182	225	87	312	10.3	4.0	14.3
1906	2,248	197	118	315	8.8	5.2	14.0
1907	2,300	160	162	322	7.0	7.0	14.0
1908	2,230	138	160	298	6.2	7.2	13.4
1909	2,301	177	139	316	7.7	6.0	13.7
1910	2,403	156	171	327	6.5	7.1	13.6
1911	2,493	174	209	383	7.0	8.4	15.4
1912	2,565	158	205	363	6.2	8.0	14.2
1913	2,717	223	233	456	8.2	8.6	16.8
1914	2,743	197	103	300	7.2	3.8	10.9

Sources: Column (1) from C.H. Feinstein, *National Income, Expenditure and Output of the United Kingdom, 1855–1965* (Cambridge U.K.: Cambridge University Press, 1972), Table 3, p. T 10. Columns (2)–(4) from Charles. H. Feinstein and Sydney Pollard (eds.), *Studies in Capital Formation in the United Kingdom, 1750–1920* (Oxford: Clarendon Press, 1988), Appendix Table XVII, pp. 462–463.

Table 2:2-3(b). *United Kingdom: Gross National Product and domestic and foreign investment (current prices)*

Years	Millions of pounds				Percents		
	Gross National Product (1)	Total domestic investment	Net investment abroad	Total domestic & foreign investment	Domestic investment rate (2)/(1)	Foreign investment rate (3)/(1)	Total domestic & foreign investment rate (4)/(1)
1870–1879	1,313.5	124.1	52.7	176.8	9.4	4.0	13.5
1880–1889	1,411.1	120.8	67.3	188.1	8.6	4.8	13.3
1890–1899	1,673.9	147.1	55.5	202.6	8.8	3.3	12.1
1900–1909	2,178.7	194.8	82.1	276.9	8.9	3.8	12.7
1910–1914	2,584.2	181.6	184.2	365.8	7.0	7.1	14.2

Source: Column (1) from C.H. Feinstein, *National Income, Expenditure and Output of the United Kingdom, 1855–1965* (Cambridge U.K.: Cambridge University Press, 1972), Table 3, p. T 10. Columns (2)–(4) from Charles. H. Feinstein and Sydney Pollard (eds.), *Studies in Capital Formation in the United Kingdom, 1750–1920* (Oxford: Clarendon Press, 1988), Appendix Table XVII, pp. 462–463.

Table 2:2-4. *United Kingdom: net national wealth*

Year	Net domestic reproducible assets	Land	Overseas assets	Net national wealth
	(millions of 1900 Pounds)			
1850	1,640	2,190	280	4,110
1860	1,950	2,190	470	4,610
1870	2,460	2,190	780	5,430
1880	3,100	2,190	1,240	6,530
1890	3,590	2,190	2,040	7,820
1900	4,420	2,190	2,550	9,160
1910	5,290	2,190	3,520	11,000
1913	5,420	2,190	4,140	11,750
	(percents)			
1850	39.9	53.3	6.8	100.0
1860	42.3	47.5	10.2	100.0
1870	45.3	40.3	14.4	100.0
1880	47.5	33.5	19.0	100.0
1890	45.9	28.0	26.1	100.0
1900	48.3	23.9	27.8	100.0
1910	48.1	19.9	32.0	100.0
1913	46.1	18.6	35.2	100.0

Source: Charles H. Feinstein and Sidney Pollard (eds.), *Studies in Capital Formation in the United Kingdom, 1750–1920* (Oxford: Clarendon Press, 1988), Table XXII, p. 469.

small totals received in the second half of the 1870s, although reflecting declines distributed across the entire industrial spectrum, were concentrated in the reduction in both private and public finance destined for railroad construction. The trough in the first quinqennium of the twentieth century reflected, at least in part, a delayed fallout from the Barings Crisis; but the decline in capital imports did not affect all industrial sectors equally. Both public and private sectors displayed ratios below their fifty-year averages (the private sector received 60 percent and the government only 40 percent of those levels). However, private railroads suffered only a 30 percent decline, and funds channeled to manufacturing actually were 12 percent above their half-century benchmark.

In 1865–69 Asian receipts were one-quarter above their fifty-year average, the result of a surge of investment in India. The Indian government did no borrowing; private firms received twice as much as their

Table 2:2-5(a). *United Kingdom: export of capital (millions of pounds)*

Year	Balance on current account	Accumulating balance of credit abroad	Year	Balance on current account	Accumulating balance of credit abroad
1815		10.0	1865	34.9	489.8
1816	14.6	24.6	1866	33.0	522.8
1817	6.3	30.9	1867	42.2	565.0
1818	4.7	35.6	1868	36.5	601.5
1819	7.3	42.9	1869	46.7	648.2
1820	3.2	46.1	1870	44.1	692.3
1821	13.8	59.9	1871	71.3	763.6
1822	13.3	73.2	1872	98.0	861.6
1823	5.9	79.1	1873	81.3	942.9
1824	16.3	95.4	1874	70.9	1,013.8
1825	2.4	97.8	1875	51.3	1,065.1
1826	2.4	100.2	1876	23.2	1,088.3
1827	0.0	100.2	1877	13.1	1,101.4
1828	3.8	104.0	1878	16.9	1,118.3
1829	6.1	110.1	1879	35.5	1,153.8
1830	0.6	110.7	1880	35.6	1,189.4
1831	2.4	113.1	1881	65.7	1,255.1
1832	6.1	119.2	1882	58.7	1,313.8
1833	3.6	122.8	1883	48.8	1,362.6
1834	7.1	129.9	1884	72.3	1,434.9
1835	12.7	142.6	1885	62.3	1,497.2
1836	5.5	148.1	1886	78.9	1,576.1
1837	2.3	150.4	1887	87.7	1,663.8
1838	4.5	154.9	1888	91.9	1,755.7
1839	3.1	158.0	1889	80.9	1,836.6
1840	−2.3	155.7	1890	98.5	1,935.1
1841	1.1	156.8	1891	69.4	2,004.5
1842	−0.6	156.2	1892	59.1	2,063.6
1843	9.3	165.5	1893	53.0	2,116.6
1844	10.4	175.9	1894	38.7	2,155.3
1845	9.3	185.2	1895	40.0	2,195.3
1846	8.0	193.2	1896	56.8	2,252.1
1847	−1.1	192.1	1897	41.6	2,293.7
1848	2.1	194.2	1898	22.9	2,316.6
1849	3.9	198.1	1899	42.4	2,359.0
1850	10.6	208.7	1900	37.9	2,396.9
1851	9.2	217.9	1901	33.9	2,430.8
1852	7.7	225.6	1902	33.3	2,464.1
1853	3.3	228.9	1903	44.8	2,508.9

Table 2:2-5(a). *(cont.)*

Year	Balance on current account	Accumulating balance of credit abroad	Year	Balance on current account	Accumulating balance of credit abroad
1854	5.8	234.7	1904	51.7	2,560.6
1855	13.9	248.6	1905	81.5	2,642.1
1856	21.8	270.4	1906	117.5	2,759.6
1857	27.1	297.5	1907	154.1	2,913.7
1858	22.4	319.9	1908	154.7	3,068.4
1859	36.1	356.0	1909	135.6	3,204.0
1860	23.7	379.7	1910	167.3	3,371.3
1861	14.4	394.1	1911	196.9	3,568.2
1862	11.5	405.6	1912	197.1	3,765.3
1863	26.5	432.1	1913	224.3	3,989.6
1864	22.8	454.9			

Source: Albert H. Imlah, *Economic Elements of the Pax Britanica: Studies in British Foreign Trade in the Nineteenth Century* (Cambridge, Mass.: Harvard University Press, 1958), Table 4, pp. 70–75.

usual share. The vast majority of finance (72 percent) was directed to railroads, but in relative terms the increase was spread more or less uniformly across the entire sector. The next Asian peak, in the second half of the 1890s, was due to foreign government borrowing. Private firms drew only 35 percent of their normal levels, but governments received more than twice their fifty-year average. The causes of decline in the region's share to less than 10 percent of the total in the 1880s can be traced to both the public and private sectors, particularly to the former. Governments together received only 15 percent of their usual allotment. Private firms continued to draw about eight-tenths of their average level, and the transfer to railroads was actually 6 percent above the norm.

In the case of Australia and New Zealand, governments were always much more important than the private sector. Over the entire period government borrowing represented more than three-quarters of all British financial infusions. Thus, it is hardly surprising that in the fifteen years 1875–89, when the region accounted for more than one-fifth of all capital created and called, the borrowing of colonial governments stood at 160 percent of its fifty-year average. The private sector, on the other hand, was a mere 7 percent above its half-century average.

Table 2:2-5(b). *United Kingdom: export of capital*

| | Millions of U.K. pounds | | | U.K. pounds per capita | |
Years	Annual average balance on current account	End of period accumulated balance of credit abroad	Years	Annual aaverage balance on current account	End of period accumulated balance of credit abroad
1816–1820	7.2	46.1	1816–1820	0.36	2.24
1821–1825	10.3	97.8	1821–1825	0.48	4.42
1826–1830	2.6	110.7	1826–1830	0.11	4.67
1831–1835	6.4	142.6	1831–1835	0.26	5.68
1836–1840	2.6	155.7	1836–1840	0.10	5.89
1841–1845	5.9	185.2	1841–1845	0.22	5.77
1846–1850	4.7	208.7	1846–1850	0.17	7.64
1851–1855	8.0	248.6	1851–1855	0.29	8.94
1856–1860	26.2	379.7	1856–1860	0.92	13.19
1861–1865	22.0	489.8	1861–1865	0.75	16.37
1866–1870	40.5	692.3	1866–1870	1.32	22.15
1871–1875	74.6	1,065.1	1871–1875	2.32	32.43
1876–1880	24.9	1,189.4	1876–1880	0.73	34.35
1881–1885	61.6	1,497.2	1881–1885	1.74	41.57
1886–1890	87.6	1,935.1	1886–1890	2.37	51.62
1891–1895	52.0	2,195.3	1891–1895	1.35	55.97
1896–1900	40.3	2,396.9	1896–1900	1.00	58.24
1901–1905	49.0	2,642.1	1901–1905	1.16	61.47
1906–1910	145.8	3,371.3	1906–1910	3.31	75.06
1911–1913	206.1	3,989.6	1911–1913	4.54	87.40

Sources: Albert H. Imlah, *Economic Elements of the Pax Britanica: Studies in British Foreign Trade in the Nineteenth Century* (Cambridge, Mass.: Harvard University Press, 1958), Table 4, pp. 70–75. Brian R. Mitchell, *European Historical Statistics, 1750–1970, Abridged Edition* (New York: Columbia University Press, 1978), Table A 1, pp. 3–11. Charles H. Feinstein, *National Income, Expenditure and Output of the United Kingdom, 1855–1865* (Cambridge U.K.: Cambridge University Press, 1972), Table 55, pp. T120–T122.

Table 2:2-6. *United Kingdom: export of capital (millions of pounds)*

Year	Nominal Values		Real Values 1913 = 100	
	Balance on current account	Accumulating credit abroad	Balance on current account	Accumulating credit abroad
1851	9.2	217.9	10.1	189.4
1852	7.7	225.6	8.4	197.8
1853	3.3	228.9	2.9	200.7
1854	5.8	234.7	4.8	205.6
1855	13.9	248.6	11.7	217.2
1856	21.8	270.4	18.3	235.6
1857	27.1	297.5	21.9	257.4
1858	22.4	319.9	20.9	278.3
1859	36.1	356.0	32.5	310.9
1860	23.7	379.7	20.4	331.3
1861	14.4	394.1	12.5	343.8
1862	11.5	405.6	9.7	353.5
1863	26.5	432.1	21.9	375.4
1864	22.8	454.9	18.4	393.8
1865	34.9	489.8	29.3	423.1
1866	33.0	522.8	27.5	450.6
1867	42.2	565.0	35.8	486.4
1868	36.5	601.5	31.5	517.8
1869	46.7	648.2	40.6	558.4
1870	44.1	692.3	39.0	597.5
1871	71.3	763.6	61.5	658.9
1872	98.0	861.6	78.4	737.3
1873	81.3	942.9	62.5	799.9
1874	70.9	1,013.8	56.3	856.1
1875	51.3	1,065.1	42.4	898.5
1876	23.2	1,088.3	19.7	918.2
1877	13.1	1,101.4	10.8	929.0
1878	16.9	1,118.3	15.0	944.0
1879	35.5	1,153.8	33.2	977.2
1880	35.6	1,189.4	32.1	1,009.2
1881	65.7	1,255.1	60.3	1,069.5
1882	58.7	1,313.8	53.4	1,122.9
1883	48.8	1,362.6	45.2	1,168.1
1884	72.3	1,434.9	73.8	1,241.8
1885	62.3	1,497.2	67.7	1,309.5
1886	78.9	1,576.1	90.7	1,400.2
1887	87.7	1,663.8	103.2	1,503.4
1888	91.9	1,755.7	105.6	1,609.0

Table 2:2-6. *(cont.)*

	Nominal Values		Real Values 1913 = 100	
Year	Balance on current account	Accumulating credit abroad	Balance on current account	Accumulating credit abroad
1889	80.9	1,836.6	90.9	1,699.9
1890	98.5	1,935.1	110.7	1,810.6
1891	69.4	2,004.5	75.4	1,886.1
1892	59.1	2,063.6	67.9	1,954.0
1893	53.0	2,116.6	62.4	2,016.3
1894	38.7	2,155.3	48.4	2,064.7
1895	40.0	2,195.3	51.3	2,116.0
1896	56.8	2,252.1	74.7	2,190.7
1897	41.6	2,293.7	54.0	2,244.8
1898	22.9	2,316.6	28.6	2,273.4
1899	42.4	2,359.0	53.7	2,327.1
1900	37.9	2,396.9	44.1	2,371.1
1901	33.9	2,430.8	40.8	2,412.0
1902	33.3	2,464.1	40.1	2,452.1
1903	44.8	2,508.9	54.0	2,506.1
1904	51.7	2,560.6	61.5	2,567.6
1905	81.5	2,642.1	97.0	2,664.6
1906	117.5	2,759.6	135.1	2,799.7
1907	154.1	2,913.7	169.3	2,969.0
1908	154.7	3,068.4	175.8	3,144.8
1909	135.6	3,204.0	152.4	3,297.2
1910	167.3	3,371.3	179.9	3,477.1
1911	196.9	3,568.2	209.5	3,686.5
1912	197.1	3,765.3	199.1	3,885.6
1913	224.3	3,989.6	224.3	4,109.9

Sources: Albert H. Imlah, *Economic Elements of the Pax Britannica: Studies in British Foreign Trade in the Nineteenth Century* (Cambridge, MA.: Harvard University Press, 1958), Table 4, pp. 70–75. B.R. Mitchell, *European Historical Statistics, 1750–1970, abridged edition* (New York: Columbia University Press, 1978), Table H 1, pp. 388–393.

Notes: Accumulated Balance in 1850 uses price index 1821–1825 = 100, and correction assumes that between 1850 and 1851 prices rose by 1.12%, the average of Belgium, France, & Germany.

Table 2:2-7. *All capital "created and called": minimum estimate by empire or foreign and by public or private ownership (percentage distribution)*

Years	Empire private	Foreign private	Total private	Empire government	Foreign government	Total government	Total empire	Total foreign
1865–1869	27.7	33.2	60.9	11.2	27.9	39.1	38.9	61.1
1870–1874	12.5	50.3	62.8	13.6	23.6	37.2	26.1	73.9
1875–1879	9.4	19.2	28.5	51.3	20.2	71.5	60.7	39.3
1880–1884	12.8	37.3	50.1	25.1	24.8	49.9	37.9	62.1
1885–1889	12.4	43.7	56.1	23.1	20.7	43.9	35.5	64.5
1890–1894	10.6	41.5	52.1	24.4	23.5	47.9	35.0	65.0
1895–1899	22.5	33.4	55.9	13.5	30.6	44.1	36.0	64.0
1900–1904	18.0	43.2	61.2	26.2	12.6	38.8	44.2	55.8
1905–1909	23.0	42.4	65.5	14.9	19.6	34.5	37.9	62.1
1910–1914	20.6	42.4	63.0	19.1	17.9	37.0	39.7	60.3
1865–1914	17.8	40.5	58.3	21.0	20.7	41.7	38.7	61.3

Sources: Lance E. Davis & Robert A. Huttenback, *Mammon and the Pursuit of Empire: The Political Economy of British Imperialism, 1860–1912,* Table 2.4, pp. 48–49.

Table 2:2-8. *All capital "created and called" by continent*

		Panel A: percentage distribution				
Years	North America	South America & Caribbean	Asia	Australia & Pacific	Europe	Africa
1865–1869	18.0	16.0	24.9	11.1	18.9	11.1
1870–1874	40.8	27.1	11.3	7.2	11.9	1.6
1875–1879	28.7	8.8	18.5	24.6	7.8	11.5
1880–1884	28.2	13.6	9.1	18.9	24.1	6.2
1885–1889	24.3	34.5	9.6	18.2	7.9	5.4
1890–1894	33.0	18.1	14.1	14.8	11.4	8.6
1895–1899	14.6	13.0	22.9	15.3	19.1	15.0
1900–1904	35.4	10.7	12.2	8.3	5.9	27.7
1905–1909	41.4	21.4	16.6	3.9	7.1	9.6
1910–1914	41.0	22.0	12.3	9.7	9.3	5.8
1865–1914	33.5	19.9	14.0	11.7	11.1	9.8
		Panel B: estimated capital flows: millions of pounds				
1865–1869	34.8	30.9	48.2	21.4	36.6	21.4
1870–1874	149.3	98.9	41.5	26.3	43.6	5.9
1875–1879	40.2	12.4	26.0	34.4	11.0	16.1
1880–1884	79.1	38.2	25.5	53.1	67.8	17.4
1885–1889	97.7	138.5	38.7	73.3	31.8	21.8
1890–1894	105.2	57.5	44.9	47.2	36.5	27.4
1895–1899	29.8	26.5	46.7	31.2	38.9	30.6
1900–1904	71.3	21.5	24.5	16.6	11.9	55.8
1905–1909	266.4	137.7	106.7	24.9	45.6	62.1
1910–1914	376.6	202.1	112.8	89.4	85.1	53.7
1865–1914	1,228.4	731.7	512.9	430.6	405.5	359.5

Sources: Lance E. Davis & Robert A. Huttenback, *Mammon and the Pursuit of Empire: The Political Economy of British Imperialism, 1860–1912*, Table 2.4, pp. 48–49. Albert H. Imlah, *Economic Elements in the Pax Britannica: Studies in British Foreign Trade in the Nineteenth Century* (Cambridge, Mass.: Harvard University Press, 1958), Table 4, pp. 70–75. C.H. Feinstein, *National Income, Expenditure and Output of the United Kingdom, 1855–1965* (Cambridge, U.K.: Cambridge University Press, 1972), Table 37, p. T 82.

In Europe receipts were about one-quarter above the fifty-year average in the first half of the 1880s and about 20 percent above in 1865–69 and again in 1895–99. In the early '80s the private sector received less than three-quarters of its usual inflow, but governments received almost three times their fifty-year average. In 1865–69, the public sector received only 28 percent and the non-rail private industries only 64 percent of their normal level of finance, but railroads received nearly twice their average flow. In the second half of the 1890s government receipts were only 10 percent above normal, and the railroads actually drew 8 percent less than their usual share. The non-rail private sector, however, drew almost twice its fifty-year average – the manufacturing and the agriculture and extractive industries were the primary beneficiaries.

Countries and colonies in Africa received 28 percent of all overseas capital created and called in the quinquennium 1900–4. A large part of that increase reflects the costs of the Boer War – the governments of the Natal and the Cape, colonies with responsible government, drew more than six times their usual level of British finance. The private sector, however, also received far more than its usual volume of finance. Overall, in the colonies with responsible government private firms received more than five times their fifty-year average. Within the private sector, the agriculture and extractive industries accounted for more than 11 percent of the continent's total, between five and six times their normal level.

2-3. The growth and evolution of the financial sector

2-3a. The banks and non-bank intermediaries: introduction
Tables 2:3-1(a), (b), and (c) and 2:3-2 provide an overview of the evolution of the nation's financial intermediaries over the three and a half decades preceding World War I.[82] Although the United Kingdom's

---

[82] There are serious questions about the level of assets held by the commercial banking sector. The data in Table 2.3-1 are taken from David K. Sheppard, *The Growth and Role of UK Financial Institutions, 1860–1962* (London: Methuen, 1971). [Hereafter cited as Sheppard, *The Growth and Role of UK Financial Institutions.*] Those data are taken from the "Banking Number" or the "Banking Supplement" of the *Economist*, a series that begins in 1878 but that does not include private banks until 1891. Even then, however, the figures for the number of banks are below those cited in Forrest Capie and Alan Weber, *A Monetary History of the United Kingdom, 1870–1892. Vol. I: Data, Sources, Methods* (London: George Allen & Unwin, 1985), appendix III, pp. 576–77. [Hereafter cited as Capie and Weber, *A Monetary History.*] The Capie and Weber study is based on a canvass of bank archives. For a comparison of the number of banks and branches reported by the two studies see Table 2.3-6. Unfortunately, the Capie and Weber study does not report the level of total assets or their

Table 2.2-9. *Percentage distribution of all capital "created and called" by continent and by user (public or private) (denominator is all capital created and called in relevant years)*

North America

Years	Empire			Foreign			All capital		
	Private	government	Total	Private	government	Total	Private	government	Total
1865–1869	2.9	0.3	3.2	13.2	1.6	14.8	16.1	1.9	18.0
1870–1874	5.8	4.8	10.6	27.3	2.9	30.2	33.1	7.8	40.8
1875–1879	4.0	9.1	13.1	13.7	1.9	15.6	17.7	11.0	28.7
1880–1884	4.1	1.2	5.3	22.8	0.1	22.9	26.9	1.3	28.2
1885–1889	5.6	2.9	8.6	15.2	0.6	15.8	20.8	3.5	24.3
1890–1894	3.7	3.2	6.9	23.1	3.0	26.1	26.8	6.2	33.0
1895–1899	1.8	1.4	3.2	10.2	1.2	11.5	12.0	2.6	14.6
1900–1904	3.1	0.6	3.7	31.6	0.1	31.7	34.7	0.7	35.4
1905–1909	15.5	4.5	20.0	20.2	1.2	21.4	35.7	5.8	41.4
1910–1914	13.0	7.0	20.0	20.4	0.5	20.9	33.4	7.5	41.0
1865–1914	8.1	3.9	12.0	20.4	1.0	21.5	28.5	5.0	33.5

South America and Caribbean

Years	Empire			Foreign			All capital		
	Private	government	Total	Private	government	Total	Private	government	Total
1865–1869	0.4	0.0	0.4	5.2	10.4	15.6	5.5	10.4	16.0
1870–1874	0.1	0.3	0.4	10.1	16.6	26.7	10.2	16.9	27.1
1875–1879	0.0	0.1	0.1	3.0	5.7	8.7	3.0	5.9	8.8
1880–1884	0.1	0.3	0.4	9.7	3.4	13.2	9.8	3.7	13.6

1885–1889	0.1	0.1	0.2	22.1	12.1	34.2	22.3	12.2	34.5
1890–1894	0.1	0.2	0.2	12.0	5.8	17.8	12.1	6.0	18.1
1895–1899	0.5	0.3	0.8	7.5	4.7	12.2	8.0	5.0	13.0
1900–1904	0.2	0.0	0.2	7.7	2.8	10.5	7.8	2.8	10.7
1905–1909	0.0	0.0	0.0	15.0	6.4	21.4	15.0	6.4	21.4
1910–1914	0.1	0.0	0.1	14.8	7.0	21.8	14.9	7.1	22.0
1865–1914	0.1	0.1	0.2	12.6	7.1	19.7	12.8	7.2	19.9

Asia

Years	Private	Empire government	Total	Private	Foreign government	Total	Private	All capital government	Total
1865–1869	22.0	0.2	22.2	1.0	1.7	2.7	23.0	1.9	24.9
1870–1874	4.3	2.9	7.3	2.1	2.0	4.1	6.4	4.9	11.3
1875–1879	2.6	13.8	16.4	0.1	2.0	2.1	2.7	15.9	18.5
1880–1884	3.9	4.6	8.5	0.6	0.0	0.6	4.4	4.7	9.1
1885–1889	2.4	5.0	7.3	1.3	1.0	2.3	3.7	6.0	9.6
1890–1894	1.8	8.0	9.8	1.9	2.4	4.3	3.7	10.4	14.1
1895–1899	6.0	3.5	9.4	0.6	12.9	13.5	6.6	16.3	22.9
1900–1904	4.4	3.0	7.4	0.5	4.3	4.7	4.9	7.3	12.2
1905–1909	3.7	4.0	7.7	1.5	7.3	8.9	5.2	11.3	16.6
1910–1914	4.1	3.0	7.2	2.0	3.1	5.1	6.1	6.1	12.3
1865–1914	4.3	4.4	8.7	1.3	3.9	5.3	5.7	8.3	14.0

(cont. on next page)

Table 2:2-9. *(cont.)*

Australia and Pacific

Year	Empire			Foreign			All capital		
	Private	government	Total	Private	government	Total	Private	government	Total
1865–1869	1.8	9.3	11.1	0.0	0.0	0.0	1.8	9.3	11.1
1870–1874	1.7	5.4	7.2	0.0	0.0	0.0	1.7	5.4	7.2
1875–1879	2.7	21.9	24.6	0.0	0.0	0.0	2.7	21.9	24.6
1880–1884	3.7	15.2	18.9	0.0	0.0	0.0	3.7	15.2	18.9
1885–1889	3.6	14.6	18.2	0.0	0.1	0.1	3.6	14.6	18.2
1890–1894	4.0	10.8	14.8	0.0	0.0	0.0	4.1	10.8	14.8
1895–1899	9.5	5.7	15.2	0.2	0.0	0.2	9.7	5.7	15.3
1900–1904	2.0	6.2	8.2	0.0	0.0	0.0	2.1	6.2	8.3
1905–1909	1.1	2.5	3.9	0.0	0.0	0.0	1.1	2.8	3.9
1910–1914	1.6	8.1	9.7	0.1	0.0	0.1	1.7	8.1	9.7
1865–1914	2.8	8.9	11.7	0.0	0.0	0.0	2.8	8.9	11.7

Europe

Year	Empire			Foreign			All capital		
	Private	government	Total	Private	government	Total	Private	government	Total
1865–1869	0.3	0.0	0.3	12.6	6.0	18.6	13.0	6.0	18.9
1870–1874	0.2	0.0	0.2	9.7	2.0	11.7	9.9	2.0	11.9
1875–1879	0.0	0.0	0.0	2.1	5.7	7.8	2.1	5.7	7.8
1880–1884	0.0	0.0	0.0	2.9	21.2	24.1	2.9	21.2	24.1
1885–1889	0.0	0.0	0.0	3.8	4.1	7.9	3.8	4.1	7.9

Year	Private	Empire government	Total	Private	Foreign government	Total	Private	All capital government	Total
1890–1894	0.1	0.0	0.1	2.2	9.1	11.3	2.3	9.1	11.4
1895–1899	0.0	0.0	0.0	8.0	11.0	19.1	8.0	11.0	19.1
1900–1904	0.0	0.0	0.0	1.1	4.8	5.9	1.1	4.8	5.9
1905–1909	0.0	0.0	0.0	2.9	4.2	7.1	2.9	4.2	7.1
1910–1914	0.0	0.0	0.0	3.2	6.1	9.3	3.2	6.1	9.3
1865–1914	0.0	0.0	0.0	3.9	7.2	11.0	3.9	7.2	11.1

Africa

Year	Empire Private	Empire government	Empire Total	Foreign Private	Foreign government	Foreign Total	All capital Private	All capital government	All capital Total
1865–1869	0.3	1.3	1.6	1.2	8.3	9.5	1.5	9.6	11.1
1870–1874	0.4	0.1	0.4	1.1	0.0	1.2	1.5	0.1	1.6
1875–1879	0.1	6.3	6.4	0.3	4.8	5.1	0.4	11.1	11.5
1880–1884	1.0	3.9	4.9	1.3	0.0	1.3	2.3	3.9	6.2
1885–1889	0.7	0.5	1.2	1.3	2.9	4.2	2.0	3.4	5.4
1890–1894	0.9	2.2	3.1	2.2	3.2	5.5	3.1	5.5	8.6
1895–1899	4.7	2.7	7.5	6.8	0.7	7.6	11.6	3.4	15.0
1900–1904	8.3	16.4	24.7	2.4	0.6	3.0	10.7	17.0	27.7
1905–1909	2.7	3.5	6.3	2.8	0.5	3.4	5.6	4.1	9.6
1910–1914	1.8	0.9	2.7	2.0	1.1	3.1	3.8	2.1	5.8
1865–1914	2.4	3.7	6.0	2.2	1.5	3.8	4.6	5.2	9.8

Source: Lance E. Davis & Robert A. Huttenback, *Mammon and the Pursuit of Empire: The Political Economy of British Imperialism, 1860–1912,* Table 2.4, pp. 48–49.

Table 2:2-10. *Percentage distribution of all capital "created and called" by continent, public or private (denominator is all capital of particular type created and called in relevant years)*

North America

Years	Empire government			Foreign government			All capital government		
	Private	government	Total	Private	government	Total	Private	government	Total
1865–1869	10.6	2.8	8.3	39.8	5.6	24.2	26.5	4.8	18.0
1870–1874	46.2	35.6	40.7	54.3	12.4	40.9	52.7	20.9	40.8
1875–1879	42.6	17.8	21.6	71.3	9.6	39.7	61.9	15.4	28.7
1880–1884	31.9	4.7	13.9	61.2	0.4	36.9	53.7	2.6	28.2
1885–1889	45.3	12.7	24.1	34.7	2.9	24.4	37.0	8.1	24.3
1890–1894	34.9	13.2	19.8	55.7	12.6	40.1	51.5	12.9	33.0
1895–1899	8.0	10.0	8.8	30.6	4.0	17.9	21.5	5.9	14.6
1900–1904	17.2	2.2	8.3	73.0	1.0	56.8	56.6	1.8	35.4
1905–1909	67.2	30.5	52.8	47.5	6.2	34.5	54.5	16.7	41.4
1910–1914	63.1	36.7	50.4	48.1	3.0	34.7	53.0	20.4	41.0
1865–1914	45.6	18.7	31.0	50.4	5.0	35.0	48.9	11.9	33.5

South America and Caribbean

Years	Empire government			Foreign government			All capital government		
	Private	government	Total	Private	government	Total	Private	government	Total
1865–1869	1.3	0.3	1.0	15.6	37.3	25.5	9.1	26.7	16.0
1870–1874	0.6	2.1	1.4	20.1	70.4	36.1	16.2	45.4	27.1
1875–1879	0.0	0.3	0.2	15.4	28.5	22.1	10.4	8.2	8.8
1880–1884	0.7	1.2	1.1	26.2	13.8	21.2	19.6	7.5	13.6

Years	Private	Empire government	Total	Private	Foreign government	Total	Private	All capital government	Total
1885–1889	1.0	0.6	0.7	50.7	58.2	53.1	39.7	27.8	34.5
1890–1894	0.8	0.6	0.7	28.9	24.7	27.4	23.2	12.4	18.1
1895–1899	2.3	2.1	2.2	22.4	15.5	19.1	14.3	11.4	13.0
1900–1904	0.9	0.1	0.4	17.7	22.4	18.8	12.8	7.3	10.7
1905–1909	0.1	0.1	0.1	35.3	32.6	34.4	22.9	18.6	21.4
1910–1914	0.5	0.2	0.4	34.9	39.3	36.2	23.7	19.1	22.0
1865–1914	0.7	0.6	0.6	31.2	34.0	32.2	21.9	17.2	19.9

Asia

Years	Private	Empire government	Total	Private	Foreign government	Total	Private	All capital government	Total
1865–1869	79.5	1.7	57.2	3.0	6.2	4.4	37.8	4.9	24.9
1870–1874	34.7	21.6	27.9	4.2	8.3	5.5	10.3	13.2	11.3
1875–1879	27.3	27.0	27.1	0.6	10.0	5.4	9.4	22.2	18.5
1880–1884	30.1	18.4	22.4	1.5	0.1	0.9	8.8	9.3	9.1
1885–1889	18.9	21.4	20.6	3.0	4.8	3.6	6.5	13.6	9.6
1890–1894	16.6	32.9	28.0	4.6	10.1	6.6	7.1	21.7	14.1
1895–1899	26.4	25.8	26.2	1.9	42.0	21.1	11.8	37.1	22.9
1900–1904	24.5	11.5	16.8	1.0	34.0	8.5	7.9	18.8	12.2
1905–1909	16.1	26.9	20.4	3.6	37.3	14.3	8.0	32.8	16.6
1910–1914	20.0	16.0	18.0	4.7	17.3	8.5	9.7	16.6	12.3
1865–1914	24.4	20.9	22.5	3.3	19.0	8.6	9.7	20.0	14.0

(cont. on next page)

Table 2:2-10. (cont.)

Australia and Pacific

Years	Empire Private	Empire government	Empire Total	Foreign Private	Foreign government	Foreign Total	All capital Private	All capital government	All capital Total
1865–1869	6.3	83.5	28.5	0.0	0.0	0.0	2.9	23.8	11.1
1870–1874	14.0	40.0	27.5	0.0	0.0	0.0	2.8	14.6	7.2
1875–1879	29.2	42.6	40.6	0.0	0.0	0.0	9.6	30.6	24.6
1880–1884	29.1	60.3	49.8	0.0	0.0	0.0	7.5	30.3	18.9
1885–1889	29.0	63.0	51.1	0.0	0.3	0.1	6.4	33.3	18.2
1890–1894	38.2	44.1	42.3	0.0	0.0	0.0	7.8	22.5	14.8
1895–1899	42.2	41.9	42.1	0.5	0.0	0.3	17.3	12.8	15.3
1900–1904	11.3	23.6	18.6	0.1	0.0	0.0	3.4	16.0	8.3
1905–1909	4.7	18.8	10.2	0.0	0.0	0.0	1.7	8.1	3.9
1910–1914	7.8	42.2	24.3	0.1	0.0	0.1	2.6	21.8	9.7
1865–1914	15.7	42.4	30.2	0.1	0.0	0.1	4.8	21.4	11.7

Europe

Years	Empire Private	Empire government	Empire Total	Foreign Private	Foreign government	Foreign Total	All capital Private	All capital government	All capital Total
1865–1869	1.2	0.0	0.9	38.1	21.4	30.4	21.3	15.3	18.9
1870–1874	1.7	0.0	0.8	19.2	8.7	15.9	15.7	5.5	11.9
1875–1879	0.3	0.0	0.0	11.0	28.3	19.9	7.5	8.0	7.8
1880–1884	0.2	0.0	0.1	7.8	85.6	38.8	5.8	42.5	24.1
1885–1889	0.3	0.0	0.1	8.6	19.9	12.2	6.8	9.4	7.9

Years	Empire			Foreign			All capital		
	Private	government	Total	Private	government	Total	Private	government	Total
1890–1894	1.1	0.0	0.3	5.3	38.8	17.4	4.5	19.0	11.4
1895–1899	0.0	0.0	0.0	24.0	36.1	29.8	14.4	25.0	19.1
1900–1904	0.0	0.0	0.0	2.6	38.0	10.6	1.8	12.3	5.9
1905–1909	0.0	0.0	0.0	6.9	21.2	11.4	4.5	12.0	7.1
1910–1914	0.0	0.0	0.0	7.5	34.0	15.4	5.0	16.4	9.3
1865–1914	0.2	0.0	0.1	9.5	34.5	18.0	6.7	17.1	11.1

Africa

Years	Empire			Foreign			All capital		
	Private	government	Total	Private	government	Total	Private	government	Total
1865–1869	1.0	11.8	4.1	3.6	29.6	15.5	2.4	24.5	11.1
1870–1874	2.9	0.6	1.7	2.3	0.2	1.6	2.4	0.4	1.6
1875–1879	0.6	12.3	10.5	1.7	23.6	12.9	1.3	15.5	11.5
1880–1884	8.0	15.3	12.9	3.4	0.1	2.1	4.6	7.8	6.2
1885–1889	5.5	2.3	3.4	3.0	13.9	6.5	3.6	7.8	5.4
1890–1894	8.3	9.2	8.9	5.4	13.8	8.4	6.0	11.4	8.6
1895–1899	21.1	20.1	20.7	20.5	2.3	11.8	20.7	7.8	15.0
1900–1904	46.1	62.5	55.8	5.6	4.5	5.3	17.5	43.7	27.7
1905–1909	11.9	23.8	16.6	6.7	2.7	5.4	8.5	11.8	9.6
1910–1914	8.7	4.9	6.9	4.6	6.4	5.2	6.0	5.6	5.8
1865–1914	13.3	17.4	15.5	5.5	7.4	6.2	7.9	12.4	9.8

Source: Lance E. Davis & Robert A. Huttenback, *Mammon and the Pursuit of Empire: The Political Economy of British Imperialism, 1860–1912*, Table 2.4, pp. 48–49.

Table 2:2-11. *Estimated distribution: all British overseas investment by continent, foreign or empire, and public or private (millions of pounds)*

North America

Years	Empire Private	Empire government	Empire Total	Foreign Private	Foreign government	Foreign Total	All capital Private	All capital government	All capital Total
1865–1869	5.7	0.6	6.3	25.5	3.0	28.6	31.2	3.6	34.8
1870–1874	21.1	17.7	38.8	99.8	10.7	110.5	120.9	28.4	149.3
1875–1879	5.6	12.7	18.3	19.1	2.7	21.8	24.7	15.5	40.2
1880–1884	11.5	3.3	14.8	64.1	0.2	64.3	75.5	3.6	79.1
1885–1889	22.6	11.8	34.4	60.9	2.4	63.3	83.5	14.2	97.7
1890–1894	11.7	10.3	22.0	73.7	9.5	83.2	85.5	19.7	105.2
1895–1899	3.7	2.8	6.4	20.8	2.5	23.3	24.5	5.3	29.8
1900–1904	6.3	1.2	7.4	63.6	0.3	63.9	69.9	1.4	71.3
1905–1909	99.6	29.2	128.7	129.8	7.8	137.7	229.4	37.0	266.4
1910–1914	119.9	64.4	184.2	187.5	4.9	192.4	307.4	69.3	376.6
1865–1914	297.2	144.0	441.2	749.0	38.3	787.2	1046.2	182.3	1228.4

South America and Caribbean

Years	Empire Private	Empire government	Empire Total	Foreign Private	Foreign government	Foreign Total	All capital Private	All capital government	All capital Total
1865–1869	0.7	0.1	0.8	10.0	20.1	30.1	10.7	20.2	30.9
1870–1874	0.3	1.1	1.3	36.9	60.7	97.6	37.2	61.8	98.9
1875–1879	0.0	0.2	0.2	4.1	8.0	12.2	4.1	8.2	12.4
1880–1884	0.2	0.9	1.1	27.4	9.6	37.0	27.6	10.5	38.2

Asia

Years	Empire Private	Empire government	Empire Total	Foreign Private	Foreign government	Foreign Total	All capital Private	All capital government	All capital Total
1885–1889	0.5	0.5	1.0	88.9	48.5	137.5	89.4	49.1	138.5
1890–1894	0.3	0.5	0.8	38.3	18.5	56.7	38.5	19.0	57.5
1895–1899	1.1	0.6	1.6	15.3	9.6	24.9	16.3	10.2	26.5
1900–1904	0.3	0.1	0.4	15.4	5.7	21.1	15.8	5.7	21.5
1905–1909	0.1	0.1	0.2	96.3	41.2	137.5	96.4	41.3	137.7
1910–1914	0.9	0.4	1.3	136.2	64.6	200.8	137.1	65.0	202.1
1865–1914	4.6	4.2	8.8	464.0	258.9	722.9	468.5	263.2	731.7

Years	Empire Private	Empire government	Empire Total	Foreign Private	Foreign government	Foreign Total	All capital Private	All capital government	All capital Total
1865–1869	42.6	0.4	43.0	1.9	3.3	5.2	44.5	3.7	48.2
1870–1874	15.9	10.8	26.6	7.7	7.2	14.9	23.6	17.9	41.5
1875–1879	3.6	19.4	23.0	0.2	2.8	3.0	3.7	22.2	26.0
1880–1884	10.8	13.0	23.9	1.6	0.1	1.6	12.4	13.1	25.5
1885–1889	9.4	19.9	29.4	5.3	4.0	9.3	14.8	23.9	38.7
1890–1894	5.6	25.6	31.2	6.1	7.6	13.7	11.7	33.2	44.9
1895–1899	12.1	7.1	19.2	1.3	26.2	27.5	13.4	33.3	46.7
1900–1904	8.9	6.1	15.0	0.9	8.6	9.5	9.8	14.7	24.5
1905–1909	23.9	25.8	49.7	9.9	47.2	57.0	33.7	73.0	106.7
1910–1914	37.9	28.0	66.0	18.3	28.5	46.8	56.2	56.5	112.8
1865–1914	159.1	161.0	320.0	48.4	144.5	192.9	207.5	305.4	512.9

(cont. on next page)

Table 2:2-11. (cont.)

Australasia and Pacific

Years	Private	Empire government	Total	Private	Foreign government	Total	Private	All capital government	Total
1865–1869	3.4	18.0	21.4	0.0	0.0	0.0	3.4	18.0	21.4
1870–1874	6.4	19.9	26.3	0.0	0.0	0.0	6.4	19.9	26.3
1875–1879	3.8	30.6	34.4	0.0	0.0	0.0	3.8	30.6	34.4
1880–1884	10.5	42.6	53.1	0.0	0.0	0.0	10.5	42.6	53.1
1885–1889	14.5	58.6	73.0	0.1	0.2	0.3	14.5	58.8	73.3
1890–1894	12.9	34.3	47.1	0.1	0.0	0.1	12.9	34.3	47.2
1895–1899	19.3	11.5	30.9	0.3	0.0	0.3	19.7	11.5	31.2
1900–1904	4.1	12.5	16.6	0.1	0.0	0.1	4.2	12.5	16.6
1905–1909	6.9	18.0	24.9	0.0	0.0	0.0	7.0	18.0	24.9
1910–1914	14.7	74.2	88.9	0.5	0.0	0.5	15.2	74.2	89.4
1865–1914	102.6	326.7	429.3	1.1	0.2	1.3	103.7	326.9	430.6

Europe

Years	Private	Empire government	Total	Private	Foreign government	Total	Private	All capital government	Total
1865–1869	0.7	0.0	0.7	24.4	11.5	36.0	25.1	11.5	36.6
1870–1874	0.8	0.0	0.8	35.4	7.5	42.8	36.1	7.5	43.6
1875–1879	0.0	0.0	0.0	3.0	8.0	10.9	3.0	8.0	11.0
1880–1884	0.1	0.0	0.1	8.1	59.6	67.8	8.2	59.6	67.8
1885–1889	0.1	0.0	0.1	15.1	16.6	31.7	15.3	16.6	31.8

Years	Empire Private	Empire government	Empire Total	Foreign Private	Foreign government	Foreign Total	All capital Private	All capital government	All capital Total
1890–1894	0.4	0.0	0.4	7.1	29.1	36.1	7.4	29.1	36.5
1895–1899	0.0	0.0	0.0	16.4	22.5	38.9	16.4	22.5	38.9
1900–1904	0.0	0.0	0.0	2.3	9.6	11.9	2.3	9.6	11.9
1905–1909	0.0	0.0	0.0	18.8	26.7	45.6	18.9	26.7	45.6
1910–1914	0.0	0.0	0.0	29.2	55.8	85.1	29.2	55.8	85.1
1865–1914	1.5	0.0	1.5	141.6	262.4	404.0	143.1	262.4	405.5

Africa

Years	Empire			Foreign			All capital		
	Private	government	Total	Private	government	Total	Private	government	Total
1865–1869	0.6	2.6	3.1	2.3	16.0	18.3	2.9	18.5	21.4
1870–1874	1.3	0.3	1.6	4.1	0.2	4.3	5.5	0.5	5.9
1875–1879	0.1	8.9	8.9	0.4	6.7	7.1	0.5	15.5	16.1
1880–1884	2.9	10.8	13.7	3.6	0.1	3.7	6.5	10.9	17.4
1885–1889	2.8	2.1	4.9	5.3	11.6	16.9	8.0	13.7	21.8
1890–1894	2.8	7.1	9.9	7.1	10.3	17.4	9.9	17.5	27.4
1895–1899	9.7	5.5	15.2	13.9	1.5	15.4	23.6	7.0	30.6
1900–1904	16.7	33.0	49.8	4.8	1.1	6.0	21.6	34.2	55.8
1905–1909	17.6	22.8	40.4	18.3	3.4	21.6	35.9	26.2	62.1
1910–1914	16.5	8.6	25.1	18.1	10.5	28.6	34.6	19.1	53.7
1865–1914	86.5	134.1	220.6	82.5	56.4	138.9	169.0	190.5	359.5

Sources: Lance E. Davis & Robert A. Huttenback, *Mammon and the Pursuit of Empire: The Political Economy of British Imperialism*, Table 2.4 pp. 48–49. Albert H. Imlah, *Economic Elements in the Pax Britannica: Studies in British Foreign Trade in the Nineteenth Century* (Cambridge Mass.: Harvard University Press, 1958), Table 4, pp. 70–75. C. H. Feinstein, *National Income, Expenditure and Output of the United Kingdom, 1855–1965* (Cambridge U.K.: Cambridge University Press, 1972), Table 37, p. T 82.

Table 2:3-1(a). *United Kingdom: assets held by financial institutions (millions of pounds)*

Year	Assets of commercial banks and discount companies	Assets of insurance companies	Assets of Post Office savings banks	Assets of trustee savings banks	Assets of building societies	Total assets of all non-bank financial institutions	Total assets of all financial institutions	Total bank loans & advances	Total investment in mortgages
1880	432	155	35	47	54	291	723	219	112
1881	453	160	37	48	59	304	757	222	116
1882	475	165	40	49	67	321	796	242	124
1883	492	170	44	49	69	332	824	239	126
1884	509	175	45	50	69	339	848	255	127
1885	517	179	49	51	70	349	866	248	129
1886	517	184	53	52	70	359	876	252	130
1887	527	190	57	52	71	370	897	259	132
1888	559	196	61	52	70	379	938	268	131
1889	586	204	65	51	70	390	976	282	132
1890	611	211	69	49	70	399	1,010	290	136
1891**	641	218	73	48	67	406	1,047	307	135
1891**	760	218	73	48	67	406	1,166	342	135
1892	777	223	79	48	64	414	1,191	339	133
1893	767	231	84	48	58	421	1,188	347	129
1894	802	240	95	49	57	441	1,243	345	126
1895	853	251	106	51	55	463	1,316	368	126
1896	872	264	120	53	56	493	1,365	392	125
1897	893	277	129	54	56	516	1,409	406	125
1898	925	289	134	56	58	537	1,462	421	128

Year									
1899	950	300	130	57	60	547	1,497	442	128
1900	983	311	134	57	60	562	1,545	456	131
1901	980	321	135	58	61	575	1,555	443	134
1902	994	337	139	59	63	598	1,592	442	137
1903	972	353	146	59	65	623	1,595	455	142
1904	985	367	149	59	67	642	1,627	450	148
1905	1,018	384	152	60	69	665	1,683	447	154
1906	1,048	396	156	61	71	684	1,732	470	158
1907	1,058	414	158	61	72	705	1,763	479	164
1908	1,080	429	161	62	73	725	1,805	464	165
1909	1,098	447	165	64	75	751	1,849	469	169
1910	1,137	467	169	65	76	777	1,914	508	171
1911	1,175	491	177	67	64	799	1,974	511	177
1912	1,219	511	182	69	64	826	2,045	532	180
1913	1,272	530	187	71	65	853	2,125	552	186
1914	1,361	551	191	72	66	880	2,241	581	187

Notes: ** In 1891 the Economist Incorporated Private Banks, the three discount houses, the Yorkshire Penny Bank, and the Cooperative Wholesale Society Bank in the series. The first 1891 figure is consistent with the 1898–1890 series, the second with the 1892–1914 series.

Source: D.K. Sheppard, *The Growth and Role of UK Financial Institutions, 1880–1962*, Table (A) 3.4, pp. 184–185.

Table 2:3-1(b). *United Kingdom: assets held by financial institutions (percent of total assets of all financial institutions)*

Year	Assets of commercial banks and discount companies	Assets of insurance companies	Assets of Post Office savings banks	Assets of trustee savings banks	Assets of building societies	Total assets of all non-bank financial institutions	Total assets of all financial institutions	Total bank loans & advances	Total investment in mortgages
1880	59.8	21.4	4.8	6.5	7.5	40.2	100.0	30.3	15.5
1881	59.8	21.1	4.9	6.3	7.8	40.2	100.0	29.3	15.3
1882	59.7	20.7	5.0	6.2	8.4	40.3	100.0	30.4	15.6
1883	59.7	20.6	5.3	5.9	8.4	40.3	100.0	29.0	15.3
1884	60.0	20.6	5.3	5.9	8.1	40.0	100.0	30.1	15.0
1885	59.7	20.7	5.7	5.9	8.1	40.3	100.0	28.6	14.9
1886	59.0	21.0	6.1	5.9	8.0	41.0	100.0	28.8	14.8
1887	58.8	21.2	6.4	5.8	7.9	41.2	100.0	28.9	14.7
1888	59.6	20.9	6.5	5.5	7.5	40.4	100.0	28.6	14.0
1889	60.0	20.9	6.7	5.2	7.2	40.0	100.0	28.9	13.5
1890	60.5	20.9	6.8	4.9	6.9	39.5	100.0	28.7	13.5
1891**	61.2	20.8	7.0	4.6	6.4	38.8	100.0	29.3	12.9
1891**	65.2	18.7	6.3	4.1	5.7	34.8	100.0	29.3	11.6
1892	65.2	18.7	6.6	4.0	5.4	34.8	100.0	28.5	11.2
1893	64.6	19.4	7.1	4.0	4.9	35.4	100.0	29.2	10.9
1894	64.5	19.3	7.6	3.9	4.6	35.5	100.0	27.8	10.1
1895	64.8	19.1	8.1	3.9	4.2	35.2	100.0	28.0	9.6
1896	63.9	19.3	8.8	3.9	4.1	36.1	100.0	28.7	9.2
1897	63.4	19.7	9.2	3.8	4.0	36.6	100.0	28.8	8.9
1898	63.3	19.8	9.2	3.8	4.0	36.7	100.0	28.8	8.8

1899	63.5	20.0	8.7	3.8	4.0	36.5	100.0	29.5	8.6
1900	63.6	20.1	8.7	3.7	3.9	36.4	100.0	29.5	8.5
1901	63.0	20.6	8.7	3.7	3.9	37.0	100.0	28.5	8.6
1902	62.4	21.2	8.7	3.7	4.0	37.6	100.0	27.8	8.6
1903	60.9	22.1	9.2	3.7	4.1	39.1	100.0	28.5	8.9
1904	60.5	22.6	9.2	3.6	4.1	39.5	100.0	27.7	9.1
1905	60.5	22.8	9.0	3.6	4.1	39.5	100.0	26.6	9.2
1906	60.5	22.9	9.0	3.5	4.1	39.5	100.0	27.1	9.1
1907	60.0	23.5	9.0	3.5	4.1	40.0	100.0	27.2	9.3
1908	59.8	23.8	8.9	3.4	4.0	40.2	100.0	25.7	9.1
1909	59.4	24.2	8.9	3.5	4.1	40.6	100.0	25.4	9.1
1910	59.4	24.4	8.8	3.4	4.0	40.6	100.0	26.5	8.9
1911	59.5	24.9	9.0	3.4	3.2	40.5	100.0	25.9	9.0
1912	59.6	25.0	8.9	3.4	3.1	40.4	100.0	26.0	8.8
1913	59.9	24.9	8.8	3.3	3.1	40.1	100.0	26.0	8.8
1914	60.7	24.6	8.5	3.2	2.9	39.3	100.0	25.9	8.3

Source: Table 2.3-1(a).

Table 2:3-1(c). *United Kingdom: assets held by financial institutions (millions of pounds)*

Year	Assets of commercial banks and discount companies	Assets of insurance companies	Assets of Post Office savings banks	Assets of trustee savings banks	Assets of building societies	Total assets of all non-bank financial institutions	Total assets of all financial institutions	Total bank loans & advances	Total investment in mortgages
1880	512	155	35	47	54	291	803	260	112
1881	537	160	37	48	59	304	841	263	116
1882	563	165	40	49	67	321	884	287	124
1883	583	170	44	49	69	332	915	283	126
1884	603	175	45	50	69	339	942	302	127
1885	613	179	49	51	70	349	962	294	129
1886	613	184	53	52	70	359	972	299	130
1887	625	190	57	52	71	370	995	307	132
1888	663	196	61	52	70	379	1,042	318	131
1889	695	204	65	51	70	390	1,085	334	132
1890	724	211	69	49	70	399	1,123	344	136
1891	760	218	73	48	67	406	1,166	364	135

(Percent of total assets of all financial institutions)

1880	63.8	19.3	4.4	5.9	6.7	36.2	100.0	32.3	13.9
1881	63.9	19.0	4.4	5.7	7.0	36.1	100.0	31.3	13.8
1882	63.7	18.7	4.5	5.5	7.6	36.3	100.0	32.5	14.0
1883	63.7	18.6	4.8	5.4	7.5	36.3	100.0	31.0	13.8
1884	64.0	18.6	4.8	5.3	7.3	36.0	100.0	32.1	13.5
1885	63.7	18.6	5.1	5.3	7.3	36.3	100.0	30.6	13.4
1886	63.1	18.9	5.5	5.3	7.2	36.9	100.0	30.7	13.4
1887	62.8	19.1	5.7	5.2	7.1	37.2	100.0	30.9	13.3
1888	63.6	18.8	5.9	5.0	6.7	36.4	100.0	30.5	12.6
1889	64.0	18.8	6.0	4.7	6.5	36.0	100.0	30.8	12.2
1890	64.5	18.8	6.1	4.4	6.2	35.5	100.0	30.6	12.1
1891	65.2	18.7	6.3	4.1	5.7	34.8	100.0	31.2	11.6

Notes: Adjusted Assets of Commercial Banks and Discount Companies and Adjusted Total Bank Loans & Advances are values reported in Table 2.3-1 times the ratio of Assets of Commercial Banks and Discount Companies in 1891 to 1891 (760/641).

Source: Table 2.3-1(a).

Table 2:3-2. *United Kingdom: per capita assets held by financial institutions (pounds per capita)*

Year	Assets of commercial banks and discount companies	Assets of insurance companies	Assets of Post Office savings banks	Assets of trustee savings banks	Assets of building societies	Total assets of all non-bank financial institutions	Total assets of all financial institutions	Total bank loans & advances	Total investment in mortgages
1880	12.51	4.49	1.01	1.36	1.56	8.42	20.93	6.34	3.24
1881	12.99	4.59	1.06	1.38	1.69	8.71	21.70	6.36	3.33
1882	13.51	4.69	1.14	1.39	1.91	9.13	22.63	6.88	3.53
1883	13.88	4.79	1.24	1.38	1.95	9.36	23.24	6.74	3.55
1884	14.24	4.90	1.26	1.40	1.93	9.49	23.73	7.13	3.55
1885	14.35	4.97	1.36	1.42	1.94	9.69	24.04	6.88	3.58
1886	14.24	5.07	1.46	1.43	1.93	9.89	24.13	6.94	3.58
1887	14.40	5.19	1.56	1.42	1.94	10.11	24.51	7.08	3.61
1888	15.16	5.31	1.65	1.41	1.90	10.28	25.43	7.27	3.55
1889	15.77	5.49	1.75	1.37	1.88	10.49	26.26	7.59	3.55
1890	16.32	5.63	1.84	1.31	1.87	10.65	26.97	7.74	3.63
1891**	16.99	5.78	1.93	1.27	1.78	10.76	27.75	8.14	3.58
1891**	20.14	5.78	1.93	1.27	1.78	10.76	30.90	9.06	3.58
1892	20.39	5.85	2.07	1.26	1.68	10.86	31.25	8.90	3.49
1893	19.93	6.00	2.18	1.25	1.51	10.94	30.87	9.02	3.35
1894	20.64	6.18	2.45	1.26	1.47	11.35	31.99	8.88	3.24
1895	21.75	6.40	2.70	1.30	1.40	11.80	33.55	9.38	3.21
1896	22.02	6.67	3.03	1.34	1.41	12.45	34.47	9.90	3.16
1897	22.34	6.93	3.23	1.35	1.40	12.91	35.25	10.16	3.13
1898	22.93	7.16	3.32	1.39	1.44	13.31	36.24	10.44	3.17

Year									
1899	23.33	7.37	3.19	1.40	1.47	13.44	36.77	10.86	3.14
1900	23.92	7.57	3.26	1.39	1.46	13.68	37.60	11.10	3.19
1901	23.64	7.74	3.26	1.40	1.47	13.87	37.51	10.69	3.23
1902	23.79	8.07	3.33	1.41	1.51	14.31	38.11	10.58	3.28
1903	23.03	8.36	3.46	1.40	1.54	14.76	37.79	10.78	3.36
1904	23.13	8.62	3.50	1.39	1.57	15.07	38.20	10.57	3.48
1905	23.69	8.94	3.54	1.40	1.61	15.48	39.17	10.40	3.58
1906	24.18	9.14	3.60	1.41	1.64	15.78	39.96	10.84	3.65
1907	24.20	9.47	3.61	1.40	1.65	16.13	40.33	10.96	3.75
1908	24.49	9.73	3.65	1.41	1.66	16.44	40.94	10.52	3.74
1909	24.69	10.05	3.71	1.44	1.69	16.89	41.58	10.55	3.80
1910	25.35	10.41	3.77	1.45	1.69	17.33	42.68	11.33	3.81
1911	25.98	10.86	3.91	1.48	1.42	17.67	43.65	11.30	3.91
1912	26.85	11.25	4.01	1.52	1.41	18.19	45.04	11.72	3.96
1913	27.90	11.63	4.10	1.56	1.43	18.71	46.61	12.11	4.08
1914	29.74	12.04	4.17	1.57	1.44	19.23	48.96	12.69	4.09

Sources: Table 2.3-1(a). B.R. Mitchell, *European Historical Statistics*, Abridged Edition (New York: Columbia University Press, 1978), pp. 5 & 8.

financial structure was relatively well developed by 1880, it continued to develop and expand.[83]

> The English financial sector of the 1870s was marked by a division of labor through specialization of function, but the parallel financial markets that this characteristic produced did, to some degree, coalesce in the 1880s. This merger came about not so much as a result of the London merchant banks taking an interest in the capital needs of provincial industry, but rather through the growing involvement on the part of the emerging nationwide joint-stock banks in overseas dealings. This expansion took a variety of forms but was marked by the commercial banks entering the international acceptance market, becoming investors in certain classes of overseas securities, underwriting foreign issues, and, finally, acting as issuing houses for international flotations.[84]

In absolute terms the sector grew by about 3 percent a year between 1880 and 1914; the per capita figure was in excess of 2 percent.

Functions may have shifted, but there were few dramatic changes in the sector's organizational structure. Commercial banks accounted for about 65 percent of total assets at the beginning of the period and about 60 percent at the end. Loans and advances by those institutions represented about one-third of all assets in 1880, and about one-quarter thirty-

---

distribution; however, since the banks unreported in the *Economist* are likely to have been small, the distortion involved may not be great. Under any conditions, reliance on the Sheppard data minimizes both the role of commercial banks in the financial sector and the total size of that sector.

Table 2.3-5 provides some information on the volume of business conducted by the commercial banks in the years between 1860 and 1880. Although the series contain no information on the distribution of investments, the volume of "public liabilities" is a good indicator of the sector's importance.

[83] Recent work by Buchinsky and Polak suggests that something akin to a national capital market had emerged in England by the end of the Napoleonic Wars. Moshe Buchinsky and Ben Polak, "The Emergence of a National Capital Market in England, 1710–1880," *The Journal of Economic History*, Vol. 53, No. 1 (March 1993), pp. 1–24. "Although other interpretations are possible, our results are consistent with the following story. London financial markets were already related (perhaps only weakly) to London real capital transactions in the mid–eighteenth century, and they became strongly related by the last part of that century. Regional capital markets – in particular those of the industrializing north and London – however, were still segmented in the mid–eighteenth century. But by the period of the Napoleonic Wars and, *a fortiori*, by the middle of the nineteenth century, regional capital market integration was in evidence" (p. 18).

[84] P.L. Cottrell, "Great Britain," in Rondo Cameron and V.I. Bovykin (eds.), with the assistance of Boris Anan'ich, A.A. Fursenko, Richard Sylla, and Mira Wilkins, *International Banking, 1870–1914* (New York: Oxford University Press, 1991), p. 27. [Hereafter cited as Cottrell, "Great Britain."]

four years later. The decline in the relative importance of the commercial banks was almost exactly offset by the increasing relative size of the insurance industry (from just less than 20 percent to about 25 percent of the total). In a similar fashion the decline in the share of building associations was almost entirely offset by the increase in the importance of Post Office Savings Banks. The former shift should have increased the relative volume of funds available for long-term investment; the latter change, however, merely involved a substitution of government bonds for mortgages in the portfolios of non-bank intermediaries – a trend that did not bode well for private domestic or international capital mobilization. To understand the full impact of the growth and the changes in the intrasectoral distribution of the financial sector, it is necessary to desegregate the data.

2-3a(1). The commercial banks:[85] "The earliest English bankers were the London money scriveners and goldsmiths," who by the middle of the seventeenth century "were in regular receipt of deposits which, in turn, were lent at interest in the normal manner of financial intermediation."[86] The loss of Britain's industrial dominance in the immediate pre–World War I era has been attributed to any number of causes, but since Alexander Gershenkron formulated his now famous hypothesis in the early 1960s, the finger has most frequently been pointed at the British capital markets in general and at the British commercial banks in particular. Gershenkron wrote, "Between the English bank essentially designed to serve as a source of short-term capital and a bank designed to finance the long-term needs of the economy, there was a complete gulf. The German banks, which may be taken as a paragon of the type of Universal bank, successfully combining the basic idea of the *credit mobilier* with the short-term activities of the commercial banks."[87] He then went on to argue that banks in Austria and Italy also established close relations with large-scale industrial enterprise, and that banks in France and certain other European countries adopted systems close to the German model. The British system, Gershenkron argued, had no equivalent institutions. Thus, he concludes that because of the failure of the commercial banking system, the process of industrialization in Britain was constrained and economic growth dampened. The

---

[85] For the basic data series for the post-1880 period – series on which most of this section is based – see Tables 2.3-1–2.3-7.
[86] Michael Collins, *Money and Banking in the UK: A History* (London: Croom Helm, 1988), p. 10. [Hereafter cited as Collins, *Money and Banking*.]
[87] Alexander Gershenkron, *Economic Backwardness in Historical Perspective* (Cambridge, Mass.: Harvard University Press, 1962), p. 13.

Table 2:3-3. *United Kingdom: number of commercial banks and their branches*

Year	Number of English & Welsh joint-stock banks*	Number of English & Welsh private banks	Total number of English & Welsh banks	Number of Scottish banks	Number of Irish banks	Total number of United Kingdom banks	Number of English & Welsh joint-stock branches*	Number of English & Welsh private branches	Total number of English & Welsh branches	Number of Scottish branches	Number of Irish branches	Total number of United Kingdom branches
1870	114	251	365	12	9	386	1,018	553	1,571	789	368	2,728
1871	114	250	364	12	9	385	1,031	552	1,583	791	370	2,744
1872	123	249	372	12	9	393	1,083	570	1,653	811	377	2,841
1873	127	237	364	12	9	385	1,154	556	1,710	843	391	2,944
1874	127	235	362	12	9	383	1,216	567	1,783	872	409	3,064
1875	131	235	366	12	9	387	1,307	568	1,875	906	424	3,205
1876	129	233	362	12	9	383	1,372	571	1,943	932	428	3,303
1877	126	227	353	12	9	374	1,419	573	1,992	948	452	3,392
1878	125	221	346	10	9	365	1,444	576	2,020	867	468	3,355
1879	126	212	338	10	9	357	1,467	577	2,044	872	470	3,386
1880	129	210	339	10	9	358	1,532	568	2,100	887	467	3,454
1881	127	211	338	10	9	357	1,553	585	2,138	890	470	3,498
1882	127	210	337	10	9	356	1,603	587	2,190	895	469	3,554
1883	124	205	329	10	9	348	1,576	599	2,175	904	461	3,540
1884	120	197	317	10	9	336	1,688	600	2,288	941	446	3,675
1885	125	193	318	10	9	337	1,743	608	2,351	946	433	3,730
1886	125	192	317	10	9	336	1,811	613	2,424	961	432	3,817
1887	122	193	315	10	9	334	1,822	626	2,448	963	434	3,845
1888	122	183	305	10	9	324	1,954	611	2,565	971	441	3,977
1889	116	175	291	10	9	310	2,077	586	2,663	976	443	4,082
1890	119	165	284	10	9	303	2,306	606	2,912	985	450	4,347
1891	120	143	263	10	9	282	2,459	579	3,038	995	471	4,504
1892	116	135	251	10	9	270	2,576	573	3,149	1,006	471	4,626
1893	115	130	245	10	9	264	2,726	557	3,283	1,013	473	4,769

1894	111	111	222	10	9	241	2,821	558	3,379	1,017	478	4,874
1895	109	109	218	10	9	237	2,914	466	3,380	1,024	484	4,888
1896	107	95	202	10	9	221	3,218	393	3,611	1,026	494	5,131
1897	104	91	195	10	9	214	3,445	340	3,785	1,042	498	5,325
1898	99	86	185	11	9	205	3,594	345	3,939	1,073	501	5,513
1899	98	84	182	11	9	202	3,841	355	4,196	1,083	508	5,787
1900	92	76	168	11	9	188	3,977	338	4,315	1,090	517	5,922
1901	86	71	157	11	9	177	4,155	317	4,472	1,097	525	6,094
1902	83	60	143	11	9	163	4,345	282	4,627	1,126	532	6,285
1903	77	55	132	11	9	152	4,567	226	4,793	1,143	560	6,496
1904	75	52	127	11	9	147	4,622	228	4,850	1,156	574	6,580
1905	70	47	117	11	9	137	4,826	198	5,024	1,170	565	6,759
1906	68	44	112	11	9	132	5,122	178	5,300	1,187	584	7,071
1907	67	40	107	10	9	126	5,150	166	5,316	1,167	591	7,074
1908	65	39	104	9	9	122	5,405	137	5,542	1,217	600	7,359
1909	63	37	100	9	9	118	5,363	131	5,494	1,227	602	7,323
1910	61	33	94	9	9	112	5,576	126	5,702	1,250	612	7,564
1911	53	32	85	9	9	103	5,762	121	5,883	1,255	613	7,751
1912	56	32	88	9	9	106	5,989	117	6,106	1,234	623	7,963
1913	53	33	86	9	9	104	6,152	107	6,259	1,249	648	8,156
1914	49	28	77	9	9	95	6,299	96	6,395	1,262	666	8,323

Notes: With the exception of Alexander Brown and Co. (1882–1888), the category "London Ephemeral Banks" has been included in Joint-Stock Banks; Alexander Brown & Co. was included in the category Private Banks.

Source: Forrest Capie and Alan Weber, *A Monetary History of the United Kingdom, 1870–1982, Volume I, Data, Sources, Methods* (London: George Allen & Unwin, 1985), Appendix III, pp. 576–577.

Table 2:3-4. *United Kingdom: number of persons served by the commercial banks and their branches*

Year	Persons per English & Welsh bank	Persons per Scottish bank	Persons per Irish bank	Persons per United Kingdom bank	Persons per English & Welsh branch	Persons per Scottish branch	Persons per Irish branch	Persons per United Kingdom branch
1870	61,500	277,517	605,633	80,902	14,289	4,221	14,812	11,447
1871	62,396	280,000	601,333	81,777	14,347	4,248	14,627	11,474
1872	61,930	283,167	598,667	80,977	13,937	4,190	14,292	11,202
1873	64,187	286,250	596,111	83,543	13,663	4,075	13,721	10,925
1874	65,442	289,417	593,444	84,867	13,287	3,983	13,059	10,608
1875	65,617	292,500	590,778	84,866	12,809	3,874	12,540	10,247
1876	67,246	295,667	588,111	86,642	12,529	3,807	12,367	10,047
1877	69,884	298,833	585,444	89,636	12,384	3,783	11,657	9,883
1878	72,240	362,300	582,889	92,778	12,374	4,179	11,209	10,094
1879	74,917	366,100	580,222	95,812	12,388	4,198	11,111	10,102
1880	75,658	369,800	577,667	96,494	12,213	4,169	11,133	10,001
1881	76,846	373,600	575,000	97,717	12,149	4,198	11,011	9,973
1882	77,973	376,500	569,778	98,792	11,999	4,207	10,934	9,896
1883	80,790	379,400	564,556	101,882	12,221	4,197	11,022	10,016
1884	84,804	382,300	559,333	106,369	11,750	4,063	11,287	9,725
1885	85,491	385,200	554,111	106,899	11,564	4,072	11,517	9,658
1886	86,716	388,100	548,889	108,065	11,340	4,039	11,435	9,513
1887	88,225	391,000	543,667	109,563	11,353	4,060	11,274	9,517
1888	92,111	393,900	538,444	113,824	10,953	4,057	10,989	9,273
1889	97,584	396,800	533,222	119,884	10,664	4,066	10,833	9,104
1890	101,056	399,700	528,000	123,594	9,856	4,058	10,560	8,615
1891	110,278	402,600	522,778	133,809	9,547	4,046	9,989	8,378

1892	116,956	407,100	520,000	141,137	9,322	4,047	9,936	8,238
1893	121,257	411,500	517,333	145,754	9,049	4,062	9,844	8,069
1894	135,410	416,000	514,556	161,212	8,896	4,090	9,688	7,971
1895	139,509	420,400	511,889	165,502	8,998	4,105	9,519	8,025
1896	152,307	424,900	509,111	179,172	8,520	4,141	9,275	7,717
1897	159,579	429,400	506,333	186,771	8,221	4,121	9,151	7,506
1898	170,114	394,364	503,667	196,790	7,990	4,043	9,048	7,318
1899	174,852	398,455	500,889	201,554	7,584	4,047	8,874	7,035
1900	191,524	402,455	498,222	218,548	7,457	4,061	8,673	6,938
1901	207,185	406,545	495,444	234,232	7,274	4,077	8,493	6,803
1902	229,524	409,182	494,667	256,288	7,094	3,997	8,368	6,647
1903	251,788	411,818	493,889	277,704	6,934	3,963	7,938	6,498
1904	264,496	414,455	493,111	289,714	6,926	3,944	7,732	6,472
1905	290,128	417,091	492,333	313,606	6,757	3,921	7,842	6,357
1906	306,241	419,727	491,667	328,341	6,472	3,890	7,577	6,129
1907	323,860	464,500	490,889	346,952	6,519	3,980	7,475	6,180
1908	336,606	519,333	490,111	361,410	6,317	3,841	7,352	5,992
1909	353,620	522,556	489,333	376,856	6,436	3,833	7,316	6,073
1910	379,957	525,778	488,556	400,402	6,264	3,786	7,185	5,929
1911	424,353	529,000	487,778	439,039	6,131	3,794	7,162	5,834
1912	411,955	530,333	486,556	428,340	5,937	3,868	7,029	5,702
1913	423,640	531,667	485,444	438,337	5,821	3,831	6,742	5,589
1914	475,519	533,000	484,222	481,789	5,726	3,801	6,544	5,499

Source: Table 2.3-3.

Table 2:3-5(a). *Net public liabilities of joint-stock banks: England and Wales, 1844–1880 (millions of pounds)*

Year	London	Provinces	Total
1844	11.0	35.4	46.4
1845	14.1	29.8	43.9
1846	12.1	32.8	44.9
1847	10.8	26.0	36.8
1848	12.0	24.9	36.9
1849	16.3	29.3	45.6
1850	19.4	30.1	49.5
1851	19.0	31.7	50.7
1852	23.1	36.3	59.4
1853	22.3	36.7	59.0
1854	25.8	36.2	62.0
1855	32.4	38.9	71.3
1856	35.7	43.2	78.9
1857	47.8	39.7	87.5
1858	34.5	42.7	77.2
1859	34.4	48.4	82.8
1860	38.5	46.6	85.1
1861	45.5	49.4	94.9
1862	44.6	55.2	99.8
1863	69.6	66.0	135.6
1864	93.1	70.1	163.2
1865	77.7	72.8	150.5
1866	84.6	85.4	170.0
1867	71.3	84.5	155.8
1868	70.5	78.1	148.6
1869	85.1	85.9	171.0
1870	80.6	79.4	160.0
1871	104.4	76.8	181.2
1872	110.0	100.1	210.1
1873	114.9	108.2	223.1
1874	120.5	115.1	235.6
1875	117.6	131.1	248.7
1876	137.4	138.1	275.5
1877	137.4	126.2	263.6
1878	124.4	157.4	281.8
1879	130.6	101.4	232.0
1880	128.3	120.4	248.7

Source: Michael Collins, "Long Term Growth of the English Banking Sector and the Money Stock," *The Economic History Review, Volume XXXVI*, Number 3, August 1983, Table 1, p. 376.

Table 2.3-5(b). *England and Wales: estimated net public liabilities of commercial banks, five-year moving averages (millions of pounds)*

	Joint-stock banks			Private Banks			
Year	London	Provinces	Total joint-stock banks	London	Provinces	Total private banks	Total All banks
1846	12.0	29.8	41.8	29.4	26.6	56.0	97.8
1847	13.1	28.6	41.7	30.3	27.3	57.6	99.3
1848	14.1	28.6	42.7	29.6	28.7	58.3	101.0
1849	15.5	28.4	43.9	30.3	29.1	59.4	103.3
1850	18.0	30.5	48.5	32.8	31.9	64.7	113.2
1851	20.0	32.8	52.8	33.6	35.2	68.8	121.6
1852	21.9	34.2	56.1	36.0	37.3	73.3	129.4
1853	24.5	35.9	60.4	38.7	39.6	78.3	138.7
1854	27.9	38.3	66.2	40.6	42.0	82.6	148.8
1855	32.8	38.9	71.7	41.5	42.0	83.5	155.2
1856	35.2	40.1	75.3	43.9	42.7	86.6	161.9
1857	37.0	42.6	79.6	44.4	44.5	88.9	168.5
1858	38.2	44.1	82.3	44.2	45.6	89.8	172.1
1859	40.2	45.3	85.5	45.7	45.8	91.5	177.0
1860	39.5	48.4	87.9	47.1	46.8	93.9	181.8
1861	46.5	53.1	99.6	49.5	47.5	97.0	196.6
1862	58.3	57.5	115.8	52.4	47.7	100.1	215.9
1863	66.1	62.7	128.8	51.3	48.1	99.4	228.2
1864	74.0	69.9	143.9	50.9	49.4	100.3	244.2
1865	79.3	75.8	155.1	50.4	50.6	101.0	256.1
1866	79.4	78.2	157.6	45.9	51.0	96.9	254.5
1867	77.8	81.3	159.1	43.4	51.5	94.9	254.0
1868	78.4	82.7	161.1	44.2	51.2	95.4	256.5
1869	82.4	81.0	163.4	46.0	50.2	96.2	259.6
1870	90.1	84.1	174.2	48.4	50.7	99.1	273.3
1871	99.0	90.1	189.1	53.7	51.3	105.0	294.1
1872	106.1	95.9	202.0	57.5	52.4	109.9	311.9
1873	113.5	106.2	219.7	60.3	56.1	116.4	336.1
1874	120.1	118.5	238.6	61.9	59.1	121.0	359.6
1875	125.6	143.7	269.3	61.6	60.3	121.9	391.2
1876	127.5	153.6	281.1	59.0	60.7	119.7	400.8
1877	129.5	150.9	280.4	56.1	58.5	114.6	395.0
1878	131.6	148.7	280.3	55.1	55.6	110.7	391.0

Source: Michael Collins, "Long Term Growth of the English Banking Sector and Money Stock, 1844–1880," *The Economic History Review, Second Series, Volume XXXVI*, Number 3, August 1983, Appendix IV, p. 394.

Table 2:3-6. *United Kingdom: number of commercial banks, two estimates*

| | All Banks | | | | | | All joint-stock banks: England and Wales | | | | | |
| | Number of banks | | | Number of branches | | | Number of banks | | | Number of branches | | |
Year	Capie & Weber (1)	Sheppard (2)	Ratio of (2)/(1) (3)	Capie & Weber (4)	Sheppard (5)	Ratio of (5)/(4) (6)	Capie & Weber (7)	Sheppard (8)	Ratio of (8)/(7) (9)	Capie & Weber (10)	Sheppard (11)	Ratio of (11)/(10) (12)
1880	358	108	0.30	3,454	2,712	0.79	129	89	0.69	1,532	1,335	0.87
1881	357	112	0.31	3,498	2,752	0.79	127	93	0.73	1,553	1,369	0.88
1882	356	119	0.33	3,554	2,869	0.81	127	100	0.79	1,603	1,487	0.93
1883	348	123	0.35	3,540	2,937	0.83	124	104	0.84	1,576	1,553	0.99
1884	336	126	0.38	3,675	2,910	0.79	120	107	0.89	1,688	1,542	0.91
1885	337	129	0.38	3,730	2,807	0.75	125	110	0.88	1,743	1,498	0.86
1886	336	128	0.38	3,817	2,918	0.76	125	109	0.87	1,811	1,546	0.85
1887	334	128	0.38	3,845	3,032	0.79	122	109	0.89	1,822	1,655	0.91
1888	324	130	0.40	3,977	3,105	0.78	122	111	0.91	1,954	1,710	0.88
1889	310	122	0.39	4,082	3,319	0.81	116	103	0.89	2,077	1,918	0.92
1890	303	123	0.41	4,347	3,634	0.84	119	104	0.87	2,306	2,203	0.96
1891	282	125	0.44	4,504	3,685	0.82	120	106	0.88	2,459	2,244	0.91
1891	282	168	0.60	4,504	3,685	0.82	120	106	0.88	2,459	2,244	0.91
1892	270	168	0.62	4,626	3,776	0.82	116	102	0.88	2,576	2,326	0.90
1893	264	166	0.63	4,769	4,003	0.84	115	99	0.86	2,726	2,515	0.92
1894	241	164	0.68	4,874	4,120	0.85	111	99	0.89	2,821	2,624	0.93
1895	237	162	0.68	4,888	4,204	0.86	109	99	0.91	2,914	2,695	0.92
1896	221	146	0.66	5,131	4,576	0.89	107	94	0.88	3,218	3,051	0.95
1897	214	137	0.64	5,325	5,180	0.97	104	90	0.87	3,445	3,454	1.00
1898	205	135	0.66	5,513	5,335	0.97	99	87	0.88	3,594	3,577	1.00

Year												
1899	202	130	0.64	5,787	5,486	0.95	98	83	0.85	3,841	3,826	1.00
1900	188	119	0.63	5,922	5,375	0.91	92	77	0.84	3,977	3,757	0.94
1901	177	115	0.65	6,094	5,679	0.93	86	74	0.86	4,155	3,935	0.95
1902	163	108	0.66	6,285	5,946	0.95	83	68	0.82	4,345	4,146	0.95
1903	152	102	0.67	6,496	6,059	0.93	77	65	0.84	4,567	4,334	0.95
1904	147	98	0.67	6,580	6,164	0.94	75	61	0.81	4,622	4,415	0.96
1905	137	95	0.69	6,759	6,344	0.94	70	59	0.84	4,826	4,558	0.94
1906	132	90	0.68	7,071	6,529	0.92	68	55	0.81	5,122	4,722	0.92
1907	126	86	0.68	7,074	6,616	0.94	67	52	0.78	5,150	4,822	0.94
1908	122	83	0.68	7,359	6,754	0.92	65	50	0.77	5,405	4,963	0.92
1909	118	77	0.65	7,323	6,862	0.94	63	46	0.73	5,363	5,022	0.94
1910	112	76	0.68	7,564	7,086	0.94	61	45	0.74	5,576	5,202	0.93
1911	103	75	0.73	7,751	7,314	0.94	53	44	0.83	5,762	5,410	0.94
1912	106	75	0.71	7,963	7,485	0.94	56	44	0.79	5,989	5,577	0.93
1913	104	71	0.68	8,156	7,747	0.95	53	43	0.81	6,152	5,797	0.94
1914	95	66	0.69	8,323	7,815	0.94	49	38	0.78	6,299	5,869	0.93

Sources: Forrest Capie and Alan Weber, *A Monetary History of the United Kingdom, 1870–1982, Volume 1*, Data, Sources, Methods (London: George Allen & Unwin, 1985), Appendix III, pp. 576–577. D.K. Sheppard, *The Growth and Role of UK Financial Institutions, 1880–1962* (London: Methuen, 1971), Table (A) 1.1, pp. 116–117 and Table (A) 1.2, pp. 118–119.

Table 2:3-7(a). *United Kingdom: combined balance sheets of commercial banks* (millions of pounds)*

| | Total liabilities | | | | | Total assets | | | Discounts | | Securities | | | |
Year	Total assets & liabilities	Deposits & other accounts	Notes in circulation	Paid-up capital & reserves	Other liabilities	Premises & other assets	Money at call & short notice	Cash	Treasury bills	Other bills	British gov't & gov't. guaranteed	Other	Loans & Advances & other accounts	Balancing item
1880*	488.8	387.1	14.4	82.0	5.3	8.5	40.3	43.5	0.0	62.8	45.2	37.7	247.5	3.4
1881*	511.7	407.1	15.8	84.8	4.0	10.9	44.4	48.1	0.0	70.7	46.5	40.0	251.3	-0.1
1882*	536.9	425.8	17.5	89.8	3.8	10.1	45.0	48.4	0.0	73.2	43.9	45.6	274.0	-3.1
1883*	556.8	443.0	15.8	93.7	4.3	14.0	46.2	49.3	0.0	79.0	48.6	47.9	270.7	1.0
1884*	575.8	459.7	15.2	96.6	2.1	12.0	45.8	48.7	0.0	71.9	51.4	61.6	288.4	4.1
1885*	584.7	468.3	14.8	97.0	0.0	13.0	49.4	51.9	0.0	70.8	51.9	65.0	280.7	1.9
1886*	584.7	468.4	14.7	97.3	4.2	12.3	50.7	53.8	0.0	70.3	53.5	59.1	284.8	0.1
1887*	595.9	480.4	14.2	97.1	4.1	12.7	52.3	54.8	0.0	68.2	51.7	64.3	292.7	-0.9
1888*	632.3	513.4	15.2	99.4	4.3	13.2	57.4	60.4	0.0	70.9	55.2	71.9	303.6	-0.3
1889*	662.0	541.2	16.1	100.1	4.6	9.5	61.2	64.2	0.0	73.2	61.4	73.0	319.0	0.6
1890*	691.3	564.0	16.2	105.2	6.0	14.6	63.2	66.3	0.0	73.8	68.2	77.9	327.3	0.0
1891*	725.2	592.2	15.7	104.6	12.7	14.4	66.5	70.6	0.0	71.0	73.2	81.9	347.6	0.2
1891	725.2	594.8	14.4	104.8	11.2	12.7	70.0	69.2	0.0	64.2	74.8	89.7	342.2	2.4
1892	739.6	608.1	14.0	106.4	11.1	15.2	73.5	71.0	0.0	66.8	79.4	92.7	339.3	1.7
1893	732.1	600.5	14.0	106.7	10.9	14.8	71.0	67.9	0.0	60.1	81.1	88.8	347.3	1.1
1894	763.3	632.2	14.2	106.5	10.4	14.8	81.8	80.0	0.0	65.2	77.7	97.7	345.1	1.0
1895	810.8	677.1	14.8	106.8	12.1	16.0	85.2	82.5	0.0	69.7	78.1	109.2	368.3	1.8

Year														
1896	834.6	700.7	14.6	106.6	12.7	17.0	82.1	81.3	0.0	69.7	77.2	115.4	392.4	-0.5
1897	856.4	721.7	14.8	106.7	13.2	17.0	85.1	85.7	0.0	67.3	74.2	121.0	405.8	0.3
1898	885.6	749.4	15.1	109.5	11.6	17.4	91.4	91.8	0.0	66.6	74.2	121.7	420.7	1.8
1899	913.7	774.3	15.5	110.8	13.1	17.8	91.7	92.2	0.0	68.6	75.0	122.9	442.4	3.1
1900	941.7	798.9	15.8	112.8	14.2	20.6	97.6	98.5	7.3	61.6	77.5	123.4	456.1	-0.9
1901	938.9	796.9	15.0	114.2	12.8	20.1	101.7	102.6	9.0	57.1	79.2	123.9	442.9	2.4
1902	954.1	808.8	15.5	115.3	14.5	21.4	106.6	108.3	9.1	62.6	81.3	120.2	442.4	2.2
1903	934.0	790.2	15.2	115.4	13.2	18.6	97.1	98.3	9.1	60.0	78.9	114.9	454.6	2.5
1904	944.4	802.0	14.6	115.2	12.6	16.8	104.8	106.7	9.1	62.2	87.8	108.9	450.0	-1.9
1905	971.6	828.0	14.0	115.6	14.0	20.8	112.1	114.1	9.1	68.4	85.4	115.2	447.4	-0.9
1906	998.1	853.8	14.5	115.8	14.0	19.6	112.6	114.6	8.4	73.3	86.3	112.8	470.1	0.4
1907	1,003.6	861.8	14.5	114.9	12.5	19.9	112.6	113.3	5.1	77.4	85.8	109.1	478.8	1.6
1908	1,023.9	883.8	14.0	115.1	11.1	19.5	120.2	123.3	5.5	81.2	86.1	121.8	464.3	2.0
1909	1,039.8	899.6	14.0	114.4	11.8	19.3	124.3	127.0	6.5	79.7	80.7	131.8	469.2	1.3
1910	1,081.1	939.4	14.5	114.3	12.9	20.1	123.5	127.2	6.4	80.7	78.9	133.3	507.8	3.2
1911	1,118.0	977.6	14.6	114.5	11.3	24.6	133.0	136.0	6.5	93.6	78.2	134.5	510.9	0.7
1912	1,156.1	1,012.3	15.1	115.2	13.5	25.6	137.7	139.6	4.1	105.0	74.2	133.8	531.5	4.6
1913	1,205.0	1,059.4	16.0	115.8	13.8	26.7	147.5	151.9	4.7	114.6	70.3	135.1	552.3	1.9
1914	1,312.6	1,163.2	20.6	114.8	14.0	28.2	121.9	224.4	6.0	109.3	100.4	140.6	581.3	0.5

Notes: (1) * Sheppard's calculations for 1880–1890 do not include Private Banks. *The Economist* only began publishing its "Private Bank Series" in 1891. To adjust for that omission the totals for the years 1880–1890 have been adjusted upward by the ratio of "Total Assets" 1891 old and "Total Assets" 1891 new (1 13065).

(2) The category "Balancing Item" has been included because the sum of Sheppard's Assets are not equal to his "Total Assets and Liabilities."

Source: D.K. Sheppard, *The Growth and Role of UK Financial Institutions, 1880–1962*, Table (A) 1.1, pp. 116–117.

Table 2:3-7(b). *United Kingdom: combined balance sheets of commercial banks* (percentage distribution)*

Year	Total assets & liabilities	Deposits & other accounts	Notes in circulation	Paid-up capital & reserves	Other liabilities	Premises & other assets	Money at call & short notice	Cash	Treasury bills	Other bills	British gov't & gov't guaranteed	Other	Loans & Advances & other accounts
	Total liabilities					Total assets			Discounts		Securities		
1880*	100.0	79.2	2.9	16.8	1.1	1.7	8.3	9.0	0.0	12.9	9.3	7.8	51.0
1881*	100.0	79.6	3.1	16.6	0.8	2.1	8.7	9.4	0.0	13.8	9.1	7.8	49.1
1882*	100.0	79.3	3.3	16.7	0.7	1.9	8.3	9.0	0.0	13.5	8.1	8.4	50.7
1883*	100.0	79.6	2.8	16.8	0.8	2.5	8.3	8.9	0.0	14.2	8.7	8.6	48.7
1884*	100.0	80.1	2.6	16.8	0.4	2.1	7.9	8.4	0.0	12.4	8.9	10.6	49.7
1885*	100.0	80.7	2.6	16.7	0.0	2.2	8.5	8.9	0.0	12.1	8.9	11.2	48.2
1886*	100.0	80.1	2.5	16.7	0.7	2.1	8.7	9.2	0.0	12.0	9.1	10.1	48.7
1887*	100.0	80.6	2.4	16.3	0.7	2.1	8.8	9.2	0.0	11.4	8.7	10.8	49.1
1888*	100.0	81.2	2.4	15.7	0.7	2.1	9.1	9.5	0.0	11.2	8.7	11.4	48.0
1889*	100.0	81.8	2.4	15.1	0.7	1.4	9.2	9.7	0.0	11.1	9.3	11.0	48.2
1890*	100.0	81.6	2.3	15.2	0.9	2.1	9.1	9.6	0.0	10.7	9.9	11.3	47.4
1891*	100.0	81.7	2.2	14.4	1.7	2.0	9.2	9.7	0.0	9.8	10.1	11.3	47.9
1891	100.0	82.0	2.0	14.5	1.5	1.8	9.7	9.6	0.0	8.9	10.3	12.4	47.3
1892	100.0	82.2	1.9	14.4	1.5	2.1	10.0	9.6	0.0	9.1	10.8	12.6	46.0
1893	100.0	82.0	1.9	14.6	1.5	2.0	9.7	9.3	0.0	8.2	11.1	12.1	47.5
1894	100.0	82.8	1.9	14.0	1.4	1.9	10.7	10.5	0.0	8.6	10.2	12.8	45.3
1895	100.0	83.5	1.8	13.2	1.5	2.0	10.5	10.2	0.0	8.6	9.7	13.5	45.5

Year													
1896	100.0	84.0	1.7	12.8	1.5	2.0	9.8	9.7	0.0	8.3	9.2	13.8	47.0
1897	100.0	84.3	1.7	12.5	1.5	2.0	9.9	10.0	0.0	7.9	8.7	14.1	47.4
1898	100.0	84.6	1.7	12.4	1.3	2.0	10.3	10.4	0.0	7.5	8.4	13.8	47.6
1899	100.0	84.7	1.7	12.1	1.4	2.0	10.1	10.1	0.0	7.5	8.2	13.5	48.6
1900	100.0	84.8	1.7	12.0	1.5	2.2	10.4	10.4	0.8	6.5	8.2	13.1	48.4
1901	100.0	84.9	1.6	12.2	1.4	2.1	10.9	11.0	1.0	6.1	8.5	13.2	47.3
1902	100.0	84.8	1.6	12.1	1.5	2.2	11.2	11.4	1.0	6.6	8.5	12.6	46.5
1903	100.0	84.6	1.6	12.4	1.4	2.0	10.4	10.6	1.0	6.4	8.5	12.3	48.8
1904	100.0	84.9	1.5	12.2	1.3	1.8	11.1	11.3	1.0	6.6	9.3	11.5	47.6
1905	100.0	85.2	1.4	11.9	1.4	2.1	11.5	11.7	0.9	7.0	8.8	11.8	46.0
1906	100.0	85.5	1.5	11.6	1.4	2.0	11.3	11.5	0.8	7.3	8.6	11.3	47.1
1907	100.0	85.9	1.4	11.4	1.2	2.0	11.2	11.3	0.5	7.7	8.6	10.9	47.8
1908	100.0	86.3	1.4	11.2	1.1	1.9	11.8	12.1	0.5	7.9	8.4	11.9	45.4
1909	100.0	86.5	1.3	11.0	1.1	1.9	12.0	12.2	0.6	7.7	7.8	12.7	45.2
1910	100.0	86.9	1.3	10.6	1.2	1.9	11.5	11.8	0.6	7.5	7.3	12.4	47.1
1911	100.0	87.4	1.3	10.2	1.0	2.2	11.9	12.2	0.6	8.4	7.0	12.0	45.7
1912	100.0	87.6	1.3	10.0	1.2	2.2	12.0	12.1	0.4	9.1	6.4	11.6	46.2
1913	100.0	87.9	1.3	9.6	1.1	2.2	12.3	12.6	0.4	9.5	5.8	11.2	45.9
1914	100.0	88.6	1.6	8.7	1.1	2.1	9.3	17.1	0.5	8.3	7.7	10.7	44.3

Notes: Percentage distribution is made on the basis of the sum of the stated assets and liabilities, since those categories seldom sum to Sheppard's "Total Assets and Total Liabilities."

Source: Table 2.3-7(a).

successful process of industrialization in the United States and Canada –
countries that, like Britain, never developed universal banks, however –
casts some doubts on that conclusion.

In the United Kingdom critics, picking up from Gershenkron, were
quick to direct their attack to the failure of British banks to accommodate domestic industry. William Kennedy, the most vocal, wrote:

> Just as the generals are often preparing to fight the next war as a con-
> tinuation of the last one, so British bankers in the late nineteenth
> century perfected a system of capital formation more appropriate to
> the age that was passing than the age that was coming. In the new con-
> ditions of increased scale, complexity and competitiveness, efficiency
> required more complete, accurate and timely information than had
> been necessary or even possible previously. The effective withdrawal of
> banks from close and risky involvement with industrial and commer-
> cial firms removed an important element of personal contact that
> had earlier permitted higher flows of information and had created
> tighter bonds of mutual interest than were subsequently to be typical.
> The bureaucratized and amalgamated Victorian banking system, with
> its rigid limitations on the initiative of the local bank managers who
> knew their borrowers best and with its equally inflexible requirements
> that loans be amply safeguarded by collateral, not only wasted infor-
> mation prodigiously but also acted to stifle any impulse to change this
> condition.[88]

Some critics have argued that the British markets were biased toward
foreign, as opposed to domestic, investments.[89] Others, including
Kennedy, have concluded that the bias was not toward foreign investment but "towards safe, well-known securities in general, a greater
number of which were foreign, and away from riskier, smaller, but ultimately from an economy-wide viewpoint, much more profitable ones."[90]
From the point of view of policy, it makes little difference which one of

---

[88] William P. Kennedy, *Industrial Structure, Capital Markets and the Origins of
British Economic Decline* (Cambridge: Cambridge University Press, 1987), p.
123. [Hereafter cited as Kennedy, *Industrial Structure, Capital Markets.*] Recently
Kennedy has widened the range of his Gershenkron-like attack on the economic
performance of the commercial banks to include much of the financial sector.
See William P. Kennedy, "Capital Markets and Industrial Structure in the Vic-
torian Economy," in J.J. Van Helten and Y. Cassis (eds.), *Capitalism in a Mature
Economy: Financial Institutions, Capital Exports and British Industry, 1870–1939*
(Aldershot, U.K.: Edward Elgar, 1990), pp. 23–51.
[89] The skeleton of the argument is succinctly summarized in Edelstein, *Overseas
Investment*, pp. 5–7.
[90] Kennedy, *Industrial Structure, Capital Markets*, p. 145.

the explanations is correct. In either case it was the seductive call of foreign alternatives that led British banks to this alleged suboptimal equilibrium. The commercial banks, however, are not without their defenders. Detailed studies by scholars such as Forrest Capie and Michael Collins have shown that British banks were much better than the critics have suggested. A very detailed rebuttal of the "bias" argument can be found in Michael Edelstein's "Foreign Investment and Accumulation, 1860–1914."[91] The academic debate still rages; here it is not possible to do more than provide a summary of those parts of the debate that focus on issues relevant to this book.

Although the London money scriveners and goldsmiths had been active for almost a century, and the Bank of England had possessed a near monopoly on note issue in London for an even longer period, historians have dated the beginning of the evolution of modern banking in the United Kingdom from the years 1825–26. In 1825 there were just over 700 banks in the United Kingdom, 650 of them in England and Wales. All of the latter – the Bank of England aside – were private (noncorporate) banks. Because none was legally permitted to have more than six partners, their capital resources were severely limited.[92] In 1825 and 1826, 93 of the 650 found themselves unable to meet their depositors' demands for cash. In an attempt to bolster the system the government introduced, and Parliament enacted, two pieces of legislation that together provided the basis for restructuring the legislative environment within which the banks were to operate.

The first law prohibited private banks in England and Wales from issuing bank notes of less than £5. That effectively extended the Bank of England's monopoly on bank note issue throughout England and Wales, and it substantially changed the way that English banks did business. The second, the Joint-Stock Bank Act of 1826, was the first in a series of

---

[91] Michael Edelstein, "Foreign Investment and Accumulation, 1860–1914," in Roderick Floud and Donald McClosky (eds.), *The Economic History of Britain Since 1706. Vol. 2: 1860–1939*, 2d ed. (Cambridge: Cambridge University Press, 1994), pp. 187–91.

[92] Legislation passed in 1708 had restricted the number of partners in all English and Welsh banks except the Bank of England and had granted joint-stock status only to that institution. Banking in Scotland was less hampered by legal restrictions. At the center of the Scottish system were the three Edinburgh public (or chartered) joint-stock banks: the Bank of Scotland, the Royal Bank of Scotland, and the British Linen Company. In 1825 those three operated a total of 173 branches. In addition there were no restrictions on the number of partners in the thirty-three private banks. In the case of Ireland, legislation similar to the English Act of 1826 was passed by Parliament in 1821. Collins, *Money and Banking*, pp. 10, 13.

legislative acts that allowed banks access to larger capital resources and that ultimately granted their shareholders some form of limited liability. In terms of the structure of the banking industry, it was the more important of the two. The act permitted the organization of banks (initially only banks located more than sixty-five miles from London) with an unlimited number of partners or shareholders. Although the Bank Charter Act of 1844 slowed the rate of new bank formation, by 1850 there were 99 joint-stock banks with 576 offices operating in England and Wales.[93] Thereafter, with the benefit of limited liability, and in 1854 with the admission of joint-stock banks to the London Clearing House, growth of what was to become the joint-stock banking sector was very rapid.[94] Ten years later, with the admission of the Bank of England to the Clearing House, an effective, national check clearing system was created "with bankers drawing on their balances with the Bank of England to settle debts among themselves."[95]

Between 1862 and 1866 "the number of joint-stock branch offices increased by over one-half; the number of banks rose by almost one-fifth; and there was a massive surge – an increase of something like eighty percent – in note and deposit liabilities."[96] By 1875, 131 English and Welsh joint-stock banks operated out of 1,438 offices (there were also 235 private banks with 568 branches). Another 21 Scottish and Irish banks with some 1,330 branches should be added to those totals.[97] By

[93] The Joint-Stock Act of 1844 placed minimum capital requirements and other restrictions (e.g., it required monthly publication of a bank's balance sheet) on new joint-stock banks; it was repealed in 1857.

[94] Initially all shareholders in United Kingdom banks (except those of the three Scottish chartered public banks) were subject to unlimited liability. The enabling legislation of 1858 and 1862 permitted the extension of limited liability to shareholders in joint-stock banks, and the Companies Act of 1879 granted all bank shareholders "reserved" liability – potential liability was restricted to a fixed sum – for all of a bank's debts and liabilities except its note issue. In 1854 the first joint-stock bank was granted admission to the London Clearing House, previously an "exclusive private banker's reserve." Collins, *Money and Banking*, pp. 74, 100–1.

[95] The Edinburgh Clearing House was established in 1865, the Dublin Clearing House in 1845. Collins, *Money and Banking*, pp. 86–87.

[96] Collins, *Money and Banking*, p. 74.

[97] The joint-stock designation was much less important in the case of the Irish and Scottish banks. The latter had never been restricted in terms of the numbers of partners and the restrictions in the former case had been lifted in 1821. Scottish banks, for example, by operating as extended co-partnerships with numerous partners, were, in reality, no different from joint-stock banks with unlimited liability. Michie, for example, in a private conversation, noted that he "could never see any difference between the North of Scotland Bank –

the turn of the century the commercial banking sector still included both joint-stock and private banks, but as Table 2:3-3 indicates, the 112 joint-stock banks with their almost 5,600 branches were what had come to dominate the industry. It is estimated that those banks held more than 90 percent of the industry's assets.[98]

The increase in the importance of joint-stock banks came at the expense of private banks. Over the four years 1862 to 1866, the assets of private banks increased by only 20 percent; by the end of the 1870s their number in England and Wales had fallen to 212, and although they still operated 577 branches, their share of English banking offices, total deposits, and note liabilities had fallen to less than one-third.[99] Thereafter, despite the potential benefits of close personal connections between bankers and borrowers, the private banking sector continued to decline, both absolutely and relatively. By 1914, when 49 English and Welsh joint-stock banks operated almost 6,300 branches, there remained fewer than 30 private banks controlling a total of less than 100 branches.

Between 1850 and 1875 real bank deposits per capita – deposits in both private and joint-stock banks – more than doubled (from £6 to £13.3). Subsequent growth was slower, but that figure had reached £20.5 by 1900.[100] The volume of aggregate assets of the commercial banking sector continued to grow, but after 1870 the structure of the sector changed dramatically.

In Scotland bankers had never been constrained by legal rules that limited capitalization, and they had always been free to open branches. As late as the 1870s, private and joint-stock banks in England and Wales were still essentially local concerns. They were, however, endowed with one important attribute: They were not restricted by law or custom from opening branches. Thus, when it came to establishing networks of branches, it was the Scots who were the innovating entrepreneurs, and the English who joined Schumpeter's "herd-like movement." In the late eighteenth century a typical Scottish banker supplemented the business of his head office by operating a small regional network of branch offices. By 1875 the number of offices per bank in Scotland (both chartered and joint-stock) was more than eight times the number being operated by joint-stock banks in England, and "by this time the main banks had established

---

Aberdeen based – and the National Provincial Bank – London based; and both were formed in the 1830s." By 1880 the Scottish and Irish banks had all acquired joint-stock status.

[98] Sheppard, *The Growth and Role of UK Financial Institutions*, appendices (A) 1.2, 1.3, and 1.4, p. 123.

[99] Collins, *Money and Banking*, pp. 9–10, 13, and 72–75, and table 2.4, p. 53.

[100] Collins, *Money and Banking*, table 2.2, p. 46.

'national' systems of branches covering most of Scotland and they were in the process of opening offices in London in order to participate in the business of the world's largest financial center."[101]

Bankers in Ireland and in England and Wales were slower to adopt the new organizational structure, although there were a few exceptions. The Northern and Central Bank of England had operated a large branch network in the 1830s, and a decade later the London-based National Provincial Bank of England had ninety branches scattered across the country. Those two were the exceptions. In the middle of the nineteenth century a typical English bank was still locally based; when it did begin to add branches, they tended to be concentrated in the local region. Gradually, as improvements in communication made it possible to expand the geographic scope of a bank's business, and thus to capture the benefits of increasing returns, the picture changed. London banks extended their networks into the provinces, provincial banks began to open offices in the City, and the initially idiosyncratic structure of the National Provincial Bank gradually became the industry's norm.

However, the movement toward national integration was more gradual than a cursory reading in banking history might suggest. Until the 1880s there were really two distinct banking systems, systems that had developed quite separately. One encompassed the commercial banks in the provinces and the other those in the City. The complete fusion of the two systems was not accomplished until after World War I, and it depended chiefly on the provincial banks' becoming City institutions rather than the London banks' "reaching out into the provinces and so encompassing the whole of the economy."[102]

Increasing firm size was not accompanied by an equivalent expansion in the size of the aggregate market. Instead, the growth of branch networks led to a reduction in the number of banks – a reduction that, while concentrated in the 1890s, has been labeled the amalgamation movement of 1870–1917.[103] There were three types of mergers. Most often the amal-

---

[101] Collins, *Money and Banking*, p. 75.

[102] Philip L. Cottrell, "The Domestic Commercial Banks and the City of London, 1870–1939," in Youssef Cassis (ed.), *Finance and Financiers in European History, 1880–1960* (Cambridge: Cambridge University Press, 1992), pp. 58–59. [Hereafter cited as Cottrell, "The Domestic Banks and the City of London."]

[103] Forrest Capie, "Structure and Performance in British Banking, 1870–1939," in P.L. Cottrell and D.E. Moggridge (eds.), *Money and Power: Essays in Honour of L.S. Pressnell* (London: Macmillan Press, 1988), p. 77. [Hereafter cited as Capie, "Structure and Performance."] Collins dates the period of greatest merger activity somewhat earlier, 1888–94, when there were 69 mergers, more than had taken place between 1870 and 1888. Collins, *Money and Banking*, pp. 78–79.

gamation involved the takeover of a private bank by a joint-stock bank. The merger of one private bank with another – a merger often triggered by a hostile takeover attempt by a joint-stock bank – was also common. Finally, there were a number of mergers between two joint-stock banks.[104]

Forrest Capie estimates that there were 387 private and joint-stock banks in the United Kingdom in 1870, by 1890 the number had fallen to 302, by 1900 to 199, and, by 1920, to 75. He estimates that over the same years the number of branches increased from 2,728 to 4,236 to 5,894 to 9,668.[105] As the number of banks fell, the average size of banks increased, but the expansion was not uniform – large banks grew more rapidly than small ones. In 1870 the five largest banks in England and Wales accounted for one-quarter of all deposits; half a century later, Barclays, Lloyds, the Midland, the National Provincial, and the Westminster together held four-fifths.[106]

The reduction in the number of firms, and the resulting increase in size and bureaucratic structure, raises three questions that bear on the role of the commercial banks in the processes of domestic capital accumulation and mobilization: (1) As the personal relations between bank officers and local borrowers shifted from owner and borrower to manager and borrower, did the banks' loan policies change? (2) Did the banking industry become more or less competitive? (3) Was the resulting industrial structure more stable than the structure that it replaced?

Any answer to the first question must be tentative; the academic jury is still out. The amalgamation movement almost certainly reduced the personal contact between the banker – a banker with local knowledge

---

[104] Capie, "Structure and Performance," p. 77; Collins, *Money and Banking*, pp. 78–79.

[105] Forrest Capie, "Prudent and Stable (But Inefficient?): Commercial Banks in Britain, 1890–1940," in Michael D. Bordo and Richard Sylla (eds.), *Anglo-American Financial Systems: Institutions and Markets in the Twentieth Century* (Burr Ridge, Ill.: Irwin Professional Publishing, 1995), table 2-2, p. 44. [Hereafter cited as Capie, "Prudent and Stable."] These figures differ somewhat from his earlier enumeration (table 2.3-3). In that work he estimated the number of banks as 386 in 1870, 303 in 1890, and 179 in 1900 and the number of branches at 2,728, 4,347, and 5,922. Sheppard puts the figures at 168 and 3,685 for 1891, 76 and 7,086 for 1910, and 44 and 9,807 for 1920. Sheppard, *The Growth and Role of UK Financial Institutions*, table (A) 1.1, pp. 116–17.

[106] Forrest Capie and Ghila Rodrik-Bali, "Concentration in British Banking, 1870–1920," *Business History*, Vol. 24 (1982), pp. 280–92. Over the same period the Herfindahl-Hirschman concentration index (low implies concentration) for banking in the U.K. fell from 74 to 11, and, for England and Wales, from 59 to 8. Capie, "Structure and Performance," p. 78.

and capable of making independent loan decisions – and local business-men. The local banker was replaced by a branch manager who was often bound to follow the strictures laid on him by the bank's London-based officers, officers who were in turn charged with producing a single corporate ethos and a standardized set of policies from a conglomeration of heretofore separate banks. Moreover, the amalgamation movement went hand in hand with the "professionalization" of bank management. Professionalization was a term used to cover the general agreement about what "constituted respectable business and acceptable practice for banks" – a set of attitudes that were "noticeably conservative and cautious" and that extolled the virtues of liquidity.[107]

One piece of evidence for the new professionalized national corporate policies was the substitution of the London-favored collateral-based (secured) loans for the overdrafts that had been standard in the country banks. As Sir Felix Schuster of the Union of London and Smith's Bank argued, "London banks were more likely to insist on the security of collateral than country banks would have been, and that, partly as the result of the conversion of private trading firms into limited liability joint-stock companies, the London based banks were tending to ask for collateral from a growing proportion of their own customers."[108]

In 1911 L. Joseph concluded that overdrafts tended to be limited in size and that "an industrial customer could not always rely on a request for such a commitment to be treated favorably." Sir Felix Schuster, when interviewed by the National Monetary Commission, argued that banks should not be providers of permanent working capital, only granters of temporary loans. Finally, Lavington predicted that bank assets would change, "as long as loans made by absorbed banks were recovered by their new managers, who would then place the resources so released in 'advances both secured and more readily available.'"[109] On the basis of

---

[107] Forrest Capie and Michael Collins, *Have Banks Failed British Industry?* (London: Institute of Economic Affairs, 1992), pp. 40–42. [Hereafter cited as Capie and Collins, *Have Banks Failed British Industry?*].

[108] C.A.E. Goodhart, *The Business of Banking, 1891–1914* (London: London School of Economics and Political Science and Weidenfeld and Nicolson, 1972), p. 154. [Hereafter cited as Goodhart, *The Business of Banking.*]

[109] L. Joseph, *Industrial Finance, A Comparison Between Home and Foreign Developments* (1911), p. 9; Lavington, *The English Capital Market*, p. 145; National Monetary Commission, *Interviews on the Banking and Currency System of England* (Washington, D.C.: G.P.O., 1910), Interview with Sir Felix Schuster, pp. 47–8. These are all cited in Philip L. Cottrell, "The Domestic Commercial Banks of the City of London, 1870–1939," in Youssef Cassis (ed.), *Finance and Financiers in European History, 1880–1960* (Cambridge: Cambridge University Press, 1992), p. 55. [Hereafter cited as Cottrell, "The Domestic Commercial Banks."]

this information, Cottrell twenty years ago concluded that the answer to the first question was yes. "The amalgamation movement led not only to more restrictive, bureaucratically controlled bank lending but also to tighter security requirements for loans."[110]

More recent research on the Midland Bank has cast doubt on that conclusion. Holmes and Green have shown that after 1900, at least, the lending limits that the bank imposed on branch managers were frequently higher than those that had been employed by the banks that it absorbed, and that with amalgamation it was possible for large corporate customers to deal directly with the London board, sidestepping the branch manager altogether.[111] Although the evidence refers to only a single bank, of all the large banks, the Midland certainly had the most centralized managerial control system.

Forrest Capie, working from a large sample of bank archival records, has found that the loan/asset ratio was stable across the years 1880–1914, and that from 1878 onward there was no decline in the ratio of the volatility of bank returns to the volatility of returns in the market as a whole.[112] If the conventional account of increasing banking conservatism were correct, given the stability of the loan/asset ratio, "we should find a steady fall in the [latter] measure." In addition, Capie finds no significant shift over time in the underlying principles that governed industrial lending. "There was an apparent constancy in the basic nature of loans to industry throughout the period, changes were largely confined to detail." He concludes that both early and late lending was largely short-term. "In particular, the banks generally refused to supply capital investment and concentrated on short-term lending (even if the loans were regularly renewed), though there may be some examples of long-term capital investment."[113] Capie's evidence does not go to the question of long-term commercial bank lending, but it does suggest that the banks

---

[110] Philip Cottrell, *Industrial Finance, 1830–1914: The Finance and Organization of the English Manufacturing System* (London: Methuen 1979), p. 278. [Hereafter cited as Cottrell, *Industrial Finance.*]

[111] A.R. Holmes and Edwin Green, *Midland: 150 Years of Banking Business* (London: Basford, 1986), pp. 115–17.

[112] In a recent publication, written with Terence Mills, he argues, "Our conclusion is that banks probably did respond to the 1878 crisis. However, the amalgamation movement, the headquarters of banks in London, and other associated factors, did not bring the increase in conservatism, and hence the fall in volatility, that has been asserted." Forrest H. Capie and Terence C. Mills, "British Bank Conservatism in the Late 19th Century," *Explorations in Economic History*, Vol. 32, No. 3 (July 1995), p. 419.

[113] Capie, "Prudent and Stable (but Inefficient)," pp. 48, 50–51, and 52.

were not becoming more conservative and that they did not discriminate against industrial borrowers.

The question of the role of the commercial banks in industrial lending in general and of the impact of amalgamation on commercial and industrial finance in particular cannot be finally answered until more micro-studies of banking loan practices and of the changes in bank/customer relationships from the 1880s to the 1920s are completed. Recently two such studies – one of shipping and one of brewing – have suggested that the loan behavior of the commercial banks does not appear to have limited industrial capital accumulation.[114] As evidence continues to accumulate, it appears unlikely that the traditional view of the conservatism of the banks and of their reluctance to finance commerce and industry can be maintained, at least not in its strictest form. Today, Cottrell agrees.[115]

The answer to the second question (did the banking industry become less competitive?) must also be tentative. At one extreme, Brian Griffith has charged that the public authorities actively colluded with the banks to produce an efficient cartel because "the Treasury and the Bank of England found it easier to implement interest rate policy when dealing with a small number of cartelized banks."[116] Michael Collins sides with Griffith. Collins cites a number of instances of formal and informal agreements among the English banks that were designed to restrict com-

---

[114] Gordon Boyce, "64thers, Syndicates, and Stock Promotions: Information Flows and Fund Raising Techniques of British Ship owners Before 1914," *The Journal of Economic History*, Vol. 52, No. 1 (March 1992), pp. 181–205. Katherine Watson, "Banks and Industrial Finance: the Experience of Brewers, 1880–1913," *The Economic History Review*, Vol. XLIX, No. 1 (February 1996), pp. 58–81. Boyce's evidence is indirect. He shows that the informal capital markets served the ocean shipping industry quite admirably, leaving relatively little need for long-term bank finance. Watson's evidence is direct. "The absence of long-term loans should not be seen as a failure of British banks to meet the needs of the brewing industry. While the public capital market was willing to provide long-term capital relatively cheaply and with few restrictions attached, banks offered a complementary source of finance for brewing companies. As public confidence in brewing collapsed during the early twentieth century, brewers placed heavier demands on banks for credit. Justifiably, bankers expressed greater reluctance to satisfy these requests, yet their response to long-standing customers was often quite accommodating particularly if their account was important to the bank" (p. 80).

[115] Philip L. Cottrell, "The Domestic Commercial Banks of the City of London," p. 55.

[116] Brian Griffiths, "The Development of Restrictive Practices in the U.K. Monetary System," *Manchester School*, Vol. 41 (1973), pp. 3–18. Cited in Collins, *Money and Banking*, p. 80.

petition. "Thus, the London joint-stock banks first agreed to pay one-percent below bank rate on deposits on current account and, then, in response to a general fall in interest rates, they abolished such payments altogether in 1877. On deposit accounts . . . they paid a common rate, set at a fixed margin of 1.5 percent below Bank rate by 1886."[117]

Forrest Capie has entered on the other side of the debate. On the basis of a careful study of banking archives, he concludes that although regional oligopolies had given way to a national oligopoly, "the banks were operating in a relatively competitive manner."[118] He finds "many instances of approaches from customers of rival banks for information on the terms available for loans. There were also many examples of implicit and explicit threat of withdrawal of accounts from existing clients who felt the terms of offer were not competitive enough (in terms of liberality of conditions and/or price)."[119] He acknowledges, however, that the banks had become "an effective cartel from the early 20th century." He dates the emergence of the effective cartel from 1920, and he attributes its success to the restrictive practices of the London Clearing House: "There was freedom of entry [into banking], but free access to the clearing house was not available."[120]

It is difficult to disguise the rates paid on deposits, but it is much more difficult for competitors to obtain information on the rates charged on loans. In the 1930s the cartel's attempt to fix a minimum 5 percent charge on overdrafts, for example, was quickly abandoned.[121] It may have been that the threat of expulsion from the clearing house was sufficient to make the banks adhere to the cartel's policies on deposit interest, but insufficient to make them adhere to its policies on loans. Such a view is certainly consistent with Capie's finding that despite the efficiency of the cartel in the deposit market, bank profitability was "certainly not higher than profitability in the rest of the economy."[122] The monopoly profits earned from the banks' market power in their deposit business may well have been eroded away by competition in the market for loans.

British economic historians will continue to debate the question of the commercial banks' failure to mobilize long-term capital for British

---

[117] Collins, *Money and Banking*, p. 98.   [118] Capie, "Prudent and Stable," p. 57.
[119] Capie, "Prudent and Stable," p. 50.
[120] Capie and Collins, *Have the Banks Failed British Industry*, p. 77; Capie, "Prudent and Stable," p. 61. In neither the United States nor Canada is there evidence of restrictions on entry into the emerging clearing houses, and, since 1914, the Federal Reserve Act has required their members to clear all checks presented by the Federal Reserve Bank at par.
[121] Capie, "Prudent and Stable," p. 58.
[122] Capie, "Prudent and Stable," p. 59, and figure II.

commerce and industry – a failure allegedly rooted in the adverse impact of bank amalgamations and the growth of national branch banking. Would local banks have been better able to overcome informational asymmetries and provide more long-term loans to industry, and would a more competitive system have expanded the volume of loans and made a larger fraction available for long-term finance to commerce and manufacturing? In short, there are two questions: Would a different set of institutions have led to more industrial loans, and if they did, would the resulting structure have necessarily been more efficient? Those questions will in large part be answered by further research into the behavior of British banks. They may also be answered, at least in part, by a comparison of British banking with commercial banking systems in other developing countries.

Recent research has raised some questions about the behavior of the German "Great Banks," the banks that provided the basis for Gershenkron's endorsement of universal banking. It now appears that those banks may well have made a much smaller contribution to early German industrial development than Gershenkron (or Kennedy) had thought.[123] Furthermore, the experiences of both the United States and Canada suggest that those countries were able to industrialize very rapidly, despite commercial banks that by law or custom were largely precluded from extending long-term loans. Moreover, Bordo, Redish, and Rockoff have demonstrated that Canadian banking, based on a system of national branches, remained at least as competitive as the American unit banks through the first half of the twentieth century, whether the measure is profits or interest charges on loans.[124]

---

[123] See, for example, Caroline Fohlin, "The Rise of Interlocking Directorates in Imperial Germany," California Institute of Technology Social Science Working Paper 931, February 1996. Caroline Fohlin, "Relationship Banking and Industrial Investment: Evidence from the Heyday of the German Universal Banks," California Institute of Technology Social Science Working Paper 913, December 1995, and Caroline Fohlin, "Bank Securities Holdings and Industrial Finance Before World War I: Britain and Germany Compared," California Institute of Technology, Social Science Working Paper 1007, May 1997. See also Jeremy Edwards and Sheilagh Oglive, "Universal Banks and German Industrialization: A Reappraisal," *The Economic History Review*, Vol. 49, No. 3 (August 1966), pp. 427–46.

[124] Michael D. Bordo, Angela Redish, and Hugh Rockoff, "A Comparison of the United States and Canadian Banking Systems in the Twentieth Century: Stability v. Efficiency," in Michael D. Bordo and Richard Sylla (eds.), *Anglo-American Financial Systems: Institutions and Markets in the Twentieth Century* (Burr Ridge Ill.: Irwin Professional Publishing, 1995), pp. 11–40.

The answer to the third question (did the banking industry become more stable?) is certainly yes, although how much of the change was due to the alteration in the structure of banking and how much to the evolution of the policies of the Bank of England is difficult to determine. As Forrest Capie writes, "Throughout the period [1890–1940] the system was enormously stable. The stability derived in good part from the structure, one that was thoroughly and increasingly branched, and therefore allowed well-diversified portfolios. And the stability was aided to an extent unknown by the mature operation of the Bank of England as a lender of last resort."[125] One feature of the British economy in the years before 1879 was the recurrence of periods of liquidity pressures "when, for short periods, public confidence in the banks' ability to meet their liabilities on demand was sorely tested." The problems of 1825 and 1826 had triggered some reform; the banking crises of 1837 and 1839 had eliminated the more adventurous, fraudulent, or simply foolhardy banks. But still, "the middle decades of the century witnessed short-lived 'runs' on the banks and notable failures in 1847, 1857, 1866, and 1878."[126] Over time the frequency and severity of the banking crises were diminishing, and in 1878, the failure of the City of Glasgow Bank triggered the last crisis marked by bank runs and suspensions. During the Barings Crisis of 1890, when one of the nation's leading merchant banks was unable to meet its immediate cash liabilities, joint action by the Bank of England and a broadly based consortium of bankers prevented suspension and possible bankruptcy.[127]

In terms of elements internal to the banking system, the causes of the change can be traced to three factors: insurance, attitude, and public policy. First, the evolution of the national oligopoly made it possible for the banks, by holding a geographically diverse portfolio, to insure their portfolios against the risk of a local economic crisis. Amalgamation also tended to winnow out the smaller and perhaps weaker banks. Second,

---

[125] Capie, "Prudent and Stable," p. 41. No one argues that the Bank of England had been formally charged with acting as lender of last resort: "the Bank's Rule of 1858 is strong evidence of formal denial." Michael Collins has shown, however, that from 1857 to 1878 the Bank, although not accepting formal responsibility, actually did make financial resources available in times of crisis. Michael Collins, "The Bank of England as Lender of Last Resort, 1857–1878," *The Economic History Review*, Vol. XLV, No. 1 (February 1992), pp. 145–53.

[126] Capie and Collins, *Have the Banks Failed British Industry*, p. 41; Collins, *Money and Banking*, p. 84.

[127] Chapter 1; see also Capie and Collins, *Have the Banks Failed British Industry?*, p. 42.

the attitudes of the bankers changed. During a banking crisis even the banks that did not go into liquidation found themselves faced with sudden demands for cash, accumulating bad debts, and damaging losses. Thus, with each successive crisis more bankers came to realize that continued operation demanded greater caution. That realization tended to reinforce their prejudice against holding too many assets that could not be readily converted into cash.[128] The change in bankers' attitude was reflected not only in the standard banking texts of the turn of the century – texts that warned "against tying up assets for long periods" and that argued for "the desirability of self-liquidating, short-term and readily saleable assets" – but also in the gradual increase in the holdings of cash reserves. Goodhart concludes that after 1900, bankers had come to accept 15 percent as the proper ratio of cash to total assets. Second, they had gradually come to agree that cash plus money at call and short notice should represent about one-third of their assets.[129] The data suggest that banks were becoming more liquid, but they had not become quite as conservative as Goodhart suggests. As Table 2:3–7 indicates, cash balances held by bankers increased from 9.1 percent of assets in the decade 1880–89 to 12.5 percent in the decade 1905–14. At the same time the percentage of total assets held as "money at call and short notice" increased from 8.6 to 11.5 percent, or an increase in their primary and secondary reserves from 17.7 to 24.0 percent.

Third, there is the issue of public policy. Unlike their American counterparts, British banks were not subject to legal reserve requirements. Banking "practice could vary a great deal from bank to bank," but there was substantially less variance than the lack of legal stricture would lead one to expect.[130] If the standard is American unregulated banking – that is, state banking before the 1840s – British bankers appear to have been amazingly conservative. Bank directors generally began to express concern "if the ratio of advances to deposits for the bank as a whole rose above 55 percent, and positive alarm would be felt if the ratio remained over 60 percent for long."[131]

---

[128] Capie and Collins, *Have the Banks Failed British Industry?*, p. 42; Collins, *Money and Banking*, pp. 84–85.

[129] Goodhart, *The Business of Banking*, pp. 139–40. The generally accepted range for the sum of cash plus money at short notice was 28 to 35 percent.

[130] Collins, *Money and Banking*, p. 103.

[131] Goodhart, *The Business of Banking*, p. 158. For the decades 1850–59 through 1870–79 the percentage of deposits held as current accounts in English banks was 63, 64, and 64. For the decades 1880–89 through 1900–9 the percentage for all U.K. banks was 61, 56, and 49. The 1850–79 data are from Collins, *Money and Banking*, p. 95, the figures for 1880–1909 from Table 2.3-2.

That attitude may have been partly the product of the directors' growing conservatism, but some may have been the product of prodding by the Bank of England. Over the course of the century the Bank had gradually emerged as "a central bank with responsibilities for the 'soundness' of the money markets in Britain." As the lender of last resort, the Bank of England may have been able to exercise considerable leverage in inducing banks to keep adequate balances. "One assumes, that the bank maintained a steady pressure on this front."[132] Evidence that the Bank did exercise pressure is weak, since informal pressure is always hard to document, and recent research casts some doubt on the Bank's ability to use moral suasion. "Firstly, it appears that it must have been very difficult for the Bank to utilize moral suasion to any great extent in this period, particularly in the late nineteenth century, because of the lack of respect it commanded among the banking community. Secondly, it seems that the Governor of the Bank of England did have some significant impact on Bank policy-making at certain points in this period, but that it was only so when the individual concerned was sufficiently able and charismatic to do justice to his position."[133] Over time, it appears that the direct influence of the bank was increasing. There is evidence that the Bank exerted its influence in 1891. More pointedly, the Bank directly requested in 1906 that "several of the joint-stock banks increase their balances at the Bank," although in general "the Bank did not dictate to the banks what the target level of their balances should be."[134]

Thus, it appears that the Bank of England may have at times imposed some binding constraints on the joint-stock and private banks' loan decisions, but such direct and indirect intervention was only a small part of the Bank's role in the evolution of British commercial banking. In the final analysis, it was the Bank's ability to manage the gold standard in a way that reduced the pressure on domestic money markets and its willingness to provide funds during periods of liquidity stress that created the fundamental element of stability that had been missing in the years before the Overend-Gurney and City of Glasgow Bank crises.[135]

[132] Goodhart, *The Business of Banking*, p. 112.

[133] Tessa Ogden, "An Analysis of Bank of England Discount and Advance Behavior 1870–1914," in James Foreman-Peck (ed.), *New Perspectives on the Victorian Economy: Essays in Quantitative Economic History, 1860–1914* (Cambridge: Cambridge University Press, 1991), p. 333. "Thus, it can be argued that many of the Bank of England's actions depended on the personalities around at the time. As mentioned previously, Lidderdale was the initiator of the Barings guarantee scheme, and it was Holden who provided leadership in the later case of the YPB" [Yorkshire Penny Bank]" (p. 334).

[134] Goodhart, *The Business of Banking*, pp. 112–13.

[135] Collins, *Money and Banking*, p. 87.

Stability is one aspect of banking. From the point of view of questions of capital accumulation and mobilization, the choice of investments made by the banks is a more important one. Between 1865 and 1914 there were significant changes in the composition of the banks' portfolios. They reflected the new role that the commercial banks were coming to play in both domestic and international finance. (The outlines of those compositional changes are displayed in Table 2:3-7.)

Putting aside such assets as the banks' premises and the cash held as a primary reserve, there were four major classes of investments: money at call and short-term, formal securities, loans and other advances, and discounts. The first, a type of secondary reserve, included some short-term transit items, but almost all of the discretionary allocations were in funds placed in the London discount market or loaned to Stock Exchange brokers, loans made to finance the purchase and sale of securities. The greatest proportion, but not all, of such call and short-notice money was lent out in London.[136] The funds advanced to the London discount market had no exact North American counterparts, but the brokers' loans were similar to money placed on call to brokers on the New York Stock Exchange or to the managers of the Canadian bond houses. In June 1914, for example, members of the London Stock Exchange owed some £81 million, and the members of the provincial exchanges an additional £11 million. Just under half was due to the London Joint Stock banks. At more or less the same time the money at call and short notice held by the London joint-stock banks totaled £90 million, a figure that would suggest that about one-half of the "volume of money at call and short notice was represented by loans on Stock Exchange security."[137]

As Table 2:3-7 indicates, investments in securities accounted for about one-fifth of the banking sector's assets; the ratio was slightly above that figure in the two decades spanning the beginning of the new century and slightly below that in the 1880s and again in the last quinquennia. Since as late as 1890 bankers still considered bills of exchange to be risky earning assets, investments in securities filled a dual role: as readily marketable secondary reserves and as earning assets.

Initially it was Consols and other government-guaranteed issues that were most sought after: "you could sleep on Consols and sell them on Sunday."[138] Over time, however, the bankers began to realize that there

---

[136] Goodhart, *The Business of Banking*, p. 119. There were also active provincial exchanges that were supported by local banks.

[137] Goodhart, *The Business of Banking*, pp. 123–24.

[138] Goodhart, *The Business of Banking*, p. 127.

was a tradeoff between the benefits of liquidity and the costs of forgone earnings.[139] The nominal interest rate on Consols had been declining since the 1820s, and by the late 1890s it had fallen to less than 2.5 percent.[140] In response bankers began to shift the emphasis of their investment portfolios away from the traditional concentration in Consols toward a "more aggressive, earnings-oriented, enterprising, outward-looking investment policy."[141] The fraction of government bonds in total investments declined by about one-fifth – from just less than one-half to less than 40 percent – over thirty-five years.

The reduction in British government issues was largely offset by an increase in the banks' holdings of other securities. In the 1890s they began to buy Indian Railroad and colonial government bonds. After the turn of the century there were very large increases in their holdings of American railroad bonds. Even those increases were dwarfed by the surge in purchases of U.S. and Canadian railway securities in the years 1907–9, a surge that represented a large fraction of the more than $100 million increase in the banks' holdings of formal securities. A large fraction it certainly was, but the $100 million increase was not limited to railroad issues. It also included Canadian government and municipal bonds, as well as the debt instruments of a number of governments and cities outside the Empire.

From 1890 onward there was a relatively steady increase in the level of the commercial banks' investments in British railway and municipal bonds – those securities remained a fairly constant share of an increasing portfolio – and toward the end of the period the banks began to absorb the bonds of privately owned domestic and foreign telephone and electric companies. The only sectors that do not appear to have benefited from the banks' increasing preference for "other" securities were commerce and manufacturing.[142]

---

[139] They also came to recognize that an asset can be liquid, but that, even in the case of government bonds, there may be substantial capital losses, if the banks attempted to liquidate their holdings at times of crisis. For example, "it had proved impossible to sell Consols at the height of the Baring crisis." In the words of one textbook, "In an acute financial crisis even English Consouls can only be realized at a tremendous sacrifice." In addition, there was always the threat of some loss, even in a non-crisis situation. R.S. Sayers, *Lloyds Bank in the History of English Banking* (Oxford: Oxford University Press, 1957), pp. 188–89, 213. E. Sykes, *Banking and Currency* (London: Butterworth, 1905), p. 121.

[140] The decade average for all classes of Consols was 2.47 percent. Homer and Sylla, *Interest Rates*, table 19, p. 197.

[141] Goodhart, *The Business of Banking*, p. 134.

[142] Goodhart, *The Business of Banking*, pp. 134–35.

The third – and from the point of view of the domestic economy, the most important – class of banking assets was advances: loans and over-drafts. Loans were for a fixed sum. They were made for a specified period, with the time pattern of repayment specified in advance, and they were almost invariably secured by formal collateral. In the case of overdrafts maximum limits were established, but the level of funds actually utilized depended on the requirements of the customer. Formal collateral was required when the limit seemed "at all large relative to the means of the client," but most often the only security was the reputation of the bor-rower. In 1900, banks in the United Kingdom held almost $500 million in loans and overdrafts. Most of the amount was domestic, although the London banks occasionally made large short-term loans to colonial gov-ernments and other public bodies and, infrequently, to foreign banks and railroads. Most domestic loans took the form of relatively small advances to business firms.[143] In 1900, for example, the branch accounts of the London and County Bank show that of a total £17,403,278 of Overdrafts, Loans, Promissory Notes, and Discounts, £10,862,871 (62 percent) was for amounts less than £5,000. Of the remaining £6,540,407, 85 percent was private; only £889,267 represented public sector advances. As Table 2:3-7 indicates, over the entire period loans and advances accounted for just less than half (47 percent) of all bank assets.

There is little evidence that the commercial banks discriminated against British industry. Just the opposite: Even the very smallest indus-trial and commercial firms had bank accounts, if only for the convenience of using normal retail banking facilities. Thus, from the point of view of theory, if an industrial firm were seeking additional funds, it would have been a simple matter to approach its local banker or branch manager. In fact, since most firms were tightly held, bank loans would have been the preferred form of finance since they did not dilute control. From the bank's point of view, given the small scale of most industrial enterprises,

---

[143] Goodhart, *The Business of Banking*, p. 154. There were, however, some excep-tions. In 1898 and 1899, for example, the London and Westminster loaned a total of £905,000 through the Crown Agents to seven colonies. The total included £500,000 to the Federated Malay States and £250,000 to Lagos. In 1904 the London and County sanctioned advances of £750,000 to the Hong Kong and Shanghai Bank and £500,000 to the London and River Plate Bank. Two years later the London and Westminster, employing the offices of Brown, Shipley and Company, advanced £100,000 to the Delaware and Hudson River Railway. Again, in 1898 the London and Westminster loaned £400,000 to the London County Council; and, in 1913, the London, County and Westminster advanced £1,000,000 to the Port of London Authority. The branches made few such large loans.

the amounts required would not be too great to carry. Moreover, since the lending bank was in a position to monitor the firm's normal trading account, the branch managers should have had relatively few problems overcoming the informational asymmetry that usually arises between lender and borrower.[144]

Industrial firms certainly did borrow, but the banks probably did not make up for the alleged inefficiency of the formal securities markets by providing medium- and long-term loans that could be used to purchase capital equipment. In most instances bank loans and overdrafts were not used to supply industry (or commerce, agriculture, or the government) with long-term finance.[145] Loans to the industrial sector appear to have followed the general established principles of nineteenth-century British bank lending. Bankers did not believe it was their function to provide fixed capital to the industrial, commercial, or agricultural sectors of the economy. Given that constraint, banks do not appear to have discriminated against new small or medium-sized firms. Although banks usually sought collateral security, they frequently lent without it. A search of the qualitative evidence in the banks' archives indicates that since they operated in a fairly competitive environment, they took a generally supportive stance toward their industrial customers. Such a stance is hardly surprising; by the late nineteenth century it was their industrial customers who provided the banks with the bulk of their profits.[146]

Three features of the banks' relations with industry stand out. First, although there is no evidence that the attraction of higher returns induced bankers to take greater risks, there is also no evidence to suggest that they were actively seeking lower risks. Second, there is no evidence of any significant shift in the principles that governed industrial lending. Both before and after the innovation of nationwide branching, there was a constancy in the basic nature of loans to industry. There are a few examples of loans made to underwrite long-term capital investment. Banks do appear to have made some medium-term loans to industry, and short-term overdrafts were routinely renewed, so that a loan might remain outstanding for many years. These were exceptions, however. In general the banks did not supply long-term finance and concentrated instead on short-term lending. Third, there "was no apparent bias toward any particular type of business activity – no one sort was favored over another. Thus, there were numerous examples of loans to novel activities – new industries, financing of new products, inventions, patents (e.g., machine

---

[144] Capie and Collins, *Have the Banks Failed British Industry?*, pp. 34–35.
[145] Capie and Collins, *Have the Banks Failed British Industry?*, p. 37.
[146] Capie, "Prudent and Stable," p. 50.

tools, electricity, cycles, and automobiles) – as well as loans to the established sectors (e.g., iron and steel, metal goods, collieries, and breweries)." Neither do the banks appear to have been biased against any particular form of business organization – sole proprietorships, partnerships, private companies, and public corporations – "although details of securities and collateral taken did differ between the types of business because of different legal positions. In fact, banks were actively engaged in the process of launching new corporations and converting established partnerships to companies. The form of involvement was to provide finance and advice for the launch; this was very common around the turn of the century."[147]

In addition, the banks' concentration at the short end of the market does not appear to have differentially injured new industrial enterprise. Even in the case of manufacturing firms, short-term capital needs were often paramount during the early stages of industrialization. The "willingness of the commercial banks and discount houses to purchase bills and provide credit created a generally supportive environment and, thus, played an important role in the financing of British economic development."[148] The short-term bias also produced a second, and perhaps an even more important, result. Even if, as some critics argue, British bank lending became increasingly inflexible (the word "ossified" has been used) – and the evidence suggests that it did not – there is no question but that the bankers' emphasis on short-term and liquid assets led to more than a half century of banking stability. It is difficult to argue that such stability was not conducive to general economic growth, nor can it be argued that British industry did not benefit tremendously from a stable economic environment.

Thus, it appears that if the domestic financial infrastructure failed to meet the capital demands of British industry, and if this failure proved detrimental to the nation's general economic growth, the fault did not lie with the commercial banks. The cause of the failure – if, indeed, there was a failure – must be sought elsewhere – a subject that will be addressed later in this chapter.[149]

Discounts represent the fourth category of bank assets. Through much of the early nineteenth century the market for inland bills served to mobilize short-term capital across regional boundaries within the United Kingdom; later in the century the commercial bill market played an equally important role in the mobilization of short-term capital across

---

[147] Capie, "Prudent and Stable," pp. 52–53.
[148] Collins, *Money and Banking*, p. 109.
[149] Collins, *Money and Banking*, pp. 116–17.

international boundaries. In many ways, in the pre–World War I years the sterling bill became the international monetary standard. That story is the subject of Section 2-3a(2).

By the late nineteenth century London had become the center of international finance, and British and Scottish bankers found themselves forced to share London's capital market with the overseas branches of a number of foreign banks as well as with the head offices of a larger number of British-owned overseas banks – the so-called imperial and international banks. In 1900 there were eighteen foreign banks with branches in the City, by 1910 that figure had risen to twenty-eight, and by 1914 to thirty-one. Although most were branches of Continental banks, other nations were represented as well. All were engaged in both foreign-exchange dealings and in the overseas remittance business.[150]

In addition to the branches of foreign banks, there were also the British-owned international and imperial Banks. The head offices of these banks were located in London, but their area of operations spanned the globe. Of the twenty-four British international banks operating in 1910, the Hong Kong and Shanghai Banking Corporation – a firm that by the turn of the century held a well-established position in both China and Japan – was probably the most successful.[151] These foreign and colonial banks sold equity and collected deposits in Britain, and their London business was almost entirely directed toward servicing financial and commercial transactions between Britain and their foreign and empire areas of operation. The primary function of the international banks was the provision of short-term mercantile credit – credit based on the sterling bill. That business in turn depended on the existence of a well-developed bill market in the home center.[152] In view of the development and dominance of the London market in the years before World War I, it is not surprising that as late as the 1930s, of the global total of 71 international Banks with 872 branches, 32 banks with 462 branches were British.

At times the international banks also carried on a traditional banking business in the foreign countries in which they operated, and when they

---

[150] Collins, *Money and Banking*, pp. 149–50. The Deutsche Bank, the Dresden Bank, Credit Lyonnais, and the Swiss Bank Verein all had branches. Because U.S. banking laws forbade American banks from opening foreign offices, there were no American banks.

[151] Collins, *Money and Banking*, p. 149; A.S.J. Baster, *The International Banks* (London: P.S. King & Son Ltd., 1929), table 1, p. 245. [Hereafter cited as Baster, *The International Banks*.] In 1910 the twenty-four banks had capital and reserves of more than £33 million and deposits of £135 million.

[152] A.S.J. Baster, *The Imperial Banks* (London: P.S. King & Son Ltd., 1935) pp. 4–5, 12. [Hereafter cited as Baster, *The Imperial Banks*.]

did they often found themselves in competition with the domestic banking sector, competition that was often not appreciated.[153] In the case of the imperial banks, the potential competitive challenge was even stronger. Although participating in the international bill market in the normal course of their business, they were primarily organized to carry on banking operations typical of the local banks in their areas of operation.[154] In this case, however, there is little evidence that they suffered at the hands of the local politicians; they were located in what was, even in the case of the colonies with self-government, a part of the British Empire.

In 1850 there was one international bank with capital of £756,000 and three branches, all in the Far East. By 1910 the number had increased to 24, capital to £19,783,000, and the number of branches to 308: 10 in Europe, 147 in the Near East, 100 in South America, 45 in the Far East, and 6 elsewhere in the world.[155] The imperial banks go back further, to 1835. Their growth was somewhat slower than that of the international banks, but it was nonetheless impressive. In 1855 there were 10 such banks, with capital of £6,193,580, operating a total of 82 branches. By 1915 their number had risen to 18, and capital to £15,381,122, and they controlled 1,169 branches scattered across the Empire.[156]

Many of the foreign- and colonial-owned banks operated deposit businesses in their London offices, but those deposits came from both British and foreign accumulations, and the proportion that represented British savings has not been estimated. In aggregate, those accounts were both large and increasing. In 1877 they totaled £107 million; in 1899, £277 million; and in 1914, £1,855.2 million – deposits equal to 21 percent, 34 percent, and 157 percent of the total deposits held by domestic U.K. banks at those dates.[157] Given those figures, it seems apparent that "by the turn

---

[153] See, for example, Baster, *The International Banks*, chap. IV, and David Joslin, *A Century of Banking in Latin America* (London: Oxford University Press, 1963), chap. 3, for a discussion of the problems of the British Bank of the River Plate.

[154] Baster, *The Imperial Banks*, pp. 49–122. In the case of the British Bank of North America, for example, the 1836 charter declared that the bank was established "for the purpose of carrying on the business of a banker in any cities, towns and places within any of the British colonies or Settlements in North America, or adjacent to British North America" (p. 83).

[155] Baster, *The International Banks*, table 3, p. 245.

[156] In 1855 there were 34 branches in Australia, 4 in New Zealand, 13 in Canada, 14 in the West Indies, and 17 in India and the Far East. In 1915 the figures were 523 in Australia, 150 in New Zealand, 99 in Canada, 19 in the West Indies, and 68 in India and the Far East. In addition there were 277 branches in South and East Africa, 26 in West Africa, and 7 elsewhere in the Empire. A.S.J. Baster, *The Imperial Banks*, appendix III, p. 269.

[157] Forrest Capie and Alan Weber, *A Monetary History* (London: George Allen & Unwin, 1985), pp. 253–54 and table 11.1.

of the century the overseas banking sector in London had become significant in quantitative terms and was growing relative to the domestic
banking community. Thus, the decisions taken by overseas banks on the
transfer of funds overseas and the purchase and sale of securities within
London could be of significance for internal monetary conditions." They
were certainly also significant for overseas enterprise both public and
private.[158] In particular, from the point of view of this book, they were to
play a major role in the evolution of the domestic financial markets in
Argentina and Australia and a lesser role in Canada.

*2-3a(2). The evolution of the market for commercial paper and the emer-
gence of the sterling bill:* The story of the evolution of the market for commercial bills, the emergence of the market for sterling bills, and the
relation of those developing markets to the nation's banks is important for
any understanding of the role of British finance in economic development,
both in the United Kingdom and in the rest of the world. In 1850, if the
demand for finance in Cleveland was relatively heavy, while the demand
in London or South Wales was less so, banks in the deficit regions could,
through the intermediation of the London discount market, sell their bills
to banks in the surplus region. The banks themselves served as the guar-
antors of the quality of the bills. Until the early years of the twentieth
century, the London joint-stock banks – the banks most heavily involved
in providing interregional mobility – limited themselves to rediscounting;
that is, the bills in their portfolios carried the endorsement of another
bank, and the bills they sold from their portfolios most often carried both
their and the originating bank's endorsement.[159]

From the accepting bank's point of view, there were really two kinds
of bills: those that were discounted directly by banks for customers, and
those that were bought in the open bill market, usually after the bills had
been accepted by a London banking house.

> Although in both cases these bills would be held by the bank until matu-
> rity, in other respects these bills were assets of markedly different char-
> acter. Essentially the discounting of bills for customers was a method
> of providing a customer with direct financial accommodation, closely

---

[158] Collins, *Money and Banking*, p. 150.
[159] W.T. King, *History of the London Discount Market* (London: George Routledge
& Sons, Ltd., 1936), p. 280. [Hereafter cited as King, *History of the London Discount Market*.] "It was considered to be the duty of the banker to avoid the
'greater risks' of the merchant, and to refrain from all transactions 'the result of
which were dependent on the rise and fall of goods.'" It might be noted that the
London offices of the Scottish banks did a large acceptance business from 1875
onward.

akin to making an advance. On the other hand, bills of exchange bought on the open market were, in a sense, anonymous (that is, there was no goodwill lost if the financial accommodation was not renewed on maturity) and possessed much greater liquidity (bearing the name of both the bill broker and acceptor as well as the drawer of the bill). The one was a risky earning asset, the other a liquid second line reserve.[160]

By the end of the nineteenth century it had become clear that liquidating even gilt-edge securities in times of crisis could involve substantial capital losses. On several occasions banks that held Consols as their secondary reserves found themselves incurring substantial losses when they attempted to liquidate their holdings. Thus, despite conventional wisdom, bankers came to realize that "a well proportioned bill case, though not marketable, would always provide a large volume of bills maturing at any time." As a result, banks began to hold self-liquidating bills – bills based on actual commercial transactions – as secondary reserves. The bills generated cash, but unlike cash they earned interest.[161]

Although the exact volume of discounts is unknown, it was clearly substantial. Based on a relatively small sample of banks, Michael Collins has shown for the four decades 1840 through 1879 that the ratio of discounts to loans and overdrafts ranged from 1.04 to 0.64, and averaged 0.89, a figure that suggests that discounted bills constituted about one-third of all bank assets.[162] In the late 1850s, however, the importance of inland bills began to decline. That decline can in part be attributed to the rediscounters' unhappy experiences during the crisis of 1857 and to the new tighter regulations imposed by the Bank of England in the wake of that crisis, in part to the increasing popularity of overdrafts, and in part to improvements in transport and communications that reduced the need for firms to hold large inventories.[163]

At the same time the expansion of nationwide branch networks provided a more than adequate alternative to the inland bill as a vehicle for interregional capital mobilization.[164] The amalgamation movement and the concomitant growth of the branch banking networks enabled the

[160] Goodhart, *The Business of Banking*, pp. 143–44.
[161] Goodhart, *The Business of Banking*, p. 133.
[162] Collins, *Money and Banking*, pp. 98, 110, table 4.4.
[163] Following the crisis there was a substantial "diminution of country bank rediscounting, the abuse of which had caused so much distress, and attracted so much censure in 1857 that regular rediscounting came to be regarded as the practice of only second rate banks. The large provincial banks therefore sought to avoid it at all normal times." King, *History of the London Discount Market*, pp. 273–74. Collins, *Money and Banking*, pp. 97–99, 106–11.
[164] King, *History of the London Discount Market*, pp. 273–74.

national banks to draw on the deposits of their agricultural branches in capital surplus regions to finance the demands of their industrial branches in capital deficit regions. The banks soon discovered that it was cheaper to finance their customers by granting loans and advances than to discount their bills: There were no commissions to be paid. In many trades the internal bill was gradually replaced by more traditional loans and advances.[165] By the 1880s all bills (domestic or international) represented less than 13 percent of bank assets, and in 1914 that figure had fallen to less than 10 percent (see Table 2:3-7).

If, in 1850, almost all the bills in the bankers' bill cases had originated in inland commerce, the same was no longer true at the century's end. Changes in the domestic economy had led to the decline in the supply of inland bills, but after the 1870s the decline was partly offset by the rise in the supply of bills originating from the finance of foreign trade. Foreign bills became steadily more important, and by 1913 inland bills accounted for hardly more than one-third of the total.[166] The inland bill had helped mobilize domestic capital, and the foreign bill played much the same role in the international market.

The international bill was in many ways similar to the earlier inland bill. In the same way that the credit requirements of a merchant in Glasgow or Leeds were met by the inland bill, the importer in Montreal or Montevideo could, at the cost of an interest charge, take possession of his goods without having to pay cash, take one to three months to sell those goods, and only then use the proceeds from the sale to pay off his debt. At the same time the exporter who had extended the credit obtained legal proof of the debt and received a bill that, once endorsed, could be sold to some individual or institution that had surplus funds to invest. That institution was most commonly a commercial bank.

Two specialist institutions – the acceptance house and the discount house – played a major role in the emergence of foreign trade as the source of large supplies of bills on London, or, as they were more commonly called, sterling bills. The more prestigious the acceptor, the more easily the bill could be sold (or discounted) and the lower the interest charge. Early in the nineteenth century a number of large London merchant banks had begun to accept bills on behalf of their customers. Over time, the London acceptance became a common guarantee for transactions throughout the world. In fact, by the end of the century, such acceptances often provided ready access to credit for international

[165] King, *History of the London Discount Market*, pp. 273–74.
[166] Collins, *Money and Banking*, p. 110. Goodhart, *The Business of Banking*, pp. 145–46.

transactions that did not directly involve Britain. "In 1913 London prime acceptances, both home and foreign, totaled £350 million of which some 60 percent, some £210 million, were finance bills arising from the working of the international gold standard. Finance bills were created to take advantage of arbitrage, their volume being related to the level of short-term interest rates prevalent on the London money market" and to the rates prevailing in the overseas market.[167]

Initially a small number of large merchant banks – Rothschild's, Barings, Kleinwort, Schroeder, Hambro, Brandt, and Gibbs – together with the London offices of overseas banks dominated the acceptance business. In the decade and a half before World War I, however, the major London clearing banks began to compete for this lucrative business. Although Rothschild's, Barings, and Hambros were all internationally recognized names, the guarantee of the London joint-stock banks greatly enhanced the attractiveness of sterling bills. On the eve of World War I the seven great merchant banks were still responsible for 45 percent of the foreign trade credit granted in London, but the shift of British domestic commercial banks into the international acceptance business – a shift that dates from the 1890s – meant that the share of those banks was a robust 24 percent.[168]

Without a ready secondary bill market, even the guarantee of the clearing banks would probably have been insufficient to induce such widespread use of sterling bills. For more than half a century, the City of London had provided a secondary market for inland bills of exchange. Initially, brokers acted as purchasing agents for their customers, but as the market expanded, they began to specialize. Ultimately, formal discount houses emerged.

The National Discount House, the first joint-stock firm to enter the market, was launched in July 1856 with paid-up capital of £200,000. It was soon joined by others.[169] In 1885, although the National remained the largest, there were competitors. Those rivals included three large firms (the General Credit Company and the United Discount Corporation, both joint-stock companies, and Alexander's, a partnership) and a number of smaller private firms.[170] In that year the two joint-stock houses

[167] Cottrell, "Great Britain," p. 33.
[168] Cottrell, "Great Britain," p. 33.
[169] King, *History of the London Discount Market*, pp. 217–29.
[170] That latter group included two firms – Brightwen, Gillett & Company and, after 1867, Gillett Bros. & Company, the forerunner of Gillett Bros. Discount Company Ltd. – that were to play an important role in the London money market for the next three-quarters of a century. King, *History of the London Discount Market*, p. 227.

merged to form the Union Discount Company of London. Within three years the new firm reported a turnover larger than the National's, and a decade later it had taken the lead in deposits as well. The success of the Union induced the partners of Alexander's to reorganize, first as a private corporation and then as a public one. "Upon Alexander's registration, the bill market assumed in general structure the form upon which it remained down to the War period, comprising three large limited companies and rather more than a score of private firms."[171] Between the end of 1891 and 1913 the balance sheets of the three joint-stock firms indicate that their assets had increased from £35 million to £68 million, funds raised from undistributed profits and from loans and deposits from £24 million to £39 million, and the level of private bills discounted from £26 million to £55 million.[172]

By the middle of the nineteenth century, the still-unincorporated brokers had begun operating as dealers, and the joint-stock companies were specifically organized to function in that way. Brokers and the new joint-stock firms bought bills for their own accounts, and as the international use of sterling bills increased, they expanded their operations to include foreign bills. The result was a large-scale, open, and competitive secondary market in discounted bills. While individuals and other institutions could and did buy bills, "it was the London discount houses which formed the main bulwark to the markets, they *always* stood ready to buy 'good' bills."[173] At the outbreak of World War I, sterling bills had become so important to international finance and to the operation of the gold standard that the economic historian Leonard Pressnell concluded that the use of the term "international gold standard" for the existing monetary regime was a misnomer; instead, it should have been called the "international bill-on-London standard."[174] By the late nineteenth century, international bills had become the mainstay of the London discount market.

2-3a(3). The non-bank intermediaries: As Table 2:3-1 indicates, the non-bank intermediaries accounted for between 35 and 40 percent of the assets held by all financial institutions. Between 1880 and 1914 the proportion of that total held by insurance companies increased gradually from just less than 20 to about 25 percent and that of post office savings banks about doubled, from 4.5 to 9 percent. At the same time the

---

[171] King, *History of the London Discount Market*, pp. 261–62.
[172] Sheppard, "The Growth and Role of UK Financial Institutions," table (A) 1.13, pp. 138–39.
[173] Collins, *Money and Banking*, pp. 151–53.
[174] Quoted in Goodhart, *The Business of Banking*, p. 149.

fraction held both by the Trustee Savings Banks and by building societies fell by half.

Although they encouraged accumulation, neither the Post Office Savings Bank nor the Trustee Savings Banks made any significant direct contribution to the process of private capital mobilization. Since both invested almost all of their funds in government securities, their only contribution was indirect: By pushing the rate of interest on government bonds down, they may have convinced some savers to redirect their accumulations to other investment opportunities.

In the case of the Post Office Savings Bank, the enabling legislation was passed, and the first deposits received in 1861 (see Table 2:3-8).[175] Between 1862 and 1914 per capita deposits increased from £0.06 to £4.14, a growth rate of over 9 percent per year. Cash and premises aside, all of the deposits were invested in government issues. In 1910, for example, deposits were £168.9 million. Out of that total, the Bank held £1.2 million in cash, £400,000 was invested in premises, £300,000 in Treasury Bills, £21.0 million in bonds of the Metropolitan Water Board, local government bonds, and temporary accommodation to local authorities, and £146.0 million in national government and government-guaranteed bonds.[176]

For most of its history, the story for the Trustee Savings Banks was similar, although it pre-dated the Post Office Savings Bank by more than half a century. The first modern savings bank in the United Kingdom dates from 1810; the first regulatory act – George Rose's Act – was passed in 1817. It required that deposits be collected and placed under the control of a government department. By 1862 there were 621 government-regulated savings banks with deposits totaling £41 million (see Table 2:3-8).[177] After the formation of the Postal Savings Bank, growth was slower – total deposits in 442 banks amounted to only £46 million in 1880. By 1914 deposits had grown to £72 million, but the number of banks had declined to fewer than 200.[178] Initially, ordinary

---

[175] The Post Office Saving Bank was the creation of Charles William Sikes, a member of the staff and later general manager of the Huddersfield Banking Company. He was knighted for his contribution in 1881. W.F. Crick and J.E. Wadsworth, *A Hundred Years of Joint Stock Banking* (London: Hodder & Stoughton, 1936), p. 224. See also Howard Robinson, *The British Post Office: A History* (Princeton: Princeton University Press, 1948), pp. 403–4.

[176] Sheppard, *The Growth and Role of UK Financial Institutions*, table (A) 2.2, pp. 144–45.

[177] H. Oliver Horne, *A History of Savings Banks* (London: Oxford University Press, 1947), pp. 76–77. [Hereafter cited as Horne, *A History of Savings Banks*.]

[178] Sheppard, *The Growth and Role of UK Financial Institutions*, table (A) 2.3, pp. 146–47.

deposits could only be turned over to the National Debt Commissioners – a government department – and invested by it in government securities.[179] Over time there was some loosening of the investment restrictions, but it did little to expand the banks' investment horizons. The Act of 1828 included one ambiguous clause that could be interpreted as giving the banks more latitude in their investment decisions. With the decline in the interest rates on Consols, and as the restriction on the maximum size of individual accounts became increasingly binding, some banks chose to interpret the clause very generously: They opened Special Investment Departments.[180] Initially, the funds raised by the new department were also invested in Consols, but the list was gradually expanded to include interest-bearing accounts in joint-stock banks and the bonds of public utilities owned by local authorities. The practice was legally recognized by the Act of 1863 (Clause 16), but it was unintentionally disallowed by the Act of 1891. When the disallowance was recognized, existing departments were grandfathered in. Finally, in 1904 the banks regained the legal right to organize Special Departments. They were, however, prohibited from investing those funds in any earning asset aside from government bonds and mortgages secured by local taxes.

The Stock Departments, a second institutional innovation, date from 1881. They also represented an attempt to overcome the constraint imposed by the limitation on the maximum size of individual deposits. Banks were permitted to purchase and hold Consols for customers whose deposits had reached the legal limit. The brief flirtation with joint-stock bank deposits aside, neither the Special Investment nor the Stock Department increased the range of Trustee Savings Banks beyond the government sector.[181]

In 1910 total deposits amounted to £65.9 million: £52.3 million in ordinary deposits, £2.7 million in the Stock Departments, and £10.9 million in deposits in the Special Investment Departments. Of the Ordinary Department's £53.7 million of assets, the National Debt Commissioners

---

[179] Charles H. Feinstein, *National Income, Expenditure and Output of the United Kingdom, 1855–1965*, Studies in the National Income and Expenditure of the United Kingdom, No. 6 (Cambridge: Cambridge University Press, 1972), p. 66.

[180] "The 1828 Act had expressly stipulated that there was nothing [in the Act] to prevent the trustees of any savings bank from receiving any sum or sums of money from any depositor for any purpose except to be paid into the Bank on account of the Commissioners for the Reduction of the National Debt, and it shall be lawful for such trustees to apply any such sum or sums of money in any manner for the benefit of the several depositors according to the rules and regulations of such Savings Banks'." Horne, *A History of Savings Banks*, pp. 221–22.

[181] Horne, *A History of Savings Banks*, pp. 221–25, 278.

Table 2:3-8. United Kingdom: trustee savings banks and the Post Office Saving Bank

| | | | Trustee Savings Banks | | | | Post Office Savings Bank | | Both Institutions | |
| | | | Sums due depositors | | | | | | | |
Year	Number of banks	Number of depositors (thousands)	Ordinary department	Stock department	Special investment department (millions of pounds)	Total	Number of open accounts (thousands)	Total sum due depositors (millions of pounds)	Total sum due depositors (millions of pounds)	Deposits in trustee banks as a percent of deposits in the Post Office Bank
1862	621	1,558.2	40.6		0.2	40.8	178.5	1.7	42.5	2,400.0
1863	603	1,556.8	41.0		0.2	41.2	319.7	3.4	44.6	1,211.8
1864	577	1,492.3	39.3		0.2	39.5	470.9	5.0	44.5	790.0
1865	561	1,468.5	38.7		0.3	39.0	611.4	6.5	45.5	600.0
1866	551	1,404.2	36.4		0.3	36.7	746.3	8.1	44.8	453.1
1867	539	1,385.8	36.5		0.3	36.8	855.0	9.7	46.5	379.4
1868	513	1,371.8	36.9		0.3	37.2	965.2	11.7	48.9	317.9
1869	507	1,377.9	37.6		0.3	37.9	1,085.8	13.5	51.4	280.7
1870	496	1,384.8	38.0		0.3	38.3	1,183.2	15.1	53.4	253.6
1871	489	1,404.1	38.8		0.5	39.3	1,303.5	17.0	56.3	231.2
1872	483	1,425.1	39.7		0.6	40.3	1,442.4	19.3	59.6	208.8
1873	481	1,445.5	40.5		0.7	41.2	1,556.6	21.2	62.4	194.3
1874	474	1,464.3	41.5		0.8	42.3	1,668.7	23.2	65.5	182.3
1875	470	1,479.2	42.4		1.1	43.5	1,777.1	25.2	68.7	172.6
1876	463	1,493.4	43.3		1.3	44.6	1,702.4	27.0	71.6	165.2
1877	458	1,509.8	44.2		1.4	45.6	1,791.2	28.7	74.3	158.9
1878	454	1,515.7	44.3		1.6	45.9	1,892.8	30.4	76.3	151.0
1879	449	1,506.7	43.8		1.8	45.6	1,988.5	32.0	77.6	142.5
1880	442	1,519.8	44.0		2.0	46.0	2,185.0	33.7	79.7	136.5
1881	437	1,532.5	44.1	0.1	2.3	46.5	2,607.6	36.2	82.7	128.5
1882	430	1,553.0	44.6	0.2	2.6	47.4	2,859.0	39.0	86.4	121.5
1883	421	1,566.2	45.0	0.4	2.8	48.2	3,105.6	41.8	90.0	115.3

Year										
1884	411	1,582.5	45.8	0.5	3.1	49.4	3,333.7	44.8	94.2	110.3
1885	409	1,593.0	46.4	0.7	3.3	50.4	3,535.7	47.7	98.1	105.7
1886	405	1,590.8	46.8	0.8	3.6	51.2	3,731.4	50.9	102.1	100.6
1887	400	1,604.6	47.3	0.9	3.8	52.0	3,951.8	54.0	106.0	96.3
1888	382	1,579.5	46.4	1.0	4.0	51.4	4,220.9	58.6	110.0	87.7
1889	346	1,551.6	44.9	1.2	4.2	50.3	4,507.8	63.0	113.3	79.8
1890	324	1,535.8	43.6	1.3	4.4	49.3	4,827.3	67.6	116.9	72.9
1891	303	1,510.3	42.9	1.3	4.1	48.3	5,118.4	71.6	119.9	67.5
1892	281	1,501.9	42.4	1.3	4.3	48.0	5,452.3	75.9	123.9	63.2
1893	267	1,470.1	42.2	1.3	4.5	48.0	5,748.2	80.6	128.6	59.6
1894	257	1,470.9	43.5	1.4	4.6	49.5	6,108.8	89.3	138.8	55.4
1895	245	1,516.2	45.3	1.3	4.7	51.3	6,453.6	97.9	149.2	52.4
1896	239	1,495.9	46.7	1.1	4.7	52.5	6,862.0	108.1	160.6	48.6
1897	232	1,527.2	48.5	1.1	4.6	54.2	7,239.8	115.9	170.1	46.8
1898	231	1,563.9	50.0	1.1	4.6	55.7	7,630.5	123.1	178.8	45.2
1899	231	1,601.5	51.4	1.1	4.6	57.1	8,046.7	130.1	187.2	43.9
1900	230	1,625.0	51.5	1.4	4.5	57.4	8,440.0	135.5	192.9	42.4
1901	230	1,647.2	52.0	1.7	4.5	58.2	8,787.7	140.4	198.6	41.5
1902	229	1,670.4	52.5	1.9	4.6	59.0	9,133.2	144.6	203.6	40.8
1903	228	1,687.7	52.5	2.1	4.7	59.3	9,403.9	146.1	205.4	40.6
1904	224	1,702.8	52.3	2.3	4.9	59.5	9,673.7	148.3	207.8	40.1
1905	224	1,730.3	52.7	2.3	5.6	60.6	9,663.0	152.1	212.7	39.8
1906	224	1,759.2	53.0	2.4	6.4	61.8	10,332.8	156.0	217.8	39.6
1907	222	1,780.2	52.1	2.5	7.1	61.7	10,692.6	157.5	219.2	39.2
1908	222	1,785.8	51.7	2.5	8.2	62.4	11,018.3	160.6	223.0	38.9
1909	222	1,804.9	52.2	2.5	9.8	64.5	7,913.3	164.6	229.1	39.2
1910	219	1,827.5	52.3	2.6	11.0	65.9	8,371.8	168.9	234.8	39.0
1911	215	1,849.0	53.0	2.7	12.2	67.9	8,453.2	176.5	244.4	38.5
1912	211	1,870.5	53.8	2.7	13.4	69.9	8,868.0	182.1	252.0	38.4
1913	202	1,912.8	54.3	2.7	14.4	71.4	9,181.0	187.2	258.6	38.1
1914	196	1,917.9	53.9	2.7	15.6	72.2	9,281.4	190.5	262.7	37.9

Source: H. Oliver Horne, *A History of Savings Banks* (London, New York, Toronto: Oxford University Press, 1947), Appendix Tables II & III, pp. 387–392.

held £52.6 million; there was £400,000 in cash and £600,000 invested in premises and other assets. Of the Special Investment Department's £11.5 million in assets, £8.6 million was invested in mortgages secured by local rates, £2.3 million in government and government-guaranteed bonds, £400,000 in municipal and local government issues, and £200,000 in cash. The Stock Departments held nothing but Consols.

Building societies directed savings into the domestic mortgage market and in the process aided private domestic capital mobilization. The societies trace their origins to the end of the eighteenth century, and they came under legal regulation in 1836. Initially they were temporary organizations, organizations that existed only until the individual members had received and repaid the advances they needed to build a house. Capital was mobilized, but it was still very personal capital.

The permanent building society was the product of organizational innovation in the late 1840s. Previously the saver and investor had been the same person or group of persons; such was no longer necessarily the case. The saver placed his accumulations with the society, and those funds were made available to qualified borrowers whether or not they were members of the organization. The building society had emerged as an institution capable of impersonally mobilizing the savings of members of the working and lower middle classes. Despite the fact that there were frequent failures, growth during the early Victorian period was rapid, and it continued until the Liberator collapse in 1893. At that time many of the societies were wound up, and the industry began to contract. The decline in the industry's fortunes was not reversed until 1911, and then only gradually.[182] In 1880, for example, there were more than 1,850 such societies with assets of £54.3 million (an average of £1.57 per capita); in 1892 the number had grown to almost 4,500 with assets of £64.1 million (£1.68 per capita); but by 1914 the number of institutions had declined to barely 1,500, and assets had increased by only £300,000 (or £1.44 per capita).[183]

Unlike the savings banks, the insurance industry made a substantial direct contribution to both the process of capital accumulation and mobilization. By 1914 there were firms selling a variety of insurance policies (insurance against railway and industrial accident, theft, legal liabilities, and even the hazards of travel by motor car had all been introduced

---

[182] G.D.H. Cole, *A Short History of the British Working Class Movement. Vol. II: 1848–1900* (New York: Macmillan, 1927), pp. 45–46.

[183] Sheppard, *The Growth and Role of UK Financial Institutions*, table (A) 2.4, pp. 150–53. The number of societies in 1892 is not reported, but there were 4,320 in 1891 and 4,485 in 1893. At their nadir, in 1911, deposits were only £63.5 million or £1.40 per capita.

between 1840 and 1910). It was, however, the life and fire sectors that dominated the industry, and life insurance accounted for the majority of the industry's assets.[184] Investments of life insurance companies amounted to about £50 million in 1856, but they had grown to £125 million by 1877. By that date, according to one contemporary, life insurance companies had become "one of the largest monetary interests in the United Kingdom."[185]

Both fire and life insurance companies date from the Industrial Revolution, although rapid growth was delayed until the nineteenth century. In 1800 there were six companies selling life insurance and fewer than twenty underwriting fire risks; since some firms did both, the total number was less than the sum of the two. Between 1790 and 1870 the sums insured by fire policies increased from £150 million to £1.500 billion, and the amount of life insurance in force rose from less than £5 million to almost £300 million, figures that suggest growth rates of something less than 3 percent a year for fire and more than 5 percent a year for life insurance. By 1870 there were about 100 companies selling life insurance, and about one-half that number writing fire policies.[186]

As Tables 2:3-9 and 2:3-10 indicate, growth continued after 1870. In the years 1880 to 1914 the insurance industry's assets increased from £155 million to £551 million, figures that indicate a rate of growth of about 3.7 percent a year – 2.9 percent in per capita terms. The life insurance component of the 1914 total was more than £350 million, and the non-life business of those companies accounted for at least an additional £66 million.[187] More importantly, life and fire insurance companies between 1870 and 1914 invested about £250 million in stock exchange securities.[188]

---

[184] In 1913, for example, premium income from both life and fire amounted to about £29 million a year, total premiums from all accident policies were about £7 million.

[185] The quotation is from Walter Brown. Barry Supple, *The Royal Exchange Assurance: A History of British Insurance, 1720–1970* (Cambridge: Cambridge University Press, 1970), p. 309. [Hereafter cited as Supple, *The Royal Exchange.*]

[186] Much of the ensuing discussion is based on Barry Supple, "Corporate Growth and Structural Change in a Service Industry: Insurance, 1870–1914," in Barry Supple (ed.), *Essays in British Business History* (Oxford: Clarendon Press [for the Economic History Society], 1977), pp. 69–87 [Hereafter cited as Supple, "Corporate Growth"], and on Supple, *The Royal Exchange*, particularly chap. 13, pp. 309–48.

[187] Supple, *The Royal Exchange*, p. 309.

[188] A.R. Hall, *The London Capital Market and Australia, 1870–1914*, Social Science monograph No. 21 (Canberra: Australian National University, 1963), p. 51. [Hereafter cited as Hall, *London and Australia.*]

Table 2:3-9(a). Assets of United Kingdom insurance companies selling life insurance: all classes of business (life, industrial, accident, bond, employer liability, and fire) (millions of pounds)

Year	Total assets	Mortgages	Loans on public rates & local government securities	Loans on policy & personal securities	British government & government guaranteed securities	Other commercial & municipal securities	Foreign government & municipal securities	Debentures	Preference, ordinary, & guaranteed stocks & shares	Land, insurance property, & ground rent	Cash & stamps	Other assets*
1880	155.1	70.9	19.5	9.0	5.0	7.1	4.4	10.6	7.9	8.1	4.5	8.1
1881	159.9	71.3	19.6	8.8	5.3	8.3	4.3	11.4	8.7	9.2	4.6	8.4
1882	165.0	72.7	21.6	8.9	5.1	8.8	4.3	11.6	9.8	9.4	3.9	8.9
1883	169.7	74.4	22.0	9.2	5.0	9.4	4.1	12.3	9.9	10.0	4.3	9.1
1884	174.8	75.0	22.6	9.3	5.3	10.8	3.9	12.6	10.4	10.7	4.7	9.5
1885	179.3	75.6	23.1	9.5	5.6	11.3	4.1	13.2	11.4	11.4	4.6	9.5
1886	184.3	77.3	23.4	9.6	5.8	11.6	4.0	14.2	11.3	12.4	4.9	9.8
1887	189.7	77.8	23.6	9.8	6.0	11.8	3.7	15.8	12.0	13.4	5.6	10.2
1888	196.0	78.2	23.6	10.0	6.2	12.6	3.6	18.1	12.5	14.4	6.6	10.2
1889	203.6	79.1	23.8	10.3	6.4	12.8	3.5	20.3	13.1	14.8	8.4	11.1
1890	211.3	83.1	22.5	10.5	6.4	12.8	3.5	23.3	13.1	15.8	8.7	11.6
1891	217.5	83.9	22.3	11.0	5.8	13.6	3.7	24.6	13.7	16.3	9.6	13.0
1892	223.4	84.8	24.7	11.3	5.5	14.4	3.9	26.5	13.6	17.2	8.9	12.6
1893	231.4	85.1	26.2	11.9	5.5	15.8	4.1	28.8	14.4	18.3	8.0	13.3
1894	240.4	84.8	27.9	12.0	5.7	17.1	4.6	30.8	16.3	19.3	8.0	13.9
1895	251.3	83.4	28.3	12.2	5.7	17.1	5.5	35.3	20.4	20.5	8.4	14.5
1896	263.8	82.0	28.9	12.6	6.2	17.4	7.0	40.9	25.1	22.0	6.9	14.8
1897	277.0	82.2	29.1	12.9	6.4	18.2	7.9	45.3	28.8	23.6	6.9	15.7
1898	288.8	84.1	28.7	13.5	6.7	18.5	9.0	47.8	32.2	25.5	6.3	16.5
1899	300.4	82.7	31.4	13.8	6.7	18.8	10.6	51.2	34.6	27.1	6.0	17.5

1900	311.1	85.2	33.1	14.4	7.7	19.3	10.9	60.0	35.1	30.0	6.1	9.3
1901	321.3	86.6	35.0	15.4	9.1	19.4	10.7	54.1	35.9	30.2	5.7	19.2
1902	336.8	88.8	37.2	16.5	9.8	19.8	10.8	58.1	38.3	31.6	6.3	19.6
1903	352.6	91.8	39.5	17.9	9.7	19.7	10.5	63.1	39.9	33.9	6.0	20.6
1904	366.7	96.1	42.6	19.3	9.4	19.9	10.4	65.3	40.5	35.8	5.9	21.5
1905	384.4	96.9	44.8	20.5	9.2	20.1	11.7	72.3	42.1	37.2	6.7	22.9
1906	395.8	99.2	45.1	21.5	7.9	20.3	12.3	77.8	42.3	39.2	7.0	23.2
1907	413.8	101.9	46.9	23.1	8.2	20.2	13.5	84.9	42.8	40.9	6.4	25.0
1908	429.3	102.3	49.6	24.8	8.0	19.1	15.0	91.8	44.5	42.7	6.9	24.6
1909	447.3	103.3	53.1	25.8	7.3	20.3	17.4	99.5	42.1	44.2	7.2	27.1
1910	467.3	102.4	31.7	27.4	6.9	38.0	29.3	108.5	44.8	44.5	6.9	26.9
1911	491.3	107.3	31.3	28.0	5.0	38.8	33.2	118.3	47.6	44.9	6.6	30.3
1912	511.0	109.7	31.4	29.3	5.8	40.3	36.6	125.8	49.3	45.6	7.4	29.8
1913	530.1	113.9	31.3	31.5	5.3	42.0	39.3	131.5	48.9	46.1	8.3	32.0
1914	551.0	114.1	30.7	32.6	6.1	44.4	44.8	137.0	49.5	46.8	11.3	33.7

Notes: (1) * Other Assets are a residual.

(2) The figures do not include the non-life insurance companies' balance sheet data. In 1922 those firms assets amounted to 39 million pounds and in 1927 to 64 million. Those figures represent 4.9 and 5.7 percent of the assets of the enumerated firms.

Source: D.K. Sheppard, *The Growth and Role of UK Financial Institutions*, Table (A) 2.5, pp. 154–156.

Table 2:3-9(b). *Percentage Distribution of assets of United Kingdom insurance companies selling life insurance: all classes of business (life, industrial, accident, bond, employer liability, and fire)*

Year	Total assets	Mortgages	Loans on public rates & local government securities	Loans on policy & personal securities	British government & government guaranteed securities	Other commercial & municipal securities	Foreign government & municipal securities	Debentures	Preference, ordinary, & guaranteed stocks & shares	Land, insurance property, & ground rent	Cash & stamps	Other assets*
1880	100.0	45.7	12.6	5.8	3.2	4.6	2.8	6.8	5.1	5.2	2.9	5.2
1881	100.0	44.6	12.3	5.5	3.3	5.2	2.7	7.1	5.4	5.8	2.9	5.3
1882	100.0	44.1	13.1	5.4	3.1	5.3	2.6	7.0	5.9	5.7	2.4	5.4
1883	100.0	43.8	13.0	5.4	2.9	5.5	2.4	7.2	5.8	5.9	2.5	5.4
1884	100.0	42.9	12.9	5.3	3.0	6.2	2.2	7.2	5.9	6.1	2.7	5.4
1885	100.0	42.2	12.9	5.3	3.1	6.3	2.3	7.4	6.4	6.4	2.6	5.3
1886	100.0	41.9	12.7	5.2	3.1	6.3	2.2	7.7	6.1	6.7	2.7	5.3
1887	100.0	41.0	12.4	5.2	3.2	6.2	2.0	8.3	6.3	7.1	3.0	5.4
1888	100.0	39.9	12.0	5.1	3.2	6.4	1.8	9.2	6.4	7.3	3.4	5.2
1889	100.0	38.9	11.7	5.1	3.1	6.3	1.7	10.0	6.4	7.3	4.1	5.5
1890	100.0	39.3	10.6	5.0	3.0	6.1	1.7	11.0	6.2	7.5	4.1	5.5
1891	100.0	38.6	10.3	5.1	2.7	6.3	1.7	11.3	6.3	7.5	4.4	6.0
1892	100.0	38.0	11.1	5.1	2.5	6.4	1.7	11.9	6.1	7.7	4.0	5.6
1893	100.0	36.8	11.3	5.1	2.4	6.8	1.8	12.4	6.2	7.9	3.5	5.7
1894	100.0	35.3	11.6	5.0	2.4	7.1	1.9	12.8	6.8	8.0	3.3	5.8
1895	100.0	33.2	11.3	4.9	2.3	6.8	2.2	14.0	8.1	8.2	3.3	5.8

Year												
1896	100.0	31.1	11.0	4.8	2.4	6.6	2.7	15.5	9.5	8.3	2.6	5.6
1897	100.0	29.7	10.5	4.7	2.3	6.6	2.9	16.4	10.4	8.5	2.5	5.7
1898	100.0	29.1	9.9	4.7	2.3	6.4	3.1	16.6	11.1	8.8	2.2	5.7
1899	100.0	27.5	10.5	4.6	2.2	6.3	3.5	17.0	11.5	9.0	2.0	5.8
1900	100.0	27.4	10.6	4.6	2.5	6.2	3.5	19.3	11.3	9.6	2.0	3.0
1901	100.0	27.0	10.9	4.8	2.8	6.0	3.3	16.8	11.2	9.4	1.8	6.0
1902	100.0	26.4	11.0	4.9	2.9	5.9	3.2	17.3	11.4	9.4	1.9	5.8
1903	100.0	26.0	11.2	5.1	2.8	5.6	3.0	17.9	11.3	9.6	1.7	5.8
1904	100.0	26.2	11.6	5.3	2.6	5.4	2.8	17.8	11.0	9.8	1.6	5.9
1905	100.0	25.2	11.7	5.3	2.4	5.2	3.0	18.8	11.0	9.7	1.7	6.0
1906	100.0	25.1	11.4	5.4	2.0	5.1	3.1	19.7	10.7	9.9	1.8	5.9
1907	100.0	24.6	11.3	5.6	2.0	4.9	3.3	20.5	10.3	9.9	1.5	6.0
1908	100.0	23.8	11.6	5.8	1.9	4.4	3.5	21.4	10.4	9.9	1.6	5.7
1909	100.0	23.1	11.9	5.8	1.6	4.5	3.9	22.2	9.4	9.9	1.6	6.1
1910	100.0	21.9	6.8	5.9	1.5	8.1	6.3	23.2	9.6	9.5	1.5	5.8
1911	100.0	21.8	6.4	5.7	1.0	7.9	6.8	24.1	9.7	9.1	1.3	6.2
1912	100.0	21.5	6.1	5.7	1.1	7.9	7.2	24.6	9.6	8.9	1.4	5.8
1913	100.0	21.5	5.9	5.9	1.0	7.9	7.4	24.8	9.2	8.7	1.6	6.0
1914	100.0	20.7	5.6	5.9	1.1	8.1	8.1	24.9	9.0	8.5	2.1	6.1

Source: Table 2.3-9(a).

141

Table 2:3-10. *United Kingdom life insurance offices: the composition of investments by sectors*

Type of investment	1870	1880	1890	1900	1905	1913
	Panel A: millions of pounds					
Mortgages	51.6	70.9	83.1	85.2	96.9	113.9
Loans to, and securities of, UK local authorities	9.2	17.6	20.4	23.5	27.5	31.4
Indian and colonial municipal securities	0.8	1.5	1.7	6.2	10.8	22.7
Foreign municipal securities	0.2	0.4	0.4	3.4	6.5	14.7
British government securities	8.2	5.0	6.4	7.7	9.2	5.3
Indian and colonial government securities	5.3	7.1	12.8	19.3	20.1	19.3
Foreign government securities	1.2	4.4	3.5	10.9	11.7	24.6
Debentures and debenture stocks	10.4	10.6	23.3	52.0	72.3	132.4
Shares and stocks	3.1	7.9	13.1	35.1	42.1	49.1
Loans on life policies	5.3	7.2	9.2	13.2	18.3	29.1
Land, house properties, ground rents	4.7	8.1	15.8	29.0	37.3	46.1
Life interests and reversions	1.7	2.7	3.5	7.5	10.0	11.6
Loans on personal security	1.8	1.9	1.3	1.3	2.3	2.4
Total Investments	103.5	145.3	194.5	294.3	365.0	502.6

Panel B: Percent of all investments

Mortgages	49.9	48.8	42.7	29.0	26.5	22.7
Loans to, and securities of, UK local authorities	8.9	12.1	10.5	8.0	7.5	6.2
Indian and colonial municipal securities	0.8	1.0	0.9	2.1	3.0	4.5
Foreign municipal securities	0.2	0.3	0.2	1.2	1.8	2.9
British government securities	7.9	3.4	3.3	2.6	2.5	1.1
Indian and colonial government securities	5.1	4.9	6.6	6.6	5.5	3.8
Foreign government securities	1.2	3.0	1.8	3.7	3.2	4.9
Debentures and debenture stocks	10.0	7.3	12.0	17.7	19.8	26.3
Shares and stocks	3.0	5.4	6.7	11.9	11.5	9.8
Loans on life policies	5.1	5.0	4.7	4.5	5.0	5.8
Land, house properties, ground rents	4.5	5.6	8.1	9.9	10.2	9.2
Life interests and reversions	1.6	1.9	1.8	2.5	2.7	2.3
Loans on personal security	1.7	1.3	0.7	0.4	0.6	0.5
Total Investments	100.0	100.0	100.0	100.0	100.0	100.0

Notes: Loans to, and Securties of, UK Local Authorities, Indian and Colonial Municipal Securities, and Foreign Municiple Securities for 1870 and 1880 on the basis of percent distribution in 1890; 1900 and 1905 extrapolated on the Basis of 1890 and 1913.

Source: Barry Supple, *The Royal Exchange Assurance: A History of British Insurance, 1720–1970* (Cambridge, U.K.: Cambridge University Press, 1970), Tables 13.3 & 13.4, pp. 332–333.

In the case of fire insurance, the post-1870 expansion did not reflect growth in the domestic market; purchasing fire insurance was a well-ingrained British habit before 1870.[189] What increase there was in new insurance on United Kingdom properties was almost solely a product of the increase in the value of buildings and other insurable assets. The industry's very substantial growth – fire premiums rose from less than £4 million in 1870 to £29 million in 1913 – was almost entirely due to a near explosion in the number of foreign policies. British companies had long operated on the Continent. After 1870 they turned their attention to South America, Australia, the Far East, and, especially, the United States. The United States alone accounted for two dollars in every five of premium income in 1900, and the rest of non-European policies generated an additional one-fifth of that total.

It was not the old-line firms (firms that could trace their histories back to the eighteenth century: the Royal Assurance, the Sun, or the Phoenix) that took the lead in opening these new markets. Instead, it was the younger companies, and their enterprise was rewarded. In 1901 four of the five largest British fire insurance companies were less than sixty years old. Moreover, success in the foreign market, coupled with near stagnation at home, meant differential rewards; by 1915 the ten largest firms had come to account for 70 percent of the industry's premium income.

The decades after 1870 also saw a revitalization of the life insurance business, but in that industry growth was rooted in the domestic market. Britain largely missed the tontine boom that drove the American industry's expansion; instead, it was two other innovations that were responsible for growth in the United Kingdom. First, between 1870 and 1914 the amount insured under ordinary life policies almost tripled (from £293 million to £870 million). Much of that growth can be traced to the addition of an endowment clause to the traditional ordinary life policy. Such clauses were seldom a part of the contract at the beginning of the period, but by 1913 they were written into two out of three of the policies then in force: Insurance had become a recognized vehicle for saving. A policy with an endowment clause provided for the payment of the amount insured either at the end of a stipulated period or at death, if that event occurred earlier.

Second, as in the United States, the period was marked by the introduction and rapid growth of industrial insurance. Industrial insurance

---

[189] It is estimated that, in 1862, of the £1,500 million in English and Welsh property, £1,000 million was covered by fire insurance, and much of the residual was in quantities too small to be insurable.

was life insurance based on the regular weekly or monthly collections of small premiums. It was a kind of insurance that was particularly suited to the needs of the relatively poor, who could not envision insuring their lives if the premium payments were large. Almost unknown in the 1860s (industrial insurance policies accounted for only about £1.5 million in premium income), the holders of such policies in 1912 paid more than £16 million in premiums. In that year, with £350 million of insurance in force, the total volume of industrial policies was about one-half as large as the amount of traditional ordinary life insurance policies. Like the Post Office, the trustee savings banks, and the building societies, the insurance industry had found a mechanism that made it possible to mobilize the savings of the industrial classes. More importantly, unlike the Post Office, the trustee savings banks, and the building societies, the savings the insurance industry channeled into investment were not monopolized by government securities and home mortgages.

In the case of fire insurance it was the younger British firms that represented the entrepreneurial element. In the case of life insurance it was American competition – particularly competition from the Equitable, the New York Life, and the Mutual of New York – that forced the British industry to revolutionize its business practices. The revolution was reflected in changes of business organization, sales techniques, and, most importantly, from the point of view of this book, portfolio policy. In the case of organizational structure the late nineteenth century and the first decade of the twentieth saw a shift from companies selling a single type of insurance to the composite company selling some combination of life, fire, accident, liability, and marine insurance. A large part of that change was the result of the amalgamation of existing firms. On average, nine firms merged with others each year between 1886 and 1900; between 1906 and 1910 the figure was thirteen. Amalgamation produced significant economies of scale, and by offering both agents and clients a wider range of services, it made the product more attractive.

Until the American invasion historians described British firms as being passive: They waited for customers to come to them. Faced by foreign competition, they became, like their American counterparts, sales organizations. It has been estimated that the number of life insurance agents in the United Kingdom increased from 6,000 to 100,000 over the first fifty years of Victoria's reign, and it is certainly true that the number of life insurance agents employed by the Royal Exchange Assurance increased from 600 in 1850, to 5,000 in 1900, and to 15,000 in 1912.

Finally, the search for profits in a highly competitive environment marked by declining returns on traditional investments induced dramatic shifts in the industry's investment portfolio (see Tables 2:3-9 and 2:3-10).

In the eighteenth century insurance companies invested a significant portion of their funds in mortgages, but by early in the next century the bulk of the industry's resources was invested in public funds. In 1838 more than 70 percent of the Royal Exchange Assurance Company's investments was in issues of the British government, another 11 percent in local authority bonds, 6 percent in the stock of the Bank of England, and only 11 percent in mortgages. By 1871, however, the combined share of the British government and the Bank of England had declined to less than one-quarter of the total. The relative holdings of local authority bonds had more than doubled, and mortgages on land and buildings had increased to almost one-third of the total. Moreover, almost one pound in eight was invested in the bonds of private companies.[190]

Those shifts were only the precursors of the policies innovated over the next four decades, as yields on investment portfolios appeared to enter a state of free fall: from 4.5 percent in the 1860s and early 1870s to 4.0 percent in 1890 and to 3.75 percent at the turn of the century.[191] The impact of the new investment policies is captured in four very marked shifts in the industry's aggregate portfolio. First, there was a dramatic decline in the proportion of funds invested in mortgages, particularly in mortgages on land and buildings in the United Kingdom. Between 1870 and 1913 the share of all mortgages in the aggregate life insurance portfolio fell from just less than one-half to less than one-fourth, and at the latter date, the share of domestic mortgages is estimated to have been only 13 percent. Second, there was a decrease in the relative proportion of British national and local government issues from 17 to 7 percent. Third, there was a very rapid increase in the fraction of funds committed to overseas investments. It rose from 7 to more than 40 percent. Fourth, there was an almost equally large increase in the proportion of private – largely railroad – stocks and bonds. By 1913 they accounted for 40 percent of all life insurance investments.

Through most of the 1870s the home building boom produced a ready demand for mortgage loans. Over the ensuing decades, as building

---

[190] Supple, *The Royal Exchange*, table 13.1, p. 315, table 13.6, p. 334.
[191] Real interest rate fell somewhat less. The Consumer Purchase Index (1913 = 100) declined from 96.0 in 1870 to 86.9 in 1896, before rising to 93.6 in 1900. Charles Feinstein, *National Income, Expenditure and Output of the United Kingdom, 1855–1965* (Cambridge: Cambridge University Press, 1972), table 61, p. 132. Supple, *The Royal Exchange*, pp. 331–2. By quinquennia beginning in 1871–75 and ending in 1911–15, the Royal Exchange's portfolio averaged 4.7, 4.5, 4.3, 4.1, 3.9, 3.8, 3.8, and 3.9 percent. The lowest return (3.72 percent) was reported in 1902. Note that these returns were earned after the firm had made its portfolio adjustments.

activity slackened, mortgage rates plummeted. At the same time, as the agricultural depression grew worse, declining land values added an increased element of risk to the already-reduced returns on mortgage loans. Mortgages no longer so clearly fulfilled the principal canon of Bailey's investment policy for insurance companies: "The first consideration should invariably be the security of capital."[192] One response to the change in the economic environment – the Scottish companies were the innovating entrepreneurs – was the expansion of the industry's investment horizons to include foreign and colonial mortgages. Such loans were thought to be at least equally safe, and they certainly were more remunerative. First negotiated in the early 1880s, the volume of such loans reached £6.4 million in 1888, £12.6 million in 1895, and £21.1 million in 1913. At the last date they accounted for just less than 30 percent of all mortgages in the industry's portfolio.[193]

Only a small part of the increase in overseas investments can be traced to regulations imposed by foreign governments as the insurance companies opened branches abroad. Although countries, provinces, and states often required some amount of local investment as a condition for permitting a company to sell insurance, most of the shift was a response to increasing interest differentials.[194] During the 1880s it was the lure of 5–5.5 percent interest on foreign and colonial mortgages that induced the Scottish Widows' Fund, the Scottish Provident Institution, and the North British and Mercantile Assurance Company to invest 15 percent of their assets in overseas mortgages.[195] The relative decline in domestic government issues was almost exactly matched by the increase in the share of colonial and foreign governments. Finally, the documents attest that it was a very pressing need to fortify their reserve position that led

---

[192] Hall, *London and Australia*, pp. 51–52.

[193] Supple, *The Royal Exchange*, pp. 343–44.

[194] In 1891, for example, the Royal Exchange was required to purchase and hold £50,000 in U.S. government bonds as a condition for opening an office in San Francisco, and in 1896 the Argentine government required the firm to invest £14,000 in their bonds. The totals, however, were never large. In 1909, for example, all deposits in the U.S. totaled only £350,000. Supple, *The Royal Exchange*, p. 242.

[195] For example, these institutions "sent special representatives to Australia for the purpose of investing some portion of the funds in suitable mortgages. It has been the practice of at least one of those offices . . . to lend from two-fifths to one-half of the value of the property, as assessed by the company's own value, at a rate of interest varying from 5 to $5\frac{1}{2}$ percent; while the security consists principally of freehold land, money has also been lent on first class city property." W.E. Wright, "Life Assurance Company Investments," *The Bankers Magazine*, 1897, pp. 71–72. Cited in Hall, *London and Australia*, p. 119.

the directors of the Royal Exchange to increase the fraction of the firm's portfolio invested in overseas governments and rails from 10 percent in 1890 to 14 percent in 1891 to 23 percent in 1909 and to 45 percent in 1913.[196]

The data in Table 2:3-10 indicate that by 1913 the life insurance companies held, at a minimum, more than £80 million in overseas investments, and that figure does not take account of the overseas portion of the industry's holdings of private debentures and preferred and ordinary shares. Hall places the latter figure at an additional £80 million. If the experience of the Royal Exchange is typical of the industry, however, the total might have been more than twice that figure. Most of those investments had been made since 1870, the same period that saw the industry investing about £25 million in overseas mortgages. Even if the total were as low as £185 million, "it is clear that life insurance companies played an important part in the mechanism whereby British capital moved overseas in this period."[197]

In 1907 all overseas investments accounted for 35.5 percent of the Royal Exchange's total investments and 66.2 percent of their holdings of formal securities; the foreign issues were drawn from a very wide geographic spectrum. The United States accounted for 38 percent and the Empire an additional 29 percent. Europe contributed 13 percent, Argentina 7 percent, and the rest of the world 12 percent. By 1914 the fraction of overseas issues in the firm's portfolio of securities had reached 85 percent, and the share of all overseas investments in the total investments of all life insurance companies exceeded two in every five pounds.[198]

The massive geographic redistribution could not have been accomplished without a concomitant shift from direct to indirect investments. In 1870 all private stock and bond issues had accounted for only 13 percent of the insurance companies' portfolios. By 1913 the figure was 36 percent, and those securities (divided in a ratio of 2.7:1 between bonds and stocks) had a nominal value of £181.5 million – more than the value of all the industry's loans. If government issues are added to the private totals, the years from 1885 to 1913 saw the proportion of securi-

---

[196] Supple, *The Royal Exchange*, pp. 345–46. Between 1893 and 1896 the company increased its holdings of U.S. rails from £81,000 to £285,000 and its investments in Indian railroads from £86,000 to £130,000.

[197] Hall, *London and Australia*, p. 54. In 1914, 85 percent of the Royal Exchange's security holdings were in overseas issues. If that fraction represented the industry average, it suggests that overseas investments represented about £170 million of the £182 million of private issues.

[198] Supple, *The Royal Exchange*, p. 346.

ties that could be traded on the London Stock Exchange increase from one-quarter to three-fifths of the life insurance industry's aggregate portfolio.

Debentures alone represented about one-half of the total, and most of the industry's debenture investments were in foreign and domestic railroad issues. There was a sprinkling of public utility bonds in the industry's portfolio; but a few domestic brewery issues and an occasional foreign bond aside, there were few commercial and industrial issues, either domestic or foreign. Accepted opinion did not consider such securities to be suitable investments for insurance companies, and in the years before 1914 many companies' articles of association prohibited such investments. Instead, it was railroads that dominated the insurance industry's investments in ordinary and preferred shares. Investment in those stocks surged during the 1890s.

As to overseas governments, the life insurance industry absorbed (net) a total of £73.6 million between 1870 and 1913: £5.9 million in the 1870s, £4.8 million over the next decade, £21.4 million in the 1890s, and £41.5 million between 1900 and 1913 (see Table 2:3-10). The colonial and Indian governments were popular investments over the last three decades of the nineteenth century; during that period they accounted for 44 percent of net additions. In 1913, however, the industry's Empire holdings were no larger than they had been at the turn of the century. The issues of foreign central governments represented more than half of the additions in the 1870s and about one-third from 1890 to 1913. In marked contrast, the industry's investments in foreign governments in the 1880s actually declined by some £1.1 million. It was the shift into foreign and colonial municipals that accounted for much of the post-1890 increase in the government section of the industry's aggregate portfolio. Between 1870 and 1890 those issues represented a very small part of the industry's net acquisition of government bonds; the Empire accounted for 8 percent and foreign countries for barely more than 2 percent of those additions. Between 1890 and 1913, however, Indian and colonial municipals represented one-third and the issues of foreign cities almost one-quarter of the £62.9 million net increase.[199]

By the first decade of the twentieth century, indirect investments had become so important to the industry's profits that, for the first time, insurance companies began to underwrite new issues.[200] The Secretary of The Royal Exchange – a firm with 62 percent of its assets tied-up in stocks and bonds – was moved to say that the company had become "an important

---

[199] Hall, *London and Australia*, pp. 53–54.
[200] Supple, *The Royal Exchange*, pp. 346–47.

item among the capitalists of the world."[201] That statement may or may not have been correct, but it is certainly true that British insurance companies had become major players in the formal securities markets.

In the formal securities market, but not in the market for domestic commercial and industrial issues, British life insurance companies did not have their American counterparts' appetite for industrial securities, although beginning in the 1870s they acquired some foreign bonds.[202] A few small holdings of domestic brewery debentures aside, they did not move into domestic or foreign industrials in any significant way before 1914. The lack of appetite was perhaps a reflection of the absence of close links between investment banks and insurance companies, a relationship that characterized U.S. and Canadian financial development. Cottrell concludes that the insurance companies, with concerns about liquidity, may have been put off by the thinness of the market for industrials, but that argument is not compelling in light of the American experience.[203] Supple points to management's prudence and caution, but he does not explain why even the increased competition provided by American firms did not lead to a more aggressive investment policy. Toward the end of the century declining returns on mortgages and government bonds led to a restructuring of the industry's portfolio, but, even then, insurance companies avoided domestic commercial or industrial securities.[204]

Recently the assault on the role of the British capital markets has been widened to include the role of the formal markets in commercial and industrial finance.[205] If there was a weakness in the British domestic capital market, it may have been centered in the supporting institutional structure. In the United States the rapidly developing life insurance industry provided a major market for new securities, including, after the 1890s, the issues of commercial and industrial firms. In Britain it did not. There were, however, two other financial institutions – finance companies and investment trusts – that could, in principle, have played an equally important role.

The finance companies were in many ways precursors of the Canadian bond houses. Like the bond houses, they acted as midwives for companies attempting to link into the market for external capital. The finance company initially mobilized capital by the sale of its own shares. It then used those funds to purchase the shares of new or newly reorganized

---

[201] Quoted in Supple, *The Royal Exchange*, p. 330.
[202] Cottrell, *Industrial Finance*, p. 183.   [203] Cottrell, *Industrial Finance*, p. 269.
[204] Supple, *The Royal Exchange Assurance*, pp. 330–48. P.G.M. Dickson, *The Sun Insurance Office, 1710–1960* (Oxford: Oxford University Press, 1960), pp. 262–63. Kennedy, *Industrial Structure, Capital Markets*, p. 133.
[205] Kennedy, "Capital Markets and Industrial Structure in the Victorian Economy."

operating companies, held those shares while a market developed, and then gradually released them on the market. The English finance companies date from the 1860s. Had the institution become firmly established, it could have provided both a channel for first issues as well as a potential secondary market for shares not quoted on the formal exchanges. During their short four-year heyday (1863–66), finance companies handled almost 15 percent of the £35.6 million in non-government public securities that were brought to the London market.[206] Despite the view of the financial press that finance companies represented an invaluable addition to the capital market, the industry never really developed. It virtually disappeared during the crisis of 1866; most of the original firms failed, and the few that remained played only a minor role in the subsequent financial process. In 1914 the shares of twenty-two finance companies were quoted on the London exchange, but the majority were newly established. Moreover, they focused their attention on overseas investment in oil, rubber, and minerals, not on domestic industry.[207]

An investment trust makes it possible to spread risks over a number of investments without seeking to exert any control over the companies in which it has equity interests.[208] A strong set of financial trusts could have helped overcome potential informational asymmetries, made it easier for an investor to diversify his portfolio, and helped widen the primary market for new issues of domestic industrial and commercial firms. The trust companies did help smooth the transition from government bonds to private issues for many security-conscious savers during the years of declining interest rates on Consols, but the evidence suggests that they did not draw many new investors into the market for domestic securities. The trusts tended to invest in high-denomination debentures – most often rails, but other industries as well – and initially they could have brought these issues within the reach of the small

---

[206] Cottrell, *Investment Banking*, p. 188.

[207] Cottrell, *Investment Banking*, pp. 660–61, 665–66, and 685–88. In 1869 the editors of the *Investors' Guardian Almanac* wrote, "The necessity for Finance Companies to manage and arrange the using of large masses of money collected together in a country like England where the profits of trade, commerce and manufactures, with the receipts from landed estates, railways, and other securities, amount to about three million a week is self-evident." Apparently it was not.

[208] Youssef Cassis, "The Emergence of a New Financial Institution: Investment Trusts in Britain, 1870–1939," in J.J. Van Helten and Y. Cassis (eds.), *Capitalism in a Mature Economy: Financial Institutions, Capital Exports and British Industry, 1870–1939* (Aldershot, U.K.: Edward Elgar, 1990), p. 140. [Hereafter cited as Cassis, "Investment Trusts."]

investor.[209] That small investor, however, does not appear to have responded. "It is questionable whether they ever succeeded in attracting small investors for their shareholders belonged to the wealthy classes or, increasingly after 1914, became institutional investors, like insurance companies and, later, pension funds."[210] However, they did have an indirect impact on capital mobilization. The trusts' support of the market for non-rail issues provided an element of stability to that sector of the market; as a result, they made those issues more attractive to wealthy investors who did not require the trusts' intermediation services.[211]

The first of these trusts, the Foreign and Colonial Government Trust, was organized in 1868. As far as domestic finance was concerned, it was really a question of too little and too late. The late 1880s saw a wave of formation of investment trusts. "On the London Stock Exchange, their total nominal capital rose from £5 million in 1887 to some £50 million in 1890 and 70 new trust companies were formed during this period. However, investment trusts suffered severely in the aftermath of the Barings Crisis. According to *Bankers Magazine*, in 1893, the net depreciation of their ordinary and preference capital was 14.45 percent; for the companies formed after 1880, the depreciation of their ordinary capital was 29.19 percent."[212] In 1903 they had about £70 million in assets, and in 1913 about £90 million. They were therefore about one-twelfth as large as the commercial banks and one-fifth as large as the insurance companies. However, they "did not hold in their portfolios more than a small fraction of the total stocks dealt in London. In 1913, their capital accounted for 0.3 percent of the total nominal value of securities traded on the London Stock Exchange."[213]

The name "Foreign and Colonial Government" turned out to be prophetic of the geographic and industrial focus of the industry's portfolio policies. The *Economist* reported that of the £14.7 million controlled by ten trusts in 1890, only £1.9 million (less than 13 percent) was invested in United Kingdom securities, and that all of the nation's trusts together owned about £50 million of overseas securities.[214] Even in the 1890s, a decade of relatively little foreign investment (the average overseas flow during that decade was less than 65 percent of the 1860–1913 mean), the

---

[209] Hall, *London and Australia*, p. 56.
[210] Cassis, "Investment Trusts," p. 154.
[211] Hall, *London and Australia*, p. 56.
[212] Cassis, "Investment Trusts," p. 141.
[213] Cassis, "Investment Trusts," p. 144.
[214] Hall, *London and Australia*, p. 56. If the same proportion held in 1914, the trusts would have been responsible for £105 million in overseas and about £15 million in domestic investment.

domestic securities in the portfolio of a typical firm – the International Investment Trust, for example – represented less than one-quarter of the total. All ordinary and preferred shares – both domestic and foreign – together constituted only 30 percent of the firm's investments. Nor did their geographic focus change before World War I. "L.E. Robinson considered that in 1914, of the £75–£100 million in investment trusts' capital, 'fully 90 percent were stuck in overseas holdings, America being the largest single claimant.' "[215] Even if the trusts had been more receptive to domestic investments, it is doubtful whether they would have had a significant impact on the aggregate market. Their principal role was in investor education, where they performed effectively, but with limited impact.[216]

Consequently, although the reasons still remain unclear, given the investment policies of the nation's insurance companies and the relative failures of the finance companies and the investment trusts, "there was no institutional floor in the domestic industrial sector of the secondary market."[217]

2-3b. The formal securities market

2-3b(1). Background and evolution: By the 1840s paper assets were gradually becoming a permanent and steadily increasing part of the British saver's portfolio. It is estimated that in 1870 there were already 250,000 such investors – about 1.5 percent of all adults over twenty – and that by 1913 the number had increased to over a million, 3.5 percent of all such adults. In 1870 those investors had for the most part limited their commitments to government and railroad issues. By the turn of the century they were holding a wide variety of other private British and foreign securities. The number of investors in domestic joint-stock companies rose from about 50,000 in 1860 to half a million in 1910. On the eve of World War I, twenty-two Canadian industrial companies reported 7,000 British investors among their shareholders. Nor did investors limit themselves to a single endeavor. A 1901 survey of 6,120 joint-stock companies with a total of 3,369,000 shareholders indicates that the typical investor held shares in between seven and eight firms. Lowenfeld

---

[215] L.E. Robinson, *Credit Facilities in the United Kingdom* (New York, 1923), p. 189. Cited in Cassis, "Investment Trusts," p. 145.

[216] H. Burton and D.C. Corner, *Investment and Unit Trusts in Britain and America* (London: Etek, 1968), pp. 39–40, 46. Kennedy, *Industrial Structure, Capital Markets*, pp. 129–33.

[217] Cottrell, *Industrial Finance*, p. 183.

concluded that in 1907 the average British portfolio contained fifteen different investments.[218]

Early on, the Board of Governors of the New York Stock Exchange recognized that savers were concerned about the problem of asymmetric information, and that if the Exchange were to flourish, it must provide signals of quality and reputation. They adopted appropriate signaling policies. In England, such concerns had been largely alleviated among a substantial class of savers by the 1870s, although they still may have affected the typical investor's choice of securities. Not only was the number of savers who were willing to invest in paper assets increasing and the scope of their portfolios broadening, but the British investor had also become more venturesome and less affected by Lavington's caveats.[219] For example, Albert Grant, company promoter, financial manager, and sometime managing director of the Credit Foncier and Mobilier of England wrote, "That was a year and era when everyone was seeking what he could make on the Stock Exchange. There was a particular fascination to some people of making money on the Stock Exchange. I know hundreds who would rather make £50 on the Stock Exchange than £250 by the exercise of their profession; there is a nameless fascination, and in the year 1871 the favorite form of making money on the Stock Exchange was by applying for shares, selling them at whatever premium they were at, and the money was considered made, and was considered honorably made."[220] Thirty years later T. E. Burton voiced similar sentiments about British overseas investments: "In addition to these influences, there has existed a spirit of boldness in enterprise, developing often into rashness, which has manifested itself in the multitude of promoters seeking capital, and even more strikingly in the great number of investors ready to furnish it."[221]

By 1914 the formal markets in the United Kingdom included the London Stock Exchange and twenty-two provincial exchanges.[222] Sup-

[218] Michie, *London and New York*, pp. 118–21.

[219] F. Lavington, *The English Capital Market*, pp. 191–92. See Chapter 1, pp. 3–4.

[220] Albert Grant, *Twycross vs Grant and Others: Speech of Albert Grant* (1876), p. 126.

[221] T.E. Burton, *Financial Crises and Periods of Industrial and Commercial Depression* (1902), pp. 41–42. Both the Grant and Burton quotations are cited in Phillip L. Cottrell, *Investment Banking in England, 1856–1881: A Case Study of the International Financial Society* (New York: Garland, 1985), pp. 692–94. [Hereafter cited as Cottrell, *Investment Banking*.]

[222] In 1909 exchanges were operating in Aberdeen, Birmingham, Bradford, Bristol, Cardiff, Dundee, Edinburgh, Glasgow, Greencock, Halifax, Huddersfield, Hull, Leeds, Leicester, Liverpool, Manchester, Newcastle, Nottingham, Oldham, Sheffield, Swansea, and York. W.A. Thomas, *The Provincial Exchanges* (London: Frank Cass, 1973), p. 327. [Hereafter cited as Thomas, *The Provincial Exchanges*.]

porting and supplementing those markets were a large number of informal arrangements linking individuals (solicitors, brokers, and company promoters) and institutions (finance companies, trust companies, and private and joint-stock banks) – individuals and institutions that occasionally, or at times frequently, were themselves involved in the issue or sale of formal securities.

Although the London Stock Exchange was only one piece of Britain's financial infrastructure, the size, rate of growth, and geographic penetration of that institution provide an index of the development of the formal securities market. On January 1, 1863, the nominal value of shares quoted on the Exchange was £1.604 billion; at the end of 1913 it was £11.2626 billion, an implied annual rate of growth of 3.8 percent. In the former year government borrowing accounted for 67 percent of the total, railroads for 28 percent, and all other activities for a mere 5 percent. By 1913 the share of government had declined to just less than one-half, the share of railroads had risen to more than one-third, and that of "others" to almost one-fifth. If the focus is narrowed to governments and railroads, the domestic share had declined from more than three-fourths to just more than one-quarter.[223] Michie has somewhat different numbers, but the story they tell is much the same (see Table 2:3-11).

How did this formal capital market operate? As Lavington pointed out seventy-five years ago, "the security market consists of two parts." The raising of capital by the sale of *new* securities was not done through the stock exchange, but through a loosely structured collage of new issue houses, company promoters and brokers, underwriters, and advertisements. The market for *old* securities – securities that had already been sold at least once – consisted of the highly organized London and provincial stock exchanges, where the active agents were jobbers and brokers. The stock exchanges provided a secondary market for investors who wanted to purchase or sell existing securities. Although individual members of the stock exchanges may have been involved in company promotion, the exchanges were not a party to those transactions. In fact, brokers on the London Stock Exchange were cautioned in the house rules "against giving the sanction of their names to the bringing out of any company without due inquiry as to the bona fides of its objects, the character of its promoters, Directors and concessionaires and of other persons connected therewith." The rule, however, was often honored only in the breach.[224]

---

[223] Morgan and Thomas, *The Stock Exchange*, table V, pp. 280–81.

[224] Lavington, *The English Capital Market*, p. 122. Michie, *London and New York*, pp. 100–1. Phillip L. Cottrell, *Industrial Finance*, p. 151.

Table 2:3-11. *Securities quoted on the London Stock Exchange: value of paid-up capital*

Industry and Location	Year						
	1853	1863	1873	1883	1893	1903	1913
	Panel A: Millions of pounds						
Governments	923.3	1,073.3	1,345.4	1,889.6	1,933.2	2,513.6	3,324.0
Domestic	853.6	901.9	858.9	914.5	901.7	1,102.2	1,290.0
Foreign	69.7	171.4	486.5	975.1	1,031.5	1,411.4	2,034.0
Railways	225.0	442.9	727.6	1,475.3	2,419.0	3,082.4	4,146.0
Domestic	193.7	245.2	374.0	658.1	854.8	1,104.6	1,217.0
Foreign	31.3	197.7	353.6	817.2	1,564.2	1,977.8	2,929.0
Urban services***	24.5	27.1	32.9	101.8	140.3	200.1	435.0
Financial services**	13.1	26.3	121.8	102.2	199.5	440.5	609.0
Commercial and industrial*	21.9	26.7	32.6	43.0	172.6	690.9	917.0
Mines	7.4	5.1	7.7	20.8	32.9	41.1	91.0
Domestic****	7.4	1.0	1.3	0.6	0.3	0.0	0.0
Foreign	0.0	4.1	6.4	20.2	32.6	41.1	91.0
Agriculture	0.0	0.0	1.1	1.6	1.7	9.7	24.0
Domestic	0.0	0.0	0.0	0.0	0.0	0.0	0.0
Foreign	0.0	0.0	1.1	1.6	1.7	9.7	24.0
Total Domestic	1,054.7	1,148.1	1,234.2	1,573.2	1,756.8	2,206.8	2,507.0
Total Foreign	101.0	373.2	847.6	1,814.1	2,630.0	3,440.0	5,078.0
Total Unidentified	59.5	80.1	187.3	247.0	512.4	1,331.5	1,961.0
Total	1,215.2	1,601.4	2,269.1	3,634.3	4,899.2	6,978.3	9,546.0

Panel B: Percents

Governments	76.0	67.0	59.3	52.0	39.5	36.0	34.8
Domestic	70.2	56.3	37.9	25.2	18.4	15.8	13.5
Foreign	5.7	10.7	21.4	26.8	21.1	20.2	21.3
Railways	18.5	27.7	32.1	40.6	49.4	44.2	43.4
Domestic	15.9	15.3	16.5	18.1	17.4	15.8	12.7
Foreign	2.6	12.3	15.6	22.5	31.9	28.3	30.7
Urban services***	2.0	1.7	1.4	2.8	2.9	2.9	4.6
Financial services**	1.1	1.6	5.4	2.8	4.1	6.3	6.4
Commercial and industrial*	1.8	1.7	1.4	1.2	3.5	9.9	9.6
Mines	0.6	0.3	0.3	0.6	0.7	0.6	1.0
Domestic****	0.6	0.1	0.1	0.0	0.0	0.0	0.0
Foreign	0.0	0.3	0.3	0.6	0.7	0.6	1.0
Agriculture	0.0	0.0	0.0	0.0	0.0	0.1	0.3
Domestic	0.0	0.0	0.0	0.0	0.0	0.0	0.0
Foreign	0.0	0.0	0.0	0.0	0.0	0.1	0.3
Total domestic	86.8	71.7	54.4	43.3	35.9	31.6	26.3
Total foreign	8.3	23.3	37.4	49.9	53.7	49.3	53.2
Total unidentified	4.9	5.0	8.3	6.8	10.5	19.1	20.5
Total	100.0	100.0	100.0	100.0	100.0	100.0	100.0

Notes: **** Excludes Domestic Coal Mines. They Are Included With Commercial & Industrial.
*** Water, Gas, Electricity, and the Provision of Urban Transport and Communication.
** Banking, Insurance, and Other Financial Intermediaries.
* Includes Shipping.

Source: Ranald Michie, *The London and New York Stock Exchanges, 1850–1914* (Edinburgh & London: Allen & Unwin, 1987), Table 2.3, p. 52.

There is no doubt that as far as foreign securities were concerned, the British markets operated very efficiently in the years between 1860 and 1914 – in Kennedy's view, they may have operated too efficiently – and it is with foreign investment that this book is primarily concerned.[225] In 1900 a partner in C.W. Morgan & Co., New York bankers and brokers, argued that "internationally listed stocks are those securities which are also 'listed' on the London Stock Exchange."[226] It was, in fact, the great upsurge in foreign lending in the third quarter of the nineteenth century that catapulted London into the undisputed position of the world's financial center.

In the mid-1850s British overseas investments probably totaled a little over £200 million; over the next twenty years they increased fivefold. In that period the bonds of Austria, Belgium, Bolivia, Brazil, Chile, China, Colombia, Costa Rica, Denmark, Egypt, France, Guatemala, Holland, Honduras, Hungary, Italy, Japan, Liberia, Mexico, Morocco, Norway, Paraguay, Peru, Portugal, Rumania, Russia, San Domingo, Spain, Sweden, Tunis, Turkey, Uruguay, the United States, and Venezuela, as well as those of a number of American states and cities – bonds with nominal values of more than £720 million – were sold on the British market. In addition, British investors purchased £160 million of the bonds of Indian and Colonial governments and railways and more than £230 million of the securities of private companies operating abroad.[227] As Walter Bagehot noted in 1873, "it is sometimes said that any foreign country can borrow in Lombard Street *at a price.* There are very few civilized Governments that could not borrow considerable sums of us if they chose, and most of them seem more and more likely to choose. If any nation wants even to make a railway – especially at all a poor nation – it is sure to come to this country – the country of banks – for the money."[228]

---

[225] "The London stock exchange offered perhaps the best choice of essentially safe securities available anywhere in the world. As a consequence, less knowledgeable risk taking (in the sense of domestic, industrial capital formation in areas of advanced technology, the real risks) took place in Britain than in any of her advanced competitors. ... A part, but only a part, of her set of capital markets operated better than anyone else's. Had Americans and Germans had the facilities to obtain such high yields with such low risks as did Britons, particularly Londoners, perhaps they too would have taken fewer of the risks that their own imperfect capital markets forced upon them." Kennedy, *Industrial Structure, Capital Markets,* pp. 145–46.

[226] Michie, *London and New York,* p. 50.

[227] Many of the foreign bonds were sold at a discount and some, although issued in London, were purchased by foreigners. The estimates put the British cash contribution at about £320 million. Morgan and Thomas, *The Stock Exchange,* p. 88.

[228] Walter Bagehot, *Lombard Street: A Description of the Money Market* (Homewood Ill.; Richard D. Irwin, 1962), p. 3.

Although the rate of increase declined, between 1880 and 1913 some £2.965 billion in new foreign issues were sold either in "London only" or "in London and Elsewhere," and the "London only" component represented more than three-quarters of the total.[229] By 1913 the foreign stocks and shares quoted in London had a nominal value of £6.8 billion, 60 percent of the value of all securities quoted anywhere in the world. Investors in the United Kingdom were estimated to have held about 40 percent of the world's foreign-owned debt.[230] Overall, British investors probably held about £3.7 billion in publicly issued foreign securities, and in addition they owned at least another £400 million in the shares of private companies operating (or with property located) outside the United Kingdom. Of the £4.1 billion total, just less than half was invested in the Empire, about one-fifth in the United States, a similar fraction in Latin America, more than 15 percent in Europe, and "the remainder scattered far and wide in relatively small amounts." Most had been directed toward developing countries in North America, Latin America, Australia, New Zealand, and South Africa. More than two-fifths of the total was invested in railways, 30 percent in government issues, 5 percent in private public utilities, 10 percent in mines and plantations, and about 8 percent in financial institutions.[231]

The formal markets' successful mobilization of domestic savings for foreign investment may or may not have been matched by success at home. Most studies have indicated that the London and provincial exchanges played an unexpectedly small role in mobilizing savings for investment in domestic industry and commerce. It appears that on the eve of World War I, although British savings were divided about evenly between home and foreign investment, the formal capital markets handled only one-third of the domestic total. The one-third figure was larger than the one-quarter estimate for 1853, but the bulk of those financial resources were still directed toward investment in transport and public utilities. The formal markets appear to have accounted for only about 10 percent of the funds made available for industrial investment.[232]

---

[229] £2,263 out of £2,965. Morgan and Thomas, *The Stock Exchange*, p. 94. *The Investors' Monthly Manual* divided issues into the two categories.

[230] Morgan and Thomas, *The Stock Exchange*, p. 97; Collins, *Money and Banking*, pp. 153–54.

[231] Morgan and Thomas, *The Stock Exchange*, pp. 79–80; Collins, *Money and Banking*, pp. 153–54.

[232] Lavington, *The English Capital Market*, pp. 204–6. Michie, *London and New York*, p. 112. A.R. Hall, "The English Capital Market Before 1914 – A Reply," *Economica*, Vol. 24, No. 4 (November 1958), p. 340. Capie and Collins put the fraction of the value of industrials to all securities listed on the London Stock

The question remains: Was the relatively small role played by the formal markets the result of a failure of the market to supply the requisite commercial and industrial finance or of a lack of demand for such finance? The policy implications are in dispute, but there is general agreement about the nature of the market for domestic industrials. From the capital market failure camp, Kennedy argues that even as late as the last quarter of the nineteenth century, 60–70 percent of industrial capital formation was financed by "small, segmented groups of men who were acquainted with each other through business or personal contacts." He concludes that "in any event, whether change occurred within firms or through the creation of new firms, it was accomplished by tapping relatively small, highly segmented pools of savings."[233] From the other side of the debate, Cottrell echoes the same words: "By 1914 there was no national perfect capital [market] for industrial needs, certainly in comparison with that provided for credit by the banking system. Instead, there was a 'Balkan-like' mosaic consisting of a number of regional bowls of savings which occasionally coalesced under special circumstances." Those occasions occurred in the 1870s, and as a result pooled finance was made available to the iron, coal, and steel industries. They occurred again two decades later when "savers' mistrust of foreign securities was so considerable that it turned their attention to domestic issues, including those issued on behalf of manufacturing concerns."[234]

> Exchange at 1 percent in 1873 and less than 5 percent in 1913. Capie and Collins, *Have Banks Failed British Industry*, p. 32. In 1913 all (domestic and foreign) commercial and industrial securities accounted for 18.5 percent of the securities listed on the London exchange. Morgan and Thomas, *The Stock Exchange*, table V, pp. 280–81. In addition, the local exchanges probably channeled funds representing 5 to 10 percent of gross domestic capital formation; and some substantial part of that total was in commercial and industrial securities. Lavington, *The English Capital Market*, p. 208. One estimate, cited approvingly by Cottrell, suggests that in 1907 no more than 10 percent of domestic industrial development was financed by public offers of securities. C.L. Ayres, *New Capital Issues on the London Money Market, 1899–1913*, Ms.C. Thesis, University of London, 1934, p. 202. Michie comes to a similar, but somewhat more optimistic conclusion. "A more realistic comparison is between securities representing real assets, such as railways, urban utilities, commercial and industrial enterprises, and all domestic real assets. The paid-up value of such securities totaled only £440.8 million in 1873, a mere 9 percent of domestic assets, while in 1913, when their value had reached £2,570, they still represented only 32 percent of the total." Michie, *London and New York*, p. 99.
>
> [233] Kennedy, *Industrial Structure, Capital Markets*, pp. 124–25.
>
> [234] Cottrell, echoing Lavington, concludes that the market for home industrials consisted, by the 1900s, of roughly three compartments, "flotations by existing, usually large, companies, some of which were rights issues and which generally faced no difficulties; private flotation's, as in the cotton industry, where the funds

The provincial nature of industrial capital is underscored by an examination of the geographic distribution of stockholders. From a random sample of firms, Cottrell finds that in 1865, 76 percent of stockholders lived within ten miles of the companies' registered offices. Twenty years later the fraction had declined, but it still stood at 47 percent, and since almost one-quarter of the shareholders lived abroad, the data indicate that 62 percent of domestic shareholders still resided within the ten-mile radius.[235]

A large part of the domestic market was clearly informal, but that conclusion does not directly translate into inefficiency. Kennedy argues that it does. He speaks of a "pervasive segmentation spawned by networks of highly localized business contacts" and argues that the provincial exchanges were no more than extensions "of the close circle of local associates," and thus that they lacked an institutional foundation adequate to collect information and support diversification.[236] That very segmentation, however, helped to allay the problems raised by Kennedy. The networks of business contacts reflected the geographical, social, and business environment within which the firms were located. It was not the public at large that was expected to bear the uncertainties, but groups of savers who, because they were operating in the same environment as the firm, possessed through personal contact and knowledge a level of insight and information that was almost certainly superior to anyone else's. "In coal-mining, iron and steel and cotton spinning the necessary finance came largely from the locality in which the operations were undertaken, and where there was the greatest concentration of informed investors. As early as 1875 it was estimated that one-fifth of the population of Oldham had been drawn upon to finance the expansion of the local spinning mills, and other networks of informed investors were evident elsewhere in the country."[237]

Moreover, there is very little evidence that commerce and industry suffered from any shortage of finance, a conclusion that perhaps provides an even more telling rebuttal to the failure argument. First, an examination of the manufacturing sector "gives little support to the hypothesis that an unduly high SPOF [Supply Price of Finance] was creating a

---

were subscribed by directors and their friends, with remaining sums being obtained through informal channels; and lastly, public, generally small or medium sized, issues made either on the provincial exchanges or the London market. It is the market conditions that these latter issues faced on which the debate has turned." Phillip L. Cottrell, *Industrial Finance*, pp. 180, 269.

[235] Cottrell, *Industrial Finance*, table 4.6, pp. 92–93.

[236] Kennedy, *Industrial Structure, Capital Markets*, pp. 124–25.

[237] Michie, *London and New York*, p. 108.

capital shortage in manufacturing or was itself much of an obstacle to growth in that sector."[238] Second, some industries were able to raise capital on the formal London market; the list included iron, coal, and steel, brewing, and chemicals.[239] Finally, even new industries were able to privately float substantial issues in London and the Midlands. Between 1870 and 1914, for example, over one hundred cycle and tire manufacturers raised, on average, about £10,000 each. Over the same period there were individual private commercial and industrial issues that exceeded £200,000.[240]

Before 1914 there is little evidence that most commercial and industrial enterprises needed to use the facilities of the formal exchanges to raise the finance they required. The actual issues were generally easily marketed, and their issue was often "more a response to the public's willingness to invest" than a reflection of the firm's need to raise capital for a further stage of development. Most firms saw little need for the services of the formal exchanges or their members.[241] Although there was a surge in the formation of joint-stock companies in the commercial and industrial sectors after 1885, there is strong evidence that the change in organizational structure was not a response to a greater demand for external finance. Among even the largest firms that adopted joint-stock

[238] R.C.O. Matthews, C.H. Feinstein, and J.C. Odling-Smee, *British Economic Growth 1856–1973* (Stanford, Calif.: Stanford University Press, 1982), p. 381. [Hereafter cited as Matthews, Feinstein, and Odling-Smee, *British Economic Growth.*]

[239] Those firms were small in number, but they represented a much larger fraction of the total demand for capital. In 1885, for example, only 1,585 of the nation's 8,955 joint-stock companies were listed on the London exchange, but that 17.7 percent, with an aggregate paid-up capital of £332 million, accounted for almost 70 percent of the total paid-up capital of all registered companies. A. Essex-Crosby, *Joint Stock Companies in Great Britain, 1890–1930*, M.C. Thesis, University of London, 1938, p. 25.

In 1880 there were twelve joint-stock breweries, and the shares of about one-half were quoted on the London Stock Exchange; by 1885 the number of quoted brewery issues had increased to eighteen. In 1886, however, Guiness successfully floated a £6 million issue – large compared even to overseas issues – through Barings', a premier merchant bank. The issue was oversubscribed many times, and its success touched off a wave of brewery flotations. By 1890, eighty-six other firms had appealed to the public for capital; and by 1906 *Burdetts Official Stock Exchange Intelligence* listed no fewer than 307 brewing companies.

Comparable in size to the larger brewery flotation's were the issues of two chemical cartels – the Salt Union established in 1888 and the United Alkali Company – a firm organized in 1890 and that went "public" the next year. Cottrell, *Industrial Finance*, pp. 168–69, 171.

[240] Michie, *London and New York*, pp. 108–9.

[241] Michie, *London and New York*, p. 110.

structure, family-based management remained common. As a result, no market in corporate control existed before 1914 for the overwhelming majority of British industrial firms.[242] Instead, the shift to joint-stock structure appears to have been partly the result of a desire by banking, insurance, and other investment firms to spread the risk by increasing the number of owners, if not the total size of the firm's net worth, partly a result of the desire to limit competition by gaining control of the operating decisions of what had heretofore been competitive firms, but overwhelmingly the result of a desire to provide the firm with unlimited life.[243]

Since Lavington, most economic historians have agreed that there is no evidence of any urgent need or desire on the part of British industrialists for use of the Stock Exchange facilities in the years before 1914.[244] Retained earnings represented the largest source of finance, and when external finance was required, industrialists tended to turn to existing shareholders. That source served to finance expansion along existing lines. In addition, established firms often diversified in order to provide the organizational basis for new lines of endeavor.[245] To the extent that there were problems, they were most often encountered when opportunities arose outside existing industries and when existing firms lacked the technical capabilities to exploit them.

Two recent studies have provided substantial evidence that the new-issues market was hardly closed to commercial and industrial firms. Katherine Watson's micro-study of the iron and steel and brewing industries proves fairly conclusively that while the relative proportion of ordinary and preference shares and debentures may have varied, firms in neither industry appear to have had any trouble raising finance by the sale of paper securities. "Iron and steel companies did not complain of a scarcity of capital." By adopting a capital structure that was appropriate for the industry they could raise funding that they perceived to be required for their business. In contrast a different financial structure appeared to be efficient for brewers during the same period. Given that there seems to be little evidence of rejected applications to the new issue market, it seems unwise to argue that the capital market "failed these

[242] Capie and Collins, *Have Banks Failed British Industry?*, pp. 31–32.
[243] Michie, *London and New York*, pp. 109–10.
[244] For example, see A.R. Hall, "A Note on the English Capital Market as a Source of Funds for Home Investment Before 1914," *Economica*, Vol. 24, No. 1 (February 1957), pp. 59–66; and Alexander K. Cairncross, "The English Capital Market Before 1914 – A Reply," *Economica*, Vol. 25, No. 2 (May 1958), pp. 142–48.
[245] Kennedy, *Industrial Structure, Capital Markets*, pp. 124–25.

industries by denying them funds."[246] Gregory Marchildon' s case study of British capital flows to Canadian industry demonstrates fairly conclusively that building on a £240,000 issue of the Dominion Brewery in 1889 and the sale of £305,200 of the debentures of the Dominion Cotton Company in 1895, no less than £23.1 million of manufacturing capital was raised by Canadian manufacturing firms between 1905 and 1913 through the aegis of the London issue market. The evidence indicates "that many lesser known British investment banks, as well as some of the largest merchant banks, were willing to channel long term capital to industry before the Great War. Moreover, there is little evidence of a systematic bias against providing capital to manufacturing companies except again in the case of Barings and Rothschilds who chose to continue raising finance for governments and large railway enterprises but eschewed industrial firms." There is no reason to believe that even if "British investment banks had a preference for foreign and colonial industry over domestic industry" that it was based on "natural preference, lack of entrepreneurial spirit, habit or predilection". Instead, it probably reflected an unwillingness by British firms to pay the requisite costs: a reflection of the availability of alternative sources or a view about potential profitability.[247]

Lavington noted that advertising and underwriting charges weigh heavier on small than on large issues, even on the provincial exchanges; moreover, the London, and increasingly the provincial, exchanges refused to list very small issues.[248] It has been suggested that the British auto and electrical machinery industries suffered somewhat from their

[246] Katherine Watson, "The New Issue Market as a Source of Finance for the UK Brewing and Iron and Steel Industries, 1870–1913," in Youssef Cassis, Gerald D. Feldman, and Ulf Olsson, *The Evolution of Financial Institutions and Markets in Twentieth-Century Europe* (Aldershot, U.K. and Brookfield, Vt.: Scolar Press and Ashgate Publishing Company, 1995), pp. 209–38. The quotation is from p. 238.

[247] Gregory P. Marchildon, "British Investment Banking and Industrial Decline Before the Great War: A Case Study of Capital Outflow to Canadian Industry," in Geoffrey Jones (ed.), *Banks and Money: International and Comparative Finance in History* (London & Portland, Ore.: Frank Cass, 1991), pp. 72–89. The quotations are from pp. 88 and 89. [Hereafter cited as Marchildon, "British Investment Banking and Industrial Decline Before the Great War."]

[248] Lavington, *The English Capital Market*, p. 219. The London Stock Exchange normally refused to quote companies with paid-up capital of less than £50,000 and, at times, £100,000. In 1890 the trustees of the Liverpool exchange decided that they would no longer provide a quotation for companies with share capital less than £50,000; and "Manchester resolved to reject quotations of small companies whose shares were 'insufficiently in public hands.'" Michie, *Money, Mania and Markets*, p. 257. Cottrell, *Industrial Finance*, pp. 182–83.

inability to establish connections with either the formal or the informal capital markets. It is certainly possible that some new industries – industries with large capital demands to support massive technological innovation – did find themselves priced out of the informal capital markets; however, given the lack of evidence of firms unable to obtain sufficient finance, the number of cases must have been quite small. It has been demonstrated that it was possible to raise £200,000 or more through the informal Edwardian arrangements. Most capital requirements continued to be modest and well within those limits, and as society was becoming more affluent, the constraints on the size limits imposed by the informal arrangements were being continuously relaxed. "Consequently, the provision of the necessary finance for most areas of economic activity continued to remain within the reach of the informal networks."[249] Even in the *rare* cases in which firms were priced out of the informal markets, it is not clear that British entrepreneurs faced problems that were any more serious than their counterparts in, for example, the United States or Canada.

2-3b(2). The formal securities markets: introduction: It is generally believed that "nearly all securities issued before 1885 were ordinary shares." However, the British habit of issuing some common shares that were not fully paid-up suggests that there was often some differentiation between one common share and another. Between 1863 and 1882 the annual average ratio of paid-up to nominal capital was 24 percent, and ranged from 13 to 40 percent. Lavington reports one – hardly typical – firm registered in 1891 with 9.6 million shares of 1/4 pence each (a paper total of £10,000) with a *total* of only 13/4 pence actually subscribed.[250] The bulk of the equities issued between 1860 and the mid-1880s had a par value of £10 or less. Smaller par values (£5) became common in the mid-1870s, and by late in that decade, the £1 share was widely used.[251]

In 1885, 12 percent of the company securities quoted on the London Stock Exchange were preference shares, and the majority had been issued by overseas railroad and finance companies. Debentures, too, had become more popular over the previous decade. By the mid-1880s they accounted for 26 percent of the aggregate value of the paid-up capital

---

[249] Michie, *London and New York*, pp. 108–9.
[250] Cottrell, *Industrial Finance*, table 4.3, p. 85; Lavington, *The English Capital Market*, p. 216.
[251] The average par value (weighted by the upper tail) was £13.2 over the years 1860–76. For the years 1876–82 it was £11.5. Cottrell, *Industrial Finance*, pp. 86–88 and table 4.1, p. 82.

quoted on the Exchange. Debenture debt had initially been innovated by overseas railway companies, by finance, land, and investment companies, and by investment trusts.

The relative importance of preference shares continued to increase throughout the period; they constituted 22 percent of the aggregate paid-up capital reported in *Burdett's* in 1895 and 30 percent in 1915. The weight of debentures in total finance also rose until the mid-1890s; they made up 41 percent of paid-up capital in 1895. Thereafter, inflation somewhat dulled the investors' appetites for any further increases in the proportions of that form of security in their portfolios. In 1915 debentures still represented two-fifths of the total. In 1884 only 227 out of the 1,585 public companies reported in *Burdett's* (15 percent) had more than one class of capital. By 1915, 75 percent of all iron, coal, and steel companies had issued both preference shares and debentures. An equal fraction of "other" public commercial and industrial companies had issued preference shares. One-half of that latter group (37.5 percent of the total) had also issued debentures.[252]

The formal secondary markets for stocks and bonds were the London and the much smaller provincial stock exchanges.[253] The market was far from complete: Lavington estimates that of the over 35,000 security issues in Great Britain, only 5,000 were officially quoted on any exchange, and even of those, "less than 400 have at any time a free market."[254] The markets, however, did continue to grow and develop. As they expanded in size and scope over the course of the late nineteenth

---

[252] Cottrell, *Industrial Finance*, pp. 164–67. The policy of issuing shares that were not fully paid-up had become less entrenched. By 1895 the unpaid liability had fallen to one-third; and, by 1915, except for financial and insurance shares, it had ceased to exist.

[253] In the case of the London Stock Exchange, the paid-up value of corporate enterprise (excluding railroads and utilities) quoted increased from £42.4 million in 1853 to £1,643.3 million in 1913. In the case of the provincial exchanges they are together estimated to have directed an annual average of about £4–5 million to those same activities in the years between 1900 and 1914. The provincial exchanges, however, although important for commercial and industrial finance before the turn of the century, were much smaller than their London counterpart. Liverpool, for example, had only 150 members, 4 percent of the London figure. Despite their size, Glasgow, a speculative market, was important for oil shares, Birmingham for cycles and rubber tires, Sheffield for iron, coal, and steel companies, and Manchester for textiles. Michie, *London and New York*, p. 108; Thomas, *The Provincial Exchanges*, pp. 114, 139; Lavington, *The English Capital Market*, pp. 220–21.

[254] Lavington admits that "these 400 are, however, constantly changing, some dropping out and others taking their place." Lavington, *The English Capital Market*, pp. 221–22.

century, the potential liquidity inherent in a security that could be bought and sold on a formal exchange made it possible to tap an increasing proportion of the nation's total savings and to direct those resources toward productive enterprise at home and abroad.

The national market was to suffer somewhat from rule changes imposed in the immediate pre-World War I years. Still the existence of securities trading at different levels, the unification between exchanges provided by shunting, and the market-making activities of the London dealers meant that by the early twentieth century, an efficient formal market served all of Britain.[255] Companies in search of capital could easily find their place in the market, and they could equally easily change places if they found that their circumstances had been altered. From the point of view of savers, the range of securities that could be readily bought and sold had expanded enormously.[256] In part, the formal market merely substituted for the existing informal market, but a substantial part of the transactions on the formal exchanges involved activities – particularly investment in infrastructure – that would have been much more difficult to finance had there been no formal markets. Such investment "was a necessary adjunct to continuing growth and change in both the British economy and numerous economies throughout the world."[257] What, then, was the structure of this new market, and how well did it perform?

2-3b(3). The primary market: promoters, underwriters, and institutions: Lavington, comparing the British market with those in Germany and France, noted that unlike those two countries, where the banks undertook the initial sale of most securities, in England, "it is broadly true that only the better classes of securities are marketed by specialized institutions of this kind. Here the marketing organization is, as a whole, much less definite in form; it includes a wide range of agencies extending from the small group of firms of high reputation who specialize in this work down to the innumerable little *ad hoc* promoting groups in London and throughout the provinces."

The firms "of high reputation" were merchant banks – the Barings, Rothschild's, Schroeder's, and Seligman's – whose major marketing focus

---

[255] The term "shunting" refers to brokers on the provincial exchanges dealing directly (by telephone or telegraph) with brokers on the London Exchange or vice versa. With competition, the existence of such links gave country brokers access to the London markets on terms that were almost as good as those enjoyed by members of the Exchange, while at the same time evading the heavy expense and responsibility of membership. Michie, *London and New York*, p. 22.

[256] Michie, *London and New York*, pp. 26–27.

[257] Michie, *London and New York*, pp. 117–18. Cottrell, *Industrial Finance*, p. 146.

was on foreign governments and railways. Next in line were some trusts, finance companies, and small "Issuing Houses," firms that were continually engaged in financial operations and that therefore had a real concern for their reputation. Finally, there were the evanescent groups, small collages of individuals and institutions most often organized to promote and sell the issues of a single venture, and usually dissolved when the shares had been sold. Not all issues involved institutional intermediation. Cities and railroads often assumed the responsibility of marketing their own securities; joint-stock companies drew additional capital by offering new issues directly to their stockholders, by advertising them in the local press, or by employing their own sales agents. It was even true that "American industrial securities used to be hawked door to door."[258]

As the data reported in Table 2:3-12 demonstrate, the routes to the British capital markets chosen by foreign and colonial borrowers were many and varied. Merchant – that is, investment – banks were a channel for more than one-third of the total, but over time their importance was declining and that of the British joint-stock banks increasing. Beginning in the 1850s the London new issues market had been dominated by the large merchant banks. By the 1890s, however, they had begun to feel competitive pressure from commercial banks and from other financial institutions.[259] Between 1815 and 1904 two merchant banks – Rothschild's and Barings – together handled 205 separate government issues totaling more than £2 billion. The banks retailed a more or less standard commodity – very large issues of fixed-interest securities – and it was important that the volumes be large enough to yield substantial economies of scale in marketing. The securities were sold through a "well-established circle of wealthy individuals and institutions, many of whom, in turn, had their own clients."[260]

The British merchant banks also played an important role in distributing corporate securities, but there were few domestic issues, and railway companies constituted a very large proportion of the total. Between 1815 and 1904, Barings and Rothschild's handled 109 private issues totaling £244 million. Corporate business, however, was not limited

---

[258] Lavington, *The English Capital Market*, pp. 183–84.
[259] In the 1860s a few joint-stock banks had entered the new issues market. Most of their operations dealt with foreign banks, but the English Joint Stock Bank brought out the Phosphate of Lime Company and the National Bank sponsored the Lundy Granite Company. However, their experience during the 1866 Overend Gurney crisis drove them out of both foreign and domestic markets for at least twenty years. Cottrell, *Industrial Finance*, p. 145.
[260] Michie, *London and New York*, p. 114.

Table 2:3-12. *The proportion of overseas new issues introduced by the main types of issuing house, 1870–1914*

Years	Official and semi-official agencies	Private (i.e., merchant) banks	Joint-stock banks	Overseas banks & agencies	Companies via their bankers	Other media*	Total amount issued
	Percents						Millions of pounds
1870–1874	1.8	53.0	4.4	9.6	18.2	13.0	390.6
1875–1879	14.5	36.5	0.8	24.7	13.0	10.5	149.2
1880–1884	6.7	38.5	3.3	14.1	26.7	10.7	355.3
1885–1889	9.9	43.7	5.3	7.5	26.1	7.5	479.2
1890–1894	10.4	46.4	9.0	8.8	19.6	5.8	349.6
1895–1899	8.7	25.1	11.2	20.3	25.2	9.5	359.6
1900–1904	27.4	19.2	17.8	14.4	16.7	4.5	258.2
1905–1909	10.3	32.7	12.2	22.4	18.7	3.7	509.9
1910–1914	8.3	35.2	17.4	18.8	17.5	2.8	783.8
1870–1914	9.8	37.2	10.3	15.4	20.5	6.8	3,636.0
Total amount issued (Millions of pounds)	355	1,354	371	562	746	248	3,636

Notes: * Other Media Comprises: (a) Investment Trusts [23m]; (b) Finance, Land and Property Companies [18m]; (c) Special Purpose Syndicates [41m]; (d) Issue Houses with Stock Exchange Connections [22m]; (e) Companies as their own issuers [13m]; and (f) miscellaneous issuers [131m]. Figures in brackets refer to the total amount introduced over the years 1870 to 1914.

Source: A.R. Hall, *The London Capital Market and Australia, 1870–1914* (Canberra: The Australian National University, 1963), Table 12, p. 72. Hall's table is based on a table prepared by W.A. Brown and published in the *Economist* (20 November, 1937) and reprinted in T. Balogh, *Studies in Financial Organization* (Cambridge, U.K.: Cambridge University Press, 1947), p. 233.

to the old-line merchant banks. By the mid-1880s a few domestic industrial issues were of sufficient size and attractiveness to permit the merchant banks to employ their mass production technology – Guinness by Baring, Salt Union by Morton, Rose, and Hotchkiss by Anthony Gibbs & Son, to cite three – but even as late as 1914 only a handful of issues met the leading banks' size and quality criteria.[261]

New merchant banks entered the field, and some were even more entrepreneurial than their older counterparts. Between 1906 and 1913, for example, Arthur Grenfell's Canadian Agency was responsible for thirty-five issues totaling £16.4 million. Of that number, more than one-quarter were Canadian industrials, 16 percent Canadian land and development companies, and 12 percent divided between South African mining and Russian oil securities.

Although "Grenfell's poor choice of issue and underwriting business (and perhaps his own incompetence) bankrupted the firm by 1914, the Canadian Agency was not alone among the younger and more entrepreneurial new generation investment banks. Almost all were based in the City of London." In the case of Canada, "Sperling & Co. was the first City investment bank to specialize in Canadian industrial flotations. It was one of the many Anglo-German houses that branched out from stockbroking activities into the general issue business. Regarded as one of the more 'reckless' firms in the City, it was consistently prepared to take on a position of great risk in floating new issues of corporate securities."[262] Other equally entrepreneurial firms competed for the same business. Between 1908 and 1914, although Sperling sold £1.5 million of the issues of Canadian General Electric, the Dominion Steel Corporation, and the British Columbia Breweries, Western Canada Trust Ltd. issued almost £4 million (£3.99 million) of the securities of the Canada Iron Company, the Canadian Car & Foundry, the Steel Company of Canada, the Canadian Steel Foundries, and the Cockshutt Plow Company. The British Empire Trust Company handled £1.364 million of Canadian Western Lumber and Canadian North Pacific Fish; the Canadian Agency, £578,000 of the issues of the Canada Cement Company and Canada Cotton; the Brazilian Canadian and General Trust Company, £760,000 of the Dominion Sawmills and Lumber; Egerton, Jones & Simpson, £326,000 of Canadian Pacific Lumber; and the British Foreign & Colonial Corporation, £153,000 of Dominion Canners. Although Barings and Rothschild's continued to resist the lure of uncertain but

---

[261] Cottrell, *Industrial Finance*, p. 181; Michie, *London and New York*, pp. 114–15.
[262] Marchildon, "British Investment Banking and Industrial Decline Before the Great War," p. 82.

high-paying Canadian industrials, having seen the profits earned by the new firms, other old-line merchant banks began to compete for the business. Speyer Brothers, for example, sold £1.116 million of Dominion Iron and Steel in 1909.[263]

Despite these notable forays, the market for new corporate issues was for the most part handled by a collection of "stockbrokers, solicitors, accountants, bankers, and numerous well connected amateurs."[264] The individuals and firms in that group were far too numerous to list. Among brokers, James Capel & Co. was involved in railway flotations in the 1840s. "Harry Panmure Gordon, the flamboyant Hatton Court broker, made quite a business out of floating home industrials. His most famous was Lipton's in 1898, and he was involved with a number of breweries including Ind Coope, Newcastle Breweries and Plymouth Breweries."[265] In the 1880s and 1890s Foster & Braithwaite concentrated on industrial firms, particularly electric power, traction, and engineering companies. Its flotations included the Anglo-American Brush Electric Lighting Corporation and the Electric Light and Traction Company of Australia. Solicitors, because of their role as investment advisors, remained important throughout the period. A few – the London firm of Ashurst, Morris, and Company, for example – specialized in company promotion. Even accountants – a newly emerging profession – were involved. Adamson, Collier, & Chadwick, a London and Manchester firm, often took part in the flotation of coal and iron companies.[266]

During the late 1880s professional promoters began playing a larger role in the market for domestic and (even at times) overseas capital. As a contemporary reported, "An entirely new class of Financiers, known as promoters, has sprung into existence."[267] The promoter of the 1880s was not a new institutional invention; instead, he was a product of an evolution that had begun at least two decades earlier with the emergence of firms like Adamson, Collier, and Chadwick. These firms acted as agents

---

[263] Marchildon, "British Investment Banking and Industrial Decline Before the Great War," table 2, p. 81. The size of issue refers to the price at which the issue was sold rather than the par value of security flotation.

[264] Mitchie, *Money, Mania, and Markets*, p. 145.

[265] John Armstrong, "The Rise and Fall of the Company Promoter and the Financing of British Industry," in J.J. Van Helten and Y. Cassis (eds.), *Capitalism in a Mature Economy: Financial Institutions, Capital Exports and British Industry, 1870–1939* (Aldershot, U.K.: Edward Elgar, 1990), pp. 115–16. [Hereafter cited as Armstrong, "The Company Promoter."]

[266] Cottrell, *Industrial Finance*, p. 181; Michie, *London and New York*, pp. 114–16; Michie, *Money, Mania and Markets*, p. 232; Morgan and Thomas, *The Stock Exchange*, pp. 96–97.

[267] Michie, *Money, Mania, and Markets*, p. 232.

"between the public and those who had property to sell," particularly companies seeking to go public. Between 1863 and 1868 Chadwick's firm successfully promoted ten companies in the iron, coal, and steel industry. Those promotions included Bolckow Vaughn & Co. Ltd. (£2.5 million in capital, £813,737 called-up), Ebbw Vale Coal and Iron Co. Ltd., and Palmers Shipbuilding and Iron Co. Ltd. David Chadwick's firm was paid only a commission; it did not underwrite the issue, nor did it hold any ownership position. Instead, it offered shares by private circular and prospectus to a list of some 5,000 clients – mostly of "eminent local connections" – who had demonstrated a willingness to invest in companies promoted by the firm. In addition, the firm frequently continued to provide business advice and auditing services long after the shares had been distributed.[268]

The second generation of promoters was very different. First, they often provided the initiative behind the organization or reorganization of the new company; that is, they approached the existing owners of a private firm with a proposal to reorganize as a public company. Second, they often took an ownership position in the new firm. Third, then, and only then, did they begin to promote the new company actively, taking their profits from some combination of sales commissions and the difference between the purchase and sale price of their shares.[269] Increasingly, after 1880 (and, after 1900, legally) they arranged to underwrite the issue.[270] Although the name of a bank was almost always prominently displayed on the prospectus, neither private nor joint-stock banks with very few exceptions took any direct role in domestic company issues. Instead, they normally did no more than agree to receive sub-

---

[268] Peter L. Payne, "The Emergence of the Large Scale Company in Great Britain, 1870–1914," *The Economic History Review*, second series, Vol. XX, No. 3 (December 1967), pp. 519–42. [Hereafter cited as Payne "Large-Scale Companies."] Other firms active in the market included Joshua Hutchison and Sons, Richardson, Chadbourne & Company, and Alfred Whitworth, Chemesha & Company. Cottrell, *Industrial Finance*, p. 115; Kennedy, *Industrial Structure, Capital Markets*, p. 133; Thomas, *The Provincial Exchanges*, p. 123.

[269] Ranald Michie, "Options, Concessions, Syndicates and the Provision of Venture Capital, 1880–1913," *Business History*, Vol. 23 (1981), pp. 147–64.

[270] Prior to 1900 the payment of an underwriting commission and brokerage out of capital was illegal; it was regarded as the equivalent of the issue of shares at a discount. Before that time the vendors could hire the promoters to underwrite an issue, but the payment could not come directly from the sale of securities. The first underwriting case (*Re. Licensed Victuallers Mutual Trading Association*, L.R. 42, Ch. D, p. 1) appeared in the courts in 1888. Earlier the law had been widely evaded by issuing shares at a premium or issuing founders shares. The Companies Act of 1900 legalized underwriting. Thomas, *The Provincial Exchanges*, pp. 136–37; Hall, *London and Australia*, p. 78.

scriptions.[271] Lavington recognized the importance of the promoter in the British infrastructure of the capital market, but he also recognized that in most instances the promoter's connections with the new company were usually severed once he had completed the flotation and sold any shares that had been allotted to him. Thus, he warned, "His [the promoter's] interests *as promoter* are quite distinct from those of the company he forms."[272]

The list of promoters was long, and ranged from those who fit Lavington's description to those who served both as midwives and pediatricians to the new firm. "It is not easy to assess the significance of company promoters in numerical terms. We cannot even identify them conclusively for many were incidentally promoters earning their incomes from a range of services, although some individuals stand out in the crowd."[273] At one extreme was Ernest Terah Hooley, a Nottingham lace manufacturer, who promoted twenty-six companies between 1895 and 1898. Many were in the burgeoning cycle industry, but the list also included Dunlop Tyre – a firm he purchased for £3 million and sold a few weeks later for £5 million – Bovril, and Schweppes. The twenty-six involved a nominal capital of £18.6 million, and Hooley's profits are estimated to have totaled £5 million. Most of his efforts, however, were not successful. By the end of 1898 he found himself faced not only by a host of unhappy investors but also by personal bankruptcy.[274] Somewhere toward the middle of the spectrum was Horatio Bottomly. He "promoted only a handful of domestic industrial companies in the late 1880s with a capital of just over £1 million, but launched over forty companies engaged in overseas mining, especially Australian gold fields between 1894 and 1903 with a nominal capital in excess of £12 million."[275]

At the other extreme were promoters in the mold of H. Osbourne O'Hagen. O'Hagen's domestic promotions included tramways in

---

[271] Morgan and Thomas, *The Stock Exchange*, p. 136.

[272] Lavington, *The English Capital Market*, pp. 213–14. "In the absence of strong intermediary agencies with machinery available for the investigation of industrial propositions and the organization requisite for efficient marketing of their securities, the work of selecting profitable new ventures, capitalizing their prospects in terms of securities and of selling these securities to the public, falls mainly on the company promoter." As Ernest Terah Hooley explained in evidence before the Bankruptcy Court in 1898, "You have to buy the business and you have to sell it, and then you are done." Cited in Payne, "Large-Scale Companies," p. 522.

[273] Armstrong, "The Company Promoter," p. 131.

[274] Thomas, *The Provincial Stock Exchange*s, p. 131. The *Economist* put his turnover at £25 million and his profits at £3 million.

[275] Armstrong, "The Company Promoter," p. 131.

London and Birmingham, an interurban system connecting the five cities of the "Potteries," the Associated Portland Cement Company, Leyland Steamships, International Tea, Eastman's, and a number of breweries. Overseas he promoted American rails, stockyards, meat packers, and breweries, the Trinidad Lake Asphalt Company, and Henry Clay and Bock, tobacco growers and cigar manufacturers. O'Hagen would secure an option, place a deposit to be forfeited should the promotion fail, arrange to underwrite the issue, and personally take a part of the issue as a "guarantee of good faith." Many of his ventures were either jointly with, or involved the good offices of, the stockbrokers, Panmure Gordon and Company. O'Hagen's underwriters included investment and trust companies and "the principal financial and moneyed men of the city of London as well as many individuals outside the City who heard of the good thing going" and who, in addition, were willing to put up one or two thousand pounds of capital. In fact, O'Hagen claimed to have invented underwriting.[276]

O'Hagen's commitment was not limited to promotion, a fact reflected in the success of his companies. He attempted to guarantee that the initial board of directors would be both qualified and willing to devote time and effort to the enterprise. On the occasions when a company did get into difficulties, he often continued to nurse it for some time after its initial promotion.[277] Although the new-issues market was still not formally institutionalized, the activities of promoters like Hooley, Bottomley, and O'Hagen and the spread of underwriting put the basic financial innovations in place. By the late nineteenth century it was possible to establish large corporations on the German and American model; in fact, a number of such companies were organized.[278]

---

[276] H. Osbourne O'Hagen, *Leaves from My Life* (London: John Lane, 1929), Vol. I, pp. 149–55. [Hereafter cited as O'Hagen, *Leaves from My Life*.]

[277] Morgan and Thomas, *The Stock Exchange*, pp. 96, 111, 137. O'Hagen, *Leaves from My Life*, *passim*, but particularly, Vol. I, pp. 150–51.

[278] Cottrell, *Industrial Finance*, p. 184; Peter L. Payne, "Large-Scale Companies," p. 523. Payne concludes, "These evolutionary changes in Great Britain created the possibility of setting up giant corporations, by using the limited-liability legislation of the 'fifties." He then goes on to note that the capital of the forty-eight largest firms in Britain ranged from £17.5 million (the Imperial Tobacco Company) to £2.0 million (the Yorkshire Wool Combers Association). In contrast, the forty-eight largest American companies in 1904 ranged in terms of capitalization from £282.5 million (U.S. Steel) to £2.1 million (the American Sewer Pipe Company). Imperial Tobacco would have ranked between the seventh (American Can) and the eighth (Corn Products Refining) American companies. A. Essex-Crosby, *Joint Stock Companies in Great Britain*, M.C. Thesis, London University, 1938, p. 47. J.B. Jeffreys, *Trends in Business Organization Since 1856*, Ph.D. Thesis, University of London, 1938.

For overseas governments and rails, promotion was much more formally institutionalized. Although there were four principal parties involved in marketing empire loans – the London representative of the various governments (the Agents General, the High Commissioner, or the Crown Agents), the financial representatives of the governments, the brokers, and the jobbers – it was the financial representatives who were the most important. They acted as agents, arranged for brokers to underwrite the issue, were responsible for advising the government's representatives on market conditions, prices, and the appropriate date of issue, advertised the issue, received subscriptions, and paid the dividends.[279]

Table 2:3-12 provides some indication of the importance of the various agencies involved in the flotation of overseas securities. In the case of colonial securities, bonds were sometimes issued and their sale managed by the Anglo-Colonial (imperial) banks and occasionally by the Bank of England; more frequently, the colonial governments used the services of the Crown Agents.[280] The category "Official and semi-official" in Table 2:3-12 refers primarily to the Bank of England and the Crown Agents for the Colonies. The Bank of England handled Indian government issues from the days of the East India Company, and it continued to act for the India Office throughout the period. In the 1870s and 1880s, with the changes in the policies of the Crown Agents, the Bank added New Zealand, Queensland, Western Australia, and South Australia to its list of clients. In the 1880s it also began to handle the issues of a selection of the state-guaranteed Indian railways. At the end of the century, when some of the self-governing Australian colonies began to establish their own agencies, the Bank attempted to make up for those losses by adding the Egyptian government to its list.

The Bank of England had begun to manage some colonial issues in the 1870s, but the actual issue remained in the hands of the Crown Agents. In 1878, under the pressure of an increased volume of business,

---

[279] The four-part classification was the result of a study by Theodore Schilling, *London als Anleihemarkt der Englischen Kolonien*. It is summarized in Lavington, *The British Capital Market*, pp. 196–97.

[280] The Crown Agents for the Colonies were established in 1858 to formalize (under the Treasury and Colonial Office) the activities of the heretofore largely independent Agent General of the Crown Colonies. They remained a public-private institution that acted as purchasing agent and loan negotiator for the Crown Colonies. See *CO 23073, Papers Explanatory of the Functions of the Crown Agents for the Colonies*, August 1881, No. 6, *Colonial Office to the Treasury*, November 26, 1880. Morgan and Thomas, *The Stock Exchange*, p. 93. Colonial issues were granted trustee status in 1900; although popular before, thereafter they became increasingly so.

the agents decided that colonies with responsible government would have to make their own financial arrangements.[281]

In the 1860s the agents advertised for tenders on colonial issues bearing fixed rates of interest; bids could be rejected, if an established minimum price were not reached. Later those bonds were offered at a fixed price, but only after the issue had been underwritten by a private agency that operated under the regulations set out in the Colonial Stocks Acts of 1877 and 1900. Underwriting arrangements were placed in the hands of one of a regular group of brokers on whom the Crown Agents thought they could rely. The brokers were not only expected to place the underwriting in "substantial hands" but also to confine it, as far as possible, to institutions that could be relied on to hold the bonds until the market could absorb them without breaking. Both underwriting and brokerage fees were fixed in advance, the former normally 1 percent, the latter one-quarter of that amount.

Between 1860 and 1914 the Crown Agents, acting through one of several private brokers (most often *Scrimegour* and Company), successfully marketed almost £85 million in long-term Empire securities. The system worked very well. Although after 1878 the Crown Agents were technically supposed to act only for colonies with dependent status, more than half of the £85 million went to colonies with responsible government. It was only under extreme pressure that those colonies were gradually forced to retain their own loan agents.[282]

Toward the end of the nineteenth century, as the British commercial banks adopted a more aggressive portfolio policy, not only did they become active dealers in the market for foreign and colonial issues, but they also came "to play a major role in the new issues market, as underwriters, and, in many cases, taking on the main responsibility for the flotation of a new issue. Some of the banks' activity in the market came as a concomitant to their role as underwriters, selling off securities from their portfolios with which they had been stuck at the time of issue. The process of arranging and underwriting new issues was a lucrative one;

---

[281] Hall, *London and Australia*, p. 73. John H. Clapham, *The Bank of England: A History*, 2 vols. (Cambridge: Cambridge University Press, 1944), Vol. II, pp. 301–5, 399–401.

[282] R.M. Kesner, *Economic Control and Colonial Development: Crown Colony Financial Management in the Age of Joseph Chamberlain* (Westport, Conn.: 1981), pp. 85–96. New Zealand marketed £21 million, the Cape, £13 million, Natal, £9 million, and Western Australia more than £1 million. The Cape continued to use the Crown Agents until 1881, New Zealand until 1883, and Natal until 1902. Davis and Huttenback, *Mammon*, pp. 184–85.

banks were continually trying to keep up influential connections," particularly with the merchant banks.[283]

The colonies with responsible government, when no longer able to use the services of the Crown Agents, often turned to the large London joint-stock banks. Glyn, Mills and Company, for example, had close connections with Canada. As a result, the Bank often acted not only for the Dominion government, but for some provinces and municipalities and even for a few of the nation's railways. The largest share of Canadian government business was, however, conducted by Canadian banks with London connections, particularly the Bank of Montreal and the Canadian Bank of Commerce. Similarly, the commercial banks provided the normal channel for linking the British market to the issues of the Australian governments. Initially these had been Australian banks with London offices, but, increasingly, as the colonies sought better recognition in the British market, those functions were taken over by British joint-stock banks. The most important of the British colonial joint-stock intermediaries was the London and Westminster Bank. In many ways the London and Westminster acted as a proto–central bank for a set of favored colonies, a set that included, among others, Tasmania, Western Australia, Victoria, New South Wales, the Transvaal, and Natal. The L&W provided loans and financial advice, organized their issues on the market, undertook the necessary paperwork, and kept the books. In carrying out its function as a "central bank," the London and Westminster maintained and even supported the market for its customers' bonds and, in times of financial pressure, occasionally acted as jobber of last resort for the jobbers and brokers on the Stock Exchange.[284]

In the case of foreign government loans, the large merchant banks (particularly Rothschild's and Barings) maintained a near monopoly of loan contracting until the 1860s. At that time the growth of the market allowed a number of middle-rank merchant banking houses to enter the lists of loan contractors, issuing houses, and financial agents for foreign governments.[285] These entrants included a number of relative newcomers to the ranks of private bankers: Bischofsheim, Elanger, Fruling & Goschen, Hambros, J.S. Morgan & Co., Raphael, Schroeder, and Stern, as well as more than a dozen other merchant and merchant banking houses.[286] Finally, in the years after 1880, as domestic yields declined,

---

[283] Goodhart, *The Business of Banking*, p. 136.
[284] Goodhart, *The Business of Banking*, pp. 138–39.
[285] Cottrell, *Investment Banking*, p. 288.
[286] Morgan and Thomas, *The Stock Exchange*, pp. 88–89.

the need to acquire overseas securities for investment "induced some London joint-stock banks to underwrite foreign issues, as it was a cheaper way of acquiring such paper." In short, those banks began to act as issuing houses. "The normally conservative London and Westminster was a leader in this field," but it was not alone. The London Joint Stock Bank was associated with German issues, Parr's, a London and provincial bank, undertook issues for China and Japan, and the Midland was involved in a number of Russian issues.[287]

The first competitors were the new generation of merchant banks, but entry did not stop there. The initial near-monopoly position in the market for foreign governments continued to erode as new institutions proved themselves equally capable of floating those issues. It was the profits attached to the burgeoning volume of issues that attracted the new competitors, but it was changes in the market conditions that smoothed their entry. On the one hand, well-placed investments speeded up the process of economic growth and development. As a result, many initially backward countries began to develop relatively mature domestic financial infrastructures. Countries that had previously found it necessary to use the services of the London merchant banks found that local domestic banks were more than capable of conducting the government's financial affairs in London. On the other hand, the structure of demand shifted away from the regions, particularly Europe, where "the family and business ties of the merchant bankers were strong and they possessed a virtual monopoly of the new issue business." Although they remained important in North and South America, even on those continents their monopoly position was undercut by local competitors, and they had never had particularly close connections with the regions that became important borrowers after 1870: Asia, Australasia, and South Africa.[288]

Over the next two decades a number of joint-stock banks, international banks, and other intermediaries also began to absorb a part of the international financial business. In the case of the international banks, entry could be viewed as merely an extension of their normal business, but a new extension nonetheless. The now-enhanced set of merchant banks found themselves also in competition with such outsiders as the Anglo-Egyptian Bank, the Anglo-Italian Bank, the Hong Kong Banking Company, and the Ottoman Bank.[289]

---

[287] Cottrell, "The Domestic Commercial Banks and the City of London," p. 51.

[288] Hall, *London and Australia*, pp. 71–73.

[289] Baster, *The International Banks*, pp. 4–5; Morgan and Thomas, *The Stock Exchange*, p. 88.

The colonial and international banks specialized in government and, to a lesser extent, railway finance. The data in Table 2:3-12 capture their role in both the Empire and foreign sectors. The decline in the banks' importance over the decade 1885–94 reflected the Australian banks' loss of the business of those colonies to the Bank of England and the London and Westminster Bank. The rapid gain in the relative role of the international and colonial banks in the years after 1894 was clearly made at the expense of the merchant banks, a substitution that was probably the result of the fallout from the Barings Crisis.[290]

In the case of the joint-stock banks, the decline in Consol yields led them to look for alternative investment outlets. Having long provided the interest-transfer mechanism between the foreign governments and their bondholders, they were well acquainted with the foreign bond market. Not surprisingly, they began buying foreign securities, initially governments' and municipals', but after 1900 railroad bonds as well. Some of the securities were acquired as by-products of the banks' underwriting operations. The two functions, when coupled together, led naturally to the next step in the evolutionary process; the banks themselves began to undertake the actual flotations.[291]

The resulting competition, although still leaving the large houses preeminent, forced even those staid institutions to broaden the scope of their activities. In the 1880s Rothschild's, for example, promoted a company mining rubies in Burma; more relevant from the point of view of this book, and more disastrous from the Bank's point of view, competition pushed Barings into promoting banking, railway, drainage, and waterworks companies in Argentina and Uruguay.[292]

As G.H. White of Barings testified before the Foreign Loan Committee in 1875, "Most generally loans were issued by the firm in London as agents of the government." The agent in his case (Barings) would prepare and issue the prospectus, and advertise in the newspapers, but "nothing more than that." In 1875 Barings was still a very conservative house doing a very high-class business – its near-monopoly position in the market had only just begun to erode – and its policies were not typical of all parts of the market for foreign government issues. Many governments were unwilling to risk the failure of a loan, and insisted that the contracting institution take the issue firm, that is, agree to take the entire

---

[290] Hall, *London and Australia*, pp. 74–75.

[291] Cottrell, *Industrial Finance*, p. 241.

[292] In the latter case, that excursion, coupled with a decision to take the shares "firm" without arranging underwriting, led to over extension, unsalable shares, a liquidity crisis, and, ultimately the need to seek assistance from the Bank of England. Morgan and Thomas, *The Stock Exchange*, p. 93.

issue at a set price and commission and then sell it for whatever the market would yield.

Finally, temporary syndicates of banks, brokers, financiers, and potential investors handled some issues, a plan with obvious parallels to modern underwriting. Syndicates organized to manage tendered issues date from the British government loans of the eighteenth century, but the institutional innovation was the syndicate organized to handle fixed-price issues. Syndicates began to figure in the more speculative government issues during the 1870s and 1880s. Such a structure, however, required close collaboration between the issuing house and the syndicate.[293] First used in the Ottoman loan of 1868, "the contractor would 'communicate to numerous capitalists, bankers, merchants, stockbrokers, private individuals and others the terms on which they could enter the syndicate.' In this way he obtained guarantees for the placing of the whole or part of the loan if subscriptions by the public were inadequate. If, on the other hand, it was fully subscribed, members of the syndicate were not asked to take stock and were paid the difference between their price and the issue price, which might be 5 or even 10 percent."[294] The fixed-price syndicate proved a valuable innovation, but it had one major disadvantage: It was relatively informal, and it often collapsed in periods of financial crisis. Crises were just the times when the borrowers had the greatest need for the syndicate, since those were the periods when the issue was most likely to fail. The formal underwriting contract provided a more effective alternative.[295]

By 1900, £1.756 billion of paid-up foreign railroad issues was quoted on the London Stock Exchange. That figure represented almost one-quarter of the total securities listed, and it was surpassed only by the £2.829 billion of foreign government bonds.[296] In the case of the U.S. railroads (no other foreign country had more listed railway securities), British investors had in the 1830s, 1840s, and 1850s bought issues that were initially floated in the United States. After the Civil War, however, the British market for American securities changed dramati-

---

[293] Hall, *London and Australia*, p. 77.

[294] Morgan and Thomas, *The Stock Exchange*, p. 89. The internal quotation is from *Bankers' Magazine*, 1876, p. 518.

[295] This form of contract was legally recognized after 1904. Hall, *London and Australia*, p. 78.

[296] Michie, *London and New York*, table 1.3(a), p. 24. In 1863 the figure had been only £198 million, and it represented only 12 percent of the total. By 1913 the figures had increased to £2,929 million and 31 percent. Table 2.3, p. 52.

cally.[297] At the center of the new marketing structure were the seven great London-based international banking houses, each with an American partner. Initially the New York and Boston-based firms were junior partners and functioned largely as agents for their London parents. Gradually they developed into at least equal partners. By the 1880s they proved more than capable of acting independently, initiating underwritings, forming syndicates among themselves, recruiting new junior partners from among smaller American investment banks, and acting for other London and European houses.[298]

The seven giants drew their strength from close and continuous relations with particular American railroads. They were, however, not the only agencies to issue American railroad securities in London. On occasion, several of the large London stockbroking firms acted independently, and a number of the investment trusts, in an attempt to expand beyond their original trust function, also floated American railroad bonds. For example, in the 1890s the Railway Share Investment Trust went through a reorganization solely because its owners wanted to participate in the syndications of railway issues.[299] The American railroads were not the only beneficiaries of British investment. In 1889, for example, more than three-fifths of the 229 shareholders in the Argentina North-Eastern railroad were British. In the same year the British also absorbed a like fraction of the railroad's £1.5 million bond issue. In a similar vein – although by 1910 the shares of the Canadian Pacific were traded in Berlin, London, New York, and a number of lesser exchanges – 65 percent of the stockholders were British.[300]

2-3b(4). The secondary markets

2-3b(4a). The London Stock Exchange: At the outbreak of World War I, the London Stock Exchange was by far the largest securities market

---

[297] British investment in American rails is estimated to have been £100 million in 1876 and, perhaps, £600 million in 1910. Dorothy R. Adler (edited by Muriel Hidy), *British Investment in American Railways, 1834–1898* (Charlottesville: University of Virginia Press, 1970), p. 152. [Hereafter cited as Adler, *American Railways.*] The 1910 figure is from Michie who cites Adler. Michie, *London and New York*, p. 53.

[298] Adler, *American Railways*, pp. 143–45. By the late 1880s, if not before, J.P. Morgan and his firm, first Drexel, Morgan, and later, after the death of Anthony Drexel, J.P. Morgan & Company, had far surpassed his father's London firm in both size and influence.

[299] Adler, *American Railways*, pp. 150–51.

[300] Michie, *London and New York*, pp. 54–55.

in the world. In 1910, when the paid-up value of *all* negotiable securities on the planet was estimated to have been £32.6 billion, no less than £10.7 billion was quoted on the London Exchange.[301] Even within the United Kingdom, however, the London Stock Exchange did not have the entire market to itself. The London market had gradually evolved from a market organized to trade in government securities to a market spanning the globe and the industrial spectrum. Even as it expanded in geographic breadth from national to international and in industrial scope from governments to rails, mines, land companies, and commercial and industrial securities, it retained some of its initial characteristics. It remained a market best suited to handle large issues marked by substantial turnover and minimal differentiation. Conversely, the provincial exchanges specialized in small issues (most often those of local joint-stock enterprises) marked by limited turnover and great variety.[302] Over time, as firms grew and their issues began to generate enough business to interest the members of the London exchange, the lines of demarcation began to blur. Thus, by 1901 almost 99 percent of all securities quoted on the Glasgow Exchange were also quoted in London. By the late nineteenth century there was an efficient integrated national securities market in which, because of the availability of rapid and continuous communication, the members of the London Stock Exchange acted as central dealers for the entire system.[303] Changes in the Exchange's rules (changes that effected shunting and dual capacity) may have adversely affected the integration of the national market in the years after 1912, but for the three decades before World War I, a national securities market operated efficiently.[304]

Initially focused largely on British Consols, the London Stock Exchange steadily expanded the scope of its operations. There had been some dealing in water, canal, and dock companies from the first days of the organized exchange, but it was 1811 before their prices were included

---

[301] Michie, *London and New York*, p. 91.

[302] The London Exchange normally refused to quote companies whose paid-up capital was less than £50,000 and even, at times, £100,000. Thus, even many small London companies sought quotation on the provincial exchanges. Michie, *Money, Mania, Markets*, pp. 256–57.

[303] Michie, *London and New York*, pp. 22–24.

[304] Ranald C. Michie, "The Stock Exchange and the British Economy, 1870–1939," in J.J. Van Helten and Y Cassis (eds.), *Capitalism in a Mature Economy: Financial Institutions, Capital Exports and British Industry, 1870–1939* (Aldershot, U.K.: Edward Elgar, 1990), pp. 110–12. [Hereafter cited as Michie, "The Stock Exchange and the British Economy."] Dual capacity involves the same firm operating as both broker and jobber.

in the official list. In 1822 quotations of foreign government securities were authorized, and in 1828 the members of the Foreign Market ceded its jurisdiction to the Exchange's Committee of General Purposes. Railway companies were first quoted on the Exchange in 1830. By 1844, sixty-six domestic railway companies were continually traded; however, the inclusion of most private non-rail joint-stock companies awaited general limited liability. Even then, with a few notable exceptions, the number of such securities listed and traded initially grew very slowly. It increased during the 1880s and grew even more rapidly between 1890 and the turn of the century:

> By the outbreak of the war, quoted joint-stock companies controlled virtually all the banks and nearly all the larger breweries; they dominated in the cement, wallpaper, soap and tobacco industries; they controlled most of the large units in iron, coal and steel and heavy engineering. In textiles they dominated the production of rayon and sewing cotton, and also several ancillary processes including combing, bleaching and dying; they owned several large sections of the heavy chemical and explosive industries and, in distribution, their influence was extending to the big London department stores, and the multiple food trades.[305]

Table 2:3-11 does not allocate the securities of Urban Services, Financial Services, and Commercial and Industrial between the Domestic and Foreign sectors, but it does trace the general outlines of the growth and shifting focus of the London Stock Exchange over the years between 1853 and 1913. A market that had been essentially domestic had, by the outbreak of World War I, become dominantly international. Even if all "Unidentified Securities" are assigned to the domestic sector (and many were foreign), that sector represented less than one-half of the total. Government securities had declined from more than three-quarters to barely one-third of the total, and the proportion of rails had more than doubled, although in 1913 they were relatively less important than they had been two decades earlier. Finally, the private, non-rail, joint-stock sector had increased from one-twentieth to one-fifth of the total. The London Stock Exchange was directing vast amounts of capital to an increasingly diverse set of economic activities located in an ever-broadening fraction of the planet's surface.

Throughout the Exchange's history, the access of individuals to membership was relatively easy. Since the proprietors' income was derived from the entrance fee of fifty guineas and the annual subscription (membership fee) of ten guineas, it is hardly surprising that in 1802 the doors

---

[305] Morgan and Thomas, *The Stock Exchange*, pp. 86, 100, 132–34.

were "open to all honorable men" proposed by two members. The requirements for membership were gradually tightened, but only gradually: In 1815 the proposers were obligated to have been members for two years; in 1821 the proposers were further required to agree to pay £250 (a sum that was gradually increased to £750 by 1874) should the new member default within two years of his appointment. Nonetheless, those requirements were never particularly onerous. In 1904 membership was somewhat further restricted. Candidates who had not served four years as a clerk were required to secure a nomination from a retiring member or from the estate of a dead member, and all candidates were required to become proprietors. Becoming a proprietor involved buying shares in the exchange, but a competitive market existed for both shares and nominations. As late as 1914 a clerk could become a member for £440 and "any honorable man" for £1,200. Those prices stand in marked contrast to the £16,000 cost of a seat on the New York Stock Exchange or the £92,000 it took to gain admission to the Paris Bourse.[306]

Although entry for individuals was relatively open, the Exchange did restrict the entry of institutions and firms that, in addition to a brokerage business, were also engaged in other business activities and it limited the number of partners in member firms. The former restriction was initially seldom enforced; a few merchant banks (Raphael's, for example) were admitted to membership, and those firms were grandfathered in when the restrictions became binding. Most foreign and merchant banks, however, were precluded from membership. Even that restriction did not prevent banks from entering the security market. Before 1912 there were no minimum commission rules. Since banks could promise a large volume of business, they found it relatively easy to hire members of the Exchange to act for them at costs that were probably no greater than those they would have had to incur had they had been able to join themselves.[307] The latter restriction, however, limited the size of the brokerage firms. Thus, unlike their American counterparts, there were no "national" firms with branches scattered across the United Kingdom.

As a result of the easy admission policies, membership in the London Stock Exchange had almost doubled within half a century, from the 550

[306] John M. Weiner, "The United Kingdom," p. 178, in David E. Spray (ed.), *The Principal Stock Exchanges of the World: Their Operation, Structure and Development* (Washington, D.C.: International Economic Publishers, 1964). In 1872 the Trustees and Managers voted to increase the entrance fee to 100 and the annual subscription to 12 Guineas. Morgan and Thomas, *The Stock Exchange*, pp. 144, 157–58.

[307] Michie, *London* and *New York*, pp. 66–67, 87–88.

who had opened Capel Court in 1802 to 1,067. Over the next thirty years it more than doubled again: There were 2,408 members in 1882. The two subsequent decades – years of increased foreign lending, of company promotion, and of speculation in South African gold stocks – pushed the figure to more than 4,000 in 1900 and to a peak of 5,567 in 1905. At that point the imposition of more stringent membership requirements produced a slight decline, but at the outbreak of World War I, membership still stood at 4,855.[308]

Although there were many changes over the course of the nineteenth century, the foundation of the unique structure of the Exchange was laid out in the original deed of settlement recorded on March 27, 1802. The deed speaks of "stock-brokers" and "stock-jobbers" – an explicit recognition that the two functions were distinct and different, although at the time it was still common for both to be carried out by the same person. A broker acted as an agent for a client and bought or sold securities on his client's account. A jobber was a principal in the transaction and bought and sold stocks and bonds on his own account. It was the jobbers who always stood ready to buy securities for, or sell securities to, brokers attempting to meet their clients' requests to buy or sell. It was the brokers' inventories that provided the padding that damped sudden price changes and smoothed market transactions. More importantly the deed recognized (1) that the building itself was a private venture to be owned and operated by a group of nine Trustees and Managers who were to represent the interests of the proprietors, the owners of the 400 £50 shares in the exchange, and (2) that the operation of the Exchange itself was to be entrusted to a Committee of General Purposes elected annually by the entire membership.[309] In 1802 there were 550 members (subscribers) but only 250 proprietors, and in 1876, when the deed was revised, there were 502 proprietors and more than 2,000 members. Most of the proprietors were members, but all were not. Until 1876 there was no rule requiring that they should be.

The split between owners and members was only gradually resolved. In 1876 the rules were changed to require that new proprietors be

---

[308] There were 1,067 members in 1853. Cottrell, *Industrial Finance*, p. 152; Thomas, *The Provincial Stock Exchanges*, p. 3; Morgan and Thomas, *The Stock Exchange*, p. 140.

[309] The nine Trustees and Managers were to be elected for life and they "were to manage it [the building] in the interest of the proprietors; to invest in government securities any reserve funds that they might accumulate, and 'fix the price at which subscribers will be admitted to attend and transact business at the Stock Exchange'". No one individual was allowed to hold more than four shares. Morgan and Thomas, *The Stock Exchange*, p. 74.

members of the Exchange and that any non-member who inherited shares in the Exchange must sell them within twelve months. In 1904 the problem of dual control was further rectified by the adoption of rules that required new members to acquire a nomination from a retired member (or from the legal representative of a deceased member) and that they also become proprietors by purchasing at least one share of the Exchange's stock. The impact of the new rules was only felt gradually, and it was 1945 before the two groups – owners and members – were formally amalgamated.[310]

Not surprisingly, there were conflicts between the two groups. The managers, in order to maximize the number of the fee-paying members, were primarily interested in assuring the dominant position of the London Stock Exchange. They would have been delighted if it had been the only formal securities market in the kingdom. Conversely, a member's income depended on the value of the securities that he bought or sold, but it did not depend on the value of the stocks and bonds he bought or sold on the Exchange. Not only was there a potential for conflict, but also the two groups often operated at cross-purposes, producing policies that were quite different from those prevailing in the provincial or many of the foreign exchanges that were operated as brokers' cooperatives.[311]

The members objected to any increase in the membership fees, and the Managers and Trustees, representing the owners, to any change that would increase public access to security quotations – an exchange telegraph, for example – and that would therefore permit brokers to deal at market prices without ever becoming members. The managers had no desire to limit membership, since their income depended on the number of fee-paying subscribers; the members had no desire to set minimum commissions, since their interests often lay in maximizing volume, a volume that might, in the presence of a minimum commission, be threatened by competition from provincial or other exchanges unconstrained by such rules. As a result of the conflicting goals, the London Stock Exchange, unlike some of its competitors, remained competitive and not cartelized.[312]

The broker-jobber distinction, increasingly honored only in the breach, was also a peculiarity of the London market. The 1847 rule book banned partnerships between brokers and dealers as being "highly inex-

[310] Hall, *London and Australia*, p. 62.
[311] Michie, *London and New York*, p. 19.
[312] Morgan and Thomas, *The Stock Exchange*, pp. 143–44; Michie, *London and New York*, p. 19.

pedient and improper," and it also prohibited brokers' clerks from acting as dealers. The broker worked for a client on commission; he did not deal with other brokers, but with a jobber who was supposedly always ready to buy or sell whatever security the broker wanted at a price. It is clear that there are potential conflicts of interest if the same person is both buying and selling securities on commission and dealing in securities on his own account. In the first case, the dealer is supposed to obtain the best deal possible for his client, but in the latter instance, he is supposed to look for the best bargain for himself. In addition to overcoming the moral hazard problem, the dichotomous system was alleged to have reduced transactions costs (since brokers with a commission to sell a security did not have to search for brokers with a commission to buy that stock or bond), broadened the market, helped to stabilize prices, facilitated large transactions, and, since it encouraged specialization, reduced informational asymmetries.[313]

When it worked – and it certainly worked in markets with high volumes and frequent transactions, the Consol market, for example – the system worked well. There were, however, continuing and growing complaints. Critics contended that when transactions in a security were less frequent, jobbers often refused either to take a position (that is, they wouldn't deal) or to set a price at which a broker could choose to buy or sell, that they tried to keep their books always balanced, thus minimizing their inventories, and that they maintained too large a spread between their buy and sell prices. High volume meant competition, and with competition these problems were minimized. Low volumes meant few jobbers and less, or no, competition.

More severe problems were raised by the growth of international business and the development of a largely unregulated after-hours exchange. "On the street" brokers dealt directly with one another, and they could sell securities obtained from sources outside the exchange: American securities from Anglo-American merchant and merchant banking firms or Rand gold stocks from South African finance houses. Jobbers, not to be outdone, built up arbitrage businesses with Continental and North American markets, and they established direct telegraph and telephone connections with brokers in the British provinces. The latter transactions – termed "shunting" – gave country brokers access to the London market on terms that were almost as good as those enjoyed by members of the Exchange, while at the same time evading the heavy expense and

---

[313] Michie, *London and New York*, pp. 84–85; Michie, *Money, Mania and Markets*, pp. 255–56; Morgan and Thomas, *The Stock Exchange*, pp. 145–47.

responsibility of membership.[314] As a result, complaints from both brokers and jobbers were growing, each group recognizing that the unregulated competition was costing it business.[315]

The Committee of General Purposes was cognizant of the benefits of the international market and recognized that its dual capacity – the ability to serve as both broker and jobber – was necessary for the conduct of intermarket arbitrage. Therefore it was very slow to respond to the complaints. Moreover, when it did agree to enforce a rule prohibiting dual capacity, it granted so many exceptions for international transactions that the prevailing de facto policies were almost unaffected.[316] For example, a new type of brokerage firm – the dummy broker who acted for the jobber – emerged. The new firm, although not in technical violation of the rules, certainly violated the spirit. In 1911 *The Economist* noted that the use of the dummy broker "was growing of late," and in 1913 the Committee of General Purposes found it necessary to take action against one such firm merely in order to establish a precedent.[317] Thus, by essentially adopting a policy of non-action, the directors of the Exchange were able to retain many of the benefits of the jobber/broker distinction for large high-volume transactions while permitting an almost equally competitive environment to exist for low-volume issues.

For most of the nineteenth century the Exchange operated without an official clearing house. The issue was first raised in the middle of the century as the number of members increased, volumes rose, and the scope of the market broadened, but nothing was done. Nature abhors a vacuum. If there is a potential for profit, institutions are often innovated to fill the perceived demand. In 1872 a voluntary cooperative group of members organized an informal clearing house. Within four years it was

---

[314] Michie, *London and New York*, p. 22.

[315] W.C. Antwerp, an American broker, writing about the friction between jobbers and brokers on the London Exchange, although admitting that the prohibition of dual capacity had advantages when the volume of business was large, commented, "fortunately there is nothing of that sort on the New York Exchange. There the result is obtained far more openly and above board by the presence in all active securities of a host of such jobbers, brokers, traders, specialists, and speculators, each actively bidding and offering, by voice and gesture, and without collusion, and each thereby contributing to the making of the freest possible market and the closest possible price". W.C. Antwerp. *The Stock Exchange from Within*, quoted in Morgan and Thomas, *The Stock Exchange*, p. 147.

[316] The Committee agreed to begin to enforce the rule in June of 1909 but their attempts were, at best, half-hearted. Morgan and Thomas, *The Stock Exchange*, pp. 145–46; Michie, *London and New York*, pp. 84–85.

[317] Hall, *London and Australia*, p. 64.

serving more than 500 firms and 1,000 members. Despite the evidence of its success, the Committee of General Purposes refused to take responsibility for its operation. However, when the informal clearing house ran into trouble in 1880, it did agree that there was a problem. In response, it established the Settlement Department, under the control of one of the Exchange's subcommittees.[318]

From the point of view of investors, governments, and private firms wishing to use the London Stock Exchange as a secondary market, the most important rules were those relating to the granting of special settlements and of quotations on issues not previously traded. Until the Committee of General Purpose had set the date for a special settlement, no one could be called on to complete a bargain, and if the Committee refused to grant a special settlement, all bargains were void. Once the initial bargains had been completed on the special setting day, the new security was treated like any other. A special settlement made it possible for members to trade in a security on the Exchange; a quotation meant that the security was entered into the Stock Exchange's Official List and that there was a price (or prices) at which a jobber was willing to buy or sell the bond or share.[319]

From 1845 onward a settlement was granted on the personal application of a member to the Committee and "on the production of a certificate from the secretary of the company that the subscription list was full, that payments had been received on two-thirds of the scrip, and that the time for signing the deed of settlement had passed." Over time the rules became somewhat more stringent. By the turn of the century, the application had to be accompanied "by a specimen of the scrip, bond, or share, a copy of the prospectus and a statutory declaration, stating the amount allotted to the general public and to others, the amount paid up, and that the securities were ready to be issued." In the case of new companies, a statement of the capital, the nominal value of the shares, and whether any shares that were authorized but not issued where vendor's shares were also required.[320]

Although investors tended to view a special settlement as a signal of quality, an even greater guarantee was associated with a quotation. As a result, the rules for granting a quotation were more demanding. In the

---

[318] The Settlement Department merely took over the operations of the existing informal clearing house; in fact, the manager of the existing clearinghouse became the manager of the newly established Department. Morgan and Thomas, *The Stock Exchange*, p. 154.

[319] Cottrell, *Industrial Finance*, p. 147; Morgan and Thomas, *The Stock Exchange*, pp. 151–53.

[320] Morgan and Thomas, *The Stock Exchange*, pp. 152–53.

case of foreign government loans, the Committee of the Foreign Stock Exchange resolved as early as 1827 that it would not "sanction or take any cognizance of bargains in new loans for a foreign state that was in default on previous obligations." That rule was adopted by the London Stock Exchange when it merged with the Foreign Stock Exchange. Like the rules for granting a settlement, the requirements for a quotation became steadily more stringent. By the end of the century, in addition to qualifying for settlement, it was also necessary

> that the prospectus must have been publicly advertised and, in the case of companies, must agree substantially with the articles of association. Not less than half the authorized capital must have been issued and 10% paid. Two-thirds of any issue must have been "subscribed for and unconditionally allotted to the public," and shares issued in lieu of money payments not to count toward this proportion. In the case of companies, the articles of association must provide, *inter alia*, that no funds of the company should be used for loans, or for purchase of its own shares; that the directors must hold a share qualification; that the borrowing powers of the board should be limited; and that accounts should be sent to shareholders, and to the secretary of the Share and Loan Department, at least seven days before the annual general meeting. New companies were also required to state the amount of shares allotted to the public and the amount paid thereon, the number of shares allotted other than for cash, the number of allottees and the largest single allotment, and to produce their allotment book and bank pass book for inspection.[321]

2-3b(4b). The provincial exchanges: Although London was the center of the world capital market, the London Stock Exchange shared the British market with the set of much smaller provincial exchanges. Between 1836 and 1903 formal exchanges were organized in seventeen cities in England and Wales, five cities in Scotland, and at least one in Ireland. In the mid-1840s the combined membership of the seventeen provincial exchanges – exchanges boasting almost 600 members – was more than half as large as that of the London Stock Exchange. There-

---

[321] Cottrell, *Industrial Finance*, p. 147. Morgan and Thomas, *The Stock Exchange*, pp. 152–53. From 1881 the Stock Exchange insisted that listed companies send to it a copy of the accounts presented to shareholders at ordinary general meetings; and, by 1901, 3,133 out of 4,166 (75%) of the companies listed on the London Stock Exchange were audited by members of the ICAEW (The Institute of Chartered Accountants in England and Wales). J.R. Edwards, *Company Legislation and Changing Patterns of Disclosure in British Company Accounts, 1900–1940* (London: Institute of Chartered Accountants in England and Wales, 1981), pp. 6, 10.

after, while London boomed, the countryside withered. By 1850, with the cooling of the railway mania, combined membership had declined by one-fifth. By 1890, although the number of exchanges in Scotland had increased from three to five, only one new exchange had been opened in England and Wales, and the total number had fallen from fifteen to eight. The local exchanges recovered only slightly with the surge of private company formations in the mid-1890s. Even as late as 1914 the fourteen existing English and Welsh exchanges could claim a total membership that was barely more than 10 percent above the figure for the exchanges that had been operating some sixty-eight years earlier.[322]

The existing fragmentary information for the small, short-lived exchanges suggests that they conducted a purely agency business with no local jobbing or shunting. In the larger markets only the Birmingham members specialized in jobbing or brokering, and even there specialization soon disappeared. There were many firms that acted as "dual capacity" brokers, jobbers, and/or shunters. Broker traditionally dealt with broker, with the market alone providing intermediation. Most markets were organized along American oral auction lines: The full list was read through once or twice a day, buy and sell orders were matched, and the price of each security was set. During the remainder of the trading period, brokers commissioned to buy made individual bargains with brokers commissioned to sell.[323]

For firms desirous of having their securities listed or quoted, access to the provincial markets was frequently easier than access to the London Stock Exchange. Applications for special settlement were seldom refused, but a company was not automatically granted a quotation. De jure, the rules for quotation were similar to those adopted in London, but de facto they were less severe. Evidence that a security was quoted in London or on another large exchange was usually sufficient to guarantee a quotation with no further questions asked. In addition, "exchange committees were very sympathetic to members requests for quotations when it was shown to be 'to the benefit of the Association.'"[324]

---

[322] The Scottish exchanges were more robust in terms of membership. The combined membership increased from 90 in 1845 to 376 in 1914, and that of the three exchanges that operated throughout the period from 90 to 350. Thomas, *The Provincial Exchanges*, pp. 72, 287, 327.

[323] Thomas, *The Provincial Exchanges*, pp. 73–74.

[324] In 1873, for example, the Manchester committee members suspended their standing orders on quotations and contented themselves with merely the last available balance sheet and the articles of association in order to attract local companies onto their list. Thomas, *The Provincial Exchanges*, p. 138.

There had always been links among provincial markets and between provincial markets and London. Initially, brokers in London and the provinces merely acted as agents for their customers, dealing with brokers operating in the primary market for the security in question. By the 1870s, however, with the innovation of the telegraph and later the telephone, the agency network was supplemented by the widespread innovation of shunting. A shunter was nothing more than a nineteenth-century ancestor of the twentieth-century *arbitrageur*; he bought securities for his own account in low-priced markets and sold them in high-priced ones. In the provinces the shunter provided price information about securities that were primarily traded in other provincial markets and in London. By linking provincial investors to London jobbers, he gave them access to the competitive facilities and breadth and depth of the main markets at near net prices. London shunters, on the other hand, provided the city's brokers both with supplies of country securities and with information about their prices in the major provincial markets. Thus, London investors had the opportunity to deal in potentially profitable country issues that were not listed on the London Stock Exchange.[325] In the United States, of course, shunting was largely unnecessary. Given "national" brokerage houses, a customer in Chicago, for example, could deal with the local branches of a firm with a seat on the New York Stock Exchange.

As a result of these intermarket links, Britain had a well-integrated capital market for almost four decades. But over time there is evidence of some erosion. On the one hand, some of the provincial exchanges, although initially very liberal in their listing policies, began to restrict access. Liverpool narrowed its list to companies with more than £50,000 in share capital, and the Manchester committee resolved to reject quotations for small companies whose shares were "insufficiently in public hands." These actions on the part of the provincial exchanges reduced the liquidity of some industrial and commercial issues and made price comparisons between new unlisted and older listed securities more difficult.[326]

---

[325] Thomas, *The Provincial Exchanges*, pp. 88–89. Most of the activity appears to have involved country funds moving into the London market rather than shifts from city to the provinces. Edward Rae, chairman of the Liverpool Stock Exchange, writing in 1909, placed the volume of business sent to London at twenty times that sent to the country. Liverpool Stock Exchange, *Minutes*, October 20, 1909. Cited in Thomas, *The Provincial Exchanges*, p. 89.

[326] Cottrell, *Industrial Finance*, pp. 182–83. Not all exchanges set such high limits. Glasgow provided quotations on firms with paid-up capital of as little as £25,000 and at Aberdeen there were firms quoted with as little as £3,500. Michie, *Money, Mania, and Markets*, pp. 233–34.

On the other hand, the Committee of General Purposes of the London Stock Exchange began to tighten its rules. To the extent that it was successful, it reduced the ability of the system to mobilize capital across geographic boundaries. Beginning in July 1909, it attempted to enforce the rule against dual capacity, and in 1912 it imposed a minimum commission. Both actions adversely affected shunting: the former by making it difficult for brokers to act as jobbers in their role as shunters, and the latter by increasing the total commission on a shunted, or agency, sale.[327] The result was a breakdown of what had been an efficient national securities market.[328]

Originally, because quotations were dependent largely on local information and industrial conditions, individual provincial exchanges had a near monopoly over industries located in their regions. Because the market did work, the provincial exchanges, drawing on their inventories of local information, were able to continue to specialize while attracting savings from all parts of Britain.[329] Among the first domestic commercial and industrial firms to turn to the formal exchanges were those in iron and steel and in shipbuilding. Between the mid-1860s and the mid-1880s, Sheffield, Manchester, and to a lesser extent Newcastle became the centers of iron and steel finance; Birmingham, Sheffield, and Bristol were the focus for railway carriages and wagon works.[330] The Liverpool market became the home of the three giants of the salt and alkali industry: Salt Union, United Alkali, and Brunner Mond.[331] Finally, Oldham became the home of a number of exchanges specializing in cotton textile stock.[332]

---

[327] Michie, *New York and London*, p. 85; Thomas, *The Provincial Exchanges*, pp. 201–2. The charge for gilt-edged was fixed at 2s. 6d. percent on stock, and for shares there was a sliding scale of minimum commissions ranging from 1–½ d. a share for those of 5s. to 15s., to 2s. 6d. on those of £20–25. For shares of higher value the charge was ½ percent of money.

[328] Ranald C. Michie, "The London and Provincial Stock Exchanges, 1799–1973: Separation, Integration, Rivalry, Unity," in D.H. Aldercroft and A. Slaven (eds.), *Enterprise and Management: Essays in Honour of Peter L. Payne* (Aldershot, U.K.: Scoler Press, 1995), pp. 206–11. [Hereafter cited on Michie, *"The London and Provincial Stock Exchanges."*]

[329] Thomas, *The Provincial Exchanges*, p. 114; Cottrell, *Industrial Finance*, p. 153.

[330] Between 1863 and 1871 twenty-five firms (including Charles Cammell & Co. Ltd. and John Brown & Co. Ltd) with a capital of £5.3 million and in 1872 and 1873 another twenty-five firms with capital of £1.4 million were granted quotations in Sheffield. The Newcastle quotations included Sir W.A. Armstrong, Mitchell & Co., Consett Iron Co. Ltd., Dorman Long & Co., and Palmer's Shipbuilding & Son Co. Ltd. Thomas, *The Provincial Exchanges*, pp. 123–24; Cottrell, *Industrial Finance*, p. 153.

[331] Thomas, *The Provincial Exchanges*, p. 135.

[332] Thomas, *The Provincial Exchanges*, chapter 7, pp. 145–64.

Although London was the home of most large breweries after the Guinness issue of 1886, by 1897, £11.7 million of "provincial only" brewery shares had been granted quotations; the main markets in those shares were Manchester, Birmingham, Bristol, and Leeds. The 1890s also saw a rapid shift in the ownership of the nation's coal mines from private to public; for that industry the main market was Cardiff.

Manufacturing cycles was the major new domestic growth industry of the late nineteenth century. Between the beginning of 1893 and the end of 1896, 441 cycle companies with a nominal capital of £31.0 million were registered (312 with £24.5 million in 1896 alone). Again it was the provincial markets, particularly Birmingham, that drew the major portion of the action.[333] The years 1897 through 1904 saw the organization of nineteen amalgamated textile firms with a total capitalization of £45.6 million by 1906; Manchester became the chief exchange for the issues of these new firms.[334] All the leading automobile manufacturers – including Daimler, British Motor Car Syndicate Ltd., Humber, and Sunbeam – were quoted on the Birmingham Exchange, where "motor shares had their main dealings."[335] Finally, Bristol was the most important market for tobacco shares, including the £14.5 million issued by the largely local Imperial Tobacco Company.[336]

Although their focus was largely domestic, the provincial exchanges were not completely immune to the lure of foreign investment. London remained by far the most important center for foreign government issues, but a few small issues of the Mexican, Egyptian, Brazilian, and Spanish governments were quoted in Liverpool and Manchester. Those exchanges were much more involved in overseas railway and mining activity. As early as the 1850s, both Leeds and Sheffield listed almost as many foreign mines as did London. From 1886 onward Leeds again became a center of overseas mining activity; during the 1894–95 mining boom, nearly fifty foreign mines were listed on that city's "Unofficial Mining Board." Because of the local interest in "Kaffirs" (South African gold stocks), that board was called every day immediately after the official reading of listed securities. Again, toward the end of the century, as American rails became increasingly popular with British investors, the

---

[333] £5 million of the £24.5 1896 total was the capital of the Dunlop Tyre Company. In 1896–97 Birmingham granted special settlement to 159 cycle companies, but quotation was granted to only 52. Thomas, *The Provincial Exchanges*, pp. 129–32.

[334] Among the largest amalgamations was the consolidation of 255 individual enterprises into seven firms with a combined capitalization of £27.8 million. Thomas, *The Provincial Exchanges*, p. 135.

[335] Thomas, *The Provincial Exchanges*, p. 134.

[336] Thomas, *The Provincial Exchanges*, p. 136.

Liverpool and, to a lesser extent, the Manchester exchanges became active centers; Liverpool, because of its position in the American trade, was actually able to compete actively with London.[337]

2-4. British investors

2-4a. Their identity

By 1913 more than 1 million U.K. residents held at least some of their assets in the form of stocks or bonds. Since most overseas capital transfers were routed through the formal exchanges, it is reasonable to look to those markets to determine (1) who those 1 million residents were, and (2) what can be deduced about their investment preferences.[338] Some clues as to the identity of these investors at the end of the period can be found in the aggregate data compiled by the Inland Revenue Service (see Tables 2:4-1 and 2:4-2). One fact stands out: Participation in the market for formal securities was an activity still largely reserved for the rich and super-rich. If the holdings of the deceased represent a reasonable sample of the holdings of all investors, almost 55 percent of all stocks, shares, and funds were held by estates valued in excess of £50,000. For estates valued at more than £25,000, such paper securities represented almost 60 percent of total assets.[339] Moreover, although they accounted for barely one-fifth of the assets of estates valued at less than £5,000, they accounted for 45 percent of the value of the assets in all classes together.

Hall, using qualitative rather than quantitative evidence, identified four groups of late-nineteenth-century individual investors: the wealthy, the commercial classes, the safe investors, and the speculators. In the case of governmental and overseas issues, the wealthy were, he argues, impersonal investors concentrating on large public issues. For domestic industrial and commercial investments, capital remained highly personalized; the wealthy seldom dealt with widely traded public issues but instead bought securities of firms in the local region through direct purchase or through the intermediation of solicitors or financial agents. Although the group's relative holdings of formal securities increased over time, their comparative importance in the market for industrial capital declined.

---

[337] Thomas, *The Provincial Exchanges*, pp. 188–90.

[338] The data and much of the analysis in this section are taken from Davis and Huttenback, *Mammon*, chapter 7, pp. 195–220. The latter, however, owes much to Hall, *London and Australia*, pp. 43–47.

[339] One caveat. These data certainly reflect some life cycle effects. The dead were on average older than the living. Thus, if every person invested the same amount in paper securities each year of their life, you would expect that older persons would have more assets than younger ones.

Table 2:4-1. *The distribution of privately held assets by wealth class, 1913–1914*

Range of assets owned	Stocks, funds, shares, etc.	Cash	Money lent on mortgages, bonds & bills	Trade assets	House & business property	Insurance policies	Other property	Net capital value of estates
Pounds	Percent of total							Thousands of pounds
100–500	5.7	6.7	1.6	11.7	45.2	8.9	20.0	5,520
500–1,000	13.3	15.4	5.9	7.2	33.8	6.9	17.5	12,589
1,000–5,000	24.2	9.8	8.0	5.9	26.7	5.2	20.2	49,968
5,000–10,000	37.3	6.7	8.2	4.9	18.8	3.7	20.4	31,884
10,000–20,000	43.5	5.6	8.3	4.5	14.0	3.4	20.7	38,125
20,000–25,000	49.6	4.8	7.1	5.3	10.8	3.3	19.1	12,293
Above 25,000	59.0	4.0	6.3	5.0	6.6	2.1	17.0	168,220
Total percent	45.5	6.5	6.8	5.3	14.2	3.5	18.2	
Total value*	148,810	21,412	22,135	17,337	46,343	11,413	60,252	327,702

Notes: * Includes estates of less than 100 pounds gross value.

Source: A.R. Hall, *The London Capital Market and Australia, 1870–1914* (Canberra: The Australian National University, 1963), Table 7, p. 40.

Table 2:4-2. *The distribution of property assessed for death duties, 1913–1914*

Panel A: Percent of total private holdings				
Range of wealth in pounds	Shares, stocks, & funds	Cash	Insurance	House & business property	Percentage of total wealth
Under 1,000	2.1	22.5	21.0	19.6	8.3
1,000–5,000	8.1	22.8	22.7	28.8	15.2
5,000–10,000	7.9	10.0	10.3	13.0	9.7
10,000–20,000	11.1	9.9	11.3	11.5	11.6
20,000–25,000	4.1	2.8	3.6	2.9	3.8
25,000–50,000	12.2	7.4	9.3	10.0	11.2
Over 50,000	54.5	24.6	21.8	14.2	40.2
Totals	100.0	100.0	100.0	100.0	100.0
Panel B: relative holdings				
Under 1,000	25	271	253	236	100
1,000–5,000	53	150	149	189	100
5,000–10,000	81	103	106	134	100
10,000–20,000	96	85	97	99	100
20,000–25,000	108	74	95	76	100
25,000–50,000	109	66	83	89	100
Over 50,000	136	61	54	35	100

Source: A.R. Hall, *The London Capital Market and Australia, 1870–1914* (Canberra: The Australian National University, 1963), Table 8, p. 42.

Initially the commercial classes concentrated their attention on domestic commercial and industrial issues. Over time, because of their knowledge and personal business connections, they became an important, probably the leading, source of finance for non-rail enterprises in the foreign and colonial sectors. While individually their relative importance in the formal capital markets continued to increase, as a group they tended to lose their cohesion. Gradually, the members aligned themselves with either the wealthy or the safe group.

The safe investors were initially drawn from the class of rentiers, but as the years passed they were gradually joined by increasing numbers of the commercial class. Over time the relative size of this enlarged group of investors increased. As investors, they valued marketability and security above all else, and they were willing to accept lower yields to obtain stocks and bonds with these characteristics. At first they restricted their investments to the issues of the British government, but by the 1870s they began to expand their investment horizons to include domestic railroads and established joint-stock banks as well as colonial central government and municipal issues. Finally, toward the end of the period, they began to invest in commercial and industrial securities. To a large extent, preferred shares and debentures were initially designed to attract the accumulations of this group.

Finally, the speculative class was made up of two distinct groups. There were the professionals – the brokers and jobbers – whose income depended on their ability to buy and sell securities at a profit. Second, during speculative booms, the financial professionals were joined by businessmen – men used to taking substantial risks and earning high returns – who attempted to cash in on their knowledge and make a fast profit on a rising market. Members of this group typified the pure impersonal investor, an investor with no personal interest in any security, who demanded only that a security be marketable.[340]

A full study of British investors would include both bond and stockholders. Given the relative importance of bonds and stocks on the exchanges, if only one group were to be selected, it should be the bondholders. Unfortunately, there is little information available about the composition of this group.[341] For stockholders there is more complete information.

The Companies Acts of 1856 and 1862 required that corporations annually file a statement of their equity structure with the Board of Trade, a statement that included the names, addresses, occupations, and the share holdings of each stockholder. Davis and Huttenback constructed a random sample of such firms divided among the geographic regions in which the firms chiefly operated. The sample contains 260 firms registered between 1883 and 1907. It includes 59 firms operating in the United Kingdom, 75 with their principal operations in the foreign sector, and 126 whose activities were focused in the Empire – in all, 79,944 stockholders (see Table 2:4-3). In an effort to restrict the sample to public stockholders – as opposed to the firms' original organizers – Davis and Huttenback selected reports that were made three to five years after registration. The sample provides a reasonable coverage of the industrial

---

[340] Hall, *London and Australia*, pp. 43–47.

[341] (1). Many of the issues were of bearer bonds. (2). There was no general register of bondholders. (3). Even for the few firms that still have records, the bondholders are identified only by name.

Table 2:4-3. *Stockholders: number of firms sampled by location and industry*

Industry	Location of firm			Total sample
	U.K.	Foreign	Empire	
Agriculture and extractive				
1. Mines	5	4	15	24
2. Tea & coffee	0	0	10	10
Commercial and industrial				
1. Breweries and distilleries	6	6	6	18
2. Miscellaneous commercial and industrial	13	9	22	44
3. Iron, coal, and steel	7	6	11	24
Finance				
1. Commercial banks	4	5	6	15
2. Financial land and development	7	10	21	38
3. Financial trusts	2	6	4	12
Public utilities				
1. Canals and docks	5	2	1	8
2. Gas and light	4	3	8	15
3. Telephones and telegraph	0	4	2	6
4. Tramways and omnibuses	5	5	5	15
5. Waterworks	0	5	3	8
Transport				
1. Railroads	0	6	11	17
2. Shipping	1	4	1	6
All industry total	59	75	126	260

Source: Lance Davis & Robert Huttenback, *Mammon and the Pursuit of Empire: The Political Economy of British Imperialism, 1860–1912* (Cambridge and London: Cambridge University Press, 1986), Table 7.1, p. 196.

spectrum (the industrial categories are those employed by the editors of the *Stock Exchange Annual Yearbook*). However, there are some gaps: There are no U.K. railroads or waterworks included in the sample (most were chartered well before 1883), and there are no tea and coffee companies in either the domestic or foreign sectors.[342]

[342] English and Welsh firms were registered in London, Scottish firms in Edinburgh. The Davis-Huttenback sample contains both English and Welsh *and* Scottish firms.

Table 2:4-4 provides a summary of the geographic distribution of sample investors. Investors living outside of the United Kingdom held less than one-half of 1 percent of the nominal value of the shares of U.K. firms, less than 3 percent of Empire firms, but almost 17 percent of foreign firms. Residents of London held only one-fifth of the nominal value of shares of domestic firms, but more than one-half of the value of equity of foreign enterprises and almost three-fifths of that of Empire firms. For investors in the rest of the country, the pattern was almost reversed. There, residents held almost 80 percent of the value of shares of U.K. firms, but less than one-third of the value of stock issued by foreign and Empire companies.

One conclusion is obvious: In Britain there was not one capital market but two. Domestic firms utilized the savings of London investors, but they could not have survived without the accumulations of residents living outside London or for that matter outside the city *and* the home counties (nonmetropolitan London represented almost three-fifths and the Celtic fringe almost an additional one-fifth of the value of domestic shares). In the case of firms operating in the foreign sector, although about 85 percent of the English population lived outside London, its total contribution was only about one-half of that of the capital city's residents. Even if the residents of Ireland, Scotland, and Wales are added to the nonmetropolitan total, the ratio is only about 0.6:1.[343] In the case of Empire firms, the story is similar; but for nonmetropolitan England the contrast is even sharper. Almost 60 percent of the total is traced to London; hardly one-third of that amount was owned by residents of the rest of England (see Table 2:4-5).

In the Celtic fringe Irish savers looked to the Empire with increasing frequency, while the Scots were enthusiastic about foreign alternatives. The Welsh restricted themselves almost entirely to investments in firms operating within the United Kingdom. The behavior of the English investors is of more interest; they accounted for 90 percent of the value of domestic equity and 80 percent of the value of all equity included in the sample. A typical London resident's portfolio of private equities was divided in a ratio of 24:37:39 between domestic, foreign, and Empire firms. Outside of London the foreign and Empire indices are about half the domestic benchmark; however, even those figures tend to overstate the affinity of many of the non-Londoners for overseas investment. The foreign percentage is inflated by the investments of the rural east and Lancashire and the Empire total by the expressed preferences of

---

[343] In 1901 the population of London was 5 million, the population of England 31 million, and the population of the United Kingdom 37 million.

Table 2:4-4. *Geographic distribution of stockholders in the sample by percent of total value held*

Stockholder's place of residence	Location of firm			Total sample
	U.K.	Foreign	Empire	
Foreign countries				
Asia	0.0%	1.1%	0.0%	0.3%
Europe	0.4	8.4	2.5	3.7
North Africa and Middle East	0.0	0.1	0.0	0.0
North America	0.0	5.5	0.0	1.6
South and Central America	0.0	1.6	0.1	0.5
Total Foreign	0.4	16.7	2.6	6.1
Empire				
Dependent Colonies	0.0	0.1	1.8	0.9
Responsible Government	0.1	0.0	4.9	2.4
India	0.0	0.0	1.8	0.9
Total Empire	0.1	0.1	8.5	4.2
London				
East Central London	9.9	33.7	38.6	30.7
Other London	10.9	17.2	19.9	17.1
Total London	20.8	50.9	58.5	47.7
England outside of London				
Home Counties	4.2	4.3	6.4	5.3
Lancashire	9.6	8.0	2.1	5.5
Midlands	8.1	2.3	2.5	3.7
Rural East	2.5	0.8	1.1	1.4
Rural West	6.4	2.8	3.2	3.7
South and Southwest	9.0	2.8	3.7	4.6
The North	5.1	1.7	0.5	1.9
Yorkshire	14.2	3.1	1.7	4.9
Total England outside of London	59.1	25.8	21.2	30.8
Total England	79.9	76.7	79.7	78.8
Ireland, Scotland, and Wales				
Ireland	1.4	1.1	0.9	1.1
Scotland	8.6	4.5	7.6	7.0
Wales	9.5	0.6	0.6	2.6
Total Ireland, Scotland, and Wales	19.5	6.2	9.1	10.7
Total United Kingdom	99.4	82.9	88.8	89.5
Total unidentified	0.0	0.3	0.1	0.2
Sample total	100.0	100.0	100.0	100.0

Source: Davis and Huttenback, *Mammon and the Pursuit of Empire*, Table 7.5, p. 209.

Table 2:4-5. *Index of relative holdings by location of the residence of the stockholder (holdings of United Kingdom firms = 100)*

Residence of stockholder	U.K.	Foreign	Empire
Foreign countries or empire			
1. Non-United Kingdom	100	1,018	471
London			
1. East Central London	100	198	164
2. Other London	100	106	154
All London	100	156	161
England outside of London			
Home Counties	100	90	176
Lancashire	100	122	47
Midlands	100	23	29
Rural East	100	229	187
Rural West	100	63	82
South and Southwest	100	48	72
The North	100	23	12
Yorkshire	100	12	12
Total England outside of London	100	50	52
England total	100	92	96
Ireland, Scotland, and Wales			
Ireland	100	86	159
Scotland	100	120	93
Wales	100	12	14
Total Ireland, Scotland, and Wales	100	58	89

Source: Davis & Huttenback, *Mammon and the Pursuit of Empire*, Table 7.8, p. 214.

residents of the rural east and the Home Counties. Clearly, London-based investors took a very different view of the investment alternatives than did most of their country cousins.

The distinctions are somewhat less sharp, but London–non-London differences appear to have carried over to the choice of investments as well (see Table 2:4-6). In terms of domestic alternatives, Londoners displayed a relative preference for mines, financial land and development companies, financial trusts, and tramways and omnibuses. In the foreign sector their attention appears to have been drawn to public utilities and railroads. They chose Empire mines and railroads, and they invested in

Table 2:4-6. *Relative attractiveness of industries to residents of London as compared with the residents of other parts of the British Isles (ratio is London/non-London)*

	United Kingdom Non-London is		Foreign Non-London is		Empire Non-London is	
Industry	England	U.K.	England	U.K.	England	U.K.
Agriculture and extractive						
1. Mines	163	170	68	59	202	143
2. Tea & coffee	nd	nd	nd	nd	61	51
Commercial and industrial						
1. Breweries and distilleries	35	43	110	116	52	68
2. Miscellaneous commercial and industrial	76	81	84	96	98	87
3. Iron, coal, and steel	56	61	104	72	83	78
Finance						
1. Commercial banks	55	73	88	95	57	67
2. Financial land and development	329	306	111	95	127	161
3. Financial trusts	184	238	38	35	93	75
Public utilities						
1. Canals and docks	54	32	422	475	282	282
2. Gas and light	82	80	244	275	62	67
3. Telephones and telegraph	nd	nd	118	133	40	56
4. Tramways and omnibuses	139	112	359	380	101	117
5. Waterworks	nd	nd	394	448	178	178
Transport						
1. Railroads	nd	nd	125	140	189	220
2. Shipping	102	81	14	16	86	107

Source: Davis and Huttenback, *Mammon and the Pursuit of Empire*, Table 7.9, p. 215.

some but not all colonial industrial sectors: financial land and development companies, but not financial trusts; canals and docks and waterworks, but not gas and light or telephone and telegraph companies. Although the boundaries are a bit fuzzy, it appears that Londoners preferred overseas investments that depended on their ability to exercise a property right directly through land ownership or indirectly through a government charter. At home the former preference appears to have dominated. For stockholders living outside of London, relative preferences appeared to support investment in tea and coffee, almost all industries in the commercial and industrial sector, no matter where the firms were located (foreign breweries and distilleries were the sole exception), commercial banks, and some domestic and Empire public utilities.

Occupation also appears to have affected a saver's choice of investments. Table 2:4-7 displays the relative holdings of U.K., foreign, and Empire shares by members of twelve occupational groups.[344] Merchants much preferred foreign to domestic investments, but businessmen as a group showed a marked preference for domestic enterprise. They appear to have been about half again as likely to choose domestic as opposed to foreign investment and almost three times as likely to have selected domestic as opposed to Empire alternatives.

The elites display a quite different set of choices. As between domestic and foreign investment, there was apparently little to choose, although within the sector there is evidence of substantial occupation-to-occupation variation. As a group, they were about one-fifth more likely to choose Empire as opposed to domestic alternatives; the choices of peers and gentlemen and of the miscellaneous elites was even more skewed.

"Others" represents such a diverse mix of investors that it is difficult to draw significant generalizations. Despite accounting for only 15 percent of domestic investment, the group supplied almost one-third of the finance directed toward foreign and Empire firms. Laborers, not surprisingly, invested primarily in domestic enterprise, but the other three subgroups appear to have looked primarily abroad. To the extent that the indices are indicative of preferences, women had a very strong preference for foreign and a moderately strong preference for Empire investment. Investors classified as "miscellaneous stockholders" slightly preferred foreign to domestic alternatives, but they much preferred Empire to domestic investments. The managers of the "miscellaneous

---

[344] In terms of occupational groups:

Businessmen were made up of (1) Merchants (merchants, sales and agency, and retail and business services); (2) Manufacturing (manufacturers, engineering and construction, and brewers and distillers); (3) Professions (management, medicine, education, creative arts, legal professions, entrepreneurs, publishing); and (4) Miscellaneous business (agriculture, marine, transportation and communication, and mining).

Elites were made up of (1) Finance (bankers); (2) Military officers; (3) Miscellaneous elites (government and civil service, ecclesiastical, members of the House of Commons – with no other occupation – and land and property owners); and (4) Peers and gentlemen.

"Others" were made up of (1) Laborers (craftsman, unskilled labor, personal service, and skilled labor); (2) Women, with no other occupation; (3) Miscellaneous public companies (other companies including banks); and (4) Miscellaneous stockholders (retired, deceased, unknown, and unknown abroad).

Table 2:4-7. *Percent of shares held and index of relative holdings by occupation*

Occupation	Location of firm			Location of firm		
	U.K.	Foreign	Empire	U.K.	Foreign	Empire
	Percent of shares held by:			Index: U.K. = 100		
Businessmen						
1. Merchants	12.8	18.1	7.7	100	142	60
2. Manufacturers	16.5	3.3	1.8	100	20	11
3. Professionals and managers	7.8	4.3	4.0	100	54	51
4. Miscellaneous businessmen	4.0	2.5	1.3	100	63	32
All businessmen	41.0	28.2	14.7	100	69	36
Elites						
1. Financiers	5.1	9.6	4.1	100	190	81
2. Military	5.0	2.6	3.0	100	52	60
3. Peers and gentlemen	31.0	25.7	40.3	100	83	130
4. Miscellaneous elites	2.3	3.7	4.6	100	158	198
All elites	43.4	41.6	52.1	100	96	120
Others						
1. Laborers	1.4	0.5	0.4	100	39	28
2. Women (no other occupation)	4.6	17.2	7.7	100	372	168
3. Miscellaneous companies	4.0	6.1	12.8	100	155	324
4. Miscellaneous occupations	5.6	6.4	12.3	100	114	220
All others	15.5	30.2	33.2	100	194	214

Source: Davis & Huttenback, *Mammon and the Pursuit of Empire*, Table 7.2, p. 199.

public companies" were about half again as likely to choose foreign as opposed to domestic alternatives, but they were more than three times as likely to choose the stock of an Empire firm.

Finally, any attempt to analyze the character of domestic and overseas investment must explore the relationship between occupations and place of residence. Did London overseas investors come from an occupational distribution similar to overseas investors outside the metropolis, or did members of the same occupational group behave differently if they resided in London? Tables 2:4-8, 2:4-9, and 2:4-10 shed some light on that question for the major categories of investors, and the answer to the question is mixed. In the case of businessmen it is apparent that London residents behaved very differently from their nonmetropolitan counterparts. With the exception of the miscellaneous businessmen's disinclination to involve themselves with foreign investments, Londoners from every occupational category were very much less willing to invest in

Table 2.4-8. *Relative attractiveness of home, foreign, and empire investment: by industry for businessmen, elites, and others (all investments = 100)*

Industry	Businessmen			Elites			Other		
	U.K.	Foreign	Empire	U.K.	Foreign	Empire	U.K.	Foreign	Empire
Agriculture and extractive									
1. Mines	58	173	172	144	69	46	132	88	85
2. Tea & coffee	nd	nd	129	nd	nd	75	nd	nd	102
Commercial and industrial									
1. Breweries and distilleries	143	68	103	63	92	108	53	144	90
2. Miscellaneous commercial and industrial	138	135	158	48	93	66	90	70	87
3. Iron, coal, and steel	102	96	91	107	111	119	83	79	87
Finance									
1. Commercial banks	112	123	79	131	105	152	23	67	61
2. Financial land and development	61	76	50	117	96	122	168	130	122
3. Financial trusts	85	79	83	117	90	92	109	142	124
Public utilities									
1. Canals and docks	117	141	73	61	112	40	121	38	193
2. Gas and light	117	101	92	70	45	124	106	73	80
3. Telephones and telegraph	nd	24	72	nd	193	127	nd	54	95
4. Tramways and omnibuses	72	73	75	133	79	76	115	135	132
5. Waterworks	nd	125	96	nd	103	120	nd	67	81
Transport									
1. Railroads	nd	116	50	nd	90	126	nd	96	116
2. Shipping	98	144	260	106	54	56	96	112	5

Source: Davis and Huttenback, *Mammon and the Pursuit of Empire*, Table 7.4, p. 206.

Table 2:4-9. *Index of the relative attactiveness of investments by industry and location; ratio is the preferences of elites to the preferences of businessmen (businessmen's preferences = 100)*

Industry	U.K.	Foreign	Empire
Agriculture and extractive			
1. Mines	285	95	60
2. Tea & coffee	nd	nd	56
Commercial and industrial			
1. Breweries and distilleries	51	135	102
2. Miscellaneous commercial and industrial	40	68	40
3. Iron, coal, and steel	121	105	127
Finance			
1. Commercial banks	135	85	188
2. Financial land and development	219	124	239
3. Financial trusts	157	123	108
Public utilities			
1. Canals and docks	59	78	53
2. Gas and light	68	44	131
3. Telephones and telegraph	nd	813	172
4. Tramways and omnibuses	213	193	172
5. Waterworks	nd	81	121
Transport			
1. Railroads	nd	77	242
2. Shipping	125	37	21

Source: Davis and Huttenback, *Mammon and the Pursuit of Empire*, Table 7.8, p. 214.

domestic enterprise and very much more willing to invest overseas, whether the opportunity was in the foreign or the Empire sector.

In the case of the elites, the urban–rural differences are much less marked. London-based members of each of the four occupational subcategories displayed a somewhat greater willingness to invest in foreign rather than domestic or Empire enterprise, but only the "miscellaneous elites" appear to have had a strong preference. Moreover, there appears to have been no uniformity of feelings as far as the choices between domestic and Empire sectors were concerned. In the former case, although the overall London–elite ratio is well below that of similar shareholders in the provinces, both the "military" and the "miscellaneous elites" tended to invest substantially more at home than did their rural

Table 2:4-10. *Relative attractiveness of home, foreign, and empire investment by occupation and residence of the stockholder, businessmen and elites only (ratio is London/non-London)*

Occupation	U.K.	Foreign	Empire
Businessmen			
1. Merchants	19	135	110
2. Manufacturers	44	140	162
3. Professionals and managers	22	114	126
4. Miscellaneous businessmen	2	40	635
All businessmen	17	122	142
Elites			
1. Financiers	61	105	103
2. Military	132	108	94
3. Peers and gentlemen	49	102	105
4. Miscellaneous elites	152	129	90
All elites	62	106	102

Source: Davis and Huttenback, *Mammon and the Pursuit of Empire*, Table 7.10, p. 21.

counterparts. In the case of elite investment in the Empire, the rates were similar for Londoners and non-Londoners. In London "financiers" and "peers and gentlemen" viewed Empire investments slightly more favorably than did their rural confreres, but the opposite was true for the "military" and the "miscellaneous elites."

"It appears that the London bias toward overseas investment, while in part accounted for by the somewhat greater concentration of elite investment in the metropolis (peers and gents accounted for about 5 percent more of London than of rural investment), can in large measure be traced to the attraction of that overseas investment for London business people. Clearly that lure was less strong outside the capital, and the farther one traveled north in England the weaker it became."[345] Thus, the overseas contingent of the "two-nations" market consisted of businessmen in London and elites everywhere, while the domestic market was largely served by businessmen living outside of the capital. From the point of view of this book, the next obvious question is: Just how much

---

[345] Davis and Huttenback, *Mammon*, p. 217. That conclusion holds until the border with Scotland is reached. Scottish savers were much inclined toward overseas investments.

did those who chose to invest overseas in the four frontier countries earn on their investments?

2-4b. The rate of return on investments in the four frontier countries[346]

Foreign issues represented more than half of the value of securities quoted on the London Stock Exchange in 1913, and between 1865 and 1914 about one-half of the foreign issues "created and called" represented government or private activity in the four frontier countries. William Kennedy has argued that the flow of savings overseas reflected the British savers' search for "safe, well known securities ... of a type that fiscally frugal, heavily industrialized Britain could no longer provide." "The conservative nature of British foreign investment, revealing a marked preference for low variance of returns at the cost of forgoing high yields, may be seen in an examination of three characteristics: (1) the infrequency of defaults of foreign investments; (2) the preponderance of fixed-interest securities in the aggregate portfolio of British foreign assets; and (3) the relative low rate of return as compared to estimates of yields on the British domestic capital stock. However, in no sense was British foreign investment, especially after 1880, thrown away. British investors got very largely the returns they paid for." "The average rates of return which the British portfolio of foreign investments yielded are consistent with a description of the aggregate portfolio as bond-laden, conservative and chosen to suit the taste of discriminating rentiers."[347]

This book deals with the impact of British capital on the evolution of the financial infrastructure in the receiving countries. Although there was some institutional investment, most of those flows came from the savings of private individuals, and they were directed by those individuals' search for profits. It therefore seems appropriate to examine the characteristics of the returns earned on both domestic and foreign investments by the allegedly conservative British savers. In earlier work real rates of return on British domestic investment have been estimated by Michael Edelstein and by J. Bradford DeLong and Richard S. Grossman. Edelstein also provides estimates of real yields on a sample of overseas investments.[348]

---

[346] This section has been prepared with the assistance of Valentina Bali, Frederick Boehmke, and Maya Federman.

[347] William P. Kennedy, *Industrial Structure, Capital Markets*, pp. 145, 149–51.

[348] The Edelstein series covers both domestic and overseas investment, but it is limited to "first- and second-class securities." "As there were no regular market-rating services during the years 1870–1913, four minimal criteria are used to define the relevant population. Briefly, these are (1) an acceptable equity share

Tables 2:4-11a through 2:4-11d display the results of an alternative series of estimates prepared for this book. Like the previous inquiries into the returns on British portfolio investment, the basic data are taken from the *Investor's Monthly Manual*. Unlike those other studies, the sample is not limited to survivors, nor, like the Grossman-DeLong sample, is it limited to large firms. The rates reported are value-weighted.

The method of selection was as follows: If an issue was listed in the monthly report of "Capital Created and Called," its entry was noted; if it was included in the end-of-year listing of securities traded on the London Stock Exchange, it was added to the sample. The interest and dividend payments were recorded, as were the end of year prices, and the nominal yield was calculated as the sum of dividends or interest plus capital gains or losses divided by the price at the end of the previous

either paid dividends regularly or manifested dividend behavior similar to that of the securities of leading companies in the same industrial group; (2) an acceptable preference or debenture share paid dividends or interest without interruption; (3) securities with long periods of heavy discounts for reasons other than nonpayment are either completely excluded or the affected portion of the securities' yield history is eliminated; (4) accepted securities had to be quoted continuously for a significant portion of the period or their term to maturity. The field is narrowed further through the use of contemporary evidence, secondary sources, and scaling procedures." The Edelstein series was first developed for his Ph.D. dissertation (*The Rate of Return on U.K. Home and Foreign Investment, 1870–1913*, Ph.D. Dissertation, University of Pennsylvania, 1970); it was first published in "Realized Rates of Return of U.K. Home and Overseas Portfolio Investment in the Age of High Imperialism," *Explorations in Economic History*, Vol. 13, No. 3 (July 1976), pp. 283–330; and it was the basis for chapters 4 and 5 of *Overseas Investment in the Age of High Imperialism: The United Kingdom, 1850–1914* (New York: Columbia University Press, 1982). The quotation is from "Realized Rates of Return on Overseas Investment in the Age of High Imperialism," pp. 287–88. The DeLong and Grossman series is reported in " 'Excess Volatility' on the London Stock Market, 1870–1990," mimeograph, January 1993. That paper, in turn, is based on a sample of firms collected by K.C. Smith and G.F. Horne and published as "An Index Number of Securities, 1867–1914", in London and Cambridge Economic Service, *The British Economy: Key Statistics* (London: London and Cambridge Economic Service, 1973), pp. 1–20. That sample includes only British firms operating in the domestic economy. "The shares selected are those for which quotations were available continuously over as long periods as possible, and cover as many industries as possible. The more important companies were selected when several were available, but in the early years the list was short, except for iron and steel and allied trades, and practically all of the data for firms of any magnitude [the nominal value of the shares in question usually exceeded £100,000] were used, subject also to their being available over a fairly long period. In 1867, 25 shares were included, in 1913 there were 77" (p. 2).

Table 2:4-11(a). *Average and variance of weighted real yields: all issues*

Years	All four countries	Argentina	Australia	Canada	United States
Panel A: Average Returns					
1870–1874	0.0784	0.1010	0.0568	0.0850	0.0787
1875–1879	0.0985	0.2233	0.0696	0.1123	0.0962
1880–1884	0.0256	0.1368	0.0607	0.0590	0.0057
1885–1889	0.0799	0.1371	0.0576	0.0733	0.0827
1890–1894	0.0280	0.0661	0.0221	0.0099	0.0287
1895–1899	0.1220	0.2277	0.0378	0.0659	0.1406
1900–1904	0.0592	0.1677	0.0140	0.0749	0.0549
1905–1909	0.0724	0.0580	0.0371	0.0408	0.0926
1910–1914	−0.0035	0.0074	0.0164	0.0004	−0.0144
1870–1884	0.0688	0.1563	0.0629	0.0832	0.0647
1885–1899	0.0798	0.1513	0.0377	0.0481	0.0903
1900–1914	0.0425	0.0635	0.0226	0.0311	0.0467
1870–1914	0.0602	0.0987	0.0338	0.0451	0.0646
Panel B: Variance of real returns					
1870–1884	0.0602	0.3926	0.0037	0.1195	0.0477
1885–1899	0.1513	0.9523	0.0063	0.0192	0.1155
1900–1914	0.5038	0.1900	0.0072	0.0180	0.8009
1870–1914	0.2945	0.4504	0.0066	0.0345	0.3939
Panel C: Coefficient of variation of real returns					
1870–1884	3.5662	4.0088	0.9671	4.1549	3.3756
1885–1899	4.8743	6.4498	2.1054	2.8807	3.7636
1900–1914	16.7009	6.8644	3.7545	4.3140	19.1634
1870–1914	9.0146	6.7996	2.4036	4.1184	9.7154

year.[349] The security (and any other issued by the same firm or government) was then followed until it disappeared from the list.

Bonds often disappeared because they were repaid, but for both bonds and equities there were also numerous other explanations for exit.

[349] The formula employed was:

$$\text{Return} = \frac{(\text{Price}_t - \text{Price}_{t-1}) + \text{dividends (or interest)}_t}{P_t - 1}$$

Table 2:4-11(b). *Average and variance of weighted real yields, all government issues*

Years	All four countries	Argentina	Australia	Canada	United States
Panel A: Average returns					
1870–1874	0.0805	0.0599	0.0493	0.0509	0.0842
1875–1879	0.0768	0.1303	0.0647	0.0724	0.0761
1880–1884	0.0663	0.0834	0.0587	0.0507	0.0687
1885–1889	0.0526	0.0756	0.0581	0.0606	0.0448
1890–1894	0.0313	0.0453	0.0377	0.0423	0.0133
1895–1899	0.0487	0.1978	0.0366	0.0243	0.0296
1900–1904	0.0229	0.1189	0.0162	0.0216	0.0167
1905–1909	0.0274	0.0616	0.0336	0.0305	0.0147
1910–1914	0.0125	0.0164	0.0148	0.0027	0.0014
1870–1884	0.0751	0.0936	0.0588	0.0580	0.0776
1885–1899	0.0450	0.1160	0.0424	0.0406	0.0315
1900–1914	0.0224	0.0628	0.0215	0.0176	0.0159
1870–1914	0.0432	0.0861	0.0339	0.0334	0.0422
Panel B: Variance of real returns					
1870–1884	0.0093	0.0254	0.0016	0.0012	0.0100
1885–1899	0.0068	0.0470	0.0012	0.0014	0.0013
1900–1914	0.0010	0.0047	0.0007	0.0008	0.0002
1870–1914	0.0054	0.0234	0.0012	0.0013	0.0048
Panel C: Coefficient of variation of real returns					
1870–1884	1.2841	1.7027	0.6803	0.5973	1.2887
1885–1899	1.8325	1.8689	0.8170	0.9216	1.1446
1900–1914	1.4117	1.0917	1.2306	1.6071	0.8894
1870–1914	1.7010	1.7767	1.0219	1.0795	1.6418

"Although many issues disappeared from the stock exchange's lists because of company failure, many left for other reasons. Companies removed themselves from the lists in order to organize themselves on a more restricted basis. Others disappeared under the threat of failure but ultimately regained profitability."[350] If possible, private securities that dis-

---

[350] Michael Edelstein, "Realized Rates of Return of the U.K. Home and Overseas Portfolio Investment in the Age of High Imperialism," p. 287.

Table 2:4-11(c). *Average and variance of real yields: all railroad issues*

Years	All four countries	Argentina	Australia	Canada	United States
	Panel A: Average returns				
1870–1874	0.0914	0.3250	0.0986	0.1063	0.0777
1875–1879	0.1997	0.6315	0.1502	0.1529	0.1989
1880–1884	−0.0361	0.3510	0.0812	0.0691	−0.0708
1885–1889	0.1149	0.2687	0.1275	0.0860	0.1137
1890–1894	0.0338	0.1106	−0.0485	−0.0136	0.0356
1895–1899	0.1946	0.2646	0.0408	0.0923	0.2056
1900–1904	0.1224	0.2171	0.0323	0.1072	0.1118
1905–1909	0.0920	0.0520	0.1594	0.0426	0.1119
1910–1914	−0.0121	0.0062	−0.0171	−0.0062	−0.0188
1870–1884	0.0615	0.4416	0.1165	0.1057	0.0376
1885–1899	0.1177	0.2070	0.0399	0.0534	0.1224
1900–1914	0.0585	0.0671	0.0581	0.0357	0.0632
1870–1914	0.0810	0.1165	0.0704	0.0508	0.0836
	Panel B: Variance of real returns				
1870–1884	0.2377	1.9001	0.0479	0.2225	0.1851
1885–1899	0.2890	2.0856	0.0273	0.0314	0.1718
1900–1914	1.0484	0.3170	0.0336	0.0184	1.4795
1870–1914	0.6714	0.8574	0.0370	0.0503	0.7995
	Panel C: Coefficient of variation of real returns				
1870–1884	7.9276	3.1215	1.8786	4.4626	11.4424
1885–1899	4.5674	6.9766	0.4141	3.3184	3.3863
1900–1914	17.5028	8.3909	3.1550	3.7996	19.2460
1870–1914	10.1159	7.9481	2.7323	4.4149	10.6955

appeared were traced through the *Register of Defunct and Other Companies Removed from the Stock Exchange Official Year Book*.[351] Appropriate values were then assigned to the firm's last year's earnings, and it was dropped from the sample.[352] If the firm could not be traced through

[351] Croydon, U.K.: Thomas Skinner & Co., 1973. [Hereafter cited as *Register*.]

[352] In the case of the U.S. American Nickel Company, for example, in 1912 it was acquired by a company of the same name. Preferred stockholders received $100 preferred stock in the new company for each $100 stock and common stockholders received $250 for each $100 stock. The 5 percent first-mortgage gold bonds were repaid on 1 April 1913 at 110%." *Register*, p. 253.

Table 2:4.4-11(d). *Average and variance of weighted real yields: all "other" issues*

Years	All four countries	Argentina	Australia	Canada	United States
Panel A: Average returns					
1870–1874	0.0623	0.0660	0.0737	0.0554	0.0614
1875–1879	0.0739	0.0857	0.0738	0.0724	0.0739
1880–1884	0.0435	0.0863	0.0631	0.0451	0.0307
1885–1889	0.0491	0.0980	0.0558	0.0561	0.0318
1890–1894	−0.0049	−0.1183	−0.0139	0.0360	−0.0119
1895–1899	0.0554	0.1304	0.0411	0.0265	0.0851
1900–1904	0.0298	0.0534	0.0084	0.0140	0.0642
1905–1909	0.1255	0.0996	0.0439	0.0555	0.2033
1910–1914	0.0037	−0.0262	0.0213	0.0259	−0.0046
1870–1884	0.0635	0.0794	0.0676	0.0583	0.0628
1885–1899	0.0331	0.0372	0.0270	0.0414	0.0356
1900–1914	0.0438	0.0265	0.0250	0.0284	0.0595
1870–1914	0.0483	0.0405	0.0332	0.0399	0.0581
Panel B: Variance of real returns					
1870–1884	0.0049	0.0164	0.0057	0.0060	0.0044
1885–1899	0.0234	0.0468	0.0174	0.0049	0.0421
1900–1914	0.0537	0.0300	0.0233	0.0455	0.0747
1870–1914	0.0289	0.0330	0.0182	0.0203	0.0356
Panel C: Coefficient of variation of real returns					
1870–1884	1.1024	1.6129	1.1168	1.3286	1.0562
1885–1899	4.6215	5.8154	4.8855	1.6908	5.7636
1900–1914	5.2907	6.5360	6.1057	7.5108	4.5935
1870–1914	3.5197	4.4854	4.0635	3.5709	3.2475

the *Register*, it was assumed that it had realized a zero return in the last year – that is, it had neither a profit nor a loss. Finally, nominal yields were converted to real yields by subtracting the percentage change in the Consumer Price Index.[353] No attempt was made to report long-term

---

[353] Technically prices and dividends were converted to real values before the gain was calculated. The Consumer Price Index is from Charles H. Feinstein, *National*

earnings from continuous reinvestments of earnings, although those estimates are available. Instead, it was assumed that securities were sold at the end of each year, and the earnings (or losses) consumed.

What, then, were the returns? At the most general level, Table 2:4-11a indicates that over the entire time period 1870–1914, real earnings on all public and private issues in the four frontier countries averaged just over 6 percent. Returns were highest in Argentina and lowest in Australia, and returns on U.S. investments were about 2 percent higher than Canadian.

There is evidence of a slight negative trend in returns, although it is largely swamped by the impact of the depression of the early 1890s. Regressions of average weighted real yields on time show a negative coefficient for the four country average as well as (U.S. "Others" aside) for each of the classes of securities and for each of the individual countries, but the coefficients are not large. Moreover, the coefficients of determination (r^2s) for the twenty regressions are – except for Australian, Canadian, and American governments and Australian "all issues" – very small. They range from 0.003 to 0.168 (see Table 2:4-19).

Trend or not, there is substantial evidence of very wide year-to-year variation. The coefficients of variation range from 2.4 for Australia to 9.7 for the United States, and the "all country" average is 9.0 (see Table 2:4-11a). The 1870s were relatively rewarding for investors in all four countries, and those who chose to invest in the United States also realized very large yields in the two quinquennia 1895–99 and 1905–9, whereas Argentine investors were particularly well rewarded in the decade 1895–1905. The first five years of the 1890s were uniformly bad for those who chose to invest in any of the four countries, as were the last five years before the outbreak of World War I.

The "all-issue" yields are in part the artifact of a changing mix of industries within countries and of differences in the intercountry composition of investment. To reduce those effects, a somewhat narrower industrial breakdown – a division into government, railroads, and "all others" – is provided in Tables 2:4-11b, 11c, and 11d.

On average, over the four-decade period, government loans to Australia and Canada averaged slightly over 3 percent, and those to the United States somewhat more than 4 percent. The Australian and Canadian returns were the least variable, but the U.S. returns were substantially more so. In the case of Argentina returns averaged more than 8.5 percent, and they were highly variable: The variance on Argentine

Income, Expenditure, and Output of the United Kingdom, 1855–1965 (Cambridge: Cambridge University Press, 1972), table 61, p. T132.

returns over the entire period was almost twenty times the Australian and Canadian average and almost five times the American.

Over time the returns on Argentine government issues show little trend; they averaged 9 percent over the first three quinquennia (1870–84), increased to almost 12 percent in the second three (1885–99), before declining to 6 percent over the first fifteen years of the twentieth century. For Australia and Canada, although the trend was not steady, real yields tended to fall from an average in the 5.5 to 6.0 percent range over the first three quinquennia to about 4 percent in the second to about 2 percent in the third (1900–14). In the case of the United States, the decline was from about 7.8 to 3.2 to 1.6 percent. At the same time, the variance of the returns for all three declined somewhat, but the coefficient of variation in general increased. That increase may, however, be nothing but a reflection of the changing mix of issues from national to state and provincial to city issues. Finally, there are significant correlations between the yields on Australian, Canadian, and U.S. government bonds and British Consols; however, returns on Argentine issues are not very closely related to the U.S. standard and at times move in the opposite directions. Of at least equal interest is the fact that there does not appear to have been any substantial improvement in the degree of association between the yields on any of those government issues over the years 1870–1914 (Table 2:4-12).

Most Australian railways were government-owned, and their finance was channeled through that sector. Thus, the Australian data are based on a small number of firms, and any conclusions should be examined with a very careful eye.[354] Returns on Canadian railroads issues averaged more than 10 percent over the first three quinquennia. They declined to half that level over the years 1885–99, and declined again to about 3.6 percent over the first fifteen years of the twentieth century (Table 2:4-11c). In the case of the United States, the returns were only 3.8 percent over the first three quinquennia. They rose to more than 12 percent between 1885 and 1899, before falling to slightly over 6 percent between 1900 and 1915. In Argentina returns were very high (44 percent) between 1870 and 1885. Although they declined to 11 percent during the first half of the 1890s, they still averaged more than 20 percent over the second three quinquennia and the first five years of the twentieth century. Thereafter, they declined to 5.2 percent between 1905 and 1909 and to a tiny 0.6 percent in the last five years before World War I.

---

[354] Only four Australian "railroads" appear in the sample: the Emu Bay and Mount Bischoff Railway (1888–1914), the Melbourne and Hobson's Bay United (1870–81), the Midland Railway of Western Australia (1892–1910), and the Tasmanian Main Line Railway (1873–90).

Table 2.4-12. *Correlation coefficients: real yields of government bonds*

	Argentina	Australia	Canada	U.S.	U.K. (consols)
Panel A: 1870–1884					
Argentina	1.000				
Australia	0.356	1.000			
Canada	0.569	0.914	1.000		
United States	0.132	0.699	0.692	1.000	
U.K.	0.395	0.821	0.785	0.636	1.000
Panel B: 1885–1899					
Argentina	1.000				
Australia	0.458	1.000			
Canada	0.324	0.690	1.000		
United States	0.348	0.564	0.594	1.000	
U.K.	−0.029	0.569	0.616	0.440	1.000
Panel C: 1900–1914					
Argentina	1.000				
Australia	−0.050	1.000			
Canada	0.225	0.815	1.000		
United States	0.419	0.371	0.448	1.000	
U.K.	−0.074	0.602	0.461	0.047	1.000
Panel D: 1870–1914					
Argentina	1.000				
Australia	0.353	1.000			
Canada	0.399	0.854	1.000		
United States	0.255	0.697	0.721	1.000	
U.K.	0.196	0.695	0.675	0.520	1.000

In Canada, but in none of the other cases, there is evidence of a secular decline in the variance of returns. Even in the case of Canada, although the coefficient of variation of the Canadian returns declines by more than 15 percent between 1870–84 and 1900–14, it rises by an almost equal amount between 1885–99 and 1900–14. Moreover, between the first sub-period and the last, the coefficient of variation for Argentina shows a more than 120 percent increase, and the U.S. estimates increased by more than two-thirds.

Unlike governments and railroads, in the case of "other" issues, Argentine yields were similar to those in the other countries. Despite the fact that "other" securities represent a polyglot mixture of firms from the agricultural and extractive, manufacturing and commercial, finance, and public utility sectors, and that the relative weights of those sectors differ from country to country, over the entire forty-five year period the average real yields in Argentina, Australia, and Canada were similar: 4.0, 3.3, and 4.0 percent respectively. Even the U.S. returns, although higher – 5.8 percent – were not markedly so. In the case of Argentina, returns fell steadily from 8 percent over the first three quinquennia to 3.7 percent in the second and to 2.7 percent in the third. For the other three countries, average returns over the whole period may have been similar, but the time patterns were different. In the first of the three subperiods, Australian yields (6.8 percent) were almost as high as those earned in Argentina. In the second, although positive, they were not high (2.7 percent). And they remained about that level (2.5 percent) in the third. In Canada, between 1870 and 1884 returns were 5.8 percent. They fell in the second subperiod but still averaged 4.1 percent, and they fell again (to 2.8 percent) over the final fifteen years. In the United States yields in the first subperiod averaged 6.3 percent. Over the second three quinquennia they declined to 3.6 percent, and despite the fact that they were negative between 1910 and 1914, because of a surge to more than 20 percent in the years 1905 to 1909, over the three quinquennia leading up to World War I they averaged more than twice the yields available in the other three countries.

Over the years 1870–85 investors interested only in the size of the average return would have chosen a portfolio of Argentine railroads; but while they would have earned almost four times as much as the next most profitable choice (Australian railroads), they would have had to accept a variance on their return that was almost forty times as high as that second alternative. Perhaps a better comparison is with Canadian rails. Their yields were about a quarter of the Argentine average, but the variance was only about one-tenth as great (see Table 2:4-13).

A similar story holds for the second three quinquennia. Although with a return of only 20 percent, the Argentine differential had declined. Argentine railroads yields were only one and two-thirds those of their closest competitors (American railroads). But to earn that return, investors would have had to accept a variance that was twelve times greater than the U.S. alternative. Finally, in the years 1900–14, Argentine railroads remained the choice of investors concerned with maximizing their yields; but if they were willing to accept one-half percent less, they could have reduced the variance in returns by almost 99 percent by choosing a portfolio of Argentine governments. It might be noted,

Table 2:4-13. *Comparative mean-variance returns: by country and industry*

Country	All governments	All railroads	All "others"
	Panel A: 1870–1884		
Argentina:			
Average Weighted Return	0.0936	0.4416	0.0794
Variance	0.0254	1.9001	0.0164
Australia:			
Average Weighted Return	0.0588	0.1165	0.0676
Variance	0.0016	0.0479	0.0057
Canada:			
Average Weighted Return	0.0580	0.1057	0.0583
Variance	0.0012	0.2225	0.0060
United States:			
Average Weighted Return	0.0776	0.0376	0.0628
Variance	0.0100	0.1851	0.0044
	Panel B: 1885–1899		
Argentina:			
Average Weighted Return	0.1160	0.2070	0.0372
Variance	0.0470	2.0856	0.0468
Australia:			
Average Weighted Return	0.0424	0.0399	0.0270
Variance	0.0012	0.0273	0.0174
Canada:			
Average Weighted Return	0.0406	0.0534	0.0414
Variance	0.0014	0.0314	0.0049
United States:			
Average Weighted Return	0.0315	0.1224	0.0356
Variance	0.0013	0.1718	0.0421
	Panel C: 1900–1914		
Argentina:			
Average Weighted Return	0.0627	0.0671	0.0265
Variance	0.0047	0.3170	0.0299
Australia:			
Average Weighted Return	0.0215	0.0581	0.0250
Variance	0.0007	0.0336	0.0232
Canada:			
Average Weighted Return	0.0176	0.0357	0.0284
Variance	0.0008	0.0184	0.0455
United States:			
Average Weighted Return	0.0159	0.0632	0.0595
Variance	0.0002	1.4795	0.0747

Table 2:4-13. *(cont.)*

Country	All governments	All railroads	All "others"
	Panel D: 1870–1914		
Argentina:			
Average Weighted Return	0.0861	0.1165	0.0405
Variance	0.0234	0.8574	0.0330
Australia:			
Average Weighted Return	0.0339	0.0704	0.0332
Variance	0.0012	0.0370	0.0182
Canada:			
Average Weighted Return	0.0334	0.0508	0.0399
Variance	0.0013	0.0503	0.0203
United States:			
Average Weighted Return	0.0422	0.0836	0.0581
Variance	0.0048	0.7995	0.0356

however, that if, they had chosen a portfolio of American railroads, the yield would have declined by only 0.4 percent, but the variance would have *increased* four and one-half times.

Even in the first quinquennia, however, there is evidence that investors were making "rational" choices, and that over time their choices, although still not "perfect," were becoming more "rational." A regression of real returns on the variance of those returns produces a positive coefficient on the variance over each of the three subperiods, as well as over the entire forty-five year period, and further evidence indicates that the coefficients were significantly different from zero, and that the coefficients of determination increased over time from 0.31 to 0.41 (Table 2:4-14).

Investors were not blessed with perfect foresight, and market signals do not always capture the future perfectly. Two questions remain. First, does the *ex post* evidence indicate that British investors chose security over returns and as a result rationally selected foreign investments over available domestic alternatives? Second, given that savers channeled half of their savings overseas, how well did their investments in the four frontier countries compare with what they might have earned had they invested in a more diversified foreign and colonial portfolio? In other words, how do the earnings in the four frontier countries compare with those available at home and with the average returns on a diversified foreign and colonial portfolio?

Table 2:4-14. *Mean-variance regressions:*
observations are country-industry

Panel A: 1870–1884	
Coefficient on the variance	0.1544
Standard error of the coefficient	0.0298
Coefficient of determination	0.3053
Panel B: 1885–1899	
Coefficient on the variance	0.0689
Standard error of the coefficient	0.0130
Coefficient of determination	0.3145
Panel C: 1900–1914	
Coefficient on the variance	0.0287
Standard error of the coefficient	0.0044
Coefficient of determination	0.4134
Panel D: 1870–1914	
Coefficient on the variance	0.0394
Standard error of the coefficient	0.0057
Coefficient of determination	0.2092

Because of the way the samples were selected, all comparisons are subject to some criticism. Some benchmarks are required, and it appears useful to attempt to compare the four country indices with the measures that have become standard in the literature. Therefore, government yields are compared with returns on British Consols and with Edelstein's series of the return to domestic bonds, a sample that contains about one-third government bonds (Consols and municipals). The private sector issues from the four countries are compared with the DeLong-Grossman and the Edelstein estimates of domestic returns and with Edelstein's series on foreign and colonial returns. Keep in mind that the DeLong-Grossman series consists of very large firms that were also very long-term survivors and that the Edelstein sample consists of firms that were survivors. One would expect those returns to display somewhat higher average yields and, almost certainly, substantially less-variable returns than the more diversified Davis-Gallman series.

In the case of government issues, if the measure is the return on Consols, it is clear that investment in the four frontier countries was more remunerative, although overseas returns were more variable – and in the case of Argentina, substantially more variable. Over the years 1870–1914, returns in the four countries averaged 4.3 percent and, Argentina aside, there were only small intercountry differences: the range was from 3.3 to 4.2 percent. Over the same years the returns on Consols averaged 2.9 percent. Of the thirty-two country-quinquennia between 1870 and 1909, returns on government issues in the four frontier countries exceeded those available on Consols in thirty cases. The exceptions were U.S. issues in the first half of the 1890s and again in the years 1905–9.

Over the entire period, investments in governments in the four frontier countries returned about 30 percent more than investments in British Consols. The difference, however, narrowed over time; those returns were, on average, 2.1 times as great over the first three quinquennia, 1.6 times over the second, but only 1.03 times over the third. At the same time the variance of returns on government issues in the four frontier countries also declined, and over the last quinquennia returns on Australian, Canadian, and American issues were all below those available on long-term British government issues. For British savers willing to absorb some risk, the government issues of Australia, Canada and the United States were obviously attractive alternatives until 1909. Argentine issues were financially even more rewarding, but they were not for the faint of heart (Table 2:4-15).

If the benchmark is Edelstein's "Home Debentures" instead of Consols, overseas investment still appears fairly attractive. Returns were more variable than those available domestically – the ratios of the coefficients of variation of the "four frontier" countries to Edelstein's U.K. bonds are 2.5, 1.5, 1.5, and 2.3 for Argentina, Australia, Canada, and the United States, respectively – but they were also more remunerative. While over the entire period Edelstein's domestic bonds returned about 15 percent more than Consols, bonds from the four overseas countries yielded over 25 percent more than those very long-term securities. Moreover, although returns were lower in all four countries during the early 1890s and again in the last pre-war quinquennia, only the yields of American issues during 1905–9 fell below those available domestically for the remainder of the period. Taken together, the issues of the four overseas countries returned 1.7 times the yield available domestically over the first three quinquennia, 1.2 times during the second, and 1.1 times during the last fourteen years.

It should not come as a surprise that if the measure is real yields in the British private sector, there are major differences between Edelstein's "Total Home" index – an index that includes both stocks and bonds – and the DeLong-Grossman U.K. real equity series (Table

2:4-16). It is more surprising that even when the Edelstein series is decomposed into its equity and debt components, the DeLong-Grossman averages are about half again those of Edelstein's equity average. The difference is particularly marked over the first decade of the twentieth century. Between 1900 and 1909 DeLong and Grossman place average returns on equity at about 9 percent; the Edelstein average is less than 1.2 percent. In both series returns on average were in the 9–11 percent range in the years 1870–85 and in the 7.9–9 percent range over the next fifteen years. Turning from equity to bonds, Edelstein's series suggest returns of something over 4 percent in the nineteenth century and about half that level in the twentieth.

The variances of the three different series – Edelstein, DeLong-Grossman, and the Davis-Gallman industries – are very different. Over the entire period, the coefficient of variation of the DeLong-Grossman series is less than one-quarter that of the Edelstein series, while the coefficients on the eight Davis-Gallman series average more than six times that of Edelstein; the range is from 3.4 to 13.5. Nor is the difference a reflection of the financial crisis of the 1890s. The average was nine times as great over the first three quinquennia, and it was more than ten times greater in the years between 1900 and 1913 (Table 2:4-17). Thus, to the extent that Edelstein and DeLong-Grossman reflect the true picture of investment opportunities in the British economy, domestic investment was much safer than the four country alternatives.

In terms of average returns, a comparison of Edelstein's "Total Home" yields with the returns on "All Railroad" issues in the four frontier countries indicates that such overseas investment must have appeared very tempting to the British saver (Table 2:4-17). Over the forty-four years surveyed, Argentine railroads were 2.7 times, Australian 1.6 times, Canadian 1.2, and U.S. railroads about 1.9 times as lucrative as Edelstein's domestic alternatives. For the first fourteen years of the twentieth century, however, the figures were 3.7, 3.2, 2.2, and 3.2 respectively.

Since neither Edelstein nor DeLong and Grossman include any railroad issues in their indices, the most symmetrical comparisons are probably between those series and the yields on the issues of private firms in the Davis-Gallman "other" category. Here again, the results depend very heavily on the choice of baseline. If the choice is the Edelstein "Total Home" series – a mix, like the Davis-Gallman series, of stocks and bonds – the comparison with overseas enterprise is mixed. In Argentina over the entire period, returns were 1.15 times those available at home, and the figure for the United States is 1.33. Such investments in Australia and Canada were, however, relatively less rewarding. The ratios of foreign to domestic yield were 0.70 and 0.85 respectively.

Table 2:4-15. *Weighted real rates of return government bonds*

Years	Four frontier countries	Argentina	Australia	Canada	United States	British Consols	Edelstein's U.K. bonds
			Panel A: Average rates of return				
1870–1874	0.0805	0.0599	0.0493	0.0509	0.0842	0.0243	0.0397
1875–1879	0.0768	0.1303	0.0647	0.0724	0.0761	0.0508	0.0448
1880–1884	0.0663	0.0834	0.0587	0.0507	0.0687	0.0304	0.0436
1885–1889	0.0526	0.0756	0.0581	0.0606	0.0448	0.0353	0.0422
1890–1894	0.0313	0.0453	0.0377	0.0423	0.0133	0.0288	0.0475
1895–1899	0.0487	0.1978	0.0366	0.0243	0.0296	0.0215	0.0219
1900–1904	0.0229	0.1189	0.0162	0.0216	0.0167	0.0150	0.0162
1905–1909	0.0274	0.0616	0.0336	0.0305	0.0147	0.0239	0.0237
1910–1914	0.0125	0.0164	0.0148	0.0027	0.0014	0.0263	0.0186
1870–1884	0.0751	0.0936	0.0588	0.0580	0.0776	0.0351	0.0427
1885–1899	0.0450	0.1160	0.0424	0.0406	0.0315	0.0285	0.0372
1910–1914	0.0224	0.0628	0.0215	0.0176	0.0159	0.0217	0.0196
1870–1914	0.0432	0.0861	0.0339	0.0334	0.0422	0.0285	0.0335

Panel B: Variance of rates of return

1870–1884	0.0093	0.0254	0.0016	0.0012	0.0100	0.0006	0.0002
1885–1899	0.0068	0.0470	0.0012	0.0014	0.0013	0.0002	0.0009
1910–1914	0.0010	0.0047	0.0007	0.0008	0.0002	0.0002	0.0003
1870–1914	0.0054	0.0234	0.0012	0.0013	0.0048	0.0004	0.0006

Panel C: Standard deviations of real rates of return

1870–1884	0.0964	0.1594	0.0400	0.0346	0.1000	0.0254	0.0130
1885–1899	0.0825	0.2168	0.0346	0.0374	0.0361	0.0123	0.0295
1910–1914	0.0316	0.0686	0.0265	0.0283	0.0141	0.0154	0.0175
1870–1914	0.0735	0.1530	0.0346	0.0361	0.0693	0.0194	0.0237

Panel D: Coefficient of variation: real rates of return

1870–1884	1.2841	1.7027	0.6803	0.5973	1.2887	0.7238	0.3039
1885–1899	1.8325	1.8689	0.8170	0.9216	1.1446	0.4324	0.7931
1910–1914	1.4117	1.0917	1.2306	1.6071	0.8894	0.7066	0.8940
1870–1914	1.7010	1.7767	1.0219	1.0795	1.6418	0.6803	0.7068

Table 2:4-16. *Estimates of real yields, U.K. domestic: Edelstein and Grossman-DeLong*

| Years | Edelstein | | | | | Grossman-DeLong U.K. equities | Ratio Grossman-DeLong to Edelstein's Common | Ratio Grossman-DeLong to Edelstein's all equities |
	All issues	Bonds	Common	Equities preferred	All equities			
1870–1874	0.0735	0.0397	0.1234	0.0839	0.1213	0.1214	98	100
1875–1879	0.0665	0.0448	0.0961	0.0779	0.0951	0.0948	99	100
1880–1884	0.0507	0.0436	0.0602	0.0546	0.0599	0.1018	169	170
1885–1889	0.0662	0.0422	0.1062	0.0647	0.1037	0.0898	85	87
1890–1894	0.0508	0.0475	0.0558	0.0515	0.0553	0.0978	175	177
1895–1899	0.0426	0.0219	0.0815	0.0337	0.0776	0.0784	96	101
1900–1904	0.0099	0.0162	-0.0042	0.0171	-0.0023	0.0942	-2,222	-4,031
1905–1909	0.0204	0.0237	0.0091	0.0312	0.0117	0.0894	985	766
1910–1913	0.0362	0.0186	0.0669	0.0328	0.0627	0.0955	143	152
1870–1884	0.0636	0.0427	0.0932	0.0722	0.0921	0.1060	114	115
1885–1899	0.0532	0.0372	0.0812	0.0500	0.0789	0.0887	109	112
1900–1913	0.0212	0.0196	0.0208	0.0266	0.0212	0.0929	446	437
1870–1913	0.0465	0.0335	0.0661	0.0501	0.0650	0.0959	145	147

As one might surmise, the comparison with the DeLong-Grossman index is much much less favorable to investment in the overseas four. Although a part of the difference can probably be traced to the difference between yields on "all issues" and those on equities alone, still, a large part of the difference must rest in the "large size" and "super survivor" characteristics of the DeLong-Grossman sample firms. The ratios of the yields in the four frontier countries to the DeLong-Grossman index are 0.56, 0.34, 0.41, and 0.64 for Argentina, Australia, Canada, and the United States respectively.

In terms of other overseas competition, a comparison with Edelstein's figures suggests that investment in the four frontier countries was sometimes better, sometimes worse, than returns available in other parts of the globe (see Tables 2:4-18(a) and 2:4-18(b)). Returns in the four countries were, however, certainly much more variable. Over the forty-four year period, the coefficients of variation on all railroad investment was 16.0, and on "Other" securities 5.5 times the comparable Edelstein standards.[355] In the case of "Railroad" investment, over the entire period, returns in Argentina were more than twice as high as the all-overseas index, Australian returns were 27 percent greater, yields on U.S. rails were almost 50 percent higher than the global average, but those in Canada were just about equal to the global benchmark. Returns in the three quinquennia 1885–99 were badly depressed by the performance in the first half of the 1890s when the yields in Australia and Canada were negative. But even then, the Argentine and American performance meant that the four-country average was still twice the "Global" index. In the first fourteen years of the twentieth century, however, although there were year-to-year variations, returns on Argentine, Australian, and U.S. railroads were all significantly above the "All overseas" benchmark, and Canadian returns were slightly above.

Finally, real yields on "Other" issues in the United States were somewhat higher than those of firms included in Edelstein's "All issues" average, but those on Australian and Canadian enterprises were substantially lower and those of Argentine companies slightly lower: 0.56, 0.68, and 0.92 respectively. Although returns from firms in Edelstein's sample fell in the first half of the 1890s (to 3.8 percent), they were very much higher than those realized in any of the frontier countries except Canada. In that quinquennium yields were negative in the three countries: 11.8 percent in Argentina, 1.2 percent in the United States, and 1.4 percent in Australia. Relative returns in the four recovered somewhat in the years after 1905, although Australian and Canadian yields were negative between 1910 and 1913.

---

[355] The railroad and "other" comparisons were with Edelstein's "Total Overseas."

Table 2:4-17(a). *Private-sector comparisons, real yields: Edelstein's U.K., Grossman-DeLong U.K., Davis-Gallman four frontier*

Years	Edelstein's U.K.	DeLong-Grossman's U.K. Equity	Davis-Gallman							
			All railroads				Other issues			
			Argentina	Australia	Canada	United States	Argentina	Australia	Canada	United States
Panel A: Average Returns										
1870–1874	0.0735	0.1214	0.3250	0.0986	0.1063	0.0777	0.0660	0.0737	0.0554	0.0614
1875–1879	0.0672	0.0948	0.6315	0.1502	0.1529	0.1989	0.0857	0.0738	0.0724	0.0739
1880–1884	0.0507	0.1018	0.3510	0.0812	0.0691	-0.0708	0.0863	0.0631	0.0451	0.0307
1885–1889	0.0662	0.0898	0.2687	0.1275	0.0860	0.1137	0.0980	0.0558	0.0561	0.0318
1890–1894	0.0508	0.0978	0.1106	-0.0485	-0.0136	0.0356	-0.1183	-0.0139	0.0360	-0.0119
1895–1899	0.0426	0.0784	0.2646	0.0408	0.0923	0.2056	0.1304	0.0411	0.0265	0.0851
1900–1904	0.0099	0.0942	0.2171	0.0323	0.1072	0.1118	0.0534	0.0084	0.0140	0.0642
1905–1909	0.0204	0.0894	0.0520	0.1594	0.0426	0.1119	0.0996	0.0439	0.0555	0.2033
1910–1913	0.0362	0.0950	0.0062	-0.0171	-0.0062	-0.0188	-0.0262	0.0213	0.0259	-0.0046
1870–1884	0.0636	0.1060	0.4416	0.1165	0.1057	0.0376	0.0794	0.0676	0.0583	0.0628
1885–1899	0.0532	0.0887	0.2070	0.0399	0.0534	0.1224	0.0372	0.0270	0.0414	0.0356
1900–1913	0.0212	0.0929	0.0791	0.0681	0.0475	0.0680	0.0533	0.0232	0.0254	0.0702
1870–1913	0.0465	0.0959	0.1287	0.0740	0.0578	0.0864	0.0534	0.0326	0.0397	0.0617
Panel B: Variance of Average Returns										
1870–1884	0.0013	0.0002	1.9001	0.0479	0.2225	0.1851	0.0164	0.0057	0.0060	0.0044
1885–1899	0.0011	0.0001	2.0856	0.0273	0.0314	0.1718	0.0468	0.0174	0.0049	0.0421
1900–1913	0.0002	0.0001	0.3548	0.0357	0.0162	1.5767	0.0264	0.0241	0.0526	0.0815
1870–1913	0.0013	0.0003	0.9273	0.0378	0.0509	0.8233	0.0314	0.0185	0.0209	0.0362
Panel C: Coefficients of Variation: Average Returns										
1870–1884	0.5672	0.1334	3.1215	1.8786	4.4626	11.4424	1.6129	1.1168	1.3286	1.0562
1885–1899	0.6235	0.1128	6.9766	0.4141	3.3184	3.3863	5.8154	4.8855	1.6908	5.7636
1900–1913	0.6671	0.1076	7.5304	2.7745	2.6796	18.4657	3.0484	6.6915	9.0294	4.0667
1870–1913	0.7754	0.1806	7.4822	2.6273	3.9033	10.5018	3.3184	4.1722	3.6415	3.0837

Table 2:4-17(b). *Private-sector comparisons: ratio of De-Long-Grossman's U.K. and Davis-Gallman's four frontier to Edelstein's U.K. index*

| Years | Edelstein's U.K. | DeLong-Grossman's U.K. Equity | Davis-Gallman sample | | | | | | | |
| | | | All railroads | | | | Other issues | | | |
			Argentina	Australia	Canada	United States	Argentina	Australia	Canada	United States
				Panel A: Average Returns						
1870–1874	100	165	442	134	145	106	90	100	75	84
1875–1879	100	141	939	223	227	296	127	110	108	110
1880–1884	100	201	692	160	136	−140	170	124	89	61
1885–1889	100	136	406	193	130	172	148	84	85	48
1890–1894	100	193	218	−96	−27	70	−233	−27	71	−23
1895–1899	100	184	621	96	217	482	306	96	62	200
1900–1904	100	948	2,184	325	1,078	1,125	537	85	141	646
1905–1909	100	438	255	781	209	549	488	215	272	997
1910–1913	100	262	17	−47	−17	−52	−72	59	72	−13
1870–1884	100	167	695	183	166	59	125	106	92	99
1885–1899	100	167	389	75	100	230	70	51	78	67
1900–1913	100	438	373	321	224	321	251	109	120	331
1870–1913	100	206	277	159	124	186	115	70	85	133
				Panel B: Variance of Average Returns						
1870–1884	100	15	146,162	3,685	17,115	14,238	1,262	438	462	338
1885–1899	100	9	189,600	2,482	2,855	15,618	4,255	1,582	445	3,827
1900–1913	100	50	177,400	17,850	8,100	788,350	13,200	12,050	26,300	40,750
1870–1913	100	23	71,331	2,908	3,915	63,331	2,415	1,423	1,608	2,785
				Panel C: Coefficients of Variation: Average Returns						
1870–1884	100	24	550	331	787	2,017	284	197	234	186
1885–1899	100	18	1,119	66	532	543	933	784	271	924
1900–1914	100	16	1,129	416	402	2,768	457	1,003	1,354	610
1870–1913	100	23	965	339	503	1,354	428	538	470	398

229

Table 2:4-18(a). *Private-sector comparison, real yields: Edelstein's overseas and Davis-Gallman's four frontier*

| | | Davis-Gallman | | | | | | | |
| | | Railroads | | | | Other issues | | | |
Years	Edelstein's overseas	Argentina	Australia	Canada	United States	Argentina	Australia	Canada	United States
					Panel A: Average Returns				
1870–1874	0.0724	0.3250	0.0986	0.1063	0.0777	0.0660	0.0737	0.0554	0.0614
1875–1879	0.0872	0.6315	0.1502	0.1529	0.1989	0.0857	0.0738	0.0724	0.0739
1880–1884	0.0610	0.3510	0.0812	0.0691	-0.0708	0.0863	0.0631	0.0451	0.0307
1885–1889	0.0697	0.2687	0.1275	0.0860	0.1137	0.0980	0.0558	0.0561	0.0318
1890–1894	0.0381	0.1106	-0.0485	-0.0136	0.0356	-0.1183	-0.0139	0.0360	-0.0119
1895–1899	0.0641	0.2646	0.0408	0.0923	0.2056	0.1304	0.0411	0.0265	0.0851
1900–1904	0.0635	0.2171	0.0323	0.1072	0.1118	0.0534	0.0084	0.0140	0.0642
1905–1909	0.0531	0.0520	0.1594	0.0426	0.1119	0.0996	0.0439	0.0555	0.2033
1910–1914	0.0180	0.0062	-0.0171	-0.0062	-0.0188	-0.0262	0.0213	0.0259	-0.0046
1870–1884	0.0743	0.4416	0.1165	0.1057	0.0376	0.0794	0.0676	0.0583	0.0628
1885–1899	0.0573	0.2070	0.0399	0.0534	0.1224	0.0372	0.0270	0.0414	0.0356
1900–1914	0.0425	0.0671	0.0581	0.0357	0.0632	0.0265	0.0250	0.0284	0.0595
1870–1914	0.0581	0.1165	0.0704	0.0508	0.0836	0.0405	0.0332	0.0399	0.0581
				Panel B: Variance of Average Returns					
1870–1884	0.0018	1.9001	0.0479	0.2225	0.1851	0.0164	0.0057	0.0060	0.0044
1885–1899	0.0007	2.0856	0.0273	0.0314	0.1718	0.0468	0.0174	0.0049	0.0421
1900–1914	0.0008	0.3170	0.0336	0.0184	1.4796	0.0264	0.0241	0.0526	0.0815
1870–1914	0.0013	0.8574	0.0370	0.0503	0.7995	0.0314	0.0185	0.0209	0.0362
			Panel C: Coefficients of Variation: Average Returns						
1870–1884	0.5741	3.1215	1.8786	4.4626	11.4424	1.6129	1.1168	1.3286	1.0562
1885–1899	0.4618	6.9766	0.4141	3.3184	3.3863	5.8154	4.8855	1.6908	5.7636
1900–1913	0.6612	8.3909	3.1550	3.7996	19.2466	6.1313	6.2097	8.0756	4.7980
1870–1914	0.6129	7.9481	2.7323	4.4149	10.6955	4.3753	4.0968	3.6233	3.2748

230

Table 2:4-18(b). *Private-sector comparison, real yields: ratio of Davis-Gallman's four frontier to Edelstein's overseas index and Davis-Gallman's four frontier index*

Years	Edelstein's overseas	Davis-Gallman							
		Railroads				Other issues			
		Argentina	Australia	Canada	United States	Argentina	Australia	Canada	United States
					Panel A: Average Returns				
1870–1874	100	449	136	147	107	91	102	76	85
1875–1879	100	724	172	175	228	98	85	83	85
1880–1884	100	575	133	113	−116	141	103	74	50
1885–1889	100	386	183	123	163	141	80	80	46
1890–1894	100	290	−127	−36	93	−310	−36	94	−31
1895–1899	100	413	64	144	321	203	64	41	133
1900–1904	100	342	51	169	176	84	13	22	101
1905–1909	100	98	300	80	211	188	83	105	383
1910–1914	100	34	−95	−34	−104	−145	118	144	−26
1870–1884	100	594	157	142	51	107	91	78	84
1885–1899	100	361	70	93	214	65	47	72	62
1900–1914	100	158	137	84	149	62	59	67	140
1870–1914	100	200	121	87	144	70	57	69	100
					Panel B: Variance of Average Returns				
1870–1884	100	104,370	2,631	12,222	10,167	901	313	330	242
1885–1899	100	297,737	3,897	4,483	24,526	6,681	2,484	700	6,010
1900–1914	100	40,120	4,252	2,329	187,262	3,341	3,050	6,657	10,315
1870–1914	100	67,517	2,914	3,961	62,958	2,473	1,457	1,646	2,851
					Panel C: Coefficients of Variation: Average Returns				
1870–1884	100	544	327	777	1,993	281	195	231	184
1885–1899	100	1,511	90	719	733	1,259	1,058	366	1,248
1900–1913	100	1,269	477	575	2,911	927	939	1,221	726
1870–1913	100	1,297	446	720	1,745	714	668	591	534

Table 2:4-19. *Rate of Return Regressions (Real yields are the dependent variable; years are the independent variable)*

	Panel A: Coefficients of determination (r2's)			
	All public & private issues	All government issues	All transport issues	All "other" issues
All four countries	0.000007	0.250851	0.023081	0.000007
Argentina	0.023943	0.006964	0.029950	0.026600
Australia	0.137201	0.187235	0.000775	0.121649
Canada	0.017357	0.234286	0.006126	0.012718
United States	0.010922	0.186467	0.021337	0.016018

	Panel B: X Coefficient			
	All public & private issues	All government issues	All transport issues	All "other" issues
All four countries	−0.000024	−0.001180	−0.001300	−0.000024
Argentina	−0.001460	−0.001130	−0.001740	−0.002700
Australia	−0.001280	−0.000870	0.000308	−0.003260
Canada	−0.000860	−0.001190	−0.001050	−0.001760
United States	−0.000680	−0.001220	−0.001320	0.001526

The overseas figures appear to conform largely to expectations. The survivor characteristics of the Edelstein averages almost certainly account for the reduced variance. Moreover, overall returns – averages that include government issues – in the frontier four were similar to the global overseas averages; however, returns on railroads were 45 percent above the Edelstein baseline, and on "other" investments, 13 percent below. That latter conclusion rests heavily on the Argentine returns. Yields from Australian and U.S. railways are higher, but Canadian yields were very slightly lower. If government bonds are included, the "frontier four" returned about 7 percent more than Edelstein's average (6.2 versus 5.8 percent). Given these comparisons, the question remains: If the Edelstein and DeLong-Grossman indices capture domestic alternatives, why did savers in the United Kingdom direct such a large fraction of their savings overseas? Clearly, *ex-post*, there is little evidence that the flow of savings overseas reflected the British savers' search for "safe, well known securities" "of a type that fiscally frugal, heavily industrialized Britain could no longer provide." In fact, although the returns on all issues appear on average to have been about one-third higher than Edelstein's domestic estimates (railroads were more than 80 percent above the domestic benchmark, and "other" issues just less than 10 percent, but governments were about 7 percent below), they were certainly more variable. Moreover, if the comparison is with the DeLong-Grossman sample, overseas investments were not only subject to more variation, but they also produced substantially lower returns.

The answer most likely has two components. The DeLong-Grossman firms were *ex ante* long and *ex post* "super survivors," and the Edelstein firms were *ex post* survivors. Thus, neither sample reflects the range of actual *ex ante* domestic investment alternatives. Although still perhaps somewhat inflated – surviving firms tend to have done better than those that failed to survive – the Edelstein series almost certainly better reflects the level of average available domestic returns than those in the DeLong-Grossman study. Investment decisions are, however, made on the margin. If the flow of overseas finance had been redirected back to the British domestic economy, marginal returns would almost certainly have declined dramatically. Thus, as large investors explored the investment margins, they may well have made very rational calculations when they chose overseas alternatives. Whatever the explanation, one conclusion appears inescapable. Savers were not searching for "safe, well known securities of a type that fiscally frugal, heavily industrialized Britain could no longer provide." They appear to have been, at least *ex ante*, quite prepared to assume a substantial level of risk or uncertainty, a conclusion that finds particular support in their experience with investment in Australia in the 1880s and early 1890s.

CHAPTER 3

International capital movements, domestic capital markets, and American economic growth, 1865–1914

3-1. Introduction

Of the four frontier countries, the United States depended least on foreign capital. Although as late as the mid-1890s the annual net change in claims on foreigners was typically negative – on balance, foreigners were lending to the United States or acquiring American assets – the story had begun to change; the country was gradually becoming a creditor nation (Table 3:1-1). From 1897 until 1905 the United States, on net, exported capital in every year, and capital exports over the nine years totaled more than $1.5 billion. Over the years 1906 through 1913, however, the country briefly returned to its heretofore traditional role of capital importer. By the standard of these measures, the United States was a very modest net importer of capital in 1906, 1907, and 1909–1913, the inflows in all of these years but one amounting to less than 2 percent of domestic capital formation. Furthermore, even in the years before the mid-1890s, when Americans were frequently experiencing numerically large net capital imports, total foreign holdings of American assets and debts were probably never as large as 10 percent of the American domestic capital stock (Table 3:1-2). Compared with the cases of Australia, Argentina, and Canada, American development was largely a result of internal finance.

Nonetheless, it would be a major mistake to treat the American experience as though it had little relationship to the international capital flows of the nineteenth and early twentieth centuries. There are several reasons for such skepticism. First, the American economy was very large – roughly six times as large as the economies of the other three taken together – and it grew rapidly. Consequently, even though foreign capital represented a small fraction of total U.S. domestic investment, the United States was the object of a very large fraction of total international investment. The American economy, then, was important to foreign investors, particularly to the British.

234

Table 3:1-1. *Change in net foreign investment in the United States as a percentage of U.S. gross capital formation, 1869–1914**

Panel A: annual data			
1869	12.4	1892	1.1
1870	7.0	1893	4.6
1871	7.6	1894	−2.5
1872	12.5	1895	5.1
1873	8.9	1896	1.7
1874	5.7	1897	−0.9
1875	6.4	1898	−10.9
1876	0.2	1899	−7.7
1877	−4.6	1900	−6.1
1878	−12.7	1901	−6.5
1879	−11.9	1902	−3.2
1880	1.6	1903	−0.5
1881	−1.8	1904	−0.2
1882	4.7	1905	−1.8
1883	2.3	1906	1.2
1884	5.0	1907	1.1
1885	1.8	1908	−0.9
1886	5.7	1909	1.0
1887	8.8	1910	4.3
1888	11.5	1911	0.9
1889	8.1	1912	0.4
1890	5.9	1913	1.4
1891	4.5	1914	−1.5

Panel B: quinquennial data			
Yearly weights		Dollar weights	
1869–1874	9.0	1869–1874	9.2
1875–1879	−4.5	1875–1879	−4.4
1880–1884	2.4	1880–1884	2.4
1885–1889	7.2	1885–1889	7.5
1890–1894	2.7	1890–1894	2.8
1895–1899	−2.5	1895–1899	−2.2
1900–1904	−3.3	1900–1904	−1.1
1905–1909	0.1	1905–1909	−1.5
1910–1914	1.1	1910–1914	−0.4

Note: * (−) Means American investments abroad exceeded foreign investments in the United States.

Sources: American Net Foreign Investment: U.S. Bureau of the Census, *Historical Statistics of the United States, Colonial Times to 1900*, Bicentennial Edition, Part I (Washington, D.C., 1975), Series U18-23.

Gross National Capital Formation, 1869–1909: Data Underlying Gallman, "Gross National Product."

Gross National Capital Formation, 1910–1914: The Gallman Series Extrapolated on Kuznets, Capital in the American Economy, Gross Capital Formation, p. 588.

Table 3:1-2. *Comparative international financial status of the U.S.,*
1840–1912

| | U.S. Net International Assets, Compared with: | | | U.S. Net International Position, Compared with: Domestic Capital Stock |
| | Domestic Capital Stock | | Railroad Capital Stock (inc. land) | |
Year	Variant A	Variant B		Variant A
1840	4.8	6.7	260.5	7.0
1850	1.0	1.4	33.2	3.7
1860	0.9	1.3	15.3	3.2
1870	5.6	7.1	57.5	7.0
1880	4.7	5.4	41.3	6.7
1890	4.3	5.0	38.4	7.4
1900	1.6	1.8	15.5	4.9
1912	−0.4	n.d.	n.d.	2.2

Notes: (1) "Net international assets" include equities, debt instruments, foreign bank balances, foreign currency, and monetary metals; "Net International Position" comprises all of the above except for monetary metals.
   (2) A minus value means that U.S. citizens' and governments' claims on foreign assets exceed foreign claims on U.S. assets.
   (3) Variant A domestic capital stock includes the value of improvements to farm land (clearing, breaking, fencing); Variant B does not.

Source: Data underlying Table 4.A.1, p. 204 (current prices) in Robert E. Gallman, "The United States Capital Stock in the Nineteenth Century," in Stanley L. Engerman and Robert E. Gallman (eds.), *Long-Term Factors in American Economic Growth Studies in Income and Wealth, Volume 51* (Chicago: University of Chicago Press).

Second, American growth was not smooth and continuous; growth and structural change were faster in some periods than in others.[356] During the years of most rapid growth, even a country marked by a high savings rate could face an investment constraint if foreign capital did not relieve the pressure. In the American case, it is clear that foreign investment permitted the extension of some boom periods and therefore helped determine the pattern of economic growth. The very large capital flows of the mid-1830s and the persistent inflows from 1849 through 1856 and 1882

---

[356] Moses Abramovitz, *Thinking About Growth* (Cambridge: Cambridge University Press, 1989), chap. 8. [Hereafter cited as Abramovitz, *Thinking about Growth*.]

to 1893 are associated with extended boom periods. Moreover, foreign capital at times almost certainly prevented what otherwise might have been an economic slowdown. In the late 1870s, for example, the federal government was faced with the task of refinancing $1.5 billion in Civil War debt, much of it foreign-held. If the government had been forced to rely on domestic savings, interest rates would have risen, and economic growth would almost certainly have been curtailed. Instead, the debt was refinanced in Europe, largely in Britain. In the long run, the debt repayment was made slowly in a manner that did not suddenly constrain growth.

Third, it is clear that although foreign investors had very catholic tastes as far as American opportunities were concerned, a very large fraction of their American investments went into railroads (see Section 3-4a). Foreign investment in the United States may have been small compared with the aggregate domestic capital stock, but it was not small compared with the requirements of the railroads (see Table 3:1-2).[357]

Finally, Americans in some respects were less sophisticated investors than were the British. Uncertainty discounts were high, and the Americans had to be given stronger assurances about quality than were required by their British counterparts. For example, the New York Stock Exchange established rules for the listing of securities – rules intended to convey to potential buyers that the listed securities were of high quality. Such strict rules were not required in the London capital markets, and American securities that could not be placed on the New York market could often be sold in London. Foreign capital was important in these cases, not because it was massive, but because it filled gaps in the American capital markets – particularly gaps in developing regions, the Midwest and the West, and to a somewhat lesser extent the South, and in industries where new technologies made mass production possible – brewing, milling, and meat packing – and where firms and industries did not have the requisite financial histories to meet the NYSE's listing requirements or to gain the imprimatur of one of the recognized investment banks. In summary, as Goldsmith concluded,

> If the United States had been limited to domestic savings, the growth of wealth would certainly have been slower until nearly the end of the nineteenth century ... because those imports were concentrated in critical areas of growth, and particularly because without them the

---

[357] On this topic, see Raymond W. Goldsmith, "The Growth of Reproducible Wealth of the United States of America," in Simon Kuznets (ed.), *Income and Wealth of the United States: Trends and Structure* (Cambridge: Bowes and Bowes, 1953), pp. 284–86. [Hereafter cited as Goldsmith, "Reproducible Wealth."]

development of the American railway system, probably the main economic achievement of the second half of the nineteenth century, would have been slowed down considerably.[358]

Foreign capital was important to American economic growth. Nonetheless, most of the savings that financed American growth came from domestic sources. To meet the enormous capital requirements efficiently, Americans were obliged to mobilize their substantial domestic savings; to that end they had to build an elaborate system of financial intermediation, a system that depended importantly on the creation and diffusion of new institutions. The American story, then, is one concerned with the interrelationships between foreign sources of finance and domestic institutional innovation.

3-2. The pattern of U.S. economic growth before World War I

Argentine, Australian, and Canadian national product series currently extend back only to the 1860s or 1870s. Reasonably robust U.S. estimates, however, begin as early as 1800. It is therefore possible to put the American experience in the years with which this book is chiefly concerned – 1870 to 1914 – into a longer term historical perspective, while keeping the argument grounded in aggregative, quantitative evidence.

For the full span of years between 1800 and 1910, the average annual U.S. rates of growth of real GNP and real GNP per capita were typical of modern economic growth: for real GNP, almost 4 percent; for real GNP per capita, about 1.3 percent. These are levels achieved by many developing countries in the nineteenth century, but not often for so long a period. This eleven-decade span was a time of rapid population growth for the United States – growth fed by high fertility and low mortality rates and, after the mid-1830s, by substantial immigration. Over the same period the physical territory of the United States more than quadrupled, and the center of gravity of the population moved steadily westward.

The pace of change was not steady. The rate of growth of population rose between 1840 and 1860, as the first great post-Revolutionary wave of immigration broke on American shores. Thereafter, however, the impact of continued pronounced immigration on the rate of population increase was offset by an accelerating decline in fertility and little, if any, improvement in mortality. In fact, mortality seems to have risen in the middle decades and to have begun its long-term decline only late in the century. Overall, population growth fell steadily from about

[358] Goldsmith, "Reproducible Wealth," p. 285.

3.1 percent per year between 1840 and 1860 to 1.9 percent between 1890 and 1910.

The rate of change of GNP, on the other hand, showed no pronounced tendency to decline. It increased quite dramatically between 1840 and 1860, although it fell during the 1860s – a decline that can be attributed to that most destructive of American wars, the Civil War – it then rose again after Appomattox.

The downward trend in the population growth rate after 1860, and the relatively level trend of real GNP, resulted in a long-term tendency for the rate of increase of real GNP per capita to rise. In the first forty years of the century, it was, on average, less than 1 percent per year. Despite the effects of the Civil War (per capita real GNP increased by less than one-half percent per year between 1860 and 1870), over the last six decades the average rose to over 1.6 percent. Focusing on the period with which this book is chiefly concerned, the average annual rate of growth across the years 1870 to 1910 was over 1.8 percent per year, a very high rate for such an extended period.

Growth proceeded in a series of decade-long surges followed by periods of slower growth. The upward surges reflect major increases to the labor force (from immigration) and to the land and capital stocks.[359] The investment components of these fluctuations were linked closely with the extension of the transportation network and with housing construction in old eastern cities and the building of new cities to the west. Although exports were never a large fraction of U.S. output, foreign demand for agricultural products played a surprisingly important role in shaping these periods of rapid expansion. Before the Civil War, cotton exports dominated American foreign trade; in the postwar years, with the opening of the Great Plains and with the development of refrigeration, the focus of agricultural exports shifted to meats and, more particularly, grains.

Agriculture had a major role to play in the story of American economic development. It contributed an important part of total U.S. output, and until World War I it absorbed a large share of U.S. labor. At the same time the structure of the economy was shifting; the country was industrializing (see Tables 3:2-1–3:2-2). By the outbreak of the war, United States GNP exceeded the sum of the GNP of three of the chief belligerents – Britain, France, and Germany – and American industry was the most productive in the world.

The modernization and expansion of the industrial sector appears to have gone forward in three major stages. The first – roughly 1820 to 1850

---

[359] Abramovitz, *Thinking About Growth*, chap. 8.

Table 3:2-1. *Sectoral distribution of value-added, labor force, and capital stock, U.S., 1800–1900*

Panel A: Value-added

	1800	1810	1820	1830	1840	1850	1860	1870	1880	1890	1900
Agriculture					41%	35%	35%	33%	28%	19%	18%
Mining, manufacturing, & hand trades					17	22	22	24	25	30	31
Transportation & public utilities					7	4	6	6	8	9	9
Commercial & all other private business					23	26	26	26	29	32	32
Government & education					2	2	2	2	2	3	3
Shelter					10	11	9	9	8	7	7
Total					100	100	100	100	100	100	100

Panel B: Labor force

	1800	1810	1820	1830	1840	1850	1860	1870	1880	1890	1900
Agriculture	74%	72%	71%	70%	67	60	56	50	50	42	39
Mining, manufacturing, & hand trades					12	17	19	25	25	27	28
Transportation & public utilities					2	2	3	4	4	7	7
Commercial & all other private business	26	28	29	30	18	19	20	19	19	21	23
Government & education					2	2	2	2	2	3	3
Total	100	100	100	100	101	100	100	100	100	100	100

Panel C: Capital stock

Agriculture	70	64	58	54	46	35	33
Mining, manufacturing, & hand trades	4	5	5	8	8	10	12
Transportation & public utilities	9	10	12	14	15	15	17
Commercial & all other private business	4	5	6	6	7	10	10
Government & education	1	2	1	1	2	2	2
Nonfarm residences	11	14	18	17	21	28	27
Total	100	100	100	100	100	100	100

Notes: (1) Columns may not sum due to rounding.
(2) Sectors are not fully comparable among panels.
(3) The years are census years. For labor and capital they refer roughly to June 1 of the year cited; for value added, they refer to the census year May 31–June 1, before the Civil War. After the War, they refer chiefly to the calandar years 1869, 1879, 1889, and 1899.

Sources: Panel A: Gallman, "The United States Capital Stock in the Nineteenth Century." Panel B: Derrived from Robert E. Gallman and Thomas J. Weiss, "The Service Industries in the Nineteenth Century," in Victor F. Fuchs (ed.), *Production and Productivity in the Service Industries, Studies in Income and Wealth,* Volume 34 (New York: National Bureau of Economic Research, 1969), pp. 299 & 303; Thomas Weiss, "U.S. Labor Force Estimates and Economic Growth, 1800–1860," in Robert E. Gallman and John J. Wallis, *American Economic Growth and Standards of Living Before the Civil War* (Chicago: University of Chicago Press, 1992), pp. 37 & 51; U.S. Bureau of the Census, *Historical Statistics of the United States, Colonial Times to 1970,* Series D 170–174, 1870–1900. Panel C: Computed from data underlying Gallman, "The United States Capital Stock."

Table 3:2-2. *Composition of the U.S. capital stock, 1774–1900*

		Panel A: Current Prices			
Year	Structures	Equipment	Inventories	Animals	Land clearing
1774	24%	8%	14%	15%	40%
1779	21	9	23	11	36
1795	26	11	24	12	28
1815	33	10	21	17	19
1840	33	10	18	12	28
1850	35	10	20	10	25
1860	42	9	17	9	22
1870	44	9	20	9	17
1880	47	10	21	8	14
1890	55	11	17	7	10
1900	55	13	18	6	8
		Panel B: 1860 Prices			
1774	17%	4%	12%	11%	56%
1779	19	5	20	13	44
1795	25	5	20	12	39
1815	27	5	19	14	36
1840	29	6	17	15	32
1850	33	7	19	12	28
1860	42	9	17	9	22
1870	44	11	18	8	19
1880	41	13	21	7	17
1890	44	22	19	5	11
1900	42	28	18	4	8

Source: Robert E. Gallman, "American Economic Growth Before the Civil War: The Testimony of Capital Stock," in Gallman & Wallis (eds.), *American Economic Growth*, p. 94.

– involved an increase in scale, labor specialization, and improved productivity but (with a few notable exceptions, such as the textile industries) little important use of machinery.[360] During the second period,

[360] See Kenneth Sokoloff, "Invention, Innovation and Manufacturing Productivity Growth in the Antebellum Northeast," in Robert Gallman and John Wallis (eds.), *American Economic Growth, and the Standards of Living Before the Civil War*, National Bureau of Economic Research Conference Report (Chicago: University of Chicago Press, 1992), pp. 345–78, and cited sources.

beginning in the 1850s, machinery was widely introduced into the industrial sector, and the supply of capital per industrial worker increased markedly. These developments can be seen very clearly in the changing structure of the capital stock. The modern sectors began to acquire consistently larger shares of capital (Table 3:2-1, Panel C). Even more striking is the dramatic increase in the fraction of the capital stock accounted for by equipment and structures (Table 3:2-2, Panel B), a relative substitution that continued at least until the end of the century.

Finally, the third stage encompasses the period from the 1880s to World War I. It was characterized by further industrial mechanization and by the achievement of substantial and widespread economies of scale. It was capped by a major industrial merger movement in the last decade of the nineteenth century and the beginning of the twentieth. The degree of market concentration realized in these few years has never again been reached – a result that at least in part, is attributable to changes in the legal environment.

3-3. **Savings-investment aggregates**

3-3a. Domestic savings and investment

From the beginning of the century, but particularly between 1840 and 1890, the capital stock increased faster than either labor or land and even faster than aggregate output.[361] The aggregate capital/output ratio rose rapidly. It had been relatively low early in the century, but by 1900 it stood at a level typical of modern experience – between three and four.

The expansion of the industrial sector did not, however, contribute directly to the deepening of capital. The capital/output ratio of that sector was low compared with the ratios in agriculture and the service sectors. Consequently, the rise of industry and the relative decline in agriculture actually tended to reduce the aggregate capital/output ratio. The forces that underlay the rise were intrasectoral in nature. The ratios in all three major sectors – agriculture, industry, and services – increased over time, but the factor that bore the principal weight was rooted in a change in the composition of the service sector. Two components of the services sector, both with very high capital/output ratios – transportation and

---

[361] The following analysis of savings, investment, and capital deepening depends importantly on Lance E. Davis and Robert E. Gallman, "Capital Formation in the United States During the Nineteenth Century," in Peter Mathias and M.M. Postan (eds.), *The Cambridge Economic History of Europe*, Vol. VII, Part 2 (Cambridge: Cambridge University Press, 1978), pp. 1–69. [Hereafter cited as Davis and Gallman, "Capital Formation."]

non-farm housing – increased in relative importance (Table 3:2-2), and taken together, drove the ratio for the sector, and thus for the economy as a whole, upward. The growth of these two parts of the service sector was closely related to the process of industrialization. The expansion of the market that made it possible to take advantage of scale economies depended on the development of the transport network, and without housing there would have been few workers to man the expanding factories. Thus indirectly, if not directly, capital deepening was influenced by the process of industrialization. Since the prices of capital goods – especially machinery and other equipment – fell relative to the GNP price index, capital deepening was particularly pronounced if output and capital are both measured in constant prices. That is, as capital goods prices declined relative to all prices, more capital could be acquired with a fixed proportion of nominal GNP.

There are at least two possible ways to explain U.S. capital deepening. One stresses biased innovation – specifically, labor-saving and capital-using innovation. Although at first blush this is an attractive explanation, it does not fit well with the main facts of the historical experience: Capital deepening was closely associated with the rise of the railroads and of non-farm housing. Certainly housing did not involve a labor saving-capital using innovation, nor is it clear that railroads did. Canals and road construction was at least as capital intensive. Even if railroad building did involve an increase in the capital/labor ratio, the innovation came long before America experienced substantial capital deepening. Alternatively, capital deepening could have been the result of the cheapening of capital – a decline in the relative price of capital, coupled with a fall in the real rate of interest. The economywide trend – a trend toward capital deepening shared by all major sectors and their components – certainly suggests that such general forces – forces operating on all elements of the economy – were at work.[362]

The explanation for the long-run decline in interest rates becomes, then, an important question. At one level, the answer is obvious: The American savings rate rose. Depending on how one measures it, it doubled or tripled, achieving ultimately, at the end of the century, a level in excess of 25 percent of GNP. Furthermore, American investors had access to international capital markets, and while the real rate was falling, American rates of return remained higher than those available on similar investments in Europe.

The cause of the rise in the savings rate has been widely discussed in the literature. Frank Lewis has shown that shifts in the age structure of

---

[362] See Robert Gallman, "The Capital Stock," manuscript.

the population and of the dependency rate were important. Jeffrey Williamson concludes that the refinance and repayment of the public debt after the Civil War shifted resources from the public to the private sector, and that shift appears in the national accounts as a rise in the savings rate. If Williamson is correct, it is not clear why the rate remained high through the rest of the century. Michael Edelstein, while granting the long-term decline of the real interest rate, argues that a short-term upward movement in the late 1860s helped to encourage increased savings. Finally, a particularly compelling case can be made for the importance of the development of an American network of financial intermediaries. These intermediaries effectively reduced the risks for investors, raised net returns to savers, lowered costs to borrowers, and enhanced the volume of savings.[363] All of these explanations almost certainly contain elements of the truth. Given the context of this book, the last is of particular interest.

3-3b. Foreign investment

3-3b(1). The temporal pattern of net foreign flows: There have been three major quantitative studies of the history of the American balance of payments. Although both their focus and their conclusions are somewhat different, their reports on the timing and magnitude of net capital imports are similar.[364] Inflows into the United States had been

---

[363] For a discussion of these issues, see the appendix to Chapter 1 and Lance E. Davis and Robert E. Gallman, "Savings, Investment and Economic Growth: The United States in the Nineteenth Century," in John James and Mark Thomas (eds.), *Capitalism in Context; Essays in Economic Development and Cultural Change* (Chicago: University of Chicago Press, 1995), pp. 202–29.

[364] Chronologically, the first was C.J. Bullock, John H. Williams, and Rufus S. Tucker, "The Balance of Trade of the United States," *The Review of Economic Statistics* (July 1919), pp. 215–54 [Hereafter cited as Bullock et al., "Balance of Trade"]; the second was Douglass C. North, "The Balance of Payments of the United States, 1790–1860," in William B. Parker (ed.), *Trends in the American Economy in the Nineteenth Century*, Vol. 24, Conference on Income and Wealth, National Bureau of Economic Research (Princeton: Princeton University Press, 1960), pp. 573–628 [Hereafter cited as North, "Balance of Payments"] and Matthew Simon, "The Balance of Payments of the United States, 1861–1900," in William B. Parker (ed.), *Trends in the American Economy in the Nineteenth Century*, Vol. 24, Conference of Income and Wealth, National Bureau of Economic Research (Princeton: Princeton University Press, 1960), pp. 629–711 [Hereafter cited as Simon, "Balance of Payments"]; and the last was Jeffrey G. Williamson, *American Growth and the Balance of Payments: A Study of the Long Saving* (Chapel Hill: University of North Carolina Press, 1962) [Hereafter cited as Williamson, *American Growth*].

particularly heavy in the 1830s. Between 1832 and 1839, as states competed to expand their banking and transport sectors, capital imports amounted to almost $12 for every man, woman, and child in the country. At the end of the decade, however, financial panic and economic depression made it difficult for the borrowing states to meet their financial obligations. The resulting default led in turn to an almost complete halt to foreign lending.[365] Thus, over the decade of the 1840s, capital exports exceeded imports by some $75 million.

The respite was short-lived. By 1850 capital again began to flow into the country, but it was the decade and a half between 1861 and 1875 that saw capital imports reach levels that were unprecedented even during the heady 1830s. Total net capital flows fell just short of $1.5 billion. They were positive in fourteen of the fifteen years (there was no discernible flow in either direction in 1862), and over the decade and a half they amounted to more than $40 per capita (Table 3:3b-1). Between 1861 and 1870 the federal government borrowed $2.4 billion – the Civil War was not cheap in either monetary or human terms – and state and local indebtedness rose by $500 million. In 1869 total American debt held abroad is estimated to have been between $1.2 and $1.5 billion, and the next six years added $780 million to that total.[366]

During the five years 1877–81, the pattern was reversed. In four of those years there was an outflow of capital as Europe experienced a delayed response to the fears engendered by the Panic of 1873. Probably $300 million in foreign-held securities were repatriated between 1876 and 1878, and by 1881 the nation's net foreign liabilities had been reduced by $390 million.[367] The respite was again short-lived. In fourteen of the next fifteen years (1882–96), foreign capital again flowed into the country. Net imports totaled more than $1.7 billion – a figure that exceeds the 1861–75 total by almost one-quarter of a billion dollars. Although there was a preponderance of railway securities, substantial quantities of foreign funds also were directed into Western mining, agriculture, and land development as well as into the emerging

---

[365] By 1842 it is estimated that $174 million in American debt held in England was either in default or had been repudiated. Williamson, *American Growth*, p. 106. For a detailed analysis of the political economy of the state debt crisis of the 1840s, see Richard Sylla and John Wallis, "The Anatomy of Sovereign Debt Crises: Lessons from the American State Defaults of the 1840s," manuscript, draft of July 1996.

[366] The $1.2 estimate is from Simon, "Balance of Payments," p. 706; the $1.5 figure is from Cleona Lewis assisted by Karl T. Shottenbeck, *America's Stake in International Investment* (Washington, D.C.: Brookings Institution, 1938), pp. 551–52. [Hereafter cited as Lewis, *America's Stake*.]

[367] Bullock et al., "Balance of Trade," p. 225.

Table 3:3b-1. *Net international capital movements: capital inflow into the United States minus capital outflow from the United States (millions of dollars)*

Year	Net capital inflow (nominal $'S)	Net capital inflow (real $'S)	Year	Net capital inflow (nominal $'S)	Net capital inflow (real $'S)
1864	111	58	1890	194	237
1865	59	32	1891	136	166
1866	95	55	1892	41	54
1867	145	90	1893	146	187
1868	73	46	1894	−66	−94
1869	176	117	1895	137	193
1870	100	74	1896	40	59
1871	101	78	1897	−23	−34
1872	242	178	1898	−279	−393
1873	167	126	1899	−229	−297
1874	82	65	1900a	−296	−361
1875	87	74	1900b	−321	−391
1876	2	2	1901	−273	−333
1877	−57	−54	1902	−82	−108
1878	−162	−178	1903	−154	−197
1879	−160	−178	1904	−117	−167
1880	30	30	1905	−94	−132
1881	−41	−40	1906	22	32
1882	110	102	1907	35	51
1883	51	50	1908	−187	−263
1884	105	113	1909	143	186
1885	34	40	1910	229	279
1886	137	167	1911	40	49
1887	231	272	1912	36	42
1888	287	334	1913	−142	−163
1889	202	249	1914	−72	−83

Notes: 1900a is comparable to earlier years; 1900b is comparable to later years.

Source: Capital Inflow: *Historical Statistics, United States* (1975), Series U, 18–25. Price Deflator: Warren & Pearson, Wholesale Prices All Commodities, 1910–14 = 100. George F. Warren and Frank A. Pearson, *Gold and Prices* (New York: John Wiley & Sons, 1935), Table 1, pp. 11–14.

manufacturing sector – both brewing and milling received substantial infusions.

The near-century-long trend in capital importation was dramatically reversed in the nine years 1897–1905. Because of the lack of comparability of the Simon and Goldsmith series, it is difficult to provide a precise estimate of the magnitudes involved, but by any measure it was substantial. Simon's data show net capital exports of $827 million between the beginning of 1897 and the end of 1900. Goldsmith estimates that long-term movements alone totaled $712 million between the beginning of 1900 and the end of 1905. The United States had become a major capital exporter. Between 1897 and 1908, American direct investments abroad rose from $635 million to $1.639 billion, and portfolio investments from $50 to $886 million. Taken together, total American financial commitments abroad rose by more than three and a half times.[368]

Contemporaries may not have realized it, but those years provided a preview of the pattern that was to hold from World War I until the 1980s; however, the last nine years of the period saw a return to the era of American borrowing. In seven of those years the nation received a net inflow of capital, and the total in 1910 reached $255 million. Overall, despite a more than 40 percent increase in American direct and portfolio investment abroad, long-term capital imports between January 1906 and December 1914 exceeded long-term capital exports by $493 million.[369] By the latter date the country's net indebtedness almost certainly again exceeded $2.5 billion.

3-3b(2). Cross-sectional evidence on the industrial structure of foreign investment and of the sources of investment: estimates of gross flows: Until the 1840s first federal and then state government loans had dominated the foreign investor's long-term portfolio. By mid-century the issues of the nation's railroads had begun to replace government debt. In 1853 the Secretary of the Treasury announced that 76 of the 244 railroads that he had canvassed reported that they had attracted some foreign investors.[370] Domestic savings rates had risen, capital markets had developed, and American investors had become sophisticated enough to absorb a substantially larger share of the much-reduced gov-

---

[368] Lewis, *America's Stake*, p. 605.

[369] Between 1908 and 1914 American direct investment abroad increased from $1.639 to $2.652 billion, although portfolio investment declined by $25 million. Lewis, *America's Stake*, p. 605.

[370] Mira Wilkins, *The History of Foreign Investment in the United States to 1914*, Harvard Studies in Business History #41 (Cambridge, Mass.: Harvard University Press, 1989), pp. 78–80. [Hereafter cited as Wilkins, *Foreign Investment*.]

ernmental offerings. Between 1850 and 1914 there were substantial changes in the composition of the foreign-held equity and debt instruments. In the former year short-term debt had accounted for 40 percent of debt held abroad; by the outbreak of World War I the figure had fallen to 6 percent. The government's role had changed in an equally dramatic fraction. In 1853 government bonds represented more than seven in every ten dollars of foreign-held securities. Inflated by Civil War finance, government issues represented more than 70 percent of all foreign investment in the United States by 1869. By 1914 the ratio had declined to less than 3 percent. The rise can be attributed to the Civil War, the decline to two largely unrelated changes. On the one hand, the federal government over the next three decades paid off almost all of its wartime debt. On the other hand, the National Banking Act required that national banks hold U.S. government bonds as reserves against their issue of national bank notes. Initially the relative gap in foreign holdings caused by the decline in the fractions of government bonds and short-term credit was filled by railroad offerings. By 1880 they accounted for two-thirds of foreign investment in the United States. By 1914, however, although foreign holdings of rails amounted to almost $4 billion, they represented hardly more than one-half of the total. Other private securities and direct investment had grown from negligible proportions to almost two dollars in every five (see Table 3:3b-2).

Who were the foreigners willing to invest their savings in the United States? Cleona Lewis begins her landmark study with the observation that "the American colonies were founded and developed with the aid of European capital; largely from Great Britain, but with funds from other countries also participating – particularly from Holland, France and Spain."[371] Technically she is correct; but in reality, investment in the United States until the 1860s was almost entirely a British preserve. Dunning estimates that in 1861 the British were responsible for 90 percent of all foreign investment in the United States. Thereafter, although the absolute magnitudes continued to rise, the relative importance of the British role began to decline; the precise timing of the decline is still an open question. According to Dunning, the British share

---

[371] During the Revolutionary War the United States received some $8.65 million in loans from the French, Dutch, and Spanish. Of that amount the French contributed in gifts and loans some $6.1 million (70.5%); the Dutch, although pledging $10 million, actually were asked to contribute only $2.0 million (23.1%); and the Spanish loaned an additional $550,000 (6.4%). In 1899 it is estimated that Dutch investments in the United States totaled some $240 million or 7.2% of the foreign total, and by 1908 the figures were $750 million and 11.7%. Lewis, *America's Stake*, pp. 7, 513, 524, 530.

Table 3:3b-2. *Industrial distribution of foreign investments in the United States*

Year	Government	Railroads	Other private securities	Direct investments	Short-term investments	Total foreign investments
Panel A: Millions of dollars						
1853	159	52	8	5	150	374
1869	1,108	243	15	25	153	1,544
1880	346	899	2	3	109	1,359
1914	213	3,934	1,607	1,210	450	7,414
Panel B: Percentages						
1853	42.5	13.9	2.1	1.3	40.1	100.0
1869	71.8	15.7	1.0	1.6	9.9	100.0
1880	25.5	66.2	0.1	0.2	8.0	100.0
1914	2.9	53.1	21.7	16.3	6.1	100.0

Notes: For 1880 other private investments, direct investments, and short-term investments are by extrapolation.

Source: 1853, 1869, 1914 are from Lewis, *America's Stake*, pp. 519–557; 1880 from Mira Wilkins, *Foreign Investment*, p. 147.

had fallen to 80 percent by 1880, to just more than 70 percent at the turn of the century, and to less than 60 percent in 1913.[372] Both Lewis and Wilkins, although agreeing with Dunning's immediate prewar estimate, place the 1900 share at 80 percent.[373] No matter which estimate is correct, it is clear that even in 1914, the British remained the nation's chief source of foreign capital. Moreover, a very large part was directed to the United States through the intermediation of the formal British capital markets.

Although British investment continued to increase, it became relatively less important. Both German and Dutch investment became relatively more important. The capital imports from those countries tended to bypass the formal markets in the United States, and in both cases they were linked to institutional innovation in the home country. In Germany the increase was in large part a result of the successful exploitation of the close personal ties that linked emigrant German merchants-cum-bankers and the banking community at home. In Holland, in an attempt to minimize the risk to individual investors, Dutch bankers organized

[372] John H. Dunning, *Studies in International Investment* (London: George Allen & Unwin, 1970), table 2, p. 151.

[373] Lewis, *America's Stake*, pp. 524, 530, 546. Wilkins, *Foreign Investment*, p. 159.

formal trusts or holding companies to invest in American securities, particularly in railroad issues.[374] Between 1908 and 1914 German investment accounted for about 15 percent of the total foreign flow, and Dutch commitments about two-thirds of that amount.[375] Richard Tilly has concluded that "the United States was the largest single recipient of German foreign investment in the late 19th century," and Augustus Veenendaal reaches a similar conclusion for the Dutch.[376]

3-4. The industrial disposition of foreign capital: micro-evidence

3-4a. The railroads

From the late 1870s until World War I, railroads received far more attention from foreign investors than any other sector of the American economy. If Civil War and Reconstruction-era finance is excluded, that conclusion holds for the period from the 1840s to World War I. The railroads were marked by high profits, but also by frequent bankruptcies, reorganizations, and skipped dividends. As a result, they became the beneficiaries of British investors with, in Michael Edelstein's view, "both an increased desire for risky, high-return assets and an absence of other sources to satisfy the demand for this type of asset." Although certainly risky in the early years, American rails paid substantially higher returns than their British counterparts, and they still returned somewhat more after 1900, when they appear to have become somewhat less risky.[377]

Between 1865 and 1914, total U.S. railroad flotations in Britain exceeded $2.7 billion, and that figure does not include securities initially

---

[374] Wilkins, *Foreign Investment*, pp. 109, 120.

[375] Lewis, *America's Stake*, pp. 520, 540, 546; and Wilkins, *Foreign Investment*, pp. 109, 120. By 1914 the other European countries accounted for about 8 percent, the Canadians 4 percent, and the rest of the world about 6 percent.

[376] Richard Tilly, "International Aspects of the Development of German Banking, 1870–1914," ms., and "Some Comments on German Foreign Portfolio Investment, 1870–1914," paper delivered in São Paolo, July 1989. Augustus J. Veenendaal, "The Kansas City Southern Railway and the Dutch Connection," *Business History Review*, Vol. 61, No. 2 (summer 1987). Tilly's data suggest that North America received about 29 percent of German portfolio investment in the years 1897–1906 and 12 percent between 1907 and 1914. "International Aspects," table 3, p. 16.

[377] It is estimated that in 1876, for example, 65 percent of all European-held American railroad securities were in default. *Bankers' Magazine*, Vol. 30 (May 1876), p. 846. Michael Edelstein, *Overseas Investment in the Age of High Imperialism: The United Kingdom, 1850–1914* (New York: Columbia University Press, 1982), pp. 93–101. The quotation is from page 96. [Hereafter cited as Edelstein, *Overseas Investment*.]

floated in New York or in a Continental market but ultimately purchased by British investors. In no year did flotations amount to less than $3.2 million, and in 1902 they reached ninety times that amount.[378] Railroad construction proceeded in a number of waves, with peaks in 1872, 1879, 1890, 1902, and 1907; the capital calls track that pattern closely, but lag it slightly. Calls reached $80 million in 1873, $79 million in 1881, $89 million in 1890, $291 million in 1902, and $210 million in 1907. Total British investment in U.S. railroads is estimated to have risen from $486 million in 1876 to $1.7 billion in 1898 and to $3.0 billion in 1913. To put this figure in perspective, Robert Gallman has estimated that the total investment in U.S. railroads in 1898 was approximately $5.2 billion.[379] In addition, access to the London Stock Exchange, the world's largest securities market, increased the mobility of both foreign and domestic savings by providing an international secondary market. The nominal value of American railroad securities quoted on that exchange rose from $403 million in 1873 to $5.394 billion in 1903, to $8.423 billion in 1913.[380]

Thus, foreign investors by 1890 held between 50 and 75 percent of the equity of the Pennsylvania, the Louisville and Nashville, the Illinois Central, the New York, Ontario, and Western, and the Philadelphia and Reading, and more than one-fifth of the stock of the Great Northern, the Baltimore and Ohio, and the Chicago, Milwaukee, and St. Paul.[381] Nor were the foreign forays limited to the major lines. Over the half-century

---

[378] For a summary of the Capital Called data on which this section is based, see Tables 3:4-1, 3:4-2, and 3:4-3.

[379] The estimate is very rough. It begins with the value (reproduction cost) of the roads (including land and equipment) in 1906, according to the estimate underlying Gallman, "The United States Capital Stock in the Nineteenth Century," in Stanley Engerman and Robert Gallman (eds.), *Long Term Factors in Economic Growth*, National Bureau of Economic Research, Studies in Income and Wealth Vol. 51 (Princeton: Princeton University Press, 1986).

[380] The figures for the values of the issues "created and called" on the London Stock Exchange, of course, include the entire amount "created and called," not just the shares initially floated or ultimately purchased in the United Kingdom. Dorothy Adler, *British Investment in American Railroads, 1834–1898* (Charlottesville: University of Virginia Press, 1970), pp. 166–68. George Paish, "Great Britain's Capital Investments in Individual, Colonial, and Foreign Countries," *Journal of the Royal Statistical Society*, Vol. LXXIV, Part II (January 1911), pp. 167–201. [Hereafter cited as Paish, "Great Britain's Capital Investments."] George Paish, "The Export of Capital and the Cost of Living," *Statist Supplement*, Vol. 79 (1914), pp. i–viii. E. Victor Morgan and W.A Thomas, *The Stock Exchange: Its History and Functions* (London: Etek Books, 1962), pp. 280–81.

[381] William Z. Ripley, *Railroads: Finance and Organization* (New York: Longman Green, 1915), p. 5.

Table 3:4-1. *U.S. capital called: British capital markets, all years 1865–1914*

Industry	Total calls (millions of dollars)		Average calls per year (millions of dollars)		Percent of Total (percent)	
Transport	2,841.7		56.8		54.4	
Government	1,603.8		32.1		30.7	
Manufacturing & Commerce	233.6		4.7		4.5	
Agriculture & Extractive	256.8		5.1		4.9	
1. Mining		103.2		2.1		2.0
2. Agriculture		30.9		0.6		0.6
3. Petroleum & chemical		22.8		0.5		0.4
4. Financial land & development		99.9		2.0		1.9
Finance	79.2		1.6		1.5	
Public Utilities	207.4		4.1		4.0	
			0.0			
Total calls	5,222.5		104.5		100.0	

Source: Davis–Gallman Capital Called tape.

Table 3:4-2. *All U.S. capital called: British capital markets by industry, 1865–1914 (thousands of dollars)*

Years	Manufacturing & commercial	Finance	Government	Agriculture & extractive	Transport	Public utilities	Total capital called
1865–1869	156	3,847	3,615	1,636	49,994	8,961	68,209
1870–1874	16,207	4,869	518,972	27,233	275,338	8,369	850,988
1875–1879	329	331	1,009,952	3,662	93,587	11,285	1,119,146
1880–1884	4,927	21,322	0	31,084	289,908	1,269	348,510
1885–1889	46,816	10,520	39	34,093	190,420	9,145	291,033
1890–1894	51,578	12,791	3,931	45,205	269,022	158	382,685
1895–1899	34,871	3,754	65,006	13,534	89,398	2,196	208,759
1900–1904	6,517	7,549	0	13,765	476,267	2,620	506,718
1905–1909	19,146	3,987	0	28,140	572,260	71,891	695,424
1910–1914	53,087	10,245	2,280	58,433	535,546	91,522	751,113
1865–1914	233,634	79,215	1,603,795	256,785	2,841,740	207,416	5,222,585

Percentages of all United States calls

Years	Manufacturing & commercial	Finance	Government	Agriculture & extractive	Transport	Public utilities	Total capital called
1865–1869	0.2	5.6	5.3	2.4	73.3	13.1	100.0
1870–1874	1.9	0.6	61.0	3.2	32.4	1.0	100.0
1875–1879	0.0	0.0	90.2	0.3	8.4	1.0	100.0
1880–1884	1.4	6.1	0.0	8.9	83.2	0.4	100.0
1885–1889	16.1	3.6	0.0	11.7	65.4	3.1	100.0
1890–1894	13.5	3.3	1.0	11.8	70.3	0.0	100.0
1895–1899	16.7	1.8	31.1	6.5	42.8	1.1	100.0
1900–1904	1.3	1.5	0.0	2.7	94.0	0.5	100.0
1905–1909	2.8	0.6	0.0	4.0	82.3	10.3	100.0
1910–1914	7.1	1.4	0.3	7.8	71.3	12.2	100.0
1865–1914	4.5	1.5	30.7	4.9	54.4	4.0	100.0

Source: Davis, Gallman Capital Called tape.

Table 3:4-3. *U.S. capital called: British capital markets, agriculture and extractive industry (thousands of dollars)*

Years	Total calls	Mining	Agriculture	Petroleum & chemicals	Financial land & development
1865–1869	1,636	1,636	0	0	0
1870–1874	27,233	20,259	670	110	6,195
1875–1879	3,662	650	146	0	2,866
1880–1884	31,084	12,455	9,936	0	8,694
1885–1889	34,093	14,549	8,115	317	11,112
1890–1894	45,206	3,922	5,161	82	36,041
1895–1899	13,534	7,765	354	73	5,342
1900–1904	13,765	3,636	292	6,877	2,960
1905–1909	28,139	13,631	326	5,834	8,348
1910–1914	58,433	24,723	5,941	9,459	18,310
1865–1914	256,785	103,226	30,941	22,752	99,868
Percentages of total United States calls					
Years					
1865–1869	2.4	2.4	0.0	0.0	0.0
1870–1874	3.2	2.4	0.1	0.0	0.7
1875–1879	0.3	0.1	0.0	0.0	0.3
1880–1884	8.9	3.6	2.9	0.0	2.5
1885–1889	11.7	5.0	2.8	0.1	3.8
1890–1894	11.8	1.0	1.3	0.0	9.4
1895–1899	6.5	3.7	0.2	0.0	2.6
1900–1904	2.7	0.7	0.1	1.4	0.6
1905–1909	4.0	2.0	0.0	0.8	1.2
1910–1914	7.8	3.3	0.8	1.3	2.4
1865–1914	4.9	2.0	0.6	0.4	1.9

Source: Davis, Gallman Capital Called tape.

the securities of a number of very small lines also found their way onto the London market. For example, the Perkiomen Railroad – a Pennsylvania line connecting Perkiomen and Emaus Junction, a distance of 38.5 miles – the Central City, Deadwood, and Eastern, and the Tonopah and Tidewater – none serving a national market – all floated security issues in London.

3-4b. Government securities

By the mid-1850s the burden of foreign-held state debt had been reduced by repudiation and repayment to about $127 million. Most states had resumed payment of principal and interest, and European savers had again shown themselves willing to hold local, state, and federal issues. Thus, the Southern states were able to take advantage of foreign capital markets to help finance the war and Reconstruction. The federal government was able to raise some military loans during the war, and in the 1870s, to refinance its war-swollen debt. Finally, the costs of the infrastructure that provided the foundation for late-nineteenth-century urbanization were also partly underwritten by foreign capital. Thus, the London market alone between 1865 and 1914 absorbed $1.6 billion in American public issues; however, more than 95 percent of those transfers occurred before 1880.

Reputation did not endear the Southern states to the European investor – critical questions were still being raised in the British Parliament in the 1930s – but the reputations of the federal government and many, particularly Northern, state and local governments were not so badly tarnished. Despite the potential availability of foreign capital and the willingness of some cities to take advantage of those opportunities, total government calls – calls that had accounted for seven in every ten dollars of American flotations in Britain in the 1860s and 1870s – constituted less than one-tenth of 1 percent of total U.S. calls in the first years of the twentieth century. Domestic savers had become sufficiently educated to meet the vast majority of government demands, and the American capital market showed evidence of rapid maturation. It should be kept in mind, however, that the speed of maturation was greatly enhanced by the national banks' demand for reserves against their note issue.

In the non-railroad private sector, domestic developments were slower, and foreign investment flowed to regions and industries that were still unable to attract depersonalized domestic finance. Foreign – particularly British – savers proved more amenable than their domestic counterparts. Over the five decades between 1865 and 1914, the British capital market channeled about 15 percent of the flows destined for the United States toward the agriculture and extractive, manufacturing and commercial, financial, and public utility sectors. Although the fraction was less than 5 percent in the first two decades, the four sectors' share of total British flows reached almost 25 percent in the 1880s and 1890s – two decades of very rapid structural transformation – and it was almost that large again in the last decade before World War I. Although these transfers were still small in relation to the total capital demands of the sectors in question, they were important on the margin, and in some industries and some regions they represented a significant fraction of total investment.

3-4c. Land-related industries

In the late nineteenth and early twentieth centuries there was a significant flow of foreign investment into the agricultural, land, and extractive sector. Those funds were directed to financial land and development companies, to firms launched to farm or raise cattle in the South and West, to investment trusts that held portfolios of American land and mortgages, to Western mines, and to oil exploration in California, Oklahoma, and Texas.[382] Although British promoters were involved in land development in Colorado and New Mexico in the late 1860s and early 1870s, it was the next decade before foreign, particularly British, funds assumed an important role – if the level of political response is a measure of importance – in the nation's attempts to push the frontier westward.[383]

Lewis reports that between 1879 and 1911 twenty-nine foreign land companies with an aggregate capital of $52 million were registered in the United States. The total number – some registered abroad – may have been twice that large.[384] Over those years the calls of land companies on the British market totaled almost $85 million – for the entire period the figure was close to $100 million – and those firms controlled between thirty and thirty-five million acres of mostly Western land.[385] By 1910 there were about sixty-four million acres in farms in the West and in the North Central regions; land companies that floated issues on the British capital market appear to have owned a significant fraction – perhaps 7 or 8 percent – of American farm land in these regions.

[382] The typical form of those investments, the investment trusts aside, involved the organization of a "free-standing company." See Mira Wilkins, "The Free-Standing Company, 1870–1914: An Important Type of British Foreign Direct Investment," *Economic History Review*, 2nd series, Vol. XLI, No. 2 (1988), pp. 259–82.

[383] In 1869 and 1870 two very large Mexican land grants, the Maxwell and the Saqre de Cristo, were purchased and development funds raised in Britain and Holland. Wilkins, *Foreign Investment*, pp. 122–24 and 232–33.

[384] Lewis, *America's Stake*, p. 85; *Philadelphia Bulletin*, December 6, 1909, p. 11.

[385] Although not all the funds were channeled through FL&D firms, studies have shown that in 1890 foreign-held mortgages represented 1 percent of the land in Iowa, 2 percent in Kansas, 3.7 percent in Minnesota, 3.8 percent in Nebraska, 9.6 percent in North Dakota, and 14.5 percent in South Dakota. Larry A McFarlane, "British Investment and the Land: Nebraska 1877–1946," *Business History Review*, Vol. LVII (summer 1983), pp. 258–92; "British Investment in Minnesota Farm Mortgages and Land, 1875–1900," unpublished ms.; "British Agricultural Investment in the Dakotas, 1857–1953," in Paul Uselding (ed.), *Business and Economic History*, 2nd series, Vol. 5 (1976), pp. 112–26; and "British Investment in Midwestern Farm Mortgages and Land, 1875–1900, A Comparison of Iowa and Kansas," *Agricultural History*, Vol. 48 (January 1974), pp. 179–98.

Land speculation was one major source of foreign investment; direct investment in agriculture was a second. A substantial fraction of that investment – nearly $31 million was channeled through the British market alone – was in Western cattle ranching, an activity that reached its peak in the 1880s. Between 1879 and 1889 no fewer than forty foreign cattle companies – firms capitalized at £4.8 million and controlling more than twenty-one million acres of land in ten states and territories – were organized.[386] Foreign investment, however, was not limited to cattle. British investors also financed rice plantations in Louisiana, cotton farms in Louisiana and Mississippi, orange groves in California, and timber companies in states as far apart as California and the Carolinas.[387]

Given the level of European interest in American, particularly Western, lands, it is not surprising that those direct capital transfers were complemented by indirect transfers routed through British and Continental mortgage companies and investment trusts. Those investments – investments that were primarily of Scottish and English origin, but that also found support among the Dutch and Germans and, somewhat later, among the Swiss and the French as well – began in the late 1870s, and they surged in the 1880s. Faced by a rising tide of anger over foreign land-holdings, they diminished somewhat after 1890. Taking all countries and both private and institutional investors together, Lewis put the total foreign holdings of American real estate mortgages in 1914 at "more than $200–250 million." Wilkins's estimate is somewhat more conservative, but she still places the figure at between $200 and $250 million, or about one-half percent of the value of U.S. farm real estate in 1914 and 6.4 percent of farm real estate in the West.[388]

There is no record of the actual number of American mines that benefited from foreign capital, but Clark Spence has estimated that between 1860 and 1914 there were 584 American mining and milling firms with a total capital of £81.2 million chartered in Britain. Edward Ashmead iden-

[386] "In 1880 there were 800,000 range cattle in Texas and 250,000 in Wyoming; by 1883 there were 5 million in Texas and 1 million in Wyoming." Wilkins, *Foreign Investment*, pp. 300, 304–5. Lewis, *America's Stake*, p. 87. For a more detailed description of the investment in cattle ranching, see Gene M. Gressley, *Bankers and Cattlemen* (New York: Knopf, 1966).

[387] Wilkins, *Foreign Investment*, p. 234. Peter J. Buckley and Brian R. Roberts, *European Direct Investment in the USA Before World War I* (New York: St. Martin's Press, 1982), p. 60. [Hereafter cited as Buckley and Roberts, *European Direct Investment.*]

[388] Lewis, *America's Stake*, pp. 86–87. Wilkins, *Foreign Investment*, pp. 502–12. *Historical Statistics U.S.*, Bicentennial Edition, Series K-11, K-66.

tified 659 British firms with nominal capital of £99.6 million that were registered between 1880 and 1904 to conduct mining operations in the United States.[389] The capital-called series indicates a total of $103 million in calls on the British capital market over the years 1865–1914. Wilkins argues that British investment represented more than one-half of all foreign investment in mining; she estimates that between 1815 and 1914, foreign capital financed between 1,500 and 2,000 mining and mineral-related companies.[390] While it was the natural endowments of coal and iron that provided the resource base for American industrialization, it was the lure of silver and gold that initially drew European investors to American mines. Gradually, however, beginning in the 1880s, investments in copper mines began to overtake those in the precious metals. Between 1905 and 1912 British mining calls totaled $34 million, and copper accounted for more than three-fifths of that total. Overall, there was also a significant level of British, French, German, and Dutch investment in the traditional non-ferrous metals – copper, lead, and zinc – as well as in aluminum, phosphate, salt, and borax.[391]

Foreign investors made little attempt to exploit American oil discoveries until the innovation of the automobile and the expansion of production into California, Oklahoma, and Texas. The British investment firm of Balfour, Williamson, and Company launched the California Oilfields Ltd. with initial capital of $1 million in 1901. With some aid from the Dutch, it financed six additional firms – two each in California, Oklahoma, and Texas – and all six were soon in operation. It was the Royal Dutch Shell group, however, that supplied the largest block of foreign capital to the petroleum industry. The Shell Transport and Trading Company began to buy American oil properties, and by 1914 the now-merged Royal Dutch Shell controlled more than one-half of the $35 million that foreigners had invested in American petroleum production.[392]

3-4d. Commerce and manufacturing

Between 1865 and 1914 there was $231 million in manufacturing and commercial calls. More importantly, in the years of rapid

[389] Clark C. Spence, "British Investment and the American Mining Frontier, 1860–1914," *New Mexico Historical Review*, Vol. 36 (April 1961), p. 121. Edward Ashmead, *Twenty-five Years of Mining, 1880–1914* (London: Mining Journal, 1909), pp. 81–90.

[390] Wilkins, *Foreign Investment*, p. 241.

[391] Lewis, *America's Stake*, pp. 93–94. Wilkins, *Foreign Investment*, pp. 264–83.

[392] Lewis, *America's Stake*, pp. 94–98. Wilkins, *Foreign Investment*, pp. 285–92.

structural transformation, 1880–95, those calls constituted more than 15 percent of total American calls. A large fraction of British finance in that decade and a half was directed toward the brewing industry. The new capital-intensive technology was characterized by substantial economies of scale; British capital permitted the Americans to benefit at a time when domestic savers were unwilling and domestic markets unable to provide the requisite finance. British savers, on the other hand, were cognizant of the opportunities offered by the new technology. In England, beginning with Bass in 1880, many brewers had successfully raised capital on the formal capital markets. For example, a £6 million issue of Guinness securities was marketed by Baring Brothers. Amounting at its peak in 1891 to about $90 million, British investment in American brewing was greater than all foreign commitments to U.S. cattle ranching, meat packing, granaries, grain elevators, and flour mills taken together.[393]

Although brewing was the dominant recipient, foreign investment was not limited to that industry; firms serving the rapidly expanding consumer market – particularly the market for flour and fresh meat – also received a significant share during the peak years. Again, these were industries where investment in new technology produced substantial economies of scale. In 1899, for example, the British purchased Pillsbury mills, the nation's largest miller, and launched Pillsbury-Washburn with a capital stock of £1 million and debentures of £635,000. In addition to substantial commitments to agricultural processing, British savers within a few years also provided finance for General Electric, Eastman's, Pullman, and Edison Photographic.[394]

Although the sector's share of the total amount of U.S. calls was only slightly over 7 percent, manufacturing and commercial firms received $53 million between 1910 and 1914. Reflecting the demands of the earlier period, the list of firms that drew funds included both the Indianapolis and the St. Louis breweries; but the list also included an additional $7 million in General Electric calls as well as more than $20 million of British American Tobacco's, $8 million of Bethlehem Steel's, and even $50,000 of Quaker Oats's. By 1914 British, Dutch, German, Swiss, and Canadian investors held $122.4 million of the common shares and $27.5 million of the preferred shares of the United States Steel Company; in addition, they had substantial holdings in both Bethlehem and Otis Steel.[395]

[393] Wilkins, *Foreign Investment*, p. 325. Lewis, *America's Stake*, p. 89.
[394] Lewis, *America's Stake*, p. 191. Wilkins, *Foreign Investment*, p. 320.
[395] Wilkins, *Foreign Investment*, pp. 247, 252, 263. Lewis, *America's Stake*, p. 101.

Table 3:5a-1. *Panel A: financial interrelations ratios, 1850–1913*
(financial assets/tangible assets)

Country	1850	1875	1895	1913
Great Britain	0.68	0.93	1.96	1.96
United States of America	0.47	0.64	0.71	0.83

Panel B: financial intermediation ratios, 1850–1913 (assets of financial intermediaries/all financial assets ×100)

Country	1850	1875	1895	1913
Great Britain	14.7	19.7	15.4	17.3
United States of America	12.5	13.6	20.0	21.3

Notes: For the United States, 1875 = 1880; 1895 = 1900; and 1913 = 1912.

Source: Raymond W. Goldsmith, *Comparative National Balance Sheets: A Study of Twenty Countries, 1688–1978* (Chicago & London: University of Chicago Press, 1985), Table 19, p. 45 & Table 47, p. 136.

3-5. The evolution of American financial markets

3-5a. Introduction

In the years before World War I the British possessed a larger and more sophisticated set of capital market institutions than did the United States. The statistical evidence provides support for that conclusion, should such support be required. Raymond Goldsmith uses two ratios to capture the size and complexity of a nation's financial structure (see Table 3:5a-1). The first, the "Financial Interrelations Ratio" – the ratio of financial to tangible assets – is designed to reflect the relative size of the financial sector; the second, the "Financial Intermediation Ratio" – the ratio of the assets of financial institutions to the total of all domestic and foreign financial assets – is designed to measure "the importance of financial institutions in terms of resources within the financial superstructure."[396]

In the case of Britain the Financial Interrelations Ratio rose from 1850 until 1895 and then remained constant at a very high level (1.96) until 1913. The American experience was quite different. The ratio also rose

[396] Raymond Goldsmith, *Comparative National Balance Sheets: A Study of Twenty Countries, 1688–1978* (Chicago: University of Chicago Press, 1985), pp. 43, 138. [Hereafter cited as Goldsmith, *Comparative National Balance Sheets*.]

persistently, but it never exceeded 0.83. Moreover, the ratio in every year is below that of Britain. It was about 70 percent of the British figure in 1850 and 1870, it had fallen to 36 percent in 1895, and still stood at only 42 percent in 1913. Finance clearly played a much larger role in Britain than it did in the United States.

The movements of the Financial Intermediation Ratio suggest that the differences between the two countries were not just a matter of size. In Britain the ratio rose from 1850 to 1875. It was relatively stable thereafter, although it was actually somewhat lower in 1913 than it had been in 1875. The U.S. ratio rose from 1850 to 1896, and was relatively stable thereafter. Although the U.S. figure was less than the British figure in 1850 and 1875 – 85 percent in 1850, 70 percent in 1875 – it was 30 percent above the British figure in 1895 and more than 20 percent above in 1913. This evidence strongly suggests that as the American capital markets matured, formal financial intermediaries played a relatively larger role and the securities markets a smaller one than in Britain.

3-5b. The commercial banks

In Britain the commercial banks, despite their strong bias toward short-term finance, appear to have played an important role in mobilizing finance both for domestic industrialization and international investment. Criticized for not providing the services of universal banks, British banks were happy to provide overdraft facilities and short-term loans secured by collateral to the manufacturing sector. Moreover, there is evidence that continued renewal at times converted short-term into long-term commitments. In the United States, despite the fact that the commercial banking sector's size, relative to that of the entire financial sector, was similar to that of its British counterpart – in fact, at the end of the period it was probably somewhat larger – the banks' role appears to have been somewhat more limited.[397] In the United States there were few branch banks to help ease problems of spatial mobilization, and they played almost no role in international finance. "The long and variegated history of U.S. joint-stock banking . . . had tended by the late nineteenth century to bind the joint stock banks in a web of regulatory constraints that made it difficult, if not impossible, to take advantage of new opportunities arising in the international sphere." "First, the sentiment against branch banking embodied in the federal and state bank laws prohibited most American joint-stock banks from establishing branches abroad as well as at home. National banks, which included the largest American

---

[397] For a comparison of the relative size, see Goldsmith, *Comparative National Balance Sheets*, table A7, pp. 232–33, and table A22, pp. 301–2.

banks and the logical candidates for foreign expansion, were prohibited by law from establishing overseas branches until the Federal Reserve Act made it possible to do so starting in 1914." Second, although the constraint may not have been binding,

> American joint-stock banks – national and state – were either legally forbidden or (what amounted to the same thing) lacked specific authorization to accept drafts or bills of exchange. Since acceptances were the main instrument by which banks participated in the finance of international trade, the inability to accept bills and drafts placed the American joint-stock banks at a competitive disadvantage relative to banks in other nations. Again, the Federal Reserve Act relaxed this restriction for national banks in 1914, as had a few state banking laws in the years immediately preceding. But it is substantially correct to say that American joint-stock banks did no accepting before 1914.

The third, and probably the most important, reason was "the absence of a central bank and a discount market for acceptances and other short term instruments such as was facilitated by the central banks of other leading nations."[398]

Between 1836 and the Civil War commercial banks were chartered and regulated exclusively by state governments. In the early years of the nineteenth century, few legal constraints were imposed on the portfolios of state banks. Gradually, however, as panics and bank suspensions became increasingly common, states began to restrict investment alternatives, and bankers became increasingly conservative. The passage of the National Banking Act and its 1864 amendments speeded up the process. The amendment – that placed a prohibitive tax on state bank notes – forced many state banks to take national charters. The Act itself was initially read to have prohibited loans on real estate, and as a result an increasing proportion of all commercial banks were forced to put more of their assets into commercial loans.[399]

---

[398] Vincent P. Carosso and Richard Sylla, "U.S. Banks in International Finance," in Rondo Cameron and V.I. Bovykin, with the assistance of Boris Anan'ich, A.A. Fursenko, Richard Sylla, and Mira Wilkins (eds.), *International Banking, 1870–1914* (New York: Oxford University Press, 1991), pp. 51–53. [Hereafter cited as Carosso and Sylla, "U.S. Banks in International Finance."]

The National City Bank opened the first foreign branch of a U.S. national bank in Argentina in November 1914. "By 1920 it would have fifty-seven foreign branches, far and away the largest number of any American bank" (p. 70).

[399] The cited statute, however, is by no means entirely clear. It gives national banks the power to negotiate "promissory notes, drafts, bills of exchange, and other evidences of debt." It also specifically indicates four ways in which such banks may "purchase and convey real estate" of which the second is germane to this discussion. "Such as shall be mortgaged to it in good faith by way of security for

In 1884, however, the Supreme Court (in the case of *Fortier vs. New Orleans National Bank*) held that a loan of money made by a national bank on security of a mortgage was not a violation of the national banking act and could be enforced.[400] Despite that ruling the Comptroller of the Currency continued to express concerns about mortgage loans, and his views may well have led national banks either to steer clear of mortgage lending or to hide their mortgage loans. The Comptroller, however, was also on record as saying that mortgage loans were legal. Keen and Smiley argue that in the West during the depression of the 1890s, real estate held by banks – obtained chiefly by foreclosure – came to 8 or 9 percent of total assets. Since not all loans were foreclosed, this figure must represent a lower bound on mortgages held by banks. Thus, it appears that the national banks probably played a somewhat larger role in the mortgage market than most economic historians have believed, but they still remained, at most, secondary players in the national mortgage market. The ambiguities were not totally resolved until the passage of the Federal Reserve Act of 1913. That Act explicitly permitted national banks to make five-year loans on farm real estate mortgages.[401]

State-chartered banks were usually under less severe strictures, and with their reemergence after the mid-1880s, they almost certainly provided some mortgage credit. The total level was probably not large, and it was almost certainly concentrated in farm mortgages. In 1896 admitted mortgage loans constituted only 7.1 percent of all commercial bank assets; by 1914 that figure had declined to 6.7 percent. It may well be that these figures are understated. Recent work has suggested that the banks' portfolios may have contained some loans that were actually supported by mortgages but that were not classified as such. In any case their contribution to long-term mortgage lending was not large. Nor did the banks invest heavily in private securities as an alternative route to long-term credit. In 1896 all non-government stocks and bonds represented only

debts already contracted." Real estate and mortgages so obtained were to be held no longer than five years. These provisions were not significantly amended until 1913.

[400] *Federal Digest, 1754 to Date*, Vol. 12 (St. Paul, Minn.: West Publishing Company, 1940).

[401] Paul Studenski and Herman E. Kroos, *Financial History of the United States: Fiscal, Monetary, Banking and Tariff, Including Financial Administration and State and Local Finance* (New York: McGraw-Hill Book Company, 1952), p. 260. [Hereafter cited as Studenski and Kroos, *Financial History*.] Richard H. Keehn and Gene Smiley, "Mortgage Lending by National Banks," *Business History Review*, Vol. LI, No. 4 (winter 1977).

6.8 percent of commercial bank assets, and the fraction even in 1914 was only 9.2 percent.[402]

It also appears that over the last third of the century, the commercial banks moved to distance themselves from other forms of long-term lending. Naomi Lamoreaux has documented a dramatic shift in the portfolios of New England banks away from the industry's traditional long-term "insider" advances and toward short-term largely anonymous commercial loans. She attributes this change in policy to two historical developments: "an expansion of the banking system that created large numbers of independent institutions whose behavior was difficult to control; and the increased interdependence that resulted from the rise of deposits as a source of lendable funds, a change that made each bank vulnerable to runs triggered by the unsound practices of other institutions. By promoting strict standards for short-term commercial loans, bank reformers sought to increase the ability of directors and stockholders to monitor the lending practices of their banks and, at the same time, to limit the damage to the system that unscrupulous bank managers could inflict."[403] Short-term commercial loans were thought to be self-liquidating, and more importantly they "were thought to make the lending process more objective: because a manufacturer had to scrutinize the wholesaler's standing before he risked his credit by endorsing the latter's note, bankers were relieved of the need to conduct further credit investigations."[404] Banker/borrower relations were to be conducted in a hands-off fashion. Long-term loans, on the other hand, "were considered *primae-facie* evidence of such potentially disastrous entanglement between borrowers and lenders." Under the new regime, banks were not supposed to furnish capital for business. "The customer should possess his own capital, and require assistance from the bank only at certain seasons and for specific purposes."[405]

"The orthodox therefore viewed this period as the golden age of banking. It was the period when lip service to the 'real bills' doctrine and the gold standard was at its peak and when bank assets were most

---

[402] *Historical Statistics U.S.* (1957), series X 98, X 100, and X 105, p. 631. The 1896 mortgage figure for non-national banks was 13.6 percent.

[403] Naomi R. Lamoreaux, " 'No Arbitrary Discretion': Specialisation in Short-term Commercial Lending by Banks in Late Nineteenth Century New England," in Geoffrey Jones (ed.), *Banks and Money: International and Comparative Finance in History* (London & Portland, Ore.: Frank Cass, 1991), pp. 93–94. [Hereafter cited as Lamoreaux, "No Arbitrary Discretion."]

[404] Lamoreaux, "No Arbitrary Discretion," p. 102.

[405] Lamoreaux, "No Arbitrary Discretion," p. 105. The latter quotation is from *Bankers' Magazine*, Vol. 57 (1898), p. 384.

distinguished for liquidity." These years were in sharp contrast with the earlier period of heavy real estate loans and the later period of large investments in government bonds.[406] As a result, in 1896 – the first year for which there are good data – the national banks had 80.2 percent of their earning assets invested in commercial loans and another 12.2 percent in government bonds; the figures for all commercial banks in that year were 72.5 percent and 9.8 percent, respectively.[407]

The rise of the national banking system as well as the near demise and later reemergence of the state system are captured in Table 3:5b-1. Clearly the nation possessed a dynamic commercial banking network, but it was spread unevenly, and the lack of branch banking made it difficult to correct the spatial imbalance. Although the data are flawed, Table 3:5b-2 suggests something about the differences in the level of banking services available across the country. If the Eastern states are taken as the standard (that is, equal to 1.00), over most of the period, bank capital per person in New England was above the Eastern benchmark. By the end of the period, however, the ratio of New England to the Eastern standard was less than 0.75. The Pacific region also compares favorably with the East – over the four dates it averaged 0.86 of the yardstick, and it exceeded that level in two of the four years. The picture in the other four regions was very different. For no region in any year does the ratio exceed 0.68, and it averages only 0.43.

In Britain branch banking made it possible to shift capital from surplus to deficit regions. From the 1860s until very recently, that institutional innovation found little favor in the United States. In 1860, in the entire country there were only 39 banks in thirteen states that had even a single branch, and the total number of branch offices was a mere 222. Moreover, those banks were not allowed to branch across state lines. In many states there was substantial resistance to intrastate, let alone interstate, branching. As a result, "during the years following the Civil War branch banking almost completely disappeared."[408]

[406] Herman E. Kroos and Martin R. Blyn, *A History of Financial Intermediaries* (New York: Random House, 1971), p. 98. [Hereafter cited as Kroos and Blyn, *A History of Financial Intermediaries*.]

[407] *Historical Statistics U.S.* (1975), Series X 635–642 and X 590–596, Vol. II, pp. 1021, 1025.

[408] John A. James, *Money and Capital Markets in Postbellum America* (Princeton: Princeton University Press, 1978), p. 90. [Hereafter cited as James, *Money and Capital Markets*.] Ray. B. Westerfield, *Historical Survey of Branch Banking in the United States* (New York: American Economists Council for the Study of Branch Banking, 1939), p. 5. For a detailed description of antebellum branch banking see John M. Chapman and Ray B. Westerfield, *Branch Banking* (New York: Harper & Brothers, 1942), pp. 22–57.

The Comptroller of the Currency surveyed state laws in 1896 and reported that although branch banking was prohibited by statute in only thirteen states, there was no legal provision in most states for branch banking. In those states it was generally held that opening a branch was illegal.[409] In 1902 only nine states definitely permitted branch banking, and in 1916 the figure was twelve. In that year the laws of twenty-seven states were silent, and branching was prohibited by statute in nine. In contrast to 1860, a survey in 1901 "revealed only forty-seven banks with a total of eighty-five branches in the entire country. New York had the largest number of branch bank systems – thirteen banks with thirty-three branches."[410]

Even if all states had legalized intrastate branching, it would not have solved the interregional mobilization problem. To solve that problem, action at the national level was required. The charter of the Second Bank of the United States coupled with the Supreme Court decision in *Marbury vs. Madison* had given the Bank the power to open branches in all parts of the country, but few bankers like competition. Even during the Civil War, with the need to find new sources of government finance a top priority, they were able to resist attempts to give the new national banks that privilege.[411] When the National Banking Act was amended in 1864, the amendment contained the following clause: "And its usual business shall be transacted at an office or banking house located in the place specified in its organization certificate." The change – a change that removed the authority for national bank branching – appears to have been made without any serious debate or consideration.[412] "Even though branch bank operations were not specifically prohibited, the implication

For a valuable discussion of legal regulations and branch banking, see Eugene N. White, *The Regulation and Reform of the American Banking System, 1900–1929* (Princeton: Princeton University Press, 1983).

[409] U.S. Comptroller of the Currency, *Annual Report, 1896* (Washington, D.C.: GPO, 1896), p. 40. Cited in James, *Money and Capital Markets*, p. 90.

[410] James, *Money and Capital Markets*, pp. 90–91. U.S. Comptroller of the Currency, *Annual Report, 1902* (Washington, D.C.: GPO, 1902), pp. 47–51. The states that permitted branching in 1902 were California, Delaware, Florida, Georgia, New York, Oregon, Rhode Island, Virginia, and Washington. The 1916 figure is from Marquis James and Bessie Rowland James, *Biography of a Bank: The Story of Bank of America NT&SA* (New York: Harper & Brothers, 1954), p. 77.

[411] The power granted to the Freedman's Savings and Trust Company in 1865 was the sole exception; after that institution went into liquidation in 1874, there were none. Paul B. Trescott, *Financing American Enterprise: The Story of Commercial Banking* (New York: Harper & Row, 1963), pp. 61–63. [Hereafter cited as Trescott, *Financing American Enterprise.*]

[412] Shirley Donald Southworth, *Branch Banking in the United States* (New York: McGraw-Hill Book Company, 1928), p. 12.

Table 3:5b-1. *Number and total assets of U.S. commercial banks*

	Number of Banks			Total Assets of Banks (millions of dollars)		
Year	Non-National Banks	National Banks	All Commercial Banks	Non-National Banks	National Banks	All Commercial Banks
1865	349	1,294	1,643	231	1,127	1,358
1870	325	1,612	1,937	215	1,566	1,781
1875	1,260	2,076	3,336	1,291	1,913	3,204
1880	1,279	2,076	3,355	1,364	2,036	3,400
1885	1,661	2,689	4,350	2,005	2,422	4,427
1890	4,717	3,484	8,201	3,296	3,062	6,358
1895	6,103	3,715	9,818	4,139	3,471	7,610
1896a	5,780	3,689	9,469	4,200	3,536	7,736
1896b	8,423	3,689	12,112	4,694	3,354	8,048
1900	9,322	3,731	13,053	6,444	4,944	11,388
1905	13,103	5,664	18,767	10,186	7,325	17,511
1910	18,013	7,138	25,151	13,030	9,892	22,922
1914	20,346	7,518	27,864	15,872	11,477	27,349

	Percents					
1865	21.2	78.8	100.0	17.0	83.0	100.0
1870	16.8	83.2	100.0	12.1	87.9	100.0
1875	37.8	62.2	100.0	40.3	59.7	100.0
1880	38.1	61.9	100.0	40.1	59.9	100.0
1885	38.2	61.8	100.0	45.3	54.7	100.0
1890	57.5	42.5	100.0	51.8	48.2	100.0
1895	62.2	37.8	100.0	54.4	45.6	100.0
1896a	61.0	39.0	100.0	54.3	45.7	100.0
1896b	69.5	30.5	100.0	58.3	41.7	100.0
1900	71.4	28.6	100.0	56.6	43.4	100.0
1905	69.8	30.2	100.0	58.2	41.8	100.0
1910	71.6	28.4	100.0	56.8	43.2	100.0
1914	73.0	27.0	100.0	58.0	42.0	100.0

Notes: (A) comparable with earlier data; (b) comparable with later data.
Source: Historical Statistics (1975), Series ×683–686, ×656–657, ×634–635.

Table 3:5b-2. *U.S. commercial banking resources per capita, by region,*
1880–1909

Region	1880	1890	1900	1909
1. *New England*				
Number of banks	662	655	655	657
Population	4,020,326	4,700,280	5,591,735	6,259,239
Persons per bank	6,073	7,176	8,537	9,527
2. *Eastern*				
Number of banks	1,773	1,266	1,591	2,477
Population	11,754,990	14,131,092	17,104,841	20,115,717
Persons per bank	6,630	11,162	10,751	8,121
3. *Southern*				
Number of banks	670	1,007	1,579	4,961
Population	15,223,740	18,327,400	22,080,736	25,484,657
Persons per bank	22,722	18,200	13,984	5,137
4. *Middle western*				
Number of banks	2,252	2,495	3,475	7,059
Population	15,779,764	19,363,695	23,074,000	25,984,179
Persons per bank	7,007	7,761	6,640	3,681
5. *Western*				
Number of banks	359	1,493	1,648	4,276
Population	1,957,268	3,817,601	5,118,688	6,726,148
Persons per bank	5,452	2,557	3,106	1,573
6. *Pacific*				
Number of banks	158	364	428	1,326
Population	1,393,718	2,268,812	3,084,168	3,749,928
Persons per bank	8,821	6,233	7,206	2,828

Notes: 1. New England is Maine, N.H., Vt., Mass., R.I., & Conn.; 2. Eastern is N.Y., N.J.,
Penn., Del., Md., & D.C.; 3. Southern is Va., W.Va., N.C., S.C., Ga., Fla., Ala., Miss., La., Tex.,
Ark., Ky., & Tenn.; 4. Mid Western is Ohio, Ind., Ill., Mich., Wisc., Minn., Iowa, & Mo.; 5.
Western is N.D., S.D., Neb., Kans., Wyo., Colo., N.M., & Okla.; 6. Pacific is Wash., Ore., Cal.,
Idaho, Utah, Nev., Ariz., & Alaska.

Source: *National Monetary Commission, Statistics for the United States, 1867–1909* (New
York: Garland Publishing Company, 1983), Table 4, pp. 24–25 & Table 6, p. 27.

to that effect is fairly clear; and, in any case, it had traditionally been held that what was not specifically authorized by the Act was prohibited. In 1892 a special act of Congress was required to allow Chicago banks to establish branches at the Columbian Exposition."[413] Only banks that had branch systems before they took out their national charter were allowed to have any branches – and they could not open new ones.[414]

As a result, of the 119 branches operating anywhere in the United States in 1900, only 5 were branches of national banks. In 1915 the nation's 27,390 commercial banks operated a total of only 785 branches. Of those, only twenty-six were branches of national banks.[415] Even as late as 1927, when the passage of the McFadden Branch Banking Act gave the national banks the power to establish "branches within the corporate limits of the places in which they were located, provided state law permitted branch banking," twenty-two states still prohibited all such branching.[416]

Soon after the turn of the century national banks had begun to attempt to finesse the restrictions on branching. "The expansion-minded National City along with other large national banks began to realize the confining character of the legal and regulatory constraints imposed by the banking laws under which they operated."

> Following the lead of New York's First National Bank, which had formed a state chartered securities affiliate in 1908, National City in 1911 launched the National City Company, a similar affiliate that was owned and managed by National City Bank but free to enter lines of business not officially authorized for national banks. The National City Company quickly became a nationwide bank holding company – holding shares in seven New York banks, eight non-New York banks, and also in the Cuban Banco de la Habana. This was the National City's way around the national banking law's prohibition of branch banking. The holding company gave National City less influence than it would have had with branches, but much more influence than it had with the 1,889 out-of-town correspondent banks with which it dealt in 1912.[417]

Branches, of course, are not necessary. The problem of the mobility of short-term capital could have been alleviated if investors in capital surplus regions had invested in banks in capital deficit regions. The

---

[413] James, *Money and Capital Markets*, p. 90.
[414] Kroos and Blyn, *A History of Financial Intermediaries*, p. 98; Studenski and Kroos, *Financial History*, p. 336.
[415] *Historical Statistics* (1975), Series X 732, Vol. II, p. 1037.
[416] Studenski and Kroos, *Financial History*, p. 336.
[417] Carosso and Sylla, "U.S. Banks in International Finance," p. 69.

National Banking Act, however, militated against that solution. The Act required that in the event of bank failure, stockholders, in addition to losing their investment, could be assessed an amount equal to the *initial par* value of their stock. Although this rule was difficult to enforce and, *ex post*, liquidators rarely collected the full *ex ante* assessment, it still presented potentially serious problems. "To avoid this danger, stockholders had to keep well informed about the condition of a bank and the character of its management – something not easy to do at a distance. Consequently, bank stock tended to remain close to home." In 1876, for example, only 10 percent of national bank stock was owned by out-of-state investors, and in the South and West – the capital deficit regions – the proportion was only slightly above that benchmark.[418]

James comes to a somewhat different conclusion. He notes that over time the fraction of bank equity held by out-of-state investors rose, particularly for banks in the high interest rate regions. He admits that out-of-state is not equivalent to out-of-region (most shares were likely held by investors in neighboring states), but he argues that some holdings were almost certainly interregional. By 1897, for example, almost 40 percent of the shares of national country banks in region eight, a quarter of those in region six, and a fifth of those in region seven were held outside the state. Thus, in the Western regions, about 15 percent of total loans and discounts was provided by funds supplied by out-of-state stockholders, and an unknown fraction could well have come from investors in capital surplus regions.[419]

By 1914 an institutional innovation had relieved the problem of spatial mobility at the short end of the capital market. In the late nineteenth century, the American economy was characterized by substantial interregional and intraregional interest differentials – rates were much higher in the South and West than they were in New England and the Middle Atlantic states, and they were higher in rural areas than in urban areas.[420] Despite complaints from local bankers, banks in low-interest regions began to seek more lucrative investment opportunities than those avail-

[418] Trescott, *Financing American Enterprise*, p. 60.
[419] Region 8 includes N.D., S.D., Ida., Mont., N.M., Az., Utah, Wyo., Washington, and Okla. Region 6 includes Ia., Minn., Mo., Kans., and Neb.; and region 7, Colo., Nev., Calif., and Ore. James, *Money and Capital Markets*, pp. 171–73.
[420] See, for example, Lance E. Davis, "The Investment Market, 1870–1914: The Evolution of a National Market," *The Journal of Economic History*, Vol. XXV, No. 3 (September 1965), pp. 355–99. [Hereafter cited as Davis, "The Investment Market."] Kenneth A. Snowden, "Mortgage Rates and American Capital Market Development in the Nineteenth Century," *The Journal of Economic History*, Vol. XLVII, No. 3 (September 1987), pp. 671–92.

able at home.[421] From a bank's point of view, commercial paper was considered an attractive secondary reserve asset: It was safe, self-liquidating, and short-term. As a result, a formal market for the purchase and sale of commercial paper had been organized in New England and the Eastern states by 1860.[422]

The development of the market received an additional fillip by the passage of the National Banking Act.

> Section 5200 of the federal code prohibited banks from loaning in excess of ten per cent of their capital to any one person or company. But there were two exceptions to this provision. The first exempted from the limit "the discount on bills of exchange drawn in good faith against actually existing values" – in other words, real commercial paper. The obvious presumption here was that, because such loans were based on tangible commodities, a bank would not be endangered by discounting large amounts from a single firm. The second exemption, "the discount of commercial or business paper actually owned by the person negotiating the same," is similarly instructive. Such persons were normally expected to be professional brokers, whose growing presence in the money markets offered reform-minded bankers another means of guarding against favoritism in loans. Not only did the brokers have the responsibility to evaluate the credit-worthiness of the notes they offered for sale, but by interposing themselves between banks and would-be borrowers, they made the lending process more impersonal and thus more objective.[423]

In the two decades after the Civil War the market began to spread westward. There were commercial paper dealers operating in Indianapolis in 1871. By the beginning of the next decade, paper was being traded in Milwaukee, Chicago, and Minneapolis, and, by the middle of the 1880s, Kansas City had been integrated into the market. By the turn of the century, brokers' offices had been opened in San Francisco, Seattle, and Los Angeles. A decade later the Midwestern market had expanded

---

[421] In the antebellum decades a number of states passed laws prohibiting bank loans to out-of-state borrowers. Albert Greef, *The Commercial Paper House in the United States* (Cambridge, Mass.: Harvard University Press, 1938), p. 18. [Hereafter cited as Greef, *The Commercial Paper House.*]

[422] This section (on the evolution of the commercial paper market) draws heavily on Davis, "The Investment Market," Greef, *The Commercial Paper House*, and John A. James, "The Rise and Fall of the Commercial Paper Market, 1900–1930," in Michael D. Bordo and Richard Sylla (eds.), *Anglo-American Financial Systems: Institutions and Markets in the Twentieth Century* (Burr Ridge, Ill. and New York City: Irwin Professional Publishers and Stern School of Business, New York University, 1995), pp. 219–60. [Hereafter cited as James, "The Rise and Fall of the Commercial Paper Market."]

[423] Lamoreaux, "No Arbitrary Discretion," p. 102.

to include Wichita and Dallas. "By 1913 it could be said that the commercial paper houses had representatives 'in all the large cities' in the United States."[424] In terms of volume, it is estimated that the market handled in excess of $1 billion in sales in 1906, and twice that amount in 1914.

The suppliers of paper were sometimes banks in the high-interest areas, but increasingly they were firms – most frequently, medium-sized firms with a net worth between $250,000 and $10 million – seeking to bypass their local banks without severing their ties with the local institutions. On occasion the ultimate demanders were individuals or corporations, but the major customers were commercial banks. By 1900 banks were buying at least 95 percent of the paper passing through the market.[425]

Between the suppliers and demanders stood the middlemen – the commercial paper dealers. The dealers' ability to expand the geographic scope of their activities and emerge as significant players in the interregional – as opposed to the intraregional – capital markets rested on a series of organizational innovations. Initially these middlemen acted simply as brokers. As late as the 1880s, a typical firm still maintained a single office. Bankers who wanted to buy bills, as well as the representatives of banks and firms with paper to sell, visited the office and left their paper or their orders. The paper dealer then attempted to match buyers and sellers and received a commission on any completed transactions.

The first organizational innovation – an innovation that led directly to the modern commercial paper house – was relatively simple: Brokers became dealers. That is, they began to solicit offerings directly from potential suppliers and aggressively search for buyers. The origins of the modern house – an American invention – can be traced to 1857 and to the firm of Henry Clews & Company. Clews described his innovation in the following terms:

> My firm became the largest dealer in mercantile paper, which business had been controlled by two other firms for at least a quarter of a century, and whose old foggy methods were by my innovation easily eclipsed. The merchants at that time would go to those discount firms and leave their receivables, bearing their endorsement, on sale there, and only when sold by piecemeal would they obtain the avails thereof. I had inaugurated the system of buying acceptances and receivables out and out.[426]

[424] Greef, *The Commercial Paper House*, pp. 39–40.
[425] James, "The Rise and Fall of the Commercial Paper Market."
[426] Cited in Kroos and Blyn, *A History of Financial Intermediaries*, p. 108.

Clews's innovation was only the first of a series. Had he still been in business, his firm would have been dwarfed by the "giants that appeared at the end of the century."[427] By that time, as Clews had foreseen, most paper was purchased outright from the borrower and then resold; but purchase and subsequent resale required both more capital and more managerial direction.

Firms became larger and more centralized. At first, the change amounted to no more than employing a few salesmen to call on prospective customers – by the turn of the century some brokers employed several score salesmen – but that expansion in scope was just beginning. There were potential economies of scale in the direct-placement market. To capture those economies, firms were forced to expand their operations into areas not previously served. The new, larger firms began to open branches in potentially lucrative markets and to establish correspondent relations in areas that could not support a branch. In its new form the firm operated out of a main office – located most often in New York, Boston, or Chicago – but it controlled branches in a number of other cities. For example, a 1920 survey of eight large firms indicates that each had, on average, just less than ten out-of-city branches.

Sales were largely the responsibility of the branch offices; their salesmen made regular visits to potential customers both in their home city and in the surrounding territory. The central office raised capital, controlled acquisitions, and directed the sales operations. The results were impressive. As early as the 1890s Western bankers were already lamenting the loss of their local monopolies. In the words of one such banker:

> Until recently, western bankers were able to maintain their loaning rates regardless of the depression of the eastern markets, but now there has arisen an element that wages constant war on the established rates. It is the festive note broker, who with his eastern capital, steps in to disturb the harmonious relations between banker and borrower, and just at the time there seems to be an opportunity to dispose of idle funds at a profitable rate, the banker is confronted with the alternative of cutting his rates or seeing his loans going to outside dealers.[428]

By the beginning of World War I, financial innovation in the purchase and sale of commercial paper outside of the South had substantially overcome short-term interregional capital immobility.

---

[427] Ibid.

[428] J.K. Deming, "Modern Methods of Soliciting Business," *Proceedings, Iowa Bankers Association*, 1892, p. 21.

By way of an epilogue, the commercial paper market could best be described as a proto-institution – an institution created to solve an important economic problem, but one that was destined to be replaced by a more efficient alternative. As banks got larger, the limits on the size of a loan to a single borrower increased. As firms got larger, they developed national reputations, and the asymmetry in information about reputations was further reduced by the emergence of a reliable financial press. As communications improved, a firm in Seattle or Portland could deal almost as easily with a bank in New York or Boston as one actually located in those cities.

There was also a second set of institutional innovations that helped alleviate the problem of the immobility of short-term capital. The post-1870 growth of checking accounts and the resulting decline in the importance of bank notes led to a resurgence of state banks. The reemergence of the state banks was given additional impetus after the mid-1880s by changes in state banking laws that made incorporation easier and reduced minimum capital requirements. Those banks, as well as the existing national banks, developed correspondent relations with banks in other regions.[429]

There is one aspect of nineteenth-century banking that seems, at first glance, somewhat perverse. Instead of banks in the low-interest East holding deposits in banks in the high-interest West, the opposite was true. Even before the passage of the National Banking Act exacerbated the problem, country and Western banks held substantial blocks of funds with their Eastern – particularly New York City – correspondents. Thus, economists – Richard Sylla, for example – have concluded that instead of alleviating the mobility problem, the correspondent system made it worse.[430] John James agrees that short-term capital mobility was certainly adversely affected, but he notes that since the funds held as bankers' balances in New York were used to finance transactions on the securities markets, and those sales promoted long-term capital transfers to firms located throughout the country, the sign of the total impact of the correspondent system on interregional capital transfers is in doubt. "The correspondent banking system, then, was an efficient means of concentrating funds in a national market to facilitate industrial financing; it does not follow, however, that it necessarily resulted in a net flow of funds

---

[429] The material in this section is drawn largely from James, *Money and Capital Markets*, chaps. IV–VI.

[430] Richard Sylla, "Federal Policy, Banking Market Structure, and Capital Mobilization in the United States, 1863–1913," *Journal of Economic History* (December 1969), pp. 657–86.

from West to East."[431] To the extent that firms raising capital on the New York markets were drawn chiefly from new industries and from developing regions, James is correct; in light of the history of the New York Stock Exchange, it is doubtful that they were.[432]

There was a second side to the correspondent relationship that may well have improved the interregional distribution of short-term capital: Banks could borrow from their correspondents, and a country bank could "only borrow from a city bank with which it carried an account. ... Thus, the provision of facilities for inter-bank borrowing was one of the principal services provided by city banks to their country correspondents, although it will be seen that it was more important to Southern banks than to Western banks."[433] The banks borrowed both by direct loans backed by collateral and by rediscounting their own customers' notes. Since the National Banking Act limited the level of such indebtedness to "an amount [not] exceeding its capital," the newly emerging state banks were the greater beneficiaries of this reverse flow. The levels of these loans and rediscounts, although not large in aggregate, were significant, particularly in the South – a region not well served by the commercial paper market.

Not all interbank loans represented interregional transfers. A bank could, and frequently did, lend to a country bank in its region. Even those transfers, however, improved capital mobility. On January 1, 1914, for example, the records of the banks in the twenty-three reserve cities showed that interbank loans represented 6.1 percent ($158.5 million) of their $2.586 billion in loans. There were, however, substantial region-to-region differences. They represented 4.7 percent of all loans in the East, 6.0 percent in the South, 6.1 percent in the West, and 10.5 percent in the Midwest.[434] Between 1897 and 1914 the South was involved in 48.9 percent of all interbank borrowing, the East in 19.0 percent, the Midwest in 12.2 percent, New England in 8.6 percent, the West in 7.0 percent, and the Pacific in 4.3 percent.[435] For the South, in some years between 1892 and 1897, interbank borrowing accounted for as much as 8.0 percent of all loans and discounts, and "if the understatement involved in that figure is considered, it would not seem unlikely that on average more than 10

[431] James, *Money and Capital Markets*, p. 124.
[432] See Section 3-5d(2).
[433] James, *Money and Capital Markets*, pp. 150–51.
[434] Calculated from James, *Money and Capital Markets*, table 24, p. 160.
[435] James, *Money and Capital Markets*, p. 161. The data are from Oliver C. Lockhart, "The Development of Interbank Borrowing in the National System, 1869–1914, II," *Journal of Political Economy*, Vol. XXIX (March 1921), p. 227.

percent of Southern loan funds were borrowed from other banks, a fairly substantial figure."[436]

Finally, by the end of the period, there was a significant level of direct interregional lending by commercial banks. The correspondent system must have played some role in overcoming informational asymmetries. For example, on September 24, 1913, the thirty largest New York bank and trust companies – firms with total loans and discounts, aside from brokers' loans, of $788 million – had directed 21 percent of those advances to banks and individuals in states outside the Eastern region.[437] Nor were direct loans limited to New York banks. A survey conducted in 1916 indicated that national banks in New England had made 23 percent of their loans to borrowers in other regions; in the East, Midwest, and West, the figure was 19 percent, in the West 14 percent, and in the South 4 percent.[438]

3-5c. Non-bank intermediaries

3-5c(1). Non-bank intermediaries: introduction: Because of the very short-term bias of the commercial banks' loan policies, and the much more serious spatial mobilization problems, American non-bank inter-mediaries played a major role in the accumulation-mobilization process. The data are weak, but a rough estimate suggests that the funds directed through those institutions increased from less than $500 million in 1865 to more than $15 billion in 1914 (see Table 3:5c-1). The five decades also saw a dramatic change in the composition of the non-bank sector. In 1870 savings banks accounted for 50 percent of the total, life insurance com-panies for about 20 percent, and the shares in building and loan compa-nies and time deposits in commercial banks divided the remaining 30 percent more or less evenly. Because of the way the data are estimated, they almost certainly minimize the contributions of savings banks and insurance companies. By 1914, however, the relative contribution of the savings banks had declined by more than 50 percent, while time deposits accounted for 30 percent, the reserves of life insurance companies for 25 percent, and trust companies for about 16 percent of the total. What factors accounted for these changes?

---

[436] James, citing data from Brekenridge, *Money and Capital Markets*, p. 163.

[437] In this case the East is defined as Maine, New Hampshire, Vermont, Massachu-setts, Connecticut, New York, New Jersey, Pennsylvania, Maryland, Delaware, and the District of Columbia. James, *Money and Capital Markets*, table 29, p. 168.

[438] James, *Money and Capital Markets*, table 28, p. 167.

3-5c(2). Savings banks: In 1865 savings banks were by far the most important of the non-bank intermediaries. Although they were originally a British innovation, their roots in this country extended back into the second decade of the century, when savings banks were opened in Boston, New York, Philadelphia, and Baltimore. Begun as semiphilanthropical efforts by the East Coast elites, the banks gradually shifted from benevolence to business. Restrictions on depositors and the size of their deposits were removed, portfolios became more diversified, and management more professional. There is some evidence that binding usury laws – laws that made it impossible for interest rates to allocate credit – may have diverted funds from their potentially best use to the uses of the directors; the directors, however, guaranteed safety. Interest payments to depositors were substantial – over the antebellum decades they averaged more than 6 percent in Boston and Baltimore and between 5 and 6 percent in New York City – and, given an absence of safe alternative investment options, growth was rapid.[439] By 1866, 336 banks nationwide served 1,067,061 depositors who held deposits of $282,455,794.[440]

The savings bank was not destined to remain the premier non-bank intermediary. Rapid expansion continued until 1873, at which time the banks together held $802 million of the savings of 2,185,832 depositors. Then problems began to emerge, and they were greatly magnified by the Panic of 1873 and its aftermath. Despite the fact that in 1873 there were savings banks in eighteen states and the District of Columbia, the institution had never really penetrated regions outside New England, New York, and the Middle Atlantic States.[441] Moreover, the banks were no

---

[439] For a more complete discussion of the rise and role of mutual savings banks see Lance E. Davis and Peter L. Payne, "From Benevolence to Business: The Story of Two Savings Banks," *Business History Review*, Vol. XXXII, No. 4 (winter 1958) [Hereafter cited as Davis and Payne, "From Benevolence to Business"]; Emerson W. Keyes, *A History of Savings Banks in the United States* (New York: Bradford Rhodes, 1876); Alan L. Olmstead, *New York City Mutual Savings Banks, 1819–1861* (Chapel Hill: University of North Carolina Press, 1976) [Hereafter cited as Olmstead, *New York Mutual Savings Banks*]; and Peter L. Payne and Lance E. Davis, *The Savings Bank of Baltimore, 1818–1866: A Historical and Analytical Study*, The Johns Hopkins University Studies in Historical and Political Science, Series LXXII, No. 2, 1954 (Baltimore: Johns Hopkins University Press, 1956).

[440] *Annual Report of the Comptroller of the Currency* to the Second Session of the Sixty-fourth Congress of the United States, December 4, 1916 (Washington, D.C.: Government Printing Office, 1917), Vol. I, pp. 85–86.

[441] In 1916, for example, the Comptroller of the Currency reported that, of the nation's 622 mutual savings banks, only 21 were located in other regions: one in

Table 3:5c-1. *Estimated accumulated savings in major types of financial intermediaries, 1865–1914 (millions of dollars)*

Year	Deposits in savings banks	Savings & time Deposits in commercial banks	Shares in savings & loan associations	Deposits in trust companies	Reserves of life insurance companies	Total savings
1865	246	124	69	nd	55	494
1870	550	163	157	nd	221	1,091
1875	924	211	264	nd	361	1,760
1880	819	230	234	150	375	1,808
1885	1,095	203	313	220	457	2,288
1890	1,525	406	400	336	703	3,370
1895	1,811	491	430	398	1,032	4,162
1900	2,130	881	400	687	1,563	5,661
1905	2,740	1,727	430	1,150	2,295	8,342
1910	3,300	3,636	610	1,700	3,226	12,472
1914	3,840	5,264	980	2,811	4,166	17,061

(Percents)

Year	(1) Savings Banks	(2) Commercial Banks	(3) Savings & Loan Associations	(4) Deposits in Trust Companies	(5) Life Insurance Reserves	Total
1865	49.8	25.1	14.0	nd	11.1	100.0
1870	50.4	14.9	14.4	nd	20.3	100.0
1875	52.5	12.0	15.0	nd	20.5	100.0
1880	45.3	12.7	12.9	8.3	20.7	100.0
1885	47.9	8.9	13.7	9.6	20.0	100.0
1890	45.3	12.0	11.9	10.0	20.9	100.0
1895	43.5	11.8	10.3	9.6	24.8	100.0
1900	37.6	15.6	7.1	12.1	27.6	100.0
1905	32.8	20.7	5.2	13.8	27.5	100.0
1910	26.5	29.2	4.9	13.6	25.9	100.0
1914	22.5	30.9	5.7	16.5	24.4	100.0

Sources: (1) Savings Banks: Historical Statistics (1975), Series ×697.

(2) Commercial Banks: 1865–1891: average of (Saving and time deposits/Total Commercial Bank Assets) for 1892–1896 x (Total Commercial Bank Assets) year in question. 1892–1914, *Historical Statistics* (1975), Series ×635, ×657, ×686, ×688, and ×694.

(3) Savings & Loan Associations: 1865–1886: average of (Saving & Loan Deposits)/(Savings Bank Deposits) for 1887–1891 × (Savings Bank Deposits) year in question. 1887–1914: *Historical Statistics* (1975), Series ×691 & ×697.

(4) Deposits in Trust Companies: Data are from Krooss & Blyn, *A History of Financial Intermediaries*, pp. 101–102 & 138 and from Conant, *Wall Street and the Country*, p. 206. 1880 = 1882; 1895 by extrapolation 1892 & 1897; 1900 by extrap olation 1899 & 1901; 1905 by extrapolation 1904 & 1910 and 1914 by extrapolation 1910 & 1919.

(5) Life Insurance Reserves: 1865–1900: (Total Assets of Life Insurance Companies) – from Pritchett, *A Study of Capital Mobilization*, Table (Policy Reserves)/(Total Assets of Life Insurance Companies) – from *Historical Statistics* (1975), Series ×908 & ×916. 1901–1914 from Series ×908 & ×916.

longer semi-philanthropic; they had become professionally managed businesses. Day-to-day operations were much improved, but there were no longer elitist directors willing to guarantee safety in times of economic stress. As a result, an industry whose history had been marked by only a handful of suspensions over the previous half century found itself faced by 123 suspensions in the five years 1875–1879. The actual losses of depositors were minute, but the long-run impact of the suspensions was very serious.[442] On the one hand, depositors no longer believed the savings banks were uniquely safe; on the other hand, government regulation of the banks' portfolios increased as states attempted to "put the savings banks into a position of impregnable safety."[443] Both factors weakened the competitive position of the savings banks relative to commercial banks (the latter had discovered that time deposits could be profitable), to the refurbished and redirected trust companies, and to the newly reinvigorated building and loan associations.

The mutuals were instrumental in mobilizing savings and in making savings available to local business. Until the end of the period, however, they played a minor role in improving spatial mobility. The New York banks began to buy the bonds of other states in the late 1820s, but until the Civil War their portfolios had a heavy local bias. In 1861, for example, 36 percent of the earning assets of the three largest New York banks (The Bank for Savings, the Seaman's, and the Bowery) were invested in local mortgages, more than 25 percent in New York City and New York State bonds, and another 25 percent in U.S. securities. The remaining 13 percent was invested in the bond issues of other states including some in the New England and Middle Atlantic regions.[444] However, by the

---

West Virginia, three in Ohio, five in Indiana, four in Wisconsin, seven in Minnesota, and one in California. *Annual Report of the Comptroller of the Currency* (1916), p. 81.

[442] The mutuals' reputation for safety was hardly undeserved. Looking back at the history of the mutual savings banks from the vantage point of the middle of the twentieth century, John Lintner wrote, "For the country as a whole, the total losses to depositors over the entire 131 year history have been less than 1/4 of 1% of the deposit balance outstanding." John Lintner, *Mutual Savings Banks in the Savings and Mortgage Markets* (Boston: Harvard University Press, 1948), p. 21.

[443] In New York, for example, laws were passed limiting deposits to $5,000 and restricting investments to United States, New York state and municipal bonds, and the bonds of those states that had not defaulted on their loans in the last ten years. Mortgage loans were limited to 50 percent of the assessed value of improved property and 40 percent of unimproved. Kroos and Blyn, *A History of Financial Intermediaries*, pp. 113–14.

[444] All banks chartered before 1848 could write mortgage loans only on property located in New York City or Brooklyn. Olmstead, *New York Mutual Savings Banks*, pp. 91, 162–71.

standards of the other early savings banks, the New York banks could be thought to have played a relatively major role in interregional mobilization. The Savings Bank of Baltimore held bonds in no other state until the mid-1850s, the Provident Institution for Savings in the Town of Boston invested in no such bonds before the Civil War, and it was the 1870s before the Philadelphia Savings Fund Society purchased its first out-of-state issue. The same local bias can be seen in their choice of other assets. In speaking about the performance of the mutuals in Boston and Baltimore, Davis and Payne write, "The investment policy of both banks was marked by a considerable degree of provincialism. It is almost as if the managers refused to invest in any asset they could not touch. The bank shares that they held were the shares of local banks; their loans were almost entirely loans to local residents; and until the mid-'fifties the state and local bonds that they held were limited to the issues of their own states."[445]

In the later years there appears to have been some weakening of the local bias. Although mortgages remained largely local and accounted for more than 45 percent of earning assets, government bonds had declined to barely more than one-fifth of the total by 1914. The mutual holdings of corporate and other securities now represented more than one-quarter of their assets (see Table 3:5c-2).

3-5c(3). Life insurance companies:[446] It is not that savings banks did not grow, it is just that they grew less rapidly than other non-bank intermediaries. In 1865 life insurance companies were fourth in size among the five major non-bank financial institutions, but by 1914 they were second only to time deposits in commercial banks. More importantly, they were without question the most important institutional force pushing toward the integration of the national long-term capital market. Like the savings banks, these firms were organized for one purpose – to sell insurance – but in the process, they accomplished another purpose: the accumulation and mobilization of capital. Even today some holders of life insurance policies probably do not realize that they are simultaneously saving and purchasing insurance. In the nineteenth century it is likely that more than half of those insured were willing to buy an insurance policy long before they were willing to trust their voluntary accumulations to a more traditional bank or non-bank intermediary.

---

[445] Davis and Payne, "From Benevolence to Business," p. 404.

[446] This section draws heavily on Kroos and Blyn, *The History of Financial Intermediaries*, pp. 82–84, 109–13; and Bruce M. Pritchett, *A Study of Capital Mobilization: The Life Insurance Industry of the Nineteenth Century* (New York: Arno Press, 1977).

Table 3:5c-2. Assets of U.S. mutual savings banks, 1896–1914 (millions of dollars)

Year	Loans		Securities			Other assets		Total
	Mortgage	Other loan	United States governments	State & local government	Corporate and other	Cash	Other	
1896	728	146	158	482	230	91	46	1,881
1900	858	169	105	567	462	121	46	2,328
1905	1,121	199	30	673	749	134	63	2,969
1910	1,500	194	13	765	906	156	64	3,598
1914	1,866	219	12	842	986	196	73	4,194
				(Percents)				
1896	38.7	7.8	8.4	25.6	12.2	4.8	2.4	100.0
1900	36.9	7.3	4.5	24.4	19.8	5.2	2.0	100.0
1905	37.8	6.7	1.0	22.7	25.2	4.5	2.1	100.0
1910	41.7	5.4	0.4	21.3	25.2	4.3	1.8	100.0
1914	44.5	5.2	0.3	20.1	23.5	4.7	1.7	100.0

Source: Historical Statistics (1975), Series ×821 to ×830.

The Presbyterian Ministers' Fund of Philadelphia and the Pennsylvania Company for Insurance of Lives and Granting Annuities were in business in the early years of the nineteenth century, but neither firm, nor any other, sold any significant quantity of insurance over the ensuing forty years.[447] The industry in the United States really dates from the 1840s, and its birth rested on two innovations: the application of the mutual principle to life insurance and the development of an adequate mortality table. Even those innovations, although making the industry economically viable, did not guarantee permanent long-run growth. In 1841 fourteen companies wrote 1,211 policies, $4 million of life insurance contracts was in force, and annual premiums totaled a little more than $250,000. A decade later the agency system had been introduced, the number of firms had tripled, the amount of life insurance in force had increased almost twenty-five times, and industry assets totaled about $9.5 million. Between 1850 and 1860 twenty-one new companies were formed, but twenty-six existing companies went out of business. Forty-three companies with assets of $35.6 million oversaw $205 million in contracts, but just five companies – Mutual of New York, Connecticut Mutual, Mutual Benefit, New York Life, and New England Mutual – were responsible for more than 60 percent of the total.

Between 1843 and 1870 the industry's assets and the amount of insurance in force grew by about 20 percent a year. Even in a growing economy markets can become saturated. Such rates could not be maintained, and even slower rates required some changes in product. The industry's continued growth over the last three decades of the century was associated with three innovations: two internal to the industry – tontine and industrial insurance – and one external – a change in the legal environment.[448]

Tontine insurance is simply the other side of the usual insurance bet. In a normal insurance contract, the company bets you live and you bet you die; in a tontine contract, you bet you live and the company bets you die. The idea of tontine insurance dates back at least to the seventeenth century and to the Neapolitan Lorenzo Tonti. Its introduction into the United States dates only to 1868 and is attributed to Henry B. Hyde and his Equitable Insurance Company. In a country without government-

---

[447] Henry Franklin Tyrrell, *Semi-Centennial History of the Northwestern Mutual Life Insurance Company of Milwaukee, Wisconsin* (Milwaukee: Privately Printed, 1908), pp. 32–35. Lester W. Zartman, *The Investments of Life Insurance Companies* (New York: Henry Holt and Co., 1906), p. 14. [Hereafter cited as Zartman, *Investments.*]

[448] Assets grew by about 6 percent per annum and insurance in force by 4 1/2.

underwritten social security and with few private pension plans, tontine insurance could provide old-age protection. The idea therefore had a very broad appeal. Between 1868 and 1905 the four largest companies selling tontine policies had contracted $5.774 billion in *new* business, while at the latter date the five largest companies selling traditional annual dividend insurance supervised only *a total* of $998 million of life insurance in force.[449] In 1905, as a result of complaints from customers and from some insurance companies, the legislature of the state of New York established a committee to investigate business practices in the life insurance industry. The New York Legislature Insurance Investigation Committee of 1905 (the Armstrong Committee) heard testimony from leaders of the industry and others and uncovered some questionable practices. In its report, the Committee recommended a number of changes in business practices, including the prohibition of further sales of tontine insurance. The Legislature adopted most of the committee's recommendations, including the prohibition of new sales on tontine insurance; other states quickly followed suit. That prohibition may have repressed the growth of the industry and its role in capital accumulation and mobilization, at least temporarily. Between 1880 and 1895 reserves of life insurance companies grew at an annual rate of 3.2 percent a year, while all intermediaries together grew at a rate of 2.7 percent. Between 1905 and 1914, the figures were 2.9 percent and 3.5 percent, respectively.[450]

The second innovation was industrial insurance. Imported from Britain in 1877 by the Prudential Insurance Company, it was designed to make insurance available to American workers. Policies with face values as low as $25 were sold door-to-door by a task force of salesmen. Weekly or monthly premiums were collected door-to-door by the same salesmen. Like the tontine companies, the firms that specialized in industrial insurance grew very rapidly. The Metropolitan – ranked eighteenth in 1875 with $25 million in force – was by 1910 the nation's largest, with the face value of the policies on its books worth more than $2 billion. The Pru-

---

[449] Kroos and Blyn label tontine insurance "a swindle," and it was outlawed in New York as a result of information uncovered by the Armstrong Committee investigation. For a favorable and more reasonable view of such insurance, see Roger L. Ransom and Richard Sutch, "Tontine Insurance and the Armstrong Investigation: A Case of Stifled Innovation, 1868–1905," *The Journal of Economic History*, Vol. XLVII, No. 2 (June 1987), pp. 379–90. [Hereafter cited as Ransom and Sutch, "Tontine Insurance and the Armstrong Investigation."]

[450] See Ransom and Sutch, "Tontine Insurance and the Armstrong Investigation"; R. Carlyle Buley, *The American Life Convention 1906–1957: A Study in the History of Life Insurance* (New York: Appleton-Century Crofts, 1953), pp. 225–44.

dential, with insurance of only $250,000 in force in 1876, had reached $139 million by 1890.[451]

Despite their rapid growth, the life insurance companies might not have played a significantly larger role in capital mobilization than the mutual savings banks had it not been for changes in the legal environment. Initially most states had laws restricting investments by insurance companies to safe government securities and to mortgages on property close to home. In the late 1860s only four states permitted investments in corporate securities; almost all had some restrictions on investment policy – most often a prohibition against investment in mortgages on out-of-state property. During the last third of the century, however, most of these laws were amended to provide a wider range of investment alternatives. Matching earlier legal revisions in New England, the New York legislature gradually expanded the area in which the state's insurance companies could invest in mortgages, until by the early 1880s they were free to invest in mortgages on property located anywhere in the United States. By 1905 only Georgia, Nebraska, Pennsylvania, and Texas retained laws prohibiting investment in out-of-state mortgages; California, Colorado, Connecticut, New Jersey, Pennsylvania, Illinois, and Wisconsin had all begun to permit at least some investment in corporate securities.[452]

The effect of these combined private and public institutional innovations can be seen in Tables 3:5c-3 and 3:5c-4. Holdings of government bonds declined from one-third of all assets in 1865 to less than 5 percent in 1914. Initially, those bonds were replaced by mortgages – they represented between 40 percent and 50 percent of all investments from 1870 to 1890 – and even in 1914 they still constituted more than one-third. Beginning in the 1880s private securities began to bulk large in the industry's portfolio. They constituted more than two-fifths of the total in the early twentieth century and represented one-third in 1914. The vast majority of the additions to the portfolio of securities were the issues of rails – from 3 percent in 1865 to 70 percent in 1914. Utilities had increased from less than 1 to almost 5 percent, and life insurance companies even held $14 million in industrial stocks and bonds.

The increasing industrial scope of the portfolios was almost matched by increases in the geographical range of investments. While developments in the securities markets and in the financial press eased the

---

[451] For an excellent discussion of both tontine and industrial insurance, see Douglass North, "Capital Accumulation in Life Insurance Between the Civil War and the Investigation of 1905," in William Miller (ed.), *Men in Business* (Cambridge, Mass.: Harvard University Press, 1952).

[452] Zartman, *Investments*, pp. 150–70, 243.

Table 3:5c-3. *Assets of U.S. life insurance companies*
(millions of dollars)

Year	Total U.S. government bonds	Total U.S. private securities	Total foreign bonds	Mortgages	Real estate	Other assets	Total assets
1865	27	2	0	21	2	30	82
1870	41	8	0	113	10	112	284
1875	65	15	0	234	25	96	435
1880	105	30	0	179	55	95	462
1885	60	135	1	222	66	80	564
1890	59	211	13	328	85	113	809
1895	115	374	26	417	128	162	1,222
1900	99	756	77	502	160	293	1,886
1905	145	1,127	112	724	171	427	2,706
1910	198	1,439	153	1,227	173	686	3,876
1914	237	1,645	183	1,706	171	993	4,935
			(percents)				
1865	32.6	2.7	0.0	25.2	2.8	36.8	100.0
1870	14.3	2.9	0.0	39.8	3.6	39.3	100.0
1875	14.9	3.4	0.1	53.9	5.8	22.0	100.0
1880	22.6	6.5	0.0	38.6	11.8	20.5	100.0
1885	10.6	23.9	0.2	39.4	11.6	14.2	100.0
1890	7.3	26.1	1.6	40.5	10.5	14.0	100.0
1895	9.4	30.6	2.1	34.1	10.5	13.3	100.0
1900	5.3	40.1	4.1	26.6	8.5	15.5	100.0
1905	5.4	41.6	4.1	26.8	6.3	15.8	100.0
1910	5.1	37.1	3.9	31.7	4.5	17.7	100.0
1914	4.8	33.3	3.7	34.6	3.5	20.1	100.0

Sources: For 1865–1900: Bruce M. Pritchett, *A Study of Capital Mobilization: The Life Insurance Industry of the Nineteenth Century* (New York: Arno Press, 1977), Table A1, pp. 290–347. For 1905–1914: *Historical Statistics* (1975). For 1905–1914 Bonds have been divided between Government and Private and Private Bonds between U.S. and foreign on the basis of the distribution in 1900.

problems of monitoring the financial status of firms far removed from New York City, Hartford, or Boston, they did not solve the problem of monitoring mortgages beyond the Hudson River. Yet another innovation was required. "In order to lend inter-regionally, intermediaries had to employ loan agents who could make and enforce mortgage contracts

Table 3:5c-4. *Industrial distribution U.S. life insurance companies holdings of securities, 1865–1910 (thousands of dollars)*

Year	United States Governments	State & local government	Railroads	Financial	Utilities	Industrials	Canal	Foreign	Other	Total bonds	Total stocks	Total securities
1865	20,832	5,928	996	1,011	63	25	91	0	0	27,698	1,248	28,946
1870	24,086	16,508	4,223	2,386	856	105	661	100	0	45,322	3,603	48,925
1875	24,800	39,882	6,658	4,253	2,496	467	618	317	131	74,510	5,112	79,622
1880	40,025	64,493	21,582	4,982	1,779	143	1,275	87	177	127,816	6,727	134,543
1885	16,159	43,860	116,702	6,359	8,630	1,380	1,286	1,374	164	176,457	19,457	195,914
1890	6,501	52,398	187,196	10,272	11,064	1,969	486	12,621	139	252,083	30,563	282,646
1895	17,036	97,954	314,978	22,196	23,322	6,475	13	25,579	7,118	455,305	59,366	514,671
1900	7,460	91,850	648,475	37,228	45,492	14,163	34	76,615	10,318	830,550	101,085	931,635
					(percents)							
1865	72.0	20.5	3.4	3.5	0.2	0.1	0.3	0.0	0.0	95.7	4.3	100.0
1870	49.2	33.7	8.6	4.9	1.7	0.2	1.4	0.2	0.0	92.6	7.4	100.0
1875	31.1	50.1	8.4	5.3	3.1	0.6	0.8	0.4	0.2	93.6	6.4	100.0
1880	29.7	47.9	16.0	3.7	1.3	0.1	0.9	0.1	0.1	95.0	5.0	100.0
1885	8.2	22.4	59.6	3.2	4.4	0.7	0.7	0.7	0.1	90.1	9.9	100.0
1890	2.3	18.5	66.2	3.6	3.9	0.7	0.2	4.5	0.0	89.2	10.8	100.0
1895	3.3	19.0	61.2	4.3	4.5	1.3	0.0	5.0	1.4	88.5	11.5	100.0
1900	0.8	9.9	69.6	4.0	4.9	1.5	0.0	8.2	1.1	89.1	10.9	100.0

Sources: Bruce M. Pritchett, *A Study of Capital Mobilization: The Life Insurance Industry of the Nineteenth Century* (New York: Arno Press, 1977), Table A1, pp. 290–347.

in distant markets. But these agents also had to be monitored."[453] Local building associations, savings banks, and commercial banks did not need such loan agents because they made mortgage loans only in their local markets. The difficulty in monitoring explains the fact that throughout the nineteenth century, the vast majority of mortgage loans were made by local lenders. For the years 1890–93, for example, Snowden places the proportion at more than three-fourths.

As the insurance companies began to exploit the national mortgage market, they were faced by a difficult monitoring problem. "A few insurance companies internalized the supervision of loan agents within elaborate branch office networks [the Northwestern Mutual, for example], but most contracted with other firms, called mortgage companies, to supervise loan agents for them."[454] Mortgage companies had begun to monitor loan agents for Eastern investors as early as the 1850s, and by the 1890s they had developed very sophisticated organizational structures that permitted them to negotiate and broker loans efficiently. When the insurance companies entered the interregional mortgage market, they contracted with those companies or with firms that were identical in structure and function to negotiate and enforce their mortgage loans. The Aetna, for example, "chose to lend through only one mortgage company in each market and relied on the exclusivity of the relationship to strengthen that agency's incentive to perform faithfully." Travelers, on the other hand, used several companies in each state.

The system did not survive the agricultural depression of the 1930s, but it worked well in the years before World War I. Most of the mortgage banks failed during the drought of the 1880s, and many individual investors were unable to cope with the problems inherent in any attempt to service the mortgage contracts of failed mortgage companies. The insurance companies were much better equipped to assume the enforcement obligations of their Western mortgage company correspondents. "In fact, the life insurance-mortgage company connection became the dominant interregional mortgage lending structure precisely because insurance companies could conduct their own property management operations if it became necessary for them to do so. . . . The unique com-

---

[453] Much of this section is drawn from Kenneth Snowden, "The Evolution of Interregional Mortgage Lending Channels, 1870–1940: The Life Insurance–Mortgage Company Connection," University of North Carolina, Greensboro, Working Papers in Business and Economics, Working Paper Series ECO94102, January, 1994. [Hereafter cited as Snowden, "The Evolution of Interregional Mortgage Lending Channels."] The quotations are all from Snowden, pp. 1, 35, 36, and 39.

[454] For a thorough discussion of the policies of the Northwestern Mutual, see Harold Williamson and Orange Smally, *Northwestern Mutual Life: A Century of Trusteeship* (Evanston, Ill.: Northwestern University Press, 1957).

bination of large size, a national market and the long-term nature of their liabilities provided insurance companies with the resources and organizational flexibility to assume substantial investments in interregional property without jeopardizing their solvency. Insurance companies came to dominate the interregional mortgage market because of their intrinsic ability to cope with contingent enforcement costs, and not because they had an advantage in negotiating and enforcing interregional mortgage loans under 'normal' circumstances."

An analysis of the interest rates earned on their portfolios by insurance companies located in different regions shows that interregional differences in rates were reduced much more rapidly than were the interregional differentials in average mortgage rates. It appears that the insurance companies, freed of their managerial and legal restrictions, were willing and able to move funds across interregional boundaries before most private investors were willing to take that step. Moreover, the data suggest that the companies' commitments to interregional mortgages were not large enough to completely arbitrage the market.[455]

An examination of the regional distribution of the earning assets of insurance companies leads to similar conclusions in the case of both mortgages and private securities (Table 3:5c-5). Standardizing for population differences, the figures suggest that until 1880 the insurance companies' investments were overwhelmingly concentrated in New England and the Middle Atlantic States. Thereafter, the South Atlantic region aside, there was a general movement toward a more equal geographic distribution. In the case of New England, the region's share had declined to the national average by 1900, although the Middle Atlantic states still received half again their normal proportions. The Northwestern and, to a lesser extent, the North Central regions had both become major beneficiaries of the life insurance companies' new investment policies.

3-5c(4). Savings and time deposits in commercial banks: It is something of a puzzle as to why it took commercial banks so long to recognize the potential profitability of time and savings accounts. The National Banking Act did not contain the favorable reserve requirements of the Federal Reserve Act, but that omission hardly made savings accounts less profitable than demand deposits, and such deposits should have provided some insurance against internal drain.[456] In the East those accounts

[455] Davis, "The Investment Market 1870–1914," pp. 383–85.

[456] The Federal Reserve Act set reserves against time deposits at 5 percent as opposed to the 18-15-12 percent requirements for demand deposits. Trescott, *Financing American Enterprise*, pp. 190–91.

Table 3:5c-5. *Life insurance company investments relative to population, by region*

	1860	1870	1880	1890	1900
Region 1* **New England**					
Percent stocks & bonds	33.8	33.0	18.1	7.9	8.8
Percent mortgages & real estate	nd	nd	6.9	3.0	2.2
Percent all earning assets	nd	nd	12.1	6.1	7.2
Percent of population	10.0	9.0	8.0	7.5	7.4
Stocks & bonds relatives	339	365	226	105	120
Mortgage and real estate relatives	nd	nd	86	40	29
All earning asset relatives	nd	nd	151	82	98
Region 2* **Middle Atlantic**					
Percent stocks & bonds	49.9	49.9	58.4	30.1	31.5
Percent mortgages & real estate	nd	nd	47.4	46.3	40.5
Percent all earning assets	nd	nd	50.6	39.9	35.4
Percent of population	26.5	25.5	23.4	22.5	22.5
Stocks & bonds relatives	188	196	249	134	140
Mortgage and real estate relatives	nd	nd	202	206	180
All earning asset relatives	nd	nd	216	178	157
Region 3* **Central Northern**					
Percent stocks & bonds	16.0	10.0	13.9	21.2	18.6
Percent mortgages & real estate	nd	nd	30.1	27.5	24.0
Percent all earning assets	nd	nd	25.4	25.0	20.9

	1860	1870	1880	1890	1900
Region 5* **Gulf and Mississippi Valley**					
Percent stocks & bonds	0.3	1.5	1.3	4.7	4.3
Percent mortgages & real estate	nd	nd	0.1	0.5	1.6
Percent all earning assets	nd	nd	0.5	2.1	3.1
Percent of population	15.0	13.3	13.0	12.0	11.8
Stocks & bonds relatives	2	11	10	39	36
Mortgage and real estate relatives	nd	nd	1	4	13
All earning asset relatives	nd	nd	4	18	26
Region 6* **Southwestern**					
Percent stocks & bonds	0.0	1.1	5.8	11.1	13.5
Percent mortgages & real estate	nd	nd	3.5	9.3	11.6
Percent all earning assets	nd	nd	4.1	10.0	12.7
Percent of population	7.8	9.1	11.7	13.2	13.8
Stocks & bonds relatives	0	12	49	84	98
Mortgage and real estate relatives	nd	nd	30	70	84
All earning asset relatives	nd	nd	35	76	92
Region 7* **Northwestern**					
Percent stocks & bonds	0.0	1.0	0.8	18.2	13.3
Percent mortgages & real estate	nd	nd	9.0	10.9	15.4
Percent all earning assets	nd	nd	6.6	13.8	14.2

Region 4*
South Atlantic

Percent of population	22.0	23.7	22.3	21.4	21.0
Stocks & bonds relatives	73	42	62	99	88
Mortgage and real estate relatives	nd	nd	135	128	114
All earning asset relatives	nd	nd	114	117	100
Percent stocks & bonds	0.0	2.2	0.7	4.6	4.7
Percent mortgages & real estate	nd	nd	0.2	0.2	0.7
Percent all earning assets	nd	nd	0.4	1.9	3.0
Percent of population	14.3	12.5	12.6	11.8	11.6
Stocks & bonds relatives	0	18	6	39	40
Mortgage and real estate relatives	nd	nd	2	1	6
All earning asset relatives	nd	nd	3	16	26

Region 8*
Pacific

Percent of population	2.8	4.7	6.1	8.0	8.0
Stocks & bonds relatives	0	21	14	228	165
Mortgage and real estate relatives	nd	nd	147	137	191
All earning asset relatives	nd	nd	109	173	176
Percent stocks & bonds	0.0	1.2	1.1	2.2	5.3
Percent mortgages & real estate	nd	nd	0.0	0.4	1.2
Percent all earning assets	nd	nd	0.3	1.1	3.5
Percent of population	1.6	2.1	2.8	3.7	4.0
Stocks & bonds relatives	0	56	38	60	133
Mortgage and real estate relatives	nd	nd	1	11	30
All earning asset relatives	nd	nd	11	30	89

Notes: *Regions:
1. New England: Conn., Mass., N. H., R. I., Vt.
2. Middle Atlantic: D. C., Del., Md., N. J., N. Y., Pa.
3. Central Northern: Ind., Ill., Mich., Ohio, Wisc.
4. South Atlantic: Fla., Ga., N. C., S. C., Va., W. Va.
5. Gulf and Missippi Valley: Ala., Ky., La., Miss., Tenn.
6. South-Western: Ark., Colo., Kans., Mo., N. M., Okla., Texas.
7. North-Western: Iowa, Mont., Minn., Neb., N. D., S. D., Wyo.
8. Ariz., Cal., Idaho, Nev., Ore., Utah, Wash.

Sources: Populations from *Historical Statistics* (1975), Series A 195, Volume 1, pp. 24–37. Regional Breakdown of Assets from B. Prichett, *A Study of Capital Mobilization*, Appendix Table A1, pp. 307–347.

had to compete against the elite-guaranteed mutuals, and that fact may have reduced the incentive to expand into the new field. Elsewhere, the competition was much less intense. Certainly after the mutual savings bank debacle of the late 1870s and the ensuing onslaught of regulations that reduced their ability to pay high rates of interest, commercial banks found themselves much more favorably placed. "[In] the West, commercial banks caught most of the savings accounts in their interest-bearing time-deposit net."[457] A decade later, the national banks, with rigid legal-reserve requirements, found themselves at a disadvantage vis à vis the trust companies, but the record suggests that once the state banks had decided to move aggressively into the market, they proved very tough competitors. In 1896 more than 50 percent of the liabilities of non-national banks consisted of time deposits, and in 1914 the ratio was still more than 45 percent. In the case of national banks, however, the comparable figures were 2 and 11 percent. By 1930, while the ratio for non-national banks had changed but little, the figure for national banks had risen to almost 30 percent.[458]

It is clear that once the non-national banks had turned their attention to time deposits, they were very successful. Between 1892 and 1914 those deposits increased from $470 million to $4.441 billion, a rate of increase of more than 10 percent a year. Their contribution to the solution of the accumulation and mobilization problems is less clear. To the extent that the existence of an intermediary, where none had existed before, increased the propensity to save, their contribution was clearly positive. To the extent that they merely substituted savings directed toward investments in commercial paper for savings that would otherwise have been directed by a savings bank to mortgages and, perhaps, non-commercial business loans, they may well have hindered the development of an efficient capital market.

3-5c(5). Trust companies: For a three-decade period between 1890 and 1920, trust companies were an important link in the nation's financial network of non-bank intermediaries, but less is known about them than about any other major American financial institution. Trusts date back to the 1820s. At that time their function was simply "to execute trusts for individuals, living and dead, and for estates and corporations."[459] Because their business was small, little attempt was made to regulate them. No

---

[457] Kroos and Blyn, *A History of Financial Intermediaries*, p. 114.

[458] *U.S. Historical Statistics* (1957), series X43, X60, X65, and X82, pp. 626–29.

[459] Charles A. Conant, *Wall Street and The Country: A Study of Recent Financial Tendencies* (New York: privately printed, 1904; reprinted by Greenwood Press, New York, 1968), p. 209. [Hereafter cited as Conant, *Wall Street and the Country*.]

regulation meant few records. With thirty-four states in the Union by 1865, state charters almost guaranteed heterogeneity. As a result, any general statement is not really general, and any conclusions are certainly open to question.[460] Until late in the nineteenth century, neither problem was very serious; there were only seven trust companies in the United States in 1865.[461] In the first decade and a half after the Civil War, there was some growth – railroad bond issues and reorganizations "created profitable trust opportunities and fiscal agency relationships" and "an increasing number of families were becoming wealthy enough to use personal trust services" – but in 1879 there were still no more trusts than states (thirty-seven).[462]

Rapid growth was delayed for another decade, but financial entrepreneurs finally recognized the implications of two quite different sets of events, and the modern trust company – "an essentially American institution" – was born.[463] First, the 1864 tax on state bank notes had forced many commercial banks to take out national bank charters, and national banks were not authorized to perform trust functions.[464] One potential source of competition had been removed, at least temporarily. Later, with the increased use of checking accounts and the general recognition that time deposits could be profitable, there was a resurgence of banks that were not constrained by federal rules. Second, the charters of the trust companies in most states had permitted them to do a general banking business – that is, to accept time and demand deposits and to make collateral loans – in the process of carrying out their primary function of managing personal and corporate trust accounts.[465] It is difficult, if not impossible, to distinguish between the exercise of such powers in pursuit of the trust business as opposed to the banking business. Thus, in spite of the intentions of the state governments, the trusts were able to act, for all intents and purposes, as commercial banks.[466]

There was one important difference. The trusts were not subject to federal regulation, and state regulation of trust companies initially was either nonexistent or much less stringent than the rules that governed

---

[460] George E. Barnett, *State Banks and Trust Companies Since the Passage of the National Bank Act* (Washington, D.C.: GPO, 1911), pp. 12–22. [Hereafter cited as Barnett, *State Banks and Trust Companies.*]

[461] Kroos and Blyn, *A History of Financial Intermediaries*, p. 102.

[462] Trescott, *Financing American Enterprise*, p. 130; Barnett, *State Banks and Trust Companies*, p. 201.

[463] The quotation is from a speech by Charles F. Phillips to the American Bankers Association in 1902. Cited in Conant, *Wall Street and the Country*, p. 205.

[464] Trescott, *Financing American Enterprise*, pp. 54–55.

[465] Kroos and Blyn, *A History of Financial Intermediaries*, p. 138.

[466] James, *Money and Capital Markets*, p. 39.

traditional commercial banks. First, reserves were often not required – there were, for example, no reserve requirements in Massachusetts until 1904 and in New York until 1906 – and when there were such requirements, they were usually substantially lower for trusts than for commercial banks. As a contemporary writer put it, "the trust companies have heretofore kept such reserves as, in the opinion of their officers, were required to meet demands upon them."[467] Second, their investment policies were much less constrained. In almost all states they were allowed to invest in mortgages – often in out-of-state mortgages. Massachusetts trusts, for example, could invest in property located anywhere in New England, New York, or Pennsylvania. In addition, trusts in most states were allowed to invest in private stocks and bonds. Third, because the trusts' deposits were not a product of their loan policies, they were much more stable.[468] Finally, in certain states, New York, for example, trust companies were allowed to have branches, including branches abroad. "The first U.S. joint-stock company to branch abroad was the Jarvis Conklin Mortgage Trust Company, which opened a branch in London in 1887." In 1912 it became the property of New York's Equitable Trust Company. The Equitable had already opened a branch in Paris in 1910. "Three additional New York trust companies also opened foreign branches before 1914: The Guarantee Trust Company (in London, 1897), the Farmers' Loan and Trust Company (in London and Paris, both in 1906), and the Empire Trust Company (in London, 1913). These trust company branches were the only foreign branches of domestic U.S. 'banks' before 1914."

Before 1914 two American corporations were chartered under state banking laws to engage solely in foreign banking. The International Banking Corporation (IBC) was chartered in Connecticut in 1901. Before 1914 the IBC had opened sixteen branches, in China, England, India, Japan, the Philippines, Panama, Singapore, and Mexico. A similar, but smaller, enterprise, the Continental Banking and Trust Company of Panama, was incorporated under West Virginia law in 1913 and opened three branches in Panama and one in Colombia.

These trust company and foreign banking company branches, numbering twenty-six in all, were the only foreign branches of American joint-stock banks established before 1914. Their late arrival and meager numbers are significant mainly in illustrating the inhibiting effects of American law on joint-stock bank expansion abroad.

---

[467] Conant, *Wall Street and the Countryside*, p. 225.
[468] Kroos and Blyn, *A History of Financial Intermediaries*, pp. 101–2, 138. Barnett, *State Bank and Trust Companies*, pp. 234–38.

In 1889 there were sixty-three trust companies in the United States, a decade later there were 276, and in 1909 there were 1,079.[469] Moreover, given their preferred position outside the normal regulatory channels, the trusts were able to pay higher rates of interest on both time and demand deposits than their more severely constrained competitors. As savers responded to these economic incentives, deposits flowed in. In 1882 deposits totaled $150 million in 1892, $400 million in 1902, $969 million, and in 1910, $1.7 billion.

These modern trusts were a far cry from their early-nineteenth-century antecedents, and "their trust services proper might be rather slight." In the words of George Barnett, many were "entirely without trust powers or chose not to use their trust powers." In 1909 twenty-six of the forty-eight trusts in Massachusetts did not even have trust departments; in Maine, in 1900, the trusts "held banking assets one hundred times as large as their trust account assets." In Massachusetts, Maine, and Vermont, no state banks – only trust companies – had been chartered for years.[470] The trusts had become de facto commercial banks – but banks unencumbered by any vestige of the real bills doctrine and with both an ability and a willingness to invest in a wide range of assets.

In the East – and most trust companies were in the East – they typically kept their liquid reserves in the call money market. In both that region and in the rest of the country, their long-term portfolios consisted largely of mortgages and increasingly of securities.[471] Once the investment banks saw the opportunities offered by the trust companies, they were quick to form alliances with this new and promising intermediary. When a syndicate was formed, the trusts provided short-term capital to support the underwriting activities. Later, when the securities were sold, they provided a ready market, particularly for railroad and utility issues. Between 1900 and 1912 the share of real estate and mortgages in the trusts' portfolios declined by about two-fifths, and the difference was made up by security purchases.[472] The trusts' connections with the formal securities markets meant that they contributed more to interregional

---

[469] Barnett, *State Bank and Trust Companies*, p. 201.
[470] Barnett, *State Bank and Trust Companies*, pp. 234–38. Trescott, *Financing American Enterprise*, p. 92.
[471] For trust companies, capital per capita ranged from $10.15 per person in the East, to $5.23 in New England, to $4.49 in the Pacific region, to $3.12 in the Midwest, to $0.92 in the South, to a low of $0.61 in the West. That distribution is even more skewed than the distribution of National Bank capital. The ratio of trust company capital to national bank capital was 63.6 percent in the East, 32.6 percent in the Midwest, 32.4 percent in New England, 29.3 percent in the Pacific region, 16.3 percent in the South, and 7.5 percent in the West.
[472] Kroos and Blyn, *A History of Financial Intermediaries*, p. 140.

mobility than their geographic concentration would suggest. However, since mortgage lending tended to be restricted to neighboring states, and since the New York security exchanges did not service all regions and industries equally, although the trust companies may well have alleviated the mobilization problem, they did not solve it.

Moreover, the commercial banks were hardly content to leave the profitable field of unregulated banking to the trust companies. The banks lobbied for change. The further the trusts moved into commercial banking, the greater the intensity of the lobbying effort, and the stricter state regulations became. At the same time, beginning with California in 1909, states gradually changed their laws to permit commercial banks to do a fiduciary business. The restrictions on the national banks, however, were not relaxed until the Federal Reserve Act, and they were not dropped completely until 1918.[473] In the case of banks too small to acquire a trust affiliate, these legal changes were important.

In the case of the large banks, neither change was really necessary. There was a simpler solution: A commercial bank could form or acquire a trust affiliate – "separately incorporated but linked by stock ownership and possible interlocking management." In 1903 the First National Bank of Chicago created the First Trust and Savings, and a group of New York banks sponsored the formation of Bankers Trust.[474] By 1911 there were already 300 trust affiliates of national banks.[475]

3-5c(6). Building and loan societies: There is general agreement that the first building and loan association was established in Oxford, Pennsylvania, a Philadelphia suburb, in 1831, but the institution really dates from the association movement of the next decade.[476] These associations were designed to provide home mortgage loans in urban areas. Prospective borrowers agreed to make regular payments for a ten-year period on a number of shares equal to the value of the loan that they expected to receive. Those payments were then used to make mortgage loans to members of the association. At some time during the life of the association, each member received a loan equal to the value of his pledge, and from that date he made interest and capital payments on the value of his loan. The association was terminated when the value of each member's

---

[473] Kroos and Blyn, *A History of Financial Intermediaries*, p. 139.
[474] Trescott, *Financing American Enterprise*, p. 130.
[475] Kroos and Blyn, *A History of Financial Intermediaries*, p. 139.
[476] Morton Bodfish, *History of the Building and Loan in the United States* (Chicago: United States Building and Loan League, 1931), pp. 32–34.

shares grew equal to the principal of his loan.[477] Since the organizations were temporary, "building and loan associations did not receive any particular notice until long after they had sprung into full growth." Although Pennsylvania was the home of a large number of these associations – 148 were chartered in the 1860s and another 317 in the early 1870s – most states had none until late in the 1870s.[478]

In the 1880s and 1890s, however, the "terminating plan" was gradually replaced by a more permanent form of organization. Initially introduced in South Carolina in the 1840s, the new structure was not widely copied until the 1880s. Under the new permanent plan members' accounts were kept separately, and they were allowed to add to their savings at any time. More importantly, under the popular Dayton variant, both share deposits and dividends could be withdrawn at any time without penalty. The associations had changed their main objective. "Before the Civil War, they had been small, temporary, and designed primarily to help would-be home owners; by the end of the century they were more involved in gathering up savings" – they had become thrift institutions.[479] After that change in mission, growth was rapid. Rotella and Snowden place the number of associations nationally at 547 located in 185 cities in 1880 and 5,597 located in 2,012 cities in 1893. They also suggest that, by the latter date, building associations were relatively ubiquitous across all regions, displaying little of the East Coast bias so apparent in the other institutions.[480]

The associations with portfolios consisting of nothing but urban mortgages played only an indirect role in interindustry mobilization. Except for a decade-long period extending from the mid-1880s until 1896, they also played almost no role in interregional mobilization. In that ten-year period, however, a number of national associations were chartered. The 240-odd nationals were designed to make loans across and within broad regional markets. They attracted savers by claiming greater safety (more

---

[477] Elyce Rotella and Kenneth Snowden, "The Building Association Movement of the Late Nineteenth Century," Working Papers in Business and Economics, University of North Carolina, Greensboro, Working Paper Series ECO940101, January, 1994. p. 3. [Hereafter cited as Rotella and Snowden, "The Building Association Movement."]

[478] Kroos and Blyn, *A History of Financial Intermediaries*, pp. 114–15, 125. The quotation is from p. 114.

[479] Kroos and Blyn, *A History of Financial Intermediaries*, pp. 115, 126.

[480] Rotella and Snowden, "The Building Association Movement," table 2. For cities under 8,000, for example, all three of the southern regions – South Atlantic, East South Central, and West South Central – display a ratio of associations to population above the U.S. average.

geographically diverse portfolios), greater earnings (loans in high-interest regions), and lower expenses (economies of scale). They faltered because they could not solve the monitoring problem. A wave of closings followed the failure of the largest national, the Southern Building and Loan Association of Knoxville, Tennessee; only six nationals survived into the twentieth century.[481]

As for the rest of the industry, although there was almost no state regulation until the failure of the nationals led to legal prohibitions against out-of-state lending, the members of some 4,000 associations had long before privately agreed to restrict their lending operations to their home counties. Despite that restriction, deposits between 1897 and 1914 more than doubled (from $420 to $890 million), and the associations directed the stream of savings to meeting the demands of one of the most capital-intensive sectors of the economy: urban housing.

3-5d. The formal securities market

3-5d(1). Investment banking:[482] Although it is generally conceded that Jay Cooke and Company was the first modern American investment bank, Cooke did not invent the institution, nor was he the first to import it into the United States. Private banks had provided some investment banking functions since early in the nineteenth century, and a number evolved into true investment banks in the post-Cooke era – some, in fact, lasted much longer than Cooke himself.

Prime, Ward and King, organized in New York in 1826, and John E. Thayer and Brother, a firm launched in Boston in 1839, are examples of brokers who moved from foreign exchange operations to become private bankers, and then assumed some of the functions of an investment bank. On an asymptotic path were certain mercantile firms, Thomas Biddle and Co. of Philadelphia and Alexander Brown and Sons of Baltimore, to cite two examples. Those firms moved first into private banking and then later into pre-modern investment banking. Both sets of firms shared one common attribute: Because of their earlier activities, they had close connections with European, particularly British, capital markets. Prime,

---

[481] Snowden, "The Evolution of Interregional Mortgage Lending Channels," p. 16.

[482] This section draws heavily on Vincent P. Carosso, *Investment Banking in America: A History*, Harvard University Studies in Business History, Vol. 25 (Cambridge, Mass.: Harvard University Press, 1970), pp. 1–136 [Hereafter cited as Carosso, *Investment Banking*]; G. Edwards, *The Evolution of Finance Capitalism* (New York: 1938); Kroos and Blyn, *A History of Financial Intermediaries*, pp. 105–8, 129–33; and Fritz Redlich, *The Molding of American Banking: Men and Ideas*, 2 Vols. (New York: 1947, 1951), Vol. II.

Ward & King had a long-standing association with Baring Brothers; Thayer dealt with the British house McCalmont & Co.; and the Browns had their own English correspondent, Brown, Shipley & Co. of Liverpool. At times the European financial connection was even more direct. The Frankfurt and Paris Rothschilds sent August Belmont to the United States to investigate financial conditions. On his arrival he organized August Belmont & Company. Similarly, Speyer & Co. was founded by members of an old German international banking family.

Although there were a few private bankers without a European financial connection, they were relatively rare. Jay Cooke's original firm – Clark & Dodge – generally depended on domestic sources of funds. Somewhat later, the Boston firm of Lee, Higginson, and Co., initially brokers and exchange dealers, drew its primary support from the group of Boston capitalists that played such an important role in textile finance.

In the United States the movement to modern investment banking was gradual. In the 1850s the firm of Winslow, Lanier & Co "probably came closer than any other to providing clients with most of the investment services associated with the great banking houses of the latter part of the nineteenth and the early twentieth centuries."[483] It was, however, the Civil War–induced financial demands of the federal government that led to the first generally recognized modern investment bank, Jay Cooke & Company.[484] The story is a familiar one. Having earlier joined with Drexel & Co. to market a $3 million Pennsylvania state defense issue, Cooke in 1862 assumed the task of marketing the federal government's 5–20's. Employing a variety of modern advertising and sales techniques, Cooke sold $362 million of those bonds before the end of 1864. At the end of the war, that effort was followed by an equally successful campaign to market a new issue, the 7–30's. "Cooke's bond drives were the first successful, large-scale effort to extend the security market to accommodate thousands of individuals with small savings, many of whom had never before owned a bond. The success of these operations made his firm the leading and most widely known banking house in the country."[485]

Cooke's attempts to emulate his wartime successes in the private sector were substantially less successful. Between 1870 and 1873 Cooke attempted to employ his wartime sales techniques to market a series of

---

[483] Carosso, *Investment Banking*, p. 12.

[484] For a detailed discussion of Jay Cooke, see Henrietta Larson, *Jay Cooke, Private Banker*, Harvard Studies in Business History, Vol. 2 (Cambridge, Mass.: Harvard University Press, 1936).

[485] Carosso, *Investment Banking*, p. 16.

bond issues for the Northern Pacific Railway. Although he was ultimately able to sell $5 million of those securities, economic conditions, inadequate financial resources, and a failure to enlist European support led to the collapse of the scheme and with it the demise of Cooke and Company. American savers, perhaps partly encouraged by feelings of patriotism, were prepared to absorb the issues of the federal government; they were not yet willing to absorb the uncertainties that marked railroad finance. A European connection was still necessary.

The Cooke failure – a failure that triggered the Panic of 1873 – and the aftermath of that panic changed the face of American investment banking. Business historians, influenced by issues of social history, have concluded that from 1873 until the first decade of the twentieth century, two groups dominated the private investment banking landscape: bankers drawn from the German-Jewish community and the so-called Yankee houses. From the point of view of ethnic studies, that conclusion is certainly correct; however, it fails to capture the economic structure of the evolving institution. With one exception, Lee, Higginson & Co., the Yankee houses were American firms that were linked with expatriate Americans who had become merchant bankers in London. With the exception of Kuhn, Loeb, the German-Jewish houses were American firms whose foreign connections were German-Jewish merchant bankers in London.[486] Nor did Kuhn, Loeb draw primarily on American capital – it was tied to European savings through the German investment banking community. Although some chartered commercial banks began to take on investment banking functions before the end of the century, it was the second-generation American junior partners of the London Yankee and German-Jewish investment banks that played the major role in mobilizing first British and then American capital and directing it to the nation's railroads.[487]

Given the reputations of the Fisks, Goulds, and Drews, the British merchant banks were hesitant to get involved in American railway finance

---

[486] Lee-Higginson acted as the banker for what were probably the most educated savers in the United States: the so-called Boston Associates. The group had provided major financial support for the New England textile industry in the 1820s and 1830s, and it was to play a major role in the finance of Western railroads and mines in the mountain states.

[487] The London merchant banks and their American partners were (1) J.S. Morgan and Drexel Morgan; (2) Brown Shipley and Brown Brothers; (3) Morton, Rose and Morton Bliss; (4) Baring Brothers and first T.W. Ward and then Baring-Magoun in New York and Kidder Peabody in Boston; (5) N.M. Rothschild and August Belmont; (6) Seligman Brothers and J&W Seligman; (7) Speyer Brothers and Phillip Speyer & Co. Note the role of family connections, which greatly eased the principal-agent problems.

because of their lack of information about the operations of the railroads and because of their inability to monitor the railroads operation. The second-generation Anglo-American investment banks were able to largely solve the problems of asymmetric information and monitoring for the British senior partners. Soon their success convinced American savers that railroad bonds endorsed by the Anglo-American investment banks were "safe," and by the 1880s they were doing as much business for domestic savers as for the British customers of the merchant banks. Moreover, it was the success of these second-generation firms in mobilizing domestic capital that spawned the third-generation American firms – Goldman-Sachs and Lehman Brothers, for example. Although still largely Yankee or German-Jewish in ownership, those American firms were to play a very important roles in the development of the American commercial and industrial sectors.

The German-Jewish connection can be traced back to Philip Speyers's arrival in the United States in 1837, but it became much more important after 1860. Between 1860 and 1890 four more firms were launched. Unlike Speyer, a trained financier and the son of an established banking family, the other original members of the group had mercantile backgrounds. In 1862 the Seligman Brothers, after successfully building a national domestic and imported dry goods firm, established the banking firm of J.&W. Seligman. Seven years later they purchased a seat on the New York Stock Exchange. In 1867 after operating general merchandise and clothing stores in Lafayette, Indiana, and Cincinnati, Ohio, Abraham Kuhn and Solomon Loeb opened a private bank in New York. Within a few years they too moved into investment banking, but the firm became important only after Jacob H. Schiff – a more recent immigrant with no mercantile background – became a partner in 1875. Schiff was the head of the firm from 1885 until after World War I. Marcus Goldman had been a peddler in Philadelphia from the time he arrived in the United States until he opened a banking and brokerage house in New York in 1869. The firm moved into investment banking in 1882, when Samuel Sachs became a partner and the firm was renamed M. Goldman & Sachs. Finally, the Lehman brothers (Henry, Emanuel, and Mayer) had been peddlers and cotton brokers in the South before and during the Civil War. After the war they expanded the scope of their brokerage business to include coffee, sugar, grain, and petroleum, as well as cotton. It was not until the 1880s, when the sons of the founders became partners, that Lehman Brothers became an investment bank. "The growth, financial strength, and durability of these German-Jewish houses rested largely on their access to European capital. Their success stemmed also from the close family, ethnic, religious, and business ties, and the care they employed in conserving their capital and maintaining its liquidity."[488]

The second group – the Yankee houses – trace their history to Junius Spencer Morgan's decision to move to London and accept a partnership in another Yankee expatriate's firm, George Peabody & Company. Upon Peabody's retirement in 1864, Morgan became the senior partner, and the firm was renamed J.S. Morgan & Co. Junius's son, John Pierpont, worked first as a clerk in the British firm and then as a clerk and accountant with the New York firm of Duncan, Sherman & Co., Peabody's representative in the United States. In 1860 he formed J. Pierpont Morgan & Co. and in 1864 Dabney, Morgan & Company. Finally, in 1871 he accepted a partnership with Drexel & Co., and Drexel, Morgan and Co. – a firm destined to be the most important investment bank in American history – was born. Drexel and Co. had been the second leading private banking house in the United States, and Morgan brought with him direct connections to British finance through J.S. Morgan & Co. and indirect connections through that firm to both the Barings and the Rothschilds. Drexel, Morgan operated in both Philadelphia and New York.[489] Morgan's influence within the firm grew steadily from 1876, when he headed the New York branch. By 1900 he was both the nation's most important investment banker and the "dominant figure in all the Drexel banks."[490]

In the same way that Jacob Schiff and his firm of Kuhn, Loeb & Co. was the most important member of the group of German-Jewish investment banks, there was little doubt that J.P. Morgan himself and Drexel Morgan the company were the senior partners in the Yankee conglomerate. The firm was, however, not the only member. In 1863 Levi Parsons Morton, a former partner of Junius Morgan in the dry-goods business, established a private bank on Wall Street – L.P. Morton & Co. Very soon, one of his partners – Walter H. Burns, J.P. Morgan's brother-in-law – moved to London and gained entry to the London financial market by establishing L.P. Morton, Burns & Co. In 1869 Levi Morton was joined by George Bliss, who had made millions in the dry-goods business, and his $2.5 million investment; the New York firm became Morton, Bliss & Co. In London John Rose became Morton's British partner, and Morton, Rose & Co. took over the business of L.P. Morton, Burns, and Co.

The other Yankee firms included two Boston firms – Lee, Higginson & Co. and Kidder, Peabody. The strength of the former rested on the

[488] Carosso, *Investment Banking*, p. 20.
[489] In New York the firm was Drexel Morgan, but in Philadelphia it remained Drexel and Co.
[490] Carosso, *Investment Banking*, pp. 21–22.

close personal connections that linked the bank's partners with "a select group of Boston investors including the officers and directors of various New England financial institutions" – that is, the Boston Associates.[491] Lee, Higginson, therefore, was the first of the very successful investment banks to depend on domestic savings since Cooke's experiments during the Civil War. Kidder, Peabody, on the other hand, was supported by more traditional foreign ties. The firm had long acted as agent and attorney for Baring Brothers.

The private investment banks did not have a complete monopoly of the new issues market – there were also commercial banks that played a significant role. By almost any measure, the most important was the First National Bank of New York. Under its founder and first president, Samuel C. Thompson, it began to buy and redistribute government bonds almost as soon as it was chartered in 1863. In the 1870s, as the market for governments began to shrink, its new president, George Fisher Baker – a friend of, and frequent collaborator with, J.P. Morgan – began to expand the scope of the bank's activities to include private sector offerings. Thereafter, it rapidly emerged as a fully-fledged investment house. "By 1900 it was one of the half dozen leading investment banking institutions in the country."[492]

Other New York banks – the National City, for example – had also begun to assume the role of investment bankers.

> Until 1907 the National City had been the junior partner of Kuhn, Loeb in their joint investment banking ventures. The bond market collapse in the panic of that year presented the opportunity for the big joint-stock bank to become an equal partner of the private banking house. The National City with its large deposit base, was able to make short-term loans to its and Kuhn Loeb's mutual client firms until the latter could sell their bonds on a reasonable basis. Kuhn, Loeb, as specialized investment bankers, did not have this short-term lending capability.[493]

Of perhaps equal importance when they are viewed as a group were the commercial banks outside the Boston-New York-Philadelphia turnpike. In the rest of the country firms too small or too local to warrant the attention of the major investment houses depended almost entirely on the services of commercial banks. The First National Bank of Chicago, for example, played a leading role in marketing Midwestern municipal and street railway bonds. At times the bank promoted the issues, at times

---

[491] Carosso, *Investment Banking*, p. 26.
[492] Carosso, *Investment Banking*, p. 23.
[493] Carosso and Sylla, "U.S. Banks in International Finance," p. 69.

it underwrote the issues, at times it organized underwriting syndicates to handle the issues, and almost at all times it distributed the issues.

Such was the industry's organizational structure. How did it operate? In the first place, the industry that emerged from Jay Cooke's experiment was designed to provide finance for America's rapidly expanding railroad network – the very task Cooke had been unable to perform – and, perhaps somewhat strangely, the new firms often chose to copy his innovations. In the 1870s the banks began to organize underwriting syndicates. In the next decade they institutionalized the long-standing ties that linked the banks and the railroads by accepting representation on the boards of directors of the railroads and by taking a more active role in management. At the same time they gradually developed long-lasting ties with particular railroads – Kuhn, Loeb with the Pennsylvania, Kidder, Peabody with the A.T. & S.F., and Morgan with the New York Central, the Northern Pacific, and a number of others.

There were also innovations that Cooke had never dreamed of. The Boston Stock Exchange had been the principal market for industrial securities through most of the nineteenth century, and the New York-based investment banks had largely ignored the manufacturing sector.[494] In the late 1890s, however, the banks' focus began to broaden. During the mid-decade depression, the preferred shares of the growing manufacturing sector had performed as well as railroad securities. Beginning in 1897 a number of those firms had gone public. Their stock issues were underwritten by private syndicates – syndicates that did not include investment banks. The potential of this new activity was not lost on J.P. Morgan and his partners. In 1898 Morgan's firm organized and managed the syndicate establishing the Federal Steel company, and he soon added both International Harvester and United States Steel to his roster of triumphs.[495] Within a very short time after Morgan's first foray into industrials, Carosso reports, "nearly all the other investment houses par-

---

[494] Much of this section is based on T. Navin and M. Sears, "The Rise of the Market for Industrial Securities, 1887–1902," *The Business History Review*, Vol. XXIX, No. 2 (June 1955), pp. 105–38. [Hereafter cited as Navin and Sears, "The Market for Industrial Securities."] Not surprisingly Kidder, Peabody and Lee, Higginson, were among the first of the major houses to establish a national reputation for distributing industrial shares. In New York the principal houses selling those shares were Baring, Magoun, and August Belmont. The former had been Kidder, Peabody's New York branch. Carosso, *Investment Banking*, p. 44.

[495] The International Harvester merger was really the work of Morgan's partner George W. Perkins. Ron Chernow, *The House of Morgan: An American Banking Dynasty and the Rise of Modern Finance* (New York: Atlantic Monthly Press, 1990), p. 109. [Hereafter cited as Chernow, *The House of Morgan*.]

ticipated in underwriting and distributing industrial bonds and preferred stock."[496]

There is one important caveat to that conclusion:

> A quarter of these *very large* [industrial] mergers was the work of investment bankers, principally those with experience in the issue of railroad securities. Eventually nearly all of the railroad houses participated in the turn-of-the-century mergers, but only J.P. Morgan with any zest. The Morgan house managed some of the largest industrial syndicates of the period and in the popular mind did much to link investment banking with the merger movement. Obscured behind the dazzling experience of the Morgans, however, is the fact that relatively few of the turn-of-the-century industrial promotions were headed by the old line railroad houses.

Those houses had been accustomed to underwriting bonds, not stocks, and they had conditioned their customers to think of bonds when they thought of investments. It was preferred stocks, however, that gained popular acceptance among industrial securities. At the same time the old-line houses had specialized in railroad finance, but it was new large-scale endeavors in commerce and industry that were the sources of the new demands for finance. In this dimension as well, the old-line houses were slow to adapt. Morgan aside, it was largely the young and hungry third-generation firms that heeded the call.

Other institutional innovations occurred during the heyday of the Drexel Morgan's and the Kuhn, Loeb's. "Not, indeed, until 1902 did industrial securities settle into the fourth stage of securities marketing – the stage when underwriting of issues came into general practice."[497] To provide $2 million for the Pennsylvania Railroad in 1870, Cooke had organized the first American underwriting syndicate. Over the next thirty-five years the nature of the syndicate changed substantially. Cooke's syndicate had acted only as an underwriter, a guarantor of last resort. By 1914 the syndicate – or increasingly the chain of syndicates – often managed all phases of the distribution: planning, purchasing or underwriting, banking, and selling.

The expansion in the number of participants in the syndicate reflected not only an increase in the number of functions undertaken, but also a deliberate attempt to broaden the market. Cooke had convinced a large number of small savers that pieces of paper issued by the government

---

[496] Carosso, *Investment Banking*, pp. 44–45. Navin and Sears, "The Market for Industrial Securities," *Business History Review*, Vol. 29, No. 2 (June 1955), pp. 135–36.

[497] Navin and Sears, "The Market for Industrial Securities," pp. 135–36, 138.

were legitimate investments, but the end of the Civil War and the Northern Pacific disaster had cooled their ardor. Thus, for the next two decades the investment bankers had been little concerned about expanding their marketing activities. They serviced the growing demands of the life insurance industry and of a relatively small group of wealthy individuals. Toward the end of the century, however, some investment bankers concluded that a larger customer base would increase their profits. N.W. Harris of Harris, Forbes, & Co. and N.W. Halsey of Halsey, Stuart and Co. were the first since Cooke to employ house-to-house salesmen. Soon after the turn of the century, James Jackson Storrow, a partner in Lee, Higginson, "began to put together a trained selling team to distribute the firm's security underwriting." By 1900 it is estimated that one out of every forty-two adult Americans held stock in the corporate sector – a percentage lower than that in the United Kingdom, but still substantial.

By that time "virtually all of the principal railroads in the country and many of the largest industrial corporations looked to the investment banker for their long-term capital requirements. The number of investment houses and commercial banks capable of meeting the financial needs of these large borrowers was very small, at most no more than a dozen institutions."[498] Those small numbers, coupled with the large size of the issues handled, created problems. The investment banks had always required both reliable access to short-term capital to cover their flotations and a ready market for the issues that they had underwritten. No one investment bank, dependent on only its own resources, was large enough to provide both short- and medium-term finance. Until the 1880s, with few exceptions, the investment banks had used their European connections to provide both short-term credit and a market for their securities. As the American savings rate rose and as the financial network improved, it became increasingly possible to solve both problems domestically. As a result there was increasing pressure to develop close ties with other domestic financial intermediaries; arm's length transactions were too uncertain.

Not surprisingly, "partners in the leading investment banks often were substantial stockholders in, or directors of, the major New York and Boston commercial banks."[499] Morgan was a vice president and director of the National Bank of Commerce, America's second largest commercial bank. So extensive was Morgan's influence at the bank that contemporaries referred to it as "J. Pierpont Morgan's bank." George R.

[498] Carosso, *Investment Banking*, p. 47.
[499] Carosso, *Investment Banking*, p. 48.

Baker, the bank's president, and his son were, together, the largest stock-holders in the First National; but Morgan's firm was the second.[500] Those banks were capable of supplying – and from the 1870s onward they did supply – the bulk of the required short-term finance; the total amount of short-term finance that the commercial banks were able to provide was increased by the provisions of the National Banking Act. Under the terms of the Act, national banks in cities were required to maintain in their own vaults a 25 percent reserve in lawful money against deposits. Banks in other cities, while also required to maintain a 25 percent reserve, could keep one-half of it on deposit in a central reserve city. Country banks had to maintain a 15 percent reserve, three-fifths of which could be deposited in a city bank. Until 1887 New York was the only central reserve city.[501]

After 1890 state-chartered trust companies grew very rapidly; the assets of New York state-chartered trust companies increased from $280 million in 1891 to $800 million a decade later. As these institutions became a major source of short-term loans, the investment banks again moved to strengthen their political and economic ties. "Private banks borrowed from them [the trust companies] regularly to carry securities being syndicated, and the trust companies themselves found these loans a favorite form of investment." "A number of trust companies closely associated themselves with certain large investment houses, commercial banks, and life insurance companies."[502] Henry Davison, partner and later chief operating executive of J.P. Morgan & Co. was a director of both the Guaranty Trust, America's largest, and Bankers Trust.[503]

A similar set of personal connections linked the investment banks with the life insurance industry. Between 1870 and 1910 the premium reserves of the nation's life insurance companies had risen nearly fifteen-fold. If those companies were to meet their obligations, the annual increase of $75 million had to be invested profitably. In 1870 less than 3 percent of life insurance assets had been invested in private corporate securities; in 1910 the figure was 37 percent: that is, each year, on average, the life insurance companies added $36 million of corporate securities to their investment portfolios.

[500] Lance E. Davis, "Capital Immobilities and Finance Capitalism: A Study of Economic Evolution in the United States, 1820–1920," *Explorations in Economic History*, Second Series, Vol. 1, No. 1 (fall 1963, p. 95). [Hereafter cited as Davis, "Capital Immobilities and Finance Capitalism."] Chernow, *The House of Morgan*, p. 153.

[501] Studenski and Kroos, *Financial History of the United States*, p. 155.

[502] Carosso, *Investment Banking*, p. 100.

[503] There were two Morgan partners on the Guaranty's voting trust. Chernow, *The House of Morgan*, p. 153.

What better investment than the securities of the nation's rapidly expanding corporate sector, and who better to supply those funds than the nation's premier investment banks? But no major investment bank, its vaults bulging with stocks and bonds from the last underwriting, wanted to depend on the vagaries of the price system to protect its market. Thus, George W. Perkins, a Morgan partner, took on the chairmanship of the New York Life Insurance Company's finance committee; Jacob Schiff, the head of Kuhn, Loeb, was a director of the Equitable; and in 1909 Morgan & Co. actually bought a controlling interest in that insurance company. None of the three – Perkins, Schiff, or Morgan – saw any conflict of interest, but Thomas Lawson, the members of the New York state Armstrong Commission, and the members of the U.S. House of Representative's Pujo Commission certainly did.[504]

Although J.P. Morgan & Co. was hardly typical, the Kroos and Blyn summary of the group with which the firm was associated dramatically captures the complex interrelations among the financial intermediaries in the investment banking community.

> In an age when foreign capital was still an important source of credit, the House of Morgan maintained excellent British and Continental ties. The Morgan partners could also call on the resources of their close allies: in Boston, Kidder, Peabody; in Philadelphia, Drexel & Co.; in New York, George Baker of the First National and James Stillman of the National City Bank of New York. One member or another of this "entente cordiale," in turn, had a controlling voice in a number of commercial banks, trust companies, and life insurance companies, including the Bank of Commerce, the Chase and Hanover National banks, the Bankers Trust, the Guaranty Trust, the New York Life, the Mutual Life, and the Equitable Life.[505]

In 1894 an advertisement in the *New York Times* listed "the fourteen greatest private banking houses." All were of either German-Jewish or Yankee origin.[506] As late as 1912 the industry was still relatively small. The Investment Bankers' Association claimed only 257 members that, "in turn, operated 280 offices located mainly in New York but also in Boston, Chicago, and Philadelphia."[507] If, at the turn of the century, someone had prepared a list of the most important investment banks, J.P. Morgan & Co. would have been at the top, and the only near competitor would have been Kuhn, Loeb. Following, in some order, would

---

[504] Thomas W. Lawson, *Frenzied Finance. Vol. I: The Crime of Amalgamated* (New York: Ridgway-Thayer Company, 1905).

[505] Kroos and Blyn, *A History of Financial Intermediaries*, p. 131.

[506] Carosso, *Investment Banking*, p. 26.

[507] Kroos and Blyn, *A History of Financial Intermediaries*, p. 129.

have been the New York firms of Speyer and Co, J.&R. Seligman, and August Belmont & Co., the Boston firms of Kidder, Peabody, and Lee, Higginson, and the Philadelphia firm of Drexel & Co. Times were, however, changing.

With the exception of Morgan the second-generation firms had moved only tentatively into industrial finance, and they moved even more tentatively into other emerging sectors of the economy. In the first decade of the twentieth century there was a growing demand for finance from companies engaged in light manufacturing, from public utilities, retail stores, and even newly emerging industries in the heavy industrial sector – automobiles, for example. Those demands were not met by the established firms; but they were increasingly met by newer, smaller, and more aggressive third-generation investment banks, firms that had not been included in the 1900 list of the nation's "greatest private banking houses." For example, beginning in 1906 with a $10 million offering of Sears, Roebuck & Co. preferred and common stock, over the next eighteen years the consortium of Goldman, Sachs & Co. and Lehman Brothers managed 114 offerings for fifty-six firms.

The new firms were both wholesalers and retailers, and most of the innovations in marketing can be traced to them. Moreover, it was largely these firms that courted, educated, and ultimately brought the small investor back into the securities market on a scale that had not been witnessed since the days of Jay Cooke. In 1911 one somewhat overly optimistic financial writer described the small investor as the "master of the investment world."[508] Years later Clarence Dillon, the head of Dillon, Read & Co., very succinctly captured the impact of those changes: "If you had relied on houses like ourselves you probably would not have had the automobile industry in this country. We would not have risked it, and we would have taken it upon ourselves as a virtue."[509]

The investment houses, both old and new, immeasurably aided the process of saver education; but initially, and probably until at least the turn of the century, they charged near-monopoly prices for the imprimatur they placed on the securities. The older bankers, Morgan and Schiff, for example, believed that banking houses should cooperate rather than compete. They deplored the aggressive sales tactics of Halsey and Harris, and they were stunned by the success of Goldman, Sachs with the issues of Sears-Roebuck, May Department Stores, and F.W. Woolworth. The educational process is seldom reversed, and competition erodes monopoly profits. Thus, it was not surprising that when in 1934,

---

[508] The writer was C.M. Keyes writing in *The World's Work*. Cited in Carosso, *Investment Banking*, p. 92.

[509] Cited in Kroos and Blyn, *A History of Financial Intermediaries*, p. 133.

after the 1929 crash, with an almost moribund securities market, and with the uncertainty of SEC regulations hanging over their head, the senior partners in J.P. Morgan & Co. were forced to choose between investment and commercial banking, all but one chose to leave the investment field.[510]

Even when most of the excess profits had been competed away, the structure of the industry changed but little. It is a structure that is far more dominated by intense interfirm rivalry – if not by competition in the economist's sense of the word – than it was a century ago. As Eugene White has pointed out, the pyramid structure of investment banking appears to be "natural." For over one hundred years, although there have been shifts in the positions of the firms within the structure, the *structure itself* has changed but little.[511]

3-5d(2). The formal securities markets: Most of the estimated 250 security exchanges that operated in the United States at some time during the nineteenth century were small, local, and short-lived.[512] The role of the formal markets in the accumulation and mobilization processes is, to a very large extent, bound up with the evolution and ultimate emergence of the New York Stock Exchange as the nation's premier exchange – impersonal, able to provide a signal of the quality of the issues traded, and nationwide in scope.

Its early history has been much publicized. The forerunner of the Exchange was initially organized in 1792, when twenty-four New York brokers joined together to agree to "not buy or sell from this date for any person whatever, any kind of public stocks at a less rate than one-quarter of one percent commission on the specie value and that we will give a preference to each other in our negotiations."[513] A more formal organization was established a quarter century later when, in 1817,

[510] Paul Sweezy, "The Decline of Investment Banking," *Antioch Review*, Vol. 1 (1941), pp. 63–68.

[511] Eugene White, "Banking and Finance in the Twentieth Century: The Domestic Financial Sector," in Stanley Engerman and Robert Gallman (eds.), *The Cambridge Economic History of the United States*, Vol. III: *The Twentieth Century* (Cambridge: Cambridge University Press, 2000).

[512] Ranald C. Michie, *The London and New York Stock Exchanges, 1850–1914* (London: Allen & Unwin, 1987), p. 167. [Hereafter cited as Michie, *London and New York*.]

[513] Cited in Francis Higginson Philip, "The Stock Exchanges of the United States: Part I," in David E. Spray (ed.), *The Principal Stock Exchanges of the World: Their Operation, Structure and Development* (Washington, D.C.: International Economic Publishers, 1964), p. 4. [Hereafter cited as Philip, "The Stock Exchanges, I."]

twenty-eight brokers representing seven firms adopted a new constitution that may have been modeled on that of the Philadelphia exchange. The constitution established an organization that was to be renamed the New York Stock and Exchange Board; it reconfirmed many of the old rules and established some new ones. It called for a $25 initiation fee and the election of members, established the offices of President and Secretary, authorized a schedule of commissions and prohibited the execution of orders for outside brokers at reduced rates, set the rules for the security auctions (the list was to be "called" at least one a day), prohibited "wash" (i.e., fictitious) sales, and required that securities be delivered on the day after their purchase, "unless expressed to the contrary" in the sales agreement.[514]

Over time the Exchange expanded both in size and in scope. Some members became full-time brokers (there had been none in 1818); the number of listed shares quadrupled between 1820 and 1835; record total volumes were set during the mid-1830s; membership increased (it reached eighty-eight in 1840 and, in response, the initiation fee was raised to $400); and the shares listed were no longer almost entirely local. During the bull market that preceded the Panic of 1837, the demand was so great that "brokers sent agents to other cities – as far as Chicago and New Orleans – to buy shares to be offered in New York." In 1835 non-local issues represented thirty-five of the 124 securities quoted. Still, the exchange was not even a shadow of its future self; on March 16, 1830, only thirty-one shares with a value of $3,470.35 were traded.[515]

In 1863 the exchange officially became "The New York Stock Exchange," and by 1867, when stock ticker tapes were first installed, the initiation fee had risen to $3,000. The next year members were granted property rights to their seats; thereafter, seats could be bought and sold. At the time there were almost 200 members, and annual business exceeded $3 billion. Perhaps most importantly, that year in response to Daniel Drew's manipulations of Erie shares, the NYSE amended its rules to require that the shares of any company using the facilities of the

---

[514] Robert Sobel, *The Big Board: A History of the New York Stock Market* (New York: Free Press, 1965), pp. 30–31. [Hereafter cited as Sobel, *The Big Board.*] E.C. Stedman and A.N. Easton, "History of the New York Stock Exchange," in Edmund Clarence Stedman (ed.), *The New York Stock Exchange: Its History, Its Contribution to National Prosperity, and Its Relation to American Finance at the Outset of the Twentieth Century* (New York: Stock Exchange Historical, 1905: reprint, New York: Greenwood Press, 1969), p. 67. [Hereafter cited as Stedman and Easton, "History of the New York Stock Exchange," and as Stedman, *The New York Stock Exchange.*]

[515] Stedman and Easton, "History of the New York Stock Exchange," pp. 84–118. Sobel, *The Big Board*, p. 43. Michie, *London and New York*, p. 171.

Exchange be registered. Despite these gains, the NYSE could still not claim to be the nation's premier exchange. Most transactions still took place on the curb, and even the Open Board, one of the competing exchanges, did more business. The Exchange retained its historic auction format, while its competitors – not only the Open Board, but also the Petroleum and Mining Board and the newly organized Gold Board – adopted continuous trading.[516]

Between 1869 and 1871 the New York financial structure was altered in a dramatic fashion. In May 1869 the 533 members of the NYSE joined with the 527 members of the Open Board and Government Bond Department, and the modern New York Stock Exchange was born. Two years later auctions were abandoned and continuous trading introduced. Although the NYSE still faced competition from other exchanges – and competition meant that the Governors were still forced to tread lightly, otherwise brokers or issuing firms might be seduced away – the results were nonetheless impressive. Between 1875 and 1909 the number of shares traded increased more than five times, and between 1879 and 1909 the real value of state and railroad bonds traded increased two and a quarter times. Even if the federal government's 1870s debt-refunding operations are included, the increase in the value of all bonds was 180 percent (see Table 3:5d-1).

The new Exchange was organized around a series of committees. At the top was the Governing Committee, the final arbiter of all problems. Article II of the 1902 Constitution and Rules for the Government of the New York Stock Exchange reads, "The government of the Exchange shall be vested in a Governing Committee, composed of the President and Treasurer of the Exchange, and of forty members, elected in the manner herein provided. The members of the Governing Committee, and the Secretary, shall be the officers of the Exchange." Although the organizational structure that was innovated in 1869 delegated final authority to a single committee, most day-to-day problems, admissions or commissions, for example, were assigned to other permanent committees.[517]

Given the competition, in 1871 the Exchange's position was still not fully secure. Between 1890 and 1900 there were two important rule changes. Both increased the strength of the Exchange's signal of quality, and both depended (at least in part) on the increasing competitive

---

[516] Sobel, *The Big Board*, pp. 83–85. Philip, "The Stock Exchanges I," p. 5.

[517] Michie, *London and New York*, pp. 250–251, "Constitution and Rules for the Government of the New York Stock Exchange, as Amended and Adopted in March, 1902," in Stedman, *The New York Stock Exchange*, pp. 485–507. The 1902 constitution lists twelve such permanent committees, Article XI, pp. 488–90.

strength of the NYSE. Despite widespread acceptance both abroad and at home (the Consolidated Exchange had employed a clearing house since it was founded in 1886) and the obvious advantages it presented in preventing frauds and attempts by brokers to renege on contracts, the NYSE had failed three times in its attempt to establish such a clearing mechanism for delivering securities. In 1892 the Governors tried again, this time with more success; by the end of the year the facilities were used for twelve securities. Before the century was over, almost the entire list of securities was included.[518]

The second change ultimately added an even greater value to the Exchange's imprimatur. In 1895 the Exchange voted to require listed companies to file annual reports, although the committee's word was still not law – they received no reports in either 1895 or 1896. By 1900 the Governing Committee felt their position more secure, and the Exchange's regulations became both more stringent and more effective: Annual reports including both balance sheets and profit and loss statements became a prerequisite for listing. It may appear that the rule changes were too long delayed, but the Exchange had moved to strengthen its guarantee of quality. For the rest of the country, full corporate disclosure was still three decades away.[519]

The NYSE was well placed to play a pivotal role in the education of the American saver, but it was a role that still left room for securities channeled through less restricted markets both at home and abroad. By the end of the Civil War, even before the merger, the NYSE had become a market that specialized in "individually large issues of securities, as represented by the borrowings of government, and this was a position it maintained thenceforth." Gone, for example, were the issues of insurance companies – issues that had constituted more than one-half the list in 1827; they were replaced by the stocks and bonds of railroads and urban transport systems and at the end of the century by the securities of large manufacturing firms.[520] Size was not the only basis on which the Exchange discriminated; "there was also a strong prejudice against volatile securities or those of unproven companies." Sudden price changes could result in the collapse of individual brokerage houses and undermine the stability of the market, "while failure or difficulties of quoted companies would reflect badly on the others, lowering their status and discouraging investment." Thus, few issues of mines or petroleum companies were handled by the Exchange, nor were the issues of

[518] Sobel, *The Big Board*, p. 131.   [519] Sobel, *The Big Board*, pp. 123, 177.
[520] In 1897 rails represented 69 percent of the transactions on the Exchange, but that figure had declined to 48 percent by 1912.

Table 3:5d-1. *Transactions on the New York Stock Exchange*

Year	Number of issues — Stocks	Bonds	Number of shares (thousands)	Average real price per share (1910–1914 $'s)	Real value of shares (millions of $'s)	Real value of government bonds (millions of $'s)	Real value of state & corporate bonds (millions of $'s)	Total real value of all bonds (millions of $'s)
1875			53,814	45.08	2,426	nd	nd	nd
1876			39,927	48.55	1,938	nd	nd	nd
1877			49,833	49.25	2,454	nd	nd	nd
1878			39,876	59.45	2,371	nd	nd	nd
1879			72,766	72.88	5,304	146	586	732
1880			95,736	69.60	6,663	59	585	644
1881			117,078	69.50	8,137	38	434	472
1882			116,734	61.22	7,147	17	255	272
1883			97,938	63.87	6,255	17	293	311
1884			95,945	66.42	6,373	16	550	567
1885			92,987	75.41	7,012	18	784	802
1886			103,953	80.00	8,316	16	776	792
1887			85,821	71.88	6,169	8	432	440
1888			65,669	72.67	4,772	8	403	411
1889			72,022	75.31	5,424	5	487	492
1890			71,410	73.41	5,243	4	459	462
1891			72,725	69.63	5,064	2	475	477
1892			86,726	81.41	7,060	2	642	644
1893			77,985	77.31	6,029	3	384	386
1894			49,276	91.71	4,519	6	500	507
1895			66,440	84.93	5,643	10	698	708
1896			54,491	95.88	5,225	40	528	568
1897			77,958	98.53	7,681	16	786	802

Year								
1898			113,466	102.39	11,618	34	1,259	1,293
1899	376		172,968	102.08	17,656	14	984	998
1900	379	827	138,989	84.39	11,729	8	779	787
1901	384	855	251,786	97.53	24,557	2	1,130	1,133
1902	383	891	186,605	92.91	17,337	2	1,105	1,106
1903	374	903	160,229	84.14	13,481	1	684	685
1904	381	907	187,312	80.34	15,050	0	1,187	1,187
1905	393	929	263,081	99.20	26,099	0	1,166	1,166
1906	389	937	284,298	104.67	29,757	0	752	752
1907	402	929	196,439	90.32	17,742	0	558	558
1908	426	984	197,206	94.13	18,563	0	1,175	1,175
1909	454	1,013	214,632	98.48	21,138	0	1,327	1,327
1910	480	1,053	164,000	nd	nd	0	617	617
1911	521	1,069	127,000	nd	nd	3	934	937
1912	511	1,083	131,000	nd	nd	1	667	668
1913	511	1,082	83,000	nd	nd	2	452	454
1914		1,096	48,000	nd	nd	1	968	969

Sources: Number of shares, 1875–1978 & 1904–1909 and average value of shares from A. Piatt Andrew, *National Monetary Commission, Statistics for the United States, 1867–1909* (New York: Garland Publishing Co., 1983). Number of shares, 1879–1903, and value of government and state and corporate bonds from Edmund Clarence Stedman, *The New York Stock Exchange*, Table IV, pp. 473–474. Number of shares, 1910–1914, and value of government and state and corporate bonds from *Historical Statistics* (1975). Series X531–X535, Volume II, p. 1007. Value of state and railroad bonds, 1904–1909, from Michie, New York and London, Table 7.1, p. 195. Number of issues, 1900–1914, from Peter Wycoff, *Wall Street and the Stock Markets: A Chronology (1644–1971)* (Philadelphia, London, and New York: Chilton Book Company, 1972), p. 155.

"industrial or commercial firms until they had proved themselves both individually and as a sector." "The Stock Exchange was not a market for small, new, or risky ventures but one for large, established and secure corporations or the issues of governments, at all levels but with unblemished records."[521]

There are at least two measures that reflect the gradual improvement in the Exchange's competitive position. First, between 1869 and 1914 the number of members was increased once: to 1,100 in December 1879. Despite that expansion, the value of seats increased. Membership in the Exchange was a valuable asset. In the first year in which seats could be freely bought and sold, on average a seat cost $7,500; by 1910 it cost $79,500; and, in real terms, the increase was not eleven- but sixteen-fold (see Table 3:5d-2). The increase was not linear. In real terms the price hovered in the $3,000–5,000 range until the end of the 1870s; it then rose into the $25,000–35,000 range, where it remained for the next two decades; then, at the turn of the century, prices more than doubled; and they remained in the $70,000–80,000 range until WWI.[522]

Second, the Exchange improved its position relative to other exchanges both in other cities and in New York. The NYSE began to expand its business well beyond the confines of Gotham. By the turn of the century it had developed a truly nationwide business. In 1901, for example, 136 New York brokerage firms with seats on the Exchange operated out-of-town branches, and another 119 member firms were actually located in other cities. Thus, by 1909 it was estimated that almost one-half of the Exchange's business originated outside the city.[523]

As the NYSE became a truly national exchange, it also erected barriers between itself and other competitive securities markets. The minimum commission requirement made intermarket arbitrage very difficult. As a result, it became increasingly difficult for other exchanges to compete. Gradually, competitors in other cities were forced to accept a secondary role. Essentially those exchanges reemerged – as they had begun a half century earlier – as markets for the issues of local firms that were still too small and unknown to attract a national business. If and when they began to attract a national business, they shifted their primary market to the NYSE. In the 1890s, for example, the market for the stocks and bonds of the Atchison, Topeka, & the Santa Fe, a railroad that had been largely Boston financed and that had long been a pillar of that city's Exchange, switched from Boston to New York. That experience was

---

[521] Michie, *London and New York*, 197–98.

[522] Between 1868 and 1877 the average was $3,609; between 1881 and 1899, $26,792; and between 1902 and 1910, $79,427.

[523] The estimate was 48 percent. Michie, *London and New York*, p. 177.

Table 3:5d-2. *Transfer valuation of a New York Stock Exchange membership, 1860–1914*

Year	Nominal price of seats			Real Price of Seats		
	High	Low ($'s)	Average of high & low	High	Low (1967 $'s)	Average of high & low
1868	8,000	7,000	7,500	20,000	17,500	18,750
1869	7,500	3,000	5,250	18,750	7,500	13,125
1870	4,500	4,000	4,250	11,842	10,526	11,184
1871	4,500	2,750	3,625	12,500	7,639	10,069
1872	6,000	4,300	5,150	16,667	11,944	14,306
1873	7,700	5,000	6,350	21,389	13,889	17,639
1874	5,000	4,250	4,625	14,706	12,500	13,603
1875	6,750	4,250	5,500	20,455	12,879	16,667
1876	5,600	4,000	4,800	17,500	12,500	15,000
1877	5,750	4,500	5,125	17,969	14,063	16,016
1878	9,500	4,000	6,750	32,759	13,793	23,276
1879	16,000	5,100	10,550	57,143	18,214	37,679
1880	26,000	14,000	20,000	89,655	48,276	68,966
1881	30,000	22,000	26,000	103,448	75,862	89,655
1882	32,500	20,000	26,250	112,069	68,966	90,517
1883	30,000	23,000	26,500	107,143	82,143	94,643
1884	27,000	20,000	23,500	100,000	74,074	87,037
1885	34,000	20,000	27,000	125,926	74,074	100,000
1886	33,000	23,000	28,000	122,222	85,185	103,704
1887	30,000	19,000	24,500	111,111	70,370	90,741
1888	24,000	17,000	20,500	88,889	62,963	75,926
1889	23,000	19,000	21,000	85,185	70,370	77,778
1890	22,500	17,000	19,750	83,333	62,963	73,148
1891	24,000	16,000	20,000	88,889	59,259	74,074
1892	22,000	17,000	19,500	81,481	62,963	72,222
1893	20,000	15,250	17,625	74,074	56,481	65,278
1894	21,250	18,000	19,625	81,731	69,231	75,481
1895	20,000	17,000	18,500	80,000	68,000	74,000
1896	20,000	14,000	17,000	80,000	56,000	68,000
1897	22,000	15,000	18,500	88,000	60,000	74,000
1898	29,750	19,000	24,375	119,000	76,000	97,500
1899	40,000	29,500	34,750	160,000	118,000	139,000
1900	47,500	37,500	42,500	190,000	150,000	170,000
1901	80,000	48,500	64,250	320,000	194,000	257,000
1902	81,000	65,000	73,000	311,538	250,000	280,769
1903	82,000	51,000	66,500	303,704	188,889	246,296
1904	81,000	57,000	69,000	300,000	211,111	255,556

Table 3:5d-2. *(cont.)*

Year	Nominal price of seats			Real Price of Seats		
	High	Low ($'s)	Average of high & low	High	Low (1967 $'s)	Average of high & low
1905	85,000	72,000	78,500	314,815	266,667	290,741
1906	95,000	78,000	86,500	351,852	288,889	320,370
1907	88,000	51,000	69,500	314,286	182,143	248,214
1908	80,000	51,000	65,500	296,296	188,889	242,593
1909	94,000	73,000	83,500	348,148	270,370	309,259
1910	94,000	65,000	79,500	335,714	232,143	283,929
1911	73,000	65,000	69,000	260,714	232,143	246,429
1912	74,000	55,000	64,500	255,172	189,655	222,414
1913	53,000	37,000	45,000	178,451	124,579	151,515
1914	55,000	34,000	44,500	182,724	112,957	147,841

Sources: Seat prices: 1868–1904, Milton J. Platt, "Annals and Statistics" in Edmund Clarence Stedman (ed.), *The New York Stock Exchanges: Its History. Its Contribution to National Prosperity, and Its Relation to American Finance at the Outset of the Twentieth Century* (New York: Greenwood Press, Publishers, 1905), p. 473. 1905–1914, Peter Wycoff, *Wall Street and the Stock Markets: A Chronology (1644–1971)* (Philadelphia, New York, London: Chilton Book Company, 1972), pp. 150–151. Price deflator: BLS Consumer Price Index, All Items; *Historical Statistics*, U.S., 1975, Senes E 135, p. 211.

repeated time and time again.[524] Thus, in 1912 the Boston Exchange, New York's most serious out-of-town competitor, listed less than one-fourth of both the number and the value of the securities that were listed on the NYSE.[525]

As in the rest of the country, so also in New York. There, in its relations with its competitors, the results were ultimately much the same. In 1868 more business had been done on the curb than on the Old Board. In the early decades of the present century some 150 to 300 unorganized brokers still handled about $500 million in stock sales annually, about 5 percent of the value of the shares traded on the NYSE. The Curb was,

[524] By 1904 the volume of A.T. & S.F. securities traded in New York were twenty-one times as large as the volume traded in Boston.

[525] Boston did remain the primary exchange for copper mining securities until after World War I. In 1912 the par value of the equity listings on that exchange were about 30 percent of those listed in New York, and the bonds were about 17 percent. Michie, *London and New York*, pp. 168, 207–9.

however, gradually becoming more organized. In 1908 operations were formalized in the New York Curb Agency. Three years later the name was changed to the New York Curb Market Association (it did not become the American Stock Exchange until 1953), and, although trading was still conducted outside (on the curb) until after World War I, an office was opened, a dues-paying membership was established, trading rules were drawn up and enforced, and a formal listing department to admit qualified stocks was organized.[526]

Since the 1870s the Curb had existed somewhat uneasily alongside the NYSE. Between 80 and 90 percent of its business was carried out on behalf of members of the more formal exchange. Gradually its relations with the NYSE became somewhat better defined. The Curb became a recognized part of the evolving securities market, an institution with a specific role to play. In 1908 one of the Curb's brokers indicated that "the curb market serves as a preliminary market for practically all stocks and bonds that are eventually listed on the New York Stock Exchange." Perhaps in a somewhat less charitable spirit, by 1909 the governing body of the Exchange itself had come to much the same conclusion: "The curb market represents, first, securities that cannot be listed; second, securities in the process of evolution from reorganization certificates to a more solid status; and third, securities of corporations which have been unwilling to submit their figures and statistics to proper committees of the Stock Exchange." A listing on the NYSE guaranteed stability; the Curb provided a market for riskier and more uncertain securities. If and when those securities were dropped because they did not find favor among the investors or when they were picked up for listing by the larger exchange, they were replaced by other issues trying to break into the market.[527]

The relationship between the NYSE and the Consolidated Stock and Petroleum Exchange was less peaceful and certainly less symbiotic. The New York and the Curb were complementary; the New York and the Consolidated were competitive. The Consolidated was the product of an 1886 merger of four smaller exchanges. It had been established specifically to exploit gaps in the NYSE's markets. As part of its attempts to signal quality, the NYSE had until the 1890s refused to trade in odd (less than 100 shares) lots. Many investors would have preferred to buy fewer than 100 shares, and the requirement probably kept many of them out

---

[526] Rolf Kaltenborn, "The United States of America, Part II: The American Stock Exchange," in Spray (ed.), *The Principal Stock Exchanges*, pp. 21–22.

[527] Michie, *London and New York*, pp. 206–7. The quotation from the Exchange is part of the reply by the NYSE to the Governor's Committee on Speculation in Securities and Commodities, p. 44.

of the market.[528] The Consolidated traded in odd lots; of its 2,403 members, some 400 were former members of the NYSE, "who broke relations with the older organization over the odd lot and other issues."[529] Moreover, unlike other local exchanges that did not directly compete, the Consolidated began to quote railroad stocks and bonds and, later, industrial securities: "With commission rates set at half of the New York level (one-sixteenth percent) and a minimum trade of only ten units," the Consolidated began to attract a substantial clientele. The extent of that competition can be seen in a comparison of the volume of shares traded on the two exchanges. They may have been on average lower valued, but over the years 1886–1913 the volume of shares traded on the Consolidated averaged 64 percent of the volume on the New York Stock Exchange. Between 1888 and 1896 the figure was 95 percent, and it exceeded 100 percent in four of those years.[530]

The New York Stock Exchange responded to this threat, in the words of the Consolidated, by, "'boycotting' more violent than the most extreme of the trade unionists," by discouraging the members of exchanges outside New York from dealing with the Consolidated, and by denying the Consolidated easy access to its (the NYSE's) prices. Although competition continued through World War I, the New York Stock Exchange's policies appear to have blunted, if not halted, the competitive threat. By 1913 membership in the Consolidated had declined to 671; there had been no bond sales since 1905; and the volume of equities traded declined to less than 30 percent of that of its larger competitor.[531]

As the economy grew and more small and medium business began to look for external finance, the Exchange's relative role in the secondary market appears to have declined somewhat, if the focus of the analysis is limited to the total number of issues listed. Although the figures are not quite comparable, it appears that in 1913 the par value of the stocks and bonds listed on the New York Stock Exchange was equal to almost 45 percent of the par value of all U.S. securities issued and still current. That figure compares with a figure of 83 percent in 1884 and 60 percent at the turn of the century.[532] The NYSE, however, increasingly concentrated on the largest and most stable equity issues and on bonds, as opposed to stocks. In 1914, for example, the average size of a railroad issue quoted on the Exchange was $21.4 million, and for an industrial and commercial issue it was $24.7 million. The comparable figures for

[528] Sobel, *The Big Board*, p. 131.   [529] Ibid.
[530] See Table 3:5d-1 and Michie, *London and New York*, table 7.2, p. 205.
[531] Michie, *London and New York*, pp. 203–5.
[532] The figure for the NYSE ($26.0 billion) is for 1913 and that for all securities ($58.1 billion) is for 1912. Michie, *London and New York*, p. 168.

Table 3:5d-3. *U.S. securities markets: sales in 1910*

Market	Stocks		Bonds	
			Par value	
	Number	Percent	(millions of $'s)	Percent
New York Stock Exchange	164,150,061	68.5	635.0	90.6
Consolidated Stock Exchange	32,238,773	13.4	0.0	0.0
New York Curb Market	18,671,438	7.8	10.8	1.5
New York Total	215,060,272	89.7	645.8	92.2
Boston Stock Exchange	15,503,336	6.5	32.7	4.7
Philadelphia Stock Exchange	8,341,599	3.5	14.6	2.1
Chicago Stock Exchange	894,362	0.4	7.4	1.1
Three City Non-New York Total	24,739,297	10.3	54.7	7.8
Six Exchange total	239,799,569	100.0	700.5	100.0

Source: Michie, *London, & New York*, p. 170.

issues that were not listed were $2.6 and $7.5 million. The NYSE's role in shares that were actively traded was much greater than the aggregate figure would suggest. In 1910, for example, taken together, the six largest exchanges in the country handled 239,799,569 shares of stock and bonds with a par value of $700.5 million. Of those totals the NYSE's shares were more than 68 percent and 90 percent respectively (see Table 3:5d-3). Moreover, it was the high-valued stable issues that provided the best vehicle for the education of the American saver. These figures, as opposed to the aggregate data on securities issued and outstanding, capture the New York Stock Exchange's role as the principal capital market link between the increasingly sophisticated saver and the private firms that were transforming the economy. By the outbreak of World War I the New York Stock Exchange was no longer the first among equals; it had become *the* American securities exchange.

3-6. The London and New York stock exchanges in the late nineteenth century[533]

Over the course of the half century before World War I American savers were becoming gradually better educated, and the formal

[533] The material in this section is largely drawn from Lance Davis and Robert Cull, *International Capital Markets and American Economic Growth, 1820–1914* (Cambridge: Cambridge University Press, 1994). [Hereafter cited as Davis and Cull, *International Capital Markets.*]

Table 3:6-1. *Number of United States stocks traded on the London and on the New York Stock Exchanges in December*

Year	Stock Exchange	Total number of U.S. stocks listed	U.S. Railroad stocks listed	U.S. Non-Railroad stocks listed
1870	1. London Stock Exchange	8	6	2
	2. New York Stock Exchange	27	12	15
1880	1. London Stock Exchange	44	19	25
	2. New York Stock Exchange	103	73	30
1890	1. London Stock Exchange	138	48	90
	2. New York Stock Exchange	118	90	28
1900	1. London Stock Exchange	145	53	92
	2. New York Stock Exchange	273	143	130
1910	1. London Stock Exchange	147	48	99
	2. New York Stock Exchange	306	146	160

Source: Lance E. Davis and Robert J. Cull, *International Capital Markets and American Economic Growth, 1820–1914* (Cambridge, New York, & Melbourne: Cambridge University Press, 1994), Table 4.1, p. 64.

Table 3:6-2. *Percentage breakdown of the U.S. stocks traded on the London and on the New York Stock Exchanges*

Year	London Railroad stocks	London Other stocks	New York Railroad stocks	New York Other stocks
1870	75	25	44	56
1880	43	57	71	29
1890	35	65	76	24
1900	37	63	52	48
1910	33	67	48	52

Source: Table 3:6-1.

securities markets were maturing. Both processes were slow. Even in 1914 some sectors of the economy were still unable to attract sufficient finance from domestic sources. Tables 3:6-1 and 3:6-2 compare the number of American securities listed on the London Stock Exchange with those listed on the premier American securities market, the New York Stock Exchange.

The list of American stocks traded in London in 1870 included six railroads, two mining companies, and one telegraph company. In New York there were twenty-seven stocks traded: twelve rails, and fifteen issues of twelve other firms – two coal companies, one mine, four express companies, Western Union, the Boston Water Power Company, and the Pacific Mail steamship line.

The increase in listings between 1870 and 1880 suggests rapid American economic expansion, and it is obvious that the financial demands engendered by that expansion placed a severe strain on the nation's still immature capital market. The total number of shares traded in New York nearly quadrupled, and those appearing on the London list increased more than five times. Among the forty-seven London listings were nineteen railroads, but it was the number of "other" issues that had increased most rapidly. By 1880 that group included two telegraph companies, two banks, four investment trusts, one wagon and railway carriage company, and eight mines.

Although there was a doubling in the number of "other" firms traded in New York, nearly three-quarters of the listings – seventy-three – were railroads. In 1870 the New York rail total had been twice that of London; ten years later it was four times as large. Conversely, in 1870 the New York listing of "other" firms had been five times the London total; in 1880 the number of New York listings was still greater than the London total, but the totals were thirty and twenty-eight.

In 1890 the total number of American shares listed in New York (118) was still slightly greater than the number traded in London (108). If, however, attention is focused on "other" issues, the London market was servicing over two and a half times the number of enterprises supported by the New York exchange. The London list included seventy-one "other" firms drawn from at least nine industries. There were the issues of two gas and waterworks, two iron, coal, and steel firms, four telephone and telegraph companies, seven land and building enterprises, one wagon and railway carriage company, three mines, and eleven breweries. In addition there were nine miscellaneous enterprises including Borax Ltd., the Chicago and Northwestern Granaries, Eastman's, J&P Coats, and the Pillsbury-Washburn Flour Mills. In New York, despite a small increase in the total number of listings (from 103 to 118), the number of "other" firms had actually declined by two. Growth obviously was straining the entire network, but that strain was particularly felt by firms in the non-railroad sectors.

The degree of strain is reflected in Table 3:6-2. In 1870 there were more "others" than rails in New York, but more rails than "others" in London. As the demand for finance for new industries – industries often located in the South and West – grew, the British exchange moved to accommodate those demands, the New York exchange responded much more slowly. By 1880 in London "other" issues constituted 60 percent of the total; in New York the percentage had declined from 56 to 29. Nor was the trend reversed over the next decade. The British proportion continued to increase (to two-thirds of the total in 1890) but the American percentage continued to decline (to less than one in four). It is clear that the London market was supplying capital to firms still either incapable or unwilling to pay the price of attracting finance on the New York Exchange.

Ten years later in 1900, the comparison strongly suggests that New York had begun to respond to the non-rail financial demands of the American economy. In London, although the number of American issues had increased by 25 percent over the decade, the share of "other" stocks in the total had actually declined. In New York the total number of listings had increased by more than 130 percent, but the number of "other" listings had risen by four and a half times. As a result their relative share had doubled. The trend away from rails continued, although more slowly, over the first decade of the next century. In 1910, for the first time since 1870, rails made up less than one-half of the New York listings.

The American market was maturing. By 1910 the list of commercial and industrial securities traded on the NYSE was expanding rapidly. Space precludes a complete compilation, but a list of the issues that begin with the word "American" appears to capture the extent to which the New York Stock Exchange had become a conduit between domestic savers and the previously neglected sectors of the economy. The list includes American Beet Sugar, American Car and Foundry, American Coal, American Cotton Oil, American District Telegraph, American Express, American Linseed, American Malting, American Smelting and Refining, American Spirits Manufacturing, American Steel Hoop, American Telegraph and Cable, American Tin Plate, American Tobacco, and American Woolen. Alphabetically the list ran from Allis Chalmers to Western Union, and it includes firms that were to remain household words for almost another century: Allis Chalmers, American Tobacco, Bethlehem Steel, International Harvester, National Biscuit, Republic Steel, Sears Roebuck, United States Rubber, and U.S. Steel.

The number of American non-railroad shares listed in New York was more than 75 percent larger than the number in London. Still there is evidence of substantial screening: the listed firms were large; they were, like International Harvester and U.S. Steel, often the product of a merger underwritten by one of the major investment banks; and there were few representatives from the South or West. Although its importance was diminishing, London still had a role to play in the capital mobilization process.

In another dimension, as well, the American market also began to display definite signs of adult behavior. In 1910 the New York list included a British firm, the Underground Electric Railways of London. The new listing joined the equity offerings of the Canadian Pacific Railway, the Cuban-American Sugar Company, the Northern Railways of Mexico, as well as the bonds of the governments of Argentina, Japan, and Panama.

The evidence seems quite conclusive: Until the end of the nineteenth century the London market served a much broader range of far more sophisticated savers than its New York counterpart.[534] The two markets did not exist in isolation, but a substantial fraction of the American securities traded in London were not even imperfect substitutes for the stocks and bonds listed on the Big Board. As a result, although the British contribution to American capital formation was not as large as the role played by the London market in Argentina, Australia, or Canada, the financial flows were not trivial. More importantly, they were often targeted at economic activities that lay outside the scope of the still embryonic American financial market. Those transfers were particularly important during the 1830s and again during the decade and a half after 1880, years when the American economy was undergoing very rapid structural transformation. In the first period British savers purchased American government securities when there was almost no formal securities market in the United States. In the second, the British exchanges complemented the American structure, filling spatial and industrial gaps that were still outside the realm of the formal American markets.

At the most general level, the relatively slow development of the New York market reflects the preferences of the savers that it served; but it was institutional differences between the markets that made it possible to translate those preferences into listings, into sales, and into capital transfers. The New York Stock Exchange was organized and owned by a collective of brokers who designed it to create a securities market, and who operated it to maintain that market. Although the London Stock Exchange was organized for ostensibly the same purposes, it was not owned nor was it operated solely by traders. The brokers shared power and authority with the owners of the Exchange, and the two groups did

---

[534] For a more extensive development of this point, see Lance E. Davis, "The Capital Markets and Industrial Concentration: The U.S. and the U.K., A Comparative Study," *Economic History Review*, Second Series, Vol. XIX, No. 2 (August 1966).

not always have the same goals. In London there was a wedge between owners and members; that wedge was absent in New York.[535]

In London two committees – the Committee of Trustees and Managers (representing owners) and the Committee for General Purposes (representing brokers) – were jointly vested with ultimate control. In New York a single committee, the Governing Committee, was the final arbiter on all issues affecting the exchange. As a collectively owned firm, the NYSE adopted policies common to collectives. Those policies were quite different from the policies embraced by the shareholder-owned London exchange.[536]

On the one hand, the rewards associated with organizing as an efficient cartel were high relative to the costs. Monopoly profits could be earned as long as there were no effective competitors. On the other hand, the cartel carefully screened its listings and implemented rules that, while providing a valuable service to some, made trading more expensive than on other competing exchanges. Firms willing and able to sustain these costs were, in effect, buying a signal that reassured the relatively unsophisticated American saver that theirs were quality securities. Given the level of sophistication and the informational asymmetries that plagued large sectors of the economy, those signals were very valuable; and some firms were willing to bear the costs – the monopoly rents earned by the brokers on the exchange – to obtain the Exchange's signal of quality. Those firms were, as a result, able to attract a fairly wide range of relatively unsophisticated investors and build a national market for their securities.

The most obvious of the NYSE's screening policies was its stringent vetting procedure, a procedure that required a firm that wanted to use its services to meet high minimum standards in terms of "size of capital, number of shareholders, and proven track record."[537] The exchange made a deliberate effort to attract large, widely held, and, price-wise, relatively stable issues. The rules also imposed additional costs on listed securities whose price fell below par or whose par value was less than $100. In the nineteenth century par value was an important component of the signal

---

[535] Michie, *London and New York*. In general, in London, traders were eager to adopt any technological advance that could facilitate increased market activity. Owners resisted many innovations – the ticker tape, for example – fearing that their innovation would make exchange quotations public property and, thus, create a disincentive for nonmembers to pay fees to join the exchange.

[536] For a discussion of the differences between collectives and traditional firms, see Lee Benham and Philip Keefer, "Voting in Firms: The Role of Agenda Control, Size, and Voter Homogeneity," *Economic Inquiry*, Vol. XXXIX (October 1991).

[537] Michie, *London and New York*, p. 198.

to the unsophisticated saver. Those rules made it virtually impossible to trade a security that did not generate the required high level of trade volume in sufficiently large trade blocks.[538]

The par value rule discriminated against firms with small capital bases. There were many such firms in the newly emerging industrial and commercial arenas, in the land, mortgage, financial sectors, and mining industries. Moreover, on the other side of the market, even if potential investors were willing to trade in normal lots (and it is likely that the small investor preferred odd lots), the par value rule made purchases or sales very expensive.

The more sophisticated investors refused to pay the charges imposed by the New York Stock Exchange, and many firms were unwilling or unable to bear the high transactions costs that listing involved. Both sophisticated savers and unwilling firms took their business to rival exchanges. The number of informed domestic savers was, however, small relative to the number of their unsophisticated peers. As late as 1910 the New York Stock Exchange provided the conduit for nearly 70 percent of the number of equities and 90 percent of the value of bonds that passed through the country's six most active formal markets (see Table 3:5d-3).[539]

Because of the relatively small number of sophisticated investors, the rival domestic exchanges were unable to mobilize sufficient capital to meet the demands of the myriad of firms whose growth transformed the nation's industrial profile. On the one hand, British entrepreneurs were given an opportunity to purchase American enterprises, reorganize them as "free-standing companies" and, through the aegis of the formal British capital market, raise finance from the relatively more sophisticated British investors. On the other hand, more than a few American entrepreneurs – Andrew Carnegie, for example – were able to tap the accumulations of British savers directly by personally exporting securities to London and the provinces.

In sum, it is quite apparent that not all American savers were equal in their abilities to evaluate uncertain investment opportunities. The evidence of the profits accrued by both the investment banks and the

---

[538] For a discussion of the role of par value, see Jonathan Barron Baskin, "The Development of Corporate Financial Markets in Britain and the United States, 1600–1914: Overcoming Asymmetric Information," *Business History Review*, Vol. 62, No. 2 (Summer 1988), p. 225.

[539] In addition to the New York Stock Exchange, there were two other important exchanges in New York (the Curb and the Consolidated). The other three were the Boston, the Philadelphia, and the Chicago. Michie, *London and New York*, p. 170.

members of the New York Stock Exchange suggests that as late as 1901 the majority – even the majority of those willing to hold paper securities at all – still demanded official certification. Again, however, times were changing. Beginning in the 1880s, at least, there had been groups of sophisticated investors (like those in Boston who were able to evaluate investment alternatives in mining and in the West or those in Philadelphia with ties to developments in the upper Midwest) who did not need the services of the NYSE to overcome informational asymmetries. Those groups were growing. Similarly, the quality stamp placed on some offerings by the large investment bankers itself furthered the process of investor education. A saver, even one who lived in Chicago, might have proved unwilling to invest in the issues of a firm like the McCormick Reaper Company, a well-established Chicago enterprise; but he jumped at the chance to buy stock in International Harvester, after J.P. Morgan & Company merged McCormick into that newly established conglomerate. The investment in International Harvester proved profitable. Having learned that paper investments were not always as uncertain as he had believed, the investor required a less strong signal for his next purchase.

Finally, the success of the New York Stock Exchange in reducing informational asymmetries helped in the long run to undercut its ability to maintain its semi-monopolistic position. Although on occasion a lesson may be lost, in general, investor education is an irreversible process, and the American saver was becoming educated. As the domestic exchanges approached maturity, there was less need to turn to London for financial support for new industries in new regions. In fact, although the educational process would continue for at least two more decades, when World War I forced Britain out of the world's financial markets, American savers were able to step in and fill at least a part of the gap.

Although there is evidence of a substantial relative expansion in the size and scope of the American market, the process of integration between the two markets – London and New York – appears to have moved less rapidly. In 1870 only a single stock – the shares of the New York Central – was traded on both exchanges (see Table 3:6-3). Twenty years later there was some evidence of increasing market integration, at least for rails. In 1890, of the thirty-seven railway shares listed in London, twenty-two were also traded in New York. There were, however, still no private non-rail issues traded on both exchanges. Despite the movement toward maturity that the New York market had demonstrated, even as late as 1910, the trend toward intermarket integration does not appear to have greatly speeded up. Some railroads aside, the same firms were seldom traded on both exchanges; in 1910 there were only four jointly

Table 3:6-3. *Percentage of Total American Stock issues that were traded on either the New York or London Stock Exchanges that were traded on both*

Year	Percentage
1870	5.6
1880	10.7
1890	20.4
1900	22.1
1910	18.2

Source: Lance E. Davis and Robert J. Cull, *International Capital Markets and American Economic Growth, 1820–1914* (Cambridge, U.K., New York, & Melbourne: Cambridge University Press, 1994), Table 5.3, p. 68.

listed American non-rail issues: U.S. Steel, A.T.& T, Anaconda Copper, and Amalgamated Copper. All were large, three were the products of mergers, and Anaconda had been owned by the British-domiciled Rothschild's.

3-7. Conclusions

The American capital markets developed quite differently both from those of the other frontier countries and from those in Britain. Although the development was largely shaped by domestic conditions, the availability of foreign capital played an important role in configuring the institutional structure. At the same time the lure of American investment opportunities caused some innovation in the financial institutions in Europe.

The majority of the foreign capital was British, but there were significant contributions from Germany and Holland as well. Although American promoters had been known to peddle securities door-to-door in London and Edinburgh, most British savers who purchased the issues of American firms or governments used the services of one of the private banking firms with American connections – J.S. Morgan or Barings, for example – or dealt in listed American securities through brokers on the London or one of the provincial exchanges. Outside of railroads, however, an alternative channel became increasingly popular over the last quarter of the nineteenth century. British promoters would purchase an American firm, reorganize it as a "free-standing company," add some well-known members of the aristocracy or the financial community to the board of directors, and sell the debentures and shares of the new – now British – company to British investors.[540] In the case of the Scots and the Dutch (and to a lesser extent the English), institutional innovation of a different type also played a role. Trusts organized to hold a portfolio of American securities provided the benefits of portfolio diversification for the saver. The German savers employed no new institutions. American securities had long been traded on the German exchanges, but the German experience underscores another lesson that might be learned from the history of evolving capital markets. Many of the transfers depended on close personal connections between German firms and financial intermediaries and German immigrants in the United States. Those connections were particularly close in the banking communities – New York on one side of the Atlantic, Hamburg and Frankfurt on the other.

Quantitatively, foreign capital was less important to American development than it was to the other frontier countries; but in the absence of such transfers development would have been slower, and it might have followed a somewhat different path. In the 1870s those foreign capital flows relieved the domestic markets of the task of refinancing the Civil War debt. Over the next several decades they financed the rapid completion of the national transport network; and they provided crucial support for the expansion of new industries and new regions during the 1880s and early 1890s, a period of rapid structural and geographic transformation.

Although there may be some question as to the exact magnitude of the change, the 1870s was a decade of very rapid growth for the American economy.[541] Domestic savings rates were in the range 15–20 percent, but the federal government was faced with a massive debt refinancing problem. If British capital markets had not provided some $1.5 billion, interest rates would have been much higher and growth undoubtedly slower. Twenty years later when the debt had to be refinanced again – albeit at a much reduced level – the refinancing could have been carried

---

[540] A "free-standing" company was one that was not directly linked with an existing concern. For a detailed discussion of this type on institutional innovation, see Mira Wilkins, "The Free-Standing Company, 1870–1914: An Important Type of British Foreign Direct Investment," *Economic History Review*, 2nd Series, Vol. 41, No. 2 (1988).

[541] Balke-Gordon, Gallman, and Romer all put the increase in GNP at more than 6 percent a year. See Chapter 3, Appendix.

out domestically with relative ease.[542] At least as far as government issues were concerned, the domestic capital market had matured very rapidly.

Most American historians agree that, in terms of its impact on economic development, the construction of the national railway network was probably the most important event of the last half of the nineteenth century.[543] Certainly it is true that the development of some national transport system was necessary if a national market was to develop. Any such system required massive infusions of capital. Although much of the capital was raised domestically, a substantial share came from Europe, particularly from Great Britain.[544] Moreover, while the major domestic exchanges concentrated on the issues of the larger roads, the British markets absorbed not only the issues of the major trunk lines but also those of much smaller railroads – the Perkiomen, the Central City, Deadwood, and Eastern, and the Tonopah and Tidewater, to cite only three – as well.

Foreign capital contributed directly to American growth, but there was an indirect contribution as well. The need for foreign infusions of railroad capital helped shape domestic financial institutions. Modern investment banking emerged in the years following the Civil War. First-generation British (and German) merchant banks spawned second-generation mostly Anglo-American investment banks to help support the flow of foreign finance; and their success in the domestic market, in turn, drew the third generation of truly American banks into the industry. Until the late 1890s investment bankers concentrated almost solely on railroad issues. With few exceptions the successful bankers initially acted largely as conduits for foreign capital. At first, although they conducted a domestic business, they used their European connections to provide short-term credit to finance their underwritings as well as to

---

[542] In 1895 the government issued a $62 million refinancing loan. Although one-half was sold abroad, the American half was oversubscribed six times. Lewis, *America's Stake*, pp. 66–67.

[543] Robert Fogel has argued that the railroads were less important in regard to the reduction of the cost of transportation than most people had believed, but his conclusion does not vitiate the more general argument. Even if canals were nearly as efficient as railroads, in the absence of railroads, there would still have been an at least equally great demand for capital to construct the necessary system of canals. Robert W. Fogel, *Railroads and American Economic Growth: Essays in Econometric History* (Baltimore: Johns Hopkins University Press, 1964), pp. 17–110.

[544] If the debt refunding operations of the 1870s are excluded, railways drew about three-quarters of the capital raised in the British market.

provide an access to a major market for the securities that they had underwritten. To that latter end, they provided on-the-spot information to help monitor and overcome informational asymmetries, and to reduce uncertainty about American investments. Much of J.P. Morgan's finance was dependent upon his connection with the British house of J.S. Morgan; Kuhn, Loeb & company exploited their relationship with the long-established banking houses in Hamburg and Frankfurt; and Kidder, Peabody had for years acted as agent and attorney for the House of Baring.

Only gradually did the investment banks shift their efforts to domestic investors. The $1.1 billion in railroad finance raised in Britain in the last prewar decade suggests that, even at the end of the period, foreign connections were still important. As American savers gradually became more sophisticated, the second- and third-generation investment banks were in a position to service the domestic as well as the foreign market. The historical record is not yet settled; but one can argue that if, indeed, Britain did suffer from a shortage of manufacturing finance in the decades before World War I, the explanation could lie in the length of institutional gestation. In Britain there was a relatively short history of *domestic* investment banking and, therefore, no well-established institutions capable of meeting the demands of new industries: autos, electricity, and chemicals, for example.

The British merchant banks' need for information led them to establish links with second-generation Anglo-American banks. That information not only helped ensure the success of the railroad issues in London, but also convinced American savers that those second-generation firms dealt in high-quality issues – that all symbolic capital was not necessarily subject to very high uncertainty discounts. With that lesson understood, it was relatively easy for the third-generation banks to build reputations sufficient to allow them to become the major channel for directing American savings into American commerce and industry.

The 1880s and early 1890s were a period of rapid geographic and structural transformation. The trans-Mississippi West had been linked to the national market. Capital was needed in primary production – in agriculture and in mining. At the same time technological developments meant that firms in brewing, milling, mining, petroleum refining, and meatpacking that were able to attract sufficient capital could invest in the new technology, achieve substantial economies of scale, reduce their prices, and dramatically increase their share of the market. The domestic capital markets were not yet mature enough to underwrite either Western growth or the requisite investment in new technologies.

In response to the first demand, British capital flowed into agriculture and mining in the Great Plains, the Mountain states, and the Pacific region. In mining there were substantial economies of scale, and, in the absence of foreign investment, development would have been much slower. Not surprisingly, in mining, foreign capital proved as welcome in the 1880s and 1890s as it had been in the railroad sector since the 1850s. In cattle ranching and corn farming, however, where there were few scale economies, American farmers resented foreign competition: They were quite prepared to exploit the nation's natural resources themselves. By the mid-1890s, in response to a rising chorus of Western agrarian complaint, the majority of states, as well as the federal government, had passed laws prohibiting or greatly restricting foreign ownership of land. In terms of American development these laws, when combined with a shortage of domestic mortgage finance in the West, almost certainly reduced investment in mining, cattle ranching, and wheat farming, and it must have slowed the development of those industries.

In the case of brewing and milling, however, the business community welcomed foreign investment. Thus, at least two decades before the American domestic markets would have been capable of mobilizing sufficient finance, Americans benefited from the new capital-intensive technologies. In the longer run, as the domestic financial structure matured, the firms and the industries became established and developed substantial reputations among the nation's savers. As a result, many companies were able to finance further growth by exploiting those now more developed markets in their appeal to the now better educated savers.

Since World War II, as the cry of economic imperialism has been heard throughout the Third World, the entire question of domestic response to foreign investment has become particularly important. In the American case two facts stand out. As long as the Europeans invested in American railroads, even when they, as creditors to a bankrupt enterprise, were forced to take over a railroad, there were few complaints. Similarly, there were no serious complaints when British capital moved into milling and brewing. Moreover, Western miners strenuously lobbied against the laws limiting foreign ownership of land; and they were sometimes successful. However, British investment in Western agricultural land brought forth one of the most strident and politically effective responses in American history. American investment in Caribbean and Central American agriculture brought forth equally strident but less effective responses, but American investment in Canadian timber and lands generated no similar reaction. How can these differences be explained? That question will be addressed in the next chapter.

It was not only in the structure of investment banking that the American and British capital markets differed. The U.S. market encompassed a more diverse set of financial institutions. By the turn of the century American intermediaries represented a larger proportion of all financial assets than their British counterparts. What causes lay behind these differences? The commercial banks were the largest intermediaries in both the United States and the United Kingdom, and until the turn of the century they appear to have been of relatively similar size. Per capita assets for U.S. banks were $67 in 1880 and $119 in 1900. The comparable figures for the United Kingdom were $61 and $111. Thereafter the American banks grew much more rapidly. By 1914 the figures were $234 for the United States and $139 for the United Kingdom. If American unit banks are compared with British bank branches, the two systems again appear to have been not dissimilar in the latter decades of the nineteenth century. In 1880 an American bank served about 15,000 people, its British branch counterpart, 13,000. Thirty-four years later the figures were 3,600 for an American bank and 5,900 for a British branch.

Despite the quantitative similarities, there were a number of very important differences. First, British banks could, and did, operate networks of branches. Not until the 1890s did the structure of commercial banking begin to devolve rapidly toward a system dominated by a handful of banks, each operating a network of branches spread throughout the country, and only at the end of World War I was the process complete. As early as 1870, however, the nation's 368 banks controlled 2,728 branches. Even though the individual branch networks tended to be localized, British banks were able to mobilize capital across some geographic boundaries; and they gained at least some of the benefits that can be obtained from holding a geographically diversified portfolio of loans.

Second, although the growth of nationwide branch systems ultimately reduced its importance, from the early nineteenth century onward, the market for inland bills provided by the London discount market made transfers from capital surplus to capital deficit regions relatively simple. Finally, the Bank of England managed the gold standard in a way that reduced the pressure on domestic money markets, and the Bank proved willing to provide funds during periods of liquidity stress. Those guarantees, combined with the safety provided by branch banking, meant that, by almost any standard, the British banks and the banking system were safe. As a corollary, the Bank's guarantee made it possible for the markets in both inland and sterling bills to operate smoothly.

The U.S. experience was very different. With neither significant branching nor a lender of last resort, the system was highly volatile. On average between 1865 and 1914, more than sixty banks suspended every year; the fifty-year total was 3,401. Even among national banks the annual figure was almost a dozen. Moreover, the widely enforced rules against branch banking meant that the commercial banking system did little to mobilize capital within, let alone between, states. Until the commercial paper houses began to reach across the country toward the end of the century, there was not even an imperfect substitute for the London Discount Market. Although it is seldom mentioned in the literature, there can be little doubt that the absence of a lender of last resort must have delayed the evolution of the commercial paper market.

As Britain moved away from inland bills, the London market shifted toward foreign paper. Over most of the last half of the nineteenth century, it was foreign bills accepted by the London discount houses that provided the secondary reserves for the ever fewer numbers of national banks. One might conclude that an institution modeled along the lines of the London Discount Market could have provided the Americans with the short-term inter-regional capital mobility that the country's size and its domestic institutional structure made it so difficult to achieve. One might also conclude that, in the absence of a domestic counterpart, the London market for sterling bills could have provided an acceptable substitute. Perhaps it could have, but it did not. The fractured nature of American commercial banking, the legal constraints, and the absence of any lender of last resort certainly slowed domestic innovation. Despite the fact that a 1907 inquiry concluded, "A study of the bills lodged by the London discount houses as security for loans is a lesson in commercial geography," the United States contributed little to that lesson.[545] Perhaps it is asking too much for the international sterling bill market to solve problems of domestic capital mobilization in the United States. First, there was clearly an insufficient supply of short-term international paper generated in the States: – Although their absolute value had increased almost threefold, the relative level of short-term transfers in all foreign investment in America had been declining since the 1850s.[546] The relative level of British exports to the United States – the source of the discounted paper – was also falling. Second, because of the structure of west-east trade, almost all foreign exports were handled by merchants in the Northeast, and there was certainly no shortage of short-term finance in that region.

[545] W.T.C. King, *History of the London Discount Market* (London: George Routledge & Sons, 1936), p. 281.

[546] It represented 40 percent of the total in 1853, 10 percent in 1869, and 6 percent in 1914. Lewis, *America's Stake*, pp. 519–57.

Banking regulation and the bias toward short-term commercial credit also imposed another constraint on the process of capital mobilization. In the expanding South and West, there was almost always an excess demand for mortgage finance to support the expansion of farms and the growth of urban housing. Until the middle of the 1880s, however, given the wording of the National Banking Act, national banks were reluctant to make mortgage loans; and, even after the Supreme Court held that such loans were legal, there appear to have been de facto constraints. At the same time bankers' adherence to something closely akin to the real bills doctrine – an adherence that can be traced either to custom or of legal regulation – also made it very difficult for state-chartered banks to fill the gap. It is hardly surprising that 2 percent of all British capital calls were directed to financial land and development companies.

At the same time the domestic intermediaries that evolved to serve the long end of the market after the commercial banks largely withdrew proved unable to transfer any significant body of finance across state lines. Both mutual savings banks and building and loan associations were to a very large extent restrained by custom and legal regulation from lending on out-of-state or, occasionally, on out-of-region mortgages. It was partly for this reason that life insurance companies came to play a particularly important role in the evolution of the American capital markets. The innovation of tontine and industrial insurance promoted an annual increase of more than 6 percent in the industry's assets over the last three decades of the nineteenth century. In 1880 the life insurance companies in the United Kingdom held $602 million of assets, while American companies held $418 million (on a per capita basis $17.39 and $8.32 respectively). Thirty-four years later the comparable total figures were $2,183 and $4,935 and the per capita estimates $47.41 and $49.79.

It was not only their size that contributed to the role the life insurance companies played in solving the American accumulation and mobilization problems. First, although their investment portfolios were almost always regulated, the degree of regulation varied from state to state. Over time there was a general easing of those regulations in almost every state. Thus, by the mid-1880s life insurance companies in most states were able to invest in mortgages in regions far removed from their home offices. In addition, their insulation from sudden and unexpected financial demands made it possible for them to hold a portfolio of mortgages safely, when institutions subject to sudden liquidity demands could not. In addition, a number of states permitted life insurance companies to invest in the securities of private corporations.

Second, the Big Five companies were all located in the Northeast and were closely connected – by ownership and interlocking directorates – to the major investment banking firms. With policy incomes generating large blocks of cash in search of investment opportunities, life insurance companies in general, and the Big Five in particular, became natural outlets for the security issues underwritten by investment bankers.

The connection between the insurance companies and the investment houses brings the discussion around once more to the chapter in American financial history that is often titled "The Money Trust." It is in the structure of investment banking that the flow of international finance almost certainly had its greatest impact on the evolution of the domestic capital markets. In Britain the railroad boom of the 1830s and 1840s had been financed in large part by the direct issue of securities (common stock and debentures) with the provincial exchanges and, especially, on the London Stock Exchange providing a secondary market.[547] Investment banks played little or no role. Since manufacturing profits were high, most industrial firms managed to finance expansion through retained earnings with only occasional appeals to the local provincial exchange. Those exchanges, like their Boston and Philadelphia counterparts in the United States, serviced local investors who were well informed about the status and prospects of the issuing firms.

In London, at least over the last third of the century, the primary security market was dominated by the great issues houses – the Rothschilds, Schroeder, or Seligman – whose main work, and therefore whose expertise, lay in marketing the issues of domestic and foreign railroads and of foreign governments. Those markets were tightly enough controlled that, before the 1890s, there was little room for second-tier firms. The great bulk of joint-stock companies were floated by "ephemeral promoting groups, usually specially formed for the purpose of selling a venture to the public, and dissolved when that purpose had been carried out."[548] The groups had no incentive to create or to retain a reputation. As a result, there was a huge gap in terms of size and quality of reputation between the second-tier American investment banks and even the very best of the British promoters, accounting firms like Chadwick, Adamson and Collier of Manchester and London (a firm that served many of the functions of a modern investment bank, but on a much smaller scale), or

---

[547] In 1842 railway companies were the largest single group of joint stock companies quoted on the London market. P.L. Cottrell, *Industrial Finance, 1830–1914: The Finance and Organization of English Manufacturing Industry* (London: Methuen, 1979), pp. 95–97. [Hereafter cited as Cottrell, *Industrial Finance.*] Thomas, *The Provincial Stock Exchanges*, p. 72.

[548] Lavington, *The English Capital Market*, pp. 183–84.

H. Osbourne O'Hagen, probably Britain's most successful nineteenth-century promoter. As the new century opened, however, the British investment market appears to have begun to take on some of the characteristics of its American counterpart. The evidence indicates "that many lesser known British investment banks, as well as some of the largest merchant banks, were willing to channel long-term capital to industry before the Great War." These City banks appear to have responded very quickly to the "demand by Canadian firms for long-term capital. Moreover, they adopted the three basic pillars of high-risk finance: they indemnified the manufacturing company by purchasing the entire issue of securities thereby acting as an issuing house; they then improved the success rate of flotations by underwriting portions of the issue before subscription was opened to the public; and finally they agreed to take their remuneration in the common shares of the company rather than a cash commission thereby staking their profit on the future viability of the enterprise."[549]

In the United States by the end of the 1890s, because of institutions established to channel foreign funds to American railroads, there were investment banking firms in place that could and did mobilize domestic savings for investment in domestic industry. Initially, the old-line firms largely served the needs of the newly merged industrial giants, U.S. Steel, for example, but there was also a demand for someone to underwrite and market the issues of middle-sized firms in commerce – Sears and Roebuck, for example – and in the new manufacturing industries; automobiles are probably the best example. J.P. Morgan aside, the old-line investment bankers were hesitant to enter these new markets; however, the industry was no longer a monopoly, if it ever had been one. There were younger, smaller, and more aggressive second-tier, third-generation, firms – Goldman, Sachs and Lehman Brothers, to cite only two – that were willing to exploit these opportunities. Thus, in large part because of an earlier dependence on foreign capital, the institutional structure was in place to speed the flow of savings from the gradually better educated domestic saver to the very frontiers of American industry.

There were also significant differences in the two major secondary markets: the London and the New York Stock Exchanges. At the beginning of the period British savers were better educated than their American counterparts, and the structure of the two markets reflects that

[549] Gregory P. Marchildon, "British Investment Banking and Industrial Decline Before the Great War: A Case Study of Capital Outflow to Canadian Industry," in Geoffrey Jones (ed.), *Banks and Money: International and Comparative Finance in History* (London and Portland, Oregon: Frank Cass, 1991), p. 88.

difference. Initially the London market was prepared to list almost any issue, at least any issue of "sufficient magnitude." The LSE granted "special settlement" rather easily. "With special settlement, transactions in the company's shares became part of the normal fortnightly account system of the house's dealings, enforced by the rules with penalties for defaulters. Originally, a company's broker could apply for special settlement as soon as the company's shares were known to be ready for delivery"; however, in the mid-1860s in an attempt to tighten up the rules, the Stock Exchange Committee ruled that, in the future, "share dealings were only to be recognized if the company involved had issued unconditionally at least half of its nominal capital, of which 10% had been paid up."[550] Gradually the Committee of the Exchange began to distinguish between a special settlement and a quotation. The rules for a quotation became substantially more demanding than the rules for special settlement. By the 1870s, for a quotation it was "also required that the prospectus must have been publicly advertised and, in the case of companies, must agree substantially with the articles of association. Not less than half the authorized capital must have been issued and 10% paid. Two-thirds of any issue must have been 'subscribed for and unconditionally allotted to the public,' any share issued in lieu of money payments not to count towards this proportion."[551]

Although these rules almost certainly were designed to provide the British saver with a stamp of quality (and there is substantial evidence that they served that function); they were a far cry from the near draconian rules that the New York Stock Exchange imposed on any issue seeking a listing.[552] Those rules included, in addition to a significant minimum size requirement, a satisfactory earnings history for both the firm and the industry, a history of price stability (a minimum of volatility), and a relatively high ($100) par value. The two sets of arrangements clearly had a twofold impact on American developments. On the one hand, the relatively loose requirements of the British market meant that there was room for American issues that could not qualify for the New York Stock Exchange. Firms in new industries and new regions benefited. On the other hand, the existence of a London alternative with effectively no minimum commission meant that it was difficult for any

---

[550] P.L. Cottrell, *Industrial Finance*, pp. 147–48. For a full explanation of the act of settlement and the granting of a quotation, see Chapter 2.

[551] Morgan and Thomas, *The Stock Exchange: Its History and Functions*, p. 153.

[552] "In practice, people do not like to invest in securities which are not brought under their notice. They would choose those securities by preference in which they saw the transactions recorded in the list." *Royal Commission on the Stock Exchange*, 1878, question 2494.

of the American local exchanges (the Consolidated and the Curb in New York and exchanges in other cities – Boston, Philadelphia, and Chicago, to cite three) to develop a level of monopoly power sufficient to permit it to successfully challenge the NYSE.

Relative to the experiences of the other three frontier countries, the flows of foreign – mainly British – capital to the United States were quite small. In a number of important ways, many quite unintentional, the transfers to the United States affected both the rate of the nation's economic growth and the structure of the American capital markets. The importance of trusts in the American financial structure was clearly the product of domestic regulations, but the importance of the investment banks in the early decades of this century was equally clearly the result of a previous dependence on foreign capital. On the other side of the issue, the success of the San Francisco branch of the Bank of British Columbia and the London and San Francisco Bank – both imperial banks – suggests how much more productive foreign capital might have been, had domestic regulations been less constraining.

Appendix: U.S. estimates of national product

The various U.S. National Product series for the period 1869–1914 currently in use all trace to the estimates by Simon Kuznets that were initially published in *National Product Since 1869*. Kuznets's estimates were chiefly in the form of overlapping decade averages.[553] His series, in turn, depended heavily on William H. Shaw's work on commodity production.[554] Kuznets marked up Shaw's benchmark (census years) final commodity flow data to allow for the costs of distribution, added estimates of consumer expenditures on services (based on budget studies), and estimated the value of changes in inventories and the value of construction. He then interpolated between benchmark dates. Those interpolations were chiefly based on Shaw's annual series for the years 1889 onward, but they were based on more fragmentary evidence for earlier years. Kuznets thought the series would be useful in the study of trends and long swings, but he had doubts with respect to their ability to properly describe business cycles, and so he never published annual series for the years before 1889. The annual series were available in mimeographed form, however, and have been used by other scholars in their work on national product.

[553] New York: National Bureau of Economic Research, 1946. More detail is available in the appendices of Kuznets's *Capital in the American Economy* (Princeton: Princeton University Press, 1961).

[554] William Howard Shaw, *Value of Commodity Output Since 1869* (New York: National Bureau of Economic Research, 1947).

The first revision of Kuznets's series was made by John Kendrick.[555] Kuznets's estimates incorporate his own concept of government, a concept that differs from the Department of Commerce concept, employed in the official U.S. series. Kendrick adjusted the Kuznets series to put them on the Department of Commerce basis. Since government was a very small sector in the United States before World War I, the Kendrick adjustments are not of great importance for present purposes.

More fundamental adjustments were advanced in a paper published in volume 30 of *Studies in Income and Wealth*.[556] The chief proposals suggested the following:

1. New estimates of firewood and animal products flowing into consumption be substituted for Shaw's. That adjustment produced a GNP series that describes a lower rate of growth than Kuznets's, throughout, but especially in the period 1869–89.
2. Harold Barger's new estimates of the cost of distribution be employed to adjust the Kuznets series.[557] The Barger work was done between the publication of Kuznets's series and the date of the volume 30 meeting.
3. The appropriate markup for heavy construction, such as railroads, differed from the markup relevant to building. Therefore, the materials flows were split and two construction series were estimated, one relating to railroad construction, and the other to building. Kuznets had estimated the value of construction by simply marking up flows of construction materials to allow for the value of construction work.
4. The volume 30 paper argued that the GNP series, at benchmark (census year) dates, be deflated by use of detailed final price indexes (base 1860) assembled by Dorothy Brady. Her price indexes are quite unusual for such an early period. They are very important, and they were not available to Kuznets.

However, there were still some open questions. The volume 30 series omitted the value of inventory changes. In this respect it is similar to the

---

[555] *Productivity Trends in the United States* (Princeton: Princeton University Press, 1961).

[556] Robert E. Gallman, "Gross National Product in the United States, 1834–1909," in Dorothy S. Brady (ed.), *Output, Employment, and Productivity in the United States After 1800*, Studies in Income and Wealth, Vol. 30 (New York: National Bureau of Economic Research, 1966).

[557] Harold Barger, *Distribution's Place in the American Economy Since 1869* (Princeton: Princeton University Press, 1955).

Urquhart series for Canada. For purposes of this book, however, Canadian decennial inventory changes were estimated by differencing estimates of elements of the capital stock.[558]

The volume 30 series were also published, like Kuznets's, only in the form of decade averages. The explanation was the same as Kuznets had used earlier. The annual series existed in typescript, however, and it was subsequently published by Friedman and Schwartz, but in a somewhat revised form.[559] Inventory changes were added back in, the deflation base was shifted to 1929, and depreciation was estimated and deducted. Thus, the series was published in the form of a national product series.

Finally, two new versions – versions produced by Christina D. Romer and Nathan S. Balke and Robert J. Gordon – have recently appeared.[560] Both sets of authors are concerned with cycles rather than trends. They adopt the Kendrick and volume 30 changes to the Kuznets series, shift the deflation base to 1982, and then reestimate the year-to-year movements of the series.[561] The two disagree with respect to the relative volatility of the prewar series, but that is a matter of no concern for this book.

The three series – volume 30, Romer, and Balke-Gordon – exhibit the following, quite similar, decennial rates of change for the decades 1869–78 to 1904–13:

	Balke-Gordon	Volume 30	Romer
1869–1878 to 1879–1888	61%	65%	62%
1874–1883 to 1884–1893	45	50	43
1879–1888 to 1889–1898	33	36	35
1884–1893 to 1894–1903	42	36	42
1889–1898 to 1899–1908	57	51	49
1894–1903 to 1904–1913	50	49	46

[558] Robert E. Gallman, "The United States Capital Stock in the Nineteenth Century," in Stanley L. Engerman and Robert E. Gallman (eds.), *Long-Term Factors in American Economic Growth*, Studies in Income and Wealth, Vol. 52 (Chicago: University of Chicago Press, 1986).

[559] Milton Friedman and Anna Jacobson Schwartz, *Monetary Trends in the United States and the United Kingdom: Their Relation to Income, Prices, and Interest Rate, 1867–1975* (Chicago: University of Chicago Press, 1982), table 4.8. pp. 122–24.

[560] Christina D. Romer, "The Prewar Business Cycle Reconsidered: New Estimates of Gross National Product, 1869–1908," and N. Balke and R. Gordon, "The Estimation of Prewar Gross National Product: Methodology and New Evidence," both in *The Journal of Political Economy*, Vol. 91, No. 1 (1989).

[561] Balke and Gordon also produce a new GNP deflator and make separate, new estimates of transportation, communications, and construction.

CHAPTER 4

Domestic savings, international capital flows, and the evolution of domestic capital markets: The Canadian experience[562]

4-1. Introduction

4-1a. Patterns of growth, 1867–1914

In 1841 the heretofore separate provinces of Upper and Lower Canada were brought together in a legislative union creating what might be termed the first Canadian confederation.[563] In 1848 the citizens of

---

[562] It is only recently that economic historians have been able to feel comfortable about their level of understanding of the quantitative measures of Canadian economic growth. That they do now feel fairly secure in their estimates is largely the product of the work of M.C. Urquhart, "New Estimates of Gross National Product, Canada, 1870–1926: Some Implications for Canadian Development," in S. Engerman and R. Gallman (eds.), *Long Term Factors in American and Economic Growth*, NBER, Studies in Income and Wealth, Vol. 51 (Chicago: University of Chicago Press, 1986); it includes M.C. Urquhart, "Canadian Economic Growth 1870–1980," Queens University, Kingston, Ontario, Working Paper No. 734, November 1988; and it culminates with the recent publication of the admirable, wide-ranging, sturdy, and very detailed compendium by M.C. Urquhart (with chapters by A.G. Green, Thomas Rymes, Marion Steel, and A.M. Sinclair, and contributions by D.M. McDougall and R.M. McInnes), *Gross National Product, Canada, 1870–1926: The Derivation of the Estimates* (Kingston: McGill-Queen's University Press, 1993). [Hereafter cited as Urquhart, *Gross National Product.*]

[563] This section is largely based on the following: Marvin McInnis, "Foundations of the Nineteenth Century Canadian Economy," manuscript chapter for Vol. II of Stanley L. Engerman and Robert E. Gallman (eds.), *Cambridge Economic History of the United States*, Vol. II (New York: Cambridge University Press, forthcoming) [Hereafter cited as McInnis, "Foundations of the Nineteenth Century Canadian Economy"]; Alan G. Green, "Twentieth Century Canadian Economic History," manuscript chapter for Vol. III of Stanley L. Engerman and Robert E. Gallman (eds.), *Cambridge Economic History of the United States*, Vol. II (New York: Cambridge University Press, forthcoming); M.C. Urquhart, "Canadian Economic Growth, 1870–1980," Queens University Discussion Paper No. 734 (1988); M.C. Urquhart, *Gross National Product, Canada, 1870–1926*

Nova Scotia were granted responsible government. That status was confirmed to Canadian residents (residents of what had been Upper and Lower Canada) a year later, and in the ensuing years it was introduced into New Brunswick, Prince Edward Island, and Newfoundland. In 1867 Nova Scotia, New Brunswick, and the now linked colonies of Upper and Lower Canada (taking the provincial names of Ontario and Quebec) joined together in a far more extensive federal union. The new commonwealth comprised 384,598 square miles; within a half dozen years it was augmented by the vast territories of the Hudson's Bay Company, British Columbia, and Prince Edward Island, the whole amounting to 3,357,348 square miles, an area almost nine times as large as was contained in the original Confederation.

The act of the British Parliament that created the Confederation was a constitutional document. Among its other features, it distributed powers and tax sources among the federal, provincial, and local governments, and, in order to open the domestic market, forbade interprovincial tariffs. The chief responsibility of the federal government was to promote peace, order, and good government; and a series of Canadian politicians have taken these goals to include policies that promote economic growth. The constitution was sufficiently detailed, in this regard, to specify that the government was to ensure that a rail line was promptly constructed between Quebec and the East Coast. Similarly, when British Columbia joined the Confederation, the government promised to support the construction of a rail link between that province and eastern Canada.

Over the years the courts weakened what had originally been envisaged as a very strong central government. Nevertheless, the promise of active governmental direction of economic growth was redeemed from the date of Confederation and strongly renewed with the electoral victory of a conservative government in 1878. However, in order to understand the imperatives that were driving Canadian actions and to appreciate the base from which economic development was to proceed,

(Kingston: McGill Queens University Press, 1993); M.C. Urquhart, "New Estimates of Gross National Product, Canada, 1870–1926: Some Implications for Canadian Development," pp. 9–88 and comments thereon by J.H. Dales, pp. 89–93, in Stanley L. Engerman and Robert E. Gallman (eds.), *Long Term Factors in American Economic Growth*, NBER, Studies in Income and Wealth, Vol. 51 (Chicago and London: University of Chicago Press, 1986); Frank Lewis and M.C. Urquhart, "Growth and the Standard of Living in a Pioneer Economy: Upper Canada, 1825–1951," paper prepared for a conference on the Economy of Early British America: The Domestic Sector, held at the Huntington Library in October, 1995.

it is necessary to briefly consider the history of Canada before Confederation.

4-1b. Growth before 1867

In 1873, when Canada was about the same size as the United States (including Alaska), the Canadian population was only about one-eleventh as great. There are three parts to the explanation for this marked contrast. First, Canada had only recently added the lands of the Hudson's Bay Company, and there had been no time to populate those new territories. Second, a much larger fraction of the total land area of the United States than of Canada is habitable. Third, the early histories of the two countries were very different. From late in the sixteenth century until 1763, Canada was inhabited and controlled by the French and their Indian allies. The Indian population was ravaged by disease and constant war, and the French population was never substantially augmented by immigration. The central economic activity of the French and their allies was the fur trade, an activity that did not require a large European population. Although the rate of natural increase of the French Canadians was high, it was probably not much higher (if at all) than that of the European and African populations of what was to become the United States; but the Americans also encouraged immigration: free, indentured, and slave.

As a result, the American population grew much more rapidly than the Canadian. Despite the substantial emigration of Loyalists from the United States to Nova Scotia and then to Quebec during and after the Revolutionary War (offset in small measure by the earlier removal of Acadians from Nova Scotia), by 1815 the combined European population of Upper and Lower Canada was only about 400,000 and that of the Maritimes about half that figure. At that time the population of the United States was almost 8.5 million and growing rapidly. Between 1815 and 1873, a period during which European immigration to Canada was officially encouraged (a policy adopted in response to fears of American expansiveness touched off by American efforts to invade Canada during the War of 1812), the Canadian-American gap narrowed slightly from a ratio of 14:1 to about 11:1.

By the end of the War of 1812, despite the earlier loss of western territory ceded to the United States by Jay's Treaty (1794), prospects for Canadian growth were bright. The British West Indies offered an excellent market for Canadian fish, barrel staves, timbers, and lumber. Timber and lumber could also bear the transport costs to Britain; they found a good market there and, eventually, in the United States as well. Land was abundant and access to it, free. Compared to the United States, the

Canadian growing season was short, but it was not short when compared to Britain. English immigrants to Upper Canada found no serious difficulty growing wheat, a crop that fit well into the conditions of the frontier. Before mechanization, wheat required little capital and could be grown and harvested with the labor available on a family farm. Under these conditions enough wheat could be produced to feed the family and provide some surplus for trade.

Initially, neither wheat nor flour could bear the costs of transportation to the British market, but there were good internal markets: the small but growing urban populations, especially in Upper Canada, and the farm population of Lower Canada. The latter colony had been settled longer and had been able to make the investments required to specialize in animal products. The products of the two colonies were complementary, and trade grew – flour moving east to Lower Canada and animal products moving west to Upper Canada. Although the end of the English corn laws meant greater competition from suppliers outside the empire, by the 1850s ocean transportation costs had fallen far enough that Canada was able to compete in the British market. Upper Canadian farmers responded by increasing their production and redirecting a part to Britain. The success of the wheat trade in this decade crowned a long period of agricultural prosperity in Canada. The lumber trade continued to be prosecuted with vigor, and wood products remained leading elements in Canadian external trade.

Geography contributed to Canadian economic promise. The St. Lawrence, the rivers that flow into it, and the Great Lakes provided a potentially magnificent east-west transportation system, but some improvements were required. As a result of the activities directed to that end, a tradition of government support for investments in social overhead capital was established. From the time Canadians were granted self-government until at least the end of the First World War, successive Canadian governments actively promoted investment in the nation's infrastructure. Ship canals were constructed around rapids and falls, and well before Confederation an all-water route to the interior had been established. To cope with the problems posed by the short navigation season on the lower St. Lawrence, in 1853 a rail line was opened between Montreal and Portland, Maine. With that rail link weather no longer shortened the west-to-east traffic season. Canadian hopes of tapping into the trade of the American West were dashed by the success of the Erie Canal, but the Canadian system could, and did, carry Canadian products from the interior to the coast. This trade became both important and profitable. At least some elements of the system – the Inter Colonial Railway (ICR), for example – were certainly built ahead of demand, and may have been ill advised given any time frame. This feature (the Canadian Pacific Railroad, perhaps, aside) continued to characterize the Canadian governments' (federal and provincial) efforts to promote transport at least until the First World War.

The Canadian River system also provided power for industrial activity. At first Canadian sawmills cut squared timber, but they soon moved to producing a more finished product, cutting boards from logs. Mills ground flour from small grains. Canadian industry was not, however, confined to processing these products of the land; instead, its scope expanded so far that some have been able to claim that the transition to modern economic growth was well under way by the 1850s and that by 1871 it had been completed.

Canadian industrial growth did not follow the patterns of Britain or the United States. Textiles and basic metals did not play a major role in the early years. Canadian strengths lay in lumber and grain milling and in the manufacture of producers' durables: ships, locomotives, rolling stock, and agricultural implements. These activities were important, but, despite these signs of industrial success, the Canadian economy remained to a large degree based on primary activities: agriculture, forestry, and fisheries (Tables 4:1-1, 4:1-2, and 4:1-3 outline the record of Canadian growth between Confederation and World War I).

4-1c. 1867–1896

By Confederation the history of the Canadian economy was already a success story. It had exhibited rapid growth in output, an ability to penetrate foreign markets, a well-developed agricultural sector, and the beginnings of industrialization. But it was not free of problems. The Reciprocal Trade Agreement, signed with the United States in 1854, was revoked by the Americans in 1866. Contemporaries certainly believed, and some scholars still argue, that the Trade Agreement improved Canadian access to American markets in important ways and contributed significantly to Canadian prosperity. The high rate of natural population increase was producing larger numbers of workers than could easily be absorbed on the farm or in urban industry. Confederation and, more particularly, the expansion of territory that was realized in 1873 came at a fortuitous time. The new land could provide opportunities both for excess eastern farm population and for new immigrants from Europe.

The opportunities, however, could not be immediately exploited. The thousands of square miles of prime wheat land on the Canadian prairies were separated from the eastern provinces by over 1,000 miles of the Canadian Shield: rock, sand, and bush. For eastern Canadians or Euro-

Table 4:1-1. *Decennial rates of the growth of population, real GNP, and real GNP per capita: Canada, U.S., and fourteen other developed countries ca. 1870–ca. 1914 (percents)*

Years	Population			Real GNP			Real GNP per capita		
	Canada	United States	14 Others	Canada	United States	14 Others	Canada	United States	14 Others
1870–1879 to 1880–1889	15.1	25.8		38.3	65.0		20.2	31.0	
1875–1884 to 1885–1894	12.7	25.2		33.7	50.0		18.7	10.0	
1880–1889 to 1890–1899	11.1	23.5		28.0	36.0		15.1	9.0	
1885–1894 to 1895–1904	11.2	21.5		42.0	36.0		26.8	13.0	
1890–1899 to 1900–1908	11.9	20.6		70.3	51.0		43.0	25.0	
1895–1904 to 1905–1914	29.6	20.7		80.1	49.0		39.0	23.0	
1870–1913	18.3	22.9	10.6	48.8	48.0	26.1	25.8	20.0	13.9

Notes: 1. The time periods for the United States are actually 1869–1878 to 1879–1888, etc.
2. The 14 are: Australia, Austria, Belgium, Denmark, Finland, France, Germany, Italy, Japan, Netherlands, Norway, Sweden, Switzerland, and the U.K., Canada and the United States are extreme outliers with respect to all three rates of growth. They are joined by Sweden with respect to the rate of growth of real GNP per capita.
3. The 1870–1913 figures for Canada are really 1870–1879 to 1905–1914 and for the United States they are 1869–1878 to 1904–1913.
4. GNP excludes the value of changes in inventories.
5. The Balke-Gordon and Romer series yield slightly different results for the United States. The largest difference is for the period 1885–1894 to 1895–1904, for which the Balke-Gordon and Romer series both yield a rate of change of 42%. Nathan S. Balke and Robert J. Gordon, "The Estimation of Prewar Gross National Product: Methodology and New Evidence" and Christina D. Romer, "The Prewar Business Cycle Reconsidered: New Estimates of Gross National Product, 1869–1908," both in the *Journal of Political Economy*, vol. 97, no. 1, 1989, pp. 1–92.

Sources: The figures were derived from: M.C. Urquart, *Gross National Product, Canada, 1870–1926*, pp. 24 & 25; *Historical Statistics of Canada*, 2nd edition, Series A1–A14; Volume 30 of Studies in Income and Wealth; *Historical Statistics of the United States*, Bicentennial Edition, Series A-7; Angus Madison, *Phases of Capitalist Development*, pp. 44–45.

Table 4:1-2. *Rates of growth of Canadian real GNP, population, and real GNP per capita (1900 prices)*

Years	Average annual percentage rates of growth		
	Real GNP	Population	Real GNP Per capita
1870–1871	4.33	1.77	2.56
1871–1872	−0.86	1.76	−2.62
1872–1873	9.37	1.92	7.45
1873–1874	1.89	1.80	0.09
1874–1875	−2.35	1.51	−3.86
1870–1875	2.37	1.75	0.62
1875–1876	−6.36	1.39	−7.75
1876–1877	6.40	1.37	5.03
1877–1878	−3.45	1.38	−4.83
1878–1879	9.65	1.58	8.07
1879–1880	4.44	1.67	2.77
1875–1880	1.98	1.48	0.50
1880–1881	14.24	1.65	12.59
1881–1882	3.96	1.16	2.80
1882–1883	−0.18	1.26	−1.44
1883–1884	8.55	1.29	7.26
1884–1885	−6.35	1.11	−7.46
1880–1885	3.88	1.29	2.59
1885–1886	0.65	0.95	−0.30
1886–1887	3.44	1.00	2.44
1887–1888	6.74	1.12	5.62
1888–1889	0.80	1.09	−0.29
1889–1890	6.11	1.06	5.05
1885–1890	3.52	1.04	2.48
1890–1891	3.05	1.01	2.04
1891–1892	−0.50	1.03	−1.53
1892–1893	−1.44	0.98	−2.42
1893–1894	5.00	0.97	4.03
1894–1895	−0.33	0.94	−1.27
1895–1896	−2.64	0.96	−3.60
1890–1896	0.49	1.00	−0.51
1870/1872–1894/1896	2.54	1.29	1.25

Sources: Computed from data in Table 16, "GNP in Constant (1900) Prices" and "Population," M.C. Urquhart, *Gross National Product Canada, 1870–1926, The Derivation of the Estimates* (Kingston and Montreal: McGill-Queens University Press, 1993), pp. 24–25.

Table 4:1-3. *The distribution of Canadian GNP among industrial sectors, 1870–1900*

Sector	1870	1880	1890	1895	1900
Primary	42.0%	37.7%	31.0%	30.9%	26.8%
Secondary	33.5	34.3	38.8	35.6	40.0
Tertiary	24.4	28.0	30.3	33.4	33.1
Total	99.9	100.0	100.1	99.9	99.9

Totals fail to sum to 100 because of rounding.

Notes: Primary sector: Agriculture, forestry, hunting and trapping, and fisheries. Secondary sector: Mining, manufacturing, manufactured gas, construction, transportation, electric light and power, and communications. Tertiary sector: Banking and finance, residential rents, government, education, trade, and services.

Source: Urquhart, *Gross National Product*, p. 16.

pean immigrants in search of land, it was easier to migrate out of Canada and into the United States, where good accessible farmland was still available, than it was to cross the Shield and establish farms on the Canadian prairies. In the United States during the period of heavy immigration that followed the Civil War, there were those who believed that the entry of the immigrants reduced opportunities for natives and thereby led natives to marry later and to have fewer children: Immigrants were replacing the natives who would have been born had there been no immigration. In Canada a similar set of ideas grew up: Immigrants were flooding the labor market and were forcing native Canadians to migrate to the United States. That immigrants can be properly blamed for what was happening in either country is doubtful, but it is certainly true that in Canada from the early 1870s to the mid-1890s emigrants typically outnumbered immigrants. For the first time migration was damping Canadian population growth.

If the projected prairie provinces were to be settled, transportation was required to carry migrants west and to ship their products east. The government planned and began to build a rail line to deal with this problem.

It was an enormous project. The railroad had to cross the Continental Shield (a region that would neither generate nor receive freight) and then cross the prairies to the Pacific coast – in total, a line running well over 2,000 miles. The project was eventually turned over to the Canadian Pacific Railway Company, and the Company was given very substantial subsidies to assist it in its task of construction. The line was completed in 1885, almost twenty years after Confederation, but another ten years were to pass before substantial settlement of the prairies began.

There were at least two other impediments to Canadian growth in the years leading up to 1896. First, the prairies posed new problems for wheat production. Solutions called for new inventions and innovations in seeds, methods of farming, and milling technologies – innovations that took time and that help explain the long delay in settlement. Second, the expansion of the Confederation to include the new lands in the West occurred in 1873, the first year of the long and deep depression of 1873–79, a depression that appears to have had a particularly unfavorable impact on Canadian industry.

For the Canadian economy the years from Confederation to the mid-1890s were less successful than the 1850s had been. Population grew more slowly, emigration exceeded immigration, both industrial and agricultural growth was sluggish, and the occupation of the prairies went forward at only a snail's pace. The annual rate of growth of population fell from 1.75 percent in the early 1870s to less than 1.50 percent in the second half of the decade, to roughly 1 percent in the late 1880s and early 1890s. The decline was persistent and pronounced. The rates of change of GNP were highly variable; the stress of the depressions of 1873–79 and of the 1890s show up very clearly in the annual rates of change. These events had more than a passing impact: The average rate of growth of real GNP per capita was only about 0.5 percent per year in the 1870s, and it was negative over the first six years of the 90s (see Table 4:1-2). Although the data on the earlier period are weak, economic performance in the 1850s was almost certainly better. Nonetheless, the years from the early 1870s through the mid-1890s was not a period of stagnation. Although the rate of population growth declined, it still averaged almost 1.3 percent a year, a rate that, if sustained, would have increased Canadian population by almost 40 percent every quarter century and by more than 250 percent every hundred years. There were hard times in the 1870s and again in the 1890s, but between 1870–72 and 1894–96 real GNP per capita grew at an annual rate of 1.25 percent, by no means a low rate. At the end of the period it was roughly 36 percent higher than it had been at the beginning, and it was among the highest in the world. Of the thirty-seven countries for which there are nineteenth-century data, the real per capita GDP of twenty-four were substantially lower than that of Canada; three more were about at the Canadian level; and

Table 4:1-4. *Distribution of Canadian gross fixed capital formation by industrial sector, 1870–1896*

Sector	1870–1879	1880–1889	1890–1896
Other business*	17.8%	20.7%	29.0%
Manufacturing	8.6	14.4	13.2
Housing construction	36.3	23.3	34.5
Railways and telegraph	24.8	33.3	12.4
Government	9.8	7.2	9.2
Public schools	2.1	1.1	1.6
Total	99.4**	100.0	99.9

Notes: * Other Business includes agriculture.
  ** Details do not sum to the total in the source document.

Source: Urquhart, *Gross National Product*, p. 16.

only ten – seven developed European countries, Australia, New Zealand, and the United States – had higher levels.[564]

There is also a clear indication that the modernization of the Canadian economy had continued. The share of output contributed by the primary sectors – agriculture, forest industries, the fisheries, hunting, and trapping – fell from 42 percent of GNP in 1870, to just under 38 percent in 1880, to 31 percent in 1890, to 27 percent in 1900 (see Table 4:1-3).

The shares of both the secondary and, particularly, the tertiary sector increased. Within the latter sector, although there were no dramatic shifts, all of the six included industries – banking and finance, residential rents, government, education, trade, and other services – gained. The secondary sector includes mining, manufacturing – by far the largest element – manufactured gas, construction, transportation, electric power, and communications; all of these, except construction, grew faster than GNP.

The data of sectoral investments provide another view of the structural changes in the economy (see Table 4:1-4). They show a very heavy commitment to railways and telegraphs (one-quarter to one-third of gross investment) in the first two decades and a decline (to about one dollar in eight) in the share of those industries in the early 1890s. The share of investment devoted to manufacturing rose by two-thirds

[564] Angus Maddison, *Monitoring the World Economy, 1820–1992* (Paris: OECD, 1995), table D-1a-D-1e.

between the 1870s and the 1880s; that directed toward "other business" (a sector that includes agriculture) increased by 16 percent over the same period, but by 40 percent between the 1880s and the early 1890s.

Investment in the Canadian economy, although dropping off somewhat in the 1890s, was substantial (see Table 4:1-5). The share of gross fixed capital in GNP averaged about 16 percent in the 1870s and 1880s before declining to 13 percent in the early 1890s. If to those totals are added the estimates for investment in inventories and in the clearing, first breaking, and fencing of farm land, the share of investment in GNP averaged more than 20 percent over the first two decades before declining to about three-quarters of that level in the 1890s. If the American experience provides a guideline, net investment probably averaged about 60 percent of gross investment, or from perhaps 12 to 14 percent of net national product in the 1870s and 1880s, 10 percent in the early and mid-1890s, and about 12 percent, on average, across the years 1870–96.

The Canadian investment record reflects both an impressive performance by Canadian savers and also a very impressive inflow of foreign – largely British – savings. Roughly two-thirds of the investment was financed by Canadians, but the remaining one-third was funded by foreigners. The aggregate figures do not, however, tell the entire story. Virtually all land clearing and investment in inventories were financed domestically, while most of the foreign contribution was directed to investment in other elements of the fixed capital stock. If investment in land clearing is ignored, total foreign investment was almost 50 percent as large as the level of gross fixed investment in the 1870s, about 40 percent in the next decade, and just less than 50 percent in the early and mid-1890s. Seen in this light, foreigners contributed enormously to Canadian growth and structural change.

Finally, while the rate of growth between 1870 and 1896 was modest by the standards of what had happened before and what was to come later, the investment in social overhead capital undertaken during this period helped prepare the way for a dramatic turnaround in the late 1890s and for the remarkable economic record of the decade and a half leading up to World War I. It should be noted that that conclusion tends to support the argument that investment in railways took place well ahead of demand, and it does not necessarily contradict the conclusion that more investment took place than could ever be economically justified. Be that as it may, transport links were established with the West; some of them were to pay off within the ensuing two decades, and even more of them in the dozen years thereafter.

Table 4:1-5. *Canadian savings and investment rates, 1870–1913*

			Percentage shares of GNP				
(1) Years	(2) Gross fixed capital formation	(3) Changes in the value of inventories	(4) Investment in farm land improvement (clearing and breaking)	(5) Total gross capital formation	(6) Capital inflow	(7) Implicit savings rate	(8) Adjusted savings rate
1870–1879	15.0	1.3	2.4	18.7	6.9	8.1	11.8
1880–1889	16.9	1.6	3.4	21.9	6.9	10.0	15.0
1890–1896	13.2	1.7	0.7	15.6	6.3	6.9	9.3
1897–1905	18.9				4.7	14.2	
1906–1913	29.3				12.8	16.5	

Sources:

Column (2): Computed from Urquhart, Gross National Product, p. 16 ("Grand Total") & pp. 24–25 ("GNP in Current Market Prices").

Column (3): Computed by differencing estimates of the value of inventories. The latter were taken to be one-half of the value of output of agriculture (exclusive of eggs, small fruits, grapes, orchard fruit, dairy products and horses), manufacturing, and mining, and one-half of the value of imports. The flow data were taken from Urquhart, Gross National Product, pp. 11–15, 19–23, 29–33, and 278–279. Outputs of hay and oats were first adjusted by multiplying them by 5 (to allow for farm consumption of animal feed, which is excluded from Urquhart's agricultural output figures). Animal inventories were not included in inventory changes, since Urquhart treats them as part of fixed capital.

Column (4): Very rough estimates. The number of acres cleared in each decade, 1871–1881, 1881–1891, 1891–1901, was computed from series M-34 in *Canadian Historical Statistics*, and average annual clearing rates were computed from the decadal values. We assumed that the average annual rate, 1890–1896, could be approximated by the average over the period 1891–1901, and the averages for the years 1870–1879 and 1880–1889, by the figures for 1871–1881 and 1881–1891. Most of the land improved in these decades was located in Ontario and other eastern provinces. We assumed that all the land was forested and that it took about one month to clear an acre. A figure derived by Martin Premack for the U.S. in the period 1860–1900. The cost of clearing was then estimated in prices of 1909 by multiplying acres cleared by the monthly farm wage rate, without board (*Canadian Historical Statistics*, series M-78). Prices of 1909 were converted into current prices by means of Urquhart's implicit GNP price index (pp. 24–25). Average decadal price indexes were computed as unweighted averages of Urquhart's figures.

Column (5): Column (2) + Column (3) + Column (4).

Column (6): Computed from Urquhart, *Gross National Product*, pp. 19–21 & 24–25. (N.B.: The printed value for current account debits in 1872, $270,851 should be $132,476.)

Column (7): Column (2)–Column (6).

Column (8): Column (5)–Column (6).

4-1d. 1897–1914

For many western nations, the end of the nineteenth century is often taken to be 1914: the assassination of the Austrian archduke and the beginning of the war that was to change western life in fundamental ways. For Canada, however, the economic history of the nineteenth century ended in 1896, not 1914. It was then that the Canadian economy experienced a pronounced upward surge; the path of growth was dramatically altered. Between 1896 and 1913 the average annual rate of growth of real GNP ran over 6.5 percent, and that of real per capita GNP, over 5.25 percent. Population took longer to turn around. In the last four years of the chronological nineteenth century, emigration exceeded immigration; and, overall, population grew by significantly less than 1 percent a year. From 1904 to 1914, however, net immigration was strongly positive; and population grew by 3 percent per year.

This dramatic increase can be attributed, ultimately, to a booming world market in wheat combined with the solution of technical problems in its production and a substantial reduction in transport costs. As a result, the prairies were opened and became the center of wheat production on a large scale. Although these factors were almost certainly the fundamental bases of the boom, the aggregate data do not clearly underscore their importance. For example, between 1895 and 1910 the share of the primary sector in GNP actually fell by more than one-quarter, while the share of the secondary sector increased by almost a like amount (see Table 4:1-3). Clearly, the boom had important industrial components as well. Moreover, although exports were important, if the boom had been solely export driven, one might have expected exports to have grown more rapidly than real GNP. Exports did grow, but the fraction of exports in GNP actually declined.[565]

The immediate driving forces in the emerging pattern of more rapid development lay in domestic investment, and much of that investment was tied to the new export opportunities (see Table 4:1-4). Those investments, however, required a long gestation period; transport surprisingly represented a very large fraction of the total. As a result, it was to be years before their total impact was reflected in the level of exports. The scale of the fundamental forces at work is neatly captured in the ratio of capital formation to GNP. In the two and a half decades before 1896, gross fixed capital formation typically accounted for about 15 percent of GNP. The investment share rose to almost 19 percent in the nine years

---

[565] For a macro-picture of the relevant sectors of the Canadian economy during the wheat boom, see Alexander K. Cairncross, *Home and Foreign Investment, 1870–1913* (Cambridge: Cambridge University Press, 1953), chap. 5.

between 1897 and 1905, and to an extraordinary 29.3 percent in the years 1906–13 (see Table 4:1-5). Some evidence that this surge in investment was largely driven by the prospects of the prairie wheat economy can be found in the sectoral distribution of that investment. In terms of its direct role, between 1897 and 1906 almost 38 percent of gross fixed capital formation flowed into the sector termed "other business," a sector dominated by agriculture (see Table 4:1-4). Over the next eight years this ratio declined, but the sector continued to account for almost one-third of total gross investment. In terms of its indirect contribution – a contribution that came through the reduction in transport costs – investment in railways recovered from the pit of 1890–96, and between 1907 and 1914 it accounted for almost one-fifth of total capital formation.

Before 1896 foreigners had typically supplied 40–45 percent of total Canadian investment; domestic savings were the source of the remainder. After 1896 the relative contribution of foreign investment fell, and the share of domestic savings rose. As a result, between 1897 and 1905 domestic savings were responsible for three-quarters of total gross capital formation; and, in addition, they accounted for all of the investment in inventories and farm formation (Table 4:1-5). Canadian savings remained high until the war; they accounted for more than 16 percent of GNP in the years 1906–13.[566] In that latter period, however, foreign investors returned in force. Their contribution amounted to almost 13 percent of GNP, and they financed 44 percent of total gross fixed capital formation. Nor did the breakdown of the traditional international capital market that followed the outbreak of World War I affect Canada in the same way that it was to impact Argentina and Australia. Canada benefited from the new high domestic savings rates, and, because of its geographic proximity, the country was able to shift its now reduced demands for foreign capital to the United States.[567]

4-1e. The institutional environment and constraints

In Canada the government played a more important role in directing economic development than it did in either the United Kingdom or the United States. Government had been involved in the early canal projects, but those contributions expanded as the economy moved into the railroad era. For example, by the early 1860s, although

---

[566] It might be noted that at least temporarily the increase in savings rate was associated with the emergence of the bond house (see Section 4-3 below).

[567] Between 1914 and 1923 American direct and portfolio investment in Canada increased almost 75 percent (from $618 million to $1.081 billion). Lewis, *America's Stake in International Investment*, p. 606.

the British had absorbed £12 million of Grand Trunk securities and despite the fact that both the ownership and management was effectively British, "the head office was in London, and the officers down to the level of management resided in that city," the Canadian government had invested substantially more.[568] In the case of the Great Western, the other major railway project of the 1850s, although the road drew extensively on British finance and it had also acquired "strong British control of its operations," by Confederation the Canadian government "had incurred a debt of almost four million dollars on behalf of the railway."[569] Nor were the government guarantees limited to the major railways.

> The method of financing small railroads stands in sharp contrast to the methods then in use in the United States. There were, it was argued, numerous opportunities for the construction of useful and profitable railroads in Canada, apart from the main trunk lines, if only the capital could be obtained to build them. The difficulty in obtaining capital arose from the fact that the potentialities of these railways, and the credit standings of the municipalities that wished to create them, was not properly appreciated outside Canada. In particular they were not appreciated in London where most of the capital would have to be raised.

In an attempt to solve this problem, parliament passed the Municipal Fund Act of 1852 – an act that permitted the government of the province or Canada to assume the role of financial intermediary and place its imprimatur on the issues of the municipal governments. The government first examined and sanctioned a subset of the proposals of the municipalities. Municipal loans were issued to cover those that survived the screen, and those securities were deposited in the Municipal Loan Fund. The government then issued debentures equal in value to the total of the pooled municipal issues, marketed those debentures in London, and transferred the funds raised to the municipalities. By 1859 Canadian municipalities had raised $9.7 million by means of this mechanism.[570] In the United States the scope of the central government was much more narrowly constrained.

The American Congress's decision that there was to be no NAFTA in the post–Civil War era induced the Canadian government to endorse

---

[568] William Robert Code, *The Spatial Dynamics of Financial Intermediaries: An Interpretation of Financial Decisionmaking in Canada*, Ph.D. dissertation, University of California, Berkeley, 1971, p. 106. [Hereafter cited as Code, *The Spatial Dynamics*.] H.A. Lovett, *Canada and the Grand Trunk, 1829–1921* (Montreal, 1924), p. 72.

[569] Code, *The Spatial Dynamics*, pp. 107–8.

[570] Code, *The Spatial Dynamics*, pp. 109–10.

Macdonald's National Policy, a policy that involved a ninety degree reorientation of the economy from its traditional north-south (that is, Canada-U.S.) orientation to an east-west one that integrated Quebec and Ontario with the Maritimes to the east and with the Prairies and British Columbia to the west.[571] That decision involved massive investment in the nation's railroads before domestic savings were anywhere nearly sufficient to finance the effort and before economic activities in the prairies and in the trans-Rocky West could possibly have underwritten the railroads' profitability; the Western railroads had to cross a thousand miles of pre-Cambrian shield before they reached the prairies, and the first east-west link was not completed until 1885.

The need for a link between Ontario and Quebec and the West Coast was only one of the challenges that faced the Canadian economy. The period from 1870 to the mid-1890s was one in which much of the infrastructure was put in place. "Most of the secular decisions at this stage of Canadian development were made by government bodies . . . and the implementation of these policies involved the exercise of initiative by

---

[571] "The Reciprocity Treaty between the British North American Provinces (Canada) and the United States was ratified in February 1855 and terminated in March 1866. It provided for free trade in all natural products, free access for the United States fisheries to the Atlantic coastal waters of British North America, and access to the St. Lawrence River for American vessels under the same tolls as native vessels.

"The classic and generally accepted view of Reciprocity is that 'an extraordinary impulse of advancement was given the provinces, particularly Ontario, by the operation of the treaty', since 'it opened the booming market of the United States [to] the natural exports of lumber, fish, coal and agricultural products [allowing them to find] wider markets and higher prices.' A country with a population of not more than three million . . . was admitted to a free market of 33 or 34 million people.

"The authoritative Canadian writers on Reciprocity are D.C. Masters (*The Reciprocity Treaty of 1854* [Toronto: Longmans, Green, 1936] and *Reciprocity, 1846–1911* [Ottawa: Canadian Historical Association, 1961]) and S.A. Saunders ("Reciprocity Treaty of 1854: A Regional Study," *Canadian Journal of Economics and Political Science*, Vol. II, February, 1936, pp. 41–53) who reach the same conclusions: 'a period of great prosperity in the colonies followed the negotiation of the treaty [as] trade between the British North American colonies and the United States showed a considerable increase,' as seen by the growth in total trade between the colonies and the United States of over 250 percent between 1853 and 1856 and an increase in Canadian exports to the United States of 364.6 percent between 1853 and 1856." Lawrence H. Officer and Lawrence B. Smith, "The Canadian-American Reciprocity Treaty of 1855 to 1866," *The Journal of Economic History*, Vol. XXVIII, No. 4, December 1968, pp. 598–99.

Officer and Smith argue that the treaty was nowhere near as important as contemporaries and earlier scholars had concluded.

the government."[572] Although politics may have led to overinvestment, "by the early part of the twentieth century, large external economies were brought about by governmental activities and a large scale boom resulted."[573]

The government's role in financing social overhead investment extended chronologically from the 1820s to at least 1920; it included railroads, roads, and canals. At times it involved government ownership, at times the direct financing of construction, and at other times the subsidization of private efforts. The history of the government's involvement with the Canadian Pacific Railway, although only one of many examples, captures the flavor of the governmental effort. It also suggests why British investors, although initially shunning the company's securities, came to feel that the Canadian government stood behind, either explicitly or implicitly, the issues of the Canadian railroads.

A transcontinental railroad had been promised to the citizens of British Columbia to salve their feelings about the increased tariffs that were implicit in the National Policy and to induce them to join the confederation. It was to be completed by 1881, but "the project stalled partly because of a corruption scandal, but mostly because of the sheer magnitude of the task." The government itself began constructing two segments of the line: the route from the Lakehead to Winnipeg and the section from the western terminus up the "tortuous Fraser Canyon." In 1880 the government signed a contract with the Canadian Pacific Railway Company, and five years later the line was complete. The government subsidy required by the company, however, was hardly insignificant. Among the provisions for financial support were "a cash subsidy of $25 million, a grant of 25 million acres of land 'fairly fit for settlement' ..., the segments already completed (valued at $40 million) to be handed over to the company, an exemption from taxes (later thought to have been worth a little over $20 million), and a guarantee that no other railway lines would be chartered south of the CPR to the border with the U.S."[574]

---

[572] Hugh G.J. Aitken, "Defensive Expansionism: The State and Economic Growth in Canada," in Hugh G.J. Aitken (ed.), *The State and Economic Growth* (New York: Social Science Research Council, 1960), p. 103.

[573] Code, *The Spatial Dynamics*, pp. 191–92.

[574] McInnis, "Foundations of the Nineteenth Century Canadian Economy," pp. 57–58. W. Kaye Lamb, *History of the Canadian Pacific Railway* (New York and London: Macmillan, 1972), pp. 1–155. James B. Hedges, *The Federal Railway Land Subsidy Policy of Canada*, Harvard Historical Monographs III (Cambridge, Mass.: Harvard University Press, 1934).

Macdonald's reorientation of the economy also involved a spatial redistribution of the claims on capital from the surplus-saving East to the savings-deficit West. In 1893, for example, per capita deposits in savings banks in the Maritime provinces ranged from $22.30 in New Brunswick, to $20.70 on Prince Edward Island, to $18.40 in Nova Scotia, while in the West the range was from $9.20 in British Columbia, to $4.30 in Manitoba, to $0.60 in the Northwest Territories: "Individual depositors may have been wealthier in the West, but it was in the populated East that the bulk of available savings were located."[575]

4-2. Foreign investment: in Canada

In the words of one student of the evolution of Canada's financial markets, "most domestic capital which was not employed directly to self-finance investment was initially tied up in the Canadian banks. Since the dominant banking institutions, the chartered banks, concentrated their assets in short-term mercantile credit, financing for industrial and infrastructure projects was largely dependent on external capital."[576]

4-2a. The temporal pattern of foreign flows

Ideally, a study of the impact of foreign capital would be based on an annual enumeration of the sectoral distribution of that capital and on the gross flows into and out of the country that linked those annual cross sections. Unfortunately, those data do not exist even today; and nineteenth-century Canada is no exception to this general rule. Instead, it is necessary to work with either annual estimates of *net* capital flows – flows derived from the balance of payments – supported by occasional cross section estimates of the sectoral distribution of the stock of foreign capital, or with the estimates of the earnings of foreigners and of the probable rates of return on those investments.

For the first part of the twentieth century, Jacob Viner and Frank Knox have estimated the total stock of foreign investment in Canada.[577] Viner's

---

[575] M. Morris, "The Land Mortgage Companies, Government Savings Banks and Private Bankers in Canada," *Journal of the Canadian Bankers Association*, Vol. 3, 1895–96, p. 254.

[576] Sheila C. Dow, *Financial Markets and Regional Economic Development: The Canadian Experience* (Aldershot: Avebury, Gower Publishing Co. Ltd., 1990), p. 60. [Hereafter cited as Dow, *Financial Markets and Regional Development*.]

[577] Jacob Viner, *Canada's Balance of International Indebtedness, 1900–1913: An Inductive Study in the Theory of International Trade*, Harvard Economic Studies, Vol. XXVI (Cambridge, Mass.: Harvard University Press, 1924), chap. IV [Hereafter cited as Viner, *Canada's Balance of International Indebtedness*]; Frank A. Knox, "Excursus: Canadian Capital Movements and the Canadian Balance of

figures cover the period 1900–13, and they rest on his carefully constructed estimate of the total stock of foreign investment in 1899. His estimates for 1900–13, then, are based on the 1899 estimate of the stock of capital and the cumulated investment component of the balance of payments for the first fourteen years of the century. As a check, he estimated the total investment stock for each of those years in a manner similar to the one he employed in constructing his 1899 baseline. The two sets of estimates differed substantially from year to year; but, for the full fourteen-year period, the totals are roughly the same, whether one employs the "cumulation" or the "direct estimates" procedure. Knox picked up the story in 1914, and he chose to base his estimates on the "direct" procedure. The Viner-Knox figures are reported in Table 4:2-1.

The first estimate of the magnitude of international capital flows for the entire period 1870 to 1914 is based on the Viner method (see Table 4:2-1, Variant 2). Annual flows were cumulated from Viner's 1899 stock estimate for the years 1900–14 and decumulated from 1898 back to 1870. The annual flows used in those calculations were, however, based on the new balance of payments figures prepared by Alasdair Sinclair for the Urquhart volume, instead of the estimates that Viner had available (see Table 4:2-2).[578] Moreover, the estimates are restricted to long-term capital flows, whereas Viner appears to have simply used the difference between "total" credits and "current account" credits. Thus, it should be no surprise that the Variant 2 series displays a flatter temporal slope than the Viner estimates, that it yields a 1913 figure well below Viner's, and that it produces a figure for 1870 that appears quite large, given the probable size of the non-agricultural capital stock in that year.[579]

Given those problems, a second set of estimates based on a different technique was constructed (see Table 4:2-1, Variant 1). Sinclair's series

International Payment, 1900–1934," in Herbert Marshall, Frank Southard, and Kenneth W. Taylor (eds.), *Canadian American Industry* (New Haven, Conn.: Yale University Press, 1936), pp. 297–99 [Hereafter cited as Knox, "Canadian Balance of Payments"].

[578] The new balance of payment series is reported in Table 4:2-2. M.C. Urquhart, *Gross National Product*, table 1.4, pp. 19–23. For a detailed discussion of the derivation of those estimates, see A.M. Sinclair, "Balance of International Payments, 1870–1925," chap. 11.

[579] The rates of return implicit in our Variant 2 series, given the interest and dividend components of the Urquhart balance of payments series, rise very steadily from very low (below 1 percent) figures in the early years to much higher figures for the later years. That apparent distortion suggests that the two series are inconsistent.

Table 4:2-1. *Estimated stock of foreign investment in Canada, 1870–1914*

| | | Millions of dollars | | Percentage distribution of variant #2 | | |
| | | Davis-Gallman | | | | |
Year	Knox-Viner	Variant #1	Variant #2	British	United States	Other
1870			587			
1871			592			
1872			618			
1873			657			
1874			671			
1875		206	688			
1876		221	699			
1877		242	710			
1878		245	724			
1879		299	737			
1880		350	762			
1881		376	773			
1882		393	791			
1883		452	815			
1884		462	862			
1885		426	897			
1886		559	913			
1887		612	980			
1888		629	1,001			
1889		720	1,023			
1890		771	1,038			
1891		747	1,067			
1892		804	1,083			
1893		811	1,114			
1894		851	1,121			
1895		849	1,131			
1896		854	1,159			
1897		932	1,176			
1898		1,030	1,175			
1899		1,135	1,200	86.7	12.5	0.8
1900	1,232	1,182	1,225	85.2	13.6	1.1
1901	1,269	1,222	1,259	83.9	14.7	1.4
1902	1,311	1,319	1,279	82.1	16.0	1.9
1903	1,366	1,350	1,309	81.0	17.0	2.0
1904	1,428	1,426	1,388	79.5	18.1	2.5
1905	1,540	1,602	1,497	78.7	18.8	2.5
1906	1,646	1,778	1,578	77.8	19.4	2.8
1907	1,741	1,577	1,648	77.3	19.8	2.9
1908	1,963	1,939	1,825	77.8	19.3	3.0

Table 4:2-1. (*cont.*)

Year	Knox-Viner	Davis-Gallman Variant #1	Davis-Gallman Variant #2	Percentage distribution of variant #2 British	United States	Other
1909	2,216	2,324	2,010	78.6	18.6	2.8
1910	2,529	2,421	2,232	77.4	19.3	3.3
1911	2,878	3,003	2,405	76.5	19.6	3.9
1912	3,199	3,164	2,683	75.6	20.2	4.3
1913	3,746	3,583	3,009	74.6	20.8	4.6
1913	3,529					
1914	3,837	4,031	3,391	72.4	23.0	4.6

Sources: (1) For the Knox-Viner estimates, Frank A, Knox, "Excursus: Canadian Capital Movements and the Canadian Balance of Payments," 1900–1934, in Marshall, Southard, and Taylor, Canadian–American Industry, pp. 297–299. The figures for 1900–1913 are from Jacob Viner, *Canada's Balance of International Indebtedness, 1900–1913*, Chapter VI.

Viner made two sets of estimates, one based on cumulations of the net foreign balance, and one based on direct estimates of investments. The two series differ markedly from year to year, but yield virtually identical totals for the increase in foreign investment 1899–1913.

  Cumulations $2,506,434 thousand
  Direct Estimates $2,545,627 thousand

Knox employed the direct estimates. He then adjusted the 1913 figure and added an estimate for 1914.

(2) The Davis–Gallman Variant #1 was estimated by capitalizing Urquhart's annual interest and dividend payments to foreigners by an estimated rate of return. The rate of return is the Ontario bond rate, 1900–1914 (*Canadian Historical Statisitics*, First Edition) linked with the Macauley series of U.S. railroad bonds – a series that tracks the Ontario series closely when the two overlap. (*Historical Statistics of the United States*, Bicentennial Edition, series × 476) and a series relating to bonded debts of Canadian railroads (Alan Green, "Growth and Productivity Change in the Canadian Railroad Sector, 1871–1926," in S. Engerman and R. Gallman (eds.), *Long Term Factors in American Economic Growth*, p. 785). Estimates were made for 1900–1913 and compared with the Viner–Knox series, but the movements of the two were not dissimilar. We reduced the interest rate series to bring our series, on average, into line with the Viner–Knox.

(3) The Davis–Gallman Variant #2 estimating procedure begins with an estimate for 1900 based on Viner–Knox. The annual long-term investments were taken from Urquhart, and they were cumulated to 1914 and decumulated to 1870.

Table 4:2-2. *Canadian balance of payments: capital items*

Year	Total (thousands of dollars)				Per capita (dollars)			
	Short-term	Long-term	War finance	Total	Short-term	Long-term	War finance	Total
1870	-5,005	3,394		-1,611	-1.38	0.94		-0.44
1871	7,350	13,290		20,640	1.99	3.60		5.60
1872	-2,341	8,019		5,678	-0.62	2.14		1.51
1873	289	22,742		23,031	0.08	5.94		6.02
1874	-5,580	38,509		32,929	-1.43	9.89		8.45
1875	3,303	14,709		18,012	0.84	3.72		4.56
1876	36	16,303		16,339	0.01	4.07		4.08
1877	1,913	10,900		12,813	0.47	2.68		3.15
1878	-2,532	11,414		8,882	-0.61	2.77		2.16
1879	-1,762	14,262		12,500	-0.42	3.41		2.99
1880	-2,409	12,358		9,949	-0.57	2.90		2.34
1881	-1,918	25,775		23,857	-0.44	5.96		5.52
1882	-584	10,310		9,726	-0.13	2.36		2.22
1883	-5,763	18,704		12,941	-1.30	4.22		2.92
1884	5,052	23,927		28,979	1.13	5.33		6.46
1885	-8,177	46,870		38,693	-1.80	10.33		8.53
1886	-2,409	35,200		32,791	-0.53	7.69		7.16
1887	-9,745	15,632		5,887	-2.11	3.38		1.27
1888	-11,900	66,519		54,619	-2.54	14.22		11.68
1889	569	21,334		21,903	0.12	4.51		4.63
1890	-2,345	22,478		20,133	-0.49	4.70		4.21
1891	-8,753	15,048		6,295	-1.81	3.11		1.30

Year						
1892	−9,953	28,625	18,672	−2.04	5.86	3.82
1893	−9,624	15,921	6,297	−1.95	3.23	1.28
1894	−4,855	31,101	26,246	−0.98	6.25	5.27
1895	−5,636	6,568	932	−1.12	1.31	0.19
1896	−11,208	10,559	−649	−2.21	2.08	−0.13
1897	−6,741	28,036	21,295	−1.32	5.47	4.16
1898	−5,312	16,722	11,410	−1.03	3.23	2.20
1899	−10,977	−1,285	−12,262	−2.10	−0.25	−2.34
1900	2,860	25,350	28,210	0.54	4.78	5.32
1901	−28,699	33,161	4,462	−5.34	6.17	0.83
1902	−3,266	20,367	17,101	−0.59	3.71	3.11
1903	16,273	30,290	46,563	2.88	5.36	8.24
1904	−21,150	79,091	57,941	−3.63	13.57	9.94
1905	−15,785	108,438	92,653	−2.63	18.07	15.44
1906	12,514	81,306	93,820	2.05	13.34	15.39
1907	21,824	69,847	91,671	3.40	10.89	14.30
1908	−92,459	177,045	84,586	−13.96	26.72	12.77
1909	33,602	185,176	218,778	4.94	27.23	32.17
1910	25,886	222,072	247,958	3.70	31.78	35.48
1911	−3,450	172,535	169,085	−0.48	23.94	23.46
1912	182	277,868	278,050	0.02	37.61	37.63
1913	−18,762	326,413	307,651	−2.46	42.77	40.31
1914	21,200	381,836	427,336	2.69	48.46	54.24
		24,300			3.08	

Source: Urquhart, Gross National Product, pp. 19–23.

on interest and dividends in the balance of payments was very carefully constructed, and it appears to be reliable. Variant 1, then, is based on the capitalized values of the interest and dividend series. The capitalization was, in turn, based on the most generally accepted series of rates of return.[580] The method was tested for the period 1900–13. For those years it yielded a good approximation of the Viner series. Although the two series differ from year to year, on average they are reasonably close, and they both display approximately the same slope. Initially, the Variant 1 estimates were a little less than Viner's; therefore, the rate of return was adjusted slightly downward to bring the two series more nearly into coincidence (Table 4:2-1). Note that the slope of the new series is more pronounced than the slope of the Variant 2 series and that the estimates of the stock of foreign capital in the early years are very much lower. The Variant 1 series, then, appears to be the more plausible; however, one conclusion appears secure regardless of the series selected: If these series are to be believed, foreign investment accounted for an enormous share of the financing of the Canadian capital stock throughout the whole period. For example, a comparison of the Viner foreign investment figures and the Urquhart GNP estimates for 1900–13 shows that the dollar value of the stock of capital financed by foreign investment was typically almost 25 percent larger than GNP.[581] Finally, if the capital/output ratio in this period was roughly three to one – the ratio exhibited by the U.S. – then the Viner and Urquhart series imply that the stock of foreign investment was equal in value to about 40 percent of the entire domestic capital stock.

The changes over time are equally striking. For example, the data clearly underscore the expanding role of domestic finance in capital formation in the ten or fifteen years before World War I: Viner's estimate of the foreign stock of investment in Canada in 1913 comes to less than the sum of gross fixed capital formation across the six years 1908–13. Both the Variant 1 and Variant 2 extensions of the foreign investment stock series also show the importance of foreign savings to Canadian capital formation; there are, however, differences between the two series in their measure of the degree of that importance and in the changes in the relative level of importance over time. According to Variant 1, the value of the stock of foreign investment in 1875 was about 45 percent as large as GNP. The ratio quickly rose to 73 percent in 1880, then drifted upward to 77 percent in 1885, and finally surged to 112 percent in 1890, and to 135 percent in 1895. Variant 2 begins at a level of 153 percent in

---

[580] We thank M.C. Urquhart, who suggested this technique.
[581] Urquhart, *Gross National Product*, p. 16.

1875, rises to 160 percent in 1880, falls slightly to 154 percent in 1885, 151 percent in 1890, and rises sharply to 179 percent in 1895, before falling to 136 percent in 1900, and trending downward to 1913. Again Variant 1 seems to tell the more plausible story.

Turning from the stock to the flow data, if the standard chosen is the American experience, once adjustments for the relative sizes of the two economies have been made, it appears that, from 1870 onwards, Canada depended much more heavily on foreign investment than did the United States. During the 1870s, on average, capital imports amounted to more than $15 million ($3.92 per capita); during the next decade that figure almost doubled – it exceeded $27 million or $6.09 per capita – before declining to its earlier level in the 1890s. Over the latter decade, the average figure exceeded $17 million, but increasing population reduced the per capita transfer to $3.50. In the twentieth century, no matter if the standard chosen is the United States, Argentina, or Australia, Canadian development was *very* heavily underwritten by foreign capital. Between 1900 and 1909, on average, the Canadian economy received more than $80 million per year ($12.98 per person); and, over the last five prewar years, even those figures pale in comparison to the average inflow of $276 million, or $36.91 for every man, woman, and child in Canada.

Knox estimated the British, American, and "other" components of foreign investment for the years 1900–14 (Table 4:2-1). He concluded that the British share declined from about 85 to 72 percent, that the American proportion rose from 14 to 23 percent, and that the percentage held by the "others" increased from less than 1 to almost 5 percent. Thus, by 1914 the British figure was about $2.8 billion, the American, $881 million, and the "others," $178 million; when compared with the 1900 baseline, in absolute terms these figures represent a 6.8 percent per year increase for the British share, an annual average 12.5 percent increment for the American, and a 20.5 percent per year addition for the "other" component.

Tables 4:2-3 and 4:2-4 offer two estimates of the composition of the foreign sources of capital for the years before 1900. The first set of estimates (#1) is based on the assumption that the years from 1870 to 1898 were characterized by the same percentage distribution that held in 1899. That estimate certainly overstates the contribution of American and "other" savers (and underestimates that of the British); it does, however, provide an upper (or, in the British case, a lower) bound on those contributions. If the distribution is applied to our Variant 1 set of estimates, then over the two and a half decade period (1815–99), the British contribution rose from about $203 million to just less than $1 billion, the American investment increased from about $3 to $142 million, and the figure for the "others" rose from essentially nothing to $9 million. These

Table 4:2-3. *Estimated stocks of foreign investment in Canada (thousands of dollars)*

Year	Estimate #1 British	Estimate #1 United States	Estimate #1 Other foreign	Estimate #2 British	Estimate #2 United States	Estimate #2 Other foreign	Total
1870	509,072	73,424	4,895	587,390	0	0	587,390
1871	516,021	74,426	4,962	595,409	0	0	595,409
1872	535,731	77,269	5,151	618,151	0	0	618,151
1873	569,106	82,083	5,472	656,660	1,470	0	656,660
1874	581,853	83,921	5,595	671,369	5,090	0	671,369
1875	595,983	85,959	5,730	687,672	8,888	0	687,672
1876	605,429	87,322	5,821	698,572	12,762	0	698,572
1877	615,321	88,748	5,916	709,986	16,763	0	709,986
1878	627,682	90,531	6,035	724,248	20,970	0	724,248
1879	638,392	92,076	6,138	736,606	25,263	0	736,606
1880	660,730	95,298	6,353	760,140	30,221	0	762,381
1881	669,666	96,586	6,439	764,431	34,758	0	772,691
1882	685,876	98,924	6,595	776,802	39,828	0	791,395
1883	706,613	101,915	6,794	793,969	45,388	0	815,322
1884	747,233	107,774	7,185	832,929	52,604	0	862,192
1885	777,740	112,174	7,478	859,980	59,546	0	897,392
1886	791,288	114,128	7,608	867,884	65,462	0	913,024
1887	848,938	122,443	8,163	923,523	75,465	0	979,543
1888	867,427	125,110	8,340	935,880	82,456	0	1,000,877
1889	886,908	127,919	8,528	948,967	89,776	0	1,023,355
1890	899,950	129,800	8,653	954,874	96,644	0	1,038,403
1891	924,758	133,379	8,892	972,927	105,009	0	1,067,028
1892	938,556	135,369	9,024	979,051	112,362	0	1,082,949
1893	965,510	139,256	9,283	998,534	121,542	0	1,114,050
1894	971,203	140,077	9,338	995,736	128,246	0	1,120,618
1895	980,354	141,397	9,426	996,352	135,498	0	1,131,177
1896	1,004,652	144,902	9,660	1,012,063	145,050	2,170	1,159,213
1897	1,019,144	146,992	9,799	1,017,548	153,425	5,032	1,175,935
1898	1,018,030	146,831	9,788	1,007,333	159,534	7,854	1,174,650
1899	1,040,000	150,000	10,000	1,040,000	150,000	10,000	1,200,000

Note: Estimate #1 is based on 1899 distribution. Estimate #2 is based on linear regression of 1899–1914 distributions. Estimate 2: Components may not add to total. The totals are the data underlying Table 3b.2, Variant 2.

Table 4:2-4. *Estimated stocks of foreign investment in Canada*

Year	Estimate #1			Estimate #2			Total
	British	United States	Other foreign	British	United States	Other foreign	
1870	86.7%	12.5%	0.8%	100.0%	0.0%	0.0%	100.0%
1871	86.7	12.5	0.8	100.0	0.0	0.0	100.0
1872	86.7	12.5	0.8	100.0	0.0	0.0	100.0
1873	86.7	12.5	0.8	99.8	0.2	0.0	100.0
1874	86.7	12.5	0.8	99.2	0.8	0.0	100.0
1875	86.7	12.5	0.8	98.7	1.3	0.0	100.0
1876	86.7	12.5	0.8	98.2	1.8	0.0	100.0
1877	86.7	12.5	0.8	97.7	2.3	0.0	100.0
1878	86.7	12.5	0.8	97.2	2.8	0.0	100.0
1879	86.7	12.5	0.8	96.7	3.3	0.0	100.0
1880	86.7	12.5	0.8	96.2	3.8	0.0	100.0
1881	86.7	12.5	0.8	95.7	4.3	0.0	100.0
1882	86.7	12.5	0.8	95.1	4.9	0.0	100.0
1883	86.7	12.5	0.8	94.6	5.4	0.0	100.0
1884	86.7	12.5	0.8	94.1	5.9	0.0	100.0
1885	86.7	12.5	0.8	93.5	6.5	0.0	100.0
1886	86.7	12.5	0.8	93.0	7.0	0.0	100.0
1887	86.7	12.5	0.8	92.4	7.6	0.0	100.0
1888	86.7	12.5	0.8	91.9	8.1	0.0	100.0
1889	86.7	12.5	0.8	91.4	8.6	0.0	100.0
1890	86.7	12.5	0.8	90.8	9.2	0.0	100.0
1891	86.7	12.5	0.8	90.3	9.7	0.0	100.0
1892	86.7	12.5	0.8	89.7	10.3	0.0	100.0
1893	86.7	12.5	0.8	89.1	10.9	0.0	100.0
1894	86.7	12.5	0.8	88.6	11.4	0.0	100.0
1895	86.7	12.5	0.8	88.0	12.0	0.0	100.0
1896	86.7	12.5	0.8	87.3	12.5	0.2	100.0
1897	86.7	12.5	0.8	86.5	13.0	0.4	100.0
1898	86.7	12.5	0.8	85.8	13.6	0.7	100.0
1899	86.7	12.5	0.8	86.7	12.5	0.8	100.0

Source: Table 4:2-3.

figures are probably too large, and the margin of error is certainly greater for the non-British than for the British investors.

The second set (#2) is based on a backward projection of the linear trends in the percentage distribution that characterized the period 1889–1914.[582] Those estimates indicate that, initially, the British were the sole source of capital and that their contribution rose from about $600 million in 1870 to more than $1 billion in 1889. American capital imports appear to date from the early 1870s, and the contribution of the "others" from the mid-1890s. The second estimates almost certainly represent a lower bound on the American and probably on "other" transfers, particularly in the early years. Although American investment was not large, it was certainly positive; and it might have represented as much as 5 percent of the total in 1870.[583] Thus, the "best guess" of the composition of foreign investment in Canada probably lies somewhere between the two estimates – most likely it lies closer to the second.

Both estimates are highly speculative, but from 1900 onwards there is enough information to provide a fairly reliable picture of the country of origin and of the size and the industrial distribution of the flows for most, if not for every, year. Moreover, in the British case, we have, in addition, detailed information on the size and industrial distribution of the annual flows of capital that passed through the British Capital Market from 1865 to 1914.

4-2(b). The investors

4-2b(1). The British contribution: Although after 1914 Canadians turned with increasing frequency to the American markets for their capital requirements, there is no question that the British had been the dominant partner over the course of the previous century.[584] In the words of a student of Canadian development, "throughout the nineteenth century Canadian capital imports originated mainly in Great Britain";

---

[582] For Britain the equation was: $15.567 - 0.00775$ (YEAR) and the $R^2 = 0.91$.
For the United States the equation was: $-10.005 + 0.00534$ (YEAR) and the $R^2 = 0.85$.
For the "others" the equation was: $-4.562 + 0.00241$ (YEAR) and the $R^2 = 0.96$.

[583] H.C. Pentland, for example, estimates the total American capital imports, prior to 1875, as under 5 percent of all capital imports. H.C. Pentland, "Further Observations of Canadian Development," *Canadian Journal of Economics and Political Science*, Vol. 19, No. 3, August 1953, p. 406.

[584] Knox's estimates indicate that the Americans overtook the British in 1922 ($2.6–$2.5 billion) and that by 1933 the ratio of American to British flows was almost 1.5:1. Knox, "Canadian Balance of Payments," p. 299.

and, again, in the words of a contemporary, "Canada's entire railroad system, for instance, has been financed practically from first to last by the British investor."[585] George Paish, one of the editors of the *Statist* and an acknowledged expert on Britain's overseas investments, placed that country's investments in Canada in 1910 at $1.89 billion and its investments in 1913 at $2.51 billion.[586] These figures stand in marked contrast to the estimates of U.S. direct and portfolio investment in Canada – $405 million in 1908 and $618 million in 1914 – and the United States was certainly the second largest foreign source of Canadian investment.[587] Similarly, Jacob Viner has placed total British investment in Canada in 1899 at $1.14 billion; in comparison, he places U.S. investment at $150 million and the financial commitments of all other countries at $10 million.[588] Although all colonies and "dominions" had access to the London capital market, because of their financial institutional structure, the Canadians were particularly well placed to exploit that market. First, both the Bank of North America and, until 1901, the Imperial Bank of British Columbia were true "imperial banks" with head offices located in London and most shareholders residing in Britain. Second, although the Canadian banks held their reserves in both New York and London, in the early years the largest share was held in the British capital. Even after 1895, that fraction was still substantial, at times more than half.[589] Third and

[585] Donald G. Paterson, *British Direct Investment in Canada, 1890–1914: Estimates and Determinants* (Toronto: University of Toronto Press, 1976), p. 23. [Hereafter cited as Paterson, *British Direct Investment.*] Fred W. Field, *Capital Investments in Canada: Some Facts and Figures Reflecting One of the Most Attractive Investment Fields in the World* (Montreal: Monetary Times of Canada, 1911), p. 9. [Hereafter cited as Field, *Capital Investment in Canada (1911).*]

[586] George Paish, "Great Britain's Capital Investments in Individual, Colonial and Foreign Countries," *Journal of the Royal Statistical Society*, Vol. 74, Part II (January 1911), pp. 176–87. George Paish, "The Export of Capital and the Cost of Living," *Statist, Supplement*, Vol. 79, February 1914. Viner argues that Paish's estimate for 1914 was not independent of his 1910 estimate coupled with the capital exports reported in the *Statist* for 1911–13. Viner, *Canada's Balance of International Indebtedness*, pp. 119–20.

[587] Lewis, *America's Stake in International Investments*, p. 606.

[588] Viner, *Canada's Balance International Indebtedness*, p. 99. Viner's estimates rest heavily on Sir Frederick Williams-Taylor's 1902 estimate of £205,405,100 for "the total investments of British capital in Canada to date." Williams-Taylor was for many years the manager of the Bank of Montreal in London. Cleona Lewis provides a somewhat higher estimate of the American contribution – $160 million in 1897 – but even that figure is still only one-seventh of the British total. Cleona Lewis, *America's Stake in International Investments*, p. 606.

[589] The New York funds were invested in stock-exchange loans, and they fluctuated with the size and success of that institution.

most importantly, well before the turn of the century the Canadian federal and provincial governments had begun to employ Canadian banks as their London fiscal agents.[590]

> Since 1891 the Dominion of Canada had floated all its long term London loans through the Bank of Montreal, its permanent fiscal agent. The bank received its expenses and a handling commission for its services. During our period [1895–1914] it handled ten loans for the Dominion, raising nearly fifty million pounds. The Bank of Montreal also handled all Ontario's London loans, most of Quebec's, and New Brunswick's single issue. The Canadian Bank of Commerce shared in the business of issuing provincial loans. It inherited the London business of British Columbia when it absorbed the old Imperial Bank of British Columbia in 1901, and it also handled most of Saskatchewan's and Manitoba's issues. These two large Canadian banks handled most of the provincial issue business. The occasional provincial loan passed through Lloyd's Bank, Parr's Bank, and the National Provincial Bank. These British firms handled £4,191,000 in provincial issues during the period. However, the issues channeled through Canadian banks were nearly three times as large. Moreover, Canadian banks also took part in the London underwriting groups which supported Dominion and provincial loans.[591]

Only Australia in the decades before the 1890s could boast of such a large institutional presence in the City.

A year-by-year comparison of four estimates of total public capital flows shows very large year-to-year differences, but the fourteen-year totals appear reasonable (Table 4:2-5).[592] Both the Field and Viner data capture British purchases on Canadian exchanges as well as purchases in London and should, therefore, be somewhat larger.

The sources of capital are important, but so are the uses that the Canadians made of those transfers. For the period after 1900, there is a substantial amount of evidence about the industrial distribution of capital

---

[590] In the early years of Confederation, the Dominion government had used Baring Brothers and Glyn, Mills as their fiscal agents. Dow, *Financial Markets and Regional Development*, pp. 60–61.

[591] Ian M. Drummond, *Capital Markets in Australia and Canada, 1895–1914: A Study of Colonial Economic History*, Ph.D. dissertation, Yale University, May 1959, pp. 16–17, 52–53. [Hereafter cited as Drummond, *Capital Markets in Australia and Canada*.]

[592] The Davis-Gallman series is dated to the month in which the call was issued; it is not clear how the other series are dated, but they may refer to the year in which the transfer actually occurred. The Simon estimates are from Matthew Simon, "New British Investment in Canada, 1965–1914," *The Canadian Journal of Economics*, Vol. III (February–November 1970), pp. 238–54.

Table 4:2-5. *Canada, public issues: four estimates of British purchases (thousands of dollars)*

Year	Field	Viner	Davis–Gallman
1900		3,068	9,109
1901		8,045	3,023
1902		4,641	18,155
1903		21,652	4,835
1904		21,934	22,272
1905	65,891	51,456	62,791
1906	31,304	42,656	50,158
1907	54,563	37,020	17,995
1908	142,959	152,478	121,977
1909	182,201	183,538	125,357
1910	187,266	177,926	184,155
1911	194,096	218,095	98,031
1912	158,064	187,140	155,825
1913	230,660	324,235	162,461
Total	1,247,005	1,433,884	1,036,144

Sources: Viner, *Canada's Balance of International Indebtedness* p. 303; Field, *Capital Investments in Canada*, p. 11; Matthew Simon, "New British Investments in Canada," *Canadian Journal of Economics*, Volume 3, Number 2, 1970, p. 248; Davis–Gallman Tape.

infusions. Viner has provided an industrial breakdown of all foreign investment in the period 1900–13, Field of all public issues floated between 1905 and 1913, and Davis and Gallman of new issues financed on the British capital market over the period 1900–13.[593] Those data are presented in Table 4:2-6. Although the numbers look different, given the way in which they were collected, they are, in fact, quite consistent. On the one hand, Field's "Public Investments" and the Davis-Gallman "New Issues" series capture gross placements; they include, therefore, some refinancing. Viner's "All Investments" series picks up direct investments and private placements; both are excluded from Field's and from the New Issues enumerations. On the other hand, government

[593] For the years 1905–10, for example, Field places total British public investment at $615 million and Viner at $645 million. Field, *Capital Investments in Canada (1911)*, p. 14. See also Viner, *Canada's Balance of International Indebtedness*, p. 126.

Table 4:2-6. *Canada, the industrial distribution of British capital, early twentieth century: three estimates*

(millions of dollars)

Estimate	Transport	Government	Public utilities, commercial, & industrial	Land, agricultural, & extractive	Financial	Unidentified & miscellaneous	Total
All investments (Viner)	670	375	420	145	32	111	1,753
Public investments (Field)	461	461	170	115	40		1,247
Capital called (Davis–Gallman)	657	176	138	91	12		1,074

(percents)

Estimate	Transport	Government	Public utilities, commercial, & industrial	Land, agricultural, & extractive	Financial	Unidentified & miscellaneous	Total
All investments (Viner)	38.2	21.4	24.0	8.3	1.8	6.3	100.0
Public investments (Field)	37.0	37.0	13.6	9.2	3.2	0.0	100.0
Capital called (Davis–Gallman)	61.2	16.4	12.8	8.5	1.1	0.0	100.0

Note: Viner & Davis & Gallman cover the years 1900–1913; Field covers the years 1905–1913.

Source: Viner, *Canada's Balance of Foreign Indebtedness*, p. 303; Field, *Capital Investments in Canada*, p. 14; Davis–Gallman Tape.

bonds issued in support of the Canadian transport network are included in "Government" in both Field's and Viner's classification, but they have been assigned to "Transport" in the Davis-Gallman taxonomy.

With the bonds issued in support of railroads assigned to "Transport," the importance of British finance to the construction of the Canadian railway network is again underscored. The differences between the contribution of capital to the "Public Utility," "Commercial," and "Industrial" sector in Viner's total capital estimates (24 percent) and the figure for that sector in the "Public Investments" (14 percent) and "New Issues" (13 percent) series reflect, in part, the importance of direct investment to those industries, an importance that is confirmed by Donald Paterson's study of direct flows (Table 4:2-7). His figures indicate that the fraction of direct investments that was channeled into distribution, public utilities, and manufacturing rose from 16 to 37 percent between 1900 and 1914.[594] Those direct investments obviously provide an the explanation for a part of the $282 million difference between the Viner and Davis-Gallman estimates, but the direct component of total transfers is not in itself large enough to explain the entire discrepancy.[595] It is possible that the residual (as well as the $111 million of Viner's "Unidentified" and "Miscellaneous" securities) represent either direct British purchases of public issues or purchases executed on the Montreal and Toronto stock exchanges, but that assertion remains highly speculative.

For the earlier period, the data are less rich, although the "Capital Called" series permit an examination, on an annual basis, of the industrial distribution of the funds that were channeled through the British capital market from 1865 onward (Tables 4:2-8 and 4:2-9). These figures, of course, exclude all direct investment, the investments of British insurance companies in Canadian assets, private placements, and any public funds that were routed through Canadian or any non-British foreign exchanges.

The importance of British portfolio investment to at least two of the Canadian sectors – transportation and government – is exhibited in Table 4:2-10. Very substantial fractions of fixed investment in these sectors appear to have been funded by calls on the London exchange. Notice, also, that the ratio of calls to total fixed investment in manufacturing increased in the early twentieth century, finally reaching a figure of over 11 percent in the years 1911–14.

---

[594] Paterson, *British Direct Investment*, p. 50.
[595] The direct flows can account for about $70 million of the $298 million difference.

Table 4:2-7. *British direct investment in Canada*

	Thousands of dollars of paid-up capital						Percents					
	1890	1895	1900	1905	1910	1914	1890	1895	1900	1905	1910	1914
Mining	7,737	8,528	92,329	58,947	40,216	54,787	18.0	19.5	64.7	55.0	33.3	27.3
Oil	1,977	3,193	4,709	1,822	4,348	3,211	4.6	7.3	3.3	1.7	3.6	1.6
Land	17,493	11,633	11,702	9,860	17,149	36,324	40.7	26.6	8.2	9.2	14.2	18.1
Timber	258	262	714	429	2,415	3,612	0.6	0.6	0.5	0.4	2.0	1.8
Finance	12,808	13,557	14,413	9,431	16,425	29,099	29.8	31.0	10.1	8.8	13.6	14.5
Distribution	0	0	143	322	242	401			0.1	0.3	0.2	0.2
Utilities	774	743	13,129	20,471	23,550	27,494	1.8	1.7	9.2	19.1	19.5	13.7
Manufacturing	1,891	5,773	9,133	6,323	16,304	45,957	4.4	13.2	6.4	5.9	13.5	22.9
Total	42,981	43,733	142,703	107,176	120,770	200,686	99.9	99.9	102.5	100.4	99.9	100.1

Source: D.G. Paterson, *British Direct Investment in Canada, 1890–1914*, p. 50.

Although Canada received a total of almost $65 million in 1888, over the first four decades the annual receipts averaged less than 45 percent of the fifty-year, $38 million mean; they were less than that benchmark in all but four of those forty years. Over the last decade, however, the Dominion received a total of $1.22 billion. The ratio of the annual average for that decade to the half-century average was 3.2 to 1, and inflows fell below that half-century average in only a single year. In terms of its attractiveness to British investors, in comparison with Argentina, Australia, and the United States, Canada was clearly a "late bloomer."

In per capita terms, Canada drew substantially more than the United States; but the average between 1865 and 1904 was "only" $3.74 a year – a figure far less than the average amount received by either Argentina or Australia. Beginning in 1905, however, the structure changed. Between then and 1914, the Dominion received, on average, $17.17 per year – far more than either Argentina or Australia, to say nothing of the United States.

As was the case in each of the other three frontier countries, Canadian railways drew the bulk of British finance – overall, more than 65 percent of the total (Table 4:2-11). There was a small surge in railroad investment between 1873 and 1877, a surge that drew more than $61 million ($15.68 per person) in 1875 and that aggregated about twice that figure. That peak was largely associated with the construction of the Grand Trunk and of two smaller lines, the Great Western and the Midland, railroads that became part of the Grand Trunk system. The total, however, also included nine other roads – some, such as the Canada, Michigan, and Chicago, that were destined to become important components of the nation's transport network, and some, the Levis and Kennebec and the St. Francis and Megantic International, for example, whose contributions were somewhat smaller. Over the five years total Canadian railroad mileage increased from 3,613 to 5,574, and a very large fraction of those miles were financed with British capital.

Despite very substantial British investments in the Canadian Pacific (they totaled $77 million between 1885 and 1896), in only eight of the twenty-six years between 1878 and 1904 did the Dominion draw as much transport finance, on a per capita basis, as the average of the four frontier countries. In ten of the eleven years between 1904 and 1914, however, transfers greatly exceeded that baseline. In seven of those years the infusion was more than $9.00 per person, the average was just less than $10.50, and it reached almost $18.50 in 1908. Although a total of thirty-one railroads received British funds, the major recipients were the Canadian Northern, the Canadian Pacific, the Inter Colonial, and, again, the Grand Trunk. Between 1901 and 1914 total Canadian railroad mileage

Table 4:2-8. *Canada: capital called on the British capital markets, 1865–1914 (thousands of dollars)*

Year	Manufacture, commercial & miscellaneous	Financial	Government	Agriculture & extractive	Transport	Public utilities	Total "called"
1865	0	0	0	180	49	0	229
1866	0	0	0	0	5,251	0	5,251
1867	0	0	0	0	0	0	0
1868	0	0	0	0	5,884	0	5,884
1869	0	0	0	0	7,769	0	7,769
1870	0	0	0	304	1,706	0	2,010
1871	1,213	0	0	0	5,630	0	6,843
1872	0	0	487	3,161	5,879	0	9,526
1873	0	0	4,729	0	17,464	0	22,193
1874	945	0	26,446	292	17,106	0	44,789
1875	0	0	3,286	426	61,994	0	65,706
1876	0	0	5,104	0	16,605	0	21,709
1877	0	0	485	707	13,998	0	15,190
1878	0	0	515	0	7,931	0	8,446
1879	0	0	2,896	0	27,091	0	29,987
1880	0	0	749	110	4,290	0	5,148
1881	0	0	0	1,098	19,384	0	20,482
1882	244	0	0	6,652	4,647	0	11,543
1883	0	0	2,737	1,975	3,581	0	8,294
1884	0	0	11,195	2,654	15,081	0	28,930
1885	0	0	671	694	45,066	0	46,431
1886	321	71	911	926	19,006	324	21,559
1887	0	0	370	179	5,052	0	5,601
1888	0	1,218	11,444	7,233	44,925	146	64,966

Year							
1889	1,680	487	6,875	3,654	12,062	596	25,354
1890	67	3,538	2,620	681	13,450	0	20,356
1891	487	218	60	489	10,651	0	11,906
1892	0	0	1,642	0	25,372	58	27,072
1893	0	0	1,049	605	7,137	740	9,531
1894	0	0	6,480	70	15,981	263	22,794
1895	975	0	79	208	668	221	2,152
1896	529	0	100	274	2,211	414	3,528
1897	1,684	0	3,352	1,387	9,326	0	15,749
1898	1,346	0	0	2,897	44	274	4,560
1899	31	0	0	2,089	24	767	2,911
1900	0	0	0	3,671	5,438	0	9,109
1901	21	0	1,007	1,176	795	24	3,023
1902	0	0	2,002	959	15,194	0	18,155
1903	63	0	0	200	4,316	256	4,835
1904	45	0	0	487	21,740	0	22,272
1905	901	1,611	19	1,696	58,175	390	62,791
1906	2,228	0	6,248	4,117	34,095	3,470	50,158
1907	487	0	2,698	768	13,116	925	17,995
1908	6,969	0	25,072	1,079	121,977	5,962	161,059
1909	11,599	0	16,111	4,338	90,601	2,708	125,357
1910	22,814	5,681	25,288	11,915	117,157	1,299	184,155
1911	16,978	1,159	17,555	24,555	31,034	6,750	98,031
1912	21,499	3,691	20,034	31,708	67,597	11,296	155,825
1913	13,186	0	60,045	4,678	76,222	8,330	162,461
1914	10,781	0	54,515	4,328	121,103	6,892	197,619

Source: Davis–Gallman tape.

Table 4:2-9. *Canada: capital called on the British capital markets, 1865–1914 (dollars per capita)*

Year	Manufacture, commercial & miscellaneous	Financial	Government	Agriculture & extractive	Transport	Public utilities	Total "called"
1865	0.00	0.00	0.00	0.05	0.01	0.00	0.07
1866	0.00	0.00	0.00	0.00	1.53	0.00	1.53
1867	0.00	0.00	0.00	0.00	0.00	0.00	0.00
1868	0.00	0.00	0.00	0.00	1.68	0.00	1.68
1869	0.00	0.00	0.00	0.00	2.18	0.00	2.18
1870	0.00	0.00	0.00	0.08	0.47	0.00	0.55
1871	0.33	0.00	0.00	0.00	1.53	0.00	1.85
1872	0.00	0.00	0.13	0.84	1.57	0.00	2.54
1873	0.00	0.00	1.24	0.00	4.56	0.00	5.80
1874	0.24	0.00	6.79	0.08	4.39	0.00	11.50
1875	0.00	0.00	0.83	0.11	15.68	0.00	16.62
1876	0.00	0.00	1.27	0.00	4.14	0.00	5.42
1877	0.00	0.00	0.12	0.17	3.44	0.00	3.74
1878	0.00	0.00	0.13	0.00	1.92	0.00	2.05
1879	0.00	0.00	0.69	0.00	6.47	0.00	7.17
1880	0.00	0.00	0.18	0.03	1.01	0.00	1.21
1881	0.00	0.00	0.00	0.25	4.48	0.00	4.74
1882	0.06	0.00	0.00	1.52	1.06	0.00	2.64
1883	0.00	0.00	0.62	0.45	0.81	0.00	1.87
1884	0.00	0.00	2.50	0.59	3.36	0.00	6.45
1885	0.00	0.00	0.15	0.15	9.93	0.00	10.23
1886	0.07	0.02	0.20	0.20	4.15	0.07	4.71
1887	0.00	0.00	0.08	0.04	1.09	0.00	1.21
1888	0.00	0.26	2.45	1.55	9.60	0.03	13.89

Year							
1889	0.36	0.10	1.45	0.77	2.55	0.13	5.36
1890	0.01	0.74	0.55	0.14	2.81	0.00	4.26
1891	0.10	0.05	0.01	0.10	2.20	0.00	2.46
1892	0.00	0.00	0.34	0.00	5.20	0.01	5.54
1893	0.00	0.00	0.21	0.12	1.45	0.15	1.93
1894	0.00	0.00	1.30	0.01	3.21	0.05	4.58
1895	0.19	0.00	0.02	0.04	0.13	0.04	0.43
1896	0.10	0.00	0.02	0.05	0.44	0.08	0.70
1897	0.33	0.00	0.65	0.27	1.82	0.00	3.07
1898	0.26	0.00	0.00	0.56	0.01	0.05	0.88
1899	0.01	0.00	0.00	0.40	0.00	0.15	0.56
1900	0.00	0.00	0.00	0.69	1.03	0.00	1.72
1901	0.00	0.00	0.19	0.22	0.15	0.00	0.56
1902	0.00	0.00	0.36	0.17	2.77	0.00	3.30
1903	0.01	0.00	0.00	0.04	0.76	0.05	0.86
1904	0.01	0.00	0.00	0.08	3.73	0.00	3.82
1905	0.15	0.27	0.00	0.28	9.69	0.06	10.46
1906	0.37	0.00	1.02	0.68	5.59	0.57	8.23
1907	0.08	0.00	0.42	0.12	2.05	0.14	2.81
1908	1.05	0.00	3.78	0.16	18.41	0.90	24.31
1909	1.71	0.00	2.37	0.64	13.32	0.40	18.43
1910	3.26	0.81	3.62	1.71	16.77	0.19	26.35
1911	2.36	0.16	2.44	3.41	4.31	0.94	13.60
1912	2.91	0.50	2.71	4.29	9.15	1.53	21.09
1913	1.73	0.00	7.87	0.61	9.99	1.09	21.29
1914	1.37	0.00	6.93	0.55	15.39	0.88	25.11

Source: Davis–Gallman tape.

Table 4:2-10. *Ratios of capital called on the British capital market to Canadian gross fixed capital formation, by sector, 1871–1880 through 1911–1914*

Years	Manufacturing	Government	Transportation
1871–1880	3.5%	64.4%	103.9%
1881–1890	1.6	52.6	55.0
1891–1900	3.2	13.7	61.2
1901–1910	7.2	29.1	62.2
1911–1914	11.5	47.3	70.7

Sources: Gross fixed capital formation is from Urquhart, *Gross National Product*, pp. 16–17, "total manufacturing," "government total," and railroad and telegraph." The data on calls is from the Davis-Gallman tape, "manufacturing, commercial and miscellaneous," "government" and "transport."

increased from 19,611 to 32,559; and, again, British capital was largely responsible. About the Canadian railway system, Jacob Viner, writing in 1924, noted:

> There is now general agreement that much of this railroad construction was unwise. Of the five great railroad systems in Canada in 1913, three, namely the Canadian Northern, the Grand Trunk, and the Grand Trunk Pacific, have since been saved from bankruptcy only by the intervention of the government – with the loss to the common stock holders in the Grand Trunk systems of their total investments. The Intercolonial Railway, as always, did not earn its fixed charges. Only the Canadian Pacific Railway was financially successful. The federal government is faced now with an annual deficit below operating charges amounting to millions of dollars on the railroads for which it is financially responsible. This overconstruction was due in large part to the moral and financial encouragement given by the government to new railroad enterprises and to its own ventures in railroad building. One motive was undoubtedly the desire of the Liberal Government to placate the western provinces for its failure to redeem its pledges to lower the tariff, by giving them additional transportation facilities for their grain.[596]

In terms of the government sector, once railroad investment has been removed, the sector's average share was about 17 percent – slightly less than Argentina but only one-half of the Australian level, even when the latter total has been adjusted for government-financed railroads. In four-

[596] Viner, *Canada's Balance of International Indebtedness*, pp. 304–5.

teen of the fifty years (including the first seven), there was no government borrowing. In no year did the sector receive more than 60 percent of the total, and in only five years was its share greater than 30 percent.

Over the half century the Canadian Agriculture and Extractive sector – a composite of agriculture, mining, petroleum, and financial land and development companies – received over 7 percent of the total, a figure that was close to the average of the four countries; however, the Canadian figures displayed a much higher variance than those of any of the others. The Canadian average includes a 79 percent share in 1865, a 58 percent share in 1882, and an average of 54 percent for the years 1898–1901; but it also includes ten years during which the sector received no British finance and an additional three years when the sector's share was less than 1 percent. Of the sector's total, financial, land, and development firms received forty-six, agriculture twenty-nine, mines twenty-three, and petroleum just less than 3 percent. The financial, land, and development calls were distributed across the half century, but the mining transfers tended to be concentrated in the years 1865–79 and in the decade and a half following 1895. The bulk of the agricultural infusions came in the last decade before the war.

Although the 79 percent figure for agriculture and extractive receipts in 1865 represented a total of only $180,000, the 1882 percentage (58 percent) translates into $6.7 million; and, between 1880 and 1894, the agriculture and extractive sector accounted for more than 10 percent of all transfers. During those three quinquennia, while the total included agricultural enterprises – the Canadian Cattle Company, the New Oxley Canada Ranches, and Quebec Timber to cite only three – and mines – Anglo Canadian Asbestos and Excelsior Copper, for example – it was heavily weighted toward financial land and development companies. Conversely, the late-nineteenth–turn-of-the-century surge to almost 20 percent of the total, although including almost half a million dollars for the Canadian Petroleum Company, was largely the product of gold discoveries in the Klondike; names such as Klondike Gold Reefs Exploration and Klondike Bonanza dominated the list of recipients.

The period 1910–14 saw transfers totaling $77 million. Although the issuing firms included mines such as Bells Asbestos, British Canadian Marble, and Ontario Porcupine Goldfield Development – to say nothing of Mond Nickel ($6.7 million between 1901 and 1914) – 46 percent of that total was directed toward timber and lumber firms in British Columbia. For example, the Upper Fraser River (British Columbia) Lumber Company alone received $19.2 million, Canadian Western Lumber, $6.5

Table 4:2-11(a). *Canada: Capital called in the British capital markets, 1865–1914 (thousands of dollars)*

Years	Manufacture, commercial, & miscellaneous	Financial	Government	Agriculture & extractive	Transport	Public utilities	Total "called"
1865–69	0	0	0	180	18,954	0	19,134
1870–74	2,157	0	31,661	3,757	47,786	0	85,361
1875–79	0	0	12,286	1,133	127,619	0	141,038
1880–84	244	0	14,681	12,489	46,984	0	74,398
1885–89	2,002	1,775	20,271	12,687	126,110	1,066	163,911
1890–94	554	3,756	11,851	1,845	72,591	1,061	91,659
1895–99	4,565	0	3,531	6,855	12,273	1,676	28,900
1900–04	130	0	3,008	6,493	47,483	280	57,394
1905–09	22,184	1,611	50,148	11,997	318,024	13,455	417,420
1910–14	85,258	10,531	177,438	77,183	413,112	34,567	798,090
Total	117,094	17,674	324,876	134,619	1,230,936	52,106	1,877,304

Table 4:2-11(b). *Canada: Capital called in the British capital markets, 1865–1914 (percents)*

Years	Manufacture, commercial, & miscellaneous	Financial	Government	Agriculture & extractive	Transport	Public utilities	Total "called"
1865–69	0.00	0.00	0.00	0.94	99.06	0.00	100.00
1870–74	2.53	0.00	37.09	4.40	55.98	0.00	100.00
1875–79	0.00	0.00	8.71	0.80	90.49	0.00	100.00
1880–84	0.33	0.00	19.73	16.79	63.15	0.00	100.00
1885–89	1.22	1.08	12.37	7.74	76.94	0.65	100.00

	Manufacture, commercial, & miscellaneous	Financial	Government	Agriculture & extractive	Transport	Public utilities	Total "called"
1890–94	0.60	4.10	12.93	2.01	79.20	1.16	100.00
1895–99	15.79	0.00	12.22	23.72	42.47	5.80	100.00
1900–04	0.23	0.00	5.24	11.31	82.73	0.49	100.00
1905–09	5.31	0.39	12.01	2.87	76.19	3.22	100.00
1910–14	10.68	1.32	22.23	9.67	51.76	4.33	100.00
Total	6.24	0.94	17.31	7.17	65.57	2.78	100.00

Table 4:2-11(c). *Canada: Capital called in the British capital markets, 1865–1914 (dollars per capita per year)*

Years	Manufacture, commercial, & miscellaneous	Financial	Government	Agriculture & extractive	Transport	Public utilities	Total "called"
1865–69	0.00	0.00	0.00	0.01	1.08	0.00	1.09
1870–74	0.11	0.00	0.00	0.02	1.17	0.00	1.19
1875–79	0.00	0.00	0.61	0.06	6.33	0.00	7.00
1880–84	0.01	0.00	0.66	0.57	2.14	0.00	3.38
1885–89	0.09	0.08	0.87	0.54	5.47	0.05	7.08
1890–94	0.02	0.16	0.48	0.08	2.97	0.04	3.76
1895–99	0.18	0.00	0.14	0.27	0.48	0.07	1.13
1900–04	0.00	0.00	0.11	0.24	1.69	0.01	2.05
1905–09	0.67	0.05	1.52	0.38	9.72	0.42	12.76
1910–14	2.33	0.29	4.71	2.11	11.12	0.92	21.49
Total	0.34	0.06	1.07	0.44	4.22	0.15	6.09

Source: Davis-Gallman Tape

million, and the British Canadian Lumber and Timber Company, $4 million. Over the fifty years those agriculture and extractive transfers averaged $0.44 per person per year; but, between 1910 and 1914 – years when the Canadian sector drew more total dollars than the American – an average share of 10 percent translated into an average per capita transfer of $2.11. The agricultural and extractive data appear to confirm the conclusion that the Canadian economy evolved more slowly than its southern counterpart. Not only is the overall proportion of investment in the land-related sectors half again as large as it was in the United States, but the Canadian peak lags the American by a decade. In the United States it was the years 1885–94 that witnessed the relative proportion of agricultural and extractive investments reaching a prewar maximum of more than 11 percent. In Canada the fraction reached 11 percent in the quinquennium 1895–99 and almost one-quarter of the total in the following five years (see Table 4:2-11b).

Although the commercial and industrial sector received, on average, slightly more than 6 percent of all funds, in one-half of the years the sector received none. Moreover, although more than $1 million was received in 1871, almost half again that figure in 1889, and more than $2 million in 1906, the periods of peak flow were 1895–98 ($4.5 million and 17 percent of the national total) and 1908–14 ($104 million and 10 percent). In the latter period, on average, the sector received $2.33 per capita. Both surges were associated with a variety of economic activities. The first, for example, included both Canada Switch and Spring ($170,000) and the Dominion Cotton Mills ($1.5 million). The recipients in the second ranged alphabetically from the Algoma Steel Corporation ($8.4 million) to the Winnipeg Paint and Glass Company ($165,000) and, in terms of the size of the British investment, from Imperial Tobacco of Canada ($12.1 million) to J.H. Sherard Manufacturing and to Swanson Bay Forests, Wood Pulp, and Lumber Mill (both firms drew just $30,000 British funds).

The Public Utilities sector received somewhat less than 3 percent of the total. There were no calls between 1865 and 1886; but thereafter, firms in the sector received funds in twenty-two of the twenty-nine years. Before 1906, however, the infusions were not large. The largest transfer was $767,000 in 1899; and, although the relative position of the industry in the years from 1893 and 1899 suggests a wave of imports – the sector's share of the total reached more than 10 percent in 1893 and more than 25 percent in 1899 – closer scrutiny indicates that these very large fractions reflect not a major surge in investment in utilities, but only the small size of total capital imports. The 1893 figures include only the calls of the Montreal Power and Water Company; and the calls of one firm – the

Canadian, British Columbia, and Dawson City Telegraph Company –
alone account for the 26 percent figure for 1899.

The flow of public utility funds to Canada increased substantially in
the years before the war. Between 1906 and 1914 the sector's share averaged only 3.5 percent, but it totaled almost $48 million. Alphabetically,
the calls ranged from Bell Telephone of Canada (ten calls for $13.7
million) to the Vancouver Power Company (seven calls totaling $6.5
million). The list includes such widely scattered enterprises as Calgary
Power, Cascade Water Power, Electrical Development of Ontario,
Kamministiquia Power, Montreal Water and Power, Northern Light,
Power and Coal, Shawinigan Water and Power, the Toronto Power
Company, and Western Canada Power. The largest single recipient was
the Toronto Power Company; the firm issued sixteen calls that totaled
$10 million.

Finance, a combination of commercial banks, insurance companies,
and investment trusts, was the smallest of the six sectors, receiving, over
the five decades, a minuscule 0.9 percent of all transfers. Despite a small
blip toward the end of the period (the sector drew $10.5 million and aver-
aged 2.5 percent of the total in 1910–12), there were no calls in forty-one
years; and the sector accounted for as much as 4 percent of the total only
once. In 1890 Colonial Securities' calls of $1.95 million, the Commercial
Bank of Manitoba's calls of $762,000, and the Bank of British
Columbia's issue of $828 thousand combined to draw $3.5 million into
the sector. The end-of-period transfers included some life insurance companies, the Union Life Assurance (Canada), for example, but it was dominated by trust companies.

Not all British funds passed through the formal London securities
market, and thus the flow data reported in the capital called series are
undercounted and the industrial distribution somewhat distorted.
Canadian land and loan companies actively solicited British investors,
and several "British companies acting under imperial legislation became
important lending institutions." Under 1874 legislation such foreign
"companies were required to be licensed by the Secretary of State to
carry on business in Canada, but apart from that virtually no restrictions
were imposed on their operations," although some restrictions may have
been imposed by their charters: "The Scottish American Investment
Trust Limited with headquarters in Edinburgh was formed in 1873
and operated in Canada until 1900. . . . The North of Scotland Canadian
Mortgage Company Limited, of Aberdeen, was formed in 1875 for the
express purpose of making loans on security of real estate in Canada and
operated in Canada for over half a century. The North British Canadian
Investment Company Limited of Glasgow, formed in 1876, was still in

operation at the beginning of the First World War."[597] Despite these forays, the distortions are almost certainly less serious than they are for the Australian data.

4-2b(2). The American contribution: As the previous discussion indicated, there is very little quantitative information about American investment in Canada until the late 1890s. The lack of an American equivalent of the "Capital Called" series leaves us with only qualitative evidence on the distribution of American investments before 1897 and even sketchier information about the years before 1870. Although in comparison with the British contributions the magnitudes were not large, there is evidence of such investments at least at far back as the 1830s. Toward the end of that decade, "speculators from Maine and New York entered the Canadian lumber industry. By the 1850's many of the Canadian lumber mills were owned by Americans." In mining, too, there is evidence of America investment: "It was American money which financed the Colonial Gold Mining Co., on the River de Loup. Nearly all the silver properties on the north shore of Lake Superior, including the prestigious Silver Islet Mine, were American owned. American money was invested in the Madoc deposit in eastern Ontario, and by 1880 all the leases were held by Americans." American capital also found its way into the Canadian transport system before Confederation. Some 70,000 shares of the Welland Canal Company were held in the United States, and there were also substantial investments in the Simcoe and Ontario, the Buffalo, Brantford and Goderich, and the Midland railways.[598] By the turn of the century American investment was still only about one-seventh of that of the British; but because of the work of Cleona Lewis, we probably have better estimates of the structure of American investment between 1897 and 1914 than we do for that of Britain or any other foreign country.[599] As Table 4:2-3 indicates, American investment appears to have become a factor in the 1870s, and it accounted for one-eighth of all foreign investment by 1899 and nearly one-quarter by 1914.

Even by that late date, however, more than 70 percent of American investment was "direct," and the figure for 1897 had been almost 85 percent (Table 4:2-12). Given the dominant position of London in the market for both Canadian rails and governments and, given the gradual

[597] E.P. Neufeld, *The Financial System of Canada: Its Growth and Development* (New York: St. Martin's Press, 1972), pp. 184–85. [Hereafter cited as Neufeld, *The Financial System of Canada.*]

[598] Code, *The Spatial Dynamics*, pp. 78–81.

[599] Lewis, *America's Stake in International Investments.*

Table 4:2-12. *American investments in Canada*

Direct investment—Type of business	1897	1908	1914	1897	1908	1914
	(millions of dollars)			(percents)		
1. Selling organization	10.0	15.0	27.0	5.3	2.2	3.1
2. Oil distribution	0.0	0.0	0.0			
3. Mining and smelting						
(a) Precious metals & precious stones	30.0	50.0	56.5	15.8	7.2	6.5
(b) Industrial minerals excluding oil	25.0	86.0	102.5	13.2	12.3	11.8
4. Oil production	6.0	15.0	25.0	3.2	2.2	2.9
5. Agriculture	18.0	25.0	101.0	9.5	3.6	11.6
6. Manufacturing						
(a) Paper and pulp	20.0	55.0	74.0	10.5	7.9	8.5
(b) All others	35.0	100.0	147.0	18.5	14.3	17.0
7. Railroads	12.7	51.4	68.0	6.7	7.4	7.8
8. Public utilities	2.0	5.0	8.0	1.1	0.7	0.9
9. Purchasing	0.3	0.6	2.2	0.2	0.1	0.3
10. Banking	0.7	2.4	7.2	0.4	0.3	0.8
Total direct investment	159.7	405.4	618.4	84.2	58.1	71.3
				0.0	0.0	0.0
Portfolio investment	30.0	291.8	248.8	15.8	41.9	28.7
Total direct and portfolio investment	189.7	697.2	867.2	100.0	100.0	100.0

Source: Cleona Lewis, *America's Stake in International Investment*, pp. 577–606.

evolution of the American market for any other type of securities, these results are hardly surprising. They are, however, important.

In comparison with the British, the Americans were much more catholic in their tastes. In 1897, for example, mining represented 29 percent of American long-term investment; but an equal proportion was invested in manufacturing. Moreover, even if railroad securities constituted all of American portfolio investment in Canada – and they certainly did not – that sector drew less than one-quarter of the total investment; and the figure was almost certainly substantially less.[600] Finally, sales agencies, oil production, and agriculture together represented almost one-fifth of the total. In short, American investors, in many

[600] In his summary of American investments in Canada for the years 1900–13, Jacob Viner estimates that railroads represented 44 percent of the sum of railroads and governments. Since those classes were the most likely candidates for portfolio investments, it does not appear unreasonable to hazard an estimate of 13.5 percent as railroad's fraction of total American investment in 1897. Viner, *Canada's Balance of International Indebtedness*, p. 303. See Table 4:3-15.

Table 4:2-13. *Total American investments in Canada industry 1900–1913*

Industry	Millions of dollars	Percent
Government		
Dominion and provincial	4	0.6
Municipal	60	9.5
Railroads	50	7.9
Industrial	180	28.6
Land and timber	145	23.0
Mining	60	9.5
Insurance	50	7.9
Miscellaneous	81	12.9
Total	630	100.0

Source: Viner, *Canada's Balance of International Indebtedness*, 1900–1913, p. 303.

ways, appear to have viewed Canada much as they viewed states such as California and Michigan: a potential market and a source of raw materials. That conclusion is underscored by both Viner's estimate and Field's enumeration of American investments in Canada (Table 4:2-13 and 4:2-14). The list includes not only mines, land companies, and manufacturing firms, but also theatrical enterprises, fox farms on Prince Edward Island, and investments in city and town property.

In terms of mines, for example, in 1877, when Boston capitalists were increasing their investments in Michigan copper, they also directed $300,000 to the Oxford Nickel and Copper Company, a firm organized to mine ore in Quebec and process it in New Jersey. Again, in 1886 Samuel Ritchie, an Ohio carriage builder and railroad entrepreneur, having paid $35,000 for 10,000 acres in Ontario, incorporated both the Canada Copper Company ($2 million) and the Anglo American Iron Company ($5 million) and arranged with the owners of Oxford Nickel to process the ore.[601]

In 1876 both the American Screw Company and the American Powder Trust opened branches in Canada; over the next decade about fifty American-chartered manufacturing companies followed suit. Although

[601] Lewis, *America's Stake in International Investments*, pp. 251–52.

Table 4:2-14. *American investments in Canada, 1909 and 1913*

Type of investment	1909	1913	1910	1913
	(millions of dollars)		(percents)	
Branch companies	105	135	37.6	23.7
Theatrical enterprises	0	3.5	0.0	0.6
Packing plants	5	6.8	1.8	1.2
Agricultural implements distributing houses	6.6	9.3	2.4	1.6
British Columbia lumber and paper mills and timber	58	71	20.8	12.5
British Columbia mines	50	62	17.9	10.9
Land deals, British Columbia	4.5	60	1.6	10.5
Land deals, Prairie Provinces	20	41	7.2	7.2
Lumber and mines, Prairie Provinces	5	10.5	1.8	1.8
Miscellaneous industrial investments	0	12.2	0.0	2.1
City and town property	0	20	0.0	3.5
Investments in maritime provinces	0	13.1	0.0	2.3
Fox Farm investments, Prince Edward Island	0	1	0.0	0.2
Purchases of government, municipal, and corporation bonds since 1905	25	123.7	9.0	21.7
Total (excluding life insurance guarantee holdings)	279.1	569.1	100.0	100.0

Note: 1909 from the *Monetary Times by Weekly Consular and Trade Reports*, No. 72, July–September 1910, p. 940. 1913 from Fred W. Field, *Capital Investments in Canada* (1914), p. 25; (1911), p. 24.

Source: Cleona Lewis, *America's Stake in International Investment*, p. 611.

those firms tended to be concentrated in textiles and woodworking, they spanned the industrial spectrum, including, for example, four drug manufacturers.[602] American insurance firms – a list that includes the "Big Three" (the New York Life, the Equitable, and the Mutual) – began selling policies in Canada at about the same time. Those sales meant, at first, investment in real estate, and then, as Canadian regulations began to bind, the investment of their reserves in a wide range of enterprises.[603]

---

[602] Lewis puts the total figure at 55 firms, Wilkins at 47. Lewis, *America's Stake in International Investments*, pp. 229, 294. Mira Wilkins, *The Emergence of Multinational Enterprise: American Business Abroad from the Colonial Era to 1914*, Harvard Studies in Business History, Vol. 34 (Cambridge, Mass.: Harvard University Press, 1970), pp. 46, 50. [Hereafter cited as Wilkins, *The Emergence of Multinational Enterprise*.] The drug manufacturers included Parke, Davis & Co.

[603] Wilkins, *The Emergence of Multinational Enterprise*, pp. 64–65.

Finally, although with the exception of some early Canadian Pacific offerings, total Canadian security sales in the United States during those early years were not large, American investors did begin to add some Canadian stocks and bonds to their portfolios. Three million dollars in Quebec bonds were sold in the United States in 1879. Over the next decade American investors purchased small blocks of the bond issues of two Canadian cities – Winnipeg (purchased by a St. Paul group) and Brandon – and of the Queen Victoria Niagara Falls Park. They also absorbed $1 million in the stock of the Northwest Land Company, and they held about one-fifth of the stock of the Great Western Railroad. In addition, Midwestern investors were the source of the majority of the funds employed in the construction of the Manitoba and Southwestern Railroad.[604]

American investment had long been significant, but the volume of annual flows erupted after 1897. Over the next seventeen years, the total increased more than four and a half times; and, while, in part, that increase was fueled by a $220 million infusion of new portfolio investment, the majority of the increase ($458 million) was in the form of direct transfers. Direct investment in agriculture rose five times, in manufacturing four times, and in mining almost three times. The agricultural component went in large part into the purchase of timberlands (in 1909 it was estimated that 90 percent of the available timberland in British Columbia was controlled by Americans or American companies), but there was some investment in western farms, and there were large speculative holdings of land in British Columbia and in the prairie provinces.[605]

In the manufacturing sector the first decade of the twentieth century saw a number of large American corporations – firms lured, in part, by

---

[604] Lewis, *America's Stake in International Investments*, pp. 335–36. The Americans sold out to the Canadian Pacific in 1884. The early financing of the C.P.R. was made difficult because of the bitter opposition of the Grand Trunk. As a result, the road's first bond issue was handled by a Montreal–New York syndicate; and its first public stock issue was underwritten in New York and Amsterdam. Overall, however, the main investors in the railroad were, since its completion, overwhelmingly British. In 1906, for example, Canadians and Americans together held slightly more than one-quarter of the common stock, while British investors held more than 60 percent. Herbert Marshall, Frank A. Southard Jr., and Kenneth W. Taylor, *Canadian-American Industry: A Study in International Investment* (New Haven, Conn.: Yale University Press, 1936), pp. 16, 114, 194.

[605] Fred W. Field, *Capital Investments in Canada: Some Facts and Figures Respecting One of the Most Attractive Investment Fields in the World* (Montreal: The Monetary Times of Canada, 1914), p. 21. [Hereafter cited as Field, *Capital Investments in Canada (1914).*] Lewis, *America's Stake in International Investments*, p. 288; Wilkins, *The Emergence of Multinational Enterprise*, p. 138.

a desire to operate behind the Canadian tariff wall – move a part of their production north of the border. General Electric and Westinghouse were among the first, but American millers and other food processors also opened plants, International Harvester began to manufacture agricultural machinery, Ford and Buick cars, and U.S. Rubber and Goodyear rubber products.[606] Moreover, the surge of industrial migration did not stop other Americans from continuing to establish and finance Canadian firms.[607] The largest American investments, however, were reserved for the pulp and paper industry. Amounting to $20 million in 1897, with the repeal of the American tariff on Canadian newsprint, the total rose to $74 million in 1914.[608]

In mining this century saw the Canadian Copper Company and the Anglo American Iron Company merge to form the International Nickel Company – a firm initially capitalized at $24 million, and a firm that instantly became the world's largest producer of nickel. In the same period Johns Manville began to mine asbestos in Quebec. In terms of precious metals, among the early lode ore mines was the American-owned Le Roi; that mine, located in British Columbia, was described in 1896 as "one of the best in the world."[609]

Less is known about the composition of American portfolio investment. It appears that such transfers represented about $33.5 million of the 1901–5 total. Of that figure $31.9 million was invested in the issues of railways and other privately controlled corporations. In 1913 American holdings of Canadian Pacific stock totaled $29 million. Between 1906 and 1914 Americans appear to have publicly purchased $153 million of the bonds of Canadian municipal and provincial governments, railways, and other private corporations that were not subject to American control. To this sum should be added the totals for private placements, a figure that Viner estimated, for the years 1905–13,

[606] Harold Underwood Faulkner, *The Decline of Laissez Faire, 1897–1917*. Vol. 7: *The Economic History of the United States* (New York: Rinehart & Company, 1951), p. 75. [Hereafter cited as Faulkner, *The Decline of Laissez Faire.*] M.J. French, "The Emergence of a U.S. Multinational Enterprise: The Goodyear Tire and Rubber Company, 1910–1939," *Economic History Review*, 2d series, Vol. 60, No. 1, 1987, pp. 69, 71.

[607] Lewis, *America's Stake in International Investments*, pp. 596–97.

[608] Lewis, *America's Stake in International Investments*, p. 595. Wilkins, *The Emergence of Multinational Enterprise*, pp. 138–39. Faulkner, *The Decline of Laissez Faire*, p. 75. Between 1900 and 1921 Canadian newsprint imports increased from 1.5 to 65 percent of American domestic production.

[609] Lewis, *America's Stake in International Investments*, pp. 208, 596. Wilkins, *The Emergence of Multinational Enterprise*, pp. 136–37. John Herbert Curle, *Gold Mines of the World* (London: Waterlow & Sons, 1896), p. 264.

Table 4:2-15. *Non-portfolio investments in Canada by countries in Continental Europe; Field's estimates*

Country	(Thousands of dollars)			Percents		
	1909	1911	1913	1909	1911	1913
France		47,250	67,250		59.0	62.5
Germany		21,725	21,725		27.1	20.2
Other continental		11,175	18,675		13.9	17.3
Total	54,450	80,150	107,650	100.0	100.0	100.0
Industry	1909	1911	1913	1909	1911	1913
Manufacturing and industrial enterprises	8,500	9,725	9,725	15.6	12.1	9.0
Land, mines, and mortgage Loans	45,950	66,425	93,925	84.4	82.9	87.3
Railways	0	4,000	4,000	0.0	5.0	3.7
Total	54,450	80,150	107,650	100.0	100.0	100.0

Source: Viner, *Canada's Balance of International Indebtedness*, p. 136.

at $73 million ($35 million of municipal and $38 million of "other" issues).[610]

4-2b(3). The contribution of other foreign investors: As Table 4:2-1 indi-cates, the contribution of "other foreign" investors was almost certainly negligible in the nineteenth century, but it became significant, if not sub-stantial, in the first decade and a half of this century. Field, writing in 1914, placed the investments of the other European countries at $55 million in 1909 and about twice that amount in 1913 (Table 4:2-15). Of those totals he assigns about three-fifths to France, between one-quarter and one-fifth to Germany, and about 15 percent to the rest of Europe. His data also indicate that the vast majority of those funds (between 80 and 90 percent) went into "Land, Mines, and Mortgage Loans," a signif-icant, but declining, fraction (from 16 to 9 percent) into "Manufacturing and Industrial Enterprises," and something less than 5 percent into the nation's "Railroads."

[610] Lewis, *America's Stake in International Investments*, pp. 341, 345, 348. Viner, *Canada's Balance of International Indebtedness*, pp. 127–28.

Although his conclusions are somewhat difficult to square with his data, Field argued that the French "were largely interested in Canadian railroad, industrial and other securities," and that, after the failure of the German-supported Sovereign Bank of Canada, that country's investors turned away from banking, but, while they showed some slight interest in the Canadian Pacific, "the chief German interest in Canadian investments is in railroad stocks affording speculative opportunities." In addition, he concluded that the Germans had invested in farming land and that "German financiers who have become interested in Canada think that land companies, for the purposes of acquiring good lands and advancing of money to settlers as an extra inducement, are good investment opportunities." "Dutch money," he wrote, "is being placed in Canada in the purchase of agricultural land and in mortgages"; and "lands, loans and to a small extent Canadian railroad securities appear to be attracting Belgian capital." Finally, "twenty shares of the Quebec Railway, Light, Heat and Power Company are held in Spain," and "the chief Russian investment is that of the Doukhobors in many acres of land in the Kootenay District, British Columbia."[611]

Viner has provided a quantitative estimate of the level of Continental investment, but he acknowledges that "practically the only information with regard to the amount of capital invested in Canada by Continental Europe is that collected by F.W. Field."[612] Thus, he based his estimate of the C.P.R.'s portion ($43.3 million) of the total Continental investment in Canadian securities on Field's assessment. To that figure, however, he added $14.5 million to capture the Canadian securities sold on the Continent in 1910–12 and $5 million to account for the increase in European holdings of Canadian bank stock from 1900 to 1913; he concluded that the "total Continental investment in Canadian securities not elsewhere accounted for will be estimated, therefore, at $62,735,000" in 1913.[613]

Turning to the other components of Continental investment in the years between 1900 and 1913, Viner placed the 1900 level of miscellaneous French investment at $15 million; and he raised Field's estimate of "the amount of German capital invested in Canada at the end of 1913, not including capital invested in Canadian railway securities by way of London," from $21.7 to $35 million. Moreover, he assumed that all but $5 million of Field's estimates of "the investments in Canada by all other countries" were made since 1900. Thus, he concluded that the total amount of miscellaneous investments was approximately $120 million,

[611] Field, *Capital Investments in Canada (1911)*, pp. 43, 51, 54, 58, 60, 61.
[612] Viner, *Canada's Balance of International Indebtedness*, pp. 135–36.
[613] Viner, *Canada's Balance of International Indebtedness*, pp. 136–37.

Table 4:2-16. *Total "Other Foreign" investments in Canada by industry 1900–1913*

Industry	Millions of dollars	Percents
Dominion and provincial governments	0	0.0
Municipal governments	0	0.0
Railroads	47	28.8
Industrial investments	30	18.4
Land and timber	80	49.1
Mining	0	0.0
Insurance	0	0.0
Miscellaneous	6	3.7
Total	163	100.0

Source: Viner, *Canada's Balance of International Indebtedness, 1900–1913*, p. 303.

of which $100 million was invested after 1899. Combining that $100 million figure with the estimate of $62.7 million for European holdings of Canadian securities, Viner concluded that the total level of Continental investment in Canada over the fourteen years was $163 million. Moreover, he argued that almost one-half that amount was directed toward investments in land and timber, 30 percent toward railroads, and just less than one-fifth toward industrial investments (Table 4:2-16).[614]

4-3. The evolution of the Canadian capital market: introduction

As an economy develops, the financial sector typically grows faster than the real sector. It is therefore reasonable to assume that a country (the United States, for example) with a substantially higher income than that of another country (say, Canada) will have a financial infrastructure that is relatively more developed than the differences in income alone would suggest. From the 1870s until sometime in the first decade of the twentieth century, Canadian per capita income was only about three-quarters of that of the United States.[615] In terms of its formal

---

[614] Viner, *Canada's Balance of International Indebtedness*, pp. 135–39.

[615] Although, during the decade 1905–14, Canadian per capita income reached more than 90 percent of that of the U.S., over the years between 1880–89 and 1900–9 the ratio fluctuated between 0.72 and 0.81; over the entire period 1880–1914, the average was 0.79. The 1880–1913 figures for the United States are really 1879–88 to 1904–13. The data are derived from M.C. Urquhart, *Gross National Product, Canada*, pp. 24–25; *Historical Statistics of Canada*, 2d edition, Series A1–A14;

Table 4:3-1. *Assets of Commercial Banks in Canada and the United States as a proportion of the Total Assets of All Financial Intermediaries*

	(selected years) Percents	
Year	Canada	United States
1860	n.d.	65
1870	73	n.d.
1880	55	59
1890	50	58
1900	53	63
1912	60	64

Source: Neufeld, *The Financial System of Canada*, Table 4:4, p. 92.

financial structure, however, Canada could hardly have been considered to have been significantly a less well-developed country than its southern neighbor. Between 1880 and 1912 the ratio of Canadian financial assets to Canadian gross national product to the ratio of U.S. financial assets to U.S. gross national product ranged from 0.87 to 1.11 and averaged 0.96.[616] Tables 4:3-1 through 4:3-5 provide some comparative data on the financial structures of the two countries. Clearly, on the statistical evidence alone, Canada's financial structure appears to have been much more developed than a comparison of per capita incomes alone would have led one to believe. In fact, however, in some dimensions the formal structure that emerges from the comparison may not precisely reflect reality.

4-3a. The chartered banks

4-3a(1). Legal rules and the growth of the chartered banks: In his report to the National Monetary Commission in 1910, Joseph French Johnson,

Robert E. Gallman, "Gross National Product in the United States, 1834–1909," in Dorothy Brady (ed.), *Output, Employment, and Productivity in the United States After 1800*, Conference on Research in Income and Wealth, Vol. 30 (New York: National Bureau of Economic Research, 1966), table A-1, p. 26; and U.S. Department of Commerce, *Historical Statistics of the United States* (1975), Series A-7.

[616] E.P. Neufeld, *The Financial System of Canada*, p. 60.

Table 4:3-2. *A comparison of commercial banks in the United States with chartered banks in Canada, 1896–1914*

Year	United States: Number of commercial banks	Canada: Number of commercial banks	United States: Number of persons. per commercial bank	Canada: Number of persons per chartered bank	Ratio of persons per bank in Canada to persons per bank in United States
1896	11,474	37	6,178	137,135	22.2
1897	11,438	37	6,311	138,432	21.9
1898	11,530	37	6,374	139,865	21.9
1899	11,835	36	6,320	145,417	23.0
1900	12,427	35	6,123	151,457	24.7
1901	13,424	35	5,780	153,457	26.6
1902	14,488	36	5,464	152,611	27.9
1903	15,814	37	5,099	152,730	30.0
1904	17,037	38	4,823	153,342	31.8
1905	18,152	37	4,618	162,216	35.1
1906	19,786	35	4,318	174,200	40.3
1907	21,361	34	4,073	188,559	46.3
1908	22,531	31	3,937	213,710	54.3
1909	23,098	30	3,918	226,667	57.9
1910	24,514	28	3,770	249,571	66.2
1911	25,183	28	3,727	257,393	69.1
1912	25,844	26	3,689	284,192	77.0
1913	26,664	24	3,646	318,000	87.2
1914	27,236	22	3,639	358,136	98.4

Sources: Historical Statistics of the United States, 1960, Series A-2, p. 7 and Series X-97, p. 632; *Historical Statistics of Canada,* Series A-1, p. 14; Neufeld, *The Financial System of Canada,* pp. 78–79.

Table 4:3-3. *Canadian assets of private Canadian intermediaries (millions of $'s)*

Year	Chartered banks	Quebec savings banks	Life insurance companies	Fraternal societies	Fire & casualty insurance companies	Building societies & mortgage loan companies	Trust companies	Total assets of private financial intermediaries
1870	103.1	5.2	3.4	0.0	4.5	13.7	0.0	129.9
1875	173.5	8.3	6.9	0.0	8.4	33.9	0.0	231.0
1880	160.7	8.9	9.8	0.0	9.1	71.4	0.0	259.9
1885	207.9	10.7	20.5	0.0	10.2	96.6	0.0	345.9
1890	246.9	12.8	43.1	1.4	17.4	122.0	0.0	443.6
1895	296.1	16.4	73.2	3.5	20.8	137.3	0.0	547.3
1900	437.3	20.8	108.7	8.5	27.6	134.7	9.6	747.2
1905	700.9	29.1	151.9	18.0	37.9	149.4	20.4	1,107.6
1910	1,060.4	37.1	212.3	32.4	58.9	193.4	34.4	1,628.9
1915	1,415.0	44.0	364.0	68.0	73.0	260.0	63.0	2,287.0
				(percents)				
1870	79.4	4.0	2.6	0.0	3.5	10.5	0.0	100.0
1875	75.1	3.6	3.0	0.0	3.6	14.7	0.0	100.0
1880	61.8	3.4	3.8	0.0	3.5	27.5	0.0	100.0
1885	60.1	3.1	5.9	0.0	2.9	27.9	0.0	100.0
1890	55.7	2.9	9.7	0.3	3.9	27.5	0.0	100.0
1895	54.1	3.0	13.4	0.6	3.8	25.1	0.0	100.0
1900	58.5	2.8	14.5	1.1	3.7	18.0	1.3	100.0
1905	63.3	2.6	13.7	1.6	3.4	13.5	1.8	100.0
1910	65.1	2.3	13.0	2.0	3.6	11.9	2.1	100.0
1915	61.9	1.9	15.9	3.0	3.2	11.4	2.8	100.0

Source: E. P. Neufeld, *The Financial System of Canada*, Appendix Table B, pp. 612–621.

Table 4:3-4. *Assets of U.S. private financial intermediaries (millions of dollars)*

Years	Commercial banks	Mutual savings banks	Life insurance companies	Fraternal societies	Fire, marine & casualty insurance companies	Savings & loan and mortgage companies	Total assets of U.S. private financial intermediaries
1850	489	43	10	1	23	1	567
1870	1,781	550	284	4	66	26	2,711
1880	2,518	882	462	6	95	43	4,006
1890	4,765	1,743	796	28	298	372	8,002
1900	10,000	2,400	1,700	50	298	700	15,350
1912	21,800	4,000	4,400	200	1,000	1,400	32,800
				(percents)			
1850	86.2	7.6	1.8	0.2	4.1	0.2	100.0
1870	65.7	20.3	10.5	0.1	2.4	1.0	100.0
1880	62.9	22.0	11.5	0.1	2.4	1.1	100.0
1890	59.5	21.8	9.9	0.3	3.7	4.6	100.0
1900	65.1	15.6	11.1	0.3	3.3	4.6	100.0
1912	66.5	12.2	13.4	0.6	3.0	4.3	100.0

Note: Goldsmith also includes the holdings of security brokers and dealers, private trusts, and private pension funds. These figures have not been included, because they appear to have no Canadian counterpart.

Source: 1900 & 1912 are from Raymond W. Goldsmith, *Financial Intermediaries in the American Economy Since 1900*, National Bureau of Economic Research, Studies in Capital Formation and Financing (Princeton, N.J.: Princeton University Press, 1958), Table 10, pp. 73–74.

The 19th century figures for Commercial Banks are from *Historical Statistics* (1960), Series X-21, p. 624; The figures for Mutual Savings Banks in the 19th century are from the annual Report of the Comptroller of the Currency, December 4, 1916 (Washington: G.P.O., 1917), Volume I, pp. 85–86. The figures for Life Insurance Companies are from Bruce Michael Pritchett, *A Study of Capital Mobilization: The Life Insurance Industry in the 19th Century* (New York: Arno Press, 1977), Table 14, pp. 87–88.

The 1850 estimates of the assets of Fraternal Societies, Fire, Marine, & Casualty Insurance Companies, Savings & Loan and Mortgage Loan Companies are estimated on the basis of Goldsmith, *Financial Intermediaries*, Chart 3, p. 61, Table 8, p. 62, and Table 9, p. 65.

Table 4:3-5. *Assets of Canadian and U.S. life insurance companies*

	(thousands of dollars) United States				
Years	Total assets less real estate	Government securities	Private stocks & bonds	Mortgages	Other non-real estate assets
1880	407,741	104,712	29,814	178,444	94,770
1890	732,620	58,769	211,186	328,086	134,579
1900	1,650,409	99,089	755,070	503,085	293,165
1917	5,762,000	562,000	2,058,000	2,021,000	1,121,000
	Canada				
1881	7,000	2,855	247	2,148	1,751
1891	23,000	3,618	1,403	9,881	8,098
1901	66,000	11,075	14,876	19,100	20,948
1911	189,000	25,515	57,456	66,849	39,180
	(percents) United States				
Years	Total assets less real estate	Government securities	Private stocks & bonds	Mortgages	Other non-real estate assets
1880	100.0	25.7	7.3	43.8	23.2
1890	100.0	8.0	28.8	44.8	18.4
1900	100.0	6.0	45.8	30.5	17.8
1917	100.0	9.8	35.7	35.1	19.5
	Canada				
1881	100.0	40.8	3.5	30.7	25.0
1891	100.0	15.7	6.1	43.0	35.2
1901	100.0	16.8	22.5	28.9	31.7
1911	100.0	13.5	30.4	35.4	20.7

Sources: Canada: R. T. Naylor, *The History of Canadian Business, 1867–1914*, Volume 1. p. 193. United States: 1880–1900, B. M. Pritchett, *Financing Growth: A Financial History of American Life Insurance Through 1900* (Huebner Foundation Monograph 13, Wharton School, University of Pennsylvania), pp. 22 & 48. 1917, from 1971 *Life Insurance Fact Book* (New York: Institute of Life Insurance, 1971), p. 68.

Dean of New York University School of Commerce, Accounts, and Finance, wrote,

> The [Canadian] chartered banks transact business which in the United States is divided among national banks, trust companies, private banks, and savings banks. They buy and sell commercial paper, discount the notes of their customers, lend money on stocks and bonds, make advances to farmers, and sometimes aid in the financing of industrial enterprises. To a Canadian the word "bank" means one of the twenty-one "chartered banks," for the law prohibits the use of the word bank by any other institutions.

> Hence, if anyone seeks to understand the financial or banking system in Canada, he must devote his attention in the main to the chartered banks. These through their branches furnish the loanable capital necessary for the support of the Dominion's trade and industry and for much of its agricultural enterprise. To them the government turns when the funds are needed for internal improvements or when the exchequer faces a deficit. The promoters of street railways, steam railways, steam railroads, and other permanent improvements take counsel with the managers of these chartered banks before they issue their securities. The banks as a rule do not invest their funds in the stocks and bonds of new enterprises, yet their managers are the men most familiar with the world's money markets and their approval, therefore, of any financial undertaking is highly esteemed.[617]

Despite the similarity in the stage of development, a comparison of the histories and the legal constraints that operated in the two countries suggests that their financial infrastructures should have been very different. In the United States, commercial banking was highly idiosyncratic, restricted by a myriad of state and, later, federal, rules that guaranteed the dominance of unit banking, a bare minimum of intrastate branching, and no branching across state boundaries.[618] If the American

[617] Joseph French Johnson, *The Canadian Banking System*, National Monetary Commission, 61st Congress, 2nd Session, Senate Document No. 583 (Washington D.C.: GPO, 1910), pp. 12, 14. [Hereafter cited as Johnson, *The Canadian Banking System*.]

[618] In 1900, for example, only 87 of the nation's 12,427 commercial banks operated any branches, and the 87, in fact, controlled only 119 branches. Of the 119 only 94 were located outside the main office city. In the nineteenth century only two states, California and North Carolina, permitted unrestricted intra-state banking; and even as late as 1960 there were only 15. Lester V. Chandler, *The Economics of Money and Banking* (New York: Harper & Brothers, 1948), p. 340. A.C.L. Day and Sterie T. Beza, *Money and Income: An Outline of Monetary Economics* (New York: Oxford University Press, 1960), p. 227. U.S. Department of Com-

system had its intellectual roots in any other country's structure, it had clearly lost a great deal in translation.

In Canada the Scottish banking system provided particularly important precedents, but "banking behavior and legislation were also influenced by Canada's economic and political ties with Britain, France and the United States."[619] Before Confederation, most banks were chartered by colonial legislatures or were granted royal charters, although a very few operated under the aegis of the Free Banking Act of 1850. The post-Confederation banking regulations were firmly rooted in the rules developed over the previous half century.

In Canada chartered banking began roughly contemporaneously in New Brunswick, Quebec, Ontario, and Nova Scotia. The first bank was formed (unchartered) in Montreal in 1792, but it failed. Soon after the end of the War of 1812 merchants in Montreal once more sought a bank charter; but, after failing three times to receive legislative sanction, they launched the Montreal Bank, or the Bank of Montreal, under articles of association in June 1817. In 1820 the Bank of New Brunswick received the first charter granted to a bank in British North America. In 1821 "charters were enacted by the Quebec legislature for each of the three banks in Lower Canada and were given the royal assent the following year. Incorporation of the Bank of Montreal was proclaimed 22 July 1822 and of the Quebec Bank and the Bank of Canada, 30 November 1822."[620] "A Bank of Upper Canada operated as a private institution in Kingston from 1818 to 1821, ending in failure, and a more permanent bank of the same name began operations in York in 1821." The merchants of Halifax organized the Halifax Banking Company, a private association, in 1825; but the first chartered bank, the Bank of Nova Scotia, did not receive its charter until 1832. "The first bank on Prince Edward Island, the Bank of Prince Edward Island, was not established until 1856, and failed in 1881; the Union Bank of Newfoundland appeared in 1854 and failed in 1894; the Bank of British Columbia was incorporated in 1862 and disappeared in a merger in 1900."[621]

merce, Bureau of the Census, *Historical Statistics of the United States: Colonial Times to 1957* (Washington D.C.: GPO, 1960), Series X 156, p. 635. [Hereafter cited as *U.S. Historical Statistics* (1960).]

[619] Sheila C. Dow, *Financial Markets and Regional Economic Development*, p. 27.

[620] The first bill to charter the Montreal Bank was dropped by the legislature in 1815. It was resubmitted in each of the next two legislative sessions, but in both cases the legislature was prorogued by the governor before the bill was considered. Bray Hammond, *Banks and Politics in America from the Revolution to the Civil War* (Princeton: Princeton University Press, 1957), pp. 645–47. [Hereafter cited as Hammond, *Banks and Politics*.]

[621] Neufeld, *The Financial System of Canada*, pp. 75–76.

The act chartering the Bank of Montreal was copied by other banks in Upper and Lower Canada, and parts of it formed the basis for banking legislation after Confederation.[622] In fact, some of its features were to become more or less permanent parts of the Canadian banking system. First, there was nothing in the charter to prohibit the Bank from opening branches; and the Bank soon established offices in Quebec City, in Kingston and York in Upper Canada, and in New York City.[623] Second, although the act allowed foreigners to own shares, it prohibited them from becoming directors. The British-subject restriction became part of the first comprehensive banking legislation of the new Dominion. Although revisions in 1890 relaxed the British-subject requirement somewhat – from 100 percent to a majority of directors – it survived otherwise intact until the early 1980s. Thus, Alexander Hamilton was the inadvertent father not only of an important part of what was to become the Canadian banking system but also of the first restriction on foreign economic control in Canada.[624]

In 1832, "with both Houses in agreement, royal assent was given to the bill incorporating 'The President, Directors, and Company of the Bank of Nova Scotia,'" since 1874, the Bank of Nova Scotia. The act called for the double liability of shareholders. It was the first instance in British North America of such a provision, and it became a continuing feature of Canadian banking legislation until 1934.[625]

In October 1833 the Committee of the Privy Council on Trade revised a set of rules to apply to bank charters. The province of Upper Canada was given to understand that no further banking act would receive royal assent unless it conformed to those rules. In brief:

> (1). Suspension of cash payments for sixty days to result in forfeiture of the charter, (2). Notes issued by any branch to be redeemable both at that branch and at the head office, (3). One-half of the capital of the bank to be immediately paid in, (4). The amount lent on paper bearing the name of a director or officer of a bank to be limited to one-third of the total discounts, (5). The bank not to hold its own shares or make advances to its shareholders on the security of their shares, (6). The statement of the affairs of the bank to be prepared weekly, and a half-

---

[622] Gordon Laxer, *Open For Business: The Roots of Foreign Ownership in Canada* (Toronto: Oxford University Press, 1989), p. 217. [Hereafter cited as Laxer, *Open for Business.*]

[623] Hammond, *Banks and Politics*, p. 647. The New York City agency had operated continuously since 1858. Neufeld, *The Financial System of Canada*, p. 481.

[624] Laxer, *Open for Business*, pp. 216–17.

[625] Joseph Schull and J. Douglas Gibson, *The Scotiabank Story: A History of the Bank of Nova Scotia, 1832–1982* (Toronto: Macmillan of Canada, 1982), p. 16.

yearly return compiled from these statements to be made to the government, (7). Shareholders to be liable for double the amount of their shares, and (8). The funds of the bank not to be lent on the security of land or other property not readily disposable, the bank to hold property only to the extent necessary to carry on their business; the bank not to own or be interested in merchandise except for the purpose of realizing on securities held; the business of the bank to be confined to the legitimate operations of banking, namely advances upon commercial paper or government securities, and dealings in money, bills of exchange and bullion.

Nearly all of these conditions were shortly afterward incorporated in the charters of the Canadian banks; several of them, third, fourth, fifth, and eighth, were virtually in operation at the time, while the first was already implied.

Again, although some were gradually modified, most became part of the Confederation's banking legislation.[626]

In 1836 the Bank of British North America, an imperial bank, opened an office in York. The bank was incorporated in Great Britain; its operations were extended to Canada by royal charter rather than by colonial legislation. "In 1837 the bank had some 600 partners in England and about 300 in the colonies, 'all of whom [were] responsible to the full extent of their fortunes for the engagements of the Bank, offering therefore unlimited security to the public.' When a charter sanctioning operations in North America was granted in 1840, the liability of the partners was specifically restricted to the amount of the capital subscribed."[627]

As a result of new entries, "at the time of the union of the two Canadian provinces, the 'recognized' banks in operation included three chartered and one unchartered bank in Lower Canada, three chartered and two unchartered banks in Upper Canada, and the Bank of British North America operating by royal charter in both provinces. Together the banking capital in Canada was £2,176,000, deposits were £811,000, and discounts £3,269,000."[628]

In 1850, in an attempt to establish small banks, to secure their circulation, and "to relieve, in part at least, the financial difficulties of the government by widening the market for its securities, and at the same time

---

[626] Victor Ross, *A History of the Canadian Bank of Commerce, With an Account of the Other Banks Which Now Form a Part of Its Organization*, 2 vols. (Toronto: Oxford University Press, 1920, 1922), Vol. 1, pp. 19–20; Vol. 2, pp. 401–2.

[627] R. Craig McIvor, *Canadian Monetary, Banking and Fiscal Development* (Toronto: Macmillan Company of Canada, 1958), p. 38. [Hereafter cited as McIvor, *Canadian Monetary Banking and Fiscal Development*.]

[628] McIvor, *Canadian Monetary, Banking and Fiscal Development*, p. 39.

so stimulating their demand as to raise their value," the Canadian parliament passed the Free Banking Act of 1850 – an act that was modeled after the free-banking laws of New York. The legislation was not a success. Only six banks took advantage of the act. To one, the British Bank of North America, the act proved of considerable value, to the others, obviously less so. In 1855 the first three Canadian banks established under the law received special charters and abandoned their free banking status. The last two struggled for three years (1856–58) "against the competition and prestige of the chartered banks and then began to retire their issues and wind up their business." In 1860 repeal was proposed, and in 1866 the "Act to establish Freedom of Banking" was repealed by the Provincial Note Act of 1866.[629]

Over the years from 1820 to 1867, the most rapid increase in the number of active bank charters occurred in two distinct periods: from 1831 to 1836, when the number increased from six to twenty-one, and from 1854 to 1859, a period of intense speculative activity, when eighteen banks opened their doors and increased the total number of banks from fifteen to thirty.[630] "Upon the day Confederation became a fact there were eighteen banks carrying on business in Ontario and Quebec under charters granted by the province of Canada, five working under Nova Scotia charters, and four under acts passed by New Brunswick. The Bank of British North America acting under its royal charter, operated in all the provinces, but it was also subject to Dominion regulation."[631]

Banks had opened, and banks had closed. From 1820 to Confederation there were nineteen failures.[632] None, however, were as important to the evolution of the Canadian banking system than the 1866 failure of the Bank of Upper Canada. The Bank had been in operation for forty-four years, for a time the province of Upper Canada had been a major shareholder, and for twelve or more years the bank had kept the Canadian government's account; it was in 1860 "the government's erstwhile banker." The Bank had, during the land speculation boom of 1857 and 1858, extended a very large amount of credit to borrowers who had pledged real estate – real estate with much inflated values – as security. By the time the boom had ended in depression, the bank owned land in

---

[629] Roeliff Morton Breckenridge, *The Canadian Banking System, 1817–1890*, Publications of the American Economic Association, Vol. X, Nos. 1–3, January, March, and May 1895 (New York: Macmillan and Company, 1895), pp. 137, 151. [Hereafter cited as Breckenridge, *The Canadian Banking System.*] Hammond, *Banks and Politics*, pp. 666–67.

[630] Neufeld, *The Financial System of Canada*, pp. 76, 81, and table 4:1, pp. 77–80.

[631] Breckenridge, *The Canadian Banking System*, pp. 222–24.

[632] Neufeld, *The Financial System of Canada*, pp. 76, 81, and table 4:1, pp. 77–80.

"practically every county in Upper Canada" and had "more assets in the form of landed property than in any other form, except discounted notes." Although banks were not supposed to lend on mortgages, there "appears to have been a loop-hole in bank charters that enabled financial institutions to lend money by the process of hypothecation on thinly disguised real-estate security."[633]

The Bank did manage to struggle on for several years. In November 1863, however, it was announced "that the Bank of Montreal should be appointed the Fiscal Agents of the Province of Canada, and that the Provincial Account should be transferred from the Bank of Upper Canada on the 1st of January." Finally, on September 14, 1866, "the directors of the Bank of Montreal were advised by their general manager 'that he had that morning in conjunction with the Bank of British North America withdrawn from the Daily Settlement between the Banks in Montreal, owing to the insecure position of the Bank of Upper Canada.' Four days later the Bank of Upper Canada stopped payment."[634]

The financial costs of the debacle were enormous. The Canadian creditors "lost at least $310,000 by the failure. The stockholders lost the whole of capital which was once $3,170,000; the government, and through it, the taxpayers lost all but $150,000 of deposits amounting to over $1,150,000. For proprietors and creditors combined the result of the failure was the disappearance of a principal which cannot be reckoned at less than five million dollars, a sum equal to 17 percent of the entire banking capital of the province." Nor was liquidation costless, for the next half decade it absorbed some $90,000 a year. The failure also had a long-term impact on the Canadian banking system. In the near term "to managers and directors it gave a wholesome warning, not only to look to the inner organization of their banks, but also to guard against any loans whatsoever on real estate security."[635] In the longer term the post-Confederation banking acts legally prohibited investment in mortgages. That legislation was molded by the bankers themselves. The legislation governing the actions of the banks confirmed to the predilection of the banks for very short-term loans; a predilection that was reinforced by the experience of the Bank of Upper Canada.[636] Neufeld concludes that there was

---

[633] Code, *The Spatial Dynamics*, pp. 127–28. McIvor, *Canadian Monetary, Banking and Fiscal Development*, p. 54. Merrill Denison, *Canada's First Bank: A History of the Bank of Montreal*, 2 vols. (Toronto: McClelland & Stewart, 1966), Vol. 2, p. 147. [Hereafter cited as Denison, *Canada's First Bank*.]

[634] Denison, *Canada's First Bank*, Vol. 2, pp. 130, 147.

[635] Breckenridge, *The Canadian Banking System*, pp. 174, 176–77.

[636] Neufeld, *The Financial System of Canada*, p. 108. R.T. Naylor, *The History of Canadian Business. Vol. I: The Banks and Finance Capitalism* (Toronto: James

probably not even a need for legal restrictions, because "the bankers themselves, until well after the Second World War, argued against their participation in mortgage lending."[637]

Confederation under the British North America Act of 1867 brought a series of new laws governing the activities of the chartered banks. An Act Respecting Banks (31 Vic., cap. 2) was the earliest statute enacted under these powers. "This was merely a temporary measure, the expiry of which was fixed at the end of the first session of Parliament after 1st January 1870. Yet some interest attaches to it as an early indication of the force with which Canadian precedents influenced the legislators of the Dominion. It first extended the powers of banks previously incorporated in any of the provinces to the territory of the whole Dominion. . . . The remainder of the law is practically a re-enactment for the Dominion of Canada of the general legislation upon banks previously in force in the province of the same name."[638] The next legislation affecting the banks – the Act Respecting Banks and Banking (33 Vic., cap. 2) – was passed in April 1870 and received the royal assent the next month. Among its provisions it required

> (a) The bank shall not issue notes or begin banking business till $200,000 of its capital shall have been *bona fide* paid up, and the fact certified to the Treasury Board; (b) Twenty percent of the subscribed capital shall be paid in each year after the beginning of business; . . . (f) No loans or discounts shall be made on the security of the bank's own stock, but the bank shall have a privileged lien for any overdue debt on the shares and unpaid dividends of its debtors, and may decline to transfer such shares until the debt is paid; (g) The paid up capital shall not be impaired by any division of profits; (h) No division of profits by way of dividend or bonus shall exceed 8 percent per annum until the rest or reserve fund, after deducting all bad and doubtful debts, shall equal 20 percent of the paid-up capital stock; . . . (s) The charter of the bank shall run to the end of the session of Parliament next after the first of January 1881, and no longer.[639]

It was, however, "An Act Relating to Banks and Banking" (34 Vic., cap. 5), passed on April 14, 1871, that was "the first general law under

Lormor & Company, 1975), p. 70. [Hereafter cited as Naylor, *The Banks and Finance Capitalism.*]

The relevant legislation is contained in 34 Victoria, 1871, Cap V., An Act Relating to Banks and Banking (passed 14 April 1871), sections 40 and 41.

[637] "Legal restrictions on bank assets, that is on bank lending, did not significantly restrict the banks' operations for most of the period of their existence." Neufeld, *The Financial System of Canada*, p. 109.

[638] Breckenridge, *The Canadian Banking System*, pp. 219–20.

[639] Breckenridge, *The Canadian Banking System*, pp. 254–56.

which the banks really worked, and may be regarded as practically the first bank act of the Dominion." The act increased the subscribed capital that was required before a bank could begin business to a bona fide $500,000, of which $100,000 must be paid up. It revised and rewrote the 1870 legislation that "allowed banks making advances to take, instead of personal security, the security of commodities stored against the time to market them, passing into, out of or through Canada, or undergoing conversion from the raw states into products such as pork, bacon, hams, malt, flour, and sawn lumber." It also declared "that a bank might acquire and hold as collateral security for any advance 'shares in the capital stock of any other bank, the bonds or debentures of municipal, or other corporations, or Dominion, Provincial, British or foreign public securities.' "[640] Finally, there were sections 40 and 41. The first required that "the Bank shall not, either directly or indirectly, lend money or make advances upon the security, mortgage or hypothecation of any lands or tenements," and the second stated that "the Bank may take, hold and dispose of mortgages and hypotheques upon personal as well as real property, by way of additional security for debts contracted to the Bank in the course of its business." These clauses were maintained in subsequent acts with the exception that, in 1880 and following, any real estate obtained (and not for use) had to be disposed of within seven years. Although these restrictions were at times honored only in the breech, "the bank failures themselves appeared to support the view that commercial banks should not 'lock-up' their funds in long credits. Nor could banks circumvent the regulations by providing loans against collateral other than real estate. Such collateral did not exist in quantity; the most important collateral was land and urban real estate."[641] Thus, while the banks were free to make short-term secured loans to farmers, it was 1967 before they could make conventional mortgage loans. "This restriction was supported by the banks, who only started petitioning for a change in legislation on mortgage lending in 1962."[642] Finally, there was nothing in the 1870 and 1871 acts or their subsequent revisions that prevented the rechartered banks from opening branches in any province in the Dominion.[643]

---

[640] Breckenridge, *The Canadian Banking System*, pp. 260–61.
[641] Neufeld, *The Financial System of Canada*, pp. 178–79.
[642] Dow, *Financial Markets and Regional Economic Development*, pp. 42–43.
[643] As early as 1868 the number of branches of Canadian chartered banks was greater (123) than the number of branches in the United States in 1900 (119). In Canada by 1900 the number of branches had grown to 2,008, and a decade later it was 2,367. Neufeld, *The Financial System of Canada*, chap. 4. The branch data are from table 4:7, p. 102. See also, Naylor, *The Banks and Finance Capital*, chap. III.

The legislation of 1870 and 1871 essentially set the structure of the Dominion's banking laws for the remainder of the pre–World War I era. The changes that were made were largely designed to correct defects in detail rather than alter general principles. For example, by 1870 "the evils of permitting the banks to loan upon shares in other chartered banks had become too manifest longer to be tolerated. The clause permitting loans upon shares was stricken out by an act taking effect upon the 15th November 1879 (42 Vic., cap. 45)."[644] The revision of 1890 greatly increased the range of the inventories of primary and intermediate products against which the banks could lend; and the revision of 1900 made bank mergers much simpler. Before then, a merger had required a special act of Parliament (there were only four between 1875 and 1900); "from the Bank Act Revision of 1900 onward mergers merely required approval of the Governor-in-Council on the recommendation of the Treasury Board." Of the thirty-six banks that disappeared over the next quarter century, no less than twenty-seven of the disappearances were results of mergers.[645]

The new legislation touched off a third round of bank formation. Between 1870 and 1874 the numbers increased from thirty-four to a record fifty-one. From the beginning of 1875 until the end of 1914, however, there was a gradual, but accelerating, decline in the number of chartered banks. Over those years seventeen new banks were chartered and opened, twenty-three failed, twenty-one merged, and two had their charters repealed. This process left the Dominion with forty-four banks in 1880, forty-one in 1890, thirty-six in 1900, thirty in 1910, and twenty-two at the end of 1914 (see Table 4:3-6).

In spite of the dissimilarities in the legal structures underlying the Canadian and U.S. banking systems, as far as their aggregate contributions to the process of capital accumulation is concerned, they appear to have been much more similar than the legal and economic structures would have suggested. Although by the first decade of the twentieth century a Canadian bank served more than thirty times as many citizens as its American counterpart, the ratios per branch were much closer. Moreover, both systems controlled very similar fractions of the financial infrastructures of their respective economies. Tables 4:3-1 and 4:3-2 provide some comparisons between the Canadian and the American commercial banking systems in the years before World War I. In 1900, for example, when there was one bank for every 6,123 Americans, there was a commercial bank branch in Canada for every 7,600 Canadians; and, a decade later, the

---

[644] Breckenridge, *The Canadian Banking System*, pp. 288–89.
[645] Neufeld, *The Financial System of Canada*, p. 97.

Table 4:3-6. *Number of Canadian chartered banks, 1820–1920*

Decade	Number active at beginning of decade	New active banks	New bank charters not used	Failures (or charters repealed)	Mergers	Number active at end of decade
1820–1829	0	6	0	0	0	6
1830–1839	6	18	0	5	2	17
1840–1849	17	1	3	3	0	15
1850–1859	15	18	6	3	0	30
1860–1869	30	15	11	9	1	35
1870–1879	35	19	10	6	4	44
1880–1889	44	5	6	7	1	41
1890–1899	41	0	2	5	0	36
1900–1909	36	9	11	5	10	30
1910–1920	30	2	3	3	11	18

Source: E. P. Neufeld, *The Financial System of Canada: Its Growth and Development* (New York: St. Martin's Press, 1972), Table 4:1, pp. 77–79.

figures were 3,770 and 3,000, respectively.[646] Similarly, the ratios of commercial bank assets to the total assets of all financial intermediaries in the two countries were quite comparable (see Table 4:3-1).

Although legal restrictions raised no barriers against national branch banking, the present Canadian system of nationwide branch banking was relatively slow to develop. In 1859 the Bank of North America opened a branch in Victoria, British Columbia. Three years later, the Bank of British Columbia began operations in that city and in New Westminster. It was, however, 1886 before the Bank of British Columbia opened a branch in Vancouver (that city's first bank), and it was the next year before it was joined by the Bank of Montreal in both Vancouver and New Westminster. In the prairies the first branch of any chartered bank was not opened until the Bank of Montreal opened an office in Winnipeg in 1878, but it was followed by the Merchants' Bank within a year.[647] In the Maritimes "the chartered banking system in the four Atlantic provinces operated more or less independently of the rest of the country until close to the turn of the century."[648]

[646] The U.S. figures are from Table 4:3-2, the Canadian branch figures from Neufeld, *The Financial System of Canada*, table 4:7, p. 102.

[647] Neufeld, *The Financial System of Canada*, pp. 91–92, 96.

[648] Dow, *Financial Markets and Regional Economic Development*, p. 29.

In 1868 the thirty-five chartered banks operated 123 branches. Despite the activity of the intervening years, in 1890 the, then, forty-one banks operated only 426 branches.[649] As late as "1895 only one Canadian bank – the Bank of Montreal – had anything like a nationwide branch system. Even its closest rival, the Canadian Bank of Commerce, operated almost exclusively in Ontario"; in the Maritimes the largest Halifax banks had only tenuous connections with Ontario.[650] Thus, even at the short end of the market, for most of the latter decades of the nineteenth century the lack of legal constraints did not substantially ease the problems of spatial mobilization.

After the mid-1890s, however, the emerging system of national branching provided an alternative to the commercial paper market, the financial innovation that helped underwrite spatial mobilization in the United States. Although by 1897 the Bank of Montreal had seven branches in British Columbia, it was only after that date that they were joined in the province by the Canadian Bank of Commerce, the Imperial Bank, the Merchants' Bank of Halifax, and Molson's Bank. In the prairies by 1898 eleven chartered banks were operating forty-six branches in Manitoba, six branches in Saskatchewan and Alberta, and two banks had a branch in the Yukon.[651] "Newfoundland's two banks both collapsed in 1894, whereupon four central Canadian banks opened up branches on the island, and the local currency was tied to the dollar. The other three Atlantic provinces experienced a decline in economic opportunities relative to the rest of Canada from the 1860s, which accelerated as new opportunities opened in the West. Eleven banks failed and the remainder attempted to protect their position with mergers. But six takeovers by banks outside the region, the removal of the Merchants' Bank of Halifax to Montreal under the new name of the Royal Bank of Canada, and the consolidation of the remaining banks in the Bank of Nova Scotia meant that by the outbreak of World War I, only the Bank of Nova Scotia remained, and even then the manager's office had been moved to Toronto" – a move that drew very little comment in the Halifax press.[652]

[649] Neufeld, *The Financial System of Canada*, pp. 101–2.
[650] Drummond, *Capital Markets in Australia and Canada*, p. 15.
[651] Neufeld, *The Financial System of Canada*, pp. 95–96.
[652] Dow, *Financial Markets and Regional Economic Development*, p. 29. "The March 23, 1900, issue of the *Acadian Recorder* simply reported that 'It has been definitely decided that the General Manager's office of the Bank of Nova Scotia is to be removed to Toronto. The staff who will leave here for Toronto on Monday are: D. Watters [sic], chief inspector, W. Caldwell, chief accountant, E. Crockett, J.W. Huggies, P.C. Robinson, C.S. Jenner, J.K. Wannamaker, W.L. Keith, S.W. Mahon, H.D. Burns.'" Schull and Gibson, *The Scotiabank Story*, pp. 80–81.

Between 1890 and 1920 the number of branches grew from 426 to 4,676.[653] By the end of World War I, with one exception (the Weyburn Security Bank of Saskatchewan, a bank that remained independent until 1931) the head offices of all nineteen chartered banks were either in Ontario or Quebec, although the titular head office of the Bank of Nova Scotia remained in Halifax.[654] As a result of the restructuring of the branch networks, by 1910 Joseph Johnson concluded,

> Taking into account the uncertainties that necessarily attach to the development of enterprises in new localities, which add to the element of risk involved in the loaning of money, it may fairly be said that Canada has only one money market and one rate of interest. In the United States great masses of loanable capital accumulate in the cities of the east and can be drawn into the country only by positive assurance of an extraordinary rate of interest. In Canada one finds no such accumulation of capital in a few cities and no such reluctance to loan it out at distant points. Banks in Montreal and Toronto lend with equal freedom in both the west and the east, and their managers have equal familiarity with the needs and credits of both sections. . . . The real nature of the Canadian system can not be understood by anyone who fails to grasp the fact that the Canadian banks are in no sense local institutions, and their managers are on the keen lookout for any chance to increase their business in any community between the Atlantic and Pacific oceans.[655]

Branching was, however, not limited to Canada proper. One of the first decisions of the management of the Bank of Montreal was to open an office in New York; and by 1870 the Bank had opened an agency in London for purposes of facilitating its foreign business, investing its surplus fund, and for payment of its dividends to foreign investors.[656] Later in the same year the Canadian Bank of Commerce followed the Bank of Montreal to the City.[657] Those connections were to play an important role in the transfer of British capital to the Dominion. Moreover, as nationwide banking institutions emerged and competition intensified, the chartered banks – particularly those with strong ties to the lagging economies of the Maritimes – pushed into the Caribbean. By 1914 both the Bank of Nova Scotia and the Royal Bank of Canada could

[653] Neufeld, *The Financial System of Canada*, pp. 101–2.
[654] Dow, *Financial Markets and Regional Economic Development*, pp. 34–35.
[655] Johnson, *The Canadian Banking System*, pp. 101–2.
[656] Neufeld, *The Financial System of Canada*, p. 480.
[657] Ross, *A History of the Canadian Bank of Commerce*, p. 58.

trace more than 10 percent of their business to operations in Jamaica, Cuba, and Puerto Rico.[658]

In Canada there were never more than fifty-one commercial banks, and by the end of 1914 the number had declined to twenty-two. Moreover, in 1870 the five largest banks controlled some 44 percent of all bank assets, and the Bank of Montreal alone almost 30 percent. By 1920 the position of the Bank of Montreal had eroded somewhat. It then represented less than 20 percent, but the five largest banks had come to control almost 65 percent of the sector's assets. The Royal Bank of Canada was now slightly larger than the Bank of Montreal, and the Canadian Bank of Commerce was only somewhat smaller.[659] The expansion into the prairies during the years of the wheat boom saw the emergence of a number of new banks (eleven opened their doors between 1900 and 1911). As the boom subsided, however, they lost the "competitive struggle with the branches of the large metropolitan banks of Toronto and Montreal." As in Britain, the economies of scale appear to have outweighed the benefits of "their somewhat greater level of independent decision-making power."[660] Despite the relatively small number of commercial banks and the skewed distribution of bank assets, there is little evidence of monopolistic restriction on the supply of bank funds. If the standard is American unit banking, it appears that "there is no evidence that cartel behavior among Canadian banks created gross differences in lending rates or other measures of bank behavior that would imply that Canada paid a high price for the stability it enjoyed."[661]

Of at least equal importance, if the goal is an assessment of the commercial banks' role in capital accumulation and mobilization, is the similarity in the structure of loans made by the banks in the two countries. In the United States contemporaries had blamed the financial debacles of 1837 and 1839–42 on the willingness of commercial banks to extend long-term credit on the basis of short-term (deposit) liabilities and on the very low ratios of note and deposit liabilities to liquid reserves. As a result, between the 1840s and the 1860s, many states and, after 1862, the

---

[658] Neil C. Quigley, "The Bank of Nova Scotia in the Caribbean, 1889–1940," *Business History Review*, Vol. 63 (winter 1989), pp. 800–1.

[659] Neufeld, *The Financial System of Canada*, table 4:6, p. 99.

[660] Code, *The Spatial Dynamics*, p. 285.

[661] Michael D. Bordo, Angela Redish, and Hugh Rockoff, "A Comparison of the United States and Canadian Banking Systems in the Twentieth Century," in Michael D. Bordo and Richard Sylla (eds.), *Anglo-American Financial Systems: Institutions and Markets in the Twentieth Century* (Burr Ridge, Ill.: Irwin Publishing Company, 1995), p. 37.

federal government imposed banking regulations that not only required that banks hold legal reserves but that also, in a number of other ways, made it increasingly difficult for commercial banks to advance any but short-term commercial credit.[662] After the 1880s some state banks did move into the mortgage loan market; but, despite a ruling by the Supreme Court, the national banks were still very hesitant. As a result, for the most part, businessmen who required long-term finance were forced to look to the newly emerging non-bank intermediaries (building and loans, savings banks, insurance companies, and, later, investment trusts) or to the formal securities markets for their external capital requirements.[663]

If American banks tended to specialize in short-term lending, the Canadian banks were legally obligated to focus their attention on the short end of the market. Naylor, for example, argues that the legal restrictions did bind in the sense that "the logic of 'real bills' concepts of banking became ossified into law."[664] Even more than in the United States, "obvious and fundamental gaps in the capital markets remained. The most obvious one was the provision of long-term credit for purposes of financing real capital investments and for facilitating the transfer of such assets."[665]

American unit banks, small, largely localized, and largely prohibited from operating overseas branches, made few attempts to attract foreign depositors. In Australia, relatively large banks with "nationwide" branch networks actively sought British deposits in order to supply mortgage finance to the agricultural and urban housing sectors. In Canada relatively large banks with nationwide branch networks, but banks restricted in their investment portfolios by the legal prohibition against mortgage lending and therefore under no pressure to provide long-term credit, did not actively seek overseas deposits. Canadian banks were involved in overseas transactions, but usually they had more foreign

---

[662] For a thorough discussion of the early American experience, see Hammond, *Banks and Politics in America*, pp. 549–630.

[663] As an example of the free-wheeling banking of the 1830s, it might be noted that the Morris Canal and Banking Company operated as a commercial bank, but almost its only liquid asset was the canal itself. In terms of state regulation, the "Forestall" system in place in Louisiana after 1842 required that the state's banks make loans of longer than ninety days only from their capital account and absolutely prohibited any renewals of short-term loans. Although the courts had ruled differently in the mid-1880s, no federal legislation was passed that specifically permitted National Banks to make mortgage loans until 1913.

[664] Naylor, *The Banks and Finance Capital*, p. 70.

[665] Neufeld, *The Financial System of Canada*, p. 78.

assets than liabilities. There were no foreign deposits in Canadian banks before 1900, and even in 1914 they accounted for less than 8 percent of the total.[666]

Few would argue that the American banking sector was particularly stable in the years before the First World War. Between 1865 and 1914 no fewer than 3,401 banks suspended payment, 1,294 in the 1890s alone. Since 1914 Canadian banks have established a reputation for great stability: there was only a single bank failure between 1915 and 1971 – but its reputation in the earlier period was hardly better than that of the United States. "Speculative activity, the lack of diversification of credit risks and in a good many instances, dishonest management, were leading factors in the liquidation of nine banks between 1880 and 1896. Between 1800 and 1910, it is estimated that approximately thirty percent of Canadian banks failed."[667] Neufeld concludes "that as a group the chartered banks have a record for solvency after Confederation that is more tarnished than that of any other financial intermediary examined."[668] In both the United States and Canada, and unlike Australia, because there were, for all intents and purposes, no foreign deposits, British savers were not injured by bank suspensions and failures; and such defaults had little direct impact on the financial links between Britain and the two North American countries.

4-3a(2). The chartered bank and the security markets: domestic and foreign: Mortgage lending aside, the investment policies of Canadian banks were little constrained by government regulations: "in their choice of investment securities the banks were not hampered by law. They may purchase not only government and provincial bonds, but also the stocks and bonds of both Canadian cities and cities of foreign countries, and the stocks and bonds of domestic and foreign railways and industrial corporations."[669] Thus, perhaps even more than many of their American counterparts, they became financial as well as commercial institutions. As a fraction of total assets, their holdings of private corporate stocks and bonds were relatively smaller than those of their American peers; but, given the differences in the level of development of the formal securities markets in the two countries, they were larger than one might have

---

[666] Urquhart and Buckley (eds.), *Historical Statistics of Canada*, Series 175, 176, 177, 178, 179, 234, and 236, pp. 240–41. In 1900, for example, 12.8 percent of chartered bank assets were held abroad, and foreign deposits represented 6.3 percent of total deposits. In 1914 the figures were 12.7 percent and 7.8 percent.

[667] McIvor, *Canadian Monetary, Banking and Fiscal Development*, p. 76.

[668] Neufeld, *The Financial System of Canada*, p. 81.

[669] Johnson, *The Canadian Banking System*, p. 74.

expected. For example, in 1909 commercial banks in the United States held 11 percent of their assets in such securities; in Canada the figure was 8 percent.[670] "These securities represent partly an investment carried on as a secondary reserve," but in Canada much more than in the United States, they also represent

> a business carried on for the benefit of their customers. In Canada the demand for long-term investment is not large, but whatever market there is for securities is mainly in the hands of the chartered banks. An investor seeks the advice of a bank manager and often is able to obtain from him securities which satisfy his needs. The banks do not publish a list of their holdings, but it is generally taken for granted that they carry only gilt-edge securities. If a customer desires to obtain second or third rate securities, being eager for a high rate of return, a bank can accommodate him, not by selling him out of its own stock, but by negotiating the purchase of the desired securities in New York or London.[671]

Even before the banks had moved into the secondary securities market, they had begun to underwrite both public and private security issues. The Bank of Montreal "became the first underwriter of significant size, and the other banks soon engaged in the activity as well – predating by many years the underwriting activities of the investment dealers." In 1874 the Bank of Montreal underwrote its first public issue.

> It participated with Morton, Rose & Co. in underwriting an £800,000 sterling issue for the Province of Quebec; it soon followed with a £750,000 City of Montreal issue, and then a £500,000 subscription to a Dominion of Canada loan. In 1876 it bought the remaining £111,000 of the City of Montreal issue and also formed a syndicate with the Imperial Bank of Toronto to purchase £100,000 worth of City of Toronto bonds. . . . In 1877 jointly with the Merchants Bank, the Bank of Montreal underwrote and distributed successfully a £200,000 Province of Quebec debenture issue and decided to join a London syndicate to underwrite the balance of the issue amounting to £400,000.[672]

On February 21, 1879,

> the General Manager reported, and the Board approved, a contract entered into between the Government of the Province of Quebec and

---

[670] Johnson, *The Canadian Banking System*, p. 51. *Historical Statistics of the United States*, Series 589 and 596, p. 1021. Urquhart and Buckley, *Historical Statistics of Canada*, Series 173, p. 238.

[671] Johnson, *The Canadian Banking System*, p. 51.

[672] Neufeld, *The Financial System of Canada*, pp. 480–82.

the Bank of Montreal [under which] the Bank undertakes the negoti-ation of an issue of Bonds representing a loan of $3,000,000 authorized by the Act of the Legislature of the Province of Quebec 41 Victoria, Cap. 1, the principal and interest of which are to be made payable at the option of the holder at the office of the Bank in London or New York.

The General Manager also stated that negotiations were in progress for the formation of a syndicate in New York City to assume the above contract at ninety-five percent net, the understanding being that the Bank would have an interest in the syndicate to the extent of $400,000.

The New York financial press was ecstatic; the financial columnist of the *New York World* reported, "The point is this: these banks have outbid the London bankers who wished to take the loan and are about to try the first experiment of placing a foreign loan in this country on its merits."[673] A Canadian bank had played a major role in an important innovation in the American capital market.

Nor were the banks' activities limited to the public sector. The Bank of Montreal was, for example, heavily involved with the financing of the Canadian Pacific Railway. Not only had they supported construction with short-term loans totaling nearly $11.5 million, but they were involved with the "$2.5 million C. Unger & Co. loan of 1883 [and] the $5 million government loan of 1885," and they provided support to the issue of "the land-grant bonds in the form of their initial purchase and later loans in connection with their sale to third parties." "In addition the Bank par-ticipated in the financing of lines which formed parts of the C.P.R. system," including the Canada Central, the Credit Valley, and the Toronto, Grey and Bruce.[674]

From the point of view of this study, however, the most significant development occurred in November 1892. Until then the Dominion had employed Glyn, Mills, Currie & Co. and Baring Brothers jointly as their fiscal agents in Britain. At a time when the Australian states were in the process of appointing new fiscal agents in London – replacing the branches of Australian domestic banks with British banks – the Domin-ion of Canada chose, as of January 1, 1893, to substitute the Bank of Mon-treal for the Glyn, Mills–Baring combination. Although "the transfer of the account was criticized in London banking circles as both injudicious and unwarranted," it greatly strengthened the financial infrastructure that linked Canada with the London capital market. Between 1906 and

[673] Denison, *Canada's First Bank*, Vol. 2, pp. 185–86.
[674] Denison, *Canada's First Bank*, Vol. 2, pp. 228–29.

1913, for example, British investment in Canada was estimated to have increased by £246,278,200; and more than 50 percent was negotiated by the Bank of Montreal.[675]

4-3b. Non-bank intermediaries: introduction

In both countries the commercial banks held relatively similar proportions of the assets of the entire financial sector – on average about 65 percent – and non-bank intermediaries supplied about equal portions of the market served by all formal bank and non-bank intermediaries (Table 4:3-1). For whatever reasons, legal or behavioral, that caused the commercial banks to act as they did, the American and Canadian non-bank intermediaries appear to have been left largely alone to serve the long-term sectors of the two capital markets.

Did the Canadian non-bank intermediaries move into the long-term market to take up the slack left by the short-term focus of the commercial banks' investment decisions? Naylor argues that they failed to do so. He writes, "The main financial requirements of the period, apart from commercial loans and discounts, were for mortgage money, long-term debt capital for business and government, and equity financing for industry. Yet despite the growth of financial institutions – which in theory should have been equipped to service those needs, in part at least – the bulk of the new financing went into mortgages, and the supply of loanable funds for long-term debt or equity in Canada remained chronically underdeveloped."[676] In part, Drummond agrees with this assessment, but only in part. He notes that, in the first decade of the twentieth century, mortgage rates rose, and this shift in yields induced loan companies to increase their foreign borrowing and for the steadily increasing flow of trustee funds to be diverted more heavily into mortgage finance. "In Canada the old established corporations moved heavily into mortgage lending as the years passed and as the wheat economy developed."[677] Between 1901 and 1914, Canadian life insurance, fire insurance, and trustee companies, together with domestic mortgage and savings banks, and building societies made more than $246 million in mortgage loans; however, even by the end of that period, for the life and fire insurance companies, the mortgage companies, and the trust companies, mortgages still represented only 42 percent of their combined assets.[678] Thus, at the most general level, Drummond's conclusions are very different from

---

[675] Denison, *Canada's First Bank*, Vol. 2, pp. 253–54, 293–94.

[676] Naylor, *The Banks and Finance Capital*, pp. 186–87.

[677] Drummond, *Capital Markets in Australia and Canada*, pp. 110–11.

[678] Drummond, *Capital Markets in Australia and Canada*, tables 1 and 2, pp. 79, 81.

Naylor's; the nation's non-bank intermediaries were apparently merely responding to market signals.

Even if Naylor is correct, the question remains: In what sense did the intermediaries fail? Was their performance in this regard better or worse than that of their American counterparts? Table 4:3-3 displays the absolute and relative size of private Canadian intermediaries at five-year intervals between 1870 and 1915, and Table 4:3-4 provides estimates of the same magnitudes for comparable institutions in the United States over much the same period. Although the commercial banks remained the dominant organization, the relative importance of the non-bank intermediaries in Canada doubled – from one-fifth to two-fifths of the total – over the forty-five-year period. Moreover, the assets that they controlled increased more than thirty times: from just over $25 million to almost $875 million. Nor were the Canadian non-bank intermediaries slow to emerge; the entire relative increase in the size of the non-bank sector vis-à-vis the U.S. occurred during the 1870s. Over the last thirty years the rate of growth of their assets matched the growth of the assets of the commercial banking sector; their relative position remained essentially unchanged. In the case of the United States, the relative growth of the non-bank intermediaries dates from a decade or two earlier (they represented only 14 percent of financial assets at mid-century); but, from 1880 onwards, the patterns in the two countries were very similar; in fact, the Canadian institutions represented a slightly higher fraction of all financial assets, although the rate of growth of assets in the two countries was almost identical.[679]

In aggregate, the non-bank sectors in the two countries appear to have been similar, but Naylor's criticism may have rested on the composition of the non-bank sector or on international behavioral differences in portfolio selection within any given type of non-bank intermediary. Table 4:3-7 was constructed to shed some light on the first of these issues. If the non-bank intermediaries are roughly grouped into three categories – savings institutions, building and loan associations and mortgage companies, and insurance companies – the marked differences between the formal financial structures of the two countries become immediately apparent.[680] In Canada building societies and mortgage loan companies

---

[679] The average Canadian proportion for the years 1880, 1890, 1900, and 1910 was 0.397. The figure for the United States for 1880, 1890, 1900, and 1912 was 0.365. The annual rate of growth of assets in the United States was 23 percent for the years 1880–1912, and for Canada 19 percent for 1880–1910 and 25 percent for 1880–1915 (two figures that suggest an extrapolated rate of 23 percent for the years 1870–1912).

[680] The savings bank figures reported in Table 4:3-5 are much larger than those that appear under the title Quebec Savings Banks in Table 4:3-3. The figures reported

– intermediaries with almost all of their resources invested in mortgages – accounted for about three dollars in five of the sector's assets while insurance companies accounted for only about one-sixth and savings banks about one-quarter of those totals. In the United States, building and loan and mortgage loan companies accounted for hardly more than 10 percent of the sector's assets, while insurance companies and savings banks divided the remaining nine out of ten dollars.

Moreover, there were also some significant intercountry differences within the latter two sectors. In the case of life insurance companies, for example, the proportion of assets invested in mortgages by firms in the two countries was very similar; but the Canadian firms held proportionately more government bonds and, until the turn of the century, substantially lower proportions of private securities (Table 4:3-5). The latter difference may, however, reflect nothing more than the relative level of development of the investment banks in the United States and of the bond houses in Canada as primary securities markets and of the formal security exchanges in the two countries as secondary markets. In addition, the Canadian mortgage bias of the insurance companies was partially offset by the much greater willingness of American savings banks to invest in those assets. In 1900, for example, non-farm mortgages represented 27 percent of the assets of the American savings banks, whereas their Canadian counterparts held none.[681]

In terms of Naylor's criticism, if the life insurance investments were typical of the entire insurance industry and the 27 percent savings bank figure for 1900 is representative of the complete period, it appears that mortgages represented almost twice as large a fraction of the assets of the non-bank intermediaries in Canada. The adjustments somewhat narrow the apparent U.S.-Canadian gap, but they certainly do not make it disappear. It is, of course, possible that the difference between the two countries is not the result of entrepreneurial failure, as Naylor suggests, but merely a reflection of legal constraints and of market signals.

First, it may have been partly due to differences in the legal environments in the two countries. Neufeld, for example, argues that "the pro-

---

in Table 4:3-5 include the Federal Post Office Savings Bank and the Dominion Government Savings Bank. With Confederation, the government largely took over the private Trustee Savings Banks. Neufeld, *The Financial System of Canada*, pp. 150–52.

[681] *United States Historical Statistics (1960)*, series X-96, p. 630 and series N-155, p. 396. The Quebec Savings Banks were not permitted to invest in mortgages until after World War II, and all of the government banks' assets were in government bonds. Neufeld, *The Financial System of Canada*, pp. 154, 162.

Table 4:3-7. Comparison of Canada and U.S.A.: Non-bank intermediaries (Millions of $'s)

	Building & loan societies, building societies, and mortgage loan companies		All insurance companies		Savings banks	
	Canada	U.S.A.	Canada	U.S.A.	Canada	U.S.A.
1870	14	26	8	354	10	550
1880	71	43	15	563	25	882
1890	122	372	19	1,122	52	1,743
1900	135	700	31	2,250	77	2,400
1912	260	1,400	62	5,600	98	4,000

(Percent of Three Industry Total in Each Country)

Year						
1870	43.6	2.8	25.2	38.1	31.2	59.1
1880	64.1	2.9	13.7	37.8	22.2	59.3
1890	63.2	11.5	9.8	34.7	27.0	53.8
1900	55.6	13.1	12.7	42.1	31.7	44.9
1912	61.9	12.7	14.7	50.9	23.3	36.4

Sources: Tables 4:4 and 4:5 and Neufeld, *The Financial System of Canada*, pp. 612–621.

Notes: (1) For Canada 1912 is 1915

(2) Canadian Savings Banks include the private Quebec Savings Banks, the Federal Post Office Savings Banks, and the Dominion Government Savings Bank.

hibition against mortgages is probably of major importance in explaining the relatively slow growth of Quebec savings banks," an observation that suggests mortgage rates must have been relatively high compared to other legal alternatives.[682] Second, since one major component of demand for mortgage credit rests on the demand for urban housing, the relative rates of growth of those two sectors provides some support for the hypothesis that differential demand accounted for at least a part of the difference. Between 1870 and 1910 the urban population of Canada grew more than half again as fast as the urban population in the United States.[683] Similarly, given the disparities between the relative sizes of the agricultural sectors in the two countries – the Canadian sector's share in the economy was about three-quarters again as large as that of the American – the relative demand for farm mortgages should have been higher as well (Table 4:3-8). Finally, the difference may be partly explained by differences in the rate at which the secondary securities markets developed in the two countries; the Canadian markets lagged their American counterparts by at least one decade and probably two. In the absence of an efficient secondary market, securities can prove to be as illiquid as mortgages; and they can hardly function as secondary reserves.

4-3b(1). Savings banks: Neufeld concludes that "the history of savings banks in Canada is interesting, not because these banks have been important, but rather because they have always been relatively unimportant."[684] In Britain and the United States the history of savings banks can be traced to the early nineteenth century, and in both countries the banks were initially organized to convince the working poor that thrift was profitable. In the process they fairly effectively mobilized the savings of the working classes and made them available to the public sector in the United Kingdom and to both the public and private sectors in the United States. In Canada savings banks appear in the second decade of the nineteenth century (only a few years after British and American banks), and the original spirit of the organizations – to help "the industrious poor" – was hardly different than that prevailing in the United States or the United Kingdom. Despite the similarity, their economic impact was much less. In the United States, in the years from 1870 to 1900, although the dominant

---

[682] Neufeld, *The Financial System of Canada*, p. 154.

[683] *United States Historical Statistics (1960)*, series A-195, M.C. Urquhart (ed.), *Historical Statistics of Canada* (Cambridge and Toronto: Cambridge University and Macmillan Company of Canada, 1971), series A-29, p. 15. Note that the U.S. figures are for urban places over 2,500; the Canadian figures are for urban places over 1,000. The figure for Canada was 666 percent, for the United States, 424 percent.

[684] Neufeld, *The Financial System of Canada*, p. 140.

Table 4:3-8. *Gross National Product by sector of origin (percents)*

Years	Agriculture	Mining	Manufacturing	Construction	Transport & public utilities	Wholesale & retail trade	Residential rents & community, business, & personal services	Banking, finance, etc.	Government
				United States					
1869–1878	20.1	1.8	13.9	5.3	11.9	15.7	14.7	11.7	4.4
1879–1888	16.1	2.1	16.6	5.5	11.9	16.6	13.6	12.6	4.9
1889–1898	17.1	2.5	18.2	4.9	10.7	16.8	11.8	12.0	6.0
1899–1908	16.7	3.1	18.4	4.5	10.7	15.3	9.6	16.0	5.6
1909–1918	17.7	3.3	20.8	3.2	10.7	14.5	8.2	15.4	6.3
				Canada					
1875	37.0	1.4	22.9	6.7	4.6	6.4	13.9	1.9	5.1
1885	34.3	1.2	24.4	4.9	5.4	7.5	14.0	2.7	5.6
1895	30.9	2.5	22.9	3.5	6.7	7.8	16.4	3.6	5.8
1905	25.7	3.4	23.8	6.0	7.9	9.0	15.1	4.3	4.8
1915	28.0	3.1	18.4	4.9	8.8	9.5	13.7	3.6	9.9

Sources: Canada:M.C. Urquhart, *Gross National Product, Canada, 1870–1926: The Derivation of the Estimates* (Kingston & Montreal: McGill-Queen's University Press, 1993), Table 1.1, pp. 11–14.

position of savings banks among non-bank intermediaries was eroding, they still held about one-fifth of the assets of all financial intermediaries. In Canada the relative holdings of the public and private savings combined banks was less than half that figure.

In Canada the Savings Bank Act of 1841 encouraged the formation of trustee savings banks, and eight banks were formed. Even then, however, problems had begun to emerge. First, in the United States the savings banks' reputation for safety was certainly deserved; in Canada the story was quite different. The trustee managers often made loans without adequate security and proved inadequate to the task of managing larger deposits and the array of local (particularly public) securities in which they invested. Second, the provincial, and later the Dominion, governments looked to the deposits as a source of governmental funds. Concerned with the difficulties of trustee management, provincial governments in the Maritimes had very early begun to "set up their own savings banks: in the 1830s in Nova Scotia and Newfoundland, in the 1840s in New Brunswick, and in the 1860s in Prince Edward Island."[685] In 1855 the Province of Canada effectively stifled new entry by imposing "impossibly high capital requirements." Sixteen years later "The Act Relating to Banks and Banking" (34 Vic., cap. 6) brought the government savings banks established in the Maritimes before Confederation under Dominion control; and it was "An Act Respecting Certain Savings Banks in the Province of Ontario and Quebec" (33 Vic. cap. 7) "that finally required the trustee savings banks either to obtain a charter and operate as limited liability joint-stock corporations or to transfer their assets to the government's new savings banks or to one of the chartered banks." The Dominion government had established the Post Office savings bank shortly after 1867, and it had inherited what became the Dominion Government's Savings Bank from the Maritime provinces at the time of Confederation.

Incorporation involved a minimum capital requirement of $200,000 with shares of at least $400, and each director required to hold at least twenty-five shares, "in complete contrast to the mutual character and voluntary management of the former trustee savings banks." "All these measures were supported by the plausible plea of guarding the public interest, but it is not unlikely that they served that interest as much by helping to find the government of the day with ample funds as by protecting individuals from loss."[686]

---

[685] Dow, *Financial Markets and Regional Economic Development*, p. 51.
[686] Neufeld, *The Financial System of Canada*, pp. 140, 151–54. Breckenridge, *The Canadian Banking System*, pp. 258–59.

Two Quebec savings banks alone elected to obtain joint-stock charters. Over time they were granted increasing freedom in their investments in papers securities and in their loan policies. They had always been permitted to make collateral loans against a wide range of securities: Canadian Dominion, provincial, and municipal government securities, British and foreign public securities, the stock of chartered banks, stocks of building societies (loan companies), bonds and debentures of institutions and corporations. They were also always allowed to invest directly in the issues of the various levels of government in Canada. In 1890 the range of allowable securities was extended to include any securities that the Government of Canada accepted from insurance companies to meet security deposit requirements; in 1897 it was again extended to the stocks and debentures of building societies, loan or investment companies, and various utilities. In 1890 they were also allowed to make unsecured loans, but this right was restricted to loans to governments (federal, provincial, and municipal) and, after 1900, to institutions and corporations with paid-up capital of $500,000 and a dividend record of 4 percent per annum for the previous five years. Until 1948, however, they were prohibited from making mortgage or personal loans.[687] The restriction against mortgage lending has been cited as one reason for their relatively slow growth.

Finally, neither the trustee savings banks that remained true to the original savings bank spirit, limited as they were to the funds of the industrious poor, nor the government banks, limited in the interest they were willing to pay, were well positioned to stave off competition. In the 1840s it was competition from a new intermediary, the building society. "This competitor appealed to the small saver without the overtones to charity, it pioneered the marvelous innovation of the contractual savings payment, it gave the saver a definite purpose for saving (the purchase of a house), and it could take full advantage of that important instrument, the real estate mortgage."[688]

Later it was the competitive pressure of the savings departments of the chartered banks that slowed the growth of both the government and Quebec savings banks. The chartered banks had apparently come to value savings accounts well before their peers in the United States. The Bank of Nova Scotia, for example, in response to the practice introduced by the British Bank of North America, began paying interest on cash deposits in 1837; and in 1868 the Canadian Bank of Commerce opened savings departments – departments paying interest at 4 percent or at 5 percent

---

[687] Neufeld, *The Financial System of Canada*, pp. 154–55, 157.
[688] Neufeld, *The Financial System of Canada*, pp. 151–52.

for sums remaining on deposit from June 20 to December 31 each year – at the bank's branches in Hamilton and Guelph.[689] The savings banks suffered further erosion of their market at the hands of the chartered banks in the 1880s; and the explosive increase in the number of chartered bank branches between 1890 and 1920 "was accompanied by the virtual disappearance of local private bankers and a substantial decline in the relative size of their Post Office Savings Bank." "Between 1875 and 1905, the banks increased their savings deposits from 19.9% to 44.2% of total liabilities."[690] In the United States the proportion of time deposits in all liabilities was 16 percent in 1900 and 26 percent in 1914.[691]

4-3b(2). Life insurance companies: In the United States insurance companies held between 35 and 40 percent of the assets of non-bank intermediaries over the last three decades of the nineteenth century, and that figure had risen to more than 50 percent by the outbreak of World War I. Of that total, life insurance companies represented about four-fifths. In Canada in the 1990s the insurance companies have grown to take second place to the chartered banks in their share of total financial assets; however, they did not hold that position in 1914. Between 1870 and 1915 the entire insurance sector accounted for hardly more than 15 percent of the assets of non-bank intermediaries. While the life insurance companies had, since the mid-1890s, held about the same share of the entire insurance industry's assets as their American counterparts, in 1869 they accounted for less than two-fifths; and, on average, between 1870 and 1895 they held far less than three-fifths of the industry's total assets (see Tables 4:3-3 and 4:3-4).[692]

The first Canadian fire insurance company was organized in Halifax in 1809 and the first in Upper Canada in 1833. The first life insurance company, the Canada Assurance Company, was organized in 1847 – only a few years after life insurance had become firmly established in the United States – but it remained the only Canadian life insurance company until the Sun Life began operations in 1871. In that interim it was British and American companies that wrote the vast majority of Canadian policies; in 1870, for example, Canada Life, although the largest

---

[689] Hull and Gibson, *The Scotiabank Story*, p. 40. Ross, *A History of the Canadian Bank of Commerce*, Vol. 2, pp. 54–55.

[690] Dow, *Financial Markets and Regional Economic Development*, pp. 51–52. Neufeld, *The Financial System of Canada*, pp. 101–2. Neufeld puts the increase from 17.5 percent in the 1873–5 period to 46.5 percent in 1896–1900, p. 117.

[691] *United States Historical Statistics* (1975), series 602 and 606, p. 1022.

[692] Dow, *Financial Markets and Regional Economic Development*, pp. 53–54.

single insurer, accounted for a mere 15 percent of life insurance in force in Canada. The remaining 85 percent was divided between 24 British and American firms.[693]

The growth in importance of Canadian life insurance companies can really be dated from the passage of two acts – one in 1875 (38 Vic., cap. 20 and 38 Vic., cap. 21) and the second in 1877 (40 Vic., cap. 40) – passed by the Canadian parliament. The acts were allegedly passed in response to evidence of malpractice, poor management, and the failure of the foreign companies; but, even if the rhetoric contained a grain of truth, the result was an opportunity for new Canadian life insurance companies. The acts required that foreign companies deposit sufficient assets to cover their Canadian liabilities with the Minister of Finance, or with a trust company approved by the Minister, while Canadian companies were only required to make nominal deposits, although they were required to hold all their assets, except those necessary for carrying on operations abroad, under their own control. Many of the British and foreign companies refused to make the deposits and, instead, withdrew from the Canadian market.[694] Many of the American firms ultimately returned, but British companies never came back in force.

Thus, between 1870 and 1900 the number of Canadian life insurance companies increased from one to seventeen (there were twenty-three a decade later); the industry's assets increased from $3.4 to $364 million (an average annual growth rate of more than 10 percent); and its share of the assets of all financial intermediaries rose from 2.6 to 15.9 percent. The industry did, however, remain fairly concentrated. In 1900 Canada Life held 38.1 percent of the industry's assets, Sun Life 17.6 percent, Confederation Life 13.1 percent, and the five largest together 84.2 percent. In 1920 the figures were 18.1, 27.3, 18.1, and 72.3 percent.[695]

One conclusion, however, is well documented: probably before, and certainly after, the turn of the century, the alleged mortgage bias of the Canadian life insurance companies was not the result of legal restrictions on their investment policies. Although the industry had been regulated by Dominion statute since 1875, these regulations never imposed stringent controls on the companies' choice of assets. The two largest companies, Sun Life and Canada Life, had, from their date of charter, possessed virtually unlimited investment powers; the newer companies

---

[693] Dow, *Financial Markets and Regional Economic Development*, pp. 53–54. Neufeld, *The Financial System of Canada*, pp. 221, 223, 225.

[694] Dow, *Financial Markets and Regional Economic Development*, pp. 53–54. Neufeld, *The Financial System of Canada*, pp. 236–37.

[695] Neufeld, *The Financial System of Canada*, table 8:2, p. 308.

Table 4:3-9. *Role of Canadian Life Insurance Companies in the New Issues Market 1900–1914 (thousands of dollars)*

Years covered from year-end to year-end	New issues of securities in Canada	Securities purchased by life insurance companies having dominion charters	Securities purchased by foreign life insurance companies	Securiuties purchased by all life insurance companies operating in Canada
1900–1905	192,591	27,877	12,533	40,410
1905–1910	272,491	29,933	5,503	35,436
1910–1914	317,130	15,630	10,874	26,504
1900–1914	782,212	73,440	28,910	102,350
(percents)				
1900–1905	100.0	14.5	6.5	21.0
1905–1910	100.0	11.0	2.0	13.0
1910–1914	100.0	4.9	3.4	8.4
1900–1914	100.0	9.4	3.7	13.1

Source: Ian M. Drummond, "Canadian Life Insurance Companies and the Capital Market, 1890–1914," *Canadian Journal of Economics and Politicial Science*, Volume 28, Number 2, May 1962, Table III, p. 224.

tended to be somewhat more sharply restricted: to municipal and government securities, mortgages, and policy loans. In 1899, however, the law was changed to grant those companies powers almost as broad as those of the two industry giants.[696] As a result, between 1900 and 1914 it appears that life insurance companies absorbed more than one-eighth of all Canadian new issues; and during the first quinquennium that fraction exceeded one-fifth (see Table 4:3-9).

Although by the end of the period Canadian insurance companies were becoming significant players in the financial markets, they still were far less important than their American counterparts. Size is not, however, the sole measure of importance. The Canadian life insurance companies were initially responsible for two innovations that contributed in a major way to the evolution of the nation's financial structure. As early as 1862 the Canada Life had begun to tender for a variety of new issues – in 1862 the whole of a $40,000 issue of Victoria debentures, and in 1865 £12,500

[696] Ian M. Drummond, "Canadian Life Insurance Companies and the Capital Market, 1890–1914," *The Canadian Journal of Economics and Political Science*, Vol. XXVIII, No. 2 (May 1962), pp. 205–6. [Hereafter cited as Drummond, "Canadian Life Insurance Companies."] The law was modified again in 1910, "although one really cannot say whether this change was an expansion of insurance companies' powers or a contraction of them."

of Montreal Harbour debentures – and they continued to do so. "These developments can be viewed as the beginning of the local institutional market for new issues, that is, the beginning of the domestic new issues market as we know it today." Also, in what almost certainly constituted one of the industry's most important contributions to the development of the Canadian capital market, almost as soon as it had begun to accumulate reserves, Canada Life began to channel these funds entirely into Canadian securities. British and American companies had invested and continued to invest largely in their own countries; and Canada Life's policy "had the effect of reversing the anomalous position of Canada's (apparently) being an exporter of capital as far as life insurance companies were concerned." Perhaps equally significantly, "it provided an institutional demand for a wide range of credit instruments."[697]

4-3b(3). Building societies, and mortgage and loan companies: In 1910 Joseph Johnson wrote,

> The only other financial institutions in Canada besides the chartered banks, which possess much importance are the mortgage and loan companies. These usually operate under charters granted by the provincial legislatures to do a business similar to farm and mortgage companies which once flourished in the United States, making loans to farmers for a term of years and taking farm mortgages as securities. They also make loans on urban and suburban real estate and thus aid in the upbuilding of the cities and suburbs. The business of these institutions is made possible by the fact that the bank act does not permit the chartered banks to accept loans secured by real estate.[698]

As Table 4:3-3 indicates, building societies and mortgage loan companies accounted for between 10 and 15 percent of the assets of private financial intermediaries in the 1870s and again between 1905 and 1915. In the intervening years, however, they held more than one-quarter of those assets.

Both the building societies and the first of the trust and loan companies date from the 1840s. "In 1843 the Trust and Loan Company of Upper Canada was incorporated by special act of the Canadian Parliament for the express purpose of lending money on the security of real property." Although the Trust and Loan Company successfully solicited funds in Britain and it remained for many years the largest company in the industry, its progress – and that of the industry's – was relatively slow.[699] It was

---

[697] Neufeld, *The Financial System of Canada*, pp. 230, 231.
[698] Johnson, *The Canadian Banking System*, p. 12.
[699] Cox, *Financial Markets and Regional Economic Development*, pp. 52–54. Neufeld, *The Financial System of Canada*, pp. 176, 180–84.

only after the turn of the century that both the company and the industry began to grow in any significant fashion. In 1912 an act (2 Geo. V, cap. 34) allowed trust companies "to take deposits as long as they were regarded as funds taken in trust with repayment and interest guaranteed and, preferably, were not called deposits; and similarly they could take funds in trust for longer periods and issue an instrument which outlined their guarantee, as long as they avoided the name debenture. To the saver, and to the capital market generally, however, the differences in practice between a trust company deposit and a bank deposit, and between a loan company debenture and a guaranteed trust certificate, were negligible."[700] By 1915, armed with these new powers to accept "deposits" and issue "debentures," the industry accounted for almost 3 percent of the assets of Canada's private financial institutions.[701]

The progress of the building societies was much more rapid. The first building society was the Port Sarnia Syndicate. In 1847, after the passage in 1846 of an act to encourage the organization of building societies in Upper Canada, it became the Port Sarnia Building Society. Like the other early societies, it was organized as a terminable building society; that is, the society's life ended when all the members' homes had been built.[702] An 1859 act was important because it permitted the capitalization of shares and legally recognized two of the societies' increasingly common practices: taking deposits and excluding borrowing members from profits. As a result, some societies became joint-stock companies, and terminable societies gradually gave way to permanent ones. In 1873 the Freehold Permanent Building Society was given the right to issue debentures, and that right was soon extended to all permanent building societies in Ontario (37 Vic., cap. 50). Debentures were a credit instrument that could be sold abroad; and, thus, it became possible for societies to begin to solicit British investors, who were attracted by the boom conditions in western Canada (one Quebec company was given monopoly access to the French capital market). "By 1874 the Ontario building societies had in every important respect become loan companies." By 1875 the Canadian building societies or loan companies had $773,000 in outstanding debentures payable in Britain, and thereafter the volume increased rapidly; by 1889 they had $40 million of such securities outstanding. Typically, the building societies approached London or Scottish intermediaries directly in an often successful attempt to recruit them to

---

[700] Neufeld, *The Financial System of Canada*, p. 298.
[701] Dow, *Financial Markets and Regional Economic Development*, pp. 52–54. Neufeld, *The Financial System of Canada*, pp. 176, 180–84.
[702] Neufeld, *The Financial System of Canada*, pp. 185–86.

sell the debentures. The building societies and loan companies were not centralized in Montreal or Toronto, but were to a large extent scattered across the smaller cities in Canada; and their approach to the British investor was usually conducted directly from the smaller cities without the use of Montreal or Toronto middlemen.[703]

The act of 1874 gave the societies access to the British financial market, but it also somewhat restricted their ability to invest in securities. Before that date their investment powers had extended to the common stock of private corporations (at that time the only readily available issues were those of the chartered banks). From 1874 until 1899, however, they were restricted by legislation to "Dominion, provincial, municipal and school securities besides mortgage loans and loans against securities eligible for investment. In 1899 Dominion legislation again permitted investment in chartered bank stock and even in securities of all Canadian and provincially incorporated companies."[704]

Prior to the turn of the century, mortgage loan companies played a very important role in the Canadian financial structure. After the turn of the century, however, their importance declined. That decline can be attributed in large part to three policies: one public and two private. First, although they were allowed to hold securities, the legislation that governed their investment behavior was generally biased toward mortgage lending; and the firms themselves did not aggressively seek investments in paper securities. Second, "they failed to develop adequately their source of funds in Canada during those years when United Kingdom funds were easy to obtain, leaving a vacuum filled by chartered banks, life insurance companies, and trust companies." Third, "they concentrated too heavily and too long on farm mortgage financing at a time when such financing was declining greatly in importance and when financing urban property (including corporate industrial property) was becoming increasingly important."[705]

There was, however, another side to the financial histories of the building society/mortgage loan companies. Their conservative borrowing and loan policies may well have led to their decline; but these policies also meant that, after the early 1870s, there is little evidence of firm failure.

> As early as 1874 the *Monetary Times* reported that "suspension or insolvency of a Canadian building society is something wholly unknown;

---

[703] Code, *The Spatial Dynamics*, pp. 112–13. W.T. Easterbrook, *Farm Credit in Canada* (Toronto: University of Toronto Press, 1938), p. 25. Neufeld, *The Financial System of Canada*, pp. 195–96.

[704] Neufeld, *The Financial System of Canada*, p. 108.

[705] Neufeld, *The Financial System of Canada*, pp. 358, 217–18.

certainly the public outside the stockholders have suffered in no single instance." In 1914 Hume Cronyn, a leading figure in the industry, wrote that "after an experience of seventy years no loan company whose business was confined to mortgage lending has failed to meet all demands, and among those few companies who through gross mismanagement or worse have collapsed, not one had in any sense contributed to its downfall through over-borrowing."[706]

The Australian story was to be very different.

4-3c. The primary and secondary securities markets

Table 4:3-8 indicates that both Canada and the United States had about equal relative concentrations in those industrial sectors – mining, manufacturing, transport and public utilities, and government – that were most likely to require long-term, non-mortgage, external finance.[707] One of the major developments in Canadian finance between 1870 and 1900 was the very rapid increase in the number and volume of the securities of industrial corporations. Data on joint-stock companies incorporated in Ontario and Quebec indicate that the shift from unincorporated to incorporated business was a product of the years after 1885. By 1890, however, the shift was well underway, "and by 1910 it had reached explosive proportions. That was a period of mergers, of takeovers of family enterprises by new corporations, and of rapid industrial development. A by-product of this development was a rise to predominance of industrial securities and with it new opportunities for brokers and underwriters." Their total numbers increased rapidly up to the First World War.[708] Still, it is clear that Canada continued to lag behind the United States.

Even if differential demand accounts for the entire intercountry difference in the ratio of mortgages to all financial assets, it would be difficult to argue that the relative demand for bond and equity finance would be significantly less in Canada than in the United States. Neufeld has shown that, as far as bank and non-bank intermediaries were concerned, the institutional structure in Canada was similar to that of the United States. Those figures, however, do not reflect the fact that, for most of the period, domestic savings rates were much lower in Canada.[709] Thus, if the

---

[706] Neufeld, *The Financial System of Canada*, p. 204.

[707] In both countries those four industrial sectors accounted for about 37 percent of their respective GNPs.

[708] Neufeld, *The Financial System of Canada*, pp. 475–76 and table 14.3, p. 475.

[709] In the United States, gross domestic savings rates were in the 20–25 percent range from at least sometime in the 1870s until World War I. In Canada, although the rate reached more than 20 percent between 1905 and 1914, it averaged only

ratio of the assets of non-bank intermediaries to GNP were similar in the two countries, once adjustment has been made for population differences, there still must have been a marked Canadian-American difference in the absolute quantities of finance directed through the formal capital markets. Such appears to have been the case.

Although the data indicate that, in a statistical sense, the financial structures of the two countries were similar, there was one very important difference: The structure in Canada was younger and less well developed. By 1900 the formal capital markets in the United States had begun to approximate the impersonal markets of the economists' ideal; however, the Canadian markets remained, for at least another decade, much more highly personalized. Drummond, in his analysis of the substitution of mortgages for securities in the portfolios of the bank and non-bank intermediaries concludes, "thus it may be possible to 'explain' the changing placement policies of the companies through an examination of relative yields and supplies of placements. However, on the Canadian scene so 'impersonal' an explanation would be singularly incomplete."[710] In a similar fashion Armstrong and Nelles use the term "the outside village," in contrast to the City, to refer to the Canadian financial community on King Street in Toronto and St. James Street in Montreal.[711]

In 1900 the "village" consisted, roughly, of the six largest banks, half a dozen insurance companies, a handful of the largest building societies and mortgage, savings, and loan companies, three or four trust companies, and about the same number of brokers and investment dealers. It was a very small world.[712] Not only was it small, but it was also highly personal, and kinship, established relations, and interlocking directorates concentrated control of these intermediaries into even fewer hands. Some sense of the small size and close relationships that linked Canadian firms can be gleaned from the personal and spatial concentration of the directors of Canada's 204 largest firms (see Table 4:3-10). On

slightly over 10 percent from 1870 to 1899. Lance Davis and Robert Gallman, "Capital Formation in the United States During the Nineteenth Century," in P. Mathias and M.M. Postan (eds.), *The Cambridge Economic History of Europe. Volume VII: The Industrial Economies: Capital, Labour, and Enterprise*, Part II (Cambridge: Cambridge University Press, 1978), pp. 1–65; see also Table 4:1-5.

[710] Drummond, "Life Insurance Companies," p. 210.

[711] Christopher Armstrong and Henry Vivian Nelles, *Southern Exposure: Canadian Promoters in Latin America and the Caribbean, 1896–1930* (Toronto: University of Toronto Press, 1988), pp. 1–23. [Hereafter cited as Armstrong and Nelles, *Southern Exposure.*]

[712] The six banks controlled more than 40 percent of all commercial bank assets, and the insurance companies accounted for $17 in every $20 of all life insurance written in Canada.

Table 4:3-10. *The forty-two persons holding the most directorships in Canada's 204 largest corporations in 1913*

Name of director	City of residence	Number of firms – Industry –					Total firms	Assets of companies of which the individual was a director (thousands of dollars)
		Financial	Insurance	Transport	Industrial	Other		
Sir Hugh Montagu Allan	Montreal	4	1	2	7	3	17	274,169
R.B. Angus	Montreal	2	0	4	1	1	8	1,432,590
Senator George A. Cox	Toronto	6	4	5	14	0	29	698,959
Senator Nathanial Curry	Montreal	2	0	0	8	0	10	102,135
George E. Drummond	Montreal	2	1	0	7	0	10	162,178
Thoms J. Drummond	Montreal	2	3	2	11	0	18	277,123
Senator W.C. Edwards	Ottawa	2	0	0	3	0	5	310,248
S.H. Ewing	Montreal	3	1	2	5	0	11	132,963
J.W. Flavelle	Toronto	2	0	0	5	0	7	266,979
Sir Rodolphe Forget, MP	Montreal	1	1	5	7	1	15	142,488
Charles B. Gordon	Montreal	1	0	2	0	0	3	276,869
E.B. Greenshields	Montreal	2	0	0	3	0	5	281,612
D.B. Hanna	Montreal	3	3	13	8	1	28	376,286
R.M. Horne-Payne	London, U.K.	0	0	5	1	0	6	398,077
H.S. Holt	Montreal	2	2	3	11	2	20	1,420,567
Charles R. Hosmer	Montreal	2	1	2	14	1	20	1,415,176
Senator Robert Jaffrey	Toronto	3	2	0	5	0	10	211,152
Senator Sir Lyman Jones	Toronto	1	0	0	2	0	3	284,251
Z.A. Lash, KC, LLD	Toronto	2	2	6	2	4	16	769,804
D. Lorne McGibbon	Montreal	1	0	0	4	0	5	36,134
D. McNichol	?	1	0	1	0	0	2	1,049,746

Name	City							
Wilmot D. Mathews	Toronto	3	1	5	5	4	18	1,281,814
Sir Donald Mann	Toronto	0	1	3	1	0	5	263,366
Sir William McKenzie	Toronto	3	1	7	8	1	20	621,639
Senator Robert Mackay	Montreal	2	0	3	13	3	21	1,609,297
S.J. Moore	Toronto	1	1	1	6	0	9	51,345
George A. Morrow	Toronto	3	4	0	3	1	11	60,772
Lieut. Carl F.S. Meighen	Montreal	1	1	0	2	1	6	57,383
Cawthra Mulock	Toronto	2	2	0	2	0	5	106,018
A.M. Nanton	Winnipeg	0	0	3	3	0	8	406,417
Frederick Nichols	Toronto	4	2	7	9	0	18	394,025
Sir Edmund B. Osler	Toronto	2	1	4	0	6	15	1,170,208
Col. Sir Henry Pellatt	Toronto	2	2	6	11	2	23	257,884
J.H. Plummer	Toronto	2	1	3	4	0	10	333,154
James Ross	Montreal	2	0	1	2	0	5	279,482
Rt. Hon Lord Strathcona	Montreal & UK	4	1	1	2	2	10	1,310,137
Sir Thomas Shaughnessy	Montreal	2	0	2	0	1	5	1,373,760
Sir William Van Horne	Montreal	1	1	9	6	3	20	1,425,274
Sir Edmund Walker	Toronto	2	1	1	3	0	7	304,408
Sir William White	?	3	2	2	3	0	10	1,127,203
D.R. Wilkey	Toronto	2	2	0	0	2	6	140,807
E.R. Wood	Toronto	4	3	6	11	0	24	824,148
Average holdings		2.1	1.1	2.8	5.0	0.9	12.0	564,715

Source: J. Castell Hopkins, *Canadian Annual Review of Public Affairs, 1913* (Toronto: Annual Review Publishing Co., 1913), pp. 57–58.

average, the forty-two most active individuals served on the boards of twelve firms with, on average, $564,000 in assets. Moreover, at least thirty-eight of the forty-two resided in either Montreal or Toronto.[713] Although on paper there appears to have been an impersonal financial structure with functionally independent intermediaries in place, most of those institutions were affiliated with one of a few distinct and well-recognized groups of companies and capitalists who did business with each other, sat on each other's boards, and often joined to promote new ventures.

A typical financial group consisted of a large bank, one or two insurance companies, a trust company, and an investment house.[714] In Toronto the most important was controlled by George C. Cox, a senator and president of both the Bank of Commerce, Canada's second largest bank, and of the Canada Life Assurance Company, the largest of its type. In addition, Cox's son-in-law was president of A.E. Ames and Company, one of the largest bond houses; his son was managing director of Imperial Life; and his protégé, E.R. Wood, headed the National Trust. In Montreal it was the directors of the Bank of Montreal, by far the country's largest bank, who integrated and coordinated most of the financial affairs of the metropolitan community. "The Bank of Montreal, bound together in loose alliance the Canadian Pacific Railway, the Sun Life and the Royal Victoria insurance company, the branches of the U.S. and British fire, life, and casualty companies, and the largest cotton manufacturers, shippers, and milling companies." As Armstrong and Nellie write, "The core consisted of approximately forty individuals, known to each other and in a few instances related by marriage. All were bound by mutual obligations and a shared understanding of business conventions." "At the top, then, the capital market was a small tribal village. Hierarchy, strict social conventions, ethnic harmony, and an elaborate code of reciprocal benefits and obligations reigned. The market process was not autonomous or impersonal; rather it was embedded in a complex social matrix."[715] Note that there were very few direct connections linking these groups to the formal securities markets in either Montreal or Toronto. What connections existed were indirect. In many ways a financial group's involvement

---

[713] Code, *The Spatial Dynamics*, pp. 304–5.

[714] The spate of trust companies formed around the turn of the century were each closely associated through interlocking directorships with the chartered banks. For example, the Royal Trust with the Bank of Montreal, the Montreal Trust with the Royal Bank of Canada, and National Trust with the Canadian Bank of Commerce. Dow, *Financial Markets and Regional Economic Development*, pp. 52–54. Neufeld, *The Financial System of Canada*, p. 295.

[715] Armstrong and Nelles, *Southern Exposure*, pp. 6–9, 11; Drummond, "Canadian Life Insurance Companies," p. 211.

with a particular company placed an imprimatur of approval that had an impact on savers similar to that in the United States produced by the decision of an investment bank like J.P. Morgan to underwrite a firm's issue.

The 1907 *Report* of the Royal Commission on Life Insurance provides yet another glance at the operations of these financial groups. In commenting on the investment decisions of the Canada Life Assurance Company, the commissioners wrote,

> The absolute control, residing in the president and general manager [Mr. G.A.Cox], and which his stockholdings and offices secure him, have to a marked extent influenced the investments of the company, which have been made to serve not only the interests of the Canada Life Assurance Company, but also his own interests and the interests of other institutions in which he is largely concerned.... The Central Canada Loan and Savings Company, in which there is a large independent shareholding, is under Mr. Cox's control to such an extent that, to use his own language, we are to treat it as being himself. This company has been very largely interested in the promotion of enterprise of more or less speculative nature, the success of which largely depends on the facilities for carrying and marketing stocks and bonds of those enterprises. Mr. Cox has, from time to time, as he frankly stated, brought about the investment of securities of this description, of the funds of the Canada Life Assurance Company, in aid of transactions in these securities on his own part and on the part of other institutions which he controls.... Upon one occasion ... when he was himself ... largely concerned in maintaining the price of a security of this description, he made use of the funds of the company to purchase the security for the express purpose of strengthening its market price.[716]

In reporting on the investment decisions of the Sun Life, the Commissioners noted:

> It was disclosed in the evidence that the company invested in the securities of a certain undertaking, and portions of these securities were handed over to certain members of the board on the same terms as the company acquired its holdings. It is reasonably clear that by this transaction the members of the board so obtaining these did so on more advantageous terms than would have been possible for them as individuals.... It had to be conceded that, if the investment had turned out to be an undesirable one, it would have been impossible to enforce ... any obligation to take any share in the venture.[717]

---

[716] Royal Commission on Life Insurance, *Report*, 1907, p. 14.

[717] Royal Commission on Life Insurance, *Report*, 1907, pp. 19–20. Both excerpts are reported in Neufeld, *The Financial System of Canada*, pp. 238–39.

Although the American bond and equity markets were still very immature, they were substantially more developed than those to the North. In the United States, by 1870, there already existed much more than an embryonic formal market structure. The New York Stock Exchange, although largely focused on government and transport issues, could trace its roots back at least into the second decade of the nineteenth century; and it could, at least since the mid-1830s, argue that it had at least some of the characteristics of a national exchange.[718] In addition, by the post-bellum decades there were less comprehensive, but partially competitive, exchanges in New York – the Curb and the Consolidated, to mention only two – as well as in such cities as Boston and Philadelphia.[719]

In Canada the exchanges were both younger and smaller. In part, that difference can be traced to the relative economic development of the two countries; but, in large part, it reflects the ready British market for Canadian government and railway issues. For example, in 1870 almost

---

[718] In 1880, for example, of the 128 bond issues admitted to the Exchange's "Official List," 97 were railroad bonds and 21 were government issues. There were only nine that were neither. Lance E. Davis and Robert J. Cull, *International Capital Markets and American Economic Growth* (New York: Cambridge University Press, 1994), Table 4.4. [Hereafter cited as Davis and Cull, *International Capital Markets.*] The original brokers organization that ultimately became the New York Stock Exchange dates from 1792, and the meeting of the stock brokers' for the organization of the present Exchange occurred on February 25, 1817. Edmund Clarence Stedman (ed.), *The New York Stock Exchange: Its History, Its Contribution to National Prosperity, and Its Relation to American Finance at the Outset of the Twentieth Century* (New York: Greenwood Press, 1969 [first published by the Stock Exchange Historical Company in 1905]), pp. 35–36, 62–66. "The biggest bull market thus far in American history began in 1834. By the end of the year, thousand-share days were common at the auctions. During the following year, trading increased five-fold. . . . Although the 1835 fire stopped the auctions for brief periods, it did not interfere with trading, which continued illegally on the streets or in local hotels. When the Exchange reopened new volume records were set and stock ran in short supply. Brokers sent agents to other cities – as far as New Orleans and Charleston – to buy shares to be offered in New York." Robert Sobel, *The Big Board: A History of the New York Stock Market* (New York: Free Press, 1965), pp. 42–43.

[719] Although the Boston Stock Exchange officially dates from 1834, the Boston Stock Market traces its roots back to 1798. Clarence W. Barron and Joseph G. Martin, *The Boston Stock Exchange: With Brief Sketches of Prominent Bankers, Brokers, Banks, and Moneyed Institutions of Boston* (Boston, 1893). Joseph G. Martin, *Seventy-three Year History of the Boston Stock Market: From January 1, 1798, to January 1, 1871* (Boston, 1871). Both are reprinted in Vincent P. Carosso and Robert Sobel (eds.), *The Boston Stock Exchange* (New York: Arno Press, 1975).

10 percent of Dominion debt was held in Canada; by 1914 that figure had fallen to less than one-half of 1 percent.[720] The Dominion Government, for example, "had never borrowed in New York and, in 1914, it had not borrowed at home for many decades."[721] "Both governments and railways could raise capital more easily and cheaply in London than in Toronto or Montreal," and experience with government and railway bonds led to a continual improvement in the British investors' knowledge of Canada. Those lessons in economic geography, in turn, produced an expansion of the British saver's investment horizon to include private non-rail issues.

The availability of Canadian securities in London created a class of British investors who could be persuaded to purchase less well-known Canadian issues; and, as a result, not only was the Canadian securities market bypassed by many potential issues, but it also lost securities for which it provided the initial market. "This process was greatly aided by the migration to London of Canadians, like, for example, J.H. Dunn, who were completely familiar with the Canadian financial environment and who had strong contacts with both British business and investors" and by the movement into Canadian securities of some of a new generation of London merchant bankers – bankers like Arthur Grenfell, the son-in-law of Earl Grey, governor general of Canada. Grenfell's Canadian Agency had by 1914 handled Canadian securities issues that totaled £11.4 million, including £4.2 million of the stocks and bonds of industrial companies. So close were these contacts that in 1907 Grenfell wrote to his father-in-law that "there is no doubt that most Canadians think they have only to arrive in London with ideas and everyone is prepared to fill their pockets with sovereigns."[722] It should not, therefore, have been surprising that when, in 1905, Canadian General Electric found that it could no longer meet its rapidly expanding capital requirements in Toronto and Montreal, it turned to the London market to sell 11,000 shares. It is, perhaps, more surprising that, in 1911, French investors had purchased 6,000 shares of Lake in the Woods Milling.[723]

---

[720] Ranald C. Michie, "The Canadian Securities Market, 1850–1914," *Business History Review*, Vol. 62 (spring 1988). p 38. [Hereafter cited as Michie, "The Canadian Securities Market."]

[721] Ian M. Drummond, "Debt and the Dominion Government, 1914–1820," paper presented at the Economic History Workshop, University of Toronto, December 7, 1992, p. 1. [Hereafter cited as Drummond, "Debt and the Dominion Government."]

[722] Michie, "The Canadian Securities Market," pp. 49–50. It should, however, also be noted that by 1914 Grenfell's firm had gone bankrupt. See Chapter, 2, p. 170.

[723] Michie, "The Canadian Securities Market," p. 46.

Canada was, however, changing. By 1900, if Canadian-registered railways like the Canadian Pacific that were almost wholly foreign owned are excluded, there were 119 joint-stock companies with $277.2 million of paid-up capital. By 1913 those figures had risen to 252 companies with $1.337 billion in paid-up capital. Moreover, while in 1900 banks and other financial intermediaries had accounted for more than 46 percent of the capitalization and mines for another 15 percent, by 1913 financial institutions accounted for less than eighteen and mines for hardly more than 5 percent of the $1.337 billion total. Over the same years the relative position of public utilities had increased from 16 to nearly 40 percent and that of industrial and commercial firms from 22 to 37 percent. It was these companies that provided the foundation for the Canadian formal securities markets.[724]

By 1914 there were formal security exchanges operating in five Canadian cities; but the Vancouver exchange was not chartered until 1907, the Calgary exchange dates from 1913, and, although the Winnipeg Exchange was chartered in 1903, it did not begin to operate until 1909.[725] Thus, for the period under review, the focus is on just two formal securities markets: Montreal and Toronto.[726]

Annual turnover of non-mining stocks on the Toronto Stock Exchange amounted to about 22,000 shares in 1879; that total increased to 340,000 in 1882. Turnover then declined to less than 100,000 shares in 1888, before beginning to increase again. It reached almost 1.7 million shares in 1902; but, despite the fact that the volume remained high by nineteenth-century standards, it never again reached a million before the outbreak of the war.[727] "Unfortunately, there are no comparable statistics for the Montreal Exchange before 1900, but the available evidence suggests a volume of turnover much in excess of that in Toronto. . . . In 1892 Montreal was reported as trading 4–5,000 shares a day, six or seven times Toronto's volume, assuming 300 working days a year."[728] Certainly Montreal remained the larger market in the years after the turn of the century. The annual volume of non-mining shares traded on that

---

[724] Michie, "The Canadian Securities Market," table 1, p. 45, 47.
[725] Huntly W.F. McKay, "The Stock Exchanges of Canada," in David E. Spray (ed.), *The Principal Stock Exchanges of the World: Their Operation, Structure and Development* (Washington, D.C.: International Economic Publishers, 1964), pp. 33–66. [Hereafter cited as McKay, "The Stock Exchanges of Canada."]
[726] There may also have been a small exchange in Quebec; the *Monetary Times* for 1869–70 lists stocks on a Quebec exchange, but it was obviously unimportant, since the exchange is not mentioned elsewhere.
[727] Michie, "The Canadian Securities Market," table 2, p. 58.
[728] Michie, "The Canadian Securities Market," p. 57.

exchange had reached more than 2 million by 1909; and, although it declined slightly below that level in the last prewar year, it totaled more than 10.6 million over the five years 1909 through 1913. Over the first fourteen years of the twentieth century, the volume of equity transactions on the Montreal exchange totaled more than 20 million. In contrast, the Toronto exchange handled 10.4 million; the comparative figures for bonds were $67.2 and $28.1 million.[729]

The evolution of the institutional structure of the two exchanges followed the British and American pattern; however, developments in Montreal usually preceded those in Toronto – an order that reflected the relative importance of the two financial centers. That order of innovation marked the shift from the call-over system – the list of securities was read out at each meeting and each was then traded in turn – to continuous trading, the use of designated areas in the exchange for dealing in specific stocks, and the creation of clearing houses to smooth the process of settling bargains between members. In both markets, however, membership remained small and turnover relatively low; as a result, the brokers had little scope for specialization. There was no development of a body of dealers who were always ready to buy and sell certain groups of securities and so create a ready market that would attract business. On the contrary, frequent complaints were made, by the brokers themselves and others, about the limitations of the market in Canadian stocks, whether traded in Montreal or Toronto.[730]

The increases and the relative volumes were, however, reflected in the increased prices that seats on the two exchanges commanded; and, as might be expected, reflecting the differences in volume, seats on the Montreal exchange were the more expensive. In 1874 a seat on the Toronto exchange was worth about $300. By 1883 the price had risen to $3,500, by 1901 to $6,400, and by 1913 to $16,000. The figures for Montreal for the same years were $800, $4,650, $12,850, and $30,000.[731]

Even then, however, stockbroking was hardly the route to fame and fortune. The *total* income from commissions on the Toronto Stock exchange fell from $24,400 in 1891 to $16,300 in 1894. Thereafter the situation improved, but not by much. Toronto brokers divided $43,200 in 1897 and more than $100,000 in 1901.[732] As Drummond points out, "It is safe to say that . . . the new issues market [for private securities] was quiescent until the new century began."[733]

[729] Michie, "The Canadian Securities Market," table 3, p. 59.
[730] Michie, "The Canadian Securities Market," pp. 64–65.
[731] Michie, "The Canadian Securities Market," pp. 59–60.
[732] Armstrong and Nelles, *Southern Exposure*, pp. 13–14.
[733] Drummond, *Capital Markets in Australia and Canada*, p. 171.

In both Toronto and Montreal organized security dealings grew out of the staple export trade. Trading in Montreal began in 1832 when a stock book was opened at the Exchange Coffee House. Weekly meetings, however, did not commence until the 1850s; it was 1863 before a Board of Brokers was organized and the Board began keeping official minutes. "In that year the Board also outlined commissions, listing fees and rules governing membership. At first the Board met daily between 12:00 and 12:30 in the office of the Board's honorary secretary, but in 1866 they rented an office especially for such meetings." It was, however, 1904 before the Exchange had its own building. In 1872 the Board was reorganized as the Montreal Stock Exchange, and in 1874 that body was incorporated.

In Toronto the Toronto Stock Exchange was organized in 1852, but regular meetings did not begin until 1861. Even then, however, there is a question of how much order the Exchange imposed on the securities market. One observer wrote, "Previous to July 1865, Toronto had a Board of Brokers which had its officers and regular meetings, and which furnished a report of the state of the market. Unfortunately it became a Board in nothing but name. There were brokers, and plenty of them, but each constituted a board in himself – each making the best bargain he could, obtaining the greatest amount of profit possible on each transaction. It opened the way for irregular, and if anyone was so disposed, for dishonest dealings, where one of the parties to the transaction was not fully posted on the state of the market." In 1871 there was a reorganization that created an exchange with daily meetings, daily lists, and a common meeting place. Five years later a scale of brokers commissions was established (0.5 percent on stocks and debentures and 0.25 percent on transactions over $2,000); the organization was formally incorporated in 1878, and in 1881 the exchange moved into permanent quarters.[734]

By 1881 the Toronto market was linked directly to the New York Stock Exchange; and fourteen years later a continuous link was provided, although it was not operated directly but rather from the telegraph office that received quotations by Morse code. "In 1906 its quotations began to be cabled to London and reported regularly in London newspapers, and in 1909 in cooperation with the North West Telegraph Company of Canada it introduced a ticker quotation service." "The Montreal Stock Exchange saw similar developments."[735]

---

[734] Naylor, *The Banks and Finance Capital*, p. 210. McKay, "The Stock Exchanges of Canada," pp. 35–38. Neufeld, *The Financial System of Canada*, pp. 471–72, 476–79. The quotation about the state of the Toronto Board before 1865 is from *The Annual Financial Review of Canada*, July 1901, Vol. 1.

[735] Neufeld, *The Financial System of Canada*, pp. 476–79, 495.

Despite these changes, there is little evidence that the business of the exchanges grew rapidly. In 1865, for example, "the listings in Toronto were for eight banks, two gas companies, three insurance companies, three building societies, plus listings for government and county debentures."[736] Nearly a decade later there had been little change. The Exchange "listed equities of banks, insurance companies, building and loan societies and one gas company. Its bond listings were all railway and city debentures and the Dominion Telegraph. Ten years later its listings were essentially the same, with not a single industrial, and over two-thirds of the business in 1880 was accounted for by bank shares, with most of the rest insurance and loan companies."[737] Nor did the next decade and a half see much change. There were fifty-seven stocks listed in 1886 and fifty-nine in 1895. Moreover, of the fifty-seven, forty-five were the shares of either commercial banks or of building or savings and loan societies; and, of the fifty-nine, forty-eight represented those two financial industries. By 1901, however, the market had begun to show signs of life. The number of listings had risen to eighty, and thirty-eight were identified as either "bonds and debentures" or as "miscellaneous" (see Tables 4:3-11 and 4:3-12).

In Montreal in 1880 the exchange listed the shares of twenty-two banks, seventeen loan and building societies, two telegraphs, two gas companies, a few railroad and government bonds, ten insurance companies, and the equity of four cotton mills. "These were the only industrials."[738] In 1900 commercial banks and savings and loan and building societies constituted 79 percent of all listings, utilities added another 10, but industrials represented a mere 9 and railroad issues only 1 percent (see Table 4:3-12). Clearly, although the exchanges had relatively long histories, they had "never handled very much business or played a key role in the process of capital formation."[739]

Nor did the two markets serve the developing mining industry any better than they did the manufacturing sector. "The Toronto and Montreal exchanges disdained most mining stocks (only two were listed on the Toronto Stock Exchange in 1898)"; however, new markets were soon organized to service the expanding industry. With the Cobalt and Klondike discoveries of the 1890s, two mining exchanges were established in Toronto; and in 1898 they merged to form the Standard Stock

---

[736] Alexander Ross, *The Traders: Inside Canada's Stock Markets* (Toronto: Collins, 1984), p. 57. [Hereafter cited as Ross, *The Traders*.]

[737] Naylor, *The Banks and Financial Capital*, p. 211.

[738] Ibid.

[739] Armstrong and Nelles, *Southern Exposure*, p. 13.

Table 4:3-11. *Toronto Stock Exchange: Number of listings by industry, 1886–1901*

Industry	1886	1891	1895	1901
Commercial banks	11	10	10	12
Building societies & savings & loans	34	39	38	30
Bonds and debentures	2	1	1	2
Miscellaneous	11	10	10	36
Total issues listed	57	60	59	80

Source: John F. Whiteside, *The Toronto Stock Exchange in 1900: Its Membership and Development of the Share Market* (M.A. dissertation, Trent University, 1979), p. 127. Reprinted in C. Armstrong & H.V. Nelles, *Southern Exposure: Canadian Promoters in Latin America and the Caribbean, 1896–1930* (Toronto: University of Toronto Press, 1988), p. 15.

Table 4:3-12. *Ratios of capital called on the British capital market to Canadian gross fixed capital formation, by Sector, 1871–1880 through 1911–1914 (percents)*

Years	Manufacturing	Government	Transportation
1871–1880	0.035	0.644	1.039
1881–1890	0.016	0.526	0.550
1891–1900	0.032	0.137	0.612
1901–1910	0.072	0.291	0.622
1911–1914	0.115	0.473	0.707

Sources: Gross fixed capital formation is from Urquhart, *Gross National Product*, pp. 16–17, "total manufacturing," "government total," and "railroad and telegraph." The data on calls are from the Davis-Gallman tape, "manufacturing, commercial and miscellaneous," "government," and "transport."

and Mining Exchange, an exchange that soon emerged as the "most important mining exchange in the world."[740]

In 1857 seven securities were traded on both the Montreal and Toronto markets; and by 1894 the number – mostly banks – had only increased to fifteen. The next two decades saw more improvement than

[740] Ross, *The Traders*, pp. 58–59. Neufeld, *The Financial System of Canada*, pp. 478–79.

a cursory glance at the listings would suggest. By 1914 the joint listings included fifty-six securities of diverse kinds; however, the data on turnover for 1913 indicate that those diverse securities represented "85 percent of the combined volume of stock transfer business done by the two exchanges." Moreover, rivalries between the two major exchanges helped slow the evolution of a truly national securities market. "The division of the Canadian securities market into two substantial components at Montreal and Toronto was a disadvantage. Communication and cooperation should have ensured that physical separation was of little importance, but in competition with each other for business, each exchange erected barriers against the other. These barriers ranged from the Montreal Exchange's refusal to recognize the validity of Toronto's prices, endorsements signed by Toronto brokers, or Toronto units of transfer to the Toronto Exchange's timing its sessions to withhold business from Montreal, preventing the circulation of Montreal prices among its membership, and discriminating against Montreal in the sharing of commissions with members of other stock exchanges. Trivial and temporary as most of these barriers were, they did prevent the members of both exchanges from coalescing to become one Canadian securities market with two principal locations; instead they remained independent bodies with their own regulations and ambitions."[741]

After the turn of the century, however, there was a change in the scope and size of the formal securities markets, and the anti-industrial bias of the two exchanges began to weaken. Savers were becoming better educated, and there was a growing tendency for Canadian individuals and institutional investors to hold securities as investments. As the managers of the Canadian Bank of Commerce commented in 1902, "During the past five years the people of Canada have grown in wealth at an unprecedented rate, and they have invested their savings in private and public securities to a degree much greater than in the past."[742]

As early as 1902, even if penny mining shares are excluded, the stocks of non-financial companies constituted a majority of the transactions on both exchanges.[743] In 1901, when data are available on both exchanges for the first time, if mining stocks trading for less than one dollar are excluded, estimates indicate that banks and financial institutions represented less than 7 percent to total activity, railways just less than one-quarter, utilities slightly more than half, and industrials and mining shares somewhat less than 10 percent each. Twelve years later the

---

[741] Michie, "The Canadian Securities Market," pp. 61–62, 71–72.

[742] Canadian Bank of Commerce, *Annual Report*, November 30, 1902.

[743] Armstrong and Nelles, *Southern Exposure*, p. 22.

share of financial institutions had declined to less than 5 percent, railways to less than 10, and mining shares to less than 0.5 percent of the total. By that latter date utilities represented almost 45 percent and industrials just less than 40. If penny securities are included, mining shares represented three-fifths of the total in 1901 and one-quarter of that figure in 1913.[744]

In part the initial redirection reflected the British Columbia mining discoveries of the late 1890s, but the long-term change clearly reflected a rising volume of listings and transactions in industrial securities: "During the next fifteen years [after 1897], the Canadian exchanges also acquired a markedly international orientation: several American tramway companies were listed and vigorously traded, there was active dealing in the stocks of the numerous Canadian companies that operated Latin-American utilities, and American investors bought heavily during mining booms."[745] Domestically, the Canadian exchanges dealt extensively in industrial bonds though the larger part of their business was in ordinary shares. "On Canadian exchanges government securities were entirely absent and the turnover was principally in mines, utilities, industrials, and transportation securities. Banks, insurance companies, and loan companies were also listed, but were rarely traded. At the same time mining shares were, at times, extraordinarily active – particularly but not exclusively on the Toronto exchange during the 'Cobalt boom' of 1904–09. At other times they excited relatively little interest, though there was always dealing in the shares of established producing mines."[746]

In the case of commercial and industrial securities, by 1899 Toronto "traded four major industrials – CCM, Commercial Cable, Carter-Crume, and Dunlop Tire." Between 1899 and 1914 the number of industrial "bonds traded rose about two-and-a-half times on both exchanges." In terms of the market for equities, industrials received an added fillip in the years after 1909, when, because of a wave of merger activity, the volume of industrials rose substantially. Between 1909 and 1912, "as businesses merged to produce companies of significant magnitude and permanence to attract investors, 58 mergers took place in the manufacturing industry, involving 275 separate firms with a combined capital of $337 million. Canada Cement, for example, formed in 1909 by the merger of twenty-three firms, was capitalized at $15 million." The result of this wave of mergers was the creation of a number of substantial Canadian corporations – a list that includes Dominion Bridge, Dominion Canners,

---

[744] The data are derived from Michie, "The Canadian Securities Markets," tables 1, 3, 4, 5, 6, 10, pp. 45, 59, 60, 61, 71.

[745] Drummond, *Capital Markets in Australia and Canada*, p. 34.

[746] Drummond, *Capital Markets in Australia and Canada*, pp. 35–36.

Dominion Steel, and Dominion Textile – corporations that were large enough to attract the attention of the Canadian financial groups, and even some British investment bankers.[747] "The industrial merger movement had the effect of introducing widespread industrial stockholding in Canada for the first time, very much as the gold rush of 1896 had for mining stocks."[748] As a result, by 1914 the Canadian formal "securities market was coming to possess certain issues that did generate a large turnover and could easily be sold in time of crisis, like the Rio de Janerio Tramway, Dominion Steel, and the perennial CPR stock."[749]

But just how wide was the wide in widespread? Looked at one way, in the case of equities, by the outbreak of the war, the evidence suggests that the educational level of the typical investor had reached grade six, even if junior high school, high school, and college were still in the future. On the basis of a survey conducted by Fred W. Field in 1914, it was estimated that Canadian shareholders held 75 percent of the common stock outstanding in Canadian non-rail corporations and about one-half of the preferred.[750] In the case of bonds, although the numbers are substantially smaller, in the years after 1900 "Canadian investors greatly increased their share of total bond investments." Between 1900 and 1914 they appear to have purchased about one-fifth of the bonds issued by Canadian public and private entities; but, given the railroads' and the Canadian governments' penchant for looking to London, the figure for private non-rail issues was almost certainly substantially higher.[751] Looked at in another way, the picture appears somewhat less rosy. Although the calculation is highly tentative, Michie puts the total number of Canadian investors who held the stocks and bonds of domestic firms in 1913 at 114,125, or a mere 1.35 percent of the population.[752] In a similar vein, in 1908 J.H. Dunn reported that, for most securities, "the market is so

[747] Michie, "The Canadian Securities Market," pp. 45–46.

[748] Naylor, *The Banks and Financial Capital*, pp. 215–16.

[749] Michie, "The Canadian Securities Market," pp. 53–54.

[750] F.W. Field, "How Canadian Stocks are Held," *The Monetary Times*, January 1915, p. 31. Cited in McKay, "The Stock Exchanges of Canada," p. 34. The survey was based on complete returns from 67 companies: 33 trust loan, and mortgage companies, 12 public utilities, and 22 industrial corporations. After Canada, "Britain was second in both cases and the United States third. According to the survey, the 22 industrial companies had 24,500 shareholders, of whom 11,000 were in Canada, 7,000 in Great Britain, and only 500 in the United States. For the public utility stocks, there were very few shareholders in Great Britain, and the United States accounted for almost as many as Canada. Most of the stock of trust, loan, and insurance companies was held in Canada but was rarely traded. The survey also estimated that one third of all the stockholders were women."

[751] Neufeld, *The Financial System of Canada*, pp. 491, 494, table 14:4, pp. 492–93.

[752] Michie, "The Canadian Securities Market," p. 48.

narrow that one or two buyers can easily advance the price of securities two or three points on very small sales."[753]

Whatever the case, the evidence suggests that there was still a long way to go before the formal capital markets would play a major role in the mobilization of Canadian domestic savings. First, the observed increase in industrial activity did not occur in a market that was likely to soon become a major competitor of New York, let alone London. In 1901 the Montreal Exchange – still the nation's largest – had forty-five members and traded about 7,000 shares a day. Thirteen years later membership had increased to seventy-five, and about 10,000 shares of the 182 stocks on the list changed hands daily. In Toronto at the turn of the century the thirty-five active brokers among the Exchange's forty members dealt in eighty issues; by 1914 the "official list" had expanded, but it still included only 200 issues.[754] Taken together, "in 1913 turnover on both exchanges totaled only 2,976,000 shares and $6,150,000 in bonds during the entire year," and even in the years of greatest turnover (1901 and 1907) only 4.7 million shares changed hands. Moreover, "because these figures include a substantial volume of transactions in very cheap mining shares, even they do not reveal how narrow the markets were."[755] In 1910 turnover on the New York Stock Exchange totaled 164.2 million shares, compared with 0.9 million in Toronto and 2.1 million in Montreal. Even combining the two, Canadian volume was less than 2 percent of that of New York Stock Exchange.[756] Clearly, the formal Canadian securities markets were of relatively minor importance within the Canadian economy at the outbreak of the war. "Neither Montreal or Toronto, separately or together, can be regarded, before 1914, as an independent national security market such as existed in Britain and the United States. They were regional components of a North American market within which New York was the primary influence, and an international securities market for which London was the dominant force."[757]

Moreover, throughout the period both Canadian exchanges remained secondary rather than new issues markets, a further reflection of the personal character of Canadian finance. New issues were almost always underwritten by syndicates whose members were drawn from one of the financial groups. "They and their institutions took large blocks of bonds

---

[753] J.H. Dunn to Dunn Fisher & Co., January 14, 1908. *Dunn Papers*, Public Archives of Canada, Ottawa.

[754] Neufeld, *The Financial System of Canada*, p. 495.

[755] Drummond, *Capital Markets in Australia and Canada*, pp. 36–37.

[756] Michie, "The Canadian Securities Market," p. 72.

[757] Michie, "The Canadian Securities Market," pp. 72–73.

to which bonus stock was attached. Once the promotion was a going concern with earnings to report, the stock could be listed and the bonus stock eased onto a carefully managed market." The finance for the entire operation – underwriting and marketing – was provided by one of the group's "in-house" financial institutions.[758] Although the Canadian "financial press normally used the terminology of London and New York to describe the much smaller events on the local exchanges, the usage can seriously obscure the fact that these markets were extremely thin. For many of the listed securities it is clear that listing itself had brought no significant increase in liquidity," and most securities were relatively illiquid. "One could easily sell large blocks of mining shares, and occasionally one could sell similar blocks of a few utility shares, without turning the market against oneself. But most of the listed securities could not be sold either quickly or easily."[759]

In contrast, in 1900 there were 273 stocks and 590 bonds listed on the New York Stock Exchange; in 1910 more than 650,000 shares and $2.5 million in bonds changed hands daily.[760] Adjusting for population differences, those figures indicate that the New York exchange alone was about three times as active as the two Canadian exchanges and that, taken together, the six most active American exchanges were more than four times as active as their Canadian counterparts.[761] Moreover, domestic issues were not the only focus of the Canadian investor's attention. In the words of the editors of Canada's leading financial newspaper, "the business in American equity done by Toronto and Montreal brokers exceeded that done in Canadian shares."[762]

Still, Naylor to the contrary and notwithstanding, in the years after 1900 there appears to have been a vigorous, although perhaps still relatively small, domestic market for Canadian securities. In 1895 it is estimated that domestic holdings represented 19 percent of total Canadian funded and non-funded debt, and that the figure had risen to 25 percent in 1905, before it declined to 19 percent in 1910 and to just less than 16 percent in 1914.[763] Again, the ratio of Canadian issues purchased domestically to those sold in London in the years 1904–13 ranged from 1.63 in

---

[758] Armstrong and Nelles, *Southern Exposure*, p. 21.

[759] Drummond, *Capital Markets in Australia and Canada*, pp. 36–37.

[760] Davis and Cull, *International Capital Markets and Economic Growth*, tables 4.1, 4.4, and 4.5.

[761] The six – the New York, the Consolidated, the Curb, the Boston, the Philadelphia, and the Chicago – had a daily average of about 960,000 shares.

[762] Naylor, *The Banks and Finance Capital*, p. 216. Naylor cites the *Monetary Times* of May 3, 1918, p. 9.

[763] Drummond, *Capital Markets in Australia and Canada*, table 7, p. 141.

1904 to 0.23 in 1908 and averaged 0.59.[764] Finally, excluding mining issues, between 1900 and 1914 more than $600 million in Canadian private securities were marketed in Canada. Moreover, even the much maligned domestic non-bank intermediaries absorbed 34 percent of the $782 million of private and government issues sold in Canada between 1901 and 1914.[765] Drummond writes, "It is perfectly true that domestic security issues were not large relative to Canadian issues on foreign markets – chiefly but not exclusively on the London market. No doubt this obvious difference has been largely responsible for creating the impression that nothing was happening on the Canadian market; faced with enormous London flotations, scholars have naturally tended to overlook the much smaller issues at home. But even here the relative size of the domestic issue-flow is much larger than might be expected."[766]

How, then, can this apparent contradictory evidence about the level of penetration of the formal security markets be explained? The answer is relatively straightforward: There was one important difference between the financial structures of Canada and the United States, and that structural difference, although only slightly altering the savers' educational curriculum, did limit the role played by the formal securities markets in the capital mobilization process. Again, as with the process of underwriting and distributing new issues, the difference was rooted in the still highly personalized nature of the Canadian capital market.

In Canada specialized bond dealers – a financial institution with no American counterpart, but soon an integral part of each "financial group" – evolved during the 1890s. Over time those dealers handled increasingly larger portions of the total volume of bond transactions, and those purchases and sales completely bypassed the formal markets. In the first decade of the twentieth century, the rapid increase in the number of bond dealers reflected the great acceleration in the volume of bond financing. "While bonds were traded on the stock exchanges, the exchanges did not really lend themselves to initial distribution of municipal issues, that is bond underwriting, and to dealing in the large number of relatively small and diverse bond issues. Bond underwriting actively developed quite separately from the exchanges, direct dealings between bond dealers and bond investors became increasingly important, and so the 'over-the-counter' market in bonds began to replace trading in bonds on the stock exchanges."[767]

---

[764] Drummond, *Capital Markets in Australia and Canada*, table 3, p. 191.
[765] Drummond, *Capital Markets in Australia and Canada*, tables 1 and 2, pp. 172 and 184.
[766] Drummond, *Capital Markets in Australia and Canada*, p. 190.
[767] Neufeld, *The Financial System of Canada*, pp. 502–3.

The Canadian exchanges had always listed and traded bonds and debentures; but, despite the fact that the two markets' trading volume in debt instruments reached a peak in 1919 – $71.6 million were traded on the Montreal and $60.5 million on the Toronto Exchange – the handwriting was already long on the wall. By 1900 the specialized dealers had begun to cut significantly into the exchanges' bond business; and as that trend continued unabated, the volume traded on the exchanges quickly declined to near insignificance.[768] In fact, Huntly McKay, writing about the Toronto Exchange in 1964 notes that "there are no bond or debenture issues listed on the Exchange, or on any other exchange in Canada."[769]

The bond houses are not an example of sudden institutional invention; instead they were the product of a gradual evolution, as an institution initially designed for one purpose took on a new shape and a new function. At the end of the process the bond houses were, in fact, new institutions, but their emergence was not the product of a sudden new invention and innovation.

Although they did not emerge as mature institutions until the last decade of the nineteenth century, the elements were in place before that time. The chartered banks had conducted a bond business at least since Confederation, and Montreal and Toronto brokers had begun buying and selling government bonds and stocks in large blocks soon thereafter. Because of the Provincial and Dominion governments' increasing preference for foreign funds, however, it was the Canadian municipalities' voracious appetite for funds to underwrite overhead investment that really underlay the growth and ultimate importance of the new institutions. In the years after the turn of the century, Canadian municipal issues totaled $309 million. Of that total $92 million were taken up in Canada. "Even in 1913 – a year of 'stringency' – Canadians took up $25 million in new municipal bonds."[770] Because of the limited chronological scope of his study, Drummond concluded that "To handle the flood of municipal debentures no institutional innovation was required – merely an enormous expansion of the existing institutional framework for long term municipal borrowing."[771] In fact, however, the new institution was quite different from the structure that existed before the mid-1880s.

---

[768] Neufeld, *The Financial System of Canada*, pp. 479, 486, 502–3.

[769] McKay, "The Stock Exchanges of Canada," p. 46.

[770] "Almost all Dominion loans, and most provincial loans, were floated abroad during the twenty years before 1914." Drummond, *Capital Markets in Australia and Canada*, pp. 142, 149.

[771] Drummond, *Capital Markets in Australia and Canada*, p. 152.

At the same time that the Canadian municipalities had begun to market their issues in a more structured fashion, there was also an increase in the volume of securities issued by private non-railroad firms.[772] To handle, first, the municipal offerings and then the private issues required a very significant expansion and a major restructuring of the existing system. "The emergence of specialized bond dealers was an important aspect of the development of underwriting facilities in Canada. They emerged both as quite new institutions, taking advantage of the acceleration of government and corporate issues that were coming on the market in the 1890s, and through the transformation of stock brokers and mortgage loan companies into investment dealers that carried on an extensive bond business as well as stock brokerage business."[773] Expansion required substantial financial support; but once the necessary finance was forthcoming, it was relatively easy to redirect a part of the activities of the newly established bond houses from municipals to private offerings.

Initially, the system used to distribute the securities generated by the new ventures that they had underwritten was the weakest link in the financial structure of the financial groups; and the new investment, or bond, houses were originally designed to strengthen those ties. The first bond houses – natural extensions of the wholesaling activities of the bond brokers – antedate the 1895 benchmark. The Central Canada Loan and Savings was founded in 1884 by G.A. Cox; and Ames and Company's role as investment bankers dates from 1889 – note again that Ames was Cox's son-in-law – when the firm underwrote its first industrial issue ($300,000 of Dunlop Tire and Rubber Company 7 percent preferred stock). After 1895, with the financial groups' encouragement and monetary support, the number of firms in the new industry increased rapidly. Most of the new firms were established by men who had close connec-

---

[772] "It used to be that a municipal treasurer, when he wanted to borrow $10,000 or $15,000 by the issue of debentures, would get the by-law passed and the debentures printed and signed on rather poor paper, and most of the debentures filled in with pen and ink, put them under his arm and come to Toronto and try to negotiate a sale with the banks or some other people who were known to be buyers. When he made his deal with banker or broker, of which latter there were perhaps three in the City of Toronto, he would go over to the solicitor and make a declaration required by the solicitor, the solicitor would give his legal opinion and the man would get his check and the deal was closed." C.H. Burgess, "Growth of Government and Municipal Financing in Canada," *Monetary Times Annual*, Vol. 78 (January 7, 1927), p. 156. Cited in Neufeld, *The Financial System of Canada*, p. 485.

[773] Neufeld, *The Financial System of Canada*, p. 486.

tions to the Toronto and Montreal financial networks. In Toronto, in addition to Ames, Cox's protégé, E.R. Wood founded Dominion securities; and W.H. White and F.H. Deacon, both from the same Methodist circle as Cox, established firms that were to become important distribution centers.[774] In Montreal it was the Hanson Brothers, E. Mackay Edgar, and F.J. Forget who operated the new bond houses, but they could not have succeeded without the financial support of the Bank of Montreal group. In 1902 a group of Halifax capitalists organized the Royal Securities Corporation, a holding and investment company, and hired Max Aitken, later Lord Beaverbrook, to operate it. In 1906 Aitken moved the company to Montreal, "and it almost immediately became the leading underwriter of industrial issues arising from mergers, reorganizations, and new ventures."[775] In both cities, Toronto and Montreal, the groups' insurance companies, banks, and savings and loans provided funds for the initial acquisitions and for the call loans that were required if the secondary markets were to operate.[776]

---

[774] Fred Deacon represents a good example of the new entrepreneur. With the encouragement of his Methodist associates he dropped out of college in 1897 and began to sell short- or medium-term debentures of Toronto-based loan and mortgage companies in rural Ontario. Through his friendship with Ames he became involved with a series of financial ventures in which the Cox institutions were involved: São Paulo Tramway Light & Power, Toronto Railway, Twin City Rapid Transit, and similar utilities in Detroit and Duluth. By 1905 he had accumulated $100,000 and had moved his base to Toronto. By 1914, and by his own estimate, he was a millionaire. John T. Saywell, "F.H. Deacon & Co., Investment Dealers: A Case Study of the Securities Industries, 1897–1945," *Ontario History*, Vol. XXXV, No. 2 (June 1993), pp. 167–91.

[775] The firm underwrote, among others, the issues of the "Porto Rico Railway Co., the Canadian Power and Calgary Power Companies, the Standard Ideal Company of Port Hope, the Robb Engineering Company, the Cape Breton Trust Company, the Montreal Trust and Deposit Company, the Camoguey Electric and Traction Company. He [Aitken] merged the Rhodes Curry Company, the Dominion Car and Foundry Company, and the Canadian Car Co. to form the Canadian Car and Foundry Company with a capital of $20 million. He formed the Western Canadian Power Company in 1909 which acquired the Slave Lake Power Co. Ltd.; he formed Steel Co. of Canada with nominal capital of $35,000,000 and under it amalgamated Hamilton Steel and Iron Co., Montreal Rolling Mills Co., Canada Screw Co., Dominion Wire Manufacturing Co., and Canadian Nut and Bolt Co.; and then in the most spectacular and notorious move of all – merging the thirteen cement companies to form the Canada Cement Company." Neufeld, *The Financial System of Canada*, pp. 488–89.

[776] In Montreal the leading investment dealers at the turn of the century were L.J. Forget and Company, Hanson Brothers, R. Wilson Smith, McCuaig and Rykert, Burnett and Company, and McDougall Brothers. The leading Toronto firms were A.E. Ames and Company, A.P. Burritt, Ferguson and Blaikie, Aemilius Jarvis and

"Canada certainly generated money that could be employed in such a fashion, especially with the large requirement for cash at harvest time and its redundancy at other periods. It is also clear that these funds were being employed to finance security purchases and holdings in Canada, though it is difficult to get precise figures"; and the financial groups were particularly well placed to direct those flows. In the case of the Canadian Bank of Commerce, for example, from 1874 to 1879 loans against securities in Canada averaged just under $0.6 million. By the years 1895–1900, that figure had risen to $3.2 million annually, "by which time 72 percent were in the form of call or short-term loans. From 1898 to 1913, Canadian Bank of Commerce call and short-term loans, for all purposes, averaged $6.6 million annually, most of it probably to brokers with securities as collateral. In addition to the banks, an increasing number of Canadian financial institutions, such as insurance, savings and loan, and trust companies, began lending on call to brokers."[777]

Although the bond houses could not have grown as they did without that financial support, they also gained from very large increases in the number of new issues of the nation's cities, their original clients. Municipalities across the continent competed for funds. Not surprisingly, Montreal and Toronto readily sold their bonds either on the London Stock Exchange or on the over-the-counter market in New York; and they would have still have been able to effect those sales, "even if no domestic financial institutions had existed." "In 1906, for example, the Montreal brokerage firm of J.H. Dunn & Company advised its London associates, Dunn Fisher & Company, that we have not been able to obtain any offer-

Company, H. O'Hara and Company, John Stock, Osler, and Hammond, Pellatt and Pellatt, F.H. Deacon, and George Stimson and Company. Armstrong and Nelles, *Southern Exposure*, pp. 10–11, 14, 21–22.

Questions were raised about the relationship between the bond houses and the supporting intermediaries. The report of the Royal Commission on Life Insurance, in commenting on Cox's use of life insurance premiums to underwrite and accommodate stock market operations in Dominion Coal, Twin City Traction, Toronto Railway, Imperial Rolling Mills, Union Electric, São Paulo Traction, and Shawinigan Power securities, notes that "In many of these transactions the conflict of Mr. Cox's interest with his duty is so apparent that the care of the insurance funds could not always have been the sole consideration." Royal Commission on Life Insurance, *Report* (Ottawa: King's Printer, Sessional Paper No. 123a, 1907), p. 17.

[777] Michie, "The Canadian Securities Market," p. 51. The business was very good for the financial groups. "The return on New York call loans was significantly less than the same loans in Canada, and it was also more volatile. Between 1901 and 1913, for example, call loans in New York yielded an average annual return of 3.65 percent, ranging from 7.68 in 1906 to 1.9 percent in 1908, whereas call loans in Montreal yielded an average 5.3 percent, with a peak of 6.26 in 1913 and a low of 4.21 in 1909" (p. 52).

ing of City of Toronto 5% bonds 1919/20. We believe these bonds were practically all held on your side and there were none offering here and there have been no dealing with them at all recently."[778] Again, three-quarters of all of the long-dated bonds that the city of Toronto issued in 1913 were taken either by the London merchant bankers (41 percent) or by Harris & Company, New York bankers and brokers (34 percent), leaving most of the remainder to small local investors like the Grand Ontario Lodge with $15,000 or Ontario Securities with $6,326.

What was true for Toronto and Montreal, however, was not true for many, "particularly the newer western cities where the desire to create social capital was particularly strong" and where "the municipalities were scattered and not equally trustworthy," those cities needed an institutional intermediary to signal potential buyers of their credit worthiness. The large blocks of municipal bonds that the London and New York markets were likely to accept "were those least likely to possess an active secondary market; the small issues, of limited duration, and often from obscure towns, characteristics that encouraged their retention until redemption rather than their use as more liquid assets."[779] Like the United States, but unlike Australia, after 1885 there were no federal or provincial government guarantees for Canadian municipals; and, even in Canada, the typical saver knew little about such strange-sounding places as Moosejaw and Saskatoon. Domestic savers, like their British counterparts, were still unwilling to purchase those issues without some further imprimatur of quality.

By 1909, however, "a Canadian municipality could expect to receive about twelve bids for an offering of securities. There were about fifty Canadian bond houses in the market as well as some dozen Canadian banks, insurance companies, and trust companies. It is interesting to note that despite the level of municipal sales, those securities were never listed on any domestic stock exchange. It is not clear why those markets did not handle the city issues, but it is clear that the existing arrangement further magnified the role of the bond houses. In the absence of a listing on an exchange, the dealers could not feed the securities 'gradually on to an impersonal market,' but had to sell each debenture by personal negotiation. Early in our period [1895–1914] this necessity had led to the growth of a nationwide sales network – and to the forming of close ties with insurance companies."[780] The bond houses' stamp of quality convinced Canadian savers of the value of municipal issues, and it also

[778] J.H. Dunn to Dunn, Fischer & Co., October 25, 1906. Dunn Papers, Public Archives of Canada, Ottawa.

[779] Michie, "The Canadian Securities Market," p. 40.

[780] Drummond, *Capital Markets in Australia and Canada*, pp. 56–57, 142–43, 149–52.

appears to have affected the views of British savers as well. In December 1910 twenty-eight issues of fourteen Canadian cities were traded on the London Stock Exchange. Although the list included Montreal, Toronto, and Quebec City, it also included Calgary, Edmonton, Hamilton, Regina, St. John, Saskatoon, Sherbrooke, Vancouver, Victoria, Winnipeg, and Woodstock, names that were hardly household words in the United Kingdom.[781]

It is not surprising that, once established, and given that they were largely free of legal or customary restrictions, the bond houses were willing and able "to move massively into the corporate securities markets whenever the prospective speculative or investment returns were sufficiently favorable."[782] Nor is it surprising that, like their second cousins, the American investment banks, they sometimes helped induce an increase in the supply of securities.

In the case of the shift into corporate securities, it is reported, for example, that "from 1900 through 1905 Dominion Securities Corporation, then the largest bond house in the country, 'purchased entire issues to the par value of $9,301,000, and participated in the purchase of, and had the selling rights on the Canadian market of, $38,767,000, or a total of $48,077,000.' "[783] Moreover, in the thirteen years after it was founded, the firm sold at least $100 million in industrial as well as approximately $15 million in municipal bonds. Despite that record, its performance was ultimately overshadowed by that of the Aitken's Royal Securities Corporation. The turnover of the Royal Securities Corporation was the largest in Canada during the last decade before the war, and its nationwide marketing organization "soon came to include a London branch."[784] The substantial and steady market for municipal securities – a result, in part, of the absence of any significant domestic funded debt – "provided the bond houses with assured though limited income and with contacts through which industrial issues could be distributed and the call money for carrying them obtained."[785]

In 1900, not only was capital still highly personal, but the entire financial network, although giving the outward appearance of a modern

---

[781] *Investors Monthly Manual*, No. 12, Vol. 40, December 1901, pp. 722–24.

[782] Drummond, *Capital Markets in Australia and Canada*, p. 243.

[783] These issues are said to exclude all industrial issues and all issues of Canadian corporations whose operations were overseas. They may or may not include the issues of public utilities. The quote is from George A. Cox, president of the Canadian Bank of Commerce, the Dominion Securities Corporation, and Canada Life. Drummond, *Capital Markets in Australia and Canada*, p. 151.

[784] Drummond, *Capital Markets in Australia and Canada*, pp. 207–8.

[785] Drummond, *Capital Markets in Australia and Canada*, p. 175.

impersonal institutional structure, still retained a highly personal flavor. As with the American investment bankers in the late nineteenth century, there were monopoly profits to be earned by providing an imprimatur of safety for bond and stock issues. In Canada, however, those profits were captured by the members of the financial groups who first innovated and then used their connections with "in-house" intermediaries to finance the operations of the "new" bond houses.

Despite the systems' deviation from "perfection," both Ian Drummond and Christopher Armstrong and H.V. Nelles have concluded that, despite some obvious conflicts of interest, the system was relatively efficient. Given the constraint imposed by small size and the close personal ties that marked the relationships between the major actors, it was perhaps the best that could have been achieved. Armstrong and Nelle write, "Bank and insurance company executives played a leading role in financing new ventures. There was nothing sinister or devious about this process. Indeed, given the small size of the Canadian market and the rather narrow band of investors, something like this socially sanctioned conflict of interest was necessary for a wider market to come into being at all."[786] Ian Drummond adds, "Of course the personal relationships could often raise the costs of finance or reduce the supply so far as outside borrowers were concerned." Those firms and individuals could use the services of a tied bond house, and they might eventually place their securities with one of the "in-house" insurance companies, but the terms were almost certainly relatively unfavorable.

> An economist might, therefore, conclude that the system produced distortions and misallocations; and it almost certainly did. Given, however, the lack of a smooth functioning capital market, it is difficult to conclude that, despite some degree of imperfection, the system performed more poorly than any alternative that was then available. Personal contacts and influence did not prevent the significant intersectoral reallocation of insurance accruals, they did not prevent companies from exploring and capitalizing on new alternatives when mortgage interest rates declined, and they did not prevent the redirection of capital to western agriculture development nor keep firms like Toronto Power or the Canadian Northern Railway off the London new issues market.

As in the American case, the existence of the London Stock Exchange – to say nothing of the formal markets in Montreal and Toronto – limited the monopoly power of the bond houses and their supporting financial groups. Thus, "one might conclude that though the capital

---

[786] Armstrong and Nelles, *Southern Exposure*, p. 22.

market was not formally efficient or highly articulated, it functioned reasonably well in the allocation of resources both between the sectors of the Canadian economy and within the industrial sector."[787]

Although there were no legal limitations on the activities of the bond houses, there appear to have been either economic or cultural constraints on the type of finance that they provided. Perhaps because of their experience, perhaps because of the biases of the contacts that they had developed in their municipal bond business, perhaps because of their customers' desire for "safe" investments, or perhaps because of the potential windfall profits from the sale of the common stock issues that were often given to the house as a bonus for their services, the bond houses traditionally limited their activities to bonds and preferred stocks. As a result, a disproportionate share of external finance in Canadian industry was bond-financed. Between 1900 and the end of 1914, issues of ordinary shares totaled $179 million, while the sale of preference shares produced $64 million and bond issues $260 million. "These bonds came from all sorts of firms, and neither the firms nor the issues were necessarily large. It was perfectly practicable to dispose of a fifty-thousand dollar issue, and it was also possible for a closely held private company to obtain external finance by a public offering of their bonds."[788] Since new companies were almost always financed by the sale of preferred stock or bonds through the intermediation of the bond houses, there was less need for ordinary share finance. Established companies raised share capital cheaply by offering new shares to their stockholders, and by 1913 these "rights" were bought and sold on both large Canadian exchanges. Before 1901 such rights had never been bought or sold on either the Toronto or the Montreal Stock Exchanges; but in 1913 they accounted for 1.3 percent of trades on the Toronto and 13.1 percent of the trades on the Montreal exchange.[789]

Like the American investment bankers in the 1880s and 1890s, the Canadian bond houses, "hungry for inventory," at the end of the first decade of the present century began to promote business mergers. The lag between developments in the United States and the parallel developments in Canada in part reflect the slower growth of the commercial and industrial sector in the latter country. In part, however, it also reflects the absence of second-generation (to say nothing of third-generation) investment banks. In some sense the explicit and implicit government

---

[787] Drummond, "Canadian Life Insurance Companies," p. 222.
[788] Drummond, *Capital Markets in Australia and Canada*, p. 176.
[789] Michie, "The Canadian Securities Exchange," table 10, p. 71.

guarantees of the nation's railroads made such innovations unnecessary. As a result, a somewhat different institution – the bond house – had to be invented and innovated; and that institution's roots were in the 1880s rather than in the 1860s and early 1870s. In fact, it is not clear how much the slower growth of the commercial and industrial sector can be attributed to the lack of formal institutional support in the financial markets. "Naturally these many mergers involved principally the industrial sector of the economy." There had been mergers before 1909, particularly in bicycles, fish-packing, textiles, furniture, and public utilities; "but not until 1908 when call money was plentiful and cheap and when Canadian financiers had observed and learned from their American mentors, did a concentrated assault on the industrial structure begin. The earlier mergers had generally been arranged by firms which entered into combinations; after 1908 an 'external' promoter generally began the work and carried it through." In most instances the external promoter was a member of one of the financial groups. There were mergers in the capital-intensive industries – trams and electric power companies – in industries serving the expanding agricultural economy – milling companies, meat packers, and dairies – and in shipping companies operating on the Great Lakes.

> During the boom years before 1914, Toronto and Montreal bond houses and promoters created seventy-seven mergers, large and small. Most of these mergers were floated between February 1909 and January 1913 – a three year period during which 248 companies were united into fifty-six consolidations. These merged concerns were capitalized at $456,938,266, including their bond issues; the public was asked to subscribe for forty issues which summed to $57,346,666, while almost $400,000,000 went to the owners of the merging companies, to the proprietors, and into other hands by private placement.[790]

Despite the relatively late start, by 1914 Canadian investors had gradually come to recognize the value of pieces of "symbolic capital." In Great Britain the process of investor education had been greatly speeded up by the experience of savers with the bonds issued by the British government during the Napoleonic Wars, and it had been reenforced during the Hudson railway mania of the 1830s and 1840s. In the northern United States a similar acceleration can be traced initially to the educational role played by the 5–20's issued by the federal government during the Civil War and to the reinforcement provided, first, by the postwar transcontinental railroad boom and, later, by the energetic efforts of J.P. Morgan

---

[790] Drummond, *Capital Markets in Australia and Canada*, pp. 178–79, 209–11.

and the other, particularly the American third-generation, investment bankers before, during, and after the "Great Merger Movement."

In Canada the scenario was somewhat different. Given the typical Canadian railway's dependence on direct and indirect government support and the proclivity of those roads to look abroad for funds, the railroads appear to have played only a minor role in the process of domestic investor education.[791] Similarly, although both the provinces and the Dominion governments were heavy borrowers, they also tended to look to London for the vast majority of their financial needs.[792] Thus, the initial educational impetus appears to have been the product of the financial groups – those groups working through their bond houses – attempting to expand the size and scope of their business. As investors became used to holding pieces of paper, capital became less personalized. As the monopoly profits began to erode, the system itself became somewhat less personal; and the institutions began to adopt a more market-oriented outlook. In the case of the "in-house" insurance firms, for example, by 1914, despite a fourfold increase in assets over the previous decade and a half, the absolute level of call loans had declined to less than 45 percent of its 1899 level; and, those loans' share of the firms' total assets had fallen from more than 8 to less than 1 percent. In addition, not only did those insurance companies begin to hold securities as long-term investments; but they also no longer turned

[791] For example, although the one Canadian Railway with a minimum of government involvement, the Canadian Pacific, was financed almost entirely with equity issues, it is estimated that Canadians contributed no more than a fifth of the total. Drummond, *Capital Markets in Australia and Canada*, p. 178.

[792] Drummond argues that, in the case of the Dominion, it was culture not economics that underlay their behavior; that is, they chose London even when domestic rates in Canada were competitive. "Furthermore and in spite of the competing attractions of direct investment, domestic finance was not always more expensive than London finance. Indeed, in 1911 and 1912 Ontario found it cheaper, while in 1909 it was no more costly." "Further it was shown that the Canadian government was obliged to borrow so heavily overseas only because it failed to exploit the potentialities of the domestic market. In other words, the senior Canadian governments went to London from choice, not solely from necessary" [sic]. In 1895 only 3 percent of Dominion and 17 percent of provincial debt was payable in Canada. In 1914 the figures were 0.2 and 12 percent. Drummond, *Capital Markets in Australia and Canada*, chapter 5, pp. 116–68. The quotations are from pp. 125 and 168, and the data from table 1, p. 117.

More likely, however, the governments recognized the thinness of the Canadian market; and they understood that even if, on the margin, rates were similar, the intramarginal rates in Canada were much higher given the scale of government borrowing; and it was the intramarginal rates that were relevant for very large issues.

exclusively to "their" bond houses, but, increasingly shopped for the "best deal."[793]

That initial impetus was, however, very strongly reenforced – but only reenforced – by the experience of domestic savers with the bonds that the Dominion government issued to finance World War I when the British market disappeared.[794] The war and the associated demand of the government for additional finance clearly had a major impact on the process of investor education. Some measure of just how far the educational process was speeded up by those events can be found in the history of the Canadian war loans. The Dominion had always been heavily dependent on London; it had never borrowed in New York; and it had not borrowed at home for many decades. Thus, it was with great trepidation that the government agreed, in 1915, to attempt to market the first war loan domestically. Between then and 1919 (the third "Victory Loan") there were a total of six such loans. The sequential response – a response in both terms of funds subscribed and the number of subscribers – provides evidence of the increasing educational levels of Canadian savers. In 1915, 24,862 subscribers offered to buy $78.73 million, an over-subscription of 57 percent; in 1916 the figures were 34,526, $169 million, and 69 percent; in 1917, 41,263, $200.8 million, 34 percent; in the fall of 1917 (1st Victory Loan), they were 820,035, $420 million, and 180 percent; in 1918, 1,139,247, $674 million and 69 percent; and, finally, in 1919 – a year after the end of the war – there were still 830,602 subscribers willing to pledge $682 million.[795]

Drummond concludes that "the facts should be sufficient to dispel the myth that there was no new issue market in Canada until the war-bond issues magically created one out of thin air." He goes on to argue that Buckley was wrong when he concluded that, "until the expansion of the bond market during the war, the domestic mortgage market was the most important market for the financing of durable capital formation in the country. In the post-war period the bond market assumed a new function. Bonds became a favorite instrument in the financing of new firms and the refinancing of old firms in manufacturing and trade. The sociological basis of an adequate market for new issues did not appear."[796]

---

[793] Drummond, "Canadian Life Insurance Companies," pp. 214, 216.

[794] For a discussion of the role of War finance in the development of the bond market, see Neufeld, *The Financial System of Canada*, pp. 505–7.

[795] Ian M. Drummond, "Debt and the Dominion Government, 1914–1920."

[796] Drummond, *Capital Markets in Australia and Canada*, p. 187. The quotation is from Kenneth Buckley, *Capital Formation in Canada 1896–1930* (Toronto: University of Toronto Press, 1956), p. 62.

Perhaps it is more correct to conclude that Buckley was half wrong. On the one hand, there was certainly a new issues market in place; and some Canadian investors had displayed a willingness to hold those paper claims on assets. On the other hand, the proportion of all domestic public and private bonds that were absorbed in Canada had averaged only 18 percent between 1904 and 1914; but the figure had risen to 67 percent by 1920.[797]

4-4. Conclusions

In the years between Canadian Confederation and World War I, the world economy passed through two clearly distinguishable periods. The first, extending to the mid-1890s, was a time of declining prices and, for many economies, chronic unemployment and slackened growth. From the mid-1890s until World War I, prices trended upward, real interest rates drifted downward; rates of investment improved, economic growth quickened, and world trade expanded.

For the Canadian economy the contrast between the first and the second periods was more pronounced than for most of economies that were marked by these general movements. During the first stage Canadian performance was robust by the standards of that period, or, for that matter, by almost any set of standards. Population, real GNP, and real GNP per capita increased rapidly. Gross domestic savings rates ran 8 to 12 percent – levels that placed them well below the levels achieved by the United States, but not below those observed in Europe. It was, however, not domestic savings alone that funded the substantial amounts of Canadian domestic capital formation that took place during the period. Foreign savings made up almost half of the resources that were directed toward domestic projects; and the chief suppliers were savers in Great Britain. Investment came both in the form of direct acquisition of Canadian productive assets and in the purchase of Canadian securities placed on foreign securities markets, especially the London market (see Table 4:4-1). By the mid-1890s foreign claims on Canadian assets, in dollar terms, were one-third to one-half again as large as the country's GNP; and, as the flow data indicate, they were probably half the value of the Canadian capital stock. The contrast with the United States – where foreign investment represented less than 10 percent of the capital stock – is very striking.

In the second stage – from the mid-1890s until World War I – the Canadian economy's performance dwarfed its hitherto robust pace:

---

[797] Neufeld, *The Financial System of Canada*, table 14.4, pp. 492–93. In the years 1940–45 the percentage had reached 98.3.

Table 4:4-1. *Canadian securities listed on the London Stock Exchange*

	December 1910			December 1900			December 1890		
	Number of gov'ts. or firms listed	Number of debt issues listed	Number of equity issues listed	Number of gov'ts. or firms listed	Number of debt issues listed	Number of equity issues listed	Number of gov'ts. or firms listed	Number of debt issues listed	Number of equity issues listed
	25	63	0	14	47	0	12	46	0
	26	57	10	18	42	12	26	50	9
	5	0	5	3	0	3	3	0	3
	6	7	7	4	3	2	0	0	0
	13	5	18	10	3	15	13	3	13
	7	4	3	4	2	3	4	0	4
	1	0	1	2	0	2	1	0	1
	83	136	44	55	97	37	59	99	30

	December 1880			December 1870		
	Number of gov'ts. or firms listed	Number of debt issues listed	Number of equity issues listed	Number of gov'ts. or firms listed	Number of debt issues listed	Number of equity issues listed
	13	13	0	3	9	0
	14	13	9	4	9	9
	2	0	2	2	0	3
	0	0	0	0	0	0
	7	0	7	5	0	5
	0	0	0	0	0	0
	3	0	3	1	0	1
	39	26	21	15	18	18

Source: Investor's Monthly Manual, December 1870, 1880, 1890, 1900, 1910.

population, real investment, real GNP, and real GNP per capita
expanded at exceptionally rapid rates. The record was remarkable, not
only by previous Canadian standards, but also by the standards of the
rest of the developing world including, perhaps surprisingly, the neighboring United States. The economic boom flowed from the buoyant
market for wheat that supported the nation's expansion into the prairies,
but wheat was by no means the full story. The manufacturing sector was
growing and modernizing; the nation began to supply the American
economy with a substantial fraction of its lumber and newsprint; and the
flow of minerals from the ground to refineries in both Canada and the
United States increased.

On the supply side the boom was supported, and its potential
exploited, by a very large increase in domestic investment. Once again,
foreign resources played a major role. This time, however, while the
British still retained the title role, American and European Continental
investors had joined the cast as more than bit players. The Americans
specialized in a wide range of direct investment; and, although the other
foreigners invested in a wide array of projects, they were particularly
interested in railways and government securities.

Although the savings of foreigners were certainly crucial to Canadian
investment, in the years after the mid-1890s domestic savings rates rose,
and Canadian savers assumed more responsibility for underwriting
Canadian investment. Perhaps the most interesting, and as yet still unanswered, question that arises out of this chapter of Canadian history
involves the explanation of the dramatic rise in savings rate. A part of
the answer probably lies in the demographic structure of the population.
In the United States the proportion of the population in the age group
twenty to fifty-nine (the ages that should produce the highest savings
rates) increased from 43 percent in 1850 to 47 percent in 1880 and
certainly accounted for a part of the increase in the savings rate that
occurred over those years. Canada experienced a similar change in the
demographic structure, but it was delayed by at least a decade. There the
proportion of the population in the twenty to fifty-nine age group rose
from 42 percent in 1870 to 46 percent in 1890 and 48 percent in 1900. By
1900 the proportions in the two countries were very similar.[798] A second
part of the explanation of the increase can likely be found in the increase
in the share of income accruing to the owners of land and capital and
the concomitant decline in the share received by wage earners. There was
a significant upward shift in the share of non-wage incomes after 1890

---

[798] *Historical Statistics of the United States* (1970), Series A 119 to 134, p. 15. *Historical Statistics of Canada*, Series A 28 to 43, p. 16.

with most of the increase occurring after the turn of the century.[799] A reasonable place to look for the remainder of the answer is in the history
of Canadian financial intermediation. At first glance, the history appears
to have been very different from developments in the United States; and
the difference seems particularly marked in the case of the two commercial banking systems. A closer look, however, suggests that not only
the two banking systems but also the two insurance industries and the
two building and loans and savings banks sectors were performing
roughly similar functions, in roughly similar ways. On further examination, however, one major difference – a difference, at least, in terms of
timing – does emerge. Although the formal institutional structures look
very similar, subsets of the Canadian institutions tended to be linked
together into a small number of highly personalized networks, or groups,
each controlled by a relatively small set of financial capitalists. In the
United States those personalized networks had begun to be transformed
into market-dominated networks before the turn of the century. In
Canada the process was delayed by at least a decade.

A second, but not unrelated, difference appears when attention is
turned to the stock and bond markets. The American markets developed
earlier and more fully. It may be that the role played by these markets
in the education of American investors was important in promoting high
American savings rates at an early date, and it certainly was important
in mobilizing those American savings. In Canada these markets played
a much more modest role; but in the second period – the mid-1890s to
World War I – the Canadian economy was the beneficiary of an important institutional innovation. Bond dealers – dealers working without the
benefit of formal securities markets – began distributing formal securities – bonds and preferred shares – on a large scale. These bond houses
were the personalized financial groups' answer to the problems of distributing the paper securities of their newly promoted ventures – initially
the bonds of Canadian municipalities, but increasingly the bonds or preferred stock of private industrial, commercial, or utility firms in Canada,
the United States, and Latin America – and providing an efficient secondary market for those issues.

Those dealers, with the monetary support of the financial groups, made
a significant contribution to the process of investor education that
opened Canadian domestic investment opportunities to domestic savers,
and they may well have helped to promote the high savings rates that
characterized the boom period. By 1914 the Canadian economy may not

---

[799] Edelstein, *Overseas Investment*, pp. 282–87.

have been quite as well developed as the American, but its financial institutional structure – although somewhat different – was becoming less personalized, and, in terms of its formal structure, it was almost as well developed. Its citizens displayed savings propensities as high as those in the United States, and, in terms of their level of investor sophistication, its savers approached the educational level of their counterparts in the lower forty-eight.

One other feature of Canadian development should be underscored. Canada drew substantial capital from abroad, even when domestic interest rates were near American levels. In terms of the importance of capital imports, the Canadian economy was much more similar to those of Argentina and Australia than to that of the United States. It differed, however, in some important respects. Unlike Argentina, most of the investment was indirect. Unlike Australia, as capital imports from Britain escalated after the turn of the century, it was a Canadian bank, the Bank of Montreal, that acted as the fiscal agent for the Dominion (and many of the provincial) governments. The signal of quality provided by that bank carried over to the private sector and eased the flow of finance from British savers to Canadian industrial and commercial firms. Thus, the number of private non-railroad securities listed on the London Stock Exchange increased from eight in 1870, to twenty-one in 1890, to thirty-two in 1910 (see Table 4:4-1).

CHAPTER 5

Domestic saving, international capital flows, and the evolution of domestic capital markets: The Australian experience

5-1. Introduction

The Australian experience stands in marked contrast to those of Canada and the United States.[800] Although all three were frontier countries, initially Australia had by far the smallest population, and, therefore, population growth over the next half century depended relatively more on immigration. In 1865 the population of the six colonies was less than 1.4 million. In contrast, the Canadian population was 3.4 million, and that of the United States, 35.7 million. Over the next five decades Canadian population grew at an annual rate of 1.7 percent, that of the United States at 2.0 percent, but that of Australia at 2.5 percent.

Initially, Australian income had been raised by the gold and silver discoveries of the 1850s, but gold can be taken out of the ground only once. Between 1860 and the Western Australian discoveries of the late 1880s, precious metal production played a steadily decreasing role in the continent's economic expansion. Given the initial high levels of income and the subsequent exhaustion of the mines, except for the fifteen years from 1889 to 1904, Australia's economic performance was remarkably good.

---

[800] Although Australia did not become a single nation until 1901, we will often treat its six states (New South Wales, Victoria, Queensland, Tasmania, South Australia, and Western Australia) as a single entity over the entire period. Moreover, although the six colonies did not officially become states until 1901, given that all, except Western Australia, had been granted self-government before 1865, we will often refer to them as states rather than colonies. The Australian Colonial Government Act of 1850 had provided the basis of separation from New South Wales of Victoria in 1851 and Queensland in 1859. Victoria, New South Wales, and Tasmania were granted self-government in 1855, South Australia in 1856, and Queensland in 1859. The Swan River settlement (Western Australia) continued under direct British control until granted self-government in 1892.

Between 1861 and 1889, when population was increasing by 3.5 percent a year, per capita real GDP rose by 1.3 percent per year; and between 1905 and 1914, when the rate of population increase was 2.3 percent, real per capita GDP was increasing by 2.9 percent (see Table 5:1-1). Given the Australian rate of population increase and the declining contribution of the gold and silver mines, domestic savings alone were unlikely to have been sufficient to continue to support such a rapid rate of growth in per capita income. It was foreign – almost entirely British – savings that provided a very large fraction of the capital needed to maintain the rate of growth. In the words of Noel Butlin, "During the thirty years 1861–90, Australian economic growth was sustained, stable and rapid. The process of economic growth rested on rapidly rising population and a fast rising stock of capital equipment. In both cases, Australian expansion depended on inflow from abroad, chiefly from Britain."[801]

Over the half century 1865 to 1914, Australia received about one-sixth of the portfolio finance that passed through the British capital market, an amount slightly less than that received by the Argentine and about four-fifths of the Canadian total. Between 1880 and 1900, however, the island continent's share soared to more than 30 percent of the four-country total. For a time – between 1883 and 1890 – the Australian colonies absorbed over one-half of total British net overseas investment.[802] Over the last two decades of the nineteenth century, the per capita gross transfers of long-term capital passing through the British capital market – the "capital called" – averaged $16.49. Although all four frontier countries received substantial infusions of British capital, relative to its size the Australian economy received much more British capital than the other three. It is safe to say that between 1865 and 1890 Australia's economic growth depended upon those flows of British capital.

[801] Noel G. Butlin, "The Shape of the Australian Economy, 1861–1900," *The Economic Record*, Vol. 34, No. 67 (April 1958), pp. 11, 13. [Hereafter cited as Butlin, "The Shape of the Australian Economy."]

Butlin estimates that, even with the rapid rise in population, between 1870 and 1914 there was an increase of 0.5 percent in real GDP per unit of labor input per annum. N.G. Butlin, "Some Perspectives on Australian Economic Development, 1890–1965," in C. Forester (ed.), *Australian Economic Development in the Twentieth Century* (London: 1970). Cited in Donald Denoon, *Settler Capitalism: The Dynamics of Dependent Development in the Southern Hemisphere* (Oxford: Clarendon Press, 1983), p. 103. [Hereafter cited as Denoon, *Settler Capitalism.*]

[802] Noel G. Butlin, *Investment in Australian Economic Development, 1861–1900* (Cambridge: Cambridge University Press, 1964), pp. 36–37. [Hereafter cited as N. Butlin, *Investment in Australian Development.*]

Table 5:1-1. *Australian economic performance indicators,*
1861–1913/1914 (annual percentage growth rates)

Years	Real GDP	Population	Real GDP per capita	GDP deflator
1861–1889	4.8	3.5	1.3	−0.4
1889–1904/1905	0.8	1.7	−0.8	−0.1
1904/1905–1913/1914	5.2	2.3	2.9	2.2

Source: Rodney Maddock and Ian W. McLean, "The Australian Economy in the Very Long Run" in Rodney Maddock and Ian W. McLean, *The Australian Economy in the Long Run* (Cambridge, New York, New Rochelle, Melbourne & Sydney: Cambridge University Press, 1987), p. 14.

5-2. Historical background

5-2a. The role of the government

Although there remain substantial questions of causality, the very heavy dependence on British capital was associated with two features of the six colonies' institutional structure: first, a very heavy dependence on government investment; and second, a relatively primitive structure of private financial institutions. The latter feature is the subject of much of this chapter. First, however, it is necessary to consider the impact of the government on the evolution of the domestic financial markets. By 1890 the Australian colonists had accumulated more public debt per capita than residents of any other country or colony in the world. The editors of *"The Bankers Magazine* torn between awe and alarm calculated that the Australian colonies had public debts of over £50 per head." In Queensland, the heaviest borrower, the figure was nearly £70; in contrast, British per capita public debt was a mere £18, the Cape's was £16, and Canada's a "frivolous" £12.[803] Given the importance of the role played by the six state and, after 1902, by the federal, governments, the Australian experience raises several questions. What was the extent of the governments' participation in the economy? What were the sectors of the economy that were dominated by government? Why was the government chosen to carry out these functions? What impact did the political structure have on government decisions? What was the relationship between the public and private sectors?

---

[803] Denoon, *Settler Capitalism*, p. 52.

Australian historians have provided satisfactory answers to many, but not all, of these questions.

In terms of the extent of the public sector, Noel Butlin notes that in Australia "the population and capital inflow was channeled into two sectors, roughly of equal size, the government and private enterprise. Between them, the institutions of these two sectors provided for the growth of Australian capital equipment, sharing expenditure about equally."[804] More precisely, in terms of capital, over the period 1865–1914, Butlin estimates that of the total of £14.1 billion of Australian gross domestic capital formation, 53 percent came from the private and 47 percent from the public sector.[805] Over those same years almost three-quarters of the funds raised by public issues floated on the formal British capital market were directed toward the government sector. Ian Drummond, writing about the last twenty years of the period, notes that "the growth in the public debt was more than six times as great as the flow of new issues to the private sector." He concludes that "this relationship reflects the dominant role of state enterprise in the Australian economy, the concentration of more capital-intensive activities in state hands."[806] In terms of the industries impacted, railroads were by far the most important. Although the private sector was responsible for the first Australian railroads, the state governments soon assumed the primary role in railroad construction; by the mid-1850s, for all intents and purposes, they had taken over all of the heretofore private railways and assumed the tasks of construction and operation of both those railroads and almost all of the ones that were to be constructed before the First World War. The story was the same for the telegraph: Initially innovated by private entrepreneurs just prior to the gold discoveries, the construction and operation of the lines were also taken over by the colonial governments during the gold boom.[807] In the 1880s the Victorian government stepped

---

[804] N. Butlin, "The Shape of the Australian Economy," p. 16.

[805] Noel G. Butlin, *Australian Domestic Product, Investment and Foreign Borrowing, 1861–1938/39* (Cambridge: Cambridge University Press, 1962), table 13, pp. 33–34; table 250, p. 422; table 265, p. 444. [Hereafter cited as N. Butlin, *Australian Domestic Product.*] N. Butlin, *Investment In Australian Development*, table 1, p. 11; appendix table II, p. 454.

[806] Ian M. Drummond, *Capital Markets in Australia and Canada, 1895–1914: A Study of Colonial Economic Development*, Ph.D. dissertation, Yale University, May 1959, pp. 171–72. [Hereafter cited as Drummond, *Capital Markets.*]

[807] "Although a Victorian [railway] company prospered, the projectors did not extend their operations and left to the government the task of more extensive railway building. In NSW the government gradually accepted increasing interest, financial responsibility, and executive control and finally, in 1854, ownership of the assets. From this time, with some exceptions, government responsibility

in to help finance the previously largely privately financed irrigation system, a step that was only the precursor of a much larger expansion of government activities in the two decades after Federation.[808] The expansion of the role of government is reflected in the doubling of the "government share in Gross Domestic Product, revenue raised, money spent and labour employed" between 1850–54 and 1890–94.[809]

In the financial sector, for example, despite the presence of an efficient publicly regulated savings bank system, both the Victoria and New South Wales governments early established competitive Post Office savings

for railway construction and operation was substantially complete." Noel G. Butlin, "Colonial Socialism in Australia, 1860–1900," in Hugh G. Aitken (ed.), *The State and Economic Growth,* Papers of a Conference held on October 11–13, 1956, under the Auspices of the Committee on Economic Growth (New York: Social Science Research Council, 1959), pp. 26–78. [Hereafter cited as N. Butlin, "Colonial Socialism."]

"Things were different in Australia, Although joint stock companies started New South Wales's and Victoria's first railways, government soon took them over. It will be recalled that in 1855 the colony of New South Wales took over private railway companies connecting Sydney and Newcastle. Melbourne's first private system fared better but the southern city's non-government railways were short suburban lines. By the middle of the 1850s it had become clear that the colony of Victoria would have to shoulder the responsibility of constructing a regional network linking the colonial capital with the growing mining centers of Ballarat and Bendigo and the agricultural districts along the Murray River." Stephen Salsbury and Kay Sweeny Salsbury, *The Bull, The Bear and the Kangaroo: The History of the Sydney Stock Exchange* (Sydney: Allen and Unwin, 1988), p. 55. [Hereafter cited as Salsbury and Sweeny, *The Bull, The Bear.*]

By the end of 1913 there were 18,592 miles of railroad in operation in Australia. A.R. Hall, *The London Capital Market and Australia, 1870–1914* Australian National University, Social Science Monograph No. 21 (Canberra: Australian National University, 1963), appendix V, table IV, p. 212. [Hereafter cited as Hall, *The London Capital Market.*]

In 1919–20, although there were thirty-two private railroads open to general traffic – fifteen in Queensland, nine in New South Wales, four in Tasmania, two in Victoria, and one each in South and Western Australia – the total mileage was only 779; and they had been built at a capital cost of less than £4,000,000. They ranged in length from the 278 miles of the Midland Railway in Western Australia to 0.83 miles of the Warwick Farm in New South Wales. *The Official Yearbook of the Commonwealth of Australia,* No. 14, 1921, p. 614.

[808] Lionel Frost, "Government and Economic Development: The Case of Irrigation in Victoria," *Australian Economic History Review,* Vol. 32, No. 1 (March 1992), pp. 63–64. [Hereafter cited as Frost, "Government and Economic Development."]

[809] H.M. Boot, "Government and the Australian Colonial Economy, 1788–1892," a chapter in Robert V. Jackson (ed.), *The Cambridge Economic History of Australia* (Cambridge: Cambridge University Press, forthcoming), ms. p. 28. [Hereafter cited as Boot, "Government and the Colonial Economy."]

banks – as did the federal government in 1912 – and by the 1860s government-owned savings banks had been established in all six states.[810] Finally, "government became drawn increasingly into financing much of Australia's farming."[811] "From 1893 onwards, most of the colonial governments entered the field of lending to farmers, sometimes by encouraging government savings banks to dispose of funds in this way, sometimes by creating special institutions such as Western Australia's Agricultural Bank of 1896. Victoria, Queensland, South Australia, Western Australia, and New Zealand all legislated in 1894 to promote state loans to farmers."[812]

---

[810] Matthew W. Butlin, "Capital Markets," in Rodney Maddock and Ian McLean, *The Australian Economy in the Long Run* (Cambridge: Cambridge University Press, 1987), p. 235. [Hereafter cited as M. Butlin, "Capital Markets."] D.T. Merrett, "Banking and Finance," in Christopher Lloyd (ed.), *Australian Institutions Transformed: Capital, Labour, and the State in the 20th Century* (forthcoming), p. 2. [Hereafter cited as Merrett, "Banking and Finance."]

[811] David Merrett, "Capital Formation and Capital Markets," in R.V. Jackson (ed.), the *Cambridge Economic History of Australia* (Cambridge: Cambridge University Press, forthcoming), ms. p. 11.

[812] Sydney J. Butlin, *Australia and New Zealand Bank: The Bank of Australasia and the Union Bank of Australia Limited, 1828–1951* (London: Longmans, Green and Company, 1961), p. 322. [Hereafter cited as S. Butlin, *Australia and New Zealand Bank.*]

"New South Wales adopted the principle of advances to settlers on 4th April, 1889 when the Advances to Settlers Act received assent." It was to be financed by a £500,000 issue of $3\frac{1}{2}$ percent inscribed stock with a maximum loan of £200, for 10 years, at 4 percent interest. In 1902 the maximum increased to £500 and the term to 31 years. In the same year the supporting securities issue was increased to £1,000,000, and the maximum loan increased to £1,500. In 1906 the above acts were repealed and the powers and loans vested in "The Commissioners of the Government Savings Bank of New South Wales." This act was amended in 1913, 1914, and 1916.

"The Advances Department of the Government Savings Bank of Victoria was established by the Savings Bank Act of 1896. . . . For the purpose of advancing money to settlers and others; a branch of the bank called the Credit Foncier Department was established, which was authorized to borrow on debentures or mortgage bonds up to the sum of £6,000,000." The lower limit on advances was £50, the upper limit £2,000. They were to be secured by a first mortgage and to bear interest at $4\frac{1}{2}$ percent. The stated purpose was "In order to assist farmers, graziers, market gardeners or other persons employed in agricultural, horticultural, viticultural, or pastoral pursuits. The Savings Bank Commissioners are empowered to make advances either by installments or otherwise, upon the security of any lands held by such persons either (a) in fee simple or (b) under a crown lease in which the rent received is taken by the Crown in part payment of the lands demised."

"The Queensland Government was authorized under the Agricultural Bank Act of 1901, to establish a bank for the purpose of promoting the occupation, cultivation, and improvement of agricultural lands of the State, and a body of

These efforts were vastly expanded by the federal government after 1910.[813]

Although it only partially involved expansion into what might be thought of as the private sector, the colonial governments either financed or operated and financed many activities that in Canada or the United

three trustees was appointed to administer the Act." The Act was amended in 1904, 1905, 1911, 1914 and 1915, and in 1916 it was repealed by the Queensland Government Savings Bank Act of 1916, when the duties of the trustees under the former act were transferred to the Commissioners of the Government Savings Bank. The original limit was to be £400 secured by a first mortgage. The limit was later raised to £1,500. The interest rate was initially set at 5 percent for the first five years. Thereafter, the loan must be repaid at the rate of £4-0s-3d per £100 each six months."

South Australia: "*Legislation*:

(1): "Under the State Advances Act of 1895, amended in 1896, 1901, and 1912 a State Bank has been established in South Australia for the purpose of making advances (i) to farmers, graziers, and other producers, and in aid of industries, upon the security of lands held in fee simple, or under Crown lease, and (ii) to local authorities, upon the security of their rates." The bank, managed by five trustees, was permitted to issue up to £3,000,000 a year in mortgage bonds. Those bonds to carry interest at $4\frac{1}{2}$ percent. The loan limit was £5,000 at an interest rate of 5 percent.

(2): In 1908 the *Advances to Settlers on Crown Lands Act* was passed. Amended in 1900, 1911, and 1912. "Treasurer authorized to set apart a sum not exceeding £200,000 a year for the purpose of loans to settlers to be administered by the Advances to Settlers Board. Maximum loan £850 for five years. Thereafter loan must be repaid in seventy half-yearly installments. Interest rate fixed but not specified."

"By the Agricultural Bank Act of 1894 the Government of Western Australia was empowered to establish a bank for the purpose of promoting the occupation, cultivation, and improvement of agricultural lands of the State." Amended from time to time and replaced in 1906 by a consolidating act. Funding was to be from the issue of mortgage bonds at rates not exceeding 4 percent. The initial limit was £1,000,000 but subsequently raised to £4,500,000. "The bank is authorized to make advances to persons engaged in the business of farming or grazing or in agricultural, horticultural, or pastoral pursuits, or in any industry that the Government may by proclamation declare to be a rural industry, for the purpose incidental to or in aid of any such business, pursuit, or industry, including the erection of dwelling houses." The limit was £2,000. Advances are made only on first mortgage, but a second mortgage may be taken as collateral security. For five years the borrower pays interest only, at such rate per annum as may be prescribed. "If the rate of interest be more than five per cent, it must not exceed by more than one per cent per annum the rate payable on funds raised by the bank." After five years the loan must be paid off at half yearly intervals over twenty-five years. "When an advance is made for any purpose other than that of effecting improvements, it must be repaid, together with interest at 6 per cent per annum, by half yearly installments within such period, not exceeding twenty-five years, as the trustees think fit."

States would most likely have been undertaken by private enterprise or by local governments. In Australia from a very early date the habit was to look to the central government: "in this case the colonial governments – rather than to local governments for help. Financially speaking, local governments in Australia have probably been weaker and less important than in any other country with an Anglo-Saxon heritage." In the words of one student of Australian public expenditure, "In summary by the end of the century the Australian people had developed strong colonial governments and comparatively weak local governments."[814]

These state government activities encompassed both public utilities and local public works, and the centralized structure of these activities remained in place and continued to expand until well into the twentieth century.

> The relative increase in government capital formation in the 20th century, and its sustained high share at almost exactly half the total, was not achieved without some important changes in the public sector. There were clearly some additions to government capital-forming outlays after 1900. New problems of power supply, particularly electricity which became important immediately before the first world war, new undertakings in the form of large scale irrigation projects and river control, dated from the end of the first decade, the development of telephonic communication in place of the primitive telegraphic equipment – these were important in sustaining government outlays. . . . Government action in the 20th century, effectively from about 1910 and most

> In Tasmania, "under the State Advances Act of 1907, an agricultural bank, administered by three trustees appointed by the Governor, was established for the purpose of making advances to promote the agricultural development of the State." Funds to be raised from the issue of debentures or inscribed stock, "for a sum not exceeding £150,000, interest at a rate determined by the Treasurer being payable on same." There were amendments in 1912, 1914, and 1916. "The trustees may make advances on the prescribed security to farmers, graziers, or persons engaged in agriculture, dairying, horticultural pursuits owning land in fee simple or holding under purchase from the Crown upon the credit system, for any of the following purposes: (a) The payment of liabilities already existing on the holding; (b) agricultural, dairying, grazing, or horticultural pursuits on the holding; (c) making or adding improvements." Loan limits: low, £25; maximum, £1,000. First mortgage, but second may be taken as collateral, security. Interest rate determined by the Treasurer. Term: five years, after five years the loan must be paid off in no more than fifty half-yearly installments. *Official Year Book of the Commonwealth of Australia*, No. 12, 1919, pp. 384–89.

[813] Drummond, *Capital Markets*, pp. 86–87.

[814] B.U. Ratchford, *Public Expenditures in Australia*, Duke University Commonwealth-Studies Center, Publication No. 11 (Durham, N.C.: Duke University Press, 1959), pp. 12–13, 15. [Hereafter cited as Ratchford, *Public Expenditures*.]

particularly during the 'twenties, was stimulated by a demand to cope with a long time lag in the provision of urban facilities, of water and sewerage and roads. In addition it had to provide "new" equipment, particularly electricity and electrification of services of transport and telephone.[815]

Some general estimate of the importance and extent of the government sector can be gleaned from Table 5:2-1. In terms of accumulated loan expenditures of all Australian states to June 1913, railways and tramways absorbed about three-fifths of the total, but the remainder was spread across a wide range of activities. Moreover, over time, the proportion of state and federal public capital formation relative to that of local authorities continued to increase. In 1872, the first year for which complete data are available, in terms of their contribution to gross capital formation, the six states spent £1.257 million on railways, £139,000 on telegraphs, £140,000 on water and sewerage, £324,000 on roads, £264,000 on bridges and harbors, £229,000 on public buildings (including schools), and £56,000 on miscellaneous capital items – a non-defense total of £2.405 million. Local authorities spent £621,000, but that figure includes subsidies from the states. In 1900 colonial governments spent £5.340 million on railways, £243,000 on telegraph, £1.532 million on water and sewerage, £785,000 on roads, £1.204 million on bridges and harbors, £941,000 on public buildings (including schools), and £582,000 on miscellaneous items – a total non-defense capital formation of £10.740 million. In the same year local and semi-government authorities spent a total of £3.120 million; but, again, a part of that total was financed by transfers from the colonial governments.[816] A little more than decade and a half later, in June 1915, the list of state and commonwealth expenditures on gross capital formation had been expanded to include electricity, industrial activity, and agriculture; and the total had reached £30.4 million. Local authorities, again with some central subsidies, were responsible for an additional £6.8 million.[817] Thus, over forty-two and a half years, ignoring state subsidies, the central government's share of public capital formation gradually increased from 72, to 77, to 82 percent.

Noel Butlin's characterization of Australia's economic system as "Colonial Socialism" certainly captures a large element of truth. It is not obvious why the voters chose so much government, although Australian

---

[815] Noel Butlin, "Some Structural Features of Australian Capital Formation, 1861–1939/39," *The Economic Record*, Vol. 35, No. 72 (December 1958), pp. 394–95. [Hereafter cited as N. Butlin, "Some Structural Features."]

[816] N. Butlin, *Australian Domestic Product*, tables 211 and 235, pp. 348, 372.

[817] N. Butlin, *Australian Domestic Product*, tables 237 and 245, pp. 391, 399.

Table 5:2-1. *The accumulated loan expenditures of all Australian states to June 30, 1913*

Heads of expenditure	Amount (1000's of pounds)	Percent of total
Railways and tramways	179,209	61.0
Water supply & sewerage	39,614	13.5
Harbors, rivers, roads, bridges, etc.	28,125	9.6
Public buildings	12,990	4.4
Land settlement & loans to local boides	14,960	5.1
All other	18,843	6.4
Total expenditures	293,741	100.0

Source: A.R. Hall, *The London Capital Market and Australia, 1870–1914*, (Canberra: The Australian National University), Table 14, p. 90.

historiography is not devoid of explanations. Three seem to have gained some degree of credence.

By the middle of the twentieth century some scholars had focused on the impact of the Australian environment on the psychology of the settlers to explain the "habit of looking to the government for leadership and assistance in economic development." Alexander Brady, for example, argued that "the traditions of centralized paternalism became entrenched and never entirely disappeared, for they were fostered by stern and unchanging facts of the geographic environment. Thus Australia, earlier and more easily than the other dominions, became a land of collectivism, accepted the state as a positive force, and relied upon it for initiative in the development of the community." A.G.L. Shaw wrote, "if the Government did much itself, it was because as yet there was no one else to do it. The time for free enterprise had not yet come; and the conditions which made freedom possible still had to be met."[818] Nor has this explanation been abandoned. In attempting to explain how, "if Australian governments were not excessively profligate or corrupt," their development policies were so often marked by failure, Lionel Frost

---

[818] Alexander Brady, *Democracy in the Dominions: A Comparative Study in Institutions*, 2nd ed. (Toronto: University of Toronto Press, 1952), p. 133. A.G.L. Shaw, *The Economic Development of Australia*, 3rd ed. (London: 1955), p. 25. Both are cited in Ratchford, *Public Expenditure*, pp. 12–13. Ratchford argues that Australians developed the habit of looking to the government for leadership and assistance in economic development.

concludes, "Australia's historical circumstances encouraged the creation of an institutional framework which frequently eschewed economic efficiency in favour of interference with the market. J.R.T. Hughes's comments on America apply with equal force to Australia: a system based on rigid economic efficiency may have been incompatible with our history, legal tradition and, indeed, whole way of life."[819]

This explanation, like most residual explanations, is not particularly satisfactory. Noel Butlin notes that no obvious motive prompted the government to preempt railway construction and operation. Moreover, in the case of the railroads, the "nation's first big business," he concludes that "except in South Australia there was no clear link with the tradition of government intervention. In fact, opinion was originally strongly opposed to government entry into railway building." Butlin, while noting that "the failure of private enterprise was, in a sense, accidental," ultimately turns to economic explanations of the choice, although he appears to be of at least two minds about just where in the economy the answer lies. On the one hand, he concludes that, "the basic fact seems to be that, at a critical time, private individuals were unable to develop adequate business organizations for railway operations." "The proposals for private railways appear to have foundered regularly, not only on the questions of the access to capital but perhaps mainly on the lack of entrepreneurial ability." As evidence he cites "Queensland's ideas on the possibility and value of attracting American railway men to Australia," and he notes that such suggestions "were symptomatic of this weakness."[820] Indirect support for that conclusion is provided by at least one other economic historian. R.V. Jackson argued that his reading of history "throws into relief the importance of colonial governments as entrepreneurs and investors."[821] Given the proven international mobility of both British and American railway entrepreneurs, this conclusion, based on entrepreneurial failure, like reliance on the Australian psyche, does not appear satisfactory.

On the other hand, Butlin also notes that railway construction had hardly begun before the discovery of gold completely altered construction conditions. "Wages rose rapidly, labor became unprocurable, and capital was devoted to gold mining and commercial ventures. These unforeseeable changes brought private construction to a standstill. It was

---

[819] Frost, "Government and Economic Development," p. 50.

[820] N. Butlin, "Colonial Socialism," pp. 39–41.

[821] R.V. Jackson, *Australian Economic Development in the Nineteenth Century* (Canberra: Australian National University Press, 1977), p. 160. [Hereafter cited as Jackson, *Australian Economic Development*.]

the belief in the superior ability of the government to raise capital, particularly in London, and to secure navies through assisted immigration that prompted the original transfer. The belief was reinforced by a sense of urgency in providing railway transport between the main ports and the gold fields."[822] This latter explanation has two quite different elements.

First, there were high short-run economic returns in those sectors that remained private and low short-run, but potentially high long-term, social returns to investment in railroads. "As the private sector became committed to residential facilities, and the more lucrative opportunities in pastoral, commercial and mining assets, governments were left with the large-scale and less profitable undertakings in railways, other land transport and communication and in less important social assets."[823]

Second, Butlin argues that the governments had access to overseas capital and the private sector did not. "The point may be illustrated by the successful flotation in London of the £8,000,000 debentures authorized by the Victorian government in 1858 – a feat beyond the imagination a few years earlier and still beyond the power of private interests in 1858."[824] Certainly the history of the ensuing three decades suggests that British investors, concerned with the security of their investments but recognizing home and colonial interest differentials, demonstrated an almost insatiable appetite for Australian government issues. Moreover, in the years between 1880 and 1890 it was the willingness of investors to subscribe to colonial government issues on the London capital market that provided an important precondition for a relaxation of railway investment criteria; and it is alleged to have been a decline in the preferences of British investors for Australian government issues that led to a sharp decline in Australian borrowing after 1892.[825]

Taken together, the trade-off between short-run private and the long-run social returns and the ability of the colonial governments to raise funds on the London market may provide an adequate explanation of the original choice of path. In the longer term, however, the explanation is not entirely convincing. It does not explain the persistence of "the governmental habit," even in the case of railroads. In Canada and Argentina,

---

[822] N. Butlin, "Colonial Socialism," pp. 39–40.

[823] N. Butlin, *Investment in Australian Development*, p. 49.

[824] N. Butlin, "Colonial Socialism," p. 40.

[825] Lionel Frost, "A Reinterpretation of Victoria's Railway Construction Boom of the 1880s," *Australian Economic History Review*, Vol. 26, No. 1 (March 1986), p. 41. [Hereafter cited as Frost, "A Reinterpretation."] N. Butlin, *Investment in Australian Development*, pp. 329–30, 360. Hall, *The Stock Exchange of Melbourne*, pp. 215–16.

for example, the government frequently guaranteed interest and capital as a means of assisting private enterprise. In Australia the device was tried without success in Victoria and New South Wales in the 1850s and, much later, briefly in Tasmania; but almost no use was made of this institutional arrangement once the gold boom had subsided. In the United States land grants played an important role in pushing the rail network across the trans-Mississippi West. In Canada, too, land grants were used to induce "private" railroads to construct lines into the west. The CPR, for example, received some twenty-five million acres. Although Queensland occasionally professed some interest in construction of a land grant railway and in Western Australia construction of such a railroad was actually begun (without, history notes, much success), the Australian states displayed little more interest in land grants than they did in subsidization.[826]

Nor does the theory explain the spread of the "habit" from railroads, to public utilities, agriculture, finance, and manufacturing. Although more work remains to be done on the question of why government ownership remained the institution of choice, politics must have played an important role. Moreover, it appears that it was the differential access to London funds, not the short-run–long-run tradeoff, that provided one key element in the explanation of the persistence and spread of "colonial socialism."

If we are to understand the role of foreign capital in the evolution of Australian financial institutions, it is necessary to assess the degree of the governments' success. Two questions are relevant: (1) How successful were government institutions in channeling overseas capital into the Australian economy? (2) Did government direct the flow of domestic and foreign savings into unproductive investment?

In terms of their initial endeavors, the governments get generally good marks. The opening of the gold fields touched off the long boom, and the railroads made a substantial contribution. In the early decades railroad receipts appear to have covered operating expenses, and, at the time, they may have also been sufficient to service the debt charges. By the end of the 1870s, however, citizens and their elected representatives had come to realize that "railways brought social and economic benefits that were not included in their earnings. The implication was that individual construction projects need not pay their way." Although the railways may have yielded unrecognized social benefits, "there was no possibility of guessing usefully at the magnitude of the benefits that were not reflected in railway earnings." Faced with substantial electoral pressure to build

---

[826] N. Butlin, "Colonial Socialism," p. 39.

additional lines, however, politicians were more than happy to accept the theoretical justification without empirical support. Thus, "once committed, government decisions to extend the [railway] system soon took on classic public choice features. Strict concern for profitability gradually gave way to less quantifiable, though 'politically' more easily justified, social and general economic considerations. By the early 1880s, even these criteria were abandoned to permit extensions of railway networks for political ends, the likelihood of any foreseeable economic return playing little or no part in decisions to enter new and larger building programs."[827] In addition, special rates were allowed on wool, grain, and certain other goods. As the railway commissioners themselves reported, these rates were set at low levels to attract business and, "*at times of drought, to provide assistance to rural producers*" (emphasis added).[828]

Given the ready access to British capital, "the new philosophy of railway building encouraged over-investment." The governments "responded to the greatly increased availability of loan funds by accelerating railway construction even though the economic criteria for individual decisions became less rigorous in the process." "The avowed purpose of most lines was still to serve existing areas of settlement, but many lines were built that linked areas with very few people and little

---

[827] H.M. Boot, "New South Wales Railways and Social Savings: On the Gravy Train or Off the Rails," paper delivered at the Economic History Society of Australia and New Zealand Annual Conference, University of Queensland, Brisbane, March 29–31, 1996, p. 2. [Hereafter cited as Boot, "On the Gravy Train or Off the Rails."]

B.R. Davidson has strongly challenged these views. He has suggested that if the indirect (i.e., social) benefits of railways are included in the cost/benefit calculation, the long-term social gains from constructing the New South Wales railway system produced an annual rate of return of 15 percent on capital invested between 1856 and 1920, or twice the average long-term bank overdraft rate. Some doubts have, however, been cast on this conclusion; and the traditional view as characterized by Boot still appears to hold sway. See B.R. Davidson, "A Benefit Cost Analysis of the New South Wales Railway System," *Australian Economic History Review*, Vol. XXII, No. 2 (September 1982), pp. 127–50, and Boot, "On the Gravy Train or Off the Rails."

[828] See, for example, *Annual Report of the New South Wales Railway Commissioners, 1893–92*, pp. 7–8, and *1894–93*, pp. 6–7. *Annual Report of the Chief Commissioner of Railways*, 1903, pp. 6–7. Losses on the routes to the Riverina and to the Central and Western Districts of New South Wales alone had reached £219,383 when first made public in 1891 and had risen to £440,697 by 1903. Boot, "On the Gravy Train or Off the Rails," p. 13.

potential trade."[829] In 1891, after some forty years of railway construction, there were some 10,206 miles of track; and almost three-fifths of that total had been built during the previous decade.[830]

Once the economic centers have been connected, the major gains from railroad construction do not come from the completion of further trunk lines. Punctiform industries such as mining aside, the gains are realized when the trunk lines are supported by a network of feeder lines.[831] Initially, Australian construction focused on trunk lines connecting population centers and traversing the colonies' most deeply populated districts: in New South Wales, for example, the Great Southern from Sydney to Albury, the Great Western from Sydney to Dubbo, and the Great Northern from Newcastle north to Wallangarra.[832] Unfortunately, that pattern continued well after the initial skeleton network had been constructed. "Apart from Queensland, building concentrated on a fan design of trunk lines spreading out from the main port cities into the interior." Even in Queensland, a somewhat similar design emerged in the 1880s. Except in part of Victoria, the period of branch-line construction lay in the future. The political pressure reflected "the struggle between the three leading commercial centers, Melbourne, Adelaide and Sydney, to dominate their respective hinterlands and to extend, regain, or retain their position in handling the growing intercolonial trade, particularly from the Riverina and western New South Wales."[833]

As for the productivity of other forms of government investment, a verdict similar to that concerning the railroads has been delivered in the case of the Victorian government's attempts to foster agriculture by subsidizing irrigation. Farmers were willing to join irrigation trusts, even

---

[829] Jackson, *Australian Economic Development*, pp. 89–90, 161–62. Sinclair, *The Process of Economic Growth*, pp. 130–31. Between 1869 and 1893 the number of miles of railroads in operation increased from 864 to 10,819, an annual compound rate of growth of 10.5 percent. B.R. Mitchell, *International Historical Statistics: The Americas and Australasia* (Detroit: Gale Research Co., 1983), table G1, p. 666. [Hereafter cited as Mitchell, *The Americas and Australasia*.]

[830] Despite the depression a further 3,229 miles were added by 1901. The total cost of construction over the first forty years was £122 million, a sum that had reached £167 million a decade later. The £122 million represented 77 percent of the nation's public debt. Boot, "Government and the Australian Colonial Economy," p. 30.

[831] W.A. Sinclair, *The Process of Economic Growth in Australia* (Melbourne: Cheshire Publishing, 1976), pp. 130–33, 137. [Hereafter cited as Sinclair, *The Process of Economic Growth.*]

[832] Salsbury and Sweeny, *The Bull, The Bear*, p. 172.

[833] Butlin, *Investment in Australian Development*, p. 293.

though they were generally uninterested in the regular use of irrigation water. If the water was free, they were willing to use it; but in general they chose to use land-extensive methods, methods that minimized their need for water. As a result, when the time came to repay the government loans, the farmers were prepared to let them go into default.[834] Thus, in the case of both rails and irrigation, political, as opposed to economic, decisions coupled with the willingness of British investors to purchase very large quantities of Australian government bonds led to substantial over-investment in government enterprise – that is, the flow of services from the investments was not commensurate with the amount of investment undertaken.[835] Over-investment in one sector has, almost by definition, a complement: under-investment in another. Noel Butlin early pointed out the inverse relation between government and private capital formation. The inversity thesis in its narrow form has found little empirical support; but the broader version, initially formulated by Butlin and fleshed out by others, seems well substantiated.[836] The broad version underscores two links between the public and private sectors' demands for finance: First, in a full employment economy, public expenditure absorbs labor, drives up wages, and reduces the demand for private investment; second, the Australian public and private sectors competed head-to-head for the limited supply of investable funds available in the British capital markets.

It is generally believed that the private sector was in a very much weaker position than the government – a sector marked in each colony by a relatively centralized machinery for decision making, an existing administrative and budgetary organization, and a set of well-established institutional structures designed to link public demand for funds to the London supply. As a result, in the inversity thesis, the government action is usually treated as the independent factor – "since the private sector was not normally in a position to exert great pressure on the government sector, we cannot avoid giving priority to government action."[837] Therefore, "it is the effects of changing government action that need be traced; the story is essentially one of government encroachment on private activity and the changing intensity of this encroachment."[838] To the extent that

---

[834] Frost, "Government and Economic Development," pp. 56–58.

[835] Jackson, *Australian Economic Development*, pp. 161–62.

[836] For a detailed discussion of the inversity thesis and the level of empirical support, see R.V. Jackson, "Short-Run Interaction of Public and Private Sectors in Australia, 1861–1890," *Australian Economic History Review*, Vol. 26, No. 1 (March 1986), pp. 59–75. [Hereafter cited as Jackson, "Short-Run Interaction."]

[837] N. Butlin, "Colonial Socialism," pp. 48–49.

[838] Jackson, "Short-Run Interaction," pp. 68–69.

the governments were in a position to dominate the flow of funds (with far from perfect private capital markets, they almost certainly were) and, to the extent that Australia accounted for more than a "small" part of the total overseas demand in the London market (in the 1880s they certainly did), over-investment in the government sector probably produced under-investment in the private sector. If capital markets had been perfect, and if Australia had accounted for only a small part of overseas demand, there may have been no impact on the supply of finance available to the private sector; however, to the extent that the government policies drove up wages and reduced the demand for private investment, there still could have been crowding out. Noel Butlin, for example, concludes that governments were able to "direct resources from the private sector to the detriment of the process of economic growth as a whole."[839]

Finally, the structure of Australian politics also affected the efficiency with which government borrowed funds were deployed. Unlike the United States, Canada, or Argentina, for most of the period there was no central government in Australia. In the words of Noel Butlin,

> The critical fact was that four separate, rival, and often mutually obstructive governments failed to make a concentrated attack on the transport needs of eastern Australia as a whole. On the contrary, confined to action within their own borders, each attempted to set in motion contrary commodity and passenger flows and a highly inefficient transport was imposed on the area. At best, transport policy was devised in isolation free of each other's planning; often each set out to divert traffic from neighboring colonies regardless of whether they were in a position to provide the most efficient transport links with the areas they attempted to serve.[840]

For example, "the New South Wales rail system was designed specifically to *limit* inter-colonial rail traffic as much as possible." The Riverina provides a particularly telling example. The region, even though it is part of New South Wales, is closer to Melbourne than to Sydney. Partly in order to capture the Riverina trade, the Victorian government built a railroad line to the Murray River, the Victoria–New South Wales boundary. The Victorian railroad was not, however, allowed to extend across the border into New South Wales. As a result, wool from the Riverina had to be hauled by road to the Murray. Moreover, New South Wales launched an expensive railway building program with the

---

[839] Cited in Jackson, "Short-Run Interaction," p. 68.
[840] N. Butlin, *Investment in Australian Development*, p. 293.

sole aim of preventing the Riverina trade going southward instead of to Sydney.[841]

The impact of intercolonial competition can be seen not only in what the states did do, but also in what they did not do. Between the 1860s and the 1890s a number of proposals were made to improve navigation on the Murray/Darling river system. Trade rivalries between Victoria and New South Wales, however, guaranteed that little would come of them. Relatively small expenditures on river improvement would have lowered transport costs significantly, but neither state government was willing to devote resources to any project that would benefit the other colony's capital city or Adelaide, even if the improvements primarily benefited farmers and pastoralists in New South Wales and Victoria.[842]

Federation might have solved this problem, and for some industries it did. In the case of banking, for example, the industry had been subject to relatively little state regulation in any of the six colonies.[843] Thus, when political pressure for regulation began to build, the bankers supported the political movement for federation, because "if there were to be regulation on banking, they preferred that it should be uniform over the whole of Australia."[844]

In the case of established regulatory practices, however, political accommodations were often made to help retain state sovereignty. For example, after federation, decisions about which new railway lines would be approved still rested with the state parliamentary committees, committees established to hear evidence on the suitability of particular extensions. At least partly because of the electoral consequences of rejecting such suggestions, in most states the committees could not be said to have required a very high standard of proof of the economic justification of any individual line. Overall, to a large extent, federation

---

[841] Jackson, *Australian Economic Development*, pp. 89–90.

[842] Boot, "On the Gravy Train or Off the Rails," pp. 8–9.

[843] The U.K. Colonial Banking Regulations of 1840 and 1846 and the charters of some of the British domiciled banks provided some regulation. "The company laws of the Australian colonies and the acts of parliament establishing banks, although permissive, did prescribe some aspects of bank behavior, most notably on the questions of financial disclosure and note issue. Both the Queensland and New South Wales governments passed laws relating to bank notes in the 1890s, the former colony making its own notes legal tender, while NSW effectively guaranteed private bank notes for a brief period." David Merrett, private correspondence, August 29, 1996.

[844] Sydney J. Butlin, *Australia and New Zealand Bank: The Bank of Australasia and the Union Bank of Australia Limited, 1828–1951* (London: Longmans, Green and Co., 1961), p. 325. [Hereafter cited as S. Butlin, *Australia and New Zealand Bank.*]

allowed for the continued operation of a political system that "permitted great pressure to be put on governments, whether state or Commonwealth, to take action"; and "an important influence on the electoral success of the parties contending for control of the various parliaments was the volume of public investment."[845]

5-2b. The long boom, depression, and after: the impact on the demand for finance

Since Noel Butlin's pathbreaking studies of the 1960s, traditional Australian historiography has divided the years from the gold discoveries of the 1850s to the beginning of the First World War into three distinct phases: the long boom running from sometime in the 1850s until about the end of the 1880s; the great depression covering the years from 1888–92 to 1897–1904, and the rest. The first two periods have been thoroughly explored; the last remains less intensely examined. Table 5:2-2 captures the movements of Gross Domestic Product, Population, and Gross Domestic Product Per Capita over the years 1861–1914, and Tables 5:2-3, 5:2-4, and 5:2-5 display the industrial structure of fixed capital formation.

Between 1865–67 and 1889–91 real Gross Domestic Product increased at 4.9 percent a year, population at 3.2, and per capita GDP at 1.5 percent. Over the next eleven years (1889–91 through 1900–2), Gross Domestic Product expanded by 0.2 percent per year, but population increased at a rate of 1.8 percent, producing a *decline* in per capita GDP of 1.6 percent a year. Finally, between 1900–2 and 1912–14, Gross Domestic Product rose at a rate of 4.0 percent per year, population by 1.7 percent, and per capita GDP by 2.2 percent.

5-2b(1). The long boom: Before the gold discoveries of the 1850s, Australia was a pastoral economy, and its fortunes rose and fell with the weather and the price of wool. Between 1860 and 1890, however, the economy became increasingly more balanced. Although the "second pastoral boom" lasted almost twenty years and lifted "pastoral investment into clear leadership, above residential and railway investment," that sector never regained its pre–gold era role as the sole and dominant "engine of growth."[846] Gold production declined slowly, but, while

---

[845] Sinclair, *The Process of Economic Growth*, pp. 184–85.

[846] "The large-scale growth of pastoral investment, concentrated in these twenty years, was achieved in three cyclical phases. In the first phase, rising from 1871 to an extreme peak in 1877 (before falling away to a trough in 1879), the level of pastoral investment increased extremely rapidly in what was, perhaps, the most profitable period of pastoral enterprise ever encountered in Australia.

Table 5:2-2. *Australia: population, Gross Domestic Product, and per capita Gross Domestic Product*

Year	Population (thousands)	Gross Domestic Product (millions of pounds)	Gross Domestic Product per capita (pounds)	Gross Domestic Product (millions of 1911 pounds)	Gross Domestic Product per capita (1911 pounds)
1861	1,166	66.8	57.29	53.4	45.80
1862	1,216	66.3	54.51	52.7	43.33
1863	1,266	65.4	51.64	54.4	42.96
1864	1,317	67.3	51.12	60.4	45.88
1865	1,367	68.3	49.97	60.2	44.04
1866	1,417	74.2	52.36	64.0	45.17
1867	1,467	74.9	51.05	71.6	48.80
1868	1,517	79.7	52.52	75.2	49.56
1869	1,568	79.8	50.91	76.0	48.48
1870	1,618	85.0	52.54	81.5	50.38
1871	1,668	82.0	49.16	78.5	47.06
1872	1,727	97.5	56.47	86.9	50.33
1873	1,785	112.9	63.25	95.9	53.73
1874	1,844	114.1	61.89	99.1	53.76
1875	1,902	123.3	64.83	109.9	57.78
1876	1,961	122.4	62.43	109.6	55.90
1877	2,019	125.2	62.01	114.1	56.51
1878	2,078	130.8	62.96	125.0	60.17
1879	2,136	133.2	62.36	126.9	59.41
1880	2,195	138.6	63.16	133.5	60.83
1881	2,253	147.8	65.60	143.2	63.56
1882	2,345	154.0	65.67	135.2	57.65
1883	2,437	171.3	70.29	155.2	63.68
1884	2,529	168.5	66.62	156.1	61.72
1885	2,621	180.1	68.70	166.3	63.44
1886	2,714	177.4	65.38	168.2	61.99
1887	2,806	195.6	69.72	192.4	68.58
1888	2,898	201.5	69.54	187.4	64.67
1889	2,990	221.4	74.05	203.3	68.00
1890	3,082	214.9	69.73	196.4	63.73
1891	3,174	211.6	66.67	211.6	66.67
1892	3,234	179.7	55.57	185.4	57.33
1893	3,294	160.6	48.76	175.3	53.22
1894	3,354	156.1	46.54	181.4	54.08
1895	3,414	148.3	43.44	171.0	50.09
1896	3,474	168.1	48.39	184.1	52.99

Table 5:2-2. (*cont.*)

Year	Population (thousands)	Gross Domestic Product (millions of pounds)	Gross Domestic Product per capita (pounds)	Gross Domestic Product (millions of 1911 pounds)	Gross Domestic Product per capita (1911 pounds)
1897	3,534	161.7	45.76	173.8	49.18
1898	3,594	186.6	51.92	200.9	55.90
1899	3,654	190.4	52.11	201.1	55.04
1900	3,714	198.3	53.39	212.9	57.32
1901	3,774	194.5	51.54	206.7	54.77
1902	3,842	197.6	51.43	208.6	54.28
1903	3,910	209.0	53.44	220.4	56.35
1904	3,978	223.1	56.08	235.4	59.16
1905	4,046	231.7	57.26	242.2	59.86
1906	4,114	254.6	61.87	259.8	63.13
1907	4,183	271.5	64.91	271.9	65.01
1908	4,251	276.6	65.06	280.1	65.90
1909	4,319	296.4	68.62	301.2	69.73
1910	4,387	321.0	73.17	321.3	73.24
1911	4,455	337.9	75.85	323.8	72.67
1912	4,553	361.5	79.40	332.9	73.12
1913	4,651	394.5	84.81	351.7	75.61
1914	4,749	392.5	82.63	323.9	68.19

Note: Data for 1901 through 1914 estimated by averaging fiscal years [i.e. 1901 = (1900/1901 + 1901/1902)/2].

Sources: Brian R. Mitchell, *International Historical Statistics: The Americas and Australia*, (Detroit: Gale Research, 1983), Table B1, p. 53. Noel G. Butlin, *Australian Domestic Product, Investment and Foreign Borrowing, 1861–1938/ 1939* (Cambridge, U.K.: Cambridge University Press, 1962), Table 1, pp. 6–7 & Table 13, pp. 33–34.

Although the methods of estimating capital formation probably exaggerated the sharpness of the second cycle, our picture of the short boom and slump during 1880–2 is amply supported by the literary evidence. During this phase a great deal of pastoral investment took the form of the equipment of entire pastoral stations, carried out by pioneers and 'developers' anxious to realize on 'monopoly' advantages through control of extensive leasehold areas or in the expectation of short-term capital gains from stations purchases and sales.

"The third phase, rising gradually from the low level of 1882, was similarly based on speculative investments designed for short-term capital gains in a rising real estate market and was reinforced by a rapidly growing demand for stock as

Table 5:2-3. *Australia: Gross domestic capital formation, overseas
borrowing, and domestic savings (millions of pounds)*

Year	Gross domestic capital formation	Gross domestic private capital formation	Gross domestic public capital formation	Net overseas borrowing	Domestic savings
1861–1875	12.03	7.27	4.76	3.81	8.22
1876–1888	18.49	10.66	7.83	7.13	11.37
1889–1897	13.36	6.41	6.95	4.22	9.15
1898–1914	14.21	7.53	6.68	0.65	13.56
1861–1888	15.03	8.84	6.18	5.35	9.68
1861–1914	14.49	8.02	6.47	3.68	10.81
1861–1870				5.69	5.98
1871–1880				1.74	13.29
1881–1890				9.45	9.38
1891–1900				2.64	9.54
1901–1910				–0.71	14.25
1911–1914				2.69	14.85
1901–1914				0.26	14.42

representing a falling fraction of total economic activity, it continued to
provide support for deficits in the remainder of the current account.
Non-pastoral farming – wheat, meat, dairy products, and beef – replaced
pastoral activities in some parts of southeastern Australia, particularly
in the late 1870s and early 1880s. City building became important as
the economy became steadily more urbanized, and the colonial governments became deeply involved in what might be labeled developmental
strategy.

the industry spread inland, particularly into Queensland and country west of
Darling in New South Wales. Accelerating in 1886 as seasons and prices began
to improve, the level of investment rose to a high, if somewhat uneven, plateau
extending until 1891. From this high point, sustained after other major sectors
of the economy had begun to contract, the level of pastoral investment fell
heavily, to touch bottom in 1897 in the major phases of pastoral and financial
reconstruction, when flocks were contracting, foreclosures were common, and
many stations were being abandoned." Noel G. Butlin, "The Growth of Rural
Capital, 1860–1890," in Alan Barnard (ed.), *The Simple Fleece: Studies in the
Australian Wool Industry* (Parkville, Victoria: Melbourne University Press in
Association with the Australian National University, 1962), pp. 325–27.

Table 5:2-4. *Australia: industrial distribution of fixed capital formation: the long boom, depression, and after*

Panel A
Thousands of pounds

Years	Government	Residential	Industrial & commercial	Mining	Shipping	Pastoral & agriculture	Total private	Total public & private
1865–1889	206,737	133,892	51,261	6,511	1,904	136,254	336,626	543,363
1890–1899	121,182	41,727	21,195	4,842	235	41,099	109,098	230,280
1900–1914	306,177	126,171	95,922	25,978	10,249	64,501	322,820	628,996
1865–1914	634,096	301,790	168,378	37,331	12,388	241,854	768,544	1,402,639

Panel B
Percent of total fixed capital formation

Years	Government	Residential	Industrial & commercial	Mining	Shipping	Pastoral & agriculture	Total private	Total public & private
1865–1889	38.0	24.6	9.4	1.2	0.4	25.1	62.0	100.0
1890–1899	52.6	18.1	9.2	2.1	0.1	17.8	47.4	100.0
1900–1914	48.7	20.1	15.3	4.1	1.6	10.3	51.3	100.0
1865–1914	45.2	21.5	12.0	2.7	0.9	17.2	54.8	100.0

Panel C
Percent of total private capital formation

Years	Government	Residential	Industrial & commercial	Mining	Shipping	Pastoral & agriculture	Total private	Total public & private
1865–1889	61.4	39.8	15.2	1.9	0.6	40.5	100.0	161.4
1890–1899	111.1	38.2	19.4	4.4	0.2	37.7	100.0	211.1
1900–1914	94.8	39.1	29.7	8.0	3.2	20.0	100.0	194.8
1865–1914	82.5	39.3	21.9	4.9	1.6	31.5	100.0	182.5

Source: Table 5:2-5.

Table 5:2-5. *Australia: the industrial distribution of fixed capital formation: the long boom, depression, and after*

Panel A
Thousands of pounds

Years	Railroads government	Other government	Total government	Residential	Industrial & commercial	Mining	Shipping	Pastoral & agriculture	Total private	Total public & private
1865–1889	98,916	107,821	206,737	133,892	51,261	6,511	1,904	136,254	336,626	543,363
1890–1899	50,135	71,047	121,182	41,727	21,195	4,842	235	41,099	109,098	230,280
1900–1914	131,957	174,220	306,177	126,171	95,922	25,978	10,249	64,501	322,820	628,996
1865–1914	281,008	353,088	634,096	301,790	168,378	37,331	12,388	241,854	768,544	1,402,639

Panel B
Percent of total fixed capital formation

Years	Railroads government	Other government	Total government	Residential	Industrial & commercial	Mining	Shipping	Pastoral & agriculture	Total private	Total public & private
1865–1889	18.2	19.8	38.0	24.6	9.4	1.2	0.4	25.1	62.0	100.0
1890–1899	21.8	30.9	52.6	18.1	9.2	2.1	0.1	17.8	47.4	100.0
1900–1914	21.0	27.7	48.7	20.1	15.3	4.1	1.6	10.3	51.3	100.0
1865–1914	20.0	25.2	45.2	21.5	12.0	2.7	0.9	17.2	54.8	100.0

Panel C
Percent of total private capital formation

Years	Railroads government	Other government	Total government	Residential	Industrial & commercial	Mining	Shipping	Pastoral & agriculture	Total private	Total public & private
1865–1889	29.4	32.0	61.4	39.8	15.2	1.9	0.6	40.5	100.0	161.4
1890–1899	46.0	65.1	111.1	38.2	19.4	4.4	0.2	37.7	100.0	211.1
1900–1914	40.9	54.0	94.8	39.1	29.7	8.0	3.2	20.0	100.0	194.8
1865–1914	36.6	45.9	82.5	39.3	21.9	4.9	1.6	31.5	100.0	182.5

Note: Data for 1901 through 1914 estimated by averaging fiscal years (e.g. 1901 = [(1900/1901 + 1901/1902)/2].

Source: N.G. Butlin, *Australian Domestic Product, Investment and Foreign Borrowing, 1861–1938/1939* (Cambridge: Cambridge University Press, 1962), Tables 4 & 5, pp. 16–19, Table 211, p. 348, & Table 237, p. 391.

Over the three decades 1860–90, Australian growth was based on four related sectors: the pastoral industry, transport, building, and the service occupations. No longer dominant, pastoral activity was still important; for example, the second boom produced an eleven-fold increase in New South Wales' wool exports. Railways superseded other transport forms, with trunk lines fanning from the major ports to the interior. The building industry expanded in the principal cities as both natural increase and surging immigration underwrote a rapid increase in population, and population became increasingly urbanized. Finally, although the impact on the demand for fixed capital was not great, there was a major increase in the service occupations: financial, commercial, personal, and governmental.[847]

The impact of these changes on the demand for capital is captured in Table 5:2-4. The service industries produced little demand for fixed capital, but the government demand drew 38 percent. Of that total, just under half was directed toward the railroads; a large fraction of the remainder was channeled into activities that, in other countries, would have been classified as local authority works. The pastoral and agricultural sector absorbed just over one-quarter, and residential construction just less than that amount. In terms of private capital formation, the latter two sectors accounted for more than four-fifths of the total. Given the role they played in pulling British investment into the subcontinent, it appears appropriate to look at each of the three sectors in more detail.[848]

The demand of the pastoral sector for external finance in the years of the long boom can be traced to the pastoralists' response to two new, but related, sets of technical opportunities: in their willingness to innovate new agricultural technology, narrowly defined, and in their reaction to changes in institutional technology. Beginning in the late 1850s the colonies began to adopt land policies designed to unlock the land from the pastoral leases and open it up to selection by small farmers, the so-called Selection Acts. In New South Wales, for example, the land legislation of 1861 allowed selectors (that is, potential farmers) to purchase up to 320 acres of Crown land, regardless of existing leases, for £1 per acre. Purchases were also subject to a residence requirement and to the

---

[847] N. Butlin, "Colonial Socialism," pp. 29–30. Rodney Maddock and Ian W. McLean, "The Australian Economy in the Very Long Run," in Rodney Maddock and Ian W. McLean, *The Australian Economy in the Long Run* (Cambridge: Cambridge University Press, 1987), p. 11. [Hereafter cited as Maddock and McLean, "The Australian Economy."] Hall, *The London Capital Market*, p. 130.

[848] N. Butlin, "The Shape of the Australian Economy," p. 17.

purchasers making minimal improvements on the property. A squatter had the right to purchase a twenty-fifth of his run and certain improved areas, but in the future squatting leases were to be limited to five years. Similar legislation was adopted in the other states.

In terms of the lawmakers' stated intentions, the laws should certainly be judged to have been failures. Nonetheless, they posed both problems and opportunities for the squatting pastoralists. Not only did purchase preempt potential agriculturists, but it also gave the pastoralist secure title. For the first time squatters were given an incentive to make permanent improvements that could increase carrying capacity and productivity; freehold title implied complete legal title to improvements, not merely the rights of compensation. Hitherto, external pastoral financial requirements had been relatively small and were easily met by merchants and local banks. With selection, however, the squatters were under substantial pressure to buy as much land as they could – either directly, through the employment of dummy selectors, or by "peacocking," an attempt to purchase key portions of a holding, thereby making surrounding areas unusable by others, and reserving them for future purchase by the squatter. As a result, Crown land sales rose steeply between 1871 and 1884. Purchase, however, required more capital than the pastoralist could command either directly or indirectly through the primitive local capital markets; but the squatters were now in legal possession of an asset that they could offer as security. New financial innovations were necessary.[849]

In the 1860s, when squatters referred to "improving their runs," they usually meant the acquisition of freehold and not the construction of fences, dams, wells, washing equipment, or homesteads.[850] Ten years later, although land purchase was still important, the meaning of the term "improvements" had been much expanded. "The character of the Australian pastoral station was transformed during the seventies. The old property of the forties, running scabby sheep, tended by shepherds, with a few rough structures erected on land to which there was no security of title, was now changed into a large, secure area on which extensive buildings, miles of fencing, and fixed paddock arrangements had been installed, water provision had been made, and in which a considerable

---

[849] Reginald Frank Holder, *Bank of New South Wales: A History*, 2 vols. (Sydney: Angus and Robertson, 1970), p. 264. [Hereafter cited as Holder, *Bank of New South Wales.*] N. Butlin, "Colonial Socialism," pp. 53–54. J.D. Bailey, *A Hundred Years of Pastoral Banking: A History of the Australian Mercantile Land & Finance Company, 1863–1963* (Oxford: Clarendon Press, 1966), p. 53. [Hereafter cited as Bailey, *A Hundred Years.*]

[850] Bailey, *A Hundred Years*, p. 53.

portion of the land might be privately owned."[851] The new technology involved a combination of fencing and water conservation, and it is difficult to unscramble the effects of the two. Fencing, by reducing labor costs, permitting better breeding, making it possible to control disease, and by permitting increased lambing percentages, raised the productivity of each acre of land. Water conservation broke the direct link between usable land and the supply of natural water and, thus, increased the number of arable acres. The well-watered lands were the first candidates for fencing, but further extension of the fence technology depended on investment in water conservation. Taken together, the two techniques made it possible to increase greatly the size of the flock as well as raise the quality of the fleece.[852] But as the margins of production were pushed into more arid land, further additions demanded ever larger investments in water conservation; and, from at least the mid-1870s, the expansion of the industry involved the development of poorly watered land well away from the main rivers. By the next decade the industry had moved into land that, *ex post*, proved incapable of supporting a high level of pastoral activity in the long run.[853] With the geographic expansion, the relative productivity of the marginal acres declined rapidly; and profits became increasingly dependent on rising wool prices.[854]

From the very beginning the industry itself had been "characterized by entrepreneurship and creative adaptability to the environment of an extremely high order."[855] At the same time evidence suggests that individual stations rarely succeeded in saving more than one-fifth of their income, and the average was closer to half that amount. Given the new demands for investment, it is clear "that the industry was incapable of providing, from its own resources, more than a small fraction of the total capital requirements."[856] This combination of low business savings

---

[851] Noel G. Butlin and A. Barnard, "Pastoral Finance and Capital Requirements, 1860–1890," chap. 26 in Alan Barnard (ed.), *The Simple Fleece: Studies in the Australian Wool Industry* (Parkville, Victoria: Melbourne University Press in Association with the Australian National University, 1962), p. 385. [Hereafter cited as Butlin and Barnard, "Pastoral Finance."]

[852] Sinclair, *The Process of Economic Growth*, p. 86.

[853] Jackson, *Australian Economic Development*, pp. 17–18.

[854] Sinclair, *The Process of Economic Growth*, pp. 129–30.

[855] John Fogarty, "Staples, Super-Staples and the Limits of Staple Theory: The Experiences of Argentina, Australia, and Canada Compared," in D.C.M. Platt and Guido di Tella (eds.), *Argentine, Australia and Canada: Studies in Comparative Development, 1870–1965* (New York: St. Martin's Press, 1985), pp. 24–25. [Hereafter cited as Fogarty, "Staples Super-Staples."]

[856] Butlin and Barnard, "Pastoral Finance," p. 388.

coupled with creative entrepreneurship led to a wave of external – largely British – finance being directed toward the industry.

In the case of residential construction, although some foreign finance was involved, particularly during the 1880s, most of the sector's connection with the international capital market was indirect. Unlike most other types of capital formation, during the long boom Australian housing was in the main financed by local Australian savings. Indirectly, however, even then British capital played a very important role. On the one hand, it kept interest rates low enough to encourage investments in this essentially long-run activity. On the other hand, it promoted a very high level of per capita income – a level of income that, in turn, generated a substantial flow of domestic savings.[857] As a result, except for the years of rapid pastoral expansion, 1874–81, residential building was the single most important field of private investment during the long boom. Moreover, the residential housing component of the capital stock surged during the decade of the 1880s when a combination of "rapid natural increase in population, heavy immigration and increased urban concentration gave rise to a burst of building activity which strained the resources of the Australian economy."[858]

The demand for housing rested on three aspects of Australian development. First, because of the very heavy immigration in the 1850s, the stock of residential housing per capita at the beginning of the long boom was very low. Noel Butlin neatly summarizes that state of affairs: "in the beginning, the Australian settlements were literally bulging at the seams of the tents in which so many were housed and the 'permanent housing' which existed was tiny and grossly overcrowded."[859] Second, in the 1880s,

---

[857] N. Butlin, *Investment in Australian Development*, p. 245. Between 1871 and 1890, Noel Butlin places the average ratio of domestic savings to gross domestic product at 12 percent. Over the same years Taylor and Williamson estimate that the domestic savings rate averaged 13.2 percent. N. Butlin, *Australian Domestic Product*, table 13, pp. 33–34; table 250, p. 422; table 265, p. 44. N. Butlin, *Investment in Australian Development*, table 1, p. 11; appendix table II, p. 454. Alan M. Taylor and Jeffrey G. Williamson, "Capital Flows to the New World as Intergenerational Transfer," National Bureau of Economic Research, Historical Factors in Long Run Growth, Working Paper No. 32, December 1991, appendix table A2, pp. 29–30.

Edelstein discusses the cause of the movement in the savings rate over the years 1861–1911. His explanation rests on a combination of secular and cyclic change. Edelstein, *Overseas Investment*, pp. 260–69.

[858] Hall, *The London Capital Market*, p. 130.

[859] N. Butlin, "Some Structural Features," pp. 399–400.

the economy experienced the first "echo" of the demographic shock of the 1850s.[860] Gold discoveries had brought large numbers of single men to Australia, and single women soon followed. Those immigration patterns left in their wake an abnormal proportion of the population in the childbearing age group.[861] Within a few years many of the immigrants had married and established families. By the 1880s their children had, in turn, grown up and begun to form their own families – the percentage of the age group twenty-five to twenty-nine in the total Australian population rose to more than 10 percent in that decade – and these young adults increased the demand for housing substantially. Allen Kelly estimates that, had the age structure been unchanged over the years 1861–1911, the demand for housing in the quinquennium 1880–85 would have been 26 percent lower than it actually was.[862] In Victoria, for example, by 1891, the proportion of the population in the house-buying age group had increased by one-third over the level of the two previous censuses.[863] Finally, immigration surged during the last decade of the long boom: Net immigration totaled 380,000 between 1881 and 1890 compared with, for example, 173,000 in the decade 1861–70, 192,000 over the years 1871–80, 25,000 over the decade of the great depression, and 41,000 over the first decade of the twentieth century.

Although the citizens of Victoria, particularly Melbourne, were treated to the most exciting ride on the speculative land boom roller coaster of the 1880s, all states received massive infusions of residential capital. Because of the notoriety it received, and because of its connection with the depression of the next decade, historians have, however, tended to focus on Melbourne. There an initial housing shortage, coupled with the city's growing wealth and population, touched off an initial spate of residential construction. When, in 1884, twice as many urban dwellings were erected as in 1883, the boom took on a life of its own. In 1888 a block of land on the corner of Collins and Elizabeth Street sold for £2,300 a foot, a sum that was, in real terms, twice as high as the most expensive piece of land in the city seven decades later. Between 1882 and 1889 investment in urban land returned over 40 percent a year to citizens, builders, and speculators who chose to commit their funds to that activity and who

---

[860] Total immigration into Australia during the 1850s was the highest of any pre–World War I decade.

[861] Sinclair, *The Process of Economic Growth*, p. 128.

[862] Allen C. Kelley, "Demographic Change and Economic Growth: Australia, 1861–1911," Working Paper, July 28, 1966. pp. 6, 23, charts II and VIII.

[863] Sinclair, *The Process of Economic Development*, p. 128.

managed to cash out before the boom collapsed.[864] In fact, Noel Butlin concluded that "Australian economic development is mainly a story of urbanization. The building of cities absorbed the greater part of Australian resources devoted to developmental purposes; the operation of enterprises in the towns employed most of the increasing population engaged in work."[865] Victorian residents employed much more than one-third share of Australia's new capital formation to build "a number of the greatest cities in the world."[866]

Speculative profits merely represent transfers of wealth from losers to winners. During the 1880s there was also a substantial level of real investment in residential housing, and those houses were largely located in urban areas. Between 1881 and 1890 residential capital formation totaled £33.8 million in Victoria, £33.6 million in New South Wales, £11.0 million in Queensland, £4.3 million in South Australia, and £1.9 million in Tasmania. In per capita terms, however, Victoria averaged £3.39, less than Queensland's £3.61 or New South Wales' £3.60, but still more that twice as much as Tasmania's £1.45 or South Australia's £1.44.[867] By 1890 there may well have been a national excess supply of housing.[868]

In 1870 there were more than 950 miles of railroads in the six colonies. Between 1870 and 1891 construction proceeded at a compound rate of more than 11 percent a year – an average annual increase of 441 miles.[869]

---

[864] Geoffrey Blainey, *Gold and Paper: A History of the National Bank of Australasia Limited* (Melbourne: Georgian House, 1958), pp. 131, 135. [Hereafter cited as Blainey, *Gold and Paper.*] R. Silberberg, "Rates of Return on Melbourne Land Investment, 1880–92," *The Economic Record*, Vol. 51, No. 134 (June 1975), table VII, p. 215. [Hereafter cited as Silberberg, "Rates of Return."] Silberberg somewhat asymmetrically compares those returns (43.1 percent) with earning for the same years on trading bank deposits (5.1), 90-day commercial paper rates (6.8), trading bank overdrafts (8.8), and mining stocks (29.7).

[865] N. Butlin, "The Shape of the Australian Economy," p. 21.

[866] Blainey, *Gold and Paper*, p. 130.

[867] N. Butlin, *Australian Domestic Product*, part III, table 156, p. 268. Population figures are from the Colonial Office, *Colonial Blue Books*, assorted years.

[868] Jackson, *Australian Economic Development*, p. 18.

[869] Hall places the 1970 figure at 994, Mitchell at 950. Hall, *The London Capital Market*, appendix V, table V, p. 212. See also Mitchell, *The Americas and Australasia*, table G1, p. 666. N. Butlin provides mileage figures for only four colonies (New South Wales, Queensland, South Australia, and Victoria). For those four the annual rate of growth was 10.7 percent, and the annual average of miles constructed was 380. To the extent that the Hall and Butlin series are comparable, it appears that Tasmania and Western Australia together had 41 miles in 1870 and 1,236 miles in 1891. N. Butlin, *Investment in Australian Development*, table 70, p. 324.

Moreover, all colonies appear to have participated in the expansion. On a per capita basis, between 1871 and 1890 annual gross railroad capital formation ranged from £0.77 in Tasmania to £3.41 in Queensland; but if the focus is narrowed to the 1880s, New South Wales, Victoria, South Australia, and Western Australia all fall between £2.38 and £2.75. Queensland, however, comes in at £4.12, and Tasmania still lags at £1.30.[870]

The railroads were much more directly involved in international capital transfers than either the pastoral or the residential construction industries. In the case of pastoral finance, although many pastoral mortgage and finance companies raised funds directly on the British market, they also drew a substantial fraction of their foreign funds indirectly through some domestic intermediary. Until the 1880s residential construction was largely domestically financed.[871] In the case of the railroads, the bulk of the construction was undertaken by the colonies, and they raised most of their loans in London, specifically for that purpose.[872]

By the end of the 1880s, except in Western Australia, the nation's basic long-term railway network was in place; however, the construction undertaken during that decade had clearly outrun the immediate needs of the economy.[873] Many of the new lines served marginal new regions and added relatively little traffic or revenue to the system. In the next century, when new innovations in wheat growing and ocean shipping technologies had come about, the railroads built in the 1880s may have played a significant role in the growth of new export industries. In 1890, however, it had become obvious that recent railway expenditures had been wasteful and that the system as a whole did not pay its own way. John B. Trivet, the government statistician, observed that "if one

---

[870] Capital formation figures are from N. Butlin, *Australian Domestic Product*, part III, table 211, p. 348.

[871] By the 1870s many Australasian banks had entered into pastoral finance, and some even established pastoral subsidiaries. "More common, however, were informal relations between banker and agent whereby the latter served as an intermediary for loans to farmers." The Bank of New South Wales, for example, dealt with a number of agent firms in both Australia and New Zealand. Those agents included Pitt, Son and Badgery in New South Wales and Wright Stevenson in New Zealand. Simon Ville, "Networks and Venture Capital in the Australasian Pastoral Sector Before World War Two," *Business History*, July 1996, pp. 50–51.

[872] In 1913 there were 952 miles of private mineral and timber lines; they represented less than 5 percent of total mileage. Hall, *The London Capital Market*, p. 122, appendix V, p. 209, and table V, p. 212.

[873] Hall, *The London Capital Market*, pp. 124–25.

added the interest charges on government borrowings to the railways' operating costs, during the nineteenth century the railways paid their way only in 1881–3 and 1889."[874]

Over most of the 1880s the Australian, and particularly the Victorian, economy had been marked by both high levels of consumption and high levels of investment.[875] That state of affairs was only possible because British savers were willing to finance a high proportion of investment outlays; over the decade 1881–90, foreign investment totaled £174.1 million and accounted for 51 percent of gross capital formation.[876] For example, in 1889 in Victoria government, local and semi-government authorities, breweries, banks, pastoral companies, building societies, land finance institutions, and a number of mines all successfully floated loans or equities in London.[877] To the north, in New South Wales, by 1890 almost half of the pastoralists were mortgaged clients of banks or brokers. Those intermediaries, in turn, drew a substantial fraction of their finance from Britain. The debts of single pastoral stations not uncommonly exceeded £500,000, and obligations of £250,000 were frequent.[878] For the economy as a whole, foreign loan commitments had created an untenable situation. "In national product terms, interest due overseas rose from about 3 percent of net national product in 1861 to about 9 percent in 1890. This matched the great fall in export values over the period. By 1890, about 40 percent of Australian exports were committed to meeting overseas interest obligations."[879]

5-2b(2). Depression: It is difficult to understand how, in 1890, any thoughtful Australian would have believed that the new decade would be as prosperous as the past four. Taking all the evidence together – the heavy foreign borrowing, the extension of the pastoral sector into increasingly arid regions, the over-building in the residential sector, and the increasing marginalization of the newly built railroads – it should

---

[874] Sinclair, *The Process of Economic Growth*, p. 169. Salsbury and Sweeny, *The Bull, The Bear*, p. 172. Trivet is quoted in *The Official Yearbook for New South Wales, 1909–10*, p. 130.

[875] All six of the colonies did not share equally in the prosperity of the decade. South Australia, for example, experienced a substantial depression in 1884–86, a depression that was strong enough to produce a decline in population and some bank failures. Blainey, *Gold and Paper*, pp. 118–19.

[876] Hall, *The Stock Exchange of Melbourne*, pp. 202–3. N. Butlin, *Australian Domestic Product*, table 13, pp. 33–34; table 250, p. 422, table 265, p. 444. N. Butlin, *Investment in Australian Development*, table 1, p. 11, appendix table II, p. 454.

[877] Hall, *The Stock Exchange of Melbourne*, p. 149.

[878] Butlin and Barnard, "Pastoral Finance," pp. 393–94.

[879] N. Butlin, "The Shape of the Australian Economy," p. 25.

have been obvious that the long boom must soon come to a halt. The end might be delayed as long as the British were content to pour funds into the six states, but such largess could not go on forever. The minute it stopped, there were certain to be problems. It was probably less clear that the depression would have been so sharp or that it would have lasted so long.

The census of 1891 reported that there were 3.174 million residents of Australia. That year, in terms of 1911 prices, the continent's gross domestic product is estimated to have been £211.6 million, or £66.7 pounds per capita. Four years later, in 1895, the figures were 3.414 million, £171.0 million, and £50.1 pounds per capita. In 1901, on the eve of Federation, population had increased to 3.714 million, but gross domestic product stood at only £206.7, or £54.8 pounds per capita (see Table 5:2-2). By the latter date, if one ignores the loss of a decade's growth, economic recovery had, in some sense, been achieved; but living standards had still not returned to the level of 1891.[880] Recovery, in that sense, was still a decade away. The Australian economy had experienced its first major recession since that of the 1840s. The early 1890s saw a very sharp reduction in the sheep population, a major shakeout in the financial sector, a cessation of immigration, and increased unemployment.[881]

As one historian has written, "the first half of the 'nineties was a period of unrelieved calamity for the Australian economy."[882] Although the effects of the Barings Crisis had a negative short-term impact on the state governments' abilities to borrow in London, the long-term roots of the depression lay in the Australian domestic economy. The crisis was a product of the collapse of domestic private investment, particularly in building and in the pastoral industry. In aggregate, gross domestic capital formation declined from an annual average of £35.3 million in the decade 1882–91 to £21.3 million in the decade 1892–1901 – a fall of more than 40 percent. Although both public and private investment suffered, the private sector fared much worse; there the decline was more than 50 percent.[883] The share of the private sector – a sector that had, between 1865 and 1890, accounted for more than 60 percent of all gross capital formation – declined to less than half of the total during the 1890s. Nor did it rebound quickly. It still accounted for barely half in the years leading up to the World War I (see Table 5:2-4).

[880] N. Butlin, "The Shape of the Australian Economy," p. 25.
[881] Maddock and McLean, "The Australian Economy," pp. 11–13.
[882] S. Butlin, *Australia and New Zealand Bank*, p. 279.
[883] The decline was from £193.7 to £95.4 million. N. Butlin, *Australian Domestic Product*, table 13, pp. 33–4, table 250, p. 422, table 265, p. 444. N. Butlin, *Investment in Australian Development*, table 1, p. 11, appendix table II, p. 454.

In the public sector nineteenth-century Australian colonial governments were expected to maintain balanced budgets but to finance the greater part of their outlays on public works through borrowing. After 1890, partly in response to the Barings crisis, and partly in response to a breakdown in existing market institutions, it became more difficult for them to issue securities in London. In 1891, for example, issues on the governments of South Australia, Victoria, and Queensland all failed badly.[884] Financial constraints did force some reductions in the states' public works programs, but the governments were in a better position than were businessmen in the private sector.[885] Between 1892 and 1900 state-financed railroad construction added only 62 percent of the mileage of the annual 1870–90 average. If, however, 1896 is ignored and 1901 included, the decline is only 17 percent.

However, the *share* of the pastoral and agriculture sectors in gross capital formation declined by almost 30 percent. Although the data on wool production and value tell a somewhat less dramatic story, of the 104 million sheep that made up the Australian flock in 1894, only half survived until 1902; and, even as late as 1914, the flock numbered only 90 million. Even after the recovery, wool exports that had commonly accounted for three-fifths of foreign earnings contributed only half that amount.[886] Similarly, the share of residential construction in additions to the capital stock declined by more than one-quarter.

The problems of the pastoral and residential construction industries were mirrored in the financial sector. The operations of the building societies, the land and mortgage banks, and the trading banks had come to be inexorably linked to investment in the two most affected sectors; and they too crumbled with the collapse of those industries. Although the crisis of the 1890s has often been linked to the most dramatic event of the period – the "great bank crash" of April–May 1893 – the actual depression began with the first clear break in the long boom. As early as 1889 the banks and non-bank intermediaries had been under pressure to contract lending, and the trading banking crisis itself extended from mid-1891 through late 1893.[887]

Although there had been earlier warnings, the first clear signal to those who were alert came at the end of 1889, when the Premier Permanent Building Association of Melbourne, a victim of the collapse of that city's

---

[884] Hall, *The London Capital Market*, p. 101. Hall, *The Stock Exchange of Melbourne*, pp. 152–53.
[885] Hall, *The Stock Exchange of Melbourne*, p. 125.
[886] Denoon, *Settler Capitalism*, pp. 100–1.
[887] Holder, *Bank of New South Wales*, pp. 442–43. S. Butlin, *Australia and New Zealand Bank*, p. 279.

residential boom, suspended payment. Unfortunately, because of the "scandalous way in which its affairs had been conducted," most of the public, although recognizing that its demise was the "most disastrous [failure] that had ever taken place in Melbourne, viewed the bankruptcy as an idiosyncratic event." Boehm argues that the evidence indicates that the banking system was becoming more vulnerable in the years immediately after 1888.[888] The ensuing financial collapse of 1890 and 1891 – a product of the puncturing of both the residential and the pastoral land booms – saw the large-scale failure of both the nation's building societies and its land banks. Ultimately, the land and mortgage failures were to include some of the nation's oldest and most trusted firms; the list included both the New Zealand Loan & Mercantile Agency and Goldsbrough Mort & Company. The land and mortgage banks discovered that their pastoral accounts were largely illiquid. They had loaned to stations whose land was "over-stocked and eaten out by rabbits and drought," that faced declining wool and livestock prices, and where the value of their accumulated debt exceeded the market value of their runs – that is, where foreclosure was not a profitable alternative.[889] Only one mortgage or land bank – the Land Mortgage Bank of Victoria – kept its doors open throughout the depression. Thirty-five such "banks" closed, "most of them permanently and most in discreditable circumstances."[890]

The building societies, although generally on sounder financial footing than the land and mortgage companies, suffered from the general loss of depositor confidence in all institutions whose assets consisted largely of land and from the withdrawals of depositors whose income had fallen or who found themselves unemployed.[891] The following two years were particularly bad for the building societies.[892] "It was the fringe banks and the building societies that succumbed first. The deluge began in late 1891 and early 1892 with widespread failures. Some of the most significant closures were by a group of companies, including the Mercantile Bank of Australia, associated with Sir Matthew Davies and his parliamentary colleagues. Public confidence in the safety of banks was severely damaged by the wayward management of this group of companies whose entire

---

[888] E.A. Boehm, *Prosperity and Depression in Australia, 1887–1897* (Oxford: Clarendon Press, 1971) [hereafter cited as Boehm, *Prosperity and Depression*], pp. 258–60, 278.

[889] Bailey, *A Hundred Years*, pp. 145–46.

[890] S. Butlin, *Australia and New Zealand Bank*, pp. 279–80.

[891] M. Butlin, "Capital Markets," pp. 229–30. Hall, *The Stock Exchange of Melbourne*, pp. 153–54.

[892] Holder, *Bank of New South Wales*, p. 443.

capital had been lost."[893] At first, in an attempt to help them cover their loss of deposits, several of the major trading banks made substantial advances to their client building societies. In December 1891, however, the management of the Commercial Bank of Australia, the banker for a large group of building societies, decided to make no further advances. As a result, a substantial fraction of the nation's building societies suspended payment.[894]

The failure of the building societies and the mortgage and land banks continued during the first half of 1892, the contagion spreading from Victoria, to New South Wales, to Queensland. The weakest and most badly managed companies were wiped out, but others were saved by government intervention.[895] Between August 1891 and February 1892, in Sydney twenty-two building societies, mortgage land banks, and other institutions soliciting public deposits failed. "In Melbourne, between July 1891 and March 1892, twenty building societies and 'banks' failed with total deposits of £10,582,806." Between the two states more than £18 million in deposits were locked up.[896]

The contagion, however, did not stop with the land and mortgage banks and the building and loan societies. The trading banks had provided substantial financial support to the land-related intermediaries, and the public's concern about their liquidity touched off a sequence of runs. If a bank is defined as "any institution which so described itself and which solicited public deposits . . . there were at least sixty-four banks in Australia in mid-1891; by mid-1893 fifty-four of them had closed, thirty-four of them permanently." Of the twenty-eight more conventionally defined banks, six suspended payment during the first crisis of 1891–92, thirteen between April 6 and May 15, 1893. Only nine remained open continuously.[897] In April and May 1893 alone, half of all the bank deposits

---

[893] David T. Merrett, "Preventing Bank Failures: Could the Commercial Bank of Australia Have Been Saved by Its Peers in 1893?" *Victorian Historical Journal*, Vol. 64, No. 2 (October 1993), *passim*, the quotation is from p. 125. [Hereafter cited as Merrett, "Preventing Bank Failures."]

[894] Hall, *The Stock Exchange of Melbourne*, pp. 153–54.

[895] Holder, *Bank of New South Wales*, pp. 445–46.

[896] S. Butlin, *Australia and New Zealand Bank*, pp. 286–87. Blainey, *Gold and Paper*, p. 147.

[897] S. Butlin, *Australia and New Zealand Bank*, pp. 279–80, 288. The nine included two London-based banks (the Bank of Australasia and the Union Bank of Australia), two with head offices in Sydney (the Bank of New South Wales and the City Bank of Sydney), and one each with headquarters in Melbourne (Royal Bank of Australia), Adelaide (Bank of Adelaide), Hobart (the Commercial Bank of Tasmania), Launceston (the National Bank of Tasmania), and Perth (the Western Australian Bank).

in the country had been frozen, and at least half of the bank notes in circulation ceased to be freely negotiable.[898]

In 1892 in Melbourne, the center of the original crisis, a joint pledge of mutual support by the voluntary Association of Banks of Melbourne was initially thought sufficient to prevent a wave of successive failures; but the Association's refusal to save the Commercial Bank of Australia, a member of the Association, demonstrated just how hollow this promise really was.[899] The March failure of the Mercantile Bank had led the state's Treasurer to urge that the Associated Banks provide some statement of joint support. On the 28th the Association complied with his wishes and issued a public statement designed to restore confidence in its member banks. "It read: 'we are authorized to state that the Associated Banks in Melbourne have agreed on mutually satisfactory conditions on which they will extend their joint support to any one of their number requiring it.' This statement has been widely interpreted as successfully allaying fears concerning the safety of banks," and to have, for the moment, reduced the risk of a potentially contagious series of bank runs. The guarantee, however, was substantially less than it appeared. The conditions attached to the statement – conditions that were not made public – included the phrase "the Associated Banks are prepared to assist any one of their number should an occasion arise to a reasonable amount upon the sound basis of approved securities." The bankers were clearly not entering into an agreement to underwrite an unfunded scheme of

---

[898] S. Butlin, *Australia and New Zealand Bank*, p. 302. B.L. Bentick has argued that in Victoria (particularly in Melbourne) the realized increase in real wealth from capital gain and expectation of future capital gains decreased the private propensity to save from personal disposable income by building up wealth, and expectations of its growth, independently of savings. He then goes on to suggest that the decrease in the propensity to save, coupled with little change in the propensity to consume, contributed to, without necessarily creating, the subsequent liquidity crisis of the financial system. B.L. Bentick, "Foreign Borrowing, Wealth, and Consumption: Victoria 1878–93," *Economic Record*, Vol. 45 (September 1969), pp. 415–29.

[899] A.S.J. Baster, *The Imperial Banks* (London: P.S. King & Son, 1929), p. 150. [Hereafter cited as Baster, *Imperial Banks*.] "The Associated Banks was a Melbourne body consisting of those banks which shared in the government banking business. The Association decided matters of common policy, but although it was the premier Australian banking organization it confined its decisions to Victoria. It consisted of four Anglo-Australian banks whose main Australian offices were in Melbourne – the Australasian, Union, London, Chartered, and the English, Scottish & Australian Chartered – and six banks whose head offices were in Melbourne – National, Commercial, Victoria, Colonial, City of Melbourne, and Federal." Blainey, *Gold and Paper*, p. 146.

deposit insurance with its attendant and nearly overwhelming problems of moral hazard.[900]

Within a year, however, the Federal and the Commercial Banks, both Associated Bank members, were "under attack from their shareholders and depositors." The Federal Bank requested no assistance and quietly closed its doors. By March 1893 pressure on the Commercial Bank again induced the state's Treasurer to appeal for a statement of support from the Associated Banks; again the banks complied. On March 14th the Associated Banks issued "their fateful statement":

> "As the maintenance of public confidence in the banking institutions of Australia is a matter of national importance, the Treasurer of Victoria, with the approval of the Cabinet, has placed himself in communication with the Associated Banks regarding unfounded and alarmist rumors which have caused disquiet in the minds of the public, and we are authorized to state that the Associated Banks, having considered the position of affairs, have agreed to act unitedly in tendering financial assistance to each other, such be required; and that the government of Victoria has resolved to afford their cordial cooperation."[901]

However, the Superintendent of the Bank of Australasia, John Sawers was absent from the meeting at which the statement had been prepared. On his return from Sydney he insisted that a supplementary statement be issued to the press. On the next morning, a very confused and anxious group of depositors read:

> "In regard to the agreement among the Associated Banks for mutual assistance referred to in yesterday's issue, the matter has been considered by Mr. John Sawers, superintendent of the Bank of Australasia, who has become a party to the understanding, and this opportunity is taken, in view of the articles which appeared in yesterday's newspapers,

---

[900] "What the Associated Banks were prepared to offer, and had offered since the late 1870s, collectively and individually, was to act as a very modest lender of last resort facility. Any bank which found itself short of gold to meet any combination of higher than anticipated withdrawals of deposits, presentation of notes or deficits at the clearing house, could swap some of their short term assets, usually short dated bills, for cash. Such a facility was given to the Colonial, City of Melbourne, the English, Scottish and Australian Chartered and the London Chartered Banks during the crisis." Merrett, "Preventing Bank Failure," pp. 125, 129.

[901] *Australasian Insurance and Banking Register*, March 1893, p. 153. [Hereafter cited as *AIBR*.] For a more complete discussion of the Commercial Bank see R.J. Wood, *The Commercial Bank of Australia Limited: History of an Australian Institution* (North Melbourne, Victoria: Hargreen Publishing Company, 1990). [Hereafter cited as Wood, *The Commerce Bank of Australia*.]

to define accurately to what extent the Associated Banks accept the obligation in question, namely: that they will in the future, as in the past, be willing to render financial assistance to each other, on such terms, and to such an extent as may seem justifiable to each of them, if, and when the occasion arises."[902]

The amended statement made it plain that no binding guarantee of mutual support existed.[903]

Recent research by David Merrett has shown that, even if the banks had wanted to provide the required support, their resources were insufficient; and, if they had tried, "treating the Commercial deficiency as a loss would have wiped out all the shareholders' funds thus causing the banking system to implode. Paradoxically, any attempt to meet the type of unconditional and blanket guarantees demanded by the banks' critics would have ensured that rather than saving the few, all would have been destroyed."[904] Merrett is undoubtedly correct, but the question remains: Would the economy have suffered less had the banks not bowed to the wishes of the Cabinet and issued a statement that, ultimately, provided depositors with a signal of the weakness of the system?

Boot has argued that, in the years before 1892, colonial government relations with domestic banking and capital markets were not governed by the need to maintain a stable banking system but "by the shifting capital needs of the different colonial governments, and by the relative advantage they believed could be gained from playing off domestic banks against each other, and against foreign banks and the London capital market."[905] In the case of the policies adopted by the governments of Victoria and New South Wales during the crisis of the early 1890s, negotiations with the Associated Banks aside, the political response proved more effective than Sidney Butlin's summary might suggest.

Although their motives have been questioned – many of the members of the several state Parliaments had close associations with the threatened building societies and mortgage banks – in 1892 several of the

---

[902] *AIBR*, March 1893, p. 153.

[903] Merrett, "Preventing Bank Failure," p. 126. For a detailed discussion of the failure and subsequent restructuring of the Commercial Bank see R.J. Wood, *The Commercial Bank of Australia*, chap. V. For a somewhat different view of the policies of the bank's general manager, Henry Gyles Turner, in the years leading up to the suspension, see Margot and Alan Beever, "Henry Gyles Turner," in R.T. Appleyard and C.B. Schedvin (eds.), *Australian Financiers: Biographic Essays* (Melbourne: Federal Reserve Bank of Australia, 1988) particularly pages 123–33.

[904] Merrett, "Preventing Bank Failure," p. 138.

[905] Boot, "Government and the Australian Colonial Economy," p. 34.

colonial governments rushed through emergency legislation designed to stop panic withdrawals from the mortgage banks and building societies. If there were reasonable grounds to believe that the majority of the institutions were illiquid rather than insolvent – and that appears to have been the case for many of the building societies, if not the mortgage banks – the New South Wales legislation was a reasonable response to the crisis. That conclusion is probably less true for Victoria, where there were mounting disclosures of "mismanagement, chicanery, falsified accounts and fraud" involving the leading members of Parliament. Despite such questions the laws were passed; creditors were largely prohibited from forcing liquidation of the insolvent institutions, and depositors and shareholders had little option but to defer claims or acquiesce in capital reconstruction. Given the success of these plans, it is not surprising that threatened trading banks found that the procedures could be readily applied to help them solve their problems during the rest of 1892 and in the aftermath of the crash of the following year.[906]

Those plans had important short-term effects on the relationship between British savers and Australian investments, and long-run effects on the structure of Australian capital markets. The first bank to be reconstructed was the Commercial Bank of Australia, and the scenario played out for the Commercial provided the outlines of the reconstruction plans that were adopted by most of the suspended banks. Negotiations between shareholders and depositors in Australia and Britain produced a reorganization plan. When it was accepted by both groups, the courts allowed the bank to reopen. A typical plan required shareholders to pay calls on shares and depositors to agree to accept repayment of their deposits at some date in the more or less distant future. Among the important variations on the scheme was the requirement that deposits be converted into preference shares or that they be converted into interminable deposit stock. In some cases depositors who refused to accept preference shares were given interest-bearing and transferable deposit receipts that were fully repayable after some number of years, often seven to twelve years. In short, "illiquid assets were made secure by making liabilities equally illiquid."[907] The plans usually met with little

[906] S. Butlin, *Australia and New Zealand Bank*, p. 286. Hall, *The Stock Exchange of Melbourne*, pp. 153–54. Holder, *Bank of New South Wales*, pp. 445–46.

[907] Hall, *The Stock Exchange of Melbourne*, pp. 207–8. Blainey, *Gold and Paper*, p. 165. In the case of the Commercial Bank, the original company was placed in liquidation and a new one formed with the same name. The new company's capital was set at £6 million fully paid (the old company's capital had been £1.2 million), of which half was to be in preference shares that could be purchased with the frozen deposits; repayment of unconverted deposits was to be deferred

initial dissent. The organizers moved quickly; shareholders and depositors were asked to agree while they were still in shock; and, fearing the loss of their investment, they were prepared to accept any alternative that offered the prospect of getting their money back.[908]

The experience of the failed and reconstructed Victorian trading banks provides some evidence about the costs of the failure to both stockholders and depositors, Australian and British. Of the twelve banks, three (the Australasia, the Royal, and the Union) survived relatively unscathed, three (the City of Melbourne, the Federal, and the Mercantile) ended in liquidation, and six (the Bank of Victoria, the Colonial, the Commercial, the English, Scottish, and Australian, the London, and the National) suspended but were ultimately reconstructed. The three surviving banks did not require additional capital, and they were not forced to convert short- and medium-run deposits into long-term deposits or preferred shares. Between March 1883 and March 1893, however, the market value of their shares declined by £5.4 million, a loss of nearly 30 percent. In the case of the three banks that went into liquidation, not only did the shareholders lose the £1.679 million of their original funds (the market value of those shares had been £2.176 million in March 1883), but they were required to pay an additional £429,000 on the uncalled portion of their holdings. Finally, of the six reconstructed banks, the shareholders had seen the market value of their stocks decline from £9.142 million in 1883 to £5.753 million in March of 1893 (a decline of 37 percent); and they had been forced to pay another £3.541 million in additional capital calls. At the same time depositors had been forced to convert their deposits into £3.316 million in newly issued preferred shares.[909]

All told, in 1893 Australian trading banks converted £57 million of deposits into deferred deposit receipts and inscribed stock; of that total at least £19 million represented British deposits.[910] Although the shareholders (British and Australian) bore the brunt of the long-run costs, depositors were not exempt. "Tens of thousands of bank depositors had a major part of their deposit claims extended for long periods –

---

for possibly five years, and "before the reconstruction scheme was completed, depositors were obliged to accept one-third of their deposits in shares." Holder, *Bank of New South Wales*, p. 454.

[908] Holder, *Bank of New South Wales*, p. 487.

[909] Merrett, "Preventing Bank Failure," pp. 135, 137.

[910] David T. Merrett, "The 1893 Bank Crash and Monetary Aggregates," Research Discussion Paper 9303, Economic Research Department, Reserve Bank of Australia, Sydney, April 1993, table 3, p. 10. [Hereafter cited as Merrett, "The 1893 Bank Crash and Monetary Aggregates."]

generally for a minimum of four years." The depositors were all eventually repaid their principal plus some, but less than market interest. Moreover, the innovation of a secondary market in deferred deposit receipts allowed depositors access to their funds, but such access was not free. Between 1893 and 1914 the discounts in the secondary Australian market ranged from 21 to 35 percent and averaged 25 percent. Thus, to the extent a British depositor had free access to the Australian secondary market, he or she would have had to sacrifice a quarter of his or her investment to realize immediate cash. Moreover, that figure reflects a relatively slow rate of conversion (in 1914 when the price in the secondary market was 76 percent of face value, there were still £2.2 million of frozen deposits held in Britain). If, in 1893, all British depositors had attempted to cash in their deposits, the losses certainly would have been much greater than the £4.458 million suggested by the Australian price in that year.[911] It goes without saying, however, that the British were not the only ones affected; the majority of the depositors and stockholders were, after all, Australian.

In terms of the vitality of the reconstructed banks, the reconstruction schemes appear to have worked fairly well, although they were not universally successful. At times the interest promised on the frozen deposits or the preferred shares proved too heavy a burden, and a number of banks were forced to attempt to renegotiate the original settlement. Despite renegotiations, the Australian Joint Stock Bank paid no dividends after 1896. The City of Melbourne Bank was unable to achieve a compromise, and it failed in 1895, as did the Standard Bank in 1898. The Queensland National Bank was ultimately rescued by direct action of that state's government. These examples aside, however, the major reconstructed banks continued, although several ultimately merged. After the early release of some current accounts, they were able to repay the deferred deposits, occasionally even ahead of the agreed time.[912]

If the structure of Australian banking had been similar to that in the United States or, even, Canada, it is doubtful that the banking crisis would have had any long-term impact on the flow of international capital. It was, however, very different. Of the twenty-eight trading banks operating at the end of the 1880s, six were British-owned imperial banks; many of the domestic banks had a significant number of British shareholders, and almost all – imperial and domestic – had actively solicited

---

[911] Merrett, "The 1893 Bank Crash and Monetary Aggregates," Tables 2 and 5, pp. 5 and 14.

[912] Holder, *Bank of New South Wales*, pp. 477–78. S. Butlin, *Australia and New Zealand Bank*, pp. 322–23.

deposits in Britain. Estimates of the level of British fixed-term deposits in Australian banks at the time of the crisis range from £19 to £40 million. Although bankers in the City had been concerned about the Australian economy, the failure of the Commercial Bank "came as a great surprise to the country, and has created consternation in the minds of share-holders and depositors in other banks."[913] Even when the banks did not fail outright, the British depositors found themselves with very illiquid assets. At the same time the British shareholders in the reconstructed banks and pastoral companies and in the unreconstructed Bank of New South Wales were required to pay calls amounting to £2.9 million.

5-2b(3). And after . . . : Except for the strain it placed on the international capital market, the depression would not have been so severe had it not coincided with a serious drought that extended over the last half of the decade. Thus, the recovery that began about the middle of the decade was dampened until the first years of the present century. By 1900 Gross Domestic Product had matched its earlier 1891 peak, but it was 1909 before per capita income had surpassed the level of that former year. The depression also undermined a part of the foundation of the traditional Australian economy and inaugurated regional and structural shifts that were to alter the nation's developmental path.

Given the effects of the drought, it was obvious that the pastoral sector had to be restructured; no longer was it possible to believe that nature would deliver water to every new acre that was fenced. At the same time new agricultural activities had become important. Technical developments in refrigeration and canning made it possible for exports of tinned and frozen meat and butter to compete in the European market with the products of Argentina, Canada, and the United States. Even more importantly, wheat, originally grown in South Australia and Victoria for domestic consumption, spread into New South Wales and Western Australia, and most of the increase was exported.[914] Despite these changes, however, the agricultural sector's share of gross fixed capital formation continued to decline: from 25 percent in the years 1865–89, to 18 percent during the depression decade, to 10 percent between the turn of the century and World War I.

Industry and commerce registered the largest gains, increasing their share of capital formation from about 9 percent in the nineteenth century

---

[913] The quotation is from a report from the Bank of New South Wales's London correspondent, David George, to the Sydney Directors. Cited in Holder, *Bank of New South Wales*, p. 478.

[914] Denoon, *Settler Capitalism*, pp. 100–1.

to more than 15 percent in the three pre-war quinquennia. It may be that Broken Hill Proprietary's Newcastle steel works symbolized the new, and soon to be protected, Australia, but the real story lay in the formation of hundreds of small- and medium-sized enterprises.[915] For example, in 1900 New South Wales recorded the registration of ninety-three new limited companies with a nominal capital value of £1.8 million; in 1912, the pre-war peak, the figures were 428 and almost £14 million. Not all of the 428 were new enterprises. The lure of unlimited life and limited liability attracted many long-established family firms, but many, including the Electric Light and Power Supply Company and the General Film Company of Australia, were.[916]

Mining too, although never regaining its relative importance in the boom of the 1850s, continued to increase in importance. Beginning in the 1890s, gold mining in Western Australia provided a powerful dynamic to that colony's growth. The seven Koolgardie companies and the two on the Murchison all paid over £1 million in dividends. Dividends from West's [WA] Mines exceeded £2 million in 1899 and again in 1903, 1904, and 1905. Through the end of 1915 total dividends exceeded £25 million; however, the riches were not evenly spread. Ten mines in the Golden Mile, a stretch that included the Great Boulder, the Ivanhoe, and the Golden Horseshoe, plus the Sons of Gwalia and the Great Fingall, paid 87 percent of all Western Australian mining dividends in the years before 1915.[917] Moreover, even with the Western Australian discoveries, the structure of industry began to shift from precious to other metals and from a sector dominated by small speculative companies to one interspersed with large, technically advanced, firms including the Sulphide Corporation, the Zinc Corporation, and Amalgamated Zinc.[918] As a result of both the gold discoveries and the expansion of the nonprecious metals sector, the industry accounted for more than 4 percent of gross fixed capital formation between 1900 and 1914.

The long boom had left the governments with unfinished business in the railroad sector. The trunk lines had been laid, but the construction

[915] The decision to build the mill was neither induced by the decline in the company's mines nor was it financed by their profits. In 1913–14 the company sold more than £1 million of new shares and debentures. Geoffrey Blainey, *The Rush that Never Ended: A History of Australian Mining* (Parkville, Victoria: Melbourne University Press, 1963), pp. 274–75. [Hereafter cited as Blainey, *The Rush That Never Ended.*]

[916] Salsbury and Sweeny, *The Bull, The Bear*, p. 178.

[917] Blainey, *The Rush That Never Ended*, p. 207.

[918] Blainey, *The Rush That Never Ended*, pp. 255–56. Salsbury and Sweeny, *The Bull, The Bear*, p. 177.

of the network of feeder lines had hardly begun. The pre-war years saw a revival of construction; and, although the rate of increase was much below that of the long boom, on average 522 miles were added each year between 1900 and 1914. "Moreover, the government had changed its view of railway construction through sparsely settled areas. Instead of being constructed more or less without regard to prospective returns, the new construction took the form of light 'pioneer' lines which could be built cheaply and made more substantial as traffic developed." One result was to reduce the capital requirements of new railway construction.[919] Although the construction of the 1880s had contributed little to the nation's productivity at that time, the system of trunk lines supported by the new network of local lines, when combined with irrigation, closer settlement policy, and technical improvements, especially in farm mechanization and wheat strains, began to yield substantial social dividends in the decade before the war.[920]

Even the cutoff of British capital flows probably yielded some tentative dividends. The states, needing a new source of finance, turned to the domestic market for the first time in several decades. They were at least partially successful, and a pale image of a formal securities market began to emerge. That development was reinforced by the financial demands of Western Australian gold mining.[921] It should be noted, however, that most of the Koolgardie stocks were floated in London; and it was to that market that the managers of the Broken Hill Proprietary Company turned to finance a substantial fraction of their excursion into steel production. Despite these positive signs, the depression left scars that may still not have healed. "The shakeout among financial institutions, particularly in Victoria, caused a long shadow over banking practices and legislation."[922] The legal complexities arising from the reconstruction policies and the litigation that arose from the renegotiation of some of those schemes increased stockholders' and depositors' concerns about the stability of the financial system. "It came to be believed that many of the banks, particularly their directors and most senior managers, had used the devices to escape the inevitable exposure, trial and convictions they so richly deserved, had they been wound up as insolvent. Greed and fraud, it was alleged, resulted in the banks' collapse and widespread loss

---

[919] Hall, *The London Capital Market*, pp. 124–25. N. Butlin, "Colonial Socialism," p. 71.

[920] N. Butlin, "Colonial Socialism," p. 71. Sinclair, *The Process of Economic Growth*, p. 169.

[921] M. Butlin, "Capital Markets," pp. 230–31.

[922] Maddock and McLean, "The Australian Economy," p. 13.

by depositors, and those responsible had used a legal device for their own protection. Banks lost their reputation and standing with the community, neither of which they have been able to regain."[923] The banks, in turn, became more cautious and increasingly conservative. "The ultimate price of the banking crisis of the 1890s was the emergence of a highly cartelized banking sector over the next 50 years."[924]

Government banks were the main beneficiaries of the tarnished image of the commercial banks. First, the reaction provided one of the best possible arguments for the establishment, in 1911, of the Commonwealth Bank – a government bank designed to compete with the private trading banks – and the expansion of government activity into the financial sector.[925] In short, first, the legislation gave the Bank, controlled and operated by the national government, both wide authority and, through its deposit function, access to a very large supply of funds. Second, the depression had wiped out a large proportion of proprietary mortgage banks and building societies, and the states moved in to fill the gap by creating state mortgage banks and by providing them with finance on especially favorable terms. Although each of the six states established some institution designed to ease agricultural credit, the activities of the state banks were concentrated in four states: Victoria, South Australia, Western Australia, and New South Wales. In 1900 the six state banks had £1.6 million in agricultural loans outstanding, and there were no non-agricultural loans. By 1914 the agricultural loans had increased to £9.0 million, and the banks in South Australia and Victoria had added an additional £2.6 million in urban mortgages to their portfolio.[926] In 1890 deposits in government savings banks had amounted to 16 percent of those in the trading banks; by 1914 the ratio had risen to 55 percent.[927]

---

[923] Merrett, "Capital Formation and Capital Markets," pp. 9–10.

[924] Merrett, "Preventing Bank Failure," pp. 139–40.

[925] It would, however, be another three decades before the Commonwealth Bank became a central bank. Baster, *Imperial Banks*, p. 157. "The powers of the Bank are extraordinarily wide: it may carry on a general banking business, acquire and hold land, receive deposits, make advances, discount bills, issue drafts, deal in exchanges, specie, gold dust and precious metals; it may borrow money and 'do anything incidental to any of its powers.' It has the power to open branches anywhere in the Commonwealth and outside this limit with the Treasurer's approval" (pp. 158–59).

Although it did not begin to operate as a commercial bank until 1914, "despite initial dissent from the states, the Commonwealth Savings Bank opened in Victoria on 7/15/12, in Queensland on 9/16/12, in the Northern Territory on 10/21/12, and in New South Wales, South Australia, and Western Australia on 1/13/13." *Official Yearbook of the Commonwealth of Australia*, Vol. 10, 1917.

[926] Drummond, *Capital Markets*, pp. 86–90, table 5, p. 89.

[927] Merrett, "Capital Formation and Capital Markets," p. 10.

Over the years 1903–14, despite the Commonwealth's return to relative prosperity, the British investor appears to have been, at minimum, largely indifferent or, more likely, actively hostile, to Australian investment opportunities. Certainly it appears to have been a much less attractive place to invest than Canada, or even Argentina. Mark Thomas suggests that the most plausible explanation of the indifference lay in a combination of risk aversion, imperfect information, and a long memory. British capital had historically been directed toward the pastoral sector, financial institutions, and, in the relatively recent past, mining. As a result, in these industries, the British saver felt he had an informational advantage. The first two had been hard hit during the depression; the pastoral economy was slow to recover; and the financial sector had reoriented its operations dramatically. Moreover, both mining and pastoral activities were marked by such extreme income and profit volatility that even Australians were hesitant to become too deeply involved. Finally, the memory of assets locked up in the trading banks, mortgage companies, and building societies was still fresh.[928]

These factors almost certainly played an important role, but the British dislike for Australian socialism was certainly an additional element helping to create the indifferent-to-hostile attitude among British investors. The Australian governments had been accused of "pandering to the working classes"; the editors of the *Investors Monthly Manual* reported that "the belief has spread among investors here that the colonies are too largely dependent on borrowed money, and the governments concerned are unfortunately greatly under the domination of labor parties, whose policy is to spend lavishly and 'make work'"; and the *Economist*'s Melbourne correspondent believed that the increased strength of the "Labour party constitutes a menace to the public credit" and that "some of its members appear to be collectivist, as well as anarchist and utterly opposed to capitalism." Given the Canadian alternative, risk aversion, imperfect information, their long memories, and these attitudes, it is not surprising that Australia was not welcomed with open arms by wealthy British investors after the turn of the century.[929]

5-3. **Income, savings, investment, and foreign finance**

The basic data are presented in Tables 5:2-2 and 5:3-1. Australian output per capita at the beginning of the period was very high by the standards of the rest of the world. Although the problems of purchasing

---

[928] Mark Thomas, "The Australian Economy in a Canadian Mirror, 1890–1913," paper delivered at the Canadian Cliometric Society Meeting, McGill University, Montreal, April 1994, pp. 29–30. [Hereafter cited as Thomas, "The Australian Economy."]

[929] Hall, *The London Capital Market*, pp. 181–82.

Table 5:3-1(a). *Australia: Gross Domestic Product, capital formation savings, overseas borrowing, and domestic savings (millions of pounds)*

Year	Gross Domestic Product	Gross Domestic capital formation	Gross Domestic private capital formation	Gross Domestic public capital formation	Net overseas borrowing	Domestic savings
1861	66.8	7.3	3.6	3.7	0.9	6.4
1862	66.3	6.6	3.1	3.5	5.6	1.0
1863	65.4	9.1	5.6	3.5	6.5	2.6
1864	67.3	8.1	5.0	3.1	4.9	3.2
1865	68.3	8.4	6.0	2.4	4.5	3.9
1866	74.2	7.8	4.7	3.1	5.3	2.5
1867	74.9	8.4	4.4	4.0	0.7	7.7
1868	79.7	10.4	6.4	4.0	3.0	7.4
1869	79.8	9.8	6.4	3.4	5.0	4.8
1870	85.0	8.9	5.4	3.5	4.4	4.5
1871	82.0	8.2	4.5	3.7	−4.6	12.8
1872	97.5	12.2	8.3	3.9	−4.2	16.4
1873	112.9	13.6	8.7	4.9	5.6	8.0
1874	114.1	15.6	9.4	6.2	2.7	12.9
1875	123.3	19.1	11.9	7.2	3.5	15.6
1876	122.4	19.8	12.9	6.9	2.6	17.2
1877	125.2	25.3	17.5	7.8	7.1	18.2
1878	130.8	22.9	13.3	9.6	7.9	15.0
1879	133.2	20.8	10.2	10.6	5.5	15.3
1880	138.6	23.7	13.8	9.9	−1.1	24.8
1881	147.8	30.2	18.7	11.5	9.7	20.5
1882	154.0	26.7	14.1	12.6	14.7	12.0
1883	171.3	30.9	16.2	14.7	12.8	18.1
1884	168.5	33.0	17.7	15.3	14.6	18.4
1885	180.1	32.2	16.0	16.2	23.6	8.6
1886	177.4	37.1	20.2	16.9	21.8	15.3
1887	195.6	38.0	23.1	14.9	14.5	23.5
1888	201.5	40.7	25.4	15.3	21.0	19.7
1889	221.4	39.6	21.8	17.8	20.3	19.3
1890	214.9	35.5	17.8	17.7	21.1	14.4
1891	211.6	39.5	21.4	18.1	11.8	27.7
1892	179.7	23.1	10.1	13.0	7.5	15.6
1893	160.6	17.1	6.7	10.4	−2.3	19.4
1894	156.1	17.7	9.6	8.1	−0.5	18.2
1895	148.3	15.6	6.4	9.2	4.1	11.5
1896	168.1	20.7	10.9	9.8	6.5	14.2
1897	161.7	15.4	4.3	11.1	7.0	8.4
1898	186.6	22.8	11.2	11.6	12.9	9.9

Table 5:3-1(a). (*cont.*)

Year	Gross Domestic product	Gross Domestic capital formation	Gross Domestic private capital formation	Gross Domestic public capital formation	Net overseas borrowing	Domestic savings
1899	190.4	23.1	10.2	12.9	−5.9	29.0
1900	198.3	22.9	9.1	13.8	7.1	15.8
1901	194.5	32.9	16.9	15.7	4.2	28.7
1902	197.6	35.8	19.0	16.6	8.7	27.1
1903	209.0	29.8	16.2	13.6	6.6	23.2
1904	223.1	25.4	14.7	10.7	−4.7	30.1
1905	231.7	26.4	15.8	10.5	−8.6	35.0
1906	254.6	30.4	19.4	11.0	−9.8	40.2
1907	271.5	34.7	21.5	13.2	−11.9	46.6
1908	276.6	37.7	20.7	17.0	−1.1	38.8
1909	296.4	41.1	21.2	19.8	−6.0	47.1
1910	321.0	47.4	23.6	23.8	−1.0	48.4
1911	337.9	58.5	28.2	30.5	−0.9	59.4
1912	361.5	68.4	33.1	35.5	12.3	56.1
1913	394.5	73.3	36.1	37.2	7.1	66.2
1914	392.5	72.3	32.8	39.5	22.9	49.4

Note: Data for 1901 through 1914 estimated by averaging fiscal years [i.e. 1901 = (1900/01 + 1901/02)/2].

Sources: N.G. Butlin. *Australian Domestic Product, Investment and Foreign Borrowing, 1861–1938/39* (Cambridge, U.K.: Cambridge University Press, 1962), Table 1, pp. 6–7; Table 4, pp. 16–17; Table 250, p. 422; Table 265, p. 444.

N.G. Butlin, *Investment in Australian Economic Development, 1861–1900* (Cambridge, U.K.: Cambridge University Press, 1964), Table 1, p. 11; Appendix Table II, p. 454.

A. Barnard & N.G. Butlin, "*Australian Public and Private Capital Formation, 1901–75.*" *The Economic Record*, Vol. 57, No. 159, December 1981, Appendix Table, p. 366.

power parity make comparisons very difficult, in the years between 1870 and 1889 Australian per capita income was almost certainly higher than that of the United States and half again that of Canada; and it may have been as much as half again that of the United States and nearly twice that of Canada.[930] Moreover, between 1861–63 and 1887–89 Australian

[930] Mark Thomas, "The Australian Economy." A very rough calculation suggests, for example, that, over the three years 1870–1872, per capita income averaged $240 as compared with $154 in the United States and $129 in Canada. N. Butlin,

Table 5:3-1(b). *Australia: Gross Domestic Product; Gross Domestic capital formation; overseas borrowing; and domestic savings as a percentage of Gross Domestic Product*

Year	Gross Domestic capital formation	Gross Domestic private capital formation	Gross Domestic public capital formation	Net overseas borrowing	Long-term capital inflow	Domestic savings
1861	10.9	5.4	5.5	1.3		9.6
1862	10.0	4.6	5.3	8.4		1.5
1863	13.9	8.6	5.3	9.9		4.0
1864	12.0	7.5	4.6	7.3		4.8
1865	12.3	8.7	3.6	6.6		5.7
1866	10.5	6.3	4.2	7.1		3.4
1867	11.2	5.9	5.3	0.9		10.3
1868	13.0	8.0	5.0	3.8		9.3
1869	12.3	8.0	4.3	6.3		6.0
1870	10.5	6.3	4.1	5.2	8.9	5.3
1871	10.0	5.5	4.5	−5.6	−4.4	15.6
1872	12.5	8.6	4.0	−4.3	−2.7	16.8
1873	12.0	7.7	4.3	5.0	4.2	7.1
1874	13.7	8.2	5.5	2.4	2.4	11.3
1875	15.5	9.6	5.9	2.8	2.8	12.7
1876	16.2	10.5	5.7	2.1	2.5	14.1
1877	20.2	14.0	6.2	5.7	4.6	14.5
1878	17.5	10.2	7.3	6.0	4.9	11.5
1879	15.6	7.6	8.0	4.1	5.6	11.5
1880	17.1	9.9	7.2	−0.8	4.1	17.9
1881	20.4	12.6	7.8	6.6	4.8	13.9
1882	17.3	9.1	8.2	9.5	5.5	7.8
1883	18.0	9.4	8.6	7.5	7.2	10.6
1884	19.6	10.5	9.1	8.7	10.6	10.9
1885	17.9	8.9	9.0	13.1	11.0	4.8
1886	20.9	11.4	9.5	12.3	9.5	8.6
1887	19.4	11.8	7.6	7.4	7.8	12.0
1888	20.2	12.6	7.6	10.4	7.6	9.8
1889	17.9	9.8	8.1	9.2	8.7	8.7
1890	16.5	8.3	8.2	9.8	8.2	6.7
1891	18.7	10.1	8.6	5.6	4.3	13.1
1892	12.9	5.6	7.2	4.2	2.3	8.7
1893	10.6	4.2	6.5	−1.4	−2.7	12.1
1894	11.3	6.1	5.2	−0.3	0.5	11.7
1895	10.5	4.3	6.2	2.8	8.2	7.8

Table 5:3-1(b). (*cont.*)

Year	Gross Domestic capital formation	Gross Domestic private capital formation	Gross Domestic public capital formation	Net overseas borrowing	Long-term capital inflow	Domestic savings
1896	12.3	6.5	5.8	3.9	4.2	8.4
1897	9.5	2.7	6.8	4.3	5.4	5.2
1898	12.2	6.0	6.2	6.9	8.9	5.3
1899	12.1	5.4	6.8	−3.1	0.4	15.2
1900	11.5	4.6	7.0	3.6	5.9	8.0
1901	16.9	8.7	8.1	2.2		14.7
1902	18.1	9.6	8.4	4.4		13.7
1903	14.3	7.8	6.5	3.2		11.1
1904	11.4	6.6	4.8	−2.1		13.5
1905	11.4	6.8	4.5	−3.7		15.1
1906	11.9	7.6	4.3	−3.8		15.8
1907	12.8	7.9	4.9	−4.4		17.2
1908	13.6	7.5	6.1	−0.4		14.0
1909	13.9	7.2	6.7	−2.0		15.9
1910	14.8	7.4	7.4	−0.3		15.1
1911	17.3	8.3	9.0	−0.3		17.6
1912	18.9	9.1	9.8	3.4		15.5
1913	18.6	9.1	9.4	1.8		16.8
1914	18.4	8.4	10.1	5.8		12.6

Note: Data for 1901 through 1914 estimated by averaging fiscal years [i.e., 1901 = (1900/01 + 1901/02)2].

Sources: N.G. Butlin, *Australian Domestic Product, Investment and Foreign Borrowing, 1861–1938/39* (Cambridge, U.K.: Cambridge University Press, 1962), Table 13, pp. 33–34; Table 250, p. 422; Table 265, p. 444; N.G. Butlin, *Investment in Australian Economic Development, 1861–1900* (Cambridge, U.K.: Cambridge University Press, 1964), Table 1, p. 11; Appendix Table II, p. 454.

income grew at a rate of 4.8 percent per annum. From the bottom of the depression in 1895–97 to 1912–14 the rate was 4.1 percent.

Australian Domestic Product, table 13, pp. 33–34. Milton Friedman and Anna J. Schwartz, *Monetary Trends in the United States and the United Kingdom: Their Relation to Income, Prices, and Interest Rates, 1867–1975*, National Bureau of Economic Research Monograph (Chicago: University of Chicago Press, 1982), table 4.8, pp. 122–29. Urquhart, *Gross National Product*, pp. 122–24. table 1.6, pp. 24–25.

Those increases were in large part driven by a high rate of gross domestic capital formation. Annual gross capital formation grew from £7.7 million (£6.33 per capita) in 1861–63 to £39.4 million (£13.60 per capita) in 1887–89, and it increased from £17.2 million (£4.95 per capita) in 1895–97 to £68.4 million (£14.71 per capita) in 1912–14. As a fraction of gross domestic product, gross capital formation averaged more than 14 percent over the years between 1861 and 1914, and a very large fraction was publicly financed. The public sector averaged more than 40 percent during the long boom; its share increased to more than one-half during the depression of the 1890s; and it remained at almost one-half throughout the remainder of the pre-war era.[931] "As recovery got under way, the public sector was left in a very much more important position than it had been in the first main phase of the expansion. In fact, private capital formation appears to have continued throughout the whole period 1900/01 to 1938/39, with very little fluctuation, at somewhat less than half the total – averaging 48% of total Australian capital formation."[932]

Investment was financed partly by domestic savings and partly by foreign – almost entirely British – savings. Domestic savings fluctuated widely, departing from the "long boom, depression, and after" scenario. Instead, they appear to have been driven by a form of life cycle behavior where savings are a function of age, income, net interest rates, and asset position. Increased incomes and innovations in the financial sector raised domestic savings in the 1860s and 1870s. The domestic savings rate more than doubled, from an average of less than 6 to almost 13 percent between the first half of the 1860s and the last quinquennia of the 1870s (see Table 5:3-1(b)). The 1880s, however, represent something of an anomaly. Increased incomes did not lead to further increases in the savings rate. Instead, rising foreign investment coupled with an asset price boom, particularly in urban land, kept interest rates relatively low and inflated the real value of existing savings. Together, they induced a sharp decline in the savings rate, to less than 10 percent. In the next decade depression reduced incomes; but the tendency for savings to decline with income was almost exactly offset by the impact of interest rates of the reduction of foreign investment, of the capital losses suffered in the collapse of asset values, and from the bankruptcies and suspensions in the financial sector. As a result, savings rates in the 1890s were almost identical to those realized over the previous ten years. The new

---

[931] The governments' share was 38 percent between 1865 and 1889, 53 percent from 1890 to 1899, and 49 percent over the years 1900–14. See Table 5:2-4.

[932] N. Butlin, "Some Structural Features," pp. 393–94.

century brought recovery, and recovery brought higher incomes. Higher incomes, "the absence of significant capital inflow (Canada being the more attractive overseas outlet for British savings), the opportunity to recover desired levels of wealth which had been eroded," and government-based institutional innovation in the financial markets combined to induce an increase in the savings rate to levels that more than restored those observed in the 1870s.[933]

Although over the entire period the contribution of domestic savers exceeded that of their foreign counterparts by a ratio of more than 3.5 : 1, the foreign contribution was very important.[934] In the 1860s net foreign borrowing accounted for just less than one-half of fixed investment, and two decades later the figure was slightly above that benchmark. At other times it was much less, but in the 1890s the fraction was still more than one-fifth, and even in the 1870s British savers accounted for almost one pound in eight of Australian investment. By the turn of the century, however, the world had changed. Between 1901 and 1914 the foreign contribution amounted to less than 2 percent of the total, and in the first decade repayments exceeded new investments.[935]

In each of the other three frontier countries, the series on issues "created and called" on the U.K. capital market provided a good proxy for the industrial distribution of British long-term investment. In the case of Australia, however, those data, although still useful, provide a less reliable substitute. First, capital market calls were augmented by British deposits in Australian banks; and from the late 1870s until the crash those deposits were recycled into long-term pastoral and urban residential finance. Second, pastoral finance companies and land mortgage banks direct solicited equity and debenture capital in England and Scotland; and in part those solicitations bypassed the formal capital markets.[936]

---

[933] McLean, "Savings in Settler Economies," p. 448.

[934] The totals for the period 1861–1914 were £306 million and £1,116 billion.

[935] See Table 5:3-1(b).

[936] Between 1880 and 1885 British deposits in Australian trading banks increased by almost £16 million ($76 million) and between that latter date and 1890 they increased by an additional £19 million ($93 million). In 1880 those banks had an excess of British assets over British liabilities of more than £6 million; by 1890, when British liabilities accounted for almost one-third of the banks' total, they had an excess of British liabilities over British assets of more than £20 million. Sydney J. Butlin, A.R. Hall, and R.C. White, *Australian Banking and Monetary Statistics, 1817–1945,* Reserve Bank of Australia, Occasional Paper 4A (Sydney: 1971), table 4(ii), p. 126. [Hereafter cited as Butlin, Hall, and White, *Australian Banking and Monetary Statistics.*]

The data on British deposits presented in Butlin, Hall, and White are only estimates. As C.V. Schedvin notes in his review, "direct estimates of external

Finally, and, perhaps, most importantly, because of the role of the state governments in the provision of railroad and public utility services, the industrial breakdown of "capital called" vastly underestimates the role of foreign capital in those sectors. Nevertheless, the data do provide some important clues on the sectoral distribution of foreign capital (see Tables 5:3-2 through 5:3-6).

If the state governments' roles in total investment set Australia apart from the other frontier countries, the separation is even greater in the case of foreign borrowing. Over the half century 1865–1914, the six governments, together with a few municipalities, absorbed almost three-quarters of the portfolio finance that passed through the formal British capital markets. In absolute terms government issues were most important in the last decade of the long boom – they amounted to $31.03 per capita in 1883 and averaged $17.83 between 1880 and 1889 – but they accounted for more than two-thirds of the total flow in every quinquennium except 1895–99 (see Table 5:3-3). Even when adjustment is made for government funds diverted to the transport sector, Australia still stands apart. Government non-railroad borrowing accounts for almost 30 percent of the total. That figure was half again as large as the figure for Argentina, and it was nearly twice the Canadian fraction (see Table 5:3-5).[937]

assets and liabilities are not available in any comprehensive form until 1926, although several indirect methods of estimation can be used for earlier periods. For this volume Dr. Hall and Mr. White have constructed a substantially new series by deducting Australian figures from aggregate balance-sheet data. The residual – net assets abroad – is apportioned between Britain and New Zealand by using New Zealand banking returns." C.V. Schedvin, "A Century of Money in Australia," *Economic Record*, Vol. 49, No. 128 (December 1973), p. 592.

Between 1880 and 1885, the ten largest incorporated non-banking pastoral finance companies increased their paid up capital by £1.9 ($9.1) million and raised an additional £8.7 ($42.4) million in debentures and deposits. Over the next quinquennia, the figures were £1.7 ($8.3) million and £6.4 ($31.3) million respectively. Over the decade from the end of 1881 to the end of 1890 the totals were £3.6 ($17.4) million and £15.1 ($74) million for a grand total of £18.7 ($91.1) million. Although all of these funds were probably not raised outside Australia, most were; and, although not all of the British contributions bypassed the formal markets, a substantial fraction certainly did. N. Butlin, *Australian Domestic Product*, table 28, p. 143; table 30, p. 151; table 31, p. 152.

[937] In the nineteenth century, colonies – even those with self-government – were expected to pay operating expenses from current revenue and borrow only for long-term investments. The adjustment, then, divides colonial expenditures on fixed investment into two parts (railroads and all other), calculates the percentage of railroad investment in the total, and assigns that fraction of borrowing to the transport sector.

Moreover, although the six states did not display equally voracious appetites for government finance, all were heavy borrowers. Between 1870 and 1913 the six states borrowed almost $1 billion. On a per capita basis, annual state borrowing ranged from a low of $4.41 in Victoria to a high of $19.31 in Western Australia; and it averaged $8.20 (see Table 5:3-7(c)).

Removing railway investment from the state totals increases the share of transport in the total of capital calls from less than 1 percent to more than 45 percent, but it still leaves it well below the averages for the other frontier countries. The levels of per capita expenditures on transport for Australia, Canada, and Argentina in the capital called series, are, however, similar – for the fifty years they are $5.43, $5.10, and $5.82 respectively; thus, the difference in the share of transport most likely reflects the Australian governments' response to the almost insatiable demand of British savers for "riskless" Australian government bonds combined with that nation's governmental habit. Once adjustment is made for differences in population, the transfers to the non-railroad government sector account for about half of the difference in the average level of capital flows between Australia and Argentina and Canada.[938]

The second largest Australian recipient of British portfolio finance was the agricultural and extractive sector. The flows to that sector were, relatively, more than twice as large as those to the same sector in Canada and more than four times as large as those to its Argentine and American counterparts. Over the half century it drew $284 million, an average of $4.4 million, or $1.75 per capita a year. Although it represented less than 5 percent of the total in the 1870s, it accounted for more than one-half in the quinquennium 1895–99, one-quarter over the next five years, and almost one-fifth between 1905 and 1909. Of those totals, the mining sector drew more than seven dollars in ten and financial, land, and development companies almost the entire residual (see Table 5:3-6).

The mining data underscore the importance of the Western Australian discoveries of the late 1880s. Foreign investment in gold mining accounted for 45 percent of the total in the years after 1885. Although Australia yielded a range of metals (the Kangarilla Proprietary Silver Mine raised almost £25,000 in 1891 and 1892), it was gold that dominated flotations in most states after 1865. Calls ranged from very small – the Glasgow Murchison Gold Mine Development raised £1,400 in 1895 and

---

[938] Over the fifty-year period, Australian per capita flows were $2.97 higher than Argentina's and $4.18 higher than Canada's. The difference in the non-railroad government "calls" account for 41 percent of the Argentine difference and 54 percent of the Canadian.

Table 5:3-2(a). *Australia: Capital created and called on the British market by industry without adjustment (i.e., all government bonds in government) (thousands of dollars)*

Year	Manufacturing, commercial & miscellaneous	Finance	Government	Agriculture & extractive	Transport	Public utilities	Total
1865	4,870	0	2,520	3,920	0	0	11,311
1866	0	0	10,496	779	0	0	11,276
1867	0	0	7,434	412	24	0	7,870
1868	292	0	7,580	0	0	0	7,872
1869	0	0	8,212	699	0	0	8,912
1870	0	0	10,540	61	0	1,315	11,915
1871	97	0	4,568	73	0	1,315	6,053
1872	985	0	662	169	3,153	0	4,970
1873	344	0	511	1,164	2,380	0	4,400
1874	15	0	10,580	280	1,668	0	12,543
1875	0	0	11,761	1,668	0	0	13,429
1876	0	0	27,088	61	0	0	27,149
1877	0	0	8,645	0	0	0	8,645
1878	0	3,922	13,630	594	0	0	18,146
1879	0	2,727	36,510	1,108	0	1,013	41,358
1880	329	487	32,029	1,758	0	288	34,890
1881	424	0	24,237	3,545	0	0	28,205
1882	0	0	10,422	2,604	0	0	13,025
1883	244	2,648	75,632	4,741	0	0	83,265
1884	49	0	56,662	12,903	0	1,342	70,956
1885	49	1,339	54,412	1,236	0	0	57,035
1886	183	1,928	73,977	4,553	463	1,505	82,607

1887	97	1,076	35,046	18,624	1,875	0	56,719
1888	614	3,666	54,508	8,419	0	0	67,207
1889	0	6,611	47,153	6,425	0	0	60,188
1890	1,187	974	34,248	5,506	0	513	41,915
1891	17	487	49,755	3,493	36	251	54,265
1892	0	0	18,150	2,962	0	0	21,398
1893	1,242	15,587	31,110	1,531	0	12	49,469
1894	183	8,910	15,999	6,615	0	0	31,719
1895	671	2,573	30,253	35,532	0	0	69,028
1896	1,216	1,997	7,422	27,348	0	0	37,983
1897	1,623	2,070	8,486	13,206	0	0	25,385
1898	2,981	761	7,183	6,755	82	61	17,823
1899	3,295	0	17,536	20,464	1,507	191	42,993
1900	372	0	17,707	10,875	828	536	30,318
1901	183	0	48,105	6,834	1,071	1,096	57,288
1902	937	348	29,890	9,738	0	0	40,913
1903	490	0	3,506	2,774	0	0	6,771
1904	0	0	0	6,529	92	0	6,620
1905	137	0	0	4,490	285	0	4,912
1906	511	0	16,758	9,566	0	0	26,835
1907	1,478	2,922	4,967	3,711	0	29	13,108
1908	804	2,313	23,896	3,777	0	0	30,789
1909	883	609	46,189	3,754	0	1,013	52,447
1910	3,021	5,479	22,875	2,442	0	260	34,076
1911	98	6,696	17,251	1,855	0	0	25,900
1912	1,640	1,975	29,495	5,384	0	1,937	40,431
1913	514	10,912	109,902	8,503	0	543	130,373
1914	780	2,392	44,283	4,161	1,023	712	53,351

Source: Davis–Gallman tape.

Table 5:3-2(b). *Australia: Capital created and called on the British market by industry without adjustment (i.e., all government bonds in government) (percent of total)*

Year	Manufacturing, commercial & miscellaneous	Finance	Government	Agriculture & extractive	Transport	Public utilities	Total
1865	43.1	0.0	22.3	34.7	0.0	0.0	100.0
1866	0.0	0.0	93.1	6.9	0.0	0.0	100.0
1867	0.0	0.0	94.5	5.2	0.3	0.0	100.0
1868	3.7	0.0	96.3	0.0	0.0	0.0	100.0
1869	0.0	0.0	92.2	7.8	0.0	0.0	100.0
1870	0.0	0.0	88.5	0.5	0.0	11.0	100.0
1871	1.6	0.0	75.5	1.2	0.0	21.7	100.0
1872	19.8	0.0	13.3	3.4	63.4	0.0	100.0
1873	7.8	0.0	11.6	26.5	54.1	0.0	100.0
1874	0.1	0.0	84.3	2.2	13.3	0.0	100.0
1875	0.0	0.0	87.6	12.4	0.0	0.0	100.0
1876	0.0	0.0	99.8	0.2	0.0	0.0	100.0
1877	0.0	0.0	100.0	0.0	0.0	0.0	100.0
1878	0.0	21.6	75.1	3.3	0.0	0.0	100.0
1879	0.0	6.6	88.3	2.7	0.0	2.4	100.0
1880	0.9	1.4	91.8	5.0	0.0	0.8	100.0
1881	1.5	0.0	85.9	12.6	0.0	0.0	100.0
1882	0.0	0.0	80.0	20.0	0.0	0.0	100.0
1883	0.3	3.2	90.8	5.7	0.0	0.0	100.0
1884	0.1	0.0	79.9	18.2	0.0	1.9	100.0
1885	0.1	2.3	95.4	2.2	0.0	0.0	100.0
1886	0.2	2.3	89.6	5.5	0.6	1.8	100.0
1887	0.2	1.9	61.8	32.8	3.3	0.0	100.0

1888	0.9	5.5	81.1	12.5	0.0	0.0	100.0
1889	0.0	11.0	78.3	10.7	0.0	0.0	100.0
1890	2.8	2.3	81.7	13.1	0.0	0.0	100.0
1891	0.0	0.9	91.7	6.4	0.0	0.9	100.0
1892	0.0	0.0	84.8	13.8	0.2	1.2	100.0
1893	2.5	31.5	62.9	3.1	0.0	0.0	100.0
1894	0.6	28.1	50.4	20.9	0.0	0.0	100.0
1895	1.0	3.7	43.8	51.5	0.0	0.0	100.0
1896	3.2	5.3	19.5	72.0	0.0	0.0	100.0
1897	6.4	8.2	33.4	52.0	0.0	0.0	100.0
1898	16.7	4.3	40.3	37.9	0.5	0.3	100.0
1899	7.7	0.0	40.8	47.6	3.5	0.4	100.0
1900	1.2	0.0	58.4	35.9	2.7	1.8	100.0
1901	0.3	0.0	84.0	11.9	1.9	1.9	100.0
1902	2.3	0.8	73.1	23.8	0.0	0.0	100.0
1903	7.2	0.0	51.8	41.0	0.0	0.0	100.0
1904	0.0	0.0	0.0	98.6	1.4	0.0	100.0
1905	2.8	0.0	0.0	91.4	5.8	0.0	100.0
1906	1.9	0.0	62.4	35.6	0.0	0.0	100.0
1907	11.3	22.3	37.9	28.3	0.0	0.2	100.0
1908	2.6	7.5	77.6	12.3	0.0	0.0	100.0
1909	1.7	1.2	88.1	7.2	0.0	1.9	100.0
1910	8.9	16.1	67.1	7.2	0.0	0.8	100.0
1911	0.4	25.9	66.6	7.2	0.0	0.0	100.0
1912	4.1	4.9	73.0	13.3	0.0	4.8	100.0
1913	0.4	8.4	84.3	6.5	0.0	0.4	100.0
1914	1.5	4.5	83.0	7.8	1.9	1.3	100.0

Source: Davis–Gallman tape.

Table 5:3-2(c). *Australia: Per capita capital created and called on the British market by industry without adjustment (i.e., all government bonds in government) (United State dollars)*

Year	Manufacturing, commercial & miscellaneous	Finance	Government	Agriculture & extractive	Transport	Public utilities	Total
1865	3.56	0.00	1.84	2.87	0.00	0.00	8.28
1866	0.00	0.00	7.41	0.55	0.00	0.00	7.96
1867	0.00	0.00	5.07	0.28	0.02	0.00	5.36
1868	0.19	0.00	5.00	0.00	0.00	0.00	5.19
1869	0.00	0.00	5.24	0.45	0.00	0.00	5.68
1870	0.00	0.00	6.51	0.04	0.00	0.81	7.37
1871	0.06	0.00	2.74	0.04	0.00	0.79	3.63
1872	0.57	0.00	0.38	0.10	1.83	0.00	2.88
1873	0.19	0.00	0.29	0.65	1.33	0.00	2.47
1874	0.01	0.00	5.74	0.15	0.90	0.00	6.80
1875	0.00	0.00	6.18	0.88	0.00	0.00	7.06
1876	0.00	0.00	13.82	0.03	0.00	0.00	13.85
1877	0.00	0.00	4.28	0.00	0.00	0.00	4.28
1878	0.00	1.89	6.56	0.29	0.00	0.00	8.73
1879	0.00	1.28	17.09	0.52	0.00	0.47	19.36
1880	0.15	0.22	14.60	0.80	0.00	0.13	15.90
1881	0.19	0.00	10.76	1.57	0.00	0.00	12.52
1882	0.00	0.00	4.44	1.11	0.00	0.00	5.55
1883	0.10	1.09	31.03	1.95	0.00	0.00	34.16
1884	0.02	0.00	22.40	5.10	0.00	0.53	28.05
1885	0.02	0.51	20.76	0.47	0.00	0.00	21.76
1886	0.07	0.71	27.26	1.68	0.17	0.55	30.44

Year							
1887	0.03	0.38	12.49	6.64	0.67	0.00	20.22
1888	0.21	1.27	18.81	2.91	0.00	0.00	23.19
1889	0.00	2.21	15.77	2.15	0.00	0.00	20.13
1890	0.39	0.32	11.11	1.79	0.00	0.00	13.60
1891	0.01	0.15	15.68	1.10	0.00	0.16	17.10
1892	0.00	0.00	5.61	0.92	0.01	0.08	6.62
1893	0.38	4.73	9.44	0.46	0.00	0.00	15.02
1894	0.05	2.66	4.77	1.97	0.00	0.00	9.46
1895	0.20	0.75	8.86	10.41	0.00	0.00	20.22
1896	0.35	0.57	2.14	7.87	0.00	0.00	10.93
1897	0.46	0.59	2.40	3.74	0.00	0.00	7.18
1898	0.83	0.21	2.00	1.88	0.02	0.02	4.96
1899	0.90	0.00	4.80	5.60	0.41	0.05	11.77
1900	0.10	0.00	4.77	2.93	0.22	0.14	8.16
1901	0.05	0.00	12.75	1.81	0.28	0.29	15.18
1902	0.24	0.09	7.78	2.53	0.00	0.00	10.65
1903	0.13	0.00	0.90	0.71	0.00	0.00	1.73
1904	0.00	0.00	0.00	1.64	0.02	0.00	1.66
1905	0.03	0.00	0.00	1.11	0.07	0.00	1.21
1906	0.12	0.00	4.07	2.32	0.00	0.00	6.52
1907	0.35	0.70	1.19	0.89	0.00	0.01	3.13
1908	0.19	0.54	5.62	0.89	0.00	0.00	7.24
1909	0.20	0.14	10.69	0.87	0.00	0.23	12.14
1910	0.69	1.25	5.21	0.56	0.00	0.06	7.77
1911	0.02	1.50	3.87	0.42	0.00	0.00	5.81
1912	0.36	0.43	6.48	1.18	0.00	0.43	8.88
1913	0.11	2.35	23.63	1.83	0.00	0.12	28.03
1914	0.16	0.50	9.32	0.88	0.22	0.15	11.23

Source: Davis–Gallman tape.

Table 5:3-3(a). *Australia: Capital created and called on the British market by industry without adjustment (i.e., all government bonds in government) (thousands of United States dollars)*

Year	Manufacturing, commercial & miscellaneous	Finance	Government	Agriculture & extractive	Transport	Public utilities	Total
1865–1869	5,162	0	36,242	5,811	24	0	47,239
1870–1874	1,442	0	26,861	1,747	7,202	2,630	39,881
1875–1879	0	6,649	97,634	3,431	0	1,013	108,727
1880–1884	1,045	3,135	198,982	25,550	0	1,630	230,342
1885–1889	942	14,620	265,096	39,257	2,338	1,505	323,757
1890–1894	2,629	25,958	149,261	20,107	36	776	198,766
1895–1899	9,785	7,401	70,881	103,305	1,589	252	193,212
1900–1904	1,982	348	99,209	36,749	1,991	1,631	141,910
1905–1909	3,813	5,844	91,809	25,297	285	1,042	128,091
1910–1914	6,052	27,454	223,806	22,345	1,023	3,452	284,131
1865–1914	32,852	91,408	1,259,780	283,599	14,487	13,931	1,696,057

Table 5:3-3(b). *Australia: Capital created and called on the British market by industry without adjustment (i.e., all government bonds in government) (thousands of United States dollars)*

Year	Manufacturing, commercial & miscellaneous	Finance	Government	Agriculture & extractive	Transport	Public utilities	Total
1865–1869	10.9	0.0	76.7	12.3	0.1	0.0	100.0
1870–1874	3.6	0.0	67.4	4.4	18.1	6.6	100.0
1875–1879	0.0	6.1	89.8	3.2	0.0	0.9	100.0
1880–1884	0.5	1.4	86.4	11.1	0.0	0.7	100.0

1885–1889	0.3	4.5	81.9	12.1	0.7	0.5	100.0
1890–1894	1.3	13.1	75.1	10.1	0.0	0.4	100.0
1895–1899	5.1	3.8	36.7	53.5	0.8	0.1	100.0
1900–1904	1.4	0.2	69.9	25.9	1.4	1.1	100.0
1905–1909	3.0	4.6	71.7	19.7	0.2	0.8	100.0
1910–1914	2.1	9.7	78.8	7.9	0.4	1.2	100.0
1865–1914	1.9	5.4	74.3	16.7	0.9	0.8	100.0

Table 5:3-3(c). *Australia: Annual average per capita Capital created and called on the British market by industry without adjustment (i.e., all government bonds in government) (United States dollars)*

Year	Manufacturing, commercial & miscellaneous	Finance	Government	Agriculture & extractive	Transport	Public utilities	Total
1865–1869	0.75	0.00	4.91	0.83	0.00	0.00	6.49
1870–1874	0.17	0.00	3.13	0.20	0.81	0.32	4.63
1875–1879	0.00	0.63	9.59	0.34	0.00	0.09	10.66
1880–1884	0.09	0.26	16.65	2.11	0.00	0.13	19.24
1885–1889	0.07	1.02	19.02	2.77	0.17	0.11	23.15
1890–1894	0.16	1.57	9.32	1.25	0.00	0.05	12.36
1895–1899	0.55	0.43	4.04	5.90	0.09	0.01	11.01
1900–1904	0.10	0.02	5.24	1.92	0.11	0.09	7.48
1905–1909	0.18	0.28	4.32	1.22	0.01	0.05	6.05
1910–1914	0.27	1.21	9.70	0.97	0.04	0.15	12.34
1865–1914	0.23	0.54	8.59	1.75	0.12	0.10	11.34

Source: Davis–Gallman tape.

Table 5:3-4(a). *Australia: capital created and called on the British market by industry with government railroads in transportation (thousands of dollars)*

Year	Manufacturing, commercial, & miscellaneous	Finance	Government	Agriculture & extractive	Transport	Public utilities	Total
1865–1869	5,162	0	28,580	5,811	7,686	0	47,239
1870–1874	1,442	0	19,394	1,747	14,668	2,630	39,881
1875–1879	0	6,649	83,170	3,431	14,464	1,013	108,727
1880–1884	1,045	3,135	169,314	25,550	29,668	1,630	230,342
1885–1889	942	14,620	263,900	39,257	3,533	1,505	323,757
1890–1894	2,629	25,958	149,261	20,107	36	776	198,766
1895–1899	9,785	7,401	70,881	103,305	1,589	252	193,212
1900–1904	1,982	348	99,209	36,749	1,991	1,631	141,910
1905–1909	3,813	5,844	91,809	25,297	285	1,042	128,091
1910–1914	6,052	27,454	223,806	22,345	1,023	3,452	284,131
1865–1914	32,852	91,408	1,199,325	283,599	74,943	13,931	1,696,057

Table 5:3-4(b). *Australia: Capital created and called on the British market by industry with government railroads in transportation (percent of total)*

Year	Manufacturing, commercial, & miscellaneous	Finance	Government	Agriculture & extractive	Transport	Public utilities	Total
1865–1869	10.9	0.0	60.5	12.3	16.3	0.0	100.0
1870–1874	3.6	0.0	48.6	4.4	36.8	6.6	100.0
1875–1879	0.0	6.1	76.5	3.2	13.3	0.9	100.0
1880–1884	0.5	1.4	73.5	11.1	12.9	0.7	100.0

Year	Manufacturing, commercial, & miscellaneous	Finance	Government	Agriculture & extractive	Transport	Public utilities	Total
1885–1889	0.3	4.5	81.5	12.1	1.1	0.5	100.0
1890–1894	1.3	13.1	75.1	10.1	0.0	0.4	100.0
1895–1899	5.1	3.8	36.7	53.5	0.8	0.1	100.0
1900–1904	1.4	0.2	69.9	25.9	1.4	1.1	100.0
1905–1909	3.0	4.6	71.7	19.7	0.2	0.8	100.0
1910–1914	2.1	9.7	78.8	7.9	0.4	1.2	100.0
1865–1914	1.9	5.4	70.7	16.7	4.4	0.8	100.0

Table 5:3-4(c). *Australia: Annual average per capita capital created and called on the British market by industry with government railroads in transportation (United States dollars)*

Year	Manufacturing, commercial, & miscellaneous	Finance	Government	Agriculture & extractive	Transport	Public utilities	Total
1865–1869	0.75	0.00	3.88	0.83	1.04	0.00	6.49
1870–1874	0.17	0.00	2.21	0.20	1.74	0.32	4.63
1875–1879	0.00	0.63	8.23	0.34	1.35	0.09	10.66
1880–1884	0.09	0.26	14.12	2.11	2.53	0.13	19.24
1885–1889	0.07	1.02	18.93	2.77	0.25	0.11	23.15
1890–1894	0.16	1.57	9.32	1.25	0.00	0.05	12.36
1895–1899	0.55	0.43	4.04	5.90	0.09	0.01	11.01
1900–1904	0.10	0.02	5.24	1.92	0.11	0.09	7.48
1905–1909	0.18	0.28	4.32	1.22	0.01	0.05	6.05
1910–1914	0.27	1.21	9.70	0.97	0.04	0.15	12.35
1865–1914	0.23	0.54	8.00	1.75	0.72	0.10	11.34

Source: Davis–Gallman tape.

Table 5:3-5(a). *Australia: Capital created and called on the British market by industry with transport and government adjusted (thousands of United States dollars)*

Year	Manufacturing, commercial & miscellaneous	Finance	Government	Agriculture & extractive	Transport	Public utilities	Total
1865–1869	5,162	0	13,990	5,811	22,276	0	47,239
1870–1874	1,442	0	9,541	1,747	24,522	2,630	39,881
1875–1879	0	6,649	35,042	3,431	62,592	1,013	108,727
1880–1884	1,045	3,135	62,575	25,550	136,407	1,630	230,342
1885–1889	942	14,620	96,378	39,257	171,055	1,505	323,757
1890–1894	2,629	25,958	63,089	20,107	86,208	776	198,766
1895–1899	9,785	7,401	40,648	103,305	31,822	252	193,212
1900–1914	1,982	348	51,755	36,749	49,444	1,631	141,910
1905–1909	3,813	5,844	41,442	25,297	50,653	1,042	128,091
1910–1914	6,052	27,454	92,528	22,345	132,300	3,452	284,131
1865–1914	32,852	91,408	506,988	283,599	767,280	13,931	1,696,057

Table 5:3-5(b). *Australia: capital created and called on the British market by industry with transport and government adjusted (percent of total)*

Year	Manufacturing, commercial & miscellaneous	Finance	Government	Agriculture & extractive	Transport	Public utilities	Total
1865–1869	10.9	0.0	29.6	12.3	47.2	0.0	100.0
1870–1874	3.6	0.0	23.9	4.4	61.5	6.6	100.0
1875–1879	0.0	6.1	32.2	3.2	57.6	0.9	100.0

	Manufacturing, commercial & miscellaneous	Finance	Government	Agriculture & extractive	Transport	Public utilities	Total
1880–1884	0.5	1.4	27.2	11.1	59.2	0.7	100.0
1885–1889	0.3	4.5	29.8	12.1	52.8	0.5	100.0
1890–1894	1.3	13.1	31.7	10.1	43.4	0.4	100.0
1895–1899	5.1	3.8	21.0	53.5	16.5	0.1	100.0
1900–1914	1.4	0.2	36.5	25.9	34.8	1.1	100.0
1905–1909	3.0	4.6	32.4	19.7	39.5	0.8	100.0
1910–1914	2.1	9.7	32.6	7.9	46.6	1.2	100.0
1865–1914	1.9	5.4	29.9	16.7	45.2	0.8	100.0

Table 5:3-5(c). *Australia: Annual average per capita capital created and called on the British market by industry with transport and government adjusted (United States dollars)*

Year	Manufacturing, commercial & miscellaneous	Finance	Government	Agriculture & extractive	Transport	Public utilities	Total
1865–1869	0.75	0.00	1.90	0.83	3.01	0.00	6.49
1870–1874	0.17	0.00	1.09	0.20	2.85	0.32	4.63
1875–1879	0.00	0.63	3.48	0.34	6.11	0.09	10.66
1880–1884	0.09	0.26	5.21	2.11	11.44	0.13	19.24
1885–1889	0.07	1.02	6.90	2.77	12.28	0.11	23.15
1890–1894	0.16	1.57	3.93	1.25	5.39	0.05	12.36
1895–1899	0.55	0.43	2.31	5.90	1.81	0.01	11.01
1900–1914	0.11	0.02	2.73	2.15	2.62	0.09	7.72
1905–1909	0.18	0.28	1.95	1.22	2.38	0.05	6.05
1910–1914	0.27	1.21	4.02	0.97	5.73	0.15	12.35
1865–1914	0.23	0.54	3.35	1.75	5.36	0.10	11.34

Source: Davis–Gallman tape.

Table 5:3-6. *Australia: Sectoral breakdown of the agricultural and extractive industry*

		Panel A: Thousands of United States dollars			
Years	Mining	Pastoral & agriculture	Chemicals & petroleum	Financial Land & development	Agriculture & extractive total
1865–1869	2,131	0	0	3,538	5,669
1870–1874	1,650	97	0	0	1,747
1875–1879	1,778	0	0	1,653	3,431
1880–1884	12,858	244	0	12,449	25,550
1885–1889	21,962	61	0	17,234	39,257
1890–1894	11,116	0	0	9,012	20,128
1895–1899	66,408	937	61	30,280	97,732
1900–1904	32,939	1,464	0	2,346	36,749
1905–1909	23,717	231	12	1,337	25,297
1910–1914	21,249	0	0	1,096	22,345
1865–1914	195,806	3,034	73	78,946	277,904
		Panel B: Percent of total			
1865–1869	37.6	0.0	0.0	62.4	100.0
1870–1874	94.4	5.6	0.0	0.0	100.0
1875–1879	51.8	0.0	0.0	48.2	100.0
1880–1884	50.3	1.0	0.0	48.7	100.0
1885–1889	55.9	0.2	0.0	43.9	100.0
1890–1894	55.2	0.0	0.0	44.8	100.0
1895–1899	67.9	1.0	0.1	31.0	100.0
1900–1904	89.6	4.0	0.0	6.4	100.0
1905–1909	93.8	0.9	0.0	5.3	100.0
1910–1914	95.1	0.0	0.0	4.9	100.0
1865–1914	70.5	1.1	0.0	28.4	100.0

Source: Davis–Gallman tape.

the Glasgow Gympie Gold Mine £3,100 three years later – to very substantial. For example, Australian Mining raised £130,000 in 1894, Eagle Hawk Consolidated Gold Mining £140,000 in that year and an additional £229,000 in 1900, and the Ivanhoe (New) Gold Corporation £375,000 in 1897. By the end of the period, however, the emphasis had moved away from the precious metals toward the more mundane industrial ones: London and Globe Deep Leads Assets raised £25,000 in 1903 and £50,000 the next year; Mount Catlin Consolidated Copper Mining floated

£150,000 in 1907; and Union Consolidated Copper followed with £30,000 four years later.

Over the fifty-year period financial land and development companies drew almost $80 million from the formal British markets, almost 30 percent of the agriculture and extractive sector's total. That figure is somewhat misleading, since it represents an average of just less than 40 percent for the years 1865–99 and an average of less than 6 percent between 1900 and 1914, the latter a reflection of the impact of the crisis on both British savers and Australian business.

An issue of the London and Australian Agency was the first recorded flotation of a financial land and development company: £120,0000 in 1865 and 1866. That foray was only the beginning. Between 1866 and 1888 the Australian Mortgage Land and Finance Company drew £680,100; over much the same period (1867–93), the Scottish Australian Investment Company Ltd. raised £565,500. It was the 1880s and 1890s, however, that saw the largest flow of funds. Over the two decades the Union Mortgage and Agency of Australia tapped the British market for £1,202,200, the Agency Land and Finance of Australia for £599,000, the Caledonian and Australian Mortgage and Agency for £551,000, the Australian Cities Investment Company £487,000, and the Australian Estate and Mortgage Company for £448,000. In the years after 1900, however, the largest issue was £50,000 by the Agency Land and Finance Company of Australia.

Although relatively small in comparison to the government and the agricultural and extractive sectors, the share of the financial sector was several times as large as it was in the other frontier countries.[939] In Australia the imperial banks were very important, and the domestic trading banks had much closer ties to the British capital markets than their counterparts in Argentina and Australia. Until the 1890s the British saver viewed the Australian banks quite favorably; but, thereafter, the majority of his contributions were not voluntary. In the years leading up to the wave of suspensions, the Australian Joint Stock Bank had raised £350,000, the Bank of Australasia £225,000, the Commercial Bank of Australia £1,014,800, the English, Scottish and Australian Chartered Bank £414,000, and the Union Bank of Australia £835,000: a total of £2,838,800. The depression, suspensions, and restructuring, however, engendered calls of £2,043,100 by the Commercial Bank of Australia, £1,526,400 by the London Chartered Bank of Australia, and £540,000 by

[939] At more than 5 percent of the total, the Australian sector was 3.5 times as large as its American counterpart and more than five times as large as those in Argentina and Canada.

Table 5:3-7. *Australia: New issues of state and local governments*

Panel A: Thousands of U.S. dollars

Year	New South Wales	Victoria	South Australia	Queensland	Tasmania	Western Australia	Municipals	Total government
1870–1874	4,841	14,698	2,717	4,461	745	0	0	27,462
1875–1879	24,481	28,343	17,157	20,415	1,670	950	1,018	94,035
1880–1884	73,513	28,270	42,520	30,418	7,597	1,894	7,704	191,917
1885–1889	86,350	64,041	24,642	42,929	9,545	3,083	18,784	249,373
1890–1894	30,306	34,202	0	23,259	4,383	7,967	16,806	116,924
1895–1899	26,176	0	10,246	13,130	2,162	26,493	0	78,207
1900–1904	32,118	4,700	4,602	16,037	2,016	23,634	0	83,107
1905–1909	28,821	7,159	0	9,448	1,442	22,816	765	70,449
1910–1913	34,041	0	8,605	31,061	0	27,145	6,117	106,970
1910–1913	340,647	181,412	110,491	191,157	29,561	113,982	51,193	1,018,444

Panel B: Percent of all state and municipal governments

Year	New South Wales	Victoria	South Australia	Queensland	Tasmania	Western Australia	Municipals	Total government
1870–1874	17.6	53.5	9.9	16.2	2.7	0.0	0.0	100.0
1875–1879	26.0	30.1	18.2	21.7	1.8	1.0	1.1	100.0
1880–1884	38.3	14.7	22.2	15.8	4.0	1.0	4.0	100.0
1885–1889	34.6	25.7	9.9	17.2	3.8	1.2	7.5	100.0
1890–1894	25.9	29.3	0.0	19.9	3.7	6.8	14.4	100.0

1895–1899	33.5	0.0	13.1	16.8	2.8	33.9	0.0	100.0
1900–1904	38.6	5.7	5.5	19.3	2.4	28.4	0.0	100.0
1905–1909	40.9	10.2	0.0	13.4	2.0	32.4	1.1	100.0
1910–1913	31.8	0.0	8.0	29.0	0.0	25.4	5.7	100.0
1910–1913	33.4	17.8	10.8	18.8	2.9	11.2	5.0	100.0

Panel C: Annual per capita average of state new issues

1870–1874	1.81	3.95	2.84	6.99	1.44	0.00		3.18
1875–1879	7.63	6.96	15.26	22.80	3.10	6.60		9.42
1880–1884	18.36	6.38	29.90	26.02	12.72	11.80		16.29
1885–1889	17.33	12.79	15.76	25.75	14.25	15.51		17.70
1890–1894	5.22	5.94	0.00	11.52	5.90	26.48		7.19
1895–1899	4.04	0.00	5.76	5.77	2.70	45.02		4.37
1900–1904	4.57	0.78	2.52	6.38	2.27	24.21		4.32
1905–1909	3.75	1.16	0.00	3.46	1.52	17.77		3.40
1910–1913	6.55	0.00	6.79	16.58	0.00	31.15		7.74
1910–1913	7.74	4.41	8.85	13.80	5.10	19.31		8.20

Sources: (1) New issues from A.R. Hall, *The London Capital Market and Australia, 1870–1914* (Canberra: The Australian National University, 1963), Appendix II, Table I, p. 209. (2) Population from E.A. Boehm, *Prosperity and Depression in Australia, 1887–1897* (Oxford: the Clarendon Press, 1971), Table 1, p. 3 and Commonwealth Bureau of Census and Statistics, *Official Yearbook of the Commonwealth of Australia, 1901–1919*, No. 13, 1920 (Melbourne, 1920), p. 97.

the Standard Bank of Australia – a total of £4,109,400. Saver confidence, however, appears to have recovered somewhat by the outbreak of the war. In 1913 and 1914, for example, the Union Bank of Australia raised £900,000, the London Chartered Bank of Australia, £491,000, and the government-owned Commonwealth Bank of Australia, £1,000,000.[940]

Because most of Australian public utilities were state owned, that industry represented a much smaller proportion of total calls than in any of the other frontier economies. In 1879 the Metropolitan Gas Company of Melbourne turned to the British market for £3,000, and in 1909 the Melbourne Electric Supply Company looked to the same source for £15,000. Between those dates the Australasian Electric Light Company raised £78,000 in 1884, the Australian Gas Light Company £309,000 in 1887 (as well as another £53,300 in 1910), and the Electric Lighting and Traction of Australia £245,400 between 1899 and 1901. International telegraph companies aside, those were the only Public Utility calls on the British market.

More surprising is the relatively minor role played by the formal British capital markets in the financing of Australian manufacturing and commerce. As in the United States and Canada there was certainly some direct investment that is not captured in the capital called data.[941] In 1865 manufacturing and commerce accounted for 18 percent of Australian GDP, and by 1914 the fraction had grown to 31 percent.[942] Over the years 1865 to 1869 the Manufacturing and Commercial sector accounted for 11 percent of calls; between 1910 and 1914 the figure was 2 percent. Over the half century, as a fraction of the total, the Australian manufacturing and commercial sector's share was only about 40 percent of the share of that sector in Canada and the United States; and it was only one-third greater than that of the Argentine. Australia's position relative to the other countries improved somewhat after the turn of the century, but it remained only one-third of that of Canada and one-half of that of the United States. There was also, of course, some British direct investment; but direct transfers appear to have played a substantially less significant

[940] Some of these banks had Australian as well as London share registers, and a part of the London issues were almost certainly taken up in Australia.

[941] For a brief nonquantitative survey of direct investment see G. Blainey, "The History of Multinational Factories in Australia," in Akio Okochi and Tadakatsu Inoue (eds.), *Overseas Business Activities*, The International Conference on Business History, No. 9 (Tokyo: University of Tokyo Press, 1984), pp. 183–210. [Hereafter cited as Blainey, "The History of Multinational Factories."]

[942] N. Butlin, *Australian Domestic Product*, table 3, pp. 12–13. In 1865 manufacturing contributed less than 5 percent, but by 1914 the sector's share was 14.3 percent.

role than they did in the United States or in Canada. Even that conclusion is tentative, since many of the firms and their records have disappeared leaving little trace. In the words of one scholar, "most of the early Australian factories have vanished," and "their main business records have vanished."

Some traces of those ventures have, however, survived. "D. Hogarth & Co., a meat canner in Aberdeen, Scotland, formed the Hogarth Australian Meat Preserving Co., Limited in 1870 with Scottish capital as well as capital subscribed by Australian colonists who had retired to live in Britain." In April 1870 the Central Queensland Meat Preserving Company Limited was formed in London and it built the biggest meat-preserving plant in Australia at Rockhampton. Of the capital subscribed before January 1873 – by then the company was heading for collapse – just over three-quarters came from English investors, and the remainder from Australians. "One of the few British firms to set up a factory in Australia in the 1880s and to leave behind some of its records, was the Bristol firm of John Lysaght Limited. About 1884 it decided to set up a factory near Sydney in order to make wire netting." Rabbits had become a major problem on Australian sheep runs, and the New South Wales government had imposed a tariff on imported wire netting. Again, in the late 1880s, John Coates, a partner in John Coates & Company, launched the Melbourne Hydraulic Power Company to build a pumping station and construct high-pressure water mains beneath the city streets in order to provide hydraulic elevators for the cities' high-rise buildings. These direct incursions appear, however, to have been fairly rare. "Tobacco was possibly the main manufacturing industry which attracted heavy overseas attention before 1900." In that industry there was also some American investment. For example, the Cameron Brothers spent about $500,000 to erect a large factory to manufacture pipe tobacco in Sydney in 1873. Overall, however, overseas direct investment does not appear to have been important in the decades leading up to World War I.[943]

The manufacturing and commercial firms that did enter the British capital market were chiefly engaged in processing the products of the Australian agricultural and mining sectors. Between 1868 and 1880, for example, the Australian Extract of Meat and Cattle Company, the Australian Meat and Agency, and the Australian Meat Importation Company drew a total of £141,500; and in 1900 the Imperial Australian Wine Company was the beneficiary of another £7,500 of British capital. In the case of mineral processing, English and Australian Copper Ltd. received £157,600 in 1886 and 1887, between 1895 and 1905 the Smelting and

---

[943] Blainey, "The History of Multinational Factories," pp. 184–94.

Refining Company of Australia drew a total of £134,500, and in 1906 and 1907 the Australian Smelting Company was the recipient of £140,000 from London calls. In 1872 Australian and Oriental Coal Ltd. raised £154,000; and some forty years later the Australian Coking and By Products Company turned to Britain for £118,000. Agriculture and mineral processing aside, only five other Manufacturing & Commercial firms appear on the list of British capital created and called: Australian Lithofracture for £37,000 in 1891, Castlemain Brewery, Melbourne, £100,000 in 1895, New Marine Rope, £8,800 in 1896, Australian Cycle and Motor, £18,800 in that year, and, finally, the Australian Cycle Agency, £49,500 in 1896 and 1897.

5-4. The evolution of the domestic capital market in Australia

5-4a. Introduction

Recently David Merrett has summarized the development of the institutional structure of the financial sector in Australia in the years before the 1890s; his summary underscores the role of British capital.

> The long period of economic expansion after the gold rush left a legacy in terms of a stock of capital skewed towards a narrow range of activities and a set of financial institutions and capital markets that, although shaped by British experience, was uniquely Australian. Despite the developments that had taken place in the financial and capital markets in the decades before the bank crashes, the narrow range of services provided by banks and other financial intermediaries, together with the colonial stock exchanges, was indicative of a relatively immature economy that was still in many respects an appendage of the United Kingdom.[944]

Throughout the period the trading banks remained by far the largest and most important financial intermediaries, although their relative position eroded after the debacle of the 1890s. On the eve of the depression they accounted for about 70 percent of the total assets of financial institutions. At that time savings banks accounted for a mere 6 percent, pastoral finance companies 12 percent, building societies 10 percent, and insurance companies 5 percent. Two decades later, in 1910, the corresponding figures were 52 percent for trading banks, 22 percent for savings banks, 2 percent for building societies, pastoral companies 9 percent, and insurance companies about 14 percent.[945] Although by 1910 the wreck-

---

[944] Merrett, "Capital Formation and Capital Markets," p. 2.

[945] David Pope, "Free Banking in Australia Before World War I," the Australian National University, Working Papers in Economic History, No. 129, December 1989. [Hereafter cited as Pope, "Free Banking."]

age of the 1890s had been cleared away and the surviving trading banks had repaired and strengthened their balance sheets, they were never again to dominate the financial markets as they had in the years before 1890. "A much reduced and different set of demands for investment funds provided opportunities for other types of financial institutions to play a larger role."[946] Despite these developments, the institutional structure that underlay the Australian financial markets remained relatively primitive. As late as 1914, for example, more than 50 percent of all financial claims were generated by the trading banks (currency and demand deposits, term deposits, and bank loans), non-bank intermediaries accounted for less than 9 percent, life insurance reserves hardly more than 5 percent, government bonds slightly more than 15 percent, and the stocks and bonds of private corporations less than one pound in five. In contrast, as early as 1900, in the United States, claims against all financial institutions comprised only 21 percent of outstanding financial instruments, whereas claims against non-financial institutions accounted for 56 percent and corporate stock 23 percent.[947]

5-4b. The trading banks

Australia, like Canada, had early recognized the value added by the Scottish banks; and all six colonies imported the Scottish banking system – a system based on branches and on short-term advances – largely intact. By 1860, however, the Australian banks had begun to take on distinctly Australian characteristics; and those characteristics were to have a significant impact on institutional development. One major difference was that, unlike the commercial banks in Britain and Scotland, the Australian trading banks did not accept savings deposits.[948]

From the date of the issue of the original bank charters in the late 1820s until the 1860s, the successful Australian banks were almost all imperial banks – banks chartered, largely owned, and directed from London.[949] The Union Bank, for example, sold 13,000 shares in Britain but reserved 7,000 for colonial investors. The Bank of Australasia, on the

---

[946] Merrett, "Capital Formation and Capital Markets," p. 5.

[947] Merrett, "Capital Formation and Capital Markets," p. 14 and table 1. Goldsmith, *Financial Structure and Development*, table 1-1, pp. 10–11.

[948] Holder, "Australia," p. 65. Technically this distinction remains true today; but, in fact, in the more recent past all of the trading banks have established savings bank subsidiaries.

[949] S. Butlin, *Australia and New Zealand Bank*, p. 3. There were domestic banks as well; but, as Butlin notes, "except for the Commercial Banking Company of Sydney, not one of these survived more than five years."

other hand, allotted only 500 of its first 5,000 shares to the colonies.[950] It should be noted that a number of the early imperial banks – banks eager to obtain a foothold in Australia as cheaply as possible – bought out an existing colonial bank, and the resulting "merger" added relatively little new banking capital.[951] From the 1860s onward, the imperial-domestic balance began to shift. The early phase of the gold boom saw three imperial banks (the Oriental Banking Corporation, the English, Scottish and Australian Bank, and the London Chartered Bank of Australia) but only one colonial bank (the Bank of Victoria) established. Between 1863 and 1888, however, no fewer than twenty-eight new banks, all incorporated in the colonies, commenced operations.[952] By the beginning of the 1870s, colonial-registered banks had "wrested majority control of the banking system in Australia from the English banks."[953] Not only were these colonial banks, but they were largely Victoria-based. Of the twenty-eight, fourteen were promoted in Melbourne and only four in Sydney. The remaining ten were spread out: three each in Brisbane and Adelaide, one each in Hobart, Launceston, Ballarat, and Rockhampton.[954]

The main offices of the imperial banks were located in London, but most of the Australian-chartered banks also maintained substantial London branches. Like the London offices of Canadian banks, the London offices of Australian banks were actively engaged in the discount and money markets, by-products of their processing their customers' trade bills. Unlike their Canadian counterparts, the Australian branches actively sought both British stockholders and British depositors. In contrast to American firms, colonial chartered banks had easy institutional access to the London capital market. An Australian firm, then, had no need to employ a British merchant bank, if it wished to tap the British capital markets. The structure, as long as it worked, reduced the role of British merchant banks in directing British capital to Australia; and it largely eliminated the need for Australian investment banks to participate in the process of international capital mobilization.[955] Despite the growing importance of the Australian chartered banks, the imperial

---

[950] Baster, *Imperial Banks*, p. 65.
[951] Examples include the amalgamations of the Bank of Australasia with the Cornwall Bank of Launceston (1835), and the Union Bank of Australia with the Tamar Bank (1837). Baster, *Imperial Banks*, p. 221.
[952] Butlin, *Australia and New Zealand Bank*, p. 174.
[953] Sinclair, *The Process of Economic Growth*, pp. 98–99.
[954] S. Butlin, *Australia and New Zealand Bank*, pp. 174–75.
[955] Salsbury and Sweeny, *The Bull, The Bear*, p. 58.

Table 5:4-1. *Australian private trading banks, 1865–1914*

Year	Number of private trading banks	Total assets of private trading banks (thousands of pounds)	Number of persons per private trading bank (thousands)	Assets per capita private trading banks (pounds per capita)
1865	14	38,947	98	28.5
1870	14	42,292	116	26.1
1876	18	67,870	111	33.9
1880	21	82,521	108	36.3
1885	23	134,876	116	50.7
1890	26	185,369	119	60.0
1895	20	154,249	171	45.2
1900	20	149,042	186	40.1
1905	20	157,114	202	38.9
1910	20	202,866	219	46.3
1914	20	244,671	237	51.5

Notes: Bank assets for 1865 and 1870 are estimated as the ratio of (Total Asset/Assets Within Australia) in 1876. 1914 assets are figures for (June 1914 + June 1915)/2.

Sources: S.J. Butlin, A.R. Hall, and R.C. White, *Australian Banking and Monetary Statistics, 1817–1945*, Reserve Bank of Australia, Occasional Paper Number 4A (Sydney, 1971), Table 1m pp. 112–113, Table 2(i), pp. 116–118, Table 2(ii), pp. 120–121, and Table 3, pp. 122–123.

banks maintained a substantial presence; and in the long run they proved more stable.[956]

As Table 5:4-1 indicates, by 1865, at least, the trading banks had become an important part of the nation's financial fabric. The number of banks grew only slowly, but assets increased at almost 4 percent a year. Despite the effects of the depression of the 1890s, assets per capita still increased at more than 1 percent a year. Thus, in terms of their relative position, Australian trading banks played a more important role

---

[956] "Of the twenty-eight banks formed during 1853–88, three failed outright before the 'nineties and eight more were taken over 'by other banks,' normally as the only alternative to failure in the formal sense. Of the other seventeen, five failed finally in the 'nineties and seven others suspended payment and reconstructed at that time. Only six of the twenty-eight reached the end of the century without temporary or final failure, and several of these never recovered from the wounds they received in 1893. By contrast, of the eight trading banks operating in Australia in 1850, five, among them the Union and the Australasia, survived all storms; one, the Bank of Van Dieman's Land, failed before the 'nineties, one, the Bank of South Australia, was forced to accept absorption in 1892, and one reconstructed after 1893." S. Butlin, *Australia and New Zealand Bank*, pp. 174–75.

in the domestic capital market than did their Canadian and U.S. counterparts.

The Scottish-based Canadian and Australian laws permitted nation-wide branching; but, from the beginning, the process went much faster in Australia. In the case of the Bank of Australasia, for example, an office in Sydney was opened in 1835, offices in Hobart and Launceston in 1836, Melbourne and Bathhurst in 1838, and Adelaide and Maitland in 1839.[957] With the exception of the Commercial Banking Company of Sydney, initially branching was a strategy only employed by the imperial banks. It was not until the 1850s that the colonial banks displayed any widespread interest in that mode of operation. Thereafter, branch banking became the Australian norm.[958]

By 1877 there were twenty-four banks of issue. Fifteen operated in only one colony, four did business in two, three in three and two (the Australasia and the Union) had become true Australian banks operating in every colony except Western Australia. A decade later there were twenty-five banks. Twelve were single colony banks; six had offices in two colonies, two in three, two in four, two (the Australasia and the Bank of New South Wales) in five, and one (the Union) in six.[959] By 1880 there were 326 branches in Victoria, one for every 2,760 people. At the same time in England and Wales the figure was one for every 12,000 residents, in Ireland one for every 11,000, and in Scotland one for every 4,000.[960] Finally, in 1892 the twenty-three largest banks of issue operated 1,512 branches – eleven in only a single colony, four in two, two in three, two in four, three in five – but the Union was still the only bank to operate in all six. Despite the widespread innovation of branching – only two of the twenty-three had only a single office – it should be kept in mind that the branches of a typical bank tended to be geographically concentrated and its loan portfolios even more narrowly focused. With the exception of the Union Bank and the English, Scottish and Australian Chartered Bank, all the large banks had both their branches and assets concentrated in the colony in which their head offices were located.[961] Thus, on the eve of the crisis the smaller bank appears to have benefited less from

---

[957] Baster, *Imperial Banks*, p. 57.
[958] S. Butlin, *Australia and New Zealand Bank*, p. 5.
[959] S. Butlin, *Australia and New Zealand Bank*, pp. 232–33.
[960] S. Butlin, *Australia and New Zealand Bank*, p. 243. The data are from the *AIBR*, December 8, 1880.
[961] Merrett, "Australian Banking Practice," p. 72 and table 1, p. 73. Note: Merrett's number of "banks of issue" differs marginally from Butlin, Hull, and White's private trading banks (Table 5:4-1).

the insurance aspect of branching than the data on branches alone might have suggested.

The rapid expansion of the banking system was achieved without a corresponding increase in the number of banks. Instead, expansion meant multiplication in the number of branches. In 1890 there were twenty-eight banks of issue, but seven of those accounted for two-thirds of all bank deposits. All seven had branches in more than one colony, and five operated in four or more.[962] Five years later, of the twenty remaining banks, four had comprehensive national branch networks; the remaining sixteen, although they operated in only a few states, all had extensive branch networks.[963] By 1911 the twenty-one banks controlled a network of more than 1,900 branches, one branch for every 2,345 persons. Moreover, faced with competition from the government-owned Commonwealth Bank with its nationwide branch network, the remaining largely localized private banks found that they could not remain economically viable, if they continued to operate in only one or two states. The result was a geographic expansion of their network of branches. Recognition of the potential competitive threat of the Commonwealth Bank was, for example, the reason for the amalgamation of the English, Scottish and Australian Bank with the London Bank of Australia, two banks with complementary branch systems.[964] Thus, by World War I the banks were better structured to benefit from the insurance features of a system based on branching.

In contrast, in Canada "as late as 1895 only one Canadian Bank – the Bank of Montreal – had anything like a nationwide branch system. Even its closest rival, the Canadian Bank of Commerce, operated almost exclusively in Ontario"; and, in the Maritimes, even the largest Halifax banks had only tenuous connections with Ontario.[965] On the other hand, despite the gains made by the Australian banks, by 1914, if the measure is based not on the number of branches per capita, but on the degree of centralization, Canada had probably passed Australia in terms of the development of its national network of branches. In Canada the networks centered in Toronto and Montreal. In Australia, although both Sydney and Victoria were important national banking centers, each state capital was still the home of at least one "national" bank.[966]

---

[962] Jackson, *Australian Economic Development*, p. 140.
[963] Drummond, *Capital Markets*, pp. 15–16.
[964] Baster, *Imperial Banks*, p. 221. Merrett, however, doubts that competition from the Commonwealth Bank was the major reason for the nine amalgamations that occurred between 1909 and 1931.
[965] Drummond, *Capital Markets*, p. 15.
[966] Drummond, *Capital Markets*, p. 16.

In terms of the impact of overseas finance, the Australian banks differed in two major respects from their counterparts in Canada and the United States: in the distribution of their assets and in the sources of their funds. In the first case the Canadian bankers' commitment to the British real bills doctrine had been legally enshrined in the Canadian banking legislation of 1871. In the United States the national banks, because of legal and administrative concerns, held relatively few mortgages. Initially, Australian bank charters also prohibited investments in mortgages. The Bank of Australasia's charter, for example, forbade loans on the security of real estate but permitted the taking of land in the settlement of debt. That provision was, however, interpreted very narrowly: Land could be foreclosed only in outright settlement of debt, it had to be sold promptly, and the bank could not lend on liens on sheep or cattle.[967] Thus, before the 1850s Australian banks had been largely forced to follow the British practice; bank loans on real estate were illegal, and, by and large, bank lending took the form of discounting commercial bills of exchange.[968] Those regulations had begun to erode as early as the 1840s. Originally passed as an emergency depression measure, the New South Wales Liens on Wool and Mortgages of Stock Act of 1843 represented the first break with the British tradition.[969] This measure gave an Australian squatter, for the first time, an effective form of security to offer as collateral for advances. Pastoralists were able to use banks, merchants, and mortgage companies to secure short-term advances.[970] The New South Wales legislation was copied in the other colonies – first in South Australia in 1847 – and, despite resistance from Britain, remained a permanent new part of the financial system. Initially, since the banks, in general, "held aloof from the new type of loan, preferring that it should be taken up by merchants whom, in turn, the banks financed by more conventional methods," the quantitative importance of the innovation was relatively slight.[971]

The next step in the evolution of long-term commercial bank lending came when the British Attorney General provided a more flexible interpretation of the bank charters – he ruled that a bank might take over land or stock to secure a doubtful debt – but he still held that it could not accept such security for a *new* loan. In yet a third break with tradition, J.J. Falconer

---

[967] S. Butlin, *Australia and New Zealand Bank*, p. 96.
[968] Jackson, *Australian Economic Development*, p. 141.
[969] Fogarty, "Staples, Super-Staples," p. 31.
[970] N. Butlin and Barnard, "Pastoral Finance," p. 384.
[971] S. Butlin, *Australia and New Zealand Bank*, pp. 92–93.

of the Bank of Australasia's Adelaide office invented the "secured account," and the courts ruled that such accounts did not violate the bank's charter. The new arrangement permitted the bank to take a lien on sheep (or cattle) as security for a new loan, the loan to be discharged when the wool was shipped. At that time the borrower sold a bill of exchange to the bank and used the payment to retire the loan.

That innovation was soon followed by a wide extension of the principle: The bank began to make loans secured by a real estate trust. The trust was created by the borrower but not in the name of the bank; however, the real estate covered by the trust could not be sold or mortgaged except to pay the debt. Thus, by 1850 the innovation of these new institutional arrangements had de facto effectively removed the legal strictures on mortgage lending that had been imposed by the original charters.[972] In fact, within a few years the practice of mortgage lending was fully accepted; and the mortgage freehold (and to a smaller degree the leasehold property) became the common form of security for bank loans.[973]

There were still de jure questions about the banks' powers, but concerns about legal niceties did not prevent the banks from moving freely and continuously into pastoral and, later, urban mortgages. The legal limitations were "practically ignored, in some cases by the special adoption of the form of entry, but frequently by the entire disregard of them."[974] Over the next years many of the banks did attempt to have their charters amended or lobbied the state legislatures to recognize their right to accept real property as security for loans, and they were more

[972] S. Butlin, *Australia and New Zealand Bank*, pp. 96–97.

[973] R.F. Holder, "Australia," in W.F. Crick, *Commonwealth Banking Systems* (Oxford: Clarendon Press, 1965), pp. 70–71. [Hereafter cited as Holder, "Australia."]

Some idea of the spread of mortgage lending can be seen in the "entry of banks, after the Act of 1858, into the field of financing the gold-mining machinery industry through the use of preferable liens and mortgages on machinery, and the gradual emergence of banking control over the gold market." In the case of the Bank of New South Wales, between 1865 and 1867, several mining companies mortgaged plant and property to secure advances (the Newcastle Coal and Copper Company and the Bulli Coal Company in New South Wales and the Peak Downs Copper Mining Company in Queensland, to cite three examples), and shipping companies borrowed against mortgages on their ships. Hall, *The Stock Exchange of Melbourne*, p. 42. Holder, *Bank of New South Wales*, pp. 368–69.

[974] The quote is from H.G. Turner, "banker, historical, and litterateur." *AIBR*, December 8, 1880.

or less successful.[975] The banks also benefited from a series of Australian court decisions that held that no one but a shareholder had the right to take action for a breach of a local act – or of a charter. That decision was interpreted to imply that a bank that had lent on land in defiance of its charter could still acquire a good title to the foreclosed land.[976]

Some banks, particularly the established imperial banks, preferred to interpose a non-bank intermediary – a merchant or a pastoral finance or mortgage company – between themselves and the squatter. In the early years these banks required the endorsement of a third party, even in the case of squatters' bills drawn on their wool. "This specialized function was often undertaken by consignment agents such as Gibbs, Ronald & Company and who, in the terminology of the City of London, acted as acceptance houses for the banks in their wool finance business."[977] Many banks, however, felt no need for the participation of a third party. Nor were their activities limited to liens on wool. They entered directly into loans for housing, for the purchase of land, and for the improvement – particularly fencing and irrigation – of pastoral runs; and the practices became more widespread as the Australian economy moved through the long boom.[978]

The impact of the shift in banking policy is clearly reflected in the balance sheets of the participating banks. For example, in the case of the Bank of New South Wales, discounted or short-dated bills – bills with a maximum maturity of 90 or 180 days – declined from 82 percent of the bank's loans in 1860, to 52 percent in 1870, to 27 percent in 1880. Somewhat more conservatively, the Bank of Australasia's proportions were roughly equal in the early 1880s. However, the share of loans secured by pastoral properties, farms, urban real estate, second mortgages, and shares in the bank itself rose from 52 percent in October 1886 to 65

---

[975] In the case of the Bank of New South Wales, for example, the state legislature of New South Wales amended the bank's Act of Incorporation in 1864 and the legislature of Queensland followed a short time later. In Victoria, however, the potential legal ambiguities were not cleaned up until the passage of the Banks and Currency Act of 1890, a change that had been recommended by a Royal Commission on Banking. Holder, *Bank of New South Wales*, pp. 368–69. Jackson, *Australian Economic Development*, p. 141.

[976] The decisions were based on Privy Council verdicts in 1870. S. Butlin, *Australia and New Zealand Bank*, pp. 249–50.

[977] Bailey, *A Hundred Years*, pp. 14–15.

[978] "Freehold land might be mortgaged, although the Australasia and Union were more chary of this than the more adventurous colonial banks; in general the English banks preferred that land mortgages be left to the mortgage companies which multiplied after 1860." S. Butlin, *Australia and New Zealand Bank*, pp. 213–15, 250. Holder, "Australia," pp. 70–71.

percent in October 1892. In both cases, even if formal mortgages are excluded, a sizable fraction of the banks' assets were committed to overdrafts and cash credits that, although allegedly repayable on the banks' demand, were actually long-term loans. "The banks' loan books became increasingly illiquid."[979] That conclusion is reflected in both the ratio of bank capital to liabilities – 24 percent in 1872, 17 percent in 1882, and 13 percent in 1892 – and in the ratio of liquid assets to deposits and notes – 32 percent in 1872 and 17 percent in 1892. In addition, banks often began to make very large loans to individual borrowers. Clearly, "it was common for banks to carry exposures that would be unacceptable under current prudential guide-lines of the Australian monetary authorities."[980]

Whether the loans were direct or indirect is not really relevant, the ultimate security was a fixed asset that could not easily be converted into cash. Real estate gradually became the most important single form of security for bank lending, not only on the farms and runs, but in the cities as well. In 1880 H.G. Turner, of the Commercial Bank of Australia, estimated that two-thirds of all bank advances in Victoria were advances against mortgages on land.[981] Speculation in urban real estate became increasingly important during the 1880s. Such loans drew an increasing proportion of the funds of the banking system, as bankers "made a virtue of necessity and rationalized the development of good modern banking, as they evaded, or had repealed, old fashioned legal restraints."[982] Turner argued that "overdrafts secured by real property were safe because . . . in a new country like Victoria, the 'unearned increment' in the value of real property offers a certain margin of security to the lender, which can always be relied upon in the long run." In a similar vein Sheppard Smith, the general manager of the Bank of New South Wales, argued that loans secured by real property were just as safe as bill transactions.[983]

Nor was it the bankers alone who provided intellectual support for the change in policies. The editors of the *Australasian Insurance and Banking Review*, for example, wrote: "The policy of Australian banking has gradually adapted itself to the requirements of a country differing widely in all essentials from the mother-land"; "conditions suited to the finance of the old world were far from adequate to the wants of the young colonies

---

[979] Merrett, "Australian Banking Practice and the Crisis of 1893," p. 71.

[980] Merrett, "Australian Banking Practice and the Crisis of 1893," pp. 74–76, 78.

[981] S. Butlin, *Australia and New Zealand Bank*, pp. 231, 249–50.

[982] S. Butlin, *Australia and New Zealand Bank*, p. 231. N. Butlin, *Investment in Australian Development*, pp. 163–64.

[983] *AIBR*, December 9, 1878; Holder, *Bank of New South Wales*, p. 366.

whose growth chiefly depended upon their profitable use of the immense territory at their disposal. No industry gives promise of such returns, and consequently there was a general desire to become possessed of land and stock.... The directors and managers of the banks fore-saw that there was scope for banking enterprise far beyond anything which the ordinary trade discounting supplied."[984] The members of the Royal Commission on Victorian Banking appear to have felt at least equally strongly about conditions in Australia. In 1887 they concluded, "here a landed estate is always marketable, subject only to the rise and fall in value. It is improbable, therefore, that a bank administered with ordinary prudence could so lock up its money in land that it would become seriously involved. Banks take care to have a margin of safety and experience shows that there are no better securities than those effected on land."[985]

There are, of course, problems arising from the extension of long-term credit on the basis of short- or medium-term liabilities. Those problems existed whether or not the bank dealt directly or through an intermediary. In particular there were potentially serious liquidity complications should the economy weaken, and weaken it did between 1888 and 1904.[986] There were also problems of potential solvency, since the prices of long-term assets can fluctuate widely.

---

[984] *AIBR*, December 8, 1880; December 9, 1878.

[985] *AIBR*, August 16, 1887. There were some voices raised against the restructuring of the banks' portfolios. John Sawers, the Bank of Australasia's superintendent, told his court of directors in 1888 that "I cannot think that all the fresh business taken by the Commercial Bank is of sound character." A year later he said, "I cannot think that the large increase shown by the Queensland National Bank can have been made without undue risk, and I confess I have an instinctive feeling that they are sowing the seeds of future trouble." In 1890 he made similar comments about the Australian Joint Stock Bank for "accepting undue risk to acquire new business." Prideux Selby, the bank's executive secretary in London, was even more pointed in his remarks. In 1888 he wrote, "you in Melbourne are riding for a bad fall," and in March he continued, "Banks which borrow freely for 6 to 12 months fixed and let it for 2 or 3 years are little better than gamblers. While things go smoothly they may make large profits and things have gone smoothly so long that the present generation looks upon banking crises as things which the world has outgrown." Again, Donald Larnach, managing director of the London office of the Bank of New South Wales, repeatedly attacked the notion in correspondence with the bank's general manager in Sydney, Shepard Smith. Merrett, "Australian Banking Practice and the Crisis of 1893," p. 67. Pope, "Free Banking in Australia," p. 16. Pope, "Bankers and Banking Business," p. 21.

[986] In the late 1860s the manager of the Perth branch of the National Bank reported that he could not even locate some of the flocks on which he had made loans in the "backblocks" of the country. "He had lent money to sheep farmers near Albany in return for a mortgage over 800 sheep, but as the customers were more

The extent of the banks' penetration into the Australian agricultural land market can be proxied by the experience of banks in New South Wales. By 1879 banks had become the registered leaseholders of 15 percent of the pastoral leases in the Central and 13 percent in the Western Division of that colony; by 1896 the figures were 24 and 23 percent, respectively.[987] Over the ten years ending in December 1892, the Bank of New South Wales took possession as mortgagee of the pastoral holdings of twenty-seven borrowers in New South Wales and Queensland. In other words, defaults on some £850,000 in the bank's loans – about 5 percent of the total portfolio – forced the bank to assume direct management and operation of these pastoral properties. In the next seven years the bank became "mortgagee in possession" of at least an additional thirty properties that, together, represented new debts of upwards of £500,000.[988] Clearly "the commercial banks had committed themselves deeply and intimately to pastoral developments, not merely by the conduct of ordinary banking business, but also by entry into wool consignment on the one hand and by a general acceptance of direct responsibility for pastoral mortgage advances beyond the limited lending on wool or livestock, that is, by fixed mortgages on station assets as a whole."[989]

Although there is no exact total level of the direct commitment of the commercial banks to mortgage lending – on both stations and stock – to Australian agriculture and pastoral activity, it is estimated that by 1883 it had reached the £35–40 million level; and that total does not include an additional £5–10 million of indirect aid through loans to pastoral finance companies.[990] In that year the Australian investments of the nation's trading banks totaled just less than £78 million.[991]

than 300 miles from the nearest National Bank, they did not take their debt seriously. Deciding to quietly move outback, they drove their flock 350 miles to Esperance Bay, and ignored the persistent letters from the Perth manager when he finally learned of their location. The bank then tried to redeem the mortgage and sell the sheep to another customer in the district, but the customer refused. The manager contemplated sending a man to take possession of the sheep, but the country was surrounded by poisonous plants and 'it would be ticklish work getting them through the poison country.' And so the sheep grazed and multiplied, and the debt stood for years on the books." Blainey, *Gold and Paper*, p. 82.

[987] Noel G. Butlin, "Company Ownership in New South Wales Pastoral Stations, 1865–1880," *Historical Studies of Australia and New Zealand*, Vol. IV, May 1950. Note that the figure for 1896 is really for the year July 1896 through June 1897.

[988] Holder, *Bank of New South Wales*, pp. 534–35.

[989] N. Butlin, *Investment in Australian Development*, p. 133.

[990] N. Butlin, *Investment in Australian Development*, pp. 133, 144–45.

[991] S. Butlin, Hall, and White, *Australian Banking and Monetary Statistics*, table 1, p. 113.

American commercial banks, with no foreign branches before 1914, had few foreign assets or liabilities; although Canadian banks were more heavily involved in overseas transactions, their foreign assets usually much exceeded their foreign liabilities.[992] In Australia, from the 1870s onward, the picture was much different. Some economists have argued against any underdeveloped country adopting a policy designed to attract external deposits for domestic investment: "it may lead to a much greater degree of financial integration between the home monetary centre and the Colony than is desirable, since the overseas banks are always exposed to the effects, at awkward moments, of sudden monetary drains at home originating from causes that have nothing to do with the Colony." The bankers, however, found that caution has a heavy price. Australian bankers realized that they could raise deposits in the United Kingdom at rates of 3.5–5 percent and lend them at home at twice those figures.[993] British savers had come to believe that British commercial banks were safe; there were no bank failures between 1878 and 1914. Moreover, Australian banks looked like British banks; some were British-owned, and almost all maintained substantial presences in the City. Add to those perceptions the fact that Australian interest rates were significantly higher than British, and normal Australian fixed-term deposit rates appeared very attractive to safety-conscious British savers. "Compared with the return on English consols, the stock of city corporations, British railways and colonial bonds on offer, the typical return on Australian fixed term deposits was much higher." "Against the 3.5 to 5 percent typically offered by Australian bankers for two or three year term deposits in the late 1880s, the return on consols was 2.75 percent, Bank of England stock at 3 percent, Liverpool Corporation at 3.25 percent, and the stock of the London and Northwestern Railway of 3.1 percent or lower. Canadian government 4 percent stock offered British investors a return of 3.1 percent, New South Wales 4 percent stock a return of 3.5 percent and the Victorian 4 percent stock a return of 3.6 percent."[994]

The idea was not new. In the 1830s the Derwent Bank had raised deposits in London for investment in the colonies, but that experiment

---

[992] In the case of Canada, in 1900, for example, 12.8 percent of the chartered banks' assets were held abroad and foreign deposits accounted for 6.3 percent of the banks' total deposits. In 1914 the figures were 12.7 and 7.8 percent. *Historical Statistics of Canada*, Series 175, 176, 177, 178, 179, 234, and 236, pp. 238, 240–41.

[993] Baster, *Imperial Banks*, pp. 154–55.

[994] David Pope, "Bankers and Banking Business, 1860–1914," Working Papers In Economic History, the Australian National University, Paper No. 85, September 1987, p. 25. [Hereafter cited as Pope, "Bankers and Banking Business."]

had proved unfortunate, and it was not repeated again for some three decades. When, in the mid-1860s, British deposits were reintroduced by the Australasia and the Union banks, the purpose was not to expand colonial business, but simply to use the deposits to offset short-term variations in London funds. By the next decade, however, the industry's goals had changed.[995] As a result, from the late 1870s until the end of the next decade, British fixed-term (usually one, two, or three years) deposits in Australian banks grew rapidly. In early 1876 the Union Bank, for example, had set a firm maximum of £250,000 on its British deposits. Within four months the board had raised the limit to £400,000, and the process did not end there.[996] The bank attracted an additional £500,000 in British deposits between 1877 and 1880. In 1885, as competition for British funds increased, the bank invented "inscribed stock deposits," instruments that were soon listed on the London Stock Exchange. The results were new deposits of £500,000 between 1885 and 1887 and an additional £250,000 in 1888.[997] Nor was the Union the only bank to adopt the new aggressive strategy in this search for funds. For example, in 1877 the Commercial Bank of Australia opened an agency in Scotland to simplify the collection of deposits from the north.

Over the next decade the quest for British deposits grew more and more intense. At first the search had been limited to the imperial banks – banks that were well positioned to exploit their British connections – but gradually all but the smallest Australian banks entered the market. By the mid-1880s it was the colonial banks that drew the lion's share of British deposits. In particular, it was the young trading banks (the Federal Bank of Australia, the Mercantile Bank of Australia, and the City of Melbourne Bank), banks that had been forced out of the Australian market by competition from the land banks. In part, this result was the product of their aggressive marketing campaigns. Most had London offices and agents; but, as the search for deposits grew more intense, they extended their connections from the city to the countryside. They appointed agents throughout Britain and supported those efforts with widespread advertising campaigns. Scotland proved particularly fruitful. They drew funds from Scots banks and from advocates administering trust funds as well as from individuals; the latter group of depositors ranged from the stylized rich and well-to-do widows to local businessmen and artisans. Looking back at the crisis, the *Australasian Insurance and Banking Review* painted this picture of the U.K. depositors:

[995] S. Butlin, *Australia and New Zealand Bank*, p. 221.
[996] S. Butlin, *Australia and New Zealand Bank*, p. 225.
[997] S. Butlin, *Australia and New Zealand Bank*, pp. 241–42.

The deposits are drawn from all sorts of classes of people. Of course the widows and the vicar, the retired colonel and the superannuated doctor, figure very largely, but often the profits of businessmen find their way in this direction. The Scottish, Irish and provincial banks, possibly from want of legitimate investment in the neighborhoods, are large depositors, and the same may be said for insurance companies, some of the latter of which are revising their articles of association in order to admit of their being able to make deposits with colonial institutions.[998]

In part the shift from imperial to colonial dominance was the product of the relatively conservative policies of the imperial banks. They established limits and were unwilling to take all the funds that were offered. The imperial banks were more aware than their colonial competitors that, faced with a financial crisis, British holders of fixed deposits were likely to be more easily frightened than Australian current account depositors or note holders.

As the institutional structure became more firmly established, and as the network of connections spread across the United Kingdom, the flow of funds increased, rising almost continuously until the early 1890s. By 1892 only two Australian banks, the City of Sydney Bank and the Bank of North Queensland, held no British deposits.[999] Although deficiencies in the data preclude a precise estimate of the volume of British deposits, it is very likely that in the peak year, 1892, they accounted for at least a quarter of all Australian bank deposits.[1000] David Pope has placed the ratio of British to domestic deposits in banks operating in Australia at 10 percent in the mid-1870s, 24 percent a decade later, and finally, on the eve of the depression, at 40 percent.[1001] Most recently, David Merrett has put the figure at £15.5 million in 1886 and £38.1 million in 1892, "a rise

[998] *AIBR*, December 20, 1904.

[999] The City of Sydney Bank survived the crash of the 1890s without closing its doors. The same can not be said for the Bank of North Queensland. S. Butlin, *Australia and New Zealand Bank*, p. 280.

[1000] Jackson, *Australian Economic Development*, pp. 142–43. Bailey, *A Hundred Years*, pp. 55–56. N. Butlin, *Investment in Australian Development*, pp. 160–61. Blainey, *Gold and Paper*, pp. 133–34. S. Butlin, *Australia and New Zealand Bank*, pp. 231, 240–41.

A.S.J. Baster puts total external deposits at £3.05 million in 1887, £14.0 million in 1899, and £16.5 million in 1914. Baster, *Imperial Banks*, p. 157. Prideaux Selbey, the Australasia's secretary with access to information from income tax deductions required by the Inland Revenue, placed the level at £14 million in 1883, £21 million in 1885, and £30 million in 1888. S. Butlin, *Australia and New Zealand Bank*, pp. 240–41.

[1001] Pope, "Free Banking in Australia," pp. 15–16.

which lifted their share of the combined Australian and United Kingdom deposits from 17 to 28 percent."[1002] For some banks the totals were much higher. The British deposits in the London Chartered and the Queensland National banks exceeded their domestic deposits, those in the Commercial Bank of Australia accounted to 45 percent of the total, and those in the Australian Joint Stock Bank represented 36 percent. Even as late as 1900, Australian banks still held some £30–35 million in British deposits.[1003] Table 5:4-2 provides one estimate of the growth of all Australian trading bank liabilities in the United Kingdom. From the point of view of the banking crisis itself, it is useful to note that the Australian banks "generally treated their British deposits as equivalent to their colonial deposits. Thus the banks accepting British deposits were able to expand credit during the eighties on a much greater scale than they would otherwise probably have done on the basis of their colonial deposits only." As a result, the ratio of bank advances to total Australian deposits rose from 0.984 in 1881 to 1.298 in September 1892.[1004]

Given the innate conservatism of British investors, one might wonder why the banks' campaigns were so successful. The explanation, however, appears relatively simple. British savers had learned that you can insure out from under risk by holding a portfolio of investments. They also had long experience with British banks, banks committed to the real bills doctrine and banks that had, at least by American and Canadian standards, a history of safety. They assumed that Australian banks were similar – some were, after all, British owned and all had London branches – and the Australians did nothing to disabuse them of that conclusion. Take, for example, the Australian Freehold Banking Corporation Ltd. When, in December 1889, William Clarke opened the London office, he

---

[1002] Merrett, "Australian Banking Practice and the Crisis of 1893," p. 75. Merrett's figures for British deposits are from E.H. Boehm, *Prosperity and Depression in Australia 1887–1897* (Oxford: Clarendon Press, 1971), table 47, p. 199. [Hereafter cited as Boehm, *Prosperity and Depression.*] By year, beginning in 1885, Boehm places British deposits at £13.1, £15.5, £19.7, £21.8, £26.2, £32.9, £35.8, £38.1, and, in 1893, £34.6 million pounds.

[1003] N. Butlin, *Investment in Australian Development*, pp. 160–62. S. Butlin, *Australia and New Zealand Bank*, pp. 306–7. N. Butlin and Barnard, "Pastoral Finance," p. 391.

[1004] Boehm, *Prosperity and Depression*, pp. 239–40, table 68, p. 280. The ratio of advances to the total of British and Australian deposits rose from 0.855 in 1881 to 0.930 in June 1892. Some banks, particularly the Union and Australasia, were more "sensitive than their colonial competitors to experience in English financial crises, which had shown that holders of fixed deposits were more easily scared than current account or note holders" and were, therefore, more conservative in their loan policies. S.J. Butlin, *Australia and New Zealand Bank*, p. 241.

Table 5:4-2. *British investment in Australia: Direct measure (minus equals an outflow) (thousands of U.K. pounds)*

Year	Banks	Pastoral finance	Other finance	Direct U.K. insurance mortgages	Mines	Miscellaneous private	Total private institutions	Total government loans	Immigrant funds	Total British transfers
1861	150	0	0	0	n.d.	n.d.	150*	1,400	-200	1,350*
1862	100	0	0	0	n.d.	n.d.	100*	2,100	200	2,400*
1863	100	0	0	0	n.d.	n.d.	100*	1,400	500	2,000*
1864	0	110	0	0	n.d.	n.d.	110*	1,200	800	2,110*
1865	270	160	0	0	n.d.	n.d.	430*	300	700	1,430*
1866	70	210	70	0	n.d.	n.d.	350*	2,800	600	3,750*
1867	30	190	70	0	n.d.	n.d.	290*	600	200	1,090*
1868	-430	-100	70	0	n.d.	n.d.	-460*	1,800	400	1,740*
1869	300	60	50	0	n.d.	n.d.	410*	1,700	400	2,510*
1870	1,620	50	50	0	10	0	1,730	2,700	400	4,830
1871	-420	40	90	0	10	10	-270	1,300	300	1,330
1872	-190	40	20	0	80	260	210	700	100	1,010
1873	-320	10	110	0	190	260	250	400	300	950
1874	-60	370	80	0	240	400	1,030	4,200	400	5,630
1875	1,290	410	100	0	190	140	2,130	2,600	500	5,230
1876	940	590	60	0	80	140	1,810	4,200	600	6,610
1877	90	550	0	0	40	0	680	1,700	900	3,280
1878	2,600	620	150	0	20	0	3,390	2,700	500	6,590
1879	820	1,630	10	160	20	50	2,690	10,800	600	14,090
1880	-1,040	1,160	20	140	10	160	450	6,200	600	7,250
1881	-1,410	810	250	200	180	240	270	4,700	700	5,670
1882	2,990	1,560	240	10	280	280	5,360	5,900	900	12,160
1883	4,490	310	1,060	170	320	210	6,560	14,100	1,700	22,360
1884	3,260	2,720	50	330	230	210	6,800	12,800	1,200	20,800
1885	3,040	1,970	300	610	160	130	6,210	13,300	900	20,410

1886	1,300	2,010	140	1,270	780	210	5,710	11,200	1,000	17,910
1887	2,170	860	900	1,330	1,610	370	7,240	7,200	800	15,240
1888	4,500	1,890	3,670	1,150	1,880	420	13,510	8,300	1,000	22,810
1889	4,960	1,130	2,020	1,330	1,350	800	11,590	9,800	600	21,990
1890	4,060	−590	2,070	1,150	620	960	8,270	6,700	600	15,570
1891	4,780	50	−4,380	740	420	910	2,520	9,400	700	12,620
1892	540	−600	0	590	440	470	1,440	4,200	0	5,640
1893	−8,840	−480	0	660	260	220	−8,180	7,400	−200	−980
1894	−2,900	−140	0	1,000	1,200	470	−370	1,400	100	1,130
1895	−2,430	900	0	−1,000	3,630	630	1,730	6,500	100	8,330
1896	−5,100	90	0	−1,000	6,410	620	1,020	800	200	2,020
1897	−2,010	−2,060	0	−1,000	6,260	940	2,130	3,700	200	6,030
1898	460	−150	0	0	4,040	1,540	5,890	1,200	0	7,090
1899	40	−110	0	0	1,600	1,940	3,470	2,500	0	5,970
1900	−1,040	−130	0	0	1,940	1,540	2,310	3,700	−200	5,810
All years	18,780	16,140	7,270	7,840	34,500	14,530	99,060	185,600	19,100	303,760*

Notes: * Data are Incomplete.

Source: N.G. Butlin, *Australian Domestic Product, Investment and Foreign Borrowing, 1861–1938/39* (Cambridge, U.K.: Cambridge University Press, 1962), Table 251, p. 424.

immediately oversaw its reincorporation as the Standard Bank of Australia Ltd. He argued that "anything suggestive of land speculation was unacceptable in the British market."[1005] Although Clarke's imaginative innovation was somewhat atypical, Australian bankers normally assisted the "educational" process – a process designed to reduce uncertainty – in two ways. "First, general managers and their representatives visited cities known to yield deposits, advertising their records of sound management. Knowledge of the 'successful management of the Australian banks' reported the *AIBR*, on November 16, 1889 'has greatly contributed to their popularity.' Evidence of successful management was seen to be the absence of failures." Second, they reduced lenders uncertainty by interposing identifiable locals between local lenders and distant projects. "Australian bankers paid commissions directly into the pockets of Scottish bank managers. The transactions costs of risk hedging were also reduced as some of the local agents of Australian banks and other brokers organized insurance cover for colonial fixed deposits."[1006] In 1893 the editors of *The Bankers', Insurance Managers', and Agents' Magazine* noted that, in answer to the magazine's query, a company that insures colonial bank deposits reported that they "were not in a position to form an estimate of the total amount of Australian deposits insured in Great Britain." They understood, however, that "from eight to a dozen companies have hitherto been insuring deposits."[1007] Those firms believed that they were offering insurance against risk but had sold policies against uncertainty.

Although the individual companies' response to the crisis varied, the results, at least from the viewpoint of most of those who had purchased insurance, were little better than the treatment received by those who declined the opportunity. A few companies, usually those with a relatively low volume of insurance in force (the Employers' Insurance Company of Great Britain, for example), announced their willingness to meet their obligations. However, "those most heavily in are ready to fight the matter out, because they are simply unable to pay or take over the securities of the suspended banks from their insured depositors."[1008] Their general response was to deny liability and, at minimum, to force their customers to litigate, litigate, litigate.

[1005] Entry for Clarke, William, in the *Australian Dictionary of Biography* (Carlton, Victoria: Melbourne University Press, various years), Vol. 3, pp. 419–20.

[1006] Pope, "Bankers and Banking Business," p. 25.

[1007] *The Bankers', Insurance Managers', and Agents' Magazine* (London: Waterlow & Sons), Vol. LV, 1893, p. 726. [Hereafter cited as *BIM&A*.]

[1008] *BIM&A*, Vol. LVI, 1893, p. 496.

Their individual strategies, however, spanned a wide range. A number of firms, including the Securities Insurance Company and the Trustee Assets & Investment Insurance Company, argued that, since the failed banks had reconstructed, they – the insurance companies – had no further liability under their policies.[1009] Some, the Mortgage Insurance Company, for example, offered their policy holders a choice between "liquidation or reconstruction, or, technically speaking, liquidation, pure and simple, or liquidation *plus* reconstruction." Needless to say the latter – "a scheme of reconstruction or *moratorium*" – "is preferred to the former."[1010] Some, the Liverpool Mortgage Insurance Company, for example, announced that they were prepared to pay, but not now. In the meantime, the policy-holders would have to continue to pay their premiums, if they wanted their policies to remain in force. One unnamed firm postponed payment, demanded that premiums continue to be paid, but sent out no premium notices in hopes that the policies would lapse.[1011] Finally, the Securities Insurance Company appealed to the courts to void their policies because the policyholders had not told them that the Real Estate Mortgage and Deposit Bank of Melbourne was in trouble.[1012]

In the words of the editors of the *Bankers', Insurance Managers', and Agents Magazine*, "it is manifestly an impossibility for the greater part of these companies to meet such claims as their limited means do not permit payments of policies being made on as great a scale as the necessities of the case require." That pronouncement was followed by a few optimistic words about the future: "The result of all such actions as we have mentioned is undoubtedly to force deposit insurance companies into liquidation, voluntary or compulsory. If the companies are to be allowed to reconstruct, will they be sure of getting new business? This is not so easy to answer. We trust, however, that with improved methods of doing business, they will avoid all the errors of the past, and proceed again on their course."[1013] That hope, however, proved overly optimistic. Finally, the editors added a few words of caution: "Since the great house of Baring stooped to underwriting foreign stocks, let the British company

---

[1009] *BIM&A*, Vol. 56, 1893, p. 494; Vol. 57, 1894, p. 132. In the case of the Securities Insurance Company, their letter to their policy holders included the following: "In order that you may reconsider this offer in all its bearings, I am to state that, from and after the dates on which the reconstruction schemes of the different banks are approved by the Supreme Courts of England and Australia, my directors will feel reluctantly obliged to disclaim any liability under their policies, in connection with the institutions that have suspended payment, and whose assets will have been transferred."

[1010] *BIM&A*, Vol. 57, 1894, p. 129.

[1011] *BIM&A*, Vol. 56, 1893, pp. 495–96.

[1012] *BIM&A*, Vol. 57, 1894, p. 622.

[1013] *BIM&A*, Vol. 57, 1894, pp. 129, 133.

which insures bank deposits and securities generally beware! It is a dangerous game, especially at present, when the formation of companies is not proceeding favorably, capital being timorous and conservative at this moment."[1014] The British savers – both those who had bought insurance and those who did not – had discovered that you can insure against risk but that you can not insure against uncertainty. They thought they were buying into a risky investment and they found they had been sold a very uncertain one. By 1894 the insurance firms had come to realize that you can provide insurance against risk; but you can not provide insurance against uncertainty. They thought they were selling insurance against risky investments and found that they were, in fact, selling insurance against very uncertain outcomes.

Some bankers certainly recognized that the asymmetry between the liquidity of their assets and their liabilities exposed the banks to danger, should the wool industry falter or the urban land boom collapse.[1015] As early as 1869, when, in response to his London manager's concern about the level of pastoral indebtedness, the General Manager of the Bank of New South Wales responded "that he would be willing to employ the whole of the Bank's resources in short-term and active investments, if it were possible; but if he was to earn a dividend, he had to accommodate himself to the business of the country and invest in the best securities offering."[1016]

The year 1889 saw the collapse of both the pastoral and urban land booms, followed, over the next two years, by the suspension of almost all, and the ultimate demise of many, of the land banks and building societies. The contagion did not stop there. The trading banks had supported, directly and indirectly, both pastoral development and urban residential construction. The suspension and bankruptcies of the land-related non-bank intermediaries, coupled with the threat of the withdrawal of British fixed-term deposits upon maturity, combined to trigger a sequence of bank runs. It was the newer domestic banks – the banks most active in soliciting British funds and making direct loans on pastoral and urban mortgages – that bore the brunt of the collapse.[1017]

The bankers, using the powers of the state courts, moved to limit the damage. Their reconstruction policies, while almost certainly ameliorating the short-term impact of the disaster, had adverse and severe long-term effects on the relationship between British savers and Australian

[1014] *BIM&A*, Vol. 57, 1893, p. 621.
[1015] Jackson, *Australian Economic Development*, p. 144.
[1016] Holder, *Bank of New South Wales*, pp. 365–66.
[1017] S. Butlin, *Australia and New Zealand Bank*, pp. 174–75.

investments and, ultimately, on the structure of the Australian capital markets. At one level the reorganizations were successful, although some banks found even those terms too difficult and never fully recovered, and a number of others were forced to mergers in order to avoid bankruptcy.[1018] At another level they were much less successful. After reconstruction, the deposit receipts and newly created preference shares became negotiable, but they initially traded at discounts of as much as one-half of their face value. It appears that many of the newly issued securities were purchased by Australian investors at very deep discounts. Although those repatriations proved very good investments for the Australian savers – in the majority of cases the securities ultimately reached par – the entire process left a permanently sour taste in the mouths of British depositors and shareholders. It was to be more than a decade before "the banks could again hope to approach the London money market with any hope of raising fresh capital." Moreover, the international deposit – the particular institutional arrangement that had played such an important role in Australian capital formation – never recovered.[1019] The peak holdings of British deposits in Australian banks "had been markedly reduced by 1900 because British depositors had sustained substantial losses in the banks forced into liquidation, because large amounts of deposits had been converted more or less compulsorily into preference and ordinary shares, and because deposits had been withdrawn in large quantities as soon as it was possible for such withdrawals to be made." As a result, in 1900 Australian banks in London had a small net balance of London funds.[1020]

In Australia the domestic capital market suffered in other ways as well. The bank managers, although still supplying some long-term credit, became increasingly cautious and displayed a high degree of risk aversion. As a result, they dramatically reduced both the volume of total loans and the fraction of those loans directed toward long-term finance.[1021] For example, beginning in 1893 the Bank of New South Wales began to invest substantial sums in first class securities that could be

---

[1018] S. Butlin, *Australia and New Zealand Bank*, pp. 322–23.

[1019] Between 1899 and 1911, the six states were marked by an *outflow* of funds totaling some £18.7 million. In the seventeen years between January 1882 and December 1899, the *net liabilities* in Britain of Australian trading banks averaged £12.8 million a year. Between January 1906 and December 1922 the *net assets* of Australian trading banks in Britain averaged £20.8 million. S. Butlin, Hall, and White, *Australian Banking and Monetary Statistics*, tables 4(ii) and 4(iii), pp. 126–27.

[1020] Hall, *The Stock Exchange of Melbourne*, pp. 214–15.

[1021] Baster, *Imperial Banks*, p. 157. M. Butlin, "Capital Markets," p. 235.

readily converted into cash on the London market. These funds became a second-line liquidity reserve, and by 1896 that reserve totaled some £960,000.[1022]

Although the banks continued to lend to the slowly recovering pastoral sector, they proved very hesitant to lend to the new industries that emerged in the post-depression restructuring of the domestic economy. The main sufferers were firms in the emerging manufacturing sector. Since the trading banks had been the major sources of private long-term credit (there had never been any Australian equivalent of the Canadian bond house or the American third-generation investment bank), those firms were forced to rely very heavily on retained earnings as a source of finance.[1023] For example, in 1912 the Bank of New South Wales had 36 percent of its advances committed to pastoral activities, 25 percent to other agricultural activities, and a total of only 23 percent to merchants, storekeepers, station agents, sawmillers, *and* manufacturers.[1024] In addition, the trading banks almost completely withdrew from their role as investment banks. The crisis did not result in a regulated banking system; the banks continued to operate without any major government involvement. Regulation proved unnecessary. The bankers became increasingly conservative and the banks much more cautious.

In the words of one economic historian, the "banks have never been able to redeem themselves in the minds of the public. They did pay out all the debts incurred to their creditors in 1893. They rebuilt their balance sheets in such a way that a repeat of the failure was highly unlikely. However, in doing so they continued to alienate customers. For decades after the 1890s Australian bankers behaved very conservatively, particularly in scrutinizing lending proposals. They were far more selective than they had been in the 1870s and 1880s. Tough minded bank managers are thought well of by their depositors and shareholders but not necessarily by those who have to take out loans."[1025] The banks' reaction to the crisis in Australia was more severe than the reaction of U.S. and U.K. banks to similar, but less severe, banking crises in the late nineteenth century. In those latter countries the banks had never been a major source of

---

[1022] Holder, *Bank of New South Wales*, p. 522.
[1023] Holder, "Australia," p. 63. Sinclair, *The Process of Economic Growth*, pp. 182–83. As evidence of the much tighter constraints on credit, it might be noted that between 1881 and 1890, the average ratio of cash plus government bonds to total advances for the trading banks equaled 0.22 (a multiplier of 4.6). Between 1905 and 1914, the ratio was 0.48 (a multiplier of 2.1). S. Butlin, Hall, and White, *Australian Banking and Monetary Statistics*, tables 2(I) and 2(ii), pp. 117, 121.
[1024] Holder, *Bank of New South Wales*, p. 547.
[1025] Merrett, "Banking and Finance," pp. 18–19.

long-term credit. The ultimate price of the banking crisis was the emergence, over the next half century, of a highly cartelized banking sector and of a large gap in the nation's financial structure as the banks narrowed the focus and shortened the length of their financial commitments.[1026] That price was paid in slow economic growth.

5-4c. The non-bank intermediaries

Most non-bank intermediaries "with the possible exception of the general life insurance companies lagged well behind the banks in maturity of organization and influence on financial flows." Even the insurance companies do not represent an important exception. Although there were life insurance companies dating from the 1850s, "the habit of buying life insurance had never become fully established in Australia."[1027] As a result, until the 1860s the trading banks faced little competition for domestic deposits; but in the 1860s two types of financial institutions – post office and general savings banks and building societies – invaded the field. By the next decade they had begun to offer some competition to the trading banks for a limited range of deposit customers. Later, particularly after 1877, building finance companies emerged. At about the same time pastoral finance companies began collecting deposits in addition to their traditional business of operating current accounts of their pastoral customers.[1028] In Australia a large part of the non-bank sector – insurance companies, trustee companies, mortgage banks, and savings banks – was constrained by either custom or law to investing only in government stock, municipal debentures, and mortgages.[1029]

The Australian data on the non-bank intermediaries are quite spotty, but they are best for the savings banks (see Table 5:4-3). The industry had its roots in the 1860s, but growth surged after the 1890s. Over the years from 1865 to 1914 deposits grew at an annual rate of 7.6 percent;

[1026] Merrett, "Preventing Bank Failure," pp. 139–40.

[1027] For example, the Australian Mutual Protective Society had an agency in Melbourne in 1850, and the Victorian Life and General Insurance Company was established in 1858. Hall, *The Stock Exchange of Melbourne*, pp. 42–43. Thus far, the only history of the Australian life insurance industry is A.C. Gray, *Life Insurance in Australia* (Melbourne: McCarron Bird, 1977). It is not very revealing on the early growth of the industry.

[1028] N. Butlin, *Investment in Australian Development*, p. 157. There had been terminable building societies earlier, but it was after 1865 before thought was given to the formation of permanent building societies. Hall, *The Stock Exchange of Melbourne*, p. 43.

[1029] Drummond, *Capital Markets*, p. 183.

Table 5:4-3. *Australian savings banks: aggregate assets and liabilities (thousands of pounds)*

| | | Deposits in other banks | | | | | | | | | Assets | Liabilities | | | Total |
| | Coin, notes, & cash on hand | Current account | Fixed deposits | Deposits with state treasury | Government securities | Local & semi-gov't securities | Mortgage loans | Bank premises | Other assets | Deposits in commonwealth bank | Securities of subsidiary banks | Reserves | Deposits | Other | Assets & liabilities |
Year															
1865	14	116	266	16	1,083	18	620	36	4			183	1,987		2,173
1870	15	376	423	257	1,235	10	840	34	5			238	2,953	2	3,195
1875	20	226	1,321	660	2,077	13	782	16	15			263	4,866		5,130
1880	28	248	1,257	895	2,181	44	1,498	15	4			393	5,778	1	6,170
1885	60	185	2,471	2,280	2,712	62	2,714	79	30			491	10,099	1	10,593
1890	84	351	3,488	2,062	3,592	110	4,755	149	8			619	13,957	6	14,599
1895	95	1,329	2,316	6,283	6,699	73	4,631	171	50			504	21,134	9	21,647
1900	170	1,799	3,191	7,442	11,595	817	5,042	181	23			682	29,407	168	30,260
1905	359	1,134	4,698	5,065	18,743	1,758	6,062	268	204			1,024	36,629	641	38,291
1910	684	2,356	6,654	3,130	33,172	3,372	6,782	455	309			1,528	55,403	780	56,914
1914	1,103	3,501	9,290	3,982	48,039	5,238	11,085	857	571	274	3,871	1,838	84,316	1,653	87,811
						(percents)									
1865	0.6	5.3	12.2	0.7	49.8	0.8	28.5	1.7	0.2	0.0	0.0	8.4	91.6	0.0	100.0
1870	0.5	11.8	13.2	8.0	38.7	0.3	26.3	1.1	0.2	0.0	0.0	7.5	92.5	0.1	100.0
1875	0.4	4.4	25.8	12.9	40.5	0.3	15.2	0.3	0.3	0.0	0.0	5.1	94.9	0.0	100.0
1880	0.5	4.0	20.4	14.5	35.3	0.7	24.3	0.2	0.1	0.0	0.0	6.4	93.6	0.0	100.0
1885	0.6	1.7	23.3	21.5	25.6	0.6	25.6	0.7	0.3	0.0	0.0	4.6	95.4	0.0	100.0
1890	0.6	2.4	23.9	14.1	24.6	0.8	32.6	1.0	0.1	0.0	0.0	4.2	95.7	0.0	100.0
1895	0.4	6.1	10.7	29.0	30.9	0.3	21.4	0.8	0.2	0.0	0.0	2.3	97.6	0.0	100.0
1900	0.6	5.9	10.5	24.6	38.3	2.7	16.7	0.6	0.1	0.0	0.0	2.3	97.2	0.6	100.0
1905	0.9	3.0	12.3	13.2	48.9	4.6	15.8	0.7	0.5	0.0	0.0	2.7	95.7	1.7	100.0
1910	1.2	4.1	11.7	5.5	58.3	5.9	11.9	0.8	0.5	0.0	0.0	2.6	96.0	1.4	100.0
1914	1.3	4.0	10.6	4.5	54.7	6.0	12.6	1.0	0.7	0.3	4.4	2.1	96.0	1.9	100.0

Source: S.J. Butlin, A.R. Hall, R.C. White, *Australian Banking and Monetary Statistics, 1817–1945*, Reserve Bank of Australia, Occasional Paper No. 4A (Sydney, 1971), Tables 53(i) & 53(ii), pp. 502–504.

over the same period per capita deposits increased from £1.45 to £10.54, a nominal rate of 4 percent. Although the rate of growth declined slightly after 1890, in terms of both its absolute or relative position, the industry grew rapidly. The savings banks appeared less affected by the depression than the trading banks, pastoral finance companies, or building societies.[1030] If the measure is the relative size of the sector, the impact of the depression is again underscored. In 1870 the aggregate assets of Australian savings banks represented 7.6 percent of those of the trading banks, and by 1890 that fraction had hardly changed; it was 7.9 percent. Thereafter, relative growth was rapid: The ratio was 20.3 percent in 1900 and 35.9 percent in 1914.

Government-owned savings banks had been established in all colonies by the 1860s. As with the private savings banks in the United States, the announced purpose of the Australian banks was to use the carrot of interest payments to encourage thrift among the poorer members of the community; but, in Australia, these banks also existed to further government programs.

> By happy coincidence for the scheme's sponsors, the accumulated funds were employed almost exclusively in the purchase of government securities and, much later, loans to farmers and home buyers at concessional rates of interest. At the margins, the products offered by these government owned savings banks and their pricing policies had an impact on the size, nature and profitability of the private banks. The savings banks' highly specialized business that provided a "captive" market for government securities and favoured some borrowers at the expense of others because of political priorities rather than commercial criterion [sic] lasted largely unchanged until the 1970s.[1031]

The explanation for the sharp change between the pre- and post-depression periods is relatively straightforward. In Australia, as in Canada but unlike in the United States, the savings banks operated largely as an arm of the government and channeled a large fraction of their deposits into government-financed activities; the governments, therefore, stood ready to cover any losses with taxpayers' funds.[1032] For

---

[1030] In the case of the trading banks, for example, assets increased at an annual rate of 6.2 percent between 1865 and 1890, but by only 1.2 percent between 1890 and 1914. In per capita terms, the comparison is even more dramatic: 2.9 percent in the first period but −0.06 percent in the second. See Table 5:4-1.

[1031] Merrett, "Banking and Finance," p. 2.

[1032] In Canada only the Quebec savings banks invested in anything beyond government securities; but, even in that province, investments in the private sector accounted for only about one-third of the total. For the years 1875, 1880, 1885, 1890, 1895, 1900, 1905, 1910, and 1914, private mortgages and loans accounted,

example, one of the largest savings banks, the Commissioners' Savings Banks of Victoria, sought and received a government guarantee of its deposit liabilities in 1893.[1033] As a result, unlike the other bank and non-bank intermediaries, the savings banks suffered no bankruptcies or suspensions during the 1890s; and their apparent safety attracted savers burned by their experience with other intermediaries. Moreover, throughout the period – both before and after the depression – the state governments had continued to encourage the expansion of the institutions that catered to household savings, while the flow of funds made it possible to extend the nation's "governmental habit." These policies slowed the development of the nation's private capital markets.[1034] In addition, since the supply price of funds to the savings banks was the artificially low rate paid on savings deposits, a rate that reflected the riskless nature of the deposits, the allocation of capital was almost certainly not economically efficient.[1035] "The government owned banks drove a wedge into the market place. These institutions whose deposits were guaranteed by the taxpayer, were more adventurous in their lending" than the post-crisis trading banks.

> Under direction from state governments in particular, government banks lent to high risk areas that the private banks eschewed, notably the rural sector that was to experience great difficulties in the inter war years. Government banks became the agents of public policy, particularly in facilitating the drive for economic development after WWI. It was the government owned savings banks that were the conduit for funds that transformed Australia into a nation of homeowners. By mid-century deposits in savings banks exceeded those in private trading banks. Government banks were more likely, at the margin, to lend and less likely to foreclose.[1036]

Their criteria, however, were political, not economic.

In Victoria, for example, there had been Commissioners' Saving banks – banks whose investment policies were closely regulated, but whose managers were allowed to invest in either government bonds or mortgages – in operation since the early 1850s. In the 1860s the state's appetite

---

on average, for 34.0 percent of all assets of the Quebec savings banks and government securities for 65.6 percent. *Historical Statistics for Canada,* Series H 303, 304, 312, and 314.

[1033] Robert Murray and Kate White, *A Bank for the People: A History of the State Bank of Victoria* (North Melbourne, Victoria: Hargreen Publishing Co., 1992), chap. 9.

[1034] M. Butlin, "Capital Markets," pp. 234–35.

[1035] Drummond, *Capital Markets,* p. 260.

[1036] Merrett, "Banking and Finance," pp. 18–19.

for funds was not satisfied, and the government established a competing post office savings bank. Those deposits – over £1 million in 1884 – completely bypassed the formal capital markets and became "directly available to government via investment trust funds."[1037] In a similar fashion, in 1871, although the Trustee Savings Bank had been in existence for four decades, the government of New South Wales established a competitive government-backed savings bank. The reasons again were apparently political; the trustees of the earlier bank, because of their opposition to the growth of public expenditures, had proved unwilling to make a sufficient fraction of the bank's funds available to the government.[1038] Nor was this lesson lost on the federal government. Almost the first official act of the governor of the newly formed government-owned and operated Commonwealth Bank was to open savings departments with offices in the now national post offices.[1039] The bank was established in 1911, the first post office branches were opened in July 1912, but it was to be at least another six months before the bank began operating as a trading bank.[1040] With the facilities of the post office now in the hands of the Commonwealth Bank, the state banks, if they were to remain in business, had to pay for new offices. Despite their desire to maintain their sources of cheap finance, the state governments found themselves in a very weak position in their competition for deposits.[1041] Within a few decades, the Commonwealth Savings Bank Department of the Commonwealth Bank of Australia had absorbed the state government savings banks in every state except Victoria and South Australia.[1042]

The State savings banks provided a large fraction of the funds employed by the government-owned mortgage banks; that is, a

---

[1037] Hall, *The Stock Exchange of Melbourne*, pp. 110–11. In 1897 the Post Office Savings Bank had been absorbed into the State Savings Bank of Victoria, and it was no longer directly available to the government as a source of funds as it had been for the previous three decades. Hall, *The Stock Exchange of Melbourne*, p. 217.

[1038] Charles Jones, "The Fiscal Motive for Monetary and Banking Legislation in Argentina, Australia and Canada Before 1914," in D.C.M. Platt and Guido deTella, *Argentine, Australia and Canada: Studies in Comparative Development, 1870–1965* (New York: St. Martin's Press, 1985), pp. 131–32. [Hereafter cited as Jones, "The Fiscal Motive."]

[1039] M. Butlin, "Capital Markets," p. 235. By 1914 (the second year of operation) those savings deposits amounted to £4,283,000, or about 5 percent of all such deposits. S. Butlin, Hall, and White, *Australian Banking and Monetary Statistics*, table 9, p. 135, and tables 54(i) and 54(ii), pp. 505–6.

[1040] Holder, *Bank of New South Wales*, p. 558.

[1041] S. Butlin, *Australia and New Zealand Bank*, p. 352.

[1042] In addition, the trustee savings banks in Hobart and Launceston also remained independent. Holder, "Australia," p. 60.

substantial fraction of the funds that the savings banks' purchases of government bonds channeled into the state treasuries also went indirectly into mortgages. The savings bank of Victoria, for example, was required to underwrite the issues of the state mortgage bank – the Victoria "Credit Foncier" – and by 1914 the bank had been forced to absorb 61 percent of the Foncier's outstanding bond issues. Again, by the end of 1913, 91 percent of the securities issued by the New South Wales Advances Department were held by the Government Savings Bank. Until the end of 1913 the Western Australia Agricultural Bank was entirely financed by the state savings bank. Only one of the state mortgage banks – that of South Australia – was not dependent, either directly or indirectly, on savings bank funds. Since the banks, with a near monopoly of the deposits of small savers, were largely insulated from the formal capital markets, their investment policies appear to have contributed substantially to an over-extension of mortgage credit, an over-extension that was the result of political, not economic, decisions.[1043]

The legal restrictions on the investments of the savings banks almost certainly induced even further misallocations of capital. After the 1890s the state governments turned increasingly to domestic savings to underwrite their seemingly ever-expanding activities. For example, a domestic new-issues market emerged in the wake of the depression. That market barely existed in 1895. It developed rapidly thereafter, but it was almost entirely centered on government securities. Moreover, although some individuals participated, 70 percent of the issues were sold to financial institutions. Among those institutions, the government savings banks were the most important.[1044] As a result, there was only a minimum of institutional spillover into the private sector; the post-depression issues of government bonds in Australia played much less of an educational role than had Britain's Napoleonic War bonds or the Civil War 5-20's in the United States.

As for the rest of the non-bank intermediaries, the Australian portrait remains somewhat clouded. Before the depression of the 1890s, building societies, land, building, and investment companies, mortgage banks, insurance companies, and incorporated non-banking pastoral finance companies were all components of the financial network. Until the very end of the long boom, the building societies, the land, building, and investment companies, and the mortgage banks were, to a very large extent, committed to the mobilization of domestic savings; but from the

---

[1043] Drummond, *Capital Markets*, pp. 109–10.
[1044] Drummond, *Capital Markets*, p. 168.

mid-1870s, the pastoral finance companies aggressively sought British funds.[1045]

It is difficult to distinguish among the three types of institutions that evolved to finance housing: building societies, land, building, and investment companies, and mortgage banks. Because of the influence of speculative real estate investment undertaken by the three institutions and, in New South Wales and Queensland, because of the legislative attempts to force building societies to register under the Companies Acts, "building societies took on banking functions, land banks made advances for house purchases and construction, and building companies adopted building society tables and procedures for financing and repayment." Moreover, the relative importance of the three institutions varied from colony to colony. Building societies were by far the most important in Victoria, South Australia, and Tasmania; in New South Wales, although building societies were important, both building companies and mortgage banks – sometimes called "fungoid banks" – had been long established. By the 1880s the former had probably become the most important. In Queensland the building societies dominated until 1886, when the government's attempt to force disclosure led many to change their registration and reemerge as building companies.[1046] In New South Wales the building societies and mortgage banks commanded about half the volume of deposits of the savings banks. In Victoria, building society deposits alone amounted to more than 85 percent of the deposits in the state savings banks; by the late 1880s they were neck and neck.[1047]

"The earliest building societies were 'terminable' societies consisting of 'investing' members who provided paid-up capital for the societies and 'borrowing' members who purchased shares as a means of securing advances made to them by the society." Over time, however, the form of the societies changed to meet new financial needs and business opportunities. Although the initial innovation occurred in New South Wales in 1850, it was the 1860s before the demand for residential capital and the level of private savings increased sufficiently to encourage widespread growth of the new form. Thereafter, however, terminating societies were relatively rapidly replaced by the now more familiar permanent society.

[1045] In the case of Victoria, for example, at the end of the 1880s, when the deposits of building societies totaled about £5 million, only £600,000 was of British origin; of that total, one society, the Modern Permanent Building Society, held £350,000, all acquired in 1889–91. N. Butlin, *Investment in Australian Development*, pp. 257–58.

[1046] N. Butlin, *Investment in Australian Development*, pp. 245–47.

[1047] N. Butlin, *Investment in Australian Development*, p. 257. In 1888 the building society deposits were actually larger.

By the beginning of the next decade, the new organization had become the norm.[1048]

It was the residential housing boom that promoted both the rapid growth and some important changes in organizational structure of the building societies. In the years between the mid-1870s and the end of the 1880s, residential construction was the most important single form of fixed capital investment, and the major sources of that industry's finance were the building societies and real estate companies. In 1888 the *Australasian Insurance and Banking Record* tabulated the balance sheet figures of sixty-nine institutions – institutions operating primarily in Melbourne – that solicited public deposits. Of the forty-nine building societies, only six antedated 1875, and twenty-nine had been organized between 1880 and 1888. By that latter date the societies held £3.3 million in shareholders' funds and £4.1 million in deposits.[1049] The new banks competed fiercely for deposits, and some drew on the trading banks for additional support. For example, the organizational structure of the Federal Bank of Australia was specifically designed to permit the bank to use an affiliated building society to lend out surplus funds. The Commercial Bank of Australia acted as the banker for a large group of building societies, and their paper constituted a substantial portion of the bank's portfolio.[1050]

The building societies were only indirectly linked to the international capital market. They were probably the largest institutional source of finance for home building; they certainly dominated the market until, at least, the final stages of the boom; and they derived almost all of their funds from local deposits. The more domestic savings they absorbed, however, the more other institutions were induced to look abroad; and those other institutions included not only the trading banks but also the mortgage banks and the land and building companies that had been formed to exploit the opportunities for speculative profits that were emerging in the subdivision of urban land. Many of these institutions "secured a significantly high proportion of their funds in Britain."[1051] For example, as early as 1881 the *A.I.B.R.* listed sixteen mortgage companies incorporated in England for operation in Australia. Some of these firms had close connections with the trading banks, banks that "welcomed

---

[1048] N. Butlin, *Investment in Australian Development*, pp. 254–56. Pope, "Free Banking in Australia," p. 2.

[1049] S. Butlin, *Australia and New Zealand Bank*, pp. 236–37.

[1050] Blainey, *Gold and Paper*, p. 148. Hall, *The Stock Exchange of Melbourne*, pp. 153–54.

[1051] Jackson, *Australian Economic Development*, pp. 142–43.

opportunities for transferring long-term loans to more suitable institutions."[1052] Some fifteen land and building companies flourished in the closing stages of the Victorian speculative boom of the 1880s, and they were responsible for a considerable volume of new advances. The 1888 enumeration of Melbourne financial institutions listed fourteen such companies with £2.6 million in shareholders' funds and an additional £1.8 million in deposits.

Mortgage banks had been operating in Australia since 1841. In Victoria, of those that ultimately became important in residential finance, the Land Mortgage Bank of Victoria was established in 1864; it was followed in the next decade by four others: the Australian Deposit and Mortgage Bank Ltd. (1874), the Land Credit Bank of Australia (1876), the Australian Freehold Banking Corporation (1879), and the Colonial Investment and Agency Company Ltd. (1879). By the peak of the mortgage boom, in 1888, the mortgage banks and mortgage companies possessed assets equal to about half of those of the building societies. The 1888 enumeration indicates that the six mortgage banks had shareholders' funds of £1.2 million and deposits of £3.1 million.[1053]

Even more than the trading banks, it was the building societies, the land and building companies, and the mortgage banks that bore the brunt of the depression. Although the Premier Permanent Building Association of Melbourne had failed at the end of 1889, that institution was not a traditional building society. The first true building society to succumb was the City of Melbourne Building Society in June of 1891. Others followed in rapid succession, and December saw widespread suspensions. The land banks began to feel the intense pressure of withdrawals at the same time as the building societies. The Imperial Banking Company Ltd. failed in July, and its failure was followed the next month by that of the British Bank of Australia and of the Anglo-Australian Bank Ltd. In the first week in December, almost simultaneously with the outburst of building society suspensions, there were several more failures as the "industrial cleansing continued."[1054] Between August 1891 and February 1892, twenty-two Sydney building societies and land banks soliciting public funds failed. In Melbourne, between July 1891 and March 1892, twenty building societies and "banks," with deposits totaling £10,582,806, collapsed. Altogether, in the space of thirteen months, forty-one land and

---

[1052] S. Butlin, *Australia and New Zealand Bank*, p. 236.
[1053] N. Butlin, *Investment in Australian Development*, pp. 247–49. S. Butlin, *Australia and New Zealand Bank*, p. 237.
[1054] Hall, *The Stock Exchange of Melbourne*, pp. 153–54.

building institutions failed in Melbourne and Sydney, locking up £18 million in deposits.[1055]

In the case of the building companies and the mortgage banks, the bankruptcies virtually wrote finis to the industry. Only one mortgage or land bank, the Land Mortgage Bank of Victoria, the oldest of all, had an unbroken record. Thirty-five "such 'banks' closed, most of them permanently, and most in discreditable circumstances."[1056] In the case of the building societies, most were illiquid rather than insolvent; and government action – action similar to that taken with the suspended trading banks – made it possible for the majority to survive. Even as late as 1914, however, they had not managed to regain their former position in the nation's financial structure. In the words of one observer writing about the state of the Australian capital market in 1914, "little can be said about Australian building societies' sources of funds; little need be said, because the societies were relatively unimportant on the Australian scene." "It is interesting to observe that Australian building societies were of small importance on the Australian scene, compared with the importance of mortgage companies on the Canadian scene"; and, in terms of their contribution to mortgage finance, he continued, "it is obvious that the contribution of the building societies was very small indeed."[1057] Such had not been the case twenty-five years earlier.

The trading banks had played a major role in pastoral finance, but between the 1870s and the early 1890s the pastoral finance companies were nearly as important. It might be noted, however, that there was a considerable level of interlocking directorships between the Anglo-Australian banks and the pastoral companies in the late nineteenth and early twentieth centuries.[1058] The first of the pastoral firms date from the 1850s, but they multiplied rapidly beginning in the mid-1870s. "They began by handling the wool and providing stores on credit, then diversified into providing investable funds to pastoralists." Most of these funds were raised by issuing company debentures in Britain and lending those funds, together with the receipts from the sale of paid-up capital, at the higher rate of interest payable in Australia. "Rural advances by pastoral companies attained a peak in 1891, those of the big five companies being

---

[1055] S. Butlin, *Australia and New Zealand Bank*, pp. 286–87. Blainey, *Gold and Paper*, p. 147.

[1056] S. Butlin, *Australia and New Zealand Bank*, pp. 279–80.

[1057] Drummond, *Capital Markets*, pp. 78–80, 102.

[1058] See, for example, Frank J.A. Boeze, *Mr. Brooks and the Australian Trade: Imperial Business in the Nineteenth Century* (Melbourne: Melbourne University Press, 1993) and David T. Merrett, *ANZ Bank: A History of the Australian and New Zealand Banking Group and Its Constituents* (Sydney: Allen & Unwin, 1985).

equal in size to about 15 percent of Australian trading banks' total advances to all customers."[1059]

Given the multiple range of their activities – in effect they undertook to meet all the financial and commercial needs of the pastoral sector (they lent money for the purchase of land, livestock, and improvements, they sold supplies to wool growers, they bought and sold wool themselves, and they acted as agents for the pastoralists) – they were unlike any financial intermediary in the United Kingdom or in any of the other three frontier countries. In Australia they were an important part of the financial infrastructure.[1060] At times they acted as intermediaries between the banks and the pastoralists, but they also were an important direct channel of finance.

The industry was still in its infancy at the end of the 1860s. Firms were relatively small, almost always unincorporated, and, although customers of the trading banks, they were largely dependent on their own financial resources. They had relatively few indebted clients. On occasion an individual might have a debt of £50,000, but such sums were rare. In fact, the average advance received by the clients of two leading firms – R. Goldborough and Company and the Australian Mortgage Land and Finance Company – were only £9,000 and £13,000, respectively.[1061]

In the late 1860s and early 1870s the Australian Mercantile Land and Finance Company was almost alone in combining limited liability, British capital, pastoral finance, and a wool consignment business.[1062] The firm was British owned, but the main source of its finance was the sale of debentures – usually short dated securities (up to five and, occasionally, ten years) – that were placed through the British stock exchanges.[1063] There were still a number of local firms, unregistered and unincorporated, supplying funds to the pastoral sector, but they were ill-equipped to provide the finance for a large-scale expansion of pastoral equipment. Their importance declined steadily from the early 1870s, and they had largely disappeared by the end of the decade.[1064]

[1059] Pope, "Free Banking in Australia," p. 2.

[1060] Drummond, *Capital Markets*, pp. 32–33.

[1061] N. Butlin and Barnard, "Pastoral Finance," p. 392.

[1062] Bailey, *A Hundred Years*, p. 70. There were a few other less well-known firms in Australia, the Australian Agency Corporation, for example; and the New Zealand Loan and Trust and Agency performed a very similar set of functions across the Tasman Sea. N. Butlin, *Investment in Australian Development*, p. 153.

[1063] N. Butlin, *Investment in Australian Development*, pp. 153–54.

[1064] Many of the smaller firms were absorbed or amalgamated with the emerging giant corporations. For example, Hastings Cunningham was absorbed by the Australian Mortgage & Agency Company in 1879, and the old Sloan firm was absorbed by the Union Mortgage & Agency Company in 1885. N. Butlin, *Investment in Australian Development*, pp. 141–42, 149, 153–54.

The disappearance of that set of competitors had been triggered by the emergence of yet another, and far more formidable, competitive threat to the Australian Mercantile Land and Finance Company. The firm found itself faced by increasing competition, not only from the entrance of the trading banks into the field of direct pastoral finance, but from other firms with organizations similar to its own, corporations with head offices in Britain. The new competitors also had similar goals: to raise capital in Britain and supply it through mortgages and overdrafts to pastoralists in Australia.[1065] The New Zealand Loan and Mercantile Agency, for example, transferred the dominant share of its business to Australia in the early 1870s. By 1876 there were three such incorporated non-banking companies; they were joined by five others between 1877 and 1880, and by two additional firms in the early years of the next decade.[1066] As early as 1879 the effects of the new competitors began to be felt, and the managers of the Australian Mercantile Land & Finance Company found themselves compelled to warn their shareholders of the adverse effects the increased competition might have on the firm's profits.[1067] Each of the ten firms competed for British funds, and from the mid-1870s their largest source of new funds was the proceeds from the sale of debentures in England and Scotland.[1068]

Between 1880 and 1891 the debentures and deposits of the ten incorporated non-banking pastoral finance companies totaled almost one-fifth more than the deposits in Australian savings banks (see Table 5:4-4).[1069] Unlike the savings banks, however, "from the beginning and throughout the whole period, these non-banking incorporated concerns relied almost entirely on British investment." Initially financed through

---

[1065] N. Butlin & Barnard, "Pastoral Finance," p. 389.

[1066] N. Butlin, *Investment in Australian Development*, pp. 128–29, 149–50.

[1067] Bailey, *A Hundred Years*, p. 70.

[1068] Jackson, *Australian Economic Development*, p. 143. "For Australia as a whole, there were in 1880 eight leading non-banking pastoral finance houses incorporated, with the South Australian Land Mortgage & Agency Co., Australian Mortgage & Agency Co., British and Australian Trust & Agency Co., Queensland Investment Land Mortgage and Agency Co., and the Australian Agency and Banking Corporation supplementing the older incorporated concerns of A.M.L. & F., the N.Z.L. & M.A. and the Trust and Agency Co. . . . The Dalgety enterprises appeared as Dalgety & Co. in 1884, as one of the giants; and the Union Mortgage & Agency Co. (later Australian Estates Ltd.) was formed in 1885, absorbing the old Sloan firm. And then there were ten." N. Butlin, *Investment in Australian Development*, p. 142.

[1069] The average figure was 1.17, but it ranged from 0.79 in 1882 to 1.45 in 1887. S. Butlin, Hall, and White, *Australian Banking and Monetary Statistics*, tables 53(i) and 53(ii), pp. 502–4. N. Butlin, *Australian Domestic Product*, table 31, p. 152.

Table 5:4-4(a). Australia: The ten incorporated non-banking pastoral finance companies, 1880–1891

	1880	1881	1882	1883	1884	1885	1886	1887	1888	1889	1890	1891
	Total paid-up capital of the ten companies											
(thousands of U.K. pounds)	1,586	1,668	1,709	1,909	3,249	3,463	3,953	4,160	4,988	5,085	5,157	5,151
	Percent of total paid-up capital of the ten companies held by											
Dalgety & Co.	0.0	0.0	0.0	0.0	30.8	28.9	25.3	24.0	20.0	19.7	19.4	19.4
New Zealand Land & Mortgage Agency	19.8	18.8	18.4	16.4	10.0	10.7	9.3	8.8	17.3	17.0	16.7	16.8
Goldsborough, Mort & Co.	7.3	12.0	11.7	10.5	6.2	5.8	5.1	6.6	7.0	6.9	8.2	8.7
Australian Mortgage, Land & Finance	22.1	21.0	20.5	21.0	14.2	13.3	11.6	12.5	10.4	10.2	10.1	10.1
Union Mortgage & Agency Co.	0.0	0.0	0.0	0.0	5.1	6.9	16.5	15.7	18.7	18.3	18.1	18.1
British & Australasian Land & Agency Co.	6.3	6.0	5.9	10.8	6.3	5.9	5.2	5.0	4.1	4.1	4.0	4.0
Australasian Mortgage & Agency Co.	11.2	10.2	9.9	8.9	6.2	5.8	6.0	6.0	5.7	5.9	5.8	5.8
Trust & Agency Company of New South Wales	12.0	11.4	11.1	10.0	5.8	6.8	6.3	6.9	4.6	6.2	6.1	6.1
South Australian Land Mortgage & Agency Co.	12.6	12.0	11.7	10.5	6.2	7.2	7.0	7.2	6.0	5.9	5.8	5.8
Queensland Investment Land Mortgage & Agency Co.	8.7	8.6	10.8	12.0	9.4	8.8	7.7	7.3	6.0	5.9	5.8	5.2
Total debentures and deposits of the ten companies												
(thousands of U.K. pounds)	6,041	6,094	7,177	8,271	11,279	12,867	14,636	15,582	16,954	18,022	17,604	17,531
	Percent of the total debentures and deposits of the ten companies held by											
Dalgety & Co.	0.0	0.0	0.0	0.0	3.7	8.1	12.0	13.2	13.0	14.1	15.0	15.3
New Zealand Land & Mortgage Agency	43.0	41.7	36.3	30.9	27.2	23.2	21.3	18.7	17.1	16.9	17.3	16.1
Goldsbrough, Mort & Co.	5.3	1.3	9.3	6.9	5.3	5.5	7.8	10.7	14.5	13.8	16.7	17.2
Australian Mortgage, Land & Finance	23.2	22.6	19.4	18.1	15.9	14.7	13.6	13.3	14.0	13.1	13.0	13.2
Union Mortgage & Agency Co.	0.0	0.0	0.0	0.0	9.1	11.3	10.2	10.2	8.9	11.0	6.6	7.5
British & Australasian Land & Agency Co.	11.6	13.1	11.1	11.6	11.4	10.5	9.9	9.5	9.0	8.8	9.1	9.6
Australasian Mortgage & Agency Co.	3.1	6.5	6.4	8.3	7.0	6.2	6.3	6.4	6.0	6.3	6.6	6.8
Trust & Agency Company of New South Wales	5.0	4.9	4.2	3.6	2.8	3.0	2.6	2.5	2.6	2.4	2.4	2.5
South Australian Land Mortgage & Agency Co.	0.0	0.0	0.0	8.0	7.1	7.1	6.8	7.1	6.8	6.6	6.3	6.3
Queensland Investment Land Mortgage & Agency Co.	8.9	9.8	13.3	12.5	10.6	10.3	9.6	8.5	8.0	7.1	6.9	6.5
Total capital, debentures, and deposits of the ten companies												
(thousands of U.K. pounds)	7,627	7,762	8,886	10,180	14,528	16,330	18,589	19,742	21,942	23,107	22,761	22,682
Total mortgage advances of the ten companies												
(thousands of U.K. pounds)	6,756	8,017	9,631	10,723	15,704	17,504	19,424	20,237	21,842	22,739	22,952	21,708

Source: N.G. Butlin, *Investment in Australian Economic Development, 1861–1900* (Cambridge: Cambridge University Press, 1964), Table 28, p. 143; Table 30, p. 151; Table 3, p. 152.

Table 5:4-4(b). *Australia: the ten incorporated non-banking pastoral finance companies: new finance, 1881–1891 (thousands of U.K. pounds)*

Company	1881	1882	1883	1884	1885	1886	1887	1888	1889	1890	1891
Dalgety & Co.	0	0	0	1,000	0	0	0	0	0	0	0
New Zealand Land & Mortgage Agency	0	0	0	10	45	0	-4	499	-1	0	0
Goldsborough, Mort & Co.	84	0	0	0	0	0	75	75	0	72	28
Australian Mortgage, Land & Finance	0	0	50	60	0	0	60	0	0	0	0
Union Mortgage & Agency Co.	0	0	0	166	73	414	0	280	0	0	0
British & Australasian Land & Agency Co.	0	0	106	0	0	0	0	0	0	0	0
Australasian Mortgage & Agency Co.	-8	0	0	30	0	37	13	34	16	0	0
Trust & Agency Company of New South Wales	0	0	0	-1	45	14	38	-55	82	0	0
South Australian Land Mortgage & Agency Co.	0	0	0	0	50	25	25	0	0	0	0
Queensland Investment Land Mortgage & Agency Co.	6	41	44	75	1	0	0	-5	0	0	-34
Total new paid-up capital (thousands of. U.K. pounds)	82	41	200	1,340	214	490	207	828	97	72	-6
Dalgety & Co.	0	0	0	415	633	702	300	149	338	106	41
New Zealand Land & Mortgage Agency	-56	60	-44	512	-80	130	-214	-4	151	-6	-222
Goldsborough, Mort & Co.	-239	587	-98	28	112	438	519	800	16	467	68
Australian Mortgage, Land & Finance	-20	16	105	290	102	102	77	311	-19	-75	23
Union Mortgage & Agency Co.	0	0	0	1,022	428	39	98	-77	464	-816	151
British & Australasian Land & Agency Co.	96	4	163	327	60	97	33	40	68	14	89
Australasian Mortgage & Agency Co.	210	60	229	100	12	127	71	14	116	32	38
Trust & Agency Company of New South Wales	0	0	0	11	80	-15	20	47	-7	-5	4
South Australian Land Mortgage & Agency Co.	0	0	664	138	115	71	111	61	22	-75	-185
Queensland Investment Land Mortgage & Agency Co.	62	356	75	165	126	78	-69	31	-81	-60	-80
Total new debentures and deposits (thousands of U.K. pounds)	53	1,083	1,094	3,008	1,588	1,769	946	1,372	1,068	-418	-73
Total new capital, debentures, and deposits (thousands of U.K. pounds)	135	1,124	1,294	4,348	1,802	2,259	1,153	2,200	1,165	-346	-79
Total new mortgage advances (thousands of U.K. pounds)	1,261	1,614	1,092	4,981	1,800	1,920	813	1,605	897	213	-1,244

Source: Table 5:4-4(a).

offerings on the London Stock Exchange, in the late 1870s and early 1880s, they "formed agencies in Britain and engaged in what was described as a house-to-house canvas for small sums. Offering high rates of interest (at least twice the deposit rates in British banks), these companies became increasingly less dependent on funds raised through the London Stock Exchange and sought much of their capital outside the Exchange."[1070]

As Table 5:4-4(b) indicates, over the decade ending in 1891, the ten firms attracted a total of more than £15 million in capital, debentures, and deposits. Although the total international flow was negative in 1890 and 1891, four of the ten firms continued to attract British funds in 1890 as did seven of the ten the next year. Despite declining wool prices, the extension of the margin of cultivation into areas with insufficient water and too many rabbits, and runs stocked with too many sheep, the pastoral houses continued to support the industry. The results were, initially, illiquid accounts and mortgaged property that was worth far less than the value of the mortgage and, ultimately, the failure of well-established firms, the New Zealand Loan & Mercantile Agency and Goldsborough, Mort & Co. to cite two examples.[1071] Those two firms were ultimately reorganized along lines similar to the ones adopted by the banks and building societies. In the pre-war decade the industry, although no longer as aggressive, continued to finance rural activities on terms broadly similar to those of the trading banks: lending to improve or purchase properties and to finance working capital with loans secured by property or future revenues. In addition, the surviving firms operated a substantial number of foreclosed properties. After 1890, however, they were forced to depend much more heavily on domestic Australian finance.[1072]

In Australia the habit of purchasing life insurance was slower to develop than in Canada and the United States. As a result, in the early years, the sector was less important. Once the habit had been established, however, given the very high levels of per capita income, the industry expanded very rapidly. Since the Australian life insurance companies

---

[1070] N. Butlin, *Investment in Australian Development*, pp. 159–60.
[1071] Bailey, *A Hundred Years*, pp. 45–46. N. Butlin and Barnard, "Pastoral Finance," p. 394.
[1072] M. Butlin, "Capital Markets," pp. 235–36. In the case of the Australian Mortgage Land & Finance Company's expansion into Queensland in the years before the war, the decision was made to sell off existing properties rather than attempt to raise funds in London where their debenture stock still sold at a discount. Bailey, *A Hundred Years*, p. 193.

viewed all of Australasia as their territory, it is difficult to estimate precisely the level of penetration in the six states alone. By 1888, for Australasia as a whole, the amount of life insurance in force per capita was £19. That figure compares with £12 for Great Britain, £8 for the United States, and £9 for Canada. In 1900 the figures were £22, £15, £17, and £15, respectively.[1073] The first Australian life insurance company is generally thought to have been the Australian General Assurance Company, a firm that was doing some life insurance business in Sydney in 1840. In 1846 it had only twenty-six life insurance policies in force. Because its directors "felt that there was not room for two life offices in Sydney," its life business was taken over by the Australian Colonial and General Life Assurance and Annuity Company, a British company.[1074] The Australian Colonial and General did not, however, prove more successful; in 1851 its life insurance business was taken over by the Liverpool and London and Globe, an even more British firm. The first successful Australian life insurance company was the Australian Mutual Provident Society. The firm was organized in Sydney in the fall of 1848 and commenced business the following January. Although growth was initially slow, the AMPS was to dominate the Australian domestic insurance market until World War I.

The organization of the AMPS did not, however, trigger a surge of competition. It was eight years before a second company, the Australasia Insurance Company, a proprietary company, opened its doors; between then and 1866, although there were to be three more such companies, none were to prove either particularly profitable or very long-lived. The Australian Mutual's success in the 1860s, however, appears to have stimulated the formation of a number of mutual life insurance companies in New South Wales and Victoria and one in South Australia. In 1869, two decades after the founding of the Australian Mutual Provident Society, a second mutual life insurance company opened its doors; and, over the next decade, life insurance became entrenched in the Australian economy. By 1881 there were nine mutual companies, and four years later Australian life insurance companies held assets totaling £8.4

[1073] A.C. Gray, *Life Insurance in Australia: An Historical and Descriptive Account* (Melbourne: McCarron Bird, 1977), p. 50 [Hereafter cited as Gray, *Life Insurance in Australia.*]

In 1891 Australia represented 84 percent of the combined population of Australia and New Zealand; in 1901 the figure was 83 percent. Brian R. Mitchell, *International Historical Statistics: The Americas and Australasia* (Detroit: Gale Research, 1983), table B1, p. 53.

[1074] The Colonial and General had two Australian directors.

million.[1075] Table 5:4-5 provides at least a partial enumeration of the largest Australasian firms selling insurance in Australia in the years before World War I.[1076] Despite the entry of a substantial number of competitors over the next four decades, the Australian Mutual Provident Society remained the dominant firm throughout the period. It represented almost three-quarters of the assets in the sample in 1877, and it still commanded more than 55 percent at the end of 1914.

Like the British industry, Australian life insurance companies were not caught up in the American tontine boom. Moreover, like the British industry, the Australian firms benefited from the innovation of endowment policies; and much of the industry's post-1870 growth can be traced to those contracts. There was, however, one important difference: the shift in the relative importance of endowment policies came earlier, and by 1900 those policies represented a higher fraction of the total in Australia than in the United Kingdom. In Great Britain endowment policies constituted about 5 percent of all life insurance policies in 1885; that figure had reached almost 10 percent five years later, and those contracts represented almost one-quarter of the total at the turn of the century. In Australia policies that included endowment clauses reached 10 percent before 1870, had exceeded 20 percent by 1873, and had passed 30 percent by the turn of the century.

In the case of industrial insurance, however, the paths of the two industries' development diverge even more markedly: Industrial insurance came later, and, in the years before World War I, it played a much less

---

[1075] The new firms included the Mutual Life Association of Australasia (Sydney, 1869), the National Mutual Life Association of Australasia Limited (Victoria, 1869), the Mutual Assurance Society of Victoria (Victoria, 1870), the Australian Widows' Fund (Victoria, 1871), the Colonial Mutual Life Assurance Society Limited (Victoria, 1873), the Australian Temperance and General Mutual Life Assurance Society Limited (Victoria, 1876), the City Mutual Life Insurance Society (Sydney, 1877), and the City Mutual Life Insurance Society (Adelaide, 1881). Gray, *Life Insurance in Australia*, pp. 18–50, 280–81. Hall, *The Stock Exchange of Melbourne*, pp. 42–43, 111–12.

[1076] The data are reported in various issues of the *Australasian Insurance and Banking Record* from 1876 through 1915. The list of firms was prepared in the following way. The *Official Yearbook of the Commonwealth of Australia* listed each year from 1907 to 1914 the firms selling life insurance in Australia. The list for 1907 was merged with the list for 1914, and firms located in Britain and the United States were removed. The result was nineteen firms: ten with head offices in Sydney, nine with head offices in Melbourne, and one (the Provident Life Assurance Company) with its head office in New Zealand. The nineteen were then traced back through their annual reports published in the *A.I.B.R.* Since the firms closed their books at various times during the year, the reports were all extrapolated to a December 31 closing.

Table 5:4-5(a). *Assets of nineteen Australasian life insurance companies (pounds sterling)*

Year	Assurance & Thrift Association	Australian Alliance Insurance	Australian Metropolitan Life Insurance	Australian Mutual Provident Society	Australian Provincial Insurance Association	Australian Temperance & General Mutual Life Assurance
1877		270,690		2,292,591		
1878		289,708		2,652,755		
1879		312,055		2,965,893		4,715
1880		342,777		3,516,497		6,161
1881		368,470		3,090,109		9,605
1882		387,017		4,420,047		13,544
1883		418,492		4,999,918		18,950
1884		421,782		5,470,628		29,962
1885		437,380		6,076,725		51,673
1886		433,549		6,731,254		55,697
1887		440,278		7,569,822		71,109
1888		531,179		8,309,595		104,782
1889		562,294		9,033,496		128,042
1890		568,069		9,855,722		163,029
1891		588,659		10,709,242		190,669
1892		602,589		11,534,576		213,063
1893		598,602		12,280,862		232,826
1894		576,016		13,006,672		240,242
1895		582,398		13,713,065		235,416
1896		586,861		14,158,617		228,395
1897		547,498		14,923,230		237,903
1898		525,387		15,728,437		252,737
1899		515,448	20,161	16,539,264		268,049
1900		501,587	21,689	17,448,878		267,265
1901		501,011	26,800	18,207,032		296,630
1902		497,532	35,826	19,243,287		339,540
1903		472,167	38,694	20,140,924		390,585
1904		460,164	38,630	20,989,017		438,339
1905		441,276	38,607	21,333,509		505,483
1906		430,009	39,534	22,783,312		593,081
1907		417,934	42,159	23,841,490		697,666
1908		384,834	47,617	24,981,528		805,222
1909		316,825	50,914	26,087,089		940,324
1910		321,831	67,135	27,425,435		1,112,745
1911	17,511	336,848	71,890	28,848,335		1,257,702
1912	23,396	337,039	76,858	30,395,931		1,491,374
1913	28,693	350,042	85,112	31,998,746	31,643	1,633,657
1914	34,432	366,294	95,489	33,736,909	60,646	1,847,576

Source: See Table 5.4-6(a).

Australian Widows' Fund Life Assurance Society	Citizens' Life Assurance	City Mutual Life Insurance Society	Colonial Mutual Life Assurance Society	Common-wealth Insurance	Co-operative Assurance	Mutual Life & Citizens' Assurance
32,471			32,401			
45,985			58,335			
60,079			95,461			
81,463			146,141			
108,544		4,246	212,360			
143,558		5,734	284,066			
191,757		8,788	368,510			
248,887		11,800	458,128			
321,900		16,166	550,091			
406,594		33,056	673,885			
504,416		34,407	743,820			
618,130	37,377	42,999	867,678			
727,404	51,169	52,931	1,053,289			
828,735	96,075	62,925	1,204,243			
946,073	116,248	97,792	1,377,542			
1,034,630	20,348	114,976	1,526,098			
1,133,696	34,957	124,978	1,666,725			
1,212,818	54,143	123,012	1,799,995			
1,273,845	81,276	133,915	1,928,933			
1,316,643	112,693	146,013	2,047,385			
1,265,958	158,156	165,224	2,159,282			
1,330,001	217,671	179,495	2,267,652			
1,389,934	301,122	205,981	2,391,882			
1,457,285	387,688	211,408	2,498,274			
1,537,705	496,215	233,532	2,600,358			
1,599,642	632,739	239,926	2,716,011			
1,664,810	778,583	254,750	2,822,062			
1,715,785	929,811	277,230	2,923,521			
1,753,632	1,065,979	309,331	2,994,668			
1,794,081	1,817,511	324,391	2,993,366			
1,845,455	2,090,718	359,540	3,085,700			
1,911,235		396,050	3,086,161			4,533,078
		434,002	3,117,515			4,904,045
		491,724	3,260,477			7,274,185
		542,142	3,413,813			6,789,727
		606,473	3,501,905		42,805	7,180,392
		717,110	3,670,785	48,504	54,199	8,759,447
		771,351	3,857,836	80,860	57,668	9,376,370

Table 5:4-5(a). (*cont.*)

Year	Mutual Life Association of Australasia	National Mutual Life Association of Australasia	Provident Life Assurance	Standard Life Association	Victoria Assurance	Victoria Life & General Insurance	Total Assets of the 19 Insurance Companies
1877	76,811	67,159				318,613	3,090,735
1878	103,326	79,212				313,886	3,543,207
1879	132,105	106,598				326,970	4,003,875
1880	168,525	156,310			160,818	344,215	4,922,906
1881	212,570	231,926			141,958	362,901	5,561,688
1882	267,073	289,811			148,586	383,302	6,342,738
1883	327,900	369,824			138,730	393,938	7,236,806
1884	390,438	455,712			137,833	404,246	8,029,414
1885	446,754	541,632			139,190	423,382	9,004,893
1886	504,713	618,350			128,063	455,445	10,040,605
1887	578,048	715,589			124,416	460,126	11,242,029
1888	661,612	832,174			129,620	447,517	12,582,662
1889	715,136	953,105			132,461	429,812	13,839,138
1890	735,065	1,078,347			142,794	403,934	15,138,938
1891	805,627	1,201,053			152,959	384,564	16,570,428
1892	888,543	1,312,602			157,430	366,277	17,771,131
1893	957,772	1,419,589			154,882	370,274	18,975,162
1894	1,011,608	1,517,453			152,646	371,492	20,066,096
1895	1,050,488	1,616,407			148,987	365,784	21,130,514
1896	1,097,324	1,954,141			147,632	365,378	22,161,082
1897	1,147,531	2,784,767			121,787	367,146	23,878,482
1898	1,200,206	2,941,550			113,140	365,817	25,122,092
1899	1,267,269	3,118,336			132,144	364,393	26,513,983
1900	1,372,331	3,274,527		14,555	136,953	360,810	27,953,249
1901	1,445,492	3,447,420		17,430	146,522	351,918	29,308,063
1902	1,545,135	3,648,989		22,695	156,835	326,514	31,004,670
1903	1,782,673	3,887,853		28,575	165,249	301,094	32,728,018
1904	1,889,415	4,159,351	15,971	34,386	168,748	289,824	34,330,190
1905	1,974,554	4,433,836	18,514	40,601	175,818	277,166	35,362,974
1906	2,088,337	4,733,425	22,453	47,790	181,752	264,601	38,113,642
1907	2,185,851	5,101,906	26,698	60,534	179,534	253,844	40,189,029
1908		5,581,948	47,589	70,360	180,839	243,707	42,270,168
1909		6,134,977	49,633		181,317	230,784	42,447,424
1910		6,499,035	53,655		193,598	213,977	46,913,797
1911		7,036,713	66,742		209,104	189,411	48,779,937
1912		7,662,836	79,392		218,554	164,008	51,780,962
1913		8,393,551	98,338		231,559	142,978	56,244,362
1914		9,108,764	115,061		251,698	130,067	59,891,021

Table 5:4-5(b). *Assets of nineteen Australasian life insurance companies (percent of total)*

Year	Assurance & Thrift Association	Australian Alliance Insurance	Australian Metropolitan Life Insurance	Australian Mutual Provident Society	Australian Provincial Insurance Association	Australian Temperance & General Mutual Life Assurance
1877	0.0%	8.8%	0.0%	74.2%	0.0%	0.0%
1878	0.0	8.2	0.0	74.9	0.0	0.0
1879	0.0	7.8	0.0	74.1	0.0	0.1
1880	0.0	7.0	0.0	71.4	0.0	0.1
1881	0.0	6.6	0.0	70.3	0.0	0.2
1882	0.0	6.1	0.0	69.7	0.0	0.2
1883	0.0	5.8	0.0	69.1	0.0	0.3
1884	0.0	5.3	0.0	68.1	0.0	0.4
1885	0.0	4.9	0.0	67.5	0.0	0.6
1886	0.0	4.3	0.0	67.0	0.0	0.6
1887	0.0	3.9	0.0	67.3	0.0	0.6
1888	0.0	4.2	0.0	66.0	0.0	0.8
1889	0.0	4.1	0.0	65.3	0.0	0.9
1890	0.0	3.8	0.0	65.1	0.0	1.1
1891	0.0	3.6	0.0	64.6	0.0	1.2
1892	0.0	3.4	0.0	64.9	0.0	1.2
1893	0.0	3.2	0.0	64.7	0.0	1.2
1894	0.0	2.9	0.0	64.8	0.0	1.2
1895	0.0	2.8	0.0	64.9	0.0	1.1
1896	0.0	2.6	0.0	63.9	0.0	1.0
1897	0.0	2.3	0.0	62.5	0.0	1.0
1898	0.0	2.1	0.0	62.6	0.0	1.0
1899	0.0	1.9	0.1	62.4	0.0	1.0
1900	0.0	1.8	0.1	62.4	0.0	1.0
1901	0.0	1.7	0.1	62.1	0.0	1.0
1902	0.0	1.6	0.1	62.1	0.0	1.1
1903	0.0	1.4	0.1	61.5	0.0	1.2
1904	0.0	1.3	0.1	61.1	0.0	1.3
1905	0.0	1.2	0.1	60.3	0.0	1.4
1906	0.0	1.1	0.1	59.8	0.0	1.6
1907	0.0	1.0	0.1	59.3	0.0	1.7
1908	0.0	0.9	0.1	59.1	0.0	1.9
1909	0.0	0.7	0.1	61.5	0.0	2.2
1910	0.0	0.7	0.1	58.5	0.0	2.4
1911	0.0	0.7	0.1	59.1	0.0	2.6
1912	0.0	0.7	0.1	58.7	0.0	2.9
1913	0.1	0.6	0.2	58.9	0.1	2.9
1914	0.1	0.6	0.2	56.3	0.1	3.1

Source: See Table 5.4-5(a).

Table 5:4-5(b). (*cont.*)

Year	Australian Widows' Fund Life Assurance Society	Citizens' Life Assurance	City Mutual Life Insurance Society	Colonial Mutual Life Assurance Society	Common-wealth Insurance	Co-operative Assurance	Mutual Life & Citizens' Assurance
1877	1.1%	0.0%	0.0%	1.0%	0.0%	0.0%	0.0%
1878	1.3	0.0	0.0	1.6	0.0	0.0	0.0
1879	1.5	0.0	0.0	2.4	0.0	0.0	0.0
1880	1.7	0.0	0.0	3.0	0.0	0.0	0.0
1881	2.0	0.0	0.1	3.8	0.0	0.0	0.0
1882	2.3	0.0	0.1	4.5	0.0	0.0	0.0
1883	2.6	0.0	0.1	5.1	0.0	0.0	0.0
1884	3.1	0.0	0.1	5.7	0.0	0.0	0.0
1885	3.6	0.0	0.2	6.1	0.0	0.0	0.0
1886	4.0	0.0	0.3	6.7	0.0	0.0	0.0
1887	4.5	0.0	0.3	6.6	0.0	0.0	0.0
1888	4.9	0.3	0.3	6.9	0.0	0.0	0.0
1889	5.3	0.4	0.4	7.6	0.0	0.0	0.0
1890	5.5	0.6	0.4	8.0	0.0	0.0	0.0
1891	5.7	0.7	0.6	8.3	0.0	0.0	0.0
1892	5.8	0.1	0.6	8.6	0.0	0.0	0.0
1893	6.0	0.2	0.7	8.8	0.0	0.0	0.0
1894	6.0	0.3	0.6	9.0	0.0	0.0	0.0
1895	6.0	0.4	0.6	9.1	0.0	0.0	0.0
1896	5.9	0.5	0.7	9.2	0.0	0.0	0.0
1897	5.3	0.7	0.7	9.0	0.0	0.0	0.0
1898	5.3	0.9	0.7	9.0	0.0	0.0	0.0
1899	5.2	1.1	0.8	9.0	0.0	0.0	0.0
1900	5.2	1.4	0.8	8.9	0.0	0.0	0.0
1901	5.2	1.7	0.8	8.9	0.0	0.0	0.0
1902	5.2	2.0	0.8	8.8	0.0	0.0	0.0
1903	5.1	2.4	0.8	8.6	0.0	0.0	0.0
1904	5.0	2.7	0.8	8.5	0.0	0.0	0.0
1905	5.0	3.0	0.9	8.5	0.0	0.0	0.0
1906	4.7	4.8	0.9	7.9	0.0	0.0	0.0
1907	4.6	5.2	0.9	7.7	0.0	0.0	0.0
1908	4.5	0.0	0.9	7.3	0.0	0.0	10.7
1909	0.0	0.0	1.0	7.3	0.0	0.0	11.6
1910	0.0	0.0	1.0	6.9	0.0	0.0	15.5
1911	0.0	0.0	1.1	7.0	0.0	0.0	13.9
1912	0.0	0.0	1.2	6.8	0.0	0.1	13.9
1913	0.0	0.0	1.3	6.5	0.1	0.1	15.6
1914	0.0	0.0	1.3	6.4	0.1	0.1	15.7

Mutual Life Association of Australasia	National Mutual Life Association of Australasia	Provident Life Assurance	Standard Life Association	Victoria Assurance	Victoria Life & General Insurance	Total Assets of the 19 Insurance Companies
2.5%	2.2%	0.0%	0.0%	0.0%	10.3%	100.0%
2.9	2.2	0.0	0.0	0.0	8.9	100.0
3.3	2.7	0.0	0.0	0.0	8.2	100.0
3.4	3.2	0.0	0.0	3.3	7.0	100.0
3.8	4.2	0.0	0.0	2.6	6.5	100.0
4.2	4.6	0.0	0.0	2.3	6.0	100.0
4.5	5.1	0.0	0.0	1.9	5.4	100.0
4.9	5.7	0.0	0.0	1.7	5.0	100.0
5.0	6.0	0.0	0.0	1.5	4.7	100.0
5.0	6.2	0.0	0.0	1.3	4.5	100.0
5.1	6.4	0.0	0.0	1.1	4.1	100.0
5.3	6.6	0.0	0.0	1.0	3.6	100.0
5.2	6.9	0.0	0.0	1.0	3.1	100.0
4.9	7.1	0.0	0.0	0.9	2.7	100.0
4.9	7.2	0.0	0.0	0.9	2.3	100.0
5.0	7.4	0.0	0.0	0.9	2.1	100.0
5.0	7.5	0.0	0.0	0.8	2.0	100.0
5.0	7.6	0.0	0.0	0.8	1.9	100.0
5.0	7.6	0.0	0.0	0.7	1.7	100.0
5.0	8.8	0.0	0.0	0.7	1.6	100.0
4.8	11.7	0.0	0.0	0.5	1.5	100.0
4.8	11.7	0.0	0.0	0.5	1.5	100.0
4.8	11.8	0.0	0.0	0.5	1.4	100.0
4.9	11.7	0.0	0.1	0.5	1.3	100.0
4.9	11.8	0.0	0.1	0.5	1.2	100.0
5.0	11.8	0.0	0.1	0.5	1.1	100.0
5.4	11.9	0.0	0.1	0.5	0.9	100.0
5.5	12.1	0.0	0.1	0.5	0.8	100.0
5.6	12.5	0.1	0.1	0.5	0.8	100.0
5.5	12.4	0.1	0.1	0.5	0.7	100.0
5.4	12.7	0.1	0.2	0.4	0.6	100.0
0.0	13.2	0.1	0.2	0.4	0.6	100.0
0.0	14.5	0.1	0.0	0.4	0.5	100.0
0.0	13.9	0.1	0.0	0.4	0.5	100.0
0.0	14.4	0.1	0.0	0.4	0.4	100.0
0.0	14.8	0.2	0.0	0.4	0.3	100.0
0.0	14.9	0.2	0.0	0.4	0.3	100.0
0.0	15.2	0.2	0.0	0.4	0.2	100.0

significant role in the development of the Australian life insurance industry. Gray concludes that the lag in development reflected the high costs that are inherent in any attempt to collect premiums house-to-house on a weekly basis in a country with as low a population density as Australia. By 1881, however, the combined population of Melbourne and Sydney exceeded 500,000; and the two cities contained almost one-quarter of the population of the six colonies. Perhaps one may have to look elsewhere for a satisfactory explanation of the slow growth of the industrial insurance business.

Although there had been some attempts to enter the market earlier, the first company to establish a permanent presence in the industrial insurance market was the City Mutual Life Assurance Society Ltd. That firm established an industrial insurance division in 1884. Two years later, with the creation of the Citizens Life Assurance Company Ltd., the division was spun off as an independent, and very successful, proprietary firm. Its success drew imitators, the Australian Temperance and General, for example, in 1886; but it was 1904 before the Australian Mutual Provident Society began to write industrial insurance policies, and 1909 before the Colonial Mutual entered the field. Despite the growth after the mid-1880s, the amount of industrial insurance in force was less than 7 percent of the ordinary life insurance in force in 1905, and that fraction was still only 11 percent a decade later.

In Victoria, where the Life Insurance Companies Act of 1873 required registration and reports, the industry's assets increased from £270,000 in 1874 to £1.4 million a decade later. Thereafter growth was more rapid. A.C. Gray puts the worldwide assets of life insurance companies with head offices in Australia at £8.4 million in 1885, £14.5 million in 1890, £28.1 million in 1900, and £46.4 million in 1910. The Australian figures would be somewhat smaller.[1077] By 1909 Australian life insurance companies commanded assets of £35.6 million, and by 1914 the total had reached £43.8 million. At that latter date, the industry was about one-half the size of the savings banks and one-quarter of the size of the trading banks.[1078] One important difference between the Australian companies and their North American counterparts remained: the Australian life insurance offices seldom expanded their portfolios far beyond gov-

---

[1077] Gray, *Life Insurance in Australia*, p. 280. The figures include the Provident Life of New Zealand.

[1078] M. Butlin, "Capital Markets," table 9.1, p. 235. The record of the "nineteen" is somewhat different. Those data suggest totals of £8.0 million in 1884, £42.4 million in 1909, and £59.8 million in 1914. Those figures, of course, include both accruals and operating property.

ernment bonds, mortgages, and other loans. Table 5:4-6 displays the asset structure of the nineteen Australasian companies in the sample. Government bonds represented just less than one-quarter of all assets in 1877 and about the same proportion in 1914. Their share, however, declined markedly from 1877 until the crisis of the 1890s; they accounted for only 2.6 percent of the total in 1891 and 1892. Mortgages, meanwhile, had increased from about one-half the total in the late 1870s to almost 60 percent in the early 1890s, before declining to just more than 40 percent in 1914. Other loans – loans on policies, personal security, and other miscellaneous collateral – rose from about 10 percent in the 1870s to about one-quarter of the total in 1914. Real estate accounted for about 10 percent of the total during the 1890s, an increase that reflected properties foreclosed during the depression.[1079]

It was not until World War II that the issues of industrial and commercial concerns began to appear in the insurance companies' portfolios.[1080] Such securities may have amounted to more than 3 percent of assets in the sample in the late 1870s (the category "Private Stocks and Bonds" includes the issues of banks, building and loan societies, railways, tramways, and pastoral companies as well as more traditionally defined commercial and industrial issues), but the proportion declined steadily over the period. In the later years, they accounted for less than one-tenth that amount. It should, however, be noted that in 1897 the Australian Alliance Insurance Company held £7,941 of the debentures of the Melbourne Cricket Club.

The industry's contribution to the mortgage market was clearly substantial. Between 1901 and 1914, despite a declining share of the industry's total investments, life insurance companies accounted for one-third of all mortgage loans – more even than the 30 percent contributed by the state mortgage banks – and almost one-half of the private total. Moreover, in 1914 they accounted for 40 percent of all outstanding

---

[1079] Gray provides a distribution of the worldwide assets of insurance companies with home offices in Australia at five-year intervals from 1885 to 1915. His figures conform closely to those of the sample of nineteen. By five-year period from 1885 through 1914 the percentage figures are the following:

1. Government and Municipal Loans: 6.5, 3.2, 3.1, 14.8, 15.9, 23.5, 23.1
2. Loans on Mortgage: 62.9, 59.8, 51.2, 47.1, 45.2, 41.8, 40.5
3. Real Estate: 8.3, 11.2, 10.8, 11.2, 7.2, 5.4, 4.7
4. Shares and Debentures: 1.2, 0.9, 0.6, 0.2, 0.3, 0.2, 0.6
5. Policy Loans: 12.0, 17.0, 20.4, 18.4, 16.4, 13.9, 13.9
6. Other Assets: 9.1, 7.9, 13.9, 8.3, 15.0, 15.2, 17.2.

Gray, *Life Insurance in Australia*, p. 280.

[1080] Hall, *The Stock Exchange of Melbourne*, pp. 111–12. Holder, "Australia," p. 63.

Table 5:4-6(a). *Assets of Australasian life insurance companies (pounds sterling)*

Year	Gov't. bonds	Loans on mortgage	Loans on personal security or policies	Misc. loans	Cash	Real estate	Private stocks & bonds	Other investments	Misc. debtors and accruals	Total assets
1877	733,606	1,055,667	302,477	0	671,670	77,079	115,288	881	134,067	3,090,735
1878	600,918	1,820,780	362,481	0	394,434	141,735	108,209	883	113,768	3,543,207
1879	610,405	2,210,445	499,473	0	306,571	151,784	100,704	1,087	123,405	4,003,875
1880	717,115	2,636,160	592,433	0	522,262	210,668	100,681	993	142,595	4,922,906
1881	583,813	3,280,026	681,362	0	448,901	276,740	96,652	1,052	193,142	5,561,688
1882	527,355	3,797,721	721,542	0	644,372	332,827	95,641	1,115	222,165	6,342,738
1883	510,401	4,498,254	798,983	0	604,918	453,290	98,499	1,182	271,278	7,236,806
1884	548,198	5,032,608	958,384	0	523,971	536,134	113,566	1,253	315,301	8,029,414
1885	586,931	5,595,152	1,171,879	0	385,461	814,161	133,682	1,328	316,298	9,004,893
1886	519,596	5,819,414	1,528,832	0	632,190	1,038,595	133,813	1,408	366,758	10,040,605
1887	476,439	6,335,581	1,858,973	0	769,233	1,284,615	141,927	1,499	373,762	11,242,029
1888	462,061	7,020,093	2,069,569	0	1,006,636	1,451,225	148,086	1,592	423,400	12,582,662
1889	447,423	8,272,941	2,362,265	0	682,477	1,502,938	147,176	4,185	419,734	13,839,138
1890	454,390	9,012,947	2,638,012	0	818,880	1,612,668	149,227	4,278	448,536	15,138,938
1891	428,295	9,800,232	2,921,962	125	973,752	1,804,398	159,438	4,384	477,842	16,570,428
1892	463,472	10,374,533	3,399,511	100,437	1,023,914	1,836,334	170,068	1,997	400,866	17,771,131
1893	565,277	10,509,166	3,968,082	119,666	996,172	2,106,788	178,137	2,117	529,757	18,975,162
1894	590,269	10,879,805	4,341,707	163,705	1,285,884	2,162,523	179,134	2,244	460,825	20,066,096
1895	889,395	10,806,704	4,479,177	421,974	1,480,102	2,412,884	183,876	2,726	453,676	21,130,514
1896	1,126,228	11,321,512	4,609,401	472,472	1,387,026	2,553,080	195,686	4,156	491,521	22,161,082
1897	1,445,285	12,169,577	4,849,297	561,725	1,327,443	2,786,991	198,766	8,136	531,261	23,878,482

Year										
1898	2,122,012	12,343,800	4,928,487	641,715	1,554,281	2,877,741	189,225	27,578	437,253	25,122,092
1899	2,841,711	12,615,179	5,076,871	754,566	1,288,244	3,112,904	164,736	63,379	596,393	26,513,983
1900	3,422,711	13,198,863	5,118,243	879,554	1,396,329	3,136,776	162,366	81,342	557,065	27,953,249
1901	4,005,980	13,874,526	5,166,386	1,190,273	1,032,670	3,164,190	161,375	104,818	607,844	29,308,063
1902	4,433,115	14,550,953	5,312,518	1,494,968	1,039,421	3,187,687	156,388	124,049	705,572	31,004,670
1903	5,102,228	15,283,919	5,511,343	1,601,386	954,102	3,210,674	152,121	121,872	790,375	32,728,018
1904	5,166,929	15,962,568	5,679,392	1,970,825	1,099,075	3,296,656	148,230	149,260	857,256	34,330,190
1905	5,509,555	16,104,745	5,537,732	2,281,851	1,203,402	3,556,623	144,451	159,249	865,364	35,362,974
1906	7,412,996	16,695,124	5,846,259	2,204,283	1,089,372	3,620,412	139,684	159,981	945,532	38,113,642
1907	8,091,596	17,106,076	5,851,753	2,680,374	1,222,834	3,703,966	133,100	152,062	1,247,268	40,189,029
1908	9,086,431	18,262,205	6,045,766	3,128,787	909,706	3,345,528	147,002	155,708	1,189,036	42,270,168
1909	9,569,831	17,715,814	6,178,203	3,370,171	1,139,068	2,939,285	135,787	155,529	1,243,735	42,447,424
1910	11,003,525	19,592,855	6,484,312	3,757,842	1,506,745	3,026,846	160,322	136,926	1,244,425	46,913,797
1911	11,665,043	20,392,425	6,554,241	4,442,263	1,279,618	2,880,529	148,924	147,794	1,269,101	48,779,937
1912	11,954,016	22,123,250	6,969,150	5,090,316	1,107,689	2,864,184	150,666	150,170	1,371,523	51,780,962
1913	12,367,428	23,995,984	7,374,167	5,891,233	1,747,789	2,891,014	182,621	162,147	1,631,979	56,244,362
1914	13,299,006	24,698,096	7,781,511	7,260,965	1,920,729	2,983,885	185,125	165,641	1,596,064	59,891,021

Source: The Australasian Insurance and Banking Record: A Supplement to "The Australasian Insurance and Banking Record." (Melbourne: Macarron, Bird & Company, 1877 through 1915).

Notes: (1). For firms with closings other than December 31, end of year balance sheets by extrapolation.

(2). For the Victoria Life and General Insurance Company, the category "Railway and Other Debentures and the Metropolitan Board of Works" has been evenly divided between Government Securities and Private Stocks and Bonds.

Table 5:4-6(b). *Assets of Australasian life insurance companies (percent of total)*

Year	Gov't. bonds	Loans on mortgage	Loans on personal security or policies	Misc. loans	Cash	Real estate	Private stocks & bonds	Other investments	Misc. debtors and accruals	Total assets
1877	23.7%	34.2%	9.8%	0.0%	21.7%	2.5%	3.7%	0.0%	4.3%	100.0%
1878	17.0	51.4	10.2	0.0	11.1	4.0	3.1	0.0	3.2	100.0
1879	15.2	55.2	12.5	0.0	7.7	3.8	2.5	0.0	3.1	100.0
1880	14.6	53.5	12.0	0.0	10.6	4.3	2.0	0.0	2.9	100.0
1881	10.5	59.0	12.3	0.0	8.1	5.0	1.7	0.0	3.5	100.0
1882	8.3	59.9	11.4	0.0	10.2	5.2	1.5	0.0	3.5	100.0
1883	7.1	62.2	11.0	0.0	8.4	6.3	1.4	0.0	3.7	100.0
1884	6.8	62.7	11.9	0.0	6.5	6.7	1.4	0.0	3.9	100.0
1885	6.5	62.1	13.0	0.0	4.3	9.0	1.5	0.0	3.5	100.0
1886	5.2	58.0	15.2	0.0	6.3	10.3	1.3	0.0	3.7	100.0
1887	4.2	56.4	16.5	0.0	6.8	11.4	1.3	0.0	3.3	100.0
1888	3.7	55.8	16.4	0.0	8.0	11.5	1.2	0.0	3.4	100.0
1889	3.2	59.8	17.1	0.0	4.9	10.9	1.1	0.0	3.0	100.0
1890	3.0	59.5	17.4	0.0	5.4	10.7	1.0	0.0	3.0	100.0
1891	2.6	59.1	17.6	0.0	5.9	10.9	1.0	0.0	2.9	100.0
1892	2.6	58.4	19.1	0.6	5.8	10.3	1.0	0.0	2.3	100.0
1893	3.0	55.4	20.9	0.6	5.2	11.1	0.9	0.0	2.8	100.0
1894	2.9	54.2	21.6	0.8	6.4	10.8	0.9	0.0	2.3	100.0
1895	4.2	51.1	21.2	2.0	7.0	11.4	0.9	0.0	2.1	100.0
1896	5.1	51.1	20.8	2.1	6.3	11.5	0.9	0.0	2.2	100.0
1897	6.1	51.0	20.3	2.4	5.6	11.7	0.8	0.0	2.2	100.0

Year										
1898	8.4	49.1	19.6	2.6	6.2	11.5	0.8	0.1	1.7	100.0
1899	10.7	47.6	19.1	2.8	4.9	11.7	0.6	0.2	2.2	100.0
1900	12.2	47.2	18.3	3.1	5.0	11.2	0.6	0.3	2.0	100.0
1901	13.7	47.3	17.6	4.1	3.5	10.8	0.6	0.4	2.1	100.0
1902	14.3	46.9	17.1	4.8	3.4	10.3	0.5	0.4	2.3	100.0
1903	15.6	46.7	16.8	4.9	2.9	9.8	0.5	0.4	2.4	100.0
1904	15.1	46.5	16.5	5.7	3.2	9.6	0.4	0.4	2.5	100.0
1905	15.6	45.5	15.7	6.5	3.4	10.1	0.4	0.5	2.4	100.0
1906	19.4	43.8	15.3	5.8	2.9	9.5	0.4	0.4	2.5	100.0
1907	20.1	42.6	14.6	6.7	3.0	9.2	0.3	0.4	3.1	100.0
1908	21.5	43.2	14.3	7.4	2.2	7.9	0.3	0.4	2.8	100.0
1909	22.5	41.7	14.6	7.9	2.7	6.9	0.3	0.4	2.9	100.0
1910	23.5	41.8	13.8	8.0	3.2	6.5	0.3	0.3	2.7	100.0
1911	23.9	41.8	13.4	9.1	2.6	5.9	0.3	0.3	2.6	100.0
1912	23.1	42.7	13.5	9.8	2.1	5.5	0.3	0.3	2.6	100.0
1913	22.0	42.7	13.1	10.5	3.1	5.1	0.3	0.3	2.9	100.0
1914	22.2	41.2	13.0	12.1	3.2	5.0	0.3	0.3	2.7	100.0

Source: Table 5.4-6(a).

595

mortgage loans.[1081] Given the problems of supplying external capital to commercial and industrial firms, it was, perhaps, unfortunate that the financial requirements of those enterprises could not be redesigned to fit within the mold of the agricultural and residential mortgages that the insurance companies offered.

The depression of the 1890s changed the structure of non-bank intermediation in Australia. Land banks, pastoral finance companies, and building societies all suspended; but most of the pastoral finance companies and the building societies were essentially sound. After reconstruction, although there were some failures and mergers, most survived. They survived, however, like the commercial banks, with very different policies in place. In fact, they appear to have been even less ready than the banks to return to the previous policy of relatively easy credit. "The specialist institutions were even more inhibited in part because they had pursued more adventurous policies before the depression than the banks and partly because they had been established to finance investment of a type, which in the case of the pastoral finance companies, was never to return to its former importance in the economy and, in the case of the building societies, was climbing only slowly from the trough."[1082]

In the case of the land and mortgage banks, the situation was much different. Beginning with the demise of the Imperial Banking Company Ltd. in July 1891, those banks failed in droves; and "by about March 1892, the process of extermination was virtually complete."[1083] "Of the 28 banking and financial institutions whose shares were listed on the Melbourne Stock Exchange in 1888, 20 were liquidated during the crisis, and six were reconstructed, while only two survived intact."[1084]

The effect of those failures did not disappear with recovery; the structure of the Australian capital markets was changed for years to come. As the wheat boom developed, the demand for mortgage credit increased in all four countries. In response to that demand in the other countries the supply response largely occurred within the existing institutional structure. In Canada, for example, the private sector expanded: Loan companies increased their foreign borrowing, there was a steady increase in the accumulation of trustee funds, and markets adjusted as changes in

---

[1081] Drummond, *Capital Markets*, tables 1 and 2, pp. 79 and 81. The comparative figures for Canada are 29 percent of the 1901–14 total and 26 percent of loans outstanding in 1914. Drummond's data for Australia are taken from the Balance Sheets of the insurance companies.

[1082] Sinclair, *The Process of Economic Development*, pp. 182–83.

[1083] Hall, *The Stock Exchange of Melbourne*, p. 154.

[1084] Drummond, *Capital Markets*, p. 79. Drummond cites H.G. Turner, *History of the Colony of Victoria*, 2 vols. (London: Longmans Green, 1904), vol. II, p. 301.

relative yields diverted funds from other sectors. In Australia the financial failures, when coupled with the Australian penchant to turn to government to solve economic problems, produced an institutional innovation that was, in the long run, to have a major impact on the economy's trajectory. Although the insurance companies and, to a lesser extent, trustee companies, banks, and building societies made some contribution, the states, by creating state mortgage banks and by providing them with finance on especially favorable terms, filled a significant portion of the gap that remained after the collapse of proprietary mortgage banks and building societies.

From 1893 onward most state governments encouraged the expansion of agricultural loans, sometimes by encouraging the government savings banks to direct their resources to that sector, sometimes by creating special institutions, Western Australia's Agricultural Bank, for example.[1085] In 1894, Victoria, Queensland, South Australia, and Western Australia all passed legislation designed to promote state loans to farmers.[1086] The depression-induced financial squeeze initially slowed the expansion of the state-subsidized programs, but after 1905 the programs grew rapidly both in terms of size and scope. For example, the Government Savings Bank of New South Wales had made no mortgage loans before 1906; and that state's existing Advance Board operated on a very small capital base. In that year the state's parliament set up a new Advance Department and gave it the power to borrow much larger sums; it also allowed the Government Savings Banks to make mortgage loans. The older Victorian Credit Foncier, the State Bank of Southern Australia, and the Agricultural Bank of Western Australia also expanded their operations. In 1910 the Credit Foncier was given permission to expand its loan activity into residential and commercial property, and three years later the New South Wales Advance Department received the same powers. Thus, even before the war, the state institutions had come to rival the insurance and trust companies in terms of the size and scope of their mortgage efforts.[1087]

Farmers, merchants, and homeowners received funds; however, because of the privileged position of the state mortgage and savings banks, the result was achieved only with a much increased risk of serious economic inefficiency. Not only were the institutions limited in terms of

---

[1085] For a general discussion of the move of state banks into agricultural lending see *Report of the Royal Commission on Monetary and Banking Systems in Australia* (Canberra: Government Printer, 1937), pp. 130–42.

[1086] Drummond, *Capital Markets*, pp. 86–87.

[1087] Drummond, *Capital Markets*, p. 258.

the scope of their investment portfolios, but also the terms of their loans were politically determined. Much of the finance came either directly or indirectly from savings deposits. Although some of the smaller banks were financed by state subventions, a high proportion of the loans offered by the larger state mortgage banks was financed by the sale of bonds to, or loans from, the state savings banks.[1088] In the market for private savings the government maintained its monopoly, and by 1914 government savings banks held almost one-third of all mortgage loans. Although the action may have been unintentional, the Australian states created institutions that did what the paralyzed indigenous mortgage companies and building societies did not do; but because politics and not economics determined the allocation, the substitution was not costless.[1089]

5-4d. The formal securities markets
    The Canadian securities markets were much less developed than the American, but both the primary and secondary markets were far more developed than the Australian. In Australia, until the 1890s the market for securities was dominated by public issues, and the market was located in London, not in Melbourne or Sydney. The United States drew importantly on British capital, but by the 1870s there was Wall Street as well as strong subsidiary markets in Boston and Philadelphia. Canada certainly absorbed its share of British – and, later, American – finance; but by the turn of the century there were also active domestic security markets with business divided between the formal stock exchanges in Montreal and Toronto and the secondary markets maintained by the bond houses in those to cities.[1090] Thus, between 1900 and 1914 Canadian firms selling shares on the domestic securities market raised more than six times as much external finance as Australian firms did. By selling bonds they raised almost thirty times as much, and in terms of total finance the ratio was almost ten to one. Even on a per capita basis the figures were four, twenty, and six (see Table 5:4-7).

[1088] Drummond, *Capital Markets*, p. 258.
[1089] Drummond, *Capital Markets*, pp. 78–80, 110–11, 273.
[1090] The financial community on King Street in Toronto and St. James Street in Montreal has been dubbed "the village" as opposed to "the City" and "the Street." Christopher Armstrong and Henry Vivian Nelles, *Southern Exposure: Canadian Promoters in Latin America and the Caribbean, 1896–1930* (Toronto: University of Toronto Press, 1988), pp. 1–23. [Hereafter cited as Armstrong and Nelles, *Southern Exposure*.]

Table 5:4-7. *Australiǎ: Annual estimates of public securities issued:
Mining shares excluded (thousands of British pounds)*

Year	Ordinary shares	Preferred shares	Debentures	Bank shares*
1900	170.8	0.0	0.0	0.0
1901	368.0	0.0	0.0	0.0
1902	195.0	292.0	300.0	25.0
1903	100.0	0.0	0.0	0.0
1904	200.0	0.0	0.0	0.0
1905	280.0	60.0	0.0	0.0
1906	155.0	68.0	275.0	1,280.0
1907	250.0	0.0	0.0	0.0
1908	370.0	0.0	170.0	0.0
1909	419.2	500.0	323.0	0.0
1910	750.9	62.1	80.0	0.0
1911	410.0	375.0	32.0	0.0
1912	151.8	24.0	0.0	2,690.0
1913	757.0	160.0	0.0	0.0
1914	301.3	346.0	746.0	0.0
Total 1900–1914	4,879.0	1,887.1	1,926.0	3,995.0

Note: * Bank shares were issued for cash.

Source: Ian M. Drummond, *Capital Markets in Australia and Canada, 1895–1914.*
PhD dissertation, Yale University, New Haven, CT, 1959, Table B, p. 293.

5-4d(1). The primary markets: If the "City" had become the "Street" in
New York and the "Village" in Canada, it might best be termed the
"corner lot" in Australia. Given the importance of the government in the
total demand for finance and the willingness of British savers to meet
those demands in the years leading up to the 1890s, mining shares aside,
there was little activity in the Australian primary issues markets. Nor was
the domestic market for governments much better developed. A quarter
century earlier, however, one might have been surprised by those conclusions, since, at that time, there appeared to be an emerging new issues
market.

   The first sign that an Australian domestic new issues market for government securities had begun to emerge was noted in 1854 when the
Bank of Australasia purchased half of two new municipal issues, one of
the city of Melbourne and one of the town of Geelong. The bank initially
bought those bonds as secondary reserves but soon sold them at a profit.

These transactions are often viewed as marking the beginning of a domestic market in government securities. It was "to be a long time before the holdings by banks of Australian securities in *Australia* was to provide them with an asset which yielded a reasonably high return, was relatively liquid, and which was in plentiful supply."[1091] Early in the next decade, faced by complaints in the newspapers about the inadequate local supply of government bonds, the Victorian government decided to meet "the want of government stocks . . . severely felt by estators, trustees and others who desire a valid security and are content with a moderate rate of interest," by issuing £250,000 in bonds. The initial issue was so successful that the government sold an additional £100,000 the next month.[1092] The Victorian experiment was repeated in New South Wales in the 1860s and early 1870s. At that time the role played by the Sydney stockbrokers, especially Lennon & Cape and Josiah Mullens, suggested that the market was beginning to take on a formal structure.[1093] In both states, however, a combination of a series of government budget surpluses and the demonstrated voracious appetite of British investors for Australian government bonds not only halted further development, but also caused the nascent infrastructure to atrophy. In 1880 the Victorian government sold £500,000 in one-, two-, and three-year Treasury bonds in Melbourne, but there was to be only one other occasion in the next dozen years when it raised new money at home. "The Victorian bond market which had not been without some vitality and significance for the economy in the 1860s and 1870s became a very anemic affair."[1094] Similarly, in New South Wales, until the 1890s, "local brokers played almost no part in raising the massive capital the government required for its railway construction."[1095]

Faced with a British market that was temporarily closed to them after the Barings Crisis of 1893, the government of Victoria turned to the country's domestic savers in an attempt to float a £750,000 bond issue. "But the bond market, which had been neglected for years, could not be expected to spring into being simply because the government now had need for it. Despite what was then an attractive rate of interest, especially in light of the government's willingness to accept tenders of £99 or above, and despite the then high community preference for safe securities, when the tenders were opened it was found that applications at or

[1091] Hall, *The Stock Exchange of Melbourne*, pp. 6–7.
[1092] Hall, *The Stock Exchange of Melbourne*, pp. 38–39.
[1093] Salsbury and Sweeny, *The Bull, The Bear*, p. 128.
[1094] Hall, *The Stock Exchange of Melbourne*, p. 106.
[1095] Salsbury and Sweeny, *The Bull, The Bear*, p. 129.

above £99 amounted to only £372,800." Although the government was ultimately bailed out by the members of the Melbourne Stock Exchange, the experience underscores the weakness of the domestic market.[1096] Moreover, it provides a telling example of the influence of foreign capital on the evolution of the domestic capital market – if foreign capital is too readily available, the domestic market may well not develop at all.

Compare the experience of Victoria in the 1890s with that of the Canadian government at the onset of World War I. The Dominion had always been heavily dependent on London; it had never borrowed in New York, and it had never borrowed at home for many decades. Thus, in 1915 it was with great trepidation that the government agreed to attempt to float its first war loan in the domestic market. At that time subscribers offered to buy $78.73 million, an over-subscription of 57 percent. By 1919, 2,142,855 subscribers had purchased almost $2,225 million in Canadian war bonds.[1097]

In Australia there were no counterparts of the American second-generation investment banks, nor any institutions that were more than a pale shadow of the Canadian bond houses. In the United States most often a railway's – and later a commercial or industrial firm's – entree into the British capital market was through one of the traditional British merchant banks or its American subsidiaries. In Canada, in the case of railroads, it was through one of the merchant banks or through the auspices of Glyn, Mills and Company or the Bank of Montreal. For commercial and industrial firms, it was usually through one of the smaller merchant banks – Arthur Grenfell, for example – often with the previous imprimatur of one of the bond houses. In Australia government loans supported the transfers of railway finance. Both the colonial and Anglo-Australian banks had London offices, and the banks used those offices as a conduit to transfer a substantial volume of private funds between Britain and Australia. In addition both the pastoral companies and the

---

[1096] Hall, *The Stock Exchange of Melbourne*, pp. 215–16. Earlier the governments had been able to float loans on the domestic market. "P.N. Lamb refers to the decade between 1869 and 1878 as a period of limited overseas borrowing. During this time the relative importance of the local market, as compared with the London market, increased. Receipts from the sales in London amounted to £3,896,000 as compared with £2,568,000 raised from local sources." Salsbury and Sweeny, *The Bull, The Bear*, p. 63. Between 1878 and 1883, however, the domestic market had all but disappeared.

[1097] Ian M. Drummond and Neil Quigley, "Debt and the Dominion Government, 1914–1920," paper presented at the Economic History Workshop, University of Toronto, December 7, 1992.

land mortgage banks marketed their securities directly to savers in England and Scotland. "As a consequence, Sydney and Melbourne saw no nineteenth century counterparts of Philadelphia's Jay Cooke & Co. or New York's Winslow, Lanier & Co., J.P. Morgan, or Henry Villard"; that is, there were no second- or third-generation investment banks to direct the flow of domestic savings toward local commerce and industry. In fact, "merchant banks, or investment banks as they are often called in America, did not appear until after the *Second* World War."[1098]

The absence of investment banking is reflected in W.D. Rubenstein's study of New South Wales' wealth holders. "A most striking feature of the New South Wales wealth structure is the absence of financiers. In Britain, bankers – the Barclays, Hoares, Martines, Rothschilds, Barings and others – were probably the largest group in the business wealth structure, and the importance of financial magnates in America is well known. The few New South Wales bankers who amassed large fortunes were, for the most part, managers or professional bankers rather than asset owning dynasts."[1099]

Despite the demise of the market for governments, private firms did float some security issues. The primary market was, however, much more informal than its American and Canadian counterparts. Well-established firms dealt directly with the banks, and those that were too small or too risky to appeal to the bankers turned first to the local stockbrokers. In New South Wales, for example, in the 1860s Sydney stockbrokers had begun to purchase government bonds for resale to local investors. The transition from public to private debt was a relatively simple matter, and within a few years brokers had begun to function as company promoters. In the New South Wales copper boom of 1872, for example, some £400–500,000 was raised on the Sydney share market.[1100] In Melbourne, beginning in 1881, there was a marked increase in the supply of "investment – that is, private non-mining – shares"; and that increase may provide "one reason why the decay of the bond market passed almost unnoticed." The increase was in part the result of existing private firms converting to public companies and offering some of their shares on the market (the Melbourne Brewing and Malting Company, Terry's West End Brewery, and the Trustees Executive and Agency Company, to cite three examples), some amalgamations and incorporations in the pastoral

---

[1098] Salsbury and Sweeny, *The Bull, The Bear*, p. 55.
[1099] W.D. Rubenstein, "The Top Wealth-Holders in New South Wales, 1817–1939," *Australian Economic History Review*, Vol. XX, No. 2 (September 1980), pp. 149–51.
[1100] Salsbury and Sweeny, *The Bull, The Bear*, p. 75.

finance industry (the amalgamation of the Australian Agency and Banking Corporation with the private firm of Richard Goldsborough), and the creation of two new trading banks.[1101] Overall, then, the new issues market grew slowly. A small market for "industrials" had emerged in both Melbourne and Sydney; it consisted largely of the issues of banks, gas companies, shipping companies, and breweries. David Merrett argues that "the list grew slowly before WWI as Australian businesses were slow to incorporate and even slower to take advantage of listing on an exchange to raise new equity. Firms continued to finance their day to day operations and their longer term expansion using a combination of their own financial resources and short term debt from banks and trade creditors."[1102] It appears likely, however, that Merrett is observing the weakness of the domestic institutional structure rather than entrepreneurial failure.

Between 1865 and 1884 there were, however, some institutional innovations in the primary markets for private securities. Of particular significance was the increased importance of the role of the broker "in the process of raising funds for borrowers who found it necessary to make use of the facilities of the stock and share market." In the early 1860s brokers' names first appeared on some company prospectuses, but they apparently functioned simply as agents.[1103] By 1865, however, their "names began to figure prominently on prospectuses, they acted as agents for accepting subscriptions in the new companies, and they appear to have accepted responsibility for a good deal of the secretarial work necessary in the initial stages of the life of a new company." At least by the early 1880s, if not before, the brokers had assumed even more responsibility for the placement of shares on the market; but there is no evidence that they were in a position to underwrite these investment issues.

A market structure was gradually evolving; but the central role of the brokers also engendered problems of moral hazard, since at the same time the broker could act as an agent for the public for the purchase of shares, "he could buy shares for himself and sell those shares to other brokers or to members of the public directly, and he could launch new companies for which he was paid in promoter's shares." The risk of a conflict between the broker and his client was enormous.[1104]

[1101] Hall, *The Stock Exchange of Melbourne*, p. 95.

[1102] Merrett, "Capital Formation and Capital Markets," p. 4.

[1103] Hall, *The Stock Exchange of Melbourne*, pp. 106–7.

[1104] Salsbury and Sweeny, *The Bull, The Bear*, pp. 55, 58, 64, 109–10. Hall, *The Stock Exchange of Melbourne*, pp. 44–45, 106–7.

Nor were the stockbrokers the only players in the Australian new issues market. By the mid-1880s stockbrokers in Victoria began to face strong competition from firms such as the Mercantile Finance Trustees and Agency Company and the Australian Financial Agency and Guarantee Company – firms that "tended to set the pace as promoters and 'issuing houses.' It was firms such as these which took the initiative in converting a number of established businesses into listed companies."[1105] Even those companies did not complete the list of competitive institutions. Although Melbourne and Sydney brokers participated in a majority of issues, both shares and debentures also found their way to market by other routes: by auction or by direct offer through the offices of the vendor company, to cite two examples. In Australia even by 1914 there were still no clear-cut channels to move new issues into the hands of the public; the new issues market remained very primitive and unstructured. Nor were the problems quickly overcome. Merrett, for example, somewhat optimistically concludes that "the domestic stock exchanges, comprising a small number of brokering firms whose partners operated with minimal capital resources and unlimited liability, managed to meet, and underwrite, the modestly expanding demands of the new issues market in the inter-war years."[1106] Again, however, there is a potential identification problem.

Throughout the period "Australian brokers were primarily brokers and not issue houses." The markets for new issues "were too thin to permit the acquisition of any considerable quantity of securities at any one time, or to permit the gradual feeding-in of a new issue; neither purchases nor large scale sales could occur without pushing price sharply up or down." Hence, investment banking on the British or American model could not really function. The brokers had taken on the task of providing a large share of the primary securities markets not because they saw it as a potential growth industry, but "because there was no one else ready to assume it – and because it fitted well with their large business in mining shares."[1107]

After the crisis of the 1890s, the domestic markets did begin to develop, but the pace was very gradual. First, a market for government bonds began to emerge. In Victoria the largest beneficiary of the new market was initially the Melbourne and Metropolitan Board of Works. Between 1893 and 1900 that authority floated bonds totaling £3,650,000 in Melbourne, and it was out of the market in only two of the seven

---

[1105] Hall, *The Stock Exchange of Melbourne*, p. 189.
[1106] Merrett, "Capital Formation and Capital Markets," p. 4.
[1107] Drummond, *Capital Markets*, pp. 192, 199.

years.[1108] The British continued to supply the bulk of state and Federation funds, but by 1914 the domestic market accounted for about one-third of the total.[1109] One might have thought that the reemergence of the market for public issues benefited from the public's suspicion of the trading banks – a suspicion that had been awakened by the widespread suspensions in 1891 and 1892 – and, for public issues, it did. Public issues were one thing, private issues another. The public's suspicion of private financial institutions carried over to the private sector in general. Those suspicions were shared by both the owners of local private enterprises who might have previously contemplated going public and by the savers who were equally suspicious of those owners. As late as 1900 very little private capital was financed through the stock exchanges.[1110]

The government had found a home. Although it took time, their issues were ultimately marketed through the local stock exchanges; however, the newly resuscitated new issues market remained to a large extent "an engine for providing long-term state loans." The rebirth of the primary market for government securities did not lead directly to more developed markets. In the case of New South Wales, "in the beginning, the politicians and treasury bureaucrats did not take the stock exchange seriously." In 1892 the members of the stock exchanges demanded a half a percent commission and a monopoly on government flotations. Ultimately, after a prolonged battle, the colonial treasurer agreed to a one-quarter percent commission, but no monopoly.[1111] Over the next five years almost all of the government issues (about 95 percent) were allotted to clients of members of the Melbourne Stock Exchange. The brokers received their one-half percent commission, but tensions remained.[1112]

In New South Wales and Victoria the governments initially saw little need for brokers. Clients could buy directly from the government; and, given the depression, the governments recognized that the brokers would sell state securities to their clients regardless of whether a commission had been paid on the initial sale. In Queensland and Western Australia, colonies with no ready access to the capital markets in Melbourne and Sydney, however, the governments recognized that

---

[1108] Hall, *The Stock Exchange of Melbourne*, p. 218.
[1109] "In 1904, Australian governments raised £39,582,000 at home. This was 17.38 percent of government loan risings in that year. Nine years later, in 1913, local borrowings were a record £90,077,000 which was 30.59 percent of the total Australian government borrowing." Salsbury and Sweeny, *The Bull, The Bear*, p. 176.
[1110] Hall, *The Stock Exchange of Melbourne*, pp. 232–33.
[1111] Salsbury and Sweeny, *The Bull, The Bear*, pp. 208–9.
[1112] Hall, *The Stock Exchange of Melbourne*, pp. 218–19.

employing brokers to intermediate increased an issue's marketability. Those governments began to work closely with the stock exchanges. In 1903, for example, both governments offered recognized brokers a one-half percent commission.[1113] Even in Melbourne, although the exchange "had not gained full acceptance of the conditions under which it wished the local bond market to operate, it had nevertheless advanced a long way towards the situation envisioned by the Chairman in 1893 when he expressed the hope that 'the Exchange will become in the future the recognized medium for the flotation of all Government and Municipal loans.' "[1114]

The primary market for private securities also began to emerge after the turn of the century, but it developed much more slowly. In New South Wales, for example, in 1900 ninety-three new limited companies with a nominal capital of £1,836,700 were promoted by brokers and registered on the stock exchange; in 1903 the figures were 154 and almost £5 million. New company promotions slowed over the next eight years, but in 1910 there was a second surge of promotions – 330 firms with nominal capital of nearly £7 million – a surge that reached a pre-war peak two years later when 428 firms with a nominal capital of almost £14 million were registered. "Some of the new companies were long-established family concerns going public, while others were attempts to raise money to underwrite new technologies."[1115] On closer examination, however, the development seems to have been more apparent than real. Over the two decades 1895 to 1914, the most striking characteristic of the Australian primary capital market was the low ratio of private to public issues. "The growth in the public debt was more than six times as great as the flow of new issues to the private sector."[1116]

Moreover, despite the emergence of the market for government securities and, after 1900, some increase in the volume of private issues, there were few institutional innovations designed to ease the marketing of those issues. The private market was still too thin to support investment banks of the Anglo-American variety, and in nineteenth-century Australia underwriting was almost unknown.

There were, however, after the turn of the century, a number of stock-broking firms either located in, or with agents in, London that dealt in Australian, particularly mining, securities. For example, the Melbourne firm of E.L. & C. Baillieu had been involved in both stockbroking in

[1113] Salsbury and Sweeny, *The Bull, The Bear*, pp. 208–9.
[1114] Hall, *The Stock Exchange of Melbourne*, p. 220.
[1115] Salsbury and Sweeny, *The Bull, The Bear*, p. 178.
[1116] Drummond, *Capital Markets*, p. 171.

Melbourne (they tended to specialize in mining shares) and in arbitraging bills of exchange between the London and Melbourne markets. The latter activity led to them appointing a London agent in 1897, and that agent not only dealt in bills but also began to sell shares in Australian mines to investors in Britain. The latter activity became sufficiently profitable that in 1902 one of the brothers (Prince Baillieu) "resigned from the Stock Exchange of Melbourne and transferred to London to become a member of the world's largest stock exchange." Again, in 1899 Lionel Robinson, an Australian share broker, moved to London and became a member of the London Stock Exchange. "In 1902 Robinson was joined in London by William Clark and the partnership was registered as Lionel Robinson, Clark & Co." The firm specialized "in buying and selling Australian stocks, especially in the very active mining section of the market." They were "also drawn into the options market and began to derive a substantial income from agency work on behalf of Australian stockbrokers." "In a remarkably short time the firm of Lionel Robinson, Clark & Co. was being transformed from a purely speculative sharebroking firm into a finance house specializing in mining, business and offering a wide range of services to clients."[1117] Thus, in mining, private institutions remained to link the London and Australian markets, but those channels were largely limited to mining enterprises.

The colonial governments had their stocks underwritten by English or continental investment bankers or through the auspices of Australian banks with London offices.[1118] Underwriting was first introduced in Australia with the Metropolitan Board of Works loan in 1898. The next year J.B. Were and Son and William Noall and Son were joint underwriters for the preference share issue of the Dunlop Pneumatic Tyre Company; and in 1914 Broken Hill Proprietary arranged underwriting for a £600,000 issue of debentures to be used to help finance their Newcastle steelworks. Some idea of the level of development is captured in the public response to the latter flotation; the size of the issue was reported to have been "unprecedented on the Australian continent." Moreover, successful underwriting of the issue required the services of both the government-owned Commonwealth Bank and four stockbroking firms.[1119] Full development, even of these relatively informal practices, did not occur until much later. Until the 1950s underwriting continued to be

---

[1117] Peter Richardson, "Collins House Financiers," in R.T. Appleyard and C.B. Schedvin, *Australian Financiers: Biographical Essays* (Melbourne: Federal Reserve Bank of Australia, 1988), pp. 231–33.

[1118] Salsbury and Sweeny, *The Bull, The Bear*, p. 213.

[1119] Salsbury and Sweeny, *The Bull, The Bear*, p. 213.

carried out on a case-by-case basis by individuals or consortiums of brokers and not by specialized investment banks.[1120] The primary market remained very undeveloped. For example, between 1899 and 1914 the paid-up capital of Australian joint-stock companies increased from about £100 million to £178 million; over the same period the public issues of Australian companies totaled only about £10.5 million, less than 15 percent of the total. Clearly, the private sector did not rely heavily on external finance.[1121] The absence of specialized investment houses was certainly a reflection of the unavailability of external corporate finance; but it was a symptom, not a cause.[1122]

What then were the causes? The Australian railroads were national-ized, and thus there was no need for investment banks to intermediate their issues in order to overcome problems of asymmetric information and moral hazard. Such intermediation had been needed in the United States. Similarly, the Australians had developed strong state but weak local governments.[1123] The states assumed many of the investment func-tions that in the United States and Canada were in the domain of local governments; and, in those cases where the investments were made by local governments, the states often guaranteed the debts. In Canada, where municipal governments borrowed far more than the Dominion or Provincial governments, the bond houses were in a position to exploit the economies of scale inherent in supplying information about the rel-ative credit worthiness of such cities as Saskatoon, Regina, and Calgary. In Australia, however, because the local governments' needs for unguar-anteed loanable funds was not great, the supply of such securities was small. As a result, the largest potential customers – the institutional investors (trust companies and insurance companies) – recognized that, since there were few economies of scale to be realized, there was no advantage in employing a specialist institution to provide information or to aid in accessing the existing supply of municipal debentures. Instead, they acquired what municipals they wanted through private placement. Gradually, "a few pale shadows of the Canadian bond houses" emerged, brokers who specialized in small municipal issues from remote munici-palities, particularly towns in Western Australia. The bond issues of these cities were both few in number and small in size. The total sales of the

[1120] Hall. *The Stock Exchange of Melbourne*, p. 237.
[1121] Drummond, *Capital Markets*, p. 172.
[1122] Drummond, *Capital Markets*, pp. 242–43.
[1123] B.U. Ratchford, *Public Expenditures in Australia*, Duke University Common-wealth Studies Center, Publication No. 11 (Durham, N.C.: Duke University Press, 1959), p. 15.

embryo bond houses were small; and their sales never provided either the financial or the client base to support an expansion of their activities into private commercial and industrial issues.[1124]

Initially the Australian banks had "spread their wings into capital market activities because there were no local equivalents of merchant banks. Consortiums of Australian banks had acted as agents to raise loans for colonial governments in London since the 1860s."[1125] It would seem to have been natural for an investment banking institutional structure to have developed. Having earned a reputation and developed a clientele in their role as the investment bankers for the colonies, the Australian banks should have been able to use that reputation and client list to provide information and underwrite sales of private Australian firms in London. They then could have used their international reputations to provide signals for domestic savers. Two factors combined to thwart this form of institutional innovation. First, because of their very large demands for London funds, the states stopped using domestic banks as British agents and turned to the Bank of England and to the London and Westminster. Second, "the loss of reputation by Australian borrowers in the London market in the early 1890s, and the subsequent downgrading of credit ratings, set in train a series of developments which were to transform local credit markets. Australian borrowers in the London market came to rely on British intermediaries, so ending the investment banking function undertaken in the late nineteenth century by the Australian banks." In Australia commercial banking and investment banking were effectively separated, and investment banks ceased to exist.[1126]

5–4d(2). The secondary market for securities: What was true for the primary market was equally true for the secondary. By British, or even American, standards the formal Canadian exchanges were both younger and smaller; by Australian standards they were both older and larger. In Australia mining shares aside – "almost throughout the nineteenth century mining shares provided the bread-and-butter business of Australian stockbrokers" – the formal securities markets played an even smaller role in the capital mobilization process than they had in Canada.[1127] In London and the provinces exchange activity revolved around the trading of British, colonial, and foreign governments and, to a lesser extent, railroad securities. "In the United States, the railroads

---

[1124] Drummond, *Capital Markets*, pp. 142–43, 152–53.
[1125] Merrett, "Banking and Finance," p. 6.
[1126] Merrett, "Capital Formation and Capital Markets," p. 2.
[1127] Hall, *The Stock Exchange of Melbourne*, p. 199.

provided the impetus for the growth of Wall Street and other subsidiary share markets." Throughout the half century leading up to World War I there were no shortages of government or railroad issues in London or of railroad issues in the United States, and the exchanges flourished. In Australia no "counterpart arose because trading there was confined largely to financial institutions, insurance companies, some industrials, and mining." In fact, mining remained both the bellwether and the lynch-pin of the Melbourne and Sydney share markets. "When rich mineral deposits were discovered and developed the market boomed and the number of brokers soared. When mining collapsed, the market con-tracted and the number of brokerage firms diminished."[1128]

In commenting on the Australian exchanges in 1964, E.L. Grimwood wrote, "Since, with the exception of the Stock Exchange of Adelaide, Limited (South Australia) incorporated in 1887 and the Hobart Stock Exchange (Tasmania) incorporated under special Act of Parliament in 1891, the other exchanges are mere voluntary associations of brokers, official dating is difficult." Although most operated loosely in the earlier years, "the 'official' dates of 'origin' are as follows": Brisbane Stock Exchange (Queensland) in 1885, the Stock Exchange of Perth (Western Australia) in 1889, Sydney (New South Wales) in 1872 "when a body known as the Associated brokers moved from Grenville's Rooms to the Sydney Stock Exchange (now the Royal Exchange) and took the name of the 'Sydney Stock Exchange,' and the Melbourne in 1884. Previously there had been several rival stock exchanges in Melbourne that differed mainly on the question of whether brokers should advertise their trans-actions in the daily press. The differences led in 1884 to the formation of the Stock Exchange of Melbourne, a body which has been in continuous existence for eighty years."[1129]

Even these tentative "official" datings are, however, really the product of hindsight. "In Sydney, for example, which had four different exchanges operating in 1890, it was still unclear which would triumph, although the Sydney Stock Exchange was the leader. Melbourne was even more chaotic, it was not until 1884 that the Stock Exchange of Melbourne was founded and, even at that late date, it had rivals."[1130] By 1895, however, there were organized securities markets in all the Australian capitals. The markets in Brisbane, Hobart, and Perth were both small and unimpor-

---

[1128] Salsbury and Sweeny, *The Bull, The Bear*, pp. 125–26.

[1129] E.L. Grimwood, "Australia," in David E. Spray (ed.), *The Principal Stock Exchanges of the World: Their Operation, Structure and Development* (Washing-ton D.C.: International Economic Publishers, 1964), pp. 352–54 [Hereafter cited as Grimwood, "Australia."]

[1130] Salsbury and Sweeny, *The Bull, The Bear*, pp. 195–98.

tant; Adelaide was somewhat more developed; but "in Sydney and especially in Melbourne the exchanges were reasonably active and fairly highly organized on the London model."[1131] Since data on transactions and turnover were never recorded in either Melbourne or Sydney, it is not possible to come to a categorical conclusion about their relative importance, "but it would nevertheless appear that the frequent contemporary comments in Melbourne sources towards the end of the 1880's to the effect that Melbourne had become the financial center of Australia are justified."[1132]

The Melbourne market traces its origins back to the 1850s. Melbourne's first broker was apparently Edward Khull, who published the city's first stock and share list in the *Argus* on October 18, 1852. Although there are questions about the actual size of the share market, the publication of the list – it continued to be published at regular intervals – is taken as the "first clear sign that the market in shares, as distinct from *ad hoc* sales, was beginning to take shape."[1133] By the end of the decade the increase in the number of brokers and in the volume of transactions made it evident that there was a need for more organized methods of conducting operations. At the beginning of 1859 there were eighteen firms on the "official" list; by the end of the year, with the addition of many mines (the product of that year's mining boom), the number had increased to forty-two; and, within a year, it had risen to almost sixty, by which time there were at least ten specialized brokerage houses operating in the city, and their members combined to start a weekly publication, *The Stock and Share Journal*. Although the journal ceased publication in April 1861, the Melbourne stockbroking community "formed what some writers have referred to as an exchange," and the members of that exchange provided the *Age* with a daily official price list. The year 1861 marks the first proto-exchange; however, the first more permanent market dates from 1865, when the Stock Exchange of Melbourne was organized; the name was soon changed to The Melbourne Stock Exchange. At that time, and for at least two decades to come, the primary business of the Exchange was in gold mining shares.[1134] The

---

[1131] Drummond, *Capital Markets*, p. 33.

[1132] Hall, *The Stock Exchange of Melbourne*, p. 197.

[1133] Hall, *The Stock Exchange of Melbourne*, p. 3.

[1134] The original 1852 list contained the names of fourteen companies, but two were British banks whose owners lived, almost entirely, in that country. The joint publication was a product of a meeting of the brokers who were concerned about "the erroneous quotations in the share lists before the public and the dissatisfaction so frequently expressed as to the manner in which business is done." Hall, *The Stock Exchange of Melbourne*, pp. 3, 22–23, 26, 33, 44–45. Salsbury and Sweeny, *The Bull, The Bear*, pp. 24, 26.

Exchange remained, until about 1880, a relatively small institution focusing on mining issues; in the early years, it was often overshadowed by provincial exchanges in such major cities as Ballarat and Bendigo.[1135] Its importance in those early years is captured in two reports on activities in the exchange that appeared in the local newspaper's commercial intelligence column in March 1874. "Scarcely any business done on this market today, the attraction of the All England-Victoria cricket match causing an early exodus from under the Verandah"; and, less than a week later, "There was scarcely even an attempt at business in this market this morning, and about noon there was a general departure for the cricket ground to share or witness a match between the brokers and brokers' clerks."[1136]

Gradually, however, the state's securities markets began to concentrate in the city. Melbourne dealt with the shares of mines in all of the gold towns, and, as a result, the exchange tended to reflect average performance and was less subject to violent fluctuations. The city was the largest in the state, and much of the state's wealth was concentrated there. Those two factors combined to produce a larger and more diverse clientele than the provincial centers. Finally, "the growth of the communications system, both railways and telegraphs, its increased efficiency and centralization in Melbourne, cheapened travel, reduced the cost of requiring reliable information, and lowered share transaction costs."[1137]

In its early years the Melbourne Exchange's business was largely centered on Victorian gold. As time passed, its focus gradually expanded. In 1868, for the first time since the previous decade, "investment" securities (the term then used to designate all non-mining private issues) actually produced almost as much income for the city's brokers as did the mines. The situation did not last, but it was indicative of future trends. Even within the mining list, the geographic focus expanded to include non-gold, non-Victorian mines, and mines in both New South Wales and Tasmania were the beneficiaries. In September 1887, the end of the first year for which we have data on new listings, the firms added to the official list included seventeen "investment" companies and seventy-five

---

[1135] Hall, *The Stock Exchange of Melbourne*, pp. 48, 59–60.

[1136] "From 1862 to 1880 the call room was situated in the Hall of Commerce, in Collins Street. It was not here, however, but under the verandah of this building that a good deal of Melbourne's share transactions too place. So much was this so that for many years it was customary to speak not of the stock exchange but of business 'under the Verandah.'" The newspaper was the *Argus*. Hall, *The Stock Exchange of Melbourne*, pp. 102, 109.

[1137] Hall, *The Stock Exchange of Melbourne*, p. 60.

mines: sixty-one gold, eleven silver, and three tin. Moreover, in the years after 1880, and particularly between 1885 and 1893, the relative importance of "investment" securities increased. In part the shift was a consequence of a continuing decline in the volume of gold-mining shares, but in part it reflected an increase in the level of transactions in the issues of firms that had been transformed from partnerships into corporations and whose shares had become available to the public. Trade in mining, however, remained an important part of the business done on the Exchange. Although the state's gold mines were gradually worked out, the Melbourne Stock Exchange benefited greatly from the discoveries of silver in Broken Hill in the late 1880s and copper at Mount Lyall, Tasmania, a decade later. Finally, as evidence of the expanding scope of the exchange's activities, in May 1883 the Melbourne firm of Clarke & Co. opened a branch managed by a resident partner in Sydney.[1138]

Between 1865 and 1889 the number of private companies listed on the Melbourne exchange increased from 158 to 231, before declining to 130 in 1900. Over the same period the value of all listed public and private securities increased from £10.2 to £80 million before declining to £65.1 million. Of the private firms, the number of non-mining enterprises increased from twenty-five in 1860 to 153 in 1889, before declining to sixty-eight in 1900. The number of listed mines declined fairly steadily from 133 in 1860 to sixty-two at the turn of the century. In terms of value, the public sector averaged slightly more than 11 percent of the total between 1865 and 1884, declined to less than 3 percent in 1889, and then rose to more than 15 percent in 1900. Mines accounted for more than 35 percent of the total in 1860, but their share had declined to less than one-third of that figure by the mid-1880s. New silver and copper discoveries led to a doubling of that share by 1889 and to a second doubling by 1900. Finally, the value of private non-mining securities accounted for 55 percent of the total in 1860 and for 83 percent in 1884; but that figure had fallen to 44 percent by 1900 (see Table 5:4-8).[1139]

These figures suggest a market that by the mid-1880s was providing strong secondary support for the private non-mining sectors, but that conclusion should be taken with a grain of salt. "Other Banks" (those with head offices outside Melbourne) accounted for 50 percent of the total listings in 1884, and they still represented almost one-quarter in 1889. Those banks were primarily owned, and their shares traded in the other colonies and in Great Britain. The "Debentures" (5 percent in 1884

[1138] Hall, *The Stock Exchange of Melbourne*, pp. 67, 98–99, 134, 137–38, 199. Blainey, *The Rush That Never Ended*, p. 223.

[1139] Hall, *The Stock Exchange of Melbourne*, tables 4, 11, and 12, pp. 58, 169, and 184.

Table 5:4-8. *Market value of stocks and shares listed on the Melbourne Stock Exchange, 1865–1900 (thousands of U.K. pounds)*

Class of Securities	1865	1870	1877	1884	1889	1900
Public						
Victorian government	988	1,371	2,314	1,957	1,478	2,798
Other Australasian governments	50	56	0	0	0	0
Local government	0	116	328	791	861	3,560
Semi-government	0	0	0	0	0	3,472
Total Public	1,038	1,543	2,642	2,748	2,339	9,830
Private						
Company debentures	243	490	625	1,539	11,578	4,561
Preference shares	0	0	0	0	653	3,075
Ordinary shares						
Melbourne banks	1,920	2,442	3,689	4,711	9,328	1,838
Other banks	2,100	1,810	15,100	16,288	17,439	10,290
Insurance	401	463	448	770	856	476
Other finance	0	196	207	695	5,554	643
Building societies	0	0	0	0	2,143	124
Pastoral	0	0	0	430	3,831	1,400
Gas companies	312	456	658	1,385	2,446	1,836
Breweries	0	0	0	333	2,502	954
Manufacturing	0	48	139	111	1,394	990
Trade	0	6	0	129	574	95
Railways	503	562	1,016	109	660	1,054
Other transport	0	0	101	408	2,855	1,010
Miscellaneous	62	36	47	98	122	466
Total nonmining ordinary shares	5,298	6,019	21,405	25,467	49,704	21,176
Base metals	0	0	0	0	0	10,185
Mining (Non-Victorian gold)	0	0	0	357	13,908	14,573
Victorian gold mines	3,626	1,716	2,093	2,470	1,775	1,667
Total ordinary shares	8,924	7,735	23,498	28,294	65,387	47,601
Total securities	10,205	9,768	26,765	32,581	79,957	65,067
Number of nonmining companies	25	32	43	62	153	68
Number of mining companies	133	118	106	93	78	62

Notes: Victorian Gold Mines in 1877 are by extrapolation between 1870 and 1884.

Source: A.R. Hall, *The Stock Exchange of Melbourne and the Victorian Economy*, (Canberra: ANU Press, 1968), Table 4, 11, & 12, pp. 58, 169, & 230.

and 15 percent in 1889) consisted mainly of the issues of pastoral land and finance companies that were sold and held in Britain; and the "Preference Shares" had been issued in London by a London-based firm.[1140] Moreover, listing did not imply that there was any substantial volume of

---

[1140] Hall, *The Stock Exchange of Melbourne*, p. 168.

transactions. Even during the years that the newly listed industrial shares outnumbered the new mining issues, mines continued to represent the vast majority of trades.[1141] Finally, the term *industrial* is also something of a misnomer. For example, of the thirty new "industrials" added to the list in calendar 1887, seventeen were financial companies of one type or another. Of the remainder, eight were existing breweries taking advantage of the euphoria spawned by the 25 percent dividend declared by the Castlemaine Brewery to capitalize their earnings at very attractive prices.[1142]

Still, the Melbourne Stock Exchange was Australia's largest and most important, and questions of its structure are important. At the time of its initial organization, in 1861, the brokers agreed to a set of rules based on those of the London and Liverpool exchanges but somewhat adapted to the local scene. These rules, sixty-three of them as published in *The Stock and Share Journal* of April 8, 1861, provided that control over activities of members of the Exchange be vested in a Committee of General Purposes (a distinct echo of the London Stock Exchange), outlined the procedures for admission to the Exchange, defined the function of brokers, jobbers, and subscribers, indicated the main procedures to be followed in buying and selling shares, provided for the treatment of defaulters and insolvents, announced the accepted scale of commissions, stated the conditions governing the issue of an official price list, and prescribed the hours of business and scale of entrance fees and annual subscriptions.[1143]

[1141] Between 1887 and 1900, the exchange added 1,426 firms to its list. Of those, 177 (14%) were industrials. Between 1887 and 1889, 442 new firms were added; of those, 134 (30%) were industrials. Over the rest of the period, however, of the 984 new listings, only 43 (4%) were not mines. From the point of view of market transactions, the figures are also misleading, because they "markedly understate the importance of the mining market. This is a consequence of the enormously greater turnover of mining securities as compared with 'investment' securities (the terms used in the market to describe non-mining securities). When turnover is taken into account, and it is this which is of prime importance to the broking community, it cannot be doubted that during these years (at least until the mid-1880's) the main business of the Melbourne share market took place in the mining section." Hall, *The Stock Exchange of Melbourne*, pp. 57–59 and appendix table 2, p. 242.

[1142] Hall, *The Stock Exchange of Melbourne*, p. 138. The promoters did not limit their brewery promotions to Victoria. Among the eight were the Swan Brewery (Perth), the Castlemaine and Quinlan Gray and Co. Ltd., both of Brisbane, and the Lion Brewery of Adelaide. p. 139.

[1143] The brokerage rates were those set in October 1860: On shares sold for £5 per share and upward, 1 percent; on shares sold for £1 and under £5, 1/per share; on shares sold for less than £1, 6d per share; on debentures, $\frac{1}{2}$ percent; on sales of

Three facets of these rules remained largely unchanged over the period. First, among the initial rules adopted was the choice of the "call system" for matching buying and selling orders, and this system was still in place a century later. The institution is a form of an auction in which each security is "called" in order. "On the occasion of each 'call,' buying and selling quotations are made by members of the Exchange assembled in the call room, and a sale is effected when the two quotations are brought together." "The strength of the system was that it provided for shares to be auctioned on the spot in full view of the brokers. Thus sellers got the true market price for their shares." In addition, at least once, and usually twice, a day (by 1886 there were three calls per day, except on Saturday), there was an opportunity for dealing with every share on the list, even those that were seldom traded.[1144]

Second, the share market was conducted in cash terms; that is, cash was paid for shares at the time they were delivered, and the normal sale was effected during three clear working days.[1145] Finally, the five members of the Committee of General Purposes were to be elected by the members of the Exchange; a proportion of the Committee was retired each year (the members were, however, eligible for reelection); and the Chairman and Deputy Chairman of the Exchange were, in turn, to be elected by the Committee.[1146]

In 1878, after almost two decades of experience, the sixty-odd rules adopted in 1861 were substantially modified and reduced to six. The change reflected a belated recognition of the fact that Melbourne was not, and was not likely to become, London. The rules still had the flavor of those that governed the London Stock Exchange, but they now clearly reflected the brokers' view of the minimum conditions required for the successful operation of a market for shares. If longevity can be taken as a measure of the success of an innovation, these rules were clearly successful. There was still a very close correspondence between the six rules and those that still governed the Exchange in the post–World War II era.

> Apart from the central rule that in all contracts between members they were to be held as principals to each other, which in effect guarantees that a transaction initiated by either a buyer or seller will be completed,

> 500 shares and upwards, the rates of brokerage may be reduced, by special agreement only, to not less than a minimum rate of 6d per share; when a brokerage at the above rates would not amount to 10/, that sum shall be charged. Hall, *The Stock Exchange of Melbourne*, pp. 26, 31–32.

[1144] Hall, *The Stock Exchange of Melbourne*, pp. 102, 137. Salsbury and Sweeny, *The Bull, The Bear*, pp. 140–41.

[1145] Hall, *The Stock Exchange of Melbourne*, p. 108.

[1146] Hall, *The Stock Exchange of Melbourne*, p. 184.

there were four basic definitions: the period within which the transaction was to be completed (three clear working days was to be allowed); the rights of purchasers; the rights of sellers; and the size of the "marketable parcel," the latter being the accepted minimum unit of volume in the securities market. The remaining rules specified the agreed rates of brokerage.[1147]

In two aspects of its micro-structure, the Melbourne Exchange differed from the London Stock Exchange. Listing was a much less formal requirement; in fact, throughout its life (1865–84), the "official list" of the Melbourne Stock Exchange was simply the list of shares called at its daily meetings. As long as the exchange faced competition, that is, as long as there was virtual freedom of entry to deal in stock market securities, there was no particular reason for firms to pay a listing fee to the Exchange. It was only when the management of the Stock Exchange could feel that its refusal to grant a quotation would carry some economic sanction that an official listing could become a signal of quality for prospective investors and, of more importance to the members, that the Exchange could charge for the service. It was not until some time after the Melbourne Stock Exchange had been replaced by the Stock Exchange of Melbourne – even in the late 1880's the Stock Exchange of Melbourne had not fully established its authority as *the* center for share trading – that those conditions were even partially met.[1148]

By 1890 the Exchange's position had changed sufficiently that the management was able to begin to conduct a stricter examination "of the *bona fides* of companies seeking inclusion on the official list." Over the next few years there was a gradual increase in the amount of

---

[1147] In investment shares the rates were to be the same as they had been since 1860. Rates on mining shares were approximately halved, "whereas the one rate of brokerage continued to be shared between buying and selling brokers of investment shares, in mining transactions the modern practice of separate payments of buying and sell brokerage had been adopted." Hall, *The Stock Exchange of Melbourne*, pp. 99–101.

[1148] In 1881 an increase in the Exchange's entrance fee to 50 guineas and a more stringent use of its balloting rules induced the entry of the Victorian Stock Exchange into the Melbourne market; and, three years later, a dispute over the "freedom of quotation in the newspaper press, or otherwise, by individual members or firms" induced the organization of the Stock Exchange of Melbourne, and that competitor underwrote the ultimate demise of the Melbourne Stock Exchange, although it remained a competitor for several years. The year 1888 saw the organization of both the Federal Stock Exchange Company Ltd. and the Public Stock Exchange Co. Ltd. The Australian Open Exchange Company was also a rival of the newly constituted Stock Exchange of Melbourne until its premises were destroyed by fire in 1891. Hall, *The Stock Exchange of Melbourne*, pp. 103–4, 173, 177–80, 186–87.

information required, and a gradual tightening up of formal conditions for listing. Progress was, however, slow. Even in 1891 when a by-law was proposed that would have meant "a radical improvement in the quantity and quality of information formally required from a company at the time of listing, the matter was simply referred to the Committee . . . this improvement in the formal listing requirements of the Exchange was not to be adopted for some years," although the Exchange did continue to move toward stricter listing requirements.[1149]

The second major source of difference in the micro-structure lay in the treatment of jobbers and brokers. As early as 1862 the question had been raised by those who believed that "brokers should operate solely as agents and never on their own account and those who believed that honest share dealing could be conducted by firms which sometimes acted as agents and sometimes dealt on their own account." Unlike the London Stock Exchange, there were no rules in Melbourne that prohibited a broker from buying and selling shares on his own account. Given the small volume of trades in all but gold mining shares that result is hardly surprising, and in that one category jobbing did emerge. As A.R. Hall wrote, "all that is necessary for the emergence of jobbers is that some individuals in the market should decide to specialize in share market operations to such an extent that the primary source of income becomes the margin between the price at which they buy and the price at which they sell shares on their own account." In periods of mining booms there tended to be few conflicts; but, when mining was experiencing one of its periodic slack periods, brokers were tempted to deal on their own account, and jobbers were often willing to earn a commission on purchases from, or sales to, the public. Until the turn of the century, conflicts continued; jobbers, unless they could qualify as brokers, could not become members of the exchange. With the opening of new quarters in 1891, however, the managers of the exchange permitted them, if they paid a fee and obtained a license, to attend and deal in the great hall. The conditions were further relaxed three years later. As the market recovered from the depths of the depression, the number of jobbers increased, to sixty-one in 1898; but the conflicts reemerged whenever the

---

[1149] In October 1891 the Chairman reported, "Your Committee considered during the year the question of having more strict supervision over the applications of Companies applying for quotation than had hitherto existed. Stringent requirements are now made in the forms of applications and the Committee carefully investigates them prior to their being submitted to the Members. Unless a Company can satisfactorily prove that it is a bona fide Coy no recommendation is made to the members for its quotation." Hall, *The Stock Exchange of Melbourne*, pp. 103–4, 167, 189–90.

volume of mining shares declined, as it did in the early years of the present century. The brokers still controlled the exchange. The rules banning undercutting on commissions were more strictly enforced, and there were few new mining discoveries. As a result jobbing became unprofitable; no new licenses were issued after 1908; and the last jobber disappeared from the Exchange in 1925.[1150]

The number of members that an exchange has and the prices that brokers are willing to pay for the right to join are the best measures of the fortunes and the importance of any stock exchange. Until the latter half of the 1880s, and the formation of the Stock Exchange of Melbourne, membership in the Melbourne Stock Exchange was small – "never more than forty and not more than twenty-five for two-thirds of its lifetime" – and, although it took an 80 percent vote of the membership to join, the membership charge was small. In 1880 there were twenty-two members, it cost only ten guineas to join, and the annual dues were only half that amount. The entrance fees were doubled in 1881, and they were increased by another five guineas in 1884. It wasn't until the Exchange was reorganized as the Stock Exchange of Melbourne, property rights in seats were created, and the Exchange began to dominate trading in Melbourne that membership began to increase and the price of a seat became a matter of some consequence. By 1884 membership had increased to sixty. The next year the entrance fee was increased to £100. In 1885 an additional fifteen seats were sold at prices ranging from £200 to £500. In 1887 there were twenty-seven more seats created, and the price had reached £1,000. In 1888 the Exchange added twenty seats; ten were sold at £1,250 and ten at £1,500. Between December of 1888 and the end of 1889, ten additional seats were sold: five at £1,650 and five at £2,000.

At that point the first effects of the onset of the depression began to be felt. Although the maximum number of seats was increased to 135 in 1891, four seats remained unsold; and for the next seventy years there were never more than 131 members. One of the new seats was sold for £2,500, but most changed hands at prices that ranged from £1,500 to £1,850. By 1892 the average price had fallen to about £1,000, by 1893 to between £350 and £500, and the next year to £200. As the economy recovered the prices again began to edge upwards, and by the turn of the century they again hovered around £1,000. It should be noted that it was almost seventy years before prospective members of the Exchange were again prepared to pay a real price for membership equal to that paid in 1891, and it was not until the second half of the twentieth century that

[1150] Hall, *The Stock Exchange of Melbourne*, pp. 27–29, 113, 172–73, 235–36.

the Exchange was again willing to increase its membership to more than 131.[1151]

Less information is available about the growth of the Sydney Stock Exchange, although it is clear that its development lagged behind its counterpart in Victoria.[1152] Initially the Sydney market focused on bank securities and industrial companies. In the early 1870s its emphasis shifted from share trading to floating mining companies. "By September 1872 the *Herald* noted that 'the greater part of 400 or 500 mining companies have been brought to the public through their means.'"[1153] Furthermore this pattern, although somewhat modified, appears to have been maintained throughout the century. On January 2, 1899, for example, the *Telegraph* calculated that the market value of all "investment" stocks that were listed on the exchange was only £23,381,200 – a figure that was less than the £23,467,250 value of the colony's leading silver mines nine years earlier.[1154]

Since the Sydney Stock Exchange was also a voluntary association of brokers, it is equally difficult to precisely date its birth. Continuous minutes of the Exchange's governing committee exist from March 1875, but fragmentary evidence places the initial organization in May 1871. The collapse of the copper mining boom in 1873 reduced the number and importance of the city's brokers and thus provided an opportunity for the Exchange to develop a formal set of rules to govern share trading in the city. Faced by three major problems – the need to develop regulations to protect brokers from one another, to shield both brokers and the public from faulty securities, and to insulate investors from the misdeeds and misfortunes of the members of the Exchange – the Exchange moved only gradually and tentatively.

The first set of rules was published in October 1872. Unlike the first rules adopted in Melbourne, "they owed little to London and much to local practice," and they addressed only a few issues.[1155] The rules established a governing body (the Standing Committee), provided procedures for selecting new members (the entrance fee was set at £5-5s), provided for a settlement procedure, set brokerage fees, and provided for the expulsion 'of any member found by the Committee to have been guilty of default or conduct unbecoming a member.'" Although they specified

---

[1151] Hall, *The Stock Exchange of Melbourne*, pp. 101, 137, 164, 167, 172–73, 180, 182–83, 193, 198, 222.

[1152] Salsbury and Sweeny, *The Bull, The Bear*, p. 24.

[1153] Salsbury and Sweeny, *The Bull, The Bear*, pp. 109–10.

[1154] Salsbury and Sweeny, *The Bull, The Bear*, p. 159.

[1155] Salsbury and Sweeny, *The Bull, The Bear*, pp. 118–19.

that there should be a meeting every day but Sunday, they said nothing about how the meeting was to be conducted; the call system was adopted much later. Initially, the chairman merely verified the business done, and a list signed by him was publicly posted. There was nothing in the original rules about listing requirements, nor was there a rule prohibiting brokers from buying and selling on their own account.[1156]

In 1876 the Exchange had still not adopted the call system. Given the fact that there were only a few transactions each week – "rare was the day when several took place" – it seemed unnecessary to have a formal meeting with the Chairman reading a long list of securities that no one was prepared to buy or sell. They did however, draw up a set of rules designed to ensure that the published quotations actually represented the business that had been done.[1157] It was thirteen years later before the Exchange began to move toward something akin to the call system that had operated in Melbourne for almost three decades. At that time it revised Rule 13 to read that, in the case of "investment stocks" at every meeting (now two each day and one on Saturday), a "list of sales and prices shall be made. The sales shall be those made since the last meeting." In the case of mining stocks, it added the requirement that "quotations of mining stock other than coal shall be only for sales made in the room." Since most of the Exchange's business was still in mining shares, this requirement centralized the bulk of the trading activity in the daily meetings "where it could be done under the watchful

---

[1156] "As regards the public, settlement was made 'with the Purchasers at the time of delivery of the Contract Note unless otherwise agreed. With Sellers on the day after the first Board day of the Company when the transfer has been, or may be assumed to have been, passed, and for debentures on the delivery of the Securities.' The settlement between members was to be made within twenty-four hours of the delivery of the Transfer, unless otherwise agreed." As to brokerage fees: "On all shares in Incorporated Registered Companies, on which consideration paid is over 25s per share, brokerage was one percent. On other share interests, the minimum brokerage was two and a half percent. The purchaser paid stamp duty and transfer fees." Salsbury and Sweeny, *The Bull, The Bear*, pp. 115–16, 103, 140–42.

[1157] Rule 11 (January 1875) required daily meetings (Saturday excepted), and it required the production of a list of bona fide sales and prices made between one meeting and another. Rule 12 was adopted in an attempt to stop false reporting. It read, "if any quotation of sale shall be challenged at the daily meeting of the Members, the Chairman of the day shall immediately accompany the Member whose quotation is doubted to his office, and there shall satisfy himself by examination of the Books and Papers of any such member as to the bonafides of the quotation, and shall report the result either to the Committee in the first instance, or direct to the Members at the daily meeting assembled." Salsbury and Sweeny, *The Bull, The Bear*, p. 142.

eyes of all the brokers. At the same time the responsibility of keeping a record of each transaction devolved from the brokerage firms to the Exchange itself, which kept a book in which was written the details of each sale."[1158]

In other dimensions institutional evolution was no more rapid. In the case of jobbing, the Exchange was never able to separate the broking and jobbing functions. "In freewheeling Sydney, a broker could perform three functions simultaneously. He could act as the traditional agent for the public for the purchase and sale of shares, he could buy shares for himself and sell those shares to other brokers or to the public directly, and he could launch new companies for which he was often paid in promoter's shares."[1159]

Somewhat more progress was made in the Exchange's attempts to "weed out" weak or fraudulent companies. Before World War I Australian company law placed the primary burden of corporation regulation in the hands of the stock exchanges, and the exchanges' main weapon in their effort to influence company behavior was the power to refuse a listing of a security.[1160] In 1876 the Exchange had begun to "remove those companies in which little or no business is doing." By 1879 the Committee routinely required companies seeking listing to provide a deed of settlement and a list of shareholders. Listing was only granted if the Committee felt that the shares were spread widely enough for them to be traded, and if it appeared that there was likely to be a minimum level of market activity. In addition, the deed of settlement was examined for objectionable features that might interfere with trading; for example, transfer fees and clauses that allowed the company to retain unclaimed dividends.[1161] The Committee soon discovered that it had the greatest leverage with mining companies: "developmental, non-dividend paying, and with promoters who desperately wanted to encourage trading in their shares." For other firms, however, their powers of persuasion were weak. Although they made continual attempts to use the threats of refusing to list or to delist in their attempts to influence company behavior, they were never more than slightly successful.[1162]

By 1890 the Governing Committee had developed a clear routine for admitting new firms to the list; however, they had made no attempt to adopt and disseminate a formal set of listing requirements. Perhaps they

[1158] Salsbury and Sweeny, *The Bull, The Bear*, p. 143.
[1159] Salsbury and Sweeny, *The Bull, The Bear*, p. 110.
[1160] Salsbury and Sweeny, *The Bull, The Bear*, p. 202.
[1161] Salsbury and Sweeny, *The Bull, The Bear*, p. 144.
[1162] Salsbury and Sweeny, *The Bull, The Bear*, pp. 144, 179.

were wise; the fallout from the crisis of the 1890s proved that the system was far from perfect. The experience was sufficient to convince the membership to adopt a formal application form to be completed by any company seeking a listing. The company was required to disclose its capital structure (distinguishing, for example, between vendor's shares and paid or subscribed funds) and cash position, and to provide a prospectus, a list of shareholders, and its articles of association. "If listed, the company agreed to provide free of charge its balance sheet and all periodical special reports, and give prompt notification of all calls, dividends, alterations of capital, and other material information." Mining companies were also required to telegraph all important operational results.[1163]

By the turn of the century the Sydney Exchange was finally in a position to exploit its monopoly position in the New South Wales securities market. In 1911 the members adopted a set of rules that would have been termed stringent had they been proposed in London. The rules regulated the applicant's prospectus, the firm was required to provide a précis of underwriting agreements and a statement of the relationship between directors and underwriters, life directorships were banned as were rules permitting the forfeiture of unclaimed dividends, and minimum rules for voting at company meetings were set out. Within the Exchange, a formal "sub-committee on listing" was established. The next year the requirements were further strengthened. Directors were not allowed to appoint their successors, company officers had to be elected by shareholders at well advertised open meetings, directors were required to disclose any personal interest that they might have in a contract or agreement entered into by their firm – the Exchange also attempted to stop them from voting on such matters – and listing was to be denied firms that allowed company directors to serve as company auditors.[1164]

In one other dimension the evolution of the Exchange's rules was equally slow. It was not until after the failures of the 1890s that the rules of the Exchange were rewritten to give the governing committee the power to complete all open transactions, including time bargains of a defaulting broker, and thus provide some protection to the public, while at the same time lessening the danger of a domino effect when the bankruptcy of one member led to the collapse of others.[1165] In terms of membership and its price, developments in the Sydney Exchange were also slower than in its counterpart in Melbourne. In 1897 the Exchange had

---

[1163] Salsbury and Sweeny, *The Bull, The Bear*, pp. 202–3.
[1164] Salsbury and Sweeny, *The Bull, The Bear*, pp. 202–7.
[1165] Salsbury and Sweeny, *The Bull, The Bear*, pp. 159, 182.

only forty-one members. Although the failure of many of the competing local exchanges encouraged fifty-two brokers to join between 1890 and 1910, in 1918 total membership was still only sixty-eight.[1166] Until 1881 the entrance fee remained at five Guineas; but in that year it was increased ten times. In the middle of the decade, the Broken Hill mining discoveries created an unprecedented demand for membership in the Exchange. In 1887 the entrance fee was increased to £210, the next year to £500, and, in November 1890, just before the economic collapse, it reached £1,000. In 1888 members were granted a property right in their seats. Over the second half of the 1890s, prices gradually rose from the depression-induced trough – some seats had been sold for less than £300 – seats were sold for £500 in 1896, and the price had reached £800 in 1898, before declining to the £500–600 range during the first decade of the present century. It was not until 1910 that the price again reached the 1890 level, but between 1911 and 1913 the Exchange created twenty new seats and sold them for £1,000 each.[1167]

There were also other signs that the nation's institutional structure was becoming more developed. By 1890 there were exchanges operating in Brisbane, Adelaide, Sydney, Hobart, Melbourne, and Perth. Although the Melbourne and Sydney exchanges concentrated largely on the public and private issues of their states, both had some pretensions of national or, perhaps, international, importance: New Zealand securities were listed in Melbourne, and a substantial business in mining stocks was done on British account in both exchanges. Moreover, if any Australian firm wished to float a substantial stock or bond issue, the firm usually found it useful to use the services of a Melbourne broker to make certain the new issue was truly intercolonial. In fact, "on numerous occasions the Melbourne brokers were wholly responsible for floating an intercolonial firm." In contrast, after the turn of the century Sydney was gradually becoming the center of a national market for government securities. Between 1900 and 1914 the exchange negotiated with both the Queensland and New Zealand governments and with the city of Freemantle, and provided advice on the issue of £250,000 in Western Australian inscribed stock.[1168]

The increasing stability of the structure was underscored by the emergence of something that, if not resembling a national securities market, at least suggested that four of the exchanges recognized each other's

[1166] Salsbury and Sweeny, *The Bull, The Bear*, pp. 82–83, 190, 241.
[1167] Salsbury and Sweeny, *The Bull, The Bear*, pp. 139, 189.
[1168] Hall, *The Stock Exchange of Melbourne*, p. 198. Drummond, *Capital Markets*, p. 33. Salsbury and Sweeny, *The Bull, The Bear*, pp. 176–77.

existence. From 1880 onwards, concerns over common problems produced a steadily increasing volume of correspondence between the several exchanges. Before the turn of the century, the individual exchanges were still too weak and divided to permit serious inter-exchange cooperation. By 1900 most of the weaker exchanges had been weeded out. In New South Wales, Queensland, South Australia, and Victoria – states that represented almost 90 percent of Australia's population – a single exchange dominated share-trading.[1169]

In 1903, faced with mounting problems common to all, officials of the four exchanges met and attempted to agree on a common set of policies regarding such matters as brokerage rates, the method for resolving disputes between members of the different exchanges, and a uniform listing policy. Some decisions were made at that time, but it was another decade before the four could agree on a uniform listing policy. Even then no effort was made to organize a single national securities market.[1170]

Despite the progress toward an efficiently operating secondary securities market, much time was to pass before the Australian formal securities markets could play an important role in the mobilization of either foreign or domestic savings. In the United States, the New York Stock Exchange as well as the Curb, the Consolidated, and a number of local exchanges dealt in a wide range of securities issues: common stock, preferred stock, mortgage bonds, and debentures. The larger part of the business of the Canadian exchanges was in ordinary shares, but they also dealt extensively in industrial bonds. In that effort they were supported by the bond houses – houses that not only provided a primary market but also served as an increasingly important secondary market. In Australia the exchanges did deal with the equity issues of local banks, pastoral companies, sugar refineries, breweries, textile mills, and steamship lines, but they seldom dealt in private debentures or bonds.

Moreover, as late as 1914, although many small companies were able to obtain a listing on one of the exchanges, even in Melbourne and Sydney the larger part of the lists consisted of shares that were infrequently traded – that were, in the vernacular of the industry, largely inactive. On both of those exchanges, transactions in private sector stocks were chiefly limited to ten or twelve issues. In fact, "the large majority

---

[1169] Salsbury and Sweeny, *The Bull, The Bear*, pp. 195–98. In 1911 the combined population of the four states was 3,976,656, 89.3 percent of the nation's 4,455,005 inhabitants.

[1170] Salsbury and Sweeny, *The Bull, The Bear*, pp. 195–98, 207. Hall, *The Stock Exchange of Melbourne*, pp. 237–38. Recent developments have, however, made Sydney the financial capital of Australia.

of local issues – both government and private – were equally illiquid. Weeks and months might pass between transactions – even in some government securities."[1171] Finally, in 1914 the directors of the Broken Hill Proprietary Company – a well-established and long profitable enterprise – required finance for their new steel mill. In the process of raising the required finance, they floated the largest issue that had ever been underwritten in Australia. Even then, however, they were forced to turn to the British market to float at least 40 percent of the more than £1 million in new shares and debentures.[1172]

5-5. **Institutional relations with the British capital market**

Britain was, for all intents and purposes, the only external supplier of capital to Australia in the years before World War I. In the nineteenth century countries that turned abroad for finance did not find themselves facing well-established international capital markets. Canada and Australia were both a part of the formal British Empire, but the institutional arrangements that emerged to link foreign lender to domestic borrower in the two countries were very different. As the data in Table 5:5-1 demonstrate, the routes into the British capital markets chosen by foreign and colonial borrowers were many and varied. Merchant banks were a channel for more than one-third of the total, but over time their importance was declining and that of British joint-stock banks increasing.

Over the course of the nineteenth century in both Canada and the United States, a diverse set of institutional links had evolved to tie governments and private firms to the British capital market. In Australia until the 1890s the links were at least as diverse and, on the surface, almost as strong. In Canada and the United States, a very large proportion of long-term British funds took the form either of portfolio or direct investment. In Australia investment largely took the form of both bank deposits and portfolio investment. Between 1884 and 1890, for example, when new private Australian issues on the London market totaled about £36 million, British deposits in Australian banks increased by £24 million.[1173] The 1880s were the period of peak British investment in Australian bank deposits; such investments were much less important before 1880 and after 1900. British deposits probably totaled less than £3 million in 1874, but they grew very rapidly thereafter. They reached £12 million

---

[1171] Drummond, *Capital Markets*, pp. 35–37.

[1172] Blainey, *The Rush That Never Ended*, pp. 274–75.

[1173] N. Butlin, *Investment in Australian Development*, pp. 160–62 and table 34. Hall, *The London Capital Market*, table 20, p. 115.

Table 5.5-1. *The proportion of oversea new issues introduced by the main types of issuing houses, 1870–1914*

	Official and semi-official agencies	Private banks*	Joint-stock banks	Overseas banks & agencies	Companies via their bankers	Other media•	Total amount issued £m
			Percentages				
1870–1874	1.8	53.0	4.4	9.6	18.2	13.0	390.6
1875–1879	14.5	36.5	0.8	24.7	13.0	10.5	149.2
1880–1884	6.7	38.5	3.3	14.1	26.7	10.7	355.3
1885–1889	9.9	43.7	5.3	7.5	26.1	7.5	479.2
1890–1894	10.4	46.4	9.0	8.8	19.6	5.8	349.6
1895–1899	8.7	25.1	11.2	20.3	25.2	9.5	359.6
1900–1904	27.4	19.2	17.8	14.4	16.7	4.5	258.2
1905–1909	10.3	32.7	12.2	22.4	18.7	3.7	509.9
1910–1914	8.3	35.2	17.4	18.8	17.5	2.8	783.8
1870–1914	9.8	37.2	10.3	15.4	20.5	6.8	
Total amount issued (£m)	355	1,354	371	562	746	248	3,636

Note: * That is, merchant bankers.

• Comprising: (a) investment trust, £23m. (b) Finance, land and property companies, £18m. (c) Special purpose syndicates £41m. (d) Issue house with Stock Exchange connections, £22m. (e) Companies as their own issuers, £13m, and (f) miscellaneous issuers, £131m.

Source: Based on a table published by A.R. Hall in *The London Capital Market and Australia 1870–1914*, (Canberra: The Australian National University, 1963).

in 1884 and surged to, perhaps, as much as almost £40 million by December 1891, before declining to about £14 million in June 1899. From then until 1914 they appear to have fluctuated between £14 and about £17 million, and in most years their volume was less than the Australian deposits in British banks. At their peak they may have represented as much as 40 percent of all deposits in Australian banks; and in 1893, at a time when all government and corporate bonds accounted for about 65 percent of the total of all British capital invested in Australia, deposits in trading banks represented 13 percent.[1174] These international deposits bypassed the formal British securities markets almost entirely; most were raised by direct solicitation of British savers.

Although London savers continued to contribute a significant proportion of the Australian deposits, the Scottish connection was particularly strong. One commentator writing in 1883 remarked that "Edinburgh seems honeycombed with agencies for collecting money not for use in Australia alone, but for India, Canada, South America, and everywhere almost, and for all purposes, on the security of pastoral and agricultural lands in Texas, California, Queensland, and Mexico."[1175] As an aside, it might be noted that it was not only individuals who chose to invest in the Australian pastoral sector: even English and Scottish insurance companies "found Australian bank deposits a convenient way of absorbing their surplus." The surplus was the product of the companies' demonstrated unwillingness to invest in stock-exchange securities, combined with the effects of the continued agricultural depression, a depression that had cut sharply into the supply of new mortgages, the Scottish insurance companies' traditional outlet for funds.[1176]

Between 1870 and 1914 about £339 million in Australian new issues passed through the London capital market. Of that total, government borrowing represented more than two-thirds. Of the less than one-third directed to the private sector, financial land and investment firms (including pastoral companies) accounted for one-third and mines for an additional two-fifths (see Table 5:5-2). The forty-five year averages, however, mask what are clearly three quite different periods of portfolio investment: the 1870s and 1880s, the 1890s, and the first years of the twentieth century.

[1174] Blainey, *Paper and Gold*, pp. 255–56. Jackson, *Australian Economic Development*, pp. 142–43. David Pope, "Free Banking in Australia Before World War I," the Australian National University, Working Papers in Economic History, No. 129, December 1989, pp. 15–16.

[1175] The quotation is from Baxter, *Banking in Australia* (London, 1883). It is cited in Baster, *The Imperial Banks*, p. 153.

[1176] Hall, *The London Capital Market*, p. 169.

Table 5:5-2. *Australian new issues in London*

Year	Banks	Financial land & investment	Mines	Other private companies	Total company issues	Government issues	Total Australian issues
				Panel A (thousands of U.K. pounds)			
1870–1889	2,813	21,829	8,378	5,329	38,349	119,228	157,577
1890–1899	0	10,824	26,352	9,615	46,791	45,068	91,859
1900–1914	3,725	1,531	10,694	6,348	22,298	66,879	89,177
1870–1914	6,538	34,184	45,424	21,292	107,438	231,175	338,613
				Panel B (thousands of U.K. pounds per year)			
1870–1889	141	1,091	419	266	1,917	5,961	7,879
1890–1899	0	1,082	2,635	962	4,679	4,507	9,186
1900–1914	248	102	713	423	1,487	4,459	5,945
1870–1914	145	760	1,009	473	2,388	5,137	7,525
				Panel C (percent of all Australian issues)			
1870–1889	1.8	13.9	5.3	3.4	24.3	75.7	100.0
1890–1899	0.0	11.8	28.7	10.5	50.9	49.1	100.0
1900–1914	4.2	1.7	12.0	7.1	25.0	75.0	100.0
1870–1914	1.9	10.1	13.4	6.3	31.7	68.3	100.0
				Panel D (percent of all company issues)			
1870–1889	7.3	56.9	21.8	13.9	100.0	310.9	410.9
1890–1899	0.0	23.1	56.3	20.5	100.0	96.3	196.3
1900–1914	16.7	6.9	48.0	28.5	100.0	299.9	399.9
1870–1914	6.1	31.8	42.3	19.8	100.0	215.2	315.2

Source: A.R. Hall, *The London Capital Market and Australia, Social Science Monograph* no. 21 (Canberra: The Australian National University, 1963), Table 15, p. 92.

In the first and last periods, the state governments dominated the Australian new issues on the London market: 76 percent in 1870–89 and 75 percent in 1900–14. The dominance was in part a reflection of political decisions within Australia, but it was also a reflection of the British saver's preference for channeling his resources into what he considered safe investments rather than into risk capital. The safety of the colonial consols had been reinforced in the late 1870s by the innovation of inscribed stock. Such stock, inscribed with the name of the purchaser, replaced the traditional debentures that, since they were essentially bearer bonds, had always presented security problems. With that innovation, and despite the fact that colonial stocks were not legally admitted to trustee status until 1900, the market for colonial government securities was greatly widened. Legally, or illegally, the innovation appears "to have brought trustee investors in large numbers into the market for colonial government stock."[1177]

The government's dominance in the first and last periods left relatively little room for the private sector. Private issues accounted for only one-quarter of the total. In the first period the private market was largely monopolized by the issues of the financial, land, and investment firms, although the nation's mines contributed a small, but significant, share. In the last period the financial, land, and development companies had largely disappeared, and mines drew almost one-half of the private total. In the depression decade the private sector accounted for slightly more than one-half of London issues, and that surge is almost entirely accounted for by a wave of new mining – largely Western Australian – flotations. Finally, it should be noted that the proportion of "other private companies" in the total, although even in the last period amounting to less than 10 percent, had doubled in both absolute volume and in its proportional share between the first and last periods.

Although the dominant role of government may have made the task of establishing institutional links to the private sector more difficult, it should not have been fatal. What made a bad situation worse was the fact that the British merchant banks had never secured a firm position in the market for Australian government issues. Barings had refused to undertake a government of Victoria issue in the mid-1850s; in 1869 Roth-

---

[1177] The Colonial Stock Act of 1877 permitted the colonial governments to issue inscribed stock – that is, securities, with the owner's name inscribed – as long as the prospectus included a statement to the effect that the United Kingdom was not responsible directly or indirectly for the loan concerned. The Colonial Stock Act of 1900 admitted colonial securities to trustee status. Hall, *The London Capital Market*, pp. 93, 95–96. N. Butlin, *Investment in Australian Development*, p. 350. N. Butlin, "Colonial Socialism," pp. 61–62.

schild's had combined with the Bank of New South Wales to offer an issue of that state's bonds; but after that date on only one occasion did a British merchant bank take part in an Australian government issue.[1178] In the United States the British merchant banks and their American partners were heavily involved in both government and railway finance. In Canada the British merchant banks also participated in a variety of railway flotations. Later they, and their younger siblings, moved into commercial and industrial finance as well. Arthur Grenfell in Britain and J.P. Morgan and Lehman Brothers in the United States are cases in point.

The commercial banks not the merchant banks provided the normal channel linking the British markets to the issues of the Australian governments. There were four principal parties involved in marketing Australian government loans: the London representative of the various governments (the Agents General, the High Commissioner, or the Crown Agents), the financial representatives of the governments, the brokers, and the jobbers. All played a role, but the financial representatives were the most important. They acted as agents, arranged for brokers to underwrite the issue, were responsible for advising the governments' representatives on market conditions, prices, and the appropriate date of issue, advertised the issue, received subscriptions, and paid the dividends.[1179] For example, Donald Lanarch, who in one capacity or another represented the Bank of New South Wales in London from 1854 until his death in 1896, in addition to helping float loans on the London market and making balances available to colonial treasurers in Australia, "floated loans for the New South Wales Government, and when debentures fell in price he arrested the decline by his own heavy purchases (from which it must be said he later gained). He also carefully managed the timing of government floats to reduce competition among issues, permitting governments cheaper accommodation."[1180]

Although New South Wales was somewhat late in employing a single financial representative, from the 1850s through the 1870s most of the states used the Anglo-colonial or colonial bank (or banks) that operated the government's accounts in Australia: the Bank of New South Wales for New South Wales and Tasmania, the Union Bank of Australia and later the Queensland National Bank for Queensland, the "Associated

---

[1178] Hall, *The London Capital Market*, p. 103. In 1910 Samuel Montague and Company was involved in an issue of the Bank of Adelaide.

[1179] The four-part classification was the result of a study by Theodore Schilling, *London als Anleihemarkt der englischen Kolonien*. It is summarized in Lavington, *The British Capital Market*, pp. 196–97. Hall, *The London Capital Market*, pp. 99–100.

[1180] Pope, "Bankers and Banking Business," pp. 22–23.

Banks" for Victoria, and the National Bank of Australasia for South Australia. Since Western Australia did not initially have representative government, its issues were, until 1890, handled by the Crown Agents.

In the mid-1880s, faced by the need for an increasing level of British funds, the colonies gradually replaced the Anglo-Australian banks with banks whose names had better recognition in the United Kingdom. As the issues became larger and more frequent, the colonial governments felt that they needed the prestige that surrounded such names as the Bank of England and the London and Westminster Bank. "To the ordinary investor their names would be a sufficient guarantee for the issue. Moreover, if the issues should strike trouble, they would be better able to meet it than the local banks." New South Wales in 1884 and Queensland in 1885 turned to the Bank of England; Victoria chose the London and Westminster in 1886, as did Tasmania at about the same time. "In 1905 New South Wales severed its twenty years' connection with the Bank of England and also transferred to the London and Westminster. By the end of the period, only South Australia still used the services of a local Australian bank. All of the others, with the exception of Queensland (Bank of England), used what was, by then, known as the London, County and Westminster."[1181]

After the crisis, the restoration of the state governments' financial standing in London "was due not only to 'sound finance' policies followed by the colonial treasurers, but by their use of the house of Nivison, a London stock broker, who came to control the applications of Australian governments to the London market." Although the colonial governments had ceased to use Australian banks as their London agents, Nivison helped to oil the wheels of the new system. As the agent for all governments, he helped eliminate the problem of competing issues. In addition, he "provided an underwriting service, which was far more successful than the previous system of having investors tender for issues."[1182]

Since the issues were government bonds, there were few problems of asymmetric information; and as a result there had never been a need for a second-generation Australian counterpart of the Bank of England or the London and Westminster. It is not clear what form institutional inno-

---

[1181] The Bank of New South Wales, for example, admitted that it had difficulty in placing £2 and £3 million loans in 1883; and the Bank of England refused to be responsible for the inscription of New South Wales stocks unless it was also allowed to issue them. Hall, *The London Capital Market*, pp. 103–4. Holder, *The Bank of New South Wales*, p. 360. For a review of early-twentieth-century developments see R.S. Gilbert, "London Financial Intermediaries and Australian Overseas Borrowing, 1900–29," *Australian Economic History Review*, Vol. 10, No. 1 (March 1971) pp. 39–47.

[1182] Merrett, "Capital Formation and Capital Markets," p. 11.

vation would have taken, if the Anglo-Australian banks had continued to be the colonial governments' financial representatives. It is clear, however, that, after the turn of the century, there was no counterpart of the merchant bank to link private Australian firms to the London capital market or to link Australian savers with Australian investors.

As the data indicate, before the 1890s it was the financial land and investment companies that drew the bulk – almost three-fifths – of the British finance that was channeled directly to the private sector. That industry was also the recipient of a substantial fraction of the indirect transfers, since it was a favorite of the banks that solicited British deposits. The importance of British investment to Australian pastoral industry dramatically increased in the 1870s, when British mortgage companies – companies like the Australian Mortgage Land and Finance Company Ltd. – were formed to channel British funds to Australia. Before the early 1880s most of these firms were pastoral land-mortgage companies, and by 1890 they had raised £20 to £25 million in Britain. By 1883, for example, five Scottish companies had a paid-up capital of £960,000 and debentures and deposits of £4,056,000; the five were only a small subset of the companies operating in Australia. After 1885 the rate of growth of the pastoral finance companies began to slow, and it was the urban land-mortgage companies that raised the majority of British funds during the second half of the decade.[1183]

"Most of the savings came from the small 'safe' British investors and one of the fascinating socio-economic aspects of the process of Australian rural development is in the transformation of a conservative British approach to foreign investment into highly venturesome undertakings which were the products of these savings in Australia."[1184] The explanation of this apparent change in attitudes of British savers, in general, and the Scottish saver, in particular, appears to lie in the distinction between uncertainty and risk. British savers had long since learned that, although ocean transport was risky, firms like the Cunard and the Royal Mail Line – firms that bundled ships and voyages – represented a form of insurance policy and that, although American rails were risky, a portfolio of American railroad bonds could provide a similar form of insurance. They also knew something of the past experience of banks and pastoral companies in the United Kingdom. Although the Overand-Gurney and the City of Glasgow Bank crises had affected

---

[1183] The ten largest incorporated pastoral finance companies grew at an annual rate of 15 percent between 1880 and 1886, but at only 4 percent between 1886 and 1891 (see Table 5:4-4(a)). Butlin and Barnard, "Pastoral Finance," p. 391. Hall, *The London Capital Market*, pp. 118–19, 167–69. Bailey, *A Hundred Years*, pp. 55–56.

[1184] N. Butlin, *Investment in Australian Development*, p. 158.

a number of banks, neither had involved the entire industry; and a stock-holder or depositor with holdings and accounts spread across a number of banks was not badly affected. At the same time British, and particularly Scottish, investors had long been involved in domestic pastoral finance; and, again, they thought that they understood the risks.

In Australia the movement of the trading banks into long-term loans – loans that were linked to pastoral finance on the geographic margins or to urban housing during the speculative boom of the 1880s – had made the future of those banks highly uncertain. Australian entrepreneurs, concerned about British finance, made it a policy to package their proposals in a manner that made British investors believe that they were buying into a risky but not an uncertain enterprise. Remember, for example, when in 1889, William Clarke established the London office of the Australian Freehold Banking Corporation Ltd. – a company that had been chartered in 1879 to take over the assets of the Australian Mutual Building society – he insisted that the firm be reincorporated as the Standard Bank of Australia, since "anything suggestive of land speculation was unacceptable in the British market." It might be noted that, after garnering some £500,000 in deposits from savers in "the main towns of England, Scotland, and Ireland," the newly renamed Standard Bank suspended in December 1891, briefly re-opened in May 1892, only to close finally in April 1893. When in December 1894 one of the Melbourne stockholders asked if Clarke had been dismissed, the chairman "replied that he had resigned, but refused any further explanation."[1185]

In the case of the Scottish connection, the main Australian borrowers were banks and finance companies. Their forays into Scotland "gathered momentum in the seventies, reached a peak of about £5 million per annum in the late eighties and continued, in smaller volume, into the early nineties, even after Australian government borrowing in London was sharply curtailed." "Australian and Anglo-Australian banks were respected and prominent institutions whose business included the managing of government accounts, the financing of trade and investing in pastoral property." The finance companies, many of which are still, today, prominent Australian wool-houses, were trading, financial, and lending institutions that handled "the multifarious financial aspects of the Australian pastoral industry." The firms were well known, and they employed well-connected local solicitors and accounts to act – for a fee – as their agents; in addition, however, they tailored their offerings to the Scottish

---

[1185] Entry for Clarke, William (born 1843) in the *Australian Dictionary of Biography* (Carlton, Victoria: Melbourne University Press, various years).

experience. "The deposit receipt, the instrument of borrowing by Australian banks, was the same type of security issued by Scottish banks and, frequently, by Scottish property companies. The maturing debentures issued by Australian finance companies were similar in form to debentures issued by Scottish investment trusts and the capital structure of these two types of company were similar."[1186]

Obviously it may take a long time to overcome the problems raised by asymmetric information; moreover, even when the system of signals has been established, unexpected events may put an entirely new meaning on those signals. In the 1880s, to the British saver the words "Australian land and mortgage company" meant, if not safe, at least, not uncertain; by the next decade the same words meant very, very uncertain. The saver had thought that he was buying securities that, although possibly risky, had an insurable return. He found instead that he was buying a set of securities with an uncertain return; his insurance premiums had been wasted.

The seemingly ever-expanding opportunities to obtain funds from these sources encouraged both individual agencies and formal institutions to begin to specialize in moving funds from British savers to Australian companies. In particular "Scottish law firms and solicitors, advising clients and handling estates, became permanent agents of Australian companies or were equally, if less directly, important in the purchase of Australian debentures. Australian firms, themselves, formed agencies in Britain that engaged in what was described as house-to-house canvass for small sums." The Australian Mercantile Land & Finance Company, for example, "maintained a list of over eighty agents to whom the company sent circulars announcing the terms at which debentures would be issued to subscribers. Fifty of these were agents in London, predominantly bankers, but including a number of stockbrokers; twenty-one were in Scotland, of whom most were solicitors; and nine were in the provinces." Although savers throughout Britain contributed, it was the Scots who – at least on a per capita basis – were the most important source of funds. Scottish domestic investment alternatives were drying up; although there is certainly an identification problem, Edinburgh, Glasgow, and Aberdeen became leading centers for the formation of these land mortgage companies.[1187]

[1186] J.D. Bailey, "Australian Borrowing in Scotland in the Nineteenth Century," *The Economic History Review*, 2nd Series, Vol. XII, No. 2 (December 1959), pp. 269, 271–72.

[1187] Bailey, *A Hundred Years*, pp. 55–56, 64–65. Hall, *The London Capital Market*, pp. 115–17, 169. N. Butlin, *Investment in Australian Development*, pp. 159–60. At times the ready availability of British funds proved something of an embarrass-

Although small investors dominated, British insurance companies contributed about £8 million to the flow of British capital into Australian land mortgages. Like the banks, these companies specialized in loans secured by pastoral freehold properties. Most of the insurance companies' investments reached the colonies in the late 1880s, when the leading investors were the Scottish Widows' Society, the Scottish Provident Institution, and the North British and Mercantile Insurance Company. In 1892, for example, the clients of the Australian Mortgage Land & Finance Company were indebted to that firm for £2,462,000; but they owed British insurance companies £547,000.[1188]

The largest blocks of pastoral finance were raised through the issue of debentures. For example, a company would issue partly paid ordinary shares with a large uncalled liability on its stockholders. The law then allowed the company to issue debentures secured by its assets *and* the uncalled liabilities of its stockholders. In the early years these debentures were typically designed to mature in three to seven years. Since they were marketed through informal arrangements with bankers and solicitors, they bypassed the formal security exchanges. These terminable debentures presented both advantages and disadvantages. On the one hand, if the interest rate fell, they could, on maturity, be replaced with debentures carrying a lower rate of interest. On the other hand, there was always the possibility that they might mature at a time that the company was in no position to repay them. As a result, beginning in the 1880s the pastoral companies began to supplement their terminable debentures with issues of perpetual debentures. Not only were the companies insulated from demands for repayment, but the issues could be listed on the London Stock Exchange. Thus, their balanced liability portfolios permitted them at least a part of the best of all worlds; they were somewhat insulated against the fluctuations on the security exchanges, they were partly hedged against changes in the interest rate, and they were at least in some degree protected against demands for repayment at something less than fortuitous moments.[1189]

The urban land-mortgage companies, many masquerading under the name "banks," that entered the market after the mid-1880s pursued policies similar to the pastoral finance companies. They reached their peak

---

ment. During 1868, the Australian Mercantile Land & Finance Company's "borrowed funds reached the £400,000 limit. Its agents in England and Scotland continued to send in money for investment in the colonies; indeed the flow was becoming an embarrassment, so the Company was obliged to subscribe temporarily to Tasmanian and New Zealand government bonds at rates below those paid on its own debentures." Bailey, *A Hundred Years*, p. 42.

[1188] Bailey, *A Hundred Years*, p. 56.

[1189] Bailey, *A Hundred Years*, pp. 62, 64–65, 67–68.

activity in the Melbourne land boom of 1888. In the subsequent depression most of these companies failed, and the British savings were lost. Many of the pastoral finance companies also went into receivership, but a fair fraction were reconstructed. In both cases, however, as with the savers who had invested in Australian bank deposits, the British shareholders (who were required to pay the uncalled portion of their shares) and the debenture holders (who either lost their savings or were required to wait a number of years before gaining access to their assets) were not anxious to repeat the experience.[1190] As a result, even after the depression had ended, at a time when the pastoral industry had recovered and the companies were again in a position to make repayments on their outstanding debentures, the survivors were no longer raising money in Britain. Instead they were repaying old loans.[1191]

In a second dimension as well, the pastoral companies had failed to establish permanent links with the British market. In both Canada and the United States, private firms had established connections – either directly or indirectly – with London merchant bankers. Despite two decades of activity, with no more than a single exception, the land-mortgage companies had been responsible for their own issues and had never established working relationships with the London merchant bankers.[1192] Thus no merchant bank had found it necessary to establish junior partners in Australia; nor did they find their profits threatened when Australian land mortgage companies were no longer able to float issues on the formal and informal British capital markets. As a result, the British merchant banks were under no pressure to search the Australian economy for private firms to replace the financial land and development companies that the British saver had come to realize were not as certain as he or, increasingly, she, had assumed.

Nor did mining finance provide the institutional structure to fill the gap after the turn of the century. The industry represented the largest share of private issues between 1895 and 1914. The Kalgoorlie-Coolgarde gold field was rich, but control of the mines was "in the hands of London

---

[1190] The reconstruction schemes adopted by the leading pastoral finance companies, Goldsborough Mort & Company and the New Zealand Loan and Mercantile Agency Company, were, for example, very similar to the plans adopted by the suspended banks. Hall, *The Stock Exchange of Melbourne*, p. 208.

[1191] Hall, *The London Capital Market*, pp. 118–19.

[1192] When Dalgety and Company (a firm that was more than a purely land mortgage company) converted into a corporation, it issued £4 million in shares through the bankers Glyn, Mills, Currie & Company. The economic historian A.R. Hall reports that "the issue of another land company (a land owning not a land mortgage company) was handled by Anthony Gibbs and Sons. The latter was the only Australian company issue, discovered by this writer, in which use was made of a merchant banker." Hall, *The London Capital Market*, p. 111.

financial groups who used the mines as speculative counters rather than business units. Not only were they over-capitalized and provided with inadequate working capital, but also they were worked with an eye to market (i.e. the Stock Exchange) considerations rather than the careful exploitation of their resources."[1193]

Since a large fraction of the ownership had originally been lodged with British owners, most of the funds raised through the new issues represented only transfers of ownership within the United Kingdom rather than new capital for Australia. In 1897, for example, "although 75 percent of gold production in Western Australia was obtained by companies controlled by British capital, of the estimated £70 million nominal capital raised for Western Australian mines probably only £7 million to £10 million actually arrived in the colony."[1194] Moreover, because of the financial manipulations – the "local managers and London directors were considered by an expert with experience in both fields, to be incompa-

---

[1193] There was little foreign investment in Australian mining until the late 1880s. The first major penetration of the London capital market occurred in 1886 when British investors became excited by the Charter Towers' (Queensland) display at the Colonial and Indian Exhibition. The display "opened the eyes of British capitalists. It also opened their purses." They agreed to float the Day Dawn Block and Wyndham Gold Mining Company and gave the Australian owners 419,000 free £1 shares in the new company and some of the £41,000 raised by selling the remaining shares to British investors. "Many Charters Towers people were so astonished at the price the shares commanded in London that they sold their own at an immense profit on their original outlay. English investors were eager to dabble in the exciting novelty of Australian gold shares and the number of shareholders of Dawn Day Block multiplied five times in three months."

The Western Australian strikes of the next decade were met with equal enthusiasm. Whitaker Wright, for example, in 1894, "floated two large Western Australian companies that yielded him £238,000 from their manipulations and operations. In 1897 he merged these two companies into the London and Globe Finance Corporation. He became managing director and held 605,000 of the 2,000,000 shares. His own shares were worth £1.2 million in that company alone, for it had large holdings in two rich Kalgoorlie mines, Lake View Consols and Ivanhoe. In 1898 he floated the Standard Exploration Company that controlled such mines as Mainland Consols and Paddington Consols from the holding company." Blainey, *The Rush That Never Ended*, pp. 100–2, 203.

Between 1900 and 1914 the British market absorbed £10.7 million of Australian mining shares. However, the volume declined steadily from £21.8 million in the quinquennia 1895–99, to £4.7 million in 1900–4, to £3.6 million in 1905–9, to £2.4 million in 1910–14. Hall, *The London Capital Market*, table 15, p. 92.

[1194] R.T. Appleyard and Mel Davies, "Financiers of Western Australia's Goldfields," in R.T. Appleyard and C.B. Schedvin (eds.), *Australian Financiers: Biographical Essays* (Melbourne: Federal Reserve Bank of Australia, 1988), p. 164. [Hereafter cited as Appleyard and Schedvin, "Financiers of Western Australia's Goldfields."] The estimate is from the *Coolgardie Miner*, May 3, 1897.

rably more 'dishonest' than had ever been the case in the Transvaal" – the vast majority of the about 500 mines in which the British were interested had still not paid a dividend by the turn of the century.[1195] Although many British financiers played a role in financing the industry, during the decade following 1894, none were as important as the London financiers Horatio Bottomly and Whitaker Wright. Their histories capture the essence of the London gold speculative fever of 1894–97. Both men "exploited the gullibility of investors, the remoteness of Western Australia and the difficulty of obtaining reliable information." Both made substantial personal fortunes, and both "were brought before the court for fraud or malfeasance."[1196] Not surprisingly, when gold production declined, little formal institutional structure – a structure that under other conditions might have provided a channel for international or domestic transfers from savers to other industries – survived.[1197]

A survey of the age of private firms listed on the London Stock Exchange in 1914 indicates that the proportion of older non-mining firms – firms that had been listed for more than twenty-five years – was much higher for Australian than for British companies. A.R. Hall argues that this demographic structure was less a tribute to the staying power of Australian companies than a sign of the stagnation in Australian company formation in London in the early twentieth century.[1198] Moreover, the evidence suggests that those missing firms had not turned to the Australian securities market as a substitute for the British exchanges. Between 1899 and 1914 the paid-up capital of Australian joint-stock companies increased from about £100 million to £178 million, but the public issues of those companies accounted for less than 15 percent of the increase.[1199]

The British saver's desire to hold uncertainty-free investments, his reaction to the financial debacle of the 1890s (the crash and the policies adopted to reconstruct the suspended financial institutions), and the Australian proclivity to choose government to carry out heavy investment projects combined to leave Australia, after the turn of the century,

---

[1195] Hall, *The London Capital Market*, pp. 120, 177. A few mines paid very large dividends. By 1915 Australian mining dividends totaled more than £25 million, but almost 90 percent of that total can be traced to twelve mines. Blainey, *The Rush That Never Ended*, p. 207.

[1196] Appleyard and Schedvin, "Financiers of Western Australia's Goldfields," p. 160.

[1197] The value of Western Australian gold production decreased from £8.8 million in 1903 to £3.7 million in 1918. *Official Yearbook*, No. 13, 1920, p. 444.

[1198] The ratio is 55 percent for Australian, and 39 percent for English and Scottish. Hall, *The London Capital Market*, table 16, pp. 93–94.

[1199] Drummond, *Capital Markets*, p. 172.

without an established institutional structure capable of transferring private finance from Britain to the island continent. As Drummond has noted, "Canadian financial institutions provided numerous channels for the importation of capital from Europe and the Australian institutions provided relatively few such channels."[1200]

5-6. Conclusions

As in the United States and Canada, the institutions designed to support international capital movements helped shape the domestic capital markets in Australia. In addition, and perhaps not surprisingly, the interplay of domestic and British preferences with the customary and legal framework that provided the structure of the financial markets led to the evolution of very different institutional structures in the capital markets of the three countries.

In Australia, at the most general level, three sets of long-run forces and a single short-term shock played important roles in shaping the institutional structure of the capital market. The long-run forces included the British saver's preference for certain investments, the Australian electorate's predilection for choosing state governmental solutions to economic problems, and the dominant role of the Anglo-Australian and the colonial trading banks in both the domestic and the international financial markets. The short-run shock was, of course, the financial crisis of 1891–93.

The search for safe, and profitable, investments led British savers to direct a very large volume of finance into Australian government bonds, into deposits in Australian trading banks, and into the shares and debentures of Australian pastoral and urban mortgage companies. That they chose government bonds, particularly after the innovation of inscribed stock, is hardly surprising. Those issues carried the imprimatur of a self-governing British colony. Even if Her Majesty eschewed ultimate responsibility, history suggested that colonial consols were safe. Similarly, although they may have been mistaken, to savers reared on the real bills doctrine, deposits in Australian banks – some actually British banks and all with offices in the City – also appeared safe, or at least not uncertain. Similarly, those savers assumed that the shares and debentures of pastoral and land mortgage companies reflected insurable risk. In the latter regards they were ultimately proven to have been wrong; but, until 1890, the evidence indicates that the British saver believed he was buying risky but not uncertain pieces of symbolic capital.

In the 1850s the Australian State governments had taken over the railroads. Within a half century they had expanded their activities to include

---

[1200] Drummond, *Capital Markets*, p. 75.

the telegraph and telephone systems, public utilities, the infrastructure for the country's rapidly growing cities, irrigation, and ultimately land banks that channeled capital to agricultural and then to residential and commercial mortgages at highly subsidized rates. The governments' assumption of responsibility for these investment decisions meant that (1) there would be a large supply of government bonds; (2) political rather than economic considerations would frequently govern the decisions about the shape and level of investment expenditures; (3) there was little need for municipalities and other local government entities to enter the financial market; and (4) with the added guarantee of the states' imprimaturs, it was not necessary to employ the services of a merchant bank to provide the British saver with a signal of quality.

The dominant position of the trading banks had implications for both the domestic and foreign capital markets. In the domestic market their importance, coupled with the absence of effective bank regulation, meant that banks were well positioned to expand their portfolios to include a substantial block of long-term mortgages and, given that those loans at times went into default, a not insubstantial number of operating pastoral properties. It also meant that the trading banks were able to compete directly or indirectly through the building societies, with the land mortgage companies for a piece of the Australian urban building boom. In the British market, initially, it meant that the banks acted as agents for state government loans and that, even after the states had shifted their allegiance to the Bank of England and the London and Westminster, although their signal may have been weakened, they were still able to act as agents for private firms seeking access to the British formal securities markets. Again, the strength of the banks meant that there was no need to utilize the services of an investment bank. Those signals, however, were lost in the wreck of 1892; they could no longer be heard in either Britain or Australia.

Finally, the end of the long boom and the financial crisis of the early 1890s meant that initial conditions had shifted abruptly; in the words of economists, there had been a major regime change. The fallout from the crisis proved that Australian issues were not immune from short-run market shocks; nor in the longer run were they insulated from the market's recognition that the investments of Australian governments – particularly investments in railroads and irrigation – may have extended well beyond the limits of economic profitability. As a result, the state governments could no longer depend on an infinitely expanding British market for their bonds. At home the public sector still required funds, but there was no domestic securities market to fall back on. Although the market did gradually develop, the process was slow. The impact of the economic collapse on the private markets was even more severe. The mortgage banks that financed the boom in urban housing were almost annihilated, and the building societies severely damaged. Many pastoral land companies failed. Many of those that did not fail, including some that were long established and British-chartered, were forced to reconstruct. The majority of the trading banks suspended, and they too required reconstruction. The results of these developments were twofold. In Britain savers learned that neither the commercial banks nor the land mortgage companies were as certain as they had thought. Some stockholders found themselves obligated to pay the uncalled portion of their shares; some savers lost their entire investments; and many of those who did not lose everything discovered that, if they did not choose to accept fractional repayment, they would be required to wait for years to recover their funds.[1201] As a result, any "sane British investor would have rather buried his money under the floor-boards than entrust it to an Australian bank."[1202] There were, however, better choices than putting their cash under the floorboards, and after the 1890's they looked elsewhere, particularly to Canada, for more certain alternatives.

In Australia the surviving financial institutions adopted a much more cautious attitude toward their investment policies. The commercial banks, for example, increased their reserve-to-loan ratios, halted their search for overseas deposits, abandoned their investment banking functions, and became very hesitant to extend their facilities to firms in the new industries that emerged from the economic restructuring that followed in the wake of the depression and Federation – wheat and dairying in the agricultural sector and the manufacturing firms expanding behind the new uniform tariff barriers. "In the Australian context, the *uneven* development of specialized financial institutions may have meant that investable funds continued to flow along established channels even when alternative uses may have been more remunerative and productive."[1203]

The loss of the long-term credit previously supplied, directly or indirectly, by the trading banks and the destruction of a substantial portion of the land mortgage industry severely constrained future economic growth. On the one hand, the government stepped into the mortgage business; and the artificially low rates charged by the government land banks almost certainly resulted in over-investment in agriculture and housing and under-investment in the private commercial and industrial

---

[1201] It is estimated that British shareholders in the reconstructed banks and pastoral companies and in the Bank of New South Wales were required to meet calls amounting to £2,900,000. Hall, *The Stock Exchange of Melbourne*, p. 208.

[1202] Blainey, *Gold and Paper*, pp. 255–56.

[1203] Jackson, *Australian Economic Development*, p. 144.

sectors. On the other hand, with the commercial banks focusing their attentions on the domestic economy, on their loan business, and on their traditional clientele, there were no British institutions with an adequate knowledge of local economic conditions to permit them to operate independently of Australian partners. There never had been any Australian equivalent of the American second-generation, let alone third-generation, investment banks. In fact, there were no investment banks. Moreover, since the colonial governments had always had their securities underwritten by English or continental investment bankers, by British joint-stock banks, or through the auspices of Australian banks with London offices, domestic underwriting was almost unknown.

Although a domestic market for government securities gradually developed, the private market evolved very much more slowly. The country was still served by a very primitive domestic securities market until well into the twentieth century.[1204] The new issues market remained very small; the great insurance and trust companies could not, or would not, buy corporate issues; and the continued attractiveness of the interest rates paid by, and the proven safety of, the government saving banks further constricted the supply of domestic private finance. Moreover, the weaker were the domestic capital market institutions, the more room there remained for government investments – investments often chosen for political rather than economic reasons. Perhaps the British investor's disenchantment with the "little socialist" of Australia was rooted in more than blind political bias.

One final lesson: Australian domestic savings rates had increased from about 9.5 percent in the decade between 1861 and 1890 to 15.0 percent in the decade 1905–14. In some ways those were decades of governmental financial innovations, and these new safer alternatives might well have induced a higher level of savings. Increased savings can lead to increased investment and, thus, higher income; but, to be the most effective, they must be mobilized and directed toward the most productive investment alternative. However, the political calculus that underlay the decisions made by the managers of the new financial structure produced the choices that were less economically profitable than those concurrently selected by the private markets in the United States, Canada and the United Kingdom.

[1204] Between 1900 and 1914, Canadian firms raised six times as much external finance as Australian firms did. Drummond, *Capital Markets*, p. 175.

CHAPTER 6

Argentine savings, investment, and economic growth before World War I

6-1. Introduction

As a result of the revolutionary movement in Spain's American empire, Argentina achieved independence early in the nineteenth century.[1205] By 1810 Buenos Aires was free, de facto, and by 1816, de jure; but the wars continued (with Argentine participation) until 1824, when the Spanish empire in America was largely liquidated. Conditions in Argentina continued unsettled until 1829, when the dictator Juan Manuel Rosas came to power.[1206] Traditional historiography treats the period of the Rosas regime as a time of political and social retrogression and economic stagnation:

> The *History of Argentina* to 1860 is still commonly framed in the mythic terms imposed by Domingo Sarmiento in his novel *Facundo*. According to Sarmiento's enduring trope, the failure by 1820 of the first Republican experiments led inexorably to a bloody conflict between "civilization and barbarism." Central to this dramatic representation of the region's history is the assertion of a fundamental rivalry between rural and urban cultures. Federalism and Unitarism were, therefore, ideological expressions of antithetical cultural traditions. The brutality, cruelty, and personalism of Juan Manuel de Rosas were natural and predictable given the brutishness, isolation, and pure physicality of life on the livestock frontier that spawned him.[1207]

[1205] Ricardo Levene, *A History of Argentina*, translated and edited by William Spence Robertson (New York: Russell and Russell, 1963), pp. 232–34. [Hereafter cited as Levene, *History of Argentina*.]

[1206] Rosas was made Governor and Captain General of Buenos Aires Province on December 8, 1829. He stepped down after one term, but was returned on March 7, 1835. His dictatorship is usually dated from 1835. Levene, *History of Argentina*, pp. 403, 410.

[1207] Lyman Johnson, "Measuring Economic Performance During the Rosa Regime," paper delivered at the January 1996 meeting of the American Historical Association in Atlanta. [Hereafter cited as Johnson, "Measuring Economic Performance."] See also Domingo Sarmiento, *Life in the Argentine Republic in the Days of the Tyrants: or, Civilization and Barbarism* (New York: Hafner Press, 1868).

No one denies the cruelty or political repression of the Rosas regime, nor even its opposition to the expansion of economic ties with Europe and North America; but modern interpreters do not find evidence of economic failure and stagnation during this period. Economic performance, in the sense of levels of income and wealth per capita, at least in Buenos Aires Province, was excellent. Furthermore, despite the efforts of Rosas to keep wages down, workers seem to have done well, and the distribution of wealth was by no means highly skewed, by relevant standards.[1208]

Economic growth proceeded at a marked rate throughout the Rosas period and for at least a dozen years thereafter. It was during this time (1829–66) that the export market for Argentine pastoral products, particularly wool, cattle hides, horse hides, and tallow, began to develop.[1209] The stimulus to the economy was substantial. New pasture was brought into production, and labor from the interior – labor formerly devoted to

---

The opposing cultural attractions of rural (domestic) and urban (internationalist) ideals – ideals that persisted – are treated in J.C.M. Ogelsby, "Who Are We? The Search for a National Identity in Argentina, Australia and Canada," in D.C.M. Platt (eds.), *Argentina, Australia and Canada: Studies in Comparative Development, 1870–1965* (Oxford: Macmillan, in Association with St. Anthony's College, 1985). A similar, but muted, theme runs through the U.S. history occasionally, as in the conflict between Andrew Jackson and the Second Bank of the United States becoming dominant.

[1208] See Johnson, "Measuring Economic Performance," for measures of wealth per capita and of the distribution of wealth. For the latter, Johnson estimates Gini coefficients slightly smaller than those obtained by Alice Jones for potential wealth-holders in the thirteen North American colonies in 1774. That the level of the wage rate was high is indicated by the fact that "In 1850 an Argentine worker could purchase a hectare of land with less than a week's wages, whereas in the United States a farm worker would need two months wages, and in England almost three years wages." Carlos Newland and Barry Poulson, "Puramente Animal, Pastoral Production and Early Argentine Economic Growth, 1825–1865" (paper delivered at Madrid, 1995), p. 9. [Hereafter cited as Newland and Poulson, "Puramente Animal."]

See also John Lynch, "From Independence to National Organization," in Leslie Bethell (ed.), *Argentina Since Independence* (Cambridge: Cambridge University Press, 1993), pp. 1–38. [Hereafter cited as Lynch, "From Independence to National Organization."]

The Bethell volume consists of essays reprinted from *The Cambridge History of Latin America*, ed. Leslie Bethell, 1985, 1986, 1991.

[1209] The trade in hides dates back to the economic reforms of the late eighteenth century. Before 1840 military activities, including European blockades of Buenos Aires, disrupted trade; but following 1840 it expanded. See Roberto Cortes Conde, "The Export Economy of Argentina, 1880–1920," in Roberto Cortes Conde and Shane J. Hunt (eds.), *The Latin American Economies: Growth and the Export Sector, 1880–1930* (New York & London: Holmes & Meier, 1985), pp. 320–1, 326–7. [Hereafter cited as Cortes Conde, "The Export Economy."]

producing food for the workers in the mines of Alto Peru – moved south and east to the new ranches. Technical changes both promoted productivity improvement and recast Argentine products in ways that allowed them to meet market demands more successfully. For example, methods of extracting tallow from cattle carcasses were improved. As a result, product per animal increased. Ranchers began to shift from raising cattle and horses to raising sheep. Local animals were bred to imported merinos to improve the quality of the wool and to bring the Argentine product better prices in world markets.[1210]

In 1854, with Rosas gone, the Republic was reconstructed, a constitution was framed, and a president elected. It took another six years to settle differences between Buenos Aires Province and the Argentine Confederation and to incorporate the province into the Confederation. Even with the basis of a stable government in place, there were, nonetheless, periodic revolutionary outbreaks, as well as military conflicts with neighboring states. Economic progress was also slowed by the long international depression of 1873–79, a depression that fell with special weight on Argentina. The final serious revolt of the nineteenth century was put down in 1880.[1211] Buenos Aires became the Argentine capital city, and a

---

[1210] Roberto Cortes Conde, "The Growth of the Argentine Economy, c. 1870–1914," in Leslie Bethell (ed.), *Argentina Since Independence* (Cambridge: Cambridge University Press, 1993), p. 48; Johnson, "Measuring Economic Performance"; Newland and Poulson, "Puramente Animal." Johnson makes the point that, although exports helped the pastoral sector and the traders in Buenos Aires, expanded foreign trade also brought in foreign imports, to the grief of local artisans.

See also Lynch, "From Independence to National Organization," pp. 38–46.

[1211] "In spite of recurrent unrest in the early 1890s, [the years 1880–1900 constituted] . . . a period when the elite's dominance remained largely unchallenged. What distinguished it from the period before 1880 was its relative stability. [The period] after 1900 saw the emergence of a pluralistic political structure under the impact of the growth of the urban sectors, and finally, in 1912, the introduction of reforms. These brought the country's institutional structure closer to a system of representative government. The main aim of the reform was to establish a coalition between the elite and the urban middle classes. . . . Rather than representing any revolutionary political change, the events of 1912 were thus more significant as a reflection of the elite's ability to adapt the political structure to new conditions, and to accommodate new groups in the political system." The whole period from 1880 until World War I was thus one of relative political stability, and was recognized as such by foreign observers and potential investors. The Argentine governments – including provincial and municipal governments – had access to international capital markets, and were able to extend their imprimaturs to certain private ventures. David Rock, *Politics in Argentina, 1890–1930: The Rise and Fall of Radicalism* (Cambridge: Cambridge University Press, 1975), ch. 2. The quotation is from p. 26. [Hereafter cited as Rock, *Politics in Argentina.*]

modern government was firmly established.[1212] A military campaign finally drove the Indians off the pampas and opened the territory to more complete exploitation. The monetary system was reformed. In place of the preexisting money supply of provincial currency, bank notes, and foreign coins, a new national system was created. Argentina adopted a bi-metallic standard, but the operation of Gresham's Law soon converted it into a gold standard. All international trade was conducted in terms of gold pesos (of roughly the value of a U.S. dollar). For internal circulation, a paper currency was provided. The 1880s seemed a propitious time for the Argentine economy. In 1883 the U.S. consul at Buenos Aires described the geographic and climatic features of each of the provinces, indicating the promise of each. The report makes clear that an unusually large fraction of Argentine surface area had productive potential, a much larger fraction than in Australia, Canada, or the United States. Consul Baker ended his review by saying that Argentine climate ranges from "subtropical to that of Northern Canada, and it is capable of maturing every variety of cereal, crop, fruit, or vegetable, which is known to earth."[1213]

[1212] Levene, *A History of Argentina*, p. 239. See also Jose Luis Romero, *A History of Argentine Political Thought* (Stanford, Calif.: Stanford University Press, 1963), ch. VI. The constitution had features similar to that of the United States, but with some important differences. The national legislature was to be bicameral; the vice president was to preside over the senate; senators were elected by provincial legislatures (two senators per province) for nine-year terms, and were to be of at least thirty years of age; deputies were to be popularly elected to terms of four years, were to be at least twenty-five years old, and citizens for at least four years. There was to be a Supreme Court and various other courts, and trial by jury was guaranteed in criminal cases. The governors and legislatures of the provinces were to be locally elected, and the provinces were to be politically independent of the federal government. There was to be a property qualification for election to the senate: a private income of 2,000 pesos a year, a figure roughly equal to $2,000 (U.S.). Candidates for President had to be native born and Roman Catholics. Secret elections were not guaranteed until 1912, when property qualifications for the vote were removed and voting became obligatory. Until 1912 the vote was restricted, and the government lay in the hands of an elite of shifting composition, but drawn chiefly from the large landed and mercantile interests. *Hand Book of the American Republics*, 1893, United States Senate, Executive Documents, 1st Session, 52nd Congress, 1891–92, Vol. 7, pp. 33–34. As late as 1910 "only about 20% of the native population actually voted. This dropped to a mere 9% if immigrants were added." Rock, *Politics in Argentina*, p. 27.

In any case, electoral fraud restricted the impact of the voters who exercised their privilege and maintained some element of the elite in political power.

[1213] United States Department of State, *Commercial Relations of the United States, Reports from the Consuls of the United States on the Commerce, Manufactures,*

He also has a word to say about Argentine political circumstances. He believed that governmental stability would persist after the long years of instability, and he praised the political and economic features of the constitution: "liberal in all provisions pertaining to trade, navigation, and commerce, and especially protective of the rights and privileges of the people in all matters of personal freedom and employment.... [they have the] right to enjoy and dispose of their property [to travel freely, to labor]."[1214] A modern commentator adds:

> British businessmen, in particular, benefited from the scale and diversity of interests in the country and from a high level of support for the Anglo-Argentine connection in the host society, at least until the 1930s. British groups applauded Argentine attempts to harmonize domestic institutions and practices with international norms. As importers and remitters, the large public utility companies and railways recognized the advantages of exchange rate stability. Although few British enterprises were registered in the country, most business groups in London were also encouraged by the tone of administrative reform and measures such as the codification and modernization of commercial legislation implemented around the mid-nineteenth century and by subsequent action designed to foster investment, immigration and trade.[1215]

Finally, in a passage eerily reminiscent of the peroration of Abraham Lincoln's second inaugural address, Consul Baker wrote:

> With the building of new lines of railway to the western and northern extremities of the nation, with new industries starting up on all sides, with annually increasing flocks and herds, with greater attention than ever paid to the agricultural development of the interior, with peace and good order throughout its borders, and with the faith and confidence of the people in the high destiny which the future so bountifully promises for it, the Argentine Republic may well be proud of the position she occupies among the republics of South America, and of the

---

Etc. of Their Consuler Districts, No. 31, July 1883 (Washington, D.C.: Government Printing Office), p. 323. [Hereafter cited as United States Department of State, *Commercial Relations.*]

Baker was correct about the area of Argentina that was potentially productive. It appears that 60 percent of the surface area of Argentina was cultivatable. See United States Department of Agriculture, Division of Statistics, Miscellaneous Series, Report No. 2, *Report on the Agriculture of South America* (Washington, D.C.: Government Printing Office, 1892), p. 24.

[1214] United States Department of State, *Commercial Relations*, p. 454.

[1215] C.L. Lewis, "British Business in Argentina," Economic History Department, London School of Economics, Working Paper No. 26/95, June 1995, p. 1.

good will which all nations feel for her in her onward movement to the place of first class power.[1216]

To interested contemporaries, Argentina in the early 1880s was rich in promise. Over the next thirty-odd years, despite some sharp checks to progress, the country seemed to be redeeming its promise.

6-2. Economic change

6-2a. The pace of growth

Virtually all of the relevant evidence indicates that Argentine economic growth in the several decades before World War I was extraordinarily rapid for that period; it was probably the most dramatic growth experience in the entire world. The most recent estimates indicate that real GDP was growing at an average rate of 6.5–6.6 percent per year (see Table 6:2-1). Over the same period the closest competitors, Australia, Canada, and the United States, recorded rates of from 3.5 to 4.0 percent per year. Argentina, thus, was the fastest growing economy by a considerable margin.[1217]

Detailed indicators show that growth was widespread. Over the period from the 1870s to 1913, hectares under wheat increased at an annual rate of 11.2 percent; hectares under maize, 8.8 percent; hectares under sugar cane, 9.6 percent; total cultivated area, 9.5 percent; exports and imports, in current gold pesos, 6.1 percent; rail cargoes, 12.4 percent. From the 1880s onward the tonnage of vessels entering Argentine ports rose 6.8 percent per year (see Table 6:2-1). The numbers of students in school and at the university also went up rapidly. The only indicators that suggest slow growth are those having to do with animal stocks and animal products, and even in those cases there is one important exception: Between 1894 and 1913, exports of frozen beef grew at the annual rate of 22.2

[1216] United States Congress, 3rd Session, H.R. Executive Document No. 98, *Report of the Commercial Relations for the Years 1880 and 1881* (Washington, D.C.: Government Printing Office, 1883), pp. 700–704, October 27, 1881.

[1217] The estimates were made by Roberto Cortes Conde, *Estimates of Argentine GDP, 1875–1935*, manuscript, October 1994. The earlier work of Gerardo Della Paolera suggests a slightly slower rate – 5.1 percent per year between 1884 and 1913 – but one still substantially above those recorded by other economies over the same period. Gerardo Della Paolera, *How the Argentine Economy Performed During the International Gold Standard*, Ph.D. dissertation, University of Chicago, December 1988. For comparative estimates for Australia, Canada, and the United States and for wider comparisons, see Angus Maddison, *Monitoring the World Economy*, Development Centre Studies (Paris: Organization for Economic Co-Operation and Development, 1995), pp. 148–60, 180–206. [Hereafter cited as Maddison, *Monitoring the World Economy*.]

Table 6:2-1. *Argentina: Long-term average annual rates of change*

	1870s–1913	1880s–1913	1890s–1913
Real Gross Domestic Product	6.5%	6.6%	6.6%
Population	3.4	3.6	3.7
Total area under cultivation	9.5	9.6	9.3
Wheat			
a. Output (tons)			5.4
b. Exports (tons)		13.6	9.8
c. Hectares cultivated	11.2	12.0	8.7
Maize			
a. Output (tons)			6.3
b. Hectares cultivated	8.8	6.8	6.9
Sugar			
a. Output (tons)			
b. Hectares cultivated	9.6	6.3	8.6
Cattle (numbers)	2.2	1.4	2.0
Sheep (numbers)	0.9	0.8	0.5
Horses (numbers)	2.3	3.2	4.2
Wool – output (tons) (1895–1913)			–2.3
Linseed oil – output			15.0
Exports & imports (in gold pesos)	6.1	7.2	6.0
Wool exported	1.0	0.9	0.5
Frozen beef exported (1900–1913)			22.2
Frozen mutton & lamb exported (1900–1913)			–1.6
Rail Cargo (tons)	12.4	12.9	9.3
Vessels clearing Argentine ports (tonnage)		6.8	4.9
Letters posted (numbers)			12.0
Telegraph messages (numbers)			8.0
University students (numbers)		8.0	
Primary school students (numbers) (1883–1904)		7.3	
Clearing house paper (1900–1913)			7.5
Central government tax revenues (in gold)	5.6	6.4	7.5
Central government expenditures (in gold)	5.3	5.9	6.9

Sources: Computed from Roberto Cortes Conde, "Estimates of Argentine GDP, 1875–1935," manuscript, October 1994; B.R. Mitchell, *International Historical Statistics for the Americas, 1750–1988*, 2nd edition (New York: Stockton Press, 1993); Ernesto Tornquist & Company, Ltd., *The Economic Development of the Argentine Republic in the Last Fifty Years* (Buenos Aires: Ernesto Tornquist & Company, Ltd., 1919).

percent. There are two explanations for the performance of the slow-growing sectors of the pastoral industries. First, and most importantly, the Argentine economy was undergoing structural change, a shift from animal to farm products (see Table 6:2-2). To take advantage of the expanding international wheat market, ranchers were plowing up part of their pampas land and selling it or, more often, renting it to grain farmers, often immigrants. The same market lifted the Canadian and, to a lesser extent, the American economies.[1218]

Second, the data on numbers of cattle understate the growth of the cattle industry. Between 1875 and 1913 the quality of beef animals improved dramatically. Thus, in 1914 an animal was worth much more, in real terms, than its opposite number of 1875. Furthermore, animals in 1913 could be slaughtered at younger ages than those of 1875, so that annual output from a herd of given size was greater at the end of the period than in the 1870s. Finally, in 1875 the chief products of the cattle industry were hides, horns, hooves, tallow, and jerky; by 1913 chilled and frozen beef had been added to this list. A larger fraction of the carcass was put to productive use, and, so far as meat was concerned, the output was of higher quality. Over this period the cattle industry, then, fared better than an inspection of the data on cattle inventories alone would suggest.

[1218] Donald Denoon, *Settler Capitalism: The Dynamics of Dependent Development in the Southern Hemisphere* (Oxford: Clarendon Press, 1983), pp. 94–95. [Hereafter cited as Denoon, *Settler Capitalism.*] Cortes Conde, "The Export Economy," pp. 343–44. James R. Scobie, *Revolution on the Pampas: A Social History of Argentine Wheat, 1860–1910* (Austin: University of Texas Press, 1964), passim. [Hereafter cited as Scobie, *Revolution on the Pampas.*] Carl E. Solberg, "Land Tenure and Land Settlement: Policy and Patterns in the Canadian Prairies and Argentine Pampas, 1880–1930," in D.C.M. Platt and Guido di Tella (eds.), *Argentina, Australia and Canada: Studies in Comparative Development, 1870–1965* (Oxford: Macmillan, 1985), pp. 61–68. [Hereafter cited as Solberg, "Land Tenure and Land Settlement."] Planting of wheat was typically the first step in the improvement of cattle feed. The farmer, usually the tenant of a rancher, would agree to raise wheat for a period of three to five years and then plant alfalfa. It was said that cattle fed on alfalfa could be brought to market a year earlier than cattle fed on the natural grass of the pampas. Alfalfa (also called lucerne) is a clover-like plant. It can be used as pasture, or it can be cut as a form of hay. See James Davenport Whelpley, *Trade Development in Argentina*, Special Agent Series, No. 43, Department of Commerce and Labor (Washington, D.C.: Government Printing Office, 1911), p. 44. Ranching and grain farming were, thus, intimately related. The development of wheat farming was in some measure a part of the long term improvement of cattle ranching. Argentina had an import surplus in grains before the early 1880s. Thereafter exports exceeded imports.

Table 6:2-2. *Sectoral division of Argentine Real Gross National Product, 1875, 1895, and 1914*

Year	Pastoral activities	Agriculture	Commercial	Industrial	Construction	Transportation	Government	Other	Total
1875	48%	3%	18%	13%	5%	1%	5%	7%	100%
1895	28	19	18	13	5	3	5	9	100
1914	15	17	19	22	8	5	5	9	100

Notes: "Other" may consist of the shelter value of houses, one of the principal items left unmentioned. The values are about the right size. Cortes Conde provides no 1875 estimates for construction and government. We assume that the shares of these sectors were the same as they were in 1895.

Source: Roberto Cortes Conde, "Estimates of Argentine GDP, 1875–1935," manuscript, October 1994.

Table 6:2-3. *Annual average rates of growth of Real Gross National Product, 1875–1913 (prices of 1914)*

Year	Percentage change
1875–1881	1.8
1881–1889	11.7
1889–1891	−6.8
1891–1896	12.3
1896–1900	−2.3
1900–1905	12.8
1905–1907	−1.6
1907–1913	8.1

Source: Roberto Cortes Conde, Estimates of Argentine GDP, 1875–1935, manuscript, October, 1994.

After 1881 the Argentine economy grew in two long surges, each followed by a relatively short period of decline (see Table 6:2-3). From 1875 to 1881 growth had been slow – GDP increased at an average rate of 1.8 percent per year – a consequence of the long international depression of 1873–79.[1219] "[I]n the River Plate alone 400 commercial houses failed"

[1219] Growth before 1875 had been vigorous. Assuming that real national wealth and real GDP grew at about the same rates, and assuming that the value of the gold peso was reasonably stable between 1857 and 1884, then between 1857 and 1885 growth was about 6.8 percent per year. See M.G. and E.T. Mulhall, *Handbook of the River Plate*, 6th edition (Buenos Aires & London: M.G. and E.T. Mulhall & Kegan Paul, Trench & Co., 1892), p. 20. [Hereafter cited as Mulhall and Mulhall, *Handbook of the River Plate*.]

This period of vigorous growth was part of a general expansion of the Western economies that affected all of Latin America. It began in the 1850s, in the time of Rosas, and carried through the collapse of the Rosas regime, the building of the Argentine state, and the war with Paraguay. The peculiarly Argentine feature of this boom was the vigorous international market for wool, hides, tallow, etc., that encouraged domestic private investment in ranching activities. Funding came from ploughing back profits, from merchant advances, and from the new and "extremely dynamic *Banco de la Provincia de Buenos Aires.*" By the standards that were to be set in the 1880s, foreign investment was modest, but there was some involvement in the nascent financial sector, and the beginning of investment in railways, some direct, and some indirect, through the purchase of government securities. Despite the heavy financial demands of the war with Paraguay, the government avoided substantial indebtedness to foreign lenders. Carlos Marichal, *A Century of Debt Crises in Latin America* (Princeton:

(between 1873 and 1877).[1220] There were also bank failures and government stringencies, but there were no government defaults on foreign loans. Argentina built a record that assured easy access to foreign credit in subsequent years. The 1880s saw an extended boom; between 1881 and 1889 real GDP increased at an average rate of 11.7 percent per year. The Barings crisis cut short the expansion. Over the two years after 1889, real GDP fell by almost 14 percent. The recovery came quickly, and it ushered in another period of rapid growth. In the five years between 1891 and 1896 the economy grew at the extraordinary rate of 12.3 percent per year. That expansion was followed by a four-year period during which the economy experienced wide fluctuations – declining, on average, by about 2.2 percent per year. From 1900 onward, however, it grew steadily and rapidly. There was a short and mild slowdown between 1905 and 1907, but from 1900 to 1913 on average real GDP grew at a rate of 8.3 percent per year. There was then a short, but sharp, decline.[1221] The Argentine experience can thus be summarized as two long periods of growth – the 1880s and the early twentieth century – divided by a decade of mixed success. That pattern was common to most of the rest of the modernizing world.

6-2b. Population change

Associated with the increase of real GDP was a very high rate of population growth. It averaged between 3.4 and 3.7 percent per year, and it rose as time passed (see Table 6:2-1). Even so, it did not absorb all of the expanded GDP. In fact, real GDP per capita increased at a rate of about 3.0 percent per year, a rate that was the highest in the

Princeton University Press, 1989), pp. 91 and ch. 3. [Hereafter cited as Marichal, *A Century of Debt Crises.*]

    For an account of the crisis and depression of the 1870s, see Marichal, *A Century of Debt Crises*, ch. 4, and Cortes Conde, "The Export Economy," pp. 328–30.

    The government of Argentina managed to ride out the depression of 1873–99 better than most Latin American governments. In 1877 those governments were in default of principal and interest of over £104 million. Argentina was not among the defaulting nations. J. Fred Rippy, "British Investments in Latin America, End of 1876," *Pacific Historical Review*, Vol. XVII, No. 1 (February 1948), p. 12.

[1220] Mulhall and Mulhall, *Handbook of the River Plate*, as quoted by Marichal, *A Century of Debt Crises*, p. 105.

[1221] For a treatment of the crisis of 1913–14, see William Lough, *Financial Developments in South American Countries*, Department of Commerce, Bureau of Foreign and Domestic Commerce, Special Agent Series, No. 103 (Washington, D.C.: Government Printing Office, 1915), pp. 7–15. [Hereafter cited as Lough, *Financial Developments.*]

world.[1222] Population growth was fed by natural increase and by exceptionally large immigration flows, flows stimulated by an aggressive government policy designed to encourage immigration. The effect on population growth was twofold. First, there was the direct impact of the arrival of the immigrants themselves. Since these people were disproportionately young adult males, their arrival immediately increased the labor force. Second, despite the fact that the sex ratio among immigrants was unbalanced, the birth rates among immigrants were unusually high. Indeed, if the Mulhalls are correct, the birth rate among native-born Argentines was quite low for the time (nineteen per thousand), and the strong overall birth rate was the result of high fertility among immigrants (for example, sixty per thousand for Italians).[1223]

Over time, immigration became an ever more important source of population growth. Leaving aside the effect on the birth rate, immigrants accounted for a little more than one-quarter of total population growth between 1869 and 1880, but for as much as 36 percent in the period 1880–1914.[1224] According to the Mulhalls, moreover, if one takes into

[1222] Maddison, *Monitoring the World Economy*, pp. 60, 62–64, 194–206.

[1223] Mulhall and Mulhall, *Handbook of the River Plate*, 1885, p. 15. The reported birth rates are for "Buenos Aires," presumably city and province. For European birth rates for the same period, see Mitchell, *European Historical Statistics*, 2nd ed., table B-6. All of the rates reported by Mitchell fall between 19 and 60. It should be noted that the Mulhalls' data refer to a period before the huge immigration of the early twentieth century. In this later period, since the sex ratio among the foreign born must have been particularly unfavorable to fertility, the birth rate among the foreign born was, presumably, lower than the figure reported by the Mulhalls.

[1224] The calculations were made by distributing the population increments between native and foreign born. Data on the native and foreign born were taken from Mulhall and Mulhall, *Handbook of the River Plate*, 1885, p. 14, 1892, p. 6, and Ernesto Tornquist and Co., *The Economic Development of the Argentine Republic in the Last Fifty Years* (Buenos Aires: Ernesto Tornquist & Co., 1919), p. 11. [Hereafter cited as Tornquist, *The Economic Development of the Argentine Economy*.]

The recorded increments to the foreign born population seem too small. Alternative estimates were computed by correcting the net-immigration streams for mortality, and then summing up the adjusted annual immigration data. We assumed an unchanging death rate of 20 per thousand. On this basis immigration accounted for almost one-third of population growth between 1869 and 1880, almost one-half between 1880 and 1891, and over four-tenths between 1891 and 1914. The adjusted estimates allowed us to judge the death rates implicit in the official data, reported in Mulhall and Mulhall, *Handbook of the River Plate*, and in Tornquist, *The Economic Development of the Argentine Republic*. Those estimates come to about 25 per thousand for the inflow from 1860 to 1880, 27 per thousand between 1880 and 1891, and 23 per thousand for 1891–1914. Bearing in mind that immigrants were disproportionately young adults and

Table 6:2-4. *Native-born as a percentage of the*
total population, Argentina, Canada, and the
United States, 1869–1914

Year	Argentina	Canada	United States
1869	87.8		
1870			82.7
1871		81.6	
1880	83.5		86.2
1881		86.1	
1890			84.6
1891	76.2	86.7	
1900			86.3
1901		87.0	
1910			84.9
1911		78.0	
1914	70.1		

Sources: U.S. *Historical Statistics*, 1957, Series C218–
283, p. 66 & Series A1–3, p. 7; Canada: Urquhart, *His-*
torical Statistics of Canada, Series A 28, p. 16 & Series
A75–113, p. 18; Argentina: Mitchell, *International His-*
torical Statistics: The Americas, 1750–1988.

account the effect of immigrants on the rate of natural increase, immigrants and their progeny (first generation only) actually were responsible for almost two-thirds of population growth between 1869 and 1882,
and no doubt for more than that in the years following 1891.[1225]

The impact of immigration on the growth of population is visible also
in the structure of the population. In 1869 and in 1880 the native born
accounted for the lion's share of the total Argentine population, 87.8
percent in 1869, and 83.5 percent, in 1880. The share then dropped
sharply across the 1880s and again between 1891 and 1914. By 1891
native-born Argentineans accounted for only three-quarters of the total
population, and by 1914 for only a little more than seven-tenths. Notice
that the role of the foreign born during this period was much greater in
Argentina than in Canada or the United States (see Table 6:2-4).

should, therefore, have experienced relatively low death rates, these figures seem
high. For comparative purposes see Mitchell, *European Historical Statistics*, 2nd
ed., table B-6.

[1225] Mulhall and Mulhall, *Handbook of the River Plate*, 1885, p. 14.

Table 6:2-5. *Argentina: average annual rates of gross immigration, emigration, and net immigration, 1875–1913 (thousands of persons)*

Years	(1) Gross immigration	(2) Emigration	(3) Net immigration	(4) (3)/(1) × 100 (percent)
1875–1879	41.5	22.3	19.2	46.3
1880–1889	102.1	17.5	84.6	82.9
1890–1899	92.9	55.2	37.7	40.6
1900–1913	238.3	117.6	120.7	50.7

Sources: Ernesto Tornquist & Company, Ltd., *The Economic Development of the Argentine Economy in the Last Fifty Years* (Buenos Aires: Ernesto Tornquist & Company, 1919).

These patterns reflect the place of immigration in the two great economic booms: the 1880s and the early twentieth century. The level of immigration during the boom of the 1880s is particularly striking (see Table 6:2-5). Gross immigration per year more than doubled over the preceding period, 1875–9. Emigration then dropped, and net immigration rose more than fourfold; it accounted for over eight-tenths of gross immigration. These developments were reversed in the 1890s: Gross immigration fell by about ten thousand per year, emigration more than tripled, and net immigration fell to a level of just over four-tenths of gross immigration. The great boom of the early twentieth century is reflected in annual gross immigration: almost one-quarter of a million per year, a figure more than twice as great as the annual flows of the 1880s and 1890s. Emigration, however, also rose. It more than doubled the annual flow of the 1890s; nonetheless, average annual net immigration reached a new peak of over 120,000 per year, over one-half of the gross flow. Net immigration has obvious long-term consequences that affect the scale and structure of the labor force as well as the rate of natural increase, but the economic impacts of those migrants who returned to their native countries should not be overlooked. A substantial migration involved the movement of farm workers following the cultivation seasons; that is, European farm workers – the *golondrinas* (swallows), as they were called – participated in the sowing, cultivation, and harvesting of crops at home, in Europe, and then after the harvest sailed for Argentina, to be in time for the growing season there. The return of workers to Europe, then, did not represent entirely a loss of labor force for Argentina, since many of the emigrants would return to Argentina at the next planting season, when they were again needed in the fields.

One important product of the immigration policy was a steady flow of workers who remained in Argentina for several years; some became permanent residents. Many of these immigrants participated in the late-nineteenth- and early-twentieth-century shift from pastoral activities to agriculture. They were the renters of the pampas land.[1226] Argentina was importing farming skills and as a result was in a position to take advantage of the large and growing world demand for bread crops.[1227] In the census year 1914 foreigners made up over 40 percent of the labor force in agriculture and ranching. Since few foreigners were engaged in ranching, a large proportion of the farmers and farm workers reported by the census must have been foreigners, chiefly Italians and Spaniards (see Table 6:2-6). Notice, however, that even more foreign workers were employed in industries and crafts than in agriculture and ranching; the difference was particularly great in 1914 (see Table 6:2-7), when there were also nearly as many foreigners in commerce as there were in agriculture and ranching. Foreigners were heavily concentrated in the capital, where they were almost as numerous as native Argentines: In 1914 there were 778,000 immigrants and 798,000 natives.[1228] Almost two-thirds of the workforce in the city was foreign born: 87 percent of tailors, 85 percent of masons, 89 percent of bakers, 67 percent of mechanics, over 75 percent of shoemakers, 66 percent of blacksmiths, and over 90 percent of day laborers, to name just a few.[1229] Almost one-third of all foreigners lived in the capital, and another 30 percent resided in Buenos Aires Province. In short, immigrants moved into those sectors of the economy that were expanding in response to international and local

[1226] See Alan M. Taylor, "Peopling the Pampa: On the Mass Migration to the River Plate, 1870–1914," *Explorations in Economic History*, Vol. 34, No. 1 (January 1997), pp. 100–32. [Hereafter cited as Taylor, "Peopling the Pampa."]

[1227] In the early stages of the migration, it was the domestic market that provided the impulse toward farming: "The first agricultural colonies of European immigrants in the provinces of Santa Fe and Entre Rios had begun to supply much of the local demand for wheat, corn, and flax." James R. Scobie, *Buenos Aires, Plaza to Suburb, 1870–1910* (New York: Oxford University Press, 1974), p. 10. [Hereafter cited as Scobie, *Buenos Aires*.]

[1228] For a quantitative treatment of the growth of the population of Buenos Aires, see Zulma L. Recchini, *The Contributions of Migration and Natural Increase to the Growth of Buenos Aires, 1855–1960*, Ph.D. dissertation, University of Pennsylvania, 1971.

[1229] Tornquist, *The Economic Development of the Argentine Republic*, p. 9; Scobie, *Buenos Aires*, p. 265.

Table 6:2-6. *Nationalities of the Argentine population, 1869, 1880, 1914 (thousands)*

Nationality	1869	1880	1914
Argentines	1,525	2,121	5,527
Italians	71	154	930
Spaniards	34	73	830
Russians	@	@	94
Uruguayans	@	@	86
French	32	69	79
Turks			64
English	11	23	28
Germans and Swiss	11	24	41
All others	53	75	206
Total	1,737	2,540	7,885

Notes: @ = Less than 500.

Sources: M.G. and E.T. *Mulhall, Handbook of the River Plate*, (Buenos Aires & London: M.G. and E.T. Mullhall & Kegan Paul, Trench & Company, 1885), p. 14; Ernesto Tornquist & Company, Ltd., *The Economic Development of the Argentine Economy in the Last Fifty Years* (Buenos Aires: Ernesto Tornquist & Company, 1919), p. 10.

demands: bread crops, industrial import substitutes, construction, and commerce.

6-2c. *Structural change*

Structural change consisted in part of shifts in the relative importance of pastoral and grain-growing activities, but it also involved the innovation and development of new agricultural products: sugar in Tucuman, tobacco, fruits, and wine in Mendoza. With the expansion of the rail network, these goods could reach a national market, where they served as import substitutes.

The industrial sector also expanded in relative terms after 1895 (see Table 6:2-2). A wide variety of activities was undertaken, running from the production of chilled and frozen meat, to candied fruit, shoes, tannin, beer, and refined sugar. As this list suggests, industrial activity was particularly focused on the processing of agricultural products, a part for export (frozen meat), but a larger part for the domestic market. In 1913

Table 6:2-7. *Argentina: distribution of the native and foreign work force among the principal industrial sectors, 1895–1914*

Panel A: Thousands of workers				
	1895		1914	
Industrial Sector	Argentine	Foreign	Argentine	Foreign
Agriculture and ranching	249	145	318	212
Industries and crafts	211	155	468	373
Commerce	55	88	112	182
Transport	29	34	56	55
Domestic service	167	56	111	108
Public administration	17	7	90	19
Total: All sectors	728	485	1,155	949

Panel B: Percent of total				
	1895		1914	
Industrial sector	Argentine	Foreign	Argentine	Foreign
Agriculture and ranching	63.2	36.8	60.0	40.0
Industries and crafts	57.7	42.3	55.6	44.4
Commerce	38.5	61.5	38.1	61.9
Transport	46.0	54.0	50.5	49.5
Domestic service	74.9	25.1	50.7	49.3
Public administration	70.8	29.2	82.6	17.4
Total: All Sectors	60.0	40.0	54.9	45.1

Source: Ernesto Tornquist & Company, Ltd., *The Economic Development of the Argentine Republic in the Last Fifty Years* (Buenos Aires: Ernesto Tornquistist & Company, Ltd., 1919), pp. 10–13.

almost two-thirds of the value of output of manufacturing industries came from food production, spinning, and weaving.[1230]

Industrial firms were typically small. For example, in 1913 the average capital of firms engaged in manufacturing and construction amounted to less than 40,000 paper pesos, the value of output to about 38,000 paper

---

[1230] Tornquist, *The Economic Development of the Argentine Republic*, p. 37. Manufacturing is defined as "industry" minus "construction"; and food, spinning, and weaving are defined as "alimentation" plus "fibre, thread, and cloth."

pesos, and the average number of employees to fewer than nine.[1231] There was not much variation in these figures from industry to industry, but there were important regional differences. In particular, in the capital, a city that in 1913 accounted for over one-third of the value of industrial output, the average industrial firm was substantially larger than the national average. It employed about fourteen workers, disposed of 50,000 paper pesos of capital, and produced 64,000 paper pesos of output.

There were also important regional differences in the rates of growth of industry. The three principal industrial areas, the capital, Buenos Aires Province, and Santa Fe Province (including the important city of Rosario), accounted for roughly two-thirds of industrial capital in both 1895 and 1913. Over those eighteen years, however, the relative importance of Buenos Aires Province increased, while that of the capital declined. The share of industrial capital located in Buenos Aires Province increased by almost 6 percent; the fraction found in the capital declined by a similar amount (see Table 6:2-8). The shifts in the relative importance of the rest of the provinces were even more marked. Among the gainers Mendoza's performance was particularly striking. It reflected the expansion of the production of wine and orchard fruits, a response to the railways' opening of the internal market. In 1895 the province contained just over 4 percent of the nation's industrial capital; in 1913 the figure was more than 9 percent.[1232]

Many industrial firms were founded by immigrants, and this helps to explain why foreigners constituted such a large fraction of the owners of industrial firms. In 1913, for example, they represented almost 65 percent.[1233] In the clothing industry, a skill-based set of activities where it was relatively easy for an unnaturalized immigrant with limited resources to get a start, roughly 84 percent of owners were foreigners.

[1231] The paper peso was worth 0.44 of a gold peso, or about 42.5 American cents.

[1232] Tornquist, *The Economic Development of the Argentine Republic*, ch. IV, part I. Scobie analyzes one rapidly growing city, Mendoza, one stagnating city, Corrientes, and one city that grew at about the average rate, Salta. James R. Scobie, *Secondary Cities of Argentina, The Social History of Corrientes, Salta, and Mendoza*, completed and edited by Samuel L. Bailey (Stanford, Calif.: Stanford University Press, 1988). [Hereafter cited as Scobie, *Secondary Cities.*]

[1233] See Herbert S. Klein, "The Integration of Italian Immigrants into the United States and Argentina: A Comparative Analysis," comments by Jorge Balan, John D. Gould, and Tulio Halperin-Donghi, and Klein's response, *American Historical Review*, 1983, pp. 317–46. In particular see Tulio Halperin-Donghi's account of the early history of Italian immigration to Argentina and the changing status of the early immigrants. Klein argues that Italian immigrants – who accounted for a substantial fraction of total immigration into both countries in the late nineteenth and early *twentieth* centuries – did better, economically, in Argentina than in the United States.

Table 6:2-8. *Argentina: regional distribution of industrial capital, 1895 and 1913*

Region	1895	1913
Federal Capital	36.0%	30.6%
Buenos Aires Province	21.6	26.3
Santa Fe Province	10.1	10.5
Mendoza Province	4.3	9.6
Tucuman Province	10.7	5.0
Entre Rios Province	7.1	4.0
Cordoba Province	2.4	4.2
The remainder of Argentina	7.8	9.8

Source: Computed from Ernesto Tornquist & Company, Ltd., *The Economic Development of the Argentine Republic in the Last Fifty Years* (Buenos Aires: Tornquist & Company, Ltd., 1919), p. 38.

In the more capital-intensive textile industry–mainly spinning and weaving–the figure was only 8 percent. However, the entrepreneurial activities of unnaturalized immigrants do not provide the whole story of foreign investment in Argentine industrialization. In metallurgy and allied industries, for example, 77 percent of owners were also foreign. Although this sector no doubt included many artisan shops with immigrant owner-operators (blacksmiths, for example), it is likely that some fraction of the foreign owners were investors living outside Argentina.[1234] The involvement of such investors, however, does not appear to have been substantial.[1235]

[1234] Donna Guy, "Dependency, the Credit Market, and Argentine Industrialization, 1860–1940," *Business History Review*, Vol. 58, No. 4 (winter 1984), pp. 551–55. [Hereafter cited as Guy, "Dependency, the Credit Market, and Argentine Industrialization."] In metal working and electrical appliances "small family-owned firms and workshops predominated until the 1950s." As to "railroad machinery, only repair workshops existed until the end of World War II. Other capital-intensive sectors, as food production or petroleum refining, were quick to develop." Maria Ines Barbero, "Argentina: Industrial Growth and Enterprise Organization, 1880s–1980s," in Alfred D. Chandler, Jr., Franco Amatori, and Takashi Hikino (eds.), *Big Business and the Wealth of Nations* (Cambridge: Cambridge University Press, 1997), p. 368. [Hereafter cited as Barbero, "Argentina: Industrial Growth."]

[1235] See Tables 6:4-4 through 6:4-7.

'The dramatic expansion of the urban population provides an indicator of both industrial and commercial growth, and of a third major structural change. In 1869 about one-quarter of the population of Argentina lived in communities of 2,000 persons or more; in 1914 the figure had risen to over half.[1236] Particularly striking was the redesign and reconstruction of Buenos Aires, both the city and the port. Between 1869 and 1914 the population increased ninefold and by the latter date accounted for 20 percent of the total population of Argentina. At roughly the same time, New York contained 5 percent of the U.S. population; New York, Chicago, and Philadelphia together 9 percent. Something over 6 percent of the Canadian population lived in Montreal; in Montreal and Toronto together, 12 percent. In terms of the level of urbanization, Buenos Aires was on a par with London: each capital accounted for about 20 percent of the population of the entire country. Buenos Aires was one of the world's great cities, larger than Moscow, Philadelphia, Glasgow – indeed, larger than every city of Europe, except for London, Paris, Berlin, Vienna, and St. Petersburg, and only substantially smaller than London.

Buenos Aires lies near the confluence of a great river system. The Argentine sections of the Uruguay, a river that drains the northeast, and the Parana, a river that drains the north, are navigable. In 1870 the Salde, a river that flows out of the northwest and joins the Parana at Santa Fe, needed further canalization before it could become a useful part of the Argentine transportation network. To the far northwest and to the west there was no water transportation system capable of bringing goods cheaply to Buenos Aires and of carrying goods from the city to the interior. Except for coastwise shipping, the same lack of water transportation also constrained trade to the south. Furthermore, the port facilities at Buenos Aires were inferior; the river was so heavily silted that goods had to be lightered to the town from vessels anchored well out in the river channel. In 1881 "a 500-ton vessel required 100 days to unload its cargo at Buenos Aires, as contrasted to ten to twelve days in most ports." It was said that "the cost of unloading at Buenos Aires was 'nearly as great as the freight from England to B. Ayres.' "[1237] Upstream the channel

---

[1236] Scobie, *Secondary Cities*, p. 225. In comparison, in 1861, 51.9 percent of the Queensland population, 41.1 percent of that of New South Wales, and 40.6 percent of that of Victoria lived in urban areas. The figures for the 1901 were 52.0, 67.8, and 64.6, respectively, N. Butlin, *Investment in Australian Economic Development*, table 38, p. 184.

[1237] Scobie, *Buenos Aires*, pp. 71–72. See chapter 3 for an account of the design and construction of new port facilities. The second quotation is attributed to Nicholas Bouwer, then an agent of Barings' in Buenos Aires. H.S. Ferns, "The Baring Crisis Revisited," *Journal of Latin American Studies*, Vol. 24, Part 2 (May 1992), p. 245. [Hereafter cited as Ferns, "The Baring Crisis Revisited."]

of the river lay close to such towns as Rosario; and effective port facilities could be, and were, constructed. These cities drew commerce away from Buenos Aires.

Efforts to deal with the port problem began in the 1870s, when deepwater facilities to the south of the city, on Riachuelo Creek, were developed. Further construction at the end of the 1880s and in the early 1890s resulted in improvements to the northern port. More importantly, new docks were built immediately east of the center of the political and commercial city. While the port continued to be less than perfectly efficient, the new works represented a marked improvement over what had previously been in place.

To the west and south, in the absence of navigable waterways, goods had been transported into and out of the city by ox cart. By 1870 this form of transportation was in the process of being replaced by railways: The Southern Railway had been constructed to Chascomuds, some seventy miles to the south, and the Western Railway, to Chilcovoy, roughly 100 miles to the west. In the mid-1870s a line was begun that would ultimately reach as far north as Rosario and there connect with existing lines to Cordoba and Tucuman, to the north, and Mercedes, San Luis, Mendoza, and San Juan, to the west. By 1898 there was a direct line west from Buenos Aires to Mercedes, and lines to the south from Chascomuds to Mar del Plata and Bahia Blanca. The line to Chilcovoy had also been extended another 175 miles to the west and south. By 1900 Buenos Aires was the hub of a national rail network – a network that tapped the provinces to the north and, particularly, the pampas to the west, north, and south. A decade later, the network was further articulated, reaching west into La Pampa and south and west of Golfo San Mattias. This network secured Buenos Aires's place as the leading city of Argentina and helped to account for the city's rapid growth. More generally, it permitted small Argentine industrial firms, such as Farga Brothers and Grimoldi Brothers – firms that formerly were confined to a local market – to expand, reap economies of scale, and sell the shoes that they produced on a national market.[1238]

The expansion of the transportation system shows up in Table 6:2-2 as a pronounced increase in the share of domestic product accounted for by the sector, from 1 percent in 1875 to 5 percent in 1914. The levels of these numbers, however – a few percentage points – do not capture the

---

[1238] Guy, "Dependency, the Credit Market, and Argentine Industrialization," p. 551. The rail lines, of course, also gave foreign firms that competed with Argentine entrepreneurs access to the interior, so that tariff policy became an important issue.

unparalleled importance of the rail and water networks to Argentine economic growth and development.[1239]

The direct and immediate impact of the growth of cities was distributed among at least three of the sectors that are recorded in Table 6:2-2: construction, government, and "other" (the latter probably including the shelter value of houses). The effects of city growth are, thus, in considerable measure obscured in the sectoral aggregates. Like the building of the rail network, the growth of cities involved extensive construction – of ports, streets, water systems, sewage systems, commercial buildings, industrial buildings, government buildings, houses, and trolley networks. In all of these activities the capital/output ratio is high. Therefore, the importance of the growth of cities – and of transportation – are more easily observed in the distribution of the capital stock among sectors than through the distribution of GDP that is exhibited in Table 6:2-2 (see Appendix Tables 13 and 14). How the investments underlying these structural changes were financed remains to be described. We begin by considering the financial intermediaries that played a role in promoting domestic savings and allocating investment drawn from domestic savings.

6-3. **Financial intermediaries**

6-3a. The banking system

6-3a(1). Commercial banking: Both private banking and commercial banking developed early in Argentina's national history. The Bank of Buenos Aires, for example, was founded in 1822. Foreign involvement also dates from the early period. Foreign banking practices influenced mercantile firms that took up banking, and banks registered and owned abroad entered the Argentine commercial banking system. The London and River Plate Bank was founded in 1862, the British Bank of South America a year later, and the German Transatlantic Bank in 1887. These three were the most important foreign financial institutions in Argentina, but they were not the only ones. By 1912 foreign banks held roughly 28 percent of Argentine deposits, and almost as large a share of discounts and advances (see Table 6:3-1).

[1239] The favorable effects were virtually confined to the direct transportation effects. Backward linkages were felt chiefly overseas, since equipment and rails were, in the main, imported. The chief backward linkages that favored Argentina came through the development of skills in the railroad repair shops. How important these effects were is apparently problematical. Barbero, "Argentine Industrial Growth," p. 372.

Table 6:3-1. *Commercial banking in Argentina as of December 31, 1912 (millions of paper pesos)*

Bank	Deposits	Discounts and Advances	Cash	Cash/ Deposits
Argentine:				
Bank of the Nation	202	177	92	46%
Bank of Buenos Aires	58	68	14	24
Italy and River Plate Bank	43	41	12	28
Spanish Bank of the River Plate	97	117	27	28
French Bank of the River Plate	36	53	11	31
New Italian Bank	18	16	4	22
Total Argentine Banks	454	472	160	35
British:				
London and River Plate Bank	68	48	29	43
British Bank of South America	24	22	10	42
Total British Banks	92	70	39	42
German:				
German Transatlantic Bank	25	26	8	32
Total German Banks	25	26	8	32
Other European	55	75	19	35
All bank total	626	643	226	36

Notes: Ford's data were converted into U.S. dollars by use of data in Ernesto Tornquist & Company Ltd., *The Economic Development of the Argentine Republic in the Last Fifty Years* (Buenos Aires: Ernesto Tornquist & Company, 1919), p. 328. Ford's data are incomplete; the details in his table are short of his totals. Comparing his data (converted into dollars) with Lough's, it is obvious that he left out European banks. Therefore, the difference between Ford's details and his totals have been assigned to "Other Europ European" banks.

Sources: A.G. Ford, *The Gold Standard, 1880–1914: Britain and Argentina* (Oxford, U.K.: Clarendon Press, 1962), p. 105. William H. Lough, *Banking Opportunities in South America*, Special Agents Series Number 106, Department of Commerce, Bureau of Foreign and Domestic Commerce (Washington, D.C.: Government Printing Office, 1915), p. 66.

Buenos Aires was a cosmopolitan city, and consequently locals, foreigners, and Portenos – foreigners of long residence in Argentina – sat together on the boards of directors and on the boards of advisors of both types of banks, foreign and domestic.[1240] A shortage of potential managers also led those banks, on occasion, to employ executives who were not nationals of the place in which the bank was registered. For a time the managers of both the Buenos Aires and the Rosario branches of the London and River Plate Bank were German nationals; on another occasion, one of the officers of the German Transatlantic Bank was an Australian.[1241] Nonetheless, each bank was likely to have a distinct national character, a character determined by the people who owned and controlled the bank and by the managers that they appointed. With few exceptions, the manager was a national of the country in which the bank was registered. In the case of the British banks, employees down to the lowest clerk were typically British or British Portenos.

Foreign banks were heavily involved with the finance of international trade, international exchange, and the generation and supply of commercial information. Note major positions occupied by bills of exchange in the balance sheet of the German Transatlantic Bank (Table 6:3-2). Unfortunately, the balance sheet of the London and Brazilian bank is less detailed, but the prominence of bills receivable and bills for collection in the balance sheet suggests the important role played by foreign trade in the activities of that bank as well (Table 6:3-3). In fact, foreign banks dominated these fields, and, throughout most of the period, domestic banks confined themselves to the finance of internal trade.

Early in its history the Bank of London and the River Plate had a series of unfortunate experiences with their loans for internal ventures (including some mortgage loans) and drew back from these activities.[1242]

[1240] The boards of directors of British banks were located in London. As a device for improving the board's grasp of the situation and as a way of monitoring the Argentine managers, a local board of advisors was often appointed. It usually included English businessmen living in Buenos Aires, perhaps some *Portenos* and sometimes Argentine businessmen who were close to the bank.

[1241] David Joslin, *A Century of Banking in Latin America* (London: Oxford University Press, 1963), p. 23. [Hereafter cited as Joslin, *A Century of Banking*.] See also Charles Jones, "Commercial Banks and Mortgage Companies," in D.C.M. Platt (ed.), *Business Imperialism, 1840–1930, An Inquiry Based on British Experience in Latin America* (Oxford: Clarendon Press, 1977), p. 40. [Hereafter cited as Jones, "Commercial Banks."] William H. Lough, *Banking Opportunities in South America*, Department of Commerce, Bureau of Foreign and Domestic Commerce, Special Agents Series, No. 106 (Washington D.C.: Government Printing Office, 1915), p. 110. [Hereafter cited as Lough, *Banking Opportunities*.]

[1242] Jones, *A Commercial Banking*, pp. 36–40.

Table 6:3-2. *Balance sheet of the German Transatlantic Bank,*
December 31, 1913 (thousands of marks)

Assets	Subtotals	Totals
1. Cash, foreign monies, and coupons		49,648
2. Due from banks		9,905
3. Bills of exchange and treasury bills without interest:		
3a. Bills of exchange and noninterest-bearing treasury bills of the German Empire and federated states	90,477	
3b. Own acceptances	31	
3c. Acceptances of clients	33,887	
Total bills of exchange and treasury bills without interest		124,395
4. Due from correspondents		12,968
5. Two name paper		1,908
6. Loans on merchandise and shipping paper		7,390
7. Owned securities:		
7a. Loans and interest-bearing treasury bills	6,998	
7b. Other securities quoted on the exchange	1,251	
7c. Other securities	36	
Total owned securities		8,285
8. Participation in syndicates		122
9. Permanent shareholder in other banks		2,480
10. Debtors in current account, secured		51,266
11. Debtors in current account, unsecured		29,607
12. Buildings		3,990
13. Other real estate		81
14. Miscellaneous accounts		156
15. Transit accounts between home office and branches		1,345
Total assets		303,546
16. Capital		30,000
17. Ordinary reserve		3,327
18. Reserve number 2		5,510
19. Correspondents		33,160
20. Deposits		
20a. Due within 7 days	41,992	
20b. Due within 3 months	21,599	
20c. Due after 3 months	52,662	
Total deposits		116,253

Table 6:3-2. *(cont.)*

Assets	Subtotals	Totals
21. Other credits		
21a. Due within 7 days	81,633	
21b. Due within 3 months	455	
21c. Due after 3 months	10,106	
Total other credits		92,194
22. Drafts to be paid		
22a. Acceptances	16,007	
22b. Checks outstanding	1,979	
Total drafts to be paid		17,986
23. Pension fund for employees		585
24. Reserves for payment of coupons		210
25. Dividends unpaid		2
26. Profit and loss		4,290
Total liabilities		303,517

Source: William H. Lough, *Banking Opportunities in South America*, Special Agents Series 106, Department of Commerce, Bureau of Foreign and Domestic Commerce (Washington, D.C.: Government Printing Office, 1915), pp. 118–119. Lough writes, "It will be convenient . . . to refer to the statement of a typical bank . . . the Deutsche Ueberseeische Bank . . . may be regarded . . . as widely representative of sound practice in South America."

Later, when the bank returned to making internal loans, they were typically limited to British-owned firms; and the conditions of the loan usually reflected the real bills doctrine – typically and usually, but not always. For example, Joslin writes that as the 1880s wore on the manager of the Rosario branch of the London and River Plate Bank became more and more certain that trouble was in the offing, although he "had striven to keep the business as close to a commercial business as he could in a city where, banking being a highly personal affair, it was quite impossible to be sure whether loans were used for speculative purposes or not."[1243] In this case it appears that the bank may have deviated from strict adherence to the real bills doctrine. At its heart, however, the bank remained true to the doctrine, in its fashion.[1244] In this respect the Bank

[1243] Joslin, *A Century of Banking*, pp. 124–5.

[1244] The Buenos Aires branch – the main branch – "continued its older traditions, with discounts, advances on promissory notes, and exchange operations as the

Table 6:3-3. *Balance sheet of the London and Brazilian Bank, January 31, 1914 (thousands of dollars)*

Assets		
1. Specie and cash	$18,690	
2. Bills receivable	17,100	
3. Bills discounted and loans	44,240	
4. Cash and remitances in transit, etc.	3,888	
5. Bills for collection as per contra	23,213	
6. Bank premises	1,362	
7. Furniture	91	
Total assets		$108,584
Liabilities		
8. Capital	6,083	
9. Reserve fund	6,813	
10. Staff pension and benevolent fund	584	
11. Current accounts and deposits in currency at branches	41,431	
12. Current accounts and deposits in currency at head office	1,098	
13. Bills Payable	23,308	
14. Agents and sundry accounts	3,425	
15. Bills for collection on Account of customers	23,213	
16. Profit & loss ($2,994,000) less interm dividend ($365,000)	2,629	
Total liabilities		108,584

Source: William H. Lough, *Banking Opportunities in South America*, Special Agents Series 106, Department of Commerce, Bureau of Foreign and Domestic Commerce (Washington, D.C.: Government Printing Office, 1915), p. 131.

of London and the Plate were typical British banks, or perhaps the better phrase would be, model British banks.

Although the balance sheet of the Transatlantic Bank suggests conservative banking – Lough refers to the bank "as widely representative of sound practice [in South America]" – it contains some items that would perhaps not be found on the balance sheet of an ultra-conservative commercial bank.[1245] Two of these items are small and

staple business." The Rosario branch may have been more closely tied to the landed interests. Joslin, *A Century of Banking*, p. 132.

[1245] Lough, *Financial Developments*, p. 118.

relatively unimportant: securities listed on the exchange and "participation in syndicates." Both the German and the British banks were known to occasionally underwrite security issues, and the two balance sheet entries probably reflect the results of those activities.[1246] More important are the entries "Debtors in Account Current," an item that refers to the provision of overdrafts. In Argentina overdrafts were a common method used by domestic banks to extend credit. European bankers tended to steer clear of such loans, if they could. When they did employ them, they typically tried to have them secured. Almost two-thirds of the current account debt held by the Transatlantic Bank was secured. Still, a substantial amount was unsecured. It is doubtful that the British banks would have extended themselves so far, although long before World War I they were involved in business with Argentine firms and may have been obliged to make some use of this form of debt.

The overdraft was a reflection of a way of doing business that differentiated Argentine from European bankers. Lough's view of the matter deserves quotation at length:

> one of the most striking features of business life in the South American cities is its strongly personal and social flavor. . . . Family ties are likely to be a controlling factor in choosing partners and employees. If one's ultimate object is to have business dealings with a firm, he must first cultivate the personal friendship of the head of the firm. . . . This is a condition which directly affects banking practice. It makes it very difficult, for example, to introduce the custom of securing full financial statements from all applicants for credit. The request for a statement is apt to be construed (as it was in this country [the U.S.] not many years ago) as a reflection on the personal honesty . . . of the applicant. Consequently, . . . bankers, are forced to rely to a great extent . . . on their personal impressions, on such information, as they are able to secure through indirect hints and questions and on business gossip. . . . It must be remembered that . . . the business communities are comparatively small and isolated. There is little opportunity . . . for long-continued fraud. . . . A man who shows traces of dishonesty is much more plainly marked than in larger communities. . . . Buenos Aires is a partial exception. Here the mercantile community is both large and active.[1247]

[1246] Joslin points out that in 1903 "[t]he bank began to take a direct interest in the long-term capital movements to Argentina." It joined in syndicates with British merchant banks, funding public utilities and government debt. But, in fact, it had been involved long before that. In 1890 it was part of the ill-fated effort by Barings' to float an issue of Buenos Aires Water Supply and Drainage Company stock, an attempt that led to the Barings' crisis. Joslin, *A Century of Banking*, pp. 131, 126.

[1247] That is, in a small community the prisoners' dilemma game will be played repeatedly, and the chances of betrayal will be more limited than in a large commu-

Given these circumstances, it is easy to see why the overdraft would be a favorite form of credit from the standpoint of the Argentine businessman, and it is easy to see why Argentine bankers would find the request for credit in the form of overdraft legitimate. For most of the period Argentine bankers exchanged very little information; they did not even have a clearinghouse until late in the period.[1248] Consequently, it was possible for a businessman to obtain his maximum credit line from each of several banks, all in secrecy. Such multiple loans did happen, and banks were frequently put in embarrassing circumstances by the failure of these businessmen.[1249] It should also be clear that, if friendship established the identity of those applicants who got credit, the allocation of resources among candidates was unlikely to be optimal from an economic point of view. The description of the role of personal contacts, of unsecured overdrafts, and of the lack of institutional structure applies to a substantial part of the history of Argentine banking. Toward the end of the period, however, there were important changes. A clearinghouse was finally founded, and it became a channel for the exchange of information.[1250] The Bank of the Nation, a bank that had never before served

nity. Lough, *Financial Developments*, p. 103. See also Lincoln Hutchinson, Special Agent of the Department of Commerce and Labor, *Report on Trade Conditions in Argentina, Paraguay, and Uruguay* (Washington D.C.: Government Printing Office, 1906), p. 24. [Hereafter cited as Hutchinson, *Report on Trade Conditions*.] "Inquiries into a man's financial standing, which are regarded as a matter of course in the United States, are here resented as a reflection on the man's personal character."

[1248] Since until quite late uttering a fraudulent check was not a criminal offense, few checks were used, so there was little need for a clearing house; but the banks, thereby, lost the access to information that could come through cooperative activities in the clearing house. The fact that checks were little used meant that making payments was extremely cumbersome. Lough, *Financial Developments*, pp. 8, 132; Joslin, *A Century of Banking*, p. 118. See also Edward N. Hurley, *Banking and Credit in Argentina, Brazil, Chile, and Peru*, Department of Commerce, Bureau of Foreign and Domestic Commerce, Special Agents series, No. 90 (Washington, D.C.: Government Printing Office, 1914), pp. 31, 33. [Hereafter cited as Hurley, *Banking and Credit*.]

[1249] "All the principal banks permit and encourage overdrafts in current account at 8 or 9 percent. It is quite possible for business houses and individuals in good standing to carry half a dozen or even 10 accounts, say for $20,000 each, in as many banks. This establishes credit in each bank, and the customer may draw from $5,000 to $20,000 on overdrafts from each one. This is freely admitted by the principal bankers [they excuse the practice on the grounds of competition.] An individual recently [ca. 1914] failed for 4,000,000 pesos. He was found to be overdrawn on many of the most important banks in the Republic. Seeking loans from several banks." Hurley, *Banking and Credit*, p. 31.

[1250] Joslin, *A Century of Banking*, p. 130.

as a central bank, provided modest discount assistance to the banking system during the crisis of 1913/14. Since the bank was both large (the seventeenth largest in the world) and strong, it was capable of substantial assistance. Most importantly, the system of providing credit was changed. In the words of Lough in 1915: "During recent years speculation has been rampant and there has been overtrading and deliberate fraud. For these reasons the inadequacy of the old-time system . . . has shown itself in its true light and has been to a considerable extent reformed. . . . The banks are more and more insisting . . . on full and accurate information."[1251]

Apart from choices among earning assets, British banks showed their conservatism by the scale of reserves they held (see Table 6:3-1). For example, in 1912 both the London and River Plate and the British Bank of South America reported cash holdings equal to over 40 percent of their deposits, a figure that is much larger than one would find in a domestic bank in Britain or America.[1252] Even more surprisingly, the British rates were exceeded by the level of reserves maintained by the Argentine Bank of the Nation. Although the remaining banks in the system kept lower cash reserves, the ratios were still high by most standards. The Argentine domestic banks kept an average of 35 percent, the German Transatlantic Bank, 32, and the remaining European banks, 35 (see Tables 6:3-2 and 6:3-3). One possible way to interpret these results is to argue that the typical bank in Argentina was conservative.[1253] A more likely explanation is that, given the nature of Argentine markets for financial assets, there were few good, liquid, secondary reserves. The substantial cash reserves, then, reflect the substitution of cash for secondary reserves. The same factor affected the practices of Argentine businessmen, who, in the absence of more lucrative financial instruments, were obliged to hold time deposits for liquidity.

[1251] Lough, *Financial Developments*, pp. 101–2.

[1252] In anticipation of trouble, in 1889 the Bank of the River Plate raised its cash reserve to almost 50 percent of its total liabilities to customers. During the crisis the bank survived a three-day run. During that time the Bank changed its opening hours from 10 A.M. to 9 A.M. in order to accommodate those customers participating in the bank run. Joslin, *A Century of Banking*, pp. 124, 128.

[1253] Some were. In the midst of the Baring Crisis, the London and River Plate Bank acquired the *Banco Carabassa*, a firm that held gold reserves of 60 percent against its gold liabilities, and 65 percent against its paper liabilities. The *Banco's* reputation was so strong that customers withdrawing funds during the run on the London and River Plate Bank, and unaware of the merger, often deposited them in the *Banco*, much to the advantage of the London and River Plate Bank. Joslin, *A Century of Banking*, pp. 127, 129.

The concentration of foreign banks, especially the British banks, on the finance of foreign trade and the concentration of domestic banks on internal lending might seem to have limited competition between the two types of banks and kept them at arm's length. That interference was however, not correct. The two sets of banks might not have competed for loans, but they certainly did compete for deposits, and this form of competition led to some serious problems. For example, the London and River Plate Bank attempted to establish a branch at Rosario, in Santa Fe Province. Initially it had considerable success luring depositors from the domestic banks. As a result of the withdrawals, the provincial banks were put under some pressure, and they sought assistance from the London and River Plate, but to no avail. The provincial banks then adopted another strategy: They brought their political power to bear. The London and River Plate attempted to respond in kind, but the British government was unwilling to expend its political capital, and it left the matter to be negotiated by the branch manager and the board of directors. The government of the Province of Santa Fe gradually increased the pressure on the bank and eventually demanded the liquidation of the branch. Matters were ultimately settled without the destruction of the branch, but the case suggests the kinds of conflicts that could arise among banks, as well as something about potential political ramifications of such conflicts.[1254]

The Argentine banking system was marked by many bank failures, particularly in the early 1890s both during and after the Barings crisis. Failures were in large measures, due to the tendency of Argentine banks – especially the political banks – to hold long-term (e.g., mortgage) assets against short-term liabilities, and to make unsecured loans, often on the basis of political, rather than economic, considerations, and for political, rather than economic, ends. The most generous interpretation of these actions is that the bankers engaging in these practices wanted their banks to perform as development banks – like the *Credit Mobilier* – rather than commercial banks. Unfortunately for them, development banks with long-term commitments and short-term liabilities do not last long. The merest rumor of trouble led depositors to withdraw their deposits and

---

[1254] Joslin, *A Century of Banking*, ch. 3. During the Barings' crisis the Republic began taxing foreign bank deposits in an attempt to drive depositors from the foreign to the domestic banks (p. 127). See also Jones, "Commercial Banks," passim. Jones argues that British bankers made enemies among Argentine bankers from their close concern for the well-being of their own banks and unwillingness to assist Argentine banks heading toward trouble. For example, British banks quickly returned Argentine bank notes to the originator and were unwilling to hold Argentine bank deposits, if this action was attended by any substantial risk.

place them in the hated, but conservative and secure, British banks.[1255] The limited indexes that we have assembled indicate that the major banks that survived the Barings crisis – as well as the two that were reconstructed after failure – seem to have done well. If the experience of the ill-fated French Bank of the River Plate is ignored, dividend rates in the last years before the war – at a time when the return on British consoles ran about 3.25 percent – varied from 6 to 20 percent and clustered between 10 and 15 percent (Table 6:3-4).[1256] The foreign banks were long-lived, had weathered the storms of major crises – for the two British banks, the great depression of the 1870s and the Barings crisis; for the German bank, the Barings crisis – and could not be fairly regarded as very risky. Their dividends suggest success. These conclusions hold less strongly for the domestic banks. Nonetheless, in the years before the war, the Spanish Bank, the Bank of Buenos Aires, the Bank of the Nation, and probably others were clearly healthy and viable; and the evidence indicates that their dividend rates reflect success rather than a risk premium.[1257]

The growth rates of the leading banks provide a second measure of success (see Tables 6:3-5 and 6:3-6). The rates fluctuated. It seems clear that the growth of the banks reflected, in part, conditions in the economy, and, in part, circumstances peculiar to the individual banks. For example, the economic depression of the 1870s is reflected in the slow growth of the two British banks.[1258] Growth rates turn around sharply in the booming 1880s; both banks exhibited exuberant growth, matching the record of real GDP. Bad times in the 1890s again went hand in hand with relatively limited bank growth. There is an exception: The German Transatlantic Bank experienced a very high rate of growth, but the Transatlantic was a new bank, chartered in 1887. In the 1890s it would have been expected either to fail – as many banks did in this period – or to grow very rapidly, from a seedling to a mature plant. It seems to have followed the latter course. The economy again turned around in the first decade of the twentieth century; the Spanish Bank of the River Plate, the Bank of the Nation, and the German Transatlantic Bank all grew

---

[1255] Jones, "Commercial Banks," passim.

[1256] Sydney Homer and Richard Sylla, *A History of Interest Rates*, 3rd ed. (New Brunswick, N.J.: Rutgers University Press, 1991), table 59, p. 444. [Hereafter cited as Homer and Sylla, *A History of Interest Rates*.]

[1257] The Bank of the Nation was not included in Table 6:3-4 because the Bank was prohibited from paying dividends (earnings went into the capital accounts).

[1258] The growth of the British Bank of South America was less impressive than its experience during the 1880s, and slightly less than its experience during the first decade of the twentieth century, but it was not extraordinarily poor.

Table 6:3-4. *Dividend rates of Argentine Banks, 1888–1914*

Year	Spanish Bank of the River Plate	Bank of Buenos Aires	Italian Bank of the River Plate	French Bank of the River Plate	London and River Plate Bank	British Bank of South America	German Transatlantic Bank
1888							5%
1890							0
1895							9
1900							8
1905					20%	9%	8
1910	12%				20	15	9
1914	11	10%	12%	In Receivership	15	12	6

Source: William H. Lough, *Banking Opportunities in South America*, Special Agents Series 106, Department of Commerce, Bureau of Foreign and Domestic Commerce (Washington, D.C.: Government Printing Office, 1915), pp. 30, 47, 70–71.

Table 6:3-5. *Principal assets and liabilities of the leading banks in Argentina, 1857–1914 (millions of dollars)*

| Bank of the Nation | | | | | Spanish Bank of the River Plate | | | | |
Year	Cash	Earning assets	Deposits	Acceptances	Year	Cash	Earning assets	Deposits	Acceptances
1857					1857			2.9	
1870					1870				
1880					1880				
1892	47.0	21.0			1892				
1900					1900			18.5	
1910					1906			58.0	
1914	208.0	205.0			1914				

| German Transatlantic Bank | | | | | London and River Plate Bank | | | | |
Year	Cash	Earning assets	Deposits	Acceptances	Year	Cash	Earning assets	Deposits	Acceptances
1870					1870	2.9	14.6	10.8	0.7
1880					1880	8.4	13.7	13.9	1.9
1890	0.7	2.5	n.a.	n.a	1890	19.7	40.1	39.2	2.7
1900	5.1	15.0	6.1	0.4	1900	43.6	63.6	97.9	25.5
1910	10.6	48.2	26.1	1.3	1910	42.7	87.4	116.8	24.4
1914	15.2	37.6	17.1	2.1	1914	52.6	83.3	92.5	29.7

| British Bank of South America | | | | | Bank of Buenos Aires | | | | |
Year	Cash	Earning assets	Deposits	Acceptances	Year	Cash	Earning assets	Deposits	Acceptances
1871	2.9	13.9	4.5	9.2	1870				
1881	1.6	17.8	2.8	13.4	1880				
1890	9.3	42.6	11.9	36.5	1890				
1900	4.5	27.7	10.2	18.3	1900				
1910	13.1	64.3	46.4	24.3	1910				
1914	16.3	52.3	40.7	18.0	1914	2.0		52.5	

Note: Earning assets of the German Transatlantic Bank consist of debits in current account, exchange, and securities.

Source: William H. Lough, *Banking Opportunities in South America*, Special Agents Series 106, Department of Commerce, Bureau of Foreign and Domestic Commerce (Washington, D.C.: Government Printing Office, 1915), pp. 33, 37, 49, 50, & 66–68.

Table 6:3-6. *Rates of growth of the real value of earning assets of leading Argentine banks 1867–1914 (percent per year)*

Bank	1857–1900	1870–1880	1880–1890	1890–1900	1900–1910
(1) Spanish Bank of the River Plate	5.1				15.8
(2) Bank of the Nation				4.0	14.8
(3) London and River Plate Bank		2.9	13.3	5.0	1.0
(4) British Bank of South America		6.2	11.1	−3.9	6.5
(5) German Transatlantic Bank				20.0	10.0

Notes: Computed from data in Table 6:4-7, deflated by a U.S. price index put together from Historical Statistics (1976), series E-23 and E-52. All of the price index numbers (except for 1890) are three year averages centered on the named year. The index for 1890 is an index for that year alone (the data for a three year average do not exist). The Bank of the Nation data refer to 1905 (standing for 1900) and 1913 (standing for 1910). The data for the British Bank of South America refer to 1871 (stand for 1870) and 1881 (standing for 1880). The Price index numbers are:

1857	103.0	1894	73.0
1870	138.7	1900	79.5
1871	133.7	1903	86.7
1880	97.7	1905	88.5
1881	103.7	1906	91.1
1890	82.0	1910	98.8
1892	78.5	1913	100.7
		1914	100.9

The base is 1910–1914 = 100. The deflator is an American index because the values in Table 6:4-7 are expressed in U.S. dollars. In the case of the Spanish Bank of the River Plate the data refer to deposits, not assets.

Source: Table 6:3-5.

rapidly. The rate of growth of the British Bank of South America was substantially lower, but it was not extraordinarily low. The London and River Plate was the major exception; deposits expanded at less than 2 percent a year, and earning assets by half that amount. In this decade the bank was expanding the number and size of its branches in other countries, and that expansion most likely accounts for the failure of the Argentine operations to grow more rapidly. By design, resources were being allocated in other directions.[1259]

[1259] Joslin gives no indication of difficulties; he leaves the impression of a most satisfactory performance on the part of the Bank.

The principal foreign banks were British and German. As we have seen, they were conservatively run, focused heavily on the finance of foreign trade, and survived the great Barings crisis. There were also a number of domestic private commercial banks, the Banco Carabassa, for example, that were also conservatively run and that survived the crisis. Failure was, however, the more common experience for the domestic banks, and that experience was shared by the two largest and most important domestic commercial banks, the Bank of the Province of Buenos Aires and the Bank of the Nation. Bank failures, however, had far less impact on Argentine growth than the Australian bank failures of the same period had on growth in the six states. British investors were heavily involved with Australian banks, but not with Argentinean banks. Insofar as the British held bank stocks or bank deposits in Argentina, they held them in British banks that survived the crisis very nicely. The losers in the collapse of the Argentine banking system were the Argentines who held deposits in domestic banks. As a result, although there were immediate repercussions, in the longer run British savers were not alienated from Argentina. Within a few years they were back with investment funds. One would think that the losses suffered by Argentines would have made them reluctant depositors in domestic banks, and initially it did. Very shortly after the crisis, however, the two giant banks – the Bank of the Nation and the Bank of the Province of Buenos Aires – were reconstituted much along a British lines, and until World War I they operated with great success. A few other domestic banks, the Spanish Bank of the River Plate, for example, also seemed to thrive in the post-crisis economy. All three became large, very powerful, well-run banks. By 1914 they operated more than 250 branches (see Table 6:3-7). Unlike the Big Three, the European banks had very few branches. According to Tulchin, in 1910 the Bank of the Nation "handled roughly one-third of all banking business directly and, through its control of foreign exchange, treasury deposits, and links with the Caja de Conversion, had indirect control over at least another third, perhaps another half of the business."[1260]

Following their restructure, although they adopted British managerial practices, both the new Bank of the Nation and the Bank of the Province of Buenos Aires appear to have allocated their loans among prospective

---

[1260] Joseph S. Tulchin, *Agricultural Credit in Argentina, 1910–1926*, Occasional Papers Series, Institute of Latin American Studies, University of North Carolina, Chapel Hill, N.C., pp. 5–6. [Hereafter cited as Tulchin, *Agricultural Credit*.] Lough has a different view: At the outbreak of World War I, a "great part of the mercantile banking business of the Argentine is in the hands of English, German, French, and other foreign banks." Lough, *Financial Developments*, p. 8.

Table 6:3-7. *Leading commercial banks in Argentina on the eve of World War I*

Name of the bank	Date founded	Number of branches in 1914
Bank of the Nation	1892	150+
Bank of Buenos Aires	1826	56
Spanish Bank of the River Plate	1886	54
London and River Plate Bank	1862	13
British Bank of South America	1863	1
German Transatlantic Bank	1887	6

Source: William H. Lough, *Banking Opportunities in South America*, Special Agents Series Number 106, Department of Commerce, Bureau of Foreign and Domestic Commerce (Washington, D.C.: Government Printing Office, 1915), pp. 30, 46, 69, and 70.

borrowers much as their predecessors had done before the catastrophe. In 1913, for example, over 57 percent of the loans of the branches of these banks in Buenos Aires Province outside the city went to ranching and agriculture, over 29 percent to commerce, and 14 percent to industry (see Table 6:3-8). If the focus of the inquiry is expanded to include the activities of the branches of these banks that were located in the city and outside Buenos Aires Province, the relative importance of loans to commercial enterprises is, of course, increased. For example, the loans of the Bank of the Nation were distributed almost equally between commerce, on the one hand, and agriculture and ranching, on the other (see Table 6:3-9). Most, but not all, of these loans were reasonably large. In 1910 only 17 percent of the funds went to loans of 10,000 paper pesos ($4,225) or less. Substantial farmers who owned their land were accommodated, and larger operators in the countryside may have retailed bank loans to small farmers and tenants. In any case the two large domestic banks seem clearly to have been servicing economic sectors – ranching, agriculture, and industry – that the big foreign banks largely ignored.

The commercial banking system, then, in the two decades before World War I was relatively well developed and provided important services to the Argentine economy. There was a variety of large, strong banks that financed foreign trade, underwrote and distributed securities (a few locally but mainly abroad, and in concert with English merchant and German industrial banks), and provided short-term internal finance

Table 6:3-8. *Lending by the Bank of the Province of Buenos Aires and the Bank of the Nation in the Province of Buenos Aires by branches located outside of the national capital, 1907–1913*

Year	Agriculture	Ranching	Industry	Commerce
Panel A: Millions of paper pesos				
1907	19.9	48.0	9.1	31.5
1908	30.0	61.3	14.2	50.8
1909	33.4	13.9	16.1	66.0
1910	40.2	86.6	17.6	65.9
1911	50.8	97.8	21.7	68.5
1912	77.8	121.6	29.1	92.6
1913	59.1	113.4	42.7	86.2
Panel B: Percents				
1907	18.3	44.2	8.4	29.0
1908	19.2	39.2	9.1	32.5
1909	25.8	10.7	12.4	51.0
1910	19.1	41.2	8.4	31.3
1911	21.3	41.0	9.1	28.7
1912	24.2	37.9	9.1	28.8
1913	19.6	37.6	14.2	28.6

Source: Jeremy Adelman, *Frontier Development: Land, Labour, and Capital on the Wheatlands of Argentina and Canada* (Oxford: Clarendon Press, 1994), p. 197.

Table 6:3-9. *Banco De La Nacion, percentage distribution of loans among industrial sectors, 1894–1914*

Years	Agriculture	Ranching	Industry	Commerce	Other
1894	10.7	19.2	11.0	45.5	5.7
1905–1909	0.1	25.5	7.0	32.9	25.3
1910–1914	8.5	24.1	6.9	36.5	23.8

Source: Laura Randall, *An Economic History of Argentina in the Twentieth Century* (New York: Columbia University Press, 1978), p. 51.

and limited mortgage credit. Before the Barings crisis, banking had been a weak element in the Argentine financial structure; after the crisis, it was greatly strengthened.[1261]

6-3a(2). Mortgage banks: Perhaps the most important – at least in quantitative terms – Argentine financial asset was the land mortgage. In view of the character of the Argentine economy, it is not surprising that mortgages were important. The other three settler economies were also rich in land, and there too mortgage credit played a major role in the mobilization of capital.

Perhaps even more than in Australia, Canada, and the United States, in Argentina individuals were also important suppliers of Argentine mortgage credit, although institutions provided the majority of finance (see Table 6:3-10). Moreover, unlike the United States and Canada, but like Australia, before the turn of the century, Argentina managed to obtain a substantial fraction of its mortgage credit from overseas.[1262] Some part of the foreign component consisted of holdings by foreign – particularly British – mortgage companies that operated in Argentina but that were registered abroad. These companies seem to have done very well financially. They were on the ground and were, therefore, in a position to carefully vet loan proposals.[1263] Such firms were important,

---

[1261] See Andres M. Regalsky, "Banking, Trade and the Rise of Capitalism in Argentina, 1850–1930," and Carlos Marichal, "Nation Building and the Origins of Banking in Latin America, 1850–1930," in Alice Teichova, Ginette Kurgan-Van Hentenryk, and Dieter Ziegler, *Banking, Trade and Industry, Europe, America and Asia from the Thirteenth to the Twentieth Century* (Cambridge: Cambridge University Press, 1997), pp. 339–77.

[1262] Table 6.3-10 relates to the years 1914 and 1915. The fraction of mortgages held overseas was almost certainly larger in the 1880s and early 1890s. Australia and, after 1900, Canada also drew foreign mortgage capital. In the case of Australia, however, many Englishmen and Scotsmen thought they were putting their money into deposits in commercial banks of the kind that they were familiar with in the United Kingdom, not into mortgages.

[1263] "Side by side with the land-mortgage banks there are operating in Argentina a number of English mortgage companies, which directly invest their own funds in land mortgages and have earned a highly satisfactory level of profits." Lough, *Financial Developments*, p. 27. "Rural credit [in New Zealand] had been provided mainly by mortgage companies such as the New Zealand Land Mortgage Company, which at the height of the depression in 1888 added 'and the River Plate' to its title and began to transfer its business to Buenos Aires." Denoon, *Settler Capitalism*, p. 150. In 1906 Argentina had "four large mortgage banks, three of which are foreign with a capital of $29,000,000." (Presumably the dollar sign refers to paper pesos.) Hutchinson, *Report on Trade Conditions*, p. 22. "Foreign capital is largely invested in mortgage loan companies and trust companies." Hurley, *Banking and Credit*, p. 25.

Table 6:3-10. *Statistics relating to Argentine land and mortgages, 1914 and 1915 (millions of dollars)*

Panel A: Land and mortgages		
Statistic	Value	Percent
Value of land, 1914	4,510.8	
Value of mortgages, 1915	1,273.9	
Value of mortgages held abroad, 1915	433.1	
Value of mortgages held in Argentina, 1915	840.8	
Value of cedulas outstanding	89.0	
Percentage of the value of land mortgaged		28.2
Percentage of value of mortgages held abroad		34.0
Percentage of mortgages in the form of cedulas		7.0

Panel B: Ownership of mortgages			
Number of owners	Identity of owners	Value of mortgages	Share in total (percent)
1	National Mortgage Bank	247.6	19.5
40	Mortgage companies and associations	368.8	29.1
19	Commercial banks	84.4	6.6
15	Insurance companies	13.9	1.1
22	Banks and companies in the interior	8.7	0.7
n.a.	Private creditors	545.9	43.0
	Total	1,269.3	100.0

Notes: (1). The values of mortgages in Panel A sum to a slightly higher total than the total in Panel B, presumably due to rounding errors in the underlying source. Tornquist (p. 237) asserts that the mortgage totals in this table understate the true totals.

Sources: Computed from Ernesto Tornquist and Company, Ltd., *The Economic Development of the Argentine Republic in the Last Fifty Years* (Buenos Aires: Ernesto Tornquist and Company, Ltd., 1919), pp. 237, 255, & 328. William H. Lough, *Banking Opportunities in South America*, Special Agents Series Number 106, Department of Commerce, Bureau of Foreign and Domestic Commerce (Washington, D.C.: Government Printing Office, 1915), p. 27.

but they almost certainly do not account for all of the foreigners operating in the Argentine mortgage market.[1264] Some of these investors must
have been individuals, rather than institutions. Why foreign individuals
were prepared to acquire an asset so charged with problems of asymmetric information and moral hazard calls for an explanation.

Large-scale foreign involvement in the mortgage market developed
during the great investment and land boom of the 1880s. It had been government policy to promote investment in social overhead capital – particularly railways – in order to open the interior to development and to
integrate those regions into the national market.[1265] Two institutions were
created to expand financial opportunities to developers of both urban
and rural land: the Mortgage Bank of the Province of Buenos Aires,
founded by the Provincial government in 1872, and the National Mortgage Bank, chartered by the Republic in 1886.[1266] The financial innovation that was chiefly responsible for smoothing the flow of foreign
finance into the Argentine mortgage market, however, was the *cedula*, a
type of instrument that had been previously employed elsewhere in
South America, but that was not introduced into Argentina until 1886.
The *cedula* was a mortgage bond, guaranteed by the bank and by the
government that had chartered the bank – the Province, in the case of
the Bank of Buenos Aires, and the Republic, in the case of the National
Bank. Three additional features made the bonds particularly attractive:
(1) collateral was to consist of land appraised at least twice the value of
the bond, (2) the bond was to be subject to an annual amortization, and
(3) the total value of *cedulas* to be issued by each bank was to be strictly
limited.

A potential borrower would go to one of the two banks to seek a loan.
If his project was approved, the bank would issue the borrower a bond
or bonds – *cedulas* – that the borrower could then sell in the open market.
The borrower was obliged to make periodic interest and amortization

---

[1264] See Table 6.3-10, Panel A, line (3) and Panel B, second line.

[1265] Much of what follows was drawn from John H. Williams, *Argentine International Trade Under Inconvertable Paper Money* (Cambridge, Mass.: Harvard Univer-sity Press, 1920), pp. 70–85 [Hereafter cited as Williams, *Argentine International Trade*]; A.G. Ford, *The Gold Standard, 1880–1914, Britain and Argentina* (Oxford: Clarendon Press, 1962), p. 99 [Hereafter cited as Ford, *The Gold Standard*]; and Lough, *Financial Developments*, pp. 26–27.

[1266] The original purpose of the two mortgage banks seems to have been to promote long term lending on farm and ranch land, but in fact substantial amounts of mortgage credit were diverted to urban ventures, both business and residential building. Jeremy Adelman, "Agricultural Credit in the Province of Buenos Aires, Argentina, 1890–1914," *Journal of Latin American Studies*, Vol. 22, Part 1 (Feb-ruary 1990), pp. 78–79. [Hereafter cited as Adelman, "Agricultural Credit."]

payments to the bank. The bank, however, was obliged to make interest and amortization payments to the bond holder, regardless of whether or not the borrower had paid. Should the bank fail to make interest or amortization payments, the debt became an obligation of the relevant governmental body. The problems of asymmetric information and moral hazard were dealt with through the imprimatur of the bank and of the government. In view of these guarantees, the lender did not have to have personal knowledge of the property on which the *cedula* was based. The rules governing the amount of collateral required and the volume of mortgage bonds that could be issued made it clear to the lender that the banks and governments took their responsibilities seriously.

The *cedula* was a great success. It permitted large amounts of finance to be funneled into Argentine landed activities. Before the great crash of the early 1890s, about 400 million paper pesos worth of *cedulas* had been sold. Of that total, some 360 million were purchased by overseas investors.[1267] But the *cedulas* did not work out exactly as planned. First, most of the *cedulas* were denominated in paper pesos, and during the latter half of the 1880s the paper peso went to a substantial discount against gold. As a result, the *cedula* became a speculative instrument; its value varied widely both with changes in the gold premium and with expectations about the future premium. Perhaps more importantly, the depreciation of the paper peso went hand in hand with a boom in land prices and with the associated speculation in land values. Price increases, however, were fragile: Any serious effort to reduce the gold premium, to stabilize the monetary system, and to return to a true gold standard would lead to a decline in land prices and, thus, reduce the collateral margin on the *cedulas*. Second, the strict limits established by government on the total permissible volume of *cedulas* were very quickly relaxed – especially in the case of the bonds guaranteed by the Provincial Bank.[1268] The volume of *cedulas* expanded rapidly at the end of the 1880s. Third, the banks' administrations – particularly the Provincial bank's – were corrupt. The appraisals of land owned by government officials and by intimates of the bank officials vastly overstated true value. More importantly, however, the banks had very limited resources. They did not need resources to float *cedulas*, but they did need them when borrowers began to default, and default they did – and on a large scale – during the crisis of the early 1890s. The Provincial Bank, a bank that had been both the more reckless and more corrupt, failed. The bank's

---

[1267] Williams, *Argentine International Trade*, pp. 83, 85.

[1268] The Provincial bank issued 275 million paper pesos worth of *cedulas* in the four years 1887–90; the National Bank created only 126.5 million. Williams, *Argentine International Trade*, pp. 82–83.

cedulas continued to be quoted on exchanges for a time at between 10 and 20 percent of par. Although it was obliged to default on some interest payments, the National Bank, after receiving some help from the Republic, weathered the storm. The National Bank continued in operation, and it continued issuing *cedulas*: 26.3 million paper pesos' worth between 1899 and 1904 (Series H), 30.0 million, between 1900 and 1905 (Series K), 38.3 million, between 1907 and 1910 (Series L), and 190 million, between 1910 and 1913. Another 21 million was authorized for 1914. The total of these five issues comes to 305 million, or 129.8 million in U.S. dollars.[1269] In 1914, 89 million U.S. dollars' worth of *cedulas* were still outstanding, and *cedulas* were still the most important assets traded on the Buenos Aires stock exchange.[1270] The National Bank held an additional 248 million dollars in direct mortgage loans. Together, the value of the bank's *cedulas* and the mortgages it held accounted for over one-quarter of the value of all Argentine mortgages, and almost precisely 40 percent of the value of mortgages that were owned domestically. If the mortgages owned by the private banker Ernesto Tornquist are included in the total, it is possible to account for over half of the value of all domestically held mortgages.

6-3a(3). Private banks: Early in the nineteenth century, in the absence of joint stock banks, many merchants added banking to their usual mercantile business. Several continued to perform these functions even as joint stock banks entered the industry. For some, banking became the most important part of their business; for a subset of these, investment banking became more important than commercial banking. As Charles A. Jones writes:

> Almost all peripheral merchants who attempted bold adaptive strategies in the second half of the nineteenth century tried their hand at banking sooner or later. Certain banking functions – a trade in commercial bills and bullion, the collection of credit information, short-term lending to government, and the receipt of deposits – had been commonplace aspects of mercantile business until the rise of joint stock banking. It made sense to try to build on accumulated skills and connections in this field. Furthermore, a bank could be used to fuel favored ventures – one's own, and those of selected clients and friends in government.[1271]

[1269] Lough, *Financial Developments*, p. 27.

[1270] Tornquist, *The Economic Development of the Argentine Republic*, pp. 213, 302–9, 328.

[1271] Charles A. Jones, *International Business in the Nineteenth Century: The Rise and Fall of a Cosmopolitan Bourgeoisie* (Brighton, Sussex: Wheatsheaf Books, 1987),

The mercantile firms from which private banks developed were part of an international coterie; many had foreign origins and long-standing overseas trading and financial connections. Perhaps the most notable of these firms was formed by Ernesto Tornquist, a leading figure in the successful reorganization of the foreign debt of the Republic in the aftermath of the Barings crisis. Consideration of his career is a useful vehicle for coming to terms with the private banking organizations of Buenos Aires. The Tornquists' origins were apparently in Switzerland, but members of the family were trained as businessmen in Germany, Belgium, and the United States (Baltimore). They engaged in the trade with Argentina from early in the nineteenth century, and part of the family then moved to Buenos Aires. Ernesto, who had gone through an apprenticeship in Germany and had worked in a mercantile house in Buenos Aires, went into business on his own in the early 1870s. He began as a foreign trader but quickly expanded into sugar production in Tucuman and investments in land. Eventually he split the firm into two independent, but related components: one to continue the original mercantile line (exporting foods and importing German and Belgian machinery), and the other to operate as an industrial bank. Tapping his sources in Antwerp for financial support, he created a sugar company and a refinery. Through the two organizations, he dealt with every level of sugar production and marketing.[1272] Next, he moved into meat processing, packaging, and both foreign and domestic sales (at one time his firm operated two hundred butcher shops in Buenos Aires). From sugar and meat he expanded into light metals, petroleum, chemicals, forestry, and fishing. His investment banking organization extended long-term credit, and it participated as a sleeping partner (limited liability) in many firms; Tornquist himself was president of eight. The firm became a major player in the mortgage market: "At the outbreak of World War I [they] controlled 1,526 mortgages worth 104,175,010.98 gold pesos."[1273] This figure is enormous. In 1914 domestic holdings of Argentine mortgages amounted to only about 871 million gold pesos. Thus, Tornquist held

---

p. 126. [Hereafter cited as Jones, *International Business.*] For a discussion of similar motivations for the creation of banks in the nineteenth-century United States, see Naomi R. Lamoreaux, *Insider Lending: Banks, Personal Connections, and Economic Development in Industrial New England* (Cambridge: Cambridge University Press, 1994).

[1272] Jones, *International Business*, pp. 137–38.

[1273] Guy, "Dependency, the Credit Market and Argentine Industrialization," pp. 546–47; Carlos Marichal, "La Gran Burguesia Comercial y Financeria de Buenos Aires, 1860–1914: Anatomia de Cinco Grupos," manuscript, October 1982, appendix. [Hereafter cited as Marichal, "La Gran Burguesia."]

better than one-ninth of the value of Argentine mortgages owned by persons or institutions domiciled in Argentina.[1274]

Tornquist is the most striking, but by no means the only, merchant-turned-financier. The founder of the Portalis firm came to Argentina from France in the 1870s and turned immediately to the import business and to land development.[1275] From these activities he moved into forestry and wood products (railway ties, for example) and then into tobacco, sugar, and tannin. In combination with Anglo-French bankers, he created the forest products firm La Forestal, a firm that owned more than one million hectares of forest land. Given that there is unlikely to have been more than sixty-five million hectares of forest land in all of Argentina, this holding is huge. Portalis also owned factories, rail lines, and port facilities. In all its activities the Portalis firm worked closely with the French Bank of Rio de la Plata.[1276]

Otto Bemberg, a firm with a German background, made its fortune in beer. Ultimately, in fact, it held a national monopoly in that drink. The Bemberg firm acquired a glass factory to make the beer bottles, and a railway line to carry raw materials to the brewery. It was also involved in sugar refining and distillery operations.[1277] Bunge and Born were both international wheat merchants and the managers of grain elevators. They bought a rail line to move the wheat and also entered the milling industry, but in Brazil, not Argentina. The firm was also heavily involved with land and mortgages. Devoto, a firm with Italian origins, was linked in business with the Bank of Italy and Rio de la Plata.[1278] Together they promoted a merger that resulted in the largest match-producing firm in Argentina – the firm employed four thousand workers. Devoto was also involved in wholesale cold storage (meat), mining, chemicals, electrical, and navigation companies.

[1274] Tornquist, *The Economic Development of the Argentine Republic*, pp. 237, 328. "By the late 1910s the [Tornquist] group controlled over fourteen industrial companies, comprising beer, sugar, meat, metullurgy, machinery, furniture, tobacco, glass, candles and soap." Barbero, "Argentina: Industrial Growth," p. 377.

[1275] The remainder of this section is drawn chiefly from Marichal, "La Gran Burguesia."

[1276] Despite the name, the Bank was domestically controlled, but it had strong links to the local French community.

[1277] Guy, "Dependency, the Credit Market, and Argentine Industrialization," pp. 546–47.

[1278] The Bank was domestically controlled, but it was deeply involved with the local Italian business community. See Barbero, "Argentina: Industrial Growth," p. 377.

These firms have certain characteristics in common. All were entre-preneurial; all were involved in complex joint undertakings with both local and foreign trading-finance firms.[1279] Some of their undertakings were very large – Tornquist's operations in sugar and in the mortgage market and Portalis's involvement with forest industries, to cite two examples – but none of them had major investments in railways, power stations, or heavy industry, the sectors that required very large supplies of finance. Unlike American investment and British merchant bankers, but like German universal bankers, they invested heavily on their own account. Unlike the American, British, and German bankers, they were not involved in the underwriting, or even in the large-scale distribution of the securities of other firms.[1280] As a result, they did not perform, at least in an important way, the prime function of the American invest-ment bankers, the British merchant bankers, and the German universal bankers: the promotion of saving by a large number and wide variety of potential savers, and the mobilization of those savings in a way that made it possible to carry out very large investment projects.

As a group these private merchant/private banking firms resemble certain private German banks that operated in the 1830s, 1880s, and 1850s. Their sources of investable funds were private, and they invested in a wide range of industrial and social overhead projects, projects linked to the "bank" by personal and family ties.[1281] There appear to be few examples of such firms in Australia, Canada, or the United States. Perhaps in Argentina there were more ethnic links to the continent than there were in the other three countries.

6-3b. Insurance companies

If the data reported by the director of the American Republics Bureau are consistent with the figures provided by Tornquist (and they seem to be), the insurance industry – chiefly fire, life, and accident – grew at a remarkable rate between the turn of the century and the years just before World War I.[1282] According to the director, these companies col-

---

[1279] For an account of these relationships, see Jones, *International Business*.

[1280] Barbero, "Argentina: Industrial Growth," pp. 376–77, argues that maybe [they were] closer to the Japanese Zaibatsu or the Korean Chaebol.

[1281] Michael Sturmer, Gabriel Teichman and Wilhelm Treue, *Striking the Balance, Sal., Oppenheimer Jr. & Cie* (London: Weidenfeld and Nicolson, 1994).

[1282] *Annual Report of the Director of the Bureau of the American Republics for the Year 1903*, 58th Congress, 2nd Session, Document No. 111, Part 1 (Washington, D.C.: Government Printing Office, 1903), p. 257. Tornquist, *The Economic Devel-opment of the Argentine Republic*, p. 252.

The distribution of total premiums collected in 1914 by type of insurance was:

lected, on average, premiums worth between 1.7 and 2.3 million U.S. dollars in the years 1897 through 1901; however, about 43 percent went to foreign companies, firms that were not investing heavily in local projects.[1283] Tôrnquist reports that premiums had risen to the equivalent of $12.1 million by 1909, and they increased further, to $19.8 million, in 1913. By 1914 there were eighty-two domestic and thirty-four foreign insurance companies of all kinds; 28 percent of the premiums went to foreign companies.

In the case of life insurance companies, a substantial fraction of premiums represent gross savings. In the case of fire and marine companies, the contribution to the savings stream is much smaller. Since even fire and marine insurance companies need to invest the premiums between the date of receipt and the date of the insurance payments, and, since the managers of fire, life, and marine insurance companies almost certainly have a more educated view of investment alternatives than do the individuals who buy the policies, all three industries do, however, contribute to the solution of the problems of capital mobilization. The data indicate that, in Argentina, this particular outlet for savings was growing rapidly. Nonetheless, it remained very small by almost any standard. For example, it was equal in value to just over 1 percent of average annual gross capital formation in the years 1910–14.[1284] It also appears that the Argentine companies were so small that no single firm was likely to have been able to finance a major undertaking in either manufacturing or public utilities. In 1914 mutual and cooperative insurance companies took in, on average, the equivalent of $170,690 U.S. dollars per firm in premiums; and they had, on average, $13.2 million U.S. dollars of insurance in force. The joint stock companies (as opposed to mutuals and cooperatives) were a little larger: On average they took in almost $200,000 U.S. dollars a year in premiums, and had $16.6 million U.S. dollars of insurance in force.

Type of Insurance	Gold Pesos	Paper Pesos
Fire	62%	45%
Life and Accident	23	52
Marine	15	3

[1283] Charles Jones, "Insurance Companies," in D.C.M. Platt (ed.), *Business Imperialism, 1840–1930, An Inquiry Based on British Experience in Latin America* (Oxford: Clarendon Press, 1977), pp. 64, 65, 71. [Hereafter cited as Jones, "Insurance Companies."]

[1284] Computed from Appendix Tables A-10 and A-11.

The asset holdings of the insurance companies are more relevant to this study, but they are less certain. If the relationships among premiums, insurance, and assets were similar to those in the United States, the assets of Argentine insurance companies – both those that were domestically and those that were foreign-owned – may, in 1914, have totaled somewhere between the equivalent of fifty and ninety million U.S. dollars, or between 0.8 percent and 1.4 percent of the total stock of Argentine tangible wealth, the capital stock plus land.[1285] The distribution of those assets between types of investment is also far from certain. A governmental investigating committee reported that insurance companies owned mortgages valued at about 13.8 million U.S. dollars in 1914.[1286] This figure represented just over 1 percent of the value of Argentine mortgages outstanding, or something over 1.5 percent of the value of domestically owned Argentine mortgages.[1287] As to the remaining assets, some part consisted of government securities. In view of the important role in the industry played by foreign companies, despite legislation requiring foreign insurance companies to acquire and deposit domestic securities – usually government bonds – a substantial fraction of the remainder was almost certainly held in the form of investments outside of Argentina.[1288]

The insurance companies, then, were not major players in the finance of Argentine economic development, nor, it seems probable, did they figure importantly in the capital formation of any substantial sector of the economy. But largely because of the vigorous activity of domestic entrepreneurs, they did provide a rapidly growing vehicle for savings.[1289]

[1285] The U.S. relationships were derived from *Historical Statistics of the United States,* 1975, Part 2, Series X-895, X-882, X-908 (all three for 1914), X-919, and X-928 (both for 1931). The Argentine statistics are from Tornquist, *The Economic Development of the Argentine Republic,* pp. 252–55.

[1286] Mortgage ownership is, however, attributed to only 15 firms out of the industry total of 116 (13 percent). That percentage seems improbably small. Tornquist believes that the value of mortgages was undercounted, but he does not specifically impugn the mortgage data for insurance companies. Nonetheless, it seems probable that insurance company holdings were substantially greater than the committee reported. Tornquist, *The Economic Development of the Argentine Republic,* p. 237.

[1287] Tornquist, *The Economic Development of the Argentine Republic,* p. 237.

[1288] By 1913 the proportion of the funds of the Royal Exchange that were invested in foreign government and municipal securities was 12 percent; in 1890 it had been 0.8 percent. A great deal, if not all, of this investment may have been specifically occasioned by deposit legislation. Jones, "Insurance Companies," p. 71. As in Canada, restrictions on foreign insurance companies seem to have led to the withdrawal of some foreign firms from the Argentine market.

[1289] Jones, "Insurance Companies," passim.

6-3c. The Stock Exchange

The Stock Exchange – The *Bolsa* of Commerce – was formed in 1854. The regulations were revised in 1886 to expand the potential lists of members and to create an associated Chamber of Commerce. Further changes were introduced on seven occasions between 1890 and 1911. Membership was extended to merchants, landowners, ship's captains, diplomats, and government officials, all of whom were given limited rights (one hour a day) to conduct transactions on the Exchange. Most trades were, however, still carried out by brokers. Early in the twentieth century, although the number of brokers was very much smaller, the membership of the Exchange totaled roughly 4,000.[1290]

Gold and silver, government securities, *cedulas*, and the stocks and bonds of joint stock companies were all traded on the Exchange. By the early twentieth century, of the financial assets, the *cedulas* were clearly the most important. In the eight years before World War I broke out, the values fluctuated between 63 and 271 million paper pesos per year, or between \$27 and \$115 million U.S. dollars. By way of comparison, in six of those years, no more than seventeen million U.S. dollars worth of all government securities were traded; in the remaining two, the figures were thirty-six and fifty-nine million U.S. dollars. In the early twentieth century the overseas debt of the Republic alone – exclusive of provincial or municipal debt – was estimated to have totaled about 290 million U.S. dollars.[1291] The *Bolsa*'s involvement with public debt was, therefore, relatively modest.[1292]

In the early twentieth century the number of joint stock companies with securities listed on the *Bolsa* typically numbered between fifty and sixty – ten banks and forty to fifty industrial firms – and trading activity seems to have been limited. For example, of the fifty securities listed on August 30, 1916, only thirty were traded on that day, and eleven had not been quoted since before the war. There were, of course, many more than

---

[1290] Tornquist, *The Economic Development of the Argentine Republic*, pp. 209–14.

[1291] Tornquist, *The Economic Development of the Argentine Republic*, pp. 213, 302–3, 328.

[1292] During the booming 1880s, *cedulas* were chiefly held abroad. Whether that distribution was still the case in the early twentieth century is not clear. In 1913 the value of *cedulas* traded was virtually equal to the value of *cedulas* outstanding. If it can be assumed that foreigners would typically have moved their holdings on foreign exchanges not on the *Bolsa*, the data on transactions could be interpreted to mean that the *cedulas* had been largely repatriated before World War I. But since there is no reason why foreigners would have to operate abroad, the assumption may not be correct. Williams, *Argentine International Trade*, pp. 84–85; Tornquist, *The Economic Development of the Argentine Republic*, p. 213; Lough, *Financial Developments*, p. 27.

fifty or sixty joint stock companies in Argentina: The census reports 679 in 1914 with capital of about 1.77 billion U.S. dollars. But over three-quarters of the value of the stocks and bonds of these companies had been issued on foreign exchanges, not the *Bolsa*; and over 85 percent were owned by persons or institutions domiciled outside Argentina. Thus, with respect to joint stock company securities, the *Bolsa*, was left with a rather limited role.[1293]

The identity of industrial firms with stocks listed on the *Bolsa* suggests something of the nature of the economy that had developed in Argentina before the war. Among the firms listed on August 30, 1916, were two sugar producers, two meat firms, one fruit merchant, two distilleries, two breweries, one dairy, one salt company, two land companies, four timber companies, one phosphorous firm, two paper companies, three firms operating warehouses and docks, two construction firms, one gas company, and two electric companies. The most important power companies, however, were German and were registered and financed overseas. The biggest land companies were also foreign-organized and funded, mainly by the English, but also by the Germans.[1294] Among the firms listed on the *Bolsa*, none was engaged in traditional heavy industry nor in the manufacture of machinery. According to J.A. Massel, writing in 1916, "Machinery manufacturing in that country is very insignificant; in fact . . . one might say that there is none at all."[1295]

[1293] Tornquist, *The Economic Development of the Argentine Republic*, pp. 250–51. The suggestion is that roughly 265 million U.S. dollars worth of the stocks and bonds of Argentine joint stock companies were held in Argentina. Most seem not to have been traded on the *Bolsa*.

[1294] "The important cities of South America are, as a rule, supplied with essential services, including street railways, water gas and electricity. Nearly all of these enterprises have been financed in England or Germany, and supplies have been furnished by English and German manufacturers. . . . In England, and to a less extent in Germany, there have been floated a number of land and cattle companies operating in Argentina and Uruguay and in one or two instances in Southern Chile and southern [sic] Brazil. One of these companies which raises sheep on a large scale . . . is now paying 40 per cent dividends. There is a possibility of further development along this line by American capital." Lough, *Financial Developments*, p. 26. See also Frederic M. Halsey, *Investments in Latin America and the British West Indies*, Department of Commerce, Bureau of Foreign and Domestic Commerce, Special Agents Series, No. 169 (Washington, D.C.: Government Printing Office, 1918), pp. 68–71, for a treatment of European investment in electric power and gas. [Hereafter cited as Halsey, *Investments in Latin America*.]

[1295] J.A. Massel, *Markets for Machines and Machine Tools in Argentina*, Department of Commerce, Bureau of Foreign and Domestic Commerce, Special Agents Series, No. 116 (Washington, D.C.: Government Printing Office, 1916), p. 18. [Hereafter cited as Massel, *Markets for Machines*.] "Investments in manufac-

The market for private securities was, thus, very thin, indeed.[1296] No doubt this situation reflected the nature of the economy, but it must also have meant that savers were given only the sketchiest education in the holding of paper assets other than mortgages, and that the potential public resources available to visionary entrepreneurs were very limited.[1297] The large projects – railways, power plants, large land companies, tram companies, packing houses – were organized and financed from abroad.

6-4. Financing development

Argentine development in the period 1870–1914 can be defined in terms of the four major components of investment that were undertaken: (1) a transportation network that tied the economy together was put in place; (2) the area of arable agricultural land was expanded, and the cattle industry was modernized; (3) there was a dramatic urban construction boom – in particular, the great, modern city of Buenos Aires was created; (4) the industrial sector – a sector concentrated in Buenos Aires province – grew rapidly, so rapidly, in fact, that it produced a continually rising fraction of national output. Two other components of investment, components that carried over from earlier times, were also important: the finance of trade and of governments. Two issues need to be addressed: first, how large, in the aggregate, was the commitment to investment? Second, what was the source of its finance?

6-4a. The aggregates

First, the scale of Argentine investment was sufficient to permit extraordinarily high rates of growth of both real GDP and real GDP per capita. In comparison with the experience of the other three settler economies, the fraction of real GDP devoted to investment was not unusually high. Leaving aside the period 1895–99, it typically ran around 20 percent gross, and 15 to 18 percent net (see Table 6:4-1). Argentina's

turing enterprises, except packing houses in Argentina and Uruguay, are not large enough to require more than local financing. The packing-house enterprise in which American capital is interested are for the present being handled directly by well-known American companies." Lough, *Financial Developments*, p. 26.

[1296] Argentina had "an economy with difficult access to long term credit." Barbero, "Argentina: Industrial Growth," p. 376.

[1297] Lough draws attention to a second problem: "Time deposits are by no means confined, as in this country [the U.S.], pretty largely to individuals, estates, and nonprofit-making corporations. Many business houses normally carry considerable sums in time deposits; this is partly due to the relative scarcity of stock and bond investments, which have a quick market." Lough, *Financial Developments*, p. 124.

Table 6:4-1. *Argentine capital formation as a percentage of domestic product, 1875–1914 (percents)*

Years	Ratio of gross capital formation to gross domestic product	Ratio of net capital formation to net domestic product
1875–1884	20.8	18.5
1885–1894	19.9	16.5
1895–1899	13.3	10.8
1900–1909	20.0	16.9
1910–1914	18.0	14.6

Source: Appendix Tables 8 and 10, conventional concepts.

record was at least the equal to those of Australia, and of Canada down to the mid-1890s. The United States had higher rates, and Canada after the 1890s, much higher.[1298]

The Argentine economy, however was growing very much faster than those of the three other settler economies, despite investment rates that were no higher, and usually lower. Relative to capital in Australia, Canada, and the United States, Argentine capital must have been very productive. Furthermore, over time it appears to have become steadily more productive. Over the same period, in the United States, at least, the productivity of capital declined.

Table 6:4-2 contains estimates of the inverse of capital productivity ratios, capital/output ratios. The capital/output ratios were computed by holding sectoral rates constant, at their putative levels in 1892, and allowing the structure of the economy to shift as it did historically. Across time, the computed ratios decline quite precipitately; sectors with high ratios were clearly losing relative importance. Investment in transportation and in urban construction, sectors with typically high ratios, was, however, increasing, not declining. Therefore, these sectors cannot have been the

[1298] It should be said that in what is more nearly a comparable period in the history of U.S. development – the antebellum decades – U.S. investment rates did not exceed the Argentine rates for the years 1875–1914. Robert Gallman, "Economic Growth and Structural Change," in Stanley Engerman and Robert Gallman (eds.), *Cambridge Economic History of the United States*, Vol. 2 (forthcoming), table 12.

Table 6:4-2. *Effects of changes in the structure of Real Gross Domestic Product on the Argentine capital/output ratios, 1884–1913*

Year	Ratio of capital to Gross Domestic Product
1884	3.38
1892	2.75
1913	2.37

Source: Appendix Tables 13 and 14.

sources of the observed reduction in the aggregate capital/output ratio. The sector that declined most dramatically – in relative terms – was the pastoral sector, and that sector was also marked by a high capital/output ratio. Here is the source of the falling aggregate capital/output ratio, or, to put it another way, the source of improvements in capital productivity. Pastoral capital consisted chiefly of animals, and the ratio of the value of the stock of animals to the value of net output was high. Consider the case of cattle raised for slaughter. For every animal killed, there were several in stock – young animals and breeding stock. The decline in the Argentine aggregate capital/output ratio was, then, in large part due to a shift in the industrial structure of real GDP away from the pastoral sector. If, in the calculation, allowance had also been made for improvements in husbandry, the pastoral sector's ratio would probably also have fallen; and that decline would have exerted further downward pressure on the aggregate ratio.[1299]

As the railways built in the nineteenth century began to be used more intensively, the transport sector almost certainly must also have contributed to the decline in the capital/output ratio.[1300] As in the case of the

[1299] Improvements in husbandry can reduce the ratio of the number of animals held in stock to the number of animals slaughtered. For example, 150 years ago in the United States, most of the cattle that were slaughtered were at least five years of age; today, they are less than one year old. The holdover stock can thus be reduced to breeding animals alone. Changes of this sort were taking place in Argentine ranching. For example, the shift of the source of cattle food from pampas grass to alfalfa meant that cattle could be brought to slaughter one year earlier than before.

[1300] Transportation firms are "faced with indivisibilities [such that] the size of the capital stock is not always a good proxy for the annual flow of services it delivers." Albert Fishlow, "Productivity and Technical Change in the Railway

Table 6:4-3. *Foreign capital as a percentage of real gross capital formation*

Years	Gross capital formation (conventional)	Gross capital formation (unconventional)
1881–1884	43.8	43.1
1885–1889	74.0	71.7
1895–1899	36.1	35.3
1900–1909	69.5	66.7
1910–1914	68.9	66.8

Source: Appendix Table 9.

United States, the industrial sector may have been marked by a rising ratio; but these movements are quite unlikely to have overbalanced the effects of structural changes and the developments within the pastoral and transportation sectors. It seems safe to conclude that the aggregate Argentine ratio did, indeed, decline.

Leaving aside the last years of the 1890s, Argentine gross investment in the thirty-nine years 1875–1914 ran about 20 percent of GDP, a value large enough to accommodate a very high rate of growth for the economy. Somewhere between one-third and one-half of this investment was derived from domestic savings, and the rest represented foreign investment (see Table 6:4-3 and the Appendix, part 4). If there was a trend in this proportion, it was downward; that is, Argentina was more dependent on foreign investment just before World War I than it had been in the almost four decades since 1875. In this respect Argentine experience differed markedly from that of Canada, where the savings rate rose strikingly in the years following the mid-1890s; from that of the United States, a country that was sometimes a net borrower and sometimes a net lender in these years, but still financed investment chiefly from savings; and even from that of Australia, forced by the reluctance of potential foreign lenders to depend mainly on domestic savings. Foreign investment came to Argentina in two great surges, surges asso-

Sector," in Dorothy S. Brady, *Output, Employment, and Productivity in the United States After 1800*, NBER Studies in Income and Wealth, Vol. 30 (New York: National Bureau of Economic Research, 1966), p. 630. Because of these indivisibilities the capital/output ratio of a railway network is likely to be highest just after it is completed. As the economy grows up to the network, the capital/output ratio will fall.

Table 6:4-4. *Distribution of foreign investment among Argentine industries in 1898*

Industry	Share of the total
Transportation	83%
Banks	6
Land companies	4
Light companies	2
Other	6
Total	101

Note: The sum reported by the Consul is in error by three million gold pesos. The error was corrected before this table was prepared.

Source: U. S. Department of State, *Consular Report for the Argentine Republic, 1898* (Washington D.C.: GPO, 1899), p. 582.

ciated with the two long booms experienced by the economy in the late 1880s and the first fourteen years of the twentieth century. This pattern appears in the aggregate data on foreign investment flows (Table 6:4-3), as well as in our series on capital called. The British are widely believed to have contributed about 60 percent of the total foreign capital invested in Argentina before World War I, and the sectoral pattern of British investment seems to have been reasonably close to the pattern shown by total foreign investment (Tables 6:4-4 and 6:4-5).[1301] The capital called series, then, may be a not unreasonable basis for studying the volume of foreign investment in Argentina, as well as the temporal and sectoral patterns of that investment (Tables 6:4-6a through 6:4-7c).

Over the fifty years between 1865 and 1914, Argentine calls totaled almost $1.86 billion U.S. dollars, an average of about $37 million per year. These flows were, however, subject to wide year-to-year fluctuations. There were two years (1877 and 1878) in which there were no calls and one year (1895) in which the total was less than $500,000. In terms of the time path, there was a small surge in the early 1870s (more than $31 million in 1871) – a surge cut off by the depression beginning in 1873 – a major run-up that began in the mid-1880s that peaked at $121 million in 1889 and that collapsed with the onset of the Barings crisis, and finally

---

[1301] C.L. Lewis, "British Business in Argentina," Economic History Department, London School of Economics, Working Paper No. 26/95, June 1995, p. 3.

Table 6:4-5. *Distribution of British investment among Argentine businesses and between the private and government sectors, 1865–1913*

Industry	1865	1875	1885	1895	1905	1913
Finance	80%	35%	19%	11%	9%	14%
Transportation	20	65	76	82	82	75
Public utilities	0	0	3	2	4	4
Commerce & industries	0	0	2	5	5	7
Total	100	100	100	100	100	100
Sector						
Private	53	36	45	54	62	64
Government	47	64	55	46	38	36
Total	100	100	100	100	100	100

Note: The summations of the data on the individual pages are somewhat greater than the total appearing on p. 145.

Source: Irving Stone, *The Composition and Distribution of British Investment in Latin America, 1865 to 1913* (New York and London: Garland Publishing Company, Inc., 1987), pp. 67A, 73A, 79, 81, 83, 85, 88, 89, 95, 97, 101A, 117, 117A, 137, and 142A.

a near tidal wave of calls in the first years of the twentieth century. Total calls reached $274 million in 1903, $126 million in 1907, and more than $135 million in 1909 before receding to an average of about $80 million over the last quinquennium before the war.

6-4b. The sectoral pattern of investment

6-4b(1). Ranching and agriculture: The decline in the Argentine capital/output ratio meant that, as time passed, a peso's worth of investment had a larger and larger impact on economic growth. Indeed, Argentina could not have generated such an extraordinary expansion and development, given the nation's net investment rates, unless the capital/output ratio had fallen. The marked shift in the structure of the economy, and the probable decline in the pastoral capital/output ratio, meant that a redeployment of new investment could take place; that is, some new investment could be directed away from what had here to fore been the most productive choices – railways and ranches – toward new

Table 6:4-6(a). *Argentine calls on the London capital market, 1865–1914 (thousands of dollars)*

Year	Manufacturing, commercial, & miscellaneous	Finance	Government	Agriculture & extractive	Transport	Public utilities	Total capital called
1865	0	1,929	0	19	5,844	0	7,792
1866	0	633	1,826	0	2,472	55	4,986
1867	0	0	0	195	4,870	0	5,065
1868	0	0	4,273	0	0	0	4,273
1869	0	0	2,612	0	110	0	2,721
1870	0	0	4,434	578	1,279	0	6,291
1871	0	0	26,388	140	4,865	0	31,393
1872	0	0	5,528	0	2,457	657	8,643
1873	0	0	1,491	0	2,739	0	4,230
1874	0	974	10,088	0	4,818	0	15,880
1875	0	0	0	0	2,265	0	2,265
1876	0	0	0	0	524	0	524
1877	0	0	0	0	0	0	0
1878	0	0	0	0	0	0	0
1879	0	0	0	0	331	0	331
1880	97	0	0	0	1,325	0	1,422
1881	358	0	0	170	1,118	341	1,987
1882	438	0	9,180	0	9,969	0	19,588
1883	0	0	4,490	3,171	13,460	0	21,122
1884	49	0	36,912	1,722	14,186	24	52,893
1885	0	0	828	24	17,028	414	18,295
1886	0	0	26,502	24	18,803	414	45,742
1887	2,951	0	23,969	341	39,522	463	67,246
1888	1,023	0	55,656	2,946	41,007	6,307	106,939
1889	3,145	1,522	37,426	637	66,068	12,243	121,042

Year							
1890	1,767	0	0	91	41,169	0	43,027
1891	0	0	0	182	30,756	0	30,938
1892	0	0	0	0	7,402	497	7,899
1893	0	1,218	0	821	1,140	0	3,178
1894	0	0	0	0	1,218	0	1,218
1895	73	0	0	0	404	0	477
1896	0	244	0	0	9,915	456	10,615
1897	0	244	0	46	6,132	1,299	7,721
1898	0	0	0	0	10,052	2,394	12,445
1899	0	0	9,740	92	5,296	400	5,788
1900	0	0	0	0	7,521	544	17,805
1901	426	0	0	141	8,118	19	8,705
1902	0	0	0	0	44,930	0	44,930
1903	0	0	6,799	0	266,244	789	273,832
1904	0	0	0	0	20,975	582	21,558
1905	53	0	72	183	36,803	0	37,110
1906	31	0	0	5,445	60,985	743	67,203
1907	0	4,140	12,250	1,308	106,773	1,778	126,248
1908	0	487	300	682	70,840	292	72,601
1909	812	0	28,822	8,729	95,544	634	134,541
1910	0	0	12,053	5,969	60,712	1,309	80,043
1911	7,213	1,218	1,320	3,160	63,298	1,948	78,157
1912	5,781	1,217	0	10,241	54,097	4,734	76,069
1913	4,624	4,724	13,070	3,668	41,835	4,105	72,027
1914	3,616	24	13,797	5,635	49,024	1,011	73,107
All years' total	32,458	18,571	349,827	56,361	1,356,241	44,452	1,857,910
annual average	649	371	6,997	1,127	27,125	889	37,158

Notes: Government railroads ($1,118,000 in 1881, $597,000 in 1882, and $3,084,000 in 1883) are included in transportation.

Source: Davis–Gallman tape.

Table 6.4-6(b). *Argentine calls on the London capital market, 1865–1914 (percent of total calls)*

Year	Manufacturing, commercial, & miscellaneous	Finance	Government	Agriculture & extractive	Transport	Public utilities	Total capital called
1865	0.00%	24.75%	0.00%	0.25%	75.00%	0.00%	100.00%
1866	0.00	12.70	36.63	0.00	49.57	1.10	100.00
1867	0.00	0.00	0.00	3.85	96.15	0.00	100.00
1868	0.00	0.00	100.00	0.00	0.00	0.00	100.00
1869	0.00	0.00	95.97	0.00	4.03	0.00	100.00
1870	0.00	0.00	70.48	9.19	20.33	0.00	100.00
1871	0.00	0.00	84.06	0.45	15.50	0.00	100.00
1872	0.00	0.00	63.97	0.00	28.43	7.61	100.00
1873	0.00	0.00	35.24	0.00	64.76	0.00	100.00
1874	0.00	6.13	63.53	0.00	30.34	0.00	100.00
1875	0.00	0.00	0.00	0.00	100.00	0.00	100.00
1876	0.00	0.00	0.00	0.00	100.00	0.00	100.00
1877	no capital called	no capital called	no capital called	no capital called	no capital called	no capital called	no capital called
1878	no capital called	no capital called	no capital called	no capital called	no capital called	no capital called	no capital called
1879	0.00	0.00	0.00	0.00	100.00	0.00	100.00
1880	6.85	0.00	0.00	0.00	93.15	0.00	100.00
1881	18.01	0.00	0.00	8.58	56.25	17.16	100.00
1882	2.24	0.00	46.87	0.00	50.90	0.00	100.00
1883	0.00	0.00	21.26	15.01	63.73	0.00	100.00
1884	0.09	0.00	69.79	3.26	26.82	0.05	100.00
1885	0.00	0.00	4.53	0.13	93.08	2.26	100.00
1886	0.00	0.00	57.94	0.05	41.11	0.90	100.00
1887	4.39	0.00	35.64	0.51	58.77	0.69	100.00
1888	0.96	0.00	52.04	2.76	38.35	5.90	100.00
1889	2.60	1.26	30.92	0.53	54.58	10.11	100.00

Year						
1890	4.11	0.00	0.00	0.21	95.68	0.00	100.00
1891	0.00	0.00	0.00	0.59	99.41	0.00	100.00
1892	0.00	0.00	0.00	0.00	93.71	6.29	100.00
1893	0.00	38.31	0.00	25.82	35.87	0.00	100.00
1894	0.00	0.00	0.00	0.00	100.00	0.00	100.00
1895	15.31	0.00	0.00	0.00	84.69	0.00	100.00
1896	0.00	2.29	0.00	0.00	93.41	4.30	100.00
1897	0.00	3.15	0.00	0.59	79.42	16.83	100.00
1898	0.00	0.00	0.00	0.00	80.77	19.23	100.00
1899	0.00	0.00	0.00	1.58	91.51	6.91	100.00
1900	0.00	0.00	54.70	0.00	42.24	3.06	100.00
1901	4.90	0.00	0.00	1.62	93.26	0.22	100.00
1902	0.00	0.00	0.00	0.00	100.00	0.00	100.00
1903	0.00	0.00	2.48	0.00	97.23	0.29	100.00
1904	0.00	0.00	0.00	0.00	97.30	2.70	100.00
1905	0.14	0.00	0.19	0.49	99.17	0.00	100.00
1906	0.05	0.00	0.00	8.10	90.75	1.11	100.00
1907	0.00	3.28	9.70	1.04	84.57	1.41	100.00
1908	0.00	0.67	0.41	0.94	97.57	0.40	100.00
1909	0.60	0.00	21.42	6.49	71.01	0.47	100.00
1910	0.00	0.00	15.06	7.46	75.85	1.64	100.00
1911	9.23	1.56	1.69	4.04	80.99	2.49	100.00
1912	7.60	1.60	0.00	13.46	71.12	6.22	100.00
1913	6.42	6.56	18.15	5.09	58.08	5.70	100.00
1914	4.95	0.03	18.87	7.71	67.06	1.38	100.00
All years' average	1.75	1.00	18.83	3.03	73.00	2.39	100.00

Notes: Government railroads ($1,118,000 in 1881, $597,000 in 1882, and $3,084,000 in 1883) are included in transportation.

Source: Davis–Gallman tape.

Table 6:4-7(a). *Argentine calls on the London capital market, 1865–1914 (thousands of dollars)*

Year	Manufacturing, commercial, & miscellaneous	Finance	Government	Agriculture & extractive	Transport	Public utilities	Total capital called
1865–1869	0	2,562	8,711	214	13,295	55	24,837
1870–1874	0	974	47,929	718	16,158	657	66,436
1875–1879	0	0	0	0	3,119	0	3,119
1880–1884	942	0	50,582	5,064	40,058	365	97,011
1885–1889	7,119	1,522	144,381	3,973	182,428	19,841	359,264
1890–1894	1,767	1,218	0	1,094	81,685	497	86,260
1895–1899	73	487	0	137	31,800	4,549	37,046
1900–1904	426	0	16,539	141	347,788	1,935	366,830
1905–1909	896	4,627	41,444	16,346	370,944	3,446	437,703
1910–1914	21,235	7,183	40,240	28,673	268,966	13,107	379,403
1865–1914	32,458	18,571	349,827	56,361	1,356,241	44,452	1,857,910

Table 6:4-7(b). *Argentine calls on the London capital market, 1865–1914 (percent of total calls)*

Year	Manufacturing, commercial, & miscellaneous	Finance	Government	Agriculture & extractive	Transport	Public utilities	Total capital called
1865–1869	0.00%	10.31%	35.07%	0.86%	53.53%	0.22%	100.00%
1870–1874	0.00	1.47	72.14	1.08	24.32	0.99	100.00
1875–1879	0.00	0.00	0.00	0.00	100.00	0.00	100.00
1880–1884	0.97	0.00	52.14	5.22	41.29	0.38	100.00
1885–1889	1.98	0.42	40.19	1.11	50.78	5.52	100.00
1890–1894	2.05	1.41	0.00	1.27	94.70	0.58	100.00
1895–1899	0.20	1.31	0.00	0.37	85.84	12.28	100.00
1900–1904	0.12	0.00	4.51	0.04	94.81	0.53	100.00
1905–1909	0.20	1.06	9.47	3.73	84.75	0.79	100.00
1910–1914	5.60	1.89	10.61	7.56	70.89	3.45	100.00
1865–1914	1.75	1.00	18.83	3.03	73.00	2.39	100.00

Table 6:4-7(c). *Argentine calls on the London capital market, 1865–1914 (dollars per capita per year)*

Year	Manufacturing, commercial, & miscellaneous	Finance	Government	Agriculture & extractive	Transport	Public utilities	Total capital called
1865–1869	0.00	0.32	0.99	0.03	1.62	0.01	2.97
1870–1874	0.00	0.09	4.86	0.08	1.61	0.07	6.71
1875–1879	0.00	0.00	0.00	0.00	0.28	0.00	0.28
1880–1884	0.07	0.00	3.67	0.37	2.95	0.03	7.09
1885–1889	0.45	0.09	9.23	0.25	11.68	1.24	22.94
1890–1894	0.10	0.07	0.00	0.06	4.74	0.03	4.99
1895–1899	0.00	0.02	0.00	0.01	1.50	0.21	1.74
1900–1904	0.02	0.00	0.70	0.01	14.04	0.08	14.84
1905–1909	0.03	0.16	1.34	0.55	12.63	0.12	14.83
1910–1914	0.58	0.20	1.10	0.80	7.53	0.36	10.57
1865–1914	0.13	0.10	2.19	0.21	5.86	0.21	8.70

Notes: Government railroads ($1,118.000 in 1881, $597,000 in 1882, and $3,084,000 in 1883) are included in transportation.

Source: Davis–Gallman tape.

opportunities in arable agriculture and industry. Fortunately for the effective allocation of Argentine capital, the principal reallocation involved directing investment away from those activities organized by the right hand of the ranchers to those organized by the left hand of the same ranchers[1302] – that is, a large part of the shift was from ranching to farming, both industries that the agricultural elites controlled.

The expansion of grain farming called for investment in fencing, machinery, animals (animals used for both power and food), housing and sheds, and the initial breaking of the pampas soil.[1303] The farmers involved were disproportionately tenants, typically immigrants, people with limited financial resources and with no experience or personal connections in the area where they were to farm. Many of them would be in the area for only three to five years. They could not finance major investments on their own, nor could they expect to tap the formal capital markets for long-term credit.

The landlord – typically a rancher – was better endowed with personal resources. He was also well known in his district – his family almost always had a history there – and, if he was rich enough, it was likely that he also had connections in Buenos Aires and in the major cities in or close to his district. He was, therefore, in a position to fund the necessary start-up costs, costs that were to be paid back by the tenant during his tenure.[1304] The landlord's financing apparently came largely from the banking system.

[1302] The flexibility displayed by the Argentine economy in permitting the relatively easy shift from pastoral to agricultural activities is treated in Solberg, "Land Tenure and Land Settlement," pp. 53–75.

[1303] The last item called for skill and effort of a much higher order than did subsequent annual plowings. In the United States plowing the prairies was a specialty, calling for much horsepower, special heavy plows, and experienced prairie plowmen. Scobie mentions the "tough sod" of the pampas. Scobie, *Buenos Aires,* p. 10.

[1304] According to Scobie, the early development of agriculture in Santa Fe Province involved the sale of land to farmers, but with the expansion of farming in Buenos Aires Province, tenancy became the usual form. By Scobie's account, the land was fenced by the owner, but the rest of the required investment seems to have been made by the tenant. Our text statement follows Adelman's description, in which everything except seasonal costs (seeds, labor) was the responsibility of the landlord. Scobie reproduces a description by a cattleman of the system by which land was put in cultivation:

The land is first divided into fenced grazing pastures of four or five thousand acres and then subdivided into surveyed numbered lots of five hundred acres each without any intervening barbed wire. These lots are rented on a three-year contract at one and a half paper pesos the acre [for comparison, wheat sold at two pesos the bushel] to Italian farmers who bring their own equipment and

There were also other sources. Farmers probably borrowed from merchants for seed and supplies, and perhaps even for advances on harvest expenses. As Lough puts it, there were "no clear-cut distinctions between dealers in commodities and bankers, for the dealers are forced to finance most of their own sales." But this system, he says, "is rapidly giving way to a more complex organization" in which the farmer borrows from a bank and pays his bills in cash.[1305] The farmers do not seem to have been borrowing from the joint-stock giants, the Bank of the Nation or the Bank of the Province of Buenos Aires; but it is possible that they were being increasingly accommodated by the local one-branch bank or by less formal local financiers. Adelman writes about a pair of brothers, the Riats, sheep ranchers who filled the gap in the credit system in their locality. They "were able to borrow from formal outlets and then re-lend it to local producers. . . . The Riats provided the small loans which banks were reluctant to furnish, setting aside almost 40 per cent of their credits to disbursements under 1,000 pesos. . . . Informal creditors occupied the institutional vacuum left by bankers, providing a service for which there was a demand but which formal networks were averse to supplying."[1306]

As Adelman points out, the difference between the rates at which ranchers could borrow in the cities and the rates at which they could relend to local farmers, many of them their tenants, was large enough to have drawn many of them into lending operations. It seems likely that a substantial part of the finance of farmers came this way, with funds from city bankers being funneled to them through the hands of local ranchers. Tulchin puts a slightly different spin on the story: "The overwhelming majority of ranchers and farmers, accounting for the most significant part of the nation's agricultural production, had to recur for credit to the local loansharks known as acopiadores. These, the retailers of agricultural credit, were financed by large commercial export houses and consignment firms in Buenos Aires, the wholesalers of agricultural credit."[1307]

supplies and agree at the end of the period to leave the land sown with alfalfa, the seed being supplied by the owner.

Scobie, *Revolution on the Pampas*, chapter III, especially pp. 45–7. Jeremy Adelman, *Frontier Development: Land, Labour, and Capital on the Wheatlands of Argentina and Canada, 1890–1914* (Oxford: Clarendon Press, 1994), chapter 6. [Hereafter cited as Adelman, *Frontier Development*.]

[1305] Lough, *Banking Opportunities*, p. 105; Tulchin, *Agricultural Credit*, p. 6; Lough, *Financial Developments*, p. 7.

[1306] Adelman, *Frontier Development*, p. 203.

[1307] Tulchin, *Agricultural Credit*, p. 1.

Foreign finance did not play an enormous direct role in the modernization of Argentine pastoral and agricultural activities, but as we have seen, some mortgage loans were made, and there was some foreign acquisition of ranches (see Tables 6:4-4, 6:4-5, 6:4-6, and 6:4-7).[1308] The British also figured in innovative activities on the land. Although the investments were small, the British were involved in the Argentine Sugar Estate and Factories and the Santiago (Argentine) Estate and Sugar Factories. The former firm raised £57,200 in London in 1883–85, and the latter £80,000 in 1884. Large flows, however, did not begin until the immediate prewar period; then the focus was on cattle, not sugar. For example, in 1909 the Argentine Estates of Bovril raised £350,000, and in 1914 its calls totaled an additional £195,000. Again, in 1911 the South American Cattle Farms turned to the London market for £350,000.

Although the first call of a land development company dates from 1870 – £65,000 by the Central Argentine Land Company – the second did not occur until 1883. Moreover, while there was a flurry of activity over the ensuing decade, there was only a single call between January 1894 and December 1905. Between 1906 and the end of 1914, however, fourteen separate companies received a total of $36,858,000 U.S. dollars (roughly seven-tenths of 1 percent of the total capital in Argentine farming and ranching in 1913). Overall, at least seventeen land development companies received funds. The list included the Argentine Colonization & Land Company (£40,000 in 1888), Argentine Eastern Land Company (£87,500 in 1911 and 1912), the Argentine Hardwood and Land Company (£246,500 between 1910 and 1914), the Argentine Northern Land Company (£317,500 between 1906 and 1913), the Argentine Southern Land Company (£165,100 between 1889 and 1897 and £73,500 in 1911), the Curamalon Land Company (£525,0000 in 1888), the Development Company of Santa Fe (£175,100 in 1909, 1910, and 1912), Leach's Argentine Estates (£1,032,600 in 1912), the Parana Land Company (£37,500 in 1887), the Rio Negro (Argentina) Land Company (£260,000 in 1907), the long-lived Santa Fe Land Company (£875,100 in 1883 and 1884 and £1,089,600 between 1906 and 1910), and the Tecka Argentine Company (£215,000 in 1910).

6-4b(2). Industry: The growth of the industrial sector appears to have been funded by an equally wide array of sources. The typical industrial firm was small and probably existed and expanded in the same way as

---

[1308] The indirect role, through the finance of the railways, was, of course, enormous.

did firms in other societies during the early stages of industrialization;[1309] that is, for many firms investment in fixed capital must have been modest: perhaps facilities to house the firm were initially rented and modified to accommodate the new venture's activities.[1310] Initially, many of these firms used little machinery; for them the pressing financial problems involved purchasing raw materials and power, collecting for finished goods sold, meeting the payroll, and funding the expansion of the business, assuming it proved successful. Materials were probably often bought on credit from the supplier, who, in turn, either borrowed from his suppliers or went to the banks. Expansion probably depended in large part on retained earnings.

Not all firms were small. Of those that were, some grew to be large; and growth often involved technological transformations that required investment in machinery. In these cases finance of a different type and on a larger scale was required, but Argentine commercial law placed barriers in the way of obtaining finance.[1311] In the Anglo countries, commercial law derives importantly from the common law; not so in Argentina. There commercial law was statute law, and colonial history provided little useful basis for such legislation. As a result, the commercial law that began to emerge was not well designed for industrial finance. A joint-stock venture could issue unsecured bonds for a value no greater than the paid in capital. Three kinds of secured loans were possible: mortgages on land, pledges (loans based on equipment or output), and loans incorporating liens on agricultural production. Of these, pledges were difficult to obtain, and the other two forms were not well suited to all the needs of industrialists:

> When finally enacted, commercial laws expressed the needs and desires of the dominant economic groups – the merchant, the rancher or farmer, the mining company, and the state.... The civil code's narrow definition of collateral was ideal for the dominant agrarian and ranch-

[1309] For discussions of the style of industrial investment in the early stages of the industrial growth of other societies, see Kenneth L. Sokoloff, "Invention, Innovation, and Manufacturing Productivity Growth in the Antebellum Northeast," in Robert E. Gallman and John Joseph Wallis (eds.), *American Economic Growth and Standards of Living Before the Civil War* (Chicago and London: University of Chicago Press, 1992), pp. 345–78. Francois Crouzet (ed.), *Capital Formation in the Industrial Revolution* (London: Methuen & Company, 1972), especially chs. 2 and 5, by Herbert Heaton and Sidney Pollard.

[1310] Machinery was also rented. For example, in 1903 the United Shoe Company began to rent machinery to Argentine shoemakers. Guy, "Dependency, Credit Markets and Argentine Industrialization," pp. 551–55.

[1311] Some foreign capital flowed into the industrial sectors, but little into manufacturing, per se. See Tables 6:4-4 and 6:4-5.

ing interests, and did not interfere with loans incurred by companies based in other countries that had more liberal credit laws. Locally organized urban industries, however, even those processing agricultural products, usually found themselves closed off from long term credit.[1312]

There were, nonetheless, sources of credit for industrialists. Some few could tap the *Bolsa*; others received finance from the private bankers. Still others were financed through foreign capital markets. Many of these firms must have been organized abroad.[1313]

In addition to the investment in industry and commerce, some British capital (about $4.5 million U.S. dollars and about one-quarter of 1 percent of all capital called) was directed to Argentine mines. The capital called data show that sixteen mining companies – borax, copper, gold, silver – entered the London market. Their names ranged alphabetically from the Anglo Argentine Mining Company to the West Argentine Gold Company. Their calls were distributed fairly evenly across the years from the first issues of the Anglo Argentine Mining Company (£40,000 in 1867) to the 1912 call of £75,000 by the Buena Tierra Mining Company. In size the issues ranged from the near sublime – the £756,500 calls of the Capillitas Copper Company in 1909 and 1910 and the £560,700 raised by the Fatima Development Company – to the absolutely ridiculous £4,000 raised by the Bueno Consols Company in 1883.

The calls of the Argentine Refinery date back to 1889 (£118,800): but, until the very end of the period, the manufacturing and commercial sector was dominated by firms processing agricultural products and exporting them. The first such calls date from the early 1880s; Delacres's Extract of Beef raised £93,500 in 1880 and 1881. It was followed by the River Plate Fresh Meat Company (£100,000 in 1882 and 1884), the Argentine Meat Preserving Company (£122,400 in 1889 and 1890), and the Entre Rios Extract of Meat Company (£50,000 in 1911). Finally, at the very end of the period, large-scale manufacturing began to command funds from

---

[1312] One way around these problems was to charter firms abroad, under foreign law. Guy argues that this strategy was by no means uncommon. Guy, "Dependency, Credit Markets, and Argentine Industrialization," especially pp. 536, 540. See also *Annual Report of the Bureau of American Republics*, 1903, pp. 64–72. Guy to the contrary, notwithstanding, mortgage credit must have played a role of some importance in the finance of large industrial firms, many of which had access to land in one form or another.

[1313] "To a great extent the industrialization process took place thanks to the supply of external resources: capital, entrepreneurs, and labor. Even though the investment of foreign capital in the manufacturing industry was very limited and mostly concentrated in the production of frozen and chilled beef, the role of the workers and entrepreneurs who remained in the country as immigrants became essential." Barbero, "Argentine Industrial Growth," p. 372.

the British market. The Argentine Iron and Steel Company raised £942,700 in 1912 and 1914, Argentine Tobacco, £1,086,000 in 1911 and 1912, and the Argentine Refinery drew an additional £270,000 in 1914.

6-4b(3). The cities: The finance of urban expansion came from a variety of sources.[1314] In the case of Buenos Aires, once it became the capital of the Republic, some part of the finance required for growth – public buildings, the port – came from the Republic. The government drew minor expenditures from current revenues but financed major projects, such as the port reconstruction, by borrowing both at home and abroad. None of the Argentine cities had substantial revenues. They had to finance some expenditures – street widening and paving – through special assessments on property, and they left other functions that are today commonly carried out by the city to religious, charitable, or private for-profit institutions. For example, the Church was responsible for the construction and management of hospitals; the Church also provided some educational services. Private for-profit institutions built and operated public utilities – trolley lines, and electrical power plants, to cite two examples. The ultimate source of funding in these cases was the domestic or foreign capital market.

Office space for private firms, warehouses, and factories must, on the whole, have been financed by their users, although some were built as rental properties by real estate operators, Bunge and Born, for example. Part of this construction must have been funded through retained earnings, but Platt stresses the vast importance of the mortgage market.[1315] Some part of mortgage finance came via the sale of *cedulas*. For developers and potential home owners "the sales of building lots on monthly payments, spread over as many as ten years" was an important innovation.[1316]

[1314] Most of this section is based on D.C.M. Platt, "The Financing of City Expansion: Buenos Aires and Montreal Compared, 1880–1914," and D.C.M. Platt, "Domestic Finance in the Growth of Buenos Aires, 1880–1914," chs. 8 and 1, in D.C.M. Platt and Guidon di Tella (eds.), *The Political Economy of Argentina, 1880–1946* (London: Macmillan, 1986). [Hereafter cited as Platt, "Domestic Finance," and Platt, "The Financing of City Expansion."]

[1315] Platt, "Domestic Finance." According to Adelman, the great Argentine mortgage banks were initially intended to promote long-term finance on the land, but credit on a large scale also went to the cities, probably for both business and residential construction. Adelman, "Agricultural Credit," pp. 78–79.

[1316] Platt, "The Financing of City Expansion." Platt cites Charles S. Sargent, who thought that this innovation "must rank with the introduction of the trolley itself as one of the major 'technical' innovations in urban residential development." Note that the *cedula* also had an important modern feature: amortization of the loan value.

The developers were presumably, financed both in the mortgage market and from joint stock and private banks.[1317]

Four cities managed to raise funds in the London market. As early as 1870 the City of Buenos Aires drew £910,400, and in 1873 and 1874 its calls totaled an additional £1,826,600. Over the booming decade of the 1880s, the City drew £9,055,000; and, although out of the market for almost the next two decades, it received an additional £6,396,100 between 1909 and 1914. In addition, the Buenos Ayres Harbour Works trust managed to issue bonds in London totaling £728,000 in 1887 and £200,000 in 1888. Most of the borrowing by the other three cities was concentrated in the 1880s: £744,900 by Cordoba in 1886 and 1888, £197,900 by Parana in 1889, and £1,337,200 by Rosario in 1887, 1888, and 1889, although the latter city also raised £14,700 in 1905.

Private firms also contributed to the development of city capital, and at times they too turned to London.[1318] The Catalinas Warehouse and Mole of Buenos Ayres (£955,400 between 1887 and 1890) and the Buenos Ayres Grain Elevators (£150,000 in 1909) improved the export infrastructure. Urban markets were also served by the Central Produce Market of Buenos Ayres (£321,000 in 1887), the Sociedad Anonima Mercado Cividad de Buenos Ayres (£10,800 in 1905), and Harrod's (BA) (£864,000 in 1913 and 1914). The public utility sector supplied gas, water, sewage disposal, electricity, and telephone service. The Bahia Blanca Gas Company turned to the British capital market for £11,300 in 1866, but the major transfers to the public utilities sector were concentrated in the second half of the 1880s and the years after 1895, particularly the years after 1909. In the first period, firms such as the Buenos Ayres (New) Gas Company (£153,500), the Belgrano Blanca (Buenos Ayres) Gas Company (£130,600), and the United River Plate Telephone Company, a company that was to serve not only Argentina but Uruguay and Paraguay as well (£170,000), all drew on British capital. The second surge reflected continued development in gas, water, and drainage (for example, the Consolidated Water Works of Rosario drew £354,500 between 1906 and 1913 and the Buenos Ayres (New) Gas Company an

---

[1317] According to Platt, a one-room artisan's cottage in Buenos Aires (toward the end of the nineteenth century) could be built for 1,000 paper pesos, presumably inclusive of the land. In good times the daily wage of an artisan was the equivalent of about 4.5 paper pesos. Assuming a 250 day work year, the cost of a cottage was less than one year's wages.

[1318] See Linda and Charles Jones and Robert Greenhill, "Public Utility Companies," in D.C.M. Platt (ed.), *Business Imperialism, 1840–1930, An Inquiry Based on British Experience in Latin America* (Oxford: Clarendon Press, 1977). [Hereafter cited as Jones, Jones, and Greenhill, "Public Utility Companies."]

additional £370,800 between 1897 and 1907); but it also reflected the widespread innovation of electricity and the continued expansion of the telephone network. The Compania de Electricidad de la Provincia de Buenos Ayres called a total of £325,000 between 1911 and 1913, the Compania Hidro-Electricia de Tucuman (Argentina), £390,000 in 1912, the Cordoba Light power and Traction, £300,000 in 1913, and the Primativa Gas & Electric of Buenos Ayres, £468,000 between 1912 and 1914. The calls of the United River Plate Telephone Company totaled £1,485,200 over the first three quinquennia of the twentieth century. Altogether, in addition to Bahia Blanca, firms from Buenos Aires City and province, Tucuman, Rosario, and Cordoba all received infusions of British funds.

6-4b(4). The Republic: According to Frederic M. Halsey, "Governmental loans of the Argentine Republic have long enjoyed wide favor among European investors. In pre-war days the bonds sold at a substantial premium, indicating the high credit of Argentina in European markets."[1319] Homer and Sylla point out that yields on long-term securities of the Republic in "the early years of the century were below those quoted for Chile and Brazil" and that "they tended to decline in the first decade, when bond yields in the great financial centers were rising."[1320] So far so good, but Homer and Sylla also point out that Argentine yields were higher than "most European yields," and Ferns mentions that

> As early as June 1893, *The Economist* called attention to an odd market phenomenon, i.e., a contradiction between the returns of Argentine railway shares and their prices on the Stock Exchange. No British railway paid profits like the Argentine railways, and yet British rails were selling on the Exchange at prices from 22 to 40% above par, whereas only one Argentine line was selling above par. What was true of Argentine rails was true of all Argentine securities.[1321]

Ferns attributes the "odd phenomenon" to the unwillingness of the market to forget, so soon, the Baring crisis; Argentine borrowers had to pay a risk premium. The forgetting took even longer: Average Argentine yields through the first ten years of the new century were, on average, one to two points above average European yields, at a time when the average European yields varied between 2.93 and 3.75 percent (see Table 6:4-8); that is, the Argentine risk premium remained relatively very large. But what about yields before the Barings Crisis?

[1319] Halsey, *Investments in Latin America*, p. 26.
[1320] Homer and Sylla, *A History of Interest Rates*, p. 626.
[1321] Ferns, "The Baring Crisis Revisited," p. 271.

Table 6:4-8. *Yields on long-term government securities, 1900–1913*

Year	Argentina	Chile	Brazil	Europe
1900	5.14%			
1907	4.90			
1908	4.86			
1909	4.81			
1900–1909	4.99	5.88%	5.20%	2.93–3.75%
1910	4.82	6.40	4.46	
1911	4.83	6.31	4.52	
1912		6.75	4.62	
1913	4.88	7.15	4.97	

Source: Sidney Homer and Richard Sylla, *A History of Interest Rates*, Third Edition (New Brunswick, N.J., and London: Rutgers University Press, 1991), pp. 463, 480, 492, 504, 622, & 629.

Argentine governmental borrowing in the international markets began with a mis-step. In 1824 the new government of the United Provinces of the Rio de la Plata working through the House of Baring borrowed £1 million pounds on the London exchange (see Table 6:4-9). The loan soon went into default, but many years later – in 1857 – another Argentine central government accepted the responsibility for the debt, issued bonds to cover the overdue interest, and ultimately liquidated the loan. That action was "a factor in establishing a reputation for Argentine 'good faith' in the minds of foreign investors."[1322] The next incursion into the London market consisted of two loans negotiated in the 1860s to finance the debilitating war with Paraguay.[1323] Thereafter, the Republic borrowed chiefly for four purposes. First, a substantial part of all borrowing was to promote development. Some was direct through investment in public works, especially railways. Some was indirect – loans and subsidies of one kind or another that were used to encourage private investment. For example, of the outstanding debts of the Republic in

---

[1322] Ferns, "The Baring Crisis Revisited," p. 242.
[1323] We focus on foreign borrowing, since such loans comprised the better part of the debt of the Republic. See Table 6:4-9. Notice that debt that was initially floated in the domestic market often ended on one or more of the European capital markets.

Table 6:4-9. *Borrowing by the Republic of Argentina before World War I*

Year	Amount & Terms	Agent	Notes
1824	£1,000,000 6% at 85	(London)	Interest defaulted in 1830. Subsequently paid off. Interest in arrears converted to bonds.
1857	£1,263,000 3%	Barings (London)	Refinance of 1824 debt.
1863, 1866*	£2,500,000 6% at 72–75	Barings (London)	To pay for the war with Paraguay. 1863 loan converted into a $3\frac{1}{2}$% Sterling bond. 1866 loan paid off in 1889.
1870	£1,034,700 6% at 88	Murietta (London)	Province of Buenos Aires. In 1880 accepted as the debt of the Rupublic.
1871	£6,122,400 6% at $88\frac{1}{2}$	Murietta (London)	Public Works.
1873	£2,040,800 6% at $89\frac{1}{2}$	Barings (London)	Public Works. Province of Buenos Aires. In 1886 accepted as debt
1876	6,000,000 pesos 9%		Internal debt. Later listed on European exchanges. In 1887 converted into an external debt at a lower rate.
1881	£2,450,000 6% at 91 1% sinking fund	Paris/Bas; Comptoir d'Escompte (Paris); Murietta (London)	Railway loan. In 1889 most of it was converted into 5% debenture stock of the Cordoba Central Railway.
1882	£817,000 6% at 90 2% sinking fund	Paris/Bas; Comptoir d'Escomte (Paris)	Military. In 1889 balance converted to $4\frac{1}{2}$% conversion bond.
1882	£2,240,000 5% at 90		Refinance.
1884	£1,714,200 5% at $84\frac{1}{2}$ 1% sinking fund	Barings (London) Paris/Bas; Comptoir (Paris)	National Bank.
1886	£4,000,000 5% at 80 1% sinking fund	Barings (London) Paris/Bas; Comptoir (Paris)	Ports and railways secured by customs duties.
1887	£4,290,000 5% at $85\frac{1}{2}$ 1% sinking fund	Barings and J.S. Morgan (London) Paris/Bas; Comptoir (Paris)	
1887	£2,017,000 5% at 90	Disconto; Nord-Deutsch; Oppenheim (Buenos Aires)	National Bank.
1887	£624,000 5% par	Murietta (London)	1876 bonds converted. £624,000 of new debt contracted.

Table 6:4-9. *(cont.)*

Year	Amount & Terms	Agent	Notes
1887–1889 1887 1888 1889	5% £1,300,000 at 91½ £1,500,000 at 94 £1,168,200 at 97	Murietta (London)	Railway extension.
1889	£5,290,000 4½% at 90	Deutsche; Disconto (Berlin) Murietta: Barings (London) Heine; Comptoir (Paris)	To refinance loans of 1871 and 1882.
1889	£2,659,500 3½% par	Stern (London)	To refinance Buenos Aires debts of 1870 and 1873.
1889	£3,933,580** 4½% at 87	Barings (London)	Internal loan, but a large part offered in Europe at 87.
1890	£2,976,000*** 5%	Cahen; Comptior (Paris) Disconto (Berlin) Stern (London)	Railway-Northern-Central

1890   Crisis Plan:
 Continue service of loans as follows:
 (1) 1886–1887: Interest and sinking fund in cash.
 (2) All others: Interest and sinking fund in cash from January 1891–January 1894 in 6% funding-loan bonds, secured by customs receipts, subject to the 1886–87 loan. Coupons receivable for customs duties.
 (3) No new loans permitted during funding period.
 (4) Surplus revenues to be used to retire paper money and create a reserve for the funding loan.
 (5) £7,630,600 funding loan bonds issues.
 [By 1906 all paid off at par.]

1892   Further Adjustment:
 (1) Interest rates on the 1886/87 loan and the B.A. water supply loan were dropped from 5% to 4%; interest on the 6% funding loan of 1891 was dropped to 5% between July 1893 and July 1898.
 (2) All other outstanding loans: Interest to be paid 60% in cash, July 1893–July 1898, and then full payment in cash. Any surplus to be used to pay holders of the 1886/87 bonds the 1% they forwent in the 5-year period.
 (3) Sinking funds not operated until January 1901.
 [N.B.: Full interest payments resumed one year ahead of schedule.]

| 1897–1900 | £31,870,890
1% sinking fund
4% | | To make good the RR guarantee areas and to settle various provincial and municipal debts.
[Mostly held in G.B., France, and Belgium.] |

Table 6:4-9. *(cont.)*

Year	Amount & Terms	Agent	Notes
1907	£7,000,000 5%		Internal gold loan, but also issued and sold in London, Berlin, and Paris.
1908	£892,857 4%		Gold bonds. Given to North Eastern Railway to fund extension.
1909	£2,976,180		London and Germany. City of B.A. secured by certain taxes. Assumed by the Republic in 1913.
1909	£10,000,000, 5% £2,960,000, 5% £3,400,000, 5% £1,640,000, 5% £2,000,000, 5% 1% sinking fund		Internal gold bonds, London. Paris Berlin New York Used for railway and public works construction.
1909	£1,209,600, 5% offered at 101		To buy the Cordoba and North Western Railway.
1910	£466,269, 4%		Given to North Eastern Railway to extend and connect with Paraguay Central Railway.
1911	350,000,000 francs 4½% 1% sinking fund		Internal gold loan. Floated in Paris and Antwerp at 99½ for public works.
1913	£5,000,000, 5%		Bonds of Port and B.A. £5 mil. Authorized. £1 mil. Sold for Port extensions.
1913	£1,367,500		Authorized to be issued to the various railway companies for the construction of irrigation works.
Dec. 31, 1915	£70,797,702 outstanding, of original loans of £86,792,658. Held mainly in G.B., but also France, Germany, the Netherlands, Belgium, and the United States. "During the Period 1911–1914 most of the 5 percent issues sold as high as 104 to 106 percent, the 4½ percent bonds as high as 102 percent, the 4 percent bonds at 91½ percent, and the 3½ percent bonds at 86½ percent."		

*   1865–1868, A/C Marichal.
** £5,263,000, A/C Marichal.
*** £3,000,000, A/C Marichal.

Sources: Fredric M. Halsey, *Investments in Latin America and the British West Indies*, Department of Commerce, Bureau of Foreign and Domestic Commerce, Special Agent Series – No. 169 (Washington, D.C.: G.P.O., 1918), 27–31.
Carlos Marichal, *A Century of Debt Crises in Latin America, From Independence to the Great Depression, 1820–1930* (Princeton: Princeton University Press, 1989), Appendices A and B.

1901, two-thirds by value went to promote public works; another 8 percent were in aid of the banking system (see Table 6:4-9).[1324]

The provinces and municipalities also were in the market for loans, usually banking or development loans.[1325] In toto, foreign borrowing by these sub-national units probably came to equal almost half as much as the foreign loans raised by the Republic. In turn, almost exactly one-half of the value of these "local" loans were issued by Buenos Aires Province and City. When Buenos Aires City became the federal capital, almost four-tenths of the Buenos Aires debts were taken over by the Republic. These assumptions of debt amounted to almost 10 percent of the total debts incurred by the Republic. Presumably they also promoted the Argentine reputation for good faith, in the same manner as the U.S. federal government's assumption of the states' Revolutionary War debts promoted the fiscal reputation of the new U.S. national government.

On occasion the Republic borrowed in Europe to pay service charges on prior debt; and, finally, the Republic borrowed to refinance debt, both to cope with the financial problems created by the Barings Crisis and to reduce the burdens of service charges, as interest rates fell in the first decade or so of the twentieth century. The Barings Crisis was triggered by an unsuccessful effort on the part of Barings to finance the private firm that had taken over and was attempting to expand and modernize the water and sewage system of Buenos Aires City.[1326] Ferns places the responsibility for the failure on extraordinary inattention to business both by Barings and by the largely European board of directors of the water and sewage firm. Barings was saved by the cooperation of Rothschilds and the London banking community, a cooperation that was orchestrated by the Bank of England. Despite the bail-out, Argentine securities came under intense pressure on the international financial markets. The timing could not have been worse. During the 1880s Argentina had experienced an enormous inflow of foreign capital. Most was directed toward investments in railroads and other public utilities, but some of the flotations were the product of the provinces' attempts to take advantage of the conditions of an ill-advised banking act of 1887. Moreover, virtually all of the finance was raised through the issue of debt

---

[1324] *Argentine Yearbook*, 1902, as reported in *Annual Report of the Director of the Bureau of the American Republic for the Year 1903*, 58th Congress, 2nd Session, Document Number 111, Part 1 (Washington, D.C.: Government Printing Office, 1903), p. 247.

[1325] Marichal, *A Century of Debt Crises*, appendices A and B.

[1326] This interpretation of the crisis comes from Ferns, "The Baring Crisis Revisited"; Marichal, *A Century of Debt Crises*; Ford, *The Gold Standard*; and Williams, *Argentine International Trade*.

instruments. These investments – at least the railway and public utility investments – might have been expected eventually to produce returns that were sufficient to service the debt. At the same time, they were expected to promote additional exports, increased exports that would, in turn, provide the necessary foreign exchange to pay off debts. These results could not be expected immediately, but the service payments were due immediately. Service obligations could, however, be met temporarily by further borrowing; and that line was followed. The Barings disaster, when coupled with a series of other crises in the Argentine economy – a sharp decline in the gold value of paper pesos, the result of the new banking act, the end of a speculative boom in land, and, most importantly, a fall in the value of Argentine exports, a fall occasioned by a major decline in prices – meant that the market for Argentine debt collapsed. The Republic – along with the other debtors – was forced to default on interest payments.

In terms of Argentine economic growth, the 1890s yielded mixed results. Given the financial debacle, it is only surprising that, on the real side, things were not worse. Perhaps the explanation lies in the actions of the Argentine government. There were two rapid changes in political leadership, and the second brought to power able people committed to solving Argentine financial problems. A plan to deal with the crisis, so far as it involved government debt, was worked out with the Bank of England, and the plan, when put in operation, proved a great success. (Table 6:4-9 provides an outline of the plan and the actions taken by the new government.) The panic ended, and yields on Argentine long-term debt declined. By 1900, through the efforts of Ernesto Tornquist and others, the banking system had been reformed, and the premium on the gold peso had been sharply reduced and stabilized.

Between 1897 and 1900 the Republic borrowed £31,870,890 from lenders in Britain and the Continent to cover arrears of railway guarantees and to meet municipal and provincial debts, but for the next seven years it stayed out of the debt market. The situation changed beginning in 1907: The Republic came back into the market to take advantage of low yield rates on its debt and, once again, to promote Argentine development. Loans were successfully sought internally, but most of the finance was raised in London, Paris, Berlin, Antwerp, and New York. These loans ran to roughly £30 million, most of which went to the acquisition of railways and to the promotion of the extension of railways. Some expenditures were made on other public utilities. Most of the loans carried 5 percent interest, but sold at a premium, a premium that provides an indication of the financial world's evaluation of the quality of the debt of the Republic.

6-4b(5). The railways: Investment in the railway system was stimulated by governmental – the Republic and the provinces – actions of various kinds: direct investment, grants of rights to construction, and grants of subsidies. Styles of support differed very markedly from those adopted in the United States, where land grants were by far the most important subsidies. In Argentina the guarantee of rates of return to investors was the most important form of encouragement.[1327] The rates that were guaranteed – 7 to 8 percent – were by no means low, and they periodically caused fiscal problems. Earned rates of return fell during cyclical downturns, so that the government was called on to make good on the guarantees at just those times that its fiscal circumstances were under most stress. Following the Barings crisis, the Republic was obliged to borrow to meet arrears in the guarantees. As in the cases of Australia, Canada, and the United States, foreign capital figured importantly in the finance of the railroads, and railway finance accounted for a very large share of foreign capital inflows (see Tables 6:4-4 through 6:4-7).[1328] There were, however, important differences. In Argentina, foreign engineers – particularly British and American – played very large roles in the design and construction of the roads; in Australia, Canada, and the United States, they did not. More important, although foreigners invested in the railroads of the other three countries, in general they did not exercise control. In Argentina, they did. By 1917 foreign-owned roads – of which many were in the hands of the British – had paid-up capital of 2,924 billion paper pesos. In contrast, the capital of the domestically controlled companies was a mere 23 million. British control of the railroads was to become a source of discontent in Argentina.[1329] The complaints against the companies were not dissimilar to those voiced in the United States about American-owned railroads. In both cases there were objections to rates and complaints that the roads paid no attention to the interests of their patrons. For example, in Argentina shippers argued that the facilities of the rail stations were inadequate to protect their goods awaiting carriage on the railroads. Finally, unlike the United States, where Anglo-American investment bankers cut their teeth on cooperative ventures with British merchant bankers – ventures that were designed to provide finance for American railways – the finance of the Argentine system

---

[1327] Tulchin has a good, brief treatment of the chief goals of governmental policy related to economic growth, and of the techniques selected to realize them. Tulchin, *Agricultural Credit*, p. 2.

[1328] Although the British were the leading Argentine foreign creditors, the claims of other lenders – chiefly the French, Belgians, and the Germans – were substantial; they held perhaps 40 percent of the Argentine foreign debt.

[1329] Tornquist, *The Economic Development of the Argentine Republic*, p. 243.

seems to have had little or no impact on the depth or sophistication of the Argentine system of intermediation.[1330]

At the end of the nineteenth century, the transport sector accounted for 83 percent of total foreign investment in Argentine business (Table 6:4-4). Most of this investment was direct, and much of it was by the British. By 1913 three-quarters of English business investment in Argentina was in transportation – chiefly railroads, but also some tramways and one navigation company – and a substantial fraction of the rail network was in British hands (Table 6:4-5).[1331] The capital called series, then, gives a fairly comprehensive account of total investment in Argentine railways. Of the sector's $1,356,241,000 (U.S. dollars) total of capital created and called, only $4,799,000 (0.35 percent) was directed to government-owned railroads. The transportation sector's fraction of total calls reached 100 percent in the quinquennium 1875–79, stood at 85 percent or more in each of the four quinquennia 1885–1889 through 1905–9, and was still over 70 percent in the last half decade.

The importance of those contributions to the Argentine railroad network is captured both in a list of the railroads that were the recipients of British savings and in the length of the time span over which those contributions were received. The list includes the Argentine Great Western (1887–1910), the Argentine North Central (1898–1903), the Argentine North-Eastern (1888–1912), Bahia Blanca & North Western (1889–1912), the Buenos Ayres & Campana (1874–75), the Buenos Ayres Central (1907–11), the Buenos Ayres & Ensanada Port (1872–91), the Buenos Ayres, Ensanada & South Coast (1873–96), the Buenos Ayres Great Southern (1865–1914), the Buenos Ayres Northern (1888), the Buenos Ayres & Pacific (1882–1908), Buenos Ayres & Rosario (1884–1907), the Buenos Ayres Western (1890–1914), the Cordoba

---

[1330] Ford makes the point that borrowing for public works construction had its basis in balance of payments considerations as much as fiscal considerations. Railroad rails, locomotives, cars, trams, machinery for power plants, etc., were either not produced at all in Argentina, or at least not in any quantity. He points out that, between 1884 and 1900, capital goods imports were about 41 percent as large, in terms of value, as imports for consumption. Ford, *The Gold Standard*, p. 142.

[1331] Almost half of the rail mileage was in British companies in 1900. By 1914 the fraction had fallen to less than 42 percent. French-owned mileage rose from almost 8 percent in 1900, to just over 11 percent in 1914. Andres M. Regalsky, "Foreign Capital, Local Interests and Railway Development in Argentina; French Investments in Railways, 1900–1914," *Journal of Latin American Studies*, Vol. 21, No. 3 (1989), p. 427.

By 1930 the English share had risen to 66 percent. Since the main lines belonged to the English, their share in the total value of investment was probably substantially higher than 66 percent. Winthrop R. Wright, *British-Owned Railways in Argentina* (Austin: University of Texas Press, 1974), pp. 5, 6, 53.

Central (1887–1914), the Cordoba Central B.A. (1905–9), the Cordoba & Rosario (1889–1910), the Cordoba & North Western (1889–90), the East Argentine (1871–1901), the Entre Rios (1885–1913), the North-West Argentine (1886–98), the Northern Colonies of Santa Fe (1884–86), the port Argentine Great Central (1911), the Port Madryn (Argentina) (1906–9), the Santa Fe & Cordoba Great Southern (1888–1912), the Santa Fe & Reconquista (1887–88), the Santa Fe, Western & Central (1887), the Villa Maria & Rufino (1889–1906), the Western & Central Colonies of Santa Fe (1887), the Western Railway of Buenos Ayres (1882–92), and the Western Railway of Santa Fe (1889).

6-5. **Conclusions**

The most striking feature of Argentine investment is that it depended so little on domestic intermediation and seems to have provided so little stimulus to the formation of elements in the system of intermediation. A very large fraction of investment was financed overseas, rather than at home; and, as we have seen in the case of the railways, foreign investment seems not to have had a major influence on the development of Argentine financial institutions. The British owned the railways, the stocks and bonds were traded on the British exchanges, and whatever short-term finance they required was typically negotiated with British-owned and -managed banks in Argentina, not with Argentine financial institutions. Argentine governments borrowed at home and abroad, but most credit was obtained abroad; even securities floated as internal debt tended to end up in the hands of foreign investors. *Cedulas* were, indeed, traded and held at home, but the lion's share of even these instruments was apparently held in Europe. The aggregate flow data suggest that between half and two-thirds of Argentine gross investment was accounted for by foreigners; the remainder – one-third to one-half – by domestic savings (see Table 6:4-3 and the Appendix). Clearly, the rapid growth of population and real GDP could not have been negotiated in the absence of foreign investment. By the standard of Argentine capital requirements, the domestic savings rate was low. It was also low by a comparative standard. The Argentine and Canadian savings experiences were similar in the years before the 1890s, but they became very dissimilar thereafter. Both economies grew rapidly in the years after 1900, but, in the case of Argentina, growth continued to reflect investment largely funded by foreigners. In the Canadian case, the domestic savings rate increased dramatically – it rose to a level of 15 percent net – and, although foreign finance continued to pour in, growth was driven by investment financed in large part from domestic savings. In the United States, developments in the two decades before World War I also differed from those of Argentina. Like Argentina, the United States experienced growth, but unlike Argentina, for the decade 1895 to 1904, the United States became a net foreign lender. Even in the last decade before the war, although the United States had again become a net capital importer, there was a very substantial volume of gross capital exports. Finally, although Australians might not have voluntarily chosen the path, the country also became a net capital exporter in the first years of the twentieth century. Argentina, however, continued to be a net foreign borrower on a large scale.

Argentina was unprepared for the collapse in the flow of foreign investment during and after the war, and the amount of investment that could be financed internally could not maintain the previous rates of growth. Alan Taylor makes a strong case that the level of the savings rate reflected a high Argentine dependency rate.[1332] The evidence on Argentine intermediation suggests that the embryonic nature and the thinness of domestic financial markets – markets that provided neither encouragement to savers nor an efficient way to mobilize capital across regional and industrial boundaries – was also a major contributory factor. The shift from cattle to wheat had been smooth in large part because the members of the agricultural elites provided personal intermediation from their old to their new business. They were not in a position to play that role in the redirection of resources from agriculture to industry. From 1870 to 1914 the economy's need to accumulate and mobilize capital had been largely met by foreign savers and foreign institutions. Their withdrawal at the outbreak of World War I left a near black hole in the Argentine financial structure.

Appendix: Estimating investment and savings series

6A-1. Introduction

This appendix deals with a number of issues relating to savings and investment in Argentina between 1875 and 1914. It begins by describing estimates of the rate of gross fixed capital formation (GFCF/GDP). It then turns to investments in inventories, develops new series measuring the fraction of GDP consisting of such investments, and combines these estimates with the GFCF/GDP ratios to yield the rate of gross capital formation: GCF/GDP. A series that measures the share of GDP accounted for by improvements (other than buildings) to

---

[1332] Alan Taylor, "External Dependence, Demographic Burdens, and Argentine Decline After the Belle Epoque," *Journal of Economic History*, Vol. 52, No. 4 (December 1992), pp. 907–35.

agricultural and pastoral lands is then added to the estimate of GCF/GDP.

A series is then assembled measuring gross foreign investment in Argentina, and, by subtraction from total gross investment, domestic savings.

Next, rough estimates of capital consumption are prepared, and these estimates are subtracted from GCF and GDP. From the adjusted investment and product data a series on net capital formation – NCF/NDP – is derived. A test of the final results of this long line of estimation is then carried out, and, finally, estimates of the capital/output ratio are computed.

Reasonably wide margins for error must be assigned to all of these estimates. In the discussion we lay out all the estimating details, and, so far as possible, we appraise data and procedures. The details are sufficiently complete so that the reader should be able to replicate our results, should he or she choose to do so.

6A-2. Real gross fixed domestic capital formation

6A-2(a). Conventional measurements: Alexander Ganz has provided estimates of GFCF/GDP for the periods 1900–1904, 1905–9, and 1910–14.[1333] By his account, the Argentine investment rate was very high, indeed: 1900–1904 = 25.9%; 1905–9 = 48.2%; 1910–14 = 42.2%. His data, however, are expressed in 1950 prices, and as Carlos F. Diaz Alejandro has remarked, they "reflect the steep increase in relative prices of capital goods that has taken place in Argentina since 1935–39."[1334] His estimated ratios, then, are much higher than estimates based on pre–World War I prices would be. For our purposes data expressed in pre-war prices are crucial, both because our interests are focused on the pre-war period and because we make use of the Cortes Conde GDP series, a series that is expressed in prices of 1914.

A closer match to our requirements are GFCF/GDP estimates prepared by Carlos F. Diaz Alejandro, 1900–1909 and 1910–14. These figures are based on series expressed in 1937 prices. Since the principal shift in the relative prices of capital goods occurred after 1935, the rates com-

---

[1333] Alexander Ganz, "Problems and Uses of National Wealth Estimates in Latin America," in Raymond Goldsmith and Christopher Saunders (eds.), *The Measurement of National Wealth*, Income and Wealth, Series VIII (Chicago: Quadrangle Books, 1959), p. 243. [Hereafter cited as Ganz, "Problems and Uses."]

[1334] Carlos F. Diaz Alejandro, *Essays on the Economic History of the Argentine Republic* (New Haven: Yale University Press, 1970) p. 28. [Hereafter cited as Diaz Alejandro, *Essays.*]

puted by Diaz Alejandro should be reasonably close to rates based on pre-war data. Certainly they are much lower than the Ganz estimates: 1900–1909 = 17.2 percent; 1910–14 = 18.7 percent. Nonetheless, they are not exactly what we require. According to Diaz Alejandro, "If we had national accounts expressed at current prices for 1900–30 they would probably show an even lower rate of gross fixed capital formation, as relative prices had already changed between 1929 and 1937 so as to increase those of manufactured goods in general, and of imported goods in particular, among which were most of the machinery and equipment used in Argentina at that time."[1335]

We decided to begin with the Diaz Alejandro figures, to project them back into the nineteenth century, and then to adjust the entire series to a 1914 base. The data are not strong enough to permit the construction of an annual series. The form of the data obliged us to restrict ourselves to estimates for 1875–84, 1885–94, and 1895–99, two decades and a quinquennium.

The Diaz Alejandro estimates of the share of GFCF/GDP are 1900–1909, 17.2 percent; 1910–14, 18.7 percent. The fixed capital formation share for 1900–1909 may be thought of as the ratio 17.2/100. One can estimate capital formation rates for earlier years by extrapolating the numerator and denominator of this ratio backward in time on appropriate series, and that is what we chose to do. The appropriate GDP series is the one prepared by Cortes Conde. The mean value of this series for the years 1900/09 is 3.1696 billion pesos of 1914. The extrapolation ratio for the denominator is, then, $100/3{,}169.6 = 0.03155$, and the estimated denominators are:

$$1900/1909 = 100.0$$
$$1895/1899 = 64.03$$
$$1885/1894 = 41.65$$
$$1875/1884 = 20.17$$

The data available to generate the numerators are mixed. Manuel Balboa and Alberto Fracchia have estimates of gross investment in: Public Works; Private Non-Agricultural Construction; Railway and Inter-Urban Ways and Installations; Railroad Rolling Stock; Agricultural Improvements and Housing; and Machinery and Motors, a comprehensive set of fixed investment series. The data for "rolling stock" are available only for 1902–15, and for "agriculture" and "machinery and motors" only for 1915. We extrapolated these data back to 1875 on the following series:

[1335] Diaz Alejandro, *Essays*, p. 29.

1. Rolling stock – the number of railroad passengers (weighted 1) and the tons of freight carried (weighted 10)
2. Agriculture – the average annual increment (in hectares) of cultivated area
3. Machinery and motors – real value added by industry

The rationale for these choices should be clear. Investment in rolling stock was probably related to passenger and freight traffic. No doubt the relationship is subject to leads and lags, but since we will use our investment estimates only in the form of quinquennial and decennial averages, leads and lags are relatively unimportant. The same remarks apply to the extrapolation of "agricultural improvements and housing" on cultivated acreage and of "machinery and motors" on value added in industry. It may well be that investment in machinery actually increased faster over time than did industrial value added; that seems to have been the case in the United States. If that interpretation is correct, our ultimate estimates of the investment rate are biased upward for the early years, but the bias should be very slight. The weights selected for rail passengers and freight are ad hoc and subject to revision.

The series on "public works," "non-agricultural construction," and "railway installations" run back only to 1885. The sum of these series in 1885 was extrapolated to 1875 on the sum of the "rolling stock," "agriculture," and "machinery" series. The assumption underlying this technique is that the basic structure of investment did not change over this decade, an assumption subject to review.

The real gross fixed capital formation series thus assembled (the sum of "public works," "non-agricultural construction," "railway installations," "rolling stock," "agricultural improvements and housing," and "machinery and motors") was then used to extrapolate backward in time the numerator of the 1900–1909 ratio of GFCF to GDP. With series representing the numerator and denominator of the GFCF to GDP ratio in each relevant time period in hand, the investment rates were computed by dividing one by the other. Tables A1-4 contain the data; the notes give the estimating details.

The series seem reasonably strong. The reader should remember, however, that the estimated investment rates are biased upward (see the remarks of Diaz Alejandro above), a point to which we will return. Second, the Balboa-Fracchia series that we employed as extrapolators are valued in 1950 prices. Thus their levels are too high; however, our interests are not in the levels of these series, but in the rates of change that can be computed from them. On standard index number reasoning, since the valuation base is much later in time (1950) than the year we

Table A-1. *Average annual gross fixed capital formation, millions of 1950 pesos, 1875/1884–1900/1909*

	(1) Public works, private nonagricultural construction, and railway and interurban ways and installations	(2) Agricultural improvements and housing	(3) Machinery and motors	(4) Rolling stock	(5) Grand totals
1875/1884		70.5	27.7	14.1	800.1
1885/1894	2,020.4	208.8	58.7	62.4	2,350.3
1895/1899	1,922.5	230.6	104.2	118.1	2,375.4
1900/1909	3,888.1	765.4	228.9	258.9	5,141.3
1915		665.8	397.2		

Sources: Col. (1): Balboa and Fracchia, 291.
Col. (2): 1915, Balboa and Fracchia, 290; 1875–1909, see Table A-2.
Col. (3): 1915, Balboa and Fracchia, 290; 1875–1909, extrapolated on Cortes Conde, value added by "Industry" (October 1994).
Col. (4): 1900/1909, Balboa and Fracchia, 290; mean of 1902–1909; 1875–1899, extrapolated on train passengers (weight of 1) and freight tonnage (weight of 10) (Tornquist, 118). See Table A-3.
Col. (5): 1900/1909, 1895/1999, 1885/1994: Sum of columns (1)–(4); 1875/84: Extrapolated on the sum of columns (2)–(4) (112.3 × 7.1243).

want to use as base (1914), it might be thought that the rates of change computed from these series would be biased downward (as compared with the rates we want), so that our estimates of the investment rates for the early years might be biased upward. But in view of the fact that markets in 1950 were subject to extensive social control, the price structure at that date is unlikely to have matched the structure that would have emerged under free market conditions. We cannot say, then, that the rates of change of these series are lower or higher than the rates that would have emerged from price weights reflecting conditions of 1914. This circumstance is one of the two chief sources of doubt that we have over the accuracy of the GFCF/GDP ratios we have estimated. The doubt, of course, is more intense with respect to the earlier estimates.

Table A-2. *Extrapolating series for "Agricultural Improvements and Housing," 1872–1914/1915*

(1) Harvested area 000 hectares		(2) Average annual increment	(3) Intervals	(4) Agricultural improvements and housing (mil. pesos)
1872	580		1875/1884	70.5
		117.4		
1888	2,459		1885/1894	208.8
		347.6		
1895	4,892		1895/1899	230.6
		383.8		
1899/1900	6,427			
1900/1901	7,311			
		1,273.9	1900/1909	765.4
1909/1910	18,776			
		1,108.2		
1914/1915	24,317		1915	665.8

Sources: Col. (1): Tornquist, 26.

Col. (2): Computed from Column (1). These figures proxy for the average annual values of the intervals identified in column (3).

Col. (3): Intervals of Table 1.

Col. (4): 1915, Balboa and Fracchia, 290; other dates extrapolated from 1915 on Column (2):

$$\frac{\text{Column 4, 1915}}{\text{Column 2, 1909/1910–1914/1915}} = 0.60079$$

The second source of doubt relates to the price bases that figure in the calculations. We want values expressed in prices of 1914, whereas Diaz Alejandro's estimates (and our extrapolations based on them) are valued in prices of 1937. Since the prices of investment goods rose relative to the GDP price index between 1914 and 1937, the investment ratios based on Diaz Alejandro's work are biased upward, compared with ratios in which numerator and denominator were expressed in prices of 1914.

The series can be adjusted by use of data fit to the following formula:

$$\frac{I_{1937} \times P_{I\,1914}}{Y_{1937} \times P_{Y\,1914}},$$

Table A-3. *Extrapolating series for "Rolling Stock," 1875/1884–1900/1909*

	(1) Average annual passenger traffic (000 passengers), divided by 10	(2) Average annual freight carried (000 tons)	(3) Sums of columns (1) and (2)
1875/1884	310	1,104	1,414
1885/1894	1,009	5,229	6,238
1895/1899	1,655	10,159	11,814
1900/1909	3,030	21,818	24,848
1915	6,740	35,655	42,395

Source: Tornquist, 118.

where

I_{1937} = Investment valued in prices of 1937
Y_{1937} = GDP valued in prices of 1937
$P_{I\,1914}$ = the 1914 price index number of investment goods, on the base 1937
$P_{Y\,1914}$ = the 1914 price index number of GDP, on the base 1937,

which equals: $\dfrac{I_{1937} \times P_{I\,1914}}{Y_{1937} \times P_{Y\,1914}}$, $\qquad\qquad$ (2)

$P_{I\,1914} = 63.74$, $\qquad\qquad$ (3)
$P_{Y\,1914} = 77.356$,

$\dfrac{P_{I\,1914} = 63.74}{P_{Y\,1914} = 77.35} = 0.8240.$ $\qquad\qquad$ (4)

Column (6) of Table A-4 was derived by multiplying each value in column (5) by 0.8240. The conversion is imperfect; for example, the investment price index covers inventory changes, as well as fixed capital formation. This problem is not serious, however. We applied the same procedures to the Ganz estimates, but the results (discussed below) were less plausible. We therefore chose to work with the Diaz Alejandro materials.

6A-2(b). Unconventional components: It is not clear that Balboa and Fracchia include in their agricultural series the clearing, first breaking,

Table A-4(a). *Estimating the gross real fixed capital formation share in GDP, 1875/1884–1910/1914*

	(1) Fixed capital formation, million pesos of 1950 (annual average)	(2) Extrapolation ratio, numerator of capital formation share	(3) Col (1) × Col (2)	(4) Denominator, capital formation share	(5) Fixed capital formation share, in prices of 1937 (percent) $\frac{\text{Col 3}}{\text{Col 4}} \times 100$	(6) Fixed capital formation share, in prices of 1914 (percent) Col 5 × 0.8240
1875/1884	807.5	0.0033454	2.7014	20.17	13.4	11.0
1885/1894	2,372.3	0.0033454	7.9363	41.65	19.1	15.6
1895/1899	2,375.4	0.0033454	7.9467	64.03	12.4	10.2
1900/1909	5,141.3	0.0033454	17.2	100	17.2	14.2
1910/1914					18.7	18.7

Sources: Col. (1): This series, taken from Column (5) of Table 1, is used as an extrapolator for the numerator of the 1900/1909 ratio of fixed capital formation to real GDP, the ratio estimated by Diaz Alejandro (29).

Col. (2): This is the extrapolating ratio for the numerator of the ratio of fixed capital formation to real GDP. It was computed by dividing the numerator of the 1900/1909 ratio, 17.2, by gross real fixed capital formation, 1900/1909, in millions of 1950 pesos (5,141.3).

Col. (3): This column shows the results of the extrapolation. In effect, these figures show the relative levels of gross real fixed capital formation in each year, as they would have been, had gross investment in 1900/1909 been 1702, instead of 5,141.3.

Col. (4): The denominator of the real fixed capital formation to real GDP ratio; the value for 1900/1909 was extrapolated backward in time on the Cortes Conde estimates of real GDP (see text).

Col. (5): 1900/1909 and 1910/1914 – Diaz Alejandro, 29. Other years – Column (3) divided by Column (4), multiplied by 100, yielding the real gross fixed capital formation share in GDP (percent), in prices of 1937.

Col. (6): See text.

Table A-4(b). *Estimating the value of clearing, breaking, and fencing arable land, as a percentage of GDP, 1875/1884–1910/1914*

	Annual increment, harvested area (mil. hectares)	Cost per hectare to break and fence (1914 pesos)	Annual investment, mil. pesos of 1914 (col. 1 × col. 2)	Share of (3) in real GDP (%)
1875/1884	0.1174	23	2.70	0.42
1885/1894	0.3476	23	7.99	0.60
1895/1899	0.3838	23	8.83	0.44
1900/1909	1.2739	23	29.30	0.92
1910/1914	1.1082	23	25.49	0.50

Sources: Col. (1): Taken from Table 2, column (2).
Col. (2): Estimated in the following way:
   (a) It took 0.04 man days per rod (5.5 yards) to put up barbed wired in the United States in 1900. (Robert E. Gallman, *Capital in the American Economy in the Nineteenth Century*, manuscript. The underlying source is Martin Primack, "Farm Formed Capital in American Agriculture, 1850 to 1910," Doctoral Dissertation, University of North Carolina, Chapel Hill, 1962.) We assumed that the expenditure of labor per rod was about the same in Argentina.
   (b) We assumed that, on average, every ten acres added to cultivation was fenced. That would have cost 20.4 man days, or 5.04 man days per hectare (2.471 acres).
   (c) In the United States in 1900 it took 0.5 man days per acre – or 1.24 man days per hectare – to break grassland for the first time. (Gallman, *Capital . . .* and Primack, "Farm Formed Capital . . ."). We assumed that the cost in labor time was the same in Argentina in 1914.
   (d) According to Diaz Alejandro (p. 42), in 1909–1914 unskilled workers in the Federal Capital earned 0.35 paper pesos per hour. In pesos of 1914 (using the price series cited in Table 5 – each year weighted equally – to put values in 1914 prices), that comes to 0.37 pesos per hour. We assumed a 10-hour day, so that daily wage is 3.7 pesos. Since wage rates outside the Federal Capital are likely to have been lower than those within the Capital, our procedure probably overstates the cost of clearing, breaking, and fencing.
   (e) From (b) and (c), above, we may infer that the labor time required to clear, break, and fence a hectare of grassland was 6.24 man days.
   (f) 6.24 man days multiplied by 3.7 pesos [(d) above] equals 23 pesos per hectare.
Col. (3): Column (1) × Column (2)
Col. (4): Column (3) divided by average GDP (pesos of 1914) + Col (3), multiplied by 100.

and the fencing of land converted to arable uses, nor is it clear that Cortes Conde includes this element in his GDP series. We suspect it was left out of the series prepared by these authors, since it is rarely included in modern national accounts. In view of the attention given to the shift of land from grassland to arable in all accounts of Argentine economic history in the several decades before 1914, we decided that an attempt should be made to estimate the impact of this development on capital formation. Details are contained in the notes to Table 4a. It will be evident to the reader that these estimates are rough, and surely could be improved. Also, the estimates cover only the value of labor consumed in this form of investment. More comprehensive figures can probably be made, but the main conclusion to be drawn from the table – the relative importance of this form of investment in the total investment picture – is probably robust.

6A-3. Investment in inventories

We estimated the real value (1914 prices) of stocks of animals and of other inventoried goods and computed investment in inventories by differencing the stocks.

In developing figures for the "other inventoried goods," we borrowed a technique of Simon Kuznets's.[1336] Kuznets estimated the value of stocks of inventories as one-half of the sum of the value of commodity production plus the value of imports. Since value added is typically close to half of the value of output of the commodity producing sectors, we used Cortes Conde's estimates of value added by agriculture and industry to represent the inventories of domestically produced goods.

Current price data on the value of imports are readily available.[1337] According to Ford, "Argentine official trade statistics prior to 1914 were by [no] means perfect," but he goes on to point out that "if Argentine estimates of their imports from U.K. are compared with U.K. estimates of exports to Argentina, both series display similar fluctuations and are of comparable magnitude if allowance is made for f.o.b./c.i.f. differences. Hence, it is concluded that they do provide a reasonable guide to both relative and absolute movements."[1338]

How the import series should be deflated is by no means clear. We chose to use a British wholesale price index (see Table A-5), on the

---

[1336] Simon Kuznets, *National Product Since 1869* (New York: National Bureau of Economic Research, 1946), pp. 108, 111.

[1337] Tornquist, *The Economic Development of the Argentine Economy*, p. 140.

[1338] A.G. Ford, *The Gold Standard, 1880–1914: Britain and Argentina* (Oxford: Clarendon Press, 1962), p. 194. [Hereafter cited as Ford, *The Gold Standard.*]

Table A-5. *Deflator for the imports series: British wholesale price index, 1875–1914 (1914 = 100)*

1875	120
1884	97
1885	91
1894	79
1895	77
1899	78
1900	85
1909	88
1910	92
1914	100

Source: B. R. Mitchell, *European Historical Statistics, 1750–1975*, Second Revised Edition (New York: Facts on File, 1980), 773, 775.

ground that Britain was Argentina's chief trading partner. A proper index would be more closely associated with the structure of Argentine imports and would employ at least German, French, and American, in addition to British, prices.

Real value added in industry and agriculture were then summed up with one-half of the real value of imports in each relevant year to produce estimates of stocks of commodities held in inventory. These estimates were then differenced and divided by the number of years between each pair of estimates to generate annual estimates of the real value of changes in commodities held in inventory. From these figures and the Cortes Conde GDP estimates, we were able to estimate the ratio of investments in inventories (of commodities) to real GDP. Details are contained in Table A-6 and its source notes.

Animal inventories – taken from B.R. Mitchell's International Historical Statistics – were valued in terms of average values for 1914, computed from data in Tornquist.[1339] The real values of total animal inventories at the inventory dates were differenced, and average annual changes were computed. From these values and Cortes Conde's real GDP data, it was possible to compute the share of investment in animal

---

[1339] Tornquist, *The Economic Development of the Argentine Economy*, pp. 263–65. N.B.: Since the *quality* of animals improved over time, the estimating technique overstates the value of animal inventories in the earlier years and, thus, *overstates* the early investment rate estimates.

Table A-6. *Estimating the share of inventory changes (excluding animals) in real GDP*

	(1) V.A. industry (millions of 1914 pesos)	(2) V.A. agriculture (millions of 1914 pesos)	(3) ½ the real value of imports (millions of 1914 pesos)	(4) Totals	(5) Δ	(6) Average annual Δ	(7) % of GDP
1875	77	17	24	118			
1884	84	64	49	197	79	8.8	1.4
1885	94	67	51	212			
1894	225	331	59	615	403	44.8	3.4
1895	249	384	62	695			
1899	349	348	75	772	77	19.3	1.0
1900	333	360	67	760			
1909	911	736	172	1819	1,059	117.7	3.7
1910	970	637	206	1813			
1914	1,011	775	161	1947	134	33.5	0.6

Sources: Cols. (1) and (2): Cortes Conde, October 1994.
Col. (3): Tornquist, 140, deflated by the price index of Table 5, and divided by 2.
Col. (7): Column 6 divided by the real GDP; e.g., Figure 8.8 (1875–1884) was divided by the mean of real GDP, 1875 through 1884.

inventories in real GDP. (Details are contained in Table A-7, and the notes thereto.)

Unfortunately, the dates for which animal inventory data are available do not correspond exactly with the intervals adopted for the measurement of the shares of other components of capital formation in real GDP. We were obliged to employ the computed annual investment rates as proxies for the investment rates for the desired intervals. Thus,

> 1875–88 proxies for 1875–84
> 1888–95 proxies for 1885–94
> 1895–8 proxies for 1895–99 and for 1900–1909
> 1911–13 proxies for 1910–14.

Given the state of the evidence, this seems to be the best choice, and since we are interested chiefly in trends, it is also a choice that is likely to produce reasonably trustworthy results.

Table A-8 contains the final version of the gross capital formation rates by type of capital.

6A-4. Foreign contribution to gross capital formation

It is well known that foreign investment flows into Argentina were large. What is less clear is just how large they were and the extent to which they varied over time.

The best data are those assembled by John H. Williams for the years 1881–91 and 1895–1900. Drawn from the Annual Reports of the Ministry of Finance, they appear to be quite comprehensive, including all foreign capital flowing into Argentina to governments and the private sector – except, perhaps, for trade credit. The values represent funds realized from sales, and therefore available for investment. The nominal values of the securities sold – that is, the debts incurred by Argentine borrowers – typically ran 15 to 20 percent higher.[1340] We assume that Williams's totals of funds realized are net of underwriting and other costs of flotation, but they may not be. Apparently such costs were highly variable but may have typically run around 10 percent.[1341]

Alberto Martinez offered an estimate of the volume of foreign capital in "commerce" (gold pesos) in 1918, a substantial fraction of which must

---

[1340] See John H. Williams, *Argentine International Trade Under Inconvertible Paper Money, 1880–1900* (Harvard Economic Studies, Vol. XXI) (Cambridge, Mass.: Harvard University Press, 1920), pp. 41, 45, 84, 94, 99, 101, 104, 152. [Hereafter Williams, *Argentine International Trade*.]

[1341] D.C.M. Platt, *Britain's Investment Overseas on the Eve of the First World War* (New York: St. Martin's Press, 1986), pp. 44–45. [Hereafter Platt, *Britain's Investment*.]

Table A-7. *Estimating the share of changes in animal inventories in real GDP*

Panel A: Animal inventories, 1875–1913 (000) and prices of 1914

	Horses	Mules	Cattle	Pigs	Sheep	Goats
1875	3,916	124	13,338	257	57,501	2,863
1888	4,263	[300]	21,964	403	66,701	[2,788]
1895	4,467	483	21,702	653	74,380	2,749
1908	7,531	465	29,117	1,404	67,212	[3,872]
1911	8,894	535	28,786	2,900	80,402	4,302
1912	9,239	556	29,123	3,045	83,546	4,431
1913	9,366	584	30,796	3,197	81,485	4,564
1914 prices (paper pesos)	54.65	47.74	84.37	22.10	10.20	5.86

Panel B: Value of animal inventories (million pesos of 1914)

	(1) Horses	(2) Mules	(3) Cattle	(4) Pigs	(5) Sheep	(6) Goats	(7) Total
1875	214.0	5.9	1,125.3	5.7	586.5	16.8	1,954.2
1888	233.0	14.3	1,853.1	8.9	680.4	16.3	2,806.0
1895	244.1	23.1	1,831.0	14.4	758.7	16.1	2,887.4
1908	411.6	22.2	2,456.6	31.0	685.6	22.7	3,629.7
1911	486.1	25.5	2,428.7	64.1	820.1	25.2	3,849.7
1912	504.9	26.5	2,457.1	67.3	852.2	26.0	3,934.0
1913	511.9	27.9	2,598.3	70.7	831.1	26.7	4,066.6

Panel C: Estimating the share of changes in animal inventories in real GDP

	(1) Average annual change in animal inventories	(2) Average annual Real GDP	(3) Share of animal inventory change in real GDP (%) $\frac{\text{Col (1)}}{\text{Col (2)}} \times 100$
	(million pesos of 1914)	(million pesos of 1914)	
1875/1888	65.5	775.8	8.4
1888/1895	11.6	1,276.4	0.9
1895/1908	57.1	2,668.8	2.1
1911/1913	108.1	5,343.7	2.0

Sources: *Panel A*: Animal inventories – B.R. Mitchell, *International Historical Statistics for the Americas, 1750–1988*, 2nd Edition (New York: Stockton Press, 1993).
Prices: Average values, computed from Tornquist, 263–265.
Panel B: Computed from the data in Panel A.
Panel C: Column (1): Computed from Panel B, Column (7).
Column (2): Computed from Cortes Conde (October 1994).

Table A-8. *Total gross capital formation as a share of real GDP,*
1875–1914 (%)

		Panel A: Conventional GDP		
	(1) GFCF	(2) Investment in animals	(3) Investment in other inventories	(4) GCF as a share of GDP
1875/1884	11.0	8.4	1.4	20.8
1885/1894	15.6	0.9	3.4	19.9
1895/1899	10.2	2.1	1.0	13.3
1900/1909	14.2	2.1	3.7	20.0
1910/1914	15.4	2.0	0.6	18.0

		Panel B: Unconventional GDP		
	$GFCF^A$	$GFCF^B$	Investment in inventories	GCF as a share of GDP
1875/1884	10.9	0.4	8.4	21.1
1885/1894	15.6	0.6	0.9	20.5
1895/1899	10.1	0.4	2.1	13.6
1900/1909	14.0	0.9	2.1	20.7
1910/1914	15.3	0.5	2.0	18.4

Sources: Panel A:
        Col. (1): Table 4, Column (6).
        Col. (2): Table 7, Panel C, Column (3).
        Col. (3): Table 6, Column (7).
        Col. (4): Sum of Columns (1)–(3).
    Panel B:
        Cols. (1), (3), (4): Data underlying Panel A, Columns (1), (2), (3), divided by real conventional GDP plus land clearing, etc. (see Table 4a).
        Col. (2): Table 4a, Column (4).
        Col. (5): Sum of Columns (1)–(4).

have been trade credit.[1342] If Martinez's estimate is somewhere near the truth, and if trade credit moved in harmony with the value of foreign trade – an assumption that seems reasonable – then it appears that trade

[1342] Reported in Frederic M. Halsey, *Investments in Latin America and the British West Indies*, Special Agents Series, No. 169, Bureau of Foreign and Domestic Commerce, Department of Commerce (Washington, D.C.: G.P.O., 1918), p. 25. [Hereafter cited as Halsey, *Investment in Latin America*.]

credit flows varied widely from year to year; but on average, over the years 1881–91, they were equal to a little more than 7 percent of total foreign capital inflows, and over the years 1895–1900 to roughly 11.5 percent; in each case total capital inflows are measured as Williams's figures plus our rough estimate of trade credit.[1343]

In other respects Williams's estimates probably overstate capital inflows. In the period in which he was interested, Argentina floated a number of conversion loans. Since these loans did not represent new capital, but simply the replacement of one set of bonds with another, they should not have been included in Williams's totals; and it appears that he quite properly excluded them. What he did with redemptions is less clear. For our purposes, they should be subtracted from capital inflows, but Williams may not have done so. How important were redemptions?

As of December 31, 1901, depending upon whether conversion issues are counted or ignored, redemptions of national, provincial, and municipal debt accounted for between 5.2 and 6.5 percent of the original value of securities floated after 1880.[1344] The small relative amount of redemptions should not be surprising. The period of time under consideration – a period that, incidentally, witnessed most of the international capital flows to Argentine governments and private firms up to 1900 – is relatively short.[1345] Sinking funds typically called for the annual accumulation of 0.5 to 1 percent of the value of the debt in question.[1346] It is also true that the 1890s was a period of government defaults, and default reduced redemptions. For private firms – overwhelmingly railroads – redemptions may have accounted for an even smaller fraction of capital, since railroads sold stocks, as well as bonds, and stocks – at least, common stocks – did not have to be redeemed. It seems likely, then, that Williams's probable (and necessary) neglect of trade credit is only partly balanced by his probable failure to net out redemptions.

Account should also be taken of defaults, defaults that Williams seems not to have deducted from his capital flows. How important they were, we do not know. Stone lists defaults of all levels of government

[1343] The values of exports plus imports, expressed in gold pesos, are taken from Tornquist, *The Economic Development of the Argentine Economy*, p. 140.

[1344] *Argentine Yearbook*, 1902, as reported in *The Annual Report of the Director of the Bureau of American Republics, for the Year 1903*, 58th Congress, 2nd Session, House of Representatives Document No. 111, Part 1 (Washington, D.C.: G.P.O., 1903), p. 247.

[1345] The effect of time is evident in data provided by Halsey (from the Report of the Corporation of Foreign Bondholders), presumably in 1918. At that time, government securities were paid down to the extent of 16.5 percent.

[1346] *The Argentine Yearbook*, 1907/8 (Buenos Aires: John Grant & Son), pp. 173–81.

securities held by the English; in the early 1890s, they amounted to £34 million sterling. Since total Argentine government foreign debt in 1901 was about £77.5 million pounds sterling, a very large fraction of government debt was thus in default. By 1905 the total had been reduced to £15.2 million, and these claims were ultimately settled by agreements with the creditors.[1347] By 1913 Stone finds nothing in default. It is clear that while foreigners suffered some losses in the collapse of 1890, Argentine governments reshaped their debt structure and finally met their obligations.[1348] Businesses failed on a large scale, but not notably in lines of activity in which foreigners had been most interested. We cannot say how important these losses were, but it is possible that Williams's inability to deal with trade credit, redemptions, and defaults wash out in their effects on capital flows over the full period 1880–1914.

In summary, if Williams's "funds realized" estimates are net of flotation costs, Williams's series is probably a reasonable set of estimates of capital flowing into Argentina; if they are not, then Williams's series probably overstates foreign capital inflows, possibly by about 10 percent.

There remains the problem of filling in the gap in Williams's series and then extending it into the twentieth century. The gap was filled by interpolating Williams's estimates between 1891 and 1895 on Ford's data on new Argentine issues in the U.K. capital markets.[1349]

For the twentieth century, there are Tornquist's estimates for 1911–12, 1912–13, and 1913–14, based on balance of payments data.[1350] We accepted these estimates and dated them to 1912, 1913, and 1914. These estimates are gross of defaults – probably few, in this period – but should be net of redemptions, discounts on securities sold, and flotation costs; they also include trade credit. Although produced in a very different way, they are probably roughly consistent with the Williams estimates for 1900 and earlier years.

The gap between the Williams and Tornquist estimates was bridged by interpolating on the Ford new issues series. This is a very shaky

---

[1347] Stone, *The Composition and Distribution*, p. 70a; Carlos Marichal, *A Century of Debt Crises*, pp. 160–70.

[1348] See Marichal, *A Century of Debt Crises*, ch. 6. Buenos Aires Province declared bankruptcy in 1891, but the debts of the Province seem to have been subsequently assumed by the national government. Williams, *Argentine International Trade*, p. 41.

[1349] Ford, *The Gold Standard*, p. 195.

[1350] Carlos A. Tornquist, El Balance de Pagos de la Republica Argentina En el Premier ano Economica Pasada Baja Loa Efectos de la Guerro Europea (Buenos Aires, 1916), as reported in V.L. Phelps, *The International Economic Position of Argentina* (Philadelphia: University of Pennsylvania Press, 1938), pp. 24, 27, 233. [Hereafter cited as Phelps, *International Position*.]

procedure, subject to major errors; alternative procedures lead to quite different results. Thus the flow series for the years 1901–11 is much weaker than the series for the years before 1901.

The new series, 1881–1914, was then converted from gold pesos to paper pesos at the rate of 1 to 2.27, and then deflated on the base 1914.[1351] The price series used for this purpose is the British wholesale price index discussed above. How the series should be deflated is by no means clear. Since Argentineans frequently used foreign capital to buy foreign capital goods, and since they bought heavily from Britain, use of the British index has some justification. But perhaps some combination of British, French, German, Belgian, Dutch, and American prices would serve better.

Table 9 contains the estimates. According to the data underlying Table 9 – hereafter, the flow series – foreign capital entering Argentina summed to about 10,262 billion paper pesos of 1914, between 1881 and 1914, or about 66 percent of total gross investment carried out in Argentina during this period. Are these reasonable figures? Here are some relevant considerations.

(1) A.B. Martinez estimated that foreign investment in Argentina came to between 4.0 and 4.5 billion gold pesos in 1918.[1352] These figures amount to 9.1 to 10.2 billion paper pesos, but the valuations presumably refer to the dates on which the securities were issued, not 1914. We developed a weighted price index number for the cumulated flow series – 0.89 – and divided this index number through the Martinez estimates, expressed in paper pesos. The results range from 10.2 billion to 11.5 billion. Foreign claims on Argentina increased little between 1914 and 1918.[1353] Martinez's estimates and the flow data seem, then, to be roughly consistent. There is one difficulty: The flow data refer to investment, whereas the Martinez data almost certainly refer to foreign claims on Argentine governments and businesses. The former are likely to be about 80 to 85 percent of the level of the latter. Adjusting the Martinez estimates to the level of investments reduces the range to something like 8.2 to 9.8 billion paper pesos. If Martinez is correct, then, the flow series may overstate foreign investment by between 4 and 24 percent, and the fraction of Argentine investment accounted for by foreigners would then be nearer 53 to 62 percent, still very large values.

[1351] Ford, *The Gold Standard*, p. 195.

[1352] Halsey, *Investments in Latin America*, p. 25.

[1353] See Halsey, *Investments in Latin America*, pp. 30–37, and Vernon Lovell Phelps, *The International Position of Argentina* (Philadelphia: University of Pennsylvania Press, 1938), p. 240. [Hereafter cited as Phelps, *International Position*.]

Table A-9. *Foreign capital flows into Argentina, and the gross savings rate, annual averages, 1881–1914*

	Panel A				
	Foreign capital				
	(1) Mil. 1914 pesos	(2) as % of conventional GDP	(3) as % of unconventional GDP	(4) Conventional savings rate (%)	(5) Unconventional savings rate (%)
1881/1884	69.0	9.1	9.1	11.7	12.0
1885/1894	195.9	14.8	14.7	5.1	5.8
1895/1899	96.5	4.8	4.8	8.5	8.8
1900/1909	441.3	13.9	13.8	6.1	6.9
1910/1914	626.3	12.4	12.3	5.6	6.1

	Panel B: Foreign capital as a percentage of real			
	(1) GCF (conventional)	(2) GCF (unconventional)	(3) GFCF (conventional)	(4) GFCF (unconventional)
1881/1884	43.8[a]	43.1[a]	82.7[a]	80.5[a]
1885/1894	74.0	71.7	94.3	90.7
1895/1899	36.1	35.3	47.1	45.7
1900/1909	69.5	66.7	97.9	92.6
1910/1914	68.9	66.8	80.5	77.8

[a] GCF and GFCF are annual averages for 1875/1884.

Panel A: Col. (1): See text.

Col. (2): Column (1) divided by annual averages of GDP, relevant years, taken from Roberto Cortes Conde, October 1994.

Col. (3): Same as Column (2), except that GDP includes all farm improvements (see Table 4a).

Col. (4): Column (4), Panel A, Table 8, minus Column (2) of Table 9.

Col. (5): Column (5), Panel B, Table 8, minus Column (3) of Table 9.

Panel B: Computed from data in Columns (2) and (3) of Panel A of this table and from Columns (1) and (4), Panel A, Table 8, and Columns (1) and (2) (summed) and (5) of Panel B of Table 8.

(2) The American consul in Buenos Aires reported that foreign investment in Argentine business in 1898 came to 614.3 million gold pesos.[1354] Foreign investment in Argentine governments, at all levels, seems to have

[1354] 56th Congress, First Session, 1899–1900, House Documents, Vol. 96, No. 481, Part 1, Commercial Relations 1899, Vol. 1, Consular Report for the Republic of Argentina, 1989, p. 582.

run 387.8 million gold pesos.[1355] Total foreign holdings around the turn of the century, then, appear to have come to about 1.0 billion gold pesos, and adjustments to allow for trade credit and to put these values in terms of 1914 prices brings the figure to 1.3 billion. Adjusting this value to put it on an investment basis brings it to the level of 1.0 to 1.1 billion paper pesos. The cumulated flows, from 1881–1900, come to about 1.2 billion. The check seems reasonably close, although, once again, the cumulated flow is high, compared with the stock.

(3) Stone's estimate of British investment in Argentina as of 1913 translates into 5,445.7 billion paper pesos.[1356] The British are widely believed to have accounted for about 60 percent of foreign investment in Argentina, an estimate that suggests that total foreign investment at that time must have run about 9.1 billion paper pesos.[1357] With an appropriate allowance for trade credit and another allowance to convert to 1914 prices, the total comes to almost 11.2 billion paper pesos, a figure that is close to the value derived by cumulating the flow series and also close to the value derived from Martinez's work. Once again, however, the stock and flow concepts are unlikely to be identical; converting the Stone-based estimate to an estimate of investment reduces it to a figure of between 9.0 and 9.5 billion paper pesos. Once again, the flow series seems high, this time by perhaps 7 to 13 percent.[1358]

The savings rates derived from our estimates compare with those prepared by Taylor and Williamson and della Paolera and Taylor, as follows:[1359]

[1355] *Bureau of the American Republics*, p. 247. The provincial and municipal debts listed were all assumed by the national government. There do not appear to have been any other provincial or municipal debts held outside Argentina. See Halsey, *Investments in Latin America*, pp. 30–37.

[1356] Stone, *The Composition and Distribution*.

[1357] C.L. Lewis, "British Business in Argentina," Economic History Department, London School of Economics, Working Paper No. 26/95, June 1995, p. 3.

[1358] See also Phelps, *International Position*, pp. 239–54. Phelps reviews a number of estimates of foreign holdings in Argentina and concludes that the Martinez estimate is too high. His preferred figures do not seem consistent with the work of Stone, if we can assume that the British really did account for about 60 percent of foreign capital in Argentina, ca. 1914.

[1359] Alan M. Taylor and Jeffrey G. Williamson, "*Capital Flows to the New World as an Intergenerational Transfer*," Working Paper Series on Historical Factors in Long Run Growth, Working Paper No. 32, National Bureau of Economic Research, December 1991, pp. 29 and 30. Gerardo della Paolera and Alan M. Taylor, "Finance and Development in an Emerging Market: Argentina in the Interwar Period," manuscript, May 1997.

Years	della Paolera and Taylor	Taylor and Williamson	Davis and Gallman
1900–1904	7%		
1905–1909	10		
1900–1909		5.4%	6.1%
1910–1914	4	5.5	5.6

The Davis and Gallman estimates are based on constant price data, whereas the ones produced by della Paolera and Taylor, and Taylor and Williamson are in current prices. Furthermore, the two sets prepared by Taylor and his collaborators rest on foreign investment figures depending on the current account balance, a somewhat different concept from the one employed by Davis and Gallman (see above). The differences are, however, probably not crucial. On the whole, then, the three sets of estimates seem to be roughly consistent: della Paolera and Taylor suggest a somewhat higher rate, 1900–9, and a lower rate, 1910–14, than do Taylor and Williamson, and Davis and Gallman. Given the nature of the data, however, the differences are very slight.

The check with della Paolera and Taylor shows a higher fraction of investment accounted for by savings in the years 1900–1909 than do Davis and Gallman, and a lower share in the years 1910–14. The unweighted della Paolera/Taylor mean rate over the full period, 1900–14, is considerably higher – 56 percent – than is the Davis/Gallman rate – 31 percent. Both accounts, however, attribute great importance to foreign investment as a source of total investment.

6A-5. Net capital formation

To estimate net capital formation, one must first compute capital consumption. Tornquist has published useful detailed evidence on the fixed capital stock for the years 1914–16.[1360] The evidence was assembled by A.E. Bunge. Converting all those estimates to 1914 values, by means of a price index of gross investment taken from *Estudios*, Cuadro 11, shifted to the base 1914, without reweighting, yields the following figures (millions of pesos):

[1360] Tornquist, *The Economic Development of the Argentine Republic*, p. 255.

	1914	1915	1915/1916	1916
Price Index	100	122.4	138.8	155.2
Fixed Installations	692[a]			1,074
Cities and Townships	4,381[a]			6,800
Railways	2,432[b]		3,375	
Tramways, Telegraphs, Telephones, Electrical and Gas Services	438[a]			680
Ports, Canals, Ships	425[a]			660
Agricultural Machinery and Implements	284			
Industrial Machinery and Implements of Labor	361[a]			440

[a] 1916 values, expressed in 1914 prices.
[b] 1915 values, expressed in 1914 prices.

We treated the results as estimates of the capital stock in 1914, and in manipulating them, we made the following assumptions:

1. "Fixed Installations" were assumed to be structures and to have useful lives of forty years; the existing stock was assumed to be ten years old, on average. Thus, capital consumption (straight line accounting) ran around 3.3 percent.
2. "Cities and Townships" (presumably residences, public buildings, and other structures), "Railways," "Tramways, Telegraphs, Telephones, Electrical and Gas Services," and "Ports, Canals, and Ships" were assumed to have useful lives of seventy-five years and to be fifteen years old, on average; thus, capital consumption ran around 1.7 percent.
3. "Agricultural Machinery and Implements" and "Industrial Machinery and the Implements of Labor" were assumed to have a useful life of fifteen years and to be five years old, on average, which implies a capital consumption rate of 10 percent.

We applied these rates to the fixed capital data, expressed in prices of 1914, and thereby derived a figure for capital consumption of 222 million paper pesos, prices of 1914. This value is 4.9 percent of GDP in 1914. However, GDP in that year was unusually low – lower than any value between 1910 and 1916. A better basis of comparison would probably be the mean of GDP in the previous two years, 1912 and 1913. On this basis, capital consumption came to 4.0 percent of GDP. This value is smaller than the 1910–14 figure implied by Ganz's work; but the reader will recall that Ganz employed data expressed in 1950 prices, data that yield a much higher ratio of investment to GDP than do data expressed in prices of 1914.[1361]

We accepted the figure of 4 percent as the ratio of capital consumption to real GDP in the period 1910–14. We extrapolated this value backward in time on the share of GFCF in GDP to allow for the effects of changes in the structure of GDP on investment. The results, together with the implied ratio of net capital formation to net domestic product, are displayed in Table A-10.

6A-6. *Test of the estimates*

The best available test of the estimates consists of computing the value of the capital stock in 1914 by accumulating the net investment flows, 1875–1914, and then comparing the result with A.E. Bunge's estimate of the capital stock in 1914, based chiefly on census data.[1362] Table A-11 shows how the cumulated investment flows were calculated.

Our estimate of the capital stock in 1914 comes to 13.000 billion pesos of 1914, a figure that is very close to the value estimated by Bunge (14.129 billion pesos). The difference between our estimate and Bunge's is also of the correct sign: since our estimate takes no account of net investment before 1875, it should be – and is – slightly smaller than the Bunge estimate. The success of the check tends to support our estimates. However, some ambiguities remain. The valuation concept we employed is net reproduction cost. Bunge's figures are more likely to be market values or net book values, or some combination of the two. Market values are likely to be close to net reproduction costs, but, depending on the movements of capital goods prices across time, book values may or may not be. The deviation between net book and net reproduction cost estimates is likely to be greater for old than for new capital. An inspection of Table A-11 will show that a substantial part of the capital stock was accumulated across the fifteen years beginning in 1900 and ending in 1914. That fact suggests that the deviation between reproduction and book costs may not have been great as far as the capital stock of 1914 is concerned.

[1361] Ganz, "Problems and Uses," p. 248, estimates that capital consumption amounted to 12.3 percent of GFCF. Since GFCF was, according to Ganz, 42.2 percent of GDP, capital consumption amounted to about 5 percent of GDP.

[1362] Reported in Tornquist, *The Economic Development of the Argentine Republic*, p. 255. The adjustment of the data, to put them all on a 1914 valuation base, is described in Section 6A-5 above.

Table A-10. *Capital consumption and net capital formation, as percentages of GDP and NDP (1875/1884–1910/1914)*

	(1) Capital consumption as a percentage of Gross Domestic Product		(2) Net capital formation as a percentage of Net Domestic Product	
	(a) Conventional measures	(b) Unconventional measures	(a) Conventional measures	(b) Unconventional measures
1875/1884	2.8	2.8	18.5	18.8
1885/1894	4.1	4.0	16.5	17.2
1895/1899	2.7	2.6	10.8	11.3
1900/1909	3.7	3.6	16.9	17.7
1910/1914	4.0	3.9	14.6	15.1

Notes: Conventional measures of capital formation and domestic product *exclude* investment in the clearing, first breaking, and fencing of arable lands; unconventional measures include them.

Sources: Col. (1): See text. Capital consumption was estimated for each period by multiplying conventional GDP by the ratio of capital consumption to GDP. No depreciation was taken for investment in the clearing, first breaking, and fencing of arable land. (The first two are not depreciable; the third is, but the adjustment required to take it into account is negligible.)

Col. (2): These figures were computed in the following way:

(a) $\dfrac{\text{GCF} - \text{capital consumption}}{\text{GDP} - \text{capital consumption}}$

(b) $\dfrac{\text{GCF} + \text{farm clearing, etc.} - \text{capital consumption}}{\text{GDP} + \text{farm clearing, etc.} - \text{capital consumption}}$

We therefore accept the test as a rough confirmation of the accuracy of our estimates.

6A-7. *A reestimation employing the GFCF series of Alexander Ganz*

Our estimates depend upon Diaz Alejandro's series of the share of GDP devoted to gross fixed capital formation. An alternative is to use instead the series prepared by Alexander Ganz. Table A-12 shows the construction of alternative investment and capital-stock estimates, based on Ganz's work. It will be observed that the cumulated capital stock value derived from the Ganz-based series is very much larger than the

Table A-11. *Estimation of the value of the capital stock, 1914*
(million 1914 pesos)

	(1) Real GDP, totals	(2) 1 minus rate of capital consumption	(3) (1) × (2) Real NNP, totals	(4) Real net capital formation
1875/1884	6,393	0.972	6,214	1,150
1885/1894	13,200	0.959	12,659	2,089
1895/1899	10,148	0.973	9,874	1,066
1900/1909	31,696	0.963	30,523	5,158
1910/1914	25,238	0.960	24,228	3,537
Total, capital stock of 1914				13,000

Note: The figures in this table are *totals*, not annual averages.

Sources: Col. (1): Computed from Cortes Conde, "Estimates of Argentina GDP, 1875–1935," October 1994.
Col. (2): Computed from data in Table 10, Col. (2) (a).
Col. (3): Col. (1) × Col. (2).
Col. (4): Col. (3) × Col. (2) (a) of Table 10.

one based on Diaz Alejandro's work. It is, of course, also very much larger than Bunge's 1914 capital stock estimates. Indeed, it is implausibly large. We conclude that our estimates depending on the Diaz Alejandro series are the more acceptable.

6A-8. *Capital/output ratios*

There are at least three ways to estimate capital/output ratios for Argentina during the period 1875–1914. First, for the year 1914 the ratio can be calculated directly from the two sets of capital stock estimates for that year – the adjusted Bunge figures and our cumulation of net flows – and our NDP estimates, derived from Cortes Conde. Second, an estimate for ca. 1914 can be derived by dividing the average net investment share in NDP, 1875–1914, by the average rate of growth of NDP over the same period. Finally, estimates can be built up from sectoral evidence for 1892, and projected to other years, including 1914.

Table A-12. *Estimates of capital formation, 1875–1914, and the capital stock, 1914, based on the work of Alexander Ganz*

	Panel A: Capital formation rates			
	(1) GFCG/GDP (%)	(2) INVΔ/ GDP × 100 (%)	(3) Capital Cons/ GDP × 100 (%)	(4) NFC/NDP × 100 (%)
1875/1884	20.5	9.8	2.8	28.3
1885/1894	29.3	4.3	4.1	30.8
1895/1899	19.0	3.1	2.7	19.9
1900/1909	26.5	5.8	3.7	29.7
1910/1914	28.3	2.6	4.0	28.0

Panel B: Net capital formation and the capital stock
(million pesos of 1914)

	(1) Real NDP (totals)	(2) Real net capital formation
1875/1884	6,214	1,759
1885/1894	12,659	3,899
1895/1899	9,874	1,965
1900/1909	30,523	9,065
1910/1914	24,228	6,784
Total, capital stock of 1914		23,472

Sources: *Panel A*: Col. (1): 1900–1914, Ganz, converted to estimates based on
1914. *1875–1899*, 1900/1909 extrapolated backward
on the series in Col. (6) of Table 4, above.
Col. (2): Col. (2) + Col. (3) of Table 8, above.
Col. (3): Col. (1) (b) of Table 10, above.
Col. (4): Cols. (1) + (2) − (3), divided by [1-Col. (3)].
Panel B: Col. (1): Col. (3) of Table 11, above.
Col. (2): Col. (1) × Panel A, Col. (4).

6A-8(a). *Direct estimates for 1913:* In 1914 real NDP was almost 20 percent below its level in the previous year. Consequently, the capital/output ratio in that year was unusually high. To get a value that is closer to expressing circumstances during full employment, we used an NDP value for 1913 to compute the required ratios. The results are as follows:

1. Capital/NDP = 2.31, where capital consists of the summation of net investment flows, 1875–1914.
2. Capital/NDP = 2.51, where capital in 1914 is the Bunge estimate, adjusted to put it on a 1914 price base.

6A-8(b). Estimate based on the net investment rate and the average rate of growth of NDP: Capital/output ratios vary from time to time and place to place, so that there is no way of judging whether the computed values are reasonable or not simply by inspecting them. There are two kinds of tests, however, that are useful. First, the ratios can be checked against alternative estimates, devised by means of different techniques. Second, the estimates can be compared with ratios relevant to other places and times.

The first alternative estimate was derived by dividing the average rate of growth of real NDP (1975/84–1910/14) by the weighted average investment rate (i.e., the share in NDP). The result, 2.39, tends to confirm the results obtained by the first method, but since both methods employ the same data, the confirmation does not have great weight. It shows only that the national accounts system devised for this purpose is coherent.

6A-8(c). A second set of direct estimates: The second set of test estimates employs some independent evidence but has other features that make it less than perfect. We begin with an estimate for 1892, based chiefly on data taken from Mulhall.[1363] Sectoral capital/output ratio estimates are assembled and then weighted by Cortes Conde's sectoral real income data to produce an aggregate ratio for 1892. The computed sectoral ratios are then applied to income data for 1884 and 1913 to check the previous estimates for 1913 and to get an impression of the trend in the capital/output ratio over time. There are three caveats. First, the sectoral ratios for 1892 come from a variety of sources, not all of them perfectly relevant. Second, the ratios for 1892 were computed from current (gold) price data, but they are projected to 1884 and 1913 on constant price data. The test would obviously be more persuasive were all estimates in either current or constant prices. Third, the projections to 1884 and 1913 allow us to see – so long as the problems touched on by the two previous caveats do not prohibit us from doing so – the effects of structural changes on the capital/output ratio; but they speak to us of the true levels

---

[1363] M.G. and E.T. Mulhall, *Handbook of the River Plate*, 6th ed. (Buenos Aires: M.G. and E.T. Mulhall; and London: Kegan Paul, Trench & Co., 1892), p. 20. The values are expressed in gold pesos.

Table A-13. *The capital/output ratio in 1892*

	(1) Gross Income originating (Y) (million of pesos 1914)	(2) K/Y	(3) Capital (K) (million of pesos 1914)
Industry Commerce Government Construction	721	1.0	721
Agriculture	218	1.1	240
Herding	400	5.1	2,040
Transportation	41	10.3	422
Housing	52	10.0	520
Totals	1,432		3,943
Weighted average		2.75	

Sources: Col. (1): Lines (1)–(4): Cortes Conde, October 1994.

Line (5): Cortes Conde does not identify the value of shelter. Presumably it is included – with income from other activities – in a residual, the difference between Cortes Conde's GDP estimate and the sum of his sectoral gross income originating estimates.

Line (6): The total here falls 31 million pesos' short of Cortes Conde's GDP estimate; presumably the difference reflects income from miscellaneous minor activities.

Col. (2): *Line (1)*: According to Davis and Gallman (L.E. Davis and R.E. Gallman, "Capital Formation in the United States During the Nineteenth Century," in Peter Malthias and M.M. Postan (eds.), *The Cambridge Economic History of Europe*, Volume VII, Part 2 (Cambridge: Cambridge University Press, 1978, 18), the U.S. K/Y ratio for mining and manufacturing ran from 0.9 to 1.0, down to 1870, when it began to rise. On that slender basis, we assigned a K/Y ratio of 1.0 to industry, construction, government, and commerce. We did not use the U.S. evidence for the years after 1870, since, in that period, the structure of U.S. industry changed in ways that must have made it increasingly unlike Argentine industry.

Table A-14. *Capital/output ratios, 1884 and 1913*

	1884		1913	
	Gross income originating (millions of 1914 pesos)	Capital (millions of 1914 pesos)	Gross income originating (millions of 1914 pesos)	Capital (million of 1914 pesos)
Industry, commerce, government construction	409	409	3,106	3,106
Agriculture	64	70	899	989
Herding	403	2,055	861	4,391
Transportation	16	165	284	2,925
Housing	47	472	105	1,053
Totals	939	3,171	5,255	12,464
K/Y	3.38		2.37	

Sources: Col. (1) and (3): Lines (1)–(4): Cortes Conde, October 1994.
    Col. (1) and (3): Line (5): Columns (2) and (4) (respectively) × 10. (See Table 13.) N. B. Line 5 is expressed in prices of 1884 [Column (1)] and 1892 [Column (3)].
    Col. (1):   *Line (7):* Column 2, Line (6) ÷ Column (1), Line 6.
    Col. (3):   *Line (7):* Column (4), Line (6) ÷ Column (3), Line (6).
    Col. (2) and (4): Lines (1)–(4): Columns (1) and (2) (respectively) multiplied by the K/Y ratios of Table 13.
    Col. (2) and (4): Line (5): Mulhall, 1892, 20.

of the ratios in these two years only if sectoral ratios were not subject to change over time, or, if so, changed in offsetting ways. We think that they may very well have changed in offsetting ways between 1892 and 1913.

Tables A-13 and A-14 and the source notes thereto explain how the estimates were made. The tables turn up at least two matters of interest. First, the capital/output ratio for 1913 checks very closely with the estimates discussed above. Given the melange of data from which this figure was constructed, and the fact that it was projected from 1892 on the assumption that intra-sectoral ratios were constant, the check has limited value. Nonetheless, it is right on the money, virtually identical with the values obtained for that date by means of the other procedures previously discussed; every little bit helps.

The other interesting feature of the tables is that they show that structural changes between the 1870s and the early twentieth century led to a quite marked reduction in the capital/output ratio. Thus, as time passed, investment in Argentina had a bigger and bigger effect on output, peso for peso, unless, of course, the tendency toward decline was offset by developments within sectors. That interference, however, seems unlikely. The ratio for industry and allied fields may have risen slightly, if U.S. experience is relevant; but the increase is quite unlikely to have had a major effect. The same conclusion is likely to have been true for agriculture. In the case of transportation between 1892 and 1913, the ratio is likely to have fallen somewhat as capacity put in place in the nineteenth century came to be more intensively used. There is no reason to suppose a major shift – up or down – in the trend for shelter. Pastoral activities may very well have experienced a downward drift in the capital/output ratio, as improvements in breeds made it possible to bring animals to slaughter at younger ages. The downward movement of the aggregate ratio, then, is probably a real phenomenon; and the fillip thereby given to Argentine growth is also real.

What of the levels of these ratios? Compared with experience elsewhere, do they seem plausible? The United States provides a reasonable comparative base, at least before the shifts in U.S. industrial structure at the end of the nineteenth century. Both Argentina and the United States had large agricultural and pastoral sectors, both were growing rapidly, and both put in place substantial rail networks in the latter decades of the nineteenth century. The U.S. capital/output ratio – exclusive of inventories – ran 2.4, in 1880, and 3.3, in 1890. Even adjusting for inventories, the two countries seem to have had capital/output ratios of similar sizes. The striking difference between the two is that, over time, in the United States the ratio was rising, while in Argentina it was falling.

CHAPTER 7

Lessons from the past: International financial flows and the evolution of capital markets, Britain and Argentina, Australia, Canada, and the United States before World War I

7-1. Introduction

Economists have tended to focus their attention on short-run issues in part because the institutional structure – the rules that are observed or enforced that govern the ways in which economic agents can compete or cooperate – can be treated as exogenous and fixed. Any economist who attempts to understand the process of long-run economic growth and development, however, must immediately confront the problem of institutional change. In the long run the institutional structure does change, and the changes are at least partly endogenous. Any successful long-run analysis must explicitly include assumptions about the nature of institutional development, but we still know little about the relationship between the institutional structure and the more traditional economic variables or about the way changes in the external environment – economic, political, social, and cultural – affect the institutional structure.

Much of what we do know about institutional change comes from the work of Nobel Prize winner Douglass North. To North, "the economies of scope, complementarities, and network externalities of an institutional matrix make institutional change overwhelmingly incremental and path dependent." Since "the static nature of economic theory ill fits us to understand that process we need to construct a theoretical framework that models economic change."[1364] Although he clearly understands the nature of the problem, we are left with a warning, an admonishment, and a number of examples. Clearly, we are not yet ready to specify a theory of institutional change; however, a taxonomy – a formal structure of

---

[1364] Douglass C. North, "Some Fundamental Puzzles in Economic History/Development," paper delivered at the Von Gremp Workshop in Entrepreneurial History, UCLA, February 21, 1996, pp. 7, 30.

753

classification and description – is a logical first step toward the development of any theory. This chapter begins the construction of a taxonomy by systematically examining the differences in processes of institutional change and development in Britain and the four frontier countries that were the focus of Chapters 2 through 6.

By the middle of the nineteenth century, there was in Britain a body of educated and sophisticated savers who had learned that investments in symbolic capital could be both rewarding and relatively safe. Their education had proceeded from their experience with government bonds during the Napoleonic Wars to the issues of domestic railroads in the 1830s and 1840s. They had learned during the Hudson panic that those private securities could be safe, even during the apparent height of unsafeness. Savers who had invested before the speculative boom became an explosion found that, in the long run, they did very well. A portfolio of railroad issues provided protection against the losses suffered by some individual firms. They also discovered that, even if ocean shipping remained very risky, the shares of firms that "bundled" ships and voyages together – Cunard and the Royal Mail Line, for example – could be safe. Moreover, for government and railway issues, the London Stock Exchange, and to a lesser extent the provincial stock exchanges, made it easy to liquidate holdings should the need occur.

At the same time savers were coming to recognize that returns on both British government securities and railway stocks and bonds were falling and were not likely to recover quickly.[1365] Overseas investments began to appear attractive, but their unfavorable experience with Latin American bonds in the 1820s and with U.S. state bonds in the 1830s and 1840s was still relatively fresh in their minds. What was required was an institutional structure that would permit them to separate questions of risk from questions of uncertainty and that would provide them with the requisite information to overcome the problems of asymmetric information, problems that appear to increase with the distance, spatially or industrially, between the saver and the investor.

Developments between the end of the American Civil War and the outbreak of World War I played a crucial role in the evolution of international financial markets. Those decades witnessed a convergence of

---

[1365] The nominal yield on 3 percent consols had fallen from 4.57 percent in the decade 1810–1819, to 3.72 percent in the 1820s, to 3.40 percent in the 1830s, to 3.26 percent in the 1840s, and to 3.16 percent in the 1850s. Correcting for changes in the price level, those yields suggest real rates of return of 8.47, 6.87, 1.84, 6.61, and 1.57 percent. Homer and Sylla, *A History of Interest Rates*, table 19, pp. 195–97. Mitchell, *Abstract of British Historical Statistics*, table Prices 3, pp. 471–72.

international interest rates – a movement promoted by the spread of the international gold standard – and the emergence of an international capital market of near modern sophistication. The years from 1870 to 1914 represent the first era of true financial globalization; and then, as now, the emerging markets were relatively free of governmental constraints on the movement of private capital. Thus, in many ways the four and a half decades can be viewed as a precursor of the modern post–Bretton Woods era.

Since economic development in each of the four settler countries depended to a substantial degree on the importation of foreign – largely British – capital, the thrust of this study is primarily directed to the differential impact of those flows on the evolution of the institutional structure of the receiving countries. That end, however, cannot be accomplished unless the effects of those transfers on the supplying economy are also analyzed. In 1870 the domestic financial structures in the four countries ranged from primitive to semi-modern. Britain, on the other hand, had, by any nineteenth-century criteria, a very highly developed financial system.

In large part the economic environment and the particular set of financial institutions that evolved in each receiving country was influenced by domestic economic and political considerations. Those considerations ranged from the policies of government, to the experiences of local businessmen, to the preferences of consumers. The evolutionary path of the economic environments and their supporting financial institutions were, however, also influenced by the availability of foreign finance. To the extent that the income, savings behavior, and the preferences of the foreign suppliers of capital were not identical to those of domestic savers, substantial gains could be, and were, realized from international capital transfers. Given economic conditions in Britain, the size of the international capital movements was largely dependent on the economic environment and on the existing set of institutions in the receiving countries. As time passed, however, the flows themselves affected both the speed of development and the structure of the emerging domestic capital market institutions. Thus a comparison of the impact of the capital flows from a single country (Britain) on the four receiving countries – countries characterized by four different sets of economic and political environments and four different sets of initial institutional structures – provides something of a natural experiment for the study of institutional invention and innovation.

Terms such as "reputational signals" and "asymmetric information" are relatively new additions to the economist's vocabulary, but their meanings and their implications were well recognized at least three-quarters of a century ago. In 1921 Frederick Lavington wrote that sellers of securities had a more intimate knowledge of the commodity with which they deal than do the buyers, and he concluded that this superior bargaining knowledge gave a wide scope for deception and that it enabled the speculator with inside knowledge to draw abnormal profits by dealing with investors who were less well informed. He had also noted that the problems of asymmetric information could be reduced by attaching the reputation of a well-regarded investment broker to the issue, by having legal disclosure requirements, and by the existence of reports in a financial press with a history of honesty.[1366]

Lavington's depiction of the British domestic and international capital markets in the pre-war era was an even better description of the British market for international securities a half century earlier. The British saver had only recently begun to direct his gaze overseas; the financial press was largely non-existent: no one (not even the well established merchant bankers) knew if there were *any* sound American, let alone Argentine, railroads; and there were few "legal enactments devised to secure the publication of essential particulars." At the most fundamental level there were questions of risk and there were questions of uncertainty.[1367] Experience with domestic railroads and trans-oceanic steamship lines in the 1830s and 1840s had shown the British saver that, even if an industry was risky, it was possible to insure against that risk by holding a portfolio of the securities of a number of firms. Experience with Latin American government bonds in the 1820s and American state bonds in the 1830s and 1840s, however, had led him to recognize that no amount of bundling can overcome the problems of uncertainty. Institutional innovation was required to solve both the problems rooted in risk and those arising from uncertainty.

The investor had to be able to distinguish between risky and uncertain investments. Since the promoter was better informed than the potential investor, problems of asymmetric information and moral hazard created additional problems of uncertainty. Uncertainty discounts can be reduced by providing more and better information, by attaching an imprimatur of quality – a signal from someone the saver recognizes and trusts – to the investment, or by innovating a better system of monitor-

---

[1366] Frederick Lavington, *The English Capital Market* (London: Methuen & Co., 1921), pp. 191–92.

[1367] The terms *risk* and *uncertainty* are used in the Knightian sense; that is, in the case of risk, while individual outcomes are unknown the distribution of those outcomes is known. In the case of uncertainty neither the individual outcomes nor their distributions are known. Frank H. Knight, *Risk, Uncertainty, and Profits* (Boston: Houghton Mifflin, 1921).

ing the agents who directed the business activities or supplied information about those activities. In the case of risk the investor had to ascertain the level of risk attached to each alternative, if he was to benefit from the insurance provided by bundling a number of investments into a single portfolio – a portfolio held by an individual or by a financial intermediary for a group of individuals.

Risk and uncertainty, however, are not the only issues. In addition, first, there were questions of transaction costs. It was necessary for the British saver to obtain information about potential foreign investments and then to acquire relatively inexpensive access to those investments. Second, it was necessary to establish some type of market to make it possible for savers or their agents to easily and speedily convert paper assets into cash at near published prices."[1368]

What was required was a set of institutions designed, first, to overcome the informational asymmetries that existed between American, Australian, Argentinean, or Canadian promoters and the British brokers and merchant bankers, second, to make it possible for British investors to monitor the behavior of overseas entrepreneurs who were operating the foreign business enterprises, and, third, to establish a market in which the pieces of paper symbolic capital could be readily traded.

Institutional innovation – particularly innovations in financial intermediation – can substantially mitigate all of these problems. In the case of transactions costs, since many of the costs associated with acquiring information are fixed, the interposition of an intermediary between saver and investor can spread those costs across a number of savers and allow each to capture the benefits of economies of scale. At the same time, by pooling savers' funds at a single well-known location, the intermediaries can reduce both the saver's and the investor's search and negotiation costs.

In the case of uncertainty, because of their experience, the managers of financial intermediaries and of formal securities markets are often better than the typical saver at selecting the most promising firms and managers. As a result, their employment will very likely produce a more efficient allocation of capital.[1369] Moreover, a well-known and trusted bank's or individual's participation in an underwriting syndicate can reduce a saver's uncertainty about the quality of an investment, as can the inclusion of a firm's securities in the portfolio of a well-regarded bank

---

[1368] Ross Levine, "Financial Development and Economic Growth: Views and Agenda," in *The Journal of Economic Literature*, Vol. XXXV, No. 2, June 1997, pp. 688–726. [Hereafter cited as Levine, "Financial Development and Economic Growth."]

[1369] Levine, "Financial Development and Economic Growth," p. 694.

or non-bank intermediary. In a similar fashion the listing of a security on a stock exchange with a known reputation for careful vetting of its listed securities can also help reduce uncertainty discounts. Reports in the financial press – a press that has a reputation for honest investigation and reporting – can have an analogous impact. Finally, firm owners can create financial arrangements that encourage managers to run "the firm in a manner that is in the best interest of the owners. In addition, "outside creditors – banks, equity and bond holders – that do not manage firms on a day-to-day basis will [attempt to] create financial arrangements to compel inside owners and managers to run firms in accordance with the interests of outside creditors. . . . Besides [the innovation of] particular types of financial contracts, financial intermediaries can reduce information costs even further" by exploiting the economies of scale inherent in obtaining the information needed to monitor distant owners and managers effectively.[1370]

In the case of risk, intermediaries can hold a portfolio of investments and provide each saver with a claim on a part of that portfolio. A formal securities market can make it possible to provide claims in relatively small denominations and therefore permit a saver to spread his limited accumulations across a number of firms in an industry or region. In the case of liquidity risk an efficient formal securities market makes it possible for any saver to turn his or her pieces of symbolic capital – be they equities or bonds – into cash at market prices, while "at the same time the capital market transforms these liquid financial instruments into long-term capital investments in illiquid production processes."[1371]

At times financial innovations occurred in the British market, at times in the receiving country, and at times they involved changes in both. Since the foreign savers were largely British, the ultimate shape of the emerging institutional structure – no matter if the new institutions were located in Britain or in the receiving country – was in part determined by those savers' view of the initial environmental conditions in the receiving country.[1372] Moreover, even when the emerging structures were located in part or entirely in Britain, they often had a significant impact on the

---

[1370] Levine, "Financial Development and Economic Growth," pp. 696–697

[1371] Levine, "Financial Development and Economic Growth," p. 692.

[1372] This conclusion was somewhat less true for Argentina than of the other three. The British were heavily into Argentine banks and railways, but very substantial contributions were also made by Continental savers, particularly those in the low countries, France, and Germany. It should also be noted that, by 1900, American capital was of more than marginal importance in Canada, and that the United States was also the recipient of some capital from continental Europe, particularly from Germany and Holland.

evolving institutional structure in the receiving country. For example, indirect finance tended to generate complementary institutions in the recipient country; but direct investment often reduced the need for such financial innovation. Again, direct investment sometimes engendered competition and conflict between domestic and foreign firms and, through the intermediation of the political process, resulted in legal constraints on future foreign investment. In the long run those constraints, in turn, affected the evolution of the domestic financial structure.

A comparison of the histories of the four frontier countries suggests something about the relationship between the economic environment and the course of domestic institutional development. The economic environment affected institutional evolution both directly through the constraints it imposed on new and evolving institutions and indirectly through the questions it raised in the minds of foreign savers, savers who, in turn, attempted to resolve those questions by institutional innovation at home or in the receiving country. In particular, three facets of the domestic economies of the receiving countries appear to have been particularly important in terms of the constraints they imposed, directly or indirectly, on the evolving structures of their capital markets. First, there are two questions involving the government of the receiving country. How large and how pervasive were the influences of the government on the local economy? What was the probability of a government meeting its financial obligations? Second, were the railroads in the receiving country financed by the private sector, the public sector, or some combination of the two? Third, what was the nature of the private non-railroad demand for finance? These questions are important, but two caveats: It is impossible to separate the three completely, and the answers to the three were not always independent of the flow of foreign capital.

Consider the problems from the point of view of a British saver looking at overseas investment alternatives sometime in the years between 1865 and 1890. Of the $4.5 billion in capital "created and called" that went to the four countries over that quarter century, government and railway issues together drew more than nine out of every ten dollars; the fraction ranged from 86 percent in Australia to 92 percent in Canada. All railroads and governments were not, however, viewed as equals. Although Canada and five of the Australian states had been granted responsible government, they were still a part of the British empire. The debt issues of the self-governing colonies in Australia and the federal and provincial governments in Canada were not guaranteed by the British Treasury; however, at least since the innovation of inscribed stock in the late 1870s, British savers had endowed those issues with de facto, if not de jure, trustee status. In 1900 such status was legally confirmed. Given those bona fides, there was little need for the innovation of a supporting infrastructure designed to provide a further stamp of quality. The government's imprimatur alone was sufficient to ease the mind of the British saver.

Not all government issues were so well received. A number of American state governments, in order to finance their financial and social overhead infrastructures, had turned to the British saver during the 1830s; and some quarter century later, the Confederate government had drawn on British resources to fight the Civil War. In the post–Civil War years many southern states had also looked to Britain for "cheap" finance. In all three cases the result had often been default, and some debts were never paid. Not surprisingly, the British saver took a very jaundiced view of American state loans after the defaults of the 1840s; he was badly burned by his experience with Confederate debt in the wake of Appomattox; and his concerns were reinforced by the post-Reconstruction defaults of many of the southern states. The federal government had not defaulted in either the 1840s or the 1860s, but its reputation still suffered. In the words of the editors of *The Times*, "The truth is the bonds of the United States are still looked upon in Europe as somewhat uncertain forms of investment."[1373] Over the 1870s the U.S. federal, state, and city government issues that were traded in London yielded, on average, 8.0 percent.[1374] In contrast, the yields on similar Aus-

---

[1373] *The Times*, December 8, 1869, p. 9b.

[1374] "A strong syndicate of international bankers failed to place the first issue of the U.S. funded loan of March 1871; 5 percent at par was too high a price, and the Americans themselves were the principal subscribers. The American Secretary of Finance was trying to reduce the interest on government securities from 6 to 5 percent, but only $75 million were subscribed to the $200 million on the market, and the subscribers were American.

"A few months later (August 1871), Jay Cooke negotiated a successful issue of the funded loan, again supported by a powerful syndicate of European bankers. He succeeded in placing $75 million on the London market, and the loan was taken up entirely by a combination of British, continental and U.S. investors. But the same syndicate was unsuccessful in placing the remaining portion of the 5 percent funded loan in London in February 1873; only $28.5 million of the $300 million on offer was sold in Europe, and very much less in the United States.

"The financial crisis that followed in the autumn of 1873 cut off further foreign investment, and no bonds were sold at a lower rate than 5 percent until 1877. Subsequent attempts during the 1870s to reduce the rate to 4 percent were a failure; American credit would not support it. John Philip Drew, a dealer on the London Stock Exchange whose business was entirely American, told the Royal Commission on the Stock Exchange in December 1877 that he did not know of

tralian and Canadian government issues average only 5.7 and 6.2 percent, respectively. The status of Argentine issues was overshadowed by the memory of the ill-fated British loan of 1823, a loan that was negotiated to build a port at Ensenada, but that was actually expended on military supplies to fight a war with Brazil. The issue was long in default and, although their concerns were partially alleviated by the Argentine government's move to reconstruct or repay the loan in the 1850s, it apparently still made subsequent Argentine issues even more suspect than their American counterparts. In the 1870s Argentine governments yielded, on average, 9.5 percent.

Given the declining returns on British domestic alternatives, it was possible for the Australian and Canadian governments to borrow at interest rates that were very low by the standards then prevailing in the private sector of their domestic economies but that still looked very attractive to British savers. Thus, in Canada and Australia there was a temptation to expand the scope of government to take advantage of this supply of cheap capital. The lure of such finance certainly influenced the Canadian government's decision to implement Macdonald's National Policy; and it even more dramatically affected the shape of Australian development, as each of the five self-governing colonial governments used British savings to expand their activities into areas – railroads, public utilities, port facilities, urban transport, and other elements of local infrastructure – that elsewhere were the province of private enterprise or of local government. Although rates on government loans were relatively higher in Argentina, they were still low by private standards; and the evidence indicates that they did not unduly discourage public borrowing. By 1890 the debt of the Republic was almost twice as large as the Canadian and almost half as large as the Australian public debt.

In Canada there was, at least, a National Plan. The American Congress's decision that there was to be no NAFTA in the post–Civil War era induced the Canadian government to endorse Macdonald's National Policy, a policy that involved a ninety degree shift in the geographic orientation of the economy from its traditional north-south (that is, Canada-U.S.) focus to an east-west one that integrated Quebec and Ontario with the Maritimes to the east and with the Prairies and British Columbia to the west. Most of "the secular decisions at this stage of Canadian development were made by government bodies; – and the

a single transaction in American 4 percents. The 4.5 percent loan had gone off well, but the attempt to reduce the borrowing rate to 4 percent had resulted in a complete fiasco." D.C.M. Platt, *Foreign Finance in Continental Europe and the USA, 1815–1870: Quantities, Origins, Functions & Distribution* (London, Boston, and Sydney: George Allen & Unwin, 1984), pp. 153–54.

implementations of those policies involved the exercise of initiative by government."[1375]

In Australia the trend toward government ownership was compounded by rivalry between the colonies as each competed for the economic domination of what local politicians, businessmen, and advocates in each colony viewed as *their* hinterlands. Unlike Canada, where the federal government designed the east-west railroad links,

> the critical fact was that four separate, rival, and often mutually obstructive governments failed to make a concentrated attack on the transport needs of eastern Australia as a whole. On the contrary, confined to action within their own borders, each attempted to set in motion contrary commodity and passenger flows and a highly inefficient transport was imposed on the area. At best, transport policy was devised in isolation free of each other's planning; often each set out to divert traffic from neighboring colonies regardless of whether they were in a position to provide the most efficient transport links with the areas they attempted to serve.[1376]

As a result, in Australia the final shape of the evolving financial institutions reflected not only a mix of public and private investment, but also the geographic scope of the colonial (later state) governments, governments that were responsible for nearly half of all public and private investment decisions.

In Argentina a mix of government promotion and guarantees, foreign intervention, and private domestic investment funded the rehabilitation of the port of Buenos Aires, the expansion of commercial and industrial activities there, and a rail network that tied Buenos Aires to the hinterland to the west, north, and south. The role of government was more limited in Argentina than in Australia, but it was relatively more important than in the United States and, railroads aside, probably also more important than in Canada.

Even today the question of the optimum scope of government activity has not been settled. In the 1990s, as in the 1890s, questions of the appropriate trade-off between the costs of political distortion of the economic process and a potentially "better" distribution of income have produced very different policies in the United States from those in Germany or France. From the point of view of the evolution of domestic capital

---

[1375] Hugh G.J. Aitken, "Defensive Expansionism: The State and Economic Growth in Canada," in Hugh G.J. Aitken (ed.), *The State and Economic Growth* (New York: Social Science Research Council, 1960), p. 103.

[1376] Noel G. Butlin, *Investment in Australian Economic Development 1861–1900* (Cambridge: Cambridge University Press, 1964), p. 293. [Hereafter cited as Butlin, *Investment in Australian Development.*]

markets, however, the issue is somewhat different. Governments with good reputations, Australia and Canada, for example, did not have to draw on the services of international financial syndicates to underwrite and market their bonds. In the case of the United States such syndicates were required. Although costly, they generated collateral economic benefits in terms of the evolution of the domestic financial structure. The American syndicates included not only well-established British and continental merchant banks, but also young U.S. investment banks; and syndicate membership improved the reputations of those American bankers both at home and abroad. In Argentina the tendency of the British to choose direct investment meant that there was only a limited role for Argentine financiers in the transfer of savings from Britain. There was a somewhat larger role in transfers from the continent; but still the impact on the domestic financial infrastructure was much less than in the United States.

The governments of Australia and Canada were able to raise loans in Britain more cheaply than their American counterparts. To the extent that those governments invested their funds wisely, they promoted domestic economic development; however, even when the policies were successful in that dimension, in the long run they tended to exacerbate some structural problems. On the one hand, they had a macro-effect. The spread between public and private rates tended to encourage the substitution of cheaper government for more expensive private investment. As a result the scope of government increased, and a smaller private sector meant that there was less need for private financial innovation. Capital markets remained primitive; private interest rates remained high; and the dominance of government enterprise was perpetuated. On the other hand, they also had a micro-impact. The better the reputation of the government issues, the less need there was for specific private institutions designed to link foreign savers to domestic investors, institutions that could, at a later date, be modified to channel domestic savings into domestic investment.

The second set of environmental constraints was linked to the composition of investment undertaken by both the government and the private sectors. Since World War II it has been potential industrial capacity that has drawn foreign capital from developed countries to the newly industrializing countries. In the nineteenth century it was the abundance of undeveloped land.[1377] Although a part of those funds was invested

---

[1377] Albert Fishlow, "Lessons from the Past: Capital Markets During the Nineteenth Century and the Interwar Period," *International Organization*, Vol. 39, No. 3 (Summer 1985), p. 435.

directly in exploiting new land and mineral resources and in firms processing the products of those farms, ranches, and mines, by far the largest fraction of foreign finance was channeled into the construction of transportation systems designed to connect the frontier developments with national and world markets. Although some resources were directed to the construction of canals and to improvements in natural river systems, the vast majority of such investment was in railroads.[1378] Because of the sector's importance, the structure of railroad finance played a particularly significant role in shaping the evolution of the capital markets in the receiving countries.

In both Britain and the United States the process of educating domestic savers in the potential profitability of a decision to commit their resources to pieces of symbolic capital – depersonalized, mobile, and easily transferable claims on real assets – proceeded from government bonds to railroad issues and, only then, to the issues of firms in agriculture, mining, commerce, and manufacturing. In the United States the Anglo-American investment banks – banks such as Drexel Morgan and Brown Shipley – that were initially established to expedite the flow of British finance to American railroads by providing on-the-spot information and helping to monitor the decisions of the managers of those railroads became, within a decade and a half, the established channels for directing American savings into investment in American railroads. Later, U.S. investment banks provided the same service for American commercial and industrial enterprises.

In Canada and Australia governments took a far greater role in underwriting transport development than in either Britain or the United States. By 1850 the Australian colonial governments had taken over the operation of most of the continent's railroads. From that point on the six states both built and operated almost all of the nation's railroads.[1379] Although the Canadian federal government did not officially nationalize the majority of the country's railroads until after World War I, it had directly financed or subsidized construction of a large fraction of the total

---

[1378] In terms of the "Capital Created and Called" in the British market, between 1865 and 1914 railroads represented 74 percent of the Argentine total, 46 percent of the Australian, 70 percent of the Canadian, and 54 percent of the U.S. totals. Davis–Gallman tape taken from the report of "capital created and called" in the *Investors' Monthly Manual*, monthly 1865–1914. [Hereafter cited as "Davis-Gallman tape."]

[1379] In 1920 there were 25,957 miles of railroad in Australia. Although there were 32 private railways open to general traffic, they accounted for only 779 miles, or about 3 percent of the total. *The Official Yearbook of Australia*, No. 14 (1921), p. 614. Brian R. Mitchell, *International Historical Statistics: The Americas and Australia* (Detroit, Mich.: Gale Research Co., 1983), table G1, p. 666.

mileage, and it had provided either de facto or de jure guarantees for a substantial portion of the debt issues of the otherwise private railways.[1380] In both countries the government's guarantees provided the British saver with signals of quality, and there was little need for Anglo-Australian or Anglo-Canadian institutions to solve problems of asymmetric information, to monitor the activities of the railroads, or to provide an independent imprimatur of quality. In Argentina the national and provincial governments were initially heavily involved in promoting the railroads as well as guaranteeing railway debt. Toward the end of the 1880s, however, the government began to privatize the state-owned railroads. For example, the previously profitable Oeste railway was sold to a British firm. The movement toward privatization antedated the construction of most of the country's railway network, and a large part of the network was primarily built and owned by British firms. There was, then, in Argentina relatively little pressure for domestic financial innovation.

Although railroads were by far the largest component of foreign investment, there was never a shortage of other Australian-, American-, and Canadian-owned and managed firms attempting to raise additional capital in the United Kingdom. At times these firms employed a British merchant bank as an intermediary, but it was not uncommon for an Australian, Canadian, or American promoter to arrive in Britain with a satchel of securities that he intended to sell directly – or through a local agent – to British savers. In these cases the problems raised by asymmetric information and the difficulty of effectively monitoring the frontier businessman emerged very quickly.

In an attempt to overcome these problems, as Mira Wilkins has demonstrated, British entrepreneurs often purchased a foreign firm, reorganized it as a British corporation – in her terms a "free standing company" – endowed it with a British board of directors, and ran its

---

[1380] In the case of the Canadian Pacific Railway, a road that escaped nationalization because of its relative success, the initial government subsidy was hardly insignificant. Among the provisions for financial support that were granted the company when it assumed the task of building a railroad to the Pacific coast were "a cash subsidy of $25 million, a grant of 25 million acres of land 'fairly fit for settlement', . . . the segments already completed (valued at $40 million) to be handed over to the company, an exemption from taxes (later thought to have been worth a little over $20 million), and a guarantee that no other railway lines would be chartered south of the CPR to the border with the U.S." Marvin McInnis, "Foundations of the Nineteenth Century Canadian Economy," manuscript chapter for Stanley L. Engerman and Robert E. Gallman (eds.), *Cambridge Economic History of the United States*, Vol. II (Cambridge: Cambridge University Press, 2000), pp. 57–58.

operations from Britain.[1381] The British directors appear to have provided an adequate signal of quality. To the extent that the Board and the British managers could provide some oversight of managerial decisions, the innovation overcame at least some of the problems arising from the asymmetry of the information possessed by the frontier operatives on one side of the world and by the British owners on the other. It should be noted, however, that this innovation did not provide a complete solution to the problems raised by the geographic distance that existed between savers in Britain and private investments in one of the four frontier countries. Despite the organizational innovation, it was still difficult to exercise effective managerial control from across an ocean. In addition, in both the United States and Argentina, the countries that made

---

[1381] Wilkins has concluded that investment in those firms should probably better be considered portfolio rather than direct investment; their shares appeared on the London and provincial exchanges. Mira Wilkins, "The Free Standing Company, 1870–1914: An Important Type of British Foreign Direct Investment," *Economic History Review*, 2nd series, Vol. XLI, No. 2 (May 1988), pp. 259–382. [Hereafter cited as Wilkins, "The Free Standing Company."]

It is therefore difficult to estimate the level of true direct investment. Wilkins concludes that "it has long been accepted that in the late nineteenth and early twentieth centuries, the value of portfolio investment far exceeded that of direct foreign investment in the United States. My research confirms this." Mira Wilkins, *The History of Foreign Investment in the United States to 1914*, Harvard Studies in Business History, Vol. XLI (Cambridge, Mass.: Harvard University Press, 1989), p. 145. [Hereafter cited as Wilkins, *Foreign Investment.*] Cleona Lewis, lumping both branches and free standing companies together, puts the level of direct investment in the U.S. in 1914 at $600 million out of a British total of $4.250 billion (14 percent). Cleona Lewis (assisted by Karl T. Schlotterbeck), *America's Stake in International Investments* (Washington D.C.: Brookings Institution, 1938), p. 546. [Hereafter cited as Lewis, *America's Stake.*] Although there is no precise quantitative estimate, it appears that, of the $600 million of direct investment, the largest fraction took the form of investment in free-standing companies. Wilkins, citing A.T. Ostrye (*Foreign Investment in the American West, 1870–1914*), puts the number of free standing companies set up to operate in the North American West between 1870 and 1914 at "roughly 1800." Wilkins, "The Free Standing Company," p. 261. A combination of Paterson's estimates of direct investment and the Viner-Knox estimates of total British investment suggests that the fraction of direct in total British investment in Canada was 11.6 percent in 1900 and 5.2 percent in 1914. Donald G. Paterson, *British Direct Investment in Canada, 1890–1914: Estimates and Determinates* (Toronto: University of Toronto Press, 1976), table 3.3, p. 49. [Hereafter cited as Patterson, *British Direct Investment in Canada.*] The issues of the definitions (direct vs. portfolio) and classification of British oversea investments are discussed in Edelstein, *Overseas Investment*, pp. 33–37 and in Irving Stone, "British Direct and Portfolio, Investment in Latin America Before 1914," *Journal of Economic History*, Vol. 37 (September 1977), pp. 690–722.

the most use of the free-standing company, those enterprises often became the target of anti-foreign prejudice.

From the point of view of the British saver, the most serious problems were raised by the lack of reliable information about foreign alternatives. That asymmetry was often coupled with moral hazard; businessmen in the receiving countries had been known to advertise oranges and deliver lemons, and their agents in the United Kingdom did not always eschew such practices. As late as 1906, for example, Arthur Grenfell, the second-generation British investment banker, discussed the problem in relation to Canadian investments: "I shall try to act as an information bureau – distributing such information as I receive from Canada to the London and especially provincial newspapers. Some such intelligence department is sadly wanted." "The truth is except for information as is given out by the C.P.R. and one or two other strong corporations, there is no commercial intelligence distributed among investors."[1382] Although Grenfell may have somewhat overstated his case for Canada in 1906, the essence of his report reflected conditions in Canada and also in Argentina, Australia, and the western United States in most of the years between 1870 and 1900. The problems faced by potential investors and the attempts to overcome those asymmetries through the innovation of new and improved institutions differed from country to country, and they affected the domestic capital markets in the receiving countries very differently.

This study of institutional innovation in the international capital markets and of the relationship between the importation of foreign capital and the evolution of domestic capital markets underscores one lesson in institutional invention: Only rarely is a new institution invented and innovated at a moment in time. Instead, like the modern computer, invention normally requires a period of experimentation, when alternative designs are tested and evaluated. Successful innovation most often demands the gradual modification of an original, almost always relatively primitive, invention.

The evidence also indicates that institutional innovation is achieved more quickly if the problem can be solved by a modification of an existing institutional technology rather than requiring the invention of an entirely new one. In such a case transition from one institution to another tends to be gradual, and the financial structure often suffers no sudden shock. Similarly, in the case of the invention and innovation of an entirely

---

[1382] Correspondence: Arthur Grenfell to Earl Grey, August 8, 1906 and November 29, 1906, Private papers of Earl Grey, Library, University of Durham. As an aside, it might be noted that Grenfell's agency went bankrupt before World War I.

new institution (even in the rare instance of rapid innovation), although there may be some elements of income redistribution (a transfer from the owners of the old institutions to those who control the new one), the transition from one structure to another is normally relatively costless; that is, the process of the substitution of the new for the old technology proceeds relatively smoothly, and there is never a discernible gap in the institutional structure. These cases may be thought of as examples of the corollary of North's theorem that "the economies of scope, complementarities, and network externalities of an institutional matrix make institutional change overwhelmingly incremental and path dependent." The same cannot be said for the effects of a sudden economic or political regime change that drastically alters the relative costs or benefits of the existing institutional structure. Under these conditions a heretofore efficient and productive institution may suddenly disappear and leave nothing in its place. The resulting gap in the financial structure may not be filled until the entire process of original invention, experimentation, and modification has been repeated, a process that can take decades. Institutional destruction is not necessarily either incremental or path dependent, institutions can be very fragile.[1383]

Over the course of the four and a half decades leading up to World War I there were continued attempts to redesign the financial structure in order to overcome informational asymmetries and reduce transaction costs. At times those attempts were very successful, at other times less so. In particular, many of the institutional innovations were designed to monitor activities in the receiving countries and to provide reputational signals for the agents involved in raising funds in Britain. At times the institutions that emerged in one country were different from those that developed in another; at times they were the same. Moreover, an institution that proved successful in one country might well prove unsuccessful in another apparently similar environment.

7-2. The data

Raymond W. Goldsmith, a leading analyst of wealth and modernization, devised a number of measures designed to describe the changes in the relative importance of, and in the structure of, the financial sector during the process of economic development. Perhaps the most useful is the ratio of financial assets to GNP. Goldsmith argued that

---

[1383] For example, it has been argued that economic crisis or skull-duggery and scandal often trigger rapid institutional change. Although that conclusion may be correct in the short run, the evidence indicates that the new institutions that emerge seldom represent long-run equilibria.

modernization brings economic activity more fully within the scope of the market and requires, if it is to proceed successfully, financial institutions and devices that ease the functioning of the market. One would, therefore, expect that, over time as modernization proceeds, the ratio of financial assets to GNP would rise. Similarly, in the cross section, one could expect to find some positive relationship between that ratio and the degree of modernization of the economies under study. The types of financial activities that Goldsmith had in mind are suggested by the financial assets that he included in the numerator of the ratio: monetary metals, currency, claims against financial institutions, mortgages, government debt, corporate stocks and bonds, and trade credit.

On the whole, Goldsmith's expectations with respect to changes over time are borne out by the evidence – the ratios rose over time for those countries experiencing economic growth, and the increase was frequently pronounced. Over the years before World War I for those countries where such measurements exist, the ratio more than doubled for the United States, France, Germany, and Italy (see Table 7:2-1). For Argentina and Japan, although the time span covered in the table is relatively short, the increase was also substantial (more than 70 percent). The exceptions were India, where development was slight, and Great Britain and Switzerland, economies that had already achieved a pronounced degree of modernization before they make their first appearance in the table.

The three frontier countries for which there are data – Argentina, Australia, and the United States – shared the general experience of modernization; their financial asset/GNP ratios rose quite markedly before World War I (see Table 7:2-1). There were, however, two periods when the secular trend in the ratio was reversed. The Australian and U.S. ratios declined between 1900 and 1913, and in both cases the drop was substantial.[1384] In the American case, the explanation may rest on the very rapid increase in GNP in the first years of the twentieth century. Over the first fourteen years GNP increased by about 6 percent a year, as compared with only 4.3 percent for the full period 1870–1913. The denominator of the ratio appears to have risen so fast that it simply outran the numerator. In the case of Australia the decline is most likely a reflection of the 1890s bank crisis, a crisis that led to a 20 percent decline in trading bank assets. The effect was, however, not visible in the period 1890–1900, a period in which one might have expected the ratio to have dropped, because of the sharp decline in the numerator of the ratio; GNP in 1900

[1384] The actual dates are 1900 and 1912 for the United States and 1901–11 for Australia.

Table 7:2-1. *Financial structure I: ratio of financial assets to GNP, various countries, circa 1850 to 1915, and the financial interrelations ratio (financial assets/tangible assets) 1913*

| Country | Financial assets/GNP | | | | | | Financial interrelations ratio 1913 |
	1850	1870	1880	1890	1900	1913	
Argentina				1.38		2.35	0.50
Australia		1.18	2.30	3.40	3.45	2.90	
United States	1.33		2.29		4.61	3.47	0.83
France	2.52		5.08			6.31	0.98
Germany	1.88		2.69		4.09	5.02	0.76
Great Britain	4.95		3.44		6.41	5.70	1.96
Italy	1.09		2.26		2.85	2.49	0.47
India	1.41		1.25		1.31	1.18	0.34
Switzerland			8.90		8.10	9.82	1.50
Japan			1.90		2.13	3.40	0.64

Notes: The concept of Financial Assets is taken from Raymond W. Goldsmith, Comparative National Balance Sheets (Chicago and London: The University of Chicago Press, 1985), pp. 82–83, 86–87, & 334–337. They include: monetary metals, currency, claims against financial institutions, loans by financial institutions, mortgages, government debt, corporate bonds, corporate stocks, trade credit, and other. In principle, holdings of foreigners should be deleted; however, Goldsmith, the source of all the figures in this table with the exception of those for Argentina and Australia, was unable to carry out this adjustment, except in the case where "government issues sold abroad," "were substantial and known." The Argentine and Australian figures are gross of "government issues sold abroad"; and, therefore, the ratios for those countries reported in the table are biased upward relative to the ratios for the other countries. In the case of Argentina for "1915," there are sufficient data to make the adjustment. The adjustment reduces the Argentine ratio from 2.35 to 2.22. Deleting all other financial assets owned abroad reduces it further to 1.59. The actual dates correspond to the dates reported in the table only in an approximate way. For example, the Argentine data refer to 1892 and 1919; the Australian data to 1871, 1881, 1891, 1901, and 1911; the U.S. data to 1850, 1880, 1900, and 1912.

Sources:
(1) Argentina: Derived from data in M.G. and E.T. Mulhall, *Handbook of the River Plate*, sixth edition (Buenos Aires & London: M.G. and E.T. Mulhall & Keegan Paul, Trench & Co., 1892); Maurice L. Munleman, *Monetary Systems of the World* (New York: 1895); Ernesto Tornquist & Co., Limited, *The Economic Development of the Argentine Republic in the Last Fifty Years* (Buenos Aires: Ernesto Tornquist & Co., 1919). Insurance company assets represent rough estimates based on premiums, losses, and the amount of insurance in force.

(cont.)

was only 85 percent of its level a decade earlier. When, after 1901, the ratio did fall, the decline can, in part, be explained by the same factor that accounted for the American experience; GNP increased very rapidly between 1901 and 1911, more rapidly than financial assets. Although those assets were also increasing, in Australia the increase was damped by the domestic and international fallout from the crisis and ensuing depression.

Goldsmith expected to find some association in the cross section between the degree of economic development and the financial asset/GNP ratio, and in this expectation he was not disappointed. The range of the ratios observed in his study of comparative national balance sheets before World War I was extraordinarily wide. At one extreme, the Italian ratio in 1850 was just over 1.0, a figure that indicates near parity between the value of financial assets and GNP. At the other end of the spectrum, the figure for Switzerland in 1913 was almost 10.0 (see Table 7:2-1).

The data indicate that there is a moderate positive statistical association in the cross section between the ratio of financial assets to GNP, on the one hand, and economic performance, as measured by real per capita GNP (an alternate index of modernization), on the other; but the degree of association is less pronounced than one might expect. For example, for 1913 the rank order correlation for the ten economies reported in

Notes to Table 7:2-1 (*cont.*)

(2) Australia: Derived from data in Munleman; Commonwealth Bureau of the Census and Statistics, *Official Yearbook of Australia, 1901–1919* (Melbourne: 1919) *and 1901–1907* (Melbourne: 1907); A.R. Hall, *The Stock Exchange of Melbourne, 1852–1900* (Canberra: Australian National University Press, 1968); Commonwealth of Australia, *Federal Handbook* Prepared in Connection with the Eighty-Fourth Meeting of the British Association for the Advancement of Science, held in Australia, August 1914 (Canberra, 1914); Noel G. Butlin, *Australian Domestic Product, Investment and Foreign Borrowing, 1861–1938/1939* (Cambridge, U.K.: Cambridge University Press, 1962), Table 1, p. 6, Gross National Product at Market Prices. The underlying data are incomplete; they include only securities listed on the Melbourne Stock Exchange (the figure for "1915" is a rough guess), mortgages are confined to those held by intermediaries, and there are no data for trade credit. To correct for these deficiencies, we raised each of the Australian ratios by 10 percent.

(3) Other countries: Raymond W. Goldsmith, *Comparative National Balance Sheets* (Chicago & London: The University of Chicago Press, 1985), Table 15, p. 37.

Table 7:2-1 is only 0.41.[1385] In some measure the differences in the ratios in the cross section appear to reflect differences in the degree of specialization in finance, rather than differences in the degree of modernization more generally defined.

The data on the financial interrelations ratio – the ratio of financial to tangible assets – provides some degree of support for that conclusion (see Table 7:2-1). The economies with the highest ratios of financial assets to GNP also have the highest financial interrelations ratios, that is, they appear to have specialized in financial activities. In addition, the degree of association between real GDP and the financial assets/GNP ratio in the cross section is reduced by the inclusion of the frontier economies, the economies that are the focus of this paper. Because of their extraordinary endowment of natural resources, the frontier economies achieved high levels of per capita GDP very early in the process of modernization. For them, economic success preceded financial sophistication.

Initially the financial assets/GNP ratios for Argentina, Australia, and the United States lie toward the bottom of the array of ratios reported for the developed countries of Western Europe. Over time the ratios for both frontier and developed economies rise, and the rough ordering remains intact. By 1913, however, although the ratio for the United States was still low by Western European standards, its financial interrelations ratio was roughly comparable to those of France and Germany. In the case of Argentina, however, the picture is somewhat different. The financial assets/GNP ratio, although it rose sharply between 1892 and 1919, remained relatively low in comparison with those for Australia and the United States, to say nothing of the ratios in the developed countries of Western Europe. Argentina's financial interrelations ratio was also relatively low; the country's level of financial sophistication was, despite its relatively high income, equivalent only to that of Italy.

Although the financial assets/GNP ratio is a useful index of financial sophistication, the driving financial force behind modernization comes from the growth and development of financial intermediaries. Their assets, however, represent only a fraction of total national financial assets. For Australia, Canada, and the United States, over the years 1870–1914 the ratio of the assets of financial intermediaries to GNP roughly doubled (see Table 7:2-2). Canada began and ended with the lowest ratios – 0.38 and 0.92 respectively – but the relative increase was greater than for either of the other two countries. By World War I all

---

[1385] The GDP data were taken from Angus Maddison, *Monitoring the World Economy, 1820–1922* (Paris: OECD, 1995), appendix D, table D-1a, pp. 194–97.

Table 7:2-2. *Financial structure II: ratio of the assets of financial intermediaries to GNP, Argentina, Australia, Canada, and the U.S., 1870–1919*

Country	1870	1880	1890	1900	1910	1914	1919
Argentina						0.69	0.57
Australia	0.56	0.84	1.38	1.23	1.03	1.09	
Canada	0.38	0.71	0.86	1.00	0.88	0.92	
United States	0.49	0.44	0.64	0.90	0.98	1.09	

Notes: (1) Argentina: Figure for 1914 is average 1913 and 1915.
　　　　(2) United States: Figure for 1870 is 1875.

Sources:
　Argentina:
　　Assets: Ernesto Tornquist & Co., *The Economic Development of the Argentine Republic in the Last Fifty Years* (Buenos Aires: Ernesto Tornquist & Co., 1919), Chapter 9, pp. 209–253.
　　GNP:　Roberto Cortes Conde, Estimates of Argentine GDP, 1875–1935, Private Communication, November 1993.
　Australia:
　　Assets: Appendix Table 2.
　　GNP:　Noel G Butlin, *Australian Domestic Product, Investment and Foreign Borrowing, 1861–1938/1939* (Cambridge, U.K.: Cambridge University Press, 1962), Table 1, p. 6.
　Canada:
　　Assets: Appendix Table 2.
　　GNP:　M.C. Urquhart et. al., *Gross National Product, Canada, 1870–1926: The Derivation of the Estimates* (Kingston & Montreal: McGill-Queen's University Press), Table 1.1, pp. 13–17.
　United States
　　Assets: Appendix Table 2.
　　GNP:　For 1870–1900, Robert E. Gallman, "Gross National Product in the United States, 1834–1909," in Dorothy S. Brady (ed.), *Output, Employment, and Productivity in the United States after 1800*, Studies in Income and Wealth, Volume 30, by the Conference on Research in Income and Wealth, National Bureau of Economic Research (New York & London: Columbia University Press, 1966), Table A-1, p. 26. For 1910 and 1914, Simon Kuznets, *Capital in the American Economy: Its Formation and Financing*, National Bureau of Economic Research, Studies in Capital Formation and Financing, Volume 9 (Princeton, N.J.: Princeton University Press, 1961), Appendix C, Table R-23, pp. 557–558.

three economies were characterized by relatively similar ratios: Canada, 0.92, Australia and the United States, 1.09.

The secular pattern of change, however, differed among the three countries. Australia began with the highest level (0.56), and the ratio rose dramatically until 1890. From then until 1910, however, the ratio declined markedly. The decline in the 1890s reflected the banking collapse: The collapse had a greater impact on the assets of intermediaries than on the larger aggregate, total national financial assets. The continued fall over the first decade of the new century can be explained by the rapid increase in GNP coupled with the withdrawal of British investments (bank deposits and the stocks and debentures of land mortgage banks and pastoral firms) and continued domestic concerns with the stability of the nation's financial institutions. As a result, in 1914 Australian financial intermediaries were relatively less important than they had been a quarter century earlier.

In Canada the ratio rose sharply early in the period, but from 1890 onward it fluctuated within fairly narrow limits. Over the latter years, the ratio appears to have averaged something slightly less, but close to 1.0; that is, the value of the assets of the nation's financial intermediaries was typically close to the value of GNP. For the United States, the secular increase in the ratio was relatively steady. Between 1870 and 1880, it fell, but only slightly. For the next two decades it increased fairly rapidly, but thereafter it rose at a more sedate pace, a pace, however, that left no doubt that the country's intermediaries were growing in relative importance.

The data for Argentina relate to a shorter time period, but the evidence is suggestive. Again it appears that Argentina was less financially sophisticated than the other three countries; at the outbreak of World War I the ratio of the assets of financial intermediaries to GNP was only 60–70 percent as high as the figures for the other three settler economies. The ratio also appears to have declined over the years of the war. That fall certainly reflects in part the differential effect of inflation on GNP and on financial assets, but the period also witnessed a sharp decline in the value of the stock of mortgages, a consequence of both foreclosures and the fact that repayments exceeded new debts.[1386]

In all four economies, commercial banks of one kind or another held more assets than all other financial intermediaries combined (see Table 7:2-3). Although the data for 1870 are less reliable than those for the

---

[1386] Ernesto Tornquist and Company, *The Economic Development of the Argentine Republic in the Last Fifty Years* (Buenos Aires: Ernesto Tornquist & Co., 1919), p. 235.

Table 7:2-3. *Financial Structure III: distribution of assets among financial intermediaries, 1870–1919*

	Argentina	Australia	Canada	United States
Panel a: 1870				
Commercial banks	97%	87%	72%	65%
Insurance companies	n.d.	n.d.	2	10
All others	3	13	26	24
Panel b: 1890				
Commercial banks	75	65	42	56
Insurance companies	n.d.	5	7	10
All others	25	30	51	34
Panel c: 1914–1915				
Commercial banks	55	56	57	58
Insurance companies	8	14	15	13
All others	37	30	28	29
Panel d: 1919				
Commercial banks	69			
Insurance companies	6			
All others	25			

Notes: 1870 data for Argentina are for 1884. Argentine "All Others" in 1870 are data for 1884 plus cedulas for 1885.

Source: Appendix Table 7.2.

later years, the picture that they reveal appears to be generally accurate. The banks probably held between 65 and 95 percent of the assets of all intermediaries, insurance companies a maximum of 10 percent, and all other institutions – chiefly firms lending on mortgages – from a few percent to about one-quarter of the total. Over time, the relative importance of the non-bank intermediaries increased, and the financial structures of the four settler economies – as measured by the structure of intermediation – converged. By 1914/15 commercial banks held about 55 percent of the assets of intermediaries, insurance companies 8–15 percent, and all other financial institutions 28–37 percent. In fact, the degree of convergence may have been even closer than the data in Table

7:2-3 indicate. The estimate of the assets of insurance companies in the outlier economy – Argentina – is very rough, and it could well be too low. Nonetheless, the broad picture sketched out by the estimates is undoubtedly correct. Commercial banks remained the most important intermediaries, but as the four economies began to commercialize and industrialize, their financial institutions became more specialized and sophisticated, and other forms of intermediation grew in relative importance.

7-3. **Britain and the four frontier countries: the primary links**

Commercial banks were the largest and most important of the formal financial intermediaries in each of the four countries (see Table 7:2-3). Although the level of their relative importance varied somewhat from country to country, over most of the period they held more assets than all of their "non-bank" competitors combined. The role of the commercial banks in the transfer of foreign capital, however, differed markedly among the four countries; and those differences led to institutional innovation proceeding along very different paths and with different trajectories. Table 7:3-1 provides a summary of the characteristics of both the British and the domestic commercial banks that operated in the four frontier countries.

In Canada and Australia the Scottish banking system initially provided important precedents, but local conditions – particularly the slow development of Western Canada and the relatively high degree of integration of the four eastern Australian colonies – influenced the evolution of the domestic structures. In Canada legal restrictions raised no barriers against national branch banking, but the present system of nationwide branch banking was relatively slow to develop. The banks were large by American standards. In 1868 the thirty-five chartered banks operated 123 branches, but, despite the growth in business activity of the intervening years, in 1890 the system's forty-one banks operated only 426 branches. As late as 1895 only the Bank of Montreal had anything approaching a national system of branches, and even its closest rival (the Canadian Bank of Commerce) operated almost exclusively in Ontario.[1387] There-

---

[1387] It was 1878 before the Bank of Montreal opened a branch in the prairies and 1887 before it moved into British Columbia. In the maritimes the banking system in the four provinces operated more or less independently of the rest of the country until the turn of the century. E.P. Neufeld, *The Financial System of Canada: Its Growth and Development* (New York: St. Martin's Press, 1972), pp. 91, 92, 96, 101–2. [Hereafter cited as Neufeld, *The Financial System of Canada.*] Sheila C. Dow, *Financial Markets and Regional Development: The Canadian Experience* (Brookfield, Vt.: Gower, 1990), p. 29. [Hereafter cited as

after, the number of banks declined; the size of the branch networks increased, and the system became more centralized. By 1920 the number of branches stood at 4,676, and, by the end of World War I, the head offices of eighteen of the nineteen chartered banks were in either Ontario or Quebec.

In Australia multi-colonial branch networks developed more rapidly. In 1877, of the twenty-four banks of issue, fifteen operated in only one colony. Four did business in two, three in three, and two (the Australian and the Union) operated in every colony except Western Australia. By 1880 there were 326 branches in Victoria alone, and in 1892 the twenty-three largest banks of issue operated 1,512 branches; eleven had branches in a single colony, four in two, two in three, two in four, three in five, and one in all six. Moreover, only two of the twenty-three had a single office.[1388] Thus, by the 1880s in Australia and by the turn of the century in Canada, inter-bank transfers effectively mobilized capital across regional boundaries. For example, in 1910 Joseph Johnson writing for the National Monetary Commission concluded that "it may fairly be said that Canada has only one money market and one rate of interest. In the United States great masses of loanable capital accumulate in the cities of the east and can be drawn on only by positive assurance of an extraordinary rate of interest. In Canada one finds no such accumulation of capital in a few cities and no such reluctance to loan it out at distant points. Banks in Montreal and Toronto lend with equal freedom in both the west and the east, and their managers have equal familiarity with the needs and credits of both sections."[1389]

In both Canada and Australia British-chartered imperial banks initially competed with the domestically chartered commercial banks, although they represented a much more important presence in Australia. In Canada there were initially four imperial banks, but the Bank of Montreal and the Quebec Bank quickly took out colonial charters. By 1870 only two remained. The Bank of British Columbia merged with the domestically chartered Canadian Bank of Commerce in 1900; and the last imperial bank, the Bank of British North America, merged with

Dow, *Financial Markets and Regional Development*.] Ian M. Drummond, *Capital Markets in Australia and Canada, 1895–1914*, Ph.D. dissertation, Yale University, May 1959, p. 15. [Hereafter cited as Drummond, *Capital Markets in Australia and Canada*.]

[1388] Sydney J. Butlin, *Australia and New Zealand Bank: The Bank of Australasia and the Union Bank of Australia Limited, 1828–1951* (London: Longmans, 1961), pp. 223–24, 243. [Hereafter cited as S. Butlin, *Australia and New Zealand Bank*.]

[1389] Joseph Johnson, *The Canadian Banking System*, National Monetary Commission, Senate, 61st Congress, 2nd Session (Washington, D.C.: GPO, 1910), pp. 101–2.

Table 7:3-1. *Outline of the characteristics of British commercial banks with overseas branches and of the domestic commercial banks in the four frontier countries*

Characteristic	Argentina	Australia	Canada	United States
	Domestically chartered banks			
1. Was branching permitted?	yes	yes	yes	no
2. Did they operate branches in the U.K.?	no	yes	yes	no
3. Did they act as agents in the U.K. for:				
(a). sub "national" units of government?	no	at times	yes for provinces & some large cities	no
(b). The "national" government?	no	yes, until the 1880s, thereafter largely British banks	no until 1893, but Bank of Montreal thereafter	no
4. Did they seek deposits in the U.K.?	no	yes	no	no
5. Was there an asset/liability mismatch?	yes	yes	no	no
6. Did bank failures in the 1890s adversely impact British savers?	no	yes	no	no
7. Did the banks combine commercial & investment banking functions?	no	yes, until the 1890s, no thereafter.	only as members of a financial group supporting a bond house	yes

	British chartered banks			
1. Was branching permitted?	yes	yes	yes	no
2. Did they operate branches in this frontier country?	yes	yes	yes, but by 1870 there were only two.	no
3. Did they act as agents in the U.K. for:				
(a). sub "national" units of the frontier country?	no	no	no	no
(b). The "national" government of the frontier country?	no	yes, after the 1880s	yes, before 1892, afterwards it was the Bank of Montreal	no
4. Did they seek deposits in the U.K.?	no	yes	no	no
5. Was there an asset/liability mismatch?	no	yes	no	no
6. Did bank failures in the 1890s adversely impact British savers?	no	yes	no	no

the Bank of Montreal in 1918. In Australia there were seven imperial banks, and they played a much longer and more important role in the country's development. In 1875 they operated 116 branches and, in 1915, 523.[1390] In both countries the imperial banks were headquartered in London. Since they competed with the domestic banks, and since there were no restrictions on branching, it is hardly surprising that many of the domestically chartered banks also maintained a major presence in London. For Australia and Canada the international institutional financial connections provided by the commercial banks were very tight.

Despite these similarities, in at least two dimensions commercial banking in the two countries developed very differently. First, in the case of Canada, the real bills doctrine was legally enshrined in the Banking Act of 1871, and it remained there until well into the twentieth century.[1391] Nor could banks easily circumvent the regulations by providing loans against collateral other than real estate; such collateral did not exist in quantity.[1392] As a result, Canadian banks, under no pressure to provide long-term credit, did not actively seek overseas deposits. Interbank balances aside, there were no foreign deposits in Canadian banks before 1900; even in 1914 they accounted for less than 8 percent of the total.[1393] Canadian mortgage companies did turn to the British, as well as the Canadian, market; but, in spite of their attempts to attract overseas funds – forays that were particularly marked during the wheat boom – they continued to seek domestic savings aggressively. The resulting

---

[1390] A.S.J. Baster, *The Imperial Banks* (London: P.S. King & Son, 1929), appendices II and III, pp. 266–68. Geoffrey Jones, *British Multinational Banking, 1830–1900* (Oxford: Clarendon Press, 1993). The imperial banks still operated 731 branches in Australia in 1927. The imperial banks operating in Australia included the Bank of Australasia, the Bank of South Australia, the Chartered Bank of India, Australia and China, the English, Scottish and Australian Bank, the London Chartered Bank of Australia, the Union Bank, and the Oriental Banking Corporation.

[1391] Section 40 required that "the Bank shall not, either directly or indirectly, lend money or make advances upon the security, mortgage or hypothecation of any lands or tenements" and section 41 that "the Bank may take, hold and dispose of mortgages and hypotheques upon personal as well as real property, by way of additional security for debts contracted to the Bank in the course of business." "An Act Relating to Banks and Banking" (34 Victoria, cap. 5). These clauses were maintained in subsequent acts with the exception that, in 1880 and following, any real estate obtained (and not for use) had to be disposed of within seven years.

[1392] Neufeld, *The Financial System of Canada*, pp. 178–79.

[1393] M.C. Urquhart and K. Buckley (eds.), *Historical Statistics of Canada* (Cambridge: Cambridge University Press, 1965), Series H 234–36, p. 240. [Hereafter cited as Urquhart and Buckley, *Historical Statistics of Canada*.]

institutional specialization – banks in the short-term market and mortgage companies and other non-bank intermediaries in the long-term market – meant that the balance sheets of the chartered banks did not reflect a structure of long-term assets supported by short-term liabilities.

Initially, the charters of the Australian trading banks had also prohibited investments in mortgages.[1394] Those regulations, however, began to erode in the 1840s. In a series of steps that culminated in the wide extension of the principle that a bank could make loans secured by a real estate trust – a trust created by the borrower not in the name of the bank but that guaranteed that the encumbered real estate could not be sold or mortgaged except to pay the debt to the bank – new institutional arrangements had de facto, if not de jure, effectively removed the legal strictures on mortgage lending that had been imposed by the original charters.[1395] In fact, within a few years the practice of mortgage lending was fully accepted, and the mortgage freehold (and to smaller degree the leasehold property) became the common form of security for bank loans. "The banks' loan books became increasingly illiquid."[1396]

Given this lucrative source of business, the trading banks aggressively sought long-term borrowers. Both the imperial and the Australian banks turned to the British market for a significant share of the savings required to support those loans. By 1890 British deposits accounted for between 25 and 30 percent of all deposits in Australian trading banks.[1397] Thus, in the Australian case, there were by 1890 two sets of financial links connecting the trading banks with the British saver: an institutional presence in Britain similar to the one maintained by the Canadian banks and

[1394] The Bank of Australasia's charter, for example, forbade loans on the security of real estate but permitted the taking of land in the settlement of debt. That provision was, however, interpreted very narrowly: land could only be foreclosed in outright settlement of debt; it must be sold promptly; and the bank could not lend on liens on sheep or cattle. S. Butlin, *Australia and New Zealand Bank*, p. 96.

[1395] S. Butlin, *Australia and New Zealand Bank*, pp. 96–97.

[1396] Reginald Frank Holder, "Australia," in W.F. Crick, *Commonwealth Banking Systems* (Oxford: Clarendon Press, 1965), pp. 70–71. [Hereafter cited as Holder, "Australia."]

[1397] Sydney J. Butlin, A.R. Hall, and R.C. White, *Australian Banking and Monetary Statistics 1817–1945*, Reserve Bank of Australia, Occasional Paper No. 4A (Sydney: 1971), tables 1 and 2(i), pp. 112, 116. [Hereafter cited as Butlin, Hall, and White, *Australian Banking and Monetary Statistics*.] David Pope puts the figure on the eve of the depression at 40 percent. David Pope, "Free Banking in Australia Before World War I," The Australian National University, Working Papers in Economic History, No. 129, December 1989, pp. 15–16. [Hereafter cited as Pope, "Free Banking in Australia."]

a deposit channel funneling savings indirectly into bank loans. In the latter case those deposits, like their domestic counterparts, represented either short- or medium-term liabilities, while the assets they supported (pastoral runs and, increasingly after 1880 as urban construction boomed, loans on residential and commercial property) were essentially illiquid long-term commitments. Not surprisingly the Canadian commercial banks suffered far less than their Australian counterparts during the economic collapse of the 1890s, and the Australian banks were much slower to recover.[1398] Perhaps more importantly in the long run, the bank failures had a very significant and negative impact on the direct deposit link that connected British savers to Australian investors, an institutional arrangement that had until the 1890s played a particularly important role in international capital mobilization.

In a second dimension, throughout the period 1870–1914 the provincial governments in Canada had, for the most part, employed Canadian banks – primarily the Bank of Montreal and the Canadian Bank of Commerce – as their fiscal agents in Britain. Initially, the federal government had employed a consortium made up of Glyn, Mills, Currie & Company and Baring Brothers as their agents; however, in 1893 the government substituted the Bank of Montreal for the Glyn, Mills–Baring combine. Although "the transfer of the account was criticized in London banking circles as both injudicious and unwarranted," it greatly strengthened the already strong financial infrastructure that linked Canada to the London capital market. As a result, as agent for both the federal and many of the provincial governments, the Canadian Bank earned a substantial amount of cachet among British investors. Between 1906 and 1913, for example, British investment in Canada was estimated to have increased by £246,278,200, and the Bank of Montreal appears to have negotiated more than half of that flow.[1399]

Certain Australian banks had originally enjoyed an equally privileged position. Although New South Wales was somewhat late in employing a single fiscal representative, from the 1850s through the mid-1880s the five self-governing colonies used the services of the colonial bank (or banks) that serviced the governments accounts in Australia: the Bank of New South Wales for New South Wales and Tasmania, first the Union Bank

---

[1398] Between 1900 and 1914 the assets of Australian trading banks grew at an annual compound rate of 3.6 percent. The figure for Canadian chartered banks was 8.7 percent. Butlin, Hall, and White, *Australian Banking and Monetary Statistics*, table 1, p. 112 & table 2(1), p. 116. Urquhart and Buckley, *Historical Statistics of Canada*, Series H 160, p. 237, and H 179, p. 238.

[1399] M. Denison, *Canada's First Bank: A History of the Bank of Montreal*, 2 vols. (Toronto & Montreal: McClelland & Stewart, 1967), vol. 2, pp. 253–54, 293–94.

of Australia and later the Queensland National Bank for Queensland, the "Associated Banks" for Victoria, and the National Bank of Australia for South Australia.[1400] Those connections earned the Australian banks, like their Canadian counterpart, a reputation for quality among the British financial community.

In the mid-1880s, however, faced by the need to increase the level of government borrowing, the colonies gradually replaced their Australian fiscal agents with banks whose names enjoyed an even better reputation in the United Kingdom. As their issues became larger and more frequent, the colonial governments concluded that they needed a signal of quality that could only be provided by well-established British banks, in particular, the Bank of England and the London and Westminster. "To the ordinary investor their names would be a sufficient guarantee for the issue. Moreover, if the issue should strike trouble, they would be better able to meet it than the local banks." New South Wales in 1884 and Queensland in 1885 turned to the Bank of England; Victoria chose the London and Westminster in 1886, as did Tasmania about the same time; and in 1905 New South Wales shifted from the Bank of England to what was now the London, County and Westminster. By that date only South Australia used the services of a local Australian bank.[1401]

The reputations of the Australian banks were undercut by the shift in allegiance of the state governments, and the reputations that remained were all but destroyed by the bank suspensions and failures of the 1890s, suspensions and failures that led to substantial losses to British depositors and investors.[1402] As a result, after the turn of the century, the

---

[1400] Since Western Australia did not have representative government, its issues were, until 1890, handled by the Crown Agents for the Colonies.

[1401] A.R. Hall, *The London Capital Market and Australia, 1870–1914*, Social Science Monograph No. 21 (Canberra: Australian National University Press, 1963), pp. 103–4. Holder, *The Bank of New South Wales*, p. 360.

[1402] Of the twelve Victorian trading banks, three survived the crisis relatively unscathed, three ended in liquidation, and six suspended but were ultimately reconstructed. The three surviving banks did not require additional capital, nor were they forced to convert short- and medium-term deposits into long-term deposits or preferred shares. Between March 1883 and March 1893, however, the market value of their shares declined by £5.4 million, a loss of nearly 30 percent. In the case of the three banks that went into liquidation, not only did their shareholders lose the £1.679 million of their original funds (the market value of those shares had been £2.176 million in March 1883), but they were required to pay an additional £429,000 on the uncalled portion of their holdings. Finally, of six reconstructed banks, the shareholders had seen the market value of their shares decline from £9.142 million in 1883 to £5.753 in 1893 (a decline of 37 percent); and they had been forced to pay another £3.5421 million in additional capital calls. At the same time depositors had been forced to convert their

Canadian-chartered banks were far better placed to provide signals of quality for British savers interested in private issues than were the Australian trading banks. In Australia, as in the United Kingdom, the Australian banks' reputations had also suffered almost irreparable harm; the ultimate price was the emergence of a highly cartelized and very conservative banking sector, a structure that lasted for the next fifty years.[1403]

Until the crisis of the 1890s destroyed the institutional connections, Australian commercial banks had looked increasingly to British savers for deposits. When that source of funds was cut off, they found it difficult to replace the British deposits with domestic ones.[1404] Still in shock, financially constrained, faced with the need to maintain higher levels of reserves, saddled with the need to pay off British depositors, and "unable to redeem themselves in the minds of the public," Australian bank managers became increasingly cautious in their loan policies. In particular, they proved unable or unwilling to maintain their previous position in the long-term mortgage market. Moreover, through much of the "long boom" that lasted from the 1850s through the 1880s, they had acted as both commercial and investment banks; but their experience in the early 1890s caused them to surrender their investment banking functions both at home and in Britain. They had, in effect, managed to invent an institutional structure similar to the one legally imposed on American investment banks by the Glass-Steagall Act. There was, however, one important difference. Unlike the American banks, the Australian banks

deposits into £3.316 million in newly issued preferred shares. On average, for all of Australia, "tens of thousands of bank depositors had a major part of their deposit claims extended for long periods – generally for a minimum of four years." A secondary market for those frozen claims did develop, but the discounts averaged 25 percent, and that figure was the norm for those claims that were still frozen in 1914. David T. Merrett, "Preventing Bank Failure: Could the Commercial Bank of Australia Have Been Saved by Its Peers in 1893," *Victorian Historical Journal*, Vol. 64, No. 2 (October 1993), pp. 135, 137. [Hereafter cited as Merrett, "Preventing Bank Failure."] David T. Merrett, "The 1893 Bank Crash and Monetary Aggregates," Research Discussion Paper 9303, Economic Research Department, Reserve Bank of Australia, Sydney, April 1993, tables 2 and 5, pp. 9 and 14.

[1403] Merrett, "Preventing Bank Failure," pp. 139–40. David T. Merrett, "Banking and Finance," in Christopher Lloyd (ed.), *Australian Institutions Transformed: Capital Labour, and the State* (forthcoming), pp. 18–19. David T. Merrett, "Capital Formation and Capital Markets," draft chapter for the *Cambridge Economic History of Australia*, vol. 2, 1890–1990, pp. 9–10. [Hereafter cited as Merrett, "Capital Formation and Capital Markets."]

[1404] It was 1909 before deposits in trading banks again reached their 1890 level. They had reached about £138 million in 1890, and they stood at about £131 million in 1908 and £142 million in 1909. Butlin, Hall, and White, *Australian Banking and Monetary Statistics*, table 1, p. 112, and table 2(i), p. 116.

did not simply split into two separate components, commercial banks on the one hand and investment banks on the other. Instead the investment banks simply disappeared from the Australian financial landscape, and they did not reappear until some four decades later.[1405]

The trading banks' partial withdrawal from the long-term mortgage market, coupled with the widespread suspensions of the building societies and the failures of the mortgage and pastoral banks, meant that there were few private domestic institutions in a position to fill what had become a gaping hole in the domestic capital market. Over time that void was filled by institutional innovation; government land banks were chartered to provide long-term credit. Their portfolio policies were, however, determined by a political rather than an economic calculus. It was to be decades before the Australian economy fully recovered.

In the United States unit banking was the order of the day. Banks, on average, were much smaller than those in Canada and Australia. There were only a handful of banks with any branches, and there were none that had branches in more than a single state.[1406] Moreover, the state governments' response to the industry's defaults of the 1840s and the initial restrictions imposed by the National Bank Act meant that, in the half century before World War I, American commercial banks were less able to make long-term loans than were the Australian banks. By 1890, however, with the reemergence and increase in the importance of state banks, and with some modifications in national bank directives, they were somewhat better placed to make such loans than were the chartered banks in Canada. Thus, over most of the period, the U.S. banks had a smaller proportion of long-term assets supported by short-term liabilities than did their Australian counterparts, but that ratio was probably still above the Canadian benchmark.

Unit banking carried with it some costs not found in countries that had adopted Scottish banking. No branches meant that the commercial banks could not easily mobilize short-term capital across state (or sometimes across county) boundaries, something that British, Argentine, Australian, and Canadian banks could do. Moreover, because there was little geographic diversity in their loan portfolios, American banks were far more likely to suffer in periods of localized economic distress. As in Australia, the explanation of the "unit banking rules" in the United States

---

[1405] Merrett, "Capital Formation and Capital Markets," p. 2.

[1406] In 1870 in Australia there were 14 banks with average assets of $14.7 million; in Canada the figures were 34 and $3.2 million; and in the United States they were 1,937 and $919,000. In 1914 the comparable figures were 20 and $59.6 million for Australia, 22 and $70.7 million for Canada, and 27,236 and $885,000 for the United States.

reflect political decisions: Most banks were state chartered; local bankers had substantial power in the state legislature; and they were, with only a few, and even then relatively late, exceptions, able to prevent competitors from invading their local monopolies. Moreover, until very recently, after their success in the battle over the re-charter of the Second Bank of the United States, they were able to prevent federally chartered banks from providing more competition than their state-chartered competitors.

It might be noted, however, that American unit banking produced one quite unanticipated positive result. Between 1865 and 1914 no fewer than 3,401 U.S. banks suspended payment; however, because there were, for all intents and purposes, no foreign deposits, British savers were not injured. Thus, the suspensions had little direct impact on the financial links between the two countries. The story was similar in the case of Argentina and of Canada, but very different in the case of Australia.[1407]

More importantly, because U.S. banks could not branch across state lines, there were no branches of American banks in London to provide reputational signals for government bonds and railroad securities. As a result, the path of institutional evolution moved along very different lines than it had in Australia or Canada. In the United States, the commercial bank-based informational links that played such a major role in Australian and Canadian development did not exist.

In the immediate post–Civil War years, British merchant bankers saw the future in terms of investment in overseas railroads. In Australia and Canada such investments appeared to pose no particular problems. In Australia the railroads were government owned and operated; in Canada most had either de facto or de jure government guarantees. In addition, there were, depending on the date, British banks or branches of the chartered and trading banks in London serving as the fiscal agents for the overseas governments, and those banks provided the British saver with signals of quality.

In the U.S. case there were more serious problems. British savers had proved willing to invest in American rails provided that the bond issues were supported by the reputation of a well-known British merchant bank. Those banks, however, were unwilling to put their reputations at risk until they were able to solve the informational and monitoring issues that separated American railroads and British savers. U.S. railroads were privately owned, and their reputations were often, to say the least, suspect. As late as 1870, for example, the editors of *The Economist* wrote,

---

[1407] Between 1870 and 1914 there were twenty-six Canadian bank failures. Neufeld, *The Financial System of Canada*, table 4:1, pp. 78–80.

"the wars between the railroad kings were ruining the property of British bond and shareholders ... there is absolutely no security, even in the state of New York, that the most solid properties may not fall into the hands of a Fisk, Gould, and Vanderbilt gang, and be applied to Opera House orgies and purposes."[1408] Moreover, there were no American commercial banks with London branches to provide signals of quality.

Although there had been a number of precursors, investment banking in the United States really can be dated to 1862 and Jay Cooke & Company's underwriting and marketing the federal government's issue of the wartime 5–20's. Cooke's attempts to emulate his wartime successes in the post-war private railroad sector were much less productive. Although he was ultimately able to sell $5 million of a Northern Pacific Railroad bond issue, his failure to enlist European support led to the collapse of the scheme and, with it, the demise of Cooke and Company. American savers, perhaps partly encouraged by feelings of patriotism, were prepared to purchase the federal government's issues of symbolic capital, but they were not yet fully willing to accept the level of uncertainty that marked railroad finance. A European connection was still necessary, but the British merchant banks were unprepared to intermediate without better information and an enhanced ability to monitor.

Institutional innovation was required. In the decade after 1865 each of seven major British merchant banks established a relationship with a junior partner – an Anglo-American investment bank – capable of providing information, on-the-spot monitoring, and administrative support.[1409] Within a decade, although these second-generation firms continued to serve as agents for their first-generation British partners, they had managed to establish independent reputations among American savers; that is, they had come to be recognized by domestic savers as firms that dealt in quality issues. As a result, they were soon doing as much or more business in underwriting and selling U.S. railroad bonds for their American customers as they were for the British customers of their senior partners in London.

Investment banking in the United States proved profitable, and profits attract competition. By 1890 the nucleus of seven British and one

---

[1408] *The Economist*, Vol. 28 (December 3, 1870), p. 1452.

[1409] The London merchant banks and their American partners were (1) J.S. Morgan/Drexel Morgan; (2) Brown Shipley/Brown Brothers; (3) Morton Rose/Morton Bliss; (4) Baring Brothers/first T.W. Ward and then Baring-Mougan in New York and Kidder Peabody in Boston; (5) N.M. Rothschild/August Belmont; (6) Seligman Brothers/J & W Seligman; (7) Speyer Brothers/Phillip Speyer & Co. Note the role of family connections – such connections eased the principal-agent problem.

German merchant banks and their Anglo-American (or Anglo-German) second generation counterparts found themselves in competition with a number of American third-generation investment banks. Some of these new firms – Goldman Sachs and Lehman Brothers, for example – although still maintaining European financial ties, were not formally connected to the European market, and they had developed a substantial American clientele. Others, Harris, Forbes, & Company and Halsey, Stuart & Company, to cite two examples, depended largely on domestic savings. Both types, however, shared two characteristics. On the one hand, they were hardly ever more than marginal players in the market for new railroad bond issues; but new railroad construction was becoming less important. On the other hand, they were very entrepreneurial.

With the exception of J.P. Morgan and Company, the second-generation firms remained committed to underwriting issues of railroad bonds and to selling those bonds to a list of traditional customers. The new firms recognized no such limits. Their investment horizons included the rapidly expanding commercial and industrial sectors (firms in light and heavy manufacturing, public utilities, and retail stores). They did not hesitate to underwrite the issues of preferred shares, and they aggressively sought out customers that the second-generation banks would never have considered approaching. As a result, they grew rapidly. For example, beginning in 1906, with a $10 million offering of Sears, Roebuck & Co. preferred and common stock, over the next eighteen years the consortium of Goldman Sachs & Co. and Lehman Brothers managed 114 offerings of fifty-six firms.

Drawing on the services of these third-generation banks, firms like Sears and Roebuck and General Motors grew and prospered. By the 1920s, Morgan aside, the third-generation banks had become the leaders in the newly transformed investment banking industry. Years later, the words of Clarence Dillon, the head of Dillon, Read & Co., captured the impact of those changes: "If you had relied on houses like ourselves you probably would not have had an automobile industry in this country. We would not have risked it, and we would have taken it upon ourselves as a virtue."[1410] New York had replaced London as the financial center of the world, and American investment banks had become more powerful than even the largest British merchant banks. The third-generation firms directed American savings into both domestic and foreign enterprise, but those firms were the product of a process of institutional innovation and

---

[1410] Cited in Herman E. Krooss and Martin R. Blyn, *A History of Financial Intermediaries* (New York: Random House, 1971), p. 133. [Hereafter cited as Krooss and Blyn, *A History of Financial Intermediaries*.]

evolution that was rooted in the earlier attempts to overcome the monitoring and informational problems that arose as British finance began to flow into the American transport sector.

Argentine banking has a long history, but the modern phase dates from the passage of Law Number 1130 in 1881. That law was intended to bring uniformity to a highly heterogeneous monetary and banking system. The money supply had consisted of bank notes, in profusion, and the coinage of neighboring states. The new law restricted the note issue (now legal tender) to four commercial banks and one private bank. A bimetallic system was introduced – a system that quickly became a de facto gold standard – and coins of other states lost their monetary status. Thus, a uniform currency was established, and the beginnings of control over the price level were put in place. The plan was, however, short-lived. The political wheel turned. In 1885 convertibility was suspended, and new legislation was enacted. The new law resembled the American National Banking Act in that it granted the power of note issue to most banks. Like in the United States, the government was a major beneficiary; banks were required to hold government securities purchased from the Republic with gold as backing for the bank notes. Many banks, however, borrowed the required gold. As a result, bank note issue expanded, and the value of bank notes fell relative to gold throughout the rest of the decade. Historians have concluded that the financial problems arising from the abandonment of the 1881 law contributed significantly to the financial collapse of the early 1890s. In the collapse most of the domestic commercial banks, including the two most powerful (the semi-official Bank of the Nation and the Bank of the Province of Buenos Aires), failed. The two banks were subsequently successfully reconstructed. In particular, the Bank of the Nation became a very successful and powerful institution. It expanded rapidly after 1900, and in 1914 it held fully half of the total of all Argentine bank deposits.

The Argentine banking system differed from those of each of the other three settler economies. Unlike the Australian banks, Argentine banks drew virtually all of their deposits from domestic sources.[1411] Unlike American banks, many Argentine banks had foreign branches that supported the finance of foreign trade and the international movement of capital.[1412] Also, unlike American banks, Argentine banks branched

---

[1411] William H. Lough, *Banking Opportunities in South America*, Department of Commerce, Bureau of Foreign and Domestic Commerce, Special Agent Series No. 106 (Washington, D.C.: Government Printing Office, 1915), p. 104. [Hereafter cited as Lough, *Banking Opportunities*.]

[1412] Argentine banks had branches in all major Latin American centers, in London, Paris, Antwerp, Madrid, and perhaps other places as well.

domestically, although the number of branches was much smaller than those in Australia or Canada.[1413] Nonetheless, they provided a system for the interregional transfer of funds that was lacking in the United States.

Argentine banks can be divided into two groups: domestic (official and private) and foreign.[1414] The official domestic banks were primarily involved in the finance of trade and of agriculture or agriculturally related industries. They were not usually officially involved in long-term finance or in the distribution of long-term debt instruments. Personal connections were often more important than a careful vetting of loan opportunities. For example, they made substantial numbers of loans – typically overdrafts – that were unsupported by any collateral.[1415] Moreover, the loans were commonly "rolled over." Although the Bank of the Nation made small movements in this direction in the decade before World War I, over most of the period, there was no central bank, nor any other institutions that stood ready to provide assistance in times of economic crisis. As a consequence banks were obliged to hold substantial reserves to weather periods of crisis. Even so, the banking system was under severe pressure during the crises of 1873–75 and the early 1890s;

[1413] In 1915 the four British banks had twenty-four branches, the two German banks, seven branches, the Spanish Bank of the River Plate, fifty-four branches, the Bank of the Nation, more than 150 branches, and the Bank of the Province of Buenos Aires, fifty-six branches. There were other foreign and domestic banks, but this list includes the largest banks and surely the largest networks.

[1414] Charles A. Jones, *International Business in the Nineteenth Century: The Rise and Fall of a Cosmopolitan Bourgeoisie* (Brighton, Sussex: Wheatsheaf Books, 1987). [Hereafter cited as Jones, *International Business*.] Fredric M. Halsey, *Investments in Latin America and the West Indies*, Special Agent Series, No. 169, Bureau of Foreign and Domestic Commerce (Washington, D.C.: GPO, 1918), pp. 484–85.

[1415] "All the principal banks permit and encourage overdrafts in current account at 8 or 9 percent. It is quite possible for business houses and individuals in good standing to carry half a dozen or even 10 accounts, say, for $20,000 each, in as many banks. This establishes a credit in each bank, and the customer may draw from $5,000 to $20,000 on overdrafts from each one. This is freely admitted by the principal bankers . . . [bankers excuse the practice on the ground that they must meet competition.] An individual failed for 4,000,000 pesos. He was found to be overdrawn on many of the most important banks in the Republic. This inspired discussion of an organization among the banks of an information service that will restrict credit extensions to parties overdrawing accounts or seeking loans from several banks. Only in 1912 did the banks of Buenos Aires establish a clearing-house association, and this is confined to the clearance of checks." Edward N. Hurley, *Banking and Credit in Argentina, Brazil, Chile, and Peru*, Department of Commerce, Bureau of Foreign and Domestic Commerce, Special Agent Series No. 90 (Washington, D.C.: Government Printing Office, 1914), p. 31.

in the latter case, even the largest, oldest, and putatively the strongest failed in large numbers.

The banking system also included domestic private banks. The most successful grew out of mercantile firms with Continental European origins. They maintained their Continental connections, but they had long histories of operations in Argentina and were thoroughly Argentine; their partners were members of the landed mercantile elite. They had begun as international traders, moving products from Argentina to Europe. With success in these activities, they turned to lending and investing in industrial undertakings, most often focusing on industries bridging landed and manufacturing activities. There they became entrepreneurs and investors on a large scale, as well as lenders, and they served as agents in approaching European merchant banks for long-term governmental, public utility, and industrial finance on a large scale. Some of them were heavily involved in mortgage finance, and all of them weathered the crisis of the 1890s successfully. Of all the Argentine financial institutions, the private banks seem to have had the most intimate connections and the closest resemblance to European institutions. Specifically, they had many of the characteristics of Continental "universal" banks. They provided equity and debt capital. With their partners serving on boards of directors, they furnished financial and managerial advice as well. Together with some of the Continental banks, they became the chief source of external domestic industrial finance. Their contributions to total industrial finance were, however, relatively small. Most domestic industrialists continued to finance expansion through ploughing back profits.

Foreign institutions, those organized and with their home offices abroad, were also an important component of the Argentine commercial banking system. Typically they performed the usual commercial banking functions, but some of the Continental banks also participated in syndicates that distributed long-term debt underwritten by merchant or private banks. Of the foreign (British, French, Italian, and Spanish) banks, British banks were both the most important and the most successful. Unlike their domestic and Continental counterparts, their loan policies were typically conservative.[1416] They followed the real bills

---

[1416] When foreign banks first began to do business in Latin America, the problem of moral hazard was serious. Domestic banking practices were very different; Argentine businessmen were likely to regard the request for evidence of credit standing or the status of their business (a balance sheet, for example) as presumptuous; they viewed their relationship with their banker as both personal and social as well as business, and the default rate was much higher than the bankers' experience in Europe had led them to expect. The evidence suggests

doctrine, largely limiting themselves to short-term loans supported by commercial paper, and held very substantial reserves, reserves that at times amounted to one-half of their total assets. Although the interest rates they charged lenders were greater than twice the rates they paid depositors – a feature that led to some discontent among depositors – their reputation for safety (they survived the collapse of the 1890s) gave them substantial advantages in the competition for deposits.

They began as dealers in international claims but moved into the finance of foreign trade. As they became more experienced, they began to provide finance for British firms operating in Argentina. Although they ultimately began to finance some local business – typically firms engaged in foreign trade – they directed the vast majority of their loans to British-controlled enterprise.[1417] Although they engaged in no long-term finance, the British commercial bankers played an important role in promoting Argentine railways and public utilities, particularly in Britain.

The British banks not only survived the 1890s, but they emerged with a much enhanced reputation among Argentine savers. Their new reputations, combined with the failure of many of their domestic competitors, meant that the British banks emerged with a significant fraction of domestic deposits.[1418] Given the pro-British bias of their loan policies, the new structure may, for a time, have actually tended to stifle the evolution of the Argentine domestic capital market. There was, however, an indirect effect. Faced with foreign competition, the reorganized domestic banks were forced to adopt similar measures in terms of loan quality and safety standards. The result was a much more stable domestic banking system.

The foreign banks were, in at least two important respects, disappointments to governments in Argentina. The expectation that these banks, especially the British, would serve as development banks was never realized, nor, indeed, was the expectation that they would bring large amounts of new capital into the domestic economy. The banks did draw some foreign capital, but most of their loans were supported by domestic savings.

that the German banks were particularly hard hit. The European managers had been transferred to an entirely new and very different business environment. Initially, they knew few people with a knowledge of local conditions upon whom they could rely for advice. As foreign bankers grew more experienced, and as the number of European personnel in Argentine banks increased, the problem receded. Lough, *Banking Opportunities*, p. 104.

[1417] Lough, *Banking Opportunities*, p. 113.

[1418] By the end of 1913 foreign banks held almost 30 percent of Argentine deposits.

Although a significant volume of foreign, largely British, capital was directed toward the industrial sector, those flows were almost entirely direct. The major Anglo-Argentine businesses were incorporated in the United Kingdom and administered by British boards of directors. British investors believed that Argentine entrepreneurial and administrative skills were not well developed, and they had much less faith in the vagaries of Argentine politics than they did in the relatively stable political structures of the other frontier countries. Nonetheless, Argentine governments were typically able to borrow long-term overseas, and at interest rates that were modest by Latin American standards.

Finally, the Argentine financial structure included two mortgage banks, the older dating from 1872. In the late 1880s these institutions began to generate a mortgage document called a *cedula*, a common form of debt instrument in Latin America but only newly innovated in Argentina. *Cedulas* were debt instruments guaranteed by the National Mortgage Banks and by the Republic, and they were distributed to borrowers on the pledge of land. The borrower then sold his *cedula* in the open market. Since *cedulas* were doubly guaranteed, buyers did not require a personal knowledge of the pledged property. In principle, they could have played a role in the domestic savers' educational process similar to that played by government bonds and railway securities in Britain and the United States. From their innovation in 1886 they became very popular in Europe, but they proved less popular at home. As a result, although their sale underwrote a fraction of the capital required to shift from sheep to cattle and grain production and provided a portion of the financial support required for urban growth, until the last decade before the war, when they began to penetrate the domestic market, they had relatively little impact on the education of the Argentine saver, and, thus, on the evolution of the domestic capital market.[1419]

7-4. Britain and the four frontier countries: secondary links and the interaction between British savers and domestic institutions

Although the reasons in the American, Argentine, Australian, and Canadian cases were quite different, the structures of the developing primary and secondary capital markets were related to the flow of foreign capital. In the case of the United States, the emergence of the second- and third-generation investment banks provided the foundation

---

[1419] D.C.M. Platt, "The Funding of City Expansion, Buenos Aires and Montreal Compared, 1880–1914" in D.C.M. Platt and Guido di Tella (eds.), *Argentina, Australia and Canada: Studies in Comparative Development, 1870–1965* (New York: St Martin's Press, 1985).

for further institutional innovation in the secondary securities market. By the 1890s an American saver on the client list of one of the large investment banks had come to recognize the quality of the securities underwritten by the bankers; he had, after all, attained a fairly high level of sophistication about the value of pieces of symbolic capital. Given the new willingness of savers to hold paper securities, the investment bankers' signals were over time reinforced by the decision of the Governors of the New York Stock Exchange to impose near-draconian listing requirements.[1420] Taken together, the resulting combination of imprimatur and a vetted listing was sufficient to convince a significant minority of American savers that investments in paper securities, although not without risk, were not subject to large uncertainty discounts. As a result, these savers began to invest in private stocks and bonds in numbers that were sufficient to yield both insurance against liquidity risk and the benefits of economies of scale in the securities markets. By the turn of the century, there existed in the United States an active secondary market for both private railroad and non-railroad securities.[1421]

The organization of an efficient secondary market, in turn, affected other parts of the nation's capital market. With a secondary market guaranteed, it was possible for insurance companies to add pieces of private symbolic capital to their portfolios, additions that greatly enhanced interindustry capital mobilization. In 1880 American life insurance companies held only $30 million in private corporate securities (7 percent of their non-real estate assets); by 1900 the figure was $756 million (44 percent); and, although that fraction had declined to 35 percent by 1914, the value of their holdings had increased to $1.645 billion. More-

---

[1420] The NYSE limited its listings to firms that met minimum standards in terms of "size of capital, number of shareholders, and proven track record." The latter restriction applied both to the firm and to the industry. The rules also imposed additional costs on listed securities whose price fell below par or whose par value was less than $100. Finally, the Exchange required that securities only be traded in large blocks. Ranald C. Michie, *The London and New York Stock Exchanges, 1850–1914* (Edinburgh & London: Allen and Unwin, 1987), p. 198. [Hereafter cited as Michie, *London and New York.*]

[1421] Between 1890 and 1900 the fraction of non-railroad to all private equity issues traded on the NYSE increased from 24 to 48 percent, and between 1880 and 1900 the fraction of non-railroad to all private bond issues increased from 8 to 11 percent. By 1910 the NYSE handled 69 percent of the value of all equities and 91 percent of the par value of all bonds traded on formal markets in the United States. Lance E. Davis and Robert J. Cull, *International Capital Markets and American Economic Growth, 1820–1914* (Cambridge: Cambridge University Press, 1994), tables 4.2, 4.4, and 4.5, pp. 64, 67, and 73. [Hereafter cited as Davis and Cull, *International Capital Markets.*]

over, although the majority of the investments were in railroad securities, by 1900 they held $45 million in utility and $14 million in industrial issues.[1422]

Shaped initially by the concerns of foreign savers, the American institutional structure developed rapidly; investment banks and the formal securities markets served a steadily increasing fraction of domestic business activity, and the two institutions mobilized an increasing fraction of American savings. In 1910, for example, the six largest securities exchanges handled almost 240 million shares of stock and bonds with a par value of $700.5 million.[1423] There were, however, still problems. Many firms were too small to attract the services of either a British merchant bank or an American investment bank; and, railroads aside, there was still a very strong East Coast bias in the regions served by the set of established British and developing American financial institutions.

The second-generation investment banks had, to a large extent, solved the problems of monitoring and asymmetric information for railroads both east and west; however, as new investment opportunities shifted to small firms, firms in the West, and firms engaged in farming, ranching, and mining – firms that did not fall within the scope of either the second- or third-generation investment banks – the problems of informational asymmetry and potential moral hazard intensified. In response, British savers began to seek out alternative organizational structures, structures that were not controlled by American entrepreneurs, whose motives were not necessarily identical to those of the British investors. The free-standing company – a company chartered in Britain with a British board of directors and, often, with British "on site" management – became the institution of choice.[1424] In the long run, however, because of the political response to the incursion of foreign firms, that choice frequently proved more costly than its innovators had predicted.

In Canada, because of the role of government in railroad finance, there were no second-generation and few third-generation investment banks. With no guaranteed clientele, the formal markets in Toronto and

---

[1422] For 1880 and 1900, Bruce M. Pritchett, *A Study of Capital Mobilization: The Life Insurance Industry in the Nineteenth Century* (New York: Arno Press, 1977), table a1, pp. 290–347. [Hereafter cited as Pritchett, *Capital Mobilization*.] For 1914, *Historical Statistics of the United States, Colonial Times to 1970* (Washington, D.C.: GPO, 1975), Series X908–X913. For the year 1914, bonds have been divided between government and private and between U.S. and foreign on the basis of the distribution in 1900.

[1423] Michie, *London and New York*, p. 170.

[1424] For a detailed discussion of the free-standing company, see Wilkins, "The Free Standing Company."

Montreal had not developed sufficiently to guarantee liquidity.[1425] "One could easily sell large blocks of mining shares, and occasionally one could sell similar blocks of a few utility shares, without turning the market against itself."[1426] The middle of the 1890s, however, witnessed an innovation in the nation's institutional structure: the bond house. A bond house was linked informally through personal connections and somewhat more formally through membership in one of the nation's major financial groups to the existing financial structure. The financial groups almost always included at least one of the nation's larger banks and at least one of the larger insurance companies. The bond house, however, played a new role. It provided both a primary and secondary market for selected commercial and industrial issues. Thus, an underwriting guarantee by one of the nation's bond houses provided initial distribution, access to an efficient secondary market, and an increasingly adequate signal to the Canadian saver.[1427] The bond houses were initially organized

[1425] By 1914 there were formal securities exchanges operating in five Canadian cities; but the Vancouver exchange was not chartered until 1907; the Calgary exchange dates only from 1913; and, although the Winnipeg exchange was chartered in 1903, it did not begin to operate until 1909. Thus, for almost all of the period under review, the focus is on just two formal securities markets, Montreal and Toronto. Huntly W.F. McKay, "The Stock Exchanges of Canada," in David E. Spray (ed.), *The Principal Stock Exchanges of the World: Their Operation and Development* (Washington, D.C.: International Publishers, 1964), pp. 33–66.

There may also at one time have been a small exchange in Quebec. The *Monetary Times* for 1869–70 lists stocks on the Quebec exchange, but, since it is not mentioned elsewhere, it was almost certainly relatively unimportant.

[1426] Drummond, *Capital Markets in Australia and Canada*, pp. 36–37.

[1427] A typical financial group consisted of a large bank, one or two insurance companies, a trust company, and a bond, or investment, house. (For example, the spate of trust companies formed around the turn of the century were each closely associated through interlocking directorships with one of the chartered banks. The Royal Trust with the Bank of Montreal, the Montreal Trust with the Royal Bank of Canada, and the National Trust with the Canadian Bank of Commerce.) In Toronto the most important financial group was controlled by George C. Cox, a senator and president of both the Bank of Commerce, Canada's second largest bank, and the Canada Life Insurance Company, the largest of its type. In addition, Cox's son-in-law was president of A.E. Ames and Company, one of the largest bond houses; his son was managing director of Imperial Life; and his protege, E.R. Wood, headed the National Trust. In Montreal, it was the directors of the Bank of Montreal, by far the country's largest bank, who integrated and coordinated most of the financial affairs of the metropolitan community. "The Bank of Montreal, bound together in loose alliance the Canadian Pacific Railway, the Sun Life and the Royal Victoria insurance companies, the branches of US and British fire, life, and casualty companies, and the largest cotton manufacturers, shippers and milling companies." Sheila C. Dow, *Financial Markets and Regional Economic Development*, pp. 52–54. Neufeld, *The Financial System*

to underwrite and distribute the bond issues of cities in western Canada, cities without established reputations. By the turn of the century, however, given that they were largely free of legal or customary restrictions, the houses were willing and able "to move massively into the corporate securities market whenever the prospective speculative or investment returns were sufficiently favorable."[1428] The times were also propitious, Canada had begun to industrialize, and that development was given an added fillip by the passage of fairly draconian tariff laws aimed at U.S. and U.K. manufactures. In both Toronto and Montreal the insurance companies, banks, and savings and loan associations that belonged to the financial group provided both the funds necessary to cover the initial underwriting and the call loans that were required if the secondary market were to operate.[1429] After 1900 the Canadian saver, having cut his teeth on the issues of western cities, turned increasingly to the stocks and bonds of private companies. In its first thirteen years of operation, for example, the Dominion Securities Corporation sold at least $100 million in industrial securities as well as $15 million in municipal bonds. Even that record was overshadowed by the performance of the Royal Securities Corporation, a firm with the largest turnover among Canadian bond houses in the last decade before the war and a firm with a nationwide marketing organization that "soon came to include a London branch."[1430] The evolution of the bond house, although impressive, lagged the developments in investment banking and the formal securities markets in the United States – the Canadian saver graduated from grade school a few years later than his American counterpart. That lag can, in large part, be traced to the views of British savers about the relative merits of Canadian and American railroad issues.

By 1912 the life insurance companies in Canada held about the same position among private financial intermediaries as did their counterparts in the United States.[1431] The secondary securities market operated by the

---

of Canada, p. 295. Christopher Armstrong and H.V. Nelles, *Southern Exposure: Canadian Promoters in Latin America and the Caribbean, 1896–1930* (Toronto: University of Toronto Press, 1988), pp. 6–9, 11. [Hereafter cited as Armstrong and Nelles, *Southern Exposure*.] Ian Drummond, "Canadian Life Insurance Companies and the Capital Markets, 1890–1914," *Canadian Journal of Economics and Political Science*, Vol. XXVIII, No. 2 (May 1962), p. 211.

[1428] Drummond, *Capital Markets in Australia and Canada*, pp. 152, 243.

[1429] Armstrong and Nelles, *Southern Exposure*, pp. 10–12, 21–22.

[1430] Drummond, *Capital Markets in Australia and Canada*, pp. 207–8.

[1431] In 1912 the assets of U.S. insurance companies represented 13.4 percent of the total assets of all private financial intermediaries. In the case of Canada the comparable figure was 12.9 percent. Raymond Goldsmith, *Financial Intermediaries in the American Economy Since 1900*, National Bureau of Economic Research,

bond houses also made it possible for Canadian life insurance companies to include the issues of corporate securities in their portfolio. Here
again, Canada lagged the United States, but in the years leading up to
World War I the gap was closing. In 1891 only 6 percent of the non-real
estate assets of the Canadian life insurance companies was invested in
private issues of symbolic capital; the American figure was 26 percent.
At the turn of the century, when the American figure was 42 percent, the
Canadian proportion had increased to almost one-quarter, and a decade
later the figures were 39 and 31 percent, respectively.[1432]

The Australian experience was very different. With the withdrawal of
the trading banks from the new issues market, there were neither investment banks nor bond houses capable of providing a signal of quality. In
addition, as late as 1900, Australian savers had had no recent experience
with colonial or local government bonds or with private railroad issues,
pieces of paper that had served to teach their British, American, and
Canadian counterparts about the potential profitability of symbolic
capital. There were, to all intents and purposes, no privately owned railroads. Although a domestic market for governments had begun to
develop in the 1860s and 1870s, the British investor's demonstrated
appetite for Australian governments caused that market to atrophy in
the 1880s.[1433] "The Victorian bond market which had not been without
some vitality and significance for the economy in the 1860s and 1870s
became an anemic affair." In New South Wales, until the 1890s, "local
brokers played almost no part in raising the massive capital the government required for its railway construction."[1434] The stock exchanges,
although slowly evolving, remained relatively primitive. As late as 1913,
only one-third of Australian government loans were floated in the

Studies in Capital Formation and Financing (Princeton: Princeton University
Press, 1958), table 10, pp. 73–74. Neufeld, *The Financial System of Canada*,
appendix table B, p. 621.

[1432] By 1921 the U.S. figure had fallen to 28 percent and the Canadian figure to 18
percent. R.T. Naylor, *The History of Canadian Business, 1867–1914*, 2 vols.
(Toronto: James Lorimer & Co., 1975), Vol. 1, *The Banks and Finance Capital*,
p. 193. [Hereafter cited as Naylor, *The Banks and Finance Capital*.] Pritchett, *A
Study of Capital Mobilization*, appendix table A1, pp. 290–347. Neufeld, *The
Financial System of Canada*, table 8:4, pp. 260–61. *1971 Life Insurance Fact Book*
(New York: Institute of Life Insurance, 1971), p. 68. The 1911 figure for the
United States are calculated by extrapolation of the 1900 and 1917 figure.

[1433] Hall, *The Stock Exchange of Melbourne*, pp. 38–39, 67. Stephen Salsbury and Kay
Sweeny, *The Bull, the Bear, and the Kangaroo: The History of the Sydney Stock
Exchange* (Sydney: Allen & Unwin, 1988), p. 128. [Hereafter cited as Salsbury
and Sweeny, *The Bull, The Bear, and the Kangaroo*.]

[1434] Hall, *The Stock Exchange of Melbourne*, p. 106. Salsbury and Sweeny, *The Bull,
the Bear, and the Kangaroo*, p. 129.

domestic market. Between 1900 and 1914, if mining issues are excluded, per capita flotations of all private issues amounted to less than one dollar a year. In contrast, the figure for Canada was more than six dollars.[1435]

The financial collapse of the 1890s had indirect effects as well. Even as late as 1914 the secondary securities markets were far too thin to provide insurance against liquidity risk, and there were no Australian equivalents of the British Rothschilds or the London and Westminster, the American J.P. Morgan and Company or Kuhn Loeb and Company, or the Canadian Dominion Securities or the Royal Securities Corporation to provide a stamp of quality. Thus, with no assurance of liquidity, it was not until the Second World War that the stocks and bonds of industrial and commercial firms began to appear in the portfolios of Australian life insurance companies.[1436] No laws or regulations prevented the insurance companies from investing in private securities. The companies had simply made a decision that from their private economic point of view was clearly rational, but it was a decision that led to at least one unrecognized external social cost: slow economic growth.

In Argentina the secondary securities market was also very thin. Although the Buenos Aires securities exchange (the *Bolsa*) was established in the mid-1850s, for many years trading was limited to gold, government securities, and bank stock. Even in those limited cases, however, the volume was never large. Corporate securities first appeared on the market in the 1870s, but by 1890 only a handful remained. The volume of transactions in corporate issues varied widely from year to year, but the range was from limited to negligible. For example, the value of trades of the securities of private corporations totaled a mere 20,000 pesos in 1908; and, although it reached a peak of 2.4 million pesos the next year, the figure was still very small by the standard of corporate securities traded on the exchanges of any of the other frontier countries or, for that matter, by the standards of the still relatively small Argentine securities market itself. In 1913, for example, twenty-nine million pesos in government bonds and 198 million pesos in *cedulas* passed through the market.

As was true in Australia, most government debt was held abroad. Even securities that had initially been floated on the domestic market frequently gravitated into the hands of foreigners and were eventually listed on foreign exchanges. The same was true for railway stocks and bonds.

[1435] The figures were $0.98 for Australia and $6.32 for Canada. Drummond, *Capital Markets in Australia and Canada*, table 1, p. 172; appendix tables 1 and 2, pp. 292–93. Salsbury and Sweeny, *The Bull, the Bear, and the Kangaroo*, p. 176.

[1436] Holder, "Australia," p. 63. Hall, *The Stock Exchange of Melbourne*, p. 112.

By World War I a substantial fraction of the rail network was owned by British interests, and the long-term debt of those railroads was also held abroad.[1437] Short-term railroad financing was typically supplied by British banks located in Argentina but managed from London. Investment in public utilities and industrial undertakings was promoted by foreign savers, but their investment was also typically direct. Exceptions were the investments of the domestic private bankers, who both promoted industrial finance and who also behaved like Continental industrial bankers, investing their own resources in industrial activities. With these exceptions the finance of neither government, nor railways, nor public utilities, nor industry provided substantial opportunities for Argentine savers to become accustomed to the holdings of paper assets.

The thinness of the formal securities markets and the shortage of domestic paper assets had a substantial impact on the evolution of non-bank intermediaries. Argentine insurance companies grew rapidly after 1900, but the industry was still small and immature when compared with the insurance sectors of the other three frontier economies. The annual premiums received by domestic companies rose from about 600,000 pesos in the years 1897 to 1901 to some twenty-three million in 1913. Much of the sector's assets, however, appear to have been channeled either directly or indirectly through the purchase of *cedulas*, into mortgage finance. Like Australia, but unlike Canada and the United States, in 1914, *cedulas* aside, the portfolios of Argentine insurance companies contained almost no private securities. Perhaps the British saver had become relatively well educated in the risks and uncertainties of investment in Argentine enterprise, although the Barings Crisis casts some doubt on that conclusion; but in Argentina the domestic saver had not advanced from kindergarten to the first grade.

One major conclusion: In each of the four countries, the ability of non-bank intermediaries, particularly life insurance companies, to effectively mobilize capital depended on the existence of a substantial and diversified list of securities that could be easily sold on a well developed formal securities market. In the case of Argentina, the reliance on foreign-owned and operated businesses meant that the flow of foreign finance had, as late as 1914, contributed little to the evolution of domestic merchant or investment banking or to a formal domestic securities markets.

[1437] In 1917, for example, foreign owned railways had a paid up capital of 2,924 million paper pesos; for domestically owned lines the figure was only 23 million.

7-5. Institutional adaptation: the case of the market for inland bills

Although institutions sometimes are invented and innovated over a very short period of time, more frequently they are the product of a period of experimentation leading to initial innovation. Initial innovation is, in turn, often followed by a process of gradual modification. It may take many years before an institution assumes its final form, but the lag involved in exporting it to a similar environment may sometimes be much shorter. At other times, however, an institution that has proved successful in one environment may not be easily transferred to an environment that appears very similar. Consider the case of institutions that evolved to mobilize short-term capital across regional boundaries.

Although commercial banks in Scotland had long operated networks of branches, as late as the 1860s in England and Wales, joint-stock banks were, with few exceptions, still essentially local concerns.[1438] Economic growth in Britain did not proceed at the same pace in all sections of the country. As a result, regional supplies of, and demands for, short-term capital were seldom balanced, and there were substantial interregional interest differentials. In Scotland branch networks provided capital mobility, but initially there was no institutional structure capable of underwriting interregional arbitrage in England and Wales (nor, for that matter, between Scotland and the rest of Britain).

Between 1820 and 1850 an inland bill market gradually evolved. Through the intermediation of a formal discount market in London, banks in deficit regions could sell their commercial bills to banks in surplus regions. Initially brokers acted as purchasing agents for their customers, but as the market expanded they began to specialize. Ultimately, formal discount houses – "houses which formed the main bulwark to the market, they always stood ready to buy good bills" – were organized to provide a formal secondary market.[1439] The endorsements of the bank in

---

[1438] The Northern and Central Bank of England had operated a large branch network in the 1830s, and a decade later the London-based National Provincial Bank of England had ninety branches scattered across the country. The two were, however, the exceptions. Michael Collins, *Money and Banking in the U.K.: A History* (London: Croom Helm, 1988), p. 75. [Hereafter cited as Collins, *Money and Banking*.] Philip L. Cottrell, "The Domestic Commercial Banks and the City of London, 1870–1939," in Youssef Cassis (ed.), *Finance and Financiers in European History, 1880–1960* (Cambridge: Cambridge University Press, 1992), pp. 58–59.

[1439] The National Discount House, the first joint-stock firm to enter the market began business in 1856. It was soon joined by others. W.T. King, *History of the London Discount Market* (London: George Routledge & Sons, 1936), pp. 217–29. [Hereafter cited as King, *History of the London Discount Market*.]

the deficit region and of one of the London banks that specialized in rediscounting provided the guarantee for the quality of the bill.[1440] For more than a quarter of a century the inland bill market performed well. Bankers came to realize that "a well proportioned bill case, though not marketable, would always provide a large volume of bills maturing at any point in time" and that such rediscounted reserves represented a safe and profitable secondary reserve.[1441] Between 1840 and 1879 it appears that discounted bills represented about one-third of the assets of all commercial banks.[1442]

Economic environments, however, change. The years after 1860 were marked by a rapid expansion of national branch banking networks in England and Wales and the penetration of Scottish banks into the London market.[1443] Despite the success of the inland bill market, the expansion of the system of nationwide branch banking provided a cheaper method of achieving interregional capital mobility. Interbank transfers did not involve the costs – costs that included the profits earned by the discount houses – of operating a central market for bills. By the end of the 1860s the London inland bill market no longer played so major a role in the interregional capital market; the institutional technology was becoming obsolete.[1444] International transportation and communications systems, however, had not developed as rapidly as their domestic counterparts. Few banks had branches in all corners of the globe. Global trade, however, was increasing.[1445] Internationally, regional supplies of, and demands for, short-term finance were seldom

---

[1440] King, *History of the London Discount Market*, p. 280.

[1441] C.A.E. Goodhart, *The Business of Banking: 1891–1914* (London: London School of Economics and Political Science & Weidenfeld & Nicolson, 1972), p. 133. [Hereafter cited as Goodhart, *The Business of Banking*.]

[1442] Collins, *Money and Banking*, p. 98 and p. 110, table 4.4.

[1443] In 1850 there were 99 joint-stock banks with 576 branches operating in England and Wales; in 1875, 131 English and Welch joint-stock banks operated 1,438 branches (in addition 21 Scottish and Irish banks controlled an additional 1,330 branches); and in 1900 the figures for the entire country were 112 joint-stock banks and almost 5,600 branches. David K. Sheppard, *The Growth and Role of U.K. Financial Institutions* (London: Methuen, 1971), appendices (A) 1.2, 1.3, and 1.4, pp. 118–23.

[1444] For a thorough discussion of the decline of the market for inland bills, see Shizuya Nishimura, *The Decline of Inland Bills of Exchange in the London Money Market, 1855–1913* (New York: Cambridge University Press, 1971).

[1445] In the case of Great Britain, for example, between 1860 and 1900 the index of the volume of imports had increased at a compound rate of 3.4 percent per year. The figure for exports was 2.3 percent. B.R. Mitchell, with the collaboration of Phyllis Deane, *Abstract of British Historical Statistics* (Cambridge: Cambridge University Press, 1962), Overseas Trade, table 13, pp. 328–29.

balanced, and there were often marked international interest differentials. As in the United Kingdom in the 1820s, there were potential profits from institutional innovation in the overseas market. This time, however, it was not necessary to invent an entirely new institution. A formal secondary market for commercial bills – a structure that now included the joint-stock discount houses as well as a number of bankers who had gained experience in discounting commercial bills – had been in place for a quarter of a century. Given the existing structure, it was a simple step for the large merchant banks with international connections to begin to accept bills drawn on merchants in Moscow, Montreal, or Montevideo.

Initially it was a small number of merchant banks – Rothschilds, Baring, Kleinwort, Schroeder, Hambro, Brandt, and Gibbs – together with the London offices of overseas banks that dominated the overseas acceptance business, but before the turn of the century the major London clearing banks had begun to compete for this lucrative business.[1446] The result was a large-scale, open, and very competitive secondary market in discounted international sterling bills. Over time the London acceptance became a common guarantee for transactions throughout the world; in fact, by the end of the century such acceptances often underwrote international transactions that did not directly involve Britain. "In 1913 London prime acceptances, both home and foreign, totaled £350 million of which about 60 percent, some £210 million, were finance bills arising from the working of the international gold standard."[1447] The market in sterling bills – a market with an institutional design that was drawn from the inland bills market of the first half of the nineteenth century – placed London at the center of the world capital market. It also led one economic historian to conclude that the system that was usually termed the "international gold standard" should instead have been called the "international bill-on-London" standard.[1448]

In Argentina, Australia, and Canada branch banking antedated the period of rapid economic growth. Given that technology, there was never a need for a commercial bill market. In 1787 British banks were local

---

[1446] On the eve of World War I, the merchant banks were responsible for 45 percent of the foreign trade commercial credit granted in London, but British domestic commercial banks accounted for an additional 24 percent. Phillip L. Cottrell, "Great Britain," in Rondo Cameron and V.I. Bovykin, with the assistance of Boris Anan'ich, A.A. Fursenk, Richard Sylla, and Mira Wilkins (eds.), *International Banking, 1870–1914* (New York & Oxford: Oxford University Press, 1991), p. 33. [Hereafter cited as Cottrell, "Great Britain."]

[1447] Cottrell, "Great Britain," p. 33.

[1448] Collins, *Money and Banking*, pp. 151–53. The quote is by L.S. Pressnell, cited in Goodhart, *The Business of Banking*, p. 149.

concerns with limited capital, and the system of unit banking that was adopted by most American states reflected the earlier British structure.[1449] East-West mobility problems had arisen almost as soon as the Erie Canal had opened the upper Midwest. Before the Civil War, however, cotton factors – most often northern or British merchants who advanced credit to southern planters in exchange for an informal lien on their crops – had served to partially solve the North-South mobility problems.[1450] The war, however, destroyed the network that linked factors to planters. Thereafter there were problems of both East-West and North-South mobility.[1451]

Given the success of the British market for inland bills, America's dedication to unit banking, the widespread recognition that self-extinguishing commercial paper constitutes an excellent secondary reserve, and the very large interregional disparities in the demand for, and the supply of, short-term capital, one might easily conclude that the innovation of some structure similar to that which had been in place in Britain by the 1850s would have occurred relatively swiftly. In fact, by 1860 a formal market for the purchase and sale of commercial paper had been organized in New England and the Middle Atlantic states.[1452] There-

---

[1449] The Bank of North America (1781) and the First (1791) and Second (1816) Banks of the United States were creatures of the central government. The First and Second Banks had interstate banking privileges, but the opposition of state banks to that structure played a significant role in the demise of both.

[1450] Bodenhorn and Rockoff find evidence of North-South capital market integration in the years before the Civil War. Howard Bodenhorn and Hugh Rockoff, "Regional Interest Rates in Antebellum America," in Claudia Goldin and Hugh Rockoff (eds.), *Strategic Factors in Nineteenth Century American Economic History: A Volume to Honor Robert W. Fogel*, a National Bureau of Economic Research Conference Report (Chicago: University of Chicago Press, 1992), pp. 172–73.

[1451] Lewis Cecil Gray, assisted by Esther Katherine Thompson, *History of Agriculture in the Southern United States to 1860*, 2 Vols. (Gloucester, Mass.: Peter Smith, 1958), Vol. 2, p. 713.

[1452] This discussion of the commercial paper market draws heavily on Lance Davis, "The Investment Market, 1870–1914: The Evolution of a National Market," *Journal of Economic History*, Vol. 25, No. 3 (September 1965, pp. 330–65); Albert Greef, *The Commercial Paper House in the United States* (Cambridge, Mass.: Harvard University Press, 1938) [Hereafter cited as Greef, *The Commercial Paper House*]; and John A. James, "The Rise and Fall of the Commercial Paper Market, 1900–1930," in Michael D. Bordo and Richard Sylla (eds.), *Anglo-American Financial Systems: Institutions and Markets in the Twentieth Century* (Burr Ridge, Ill. & New York: Irwin Professional Publishers and Stern School of Business, New York University, 1995, pp. 219–60) [Hereafter cited as James, "The Rise and Fall of the Commercial Paper Market"].

after, however, the market spread much more slowly. It reached Indianapolis in 1871, but it was the next decade before paper originating in Milwaukee, Chicago, or Minneapolis was widely traded, the middle of that decade before the market had grown to encompass Kansas City, the turn of the century before brokers' offices were opened in San Francisco, Los Angeles, and Seattle, and another ten years before Wichita and Dallas were integrated into the national mosaic. Moreover, "by 1913 it could be said that the commercial paper market had representatives 'in all the large cities' in the United States," but the market never penetrated the South in any significant way.[1453] The slow adoption of the institutional structure remains something of a puzzle. The first American modern commercial paper house dates back almost as far as the National Discount house, but widespread innovation was slow.[1454] As late as the 1880s, a typical firm still maintained only a single office. Bankers who wanted to buy bills, as well as the representatives of banks and firms with paper to sell, personally visited that office with their paper or their orders. It was only later that new and larger firms began to open branches in potentially lucrative markets and to establish correspondent relations in areas that could not support a branch. By 1920 eight of the larger firms with head offices in New York, Boston, and Chicago had, on average, just less than ten out-of-city branches.

Research has yet to uncover the full explanation of the relatively slow development of the American market, but it probably can be at least partially explained by four characteristics of that market that set it apart from the British. First, the spatial distances were substantially greater than in the United Kingdom. In addition, the high-interest areas tended to be West-North Central, the Mountain, and the Pacific regions, regions where, from the point of view of eastern banks, the problems of asymmetric information appeared particularly critical. Second, unit banking meant that, from the point of view of an eastern banker, there was often a question of the credit worthiness of the endorsing bank – again, a question of asymmetric information. Third, although some 95 percent of the commercial paper that passed through the market was purchased by commercial banks, most U.S. banks, unlike their British counterparts,

---

[1453] Greef, *The Commercial Paper House*, pp. 39–40. It should be noted that, although the market in its early years dealt, like its British counterpart, in two-name paper, the American market in the years after the turn of the century was dominated by single-name paper. James, "The Rise and Fall of the Commercial Paper Market," pp. 221–22.

[1454] Henry Clews & Company, generally regarded as the prototype of the modern commercial paper house, began business in 1857. Kroos and Blyn, *A History of Financial Intermediaries*, p. 108.

were faced by legal reserve requirements. As a result, they may have faced a less pressing demand for secondary reserves. Moreover, unlike in Britain, before the Federal Reserve Act there was no secondary market for commercial paper. As a result, such paper may well have been considered an inferior secondary reserve. Of course, the question remains: Why did the secondary market not develop?[1455] Finally, as the early experiences of the Federal Reserve Banks underscored, American commercial bankers traditionally appear to have been loath to discount their customer's commercial paper. That last conclusion receives some support from the nature of the firms that did enter the market as suppliers of commercial paper. Although the suppliers were sometimes banks in high-interest areas, they were increasingly commercial and industrial firms – most frequently medium-sized firms with a net worth between $250,000 and $10 million – seeking an anonymous way to bypass their local banks and thus gain additional capital without damaging their ties to the local institution.[1456] None of the four explanations, however, satisfactorily explains the almost complete failure of the commercial paper market, even during its post–World War I heyday, to penetrate the South. We clearly still have much to learn about institutional transfer.

7-6. Institutional fragility: obsolescence, structural weakness, and regime changes

In Britain the growth of joint-stock banks with national branch networks had made the inland bill and its supporting institutional structure nearly obsolete. Short-term capital mobilization within the United Kingdom could be effected more cheaply with the new technology, but the old institutional technology was still competitive in some parts of the domestic market, and it became the basis for international capital short-term mobility between most of the world's major ports. It should be noted, however, that in the international market, it performed less well as the distance from the port to the hinterland increased. In the United States, something akin to the old British technology provided the foundation for a market in commercial paper. By the first decade of the twentieth century, that market had largely solved the problems of East-West short-term capital mobility, but, despite the nation's continued reliance on unit banking, it too became obsolete. In 1906 sales of commercial paper were estimated to have been in the $500 million to $1 billion range; by 1914 they may have reached twice that figure; and by 1920 the volume

---

[1455] James, "The Rise and Fall of the Commercial Paper Market," pp. 223–24.
[1456] James, "The Rise and Fall of the Commercial Paper Market," p. 223.

of commercial paper outstanding had reached $1.296 billion, a figure that implies annual sales of about $7 billion.[1457]

Thereafter, however, the volume began to decline. By 1929 it had fallen to $265 million, and *Business Week* observed that commercial paper "was widely held to be going out of use." The decline reflected both the growth in the size of banks and in the size of the borrowing firms. The greater the volume of assets held by a bank, the larger the limit on the size of loans that the bank could make to a single borrower without pushing against the regulatory constraints imposed by the National Banking Act. Moreover, the Federal Reserve Act excluded some commercial paper from the single borrower constraints.[1458] At the same time the evolution of a national market for goods and services was linked to the growth of firm size and the emergence of firms with nationally recognized reputations, firms capable of borrowing in almost any local market.[1459] National branch banking spelled the end of the inland bill market in the United Kingdom, but in the United States the story was just the opposite: Although there were still no banks with nationwide branch networks, there were firms with both the reputations and the network of branches that permitted them to borrow nationwide. In both cases, however, the institutional substitution was based on changes in relative prices; the new technology was simply cheaper than the old.

It is not always the competition from alternative institutions that weakens an institution. Moreover, at times exogenous changes can produce a form of technological regression. Take, for example, the London Stock Exchange. In 1914 it was the world's premier formal securities market. Since the 1830s, however, it had not been the only formal exchange in Great Britain; there were also a number of provincial exchanges.[1460] Like their American counterparts, they dealt in some local

---

[1457] Greef, *The Commercial Paper House*, pp. 56, 58–60, 115.

[1458] Section 5200 of the federal code prohibited banks from lending in excess of ten percent of their capital to any one person or company. There were, however, exceptions that permitted a bank to exceed the limit for brokered commercial paper. That exemption clearly supported the commercial paper market. Naomi R. Lamoreaux, "'No Arbitrary Discretion': Specialisation in Short-Term Commercial Lending by Banks in Late Nineteenth Century New England," in Geoffrey Jones (ed.), *Banks and Money: International and Comparative Finance in History* (London: Frank Cass, 1991), p. 102.

[1459] James, "The Rise and Fall of the Commercial Paper Market," p. 232.

[1460] Although all did not survive nor operate continuously, between 1836 and 1903 formal exchanges were organized in seventeen cities in England and Wales, in five cities in Scotland, and in at least one Irish city. For a history of the provincial exchanges, see W.A. Thomas, *The Provincial Exchanges* (London: Frank Cass, 1973), especially pp. 72, 287, 327.

securities that were not listed elsewhere, but because of the LSE's restrictions on the size of brokerage firms, they also served as effective "substations" for the London Stock Exchange. "Until the years immediately before World War I all of these exchanges had existed in relative harmony, mainly because London did not impose any minimum commission rates and was lax in the implementation of rules which would have restricted inter-market dealing – rules that forbade jobbers to transact business with non-members, for example. Thus an integrated securities market had developed – a market that facilitated active nationwide trading in all types of securities, including increasingly numerous industrial and commercial issues."[1461] In the years immediately before the war, however, some members of the London Stock Exchange became convinced that their business was slipping away to the provincial markets. "In essence, brokers saw their commissions being threatened by jobbers' direct contacts outside the stock exchange while jobbers felt their livelihoods threatened by brokers making markets. The consequence was a steady build up of hostility to the whole way that the London and provincial business was being conducted because of its potential ability to undermine the value of the London Stock Exchange to its members." In response, those members attempted to erect a series of barriers between the London and the other domestic exchanges. In 1909 "jobbers were prohibited from trading with non-members, within the United Kingdom, and brokers were banned from making markets, again in the United Kingdom." Those rules became binding when, in 1912, minimum commission rates were introduced.[1462] These rules were adopted with far from the unanimous approval of the members, and they would most likely have been repealed had not the war undermined the Exchange's international position and convinced the large majority of members of the necessity of preserving their position against all rivals, no matter what the consequences. The provincial exchanges, however, proved more resilient than the London brokers and jobbers had imagined; far from insulating the London Exchange from provincial incursions, the most significant outcome of the new institutional regime was a weakening of the

---

[1461] Ranald C. Michie, "The Stock Exchange and the British Economy, 1870–1939," in J.J. Van Helten and Y. Cassis (eds.), *Capitalism in a Mature Economy: Financial Institutions, Capital Exports and British Industry, 1870–1939* (Aldershot, U.K. and Brookfield, Vt.: Edward Elgar, 1990), p. 111. [Hereafter cited as Michie, "The Stock Exchange and the British Economy."]

[1462] Ranald C. Michie, "The London and Provincial Stock Exchanges, 1799–1973: Separation, Integration, Rivalry, Unity," chapter 8 in D.H. Aldercroft and A. Slaven (eds.), *Enterprise and Management: Essays in Honour of Peter Payne* (Aldershot: Scola Press, 1995), pp. 208–9.

position of the London Exchange itself. The weakening, in turn, left the national capital market fractured. The provincial exchanges developed their own parallel marketing mechanisms, and "inevitably the result was to weaken the national securities market by raising costs and increasing dealing times."[1463] The division between brokers and proprietors on the London Stock Exchange had retarded innovation in the late nineteenth century, and the search of the now owner-proprietors for increased profits in the early twentieth century led to the breakdown of what had been for more than three decades, an efficient national market for symbolic capital.[1464]

The moral of the story is clear: There is no reason to believe that an institution designed for the profits of a few, even though it initially serves to improve overall efficiency, will always prove beneficial to the economy more broadly defined if the regime suddenly changes. Moreover, when the institutional structure is not based on the coercive power of the government, if the benefits narrow, the institution may weaken, or, like the investment banking functions of the Australian trading banks, disappear altogether. In the case of the New York Stock Exchange, the very strict listing ∤ requirements yielded substantial monopoly profits to the members, but they also provided a signal of quality that greatly aided the process of investor education across the economy as a whole. At the same time, the social costs of the Exchange's policies were minimized because firms and investors who concluded that the signal was unnecessary had a ready access to less stringently regulated exchanges in London, on the Curb and the Consolidated exchanges in New York, and in cities like Boston or Philadelphia, or to the informal solicitor- or broker-intermediated markets in England and Scotland.

The attempt to provide deposit insurance for the British holders of Australian bank deposits provides another example of the causes of

---

[1463] Michie, "The Stock Exchange and the British Economy," p. 111.

[1464] The initial deed of settlement had recognized two distinct groups: (1) the proprietors who were the owners of the 400 £50 shares and who owned the physical exchange; they were represented by nine Trustees and Managers who set the general rules for the exchange; and (2) the members of the Exchange, the brokers and jobbers who paid to be allowed to use the facilities of the Exchange. They were represented by the Committee of General Purposes; that committee operated the Exchange. In 1876, for example, there were 502 proprietors and more than 2,000 members. Although most of the proprietors were members, not all were. The split between owners and members was only gradually resolved. Although it was to be 1945 before the two groups were formally amalgamated, the problems had largely been solved by World War I. Victor E. Morgan and W.A. Thomas, *The Stock Exchange: Its History and Functions* (London: Etek Books, 1962), pp. 74, 140. Michie, *London and New York*, p. 19.

institutional fragility. As late as 1891 some eight to twelve British firms were actively selling such insurance policies.[1465] Those firms believed that they were offering insurance against risk, but in fact the status of the Australian bank deposits was one of uncertainty, not risk. Although the individual companies' response to the 1890s crisis varied, from the point of view of the depositors who had purchased insurance, the results, with few exceptions, were similar: By 1894 almost all of those firms had either refused to meet their legal obligations or failed completely. A few companies, usually those with a relatively low volume of insurance in force, announced their willingness to meet their obligations; however, "those most heavily in are ready to fight the matter out, because they are simply unable to pay or take over the securities of the suspended banks from their insured depositors."[1466] Their general response was to deny liability and, at minimum, to force their customers to litigate, litigate, litigate.[1467]

Even the commercial press failed to recognize the underlying situation. The editors of the *Bankers', Insurance Managers, and Agents' Magazine* correctly concluded that "it is manifestly an impossibility for the greater part of these companies to meet such claims as their limited means do not permit the payments of policies being made on as great a scale as the necessities of the case require." The pronouncement was followed by what proved to be a few overly optimistic words about the future, words that suggested a lack of understanding of the underlying

---

[1465] *Bankers', Insurance Managers, and Agents' Magazine* (London: Waterlow & Sons), Vol. 55 (1893), p. 726. [Hereafter cited as *BIM&A*.]

[1466] *BIM&AM*, Vol. 56 (1893), p. 496.

[1467] The individual strategies spanned a wide range. A number, including the Securities Insurance Company and the Trustee Assets & Investment Insurance Company, argued that, since the failed banks had reconstructed, they – the insurance companies – had no further liabilities under their policies. Some, the Mortgage Insurance Company, for example, offered their policy holders a choice between "liquidation or reconstruction, or, technically, liquidation, pure and simple, or liquidation *plus* reconstruction. Needless to say the latter – a scheme of reconstruction or *moratorium*, is preferred to the former." Some, the Liverpool Mortgage Insurance Company, for example, announced that they were prepared to pay, but not now; and in the meantime the policy holders would have to continue to pay their premiums, if they wanted their policies to remain in force. One unnamed firm postponed payment, demanded that premiums continue to be paid, but sent out no premium notices in hope that the policies would lapse. Finally, the Securities Insurance Company appealed to the courts to void their policies because the policy holders had not told them that the Real Estate Mortgage and Deposit Bank of Melbourne was in trouble. *BIM&AM*, Vol. 56 (1893), p. 494; Vol. 57 (1894), p. 132; Vol. 57 (1894), p. 129; Vol. 56 (1893), pp. 495–96; Vol. 57 (1894), p. 622.

problem. "The result of all such actions as we have mentioned is undoubtedly to force deposit insurance companies into liquidation, voluntary or compulsory. If the companies are to reconstruct, will they be sure of getting new business? This is not easy to answer. We trust, however, that with improved methods of doing business, they will avoid all the errors of the past, and proceed again on their course."[1468] British savers – both those who had bought insurance and those who did not – had learned that you can insure against risk but that you cannot insure against uncertainty, but the lesson was costly. They had thought they were buying into a risky situation, but they found that they had been sold a very uncertain one. By 1894 the insurance firms had come to realize that they can provide insurance against risk, but you can not provide insurance against uncertainty. The firms may well have thought they were selling insurance against risky investments, but they found that they were selling insurance against very uncertain outcomes. Like the experience of the savers, the lesson did not come cheaply.

Finally, a change of regime in the economic environment can destroy a functioning and apparently efficient institutional structure. Australia in the years after 1890 provides a classic example of the impact of total breakdown of the institutional structure. Over the decade and a half leading up to the crisis of 1893, British capital had financed a substantial proportion – probably more than 40 percent – of Australian long-term capital formation.[1469] Although government loans represented a large part of the foreign (almost entirely British) capital imports, Australian pastoral firms appealed directly to the British saver, and those firms directed funds into land purchases, buildings, fencing, and irrigation. Land and mortgage banks solicited funds to underwrite the urban mortgage boom. Finally the trading banks solicited medium-term deposits in Britain, and those deposits were quickly recycled into investments in agriculture and urban housing.[1470]

[1468] *BIM&AM*, Vol. 57 (1894), pp. 129, 133.

[1469] Noel Butlin's estimates put the figure at 41 percent. See Noel G. Butlin, *Australian Domestic Product, Investment and Foreign Borrowing, 1861–1938/39* (Cambridge: Cambridge University Press, 1962) [hereafter cited as N. Butlin, *Australian Domestic Product*], table 1, pp. 6–7, table 4, pp. 16–17, table 250, p. 422, table 265, p. 444. Butlin, *Investment in Australian Development*, table 1, p. 11, appendix table II, p. 454.

[1470] The mortgage banks and the land and building companies had been formed to exploit the opportunities for speculative profits that were emerging in the subdivision of urban land. Many of these institutions "secured a significantly high proportion of their funds in Britain." For example, as early as 1881, the *Australasian Insurance and Banking Review* listed sixteen mortgage companies incorporated in England for operation in Australia. Some of these firms had

The experience of the British savers with their investment in the Australian private sector – there were no public sector defaults – destroyed the existing institutional structure. British depositors as well as equity and bond holders bore a substantial fraction of the Australian losses, and even those who ultimately were repaid were forced to wait

close connections with the trading banks, banks that "welcomed opportunities for transferring long-term loans to more suitable institutions." Jackson, *Australian Economic Development*, pp. 142–43. S. Butlin, *Australia and New Zealand Bank*, p. 236.

The first of the pastoral firms date from the 1850s, but they multiplied rapidly from the mid-1870s. "They began by handling wool and providing stores on credit, then diversified into providing investable funds to pastoralists." Most of the funds were raised by issuing company debentures in Britain and lending those funds, together with the receipts from the sale of paid-up capital, at the higher rate of interest payable in Australia. "Rural advances by pastoral companies attained a peak in 1891, those of the big five companies being equal in size to about 15 per cent of Australian trading banks' total advances to all customers." Pope, "Free Banking in Australia," p. 2.

In the case of the trading banks, it is estimated that as early as 1883 mortgage lending had reached the £35 to £40 million level, and that total does not include an additional £5 to £10 million in indirect aid through loans to pastoral finance companies. In that year the Australian investments of the nation's trading banks totaled just less than £78 million. S. Butlin, Hall, and White, *Australian Banking and Monetary Statistics*, table 1, p. 113.

Even the official Australian wisdom was that long-term investments by commercial banks in land-related enterprises were not a subject of concern. The editors of the *Australasian Insurance and Banking Review*, for example, wrote, "the policy of Australian banking has gradually adapted itself to the requirements of a country differing widely in all essentials from the mother-land"; "conditions suited to the finance of the old world were far from adequate to the wants of the young colonies whose growth chiefly depended upon their profitable use of the immense territory at their disposal. No industry gives promise of such returns, and consequently there was a general desire to become possessed of land and stock. . . . The directors and managers of the banks fore-saw that there was scope for banking enterprise far beyond anything which the ordinary trade discounting supplied." The members of the Royal Commission on Victorian Banking appear to have felt equally strongly about conditions in Australia. In 1887 they concluded, "here a landed estate is always marketable, subject only to the rise and fall in value. It is improbable, therefore, that a bank administered with ordinary prudence could so lock up its money in land that it would become seriously involved. Banks take care to have a margin of safety, and experience shows that there are no better securities than those effected on land." *AIBR*, December 8, 1880, December 9, 1878, and August 16, 1887.

In the case of British deposits in those trading banks, by 1892 only two Australian banks held no British deposits. The data are weak, but it appears very likely that in 1892 such deposits accounted for at least one-quarter of all Australian bank deposits. Prideaux Selbey, the Bank of Australasia's secretary, placed the level at £14 million in 1883, £21 million in 1885, and £30 million in

for an extended period. Those savers had long memories, and after 1893 it was almost impossible to sell private stocks or bonds or to successfully solicit bank deposits in the United Kingdom. After suffering substantial losses, British savers looked elsewhere – particularly to Canada – for less uncertain private alternatives. The existing structure disappeared. It was to be decades before overseas lenders were willing to turn their accumulations over to firms in the Commonwealth's private sector.

Perhaps more importantly, other private domestic institutions did not quickly emerge to fill the gap. It was the end of World War II before a new set of private Australian financial institutions had evolved sufficiently to effectively mobilize domestic savings. In the decade leading up to World War I, the Australian economy was faced by a series of new economic opportunities. In agriculture, wheat and dairying were in a position to undercut the traditional specialization in wool, and there were substantial opportunities to expand the manufacturing sector behind the new higher and uniform tariff barriers. Since British savers were unwilling to finance those changes, and because the private domestic markets were in tatters, the pace of change was slow. Government credit, however, had not been damaged; there had been no public defaults. Both the states and the Commonwealth government found that they could still borrow abroad. At the same time domestic savers – savers who no longer trusted even those private financial institutions that had survived relatively intact – proved willing to purchase government bonds and to place their savings in government savings banks.[1471] Farmers in

1888. David Pope has placed the ratio of British to domestic deposits at 10 percent in the mid-1870s, 24 percent a decade later, and at 40 percent on the eve of the depression. Most recently, David Merrett has put the figure at £15.5 million in 1886 and £38.1 million in 1892, "a rise which lifted their share of the combined Australian and United Kingdom deposits from 17 to 28 percent." S. Butlin, *Australia and New Zealand Bank*, pp. 240–41. Pope, "Free Banking in Australia," pp. 15–16. David Merrett, "Australian Banking Practice and the Crisis of 1893," p. 75.

[1471] In the decade leading up to the crisis, none of the six colonies had issued a loan in the domestic market. Although the British continued to supply the bulk of state and Federation funds after 1900, by 1914 the domestic market accounted for about one-third of the total. In 1904 Australian governments raised £39.6 million at home, 17 percent of the total. In 1913 government borrowing was a record £90.6 million, and 31 percent was raised domestically. Salsbury and Sweeny, *The Bull, the Bear and the Kangaroo*, p. 176.

In 1900 the six states had £1.6 million in agricultural loans outstanding, and there were no nonagricultural loans. By 1914 the agricultural loans had increased to £9 million, and banks in South Australia and Victoria had added an additional £2.6 million in urban mortgages to their portfolios. In 1890 deposits in government savings banks had amounted to 16 percent of those in the trading banks;

the expanding wheat and dairy industries received some help from the state-run mortgage banks, but probably less than they would have received in a market directed by economic rather than political criteria. Manufacturing firms, on the other hand, were forced to depend largely on retained earnings for their long-term finance.[1472] Political decisions are almost always made on the basis of where the voters are, rather than on where they might be sometime in the future. Thus, although it is not clear what the precise mobilization channels would have been in the absence of government action, over time there almost certainly had been some private institutional innovation; and, thus, in the long run at least, it is highly likely that the subsidized government loans did, in fact, "crowd out" economically more productive investments. Given the attitude of domestic savers, there was little economic incentive to design and innovate a new private institutional structure. It is not that the government guessed wrong, it is simply that vote maximization is not equivalent to income maximization.

7-7. Asymmetric information and institutional innovation: whose signals do you trust?

Financial institutions can help overcome informational asymmetries, make it easier to monitor business firms operating outside the saver's immediate ken, and reduce the level of the saver's uncertainty discounts. The second-generation Anglo-American investment banks were originally established to monitor American rails for British merchant banks and, indirectly, for British savers who were highly uncertain about the American enterprises. By and large, they were successful. Moreover, those second-generation banks soon emerged as major players in the domestic financial structure. The American economic landscape would have been much different had it not been for the contributions of investment banks like J.P. Morgan in New York or Kidder Peabody in Boston. To the north, the Canadian bond houses played a similar and equally productive role, although they were slower to develop and the order of their impact on the mobilization problem was

by 1914, the ratio was 55 percent. Drummond, *Capital Markets in Australia and Canada*, pp. 86–90, table 5, p. 89. Merrett, "Capital Formation and Capital Markets," p. 10.

[1472] A small market for industrials had emerged in both Melbourne and Sydney, "but the list grew slowly before WWI as Australian businesses were slow to incorporate and even slower to take advantage of listing on an exchange to raise new equity. Firms continued to finance their day-to-day operations and their longer term expansion using a combination of their own financial resources and short term debt from banks and trade creditors." Merrett, "Capital Formation and Capital Markets," p. 4.

reversed: They first mobilized domestic and then foreign savings. Their imprimatur of quality convinced domestic savers that the pieces of symbolic capital they offered (originally the bonds of western cities and later the debentures of commercial and industrial firms) were safe, but only later was the quality signal accepted by British savers. Despite the delay, those signals played an important role in motivating the massive transfers of private capital from Britain to Canada during the wheat boom years.[1473] Similarly, Canadian chartered banks gained an extra level of cachet with British savers when, in January 1893, the Dominion government replaced the combine of Glyn, Mills, Currie & Co. and Baring Brothers with the Bank of Montreal as their fiscal agents in London. All innovations were not, however, equally successful, as the Australian experience underscored. In the short run the implementation of the policy that shifted the colonies' fiscal agents from domestic to British banks was successful. In the longer term, however, it weakened the reputational signals attached to the Australian banks in Britain; and it certainly weakened the Australian depositors' perception of the British depositors' view of those signals: In the minds of the Australians, it increased the likelihood that British deposits would be withdrawn at the first sign of trouble. That fear, in turn, helped precipitate the domestic runs on Australian banks in 1892 and 1893, and, thus, it contributed in a major way to the near-collapse of the Australian financial structure. Moreover, it left private Australian firms with few institutional links to the British capital market.

Signals can also transmit false or misleading information. English and Scottish savers had learned that you can insure out from under risk, and they thought that they understood the riskiness of Australian trading banks and land mortgage companies. They were certainly more than familiar with the distribution of returns from their domestic counterparts. Australian entrepreneurs were anxious to attract British capital. They attempted to package their proposals in manners that were familiar to the British saver, and they attempted to disguise uncertain as

---

[1473] Between 1905 and 1914 net capital inflows to Canada as a percentage of GNP ranged from a low of 5.1 percent to a high of 17.5 percent and averaged 10.7 percent. M.C. Urquhart, *Gross National Product, Canada, 1870–1926: The Derivation of the Estimates* (Kingston: McGill-Queen's University Press, 1993), table 1.1, pp. 11–15, table 1.4, pp. 19–23. [Hereafter cited as Urquhart, *Gross National Product, Canada.*] Moreover, to the extent that the data from "capital created and called" on the London market reflect the composition of the new investment, more than one-fifth (21.2%) was directed toward the Manufacturing and Commercial (8.9%), the Financial (1.0%), the Agricultural and Extractive (7.3%), and the Public Utility (4.0%) sectors, while transport drew 60.1% and the Governments 18.7%. Davis–Gallman Tape.

risky alternatives. In the case of banks, British savers were very familiar with the policies of British banks, banks committed to the real bills doctrine and banks that had, at least by American and Canadian standards, a history of relative safety. They assumed that Australian banks were similar; some were, after all, British owned, and many had branches in London. The Australians did nothing to disabuse them of that conclusion. For example, before William Clarke established a London office of the Australian Freehold Banking Corporation Ltd. (a firm formed in 1879 to take over the assets of the Australian Mutual Building Society), he insisted that the firm be reincorporated as the Standard Bank of Australia. He argued that "anything suggestive of land speculation was unacceptable in the British market."[1474] The British savers thought they were depositing their funds in a commercial, not a mortgage, bank. It wasn't; not surprisingly, the Standard Bank was one of the first to fail in the crisis of the 1890s.[1475] Although Clarke's imaginative innovation was somewhat atypical, Australian bankers normally assisted the educational process – a process designed to convert uncertainty into risk in the minds of investors – in two ways. "First, general managers and their representatives visited cities known to yield deposits, advertising their records of sound management. Knowledge of the 'successful management of Australian banks', reported the *AIBR*, on November 16, 1889, 'has successfully contributed to their popularity.' Evidence of successful management was seen to be the absence of failures." Second, the bankers attempted to further reduce uncertainty by interposing identifiable local bankers between lenders and distant projects. "Australian bankers paid commissions directly into the pockets of Scottish bank managers."[1476]

In the case of both Australian banks and finance companies, those firms attempted, first, to provide savers with recognized signals of quality in order to minimize uncertainty and, second, to tailor their offerings to the British experience in order to mask uncertainty as risk. On the one hand, the firms were well known; and they employed well-connected local solicitors and accountants to act – for a fee – as their agents.[1477] On

---

[1474] Entry for Clarke, William, in the *Australian Dictionary of Biography* (Carlton, Victoria: Melbourne University Press, various years), Vol. 3, pp. 419–20.

[1475] It suspended in December 1891, briefly re-opened in May 1892, only to close finally in April 1893.

[1476] Pope, "Bankers and Banking Business, 1860–1914," Australian National University Working Papers in Economic History, No. 85, September 1987.

[1477] "Australian and Anglo-Australian banks were respected and prominent institutions whose business included the managing of government accounts, the financing of trade and investing in pastoral property. The finance companies, many of them, which are still, today, prominent Australian wool-houses, were trading,

the other hand, "the deposit receipt, the instrument of borrowing by Australian banks, was the same type of security issued by Scottish banks and, frequently, by Scottish property companies. The maturing debentures issued by Australian finance companies were similar in form to the debentures issued by Scottish investment trusts, and the capital structure of these two types of companies was similar."[1478] The British investors thought they were buying into risky situations; time proved that they were placing their accumulations in very uncertain alternatives.

If there is a lesson in institutional design to be learned from the American, Canadian, and Australian examples, it is probably the following: Your agents certainly require careful monitoring, but their incentives are probably at least somewhat aligned with yours. Their agents, however, are very unlikely to have their incentives aligned with yours and more than likely to have them aligned with those of their principals.

7-8. The political response to foreign investment

Imported capital can produce benefits to the receiving country, but it may also lead to increased competition for domestic businesses and for domestic businessmen. To the extent that businessmen have a voice in the local political process, they may turn to political solutions to the problems raised by the unwanted and, in their view, certainly unwarranted competition. The histories of the four countries provide a spectrum of political responses to capital imports, and they underscore the relationship between the form of the transfer and the intensity of the response. The status of Australia and Canada within the British Empire did, of course, provide some legal constraints on the level of potential political response.

Australia stands at one end of the spectrum. On that continent there is little evidence of any adverse response to the importation of British capital. Over the years 1870–1914 government bonds represented just less than three-quarters of the Australian capital created and called on the British capital market, and the government sector accounted for 45 percent of all new fixed capital formation.[1479] With the exception of

---

financial and lending institutions that handled the multifarious financial aspects of the Australian pastoral industry." Bailey, "Australian Borrowing in Scotland in the Nineteenth Century," pp. 269, 271–72.

[1478] Bailey, "Australian Borrowing in Scotland in the Nineteenth Century," pp. 271–72.

[1479] Government bonds represented 74.3 percent of the capital created and called on the British market. Davis-Gallman Tape. The figure for the government's proportion of all fixed capital formation was £634.1 million out of £1.4026 billion, or 45.2 percent. N. Butlin, *Australian Domestic Product*, tables 4 and 5, pp. 16–19.

Western Australia, the six colonies had been granted representative government before 1860. Thus, the distribution of the lion's share of foreign capital was in the hands of the elected representatives of the Australian voters. While the economic productivity of some of the government expenditures may be questioned, there is no reason to believe that they were directed towards enterprises of which the voters disapproved.

Only a tiny fraction of the long-term non-governmental transfers represented either traditional direct investment or investment in freestanding companies. Most went to Australian companies, and a large fraction was channeled through Australian intermediaries. In the 1880s British capital flowed into investments designed to improve sheep runs and to produce urban housing. The runs and the land development companies were not operated by foreign nationals in competition with Australian citizens; they were Australian owned and operated. There were British-owned imperial banks, but few Australians viewed them as foreign. Their loans went to Australian enterprise, even if a majority of their capital came from abroad; and it was almost impossible to distinguish their behavior from that of their Australian competitors. The same was true for the few British-chartered pastoral firms. In the case of both the imperial and domestic banks, in 1892 it was the Australian depositors, operating on the basis of local information, who triggered the crisis of 1892–93 by withdrawing their deposits before the British time deposits became due and left the British depositors holding the bag. It was also largely Australians who later purchased the British deposit receipts and preferred shares – the products of the post-crisis reorganizations – at deep discounts. There was little room for Australian complaints on those scores.

The story was similar for the British capital that financed urban residential construction. The mortgage banks and land development companies that intermediated the flow were Australian; the construction was undertaken by Australian domestic firms; and the final owners were residents of Adelaide, Brisbane, Melbourne, and Sydney. In a similar fashion, although Western Australian mining enterprises were often organized as free-standing companies, the mining claims had almost all been sold to the British entrepreneurs by the original Australian owners. It should, perhaps, surprise no one that, while a few mines paid very handsome dividends, most returned little or nothing to the British investors.[1480] In the case of British investment in the commercial banks,

---

[1480] In the case of the Western Australian gold boom of the late 1890s and first decade of the twentieth century, the seven Koolgardie companies and the two on the Murchison all paid over £1 million in dividends. Dividends from West's [WA] Mines, alone, exceeded £2 million in 1899 and again in the three years 1903–5.

in building and loan societies and mortgage banks, in the Western Australian gold mines, and in the pastoral finance companies, there was little reason for the Australians to resent the presence of foreign capital. In fact, their reaction was almost certainly just the opposite: If someone wants to give you something free, take it.

Given the recent level of nationalistic rhetoric directed against foreign, largely American, investment, it might seem surprising that there is little evidence of such feelings among Canadians in the years before 1914.[1481] Until the turn of the century the Canadians received substantially less foreign capital than the Australians. Nonetheless, the flows were large; and they played an important role in Canadian development.[1482]

In the case of British capital, the explanation of the absence of rhetoric or political response lies chiefly in the nature of the investments. In Canada, as in Australia, most of those investments were not very visible. Government issues constituted a much smaller fraction of the total flow of capital in Canada; however, almost 90 percent of the capital imported into the private sector was placed indirectly.[1483] Transport represented about half of the portfolio issues floated in Britain, but most of those railroads were incorporated in Canada, and most were managed by Canadians.[1484] In the remainder of the private sector, "British investors

Through the end of 1915, total dividends from the state's mines exceeded £25 million; however, the riches were not evenly spread. Although the total number of Australian and British mining companies numbered in the thousands, ten mines in the "Golden Mile," a stretch that included the Great Boulder, the Ivanhoe, the Golden Horseshoe, plus the Sons of Gwalia and the Great Finigall, paid 87 percent of all Western Australian mining dividends in the years before 1915. As for the rest, no more than ninety ever paid a single dividend, "and some of those paid only one and some had no right to pay even that." Geoffrey Blainey, *The Rush That Never Ended: A History of Australian Mining* (Parkville, Victoria: Melbourne University Press, 1963), p. 207.

[1481] For an example of recent anti-American rhetoric, see Kari Levitt, *Silent Surrender: The American Economic Empire in Canada* (New York: Liveright, 1970).

[1482] Between 1870 and 1900 the current account deficit amounted, on average, to about 43 percent of Gross Domestic Capital Formation. Urquart, *Gross National Product, Canada*, pp. 16, 17, 19–22, 25. In terms of capital created and called in Britain, over the years 1865–99, the annual per capita figure for Canada was $3.99. The comparative figure for Australia was $12.47.

[1483] Donald G. Paterson, *British Direct Investment in Canada*, p. 9. Jacob Viner, *Canada's Balance of International Indebtedness, 1900–1913* (Cambridge, Mass.: Harvard University Press, 1924), p. 28.

[1484] The major exception was the Grand Trunk, a railroad that was initially supervised by two boards of directors, one in London and one in Canada. It was built by the British firm of Brassy, Peto, Jackson and Betts, a firm that had built nearly

had long been content to assume a conservative role – ordinarily they did not actually establish branches of British companies, nor did they incorporate the Canadian businesses in which they invested as British firms administered from London. . . . In other words, British investors purchased securities of Canadian companies that Canadian management operated from head offices in Montreal or Toronto."[1485]

Given the long-standing Canadian fear of American territorial expansion, the Canadian response to American investments is somewhat more difficult to explain. Although far less important than the British transfers, American investment became a factor in the 1870s, and it accounted for nearly one-quarter of all foreign investment by 1914.[1486]

Moreover, those capital flows were largely direct.[1487] In 1913, for example, American investments in Canada totaled almost $600 million. Of that sum, branches of American firms established to operate behind the Canadian tariff barriers represented just less than one-quarter; American-owned land-related enterprises (lumber and paper mills and timber, mines, and land development companies) in British Columbia and the prairies constituted something more than 40 percent.[1488]

one-third of the English railways of the period. In 1862 "the railroad was completely reorganized, at which time the anxious British bondholders not only tried to secure some voting power but also effected the transfer of its headquarters from Canada to London in an attempt to increase their influence." Even in this case, however, it was the Canadians who managed to effect a transfer of rents from British investors to Canadian businessmen. A special report in 1860 "unveiled the degree to which the line had been deliberately mismanaged by its Canadian board and illegal and ruinously expensive arrangements with other Canadian companies undertaken." W. Kaye Lamb, *History of the Canadian Pacific Railway* (New York: Macmillan Publishing Company, 1977), pp. 3–4. Naylor, *The Banks and Finance Capital*, pp. 24, 26.

[1485] Carl E. Solberg, *The Prairies and the Pampas: Agrarian Policy in Canada and Argentina, 1880–1930* (Stanford, Calif.: Stanford University Press, 1987), p. 38. [Hereafter cited as Solberg, *The Prairies and the Pampas*.]

[1486] Knox puts total foreign investment in Canada in 1914 at $3.8369 billion, of which $2.7785 billion (72.4%) was British, $880.7 million (23.0%) was American, and $177.7 million (4.6%) was from the rest of the world. Frank A. Knox, "*Excursus*: Canadian Capital Movements and the Canadian Balance of International Payments, 1900–1934," in Herbert Marshall, Frank A. Southard, Jr., and Kenneth W. Taylor, *Canadian-American Industry: A Study in International Investment*, for the Carnegie Endowment for International Peace: Division of Economics and History (New Haven & Toronto: Yale University Press and Ryerson Press, 1936), p. 299. [Hereafter cited as Knox, "Excursus."]

[1487] Such transfers are estimated to have constituted almost 85 percent of the American total in 1897, and they still accounted for more than 70 percent in 1914. Lewis, *America's Stake*, pp. 577–606.

[1488] Lewis, *America's Stake*, p. 611.

It is hardly surprising that the Canadians did not object to the American investments in manufacturing; the tariff barriers had, after all, been erected to encourage such investments. Similarly, Canadian miners, like their Australian and American counterparts, may well have been delighted at the prospect of selling their claims to foreigners at insider prices.[1489] Still the question remains: Why didn't the funds channeled into British Columbia timber lands – in 1909, it was estimated that 90 percent of the available timberland in that province was controlled by Americans or American companies – or into land development in British Columbia and the prairies trigger a political response similar to that witnessed in the American West and Midwest?[1490]

The explanation is not clear, but it probably has at least three components. First, Canadian savings rates averaged about 10 percent in the years between 1870 and 1896; in contrast, the figure for the United States was nearly twice that high. Those were years in which the annual growth rate of Canadian real GNP per capita was only 1.06 percent.[1491] Given the relatively low level of domestic savings, foreign capital inflows were required to promote growth. Although these facts may not have been known to the man in the street, Canadian politicians were almost certainly well aware of them. As a result, foreign capital may have been viewed more favorably in Canada, where it was a near necessity, than in the United States, where it represented only a sometimes welcome luxury. Second, in western Canada, it may not have been clear that foreign capital was really foreign. Western Canada was sorely under-populated, and American immigrants to British Columbia and the Prairies had been welcomed with open arms. As late as 1911 at least one in seven (and perhaps as many as one in five) of the residents had been born in the United States, and a substantial fraction of the native-born were direct descendants of earlier American immigrants. Thus, while a

---

[1489] In 1894 three British Columbian miners "went over the mountain" on their day off and discovered four gold mines. Upon their return, they gave their claim on one to the owner of the road house in return for the $25 needed to file their claims. The mine was the Le Roi, which, in 1899, was described as "one of the best in the world." It was soon sold to American investors at a healthy profit. J.U. Curle, *Gold Mines of the World* (London: Waterlow and Sons, 1896), p. 264.

[1490] Fred W. Field, *Capital Investments in Canada: Some Facts and Figures Respecting One of the Most Attractive Investment Fields in the World* (Montreal: Monetary Times of Canada, 1914), p. 21. Lewis, *America's Stake*, p. 278. Mira Wilkins, *The Emergence of Multinational Enterprise: American Business Abroad from the Colonial Era to 1914* (Cambridge, Mass.: Harvard University Press, 1970), p. 138.

[1491] Urquhart, *Gross National Product, Canada*, table 1.6, pp. 24–25.

majority of Canadians – particularly those living in the East – feared American expansion, western Canadians may well have taken a more sanguine view of their neighbor's intentions. Finally, throughout the nineteenth century, Canadian policy was directed toward maintaining a balancing act between threats of domination by the British and by the Americans; "the competing pulls of the United States and Great Britain provided opportunities for channeling external pressures in directions congenial to Canadian goals."[1492] In the more recent past, as the threat of British dominance declined, as the importance of American investment increased, as American immigrants came to represent a smaller fraction of the population, and as the geographic focus of American investment shifted eastward, the level of anti-American rhetoric has increased substantially.[1493]

In Australia there were few rhetorical attacks on foreign capital. In Canada such rhetoric did not become common until well into the twentieth century, and in neither country did the rhetoric produce a strong political response. In Argentina the anti-British attacks were almost as vigorous as they were in the United States, but in the years leading up to World War I the political response was muted. British investment in Argentina was primarily direct; the major British businesses were incorporated in the United Kingdom and administered by British boards of directors. As a result, in Argentina British capital was very visible and much more open to nationalistic attack.[1494]

For example, consider the conflict between the British-owned and -managed London and River Plate Bank and the domestic bankers and the Province of Santa Fe. The bank opened a branch in Rosario and quickly came into sharp competition for deposits with the local domestic banks. As their deposits declined, the local banks began to experience pressure on their reserves. Appeals for assistance fell on the deaf ears of the manager of the British bank. Pushed by the local bankers, the Provincial government brought pressure to bear by, first, taking away the British bank's note-issuing privileges and, then, as part of a proposed liquidation of the bank, by confiscating the bank's gold reserves. Eventually, a compromise solution was reached, but not before trade in the Province was disrupted. That disruption, in turn, raised the "possibility that a des-

---

[1492] Hugh G.J. Aitken, *American Capital and Canadian Resources* (Cambridge, Mass.: Harvard University Press, 1961), p. 130.

[1493] In 1900 American investment represented 14 percent of all foreign capital invested in Canada; in 1915 the fraction was 27 percent; and in 1930 it was 59 percent. Knox, *Excursus*, p. 299.

[1494] Solberg, *The Prairies and the Pampas*, p. 38.

perate treasury would be called upon to honor its railway guarantees to the British stockholders."[1495]

The largest fraction of British investment was in railroads, and three problems existed. First, customers believed that their interests were not considered. In part these criticisms reflected populist arguments about monopoly profits and external control. In part they were directed to the storage facilities provided by the railroads; wheat farmers complained that the grain was not protected from the weather while awaiting shipment. Second, most of the British railroads had government guarantees that assured the owners dividends of 7 or 8 percent. The Argentine critics argued that the British management did not have to be efficient to be profitable; if there were no profits, the government would pay. Third, the network had been built piecemeal, and it included both wide gauge and narrow gauge sections. The Argentine users felt that it was not designed to operate as an efficient system. Outside of the railroads, since British firms were often in direct competition with Argentine businesses, and, because they tended to limit their choice of suppliers and sales agents to other British firms, there was little love lost between the British and Argentinean commercial communities.

In the cities resentment against both foreign investors and the liberal economic system developed shortly after external capital began to flow into the country. "Criticisms were levied first against specific features of that system, but gradually spread to a general condemnation of British-Argentine ties. Railroads, meat-packing plants, and public utilities were accused of making exorbitant profits by taking advantage of monopolistic or oligopolistic power"; "and agitation for a congressional investigation became acute every time the meat trade became depressed."[1496]

To some extent, the political response to these conflicts was muted by the continuing industrial cleavage between native Argentineans and European immigrants. The majority of the Argentine elites, the citizens who held the bulk of political power, remained on the land. Many of the remainder were well-to-do merchants in Buenos Aires. Those merchants had gotten their start in financing the movement of farm products, particularly wheat, from the pampas to the ports. They also had landed interests – sugar growing and processing, for example – and many owned ranches as well. Both groups enjoyed the benefits of complementary

---

[1495] David Joslin, *A Century of Banking in Latin America* (London: Oxford University Press, 1963), pp. 43–50.

[1496] Carlos F. Díaz Alejandro, *Essays on the Economic History of the Argentine Republic* (New Haven: Yale University Press, 1970), p. 60. [Hereafter cited as Díaz Alejandro, *Essays on the Economic History of the Argentine Republic*.]

British capital. Thus, although there were divisions among the landed and mercantile elite that ran the country, there was no fundamental difference with respect to economic policy. All factions favored immigration, foreign investment, and the export economy.

Outside of agriculture and agriculturally related commercial enterprises, the majority of the nation's commerce and industry – enterprises that faced both competitive British capital and British imports – remained largely in the hands of immigrants.[1497] The immigrant industrialists were on the whole small operators who built their firms on the basis of a skill; baking, tailoring, shoemaking were all immigrant bastions. Compared with Canada and the United States, most Argentine industrial firms operated on a relatively small scale; but, like their counterparts to the north, they produced goods for the domestic market. Their economic interests were by no means identical with those of the elite. The immigrants could complain, but, as late as 1912, they still commanded little political power, since only the native-born could vote. It is hardly surprising that over time they became the source of both reformist and radical sentiments, sentiments that were ultimately to have an impact on the flows of foreign capital. In 1912 the government attempted to co-opt the middle class industrial entrepreneurs by changing the voting laws to permit immigrants to vote and by attempting to control the fraud that usually marked Argentine elections. History suggests that, in the long run, the policies may not have proved effective; but the political system did remain stable for at least a few more years.[1498]

There was some political response, but the rising volume of criticism was not translated into political action until much later. The British-owned railways, for example, were extremely powerful, both economically and politically. "Because Argentine governments traditionally had attempted to attract foreign investment, the railroads long received favorable official treatment. The Conservative administrations that controlled Argentine politics until 1916 believed that the British railways were fundamental to Argentine prosperity and growth, and that their interests must be respected." Such respect was written into law in 1907. The law exempted the railroads from import duties as well as from state

---

[1497] For example, in 1895, only 19 percent of industrial establishments were owned by native born Argentineans; as late as 1935 the figure was only 39 percent. Díaz Alejandro, *Essays on the Economic History of the Argentine Republic*, pp. 214–15. See also Chapter 6.

[1498] David Rock, *Politics in Argentina, 1890–1930* (Cambridge: Cambridge University Press, 1975), chapters 1–4. Among other reforms the secret ballot was introduced.

and city taxes. It limited federal taxes to 3 percent of the net income of the railroads, required that those levies be used only for further railroad construction, and largely precluded future effective rate regulation.[1499] The legislation aroused a storm of controversy, but it was more than two decades before the sons and daughters of the immigrant merchants and industrialists gained effective political power.

If Australia occupied one end, the United States represented the other end of the spectrum of political reaction. In the United States the response was initially rhetorical; but it soon was translated into effective political action. Over most of the nineteenth century there had been a general recognition that foreign investment made a substantial contribution to economic growth. In the words of the financial editor of the *New York Evening Mail* in 1907, "Without the accumulated and unemployed pound sterling of the Englishman, the francs of the Frenchman, the Belgians, and the Swiss, the gilders of the Dutchman and the marks of the German, the material progress that has been the lot of the United States ever since the close of the Civil War could not continue."[1500]

As long as the capital was channeled through American firms, most of the complaints appeared to be arise on the other side of the ocean. Despite the intermediating presence of the American investment banks, until the 1880s, the problems of monitoring and asymmetric information had not been completely solved. As British investment shifted westward and toward land developing enterprises, those problems intensified. In response, British savers began to seek alternative channels that were not American controlled. The free-standing company became the British institution of choice. The free-standing company, however, was hardly considered the institution of choice by potential American competitors. Unlike their Argentinean counterparts, a substantial fraction of the businessmen confronted by direct foreign competition were farmers and ranchers. For them, foreign investment was competitive not complementary; and, like the Argentine ranchers, they did have a strong voice in the political process. British investments in railroads or government debt had raised few American objections. Such investments were largely impersonal, and they were subject to the same general economic influences that affected domestic investors. Furthermore, the decisions of the borrowers reflected American concerns, not the preferences of foreign owners. Between 1870 and 1890, however, British investment in the trans-Mississippi West "consisted much more of enterprises that

---

[1499] Solberg, *The Prairie and the Pampas*, pp. 120–21.

[1500] Quoted in Charles F. Speare, "Selling American Bonds in Europe," *Annals of the American Academy of Political and Social Science*, Vol. 30 (1907), p. 269.

made western development bend to British purpose and interest."[1501]
Despite the fact that both mining and manufacturing were the recipients
of substantial British investment, aside from a demand that foreign
capital not be given any special treatment, there was little evidence of
complaint from either western miners or from the western industrial and
commercial firms engaged in processing and marketing agricultural
products.[1502]

The reaction from western and Midwestern farmers and ranchers was,
however, much different. They found themselves in direct competition
with foreign investors for western lands. As a group they were almost
unanimous, and they were certainly vociferous in their complaints about
British direct investment. "A passionate, hitherto unmatched fury
mounted against foreign investment in the United States." The reaction
was so intense that in 1892 the partners in an American law firm doubted
that a British client could obtain fair treatment in the Illinois courts,
because "of the prejudices of the West against English capital."[1503] Unlike
the complaints of the Argentine business community, those accusations
were soon translated into political action. At the federal level, in March
1887 a bill forbidding "any absentee alien, or resident alien who had not
declared their intention of becoming a citizen, to gain possession in the
future of real property in the territories, except property acquired by
inheritance or through the collection of debts previously contracted"
and, in addition, requiring that "at least four-fifths of the stock of any
corporation thereafter acquiring real estate in the territories had to be
held by citizens" was passed by both houses of Congress and signed into

[1501] Roger V. Clements, "British Controlled Enterprise in the West Between 1870
and 1890, and Some Agrarian Reactions," *Agricultural History*, Vol. 27, No. 4
(October 1953), p. 135.

[1502] In the mining regions there was a widespread belief "that foreign investors in
mines in the territories had 'facilitated the development of the country, enabled
farmers to find a market, and all industries to prosper.'" As a result, "although
Colorado passed a law prohibiting alien ownership of property, mineral lands
were excluded (the law itself was soon repealed), and in Montana, Idaho, and
Utah, among the strongest arguments for statehood was the claim that the new
political regime would make it possible to abolish the ownership restrictions
imposed by the federal law of 1887." Wilkins, *Foreign Investment*, p. 158. For a
thorough discussion of the position of the mining states and territories see Roger
V. Clements, "British Investment and American Legislative Restrictions in the
Trans-Mississippi West, 1880–1900," *Mississippi Valley Historical Review*, Vol. 42
(October 1955), pp. 207–27.

[1503] Wilkins, *Foreign Investment*, p. 566. Letter of April 17, 1892, cited in Robert
T. Swaine, *The Cravath Firm and Its Predecessors*, 2 vols. (New York:
Privately Printed, 1946), Vol. I, p. 467. This issue was related to the Chicago
stockyard.

law.[1504] Beginning with Indiana, similar laws were passed by the majority of the western and Midwestern states; and by 1900 thirty of the forty-five states had passed laws that in some way restricted alien ownership of land. "The laws in Nebraska, Missouri, Oklahoma, Texas, Iowa, and Washington were the most stringent; but anti-foreign feelings were so intense that voters in both California and Kansas demanded that their state's constitution be amended to remove long standing guarantees of property rights."[1505] The histories of the four countries contain at least two lessons of interest to twentieth-century policy makers. First, indirect investment is unlikely to trigger any serious complaints by the residents of the receiving countries; however, because of the problem of asymmetric information and because of the difficulty of monitoring business decisions, such investments often appear highly uncertain to the overseas saver. Attempts to overcome informational and monitoring problems by the exercise of control through the innovation of directly controlled organizational structures (the free-standing company, for example) are, however, likely to raise different, but equally important, issues. In the nineteenth century such organizational innovations proved a failure in the American farming and ranching sectors, and the recent experience of ENCOR with the state government of Maharashtra suggests that the world has not yet changed completely.

Second, investments are less likely to induce a political response, if the interests of the overseas savers are aligned with those who exercise political power in the receiving country. One must recognize, however, that today's ins may become tomorrow's outs. Only time will tell if joint ventures between foreign investors and the governments of the receiving companies – between U.S. corporations and the People's Republic of China, for example – will solve the informational and monitoring problems without inducing political repercussions or rent-seeking behavior on the part of those who hold a monopoly of political power.

7-9. **Conclusions**

This exercise in natural experimentation has produced some suggestive insights into the process of institutional change. To a significant extent, Douglass North's initial conclusions that "the economies of scope, complementarities, and network externalities of an institutional

---

[1504] *Statutes at Large of the United States*, Vol. XXIV (1887), 476–77.

[1505] Davis and Cull, *International Capital Markets*, p. 52. Although there may have been some way for foreigners to exploit loopholes, there is little evidence that such evasions were important. Certainly the position of Japanese farmers in California during World War II suggests that it was not easy to distinguish ownership by noncitizens, even for long-standing legal residents.

matrix make institutional change overwhelmingly incremental and path dependent" have been confirmed. The exercise has added some additional twists to that conclusion, and it has also, hopefully, substantially expanded the scope of our knowledge.

The history of capital market development underscores the path dependency and incremental nature of institutional evolution, but it also suggests that the logical argument underpinning the conclusion may be more complex than originally thought. First, the evidence indicates that – at least in the case of private institutions – institutional innovation was often the product of a process of invention, initial innovation, modification, and re-innovation, with the last two steps often repeated several times. That process, since it was seldom repeated in two different environments, may provide a large part of the explanation for the path dependency observed by North. Two examples stand out. In the case of the Australian trading and the Canadian chartered banks, initially both countries imported the Scottish-based British system almost intact. That system had two important characteristics: It permitted branch banking, and it was based on the real bills doctrine. In Canada the restrictions against long-term lending were legally enshrined in the Banking Act of 1871.[1506] Although the system of nationwide branches dominated by a very few banks only gradually emerged, Canadian banks, restricted to the short-term market, never found it profitable to turn to Britain as a source of funds. British savers were never involved directly with the portfolio decisions of the chartered banks, and bank failures had little impact on British investment in the Dominion. At the same time profit opportunities in the long-term market promoted the growth of mortgage banks and insurance companies. In Australia, through both legal and extra-legal means, the original legal restrictions on long-term lending gradually eroded; by the 1880s the trading banks had moved heavily into mortgage finance. To support that activity they turned increasingly to British savers, but the fallout from the banking collapse of the 1890s destroyed the international link. The banks that emerged in the early years of the twentieth century were very different from those that had entered the 1890s. Until some institutional substitutes emerged – and that process took decades – the Australian economy suffered while the Canadian economy boomed.

A similar pattern of invention, innovation, modification, and re-innovation characterizes the history of investment banking in the United States. The first-generation British merchant banks wanted to invest in American railroads but were faced by severe problems of asymmetric

---

[1506] 34 Vic. cap 5.

information and moral hazard. To solve those problems they established relations with second-generation American investment banks, and over time those banks used the reputations they earned from their trans-Atlantic associations to become dominant players in the domestic market for American railroad bonds. Their success attracted third-generation competitors, firms that, while no more than fringe competitors in the domestic market for railroad bonds, quickly became the established leaders in the mobilization of domestic savings for investment in commerce and industry in the United States. The entire process from British merchant to American third-generation investment banks, however, spanned half a century.

Second, the evidence clearly indicates that the process of innovation can be speeded up if, instead of requiring the invention and innovation of a new institution, an existing institution can be modified to serve a new purpose. The emergence of the Canadian bond house, for example, was made much simpler by earlier developments. The chartered banks had conducted a bond business at least since Confederation, and Montreal and Toronto brokers had begun buying and selling government bonds in large blocks soon thereafter. It was, therefore, at least by the standards of institutional invention and innovation, a relatively simple step to consolidate those activities in a formal bond house linked to, and provided with financial support by, one of the large financial groups. In fact, Ian Drummond concluded that "to handle the flood of municipal debentures no institutional innovation was required – merely an enormous expansion of the existing institutional framework for long term municipal borrowing."[1507] Despite Drummond's conclusion – a conclusion almost certainly influenced by the relatively short chronological focus of his study – the new institution was very different from the structure it replaced; but the speed with which the substitution was made (in less than two decades) was, in large part, a function of the fact that both bond brokers and the financial groups had been in existence before the mid-1880s. Similarly, the fact that, in the eighteenth century, Scottish banks that had access to largely unrestricted supplies of capital and were legally allowed to operate branch networks provided a model that made it relatively easier for the British Parliament, in response to the banking crisis of 1825, to write and legislate the Joint-Stock Bank Act of 1826.[1508] Although the growth of banks with nationwide branch networks was

---

[1507] Drummond, *Capital Markets in Australia and Canada*, p. 152.
[1508] In Scotland there were three public joint-stock banks, and there was no restriction on the number of partners that a private bank could have. Collins, *Money and Banking*, pp. 10, 13.

slow, no longer was a bank limited to the financial resources that could be provided by a maximum of six partners.

Across the oceans, in both Canada and Australia, the Scottish banking system (with British innovations) was imported largely intact. In the United States, however, the Revolution had occurred a half century before the Banking Act, and by the 1830s the model appears to have provided little guide for American policy makers. Although largely untethered joint-stock banking had come to New York and Michigan with the free banking legislation of 1838, and to most of the rest of the nation by 1860, American politicians were still debating the desirability of nationwide branch networks in the 1990s.

Finally, although the evolution of institutions does generally appear to have been incremental, the same cannot be said for their destruction. One lesson is obvious from the Australian experience: Even a well-functioning institutional structure can prove very fragile in the face of a sudden regime change. The fallout from the crisis of the 1890s almost totally severed the private financial links between Britain and the six colonies, links that had accounted for a substantial portion of capital formation over the previous decades. In addition, it engendered a substantial level of distrust of the existing private financial structure among domestic savers, and it caused them to redirect their accumulations toward governmental institutions.

In a similar vein, although it has been argued by some that economic crisis or skullduggery and scandal often trigger rapid institutional change, the evidence suggests a somewhat different story. If the substitution of the government for private enterprise in the Australian mortgage market after the debacle of the 1890s or the legislation passed in the United States in response to the British innovation of the free-standing company can be generalized, it appears that the new institutions that emerge in the short run seldom represent long-run equilibria. One path may be broken, but it takes time to discover a new relatively efficient path.

As North has indicated, economies of scope also played an important role in the evolution of the financial markets in both Britain and in the four frontier countries. The institutional structure supporting the market for inland bills in the United Kingdom substantially reduced the costs of operating a market for foreign bills of exchange. The development of that market, in turn, assured Britain of a central position in the world capital market in the pre–World War I era. The signals provided by American investment banks reassured domestic savers about the quality of some pieces of symbolic capital. Their willingness to hold such pieces of paper, in turn, made it possible for the New York Stock Exchange to provide a highly efficient secondary market for a wide range of thoroughly vetted securities; and the existence of that market made it possible for the nation's life insurance companies to hold substantial blocks of private stocks and bonds in their investment portfolios. In Canada the bond houses alone played the role of both the investment banks and the New York Stock Exchange, but the effect on the portfolio decisions of the management of that nation's life insurance companies was much the same. In Australia and Argentina the story was very different. In a similar fashion the fact that each of the Australian states had long operated government savings banks made it possible for those same state governments to generate the funds needed to organize and operate the government mortgage banks in the years after 1900. Given that there had been no savings bank failures, their reputations had not been jeopardized. It was a simple matter for them to direct the suddenly greatly increased flow of deposits into the new government-owned mortgage banks.

The study has also underscored some issues that North has not directly emphasized. First, it has pointed up the need for institutional innovation to overcome asymmetric information and potential moral hazard. In particular, it has demonstrated the need for savers to be able to distinguish between risk and uncertainty and to be able to assess the quality of the signals provided by the managers of distant enterprises. In addition, it has emphasized the need of principals to monitor the behavior of their agents even when it is not totally clear who the principals are.

British savers thought they were investing in risky alternatives when they chose to put their resources into Australian trading banks and pastoral and mortgage companies. Hardly surprisingly, the Australian companies often made no effort to disabuse them of that idea; in fact, it was not unheard of for those firms to attempt to package their offerings as risky rather than uncertain alternatives. All American railroad securities were not equal, but how was the British saver to discover into which risk class each should be assigned? The innovation of formal financial intermediaries can often help overcome both sets of informational questions, a function performed by British merchant banks, American investment banks, and Canadian bond houses. The imprimatur of a formal securities market with a reputation for carefully vetting their listed securities – a market like the New York Stock Exchange – can also perform a similar function.

The attempts by British firms to sell insurance to depositors in Australian banks, however, suggests that although it may often be true that an intermediary is in a position to capture economies of scale in the acquisition of information and that its managers may be more expert than the average individual in discriminating between risk and uncertainty and in properly assigning particular issues to the appropriate risk classes, that conclusion is not always correct. To the extent that they were honest not fraudulent enterprises, those companies thought they were selling insurance against a risky situation; but they discovered that they were selling insurance against an uncertain one.[1509] The result was unfortunate for both the companies and their clients. If, however, the managers knew they were selling insurance against uninsurable risk, the results were unfortunate only to their clients.

The British savers who purchased the Australian offerings often thought they were operating on the advice of their agents – local bankers and solicitors – but later discovered that those worthies were actually the agents of Australian firms. The early investors in the Canadian Grand Trunk Railway thought that they were investing in a British-chartered and -managed firm, only to discover that the actual operating decisions were being made by the Canadian board whose interests were hardly aligned with those of the savers. In the United States and in Argentina the institutional response to these problems often took the form of reorganization on the basis of a free-standing company; but even that innovation, as the history of many mining enterprises in the American West attests, was no certain guarantee that British investors possessed the same information as American entrepreneurs.

Second, the study suggests something of the nature of political – as opposed to private – institutions. The Australian case provides a particularly powerful example of the impact of the government on the evolution of a capital market. On the one hand, the decisions about the allocation of resources effected by the government decision maker tend to be made on the basis of a political rather than an economic calculus. The Australian nineteenth-century transport network is only one case in point. On the other hand, the fact that the government tax base stands behind the institutions may well mean that non-economic allocation decisions may be rewarded rather than punished. The Australian state savings banks provide a particularly telling example. Moreover, politics can operate even in the absence of government organizations. In the American West agrarian opposition to the competition of British free-standing companies led to the passage of laws that prohibited foreign investment.

[1509] Britain had witnessed financial crises that produced bank failures, but there was nothing in their historical experience that prepared them for the fallout from the Australian crisis of the 1890s.

Finally, the study offers some insights into the nature of legal rules versus private structures, and it raises some questions about both. In the case of a legal rule (the prohibition against branch banking in the United States, for example), the political power of a group may make it possible to prevent, or at least delay, relaxing the legal constraints, even when changes in the economic environment would make such institutional innovations highly productive. Conversely, as in the case of the prohibitions against Australian trading banks making long-term loans, political power can make it possible to revise those rules (either de facto or de jure) even though the reasons for their original imposition have not changed.

In the case of institutions based on voluntary cooperative decisions, there is no reason to expect that a socially efficient institutional arrangement will endure should the private benefits evaporate. The erosion of the position of the London Stock Exchange after 1912 – at that time the world's largest and, internationally, by far the most important – attests to the inherent weaknesses of such arrangements. New insights, perhaps, but it is clear that we still have much to learn about the process of institutional change.

Table 7A.1. *Basic data on capital flows to the four frontier countries*

	Argentina				Australia			
Year	Population (000's)	Real GDP ($000's)	Net capital inflow ($000's)	Capital created & called ($000's)	Population (000's)	Real GDP ($000's)	Net capital inflow ($000's)	Capital created & called ($000's)
1870	1,882			6,291	1,618	485,018	21,428	11,915
1871	1,936			31,393	1,668	467,164	−22,402	6,053
1872	1,989			8,643	1,727	517,154	−20,454	1,817
1873	2,045			4,230	1,785	570,714	27,272	2,020
1874	2,102			15,880	1,844	589,758	13,149	10,875
1875	2,161			2,265	1,902	654,030	17,045	13,395
1876	2,223	234,820		524	1,961	652,245	12,662	27,149
1877	2,287	246,285		0	2,019	679,025	34,577	8,645
1878	2,353	273,461		0	2,078	743,893	38,473	18,146
1879	2,421	265,817		331	2,136	755,200	26,785	41,358
1880	2,492	249,257		1,422	2,195	794,477	−5,357	34,890
1881	2,565	244,161		1,987	2,253	852,203	47,239	28,205
1882	2,639	247,983		19,588	2,345	804,594	71,589	13,025
1883	2,716	312,527		21,122	2,437	923,617	62,336	82,036
1884	2,797	350,318		52,893	2,529	928,973	71,102	68,338
1885	2,880	374,947		18,295	2,621	989,675	114,932	56,914
1886	2,966	439,915		45,742	2,714	1,000,982	106,166	79,612
1887	3,056	441,614		67,246	2,806	1,144,999	70,615	54,844
1888	3,158	471,762		106,939	2,898	1,115,244	102,270	63,761
1889	3,265	547,346		121,042	2,990	1,209,867	98,861	57,648
1890	3,377	600,425		43,027	3,082	1,168,804	102,757	41,915
1891	3,490	550,743		30,938	3,174	1,259,261	57,466	50,064
1892	3,607	521,444		7,899	3,234	1,103,341	36,525	16,736
1893	3,729	622,505		3,178	3,294	1,043,235	−11,201	49,469
1894	3,856	659,448		1,218	3,354	1,079,537	−2,435	31,719
1895	3,956	760,085		477	3,414	1,017,645	19,967	69,028
1896	4,071	842,887		10,615	3,474	1,095,605	31,655	37,972
1897	4,233	932,059		7,721	3,535	1,034,308	34,090	25,385
1898	4,357	756,263		12,445	3,594	1,195,584	62,823	17,733
1899	4,477	819,958		5,788	3,654	1,196,774	−28,733	41,494
1900	4,607	964,756		17,805	3,714	1,266,998	34,577	29,538
1901	4,740	851,380		8,705	3,774	1,230,101	20,454	56,217
1902	4,871	926,539		44,930	3,842	1,241,110	42,369	40,913
1903	4,976	956,263		273,832	3,910	1,311,334	32,142	6,771
1904	5,103	1,138,429		21,558	3,978	1,400,601	−22,889	6,529
1905	5,289	1,326,964		37,110	4,046	1,441,366	−41,882	4,648
1906	5,524	1,554,140		67,203	4,115	1,545,809	−47,726	26,835
1907	5,821	1,537,580		126,248	4,183	1,618,115	−57,953	13,108
1908	6,046	1,503,609		72,602	4,251	1,666,914	−5,357	30,789
1909	6,331	1,768,577		134,541	4,319	1,792,186	−29,220	52,447
1910	6,586	1,903,609		80,043	4,387	1,912,101	−4,870	34,076
1911	6,913	1,981,316		78,157	4,455	1,926,682	−4,383	25,900
1912	7,147	2,048,832		76,069	4,553	1,981,135	59,901	40,490
1913	7,482	2,370,276		72,027	4,651	2,093,016	34,577	130,373
1914	7,996	2,394,055		73,107	4,749	1,927,277	111,523	52,328

Canada				United States			
Population (000's)	Real GNP ($000's)	Net capital inflow ($000's)	Capital created & called ($000's)	Population (000's)	Real GNP ($000's)	Net capital inflow ($000's)	Capital created & called ($000's)
3,625	491,302	−1,611	2,010	39,905	7,171,253	100,000	24,706
3,689	512,582	20,640	6,843	40,938	7,500,193	101,000	262,417
3,754	508,193	5,678	6,682	41,972	7,809,698	242,000	117,039
3,826	555,807	23,031	22,193	43,006	8,205,752	167,000	365,434
3,895	566,314	32,929	44,789	44,040	8,142,000	82,000	81,392
3,954	552,216	18,012	65,706	45,073	8,577,311	87,000	52,898
4,009	517,104	16,339	21,709	46,107	8,680,000	2,000	250,388
4,064	550,221	12,813	15,190	47,141	8,956,828	−57,000	793,772
4,120	531,867	8,882	8,446	48,174	9,331,804	−162,000	14,360
4,185	583,205	12,500	29,987	49,208	10,481,558	−160,000	7,729
4,255	609,007	9,949	5,148	50,262	11,721,121	30,000	55,542
4,325	695,723	23,857	20,482	51,542	12,131,277	−41,000	86,798
4,375	723,254	9,726	11,543	52,821	12,900,576	110,000	65,845
4,430	721,924	12,941	8,294	54,100	13,218,579	51,000	83,951
4,487	783,636	28,979	28,930	55,379	13,471,341	105,000	56,374
4,537	736,820	38,693	46,431	56,658	13,558,109	34,000	21,951
4,580	741,608	32,791	21,559	57,938	13,963,347	137,000	25,185
4,626	767,144	5,887	5,601	59,217	14,600,150	231,000	56,565
4,678	818,881	54,619	64,966	60,496	14,525,100	287,000	99,321
4,729	825,398	21,903	25,354	61,775	15,438,596	202,000	88,011
4,779	875,805	20,133	20,159	63,056	15,667,726	194,000	153,689
4,833	902,538	6,295	11,906	64,361	16,157,342	136,000	107,563
4,883	898,016	18,672	27,072	65,666	16,913,773	41,000	20,278
4,931	885,248	6,297	9,628	66,970	16,914,066	146,000	72,726
4,979	929,537	26,246	22,794	68,275	16,411,255	−66,000	28,430
5,026	926,478	932	2,152	69,580	18,345,742	137,000	102,008
5,074	902,006	−649	3,732	70,885	17,938,979	40,000	31,149
5,122	1,002,820	21,295	15,895	72,189	19,396,667	−23,000	19,722
5,175	1,040,991	11,410	4,572	73,494	19,844,059	−279,000	39,529
5,235	1,134,756	−12,262	3,398	74,799	22,143,367	−229,000	16,352
5,301	1,199,793	28,210	9,109	76,094	22,587,971	−321,000	28,430
5,371	1,301,538	4,462	3,023	77,585	25,348,679	−273,000	36,281
5,494	1,420,706	17,101	18,950	79,160	25,804,132	−82,000	302,092
5,651	1,474,039	46,563	4,835	80,632	26,528,445	−154,000	8,904
5,827	1,498,777	57,941	22,272	82,165	27,556,739	−117,000	131,011
6,002	1,654,520	92,653	62,791	83,820	30,038,000	−94,000	47,006
6,097	1,831,543	93,820	50,158	85,437	31,299,869	22,000	60,729
6,411	1,932,490	91,671	22,037	87,000	30,798,095	35,000	264,165
6,625	1,836,730	84,586	385,939	88,709	29,114,878	−187,000	183,128
6,800	2,021,334	218,778	127,013	90,492	32,516,471	143,000	140,397
6,988	2,200,618	247,958	184,751	92,407	32,660,000	229,000	132,699
7,207	2,353,967	169,085	98,031	93,868	33,704,631	40,000	95,832
7,389	2,532,586	278,050	155,825	95,331	35,645,853	36,000	140,297
7,632	2,631,272	307,651	162,461	97,227	37,038,762	−142,000	210,650
7,869	2,440,284	427,336	197,619	99,118	34,250,000	−72,000	171,636

Table 7A.2. *Estimated assets of selected financial intermediaries (millions of dollars)*

Panel A: United States					
Year	Commercial banks	Savings banks	Building & loan associations	Trust companies	Life insurance companies	Total
1870	1,781	533	131	n.d.	266	2,711
1875	2,308	896	220	n.d.	403	3,827
1880	2,518	882	216	195	418	4,229
1885	3,224	1,203	295	294	525	5,541
1890	4,437	1,743	428	524	771	7,903
1895	5,425	2,054	504	704	1,160	9,847
1900	8,552	2,328	571	1,371	1,742	14,564
1905	13,970	2,969	629	3,730	2,706	24,004
1910	18,734	3,598	932	4,492	3,876	31,632
1914	22,546	4,194	1,358	5,727	4,935	38,760

Panel B: Canada					
Year	Chartered banks	Savings banks	Building societies & mortgage loan companies	Trust companies & fraternal societies	Life insurance companies	Total
1870	103.1	9.8	13.7	13.7	3.4	143.7
1875	173.5	15.3	33.9	33.9	6.9	263.5
1880	160.7	24.7	71.4	71.4	9.8	338.0
1885	207.9	47.9	96.6	96.6	20.5	469.5
1890	246.9	52.2	122.0	123.4	43.1	587.6
1895	296.1	63.2	137.3	140.8	73.2	710.6
1900	437.3	76.9	134.7	143.2	108.7	900.8
1905	700.9	91.0	149.4	167.4	151.9	1,260.6
1910	1,060.4	95.1	193.4	225.8	212.3	1,787.0
1915	1,415.0	99.0	260.0	328.0	364.0	2,466.0

Panel C: Australia					
Year	Trading banks	Savings banks	Building societies & mortgage loan companies	pastoral finance companies	Life insurance companies	Total
1870	206.0	15.6	n.d.	14.0	n.d.	235.6
1875	330.7	24.8	47.7	14.4	14.1	431.7
1880	401.8	30.2	58.4	51.8	22.4	564.6
1885	657.0	51.6	105.7	110.9	41.1	966.3
1890	902.9	71.1	200.2	154.6	70.5	1,399.3
1895	751.0	105.2	67.5	113.7	107.7	1,145.1
1900	725.6	147.6	48.4	95.6	136.9	1,154.1
1905	765.1	186.5	29.3	105.1	175.3	1,261.4
1910	988.1	277.1	21.4	147.7	226.2	1,660.6
1914	1,191.7	427.6	30.7	178.5	305.9	2,134.4

Table 7A.3. *Capital created and called London Stock Exchange, 1865–1914, by industry (government railroad calls in transport) (thousands of dollars)*

Years	Manufacturing, commercial & miscellaneous	Finance	Government	Agriculture & extractive	Transportation	Public utilities	Total
			Panel A: Argentina				
1865–1869	0	2,581	8,711	195	13,295	55	24,837
1870–1874	0	974	47,929	718	16,158	657	66,436
1875–1879	0	0	0	0	3,119	0	3,119
1880–1884	942	0	50,582	5,064	40,058	365	97,011
1885–1889	7,703	1,522	144,381	3,973	182,428	19,256	359,263
1890–1894	1,767	1,218	0	1,094	82,415	497	86,991
1895–1899	73	487	0	137	31,800	4,549	37,046
1900–1904	426	0	16,539	141	353,048	1,935	372,089
1905–1909	871	4,627	41,444	16,371	374,551	3,471	441,335
1910–1914	15,946	7,183	40,240	33,961	298,106	13,107	408,543
1865–1914	27,728	18,592	349,826	61,654	1,394,978	43,892	1,896,670
			Panel B: Australia				
1865–1869	292	0	14,067	5,799	23,947	0	44,105
1870–1874	1,439	0	9,670	1,744	24,323	2,624	39,800
1875–1879	0	6,635	34,837	3,424	62,597	1,011	108,504
1880–1884	799	3,129	61,885	25,741	139,887	1,626	233,067
1885–1889	940	14,650	96,586	39,116	170,298	1,502	323,092
1890–1894	2,623	25,904	64,881	18,364	84,109	774	196,655
1895–1899	8,311	7,386	37,779	104,536	34,542	251	192,805
1900–1904	1,489	347	49,399	37,212	51,593	1,628	141,668
1905–1909	816	6,166	42,867	27,921	49,039	1,040	127,849
1910–1914	1,825	28,005	94,604	25,965	131,465	3,445	285,309
1865–1914	18,534	92,222	506,575	289,822	771,800	13,901	1,692,854

Table 7A.3. (cont.)

Years	Manufacturing, commercial & miscellaneous	Finance	Government	Agriculture & extractive	Transportation	Public utilities	Total
			Panel C: Canada				
1865–1869	0	0	0	180	18,954	0	19,134
1870–1874	2,157	0	31,661	3,757	47,786	0	85,361
1875–1879	0	0	12,286	1,133	127,619	0	141,038
1880–1884	244	0	14,681	12,489	46,984	0	74,398
1885–1889	2,002	1,775	20,271	12,687	126,110	1,066	163,911
1890–1894	554	3,756	11,851	1,845	72,591	1,061	91,658
1895–1899	4,565	0	3,531	6,855	12,273	1,676	28,900
1900–1904	130	0	3,008	6,493	47,483	280	57,394
1905–1909	22,184	1,611	50,148	11,997	317,964	13,455	417,359
1910–1914	85,258	10,531	177,438	77,183	413,112	34,567	798,089
1865–1914	117,094	17,673	324,875	134,619	1,230,876	52,105	1,877,242
			Panel D: United States				
1865–1869	156	3,847	3,615	1,636	49,994	8,961	68,209
1870–1874	16,207	4,869	518,972	27,233	275,338	8,369	850,988
1875–1879	329	331	1,009,952	3,662	93,587	11,285	1,119,146
1880–1884	4,927	21,322	0	31,084	289,908	1,269	348,510
1885–1889	46,816	10,520	39	34,093	190,420	9,145	291,033
1890–1894	51,578	12,791	3,931	45,205	269,022	158	382,685
1895–1899	34,871	3,754	65,006	13,534	89,398	2,196	208,759
1900–1904	6,517	7,549	0	13,765	476,267	2,620	506,718
1905–1909	19,146	3,987	0	28,140	572,260	71,891	695,424
1910–1914	53,087	10,245	2,280	58,433	535,546	91,522	751,113
1865–1914	233,634	79,215	1,603,795	256,785	2,841,740	207,416	5,222,585

Skipping ahead: The evolution of the world's finance markets 1914–1990 – A brief sketch

8-1. Introduction

When World War I broke out, Britain and the four frontier countries were among the richest in the world. Britain was the most fully developed, had the best articulated and most comprehensive set of financial intermediaries, and was the world's leading creditor. Per capita income was at least as high in the United States as in Britain, and the American economy was very much the larger – in fact, the largest in the world. The financial system was also well developed; American savings had begun to exceed domestic investment requirements; and the United States had taken up the role of an international lender. Canada had experienced an exceptionally high rate of growth in the two decades before the war, a rate sustained by an unusually large Canadian capacity (and willingness) to save and invest, and by a steady inflow of foreign capital. The Canadian economy was much smaller than the American, but per capita income was gaining on that of the United States. The banking system was strong; the securities markets were small, but effective and growing; and in other respects the system of intermediation was gaining in depth and strength. These countries seemed set on a course of successful modern economic growth.

The prospects of the other two were more problematical. Australia, with abundant resources and a small modern population, may well have been the richest country in the world in 1870, and, perhaps in 1890, if richness is measured by per capita aggregate product of the population of European origin. By 1913, however, as a result of a pace of growth slower than those exhibited by the other four and of the very damaging effects of the crisis of the early 1890s, Australia, while still rich, had lost much of the advantage it had held in 1870. More troubling, financial intermediation was not well developed; and the principal private financial institutions – commercial and mortgage banks – had suffered very damaging blows in the 1890s, blows with enduring consequences. English lenders, severely hurt in the Australian financial collapse, were reluctant to resume lending to the private sector.

Argentina, in the four decades before the war, had experienced the highest rate of growth of the five, and by 1913 per capita income was roughly three-quarters of the U.S. level. The last decade was particularly favorable; in addition to the vigorous expansion of the real economy, Argentina had managed successfully to reform the commercial banking system, a system that had been a continuing source of financial and economic problems.[1510] What made future Argentine prospects at least slightly problematical was the mode by which domestic investment was financed; down to the outbreak of the war, Argentina depended very heavily on foreign capital. Contemporaries worried about what would happen if the tap of foreign finance were turned off. Furthermore, a large fraction of foreign investment was direct, and it had done little to help develop the domestic financial system. Apart from commercial banking, the financial infrastructure was not well developed.

The first seven chapters of this book leave two sets of questions unanswered. First, although we know what the prospects of the five countries were on the eve of the war, the questions remain; how did the five actually fare in the years following 1913? That question is briefly addressed in Section 8-2; that section chiefly focuses on the real side of the five economies, and it leaves financial considerations largely aside. Second, although the first seven chapters treat only five countries, the five were central to the development of international finance in the late nineteenth century. Britain was very much the largest international creditor, and Argentina, Australia, Canada, and the United States were very much the largest international debtors. Conditions began to change during World War I, and since then they have gone through a sequence of pronounced shifts. New, important players have entered the game, on both the creditor and debtor sides. What then were the developments in the international capital markets between 1914 and 1999? The last section of Chapter 8 brings the world financial story up to date. It could not, however, be restricted to accounts of the five economies treated in the first seven chapters. The focus of the remainder of the chapter is on the international markets for capital. The five original countries appear in this story – the United States and the United Kingdom playing major roles – but the interest is less in these countries, per se, than on the changes in the international financial infrastructure and its supporting

---

[1510] The reform did not solve all of Argentina's financial problems, nor did it solve the banking problem in its entirety and for all time: Valeriano F. Garcia, *A Critical Inquiry into Argentine Economic History, 1946–1970* (New York: Garland Publishing, 1987), pp. 102–3; Barry Eichengreen and Albert Fishlow, *Contending with Capital Flows: What Is Different About the 1990s?* (New York: Council on Foreign Relations, 1996), pp. 42–43.

institutions, a structure and agent of institutions that were rooted in the previous half century.

8-2. **How did the five fare after 1913?**

The impact of World War I on the five differed markedly from country to country. For Argentina the war was an economic disaster. By 1917 per capita real income was less than three-quarters that of 1913, and, while it subsequently recovered in some measure, as late as 1919, it was still 13 percent below the 1913 level (see Table 8:2-1, Panel A). The source of the problem may have been the extremely low gross investment rate, a rate that fell from 10 percent of GDP in 1914, to as little as 4.9 percent, in the last year of the war, and a rate that did not again reach the pre-war level until 1922 (see Table 8:2-2). Since Argentina maintained a favorable trade balance in all years but one between 1914 and 1919, it is unlikely that Argentina received much, if any, net foreign investment; and the domestic savings rate remained low, as it had been in pre-war times.

The Australian savings rate in the first three years of the war was very small – indeed, even minuscule, in 1915/16 – but it increased to a respectable level in the next several years; and, as far as gross investment is concerned, domestic savings were supported by an inflow of capital that was quite large (Table 8:2-3). Australia's performance during the war was, then, somewhat better than Argentina's, although by 1919 as compared with 1913, the two had at about the same relative level of per capita income (Table 8:2-1, Panel A). The other three countries weathered the war more successfully. They were among the chief suppliers of war materials to the Allies, and war demands stimulated production (Table 8:2-1, Panel A).

Capital inflows into Canada dropped off sharply during the war, but the savings rate remained high and supported a healthy rate of capital formation (Table 8:2-4). In the 1920s, in terms of savings, Canada continued to perform well, well enough to generate a strong domestic investment record despite very little help in the form of transfusions of foreign capital (Tables 8:2-1, Panel A, and 8:2-4).[1511] After a sharp post-war recession, for the rest of the 1920s the Canadian growth rate was even higher than the American, as satisfactory as that latter rate was.

[1511] Indeed, as Table 8:2-4 shows, Canada was a net international lender from 1923 through 1926. From 1926 to 1930 Canadian net foreign debts rose very slightly, from $5.966 billion to $6.003 billion. Statistics Canada, *Historical Statistics of Canada*, 2nd ed. (Ottawa: Statistics Canada and the Social Science Federation of Canada, 1983), series G-190.

Table 8:2-1. *Indexes of real GDP per capita, 1913–1994*

		Panel A: Annual estimates		
Year	Argentina	Australia	Canada	United States	United Kingdom
		Base 1913			
1913	100	100	100	100	100
1914	87	90	91	91	100
1915	85	84	95	92	107
1916	81	90	104	103	109
1917	73	93	108	99	110
1918	86	92	100	107	111
1919	87	88	90	107	99
		Base 1920			
1920	100	100	100	100	100
1921	100	108	87	96	91
1922	105	106	98	100	95
1923	112	106	103	111	98
1924	117	111	103	112	101
1925	113	113	112	113	106
1926	115	110	116	119	101
1927	120	107	126	118	109
1928	124	103	134	118	110
1929	126	101	131	124	113
		Base 1930			
1930	100	100	100	100	100
1931	91	95	83	92	94
1932	86	97	76	79	95
1933	89	102	70	77	97
1934	94	105	77	82	103
1935	97	109	82	88	107
1936	96	113	86	100	111
1937	101	119	93	104	114
1938	100	118	94	99	115
1939	102	118	99	106	115
		Base 1940			
1940	100	100	100	100	100
1941	103	110	113	117	109
1942	103	122	131	139	111
1943	101	125	135	164	113
1944	110	119	139	176	108
1945	105	112	133	167	103
1946	112	107	129	131	98

Table 8:2-1. *(cont.)*

Panel A: Annual estimates				
Year	Argentina	Australia	Canada	United States	United Kingdom
			Base 1947		
1947	100	100	100	100	100
1948	103	105	100	102	102
1949	99	109	100	101	105
1950	98	112	105	108	109
1951	100	114	108	116	111
1952	93	112	113	119	111
1953	96	113	115	122	115
1954	98	118	111	119	119
1955	103	121	118	123	123
1956	104	123	124	123	124
1957	107	122	124	123	125
1958	112	126	123	121	125
1959	103	130	125	125	129
			Base 1960		
1960	100	100	100	100	100
1961	106	97	114	101	102
1962	102	102	106	105	103
1963	98	106	110	108	106
1964	107	111	115	113	111
1965	115	115	120	119	113
1966	114	115	126	125	114
1967	115	121	128	127	116
1968	118	126	132	132	120
1969	127	131	137	134	122
			Base 1970		
1970	100	100	100	100	100
1971	103	101	104	102	101
1972	105	103	109	107	105
1973	109	107	116	112	112
1974	114	107	119	110	110
1975	111	109	120	108	109
1976	109	112	127	113	112
1977	114	112	130	118	115
1978	107	114	134	122	119
1979	113	117	138	124	122

Table 8:2-1. *(cont.)*

		Panel A: Annual estimates			
Year	Argentina	Australia	Canada	United States	United Kingdom
			Base 1980		
1980	100	100	100	100	100
1981	93	102	102	102	99
1982	89	100	98	99	100
1983	90	100	101	102	104
1984	91	105	106	107	106
1985	84	109	110	110	110
1986	89	111	113	112	114
1987	90	113	116	116	119
1988	87	117	121	117	125
1989	81	119	122	119	127
			Base 1990		
1990	100	100	100	100	100
1991	108	99	97	98	97
1992	116	99	93	99	97
1993	121	101	93	100	98
1994	127	104	94	103	100
		Panel B: Benchmark dates			
			Base 1913		
1913	100	100	100	100	100
1919	87	88	90	107	99
1929	115	93	114	130	104
1939	109	102	107	124	119
1946	123	115	156	174	128
1959	138	152	199	210	162
1969	185	203	276	283	208
1979	217	248	386	348	260
1989	175	299	472	410	324
1994	221	311	436	425	325

Panel C: Real GDP per capita, Argentina, Australia, Canada, and the United Kingdom, as a percentage of Real GDP per capita in the United States, benchmark dates

1913	71.5	103.7	79.4	100.0	94.8
1920	62.5	90.8	65.8	100.0	83.7
1930	65.6	77.0	73.3	100.0	83.5
1940	59.2	84.5	72.5	100.0	93.2
1947	57.2	72.2	75.5	100.0	70.9
1950	52.1	75.4	73.6	100.0	71.5
1960	49.7	76.3	75.6	100.0	76.6
1970	49.2	78.3	79.2	100.0	72.0
1980	45.1	75.6	89.1	100.0	69.9
1990	30.1	75.1	89.6	100.0	74.6
1994	37.1	75.8	81.3	100.0	72.5

Source: Derived from Angus Maddison, *Monitoring the World Economy 1920–1992* (Paris: OECD, 1995), Tables C-16a (pp. 180–183) and C-16d (pp. 188–189).

Table 8:2-2. *Argentine gross investment and the net trade balance (exports minus imports) expressed as a percentage of GDP, 1914–1945*

Year	Gross investment	The trade balance
1914	10.0	+9.3
1915	7.2	+17.1
1916	7.2	+3.0
1917	6.7	−0.7
1918	4.9	+2.5
1919	5.7	+6.9
1920	7.5	−10.5
1921	8.3	−18.0
1922	10.0	−9.7
1923	12.4	−16.5
1924	11.4	−5.9
1925	11.5	−16.1
1926	11.3	−15.8
1927	11.9	−12.0
1928	12.6	−1.4
1929	14.1	−5.8
1930	12.9	−9.0
1931	9.9	+3.8
1932	8.0	+8.6
1933	7.8	+1.0
1934	10.7	+3.9
1935	12.2	+3.0
1936	13.1	+4.0
1937	11.3	+5.4
1938	12.5	−1.9
1939	10.6	+3.4
1940	10.5	+3.2
1941	9.7	+6.1
1942	11.4	+6.4
1943	11.5	+10.5
1944	8.4	+10.0
1945	12.1	+7.4

Source: *Estudios*, Ano IX – No. 39 – Julio/Septembre 1986. Guardo 13.

Table 8:2-3. *Australian gross investment, foreign capital inflows, and implied savings, expressed as a percentage of GNP, 1914/1915–1935/1936*

Years	Gross Investment	Foreign Capital Inflow	Implied Savings
1914/1915	11.6	8.9	2.7
1915/1916	11.1	11.0	less than 1/2%
1916/1917	18.6	13.4	5.2
1917/1918	18.0	5.1	12.8
1918/1919	15.7	5.6	10.0
1919/1920	14.4	−3.1	17.5
1920/1921	19.6	6.2	13.4
1921/1922	20.9	−0.9	21.9
1922/1923	17.9	4.5	13.4
1923/1924	18.3	5.8	12.5
1924/1925	19.6	1.1	18.5
1925/1926	20.2	4.9	15.4
1926/1927	19.3	7.3	11.7
1927/1928	19.0	5.4	13.6
1928/1929	19.1	5.2	14.6
1929/1930	16.3	11.0	5.3
1930/1931	15.0	3.9	11.1
1931/1932	11.3	−1.7	13.0
1932/1933	12.1	0.7	11.5
1933/1934	12.7	−1.3	14.0
1934/1935	15.3	2.5	12.7
1935/1936	14.8	1.2	13.6

Source: N.G. Butlin, *Australian Domestic Product, Investment and Foreign Borrowing, 1861–1938/1939* (Cambridge, U.K.: Cambridge University Press, 1962), p. 7 for Gross National Product at Market Prices, Gross Domestic Capital Accumulation, and Gross National Capital Accumulation. Foreign capital inflow is Gross Domestic Capital Accumulation minus Gross National Capital Accumulation. Capital accumulation includes changes in animal inventories; GNP apparently does not. Between 1914/1915 and 1918/1919, capital accumulation exceeded capital formation by 10%; between 1919/1920 and 1928/1929, the two were virtually identical; between 1929/1930 and 1935/1936, Capital Accumulation exceeded Capital Formation by 3%. Thus, the proportions given in columns (1) and (3) are biased upward slightly, because the concepts of GNP and Capital Accumulation are not identical.

Table 8:2-4. *Canadian gross investment, foreign capital inflows, and implied savings, expressed as a percentage of GNP, 1914–1926*

Year	Gross investment	Foreign capital inflow	Implied savings
1914	27.0	10.3	16.7
1915	17.5	2.5	15.0
1916	15.5	0.8	14.7
1917	14.8	−3.4	18.2
1918	12.9	−0.6	13.5
1919	15.1	0.3	14.8
1920	16.6	3.1	13.5
1921	18.0	4.1	13.9
1922	15.9	3.0	12.9
1923	19.0	−1.2	20.2
1924	17.0	−1.8	18.8
1925	15.4	−3.9	19.3
1926	15.1	−2.4	17.5

Source: M.C. Urquhart, *Gross National Product, Canada, 1870–1926: The Derivation of the Estmates* (Kingston and Montreal: McGill-Queen's University Press, 1993), p. 28.

In the United States, unlike the other four, per capita GDP grew moderately during the war; it was 7 percent higher in 1919 than it had been in 1913. Growth continued over the next decade, and in 1929 per capita GDP was 24 percent above the 1920 benchmark.

During the 1920s the Argentine gross investment rate improved over the wartime years, and aggregate economic growth very nearly matched the Canadian performance. It was, in fact, actually somewhat better than the American. Since the Argentine trade balance was heavily unfavorable throughout the decade, it is likely that foreign investment inflows were substantial; and, as was the case before the war, domestic investment depended but little on Argentine savings (Table 8:2-2).

Australia made the transition from war to peace more quickly than did any of the other four; but the downturn at the end of the 1920s came earlier; at the end of the decade, Australia's position, relative to that of 1920, was weaker than that of any of the other four. The well-known economic troubles of the United Kingdom are clearly visible in the decline of per capita GDP after 1920, in its failure to re-achieve the 1920 level before 1924, and in a further dip from 1925 to 1926.

In the 1930s it was America's turn to stumble economically. Both Canada and the United States did badly, especially in the early years;

and, although Argentina avoided the very sharp decline that marked the other two countries, growth was limited. At the end of the decade Australian per capita product was only 2 percent higher than it had been in 1930 (Table 8:2-1, Panel A). In Australia and the United Kingdom income growth was slightly higher than the poor performance of the 1920s; but it was not much higher. None of the five countries really escaped the disaster of the 1930s.

In terms of per capita product, both Canada and the United States prospered during World War II (Table 8:2-1, Panel C). The gains for this period far exceed those of the late 1910s, the 1920s, or the 1930s; a part of these gains was, of course, devoted to the prosecution of the war, not to ministering to the other wants of the Canadian and U.S. populations. But these two countries at least avoided the fate of the chief Continental countries, whose economies ended the war in a shambles. The United Kingdom raised per capita output from 1940 through 1943 and ended the war with this index only 2 percent below the level of 1940. Whatever gains that were achieved, however, went to the fighting of the war; civilian material well-being almost certainly deteriorated. The Australian pattern is similar to the British, except that the early surge of growth is more prominent, and the subsequent decline, less drastic; but, compared with Canada, the gains are less and the losses greater. Throughout the war Argentina's output per capita changed little, except for upward surges in 1944 and 1946.

In the late 1940s and the 1950s, Argentinean income made no major gains; however, income in Australia, Canada, the United States, and the United Kingdom all rose. In the 1960s all five did well, but in the 1970s, less well. The Argentine and Australian data reflect no large gains for the 1970s, but, for Canada, the advance was pronounced. The records for the United States and United Kingdom are closer to those of Argentina and Australia than to that of Canada. Australia, the United States, and the United Kingdom experienced about the same improvement across the 1980s as they had during the previous decade; but the Canadian increase was somewhat less. In Argentina there was a pronounced drop – a drop concentrated in the early years of the decade – and again in 1985 and 1989. Between 1990 and 1994, Argentinean growth rebounded strongly; for the other four, there were no big gains or losses.

So much for short-term changes, but what of long-term developments? The unsatisfactory quality of the inter-war period is reflected in the data for Argentina, Australia, and Canada; in 1939 per capita income levels were only slightly higher than they had been over a quarter century earlier (Table 8:2-1, Panel B). The experiences of the United States and the United Kingdom were better, but both had still generated very modest income gains. The post-war growth, of course, was much more satisfactory: by 1994 Canadian per capita product was over four times its 1913 level, that of the United States, about the same. Australia and the United Kingdom, although exhibiting pronounced growth, lagged behind Canada and the United States; however, the levels of their per capita real GDP were still over three times as high as in 1913. Argentina was farthest behind. The lag was due chiefly, but not entirely, to poor post–World War II performance, particularly in the 1980s. Still, by 1994, Argentine real GDP per head was over twice as high as it had been in 1913.

Perhaps the most telling figures appear in Panel C of Table 8:2-1. There estimates of real GDP per capita are expressed as percentages of the U.S. level. By these calculations, Canada, behind the United States in 1913, fell farther behind during World War I and did not achieve its pre-war relative level again until 1970. In the 1970s and 1980s Canada grew faster than the United States, but by 1994 it was in about the same relative position as in 1913. Australia enjoyed a very slightly higher real GDP per capita than the United States in 1913, but that country fell dramatically behind during World War I, lost further ground during the 1920s, and from then until 1994 remained in about the same relative position. At the beginning of World War II, British real per capita GDP was a little more than 93 percent of the U.S. level, roughly the same as at the outbreak of World War I; but by 1947 the figure had fallen to roughly 71 percent, and it stayed at about that level until 1994. As in the case of real GDP, Argentina had the worst record. In 1913 real GDP per capita was better than seven-tenths as high as that of the United States. World War I led to a relative decline to a little more than six-tenths of the U.S. level. That figure then drifted downward, until, in 1980, it was only 45 percent of the U.S. standard. In the 1980s there was a major further relative decline, to just over 30 percent of the American level. There was then a recovery in the 1990s, but the level achieved as late as 1994 was still only 37 percent of the U.S. benchmark.

In summary, according to these measures of performance, between 1913 and 1994, there were both good times and bad times for all five countries. The long-term records of all show substantial growth, but for Argentina the story has distressing elements. There are the losses sustained during World War I, the fifty-year period of relative decline between 1930 and 1980, and the pronounced drop in the 1980s, a drop associated with political turmoil. By 1990 per capita product was less than one-third the U.S. level. Australia and the United Kingdom also lost ground when compared with the United States – the world leader – but by 1994 each had a per capita product three times its level in 1913. Canada, alone, matched the U.S. growth, and by 1994 it had a real GDP per capita over four and one-third times as high as its level in 1913.

8-3. World financial developments after 1913

8-3a. World War I

World War I was an unprecedented epic of destruction. But as John Hughes points out:

> Oddly enough, even though the only irretrievable loss by war is human life, no aspect of the economic impact of modern war is more shunned by historians and economists. It is as if machines, coal mines, railroads, and wheat fields were lost forever, while the dead were "replaced" in economic life by the next round of people sprung from the loins of the survivors. It cannot be shown, really, to have been otherwise, but one suspects that it could have been . . . one wonders what great economic talents were lost forever in the twentieth century fields of slaughter?[1512]

The issue is not purely or chiefly a numerical one, but it is true that the numbers killed were enormous. Hughes estimates military deaths at 8.5 million; Maddison puts the figure at 8.8 million. Hughes adds 5.0 million for civilian deaths by military causes. No doubt civilian deaths indirectly due to the war were also high.[1513] At a guess, total numbers killed may have come to 15 or 16 million, or roughly the size of the combined populations of Canada and Austria (14.9 million) or Canada and Belgium (15.8 million). In Germany military deaths alone took 5 percent of the prewar population.[1514] Since deaths were concentrated among young adult males, the structures of the populations of the chief belligerents were distorted by the war; and the relative size and quality of the labor force of these countries were diminished.

The term "lost generation" – a term applied to the generation that had fought the war – could well have referred to those killed or missing

---

[1512] Johnathan Hughes, *Industrialization and Economic History: Theses and Conjectures* (New York: McGraw-Hill Book Company, 1970), p. 240.

[1513] Ibid., pp. 240–41; Angus Maddison, "Economic Policy and Performance in Europe, 1913–1970," in Carlo M. Cipolla (ed.), *The Fontana Economic History of Europe, Vol. 5, The Twentieth Century Part Two* (N.P.: Harvester Press Limited/Barnes and Noble Import Division, by agreement with Fontana Books, 1977), p. 447. [Hereafter cited as Maddison, "Economic Policy and Performance."]

[1514] The population data are from Angus Maddison, *Monitoring the World Economy, 1820–1992* (Paris: OECD, 1995), pp. 104–6. The Austrian figure refers to population within the borders of Austria as these borders were established after the war. The German war deaths are from Maddison, "Economic Policy and Performance," p. 447.

during the war. It was, however, intended to describe the emotional state of the survivors, who were believed to have lost confidence that the world was ordered in a reasonable way, a way that yielded fundamentally benign results.[1515] With this disenchantment went a loss of faith in the strength of the cement holding society together, or at least the cement that was holding it together in the old forms.

Large-scale conscription had meant that the scope of discontent among working and lower middle class people was more readily identified as a general malaise, not a disease confined to the small group of friends the soldier had known before the war. Military service also meant that these groups learned to cooperate in ways that became relevant to post-war political and labor organizations. These effects of the war on the structure of society, together with the example of alternatives provided by the Russian Revolution, accounted for "the almost universal explosion of working class struggles and protests after the war" and made the European working class unwilling to submit easily to the discipline of economic policy, if that policy had unfavorable impacts on wage rates or employment. Worker militancy was one of the factors that promoted the increased rigidity in post-war labor markets that was observed by Svennilson.[1516] The war also destroyed capital. The belligerents were not equally affected; fighting had taken place chiefly in Belgium and France.

In the regions where battles were fought, losses of structures, both business and residential, were heavy, and so was the destruction of transport, mines, and farm land. The war at sea cost many tons of merchant shipping, and the British were particularly affected. As Maddison points out, private investment rates were reduced during the war. The low investment rates, together with the destruction of capital, meant that the capital stocks of most of the belligerents were almost certainly lower in 1919 than they would have been had there been no war – perhaps, in some cases, lower than they had been before the war. Keynes estimated war damage to capital stock (at pre-war prices) at £150 million in Belgium, £500 million in France, £260 million in the United Kingdom (mostly shipping), and between £50 and £100 million in Italy. He did not

---

[1515] "'You are all a lost generation.' Gertrude Stein, in conversation." Headnote to Ernest Hemingway, *The Sun Also Rises*.

[1516] Charles H. Feinstein, Peter Temin, and Gianni Toniolo, *The European Economy Between the Wars* (Oxford: Oxford University Press, 1997), pp. 26–27. [Hereafter cited as Feinstein, Temin, and Toniolo, *The European Economy Between the Wars*.] Inavar Svennilson, *Growth and Stagnation in the European Economy* (Geneva: United Nations Economic Commission for Europe, 1954), as cited in Feinstein, Temin, and Toniolo, p. 14.

express the figures in relation to pre-war capital stock, except for Belgium, where the loss appears to have been about 12 percent.[1517]

The belligerents also lost financial assets that had contributed to pre-war income. Some were liquidated to help finance the war, and some – notably French credits against Russia – were lost by default; the loss of financial assets through default, of course, resulted only in a transfer of income from the holders to the defaulter unless, as appears likely, the defaulter had used the resource to finance the war. The loss through liquidation involved a portfolio shift from earning assets to war material. The United Kingdom was said to have liquidated 15 percent of the overseas financial assets owned by its citizens, while defaults of debtors to French creditors reduced French foreign financial holdings by two-thirds. In addition, substantial debts were incurred by the British who borrowed from the Americans and by the Continental Allies – especially France – who borrowed from the British. This maze of obligations was ultimately eliminated (forgiven) during the 1930s. German foreign financial assets fell by about £1.2 billion – virtually all of German pre-war holdings of foreign financial assets – a figure five or six times the losses suffered by the British. German assets were in part liquidated during the war, but they were in part removed by reparations. Thus, unlike the French and British losses, a part of these assets may have remained in European hands.[1518]

Although the capital losses – both physical and financial – were serious, other aspects of the war experience are widely believed to have figured more importantly in the economic problems that emerged in the 1920s and 1930s. In 1914 only one of the belligerents – the United States – had fought a full-fledged war involving the extensive mobilization of fiscal and material resources within the past century, and even that

---

[1517] Maddison, "Economic Policy and Performance," pp. 448–49. Using Goldsmith's measure of "Tangible Assets" as a measure of the capital stock the losses suppressed appear to represent 11.3 percent of Belgium's, 4.9 percent of France's, 2.3 percent of Britain's, and between 0.8 and 1.6 percent of Italy's Tangible Assets. Raymond W. Goldsmith, *Comparative National Balance Sheets; A Study of Twenty Countries, 1688–1978* (Chicago: University of Chicago Press, 1985), tables A2, p. 199; A5, pp. 216–17; A7, pp. 232–33; and A11, pp. 248–49. Exchange rates from *The Statesman's Yearbook, 1913* (London: Macmillan and Co., 1914), pp. 697, 806, and 1040.

[1518] Kathleen Burk, "Money and Power: The Shift from Great Britain to the United States," in Youssef Cassis (ed.), *Finance and Financiers in European History, 1880–1960*, Editions de la Maison des Sciences de L'Homme, Paris (Cambridge: Cambridge University Press, 1992), p. 363. [Hereafter cited as Burke, "Money and Power."] Maddison, "Economic Policy and Performance," p. 449; Feinstein, Temin, and Toniolo, *The European Economy Between the Wars*, p. 22.

experience was five decades in the past.[1519] The problems of organizing and financing war production and raising a military force were enormous, and methods for coping with these problems had to be invented. As Feinstein, Temin, and Toniolo point out, the belligerents had been accustomed to devoting roughly 15 percent of GDP to governmental objects; between 1914 and 1918 the share of government grew to over one-half of GDP. Two major interrelated tasks faced policy makers and bureaucrats: to reallocate labor from peacetime pursuits to the military and to the arms industries, and to do so without triggering serious inflation. All failed to cope successfully with the latter, but the degree of failure varied from one economy to the next. As a part of the joint task, controls had to be imposed on internal and international transactions. At the end of the war the warring nations were faced with the problems of reconverting back from military to peacetime production, of releasing soldiers into civilian life and civilian pursuits in an orderly way, and of removing wartime controls at such a time and in such a manner as to minimize the unfavorable shocks to the economy.[1520] In the context of world – as opposed to domestic – production, there were additional changes that would cause post-war problems. During the war some customary European sources of food and non-food staples had been blocked off or reduced – grain supplies from Central and Eastern to Western Europe, for example – and European nations had encouraged alternative suppliers. U.S. and Canadian farmers, among other overseas producers, were accustomed to rising prices in the pre-war years; and they were confident enough in the buoyant wartime world markets to expand their operations, expansion often based on extensive borrowing. With the end of the war, European production came back on line; trade between eastern and central Europe, on the one hand, and the west, on the other, was renewed; farm prices fell; the debts of overseas wartime suppliers became weighty; and the new suppliers experienced a decade of bad times, a decade to be followed by a second associated with a great depression that was to prove as bad or worse.

At the same time, the war effort reduced the ability of European – especially British – manufacturers to supply their accustomed

---

[1519] For a careful assessment of the nature of the Civil War (Was it a total war? Was it a modern war?) see Stanley Engerman and J. Matthew Gallman, "The Civil War Economy: A Modern View," in Stig Forster and Jorge Nagler (eds.), *On the Road to Total War: The American Civil War and the German Wars of Unification, 1861–1871* (Cambridge: Cambridge University Press, 1997), pp. 217–48.

[1520] Feinstein, Temin, and Toniolo, *The European Economy Between the Wars*, chapter 2.

overseas markets. Local manufacturers expanded production to provide substitutes for the lost imports. When the war ended, European producers found these markets difficult to re-enter. Domestic producers had had several years to build expertise, and they were formidable competitors. Moreover, when their ability to compete proved inadequate, they had become important enough domestically to call for tariff protection and powerful enough to have governments listen to their cries for help. These developments represented a major source of British export problems in the post-war years, and they were exacerbated by a demonstrated unwillingness or inability to develop new lines of manufactured exports.[1521]

Changes that had occurred just before and during the war presaged a shift in financial predominance from London to New York. Unfortunately, the inexperience of New York as a world financial leader may have contributed to the financial collapse at the end of the 1920s.[1522] Just how thin American experience in world finance was at the end of the 1920s, when pressures on the U.S. financial system were building,

---

[1521] Ibid.

[1522] American inexperience, in the sense that the country was hesitant to become the world's central banker, may have contributed to the crash; but Kindleberger, among others, argues that the crash, its depth, and duration were not primarily of American origin or American responsibility. Charles P. Kindleberger, *A Financial History of Western Europe*, 2nd ed. (New York and Oxford: Oxford University Press, 1993), pp. 353–54. [Hereafter cited as Kindleberger, *A Financial History of Western Europe*.]

"It was however, in the international dimension that the lender of last resort was most conspicuously missing. The task is a difficult one at best, but Britain tried, up to the last 50 million schillings for Austria in June 1931, when the rest of the world backed out. After that setback, Britain stood aside from a loan to Germany, while the French and Americans undertook one – 'too little and too late' not to mention the stringent French political conditions. When it came England's turn to seek help, the United States and France proceeded with one loan at a time – salami tactics, when the Bagehot prescription was lend freely – and attached economic conditions to a second loan so severe that they brought the Labour government down. . . .

"The United States was uncertain in its international role. It felt that the British were shrewder, more sophisticated, more devious in their negotiating tactics, . . . Stimson would have been willing to undertake a major discounting operation to rescue the Reichsmark in 1931; Hoover, Mellon, and (though from New York) Mills were opposed to sending good money after bad, as discounting calls for. In 1933 James Warburg, Moley and presumably Woodin and Roosevelt still resisted sending good money after bad." Charles P. Kindleberger, *The World in Depression, 1929–1939*, revised and enlarged edition (Berkeley: University of California Press, 1986), pp. 295, 297.

is suggested by the importance given to the death of one man, Benjamin Strong.[1523] If one financial leader could have been thought to be so important, quality financial leadership must have been thin indeed. More broadly, the results of inexperience showed up in the record assembled by the commercial banking system. For example, in the 1930s a commercial bank's experience in foreign bond holding was inversely associated with the level of its investment in defaulted bonded debt.[1524]

Two developments – one just before and the other during the war – were particularly important in underwriting the financial shift from London to New York. First was the passage of the Federal Reserve Act, an act that for the first time gave the United States a true central bank and that also permitted large national banks to establish foreign branches. In particular, by making trade acceptances generated in the finance of foreign trade eligible for rediscount, banks were encouraged to acquire such acceptances. The intention of these provisions was to permit New York to replicate the London bill market and, thereby, to secure for that city at least some of the business of financing international trade, a business that London had dominated for more than a half century. The U.K.'s wartime financial problems created opportunities for the United States. "The result was that the dollar largely replaced the pound as the means of paying not only for American exports and imports – a source of commissions which the City never really recovered – but also for more of Europe's trade with Latin America and the Far East."[1525]

A second development that was to have important post-war consequences for foreign lending involved the expansion of the New York bond market. At the end of the nineteenth century, about 90 percent of

[1523] Stephen V.O. Clarke, *Central Bank Cooperation, 1924–1931* (New York: Federal Reserve Bank of New York, 1967), as cited in Feinstein, Temin, and Toniolo, *The European Economy Between the Wars*, p. 15; Milton Friedman and Anna J. Schwartz, *A Monetary History of the United States, 1867–1960* (Princeton: Princeton University Press, 1963), as cited in Barry Eichengreen, *Golden Fetters: The Gold Standard and the Great Depression, 1919–1939* (New York and Oxford: Oxford University Press, 1992), pp. 251–52. [Hereafter cited as Eichengreen, *Golden Fetters*.]

[1524] Ilse Mintz, *Deterioration in the Quality of Foreign Bonds Issued in the United States* (New York: National Bureau of Economic Research, 1951), as cited by Barry Eichengreen and Albert Fishlow, *Contending with Capital Flows: What Is Different About the 1990s?* (New York: Council on Foreign Relations, 1996), p. 7. [Hereafter cited as Eichengreen and Fishlow, *Contending with Capital Flows*.]

[1525] Burk, "Money and Power," p. 361.

U.S. foreign investment had been direct; by the end of the 1920s, however, about half was portfolio investment.[1526] This change can be, at least in part, attributed to war-related events that led to a dramatic expansion of the bond market. In part the stimulus came from the flotation of bonds for the Allied governments; however, as the war went on, much of the U.S.-held Allied debt had been acquired directly by the federal government, completely bypassing private agencies and markets. As a result, after 1917 the more important stimulus to the domestic market came from the sales of U.S. government bonds. These bonds were eagerly absorbed by American buyers, and an enlarged and permanent cadre of bond buyers was thereby created. The experience was similar to that of the Civil War, when sales of federal bonds expanded the capacity of the bond market by increasing investor sophistication and producing a generation of savers who were willing to invest first in government, and then in private U.S. railway bonds. "[W]hereas in 1914 there had been no more than 200,000 bond buyers in the country as a whole, wartime Liberty Loan campaigns raised that number to the millions. Once jarred from its slumber, the bond market was awake for good."[1527] Moreover, once the war was over, Americans became willing, indeed eager, to acquire foreign bonds to go with or to replace the U.S. securities purchased during the war.

8-3b. The interwar period

The interwar years were divided into two almost equal parts by the great financial and economic collapse of 1927–33.[1528] In terms of the development of financial markets, the leading consequence of the collapse was the rise of autarky. The capital flight that in 1931 put Britain off the gold standard and that was the harbinger of the final abandonment of that system by the rest of the world led to the adoption of

---

[1526] In 1897 portfolio investment represented only $50 million of a total of $684.5 million of U.S. long-term foreign investment (8.6 percent). In 1929 the figure was $7.8393 billion out of a total of $15.3926 (50.9 percent). Lewis, *America's Stake in International Investments*, p. 605.

[1527] Eichengreen and Fishlow, *Contending with Capital Flows*; Burk, "Money and Power," p. 361.

[1528] "The Great Depression is typically thought to have started in August 1929. But well before that summer, economic activity was already in decline over significant parts of the globe. In Australia and the Netherlands East Indies the deterioration of business conditions was visible at the end of 1927. Recession spread next to Germany and Brazil in 1928 and to Argentina, Canada, and Poland in the first half of 1929." Eichengreen, *Golden Fetters*, p. 222, citing John Dell Condliffe, *World Economic Survey 1931–32* (Geneva: League of Nations, 1932).

controls over private capital movements and to the virtual disappearance of long-term international capital movements for three decades. A full return to the free movements of the pre–World War I period took even longer than that. Thus, the capital markets that had grown to such prominence in the forty or fifty years before World War I – markets that had weathered periodic international financial crises – were virtually destroyed in the early 1930s; and they were not reestablished for a period of almost equal length. "The prewar record was checkered. . . . But while lending was interrupted periodically, there was no extended hiatus similar to that which began in the 1930s, perhaps because each wave of default was confined to a relatively small number of countries [and thus] experience was reasonably satisfactory."[1529]

Capital markets were not all that disappeared. Countries, attempting to shelter themselves from the effects of the deep depression that had engulfed their trading partners and to promote recovery by import substitution, opted for a policy of tariffs and exchange and import controls. Exports declined.[1530] More generally, domestic economic concerns came to dominate the thoughts of policy makers. The lessons taught by the experience of the British during the 1920s were, perhaps, too well learned: domestic well-being would not again be sacrificed to international goals that would yield, at best, domestic gains that could only be reaped in the long run. Although there may have been some international fallout, the notion of public works as a device for attacking unemployment – an idea promoted by the work of J.M. Clark – had a clearly domestic focus, as did Keynesian ideas, ideas

[1529] Eichengreen and Fishlow, *Contending with Capital Flows*, p. 6. For an account of the nature of the change in capital markets, see Feinstein, Temin, and Toniolo, *The European Economy Between the Wars*, pp. 166–69. The movement of capital in the 1930s reflected financial and, later, political fears. Thus, capital, instead of flowing, as before, from rich countries to developing countries, to promote export growth, moved from poor to rich countries, shifting among the latter as appraisals of financial and political safety changed. Capital movements, then, did not involve long-term investments on a large scale; they consisted of short-term, "hot-money" transfers. The ultimate result, once Hitler's plans became clear and as war loomed, was the concentration of "hot money" – and gold stocks – in the United States. According to Burk, British capital flows stopped in 1930–31; and in 1933 "a strict embargo on overseas loans was imposed, although loans to the Empire were still allowed." Burk, "Money and Power," p. 362.

[1530] See Maddison, "Economic Policy and Performance," pp. 462–63. Citing the Woytinskys, Maddison finds that the average "ad valorem incidence of import duties in 1931" in Continental Europe came to 48 percent. W.S. and E.S. Woytinsky, *World Commerce and Governments* (New York, 1955), p. 277. As late as 1937, European exports were 13 percent lower than in 1913.

that began to have a major influence on policy in the late 1930s and in the 1940s.[1531]

The seeds of economic collapse were planted during the war and brought to maturity during the 1920s. Although the causal lines among them and the weight each should bear remain subject to debate, the chief events of the 1920s that ultimately led to the economic and financial collapse – and, indeed, international and domestic political collapses – are well known. First, the defeated Central Powers suffered hyperinflation; and, although inflation was brought under control by the mid-1920s, price increases and the policies adopted to suppress them carried a substantial political and social cost. The remaining European countries were subject to more modest rates of price increases, but, although the extent varies from one country to another, inflation was widespread. Thus in 1924 (on a 1914 base of 100) the price index was 1,055 in Finland, 481 in Italy, 469 in Belgium, 395 in France, 176 in the United Kingdom, 169 in Switzerland, and 145 in the Netherlands.[1532] Under these circumstances the return to a system of free exchanges posed serious problems. At one extreme, each country could force down domestic prices until its currency could be marketed at its pre-war gold-standard value. At the other extreme, countries could devalue sufficiently to bring the gold exchange

---

[1531] See, for example, the treatments of the Keynesian model by Joseph A. Schumpeter in *Ten Great Economists from Marx to Keynes* (New York: Oxford University Press, 1965), chapter 10, and Don Patinkin, "Keynes, John Maynard," in John Eatwell, Murray Milgate, and Peter Newman, *The New Palgrave: A Dictionary of Economics* (London: Macmillan Press, 1987), Vol. 3, K to P, pp. 19–41. The international sector figures not at all in these accounts. It would be fair to say that wide acceptance of the Keynesian model in the 1930s and 1940s involved also an acceptance of the notion that domestic well-being should never again be sacrificed to international goals. John Maurice Clark, *Economics of Planning Public Works*, a study made for the National Planning Board of the Federal Emergency Administration of Public Works (Washington, D.C.: GPO, 1935). Clark devotes just over one of his 194 pages to international issues. It should be noted, however, that in 1951 Alvin Hansen devoted an entire chapter (12 out of 616 pages) in his *Business Cycles and National Income* (New York: W.A. Norton, 1951) to international aspects of business cycles.

[1532] Feinstein, Temin, and Toniolo, *The European Economy Between the Wars*, p. 39. Inflation was also widespread after World War II. Thus in 1951 (on a 1939 base of 100) the price index was 936 in Finland, 3,533 in Italy, 353 in Belgium, 1,428 in France, 226 in the United Kingdom, 134 in Switzerland, and 274 in the Netherlands. The index for Germany was 222. For the years 1939–48 the price index in 1948 (1939 = 100) was Finland 900, Italy 5,228, Belgium 380, France 1,573, United Kingdom 214, Switzerland 209, and the Netherlands 268. B.R. Mitchell, *European Historical Statistics, 1750–1970*, abridged edition (New York: Columbia University Press, 1978), pp. 387–592.

rate in line with domestic prices.[1533] These decisions should ideally have been made in concert, so that the return to gold could have been managed without substantial losses to some countries and gains to others. There was, however, no such cooperation. In fact, there was not even a willingness among central banks to follow the rules of the gold standard game, much less to cooperate in other respects. When gold flowed in, central banks did not automatically expand the money supply; instead, they tended to neutralize the gold flow.[1534]

As a result of these central bank practices, countries returned to gold at different times and in different ways. The contrast between policies adopted by Britain and France was particularly sharp. The British employed a tight monetary policy to force down prices and wages in order to permit a return to gold at the pre-war par. The French devalued. As a consequence, through the first half of the 1920s the British economy suffered from heavy unemployment and labor unrest, and policy makers were obliged to restrict capital outflows. In France current economic conditions were better; the French central bank accumulated gold, but the inflation-induced income redistribution remained.[1535]

In the United States, as the Federal Reserve Banks sought to control the price level, interest rates rose; but, after 1923, they began to fall, reaching a nadir in 1928. The reduction in interest rates, the revival of the New York bond market, and the appearance of an important financial innovation – the investment trust – led to an outflow of American long-term capital. Investment trusts played the same role in the 1920s as emerging-market mutual funds were to perform in the 1990s:

[1533] An elegant treatment of the pros and cons of each of these possible choices can be found in John Maynard Keynes, *Monetary Reform* (New York: Harcourt, Brace and Company, 1924), chapter IV.

[1534] Feinstein, Temin, and Toniolo, *The European Economy Between the Wars*, p. 15; Eichengreen, *Golden Fetters*, pp. 253–54. Marc Flandreau argues that, contrary to some scholarly opinion, the failure of central banks to cooperate was nothing new; they also failed to do so before the war. For present purposes, however, it is sufficient to note that during the post-war period, the failure of the central banks to cooperate is undoubted. Marc Flandreau, "Central Bank Cooperation in Historical Perspective: A Skeptical View," *Economic History Review*, Vol. L, No. 4 (November 1997), pp. 735–63.

[1535] Burk, "Money and Power," p. 362. "From 1920 to 1925 Montagu Norman, the Governor of the Bank of England, imposed an 'embargo' of sorts on foreign loans. [On the return to gold,] the Chancellor of the Exchequer, Winston Churchill, told Norman that he hoped no loan would be floated on behalf of any country which had not settled its war debts with Britain, and an embargo in this form remained until October 1928."

They pooled the subscriptions of their clients, placed their management in the hands of specialists, and issued claims entitling holders to a share of their earnings. They facilitated position-taking in foreign securities by investors who would have been deterred otherwise by transaction and information costs. Commercial banks established bond departments and securities affiliates, much in the manner that commercial banks in the 1990s created their own mutual funds.[1536]

Like the Keating-directed savings and loans in the 1980s, the bank bond departments and investment trusts often pressed their salesmen to unload bonds and shares without fully informing buyers of the extent of the difference between the risks associated with foreign and U.S. government securities. Unlike the pre-war long-term capital flows – flows that were almost always invested in transportation or other social overhead capital and flows that ultimately promoted exports that generated the funds needed for servicing the debt – in the 1920s, American foreign loans were frequently used to underwrite current government expenditures rather than productive public investment.[1537] The resulting failure of investment trusts and bank bond departments during the great collapse was the chief reason for the passage of U.S. banking legislation (the Glass-Steagall Act) that separated commercial banks from their securities operations.

At the end of the 1920s, the value of foreign securities listed in London was still greater than those listed in New York, but that ordering was no longer true for new listings. "Comparing foreign capital issues publicly offered in New York (excluding refunding issues) with overseas issues on the London market, in 1924 the values were $969 million versus £134 million [$653 million], in 1927 $1,337 million versus £139 [$677 million]." In some sense, then, New York had emerged as the premier world financial center. Furthermore, by 1931 the pound had "resigned its former position as a trading currency."[1538] Thus, for a time, London gave up the roles that it had formerly played both in the finance of foreign trade and in the direction it gave of long-term capital flows.

The great American overseas investment boom came to an end in 1928. In that year the Federal Reserve, in an effort to cool down the stock market boom, tightened credit. It was a clear case of domestic

---

[1536] Eichengreen and Fishlow, *Contending with Capital Flows*, p. 7.

[1537] Ibid., p. 9. See also Carlo Zacchia, "International Trade and Capital Movements 1920–1970," in Carlo Cipolla (ed.), *The Twentieth Century*, pp. 573–82.

[1538] Burk, "Money and Power," p. 364. See also Eichengreen and Fishlow, *Contending with Capital Flows*, p. 10: "Net portfolio lending by the United States declined from more than $1 billion in 1927 to less than $700 million in 1928, with virtually all lending in 1928 concentrated in the first half of the year."

desiderata being placed ahead of the well being of the international system. The increase in the rate of interest induced a backflow of American capital invested overseas, and it attracted foreign investors as well. By 1929 new foreign listings in New York had fallen to a level little more than half what they had been two years earlier. Although there is disagreement as to the importance of the decline (some argue that the German economy was already moving into a depression before the impact of American interest rate policy was felt), it is true that German reparation payments had been partly financed by inflows of American capital; and, even if the German economy had already begun to slide, it was certainly inconvenient, to say the least, to have American capital inflows reduced so sharply over such a short period of time.

The depression of the early 1930s was felt throughout the world, although the magnitude and length of the crisis varied widely from country to country. At one extreme were countries like the United States and Canada. In the former, real GNP declined by 23 percent between 1930 and 1933; and the 1930 level was not again reached permanently until 1939. In Canada the decline was 30 percent; and recovery to the 1930 level was delayed until 1940. At the other end of the spectrum were countries like the United Kingdom and Australia, two countries marked by only a 5 percent decline between 1930 and 1931. In Australia the 1930 level was again reached in 1933, although in Britain recovery was delayed until 1935. Between these extremes were countries like France (a 17 percent decline between 1930 and 1936), Germany (a 15 percent fall between 1930 and 1932), and Argentina (14 percent between 1930 and 1932). Even in those countries, however, there were differences in the length of the depression. In Germany the 1930 level was again achieved in 1934; in Argentina it was 1937; but, in the case of France, it was 1950, five years after the end of World War II.

Precisely how this collage of developments in the United States and abroad and the sequence of financial events of the late 1920s and early 1930s led to the collapse of the 1930s is not part of this story.[1539] The focus here is in the growing disorder of international markets, in its consequences for the collapse of the 1930s, and in the effects of the collapse on the nature of international capital markets during the ensuing seven decades. To that end, it is important to understand that the capital flights of the early 1930s so impressed themselves on the minds of both economists and those politicians responsible for public policy that, a decade

---

[1539] See Michael D. Bordo and Anna J. Schwartz, "Monetary Policy Regimes and Economic Performance: The Historical Record," Working Paper 6201, September 1997, National Bureau of Economic Research, p. 83.

and a half later, one foundation block of the plan adopted for the reconstruction of the international financial system after World War II (the Bretton Woods Agreement) was a commitment to prevent such events in the future, even at the cost of nearly stifling the reemergence of private international capital markets. Extra-market controls were placed on international capital flows.

8-3c. World War II and the Bretton Woods era

Between 1939 and 1945, war once again placed strains on the world financial system. This time, however, the Allies made no effort to maintain free markets or to arrange financial flows based on formal debt. It was intended that the post–World War I agonies over the payment of debt and the related issues surrounding reparations were to be avoided. The plan was at least partially successful. Britain was, however, an exception. It borrowed heavily from Commonwealth countries during the war and from Canada and the United States just after the war (before the Marshall Plan). Britain was also obliged, once again, to liquidate 15 percent of its foreign assets, and therefore, it entered the post-war world in difficult financial straits. In general, the net international position of the other leading European pre-war creditors had also deteriorated, but none so seriously as that of the British.[1540]

Immediately after World War II, substantial inter-government capital flows – flows chiefly from the United States to European countries – were substituted for the large private capital flows from Britain to the settlement economies that had dominated global financial markets before World War I. These new flows were initially associated with Marshall Plan recovery aid, but they were soon followed by development grants to third world countries and by military aid to allies in the Cold War.[1541] As the Cold War changed to a hot war in Korea and Vietnam, these military grants became of overwhelming importance; from 1963 through 1970 they totaled more than $14.9 billion, an average of almost $1.9

[1540] Maddison, "Economic Policy and Performance," pp. 471–72. "As a result its net asset position declined from a positive balance of $21 billion in 1938 to a negative one of $2 billion in 1947. Unlike the situation after the First World War, these debts were honored in full and have been a very heavy burden for the U.K." The French losses were substantially less, but they amounted to the whole of French pre-war foreign holdings; the Dutch lost something over half of their foreign assets, the Belgians, very much less. Of this group, only the Germans improved their international position from the war, entering it as a debtor and coming out of it, eventually, as a creditor.

[1541] U.S. government transfers abroad averaged almost $2 billion a year between 1945 and 1949 and still amounted to $408 million a year over the decade 1950–59. *Historical Statistics of the United States, 1970*, Series U 15 to 25, p. 866.

billion a year.[1542] Government grants, together with expanding American private investment, soon eroded what had been an overwhelming American foreign credit position, converting a "dollar shortage" into a dollar superabundance, and ultimately, in the 1970s, upsetting the financial system put in place by Bretton Woods.[1543]

The formal structure of that system reflected the lessons that economists and politicians had thought that they learned in the inter-war period. Given their assumptions – assumptions that time was to prove were seriously flawed – the system was designed to assure the stability of exchange rates, but not at the cost of serious deterioration of domestic well-being. The importance of both domains – international and domestic – was recognized, and an institutional apparatus was set in place that, it was hoped, could adjudicate between the two. It should be noted, however, that, both de facto and de jure, the bias in the system was heavily weighted toward domestic considerations.

Bretton Woods required that the United States peg the dollar to gold (initially at $35 an ounce) and that other countries peg their currencies to the dollar. In its original design, however, Bretton Woods was not a fixed exchange rate system. Just as the gold standard had an escape clause for certain economic contingencies, a country other than the United States was permitted to change its currency's par value to correct a fundamental disequilibrium. Although left undefined, the term "fundamental disequilibrium" was "intended to refer to disturbances other than government policies that justified a change in par." Examples of such disturbances included changes in the terms of trade or in productivity. The countries were, however, supposed to obtain agreement in advance from the IMF to ensure that the change was not a response to a change in government policy.[1544]

Although the Bretton Woods agreement was signed in 1944, because of governmental controls on international capital movements, the system

---

[1542] Ibid.

[1543] But see Kindleberger, *A Financial History of Western Europe*, p. 424, for objections to the term "dollar shortage."

[1544] Michael D. Bordo and Anna J. Schwartz, "The Specie Standard as a Contingent Rule: Some Evidence for Core and Peripheral Countries, 1880–1990," paper prepared for the Conference: *Historical Perspectives on the Gold Standard: Portugal and the World*, Arrabida, Portugal, June 3/4 1994, p. 27. Michael D. Bordo, "The Bretton Woods International Monetary System: A Historical Overview," in Michael D. Bordo and Barry Eichengreen (eds.), *A Retrospective on the Bretton Woods System: Lessons for International Monetary Reform*, National Bureau of Economic Research Project Report (Chicago: University of Chicago Press, 1993), pp. 49–50. [Hereafter cited as Bordo, "The Bretton Woods International Monetary System."]

did not become fully operational until full convertibility on current account transactions was finally achieved in 1959.[1545] Although the system was to operate fairly well until the late 1960s, and although it was to formally survive until 1973, in 1959 the system differed in several dimensions from the structure that its architects had intended. These differences included the initial dominance of the United States in the international monetary institutional structure – a dominance soon to be challenged by a reemerging continental Europe – "the reduced prestige of the IMF, the rise of the dollar as a key currency and the decline of sterling, a shift from the adjustable peg system toward a de facto fixed exchange rate regime, and, finally, growing capital mobility."[1546] As a result, already by 1959 emerging signs of weakness had become apparent. A combination of the growth of liquid dollar claims in the hands of foreigners and the reduction in official, and especially U.S., gold holdings increasingly "convinced policymakers that, barring some alteration, the system was on a trajectory headed toward collapse."[1547]

The problems created by this new institutional structure – problems captured by the now-classic taxonomy *adjustment*, *liquidity*, and *confidence* – intensified during the 1960s. In terms of the first, the original Bretton Woods system allowed for adjustment in circumstances of fundamental disequilibrium, but countries chose not to adjust. On the one hand, some countries (particularly Germany) did not wish to appreciate because of concern for their export industries and the United States did not wish to devalue because it felt that other countries, concerned about their export industries, would be expected to follow.[1548] On the other hand, some countries avoided devaluation because of their expectation that devaluation might generate further devaluations and, thus, generate further speculation against their currency.[1549]

[1545] Peter M. Garber, "The Collapse of the Bretton Woods Fixed Exchange Rate System," in Michael D. Bordo and Barry Eichengreen (eds.), *A Retrospective on the Bretton Woods System: Lessons for International Monetary Reform*, National Bureau of Economic Research Project Report (Chicago: University of Chicago Press, 1993), p. 461. [Hereafter cited as Garber, "The Collapse of the Bretton Woods Fixed Exchange Rate System."]

[1546] Bordo, "The Bretton Woods International Monetary System," p. 48.

[1547] Garber, "The Collapse of the Bretton Woods Fixed Exchange Rate System," p. 461.

[1548] The exchange rate between dollars and gold remained at $35 an ounce until 1971.

[1549] W. Max Cordon, "Why Did the Bretton Woods System Break Down?" in Michael D. Bordo and Barry Eichengreen (eds.), *A Retrospective on the Bretton Woods System: Lesson for International Monetary Reform*, National Bureau of Economic Research Report (Chicago: University of Chicago Press, 1993), p. 506. [Hereafter cited as Cordon, "Why Did the Bretton Woods System Break Down?"]

In terms of the liquidity problem, the years after 1960 were marked by sources of liquidity "that were not adequate or reliable enough to finance the growth of output and trade. The world's monetary stock was insufficient by the late 1950s, IMF unconditional drawing rights were meager, and the supply of U.S. dollars depended on the U.S. balance of payments, which, in turn was related to the vagaries of government policy and the confidence problem."[1550] Although the United States maintained a surplus of exports over imports throughout the 1960s, the surplus declined from an average of $6.5 billion over the years 1961–5 to only $3.6 billion over the next half decade. Over the ten years 1961–70, American net investment abroad skyrocketed from an annual average of $1.0 billion in 1951–60 to $5.5 billion. In part this deficit was covered by a decline in the U.S. stock of gold; after falling by $5.5 billion between 1958 and 1960, it declined by another $4.9 billion over the next decade.[1551] In part, however, it was covered by the build up of U.S. dollar holdings abroad, particularly in Europe (the so-called Eurodollars).

The accumulation of U.S. and other foreign currency deposits in London banks was not new. Such deposits had existed in the interwar period and had only ended with the collapse of the international monetary system and the imposition of exchange controls during the 1930s. By the early 1960s the relaxation of exchange controls underwrote the reemergence of these dollar deposits, mainly deposits by European banks in banks in London. These deposits were, however, much larger than those of the 1920s; and, equally importantly, they were not immediately remitted to the Federal Reserve Bank of New York nor deposited in American banks, but instead were loaned to third parties in the United Kingdom or abroad.[1552] In London the management of the Midland Bank recognized a potential profit opportunity; and, in mid-1955, it moved to seek such dollar denominated deposits by offering 1 7/8 percent interest on thirty-day deposits (a rate that was 7/8 percent more than the maximum payable in the United States under regulation Q), selling those dollars for sterling on the spot market, and then, at the same time, buying them back in the forward market at a premium of 2 1/8 percent. They were thus able to attract sterling deposits at a cost of 4 percent at a time when the bank rate was 4.5 percent. These were the first "Eurodollars," but they were not the last; the financial innovation was quickly copied,

---

[1550] Bordo, "The Bretton Woods International Monetary System," pp. 50–51.

[1551] *United States Historical Statistics, 1970*, Series U 18–25, p. 866. In the 1960s gross private foreign investment totaled $47.5 (out of a total of $64.5) billion.

[1552] Catherine R. Schenk, "The Origins of the Eurodollar Market in London: 1955–1963," *Explorations in Economic History*, Vol. 35, No. 2 (April 1998), p. 221. [Hereafter cited as Schenk, "The Origins of the Eurodollar Market."]

first in the City and later throughout the world. In mid-1956 the Midland probably still accounted for at least half of all Eurodollar deposits, but seven years later they held only 3 percent of the U.K. banks' Eurocurrency deposits. Nor were U.K. banks alone in their attempts to attract dollar deposits. By the end of 1962, U.S. banks in London, British overseas banks, accepting houses, and Japanese banks had taken over the market; and U.S. banks accounted for almost one-third of the total. By March 1963 such deposits amounted to £1.17 billion, of which 85 percent represented Eurodollar transactions.[1553]

Although there is still some question of the origins of the deposits, it appears that there were probably three major sources. First, European commercial banks – banks seeking to employ liquid funds produced by America's accumulating balance of payment deficits – are believed to have been the main source of deposits. The second largest category of depositors was the European central banks themselves – banks also awash with dollars generated by the U.S. balance of payment deficits – and the Bank for International Settlement. The BIS sought to deposit its U.S. dollar surpluses in order to minimize the accounting of its official reserves. Finally, other sources, including U.S. corporations, probably accounted for something less than one-third of the total. The geographic distribution of the loans based on the Eurodollar deposits also shifted dramatically between 1955 and 1963. Initially almost all the funds had been employed in Britain; by the end of the period, however, the U.K. accounted for only about 10 percent of the total, while 40 percent were loaned in Europe, 40 percent in the U.S., and the last 10 percent as far away as Japan.[1554]

The liquidity problem led, in turn, to the problem of confidence, a problem that involved shifts between dollars and gold. "As outstanding dollar liabilities held by the rest of the world monetary authorities increased relative to the U.S. monetary gold stock, the likelihood of a run on the 'bank' increased. The probability of all dollar holders being able to convert their dollars into gold at the fixed price declined."[1555] The problem was intensified as the free market price of gold rose above the "fixed price" of $35 an ounce, and the holders of dollar balances abroad had an ever increasing incentive to turn those balances into $35 dollar gold and then resell that gold at the free market price. Still, there were policy makers who remained committed to Bretton Woods; and for three years, and despite the increasing level of exchange risk, Europe

---

[1553] Schenk, "The Origins of the Eurodollar Market," pp. 225–26, 229–30.
[1554] Schenk, "The Origins of the Eurodollar Market," pp. 231–32.
[1555] Bordo, "The Bretton Woods International Monetary System," pp. 50–51.

continued to absorb dollar claims, perhaps as much as $70 billion between 1968 and 1971.[1556] However, given the decisions of Presidents Johnson and Nixon to finance the Vietnam War by inflation rather than raising taxes, the structure could not be maintained; at some point a speculative attack on the dollar was inevitable.

The dollar flood increased the reserves of the surplus countries, triggering rapid money growth and inflation. In April 1971 the dollar inflow to West Germany reached $3 billion, and domestic pressure mounted for a revaluation of the mark. In the same month the U.S. balance of trade turned to a deficit for the first time, and influential voices in that country began urging dollar devaluation. On May 5, 1971, "the German central bank suspended official operations in the foreign exchange market and allowed the deutsche mark to float." Austria, Belgium, the Netherlands, and Switzerland soon followed suit. In the following months both France and the United Kingdom announced their intention to convert dollars into gold. The final act was inevitable. "On 15 August, at Camp David, President Nixon announced that he had directed Secretary Connolly 'to suspend temporarily the convertibility of the dollar into gold or other reserve assets.'" Nixon's decision ended what had become a key component of the Bretton Woods system; the remaining part – the adjustable peg – disappeared nineteen months later.[1557]

Since that time there has been substantial finger pointing within the academic community as to who was responsible for the demise of an institution that had worked well for more than a decade. At one extreme, some have argued that the breakdown of Bretton Woods was largely or entirely the fault of a hegemonic power's political decisions about fiscal and monetary policy, decisions that reflected solely domestic concerns and ignored their international implications. Those scholars argue that

> adjustment to the U.S. expansion was not comparable to adjustment to other kinds of shocks and more country-specific developments. The United States was the center of the system. It was unreasonable to expect numerous countries to appreciate – and to expect them to do so in a timely fashion – when even the full nature of the developments was not understood and a fixed exchange rate habit had developed. Furthermore, the surplus countries would have had to appreciate collectively since, if any one of them did on its own, it would lose competitiveness relative to the others. Thus, the U.S. expansion did put the system under an exceptional degree of strain. To that extent, special

[1556] Garber, "The Collapse of the Bretton Woods Fixed Exchange Rate System," pp. 483–84.

[1557] Bordo, "The Bretton Woods International Monetary System," p. 80.

blame attaches to U.S. policies. Given that the system had evolved into a dollar standard, the United States had an obligation to maintain conservative monetary policies that would avoid the need for many other countries to appreciate relative to the dollar.[1558]

At the other end of the spectrum are those who argue that, although

the breakdown in August 1971 resulted from a determined attempt by the U.S. authorities to bring about the real devaluation of the dollar to improve U.S. competitiveness, which had been eroded, it would have happened within the system if other countries had been more cooperative, appreciating their currencies sufficiently relative to gold while the dollar price of gold stayed unchanged, or agreeing to maintain their gold par values if the United States devalued the dollar. . . . The aim was, essentially, to force adjustment. The concern was not primarily with the accumulation of dollar assets by foreigners, but with the competitiveness of U.S. export- and import-competing industries.

"To summarize, this category of explanations essentially places the blame on countries other than the United States for failing to operate the system properly by adjusting appropriately at intervals."[1559]

Although the jury is still out, a more centrist view seems more reasonable than either extreme position; but it may be that the entire question is really irrelevant. "There will always be a need for adjustment. And, if there is a sustained reluctance to adjust, the system will eventually break down because of the confidence problem. Presumably, if the system had not broken down in March 1973 as a result of U.S. expansionary policies, it would have done so later as a result of the first oil shock and its consequences and, if not then, in the early 1980s."[1560]

In short, a system of fixed but occasionally adjusted exchange rates is incompatible with a high degree of capital mobility – in the years from the mid-1960s to the 1990s capital was becoming very mobile – and with domestic economic considerations dominating international considerations. Today economists talk about a trilemma; you can have only two out of the following: fixed exchange rates, free capital mobility, and independent domestic monetary policy.

In the words of Richard Cooper, Bretton Woods broke down because it was fundamentally flawed. The architects of the system had assumed that international mobility of capital would be low in the post-war era. The assumption was based on the notion that private investors would

---

[1558] Cordon, "Why Did the Bretton Woods System Break Down?" p. 508.
[1559] Cordon, "Why Did the Bretton Woods System Break Down?" p. 507. In particular it has been argued that Germany and Japan had not played by the rules.
[1560] Cordon, "Why Did the Bretton Woods System Break Down?" p. 508.

shy away from foreign investments after the experience of the 1930s and that many countries, including the United Kingdom, concerned with their outstanding sterling balances, would maintain controls on the movement of short-term capital. In fact, the IMF's Articles of Agreement enjoin all member countries to assist in enforcing the capital controls of those countries maintaining them. This provision, however, remained a dead letter.[1561] The major culprits were the increasingly efficient international capital market and each country's concerns about its domestic economy.

8-3d. The return to the global economy: the 1970s to the 1990s

Even more than the reconstruction of the gold standard in 1925 or the restoration of convertibility in 1958, the demise of Bretton Woods was a watershed. It transformed international monetary affairs in a way that neither of the others had done. Since central banks had first begun to use monetary policy to affect the macro-economy, the stability of exchange rates had been a major policy goal. Monetary policy was used to peg the exchange rate except during exceptional periods of war, reconstruction, and depression. As a consequence of international capital mobility, in 1973 economic policy was cut loose from these moorings, and exchange rates were ultimately allowed to float. Japan and the United States, for whom the importance of international transactions was still limited, opted to float immediately. In an effort to support currency pegs against major trading partners, for a time some countries continued to maintain tight capital controls. "The countries of Western Europe, for whom intra-European trade was exceptionally important and whose Common Agricultural Policy could be seriously disrupted by exchange rate controls, also sought to peg their currencies to one another, behind the shelter of legislative controls. Although they created new institutions to structure the international cooperation needed to support a collective currency peg, there was no going back. The continued development of financial markets, powered by advances in telecommunications and information-processing technologies, gravely hampered any effort to contain international financial flows. Such efforts were not only difficult, but they became increasingly costly; with the development of competing financial centers, countries imposing onerous controls risked losing their financial business to offshore markets. It was not only industrialized

---

[1561] Richard N Cooper, "Comment," in Michael D. Bordo and Barry Eichengreen, *A Retrospective on the Bretton Woods System: Lessons for International Monetary Reform*, National Bureau of Economic Research Project Report (Chicago: University of Chicago Press, 1993), pp. 104–5.

countries that were affected, developing countries that failed to liberalize risked being passed over by foreign investors. Liberalization, though inevitable, exacerbated the difficulty of pegging the exchange rate, leading a growing number of countries to float their currencies."[1562]

Although it is difficult to measure the level of international integration of the world's capital market, there can be little doubt that it increased substantially from the mid-1960s to the 1990s. For fifteen advanced industrial countries, the average of annual exports plus imports as a fraction of Gross Domestic product increased from 45 to 60 percent.[1563] Moreover, much of the growth was based on trade with countries outside the developed world. For example, in Europe imports from the newly industrializing countries in Asia and Latin America grew steadily; and, by the end of the 1980s, they constituted almost 10 percent of all OECD imports.[1564] Again, for a similar set of fifteen countries, on average, the ratio of their current account balance to national income doubled (from 0.013 to 0.026) between the years 1960 through 1973 and the years 1989 through 1996. In only two of the fifteen cases did the ratio decline.[1565]

Still, economists have recognized that the rise in international capital flows could have been the product of any number of changes in the investment environment. The causes of such an increase are not limited to reductions in the barriers to cross-border capital movements.[1566] In terms of alternative measures of "perfect capital mobility" Jeffrey Frankel has suggested that there are four definitions in widespread use:

> (1) The *Feldstein-Horioka* definition: exogenous changes in national savings (i.e. in either private savings or government budgets) can be easily financed by borrowing from abroad at the going real interest rate, and thus need not crowd out investment in the originating country (except perhaps to the extent that the country is large in world

---

[1562] Eichengreen, *Globalizing Capital*, pp. 130–38.

[1563] The fifteen are Australia, Austria, Belgium, Canada, Denmark, Finland, France, Germany, Italy, Japan, Netherlands, Norway, Sweden, the United Kingdom, and the United States.

[1564] Geoffrey Garrett, "Capital Mobility, Trade and Domestic Politics of Economic Policy," draft, November 1994, forthcoming in *International Organization*, p. 4. [Hereafter cited as Garrett, "Capital Mobility."]

[1565] The fifteen are Argentina (0.010 to 0.020), Australia (0.023 to 0.045), Canada (0.012 to 0.040), Denmark (0.019 to 0.018), Finland (0.017 to 0.051), France (0.006 to 0.007), Germany (0.010 to 0.027), Italy (0.021 to 0.016), Japan (0.010 to 0.021), Netherlands (0.013 to 0.030), Norway (0.024 to 0.029), Spain (0.012 to 0.032), Sweden (0.007 to 0.020), Great Britain (0.008 to 0.026), and the United States (0.005 to 0.012). Maurice Obstfeld and Alan M. Taylor, "World Capital Market: Integration, Crisis, and Growth," manuscript, June 1998, table 3.2, p. 64.

[1566] Garrett, "Capital Mobility," p. 4.

financial markets). (2) *Real interest parity*: International capital flows equalize real interest rates across countries. (3) *Uncovered interest parity*: Capital flows equalize expected rates of return on countries' bonds, despite exposure to exchange risk. (4) *Closed interest parity*: Capital flows equalize interest rates across countries when contracted in a common currency.[1567]

Because of data problems, it is somewhat difficult to completely operationalize these definitions; however, the evidence suggests that, popular notions aside, the international market was far from perfect in the 1970s, that there were major improvements during the 1980s, but that, under the strictest definition (closed interest parity), the international market was still not "perfect" in the 1990s. "Capital controls and other barriers to the movement of capital across national boundaries remained for such countries as the United Kingdom and Japan as recently as 1979, and France and Italy as late as 1986."[1568] The 1980s, however, saw a major shift of policies in the direction of greater mobility. Between 1975 and 1990 the correlation between private domestic savings and private domestic investment in the fifteen industrialized countries declined from 0.85 to 0.20, and the number of government restrictions imposed on cross-border capital flows fell by a similar amount.[1569] Thus, over the 1980s, worldwide trends had all but eliminated short-term interest differentials for the major industrialized countries. However, a currency premium – a combination of exchange rate risk premiums plus expected real currency depreciation – still remains; and, thus, even with the equalization of covered interest rates, large differentials in real interest rates remain. Moreover, "there is a further gap that separates real interest parity from the proposition that changes in national saving do not crowd out investment because they are readily financed by borrowing from abroad. Bonds are not perfect substitutes for equities, and equities are not perfect substitutes for plant and equipment. Thus at each stage, there are good reasons to think that shortfalls in national saving continue to be capable of crowding out [at least some] investment."[1570]

[1567] Jeffrey A. Frankel, "Quantifying International Capital Mobility in the 1980s," in B. Douglas Bernheim and John B. Shoven, *National Saving and Economic Performance*, National Bureau of Economic Research Project Report (Chicago: University of Chicago Press, 1991), pp. 228–29. [Hereafter cited as Frankel, "Quantifying International Capital Mobility."]

[1568] Frankel, "Quantifying International Capital Mobility," p. 252.

[1569] Garrett, "Capital Mobility," pp. 4–5 and figure 2. The categories are restrictions on the capital account, on bilateral payments with IMF members, on bilateral payments with nonmembers, and on foreign deposits. For the period 1967 to 1990 the correlation between the two series is 0.77.

[1570] Frankel, "Quantifying International Capital Mobility in the 1980s", pp. 252–53.

The increasing level of internationalization of the world's financial markets can also be seen in the spread of "international banking centers." Basing his rating largely on the presence in the financial center of local bank headquarters of large internationally active commercial banks, Howard Reed has provided an index of the relative importance of international banking centers over the eight decades between 1900 and 1980.[1571] In 1900 only three cities achieved a rank score of 85 or over: London (100), New York (87), and Paris (85). By 1930 the number had fallen to two – London (100) and New York (93) – and that ranking still held in 1947: London (100) and New York (92). By 1960 Paris had rejoined the elite circle – London (100), New York (97), Paris (85) – but fifteen years later the 1900 set of cities had been supplemented only by the addition of Tokyo: London (100), New York (99), Tokyo (96), and Paris (93). By 1980, however, the movement toward globalization was clear; eleven cities scored 85 or more: London (100), New York (100), Paris, Frankfurt, and Tokyo (each 90), Hamburg and Hong Kong (both 89), Zurich (88), San Francisco and Chicago (both 87), and Amsterdam (86).

Reed has also produced a similar listing for "international financial centers" in the years since 1955. The results are similar, but there are some important differences. Using the same criteria of 85 or more in the rank score, in 1955 there were three such centers: New York (100), London (99), and Paris (86). A decade later, London had supplanted New York as the leading center; and the number of cities in the set had fallen to two: London (100) and New York (96). By 1975, however, the list of qualifying centers had grown to five: London (100), New York (95), Tokyo (90), Paris (90), and Frankfurt (87). Until then the banking center and the financial center stories are much the same, but over the next five years the two scenarios diverged sharply. While the number of banking centers had soared to eleven, the number of financial centers surpassing the 85 criteria had declined to two – London and New York – and London (100) had far outpaced New York (85).[1572] Thus, it appears that, although the financial markets were rapidly becoming global, as in the years leading up to World War I, London was once again the undisputed international financial capital of the world. For example, although the volume of trading on the New York Stock Exchange remained higher than that on the London market, and although in the

[1571] Howard Curtis Reed, *The Preeminence of International Financial Centers* (New York: Praeger Publishers, 1981), table 2.2, pp. 20–21. [Hereafter cited as Reed, *International Financial Centers*.]

[1572] Reed, *International Financial Centers*, table 2.4, pp. 28–29.

early 1980s London's second position among securities exchanges was briefly challenged by Tokyo, after the mid-1970s, as in the years before 1914, London was unchallenged as the premier market in international securities.

What events triggered the resurgence of London and the relative decline of New York? At the end of World War II most experts would have assumed that New York would remain the world's leading financial center for the foreseeable future. Bretton Woods had made the U.S. dollar the world's reserve currency; the country owned two-thirds of the world's gold reserves; its GNP was as large as the combined GNP of the rest of the Western world; it was the principal source of international investment; and its banks were the largest and soundest. In the literature New York's inability to hold its dominant position has been attributed to two factors: the U.S. government's legal attempts to control capital flows and the state of New York's restrictions on foreign branch banking. Neither explanation, however, appears sufficient to account for the rapid decline in the relative position of New York. Almost certainly of more importance was, initially, the adverse U.S. balance of payments that led, first, to the innovation of the Eurodollar and ultimately, in 1971, to the breakdown of the Bretton Woods system of fixed exchange rates; and, second, the not completely unrelated erosion of the U.S. position as undisputed leader of the non-communist world. In particular, when OPEC decisions triggered a fourfold increase in petroleum prices and transferred billions of dollars in wealth from the industrialized West to the oil producing countries, the employment of those funds for recycling through the international system was overwhelmingly centered in London, even though interest rates on day deposits were higher in New York. The OPEC nations apparently feared that the U.S. authorities might somehow, use their control of the deposits to obtain price concessions on oil or political concessions from Arab states over territorial disputes with Israel. Given the later American decision to freeze Iranian government assets, such fears may not have been unreasonable. Under any conditions, with the decline in U.S. political dominance, there were other countries (including the United Kingdom) that were more than ready to enjoy the benefits of the OPEC deposits.

In the case of London, its role as an international finance center in the immediate post-war years appears to have rested on the residual leadership emanating from the international banking and financial legacies of the earlier colonial era. The City still retained close ties with financial markets in Bombay, Calcutta, Hong Kong, Shanghai, Singapore, Tientsin, Johannesburg, Kuala Lumpur, Melbourne, Sydney, and Rangoon as well as vestigial ties with centers in Latin America. The innovation of the

Eurodollar gave London banks access to additional capital, and the OPEC decision to keep their deposits in London solidified the City's claim of dominance.[1573]

8-4. Conclusions

Thus, as the twentieth century nears its end, the emerging international capital market has come to resemble an institutional structure that the ghosts of the partners in such firms as Glyn-Mills and J.P. Morgan might well recognize as an infrastructure similar to the one that had directed and channeled the flows of savings from the developed to the developing world in the years and months leading up to August 1914. As in 1914, it is an integrated market with few barriers to the international movement of capital, and a market with its center in London. Closer inspection, however, would reveal that it is quite a different market. It is no longer held together by an international commitment to the gold standard; instead, exchange rates were largely free to fluctuate. London is no longer supported by just three major international banking centers (London, New York, and Paris), but by nearly a dozen such nodes; new centers have developed not only in European cities like Amsterdam and Zurich, but also in such distant places as San Francisco, Hong Kong, and Tokyo. Moreover, the network was much larger – it encompassed a much larger population of savers and investors and many more political regimes – and those people and politicians were served, on average, by a much more well-developed set of domestic financial institutions.

The world market is obviously much nearer to the economists' definition of perfection, but it is also an economic regime that has been marked by a series of economic crises, crises that, from some viewpoints, appear more like those of the 1920s and 1930s than those of the decades leading up to World War I. Is it possible that there are still lessons to be learned from the events of a century ago, when world financial markets were less well developed and were bound together by the "fetters" of the international gold standard?

[1573] Reed, *International Financial Centers*, pp. 32–33, 58.

CHAPTER 9

Lessons from the past

9-1. Introduction

In 1999 the international capital market, although still not a perfect market by an economist's definition of the term, is certainly much broader and almost certainly more efficient than it was two and a half decades ago. In fact, its breadth and efficiency have caused a number of highly respectable economists to suggest arguments that almost certainly would, only recently, have been considered heresy: namely, that "perfection" carries with it some serious problems and that, at times, it may constitute a considerably less than perfect institutional structure. There have been financial crises in Mexico and Latin America in the early 1980s, and again in the mid-1990s. Since the mid-1990s the Japanese miracle has become a bad dream. In 1998 and 1999 a major Asian crisis – a crisis that has already begun to impact Brazil and threatens to engulf markets throughout the western world – has had a dramatic effect on the financial infrastructure of developing Asian countries, countries like Korea, Thailand, Indonesia, and Malaysia. Given these apparently continuing problems, could policy makers have learned anything from the history of the world's financial markets in the years leading up to World War I?

In a recent article in *The Economist*, Jeffrey Sachs, citing dramatic declines in GDP in Indonesia, in Thailand, South Korea, and Hong Kong, a near breakdown – that is, collapses of share prices of nearly 50 percent or more – of the stock markets of Indonesia, Brazil, South Korea, Hong Kong, and Thailand, and the dramatic erosion of the Thai baht, the South Korean won, and the Indonesian rupiah, concludes that "the collapse of the emerging markets and its ricochet effect on advanced economies may not be the end of globalization. But it is certainly the end of an era."[1574] In a similar vein, the normally staid *Los Angeles Times* published a

---

[1574] Jeffery Sachs "Global Capitalism," *The Economist*, September 12–18, 1998, pp. 23–24. Sachs is a professor of international trade at Harvard and director of the Harvard Institute for International Development.

special report on the world economy entitled "Are Free Markets Failing"; the author concludes: "Not necessarily. But they urgently need help."[1575] And the advice (even from economists) on what form that help should take frequently involves recommendations for direct government interference in the operation of those free markets. Sachs argues that "the best idea around is that developing countries should impose their own supervisory controls on short-term international borrowing by domestic financial institutions." Similar conclusions have been reached by both Joseph Stiglitz, the World Bank's chief economist, and MIT economist Paul Krugman. Those conclusions constitute a conspicuous departure from the free-market doctrine that Western policy makers and economists have long been preaching and that have been near articles of faith among mainstream economists. Krugman, for example, is quoted as saying "that while currency controls inevitably cause distortions and work badly if kept in place too long, when you face the kind of disaster now occurring in Asia, the question has to be: badly compared to what."[1576]

Nor have pleas for intervention during this world crisis been limited to underdeveloped and developing countries. In the United States the New York Federal Reserve Bank found it necessary to organize a bailout of Long-Term Capital Management, a firm "whose senior partners included John W. Meriwether, once a near-legendary trader at Salomon Brothers, and Myron S. Sholes and Robert C. Merton, who shared the 1997 Nobel Prize in economics for co-inventing the fundamental mathematical techniques of modern risk management." Although subject to criticism for its actions, the New York Fed concluded that the firm was "too big to fail," a conclusion that should remind the reader of two decisions of the Bank of England: first, to organize a bailout of Baring Brothers in the 1890s, and, second, to refuse to intervene in a similar Baring debacle a century later.[1577] Perhaps, then, history may cast some light on contemporary problems.

[1575] James Flanigan, A *Los Angeles Times* Special Report, "The World Economy: Are Free Markets Failing," *Los Angeles Times*, Section S, Wednesday, September 16, 1998, pp. S1–S4.

[1576] Ibid., p. S3. Not all economists, however, have adopted this heretofore heretical position. Sebastian Edwards, comparing the experiences of Argentina, Brazil, and Mexico with those of Chile and Colombia during the 1980 debt crisis, concludes that "capital outflow limits don't work." Sebastian Edwards, "Capital Outflow Limits Don't Work," *Los Angeles Times*, Monday, October 12, 1998, p. B5.

[1577] Charles R. Morris, "Financial Follies," *Los Angeles Times*, Section M, Sunday October 4, 1998, pp. M1, M6. *The Wall Street Journal* on October 8, 1998, reported that Long Term Capital had already used up $1.9 billion of the $3.625 billion

9-2. **Japan**

*9-2a. Introduction: Japanese foreign investment in the
past thirty years*
Although the world crisis of the late 1990s has had its most devastating impact on countries like Indonesia, in terms of the world's financial infrastructure, it is Japan's problems that probably present the most serious long-term threat to international stability. In the nineteenth century, Britain was the largest source of the savings that were channeled into world capital markets. From 1914 until the early 1980s that position was held by the United States. From the early 1980s to the mid-1990s, however, Japan was the world's largest exporter of capital. "Despite having the highest investment rate of all major industrial countries, Japan has invested less at home than it has saved," transferring a substantial part of its savings abroad.[1578] That country's annual net long-term capital flows averaged only $7.4 billion in 1980–82; but that figure had risen to $133.0 billion in the years 1986–88, and, despite a net import of long term capital in 1991, still averaged $47.9 billion in the years 1991–93.[1579]

Over the entire fourteen-year period, developments in Japan's capital account can be divided into three different phases. "In the first half of the decade, long-term capital flows (gross and net) grew rapidly, albeit from a low base, while short-term flows were relatively small and stable." The increase in the long-term flows can, in large part, be traced to the liberalization of government controls that began with the 1980 revision of the Foreign Exchange and Transactions Control Law, a revision that, among other changes, abolished the requirement that the government give prior approval of investments in foreign securities. In the second half of the decade, "long-term capital outflows continued their rapid rise, with foreign direct investment becoming an important component of capital exports"; however, unlike the earlier period, there was, at the same time, a net inflow of short-term capital. Finally, in the early 1990s, although the gross outflow of long-term capital declined dramatically, Japan, having borrowed large amounts of short-term capital in the late

---

bailout injected the previous week by the Fed-organized consortium of financial institutions (pp. C1, C15).

[1578] Juha Kähkönen, "Japan's Capital Flows," in Ulrich Baumgartner and Guy Meredith, *Savings Behavior and the Asset Price "Bubble" in Japan: Analytical Studies*, International Monetary Fund, Occasional Paper No. 124, April 1995 (Washington, D.C.: International Monetary Fund, 1995), p. 16. [Hereafter cited as Kähkönen, "Japan's Capital Flows."]

[1579] Kähkönen, "Japan's Capital Flows," table 3.1, p. 18.

1980s, began to repay those debts and became a net exporter of short-term finance. In part, the decline in long-term capital exports can be simply traced to the educational effects of the passage of time: "Japanese investors having had sufficient time to reach a desired degree of intentional diversification." More importantly, however, were, first, the fact that the collapse of the asset price bubble in 1990 had reduced the level of the financial system's unrealized capital gains – gains that had never been reported on the balance sheets of those institutions – and, second, the fact that, as banks attempted to meet BIS guidelines, there was a growing concern about the adequacy of their capital base.[1580]

During the late 1980s and early 1990s the overseas flows of Japanese long-term capital were largely directed toward the developed world. Between 1988 and 1993 the United States received 32 percent of the total; the United Kingdom and other countries in the European Union were the beneficiaries of 43 percent. Of the 26 percent channeled to the rest of the world, Hong Kong, Korea, Singapore, and Taiwan received less than 2 percent.

Japan's total net financial flows to developing countries have, from the mid-1980s until recently, averaged about $20 billion annually. About half has come from governmental development assistance (contributions to multilateral financial institutions, bilateral loans, grants, and technical assistance); other official flows, including loans from the Export-Import Bank of Japan, accounted for an additional 10 percent; and the remainder came from the private sector (loans from commercial banks, direct investment, and commercial bank co-financing with the Export-Import Bank and with multilateral development institutions).[1581]

In the aggregate, long-term investment took a variety of forms: 56 percent represented purchases of securities, 26 percent was direct, 12 percent was in the form of loans, and the remaining 6 percent took "other" forms.[1582] Securities were clearly the most important vehicle for transferring Japan's savings abroad. "Investment by Japanese residents in foreign securities grew more than tenfold between 1982 and 1986, reaching a peak of $113 billion in 1989. The rapid rise in securities investment was almost entirely in the form of bonds." During the 1980s and early 1990s investment in securities other than bonds was relatively limited. Between 1985 and 1992 investment in stocks and shares represented, on average, less than 8 percent of the total investment in securities and exceeded $10 billion only in 1987 and 1989. It did, however,

---

[1580] Kähkönen, "Japan's Capital Flows," pp. 16–19.
[1581] Kähkönen, "Japan's Capital Flows," pp. 23–24.
[1582] Kähkönen, "Japan's Capital Flows," table 3.3, p. 21.

reach almost 30 percent of the total in 1993, but, at that time, the total value invested in equities was less than it had been in either 1987 or 1988.[1583]

In the years after World War II, in part because of stringent government regulations, annual outflows of direct foreign investment rose only slowly, to an average of $150 million per year in the second half of the 1960s. In those early post-war years, foreign direct investment was primarily for two purposes: to secure supplies of fuel and of the raw materials that were required by the manufacturing sector and to take advantage of cheaper skilled workers in labor-intensive manufacturing industries in nearby Asian countries. In the 1950s and 1960s about two-thirds of direct investment was channeled toward developing countries in Asia and Latin America, countries that included Hong Kong, South Korea, Indonesia, and Brazil.

In the years immediately after 1970, direct investment increased sharply. It rose fivefold in the first three years, and it then stabilized at about $2 billion annually for the rest of the decade. The increase was, in large part, a response to changes in government policy. Not only were the regulations on overseas investment eased, but the new policies actively promoted such investments. In that decade, although investment in mining declined and large investments were made in the United States – investments intended to aid the distribution of automobiles and other consumer durables – the bias toward underdeveloped countries in Japan's capital exports was still evident.

That bias did not, however, survive the next decade, a decade that saw Japan's direct foreign investment growing spectacularly (from $4.6 billion in 1980 to a peak of $67.5 billion in 1989). First, as the nation's industrialized trading partners became more protectionist, it became necessary for exporting firms to make defensive investments, if they were to protect their market share. In particular, Japanese auto and consumer electronics firms established plants in Europe and North America. Second, Japanese firms, responding in part to the oil crisis, became more knowledge intensive; as a result, raw materials became relatively less important and investment in Asian manufacturing declined. Finally, Japanese banks and investment firms utilized excess funds to expand their presence abroad, especially in the developed world. Investments in finance, insurance, transport, and real estate increased particularly fast; the share of the tertiary sector in total direct investment reached 70 percent; and service-oriented industries tend to be located near their markets. As a result of these changes in the industrial structure of the

---

[1583] Kähkönen, "Japan's Capital Flows," pp. 19–20, table 3.3, p. 21.

investment flows, the regional distribution changed as well. The share of developing countries declined sharply: industrialized countries absorbed over two-thirds of the total; in 1988–90 the United States received over one-half of that total. The overseas boom in direct investment came to an end in the early 1990s, but, although the total declined, the regional and sectoral pattern remained broadly the same as in the years of rapid growth.[1584]

"During the 1980s the Japanese financial system was widely regarded as a model to be emulated both by developed countries and emerging economies." Economists and businessmen believed that the "main bank system" – a system that saw most non-financial firms securely attached by both custom and economic links to a major bank – provided close monitoring to guarantee that the bank's funds were not wasted but invested profitably for the long term, assured the world that, if management got out of line they could be disciplined, and convinced potential stockholders that adequate funds were available to see a company through difficult times. The "true believers" argued that the U.S. economy would function better, if only it were redesigned along Japanese lines. "By the middle of the 90s these perceptions of the Japanese and U.S. financial systems had apparently been reversed."[1585]

9-2b. The evolution of the Japanese financial infrastructure, 1870–1970

9-2b(1). Introduction: Given the beliefs of the 1980s as well as Japan's recent role in international finance, it seems appropriate to examine that country's financial structure in light of possible "lessons of the past." What do we know about the history of the evolution of Japanese financial markets? In the years of the "miracle," the Japanese financial infrastructure displayed two characteristics that set it apart from both Britain and the United States. First, the dominance of intermediated markets, and, within those markets, the dominance of bank intermediation; and a corollary to that dominance: the relatively minor role played by direct

[1584] Robert C. Hsu, "Direct Overseas Investment," *MIT Encyclopedia of the Japanese Economy* (Cambridge, Mass.: MIT Press, 1994), pp. 101–3. Kähkönen, "Japan's Capital Flows," pp. 26–27. Marumi Ichiki, "Japanese Overseas Investments," in Foundation for Advanced Information and Research, Japan (FAIR), *Japan's Financial Markets*, Fair Fact Series II (Singapore: Look Japan Publishing, 1991), pp. 308–9.

[1585] Franklin Allen, "The Future of the Japanese Financial System," the Wharton School, University of Pennsylvania, Financial Institutions Center, Working Paper 96–56, August 1996, pp. 1–2. [Hereafter cited as Allen, "Japanese Financial System."]

finance. Second, the pervasive influence (both direct and indirect) of the government in the process of financial decision making.[1586]

In the quinquennia 1981–85, of the total flow of funds passing through the financial sector, the banks, both public and private, were responsible for 54 percent in Japan but for only 36 percent in the United States.[1587] Although the data are not strictly comparable, a similar pattern can be seen in the organizational structure of the two financial systems. In Japan in 1950, the "Banking System" accounted for 97 percent of the total assets of the "Main Types of Financial Institutions"; in the United States the figure was 50 percent in 1949 and 48 percent in 1952. In 1977 the Japanese figure was still 92 percent; in 1975 the U.S proportion was 50 percent.[1588]

In terms of the relative role of direct investment, two pieces of evidence underscore the difference between Japan and the United States. In the late 1970s in Japan, loans by financial institutions accounted for 23 percent of the total of all financial assets; but such loans represented less than 8 percent in the United States.[1589] A similar picture emerges from a 1993 study of the distribution of corporate equity among different categories of shareholders. In Japan, banks and "other financial institutions" held 23 percent, insurance companies, pension funds, and mutual funds 21 percent, and individuals only 24 percent. In the United States the figure for "banks and other financial institutions" was 4 percent, that for insurance companies, pension funds, and mutual funds 42 percent, and for individuals 49 percent.[1590]

[1586] Thomas F. Cargill and Shoichi Royama, *The Transition of Finance in Japan and the United States: A Comparative Study* (Stanford, Calif.: Hoover Institution Press, Stanford University, 1988), p. 22. [Hereafter cited as Cargill and Royama, *The Transition of Finance.*]

[1587] Ibid., tables 2.3 and 2.4, pp. 26–29.

[1588] Raymond W. Goldsmith, *The Financial Development of Japan, 1868–1977* (New Haven: Yale University Press, 1983), table 7–10, p. 166. [Hereafter cited as Goldsmith, *Japan.*] Raymond W. Goldsmith, *Financial Intermediaries in the American Economy Since 1900*, Study of the National Bureau of Economic Research (Princeton: Princeton University Press, 1958), table 11, p. 75. [Hereafter cited as Goldsmith, *Financial Intermediaries.*] Raymond W. Goldsmith, *The National Balance Sheet of the United States, 1953–1980*, National Bureau of Economic Research Monograph (Chicago: University of Chicago Press, 1982), p. 42. [Hereafter cited as Goldsmith, *National Balance Sheet of the United States.*]

[1589] Raymond W. Goldsmith, *Comparative National Balance Sheets: A Study of Twenty Countries, 1688–1978* (Chicago: University of Chicago Press, 1985), table A 12, pp. 255–56 and table A 22, pp. 300–1.

[1590] Allen, "The Japanese Financial System," figure 5. The source of the data was *Organization for Economic Co-Operation and Development – Financial Market Trends*, Number 62, November 1995.

Finally, although the indirect role of the government in the two countries is difficult to quantify, their direct importance can be measured by the relative size of government institutions in each nation's banking sector. In the U.S. case, the Federal Reserve Banks and the Postal Savings System accounted for 20 percent of the system's assets in 1952, and that figure had fallen to less than 10 percent by 1975. In Japan, even if the cooperative agricultural banks and the cooperative nonagricultural banks are classified as private, government institutions accounted for 37 percent of the sector's assets in 1950 and 36 percent in 1977.[1591] Both characteristics – bank dominance and the role of the government – have strong historical precedents.

9-2b(2). The private banks: Given the importance of banks in the financial structure, it appears reasonable to begin the examination of the financial system with those institutions. Today the Japanese banking system consists, in addition to the Bank of Japan, of seven different types of institutions: city banks, regional or local banks, long-term credit banks, trust banks, foreign banks, and other financial institutions specializing in providing banking services for small business.[1592] That structure is a product of more than a century of institutional innovation and evolution.

In 1868 in the wake of the Meiji restoration, the Japanese government moved to establish a modern industrial economy. As part of that attempt, western financial institutions were introduced. Although initially entry into the banking system was easy and there was little government regulation, the regulatory environment soon changed.[1593] The National Bank Decree of 1871 introduced a series of tight regulations that were to govern the newly established national banks, regulations that "thereafter, were to characterize the interventionist character of Japanese financial authority."[1594] The banks quickly took advantage of their new right to issue bank notes and rapidly expanded both loans *and* the money supply; however, the increase in bank notes touched off a paper money inflation that weakened the Japanese economy. In 1881 Masayoshi Matsuka

---

[1591] Goldsmith, *Financial Intermediaries*, table 11, p. 75. Goldsmith, *National Balance Sheet of the United States*, p. 42. Goldsmith, *Japan*, table 7–10, p. 166.

[1592] Cargill and Royama, *The Transition of Finance*, p. 23.

[1593] Allen, "Japanese Financial System," p. 3.

[1594] The decree established minimum capital requirements, suggested that a 25 percent reserve (in the form of national bonds) be held against all deposits, prohibited lending against the security of its own stock, and permitted bank loans to be made in the form of bank notes. Norio Tamaki, *Japanese Banking: A History, 1859–1959* (Cambridge: Cambridge University Press, 1995), p. 31. [Hereafter cited as Tamaki, *Japanese Banking*.]

became Finance Minister and moved to restructure the financial system. Over the next two decades he oversaw the establishment of a central bank (the Bank of Japan), restored convertibility between paper money and silver, restructured the commercial banking system, privatized government-owned firms, and encouraged infrastructure and industrial development by fostering securities markets and by establishing the first of the special (long-term credit) banks. In 1897 he was largely responsible for Japan's adopting the gold standard.

Convertibility involved the replacement of both the government's fiat issues and the private bank notes with notes of the Bank of Japan. In the process of reaching that goal, in 1883 Matsuka oversaw the withdrawal of the right of private bank note issue. Thus, by the end of the 1880s, the national banks were gone. Most had become "ordinary banks" joining the previously established, more numerous, and successful private banks and the so-called quasi banks. By the end of the 1890s the country had some 1,500 ordinary commercial banks with more than 1,000 branches.[1595]

The agricultural and stock market crisis of 1896 led the Bank of Japan to begin "discounting bills covered by specified brands of stocks and shares," and that action provided evidence that the bank would, in the future, act as lender of last resort. The change required that the Bank of Japan's by-laws be changed to permit such discounting, and with that change the Bank was "thus qualified fully and finally as the modern central bank."[1596]

In terms of the establishment of special banks, Matsukata pushed the Bank of Japan to develop a tight working relationship with the Yokohama Specie Bank – a bank originally established to organize a market for silver and gold bullion – and he tied both institutions to the Ministry of Finance.[1597] But more was to come; Matsukata's name became almost synonymous with government banking. In rapid succession, beginning in 1896, the government established the Hypothec Bank, the supporting Agri-Industrial and the Hokkaido Development Banks, and finally, in 1900, the Industrial Bank of Japan.[1598]

[1595] Richard Sylla, "Emerging Markets in History: The United States, Japan, and Argentina," in R. Sato and R. Rama Chandran, and K. Miño (eds.), *Global Competition and Integration* (Boston: Kluwer Academic Publishers, December 1998), chapter 19, pp. 427–46. [Hereafter cited as Sylla, "Emerging Markets."]

[1596] Tamaki, *Japanese Banking*, pp. 66–67.

[1597] Richard Sylla, "Emerging Markets," p. 432–33. Tamaki, *Japanese Banking*, pp. 46–47.

[1598] Tamaki, *Japanese Banking*, pp. 98–101. For a discussion of the role of the new government banks, see below.

Despite the size and influence of the government banks, private banks have always been the largest single component of the Japanese financial system. At the end of the nineteenth century, the commercial banks began to make long-term, as well as short-term, loans to industrial firms, but "contrary to the long-maintained proposition that the banks, especially the large ones, were a dominant factor in providing industrial capital," the evidence indicates that "the importance of large banks as owners of individual shares and as individual financiers has been significantly overstated." The bank records reveal that the industrial finance provided by the large banks was limited in magnitude to no more than 15 percent of the total paid-in industrial capital; often it was much less; and it was certainly insufficient to justify the conclusion that "the banks were the major source of industrial financing by the end of the [nineteenth] century." Despite the relatively small size of the financial infusions, these early years saw the beginning of the bank/zaibatsu connection that was later to become a major characteristic of the Japanese economy. "Many of the long-term loans made by the largest banks went to a small number of firms which were closely connected with these banks or ventures which were organized by the bankers themselves. These were the zaibatsu industrial firms in mining, shipbuilding, and other industries, and they were in many instances firms which were established from the former government [owned] plants." During the 1897–98 recession, for example, both the Mitsui and the Mitsubishi banks "curtailed loans as much as possible to general borrowers" and confined large loans to firms that were bank related. The firms that did receive long-term credit were, however, still "small in number compared to the large number of firms which lamented the lack of long-term credit."[1599]

Thus by 1914 the skeleton of what was to become the pre–World War II Japanese banking system was in place; however, it was the economic boom touched off by World War I and the problems of the 1920s that were to have the most profound impact on Japanese banking practices. It was during the war that the largest banks (now called zaibatsu banks) "began to advance significant sums in long-term loans to industrial firms in such capital-using industries as the heavy chemical and utility industries." Moreover, these new recipients were not firms that previously had had a zaibatsu connection; those "first-generation" recipients had, by the end of the boom, become largely financially self-sufficient.

[1599] Kozo Yamamura, "Entrepreneurship, Ownership, and Management in Japan," in Kozo Yamamura (ed.), *The Economic Emergence of Modern Japan* (Cambridge: Cambridge University Press, 1997), pp. 326–28. [Hereafter cited as Yamamura, "Entrepreneurship, Ownership, and Management."]

The 1920s were marked by a series of financial crises, in 1920, 1923, and 1927. The first of these was triggered by the end of the wartime boom; the second, was associated with the immediate problems arising from the great earthquake; the last and largest, although it too had its roots in earthquake, did not really impact the economy until 1927 when "the number of closed, nearly closed, and officially suspended banks reached 126."[1600] The bank managers' ability to make sound business decisions in the immediate post-war environment had been badly warped by the profits they had earned from their aggressive behavior during the war boom; but, under any conditions, it would have been difficult to painlessly contract their over-extended businesses.[1601] The underlying causes of the period of financial turbulence that began in 1923 certainly included the earthquake. In addition to the massive physical damage, the quake also produced the "Earthquake bills," notes that many borrowers were unable to pay, but notes that were supposed to be guaranteed by the Bank of Japan. On the one hand, the "guarantee" limited the Bank's ability to exercise effective monetary policy. On the other hand, it "constrained the activities of banks because the banks had to depend on heel-dragging political decisions by the government as to the amount of loans to be made to banks holding these bills." The problems were also compounded by the many banks that had become "organs" of their clients. Those banks had committed a large fraction of their assets to a small set of firms; and, since a client's bankruptcy would have meant the end of the bank itself, they found themselves forced to make further unsound loans to those same, mostly industrial firms. The "organ" banks became the particular targets of a series of nationwide bank runs.[1602] Clearly the banks had concentrated too large a fraction of their assets in too few firms, particularly firms owned by directors or shareholders. In supplying such large amounts of capital, the banks failed to secure a sufficient guarantee of the borrowing firms' ability to repay. In addition, all too often, the banks either ignored, or even sabotaged, attempts to audit their business conduct.[1603]

As a result of the crises, depositors sought the safety of the largest banks, particularly the giant zaibatsu banks. Those banks had survived the crises with only an occasional run on their branches, runs similar to those that, in other cases, had caused many of the smaller banks to close

---

[1600] Tamaki, *Japanese Banking*, pp. 147–54. Allen, "Japanese Financial System," p. 3.
[1601] Tamaki, *Japanese Banking*, p. 153.
[1602] Yamamura, "Entrepreneurship, Ownership, and Management," p. 336.
[1603] Tamaki, *Japanese Banking*, p. 153.

their doors.[1604] Investors, too, lured by the apparent safety of the zaibatsu banks, turned their attention to those institutions. Finally, government policy also contributed to rapid concentration of banking during the 1920s. First, the Ministry of Finance, acting on the government's desire to stabilize the financial markets, "actively promoted mergers and unification's of weaker (small and/or local) banks." Beginning in 1924 the Ministry "engaged in an active program to reduce the number of banks in each prefecture, to extend assistance in the evaluation of assets at the time of merger, and to help select the best-qualified managers for the newly unified banks." "The Ministry's 'persuasion' was extremely effective in numerous instances." Second, the fallout from the 1927 crisis produced the Bank Act of 1927, an act that dramatically increased the capitalization required for an "ordinary" bank. Since 809 of the 1,422 ordinary banks proved to have insufficient capital to qualify, the new law touched off another surge of bank amalgamations. Thus, the giant banks grew rapidly in strength, in absolute and in relative terms, both through increases in their capital and deposits and through mergers with the smaller weaker banks. "One could say that the zaibatsu banks became, during the 1920s, investment banks of the German type."[1605]

Between 1919 and 1927 the zaibatsu banks increased their share of total bank deposits from 25 to 31 percent; and, by the latter date, the eight zaibatsu (including banks, insurance companies, and credit companies) accounted for 46 percent of the total capital, deposits, and reserves of all private banks. More and more the zaibatsu banks moved to provide long-term capital not only to firms within the family but also, increasingly, to non-zaibatsu firms. Although much of the investments in non-zaibatsu firms took the form of bond purchases (in 1929 the zaibatsu banks held more than one-quarter of all outstanding bonds), the long-term loans made by those banks also increased rapidly, particularly in the latter half of the decade. For example, the Mitsui Bank's ratio of long-term loans to total assets increased from 24 percent in 1912 to 44 percent in 1930.[1606]

[1604] The eight zaibatsu include the "big five" – Mitsui, Mitsubishi, Sumitomo, Yasuda, Daiichi – and the smaller three – Kawasaki, Yamaguchi, and Konoike – groups. Yamamura, "Entrepreneurship, Ownership, and Management," p. 336.

[1605] Yamamura, "Entrepreneurship, Ownership, and Management," pp. 330, 336–37. Tamaki, *Japanese Banking*, pp. 157–58. The minimum capital requirements were set at ¥1 million except in Tokyo and Osaka where the minimum was ¥2 million. In 1927 there had been 1,280 ordinary banks; by 1932 that figure had declined to 538. Statistics principal accounts of private/ordinary banks, 1876–1945, p. 229.

[1606] Yamamura, "Entrepreneurship, Ownership, and Management," pp. 335–36.

The zaibatsu banks continued to expand their financial power throughout the 1930s, and, by 1942, the four largest accounted for almost one half of the total paid-in capital of the banking, insurance, and credit industries. In other parts of the economy, the four owned one-third of the total paid-in capital of the heavy industries, 11 percent of the light industries, and 13 percent of that of the utility, transport, and real estate sectors. Moreover, in 1944 the four were responsible for three-quarters of *all* loans made in Japan. Similarly, the size of the individual families (the number of firms, both financial and non-financial, that were interconnected) continued to increase as each zaibatsu wove an apparently ever widening net of interlocking directorships. "For example, Mitsui alone commanded the fate of nearly two hundred large firms in which it placed key executive officers."[1607]

On September 2, 1945, Japan surrendered, and the American occupation began. As *Newsweek* concluded two years later, "One of the basic objectives of the American occupation of Japan has been to break up the *zaibatsu*, the great family monopolies that controlled most of the country's economic life and were used to finance Japanese aggression." To that end, the Mitsui and Mitsubishi Trading companies were dissolved, and the Supreme Commander of the Allied Powers (SCAP) directed the government to consider enactment of "a bill of dissolution of excessive private concentration of economic power." The bill was passed and was to become effective in December 1947; however, objections about aims and costs were raised by critics in the United States; and, probably more importantly, the onset of the Cold War led U.S. policy makers to decide that political goals were more important than economic ones. What was now required was an alliance with a strong Japanese economy. Thus, the "implementation of the Act for the Dissolution of Excessive Private Concentration of Economic Power, which was well in hand, suddenly came to a standstill." In sharp contrast to the German experience, the Japanese banks recovered their institutional identity within a decade of 1945. Moreover, the policies of the intervening years had given the banks a large measure of independence from the *zaibatsu* industrial groups, and that independence allowed the banks to assume a central role in the Japanese economy.[1608]

[1607] Yamamura, "Entrepreneurship, Ownership, and Management," pp. 336–37.

[1608] Tamaki, *Japanese Banking*, pp. 190–92. In terms of critics, James L Kauffman wrote, "SCAP proposes to create in Japan what it terms a 'democratic Japanese economy' . . ." There is no definition in writing, as far as I have been able to learn, of what is meant by a "democratic Japanese economy." And, similarly, W.H. Draper, Under-Secretary of the Army, warned the State Department that the

The problems associated with the allocation of credit had established close relationships between firms and banks, and those ties, combined with the enhanced position of the banks, led to the evolution of what has come to be known as the "main" bank system. "The main characteristics of this system are the long-term relationship between a bank and its client firm, the holding of both debt and equity by the bank and the active intervention of the bank should its client become financially distressed." At the same time the need of firms for long-term funds was, at least in part, answered by the 1952 enactment of the Law of Long-Term Credit Banks, an act that allowed some special banks to raise funds by issuing long-term debentures rather than taking short-term deposits.[1609] The new structure, now termed *keiretsu* rather than *zaibatsu*, consisted of both vertical and horizontal groupings of firms. The former were merely a reflection of the profitability of vertical integration. The latter, however, appeared to reflect historic legacies as much as economic rationale. The legacy of the past led former *zaibatsu* firms to seek out other firms that previously had been members of their group. Those historic ties reestablished long-existing personal connections and brought together firms that were well acquainted with each other's operations; both connections and familiarity helped solve problems of asymmetric information.[1610]

From the 1950s through the 1970s, although the government employed its special banks to direct resources to "chosen" industries, the majority of capital was mobilized through the private sector. Moreover, the evidence suggests that the main bank system provided a reasonable method of allocating resources to those industries where the basic technology had been developed in the United States or Western Europe; and those were, after all, the industries that provided the basis for the original "Japanese miracle." Certainly the main banks provided a vital channel in the transfer of savings into investment, but that did not mean that they could totally disregard market forces in distributing capital or that they had complete discretionary powers in deciding to whom they would lend. There were many banks, and they had to compete for customers. Other financial institutions (long-term credit banks and insurance companies, for example) were alternative sources of capital; and, as firms grew, they were increasingly able to finance themselves. "Although the banks cultivated long-term relationships with firms under the system of indirect financing, that does not mean that the banks distributed capital or set

Dissolution Act, if really carried out, would virtually destroy the Japanese economy.

[1609] Allen, "Japanese Financial System," pp. 5–6.

[1610] Yamamura, "Entrepreneurship, Ownership and Management," pp. 339–41.

interest rates unilaterally as they wished. Some of the mechanisms of a competitive market were still at work."[1611] In the words of one student, the private "financial system did not hinder and may have been at least partially responsible for the spectacular performance of the Japanese economy from the 1950s to the 1970s."[1612]

The cold war had interfered with the Americans' attempt to "reform" the Japanese banking system and had left in place a close copy of the system that had begun to evolve at the turn of the century and that had reached something close to its final form in the troubles of the 1920s. There was however, one important difference – it was the banks, not the industrial zaibatsus, that were at the center of the new networks. It was a system that was to serve the Japanese reasonably well for the next quarter century; however, other forces were at work, forces that were to test the flexibility of the system in a world where the economic environment was subject to major regime changes. In the 1960s the government, bowing to international pressure, had begun to relax its control of the financial system. Over the ensuing decade and a half, controls continued to be eased, and, in fact, the process gathered speed. In the 1970s the government began issuing bonds on a large scale, and, if those issues were to be floated successfully, it was necessary to deregulate the secondary market for government bonds. Deregulation of the secondary government market put pressure on the secondary market for private corporate bonds and led, in time, to the deregulation of that latter market as well.

In the next decade, as foreign exchange controls were eased, Japanese firms were able to turn to foreign financial sources. Foreign competition, together with the domestic competition offered by the new market for unsecured corporate bonds, forced domestic banks to offer better terms to their customers and placed main bank relationships under increasing pressure. By the 1980s competition had reduced the demand for the banks' traditional business, supplying long-term loans to industry; and, to fill the gap, the banks "increased their lending to real estate development companies and to non-bank financial intermediaries such as the *jusan*, which in turn lent for real estate speculation, and to industrial companies for their financial and real estate speculation." The resulting infusion of funds into the real estate market led to rapid increases in land and building prices; and, as a result, share prices in real

---

[1611] Yutaka Kosai, "The Postwar Japanese Economy, 1945–1973," in Kozo Yamamura (ed.), *The Economic Emergence of Modern Japan* (Cambridge: Cambridge University Press, 1997), pp. 193–95. [Hereafter cited as Kosai, "The Postwar Japanese Economy."]

[1612] Allen, "Japanese Financial System," pp. 6–7.

estate associated firms rose spectacularly. In 1990, however, the bubble burst.[1613]

Since then, the banking system has been under ever increasing strain; but politics, the historic old-boy network, and the question of how much of the bill should be assumed by the taxpayers had, until recently, led to near-legislative paralysis and to continued domestic default and depression. Over the decade the banking system staggered under an estimated $1 trillion in bad debts; however, it was not until October 1998 that the legislature agreed to a $520 billion bank bailout plan and to the passage of eight other bills that, together, outlined the method of dealing with insolvent institutions. Despite the spate of legislation, the answers to at least two questions still remain in doubt. Will the $520 billion of taxpayer money ($217 billion to be channeled into weak but viable banks and $303 billion to be used to buy the stock or guarantee the deposits of failed banks) be sufficient? Does the legislature have the political will to enforce the closure procedures? The evidence is clear, but its interpretation is ambiguous. On the one hand, despite the failure to pass more substantial reforms, the continued antagonism of the main opposition party, and the general consensus that, even if the reforms are sufficient, it may be years before the economy returns to full employment, the Nikkei-225 index jumped 2.2 percent on the news of the bill's passage. On the other hand, since the Hong Kong and Singapore indices rose by 9 percent on the same day, it is possible that the typical Japanese investor still remained unconvinced.[1614]

9-2b(3). The government banks: Nor were changes limited to the private sector. Although the private banks still remain the dominant financial institutions, there are other parts of the infrastructure that, in the long term, have contributed heavily to the current crisis. In particular, there were, and are, the "government" banks. Foremost among the government banks, of course, was the Bank of Japan. From the 1890s until World War II, it acted largely as Matsuka had visualized, as a central bank. In February 1942 a new Bank of Japan Act replaced all previous legislation regarding that institution; included were some revisions in regulations that had been in place since 1882. The Act made three substantial changes in the operation of the Bank. First, the Bank became solely a servant of the government – any notion of independence was abandoned – and was required to lend to the government without security. Second, its business was extended, and it was required to make advances when

---

[1613] Allen, "Japanese Financial System," pp. 7–8.

[1614] *Los Angeles Times*, pp. C1–2, C4, October 17, 1998.

eligible securities were available, to lend to overseas institutions, and to generally support the Japanese system as a whole. Third, the Bank was granted the freedom to issue any amount of bank notes that it deemed proper. Thus, it was empowered and required to work solely for national goals, and this structure was to remain in place in the post-war period.[1615]

Although there were private savings banks – banks modeled after the British savings banks – from the 1890s until their final disappearance in the post-war inflation, government-sponsored savings institutions date from the 1870s. Initially termed as "savings" by the Ministry, in 1880 the system was renamed *ekitei*, or stage savings, and in 1887, the name was changed again to the postal savings system (*yucho*), a system with branches in post offices throughout the nation. The deposits were entrusted to the deposit department of the Finance Ministry, and the creation of the system was to prove a boon to the government's financial resources. Over the years the system became an important savings vehicle for many households; even in this early period, deposits amounted to 9 percent of total national bank deposits. By 1897 the system's deposits were equal to 13 percent of the total deposits of the ordinary banking system. Those deposits were invested in government bonds, and by 1919 the post office savings system had become the largest contributor to the government's direct financial requirements. At that time the pool of resources amounted to ¥731 million, a sum equivalent to 15 percent of the total deposits in ordinary banks. The financial turbulence of the 1920s saw further increases in the system as savers, in addition to their move to the large Zaibatsu banks, also switched to the "safer" postal savings banks. That shift was to continue during the depression of the next decade. Deposits increased from ¥2,664 billion in 1931 to ¥4,013 billion in 1937. In both years they constituted a little more than 70 percent of the total funds available to the Ministry of Finance. In the wartime years deposits continued to surge. While the total assets of all banks increased sevenfold between 1937 and 1945, those of the post office system increased twelvefold, to ¥47,200 billion, one-quarter of all bank deposits.[1616] In the post-war years the majority of the funds used by the Reconstruction Financing Bank, the Japanese Development Bank, and other quasi-government institutions came from the postal savings system. The system, because of its implicit government guarantees and various taxes, and other advantages constituted a key mechanism in the

---

[1615] Tamaki, *Japanese Banking*, p. 175.
[1616] Allen, "Japanese Financial System," p. 3. Richard Sylla, "Emerging Markets," p. 432. Tamaki, *Japanese Banking*, pp. 77, 134, 154, 164, 180, 245.

implementation of the government's policy of continued intervention in the allocation of financial resources.[1617]

The Act of 1896 established the Hypothec Bank and stipulated that it supply funds for the development and improvement of agriculture and manufacturing. Moreover, the government appointed the managers who were to direct the Bank's business. The Bank was not allowed to accept deposits, but, in order to provide it with lending resources, it was permitted to issue debentures. It was the first of the debenture-issuing banks that were to become an important component of the Japanese banking system. Since the Hypothec Bank had only a single Tokyo office, further innovations were required if the Bank was to successfully channel its resources into economic activity in other parts of the country. To solve the distribution problem, the Agri-Industrial Bank was established in 1896, and three years later the government organized the Hokkaido Development Bank. By 1900 the Agri-Industrial Bank had established branches in all forty-six prefectures. In addition to the debenture-issuing business, with the sanction of the Ministry of Finance, these development banks were not only permitted to open branches, but they were allowed to accept deposits. Their debentures were, in turn, accepted by the Hypothec Bank as security for loans, loans that were then recycled by the local special banks to finance development throughout Japan.

By the end of World War I, even though ordinary banks were not permitted to draw on debenture-based finance, the Hypothec Bank began to transform itself a somewhat special "ordinary" bank. That transformation was speeded up by the passage of the Hypothec/Agri-Industrial Bank Amalgamation Act in 1921, an act designed, in the face of the postwar depression, to produce an expanded reservoir of industrial finance in a remodeled bank that could make more loans at lower interest rates. By 1923 nineteen of the forty-six Agri-Industrial Banks had aligned themselves with the Hypothec; the result was an increase in advances from ¥285 million in 1919 to ¥633 million in 1923, a sixfold increase in deposits, and a doubling of the value of outstanding debentures. By that date the "new" bank's loans were more than one and a half times those of the twenty-seven still independent Agri-Industrial Banks, deposits were nearly twice as large, and outstanding debentures more than twice the figure for the "independents."[1618]

Finally, the Industrial Bank of Japan Act of 1900 established yet another special bank. The Act specified that the Industrial Bank would

[1617] Allen, "Japanese Financial System," p. 5.
[1618] Tamaki, *Japanese Banking*, pp. 123, 145.

be allowed to make advances on local bonds, debentures, and equities. "The business of the Bank was to be exactly the same as that done by the Yokohama Specie Bank since the 1880s." The government encouraged non-governmental transactions, appropriated the specie itself, and, thus, augmented its own reserves. In sum, the Industrial Bank was charged with mobilizing any unemployed monetary sources, whether domestic or foreign, and with providing liquidity for the securities that were already in the hands of other financial institutions. When, in 1902, the Industrial Bank first entered the London money market, "it operated in exactly the same way as the senior Specie Bank." From 1902 to 1911 it floated more than £27 million in securities (national bonds, the bank's own debentures and equities, city municipal bonds, and South Manchurian Railway debentures) on the London market.[1619]

Between 1911 and the end of the war, however, the regulations governing the Industrial Bank were revised substantially. Those revisions permitted it to conduct a much broader range of business and resulted in an institution that was similar, in many ways, to the Hypothec Bank. In 1911 it was allowed to discount bills, make advances on property, and buy and sell securities; in short, it also was allowed to operate as a somewhat special "ordinary" bank. In 1914 it was sanctioned to undertake foreign exchange operations; and, in 1917, it was authorized to make loans to industrial associations, particularly associations located in urban areas that had previously done business entirely with the Hypothec and its subordinate Agri-Industrial Banks. With the expanded powers, the Bank was able to support the Ministry of Finance in its attempts to supply emergency funds to the securities exchanges during the stock market collapse of 1916, to provide financial backing to the shipping and shipbuilding industries, first, during the post-war slump and, then, through the industries' continuing depression, and, finally, in 1917 and 1918, to issue securities in support of, and to help arrange, a ¥180 million loan to protect Japanese investments in China.[1620]

Despite its new powers, unlike the Hypothec Bank, the Industrial Bank of Japan remained largely a special bank. With only three branch offices in 1918, the Bank did not rely on the deposits of ordinary customers. Instead, it continued to serve as an arm of the Ministry of Finance. That relationship was underscored by the location of its main Tokyo office; the office was not in the city's banking center, but, instead, within the inner moat surrounding the Emperor's palace and very close to the Ministry. Moreover, the Bank continued to conduct its overseas

---

[1619] Tamaki, *Japanese Banking*, pp. 98–101.
[1620] Tamaki, *Japanese Banking*, pp. 122–23.

business through the offices of the Specie Bank, a connection that suggests a lack of independence from that more senior creature of the Ministry.

Over the years 1919–23 the Industrial Bank grew much more slowly than the Hypothec Bank, but it continued to act effectively as an arm of government policy. In 1920 it led a successful operation to rescue the collapsing securities market. In the same year the Bank organized and led a national bond underwriting syndicate, an effort that produced funds that could be used to support industrial sectors suffering from the demise of the wartime boom. The syndicate actually distributed almost ¥50 million to firms in a variety of industries including telecommunications, electricity, paper, flour, chemicals, brewing, mining, textiles, railway transport, shipping, shipbuilding, iron and steel, machinery, and sugar refining; in addition, the Bank used its own funds to support firms in shipping and shipbuilding, copper mining, silk manufacture, and other small industrial sectors that were particularly impacted by the depression. For example, the Bank provided the shipping and shipbuilding industry with sums that ranged from ¥30 million to more than ¥50 million in every year between 1921 and 1925.[1621]

The special banks continued to operate through the 1930s, but the government's need to mobilize the nation's financial resources to conduct World War II and the American occupation temporarily put to an end the operations of those banks as Masayosi Matsukata had visualized them. The report of their demise, however, proved to be somewhat exaggerated. They reemerged, although in somewhat different form, soon after the Cold War had begun and occupation had ended.

The Industrial Bank of Japan was probably the most severely exploited by the government during the war. It was commissioned to issue bonds, to gather funds, and to lend them together with money created by the Bank of Japan to the munitions industries. The Hypothec Bank had, by 1937, absorbed most of Agri-Industrial branches; during the war both it and the Hokkaido Development Bank were subject to much the same government orders as the Industrial Bank. Overseas, the Yokohama Specie Bank was ordered to closely follow the army and navy; and, with offices throughout occupied Asia, it functioned as a cash and remittance office for the Japanese military.[1622]

At war's end the special banks came under American attack. The Americans felt that the Yokohama Specie Bank had been part of

---

[1621] Tamaki, *Japanese Banking*, pp. 145–46.
[1622] Tamaki, *Japanese Banking*, p. 178.

Japan's war effort, and insisted that it convert itself into a small, harmless bank, the Bank of Tokyo. The three other industrial banks, the Industrial Bank of Japan, the Hypothec Bank, and the Hokkaido Development Bank were also vulnerable. SCAP first required that the special banks choose between becoming either ordinary banks or debenture-issuing institutions. Then, in 1948, it issued a memorandum on an "Overall Revision of Banking Structure" that outlined a policy designed to erase any trace of the special banks. The Americans' need for allies in the soon-to-be hot Cold War, however, almost immediately caused SCAP to shift its position.[1623] First, in 1950 the government was allowed to promulgate the Act of Issuing Bank Debentures; and the Industrial Bank was included. Next, although the Americans demanded that the institution be focused solely on financing exports and that it be independent of the government, they agreed to the organization of the Export Finance Bank. Clearly, even today, no one knows how, in the Japanese economic environment, that such a bank could have been independent of the government; and, in fact, when the bank opened its doors the paid-in capital of ¥5 trillion came half from counterpart funds and half from the general budget account. A year later, again with American acquiescence, the Japan Development Bank Act was passed. The Development Bank – a bank funded by ¥2.5 trillion in counterpart funds drawn from the United States' "Government Appropriations for Relief in Occupied Areas" and "Economic Rehabilitation of Occupied Areas" accounts – was allowed to finance equipment loans to industries for a period longer than one year. Because of concerns about inflation, it was prohibited from issuing debentures. It was, however, sanctioned as a long-term finance institution, to "refinance the long term loans made by city banks," but the Bank was warned not to compete with those banks.

With the end of occupation in sight, the regulations governing the Japan Export Finance Bank were amended to permit the Bank to finance imports and to allow it to enter the guarantee business with both borrowed foreign currency and funds from the Bank of Japan. Shortly thereafter, the Japan Development Bank Act was revised to allow it to issue debentures and to permit it to enter the guarantee business using foreign loans, borrowed foreign currency, and government money. "Special Banking was *de facto* revived." In fact, over the next few years no fewer than five more corporations, all with specific banking tasks, were chartered. Despite the initial American plans for the innovation of an entirely private Japanese financial system, by the late 1950s "there was an

---

[1623] Tamaki, *Japanese Banking*, p. 198.

enormous government banking workforce ready and waiting to finance new demands."[1624] Masayoshi Matsukata would have been pleased.

9-2b(4). The securities exchange: In the 1980s the Tokyo Stock Exchange had, at least in terms of volume, challenged the leadership of both the New York and London exchanges. However, largely because of the banks' domination of the financial system, it has played a smaller role in the Japanese financial infrastructure than the securities markets in either of the other two cities. The Exchange was founded in 1878, but, while its role increased somewhat after 1885, it was still of only marginal importance at the turn of the century.[1625] By the 1930s, however, although it still financed relatively little direct investment, it provided liquidity for investments that accounted for about one-third of the funds directed toward industry; however, that share probably declined in the immediate post war period, as the contributions of non-bank institutions and retained earnings increased substantially.[1626]

The Allies had wanted Japan to develop an American-style securities market, a market that focused on supplying long-term capital, while the banks focused on supplying short-term finance. As a practical matter, however, with a well-established banking system in place – a system with banks heavily committed to long-term finance – it was very difficult to implement such a plan. It was, for example, the late 1980s before even large firms were able to gain more than limited access to the bond market. Not only was the market regulated until relatively late, but also only secured bonds could be issued; and, under the law, only banks could manage collateral. Thus, banks were able to charge substantial fees, and those charges made the use of even the relatively deregulated securities markets very expensive.[1627] Deregulation and some rule changes did help reduce costs. In the 1980s firms began to raise an increasing proportion of their funds through the issue of securities, and, as a result, the Tokyo Exchange began to provide liquidity for a broader range of securities. Despite these gains, in 1993, although the of the value of market capitalization of equity as a percentage of GDP was about the same in Japan as it was in the United States, the distribution of the paper claims on

---

[1624] Tamaki, *Japanese Banking*, p. 198. In 1952 the Industrial Bank of Japan, taking advantage of the Long-term Credit Bank Act that permitted banks to issue debentures rather than taking deposits, also managed to resume its traditional business (p. 204).

[1625] Tamaki, *Japanese Banking*, p. 66.

[1626] Allen, "Japanese Financial System," pp. 3–5. Kosai, "The Postwar Japanese Economy," pp. 192–93.

[1627] Allen, "Japanese Financial System," p. 6.

capital was much different. The cross-holdings of non-financial firms was much higher (the U.S. data do not even report such holdings). In addition, the fraction of shares held by the banks and insurance companies was much greater. Together, banks and insurance companies held about 40 percent of Japanese equity. The liabilities of those financial institutions were, to a large extent, fixed; thus, everything else equal, volatility in the stock market was more likely to cause significant problems for the stability of those financial institutions. As a result, the Japanese financial system may be somewhat more prone to instability than its U.S. counterpart.[1628]

9-2b(5). Government regulations: Finally, since the late 1920s, in addition to exercising central banking powers and directing the activities of the special banks, the Japanese government has played a greater direct and indirect role in the economy than was common in other industrialized western countries. Although many of the government policies can be traced to the needs of wartime mobilization, the initial entry was a product of the financial turbulence of the 1920s. In 1928 the Ministry of Finance was charged with administering the new banking law; and, at least since then, the Ministry has had a very strong influence on the Japanese financial infrastructure. For example, following the passage of the law, the Ministry moved to significantly reduce the number of banks by introducing the principle of "one bank one prefecture," that is, a policy designed to reduce the number of banks and give each remaining bank a monopoly in a limited area. The required reduction in the number of banks was effected through government-facilitated mergers, and public funds were used to underwrite the process. Although wartime measures pushed the Ministry's policies farther and farther into the financial sector, its role in shaping the financial system can be traced back nearly a decade before the outbreak of the war with China.[1629]

The war that began in 1937 did, however, dramatically increased the scope and intensity of government involvement. During the first three months of 1937 military expenditures were ¥2.5 billion, and the government, faced with the need to reduce imports and the desire to expand the money supply, passed the Temporary Capital Adjustment Law. The law was designed to ensure strict regulatory control of all new investments, and it particularly favored investments in munitions. Government permission was required for any large firm to increase its equity base or

---

[1628] Allen, "Japanese Financial System," pp. 7–8, 13–14, 18.
[1629] Allen, "Japanese Financial Institutions," p. 3.

merge. The law also controlled loans to firms – firms that were catego-
rized as either "favored," "permitted," or "proscribed." Under this Act
the government was given extraordinary powers to examine every aspect
of the nation's financial structure in order to pressure financial institutions to search for and find additional funds to supply wartime needs.
Between 1937 and 1942 the Act raised ¥18.454 billion of new money, a
sum equivalent to more than 60 percent of the aggregate level of lending
then outstanding by all banks, trust companies, and the trust fund department of the Finance Ministry.[1630]

In March 1938 the Diet enacted the National General Mobilization
Law – a law that gave the government widely sweeping powers to control
the economy, in general, and the financial sector, in particular. The establishment of firms, capital increases, bond flotations, and long-term
loans came under a licensing system; the government was empowered
to regulate the manufacture, distribution, transfer, use, and consumption
of materials connected with imports and exports, particularly their
restriction or prohibition; and it was charged with conscripting labor,
establishing working conditions, and directing the disposition of private-
sector profits and of the funds of financial institutions. In addition,
it assumed the tasks of administration, use, and expropriation of factories and mines, as well as the formation of cartels. "These measures
were invoked one after another as the war situation became more
grave."[1631]

The provisions of the Temporary Capital Adjustment Law were
designed to assure a flow of funds to the munitions industry, since the
major banks belonging to the *zaibatsu* groups had resisted concentrating their loans among these companies, companies that the banks
regarded as poor risks. Over the next six years these regulations gradually evolved into a system of central control of financial resources; and
the Bank of Japan played a pivotal role in the allocation decisions. The
process culminated in 1944 with the passage of the Munitions Companies Designated Financial Institutions System Act, an act that assigned
each munitions company to a major bank and that charged that bank
with taking care of the firm's financial needs. After the war these
government-prescribed links evolved into what was to become the "main

---

[1630] Takafusa Nakamura, "Depression, Recovery, and War 1920–1945," in Kozo
Yamamura (ed.), *The Economic Emergence of Modern Japan* (Cambridge:
Cambridge University Press, 1997), p. 146. [Hereafter cited as Nakamura,
"Depression, Recovery, and War."] Allen, "Japanese Financial System," pp. 3–5.
Tamaki, *Japanese Banking*, pp. 174–75.

[1631] Nakamura, "Depression, Recovery, and War," p. 146. Allen, "Japanese Financial
System," pp. 3–5.

bank" system.[1632] Three other institutions were established in the wake of the war. The War Cash Office, under direct government control, supplied funds to strategically placed manufacturing industries and was authorized to support the securities market. The Southern District Cash Office supplied funds to the same manufacturing industries in the Japanese-occupied areas in Southeast Asia the South Pacific. The powers granted the National Financial Control Association placed almost all of the "government" financial institutions (the Bank of Japan, the Yokohama Specie Bank, the Industrial Bank of Japan, the Hokkaido Development Bank, the Bank of Taiwan, the Bank of Korea, the Korean Development Bank), all ordinary and savings banks, the War Cash Office, and the Central Cash Office for Industrial Associations under direct government control. Later the Central Cash Office for Small Commercial and Industrial Associations, the Pension Cash Office, and the People's Cash Office, all founded about the time of the "China Incident," and all designed to finance small businesses and firms that were experiencing increasing difficulties in borrowing, were also put under the Control Association.[1633]

Nor did the end of the war lead to a significant "privatization" of the financial system. On the one hand, the government continued to intervene directly through institutions like the Reconstruction Finance Bank and the Japan Development Bank. On the other hand, industrial rationalization plans – plans that were nominally characterized as independent plans carried out by private business enterprise – contained large elements of government support. "To be sure, the government intervened in the process, making it a kind of joint venture between the government and key private enterprises, but the government did not use price controls (price subsidies) or commodity controls to achieve its ends." Instead, it relied on other methods.

Indirectly, in the 1950s and 1960s, it kept interest rates low; a policy that provided rents for banks, rents that helped ensure the solvency of the banks and contributed to the stability of the system. In addition, with the 1952 passage of the Enterprises Rationalization Act and the amendment of the Special Tax Measures Law, the government was able to directly employ an arsenal of special techniques designed to promote the development of industries that were specially targeted for rationalization. These techniques included special tax treatment, a subsidy of interest on loans to shipbuilding, direct loans of government funds through

---

[1632] Nakamura, "Depression, Recovery, and War," p. 146. Allen, "Japanese Financial System," pp. 3–5. Tamaki, *Japanese Banking*, pp. 174–75.
[1633] Tamaki, *Japanese Banking*, pp. 175–76.

institutions like the development banks, the establishment of the Electrical Power Source Development Company, the use of import quotas, controls over the import of foreign capital, and "administrative guidance."

The popular notion that there was a so-called Japan Incorporated, a close alliance between government and business, with the government directly guiding the activities of private firms, is probably somewhat over-drawn. Japan was not a planned economy; the financial investment deci-sions were in the hands of the business firms; however, the relative prices that they faced and the forces that determined the relative profits of alternative investments were certainly subject to government manipula-tion.[1634] It might be said that, during World War II, the government con-trolled the economy by fiat, but in the post-war decades the government largely controlled the signals that guided private investment.

9-2b(6). Are there lessons to be learned from history? It is an interest-ing historical anomaly that, at the same time that Masayoshi Matsukata was designing and implementing the financial infrastructure that was to guide Japan for most of the next century, the Australians had developed a system that was a remarkably similar to the one that evolved from the "Matsukata model." In the years 1870–90 the commercial banks played as central a role in the financial structure as they did in twentieth-century Japan. Moreover, although there was no equivalent of the zaibatsu, those banks did oversee something akin to the "main bank" system. The banks took short-term deposits and converted them to long-term loans, and they developed close relations with the borrowing firms: both "indus-trial" (usually agricultural) enterprises and non-bank intermediaries that stood between the bank and the final demander. Given the temporal asset/liability mismatch, the system was relatively illiquid and, thus, subject to runs should the economy begin to decline; and, given the relative size of the loans to individual firms and the close bank/firm relationships that had developed, the banks often felt required to con-tinue to support operating firms, especially when the economic prospects for those firms became increasingly uncertain. During the "Great Boom" from the 1850s through the 1880s, the system worked well; but it collapsed completely with the economic debacle of the 1890s.

The American experience, too, offers some lessons that might have affected Japanese policies toward commercial banks. In the first half of the nineteenth century, banks in New England had developed a struc-

---

[1634] Kosai, "The Postwar Japanese Economy," pp. 182–83. Allen, "Japanese Financial System," p. 6.

ture closely akin to the "crony capitalism" of Japan a century later. There, "directors often funneled the bulk of the funds under their control to themselves, their relatives or others with personal ties to the board. Though not all directors indulged in this behavior, insider lending was widespread during the early nineteenth century." However, in the post–Civil War era, increased competition, the rapid expansion of the geographic market, the increased ability to monitor borrowers operating outside the immediate area, and the fragility of the institution in the face of economic crisis combined to convince bank managers that profitability dictated that they abandon their traditional "insider" loan policies and open their business to non-connected customers.[1635] Toward the end of the century, the emergence of the investment bank with its connected commercial bank or trust company produced an institution that was also somewhat similar to the Japanese main bank. From the 1890s to the 1930s the institution performed well, but it foundered in the wake of the stock market crash of 1929 and the ensuing depression. Because of the effect of the crisis on the "tied commercial banks," the economic reforms of the 1930s included the passage of the Glass-Steagall Act – an act that required investment banks divest their commercial bank subsidiaries.

Finally, a reading of Canadian history might well have alerted the Japanese banks to the dangers of funding a speculative land boom; such funding was, of course, the immediate cause of the banking systems' current massive problems. Until 1863 the forty-four-year-old Bank of Upper Canada had not only been the largest bank in what is now Ontario, but it had served as the Canadian government's "erstwhile banker." During the speculative land boom of 1857–58, however, it had extended large loans to borrowers who had pledged real estate – real estate with much inflated value – as collateral. Although the Bank struggled along for nearly a decade, it collapsed in 1866. The cost of the debacle was enormous: immediate losses to creditors, stockholders, and the government came to almost $5 million (one-fifth of the colony's banking capital), and the longer-term costs added nearly another $1 million to the total.

After 1900 the Australian financial system became increasingly dependent on the government for direction. Although government involvement had begun with the initial railway boom – at that time the gold rush may well have left the government as the only possible

---

[1635] Naomi Lamoureaux, *Insider Lending: Banks, Personal Connections, and Economic Development in Industrial New England* (Cambridge: Cambridge University Press for the National Bureau of Economics Research, 1994), Introduction, chapters 1 and 4, particularly pp. 4, 84.

supplier of labor and finance – it expanded dramatically with the commercial bank failures of the 1890s. Just as Japanese depositors were to do three decades later, because the government banks appeared "safe" – they had de jure government guarantees and were supported by the tax system – Australian savers increasingly placed their accumulations with government rather than private banks. The governments, awash in funds, then took it upon themselves to allocate those funds among competing industrial uses. Just as government direction of railway investment had earlier been biased toward where the voters were, rather than where they might be in the future, the post-1900 decisions were heavily influenced by the industrial (and voter) distribution at the turn of the century rather than by what that distribution might have become in the years 1910–40 had the economically most profitable alternatives received the funds that an economic, rather than a political, calculus would have dictated.

A succession of Australian governments failed to support both industrial and new agricultural developments in wheat and dairy farming; and Australia, with what was probably the highest GDP per capita in the world in 1890, struggled throughout the first half of the twentieth century to remain among the top twenty. In a similar fashion, in Japan the Reconstruction Finance Bank and Japanese Development Bank, while continuing in the 1950s and 1960s to direct capital to coal mining, agriculture, forestry and fishing, and marine transportation, rejected the requests for support from such firms as Toyota and Sony.[1636] The question remains, if Matsukata had been aware of the Australian experience of 1890–1910, would he have retained his vision of the appropriate Japanese financial structure?

9-3. History and current events: developing economies in Latin America and Asia: problems of the 1980s and 1990s

9-3a. Latin America

9-3a(1). Latin America: introduction: In 1982 the Mexican government's moratorium on service on its debt "sent powerful shock waves through the global financial system." New loans to developing countries quickly dried up, and those countries began to develop severe debt-servicing problems. What was initially labeled as a short-term liquidity crisis exploded into a long-term crisis of global proportions. In the developing world it was marked by economic stagnation and the demise or near

---

[1636] Allen, "Japanese Financial System," p. 3.

demise of many of those countries' financial institutions.[1637] Hardly more than a decade later the scenario was repeated as the "Tequila Crisis" spread across Latin America.

9-3a(2). The financial infrastructure: Banks have long played a key role in economic development in Latin America. It is, however, true that banks perform best in an economic environment endowed with efficient and effective institutions, an environment characterized by an independent central bank, a judiciary that responsibly enforces statute and common law, and a legal structure that demands fiscal accountability. Unfortunately, such political and economic institutions have traditionally been in short supply across Latin America. In addition, at least since World War II the Latin American environment had been marred by fiscal mismanagement, high inflation, and protectionist policies. Hardly surprisingly, the banks have also developed endogenous problems: protected against foreign competition, they became bloated and inefficient, loan relationships were personalized or relationship driven, regulation was virtually nonexistent, and state banks were managed in a way that optimized political, rather than economic, objectives. The banking systems operating within such environments were clearly disasters waiting to happen.[1638]

In Latin America, as in other emerging markets, when interest rates are high relative to those in the developed world, there is a strong temptation for both the banks and their customers to denominate debts in foreign currency. Because they have less access to longer-term sources of funding than do their developed neighbors, all too often they turn to short-term, foreign-currency-denominated, borrowing in the interbank market; and they then use those resources to fund long-term loans at home. Not only does such a strategy produce serious maturity mismatches, but it can quickly be derailed by any subsequent devaluation.[1639]

In many Latin American countries, each banking crisis brought with it increased government regulation. Often, however, the new regulations

---

[1637] Walter T. Molano, "From Bad Debts to Healthy Securities': The Theory and Financial Techniques of the Brady Plan," Swiss Bank Corporation, manuscript, December 1996, p. 1. [Hereafter cited as Molano, "From Bad Debts to Healthy Securities."]

[1638] Walter T. Molano, "Financial Reverberations: The Latin American Banking System During the Mid-1990s," manuscript, August 1997, pp. 1–2. [Hereafter cited as Molano, "Financial Reverations."]

[1639] Morris Goldstein and Philip Turner, "Banking Crises in Emerging Economies: Origins and Policy Options," Bank for International Settlements, Monetary and Economic Department, Basle, BIS Economic Papers, No. 46, October 1996, pp. 15–16. [Hereafter cited as Goldstein and Turner, "Banking Crisis."]

were designed, not to strengthen the banking systems, but, instead, to impose credit allocation schemes that were tied to government finance and government-sponsored programs. For example, "in Argentina and Peru when the authorities were unable to pay off their debts to the banks, they imposed interest rate controls on banks and resorted to highly inflationary policies"; and, as the depositors' real wealth declined, those policies led to flight from bank deposits. "The experiences of Argentina, Mexico, and Peru in the mid-1980s strongly indicate that financial regulation in Latin America often leads to instability rather than stability."[1640]

In addition, despite increased privatization, state-owned banks have retained a significant share of bank assets. Most state-owned banks were established to allocate credit to favored sectors; as a result, they were likely to be subject to government, rather than market, direction; and, very often, the economic creditworthiness of the borrower did not weigh heavily in the banks' lending decision. The government's connections with favored businesses, taken together with its explicit or implicit guarantee against bank failure, often led to "connected lending," careless monitoring, inefficient operations, and high levels of nonperforming loans. In 1994 one-third of the total loans of Argentina's state banks were in default; for the country's private banks, the figure was only 10 percent. In Brazil more than half of the $20 billion of non-performing loans held by Banesa – the state bank of São Paulo – were owed by the state itself.[1641]

9-3a(3). Mexico: a case study in bank/government relations: The history of the Mexican government's relations with the country's banks in the aftermath of the crisis of the early 1980s, although not duplicated elsewhere, does suggest something about bank/government relations, more generally, and about the chaotic state of the Latin American institutional environment, in particular. On September 1, 1982, the Mexican President announced the government's expropriation of almost all-private banks.[1642] President Portillo argued that the banks had generated excessive profits, that amalgamations had created monopolistic markets, and that they had facilitated the massive capital flight that had prolonged and

---

[1640] Lillian Rojas-Suarez and Steven R. Weisbrod, "Banking Crisis in Latin America: Experience and Issues," Inter-American Development Bank, Office of the Chief Economist, Working Paper Series 321, February 1996, p. 12. [Hereafter cited as Rojas-Suarez and Wesibrod, "Banking Crisis in Latin America."]

[1641] Goldstein and Turner, "Banking Crises," pp. 18–21.

[1642] Banco Obrero, owned by a labor union, and Citibank Mexico, the only foreign bank that had been permitted to operate branches, were the only exceptions to the nationalization order.

magnified the effects of the crisis. Moreover, in order to prevent a future reversal of the decision, the Mexican constitution was amended to prohibit private ownership of banks.

Between 1983 and 1986 the banking system was restructured. First, the total number of banks in the country was reduced from forty-nine, to twenty-nine, to nineteen, and finally to eighteen. Second, the legal structure of the banks was changed from corporations to "national credit associations"; their shares were converted into *certificados de aportacion patrimonial* (CAPS); in 1987 34 percent of the CAPS were offered for sale to the private sector. Third, the now-nationalized commercial banks divested their non-bank subsidiaries; and the former bank owners were allowed to use their bank indemnification bonds to purchase those subsidiaries. Finally, the law required that the banks lend almost exclusively to the government. In 1972, for example, bank credit to the private sector amounted to almost 20 percent of GDP; by 1988 this percentage had fallen to 7. Triggered by the crowding out of the private sector, "a new informal financial system developed: stock-brokerage houses and investment banks began to perform banking functions under fancy names such as 'financial engineering firms' and helped private companies obtain financing."

Given the need for a stable institutional environment, this regime change appears to have little to recommend it; but it was at least possible that the efficiency gains from the new structure might be greater than the turbulence losses. Unfortunately, no sooner was the revolution over and victory declared, than the counter-revolution began. In 1989 the government, in an attempt to get its fiscal house in order and to increase efficiency and stimulate the economy through large-scale privatization, moved to denationalize the banking system. Although the nationalized banks had been profitable, the need for large capital investments loomed on the horizon; and the divestiture increased government revenues both directly, through the sale of the banks (eighteen banks were auctioned off for a total of $12.4 billion), and indirectly, by bringing the banks into the government tax network. On May 2, 1990, the President submitted and Congress passed a second constitutional amendment – an amendment that excluded banking from the list of activities that were reserved exclusively for the state.[1643]

Initially, it appeared that the new government policies – policies designed to deregulate markets, liberalize trade, reduce the govern-

---

[1643] Haluk Unal and Miguel Navarro, "The Technical Process of Bank Privatization in Mexico," the Wharton School, University of Pennsylvania, Financial Institutions Center, Working Paper No. 97-42, pp. 2–6 and table 6, p. 32.

ment's role in productive processes, and renew fiscal discipline – were a success; GDP rose for most of the next half decade.[1644] In the long run liberalization can lead to rapid growth; however, in the shorter term, liberalization is often accompanied by an increased level of aggressive behavior on the part of the bank managers – they raise deposit rates in order to increase their supply of loanable funds, and, then, to find outlets for those more expensive resources, they begin to fund more risky projects – and in the early 1990s Mexican banks proved very aggressive.[1645] The new regime touched off a boom in bank lending to the private sector, and the resulting increases in the money supply touched off inflation. Inflation, in turn, both raised the banking system's demand for domestic bank deposits and encouraged capital inflows, inflows that were partly intermediated through the banks. During a lending boom banks often increase the fraction of their loans to leveraged firms, firms that will have difficulty servicing their debts if growth slows, interest rates rise, or the banks are forced to curtail lending and demand that loans be repaid rather than "rolled over." If the banks' portfolios are heavily weighted toward such loans, they become vulnerable. Moreover, during a boom, banks often expand lending to new customers, about whom the banks have very little evidence concerning their long-term economic viability. Thus, there is often an increase in the fragility of bank balance sheets, a fragility that would further compound the problems of the banking system, should the boom become a bust.[1646]

Mexican regulators did not require reserves against deposits, and that policy almost certainly amplified the boom and left the banks susceptible to possible runs. In addition, the general weakness of the banking system raised the potential cost of implementing a tight money policy, a policy that might have slowed economic activity and defused the crisis.

[1644] Nancy Birdsall, Michael Gavin, and Ricardo Hausman, "Lessons from the Mexico Crisis," February 25, 1997, draft of a paper to be included in Sebastion Edwards and Moises Naim (eds.), *Mexico 1994: Anatomy of an Emerging-Market Crash* (Washington, D.C.: Brookings Institution Press for the Carnegie Endowment for International Peace, December 1997), p. 2. [Hereafter cited as Birdsall, Gavin, and Hausman, "Lessons from the Mexico Crisis."]

[1645] Jeffrey Sachs, Aaron Tornell, and Andres Velasco, "Financial Crises in Emerging Markets: The Lessons From 1995," National Bureau of Economic Research, Working Paper No. 5576, May 1996, p. 26. [Hereafter cited as Sachs, Tornell, and Velasco, "Financial Crises."]

[1646] Birdsall, Gavin, and Hausman, "Lessons from the Mexico Crisis," p. 4. "Rapid growth in the ratio of bank credit to GDP preceded financial troubles in Argentina (1981), Chile (1981–82), Colombia (1982–83), Uruguay (1982), Norway (1987), Finland (1991–92), Japan (1992–93), and Sweden (1991)." Sachs, Tornell, and Velasco, "Financial Crisis," p. 25.

The central bank's concern for the financial health of the banks had been growing since 1992. In 1990 non-performing loans amounted to only 2 percent of all bank loans; by 1992 that figure had increased to almost 5 percent; it rose to more than 7 percent the next year, and to more than 8 percent in 1994. In that year, with the Banco Cremi, the nation's fourth largest bank, in serious trouble, politicians and central bankers agreed that higher interest rates would badly damage the already weakened banking system.[1647] The combination of increased private loans, weak banks, and a paralyzed monetary authority, left Mexico vulnerable to a speculative attack.

That attack was launched in December 1994, and it produced what was originally called the Mexican Peso Crisis, an economic collapse that, as it spread south from Mexico, was soon renamed the *Tequila Crisis*. The collapse left the government in undeclared insolvency; in addition, with upwards of 30 percent of private bank credits in technical default, the private banking system was equally insolvent. For all intents and purposes, the country's financial system – public and private – was bankrupt. As the crisis grew, Mexico lost its external sources of finance, and then, as domestic depositors fled, its internal sources as well. Even at interest rates in excess of 50 percent, there was little domestic lending for productive investment. In 1995 real GDP declined by 8 percent, virtually eliminating the growth that had occurred since the reforms were first introduced.[1648]

9-3a(4). The Tequila Crisis: would a reading of history have helped? The Mexican crisis triggered reverberations – the so-called *Tequila Effect* – in the financial markets of developing countries around the world. As in Mexico, depositors, fearing that others would lose their nerve, rushed to withdraw their funds from the banks. In Latin America, in countries like Brazil and Argentina, and, in Asia, in the Philippines, financial institutions succumbed to their own self-induced speculative panics.[1649] Most of the academic rhetoric about the Tequila Crisis has focused on the role of short-term capital flows and questions of bank regulation. Putting

---

[1647] Birdsall, Gavin, and Hausman, "Lessons from the Mexico Crisis," pp. 6–7, 10. In 1993 net capital inflows – mostly short-term and channeled into the stock market – exceeded 8 percent of GDP. Sebastian Edwards, "The Mexican Peso Crisis: How Much Did We Know? When Did We Know It?" National Bureau of Economic Research, Working Paper No. 6334, December 1997, pp. 10–11, 21–22.

[1648] Andrew Cornfeld and Jan Kregel, "Globalization, Capital Flows and International Regulation," the Jerome Levy Economic Institute of Bard College, Working Paper No. 161, May 1996, p. 16.

[1649] Sachs, Tornell, and Velasco, "Financial Crises," pp. 1–3.

aside such questions as whether or not some form of short-term capital controls would be effective, and admitting that better regulation – regulation based on more exact accounting and legal standards – would have improved the financial structure, the experience of the "frontier four" in the late nineteenth century appears to furnish some additional lessons for the Latin American economies of the late twentieth century.

As in the case of Japan, government banks in Latin America have tended to direct resources to favored industries and have supported high levels of government spending. In addition, where the government has operated the savings banks, those banks have stifled private capital mobilization. In Argentina, for example, in June 1995 provincial banks accounted for 42 percent of total loans and 33 percent of all bank employees. These institutions were used by the provincial governments to channel loans to political allies and to finance state deficits. Moreover, although by international standards most of the banks were insolvent, political decisions forced the central bank to use loans and guarantees to keep them afloat. In addition, the government nationalized savings accounts. These government policies led to low mobilization of bank deposits, scarcity of credit, and high levels of inefficiency.[1650]

Similarly, many private banks – in countries like Argentina, Brazil, and Chile – have made it a practice to direct a significant proportion of their financial resources to "connected" borrowers, particularly to bank owners or managers and their related businesses. In 1921, although he did not use the word, Lavington underscored the importance of solving problems of asymmetric information, if capital markets are to operate efficiently. No one doubts the issue remains important today. As the debate over the role of universal banking continues, participants on both sides have recognized that, in principle, that problem can be alleviated by universal banks – banks that make long-term loans to commercial and industrial firms – if the bankers maintain a proper arm's length relationship with their customers. Those banks are particularly well placed to obtain information about the firms that use the banks' resources – information that other outsiders are most often not able to access – and to otherwise monitor those firms' activities. The problem, however, lies in the fine line between responsible connections with bank-loan customers and irresponsible and disastrous connections. "Cronyism" or "connected borrowing" are just ways of describing the latter relationship. There is, after all, a great temptation for a bank manager to transfer profits from the bank to a borrowing firm, when that firm is owned by the manager, his relatives, his friends, or his political allies. As a result,

---

[1650] Molano, "Financial Reverberations," pp. 11–12.

despite the potential benefits, connected borrowing is often marked by a lack of objectivity (or, perhaps, outright fraud) in the determination of the borrower's creditworthiness; and it has produced not only flimsy bank balance sheets, but also an undue concentration of loans. Thus, the failure of a few large related borrowers, or the collapse of a particular sector of the economy, can wipe out a bank's capital. The problem is compounded by the fact that, in many Latin American countries, the less exact accounting and legal standards made it all but impossible for the regulating authority to determine whether the borrower had a personal relationship with the bank.[1651] These are hardly new problems; they were problems that produced the Australian crisis of the 1890s and, in the wake of that crisis, a half century of slow growth for what had been the world's richest country.

There is at least one other insight into Latin American problems that can be gleaned from the reading of the histories of the "frontier four." Even more than Japan, the Latin American countries tend to be "bank heavy"; and, even more than Japan, since the Latin American banks tend not to raise funds through the issue of debentures, the banks in those countries suffer from chronic asset/liability mismatches. Although there are certain chicken-egg questions, the problem of bank dominance and the resulting asset/liability mismatches is self-reinforcing. In the United States during the 1820s and 1830s, commercial banks were the source of long-term capital for canals and railroads. However, the fallout from the Panic of 1837 and the subsequent Depression of 1839–41 set in motion the adoption of new rules – both legal and cultural – that increasingly forced banks to focus their lending activities in the short end of the market. Those rules were further strengthened by the passage of the National Banking Act and its subsequent amendment, an amendment that placed a prohibitive federal tax on state bank notes. Similarly, in Canada, banking legislation – legislation that remained in force until relatively recently – largely restricted banks to making short-term loans.

These rules had a major impact on the subsequent structure of financial intermediation. Given that banks were largely precluded from making long-term loans, other financial intermediaries – private savings banks, life insurance companies, and building and loan societies – moved

---

[1651] Goldstein and Turner, "Banking Crises," pp. 20–21. Rojas-Suarez and Weisbrod, "Banking Crisis in Latin America," p. 16. The temptation may, of course, be reduced if the loans are truly short-term and/or are supported by the collateral that can be easily realized. Too often, however, neither constraint was met in the majority of the Latin American cases; the same was true in Australia in the 1890s.

to service the needs of firms requiring long-term capital. To a large extent, these "other" institutions were less subject to potential asset/ liability mismatches. In the United States the imprimatur of approval placed on the mutual savings banks by the local business and social elites insulated those banks from potential runs; with a mortality table in hand, life insurance companies were able to gauge the temporal distribution of their potential payouts; and the required "deposits" in building and loan associations were spelled out in advance.

The absence of banks in the long-term market also meant that there was more room for the development of formal securities markets. In the United States not only the New York Stock Exchange but also local securities markets grew and flourished. In Canada viable securities markets emerged in both Montreal and Toronto, and, in addition, the bond house proved to be a profitable institutional innovation. Finally, in the United States international capital flows were not interemediated by the commercial banks; instead there was a profitable role for the second-generation Anglo-American investment banks – the junior partners of the British merchant banks – and, later, for the third-generation truly American investment banks. In Argentina in the late nineteenth century, as in much of Latin America in the late twentieth century, banks were able to supply long-term credit; financial innovation in the formal securities markets and in supporting institutions was less profitable; and the threat that asset/liability mismatches could trigger new financial crises – a threat that is currently compounded by the globalization of short-term capital movements – still remains today.

9-3b. *From tigers to pussycats: the Asian NICS, 1996–1999*

9-3b(1). Introduction: If the economic problems of the 1980s and mid-1990s were largely rooted in Latin America, the more recent "world crisis" began in the developing countries of Asia. The Asian NICS – Indonesia, Korea, Malaysia, the Philippines, Singapore, Taiwan, and Thailand – had been the economic stars of the two decades between 1976 and 1996. While world GDP growth had averaged 2.8 percent per year, the "Tigers" had come in at 6.6 percent.[1652] In those countries the 1980s and early 1990s had witnessed major changes in the legal rules governing the financial sector, rule changes that linked those economies more closely with the rest of the world. In 1970 the financial sector represented 4.1

[1652] Ross C. DeVol, "The Asian Crisis Tsunami: Trade and Other Impacts on California and the United States," Milken Institute, Policy Brief, September 1988, p. 3. [Hereafter cited as DeVol, "Tsunami."] The individual figures were 5.5, 8.4, 7.3, 3.1, 7.9, 8.2, and 6.1 percent respectively.

percent of GDP in the United States and 4.7 percent in Japan. The comparable figure for Indonesia was 1.8 percent, for Korea 2.5, for the P hilippines and Taiwan 3.0, and for Thailand 3.5. By 1990, the Philippines aside, the gap had closed substantially. With the United States at 6.1 percent and Japan at 5.9, the figure for Indonesia was 4.2, for Korea 5.0, for the Philippines 4.0, for Taiwan 10.5, and for Thailand 5.5 percent.[1653] Although private commercial banks remained a more dominant part of the Asian financial infrastructures than they were in the United States, by 1994 they had come to play a lesser role than in either Latin America or in Japan. In the United States private commercial banks held 23 percent of the assets of all financial institutions; in Japan the figure was 79, and in the six Latin American countries 57 percent. In the NICS it averaged 43 percent, although the figure ranged from 23 percent in Taiwan to 71 percent in Singapore.[1654]

9-3b(2). The financial infrastructure before 1980: By the 1970s Indonesia, Korea, and Taiwan had nationalized most or all of their commercial banks; and, in the Philippines and Thailand, government-owned banks or similar depositories had a substantial minority presence. Moreover, regardless of ownership, governments had established elaborate regulatory systems designed to constrain bank behavior. There were rules governing both the sectors that were eligible for loans and the terms at which those loans could be made. In Indonesia, Korea, Malaysia, the Philippines, and Thailand, the government either required or pressured banks to allocate fixed proportions of their loan portfolios to particular economic sectors. In Korea, for example, even a decade after the banks had been privatized, policy loans – loans made in response to a government policy – accounted for almost one-half of all bank loans. In addition, reserve and liquidity requirements were often used to force banks to hold significant quantities of government bonds. Deposits, too, were subject to interest ceilings, ceilings that were, at times, below the rate of inflation. Finally, even in the private banking sector, entry of new firms was usually forbidden; and, although some established foreign banks were allowed to continue limited operations, the entry of new foreign-based banks was largely prohibited. In contrast, despite the extensive network of economic regulation, rules relating to safety and soundness were largely or entirely neglected. "Concerns about prudent lending

---

[1653] Lawrence J. White, "Structure of Finance in Selected Asian Economies," in Shahid N. Zahid (ed.), *Financial Sector Development in Asia* (Hong Kong: Oxford University Press [for the Asian Development Bank], 1995), table 2.1, p. 36. [Hereafter cited as White, "Structure of Finance."]

[1654] Goldstein and Turner, "Banking Crises," table 2, p. 19.

practices, profitable operation, and accurate representation of balance sheet values were secondary considerations (if they were given consideration at all) to the goals of ensuring that specified sectors of the economy received credit on specified favorable terms."[1655]

With respect to the rest of the financial sector, in most of the NICS governments had created special development banks – banks established to make long-term loans to industry – and most non-bank intermediaries had either been nationalized or subjected to intensive economic regulation, regulations similar to those imposed on the banks. Although securities markets tend to be relatively unimportant in the early stages of development, the governments had also moved to control those markets both through the imposition of direct controls – restrictions on the existence and operation of private mutual funds, specification of the prices at which initial public offerings of shares could be sold, exclusion of foreign securities firms from domestic securities markets, and prohibitions on foreign investment in domestic securities – and through taxes levied on specific types of financial instruments and transactions.[1656]

During the 1970s, Korea, Singapore, and Taiwan all drew on overseas capital to underwrite their development. Despite the importance of foreign capital, although government policies varied in terms of severity, the three countries continued to place very significant restrictions on the participation of foreign financial institutions in their domestic markets. As a result, domestic financial institutions continued to dominate the financial markets in Korea and Taiwan; and, in Singapore, that domination continued in the domestic (as opposed to the international) market.[1657]

In the case of foreign financial institutions, as in the case of private commercial banks, Singapore represented something of an exception. The country had become independent from Malaysia in 1965. Almost immediately it had moved to become an international financial center. In 1968 offshore financial markets were established, and in 1970 new government policies designed to attract branches of foreign banks were implemented.[1658] The country moved to a free-floating exchange rate in 1973; two years later the government issued Singapore dollar-negotiable

[1655] White, "Structure of Finance," pp. 134–35.
[1656] White, "Structure of Finance," pp. 135–36. Goldstein and Turner, "Banking Crises," pp. 20–21.
[1657] Masumi Kishi, "Financial Markets and Policies in Newly Industrializing Economies," in Shahid N. Zahid (ed.), *Financial Sector Development in Asia* (Hong Kong: Oxford University Press [for the Asian Development Bank], 1995), p. 174. [Hereafter cited as Kishi, "Financial Markets and Policies."]
[1658] Kishi, "Financial Markets and Policies," p. 174.

certificates of deposit, although the privilege was given to only certain banks, and completed deregulation of interest rates on domestic deposits and lending; finally, in 1978 foreign exchange controls were lifted.[1659]

In one dimension, however, through the 1970s Singapore followed (and still, to some extent, does follow) what might be called the "Asian pattern," and, given the role of the banks in the economy, it was an important exception to the post-1970s liberalization. In Singapore commercial banking is still dominated by four banks, and those banks act together to create an effectively monopolized market. Moreover, at the same time that the government, in its attempt to develop an international financial center, was concentrating on attracting foreign banks, it moved to protect local banks. Domestic banks were of three kinds: full license, restricted license, and offshore. Full license banks could, with no restrictions, carry on all banking operations in the Singapore domestic market, but restricted license banks and offshore banks as well as foreign banks were severely limited in the scope of their domestic activities. In addition, the government controlled the Post Office Savings Bank, one of the country's major financial institutions.[1660]

9-3b(3). The liberalization of the 1980s and early 1990s: Singapore somewhat aside, the Asian NICS entered the 1980s with heavily regulated financial sectors; but, although the extent of deregulation varied from country to country, the next decade and a half were marked by some degree of liberalization in all seven. For example, the governments of Indonesia, Korea, the Philippines, Taiwan, and Thailand encouraged the expansion of private sector non-bank financial intermediaries (finance companies, leasing companies, and investment trusts), while de-emphasizing the role of government-owned development banks and development finance institutions. In addition, by the early 1990s all five were prepared to accept some level of foreign participation and investment in their securities markets.[1661]

In Indonesia between 1982 and 1991 the structure of the banking system changed significantly. The government eliminated most of its interest rate restrictions on bank loans and deposits, and it reduced its sectoral loan requirements on the state banks, while, at the same time,

[1659] Kishi, "Financial Markets and Policies," p. 202.
[1660] Kishi, "Financial Markets and Policies," p. 182. The four dominant domestic banks were the Overseas Chinese Banking Corporation, United Overseas Bank, Overseas Union Bank, and the Development Bank of Singapore. In 1991 the deposits in the Post Office savings Bank represented 22 percent of the deposits of nonbank customers in the commercial banks.
[1661] White, "Structure of Finance," p. 136.

encouraging the expansion of private banks. In response, the share of the government-owned banks in total financial assets dropped, and the share of privately owned banks (including some foreign banks) rose sharply. The relaxation of government restrictions on interest rates, credit ceilings, entry, and branching also induced some changes in the structure of non-bank intermediation: a decline in the share of merchant banks in financial assets – most of the merchant banks had been joint ventures affiliated with the government-owned banks – and an increase in the importance of insurance and leasing companies. At the time of the 1988 reforms – reforms that opened entry to new banks and encouraged branching of existing banks – the authorities expressed little interest in protecting the government-owned banks and, if anything, sought to reduce preferential treatment. The government also moved to encourage the expansion of the formal securities markets. The underlying thrust of these policies was to curtail preferential directed-credit programs, programs that had been channeled mainly through the government banks, to increase competition throughout the banking industry and to open the way for both non-Chinese Indonesians and foreigners to expand their activities.[1662]

"In Korea, industrialization had been initially led by the Government with significant involvement of large companies, particularly corporate groups."[1663] But by 1990 that structure had begun to erode. In fact, it has been argued recently that "if America's brand of cowboy capitalism and free-market ideology is to work anyplace in East Asia, it will be in South Korea."[1664] Korea began by deregulating its interest rate controls and its sectoral loan allocations for banks. Deregulation was characterized by an emphasis on policies that promoted competitiveness through privatization, that relaxed direct controls over financial institutions, and that eased the regulations covering financial assets and interest rates. Since these latter policies gave preference to nonbank intermediaries, secondary financial institutions grew more rapidly than the banking sector. Over the decade there was an easing of controls on foreign investment: international trust funds were established, foreign brokers were

---

[1662] White, "Structure of Finance," p. 136. David C. Cole, "Financial Sector Development in Southeast Asia," in Shahid N. Zahid (ed.), *Financial Sector Development in Asia* (Hong Long: Oxford University Press [for the Asian Development Bank], 1995, pp. 230–39. [Hereafter cited as Cole, "Financial Sector Development."] Foreign participation in banking was still confined to joint ventures, but the foreign participation could reach 85 percent.

[1663] Kishi, "Financial Markets and Policies," p. 173.

[1664] Mark Magnier, "S. Korea a Model Student in US Schools of Economics," *Los Angeles Times*, November 23, 1998, p. A8.

allowed to open branches and establish joint ventures, and in 1992 the government allowed foreign brokers, firms, and individuals to invest in the local market. The commercial banks were privatized, and two new banks established. In addition, restrictions on nonbank intermediaries were lifted, and, as a result, the number of investment finance companies and mutual deposit and finance companies rose. There were also attempts to release interest rates from political control; however, since government "guidance" continued to keep rates low, "it is not really possible to say that liberalization was in fact implemented." Finally, the government turned its attention to the securities markets; some of the restrictive economic regulations were removed, and some rules designed to increase disclosure and augment investor protections were strengthened.[1665]

Of the seven Asian NICS, Malaysia underwent the least liberalization in the post-1980 years. In light of its government's recent response to the 1998 crisis, that should come as no surprise. Between 1980 and 1990 there were no dramatic changes in its financial structure. There was a moderate 7 percent decline in the share of commercial banks and in the government's Provident Fund, a decline that was largely offset by an increase in the share of finance companies, unit trusts, building societies, and housing bonds. Throughout the period, however, in a government-led attempt to expand the role of domestic banks, a series of policies designed to curtail the activities of foreign banks were implemented. In addition, within the domestic banking sector there has been a continued government policy bias toward government- and Malay-owned banks and against non-Malay, particularly Chinese, ownership.[1666]

Between 1986 and 1991 there was little change in the structure of Philippine financial intermediation. There was a small decline in the share of foreign-owned banks (from 9 to 7 percent of the assets of all financial institutions) and a corresponding increase in the share of private domestic banks. Like Indonesia, the Philippines eliminated most of the interest rate restrictions that had applied to loans and deposits. In addition, the government loosened some of the restrictions on the commercial banks, and it focused more attention on its securities markets. The government continued to attempt to curtail the activities of the existing foreign-owned banks and to expand the role of their domestic counterparts. During the 1980s government policy encouraged the merger and consolidation of domestic banking institutions, and those

---

[1665] White, "Structure of Finance," p. 136; Kishi, "Financial Markets and Policies," pp. 200–1.

[1666] Cole, "Financial Sector Development," table 5.3, pp. 228, 230, 238. The decline was from 53 to 46 percent.

efforts led to significantly increased concentration. The rules on bank entry and branching were relaxed in 1989, but they were still relatively restrictive. For example, approval of new bank licenses takes from one to three years. Moreover, entry of wholly owned foreign banks was still prohibited, and foreign participation in joint ventures was limited to 40 percent.[1667]

In the "decade of liberalization" Singapore continued to be half out of step with its Asian peers. On the one hand, financial deregulation designed to bolster the city-state's role as an international financial center continued. On the other hand, the government tightened its controls on the domestic financial system. At the beginning of the 1980s the government took further steps to internationalize its offshore financial and capital markets. In 1983, for example, it granted certain tax exemptions to the offshore income of nonresidents. In the second half of the decade, with an aim at further developing its capital markets, it largely deregulated the stock exchange. In 1987 the Stock Exchange of Singapore permitted foreign financial institutions and securities brokers to acquire 49 percent of local brokers, and the Monetary Authority opened the government securities market to foreigners. Three years later further reforms included scrapping the overlapping listing system at the Singapore Securities Exchange Market and the Malaysian Securities Exchange Market. Two steps forward, at least one step back. In 1984 the Monetary Authority of Singapore Amendment Act became binding. That law effectively granted the Monetary Authority much greater powers to regulate and control the financial system. At the same time it increased the role of the banking system in the nation's financial infrastructure, and, by enhancing the Authority's position as advisor to the government, it tightened the connections between the government and the infrastructure.[1668]

Liberalization came earliest to Taiwan. In many dimensions the market had been liberalized before the 1970s. Beginning in the 1970s, further financial deregulation was aimed at improving the infrastructure's efficiency in allocating funds, at enhancing the managerial efficiency of the commercial banks, and at attempting to adjust the competitive balance between the public and private sectors, a balance that had been heavily tilted toward public institutions. The central features of the reforms involved lifting the restrictions on interest rates and foreign exchange and the Central Bank's shift from policies of direct to

---

[1667] White, "Structure of Finance," p. 136. Cole, "Financial Sector Development," pp. 230, 238–39.
[1668] Kishi, "Financial Markets and Policies," pp. 202–3.

policies of indirect financial control. Lending rate liberalization began in the mid-1970s; however, the government, to avoid "excessive" competition between financial institutions and to ensure "stability" in the financial system, promulgated the "essentials of interest rate adjustment" in 1980. The 1980s did, however, see some further liberalization. In 1985 commercial banks were obliged to set a prime rate; the next year the Central Bank reduced the number of categories of deposit rate ceilings from thirteen to four; and the government partially liberalized interest rates on domestic and foreign currency deposits. In 1987 controls on most foreign exchange transactions were eliminated, and currency account transactions were almost totally liberalized. Finally, in 1989 the Revised Banking Law further extended the liberalization of interest rates for both deposits and lending: and a foreign currency call loan market was established. During the 1980s and early 1990s, the Taiwanese government also permitted the entry and expansion of both new domestic and foreign banks.[1669]

In Thailand, between 1983 and 1992, there is very little evidence of any substantial change in the financial infrastructure. The share of commercial banks in all financial sector assets remained constant at slightly less than 70 percent. There was, however, a small increase in the share of finance companies, while the share of pawnshops, credit companies, and the government savings bank declined. Until recently government policy continued to restrict new bank entry and prevented foreign banks from branching, but it did encourage the growth and branching of domestic banks. Those policies, however, resulted in strengthening the already existing oligopolistic cartel; to partially offset that structure, the authorities permitted non-banks to engage what had, theretofore, been regarded as traditional commercial banks preserves. Unfortunately, this new policy has created major regulatory problems, and it has not seriously affected the behavior of the cartelized banking system. In the mid-1990s the government, in an attempt to encourage more foreign participation and a more active international banking system, approved the organization of the Bangkok International Banking Facilities. Four years later, it is still unclear if this action will help alleviate the cartel problems.[1670]

Overall, a snapshot of the financial sectors of the seven countries in the mid-1990s showed substantially more variation among both regulatory policies and institutional structures than had been true two decades

---

[1669] White, "Structure of Finance," p. 136. Kishi, "Financial Markets and Policies," p. 203.

[1670] Cole, "Financial Sector Development," table 5.3, p. 232, pp. 231, 239.

earlier. Although governments remained extensively involved in the financial sectors of all seven, the extent of economic regulation was reduced from the levels of the 1970s, with Indonesia probably the furthest along the path to complete liberalization. There were significant intercountry differences in the extent of government ownership of banks, in the residual influences over interest rates and sectoral loan allocations, in the role of foreign-based banks, and in the relative importance of securities markets and the degree of foreign participation in those markets. Indonesia aside, all tended to remain wary of foreign involvement and continued to place some barriers to the entry of foreign-based firms into their banking, insurance, and securities markets. At the same time they sought to protect the positions of existing firms. Finally, the role of government-owned banks had been diminished, but it had not been eliminated.[1671]

9-3b(4). The Asian crisis: On the one hand, foreign financial institutions – institutions from well-supervised financial markets in developed countries – bring to local markets the benefits of global diversification, the financial support of their main offices, and, perhaps, most importantly, the "best-practice" standards of disclosure, accounting, and prudent behavior.[1672] In 1995 those benefits had not been fully realized. On the other hand, "managers of state banks are unusually susceptible to political pressures to engage in directed lending; if supervisors see the allocation of loans as a device for furthering political objectives rather than maximizing return on bank capital, problems of bank insolvency and liquidity can result." A deposit insurance scheme, either implicit or explicit, in conjunction with a regulator who subscribes to either the "too-big-to-fail" or the "too-well-connected-to-fail" principle will encourage bank managers to assume excessive risk; and at the same time it will relieve customers and shareholders of their incentive to monitor the bank's behavior.[1673] In most of the Asian NICS, state banks were still operating in 1995; for example, they represented 57 percent of bank assets in

---

[1671] White, "Structure of Finance," pp. 137, 141. Cole, "Financial Sector Development," p. 239.

[1672] Nancy Birdsall, Michael Gavin, and Ricardo Hausman, "The East Asian Financial Crisis: A View from Latin America," Working Paper, Office of the Chief Economist, Inter-American Development Bank, February 1988, p. 13. [Hereafter cited as Birdsall, Gain, and Hausman, "The East Asian Financial Crisis."]

[1673] Barry Eichengreen and Andrew Rose, "Staying Afloat When the Wind Shifts: External Factors and Emerging-Market Banking Crises," manuscript, December 10, 1997, p. 16. [Hereafter cited as Eichengreen and Rose, "Staying Afloat."]

Taiwan, 46 percent in Indonesia, 13 percent in Korea, and just less than 10 percent in Malaysia and Thailand.[1674]

By 1996 the partially reformed Asian NICS had experienced a major lending boom. In Indonesia, the Philippines, and Thailand, for example, bank credit growth had exceeded the corresponding GDP growth rates by 60 percent or more; and, in Malaysia, it was only slightly less.[1675] Such a lending boom tends to weaken domestic financial systems and leave in its wake a large stock of undisclosed bad debts on lenders' balance sheets. The extent of the deterioration is often not apparent until the boom subsides and debtors – debtors who had appeared creditworthy during the period of economic buoyancy and easy credit – begin to experience economic difficulties.[1676] Asia in the mid-1990s was no exception to this general rule. As domestic borrowers began to experience financial difficulties, lenders forced them to rely more and more heavily on short-term debt and left them with an increasing level of maturity mismatches.[1677] The larger an economic shock, the more the maturity mismatches will prove inconsistent with financial stability. Financial institutions, particularly banks in highly volatile developing economies, should attempt to closely match the maturity of their assets and liabilities. The opposite, however, is usually true. Not only do the banks often play a greater role in those developing economies, but they typically have poorer access to long-term funding than their counterparts in the more developed world. As a result, the average maturity of their liabilities is much shorter.[1678] Such was the case in Asia in the mid-1990s. In Indonesia, Korea, Taiwan, and Thailand, for example, bank assets as a percentage of GDP were greater and in some cases much greater than the volume of bonds listed on the countries' exchanges or the total capitalization of their equity markets. Unfortunately, in 1996 the Asian

---

[1674] James R. Barth, R. Dan Brumbaugh, Lalita Ramesh, and Glen Yago, "The East Asian Banking Crisis: Governments vs. Markets: Does the I.M.F. Create Incentives That Exacerbate Crises?" Milken Institute, *Jobs and Capital*, Vol. VII, No. 3/4 (summer-fall 1998), figure 7, p. 38. [Hereafter cited as Barth et al., "The East Asian Banking Crisis."] James R. Barth, R. Dan Brumbaugh, Jr., Lalita Ramesh, and Glenn Yago, "The Role of Governments and Markets in International Banking Crises: The Case of East Asia," paper delivered at the 73rd Annual Western Economic Association International Conference, Lake Tahoe, June 28–July 2, 1998, p. 34. [Hereafter cited as Barth et al., "The Role of Governments and Markets."]

[1675] Barth et al., "The Role of Governments and Markets," p. 18.

[1676] Birdsall, Gavin, and Hausman, "The East Asian Financial Crisis," p. 4.

[1677] Ibid.

[1678] Eichengreen and Rose, "Staying Afloat," p. 14.

economy was about to receive the first of a series of severe economic shocks.[1679] The initial shock, coupled with the maturity mismatches, touched off a self-fulfilling financial crisis.[1680]

Between 1997 and 2000, the term "Tigers" has been seldom used; better labels range, depending on the country, from lynxes to kittens or, perhaps, even to skunks. At the end of 1998 Indonesia was the basket case of Asia. The economy was in free-fall, declining at an annual rate of 14 percent in the first two quarters of the year, and inflation was nearing 50 percent. Korea was in the midst of a severe depression; real GNP declined almost 6 percent in the first quarter of 1998 (the first decline in seventeen years); and in May industrial production was down 10 percent over the previous year. While Malaysia at first appeared to have avoided the contagion, recent events suggest that it also has not been immune. In the first quarter of 1998 real economic output was down by almost 2 percent over its level of a year ago, and the stock market has lost 40 percent of its value since the year began. The Philippines have been affected, but much less than most of the other NICS. An initial shock was felt in the foreign exchange and stock markets; but in 1998, although economic growth declined to about 2 percent (down from 5 percent in 1997), it was still positive. In Singapore economic conditions deteriorated, the region's demand for the country's exports plummeted, and GDP contracted by 3.6 percent between the fourth quarter of 1997 and the third quarter of 1998. Taiwan remains at least a mountain lion, if not a full-fledged tiger. Economic growth is slowed, but it remained firmly positive; real GDP rose at a rate of 5.8 percent in the first half of 1998 (down, however, from 6.7 percent in 1997). Recession in the region, however, has adversely impacted exports, and foreign direct investment in the first quarter of 1998 was the lowest in a half decade. The Thailand economy was in deep recession. The economy contracted by 8 percent in the first half of 1998; capital flight continued; and, because of questionable lending practices at the end of the year, non-performing bank loans probably accounted for 40 percent of all outstanding loans.[1681]

9-3b(5). History has a way of repeating itself: Recently Nobel Laureate Gary Becker attempted to explain the Asian crisis. He is quoted as saying that "obtrusive regulations and excessive government control over the financial sector are the weakest links in the economic superstructure of Indonesia, Malaysia, Thailand, and South Korea." Their governments, he continued, "have regularly steered subsidies and other assistance to

---

[1679] Barth et al., "The Role of Government and Markets," p. 39.
[1680] Birdsall, Gavin, and Hausman, "The East Asian Financial Crisis," pp. 4–5.
[1681] DeVol, "Tsunami," pp. 15–16.

favored customers and bailed out those that got into financial difficulties."[1682] Nor has Becker been alone in suggesting government policies as the primary source of weaknesses in the financial infrastructures of the Asian economies. Given the general consensus about the causes of the Asian turmoil, it seems reasonable to ask if a study of history could have provided warnings to the governments of the Asian NICS?

It is probably unnecessary, but it should be noted that, through the early 1990s, most of the NICS were making serious efforts to liberalize their economies, but, Indonesia perhaps aside, all still had a long way to go. An examination of the Asian countries' financial structures in 1996 underscores many of the same problems that have become evident in Japan, problems rooted in the direct government controls that Becker complains about. Even more than in Japan, both the government-owned development banks and the sometimes "private," sometimes nationalized, banks were subject to direct government regulations designed to allocate credit to favored sectors. In Japan in the decades following World War II, the private banks, although subject to charges of "crony capitalism" and with their decision making partially constrained by indirect government policies, still retained a substantial degree of freedom in their investment policies. In the Tigers, however, governments continued to exercise a substantial level of direct control; and, as a result, probably even more than in Australia in the nineteenth century, governments directed investments toward activities that maximized political, rather than economic, profits.

As in Japan, the government savings banks in the NICS were a major source of government finance. Here, too, an examination of the comparative histories of savings banks in Australia, Canada, the United Kingdom, and a willingness to learn from the U.S. experience might have led to very different policies. In Australia the banks became the source of the funds that the government directed toward politically determined sectors. In the United Kingdom and in most of Canada, the banks' investments were limited to government bonds. Those purchases provided interest relief for government finances and may, by reducing general interest rates, have indirectly released resources for private investment; but the savings banks played little direct role in the accumulation and mobilization of capital for the private sector. Only in the United States did the savings banks perform that function. Although the regulations governing investments differed from state to state, until the 1870s the mutual savings banks supplied funds for a multitude of market-driven economic activities: In Maryland they supplied funds for both local

---

[1682] Cited in Barth et al., "The Role of Governments and Markets," p. 45.

private business and for larger enterprises like the Baltimore & Ohio Railway, in New York for the Erie Canal, and in Massachusetts for both private railroads and for the developing cotton textile industry. Where state regulations permitted such investments, the banks proved important in both the accumulation and the mobilization of private-sector capital. Although their area of operations was to a large extent limited to New York, New England, and the Middle Atlantic states, taken together, American mutual savings banks remained, until the 1870s, the nation's largest and most important non-bank intermediary. Moreover, had it not been for the rush to pass regulatory legislation after the fallout from the panic of 1872, they might well have continued their major role.

Finally, in the developing countries of Asia, direct controls were frequently extended to the securities markets; and, again, there was a historical lesson that could have been learned. In Australia, Canada, the United Kingdom, and the United States the securities markets were private organizations (mostly partnerships) subject only to rules governing all such private organizations. Entry into the industry was free. Thus, in the United States, for example, not only were there exchanges in cities like Boston, Chicago, and San Francisco (more than 250 in all), but also, because of the rules imposed by the New York Stock Exchange, there were competitive exchanges (the Curb and the Consolidated, to cite only two examples) within shouting distance of the NYSE. In the United Kingdom there was only a single exchange in London, but that fact reflected not a protected market, but the rules of the Exchange: no minimum commission, very loose rules governing the types of securities traded, and a carefully drawn distinction between securities granted a special settlement and those "quoted." Moreover, like in the United States, there were local exchanges (at least seventeen in England and Wales, five in Scotland, and one in Ireland). Thus, in both countries, whatever were the listing rules of a specific exchange, it was almost always possible to find some market on which the stocks and bonds of an enterprise could be traded. Moreover, the varying quality of the markets' imprimaturs was used as a signal by those savers who were still not very well educated about their paper investment alternatives. Nor was there any effective way for the government to influence the industrial composition or the types of the securities traded on these private markets. Since either the brokers or some set of investors owned the exchanges, the operators were primarily interested in selling securities; and, given the reputational demands for repeat business, the potential profitability of the issuing companies was a major determinant in their decisions to list or trade. Contrast nineteenth-century London and New

York with Paris. On the Paris Bourse, in a manner much like the rules that currently regulate the securities markets of the NICS, the government controlled entry, established trading rules, and determined the composition of the securities traded. Not surprisingly, in Paris that screening was frequently based on a political rather than an economic calculus. The monopolistic characteristics of the market kept costs high, and the exchange played only a limited role in private capital accumulation and mobilization.

In Asia government policies also indirectly impacted the financial infrastructures. In almost every country (Indonesia again an exception), the government moved to protect private bankers from competition, domestic as well as foreign. Domestically, such policies tended to lead to effective cartelization – lower deposit and higher lending rates – as well as "crony capitalism." Again, as in Japan and Latin America, although the bank managers might have effectively monitored their customers' activities and, thus, helped solve the problem of asymmetric information, they appear more often to have used their power to transfer profits from the banks to themselves, relatives, friends or, perhaps, to political allies. Contrast the Asian banking structures with the relatively "free-wheeling" experience of the United Kingdom and Canada and the somewhat different American experience. In the case of Britain and Canada, at least after midcentury, entry into banking was largely unrestricted. Over time the potential economies of scale inherent in large branch networks worked to reduce the number of banks, but there is no evidence that in Canada there was ever any effective cartelization. In the United Kingdom competition held sway, at least through World War I and probably through the 1920s. As a result, capital accumulation was promoted, and the banking networks speeded mobilization; they channeled savings both to new industries and to newly developing regions. In the United States, with the emergence of "free banking" in the 1830s and 1840s, entry was easy. Restrictions on branching, however, left many bankers in small towns and the countryside in a semi-monopolistic position; and even when there was local competition, interregional mobilization was difficult. As a result, large parts of the nation, particularly areas in the South and West, were marked by low rates of interest on deposits and high rates on loans; and the country did not develop a truly national capital market until almost the end of the nineteenth century. A comparison of the three systems should have warned Asian policy makers that, although the U.S. system with free local entry was clearly better than the system of restricted entry that it replaced – a system similar to those of the NICS – it was certainly inferior to a system of unrestricted national entry that characterized banking in Canada and the United Kingdom.

Similar lessons can also be drawn from the role of foreign banks in the economic development of the frontier economies in the nineteenth century. Such banks not only bring added resources, but equally importantly, they often introduce better business and accounting practices, practices that both make the system less fragile and provide imprimaturs of quality that can help educate domestic savers. The importance of the first-generation Anglo-American merchant/investment banks in the evolution of the American financial infrastructure has already been noted. Similarly, the success of the British banks in Argentina during the crisis of the 1890s played a similar educational role in that South American country. The Argentine savers' response to the success of the British banks forced the managers of their domestic competitors to adopt stricter loan policies; and, as a result, both the management and institutional structure of the domestic commercial banks emerged from the crisis much stronger. Elsewhere in the late nineteenth century, the British imperial and international banks played analogous roles both in the empire and in other developing countries. Nor was Britain alone in providing "aid" to countries with underdeveloped financial markets. In the case of California the branches of both British and Canadian banks helped to partially overcome the problems of national capital mobility that were rooted in the American unit banking system. Despite the fact that their entry may erode the profits of politically connected domestic bankers, if a country wants to provide at least a high school education for its savers, while at the same time developing a strong financial infrastructure, foreign banks – banks subject to significant levels of managerial oversight and accounting regulations in their home countries – should be viewed as assets, not liabilities.

9-4. Conclusions

Clearly, if economic efficiency is the desired goal, policy makers can find useful lessons in history. But, as recent political events in Russia and economic events in both Asia and Latin America have underscored, time itself may also be important. Although both Canada and the United States only gradually received the benefits of a modern financial structure, at one level both benefited from the gradual evolution of their financial systems. In Australia in the 1890s, a sudden regime change not only exposed an undetected fragility in the financial structure, but also yielded financial innovations that, although perhaps useful during the period of crises, proved both very inefficient in the longer term and very difficult to replace. There is, therefore, an extra lesson that the Asian and Latin American countries should heed: if the government attempts to introduce new financial innovations to "stabilize" the economy, at a later date it may prove difficult to later replace those new institutions. Thus, while developing and underdeveloped countries can benefit from the "Lessons of the Past," their governments should be willing to let the market test any innovations that either those lessons or local politicians may suggest.

One final word: as Lavington pointed out more than three-quarters of a century ago, issues of monitoring and asymmetric information are crucially important if financial markets are to efficiently solve the problems of capital accumulation and mobilization. The history of the impact of foreign capital on the evolution of the domestic capital markets in underdeveloped frontier countries in the nineteenth century again demonstrates that the issues Lavington raised were not new, even in 1921, and that they are still relevant today. Finally, the current Asian crisis indicates that, although the past has provided valuable lessons, it does not appear that, even a century later, those lessons have been learned.

BIBLIOGRAPHY

Abramovitz, Moses. "The Monetary Side of Long Swings in U.S. Economic Growth," Center for Research in Economic Growth, Memorandum No. 146, Stanford University, April 1973.

Thinking About Growth (Cambridge: Cambridge University Press, 1989).

Abramovitz, Moses, and Paul A. David. "Economic Growth in America: Historical Parallels and Realities," *The Economist*, 1973.

"Reinterpreting Economic Growth: Parallels and Realities of the American Experience," *American Economic Review, Papers and Proceedings*, May 1973.

Adelman, Jeremy. "Agricultural Credit in the Province of Buenos Aires, Argentina, 1890–1914," *Journal of Latin American Studies*, Vol. 22, Part 1 (February 1990).

Adler, Dorothy. *British Investment in American Railways, 1824–1898* (Charlottesville: University Press of Virginia, 1970).

Adler, John H., ed. *Capital Movements and Economic Development*, Proceedings of a Conference held by the International Economic Association, July 1965 (London: Macmillan, 1967).

Aitken, Hugh G.J. *American Capital and Canadian Resources* (Cambridge, Mass.: Harvard University Press, 1961).

"Defensive Expansionism: The State and Economic Growth in Canada," in Hugh G.J. Aitken (ed.), *The State and Economic Growth*, Papers of a Conference Held on October 11–13, 1956, under the Auspices of the Committee on Economic Growth (New York: Social Science Research Council, 1959).

"A New Way to Pay Old Debts: A Canadian Experience," in W. Miller (ed.), *Men in Business* (New York: Harper and Row, 1952), pp. 71–90.

Allen, Franklin. "The Future of the Japanese Financial System," Wharton School Working Paper, August 19, 1996.

Allen, Frederick Lewis. *The Great Pierpont Morgan* (New York: Harper & Bros., 1949).

Annual Report of the Controller of the Currency to the Second Session of the Sixty-fourth Congress of the United States, December 4, 1916 (Washington, D.C.: GPO, 1917).

Anonymous. "British Bank Conservatism in the Late Nineteenth Century," manuscript, 1994.

Appleyard, R.T., and C.B. Schedvin. *Australian Financiers: Biographical Essays* (South Melbourne, Australia: Macmillan, 1988).

Argentine Yearbook. 1903, 1907–8 (Buenos Aires: John Grant and Son, various years).

Armstrong, Christopher, and H.V. Nelles. *Southern Exposure: Canadian Promoters in Latin America and the Caribbean, 1896–1930* (Toronto: University of Toronto Press, 1988).

Armstrong, John. "The Rise and Fall of the Company Promoter in the Financing of British Industry," in J.J. Van Helten and Y. Cassis, *Capitalism in a Mature Economy: Financial Institutions, Capital Exports and British Industry, 1837–1939* (Aldershot, U.K.: Edward Elgar, 1990).

Armstrong, Warwick. "The Social Origins of Industrial Growth: Canada, Argentina and Australia, 1870–1930," in D.C.M. Platt and Guido di Tella (eds.), *Argentina, Australia, and Canada: Studies in Comparative Development 1870–1965* (New York: St. Martin's Press, 1985).

Ashmead, Edward. *Twenty-five Years of Mining, 1880–1914* (London: Mining Journal, 1909).

Australian Dictionary of Biography (Carlton, Victoria: Melbourne University Press, various years).

Ayres, C.L. *New Capital Issues on the London Money Market, 1899–1913*. Ms. C. thesis, University of London, 1934.

Bacon, Nathaniel C. "American International Indebtedness," *Yale Review*, Vol. 9 (November 1900).

Bagehot, Walter. *Lombard Street, A Description of the Money Market* (Homewood, Ill.: Richard D. Irwin, 1962).

Bailey, J.D. "Australian Borrowing in Scotland in the Nineteenth Century," *Economic History Review*, Second Series, Vol. XII, No. 2 (December 1959).

A Hundred Years of Pastoral Banking: A History of the Australian Mercantile Land & Finance Company, 1863–1963 (Oxford: Clarendon Press, 1966).

Balboa, Manuel, and Alberto Fracchia. "Fixed Reproducible Capital in Argentina, 1935–55," in Raymond Goldsmith and Christopher Sanders (eds.), *The Measurement of National Wealth, Income and Wealth*, Series VIII (Chicago: Quadrangle Books, 1959).

Balke, Nathan S., and Robert J. Gordon. "The Estimation of Prewar Gross National Product: Methodology and New Evidence," *Journal of Political Economy*, Vol. 97, No. 1 (February 1989).

Bankers', Insurance Managers, and Agents' Magazine (London: Waterlow & Sons), Vol. 55 (1893).

Barbero, Maria Ines. "Argentina: Industrial Growth and Enterprise Organization, 1880s–1980s," in Alfred D. Chandler, Jr., Franco Amatori, and Takashi Hikino (eds.), *Big Business and the Wealth of Nations* (Cambridge: Cambridge University Press, 1997).

Barclay's Bank. Chapter 6, "Barclay's Abroad: *The Transition to Global Banking (1945–1990)*" (1995).

Bardham, Anab, Jere Behrman, and Albert Fishlow. *International Trade, Investment, Macro Policy and History: Essays in Memory of Carlos F. Diaz-Alejandro* (North-Holland: Elsevier Science Publishers, 1987).

Barger, Harold. *Distribution's Place in the American Economy Since 1869* (Princeton: Princeton University Press, 1955).

Barnard, A., and Noel G. Butlin. "Australian Public and Private Capital Formation, 1901–75," *The Economic Record*, Vol. 57, No. 159 (December 1981).

Barnett, George C. *State Banks and Trust Companies*, Senate Document No. 659, 61st Congress, 3d Session (Washington, D.C.: GPO, 1911).

Barth, James R., R. Dan Brumbaugh, Lalita Ramesh, and Glen Yago. "The East Asian Banking Crisis: Governments vs. Markets: Does the I.M.F. Create Incentives That Exacerbate Crises?" Milken Institute, *Jobs and Capital*, Vol. VII, No. 3–4 (summer-fall 1998).

"The Role of Governments and Markets in International Banking Crises: The Case of East Asia," paper delivered at the 73rd Annual Western Economic Association International Conference, Lake Tahoe, Nev., June 1998.

Baskerville, Peter. "Americans in Britain's Backyard: The Railway Era in Upper Canada, 1850–1880," *Business History Review*, Vol. LV, No. 3 (autumn 1981).

Baskin, Jonathan Barron. "The Development of Corporate Financial Markets in Britain and the United States, 1600–1940: Overcoming Asymmetric Information," *Business History Review*, Vol. 62, No. 2 (summer 1988).

Baster, A.S.J. *The Imperial Banks* (London: P.S. King & Son, 1929).

The International Banks (London: P.S. King & Son, 1935).

Batchelor, Roy A. "The Avoidance of Catastrophe: Two Nineteenth-Century Banking Crises," in Forrest Capie and Geoffrey E. Wood (eds.), *Financial Crises and the World Banking System* (Houndsmills: Macmillan Press, 1986).

Bechart, Benjamin H. *The Banking System of Canada* (New York: Henry Holt, 1929).

Beever, Margot, and Alan Beever. "Henry Giles Turned," in R.T. Appleyard and C.D. Schedvin (eds.), *Australian Financiers: Biographic Essays* (Melbourne: Federal Reserve Bank of Australia, 1988).

Bennett, Robert L. "Financial Innovation and Structural Change in the Early Stages of Industrialization: Mexico, 1945–59," *Journal of Finance*, Vol. XVIII, No. 4 (December 1963).

Bentick, B.L. "Foreign Borrowing, Wealth and Consumption: Victoria 1873–93," *Economic Record*, Vol. 45 (September 1969).

Bercuson, David, and Howard Palmer. *Settling the Canadian West*, Focus on Canada History Series (Toronto: Grolier, 1984).

Best, Michael, and Jane Humphries. "The City and Industrial Decline," in Bernard Elbaum and William Lazonick (eds.), *The Decline of the British Economy* (Oxford: Oxford University Press, 1986).

Birch, A.H. *Federalism, Finance and Social Legislation in Canada, Australia, and the United States* (Oxford: Oxford University Press, 1955).

Birdsall, Nancy, Michael Gavin, and Ricardo Hausman. "The East Asian Financial Crisis – A View from Latin America," Working Paper, Office of the Chief Economist, Inter-American Development Bank, February 1988.

"Lessons from the Mexico Crisis," in Sebastian Edwards and Moises Naim (eds.), *Mexico 1994: Anatomy of an Emerging-Market Crash* (Washington, D.C.: Brookings Institute Press for the Carnegie Endowment for International Peace, 1997).

Blainey, Geoffrey. *Gold and Paper: A History of the National Bank of Australasia Limited* (Melbourne: Georgian House, 1958).

"A History of Multinational Factories in Australia," in Akio Okochi and Tadakatsu Inoue (eds.), *Overseas Business Activities*, International Conference of Business History, No. 9 (Tokyo: University of Tokyo Press, 1983).

The Rush That Never Ended: A History of Australian Mining (Parkville, Victoria: Melbourne University Press, 1963).

Bliss Michael. *A Canadian Millionaire: The Life and Business Times of Sir Joseph Flavelle, Bart, 1858–1939* (Toronto: Macmillan, 1978).

Northern Enterprise: Five Centuries of Canadian Business (Toronto: McClelland and Stewart, 1987).

Bloomfield, Arthur I. *Patterns of Infrastructure in International Investment Before 1914*, Princeton Studies in International Finance, No. 21, 1968 (Princeton: Princeton University Press, 1968).

Short Term Capital Movements Under the Pre-1914 Gold Standard, Princeton Studies in International Finance, No. 11 (Princeton: Princeton University Press, 1963).

Bodenhorn, Howard. "Capital Mobility and Financial Integration in Antebellum America," *The Journal of Economic History*, Vol. 57, No. 3 (September 1992).

"A More Perfect Union: Regional Interest Rates in the United States, 1880–1960," in Michael D. Bordo and Richard Sylla (eds.), *Anglo-American Financial Systems: Institutions and Markets in the Twentieth Century* (Burr Ridge, Ill.: Irwin Professional Publishing, 1995).

Bodfish, Morton. *History of the Building and Loan in the United States* (Chicago: United States Building and Loan League, 1931).

Boehm, E.A. "Measuring Australian Economic Growth, 1861–1938–39," *The Economic Record*, Vol. 41, No. 93 (March 1965).

Prosperity and Depression in Australia, 1887–1897 (Oxford: Clarendon Press, 1971).

Boeze, Frank J.A. *Mr. Brooks and the Australian Trade: Imperial Business in the Nineteenth Century* (Melbourne: Melbourne University Press, 1993).

Bond, D.E., and R.A. Shearer. *The Economics of the Canadian Financial System: Theory, Policy and Institutions* (Scarborough, N.Y.: Prentice Hall, 1972).

Boot, H.M. "Debts, Drought, and Foreclosure: Wool Producers in Queensland and New South Wales, 1870–1905," *Australian Economic History Review*, Vol. 28, No. 2 (September 1988), pp. 33–52.

"Government and the Australian Colonial Economy, 1788–1892," chapter prepared for the *Cambridge Economic History of Australia* (forthcoming).

"New South Wales Railways and Social Savings: On the Gravy Train or Off the Rails," paper delivered at the Annual Meetings of the Economic History Society of Australia and New Zealand, University of Queensland, Brisbane, March 29–31, 1996.

Bordo, Michael D. "The Bretton Woods International Monetary System: A Historical Overview," in Michael D. Bordo and Barry Eichengreen (eds.), *A Retrospective on the Bretton Woods System: Lessons for International Monetary Reform*, National Bureau of Economic Research Project Report (Chicago: University of Chicago Press, 1993).

"Financial Crises, Banking Crises, Stock Market Crashes and the Money Supply: Some International Evidence, 1870–1933," in Forrest Capie and Geoffrey E. Wood (eds.), *Financial Crises and the World Banking System* (London: Macmillan, in association with the Centre for Banking and International Finance, the City University, 1986).

Bordo, Michael D., and Finn E. Kydland. "The Gold Standard as a Commitment Mechanism" (1993). Paper prepared for the volume. Tanin Bayoumi, Barry Eichengreen, and Mark Taylor (eds.), *Modern Perspectives on the Gold Standard*.

Bordo, Michael D., and Angela Redish. "Why Did the Bank of Canada Emerge in 1935?" paper presented to the 46th Annual Meeting of the Economic History Association, Hartford, Conn., September 1896.

Bordo, Michael D., Angela Redish, and Hugh Rockoff. "A Comparison of the United States and Canadian Banking Systems in the Twentieth Century: Stability vs. Efficiency," in Michael D. Bordo and Richard Sylla (eds.), *Anglo-American Financial Systems: Institutions and Markets in the Twentieth Century* (Burr Ridge, Ill.: Irwin Professional Publishing, 1995).

"A Comparison of the Stability and Efficiency of the Canadian and American Banking Systems, 1870–1925," National Bureau of Economic Research, Historical Paper No. 67, January 1995.

Bordo, Michael D., and Carlos A. Végh. "If Only Alexander Hamilton Had Been Argentinean: A Comparison of the Early Monetary Experiences of Argentina and the United States," Working paper, delivered at National Bureau of Economic Research, Monetary Group's Summer Meetings, July 1995.

Bordo, Michael D., and Hugh Rockoff. "The Gold Standard as a 'Good Housekeeping Seal of Approval,'" National Bureau of Economic Research, Working Paper 5340, November 1995.

Bordo, Michael D., and Anna J. Schwartz. "Monetary Policy Regimes and Economic Performance: The Historical Record," Working Paper 6201, September 1997, National Bureau of Economic Research.

"The Specie Standard as a Contingent Rule: Some Evidence for Core and Peripheral Countries, 1880–1990," paper prepared for the conference *Historical Perspectives on the Gold Standard: Portugal and the World*, Arrabida, Portugal, June 1994.

Bordo, Michael D., and Richard Sylla. "North American Financial Institutions and Markets: The United States and Canada in the Twentieth Century," working paper, July 1993.

Boulding, Kenneth E. "Internal and External Influences on Development," in Dingle, A.E. and Merritt, D.T. (eds.), *Argentina and Australia: Essays in Comparative Economic Development*, Economic History Society of Australia and New Zealand, Occasional Paper No. 1, 1985.

Bowen, H.P., and P.H. Cottrell. "Banking Commerce, and Industry in Great Britain, 1694–1878," working paper, University of Leicester.

Boyce, Gordon. "64thers, Syndicates, and Stock Promotions: Information Flows and Fund-raising Techniques of British Ship Owners Before 1914," *The Journal of Economic History*, Vol. 52, No. 1 (March 1992).

Brady, Alexander. *Democracy in the Dominions: A Comparative Study in Institutions*, 2nd edition (Toronto, 1952).

Brecher, I. *Capital Flows Between Canada and the United States* (Montreal: Canadian-American Committee, 1965).

Monetary and Fiscal Thought in Canada, 1919–1939 (Toronto: University of Toronto Press, 1957).

Breckenridge, Roelift M. *The Canadian Banking System, 1817–1890* (New York: Macmillan, 1895).

The History of Banking in Canada, Senate Document Number 332, 61st Congress, 2nd session (Washington, D.C.: GPO, 1910).

Brezis, Elise S. "Foreign Capital Flows in the Century of Britain's Industrial Revolution: New Estimates, Controlled Conjectures," *The Economic History Review*, Vol. XLVIII, No. 1 (February 1995).

Briggs, Asa. *The Making of Modern England: 1783–1867, The Age of Improvement* (New York: Harper and Row, 1959).

The British Economy: Key Statistics, 1900–1970. The Statistician, London and Cambridge Economic Service, Department of Applied Economics, Sidgwick Avenue, Cambridge.

Buchinsky, Moshe, and Ben Polack. "The Emergence of a National Capital Market in England, 1710–1880," *The Journal of Economic History*, Vol. 53, No. 1 (March 1993).

Buckley, Kenneth. *Capital Formation in Canada*. Canadian Social Science Research Council, Canadian Studies in Economics, Vol. 2 (Toronto: University of Toronto Press, 1955).

"Capital Formation in Canada, 1896–1930," in T. Easterbrook and M.H. Watkins (eds.), *Approaches to Canadian Economic History* (Toronto: McClelland & Stuart, 1967).

"Capital Formation in Railway Transport and Telegraphs in Canada, 1850 to 1930," paper given at the Canadian Political Science Association Conference on Statistics, McMaster University, Hamilton, Ontario, June 10–11, 1962.

Buckley, Peter J., and Brian R. Roberts. *European Direct Investment in the USA Before World War I* (New York: St. Martin's Press, 1982).

Bullock, Charles J., Tucker Williams, and S. Rufus. "The Balance of Trade of the United States," *The Review of Economic Statistics*, Preliminary Vol. 1 (July 1919).

Burgess, C.H. "Growth of Government and Municipal Financing in Canada," *Monetary Times Annual*, Vol. 78 (January 7, 1927).

Burk, Kathleen. "Money and Power: The Shift from Great Britain to the United States," in Youssef Cassis (ed.), *Finance and Financiers in European History, 1880–1960*, Editions de la Maison des Sciences de L'Homme, Paris (Cambridge: Cambridge University Press, 1992).

Morgan Grenfell, 1938–1988: The Biography of a Merchant Bank (Oxford: Oxford University Press, 1989).

Burton, H., and D.C. Corner. *Investment and Unit Trusts in Britain and America* (London: Elek Books, 1968).

Burton, T.E. *Financial Crises and Periods of Industrial and Commercial Depression* (1902), in Phillip Cottrell (ed.), *Investment Banking in England, 1856–1881: A Case Study of the International Financial Society* (New York: Garland Publishing Company, 1985).

Butlin, Matthew W. "Capital Markets," in Rodney Maddock and Ian W. Mclean (eds.), *The Australian Economy in the Long Run* (Cambridge: Cambridge University Press, 1987).

Butlin, Noel G. *Australian Domestic Product, Investment and Foreign Borrowing, 1861–1938/39* (Cambridge: Cambridge University Press, 1962).

"Colonial Socialism in Australia, 1860–1900," in Hugh G. Aitken (ed.), *The State and Economic Growth*, Papers of a Conference Held on October 11–13, 1956, under the Auspices of the Committee on Economic Growth (New York: Social Science Research Council, 1959).

"The Growth of Rural Capital, 1860–1890," in Alan Barnard (ed.), *The Simple Fleece: Studies in the Australian Wool Industry* (Parkville, Victoria: Melbourne University Press, 1962).

Investment in Australian Economic Development 1861–1914 (Cambridge: Cambridge University Press, 1964).

"The Shape of the Australian Economy, 1861–1900," *Economic Record*, Vol. 34, No. 67 (April 1958).

"Some Structural Features of Australian Capital Formation, 1861–1938/39," *The Economic Record*, Vol. 35, No. 72 (December 1959).

Butlin, Noel G., and A. Barnard. "Pastoral Finance and Capital Requirements, 1860–1960," in Alan Barnard (ed.), *The Simple Fleece: Studies in the Australian Wool Industry* (Parkville, Victoria: Melbourne University Press, 1962).

Butlin, Sydney J. *Australia and New Zealand Bank: The Bank of Australasia and the Union Bank of Australia Limited, 1828–1951* (London: Longmans, 1961).

Butlin, Sydney J., A.R. Hall, and R.C. White. *Australian Banking and Monetary Statistics, 1817–1945*, Reserve Bank of Australia, Occasional Paper 4A (Sydney, 1971).

Cairncross, Alexander K. "The English Capital Market Before 1914 – A Reply," *Economica*, Vol. 25, No. 2 (May 1958).

Home and Foreign Investment 1870–1913 (Cambridge: Cambridge University Press, 1953).

"Investment in Canada, 1900–13," in A.R. Hall (ed.), *The Export of Capital from Britain 1870–1914* (London: Methuen & Co., 1968).

Calomiris, Charles W. "Corporate-Finance Benefits from Universal Banking: Germany and the United States, 1870–1914," National Bureau of Economic Research, Working Paper No. 4408, July 1993.

"The Costs of Rejecting Universal Banking: American Finance in the German Mirror, 1870–1914," in Naomi Lamoreaux and Dan Raff (eds.), *The Coordination of Economic Activity Within and Between Firms: Historical Perspective on the Organization of Enterprise* (Chicago: University of Chicago Press, 1995).

Calomiris, Charles W., and Charles M. Kahn. "The Efficiency of Self-regulated Payments Systems: Learning from the Suffolk System," National Bureau of Economic Research, Working Paper 5442, January 1996.

Calomiris, Charles W., and Carlos D. Ramirez. "Financing the American Corporation: The Changing Menu of Financial Relationships," NBER, DAE Working Paper No. 79.

Cameron, Rondo. *Banking in the Early Stages of Industrialization. A Study of Comparative Economic History* (New York: Oxford University Press, 1967).

ed. *Financing Industrialization*, 2 vols. International Library of Macroeconomic and Financial History Series, Vol. 4 (Aldershot, U.K.: Edward Elgar).

Cameron, Rondo, and V.I. Bovykin, assisted by Boris Anan'ich. *International Banking, 1870–1914* (New York: Oxford University Press, 1991).

Canadian Manufacturers Association. *Industrial Canada*, Toronto, Various monthly issues, 1907–14.

Capie, Forrest. "Prudent and Stable (But Inefficient?): Commercial Banks in Britain, 1890–1940," in Michael Bordo and Richard Sylla (eds.), *Anglo-American Financial Systems: Institutions and Markets in the Twentieth Century* (Burr Ridge, Ill.: Irwin Professional Publishing, 1995).

"Structure and Performance in British Banking, 1870–1913," in P.L. Cottrell and D.E. Moggridge (eds.), *Money and Power: Essays in Honour of L.S. Pressnell* (London: Macmillan Press, 1988).

Capie, Forrest, and Michael Collins. *Have the Banks Failed British Industry? A Historical Survey of Bank/Industry Relations in Britain, 1870–1990*, Hobart Paper (London: Institute of Economic Affairs, 1992).

Capie, Forrest, and Terrence C. Mills. "British Bank Conservatism in the Late 19th Century," *Explorations in Economic History*, Vol. 32, No. 3 (July 1995).

Capie, Forrest, Terrence C. Mills, and Geoffrey E. Wood. "Money, Interest Rates and the Great Depression: Britain from 1870 to 1913," in James Foreman-Peck (ed.), *New Perspectives in the Late Victorian Economy: Essays in Quantitative Economic History, 1860–1914* (Cambridge: Cambridge University Press, 1991).

Cargill, Thomas F., and Shoichi Royama. *The Transition of Finance in Japan and the United States: A Comparative Study* (Stanford, Calif.: Hoover Institution Press, Stanford University, 1988).

Carlos, Ann M., and Frank Lewis. "The Creative Financing of an Unprofitable Enterprise: The Grand Trunk Railway of Canada, 1853–1881," *Explorations in Economic History*, Vol. 32, No. 3 (July 1995).

"International Financing of Canadian Railroads: The Role of Information," in Michael D. Bordo and Richard Sylla (eds.), *Anglo-American Financial Systems: Institutions and Markets in the Twentieth Century* (Burr Ridge, Ill.: Irwin Professional Publishing, 1995).

Carosso, Vincent P. *Investment Banking in America* (Cambridge, Mass.: Harvard University Press, 1970).

Carosso, Vincent P., and Richard Sylla. "U.S. Banks in International Finance," in Rondo Cameron and V.I. Bovykin (with the assistance of Boris Anan'ich, A.A. Fursenk, Richard Sylla, and Mira Wilkins) (eds.), *International Banking, 1870–1914* (New York: Oxford University Press, 1991).

Carroll, Chris, and L.H. Summers. "Why Have Private Savings Rates in the U.S. and Canada Diverged?" *Journal of Monetary Economics*, Vol. 20, No. 2 (September 1987).

Cassis, Youssef. "The Emergence of a New Financial Institution: Investment Trusts in Britain, 1870–1939," in J.J. Van Helten and Y. Cassis, *Capitalism in a Mature Economy: Financial Institutions, Capital Exports and British Industry, 1837–1939* (Aldershot, U.K.: Edward Elgar, 1990).

"Financial Elites in Three European Centers: London, Paris, Berlin, 1880s-1930s," in Geoffrey Jones (ed.), *Banks and Money: International and Comparative Finance in History* (London: Frank Cass, 1991).

Chandler, Lester V. *The Economics of Money and Banking* (New York: Harper and Brothers, 1948).

Chernow, Ron. *The House of Morgan: An American Dynasty and the Rise of Modern Finance* (New York: Atlantic Monthly Press, 1990).

Clapham, John H. *The Bank of England: A History*, 2 vols. (Cambridge: Cambridge University Press, 1944).

An Economic History of Modern Britain. Vol. II: Free Trade and Steel (Cambridge: Cambridge University Press, 1963).

Clark, Gregory. "Government Debt and Private Capital Markets in England, 1720–1837," Papers of the *34th Annual Cliometrics Conference*, University of Arizona, Tucson, May 20–22, 1994.

Clark, John Maurice. *Economics of Planning of Public Works*, a study made for the National Planning Board of the Federal Emergency Administration of Public Works (Washington, D.C.: GPO, 1935).

Clark, William, and Charlie Turner. "International Trade and the Evolution of the American Capital Market 1888–1911," *The Journal of Economic History*, Vol. 65, No. 2 (June 1985).

Clarke, Stephen V.O. *Central Bank Cooperation, 1924–1931* (New York: Federal Reserve Bank of New York, 1967).

Clements, Roger V. "British Controlled Enterprise in the West Between 1870 and 1890 and Some Agrarian Response," *Agricultural History*, Vol. 27 (1955).

"British Investment and American Legislative Restrictions in the Trans-Mississippi West, 1880–1900," *Mississippi Valley Historical Review*, Vol. 42 (1955).

"The Farmers' Attitude Toward British Investment in American Industry," *The Journal of Economic History*, Vol. 15, No. 2 (1955).

Cleveland, Frederick A., and Fred W. Powell. *Railroad Promotion and Capitalization in the United States* (New York: B. Appleton, 1909).

Code, William. *The Spatial Dynamics of Financial Development in Nineteenth Century Canada*. Ph.D. dissertation, U.C. Berkeley, 1971.

Cole, David C. "Financial Sector Development in Southeast Asia," in Shahid N. Zahid (ed.), *Financial Sector Development in Asia* (Hong Kong: Oxford University Press, 1995).

Cole, G.D.H. *A Short History of the British Working Class Movement. Vol. II: 1848–1900* (New York: Macmillan Company, 1927).

Collins, Michael. "The Bank of England as Lender of Last Resort, 1857–1878," *The Economic History Review*, Vol. XLV, No. 1 (February 1992).

Banks and Industrial Finance in Britain 1800–1939 (London: Macmillan, 1990).

"Long-Term Growth in the English Banking Sector and the Money Stock, 1844–1880," *The Economic History Review*, Second Series, Vol. XXXVI, No. 3 (August 1983).

Money and Banking in the U.K.: A History (London: Croom Helm, 1988).

"The Nature of Bank/Client Relations and Industrial Lending by English Commercial Banks Before World War I," paper given at Seville Pre-Conference at the Center for German and European Studies, University of California, Berkeley, April 17–20, 1997.

"Colonial Bank Deposit Insurance Companies." *The Bankers', Insurance Managers', and Agents' Magazine* (London: Waterlow and Sons), January–June 1893, p. 726; July–December 1893, pp. 493–497; Vol. LVII, 1894, pp. 129–33; and Vol. LVII, 1894, pp. 621–27.

Commercial Relations of the United States: Reports from the Consuls of the United States on the Commerce, Manufacture, Etc. of Their Consular Districts, No. 31, July 1883, Published by the Department of State (Washington D.C.: GPO, 1883).

Conant, Charles A. *Wall Street and the Country: A Study of Recent Financial Tendencies* (New York: Greenwood Press, 1968).

Consular Report for the Republic of Argentina. 56th Congress, First Session, 1899–1900, House Documents, Vol. 96, No. 481, Part 1, Commercial Relations 1899, Vol. 1.

Cooper, Richard N. "Comment," in Michael D. Bordo and Barry Eichengreen. *A Retrospective on the Bretton Woods System: Lessons for International Monetary Reform*, National Bureau of Economic Research Project Report (Chicago: University of Chicago Press, 1993).

Cordon, W. Max. "Why Did the Bretton Woods System Break Down?" in Michael D. Bordo and Barry Eichengreen (eds.), *A Retrospective on the Bretton Woods System: Lessons for International Monetary Reform*, National Bureau of Economic Research Project Report (Chicago: University of Chicago Press, 1993).

Cornfeld, Andrew, and Jan Kregel. "Globalization, Capital Flows and International Regulation," Jerome Levy Economic Institute of Bard College, Working Paper No. 161, May 1996.

Cortes Conde, Roberto. *Dinero, deuda, y crisis: evolución fiscal y monetaria en la Argentina, 1862–1890* (Buenos Aires: Editorial Sudamericana, Instituto Torcuato Di Tella, 1989).

"Estimaciones del PBI en la Argentina, 1875–1935," Ciclo de Seminarios, Departamento de Economia, Universidad de San Andres, March 1994.

"Estimates of Argentine GDP, 1875–1935." October 1994, private communication, November (24) 1994.

"The Export Economy of Argentina, 1880–1920," in Roberto Cortes Conde and Shane J. Hunt (eds.), *The Latin American Economies: Growth and the Export Sector, 1880–1930* (New York: Holmes and Meier, 1985).

Money, Debt and Crisis: Fiscal and Monetary Evolution in Argentina, 1862–1890, translated by Dan Newland, manuscript.

Cottrell, Phillip L. "The Coalescence of a Cluster of Corporate International Banks, 1855–75," in Geoffrey Jones (ed.), *Banks and Money: International and Comparative Finance in History* (London: Frank Cass, 1991).

"The Domestic Commercial Banks in the City of London, 1870–1939," in Youssef Cassis (ed.), *Finance and Financiers in European History, 1880–1960* (Cambridge: Cambridge University Press, 1992).

"Great Britain," in Rondo Cameron and V.I. Bovykin (with the assistance of Boris Anan'ich, A.A. Fursenk, Richard Sylla, and Mira Wilkins) (eds.), *International Banking, 1870–1914* (New York: Oxford University Press, 1991).

Industrial Finance, 1830–1914: The Finance and Organization of English Manufacturing Industry (London: Methuen, 1979).

Investment Banking in England, 1856–1881: A Case Study of the International Financial Society (New York: Garland Publishing, 1980).

Craig, Lee A., and Douglas Fisher. "Integration of the European Business Cycle: 1871–1910," *Explorations in Economic History*, Vol. 29, No. 2 (April 1992).

Crapol, Edward P., *America for Americans: Economic Nationalism and Anglophobia in the Late Nineteenth Century*, Contributions in American History, No. 28 (Westport, Conn.: Greenwood Press, 1973).

Crick, W.F., and J.E. Wadsworth. *A Hundred Years of Joint Stock Banking*, 4th edition (London: Hodder & Stoughton, 1964).

Cull, Robert J. *Capital Market Failure and Institutional Innovation*, Ph.D. dissertation, California Institute of Technology, 1992.

Cull, Robert J., and Lance E. Davis. "Un, deux, trois, quatre marchés? L'Intégration du marché du États-Unis et Grande-Bretagne, 1865–1913," *Annales: Économies Sociétiés Civilizations*, No. 3 (May–June 1992).

Curioni, Stefano Baia. "The Telegraph and the Creation of an Integrated System of Securities Markets in Italy (1888–1905)," Mimeograph, May 1993.

Curle, J.H. *The Gold Mines of the World: Containing Concise and Practical Advice for Investors Gathered from a Personal Inspection of the Mines of the Transvaal, India, West Australia, Queensland, New Zealand, British Columbia and Rhodesia* (London: Waterlow & Sons, 1899).

Curtis, E.A. "Evolution of Canadian Banking," *Annals of the American Academy of Political and Social Science*, Vol. 253.

David, Paul A. "Invention and Accumulation in America's Economic Growth: A Nineteenth Century Parable," in K. Brunner and A. Meltzer (eds.), *International Organization, Public Policies and Economic Development* (Amsterdam: North Holland Press, 1977).

David, Paul A., and John L. Scadding. "Private Savings: Ultrarationality, Aggregation, and 'Denison's Law'," *Journal of Political Economy*, Vol. 82, No. 2, Part 1 (March/April 1974).

Davis, Lance E. "Capital Immobilities and Finance Capitalism: A Study of Economic Evolution in the United States, 1820–1920," *Explorations in Entrepreneurial History*, Second Series, Vol. 1, No. 1 (fall 1963).

"The Capital Markets and Industrial Concentration: The U.S. and the U.K., A Comparative Study," *Economic History Review*, Second Series, Vol. 19, No. 2 (1966).

"Comments on Session IV – Intermediation, Foreign Investment, and Financial Integration," in Micahel D. Bordo and Richard Sylla (eds.), *Anglo-American Financial System's: Institutions and Markets in the 20th-Century* (Burr Ridge, Ill.: Irwin Professional Publishing, 1995).

The Evolution of the American Capital Market, 1860–1940: A Case Study in Institutional Change," in W. Silber (ed.), *Financial Innovation* (Lexington, Mass.: Lexington Books, 1975).

"The Investment Market, 1870–1914: The Evolution of a National Market," *The Journal of Economic History*, Vol. 25, No. 3 (September 1965).

"The New England Textile Mills and the Capital Markets: A Study of Industrial Borrowing, 1840–60," *Journal of Economic History*, Vol. XX, No. 1 (March 1960), pp. 1–30.

"Sources of Industrial Finance: The American Textile Industry – A Case Study," in *Purdue Faculty Papers in Economic History, 1956–66* (Homewood, Ill.: Richard D. Irwin, 1967).

"Stock Ownership in the Early New England Textile Industry," *Business History Review*, Vol. XXXII, No. 2 (summer 1958), pp. 204–22.

Davis, Lance E., and Robert J. Cull. *International Capital Markets and American Economic Growth, 1820–1914* (New York: Cambridge University Press, 1994).

"International Capital Movements, Domestic Capital Markets, and American Growth," in Robert Gallman and Stanley Engerman (eds.), *The Cambridge Economic History of the United States*, Vol. II (New York: Cambridge University Press, 2000).

Davis, Lance E., Robert J. Cull, and Robert E. Gallman. "Sophisticates, Rubes, Financiers, and the Evolution of Capital Markets: US–UK Finance, 1865–1914," paper presented at the NBER Franco-American Conference, Cambridge, Mass., July 15–16, 1993.

Davis, Lance E., and Robert E. Gallman. "Savings, Investment, and Economic Growth: The United States in the Nineteenth Century," in John James and Mark Thomas (eds.), *Capitalism in Context* (Chicago: University of Chicago Press, 1993).

Davis, Lance E., and Jonathan R.T Hughes. "A Dollar-Sterling Exchange, 1803–95," *Economic History Review*, Vol. XIII, No. 1 (August 1960).

Davis, Lance E., Jonathan R.T. Hughes, and Stanley Reiter. "Aspects of Quantitative Research in Economic History," *Journal of Economic History*, Vol. XX, No. 4 (December 1960).

Davis, Lance E., and Robert A. Huttenback. *Mammon and the Pursuit of Empire: The Political Economy of British Imperialism, 1860–1912* (Cambridge: Cambridge University Press, 1986).

Davis, Lance E., and Peter L. Payne. "From Benevolence to Business: The Story of Two Savings Banks," *Business History Review*, Vol. XXXII, No. 2 (winter 1958).

Davis, Lance E., and H. Louis Stettler III. "The New England Textile Industry, 1825–60: Trends and Fluctuations," in *Output, Employment, and Productivity in the United States After 1800*. Studies in Income and Wealth, Vol. 30, National Bureau of Economic Research, Conference on Income and Wealth (New York: NBER, 1966).

Day, A.C.L., and Sterie T. Beza. *Money and Income: An Outline of Monetary Economics* (New York: Oxford University Press, 1960).

De Bever, Leo J., and Jeffrey G. Williamson. "Savings, Accumulation and Modern Economic Growth: The Contemporary Relevance of Japanese History," *Journal of Japanese Studies*, Vol. 4, No. 1 (fall 1977).

De Vol, Ross C. "The Asian Crisis Tsunami: Trade and Other Impacts on California and the United States," Milken Institute, Policy Brief, September 1988.

Dean, Phyllis, and W.A. Cole. *British Economic Growth, 1688–1969: Trends and Structure* (Cambridge: Cambridge University Press, 1962).

Della Paolera, Gerardo. *How the Argentine Economy Performed During the International Gold Standard*, Ph.D. dissertation, University of Chicago, 1988.

Della Paolera, Gerardo, and Alan M. Taylor. "Finance and Development in an Emerging Market: Argentina in the Interwar Period," manuscript, May 1997.

Delong, J. Bradford. "Did Morgan's Men Add Value? A Historical Perspective on Financial Capitalism," in Peter Temin (ed.), *Inside the Business Enterprise: Historical Perspectives on the Use of Information* (Chicago: University of Chicago Press, 1991).

Delong, J. Bradford, and Richard S. Grossman. "Excess Volatility on the London Stock Market, 1870–1990," working paper, January 1993.

Deming, J.K. "Modern Methods of Soliciting Business," *Proceedings, Iowa Bankers Association*, 1892.

Denison, M. *Canada's First Bank: A History of the Bank of Montreal*, 2 vols. (Toronto: McClelland & Stewart, 1967).

Denoon, Donald. *Settler Capitalism: The Dynamics of Dependent Development in the Southern Hemisphere* (Oxford: Clarendon Press, 1983).

Dewey, Davis R. *Financial History of the United States* (New York: Longmans, Green, and Co., 1903).

Dewing, Arthur Stone. *The Financial Policy of Corporations*, 2 vol. in one, 4th edition (New York, 1941).

Di Tella, Guido D., and D.C.M. Platt, eds. *The Political Economy of Argentina, 1880–1946* (Oxford: Macmillan, 1986).

Diaz-Alejandro, Carlos F. "Argentina, Australia and Brazil Before 1929," in D.C.M. Platt and Guido di Tella (eds.), *Argentina, Australia, and Canada: Studies in Comparative Development 1870–1965* (New York: St. Martin's Press, 1985).

Essays on the Economic History of the Argentine Republic (New Haven: Yale University Press, 1970).

"No Less than One Hundred Years of Argentine History Plus Some Comparisons" in A. Velasco, *Development and the World Economy: Selected Essays of Carlos F. Diaz-Alejandro* (Oxford: Basil Blackwell, 1988).

Dick, Trevor J.O., and John E. Floyd. "Balance of Payment Adjustments Under the International Gold Standard: Canada, 1871–1913," *Explorations in Economic History*, Vol. 28, No. 2 (April 1991).

Dickens, Paul D. *The Transitional Period In American International Financing, 1897–1914*, Ph.D. dissertation, George Washington University, 1933.

Dickson, P.G.M. *The Sun Insurance Office, 1710–1960* (Oxford: Oxford University Press, 1960).

Dingle, A.E., and D.T. Merrett. *Argentina and Australia: Essays in Comparative Economic Development*, Economic History Society of Australia and New Zealand, Occasional Paper No. 1, 1985.

Dow, Sheila C. *Financial Markets and Regional Economic Development: The Canadian Experience* (Brookfield, Vt.: Gower, 1990).

Drake, Paul W., ed. *Money Doctors, Foreign Debts, and Economic Reforms in Latin America from the 1890s to the Present* (Wilmington, Del.: SR Books, 1993).

Draper, Stephanie. "The Sperling Combine and the Shipbuilding Industry: Merchant Banking and Industrial Finance in the 1920s," in J.J. Van Helten and Y. Cassis, *Capitalism in a Mature Economy: Financial Institutions, Capital Exports and British Industry, 1870–1939* (Aldershot, U.K. and Brookfield, Vt.: Edward Elgar, 1990).

Drummond, Ian M. "Banks and Banking in Canada and Australia," in Rondo Cameron and V.I. Bovykin (with the assistance of Boris Anan'ich, A.A. Fursenk, Richard Sylla, and Mira Wilkins) (eds.), *International Banking, 1870–1914* (New York: Oxford University Press, 1991).

"Canadian Life Insurance Companies and the Capital Market, 1890–1914," *The Canadian Journal of Economics and Political Science*, Vol. XXVIII, No. 2 (May 1962).

Capital Markets in Australia and Canada, 1895–1914, Ph.D. dissertation, Yale University, 1959.

"Debt and the Dominion Government, 1914–1920," working paper, Economic History Workshop, University of Toronto, December 1992.

"Government Securities on Colonial New Issues Markets," *Yale Economic Essays*, Vol. I (spring 1961).

Drummond, Ian M., and Neil Quigley. "Debt and the Dominion Government, 1914–1920," Paper presented at the Economic History Workshop, University of Toronto, December 7, 1992.

Duncan, Tim. "Australia and Argentina: A Tale of Two Political Cultures," in A.E. Dingle and D.T. Merrett (eds.), *Argentina and Australia: Essays in Comparative Economic Development*, Economic History Society of Australia and New Zealand, Occasional Paper No. 1, 1985.

Duncan, Tim, and John Fogarty. *Australia and Argentina, On Parallel Paths* (Melbourne: Melbourne University Press, 1984).

Dunn, J.H. to Dunn Fisher and Co., January 14, 1908. *Dunn Papers*, Public Archives of Canada, Ottawa.

Dunning, John H. *Studies in International Investment* (London: George Allen & Unwin, 1970).

Easterbrook, W. Thomas. *Farm Credit in Canada* (Toronto: University of Toronto Press, 1938).

Easterbrook, W. Thomas, and Hugh G.J. Aitken. *Canadian Economic History* (Toronto: Macmillan, 1958).

Edelstein, Michael. "Foreign Investment and Accumulation, 1860–1914," in Roderick Floud and Donald McClosky (eds.), *The Economic History of Britain Since 1706. Vol. 2: 1860–1939*, 2nd edition (Cambridge: Cambridge University Press, 1994).

——— *Overseas Investment in the Age of High Imperialism: The United Kingdom, 1850–1914* (London: Methuen & Co., 1982).

——— "Were U.S. Rates of Accumulation in the 20th Century Investment or Savings Driven?" *Research in Economic History*, Vol. 13 (Westport, Conn.: JAI Press, 1991).

Edwards, G. *The Evolution of Finance Capitalism* (New York, 1908).

Edwards, Jeremy, and Sheilagh Oglive. "Universal Banks and German Industrialization: A Reappraisal," *The Economic History Review*, Vol. 49, No. 3 (August 1996).

Edwards, J.R. *Company Legislation and Changing Patterns of Disclosure in British Company Accounts, 1900–1940* (London: Institute of Chartered Accountants, 1981).

Edwards, Sebastian. "Capital Outflow Limits Don't Work," *Los Angeles Times*, October 12, 1998.

——— "The Mexican Peso Crisis: How Much Did We Know? When Did We Know It?" National Bureau of Economic Research, Working Paper No. 6334, December 1997.

Eichengreen, Barry. "Financing Infrastructure in Developing Countries: An Historical Perspective from the Nineteenth Century," September 1993, background paper prepared for World Bank's 1993 *World Development Report*.

——— *Golden Fetters: The Gold Standard and the Great Depression, 1919–1939* (New York: Oxford University Press, 1992).

——— "Mortgage Rates in the Populist Era," *American Economic Review*, Vol. 74, No. 5 (December 1984).

Eichengreen, Barry, and Albert Fishlow. *Contending with Capital Flows: What Is Different About the 1990s?* (New York: Council on Foreign Relations, 1996).

Eichengreen, Barry, and Peter H. Lindert, eds. *The International Debt Crisis in Historical Perspective* (Cambridge, Mass.: MIT Press, 1989).

Eichengreen, Barry, and Andrew Rose. "Staying Afloat When the Wind Shifts: External Factors and Emerging-Market Banking Crises," manuscript, December 10, 1997.

Engerman, Stanley and J. Matthew Gallman. "The Civil War Economy: A Modern View," in Stig Forster and Jorge Nagler (eds.), *On the Road to Total War: The American Civil War and the German Wars of Unification, 1861–1871* (Cambridge: Cambridge University Press, 1997).

Essex-Crosby, A. *Joint Stock Companies in Great Britain*, M. Comm. thesis, London University, 1938.

Evans, L.T., and Neil Quigley. "Discrimination in Bank Lending Policies: A Test Using Data from the Bank of Nova Scotia, 1900–1937," *Canadian Journal of Economics*, Vol. XXIII, No. 1 (February 1990).

Faulkner, Harold Underwood. *The Decline of Laissez Faire*. Vol. 7, *The Economic History of the United States* (New York: Rinehart & Company, 1951).

Federal Digest, 1754 to Date. Vol. 12 (St. Paul, Minn.: West Publishing Company, 1940).

Feinstein, Charles H. "Britain's Overseas Investments in 1913," *The Economic History Review*, 2nd Series, Vol. 63, No. 2 (March 1990).

——— *National Income, Expenditure and Output of the United Kingdom 1855–1965*, Studies in the National Income and Expenditure of the United Kingdom, No. 6 (Cambridge: Cambridge University Press, 1972).

Feinstein, Charles H., Peter Temin, and Gianni Toniolo. *The European Economy Between the Wars* (Oxford: Oxford University Press, 1997).

Feis, Herbert. *Europe the World's Banker, 1870–1914: An Account of European Foreign Investment and the Connection of World Finance with Diplomacy Before 1914* (New Haven: Yale University Press, 1930).

Feldstein, Martin, and Charles Horioka. "Domestic Savings and International Capital Flows," *Economic Journal*, Vol. 90 (June 1980).

Ferns, Henry Stanley. "Britain's Informal Empire in Argentina, 1806–1914," *Past and Present*, No. 4, November 1953.

Britain and Argentina in the Nineteenth Century (Oxford: Clarendon Press, 1960).

Ferrer, A. *The Argentine Economy* (Berkeley: University of California Press, 1967).

Field, Fred. W. *Capital Investments in Canada: Some Facts and Figures Respecting One of the Most Attractive Investment Fields in the World* (Montreal: Monetary Times of Canada, 1911).

Capital Investments in Canada: Some Facts and Figures Respecting One of the Most Attractive Investment Fields in the World (Montreal: Monetary Times of Canada, 1914).

"How Canadian Stocks Are Held," *The Monetary Times*, January 1915.

Firestone, O.J. "Canada's External Trade and Net Foreign Balance, 1851–1900," in William Parker (ed.), *Trends in the American Economy in the Nineteenth Century*, Studies in Income and Wealth, Vol. 24, NBER Conference on Research in Income and Wealth (Princeton: Princeton University Press, 1960).

Fishlow, Albert. "Lessons from the Past: Capital Markets During the 19th Century and the Inter-war Period," *Industrial Organization*, Vol. 39, No. 3 (summer 1985).

"Productivity and Technological Change in the Railroad Sector, 1840–1910," in Dorothy Brady (ed.), *Output, Employment, and Productivity in the United States After 1800*, Studies in Income and Wealth, Vol. 30 (New York: National Bureau of Economic Research, 1966).

Fitzpatrick, B. *The British Empire in Australia, 1834–1939* (Sydney: Macmillan, 1969).

Flandreau, Marc. "Central Bank Cooperation in Historical Perspective: A Skeptical View," *The Economic History Review*, Vol. L, No. 4 (November 1997).

Flanigan, James. *Los Angeles Times* Special Report, "The World Economy: Are Free Markets Failing," *Los Angeles Times*, Section S, September 16, 1998.

Fogarty, John. "The Role of the Export Sector in Industrialization: The Australian and Argentine Experience Compared," in A.E. Dingle and D.T. Merrett (eds.), *Argentina and Australia: Essays in Comparative Economic Development*, Economic History Society of Australia and New Zealand, Occasional Paper No. 1, 1985.

"Staples, Super-Staples and the Limits of the Staple Theory: The Experiences of Argentina, Australia and Canada Compared," in D.C.M. Platt and Guido di Tella (eds.), *Argentina, Australia, and Canada: Studies in Comparative Development 1870–1965* (New York: St. Martin's Press, 1985).

Fogel, Robert W. *Railroads and American Economic Growth: Essays in Econometric History* (Baltimore: Johns Hopkins University Press, 1964).

Fohlin, Caroline M. "Bank Securities Holdings and Industrial Finance Before World War I: Britain and Germany Compared," California Institute of Technology Social Science Working Paper 1007, May 1997.

"Relationship Banking and Industrial Investment: Evidence from the Heyday of the German Universal Banks," California Institute of Technology Social Science Working Paper 913, December 1995.

"The Rise of Interlocking Directorates in Imperial Germany," California Institute of Technology Social Science Working Paper 931, February 1996.

"The Role of Financial Intermediation in Industrial Development: The Case of the German *Kreditbanken*, 1871–1914," manuscript, University of California, Berkeley, October 1933.

Ford, A.G. "British Investment in Argentina and Long Swings," *Journal of Economic History*, Vol. 31 (September 1971).

The Gold Standard, 1880–1914: Britain and Argentina (Oxford: Clarendon Press, 1962).

Frankel, Jeffrey A. "Quantifying International Capital Mobility in the 1980s," in B. Douglas Bernheim and John B. Shoven (eds.), *National Saving and Economic Performance*, National Bureau of Economic Research Project Report (Chicago: University of Chicago Press, 1991).

Freedeman, Charles Elton. *Joint Stock Enterprise in France, 1807–1867: From Privileged Company to Modern Corporation* (Chapel Hill: University of North Carolina Press, 1979).

French, M.J. "The Emergence of a US Multinational Enterprise: The Goodyear Tire and Rubber Company," *Economic History Review*, 2nd Series, Vol. XL, No. 1 (1987).

Frieden, Jeffry A. "The Economics of Colonialism and Decolonization: American Relations with Underdeveloped Areas, 1890–1950," mimeograph, October 1986.

"The Economics of Intervention: American Overseas Investments and Relations with Underdeveloped Areas, 1890–1950," *Comparative Studies in Society and History*, Vol. 31, No. 1 (January 1989).

Friedman, Milton, and Anna J. Schwartz. *A Monetary History of the United States, 1867–1960* (Princeton: Princeton University Press, 1963).

Monetary Trends in the United States and the United Kingdom: Their Relation to Income, Prices, and Interest Rates, 1867–1975 (Chicago: University of Chicago Press, 1982).

Frost, Lionel E. "Government and Economic Development: The Case of Irrigation in Victoria," *Australian Economic History Review*, Vol. 32, No. 1 (March 1992).

"A Reinterpretation of Victoria's Railway Construction Boom of the 1880s," *Australian Economic History Review*, Vol. 26, No. 1 (March 1986).

Fullerton, Douglas H. *The Bond Market in Canada* (Toronto: Carswell Co., 1962).

Gallman, Robert E. "American Economic Growth Before the Civil War: The Testimony of the Capital Stock," in Robert E. Gallman and John J. Wallis (eds.), *American Economic Growth and the Standard of Living Before the Civil War* (Chicago: University of Chicago Press, 1992).

Appendix A to "Gross National Product in the United States, 1834–1909," mimeograph.

"Gross National Product in the United States, 1834–1909," in Dorothy S. Brady (ed.), *Output, Employment, and Productivity in the United States After 1800*, National Bureau of Economic Research, Studies in Income and Wealth by the Conference on Research in Income and Wealth, Vol. 30 (New York: Columbia University Press, 1966).

"The United States Capital Stock in the Nineteenth Century," in Stanley Engerman and Robert Gallman (eds.), *Long-Term Factors in Economic Growth*, National Bureau of Economic Research, Studies in Income and Wealth, Vol. 51 (Princeton: Princeton University Press, 1986).

"United States Income Estimates," manuscript, 1994.

Ganz, Alexander. "Problems and Uses of National Income Estimates in Latin America," in Raymond Goldsmith and Christopher Saunders (eds.), *The Measurement of National Wealth*, Income and Wealth Series Vol. VIII (Chicago: Quandrangle Books, 1959).

Garber, Peter M. "The Collapse of Bretton Woods Fixed Exchange Rate System," in Michael Bordo and Barry Eichengreen (eds.), *A Retrospective on the Bretton Woods System: Lessons for International Monetary Reform*, National Bureau of Economic Research Project Report (Chicago: University of Chicago Press, 1993).

Garcia, Valeriano F. *A Critical Inquiry into Argentine Economic History, 1946–1970* (New York: Garland Publishing, 1987).

Garland, N. Surrey, ed. *Banks and Bankers in Canada* (Ottawa: Mortimer & Company, 1890).

Garrett, Geoffrey. "Capital Mobility, Trade and Domestic Politics of Economic Policy," draft, November 1994, forthcoming in *International Organization*, Vol. 49, No. 4, Autumn 1995.

George, Peter J. "Rates of Return in Railway Investment and Implications for Government Subsidization of the Canadian Pacific Railway: Some Preliminary Results," *Canadian Journal of Economics*, Vol. 1, No. 4 (November 1968).

Gerardi, R.E. *Australia, Argentina, and World Capitalism: A Comparative Analysis 1830–1946*, Transnational Corporations Research Project, Occasional Paper No. 8, Faculty of Economics, University of Sydney, May 1985.

Gerber, Peter M. "Alexander Hamilton's Market-Based Debt Reduction Plan," *Carnegie-Rochester Conference Series on Public Policy*, Vol. 35 (1991).

"The Collapse of the Bretton Woods Fixed Exchange Rate System," in Michael D. Bordo and Barry Eichengreen (eds.), *A Retrospective on the Bretton Woods System: Lessons for International Monetary Reform*, National Bureau of Economic Research Project Report (Chicago: University of Chicago Press, 1993).

Gershenkron, Alexander. *Economic Backwardness in Historical Perspective* (Cambridge, Mass.: Harvard University Press, 1962).

Gilbert, R.S. "London Financial Intermediaries and Australian Overseas Borrowing, 1900–29," *Australian Economic History Review*, Vol. 10, No. 1 (March 1971).

Gillespie, W. Irwin. *Tax, Borrow and Spend: Financing Federal Spending in Canada, 1867–1990* (Ottawa: Carlton University Press, 1991).

"Glyns and the Bank of England." *Three Banks Review*, No. 40 (December 1958).

Goetznann, William N., and Roger G. Ibbotson. "An Emerging Market: The NYSE from 1815 to 1871," Yale School of Management, working paper, December 1994.

Goldsmith, Raymond W. *Comparative National Balance Sheets: A Study of Twenty Countries, 1688–1978* (Chicago: University of Chicago Press, 1985).

The Financial Development of Japan, 1868–1977 (New Haven: Yale University Press, 1983).

Financial Intermediaries in the American Economy Since 1900 (Princeton: Princeton University Press, 1958).

"The Growth of Reproducible Wealth of the United States of America," in Simon Kuznets, *Income and Wealth of the United States: Trends and Structures*, International Association for Research in Income and Wealth, Series II (Cambridge: Bowes & Bowes, 1953).

The National Balance Sheet of the United States, 1953–1980, National Bureau of Economic Research Monograph (Chicago: University of Chicago Press, 1982).

A Study of Savings, 3 vols. (Princeton: Princeton University Press, 1955).

Goldstein, Morris, and Phillip Turner. "Banking Crises in Emerging Economies: Origins and Policy Options," Bank for International Settlements, Monetary and Economic Department, Basle, BIS Economic Papers, No. 46, October 1996.

Goodhart, C.A.E. *The Business of Banking, 1891–1914* (London: London School of Economics and Political Science and Weidenfeld & Nicolson, 1972).

The New York Money Market and the Finance of Trade (Cambridge, Mass.: Harvard University Press, 1965).

Grant, Albert. *Twycross vs. Grant and Others: Speech of Albert Grant* (1876).

Gravil, R. *The Anglo-Argentine Connection, 1900–1939* (Boulder: Westview Press, 1965).

Gray, A.C. *Life Insurance in Australia: An Historical and Descriptive Account* (Melbourne: McCarron Bird, 1977).

Gray, Lewis Cecil, assisted by Esther Katherine Thompson. *History of Agriculture in the Southern United States to 1860* (Gloucester, Mass.: Peter Smith, 1958).

Greef, Albert. *The Commercial Paper House in the United States* (Cambridge, Mass.: Harvard Unviersity Press, 1938).

Green, Alan G. "Growth and Productivity Change in the Canadian Railway Sector, 1871–1926," in Stanley Engerman and Robert Gallman (eds.), *Long Term Factors in Economic Growth*, National Bureau of Economic Research, Studies in Income and Wealth, Vol. 51 (Princeton: Princeton University Press, 1986).

Green, Alan G., and David A. Green. "Balanced Growth and the Geographical Distribution of European Immigrant Arrivals to Canada, 1900–1912," *Explorations in Economic History*, Vol. 30, No. 1 (January 1993).

Green Alan G., and Gordon R. Sparks. "Population Growth and the Dynamics of Canadian Development: A Multivariate Time Series Approach," London School of Economics and Political Science, Working Papers in Economic History, No. 32/96, June 1996.

Green, Alan G., and M.C. Urquhart. "Factor and Commodity Flows in the International Economy of 1870–1914: A Multi-Country View," *Journal of Economic History*, Vol. 36, No. 1 (March 1976).

Greenwood, E.L. "Australia," in David E. Spray (ed.), *The Principal Stock Exchanges of the World: Their Operation, Structure and Development* (Washington, D.C.: International Economic Publishers, 1964).

Griffiths, Brian. "The Development of Restrictive Practices in the U.K. Monetary System," *Manchester School*, Vol. 41 (1973).

Grimwood, E.L. "Australia," in David E. Spay (ed.), *The Principal Stock Exchanges of the World: Their Operation, Structure and Development* (Washington D.C.: International Economic Publishers, 1964).

Grinath, Arthur, John Joseph Wallis, and Richard E. Sylla. "Debt, Default, and Revenue Structure: The American State Debt Crisis in the Early 1840s," working paper.

Grossman, Richard S. "Rearranging the Deck Chairs on the Titanic: English Banking Concentration and Efficiency, 1870–1914," mimeograph, June 16, 1995.

Grossman, Richard S., and J. Branford DeLong. "The Pre-WWI British Stock Market and Industrial Decline," National Science Foundation Proposal, 1994.

Guy, Donna S. "Dependency, the Credit Market, and Argentine Industrialization, 1860–1940," *Business History Review*, Vol. 58, No. 4 (winter 1984).

Haber, Stephen H. "Capital Immobilities and Industrial Development: A Comparative Study of Productivity Growth and Concentration in Brazil, Mexico, and the United States, 1840–1930," mimeograph.

"Capital Markets and Industrial Development: A Comparative Study of Brazil, India, Mexico, and the United States, 1840–1930," paper presented at the LIII Meeting of the Economic History Association, Tucson, Arizona, October 1–3, 1993.

"The Efficiency and Consequences of Institutional Change: Capital Market Regulation and Industrial Productivity Growth in Brazil, 1866–1934," Paper Delivered at the All-UC Conference in Economic History, UCLA, June 7–9, 1996.

"Industrial Concentration and the Capital Markets: A Comparative Study of Brazil, Mexico, and the United States, 1840–1930," Paper Presented at the Von Gremp Workshop in History of Entrepreneurship in the U.S. Economy, UCLA, October 17, 1990.

"Industrial Concentration and the Capital Markets: The United States and Latin America, 1840–1930," Paper presented at the NBER, Institute on the Development of the American Economy, Cambridge, Mass., July 1990.

Haggard, Stephan. "The Politics of Adjustment: Lessons from the IMF's Extended Fund Facility," *International Organization*, Vol. 39, No. 3 (summer 1985).

Hall, A.R. "The English Capital Market Before 1914 – A Reply," *Economica*, Vol. 25, No. 4 (November 1958).
    The London Capital Market and Australia 1870–1914, Social Science Monograph No. 21 (Canberra: Australian National University, 1963).
    "A Note on the English Capital Market as a Source of Funds for Home Investment Before 1914," *Economica*, Vol. 24, No. 1 (February 1957).
    The Stock Exchange of Melbourne and the Victorian Economy (Canberra: Australian National University Press, 1968).
    ed. *The Export of Capital from Britain, 1870–1914* (London: Methuen, 1968).
Halsey, Frederic M. "Investments in Latin America and the British West Indies," Special Agents Series, No. 169, Bureau of Foreign and Domestic Commerce, Department of Commerce (Washington, D.C.: GPO 1918).
Hammond, Bray. *Banks and Politics in America from the Revolution to the Civil War* (Princeton: Princeton University Press, 1957).
Hand Book of the American Republics. Senate Executive Documents, 1st Session, 52nd Congress, 1891/92, Vol. 7.
Hansen, Alvin. *Business Cycles and National Income* (New York: W.W. Norton, 1951).
Harley, C.K. "Goschen's Conversion of the National Debt and the Yield on Consols," *Economic History Review*, 2nd Series, Vol. XXIX, No. 1 (February 1976), pp. 101–6.
Hartland, Penelope. "Canadian Balance of Payments Since 1868," in William N. Parker (ed.), *Trends in the American Economy in the Nineteenth Century*, National Bureau of Economic Research, Conference on Income and Wealth, Studies in Income and Wealth, Vol. 24 (Princeton: Princeton University Press, 1960).
Hatton, Timothy, and Jeffrey G. Williamson. "Late-Comers To Mass Emigration: The Latin Experience," National Bureau of Economic Research, Working Paper Series on Historical Factors in Long Run Growth, Historical Paper No. 47, June 1993.
Hautcoeur, Pierre-Cyrille. "Information Asymmetries, Agency Costs and the Financing of French Firms," Working Paper, Rutgers, 1996.
Hidy, Ralph W. *House of Baring in American Trade and Finance: English Merchant Bankers at Work*, Harvard Studies in Business History, No. XIV (Cambridge, Mass.: Harvard University Press, 1949).
Higgins, Matthew, and Jeffrey G. Williamson. "Asian Demography and Foreign Capital Dependence," NBER, Working Paper Series No. 5560.
U.S. Bureau of the Census, *Historical Statistics of the United States: Colonial Times to 1970* (Washington, D.C.: GPO, 1975), Seven X732, p. 1037.
Hobson, Charles Kenneth. *The Export of Capital* (London: Constable and Company, 1914).
Holder, Reginald Frank. "Australia," in W.F. Crick (ed.), *Commonwealth Banking Systems* (Oxford: Clarendon Press, 1965), pp. 68–95.
    Bank of New South Wales: A History, 2 vols. (Sydney: Angus and Robertson, 1970).
Holmes, A.R., and Edward Green. *Midland: 150 Years of Banking Business* (London: 1986).
Homer, Sydney, and Richard Sylla. *A History of Interest Rates*, 3rd edition (New Brunswick, N.J.: Rutgers University Press, 1991).
Hood, W.C. *Financing Economic Activity in Canada*, Royal Commission on Canada's Economic Prospects (Ottawa: Queen's Printer, 1959).
Horne, H. Oliver. *A History of Savings Banks* (London: Oxford University Press, 1947).
Hsu, Robert C. "Direct Overseas Investment," *MIT Encyclopedia of the Japanese Economy* (Cambridge, Mass.: MIT Press, 1994).
Hughes, Jonathan. *Industrialization and Economic History: Theses and Conjectures* (New York: McGraw-Hill, 1970).

Hurley, Edward. *Banks and Credit in Argentina, Brazil, Chile and Peru*, Department of Commerce, Bureau of Foreign and Domestic Commerce, Special Agents Series, No. 90 (Washington, D.C.: GPO, 1914).

Hutchinson, Lincoln. Special Agent of the Department of Commerce and Labor, *Report on Trade Conditions in Argentina, Paraguay, and Uruguay* (Wash., D.C.: Government Printing Office, 1906).

Ichiki, Marumi. "Japanese Overseas Investments," in Foundation for Advanced Information and Research, Japan (FAIR), *Japan's Financial Markets*, Fair Fact Series II (Singapore: Look Japan Publishing Pte., 1991).

Imlah, A.H. *Economic Elements of the Pax Britannica: Studies in British Foreign Trade in the Nineteenth Century* (Cambridge, Mass.: Harvard University Press, 1958).

Industrial Canada. Published Monthly by the Canadian Manufacturers Association, Inc., head office in Toronto. Includes various short essays on Canadian industry and finance. Various issues, Vol. VIII (1907–8) through Vol. 14 (1913–14).

Innis, Harold A. *Essays in Canadian Economic History* (Toronto: University of Toronto Press, 1956).

Institute of Life Insurance. *The Historical Statistics of Life Insurance in the United States, 1759–1958* (New York: Institute of Life Insurance, 1960).

Investors Monthly Manual, No. 12, Vol. 40 (December 1901).

Inwood, Kris, and Thanasis Stengos. "Discontinuities in Canadian Economic Growth," *Explorations in Economic History*, Vol. 28, No. 3 (July 1991).

Jackson, R.V. *Australian Economic Development in the Nineteenth Century* (Canberra: Australian National University Press, 1977).

"Short-Run Interaction of Public and Private Sectors in Australia, 1861–90," *Australian Economic History Review*, Vol. 26, No. 1 (March 1986).

Jackson, W. Turrentine. *The Enterprising Scot: Investors in the American West After 1873*, Edinburgh University Publications in History, Philosophy, Economics, No. 22 (Edinburgh: Edinburgh University Press, 1968).

James, John. "The Development of the National Money Market, 1893–1911," *The Journal of Economic History*, Vol. 36, No. 4 (December 1976).

Money and Capital Markets in Postbellum America (Princeton: Princeton University Press, 1978).

"The Rise and Fall of the Commercial Paper Market, 1900–1930," in Michael D. Bordo and Richard Sylla (eds.), *Anglo-American Financial Systems: Institutions and Markets in the Twentieth Century* (Burr Ridge, Ill.: Irwin Professional Publishing, 1995).

James, John A., and Jonathan Skinner. "Sources of Savings in the Nineteenth Century United States," in P. Kilby (ed.), *Quantity and Quidity, Essays in U.S. Economic History* (Middletown, Conn.: Wesleyan University Press, 1987).

Jeffreys, J.B. *Trends in Business Organization Since 1856*, Ph.D. thesis, University of London, 1938.

Jenks, Leland. *The Migration of British Capital to 1875* (London: Thomas Nelson & Sons, 1963).

Johnson, Arthur M., and Barry E. Supple. *Boston Capitalists and Western Railroads: A Study in the Nineteenth Century Railroad Improvement Process* (Cambridge, Mass.: Harvard University Press, 1967).

Johnson, J.F. *The Canadian Banking System*, National Monetary Commission, Senate, 61st Congress, 2nd Session (Washington, D.C.: GPO, 1910).

Johnson, Lyman. "Measuring Economic Performance During the Rosas Regime," Paper Delivered at the January 1996 meeting of the American Historical Society, Atlanta.

Johnson, Paul. "Creditors, Debtors and the Law in Victorian and Edwardian England," London School of Economics and Political Science, Working Papers in Economic History, No. 31/96, May 1996.

Jones, Charles. "The Fiscal Motive for Monetary and Banking Legislation in Argentina, Australia and Canada Before 1914," in D.C.M. Platt and Guido di Tella (eds.), *Argentina, Australia, and Canada: Studies in Comparative Development 1870–1965* (New York: St. Martin's Press, 1985).

"Insurance Companies," in D.C.M. Platt (ed.), *Business Imperialism, 1840–1930: An Inquiry Based on British Experience in Latin America* (Oxford: Clarendon Press, 1977).

Jones, Geoffrey. *British Multinational Banking, 1830–1990* (Oxford: Clarendon Press, 1993).

Joseph, L. *Industrial Finance, A Comparison Between Home and Foreign Developments* (1911).

Joslin, David. *A Century of Banking in Latin America* (London: Oxford University Press, 1963).

Jun, Kwang W. Frank Sader, Haruom Horaguchi, and Kwak Hyuntai. "Japanese Foreign Direct Investment: Recent Trends, Determinants, and Prospects," World Bank, International Economics Department, Debt and International Finance Division, Policy Research Working Paper No. 1213, November 1993.

Kähkönen, Juha. "Japan's Capital Flows," in Ulrich Baumgartner and Guy Meredith, *Savings Behavior and the Asset Price "Bubble" in Japan: Analytical Studies*, International Monetary Fund, Occasional Paper No. 124, April 1995 (Washington, D.C.: International Monetary Fund, 1995).

Kahler, Miles. "Politics and International Debt: Explaining the Crisis," *International Organization*, Vol. 39, No. 3 (summer 1985).

Kaltenborn, Rolf. "The United States of America, Part II: The American Stock Exchange," in D.E. Spray (ed.), *The Principal Stock Exchanges of the World* (Washington, D.C.: International Economic Publishers, 1964).

Kaufman, Robert R. "Democratic and Authoritarian Responses to the Debt Issue, Argentina, Brazil, Mexico," *International Organization*, Vol. 39, No. 3 (summer 1985).

Keehn, Richard H., and Gene Smiley. "Mortgage Lending by National Banks," *Business History Review*, Vol. LI, No. 4 (winter 1977).

Kelley, Allen C. "Demographic Change and Economic Growth: Australia, 1861–1911," mimeograph, July 28, 1966.

"International Migration and Economic Growth: Australia, 1865–1935," Research Center in Economic Growth, Stanford University, Memorandum No. 29, July 1964.

Kennedy, William P. "Capital Markets and Industrial Structure in the Victorian Economy," in J.J. Van Helten and Y. Cassis, *Capitalism in a Mature Economy: Financial Institutions, Capital Exports and British Industry, 1870–1939* (Aldershot, U.K.: Edward Elgar, 1990).

"Economic Growth and Structural Change in the U.K., 1870–1914," mimeograph.

Industrial Structure, Capital Markets and the Origins of British Economic Decline (Cambridge: Cambridge University Press, 1987).

"Notes on Economic Efficiency in Historical Perspective," London School of Economics, mimeograph, May 1981.

Kesner, R.M. *Economic Control and Colonial Development: Crown Colony Financial Management in the Age of Joseph Chamberlain* (Westport, Conn., 1981).

Keyes, Emerson W. *A History of Savings Banks in the United States* (New York: Bradford Rhodes, 1876).

Keynes, John Maynard. *Monetary Reform* (New York: Harcourt, Brace and Company, 1924).

Kindleberger, Charles P. *A Financial History of Western Europe*, 2nd edition (New York: Oxford University Press, 1993).

The World Depression, 1929–1939 (Berkeley: University of California Press, 1986).

King, W.T.C. *History of the London Discount Market* (London: George Routledge & Sons, 1936).

Kishi, Masumi. "Financial Markets and Policies in Newly Industrializing Economies," in Shahid N. Zahid (ed.), *Financial Sector Development in Asia* (Hong Kong: Oxford University Press, 1995).

Klein, Herbert S. "The Integration of Italian Immigrants into the United States and Argentina: A Comparative Analysis," *American Historical Review*, 1983.

Knight, Frank H. *Risk, Uncertainty, and Profit* (Boston: Houghton Mifflin, 1921).

Knowles, Charles E. *History of the Bank for Savings in the City of New York, 1819–1929* (New York: Bank for Savings, 1929).

Knox, Frank A. "*Excursus:* Canadian Capital Movements and the Canadian Balance of International Payments, 1900–1934," in Herbert Marshall, Frank A. Southard Jr. & Kenneth W. Taylor (eds.), *Canadian-American Industry: A Study in International Investment*, for the Carnegie Endowment for International Peace: Division of Economics and History (New Haven and Toronto: Yale University Press and Ryerson Press, 1936).

Kosai, Yutaka. "The Postwar Japanese Economy, 1945–1973," in Kozo Yamamura (ed.), *The Economic Emergence of Modern Japan* (Cambridge: Cambridge University Press, 1997).

Kreps, David M. *A Course in Microeconomic Theory*, ch. 17, "Adverse Selection and Market Signaling" (Princeton: Princeton University Press, 1990).

Krooss, Herman E., and Martin R. Blyn. *A History of Financial Intermediaries* (New York: Random House, 1971).

Kuznets, Simon. *Capital in the American Economy* (Princeton: Princeton University Press, 1961).

"Foreign Economic Relations of the United States and Their Impact on the Domestic Economy: A Review of Long Term Trends," *Proceedings of the American Philosophical Society*, Vol. 92, No. 4 (1948).

National Product Since 1869 (New York: National Bureau of Economic Research, 1946).

Lamb, W. Kaye. *History of the Canadian Pacific Railway* (New York: Macmillan Publishing Company, 1977).

Lamoreaux, Naomi R. "Banks, Kinship, and Economic Development: The New England Case," *The Journal of Economic History*, Vol. XLVI, No. 3 (September 1986).

"Information Problems and Banks' Specialization in Short-Term Commercial Lending: New England in the Nineteenth Century," in Peter Temin (ed.), *Inside the Business Enterprise: Historical Perspective on the Use of Information* (Chicago: University of Chicago Press, 1991).

Insider Lending: Banks, Personal Connections, and Economic Development in New England (New York: Cambridge University Press, 1994).

" 'No Arbitrary Discretion': Specialization in Short-Term Commercial Lending by Banks in Late Nineteenth Century New England," in Geoffrey Jones (ed.), *Banks and Money: International and Comparative Finance in History* (London: Frank Cass, 1991).

Larson, Henrietta. *Jay Cooke, Private Banker*, Harvard Studies in Business History, Vol. 2 (Cambridge, Mass.: Harvard University Press, 1936).

Lavington, F. *The English Capital Market* (London: Methuen & Co., 1921).

Lawson, Thomas W. *Frenzied Finance: Vol. I, The Crime of Amalgamated* (New York: Ridgeway-Thayer Company, 1905).

Laxer, Gordon. *The Roots of Foreign Ownership in Canada* (Toronto: Oxford University Press, 1989).

Levene, Ricardo. *A History of Argentina*, translated and edited by William Spence Robertson (New York: Russell and Russell. 1963).

Levine, Ross. "Financial Development and Economic Growth," World Bank, February 1996, in *The Journal of Economic Literature*, Vol. XXXV, No. 2, June 1997.

Levitt, Kari. *Silent Surrender, The American Economic Empire in Canada* (New York: Liveright, 1970).

Lewis, Cleona, assisted by Karl T. Schottenbeck. *America's Stake in International Investments* (Washington, D.C.: Brookings Institution, 1938).

Lewis, Colin M. "British Business in Argentina," London School of Economics and Political Science, Working Papers in Economic History, No. 26/95, June 1995.

Lewis, Frank. "Fertility and Savings in the United States: 1830–1900," *Journal of Political Economy*, Vol. 91, No. 5 (October 1983).

Lewis, Paul H. *The Crisis of Argentine Capitalism* (Chapel Hill: University of North Carolina Press, 1990).

Lindert, Peter H. "Key Currencies and Gold 1900–1913," Princeton Studies in International Finance, No. 24, August 1969.

Lintner, John. *Mutual Savings Banks in the Savings and Mortgage Markets* (Boston: Harvard University Press, 1948).

Lipsey, Robert E. "U.S. Foreign Trade and the Balance of Payments, 1800–1913," National Bureau of Economic Research, Working Paper No. 4710, April 1994.

Litan, Robert E. *The Revolution in U.S. Finance* (Washington, D.C.: Brookings Institution, 1991).

Lockhart, Oliver C. "The Development of Interbank Borrowing in the National System, 1869–1914, II," *Journal of Political Economy*, Vol. XXIX (March 1921).

Lothian, James R. "Capital Market Integration and Exchange-Rate Regimes in Historical Perspective," paper Delivered at the Cliometric Society Sessions at the ASSA Meetings, San Francisco, Calif., January 5–7, 1996.

Lough, William. *Banking Opportunities in South America*, Department of Commerce, Bureau of Foreign and Domestic Commerce, Special Agents Series, No. 106 (Washington, D.C.: GPO, 1915).

   Financial Developments in South American Countries, Department of Commerce, Bureau of Foreign and Domestic Commerce, Special Agent Series, No. 103 (Washington, D.C.: GPO, 1915).

Madden, John J. *British Investment in the United States*, Ph.D. dissertation, Cambridge University, 1958 (New York: Garland Press, 1985).

Maddison, Angus. "Economic Policy and Performance in Europe, 1913–1970," in Carlo M. Cipolla (ed.), *The Fontana Economic History of Europe. Vol. 5: The Twentieth Century Part Two* (N.P.: Harvester Press Limited/Barnes & Noble Import Division, by agreement with Fontana Books, 1977).

   Monitoring the World Economy, 1820–1992 (Paris: OECD, 1995).

   Phases of Capitalist Development (Oxford: Oxford University Press, 1982).

Maddock, Rodney, and Ian W. McLean. "The Australian Economy in the Very Long Run," in Rodney Maddock and Ian W. McLain, *The Australian Economy in the Long Run* (Cambridge: Cambridge University Press, 1987).

   "Supply-Side Shocks: The Case of Australian Gold," *The Journal of Economic History*, Vol. 43, No. 4 (December 1984).

Magnier, Mark. "S. Korea a Model Structure in U.S. School of Economics," *Los Angeles Times*, November 23, 1998.

Marchildon, Gregory P. "British Investment Banking and Industrial Decline Before the Great War: A Case Study of Capital Outflow to Canadian Industry," in Geoffrey Jones (ed.), *Banks and Money: International and Comparative Finance in History* (London: Frank Cass, 1991).

Marichal, Carlos. *A Century of Debt Crises in Latin America* (Princeton: Princeton University Press, 1989).

"Elite Mercantile y Financiera, B.A. 1880–1914," manuscript.

"Introduction," in Carlos Marichal (ed.), *Foreign Investment in Latin America: Impact on Economic Development, 1850–1930*, Proceedings of the Eleventh International Economic History Congress, Milan, September 1994 (Milan: Universita Bocconi, 1994).

"Los banqueros Europeos y los emprestitos Argentinos: rivaladid y colaboracion: 1880–1990," *Revista ta da Historia Económica*, Vol. II, No. 1 (1984).

"Políticas de dessarollo económico y deuda externa en Argentina (1868–1880)," *Revista ta de Historia* (Sig Lo XIX), Vol. III, No. 5 (1988).

Marr, W.L., and D.G. Paterson. *Canada: An Economic History* (Toronto: Macmillan, 1980).

Marshall, Herbert, Frank A. Southard, Jr., and Kenneth W. Taylor. *Canadian-American Industry: A Study in International Investment*, with an excursus on *The Canadian Balance of Payments*, by Frank A. Knox (New Haven: Yale University Press, 1936).

Martin, Joseph G. *A Century of Finance: Martin's History of the Boston Stock and Money Markets, One Hundred Years. From January 1798 to January 1898* (Boston: Published by the Author, 1898).

"Seventy-three Years' History of the Boston Stock Market: From January 1, 1798, to January 1, 1871," in Vincent P. Carosso and Robert Sobel (eds.), *Wall Street and the Security Markets* (New York: Arno Press, 1975).

Mason, Mark. "The Origins and Evolution of Japanese Direct Investment in Europe," *Business History Review*, Vol. 66, No. 3 (Autumn 1992).

Massel, J.A. *Markets for Machines and Machine Tools in Argentina*, Department of Commerce, Bureau of Domestic and Foreign Commerce, Special Agents Series No. 116 (Washington, D.C.: GPO, 1916).

Masters, Donald C. *Reciprocity, 1846–1911* (Ottawa: Canadian Historical Association, 1961).

The Reciprocity Treaty of 1854 (Toronto: McLelland and Stewart, 1963).

Matthews, R.C.O. C.H. Feinstein, and J.C. Odling-Smee. *British Economic Growth 1856–1973* (Stanford, Calif.: Stanford University Press, 1982).

Maurer, Noel H. "The Profitability of the Porfiriato: Returns, Rents, and Risk in Porfirian Mexico, 1898–1911," mimeograph, 1996.

Meier, G.M. "Economic Development and the Transfer Mechanism: Canada, 1895–1918," *Canadian Journal of Economics and Political Science*, Vol. 19, No. 1 (1953).

McCalla, Douglas. "Fire and Marine Insurance in Upper Canada: The Establishment of a Service Industry, 1832–1868," in Peter Baskerville (ed.), *Canadian Papers in Business History*, Vol. I (Victoria, B.C.: Public History Group of the University of Victoria, 1989).

McFarlane, Larry A. "British Agricultural Investment in the Dakotas, 1877–1953," *Business and Economic History*, 2nd Series, Vol. 5 (1976).

"British Investment in the Land: Nebraska, 1877–1946," *Business History Review*, Vol. LVII (summer 1983).

"British Investment in Midwestern Farm Mortgages and Land, 1875–1900: A Comparison of Iowa and Kansas," *Agricultural History*, Vol. 48 (January 1974).

"British Investment in Minnesota Farm Mortgages and Land, 1875–1900," mimeograph, 1978.

McGrane, Reginald C. *Foreign Bondholders and American State Debts* (New York: Macmillan, 1935).

McInnes, R. Marvin. "Foundations of the Nineteenth Century Canadian Economy," in S. Engerman and R. Gallman (eds.), *The Cambridge Economic History of the United States, Vol. II: The Nineteenth Century* (Cambridge: Cambridge University Press, 2000).

"Output and Productivity in Canadian Agriculture, 1870–71 to 1926–27," in Stanley Engerman and Robert Gallman (eds.), *Long-Term Factors in Economic Growth*, National Bureau of Economic Research, Studies in Income and Wealth, Vol. 51 (Princeton: Princeton University Press, 1986).

McIvor, R. Craig. *Canadian Monetary, Banking and Fiscal Development* (Toronto: Macmillan of Canada, 1958).

McKay, Huntley W. "The Stock Exchanges in Canada," in David E. Spray (ed.), *The Principal Stock Exchanges of the World* (Washington, D.C.: International Economic Publishers, 1964).

McLean, Ian W. "Australian Savings Since 1861," in Peter J. Stemp (ed.), *Savings and Policy: Proceedings of a Conference* (Canberra: Center for Economic Policy Research, Australian National University, 1991).

"Recovery from the 1890s Depression: Australia in an Argentine Mirror," paper delivered at the All-UC Conference on Economic History, UCLA, June 7–9, 1996.

"Savings in Settler Economies: Australian and North American Comparisons," University of Adelaide, August 1991, photocopy.

"Savings in Settler Economies: Australian and North American Comparisons," manuscript, version 1, September 20, 1991, version 2, November 11, 1992.

"Savings in Settler Economies: Australian and North American Comparisons," *Explorations in Economic History*, Vol. 31, No. 4 (October 1994).

McLean, Ian W., and Jonathan J. Pincus. "Did Australian Living Standards Stagnate Between 1890 and 1940?" *Journal of Economic History*, Vol. 43, No. 1 (March 1983).

Menzies, William John. *America as a Field for Investment*, Lecture Delivered to the Chartered Accountants Student's Society, February 18, 1892 (Edinburgh: William Blackwood & Sons, 1892).

Mercer, Lloyd J. "Rates of Return and Government Subsidization of the Canadian Pacific Railway: An Alternative View," mimeograph, Santa Barbara, Calif., February 1972.

Merrett, David T. *ANZ Bank: A History of the Australian and New Zealand Banking Group and Its Constituents* (Sydney: Allen & Unwin, 1985).

"Australian Banking Practice and the Crisis of 1893," *Australian Economic History Review*, Vol. 29, No. 1 (March 1989).

"Banking and Finance," in Christopher Lloyd (ed.), *Australian Institutions Transformed: Capital Labour, and the State* (forthcoming).

"Capital Formation and Capital Markets," draft chapter for the *Cambridge Economic History of Australia*, Vol. 2, 1890–1990.

"Financial Institutions and Pressure: Are the Right Lessons Being Learnt from the 1890s," *Economic Papers*, Vol. 10, No. 1 (March 1991).

"Global Reach by Australian Banks: Correspondent Banking Networks, 1830–1960," *Business History*, Vol. 37, No. 3 (1995).

"Paradise Lost? British Banks in Australia," in Geoffrey Jones (eds.), *Banks as Multinationals* (London: Routledge, 1990).

"Preventing Bank Failure: Could the Commercial Bank of Australia Have Been Saved by Its Peers in 1893?" *Victorian Historical Journal*, Vol. 64, No. 2 (October 1993).

"The 1893 Bank Crash and Monetary Aggregates," Economic Research Department, Reserve Bank of Australia, Research Discussion Paper No. 9303, April 1993.

Michie, Ranald C. "The Canadian Securities Market, 1850–1914," *Business History Review*, Vol. 62, No. 1 (spring 1988).

The City of London, Continuity and Change, 1850–1990 (Edinburgh: John Donald Publishers, n.d.).

"Introduction," in Ranald C. Michie (ed.), *The Industrial Revolution. Vol. II: Financial and Commercial Services* (Oxford: Basil Blackwell, 1994).

The London and New York Stock Exchanges, 1850–1914 (Edinburgh: Allen and Unwin, 1987).

"The London and Provincial Stock Exchanges, 1799–1973: Separation, Integration, Rivalry, Unity," in D.H. Aldercroft and A. Slaven (eds.), *Enterprise and Management: Essays in Honour of Peter L. Payne* (Aldershot, U.K.: Scola Press, 1995).

Money, Mania and Markets: Investment Company Formation and the Stock Exchange in Nineteenth-Century Scotland (Edinburgh, John Donald Publishers, n.d.).

"Options, Concessions, Syndicates and the Provision of Venture Capital, 1880–1913," *Business History*, Vol. 23 (1981).

"The Stock Exchange and the British Economy, 1870–1939," in J.J. Van Helten and Y. Cassis, *Capitalism in a Mature Economy: Financial Institutions, Capital Exports and British Industry, 1870–1939* (Aldershot, U.K.: Edward Elgar, 1990).

Mintz, Ilse. *Deterioration in the Quality of Foreign Bonds Issued in the United States* (New York: National Bureau of Economic Research, 1951).

Mitchell, Brian R. *European Historical Statistics, 1750–1970*, abridged edition (New York: Columbia University Press, 1978).

International Historical Statistics: The Americas and Australia (Detroit: Gale Research, 1983).

Mitchell, Brian R., with the collaboration of Phyllis Dean. *Abstract of British Historical Statistics* (Cambridge: Cambridge University Press, 1962).

Modigliani, F., and R. Brumberg. "Utility Analysis and the Consumption Function: An Interpretation of Cross-section Data," in K.K. Kurihara (ed.), *Post-Keynsion Economics* (New Brunswick, N.J.: Rutgers University Press, 1954).

Mole, D. "Financial Development and Capital Formation," in M.H. Watkins and H.M. Grant (eds.), *Canadian Economic History: Classic and Contemporary Approaches* (Ottawa: Carlton University Press, 1993).

Moore, E.S. *American Influences on Canadian Mining* (Toronto: University of Toronto Press, 1941).

Morgan, Victor E., and W.A. Thomas. *The Stock Exchange: Its History and Functions* (London: Etek Books, 1962).

Morgenstern, Oskar. *International Financial Transactions and Business Cycles*, National Bureau of Economic Research, Studies in Business Cycles (Princeton: Princeton University Press, 1959).

Morris, Charles R. "Financial Follies," *Los Angeles Times*, Section M, October 4, 1998.

Morris, M. "The Land Mortgage Companies, Government Savings Banks and Private Bankers in Canada," *Journal of the Canadian Bankers Association*, Vol. 3 (1895–96).

Mulhall, M.G., and E.T. Mulhall. *Handbook of the River Plate*, 6th edition (Buenos Aires and London: M.G. and E.T. Mulhall & Paul Kegan, Trench & Co., 1892).

Murray, Robert, and Kate White. *A Bank of the People: A History of the State Bank of Victoria* (North Melbourne: Hargreen Publishing Company, 1992).

Nakamura, Takafusa. "Depression, Recovery, and War 1920–1945," in Kozo Yamamura (ed.), *The Economic Emergence of Modern Japan* (Cambridge: Cambridge University Press, 1997).

Nash, R.C. "The Balance of Payments and Foreign Capital Flows in Eighteenth-Century England: A Comment," *Economic History Review*, Vol. 50, No. 1 (February 1997).

Nash, Robert Lucas. *Banking Institutions of Australasia: A Reprint of Articles Published in The British Australasian, Australian Times and Anglo-New-Zealander* (London and Melbourne: British Australasian Company, and McCarron, Bird and Co., 1889).

National Monetary Commission. *Statistics for the United States: 1867–1909* (New York: Garland Publishing, 1983).

Navin, T., and M. Sears. "The Rise of a Market for Industrial Securities," *Business History Review*, Vol. 29, No. 2 (June 1955).

Naylor, R.T. *Canada and the European Age, 1453–1919* (Vancouver: New Star Books, 1987), chapter 26, "Canada and the Cross of Gold."

  The History of Canadian Business, 1867–1914, 2 vols. (Toronto: James Lorimer & Co., 1975). Vol. I, *The Banks and Finance Capital*, Vol. II, *Industrial Development*.

Neal, Larry. "The Disintegration and Re-integration of International Capital Markets in the 19th Century," University of Illinois, mimeograph, February 29, 1992.

  "The Emergence of Stock Markets: Past and Present," Paper Delivered at the All-UC Conference on Economic History, UCLA, June 7–9, 1996.

  "The First Latin American Debt Crisis and the Stock Market Crash of 1825," Paper Delivered at the Economic History Workshops, UC Davis, May 28, 1996, and Stanford University, May 29, 1996.

  "The Response of the London Stock Market to New Issues: Canals, Railways and Empire in the 19th Century," paper given at the Social Science History Association meetings, Baltimore, November 6–9, 1993.

  "Trust Companies and Financial Innovation, 1897–1914," *Business History Review*, Vol. XLV, No. 1 (spring 1971).

Neal, Larry, and Paul Uselding. "Immigration, a Neglected Source of American Economic Growth: 1790 to 1912," *Oxford Economic Papers*, Vol. 24, New Series (1972).

Neufeld, E.P. *The Financial System of Canada: Its Growth and Development* (New York: St. Martin's Press, 1972).

Newland, Carlos, and Barry Poulson. "Puramente Animal, Pastoral Production and Early Argentine Economic Growth, 1825–1865," Paper delivered at Madrid, 1995.

Newton, Lucy. "Domestic Institutional Change: English and Welsh Joint Stock Banking, 1826–1860," Paper given at Seville Pre-Conference at the Center for German and European Studies, University of California, Berkeley, April 17–20, 1997.

Nishimura, Shizuya. *The Decline of Inland Bills of Exchange in the London Money Market, 1855–1913* (New York: Cambridge University Press, 1971).

Norries, K.H. "Tariffs and the Distribution of Prairie Incomes," *Canadian Journal of Economics*, Vol. 7 (1974).

North, Douglass C. "The Balance of Payments of the United States, 1790–1860," in William B. Parker (ed.), *Trends in the American Economy in the Nineteenth Century*, Studies in Income and Wealth, Vol. 24, by the Conference on Income and Wealth, National Bureau of Economic Research (Princeton: Princeton University Press, 1960).

  "Capital Accumulation in Life Insurance Between the Civil War and the Investigation of 1905," in William Miller (ed.), *Men in Business* (Cambridge, Mass.: Harvard University Press, 1952).

  "Order, Disorder and Economic Change," Working manuscript, February 1996.

"Some Fundamental Puzzles in Economic History/Development," Paper Presented to the Von Gremp Workshop in Entrepreneurial History, UCLA, February 21, 1996.

O'Hagen, H. Osbourne. *Leaves from My Life* (London: John Lane, 1929).

O'Rourke, Kevin H., Alan M. Taylor, and Jeffrey G. Williamson. "Factor Price Convergence in the Late Nineteenth Century," *International Economic Review*, Vol. 37, No. 3 (August 1996).

O'Rourke, Kevin, Jeffrey G. Williamson, and Timothy J. Hatton. "Mass Migration, Commodity Market Integration, and Real Wage Convergence: The Late Nineteenth Century Atlantic Economy," Harvard Institute of Economic Research, Harvard University, Discussion Paper No. 1640, May 1993.

Obstfeld, Maurice, and Alan M. Taylor. "World Capital Market: Integration, Crisis, and Growth," manuscript, June 1998.

Odell, Kerry A. "The Integration of Regional and Interregional Capital Markets: Evidence from the Pacific Coast, 1883–1913," The *Journal of Economic History*, Vol. 49, No. 2 (June 1989).

Officer, Lawrence A., and Lawrence B. Smith. "The Canadian-American Reciprocity Treaty of 1855 to 1866," *The Journal of Economic History*, Vol. 28, No. 4 (December 1968).

Official Yearbook of the Commonwealth of Australia, Vol. 1, 1907, through Vol. 12, 1919.

Ogden, Tessa. "An Analysis of Bank of England Discount and Advance Behavior 1870–1914," in James Foreman-Peck (ed.), *New Perspectives on the Victorian Economy: Essays in Quantitative Economic History, 1860–1914* (Cambridge: Cambridge University Press, 1991).

Ogelsby, J.C.M. *Gringos from the Far North: Essays in the History of Canadian-Latin American Relations, 1866–1968* (Toronto: Macmillan, 1976).

Okochi, Akio, and Tadakatsu Inoue, eds. *Overseas Business Activities*, Proceedings of the Fuji International Conference on Business History (Tokyo: University of Tokyo Press, 1984).

Olmstead, Alan L. *New York City, Mutual Savings Banks, 1819–1961* (Chapel Hill: University of North Carolina Press, 1976).

Olson, Mancer. "Why Are Differences in Per-Capital Incomes So Large and Persistent?" mimeograph, 1993.

Oneal, John R. "Foreign Investments in Less Developed Regions," *Political Science Quarterly*, Vol. 103, No. 1 (spring 1988).

Oneal, John R., and Frances H. Oneal. "Hegemony, Imperialism, and the Profitability of Foreign Investments," *International Organization*, Vol. 42, No. 2 (spring 1988).

Oxley, Les, and David Greasley. "A Tale of Two Dominions: Australia, Canada and the Convergence Hypothesis," paper presented to the Australian National University, Economic History Seminar, RSSS, August 25, 1995.

"A Time Series Perspective on Convergence: Australia, UK and USA Since 1870," *The Economic Record*, Vol. 71, No. 214 (September 1995).

Paish, George. "The Export of Capital and the Cost of Living," *Statist Supplement*, Vol. 79 (1914).

"Great Britain's Capital Investments in Individual, Colonial and Foreign Countries," *Journal of the Royal Statistical Society*, Vol. 74, Part II (January 1911).

"Great Britain's Capital Investments in Other Lands," *Journal of the Royal Statistical Society*, Vol. 72, Part III (September 1909).

"Our New Investments in 1908," *Statist*, Vol. 63 (January 1909).

"Trade Balances of the United States," U.S. Senate, *National Monetary Commission*, 61st Congress, 2nd Session, 1910, Senate Document 579.

Paterson, Donald G. *British Direct Investment in Canada, 1890–1914: Estimates and Determinates* (Toronto: University of Toronto Press, 1976).

Patinkin, Don. "Keynes, John Maynard," in John Eatwell, Murray Milgate, and Peter Newman, *The New Palgrave: A Dictionary of Economics* (London: Macmillan Press, 1987).

Payne, Peter Lester. "The Emergence of the Large-Scale Company in Great Britain, 1870–1914," *Economic History Review*, Vol. XX, No. 3 (December 1967).

Payne, Peter L., and Lance E. Davis. *The Savings Bank of Baltimore, 1818–1866: A Historical Analytical Study*, Johns Hopkins University Studies in Historical and Political Science, Series LXXII, No. 2,954 (Baltimore: Johns Hopkins University Press, 1956).

Pentland, H.C. "Further Observations on Canadian Development," *Canadian Journal of Economics and Political Science*, Vol. 19, No. 3 (August 1953).

"The Role of Capital in Canadian Economic Development Before 1875," *Canadian Journal of Economics and Political Science*, Vol. XVI, No. 4 (November 1950).

Perkins, Edwin J. *American Public Finance and Financial Services* (Columbus: Ohio State University Press, 1994).

Peters, Harold Edwin. *The Foreign Debt of the Argentine Republic* (Baltimore: Johns Hopkins University Press, 1934).

Phelps, Vernon Lovell. *The International Economic Position of Argentina* (Philadelphia: University of Pennsylvania Press, 1938).

Phillip, Francis Higginson. "The Stock Exchanges of the United States: Part I," in David E. Spray (ed.), *The Principal Stock Exchanges of the World – Their Operation, Structure and Development* (Washington, D.C.: International Economic Publishers, 1964).

Picket, J. "Residential Capital Formation in Canada, 1865–1914," *Canadian Journal of Economics and Political Science*, Vol. 29, No. 1 (1963).

Piva, Michael J. *The Borrowing Process: Public Finance in the Province of Canada, 1840–1867* (Ottawa: University of Ottawa Press, 1992).

Platt, D.C.M. *Britain's Investment Overseas on the Eve of the First World War* (New York: St. Martin's Press, 1986).

"British Portfolio Investment Before 1870: Some Doubts," *The Economic History Review*, 2nd Series, Vol. 33, No. 1 (February 1980).

Foreign Finance in Continental Europe and the United States, 1815–1870: Quantities, Origins, Functions and Distributions (London: George Allen & Unwin, 1984).

Platt, D.C.M., and Guido di Tella, eds. *Argentina, Australia, and Canada: Studies in Comparative Development 1870–1965* (New York: St. Martin's Press, 1985).

Platt, Milton J. "Annals and Statistics," in E.C. Stedman (ed.), *The New York Stock Exchange* (New York: Greenwood Press, 1969).

Poapst, James V. "Life Insurance Savings in Canada," *Canadian Journal of Economics and Political Science*, Vol. 19, No. 2 (May 1958).

Pomfret, Richard. "Capital Formation in Canada, 1870–1900," *Explorations in Economic History*, Vol. 18, No. 1 (January 1981).

The Economic Development of Canada (Toronto: Methuen, 1981).

Pope, David. "Australian Money and Banking Statistics," Australian National University, Source Papers in Economic History, No. 11, March 1986.

"Australian Trading Bank Interest Rates," Manuscript, Australian National University, May 1996.

"Bank Deregulation in Historical Perspective," in Michael R. Johnson, Peter Kriesler, and Anthony Owen, *Issues in Australian Economics* (St. Leonardo, Australia: Allen & Unwin 1994).

"Bankers and Banking Business, 1860–1914," Australian National University, Working Papers in Economic History, No. 85, September 1987.

"Free Banking in Australia Before World War I," Australian National University, Working Papers in Economic History, No. 129, December 1989.

"Protection and Australian Manufacturers' International Competitiveness, 1901–1930," *Australian Economic History Review*, Vol. 26, No. 1 (March 1986).

Postan, M.M. "Some Recent Problems in the Accumulation of Capital," *Economic History Review*, Vol. VI, No. 1 (February 1935).

Powrie, T. *The Contribution of Foreign Capital to Canadian Economic Growth* (Edmonton: Hurtig, 1978).

Pratt, Sereno S. *The Work of Wall Street* (New York: D. Appleton and Company, 1903).

Pritchett, Bruce M. *A Study of Capital Mobilization: The Life Insurance Industry of the Nineteenth Century* (New York: Arno Press, 1977).

Productivity Trends in the United States (Princeton: Princeton University Press, 1961).

Pursell, G. "Australian Non-Life Insurance Since 1909," *The Economic Record*, Vol. 44 (December 1968).

Quigley, Neil C. *Bank Credit and the Structure of the Canadian Space Economy, 1890–1935*, Ph.D. dissertation, University of Toronto, 1986.

"The Bank of Nova Scotia in the Caribbean, 1889–1940," *Business History Review*, Vol. 63, No. 4 (winter 1989).

Ramirez, Carlos D. "Did J.P. Morgan's Men Add Liquidity? Corporate Investment, Cash Flow and Financial Structure at the Turn of the Twentieth Century," paper presented at the July 1992 meeting of the NBER's Research Group on the Development of the American Economy, Cambridge, Mass.

Randall, Laura. *An Economic History of Argentina in the Twentieth Century* (New York: Columbia University Press, 1978).

Ransom, Roger L., and Richard Sutch. "Tontine Insurance and the Armstrong Investigation: A Case of Stifled Innovation, 1868–1905," *The Journal of Economic History*, Vol. XLVIII, No. 2 (June 1987).

Ratchford, B.U. *American State Debts* (Durham: Duke University Press, 1941).

Public Expenditures in Australia, the Duke University Commonwealth-Studies Center, No. 11 (London: Cambridge University Press, 1959).

Recchini, Zulma L. *The Contributions of Migration and Natural Increase to the Growth of Buenos Aires, 1855–1960*. Ph.D. dissertation, University of Pennsylvania, 1971.

Reed, Howard Curtis. *The Preeminence of International Financial Centers* (New York: Praeger Publishers, 1981).

Reed, M.C. *Investment in Railways in Britain, 1820–1844: A Study in the Development of Capital Markets* (London: Oxford University Press, 1975).

Regalsky, Andres M. "Banking, Trade and the Rise of Capitalism in Argentina, 1850–1930," in Alice Teichova, Ginette Kurgan-Van Hentenryk, and Dieter Ziegler (eds.), *Banking, Trade and Industry, Europe, America and Asia from the Thirteenth to the Twentieth Century* (Cambridge: Cambridge University Press, 1997).

Report of the Commercial Relations of the United States with Foreign Countries for the Years 1880 and 1881, 46th Congress, 3rd Session, House of Representative Executive Document No. 98 (Washington, D.C.: GPO, 1883).

Rich, George. *The Cross of Gold: Money and the Canadian Business Cycle* (Ottawa: Carlton University Press, 1988).

Richardson, H.W. "British Emigration and Overseas Investment, 1870–1914," *The Economic History Review*, Vol. 25 (February 1972).

Richardson, Peter. "Collins House Financiers," in R.T. Appleyard and C.B. Schedvin (eds.), *Australian Financiers: Biographical Essays* (Melbourne: Federal Reserve Bank of Australia, 1988).

Riegel, Robert E. *The Story of the Western Railroads* (Lincoln: University of Nebraska Press, 1926).

Ripley, William Z. *Railroads: Finances and Organization* (New York: Longman Green, 1915).

Rippy, J. Fred. *British Investments in Latin America, 1822–1949: A Case Study of Private Enterprise in Retarded Regions* (Minneapolis: University of Minnesota Press, 1959).

Roberts, Charles A. "North-South Exchange Rate Differences: 1820–1830," paper given at the Southern Economic Association meeting, New Orleans, November 1993.

Robinson, Howard. *The British Post Office: A History* (Princeton: Princeton University Press, 1948).

Robinson, L.E. *Credit Facilities in the United Kingdom* (New York, 1923).

Rock, David. *Argentina, 1516–1982: From Spanish Colonization to the Falklands War* (Berkeley: University of California Press, 1985).

Politics in Argentina, 1890–1930 (Cambridge: Cambridge University Press, 1975).

Rockoff, Hugh. "The Capital Market in the 1850's," National Bureau of Economic Research, Working Paper Series on Historical Factors in Long Run Growth, Working Paper No. 11.

"Walter Bagehot and the Theory of Central Banking," in Forrest Capie and Geoffrey E. Wood, *Financial Crises and the World Banking System* (London: Macmillan [in association with the Centre for Banking and International Finance, the City University], 1986).

Rockoff Hugh, and Howard Bodenhorn. "Regional Interest Rates in Antebellum America," in Claudia Golden and Hugh Rockoff (eds.), *Strategic Factors in Nineteenth-Century American Economic History* (Chicago: University of Chicago Press, 1992).

"The Role and Functions of the Australian Stock Exchange." A Submission to the [Australian] Trade Practices Commission, November 1981.

Rojas-Suarez, Lillian, and Steven R. Weisbrod. "Banking Crisis in Latin America: Experience and Issues," Inter-American Development Bank, Office of the Chief Economist, Working Paper Series 321, February 1996.

Romer, Christina D. "The Prewar Business Cycle Reconsidered: New Estimates of Gross National Product, 1869–1908," *Journal of Political Economy*, Vol. 97, No. 1 (February 1989).

Romero, Jose Luis. *A History of Argentine Political Thought* (Stanford, Calif.: Stanford University Press, 1963).

Ross, Alexander. *The Traders: Inside Canada's Stock Markets* (Toronto: Collins, 1984).

Ross, Victor A., and A. St. Louis Trigge. *A History of the Canadian Bank of Commerce*, 3 vols. (Toronto: Oxford University Press, 1920–1934).

Rotella, Elyce, and Kenneth Snowden. "The Building Association Movement of the Late Nineteenth Century," *Working Papers in Business and Economics, Center for Applied Research, Joseph M. Bryan School of Business and Economics*, University of North Carolina, Greensboro, Working Paper Series ECO940101, January 1994.

Rowthorn, R.E., and S.N. Solomon. "The Macroeconomic Effects of Overseas Investment and the U.K. Balance of Payments, 1870–1913," *Economic History Review*, Vol. 44 (November 1991).

Royal Commission on Life Insurance. *Report*, London, 1907.

Rubenstein, W.D. "Men of Wealth," *Australian Cultural History*, No. 3, 1984.

"The Top Wealth-Holders in New South Wales, 1817–1939," *Australian Economic History Review*, Vol. XX, No. 2 (September 1980).

Sachs, Jeffrey. "Global Capitalism," *The Economist*, September 12–18, 1998.

Sachs, Jeffrey, Aaron Tornell, and Andres Velasco. "Financial Crises in Emerging Markets: The Lessons from 1995," National Bureau of Economic Research, Working Paper No. 5576, May 1996.

Safarian, A.E. *Foreign Ownership of Canadian Industry* (Toronto: McGraw-Hill, 1966).

Salsbury, Stephen, and Kay Sweeney. *The Bull, the Bear, and the Kangaroo: The History of the Sydney Stock Exchange* (Sydney: Allen and Unwin, 1988).

Sarmiento, Domingo. *Life in the Argentine Republic in the Days of the Tyrants: Or, Civilization and Barbarism*, with a Biographical Sketch of the Author by Mrs. Horace Mann (New York: Hafner Press; first published 1868).

Saunders, S.A. "Reciprocity Treaty of 1854: A Regional Study," *Canadian Journal of Economics and Political Science*, Vol. 2, February 1936.

Sayers, R.S. *Lloyd Bank in the History of English Banking* (Oxford: Clarendon Press, 1957).

Saywell, John T. "F.H. Deacon and Co., Investment Dealers: A Case Study of the Securities Industry, 1897–1945," *Ontario History*, Vol. LXXXV, No. 2 (June 1993).

Schedvin, C.B. "Argentina and Australia: Responses to Instability and Industrialization 1930–1960," in A.E. Dingle and D.T. Merrett (eds.), *Argentina and Australia: Essays in Comparative Economic Development*, Economic History Society of Australia and New Zealand, Occasional Paper No. 1, 1985.

"A Century of Money in Australia," *Economic Record*, Vol. 49, No. 128 (December 1973).

"Midas and Marino: A Perspective on Australian Economic History," *The Economic History Review*, Vol. 32, No. 4 (November 1979).

Schenk, Catherine R. "The Origins of the Eurodollar Market in London: 1955–1963," *Explorations in Economic History*, Vol. 35, No. 2 (April 1998).

Schmitz, Christopher J. "Patterns of Scottish Portfolio Foreign Investment, 1860–1914," Manuscript, 1993.

Schull, Joseph, and J. Douglas Gibson. *The Scotiabank Story: A History of the Bank of Nova Scotia, 1832–1932* (Toronto: Macmillan, 1982).

Schumpeter, Joseph A. *Ten Great Economists from Marx to Keynes* (New York: Oxford University Press, 1965).

Scobie, James R. *Buenos Aires, Plaza to Suburb, 1870–1910* (New York: Oxford University Press, 1974).

Revolution on the Pampas: A Social History of Argentine Wheat, 1860–1910 (Austin: University of Texas Press, 1964).

Segal, Harry H., and Matthew Simon. "British Foreign Capital Issues, 1865–1914," *The Journal of Economic History*, Vol. XXI, No. 4 (December 1961).

Shaw, William Howard. *Value of Commodity Output Since 1869* (New York: National Bureau of Economic Research, 1947).

Sheppard, David K. *The Growth and Role of UK Financial Institutions* (London: Methuen, 1971).

Sheppard, D.K. "The New England Investment Banker – Ephor or Entrepreneur in the Nineteenth Century," University of Birmingham, Faculty of Commerce, Series D, No. 2 (December 1963).

Silber, W. "Technology, Communication and the Performance of Financial Markets: 1840–1975," Mimeograph, February 1977.

Silberberg, R. "Rates of Return on Melbourne Land Investment, 1880–92," *The Economic Record*, Vol. 51, No. 134 (June 1975).

Simon, Matthew. "The Balance of Payments of the United States, 1861–1900," in William B. Parker (ed.), *Trends in the American Economy in the Nineteenth Century*, Studies in Income and Wealth, Vol. 24, by the Conference on Income and Wealth, National Bureau of Economic Research (Princeton: Princeton University Press, 1960).

"New British Investment in Canada," *Canadian Journal of Economics*, Vol. 3, No. 2 (1970).

"The Pattern of New British Portfolio Foreign Investment, 1865–1914," in John H. Adler (ed.), *Capital Movements and Economic Development*, Proceedings of a Conference held by the International Economic Association, July, 1965 (London: Macmillan, 1967), pp. 33–70. Reprinted in A.R. Hall, *The Export of Capital from Britain, 1870–1914* (London: Metheun, 1968).

Sinclair, W.A. "Capital Formation," in Colin Foster (ed.), *Australian Economic Development in the Twentieth Century* (London: Allen and Unwin, 1970).

The Process of Economic Growth in Australia (Melbourne: Longmans Cheshire, 1976).

Sinkovich, Boris A., Alan M. Taylor, and Jeffery G. Williamson. "Appendix Materials" [to Jeffery G. Williamson, "Evolution of Global Labor Markets Since 1930: Background Evidence and Hypotheses," NBER/DAE Working Paper No. 36 (February 1992)], Harvard University, mimeograph, September 1992.

Smith, K.C., and G.F. Horne. "An Index Number of Securities, 1867–1914," *London and Cambridge Economic Service*, Memorandum No. 47, London, Royal Economic Society, 1934.

Snowden, Kenneth A. "American Stock Market Development and Performance, 1871–1921," *Explorations in Economic History*, Vol. 24, No. 4 (October 1987).

"The Evolution of Interregional Mortgage Lending Channels, 1870–1940: The Life Insurance-Mortgage Company Connection," in Naomi R. Lamoreaux and Daniel M.G. Raff, *Coordination and Information: Historical Perspectives on the Organization of Enterprise*, National Bureau of Economic Research Conference Volume (Chicago: University of Chicago Press, 1995).

"Historical Returns and Security Market Developments, 1872–1925," *Explorations in Economic History*, Vol. 27, No. 4 (October 1990).

"Innovation in the Nineteenth Century Mortgage Market: A Tale of Two Failures," paper Delivered to the Economic History Association Annual Meeting, Boulder, September 27–29, 1991.

"Mortgage Lending and American Urbanization, 1880–1890," *Journal of Economic History*, Vol. 48, No. 2 (June 1988).

"Mortgage Rates and American Capital Market Development in the Nineteenth Century," *Journal of Economic History*, Vol. XLVII, No. 3 (September 1987).

"Mortgage Securitization in the United States: 20th Century Developments in Historical Perspective," paper presented at the New York University Salomon Center, Leonard N. Stern School of Business, Conference on *Anglo-American Finance: Financial Markets and Institutions in 20th-Century North America and the U.K.*, December 10, 1993.

"Mortgage Securization in the United States: 20th Century Developments in Historical Perspective," *Working Papers in Business and Economics, Center for Applied Research, Joseph M. Bryan School of Business and Economics*, University of North Carolina, Greensboro, Working Paper Series ECO940104, January 1994.

"Why Did Late Nineteenth Century American Mortgage Banking Fail?" *Working Papers in Business and Economics, Center for Applied Research, Joseph M. Bryan School of*

Business and Economics, University of North Carolina, Greensboro, Working Paper Series ECO940103, January 1994.

Snowden, Kenneth A., and Nidal Abu-Saba. "Why Did Late Nineteenth Century Mortgage Banking Fail?" Paper presented at the National Bureau of Economic Research, Franco-American Conference, Cambridge, Mass., July 15–16, 1993.

Sobel, Robert. *The Big Board: A History of the New York Stock Market* (New York: Free Press, 1965).

Sokoloff, Kenneth. "Invention, Innovation and Manufacturing Productivity in the Antebellum Northeast," in Robert Gallman and John Wallis (eds.), *American Economic Growth, and the Standards of Living Before the Civil War*, National Bureau of Economic Research Conference Report (Chicago: University of Chicago Press, 1992).

Solberg, Carl H. *The Prairies and the Pampas: Agricultural Policy in Canada and Argentina, 1880–1930* (Stanford, Calif.: Stanford University Press, 1987).

Southworth, Constance. "The American-Canadian Newsprint Industry and the Tariff," *The Journal of Political Economy*, Vol. 30 (October 1992).

Southworth, Shirley D. *Branch Banking in the United States*, Chapters I, III (New York: McGraw-Hill, 1928).

Speare, Charles F. "Selling American Bonds in Europe," *Annals of the American Academy of Political and Social Science*, Vol. 30 (1907).

Spence, Clark C. *British Investments and the American Mining Frontier 1860–1901* (Ithaca, N.Y.: Cornell University Press, 1958).

"British Investment and the American Mining Frontier, 1860–1901," *New Mexico Historical Review*, Vol. 36 (April 1961).

Spray, David E., ed. *The Principal Stock Exchanges of the World: Their Operation, Structure and Development* (Washington, D.C.: International Economic Publishers, 1964).

Statutes at Large of the United States, Vol. xxiv (1887).

Stedman, Edmund C., ed. *The New York Stock Exchange: Its History, Its Contribution to National Prosperity, and Its Relation to American Finance at the Outset of the Twentieth Century* (New York: Greenwood Press, 1969); first published 1905.

Stedman, E.C., and Easton, A.N. "History of the New York Stock Exchange," in E.C. Stedman, *The New York Stock Exchange* (New York: Greenwood Press, 1969).

Stone, Irving. *The Composition and Distribution of British Investment in Latin America, 1865–1913* (New York: Garland Publishing, 1987).

Studenski, Paul, and Herman E. Krooss. *Financial History of the United States: Fiscal, Monetary, Banking, and Tariff, Including Financial Administration and State and Local Finance* (New York: McGraw-Hill, 1952).

Sullivan, Emmett. "Expressing a Preference: Tariff Legislation in Canada & Australia, 1910–11," Manuscript, La Trobe University, 1995.

Supple, Barry. "Corporate Growth and Structural Change in a Service Industry: Insurance 1870–1914," in Barry Supple (ed. for the Economic History Society), *Essays in British Economic History* (Oxford: Clarendon Press, 1977).

The Royal Exchange Assurance: A History of British Insurance, 1720–1970 (Cambridge: Cambridge University Press, 1970).

Svennilson, Lars., *Growth and Stagnation in the European Economy* (Geneva: United Nations Economic Commission for Europe, 1954).

Swan, T.W. "Economic Growth and Capital Accumulation," *Economic Record*, Vol. 32 (November 1956).

Sweezy, Paul. "The Decline of Investment Banking," *Antioch Review*, Vol. I (1941).

Sylla, Richard. "Emerging Markets in History: The United States, Japan, and Argentina," in R. Sato, R. Rama Chandran, and K. Miño (eds.), *Global Competition and Integration* (Boston: Kluwer Academic Publishers, 1995).

"Federal Policy, Banking Market Structure, and Capital Mobilization in the United States, 1863–1913," *The Journal of Economic History*, Vol. 29, No. 4 (December 1969).

"Financial Intermediaries in Economic History: Quantitative Research on the Seminal Hypotheses of Lance Davis and Alexander Gerschenkron," in Robert Gallman (ed.), *Recent Developments in Business and Economic History: Essays in Memory of Herman E. Kroos* (Greenwich, Conn.: JAI Press, 1977).

Sylla, Richard, and Smith, George David. "Information and Capital Market Regulation in Anglo-American Finance," in Michael D. Bordo and Richard Sylla (eds.), *Anglo-American Financial Systems: Institutions and Markets in the Twentieth Century* (Burr Ridge, Ill.: Irwin Professional Publishing, 1995).

Sylla, Richard, and John Wallis. "The Anatomy of Sovereign Debt Crisis: Lessons from the American State Defaults of the 1840s," manuscript draft, July 1996.

Sylla, Richard, Wilson, Jack W., and Jones, Charles P. "Financial Markets and the Great Merger Movement of 1895–1904," Mimeograph.

Sylla, Richard, Jack W. Wilson, and Charles P. Jones. "U.S. Financial Markets and Long-Term Economic Growth, 1790–1989," in Thomas Weiss and Donald Schaefer (eds.), *Economic Development in Historical Perspective* (Stanford, Calif.: Stanford University Press, 1993).

Tamaki, Norio. *Japanese Banking: A History, 1859–1959* (Cambridge: Cambridge University Press, 1995).

Tassonyi, Almos. "Debt Limits and Supervision: An Issue in Provincial-Municipal Relationships in Times of Fiscal Crisis; A Comparison of the 1930's and the 1980's," paper prepared for the Government and Competitiveness Discussion Paper Series.

Taylor, Alan M. *Argentine Economic Growth in Historical Perspective*, Ph.D. thesis, Harvard University, July 1992.

"Convergence and International Factor Flows in Theory and History," NBER Working Paper No. 5798, October 1996.

"Domestic Saving and International Capital Flows Reconsidered," paper presented to the Von Gremp Workshop, UCLA, October 18, 1995.

"External Dependence, Demographic Burdens, and Argentine Economic Decline After the *Belle Époque*," Paper for NBER/DAE conference, July 1992, mimeograph.

"External Dependence, Demographic Burdens, and Argentine Economic Decline After the Belle Époque," *The Journal of Economic History*, Vol. 52, No. 4 (December 1992).

"International Capital Mobility in History: Purchasing Power Parity in the Long Run," NBER Working Paper No. 5742, September 1996.

"International Capital Mobility in History: The Savings-Investment Relationship," NBER Working Paper No. 5743, September 1996.

"Peopling the Pampa: On the Impact of Mass Migration to the River Plate, 1870–1914," NBER, DAE, Working Paper No. 68, May 1995.

"Sources of Convergence in the Late Nineteenth Century," NBER Working Paper No. 5806, October 1996.

Taylor, Alan M., and Jeffrey G. Williamson.

"Capital Flows to the New World as an Intergenerational Transfer," NBER, DAE Working Paper Series on Historical Factors in Long Run Growth No. 32, December 1991.

"Convergence in the Age of Mass Migration," National Bureau of Economic Research, Working Paper No. 4711, April 1994.

Tesar, Linda L., and Ingrid M. Werner. "International Equity Transactions and U.S. Portfolio Choice," Manuscript, September 1993.

The Annual Financial Review of Canada, July 1901, Vol. 1.

The Economist, Vol. 28 (December 3, 1870).

Thomas, Mark. "The Australian Economy in the Canadian Mirror, 1890–1913," Paper delivered at the Canadian Cliometric Society Meeting, McGill University, Montreal, April 1994.

"Frontier Economies and the Diffusion of Growth," in John A. James and Mark Thomas (eds.), *Capitalism in Context: Essays on Economic Development and Cultural Change in Honor of R.M. Hartwell* (Chicago: University of Chicago Press, 1994).

Thomas, W.A. *The Provincial Exchanges* (London: Frank Cass, 1973).

Thorne, H.O. *A History of Savings Banks* (London: Oxford University Press, 1947).

Tilly, Richard. *Financial Institutions and Industrialization in the Rhineland, 1815–1870* (Madison: University of Wisconsin Press, 1966).

"International Aspects of the Development of German Banking 1870–1914," mimeograph.

"Some Comments on German Foreign Portfolio Investment, 1870–1914," paper delivered at a conference in São Paulo, Brazil, July 1989.

Tornquist, Carlos A. *El Balance de pagos de la Republica Argentina en el premier ano economica pasado baja los efectoa de la guerro Europea* (Buenos Aires: 1916), as reported in V.L. Phelps, *The International Economic Position of Argentina* (Philadelphia: University of Pennsylvania Press, 1938).

Tornquist, Ernesto, and Company. *The Economic Development of the Argentine Republic in the Last Fifty Years* (Buenos Aires: Ernesto Tornquist & Co., 1919).

Trescott, Paul B. *Financing American Enterprise: The Story of Commercial Banking* (New York: Harper & Row, 1963).

Triner, Gail D. "Banking on the Periphery: Brazil, 1906–1930," paper presented at the Cliometrics Panel, ASSA Conference, San Francisco, January 7–9, 1996.

Tulchin, Joseph S. *Agricultural Credit in Argentina, 1910–1926*, Occasional Papers Series, Institute of Latin American Studies, University of North Carolina, Chapel Hill.

Turner, Paul. "The U.K. Demand for Money, Commercial Bills and Quasi-Money Assets, 1871–1913," in James Foreman-Peck (ed.), *New Perspectives in the Late Victorian Economy: Essays in Quantitative Economic History, 1860–1914* (Cambridge: Cambridge University Press, 1991).

Twomey, Michael J. "Foreign Investment and the Capital Stock in Canada Before 1926," Paper, June 1995.

Tyrrell, Henry Franklin. *Semi-centennial History of the Northwestern Mutual Life Insurance Company of Milwaukee, Wisconsin* (Milwaukee, 1908).

Unal, Haluk, and Miguel Navarro. "The Technical Process of Bank Privatization in Mexico," Wharton School, University of Pennsylvania, Financial Institutions Center, Working Paper No. 97–42.

United Nations, Economic Commission for Latin America. *Economic Development and Income Distribution in Argentina* (New York: United Nations, 1969).

United States Congress, 3rd Session, H.R. Executive Document Number 98. *Report of the Commercial Relations for the Years 1880 and 1881* (Washington, D.C.: GPO, 1883).

Urquhart M.C., ed. *Historical Statistics of Canada* (Cambridge and Toronto: Cambridge University Press and the Macmillan Company, 1971).

"Canadian Economic Growth, 1870–1980," Discussion Paper No. 734, Institute for Economic Research, Queens University, Kingston, Ontario, November 1988.

Capital Accumulation, Technological Change, and Economic Growth, mimeograph, about 1953.

(with chapters by A.G. Green, Thomas Rymes, Marion Steel, and A.M. Sinclair, and contributions by D.M. McDougall and R.M. McInnes). *Gross National Product, Canada, 1870–1926: The Derivation of the Estimates* (Kingston: McGill-Queen's University Press, 1993).

"New Estimates of Gross National Product, Canada, 1870–1926: Some Implications for Canadian Development," in Stanley Engerman and Robert Gallman (eds.), *Long Term Factors in American Economic Growth*, National Bureau of Economic Research: Studies in Income and Wealth, Vol. 51 (Chicago: University of Chicago Press, 1986).

Urquhart, M.C., and K.A.H. Buckley. *Historical Statistics of Canada* (Cambridge: Cambridge University Press, 1965).

U.S. Department of Agriculture, Division of Statistics, Miscellaneous Services, Report No. 2, *Report on the Agriculture of South America* (Washington D.C.: GPO, 1892).

U.S. Department of Commerce, Bureau of the Census. *Historical Statistics of the United States, Colonial Times to 1970*, 2 vols. (Washington, D.C.: GPO, 1975).

Historical Statistics of the United States: Colonial Times to 1957 (Washington, D.C. GPO, 1960) Series A-195.

U.S. Department of State. *Commercial Relations of the United States, Reports from the Consuls of the United States on the Commerce, Manufactures, Etc. of Their Consular Districts*, No. 31, July 1883 (Washington, D.C.: GPO).

Van Oss, Salomon F. *Railroads as Investments* (New York: Arno Press, 1977).

Veenendaal, Augustus J. Jr. "The Kansas City Southern Railway and the Dutch Connection," *Business History Review*, Vol. 61, No. 2 (summer 1987).

Slow Train to Paradise: How Dutch Investment Helped Build American Railroads (Stanford, Calif.: Stanford University Press, 1996).

Ville, Simon. "Networks and Venture Capital in the Australasian Pastoral Sector Before World War II," *Business History*, Vol. 38, No. 3, July 1996.

"The Role of Agents in Australasian Economic Development Before World War II," paper delivered at a conference at the University of New England, 1994.

Viner, Jacob. *Canada's Balance of International Indebtedness, 1900–1913: An Inductive Study in the Theory of International Trade*, Harvard Economic Studies, Vol. XXVI (Cambridge, Mass.: Harvard University Press, 1924).

Wachtel, Paul, and Peter Rousseau. "Financial Intermediation and Economic Growth: A Historical Comparison of the U.S., U.K., and Canada," Paper presented at the New York University Salomon Center, Leonard N. Stern School of Business, Conference on *Anglo-American Finance: Financial Markets and Institutions in 20th-Century North America and the U.K.*, December 10, 1993.

Wall Street Journal, February 27, 1995.

Ward, Tony. "The Origins of the Canadian Wheat Boom, 1880–1910," *Canadian Journal of Economics*, Vol. XXVII, No. 4 (October 1990).

Warren, George F., and Frank A. Pearson. *Gold and Prices* (New York: Garland Publishing, 1983); first published 1935.

Watson, Katherine. "Banks and Industrial Finance: The Experience of Brewers, 1880–1913," *The Economic History Review*, Vol. XLIX, No. 1 (February 1996).

"The New Issue Market as a Source for Finance for the UK Brewing and Iron and Steel Industries, 1870–1913," in Youseff Cassis, Gerald D. Feldman, and Ulf Olsson (eds.), *The Evolution of Financial Markets and Institutions in Twentieth-Century Europe* (Aldershot, U.K., and Brookfield, Vt.: Scolar Press and Ashgate Publishing Company, 1995).

Watson, N.L. *Argentine as a Market* (Manchester: Manchester University Press, 1908).

Weiner, John M. "The United Kingdom" in David Spray (ed.), *The Principal Stock Exchanges of the World: Their Operation, Structure and Development* (Washington, D.C.: International Economic Publishers, 1964).

Wellons, Philip A. "International Debt: The Behavior of Banks in a Politicized Environment," *International Organization*, Vol. 39, No. 3 (summer 1995).

Westerfield, Ray B. *Banking Principles and Practice*, chapter XV (New York: Ronald Press Company, 1924).

"Historical Survey of Branch Banking in the United States," American Economists Council for the Study of Branch Banking, 1939.

Whelpley, James D. *Trade Development in Argentina*, Special Agent Series, No. 43, Dept. of Commerce and Labor (Washington, D.C.: GPO, 1911).

White, Eugene N. "Banking and Finance in the Twentieth Century: The Domestic Financial Sector," in Stanley Engerman and Robert Gallman (eds.), *The Cambridge Economic History of the United States. Vol. III: The Twentieth Century* (Cambridge: Cambridge University Press, 2000).

The Regulation and Reform of the American Banking System, 1900–1929 (Princeton: Princeton University Press, 1983).

White, Lawrence J. "Structure of Finance in Selected Asian Economies," in Shahid N. Zahid (ed.), *Financial Sector Development in Asia* (Hong Kong: Oxford University Press, 1995).

Wigmore, Barrie E. *The Crash and Its Aftermath: A History of Securities Markets in the United States, 1929–1933* (Westport, Conn.: Greenwood Press, 1985).

Wilkins, Mira. *The Emergence of Multinational Enterprise: American Business Abroad from the Colonial Era to 1914*, Harvard Studies in Business History, Vol. XXXIV (Cambridge, Mass.: Harvard University Press, 1970).

"'Flows Do Not Stock Make': Guidelines for Determining the Level of Long Term Foreign Investments in the United States – Methodological Quandaries in Handling Pre-1914 Data," Mimeograph, 1986.

"The Free-Standing Company, 1870–1914: An Important Type of British Foreign Direct Investment," *Economic History Review*, Second Series, Vol. XLI, No. 2 (1988).

The History of Foreign Investment in the United States to 1914, Harvard Studies in Business History, Vol. XLI (Cambridge, Mass.: Harvard University Press, 1989).

"Japanese Multinational Enterprises Before 1914," *Business History Review*, Vol. 60 (summer 1986).

"Japanese Multinationals in the United States: Continuity and Change, 1879–1990," *Business History Review*, Vol. 64 (winter 1990).

ed. *The Growth of Multinationals* (Bookfield, Vt.: Edward Elgar, 1991).

Williams, John H. *Argentine International Trade Under Inconvertible Paper Money, 1880–1900*, Harvard Economic Studies, Vol. XXII (Cambridge, Mass.: Harvard University Press, 1920).

Williamson, Harold, and Orange Smalley. *The Northwestern Mutual Life: A Century of Trusteeship* (Evanston, Ill.: Northwestern University Press, 1957).

Williamson, Jeffrey G. *American Growth and the Balance of Payments: A Study of the Long Swing* (Chapel Hill: University of North Carolina Press, 1962).

"The Evolution of Global Labor Markets in the First and Second World Since 1830: Background Evidence and Hypotheses," NBER/DAE Working Paper No. 36, February 1992.

"Globalization, Convergence, and History," *The Journal of Economic History*, Vol. 56, No. 2 (June 1996).

"Government Debt Management, Taxation, and Private Capital Formation, 1849–1878: Another Look at the Impact of the Civil War," Discussion Paper Series, Economic History, University of Wisconsin, Madison, March 1973.

Inequality, Poverty, and History: The Kuznets Memorial Lectures of the Economic Growth Center, Yale University (Oxford: Basil Blackwell, 1991).

Winslade, S. "Wire Fencing Investment in Eastern Australia: 1858–1914," *Australian Economic History Review*, Vol. XXXIV, No. 1 (March 1994).

Wood, Gordon. *Borrowing and Business in Australia: A Study of the Correlation Between Imports of Capital and Changes in National Prosperity* (New York: Arno Press, 1977).

Wood, R.J. *The Commercial Bank of Australia Limited: History of an Australian Institution* (North Melbourne, Victoria: Hargreen Publishing Company, 1990).

Woytinsky, W.S. and E.S. *World Commerce and Govenments* (New York, 1955).

Wright, J.F. "The Contribution of Overseas Savings to the Funded National Debt of Great Britain, 1750–1815," *The Economic History Review*, Vol. L, No. 4 (November 1997).

Wright, W.E. "Life Assurance Company Investments," *The Bankers Magazine*, Vol. 32 (1897).

Wyckoff, Peter. *Wall Street and the Stock Markets: A Chronology (1644–1971)* (Philadelphia: Chilton Book Company, 1982).

Yamamura, Kozo. "Entrepreneurship, Ownership, and Management in Japan," in Kozo Yamamura (ed.), *The Economic Emergence of Modern Japan* (Cambridge: Cambridge University Press, 1997).

Young, Ralph A. *A Handbook of American Underwriting of Foreign Securities*, U.S. Department of Commerce, Trade Promotion Series, No. 104 (Washington, D.C.: GPO, 1930).

Zacchia, Carlo. "International Trade and Capital Movements 1920–1970," in Carlo Cipolla (ed.), *The Twentieth Century* (New York: Harvester Press, 1977).

Zartman, Lester W. *The Investments of Life Insurance Companies* (New York: Henry Holt and Co., 1906).

INDEX

A.E. Ames and Company, 440
Acceptance market, of London, 129–130,
    803
Acopidores, 707
Act of 1828, 133
Act of 1863, 133
Act of 1891, 133
Act of 1896 (Japan), 892
Act Relating to Banks and Banking,
    410–412, 428
Adamson, Collier, & Chadwick, 171–172
Adelman, Jeremy, 707
Aetna, The, 290
Africa, British overseas investment in, 70t,
    71, 75t, 79t, 83t
Agency Land and Finance of Australia,
    539
Agri-Industrial Bank, 883, 892
Agricultural Bank of Western Australia,
    597
Agriculture
  in Argentina
    financing development of, 698t, 699,
        699t–705t, 706–708
    growth rate of, 649–651, 650t
  in Australia, 535, 538t
    during boom years, 489, 492, 495–
        497
    government subsidy of, 485–486,
        597–598
    during post-depression years, 513
  in Canada, 347–348, 349, 352, 385, 388,
    394
  capital called, in British capital markets,
    31t
Aitken, Max, 457, 460
Alexander Brown and Sons, 300–301
Alexanders, 130–131
Algoma Steel Company, 388
Alliance Insurance Company, 591
Amalgamated Zinc, 514
America: see North America; South
    America; United States
American Powder Trust, 392
American Republics Bureau, 689
American Screw Company, 392

Ames and Company, 456
Anaconda Copper, 331
Anglo-American Iron Company, 392, 395
Anglo-Argentine Mining Company, 710
Anglo-Australian Bank Ltd., 575
Anglo-Canadian Asbestos, 385
Anglo-Egyptian Bank, 178
Anglo-Italian Bank, 178
Argentina, 644–752
  appendices for, 723–752, 749
    capital formation in, domestic, real
        gross fixed
      conventional measurements of,
          724–729, 727t–729t
      unconventional components of,
          729–732, 730t–731t
    capital formation in, foreign
        contribution to, 735–743,
        736t–737t, 741t
    capital formation in, net, 743–745
    capital/output ratios, 747–749
      direct estimates, 749–752, 750t–751t
      for 1913, 748–749
      estimate based on net investment
          rate, 749
    inventory investment in, 732–735,
        733t–734t
    reestimation of GFCF series, 746–747,
        748t
    test of the estimates, 745–746, 747t
  Britain overseas investments in, 10,
    27t–33t, 35t
  British savers' link to domestic
      institutions in, 799–800
  capital flows to, 834t
  concluding summary of, 722–723
  economic change in, 649–665
    growth rate in, 649–654
      agriculture in, 649–651, 650t
      average annual, 650t
      depression on, 653–654
      GNP, by sector, 652t
      GNP, growth rate of, 653t
    population change in, 654–659
      immigration on, 655–659, 657t
      nationality mix and, 659t

964

native born *vs.* total, 656t
structural change in, 659–665
immigrants and, 661–662
by industrial sector, 1895 *vs.* 1914, 660t
by region, 661, 662t
transportation system and, 663–665
urban population and, 663, 665
financial intermediaries in, 665–694
banking system in, 23, 665–689
British banks and, 789–793
commercial banking in, 665–682, 789–793 (*see also under* Commercial banks)
government influence on, 908
mortgage banks in, 682–686, 683t
private banks in, 686–689
insurance companies in, 689–691, 800
stock exchange in, 692–694
financial markets of, 1914–1945, 845t
financing development in, 694–722
aggregates in, 694–699
calls on London capital market, in dollars, 700t–701t, 704t–705t
calls on London capital market, in percentages, 702t–703t, 704t
capital formation in, as a percent of domestic product, 695t
foreign capital, as percent of gross capital formation, 697t
foreign capital, British, 699t
foreign capital, by sector, 698t
GDP and capital/output ratios, 696t
the Argentine Republic in, 713–719, 762
borrowings of, 715t–717t
government securities yields of, 714t
cities in, 711–713
industry in, 708–711
railways in, 720–722
ranching and agriculture in, 698t, 699, 699t–705t, 706–708
foreign investment in, political response to, 822–825
GDP per capita, 1913–1994, 842t–844t
government issues of, 216
gross investment and trade balance in, 1914–1945, 845t, 847–849
inventory investment in, 732
rates of return in, 218
ratio of financial assets to GNP in, 668–776, 770t, 773, 775t
savings rate in, 20
World War I on, 841
Argentine Bank of the Nation, 673

Argentine Estates of Bovril, 708
Argentine Iron and Steel Company, 710
Argentine Land Companies, 708
Argentine Meat Preserving Company, 710
Argentine Refinery, 710, 711
Argentine Sugar Estate and Factories, 708
Argentine Tobacco, 711
Argus, 611
Armstrong, Christopher, 437, 440
on bond underwriting, 461
Armstrong Committee, 286, 310
Arthur Grenfell, 631
Arthur Grenfell's Canadian Agency, 170, 601
Ashmead, Edward, 258–259
Ashurst, Morris and Company, 171
Asia
British overseas investment in, 63–65, 70t, 73t, 77t, 81t–82t
NICS in, 1996–1999, 910–925
Asian crisis of, 918–924
conclusions from, 924–925
introduction to, 910–913
liberalization of the 1980s and 1990s on, 913–918
Associates, 16
Association of Banks of Melbourne, 507
Asymmetric information, 755–756, 814–817
August Belmont & Company, 301
Australasian Insurance and Banking Review, 553–554, 557–558, 562, 574, 816
Australia, 471–643
British capital market and, institutional ties to, 626–640, 777–780, 778t–779t
Australian new issues in London, 629t
government sector and, 628, 630–632
private sector and, 633–640
routes to, 627t
British overseas investments in, 9–10, 27t–33t, 35t, 65, 70t, 74t, 78t
British savers' link to domestic institutions in, 798–799
capital market evolution in, 544–626
capital flows to, 834t
introduction to, 544–545
non-bank intermediaries in, 567–598, 836t
building societies in, 573–575
depression on, 569–570, 596–597
government encouragement of, 597–598

Australia *(cont.)*
life insurance companies in,
581–583, 590–591
life insurance company assets in, in
percentages, 587t–589t
life insurance company assets in, in
pounds, 584t–586t
life insurance company portfolio
mix, in percentages, 594t–595t
life insurance company portfolio
mix, in pounds, 592t–593t
mortgage banks in, 575–576
pastoral finance companies in,
576–578, 580t, 581
savings banks in, assets and
liabilities of, 568t
savings banks in, government-
related, 569–572
securities markets in, formal, 598–626
(*see also under* Securities
markets)
primary, 599–609
secondary, 609–626
trading banks in, 545–567, 836t
branch system of, 548–549
British investment in, 560t–561t,
564–566
deposit insurance and, 562–564,
809–811
foreign assets of, 556–559, 562
imperial banks in, 545–547
land boom collapse on, 564–567,
784–785
number of, 547t
real estate lending of, 550–555,
784–785, 828
Scottish system and, 545, 828
concluding summary of, 640–643
financial markets of, 1914–1945, 846t
foreign investment in, political response
to, 817–819
GDP per capita, 1913–1994, 842t–844t
gross investment, foreign capital flows
and savings in, 1914–1936, 846t,
847–849
gross national product of, 472, 473t, 489,
490t–491t, 513, 542
financial asset ratio to, 668–776, 770t,
773, 775t
historical background of, 473–517
boom years, 489–502
British investment and, 502
construction sector in, 498–500
growth sectors in, 495
industrial sector in, 497–498
pastoral sector in, 489, 492, 495–497

transport sector in, 500–502
capital formation in, 492t–494t
depression years, 502–513
banks and, 506–513
British investment and, 502–503
building societies and, 505–506
private *vs.* public sector in, 503
warnings of, 504–505
government role in, 473–489, 901–902
"colonial socialism" and, 479–483
colonial *vs.* local government in,
476–479
investment efficiency and, 483–489
per capita debt and, 473
public *vs.* private sectors and,
474–476
railroads and, 762
post-depression years, 513–517
income, savings, investment, and foreign
finance in, 517–544
agriculture in, 525, 538t
capital created and called on British
markets
in dollars, 526t–527t
by industry, in dollars, 532t–533t,
534t, 536t
by industry, per capita, 530t–531t,
535t, 537t
in percentages, 528t–529t,
534t–535t, 536t–537t
capital formation in, 522–523
extractive industry in, 525, 538–539,
538t
financial sector in, 539, 542
government new issues in, 540t–541t
gross domestic product in, 518t–519t
in percentages, 520t–521t
in pounds, 518t–519t
industrial sector in, 542–544
state government role in, 524–525
utility companies in, 542
introduction to, 471–472, 473t
Matsukata banking model in, 900
pastoral sector defaults and, 811–814
rates of return in, 216, 218
savings banks in, 19, 22–23
savings rates on, 21
World War I on, 841
Australian and Oriental Coal Ltd., 544
Australian Cities Investment Company,
539
Australian Coking and By Products, 544
Australian Colonial and General Life
Assurance, 582
Australian Deposit and Mortgage Bank
Ltd., 575

Australian Estate and Mortgage Company, 539
Australian Extract of Meat and Cattle Company, 543
Australian Financial Agency and Guarantee Company, 604
Australian Freehold Banking Corporation Ltd., 559, 575, 634, 816
Australian General Assurance Company, 582
Australian Joint Stock Bank, 512, 539
Australian Meat and Agency, 543
Australian Meat Importation Company, 543
Australian Mercantile Land and Finance Company, 577, 578
    United Kingdom agents of, 635
Australian Mining, 538
Australian Mortgage Land and Finance Company, 539, 577, 633, 636
Australian Mutual Building Society, 634, 816
Australian Mutual Provident Society, 582, 590
Australian Temperance and General, 590
Automobile manufacturers, 194

Bagehot, Walter, 158
Bahia Blanca Gas Company, 712
Bailey's investment policy, 147
Baker, 647–649
Baker, George F., 305, 308–309
Balance of payments
    in United States, 245–248, 247t
Balboa, Manuel, 725, 729, 730t–731t, 732
Balfour, Williamson, and Company, 259
Balke, Nathan S., 344
Banco Carabassa, 679
Banco Cremi, 907
Banesa, 904
Bank Act of 1927 (Japan), 886
Bank Charter Act of 1844, 108
Bank for International Settlements, 866
The Bank for Savings, 282
Bank of Australasia, 539, 545–546, 548, 549, 551, 552
    in new issues market, 599
Bank of British Columbia, 342, 389, 415, 777
Bank of British North America, 409, 411
Bank of Buenos Aires, 665, 666t, 675
    assets and liabilities of, 677t
    dividend rate of, 676t
Bank of Commerce, 440

Bank of England
    as Australian bank agent, 632
    as Australian government's agent, 609, 783
    on British commercial paper markets, 128
    on commercial bank reserve requirements, 119–120
    gold standard and, 336
    in House of Barings crisis, 2–3
    note issue monopoly of, 107
    underwriting activities of, 175, 179
Bank of Italy, 688
Bank of Japan, 882–883, 894, 898, 899
    central bank role of, 890–891
    guarantees of, 885
Bank of Korea, 899
Bank of Montreal, 177, 374, 405, 406, 409, 413, 457, 601, 780
    branch operations of, 415, 776–780
    dominance of, 440
    London agency of, 782
    market share of, 416
    underwriting of, 419–420
Bank of New Brunswick, 405
Bank of New South Wales, 513, 552, 553, 555, 565–566
    London representative of, 631, 782
Bank of North America, 373, 413
Bank of North Queensland, 558
Bank of Nova Scotia, 414, 415, 429
Bank of Rio de la Plata, 688
Bank of Taiwan, 899
Bank of the Nation, 672–673, 675, 679
    agricultural finance and, 707
    assets and liabilities of, 677t
    failure and reconstruction of, 789
    loans of, 680, 681t
Bank of the Province of Buenos Aires, 679, 681t
    agricultural finance and, 707
    failure and reconstruction of, 789
Bank of Tokyo, 895
Bank of Upper Canada, 405, 408–409, 901
Bank of Victoria, 546
The Bankers', Insurance Managers', and Agents' Magazine, 473, 562, 563–564, 810
    on Barings crisis of 1890, 152
Bankers Trust, 298, 309
Banking Act of 1871 (Canada), 780, 828
Banking centers, international, 872
Banks, commercial: see Commercial banks
Barclays Bank, 111
Barger, Harold, 343
Baring Brothers, 301, 305, 420, 782, 815

Barings Bank, 1–3
  in American markets, 331, 334
  Guiness securities and, 260
  in London acceptance market, 130
  as underwriters, 167–168, 177
Barings Crisis of 1890, 117
  on Argentina
    bank failures, 674–675
    bond yields, 713
    cedulas, 685–686
    debt of, 718–719, 720
    growth rates, 654, 698–699
  on Australia, 503, 600, 604
  on investment trusts, 152
  on underwriting markets, 179
Barnett, George, 297
Beaverbrook, Lord, 457
Becker, Gary, 920–921
Belgium, World War I on, 851–852
Belgrano Blanca Gas Company, 712
Bell Telephone of Canada, 389
Bethlehem Steel, 260
Bliss, George, 304
Blyn, Martin R., 310
Boehm, E.A., 505
Bolsa of Commerce, 692–694, 799
Bonds
  Argentine government, 714, 714t–717t,
    718–719
  Australian government, 599–600
  Canadian underwriting of, 454–466,
    469–470, 796–797
  New York market for, 855–856
Boot, H.M., 509
Bordo, Michael, 116
Boskin, Michael, 47
Boston Associates, 305
Boston Stock Exchange, 306
Bottomly, Horatio, 173, 639
Bowery Bank, 282
Brady, Alexander, 480
Brady, Dorothy, 343
Branch banking
  in Argentina, 674
  in Australia, 548–549
  of British commercial banks, 776–780,
    778t–779t
  in Canada, 413–416, 776–777
  in United States, 266–267, 271–272,
    785–786, 830
Brandt Bank, in London acceptance
    market, 130
Brazilian Canadian and General Trust
    Company, 170
Bretton Woods era, on frontier economies,
    862–869

Brewing, 260, 335, 615
Brezis, Elise, 50
Britain: *see also* United Kingdom
  capital market evolution in
  history and current events in, 1–3
  overseas investments in frontier
    countries and, 5–6, 9–10, 19–25,
    34–35
    agricultural and extractive capital
      called, 31t
    in Australia, 472
    finance capital called, 29t
    government capital called, 30t
    manufacturing and commercial
      capital called, 28t
    public utility capital called, 33t
    total capital called, 27t
    transport capital called, 32t
  foreign investment into, 51
  savings in
    and Canadian investments, 355
    during Industrial revolution, 15–16, 51
British Bank of Australia, 575
British Bank of North America, 429
British Bank of South America, 678
  assets and liabilities of, 677t
  dividend rate of, 676t
British Empire Trust, 170
British Foreign & Colonial Corporation,
    170
British Gross National Product, 56, 57t
British West Indies, 347
Broken Hill Proprietary, 514, 607
  securities of, 626
Brown, Shipley & Co., 301, 764
Buckley, Kenneth, 465–466
Buena Tierra Mining Company, 710
Bueno Consols Company, 710
Buenos Aires City, 718
Buenos Aires Harbor Works, 712
Buenos Aires securities exchange,
    692–694, 799
Buenos Ayres Gas Company, 712
Buenos Ayres Grain Elevators, 712
Building and loan societies
  in Australia, 573–575
    during depression years, 505–506
  in Canada, 422–423, 424t–425t, 433–436
  in United Kingdom, 136
  in United States, 298–300, 424t–425t
Bunge, A.E., 743, 745, 747
Bunge and Born, 688, 711
Burdett's, 166
Burns, Walter H., 304
Burton, T.E., 154
Butlin, Noel, on Australia, 472

capital formation in, 474, 487
Colonial Socialism in, 479–480, 481–482
housing sector in, 498–499

C. Unger and Company, 422
C.W. Morgan & Company, 158
Caledonian and Australian Mortgage and
Agency, 539
California Oilfields, Ltd., 259
Call system, on Melbourne Stock
Exchange, 621
Cameron Brothers, 543
Canada, 345–369
bond houses in, 796–797
Britain overseas investments in, 27t–33t,
35t, 359
British savers' link to domestic
institutions in, 795–798
capital markets in, 398–470
capital flows to, 835t
chartered banks in, growth of,
399–418, 836t
1820–1920, 413t
An Act Relating to Banks and
Banking on, 410–412
asset growth of, 399t
Bank of Upper Canada failure on,
408–409
branch banking and, 413–416,
776–777
British North America Act of 1867
on, 410
early development of, 405–408
loan structure of, 416–418, 780–781
as London agents, 782
private intermediary assets in,
401t
Scottish precedents in, 405, 776–777
stability of, 418
vs. United States banks, 400t, 402t,
404, 412
chartered banks in, security markets
and, 418–421
non-bank intermediaries in, 421–470,
424t–425t, 836t
building societies, 433–436
introduction to, 421–426
life insurance companies, 430–433,
797–798
long-term loans and, 909–910
mortgage and loan companies,
433–436
savings banks, 426–430
securities markets, 436–466, 467t
(*see also* Securities market)
summary of, 466–470

financial markets of, 1914–1926, 847t
foreign investment in, 362–398
American, 390–396
in 1909 and 1913, 392t
direct, 391t
total, 392t
British, 9, 27t–33t, 35t, 359, 372–390,
466, 470
called on British capital markets, by
sector, 384t
called on British capital markets, in
dollars, 379, 380t–381t, 386t–387t
called on British capital markets,
per capita, 379, 382t–383t
direct, 377, 378t
industrial distribution of, 376t
European, 396–398, 396t, 398t
political response to, 819–822
temporal pattern of, 362–372
in balance of payments, 366t–367t
in stock of foreign investment,
364t–365t, 370t–371t
GDP per capita, 1913–1994, 842t–844t
gross investment, foreign capital flows
and savings in, 1914–1926,
847–849, 847t
gross national product of, 350t–352t,
353–355, 466, 468
from 1897–1914, 352t, 357–358
by sector, 427t
overview of
growth patterns, 1867–1896, 349–355,
351t, 352t
growth patterns, 1867–1914, 345–347,
350t, 356t
growth patterns, 1897–1914, 357–358
growth patterns, before 1867, 347–349
institutional environment, 358–362
population of, native born *vs.* total, 656t
rates of return in, 216–217
savings banks in, 19, 20–21, 22
savings in, 355, 356t, 362
World War I on, 841
Canada Assurance Company, 430
Canada Cement, 450
Canada Copper Company, 392
Canada Life Assurance Company,
430–431, 432–433, 440, 441
Canada Switch and Spring, 388
Canadian Agency, of Arthur Grenfell, 170
Canadian Bank of Commerce, 177, 374,
414, 429–430, 449
branch operations of, 415
call and short term loans of, 458
London agency of, 782
market share of, 416

Canadian Cattle Company, 385
Canadian Confederation, 345–347
Canadian Copper Company, 395
Canadian General Electric, 443
Canadian Grand Trunk Railway, 832
Canadian Pacific Railway Company, 353,
     361, 379, 384, 451
  Bank of Montreal and, 420
Canadian Petroleum Company, 385
Canadian River System, 349
Capie, Forest, 107, 111, 113–114, 115, 117
Capillitas Copper Company, 710
Capital markets: *see also under* specific
     countries, e.g. Australia
  Bretton Woods era on, 862–869
  evolution of, 1–49, 762–763
     Britain and four frontier countries in,
        19–25
     British long-term capital transfers in,
        25–35, 27t–33t, 35t
     capital accumulation and mobilization
        in, 8–19
     capital market formation in, 3–8
     concluding summary of, 35–41
     history and current events in, 1–3
     saving and investing decisions in,
        42–49, 200, 204
  and global economy, 1970s to 1990s,
     869–874
  institutional innovation in (*see*
     Institutional change)
  interwar period on, 856–862
Capital mobility, 870–871
Capital stock, World War I on, 851–852
CAPS (*certificados de aportacion
     patrimonial*), 905
Carnegie, Andrew, 329
Carosso, Vincent P., 306–307
Carter-Crume, 450
Castlemaine Brewery, 615
Catalinas Warehouse and Mole of Buenos
     Ayres, 712
Cattle industry, in Argentina, 651
CCM, 450
Cedulas, 684–686, 711, 793, 799, 800
Central Argentine Land Company, 708
Central Canada Savings and Loan, 456
Central Cash Office for Small Commercial
     and Industrial Associations, 899
Central Produce Market of Buenos Ayres,
     712
Central Queensland Meat Preserving
     Company, 543
Certificados de aportacion patrimonial
     (CAPS), 905
Chadwick, Adamson, and Collier, 339

Citizens Life Assurance Company Ltd.,
     590
City Mutual Life Assurance Society Ltd.,
     590
City of Glasgow Bank, 117, 119, 633–634
City of London, secondary bill market of,
     130
City of Melbourne Bank, 512, 557
City of Melbourne Building Society, 575
City of Sydney Bank, 558
Civil War (American)
  on capital flows, 246, 249
  foreign financing of, 332
  on investment banking, 301
Clark, J.M., 857
Clark & Company, 613
Clark & Dodge, 301
Clarke, William, 559, 562, 607, 634, 816
Clearing house, for London Stock
     Exchange, 188–189
Clews, Henry, 274–275
Coates, John, 543
Collateral-based loans, *vs.* overdrafts,
     112–113
Collins, Michael, 114–115
  on British commercial banks, 107
  on British commercial paper markets,
     128
Colonial Gold Mining Co., 390
Colonial Investment and Agency
     Company, Ltd., 575
Colonial Securities, 389
"Colonial socialism," in Australia, 479–483
Colonial Stocks Act, 176
Commercial Bank of Australia, 506, 507,
     510, 513, 539, 553, 574
Commercial Bank of Manitoba, 389
Commercial Banking Company of Sydney,
     548
Commercial banks
  in Argentina, 665–682
     as of 1912, 666t
     assets and liabilities of, 677t
     dividend rates of, 676t
     failures of, 674–675
     foreign involvement in, 665–671, 674,
        679–680
     German Transatlantic Bank in,
        668t–669t
     growth of, 675–678, 678t
     lending activity of, 681t
     London and Brazil Bank in, 670t
     overdraft facility of, 671–673
     primary, 680t
     reserves of, 673
  in Asian NICS

before 1980, 911–913
during 1980s to 1990s, 913–918
in Australia, 545–567
branch system of, 548–549
British investment in, 560t–561t,
564–566
deposit insurance and, 562–564
foreign assets of, 556–559, 562
imperial banks in, 545–547
land boom collapse on, 564–567
number of, 547t
real estate lending of, 550–555
Scottish system and, 545
in frontier economies institutional
change, 776–793, 778t–779t (*see
also under* Institutional change
and development)
in Mexico, 904–907
in United Kingdom (*see under* United
Kingdom, financial sector
growth)
in United States, 262–278
branch banking and, 266–267,
271–272, 785–786
vs. British banks, 262, 266
commercial paper market and,
273–276, 804–807
correspondent system of, 276–278
international opportunities and,
262–263
loan length of, 265–266, 338
mortgage lending and, 263–264
numbers of, 268t–269t
by region, 270t
state banks and, 273–276
total assets of, 268t–269t
trust companies and, 298
Commercial Cable, 450
Commercial law, in Argentina, 709–710
Commercial paper markets
in United Kingdom, 127–131
in United States, 273–276, 804–807
Commissioners' Savings Banks of Victoria,
570–571, 572
Commonwealth Bank of Australia, 516,
542, 548, 607
Compania de Electricidad de la Pronincia
de Buenos Ayres, 713
Compania Hidro-Electricia de Tucuman,
713
Companies Act of 1856 and 1862, 198
Conde, Cortes, 725, 732, 733, 749
Confederation Life, 431
Confidence, in U. S. dollar, 866–868
Consolidated Stock and Petroleum
Exchange, 321–322

Consolidated Water Works of Rosario,
712
Consols, debt market in, 120–121
Continental Banking and Trust Company
of Panama, 296
Cooke, Jay, 300, 301–302, 307–308
Cooper, Richard, 868
Copper boom, in New South Wales, 602
Cottrell, Phillip, 113, 114
on British securities markets, 160–161
on insurance company liquidity, 150
Cox, George C., 440, 441, 456
Credit Foncier and Mobilier, 154, 674
"Crony capitalism"
in Asian NICS, 921
in Latin America, 908–909
in United States, 900–901
Cronyn, Hume, 436
Crown Agents, 175–176, 177, 631, 632
Cunard Line, 633
Curamalon Land Company, 708
Currency, in Argentina, 685, 789

David, Paul, 44
Davies, Matthew, 505
Davis, Lance, 14–15, 58–59, 375–377, 376t,
689, 739, 743
on British capital markets, 253t–255t
on British stockholders, 198–199, 199t,
223
on savings banks, 283
Davison, Henry, 309
Dawson City Telegraph Company, 389
Deacon, F.H., 457
Delacres's Extract of Beef, 710
della Paolera, 743
DeLong, Bradford, 15
on British domestic rates of return, 209,
221, 222–223, 226t
Department of Commerce, 343
Deposit insurance, in Australia, 562–564,
809–811
Depreciation, of Argentine currency, 685
Depression
in Argentina, 1873–1879, 646, 653–654
in Australia, 502–513
banks and, 506–513
British investment and, 502–503
building societies and, 505–506
on non-bank intermediaries, 569, 572,
596–597
private *vs.* public sector in, 503
warnings of, 504–505
of 1930's, causes of, 857–862
Derwent Bank, 556–557
Devaluation, of U. S. dollar, 867–868

Developing economies: *see also* Frontier economies
  capital market evolution in, 14–16
Development Company of Santa Fe, 708
Devoto, 688
Diaz Alejandro, Carlos F., 724–725, 728, 747
Dillon, Clarence, 311, 788
Dillon, Read & Co., 788
Discount houses, British, 130–131, 337, 802
Dominion Brewery, 164
Dominion Bridge, 450
Dominion Canners, 450
Dominion Cotton Company, 164, 388
Dominion Securities Corporation, 457, 460, 797
Dominion Steel, 451
Dominion Textile, 451
Drew, Daniel, 313
Drexel & Co., 301, 304
Drexel Morgan, 764
Drummond, Ian, 421–422, 437, 445
  on Australian capital formation, 474
  on bond underwriting, 455, 461, 465, 829
Ducan, Sherman & Co., 304
Dunlop Pneumatic Tyre Company, 607
Dunlop Tire, 450, 456
Dunn, John H., 443, 451–452
Dunn Fisher & Company, 458–459
Dunning, John H., 249–250

E.L. & Baillieu, 606–607
Eagle Hawk Consolidated Gold Mining, 538
Earthquake bills, 885
East India Company, 175
The Economist, 713
  on Australian socialism, 517
  on dummy brokers, 188
  on investment trust portfolios, 152
  on Southeast Asia GDP, 875
  on United States railroad financing, 786–787
Edelstein, Michael, 11–12, 45
  on British commercial banks, 107
  on British domestic rates of return, 209, 221–223
  on British foreign investment, in United States, 251
  on United States savings rates, 245
Edgar, E. Mackay, 457
Egerton, Jones & Simpson, 170
Eichengreen, Barry, 14
Ekitei, 891
Electric Light and Power Supply Company, 514

Electrical Power Source Development Company, 900
Empire Trust Company, 296
English, Scottish and Australian Chartered Bank, 539, 546, 548
English and Australian Copper, Ltd., 543
Enterprises Rationalization Act, 899
Entre Rios Extract of Meat Company, 710
Equitable Insurance, 145, 310
  tontine insurance and, 285–286
Equitable Trust Company, 296
Eurodollars, 865–866
Europe
  British overseas investments in, 74t–75t, 78t–79t, 82t–83t
  Canadian investments of, 396–398, 396t, 398t
Exchange Coffee House, 446
Export Finance Bank, 895
Export-Import Bank of Japan, 878
Extractive industries
  in Australia, 514, 515, 525, 538–539, 538t
    stock exchange listings and, 611–613, 637–639
  in Canada, 385, 388, 395
  capital called, in British capital markets, 31t
  in United States, 258–259, 335

Falconer, J.J., 548–549
Farmers Loan and Trust Company, 296
Fatima Development Company, 710
Federal Bank of Australia, 557, 574
Federal Reserve Act (U. S.), 263, 264
  on commercial paper market, 807
  on financial shift from London to New York, 855
Federal Reserve Bank, 806
  pre-depression policies of, 859–861
Federal Steel Company, 306
Feinstein, Charles H., 853
Ferns, Henry Stanley, 713
Field, Fred W., 374, 375t, 377, 396–397
Finance capital called, in British capital markets, 29t
Finance companies, as nonbank intermediaries, 150–151
Financial assets/GNP ratio, 768–776, 770t, 773t, 775t
Financial intermediaries: *see* Intermediaries, financial
Financial intermediation ratio, 261–262, 261t
Financial interrelations ratio, 261–262, 261t
Fire insurance, 144
  in Canada, 430–431

First National Bank of Chicago, 298, 305–306
First National Bank of New York, 305
First Trust and Savings, 298
Fishlow, Albert, 39, 40
Ford, A.G., 732, 739
Ford Motors, 395
Foreign and Colonial Government Trust, 152–153
Foreign Exchange and Transactions Control Law, 877
Foreign government loans, British underwriting of, 177
Forget, F.J., 457
Fortier vs. New Orleans National Bank, 264
Foster & Braithwaite, 171
Fracchia, Alberto, 725, 729, 730t–731t, 732
France
    Canadian investments of, 396–398, 396t
    World War I on, 851–852
Frankel, Jeffrey, 870–871
Free Banking Act of 1850, 405, 408
Freehold Permanent Building Society, 434
Friedman, Milton, 11
Frontier economies, 5–6, 9–10, 19–25; *see also* Institutional change and development; specific countries, e.g., United States
    British commercial banks and, 776–793, 778t–779t (*see also under* Institutional change and development)
    capital flows to, 834t–835t
    financial markets of, 1914–1990, 839–874
    Argentina in, 1914–1945, 845t
    Australia in, 1914–1945, 846t
    Canada in, 1914–1926, 847t
    GDP per capita in, 842t–844t, 847–850
    global economy period on, 1970–1990s, 869–874
    interwar period on, 856–862
    introduction to, 839–841
    World War I on, 850–856
    World War II and Bretton Woods era on, 862–869
    investment return rates in, 209–233
    political response to foreign investment in, 817–827 (*see also under* Institutional change and development)
    ratio of financial assets to GNP in, 768–776, 770t, 773t, 775t
Frost, Lionel, 480–481
Fungoid Banks, 573

Gallman, Robert, 375–377, 376t
    on Argentina, 743, 743t
    on British capital markets, 252, 253t–255t
    on United States railroad investment, 252
Ganz, Alexander, 729, 745, 746
General Credit Company, 130
General Electric, 260, 395
    of Canada, 443
General Film Company of Australia, 514
George, Eddie, 2
George Rose's Act, 132
German Transatlantic Bank, 667
    in Argentina, 668t–669t
    assets and liabilities of, 677t
    balance sheet of, 668t–669t
    dividend rate of, 676t
    growth of, 675
Germany
    investments in Canada, 396–398, 396t
    investments in United States, 250–251, 332
    World War I on, 852
Gershenkron, Alexander, 14
    on British commercial banks, 93, 106
Gibbs, Ronald & Company, 552
Gibbs Bank, in London acceptance market, 130
Gillan, Reverend, 48
Glasgow Exchange, 182
Glasgow Gympie Gold Mine, 538
Glasgow Murchison Gold Mine Development, 525
Glass-Steagal Act, 901
Global economy, 1970s to 1990s, 869–874
Glyn, Mills, Currie & Co., 420, 601, 782, 815
Gold Board, 314
Gold standard, 858–859
    Bretton Woods and, 863
    U. S. dollar and, 866–868
Goldman, Marcus, 303
Goldman, Sachs, 303, 311, 340, 788
Goldsbrough Mort & Company, 505, 581
Goldsmith, Raymond, 11, 12–13
    on financial innovation hypothesis, 47
    on foreign capital in United States, 237–238, 248
    on ratio of financial assets to GNP, 768–769, 771
Golondrinas, 657–658
Goodhart, C.A.E., 118
Goodyear, 395
Gordon, Harry Panmure, 171
Gordon, Robert J., 344

Government capital, called in British capital markets, 30t
Government issues
  of Argentina, 713–719
    borrowings of, 715t–717t
    yields on, 714t
  Australian, 482, 540t–541t, 599–601
  British investor viewpoint on, 760–761
  United States
    British view of, 760–761
    foreign held, 255–256
    Jay Cooke & Co. in, 301
    yields of, 212t
Government Savings Bank (Australia), 572
Government Savings Bank of New South Wales, 597
Grand Trunk, 379, 384
  securities of, 359
Grant, Albert, 154
Gray, A.C., 590
Great Western Railroad, 359, 379, 394
Green, Edwin, 113
Grenfell, Arthur, 170, 443, 601, 767
Gresham's Law, in Argentina, 647
Griffith, Brian, 114
Grimwood, E.L., 610
Gross national product (GNP)
  of Argentina, 649–654, 723–732
    average annual rates of, 650t, 653t
    by sector, 652t
  of Asian NICS, 910–911
  of Australia, 472, 473t, 489, 490t–491t, 513
  of Britain, 56, 57t
  of Canada, 350t–352t, 353–355, 466, 468
    from 1897–1914, 352t, 357–358
    by sector, 427t
  financial asset ratios and, 768–776, 770t, 773t, 775t
  of frontier economies, per capita 1914–1990, 842t–844t
  great depression on, 861
  of United States, 342–344
Grossman, S., 209, 221, 222–223, 226t
Growth rates
  in frontier economies, 6–7, 7t
  in United Kingdom 1870–1914, 56, 58t
Guarantee Trust Company, 296, 309
Guiness, 260

H. Osbourne O'Hagen, 340
Hall, A.R., 618
  on Australian issues on London Stock Exchange, 639
  on British investors, 195

  on insurance overseas investments, 148
Halsey, Frederick M., 713
Halsey, N.W., 308
Halsey, Stuart and Co., 308, 788
Hambro Bank, in London acceptance market, 130
Hamilton, Alexander, 35–36
  Canadian banking and, 406
Hanson Brothers, 457
Harris, Forbes & Co., 308, 788
Harris, N.W., 308
Harris & Company, 459
Harrod's, 712
Hatton Court, 171
Henry Clews & Company, 274–275
Henry Villard, 602
Herald, 620
Hogarth Australian Meat Preserving Co., 543
Hokkaido Development Bank, 883, 892, 894, 895, 899
Holland, United States investments of, 250–251
Holmes, A.R., 113
Homer, Sydney, 713
Hong Kong and Shanghai Banking Corporation, 125
Hong Kong Banking Company, 178
Hooley, Ernest T., 173
House of Baring, 1–3; *see also* Barings Bank; Barings Crisis of 1890
  Argentine financing of, 714
  and crisis of 1890, 117
Hudson's Bay Company, 347
Hughes, John R.T., 481, 850
Huttenback, Robert, 58–59
  on British stockholders, 198–199, 199t
Hyde, Henry B., 285–286
Hypothec Bank, 883, 892, 893, 894, 895

Immigration
  to Argentina, 655–659, 657t
  to Australia, 498–499
  to Canada, 347, 352, 353
Imperial Australian Wine Company, 543
Imperial Bank, 414
Imperial Bank of British Columbia, 373
Imperial Banking Company, Ltd., 575, 596
Imperial Life, 440
Imperial Tobacco of Canada, 388
Indonesia, 913–914; *see also* Asia, NICS in
Industrial Bank of Japan, 883, 893, 894, 895, 899
Industrial Bank of Japan Act of 1900, 892–893
Industrial insurance, 144–145

in Australia, 583, 590
in United States, 286–287
Industrial revolution
  British financing of, 50
  British savings in, 15–16
Industrial sector
  in Argentina
    expansion of, 659–662, 660t
    financing development in, 708–711
  in Australia, 542–544
    during boom years, 497–498
    during post-depression years, 513–514
  British commercial bank financing of, 122–124
  in Canada, 349
  in United States, on savings-investment aggregates, 243–244
Inflation
  in Mexico, 906
  in 1920's, 858
Inland bills market, 801–806
Inland Revenue Service, 195
Inscribed stock, 630
  on London Stock Exchange, 557
Insider lending, in United States, 901
Institutional change and development, in frontier economies
  asymmetric information and, 814–817
  British commercial banks in, 776–793, 778t–779t
    Argentina and, 789–793
    branch networks of, 776–780, 778t–779t
    as London fiscal agents, 782–783
    real bills doctrine on, 780–781
    real estate lending and, 781–782, 784–785
    unit banking and, 785–786
    United States and, 786–789
  British savers' link to domestic institutions in, 793–800
    in Argentina, 799–800
    in Australia, 798–799
    in Canada, 795–798
    in United States, 793–795
  conclusions from, 827–833, 834t–838t
  data in, 768–776
    financial assets to GNP, 770t
    financial intermediary asset distribution, 775t
    financial intermediary assets to GNP, 773t
  fragility and obsolescence in, 806–814
    Australian deposit insurance and, 809–811

Australian pastoral sector defaults and, 811–814
    London Stock Exchange and, 807–809
    United States commercial paper market and, 806–807
  inland bills market in, 801–806
  introduction to, 753–768
    British savers in, 754
    financial intermediaries in, 757–759
    government issues in, 760–763
    information asymmetries in, 755–757
    innovation process in, 767–768
    international interest rate convergence in, 754–755
    organizational innovation in, 765–767, 795
    transportation development in, 764–765
  political response to foreign investment and, 817–827
    in Argentina, 822–825
    in Australia, 817–819
    in Canada, 819–822
    in United States, 825–827
Insurance companies: *see also* Life insurance
  in Argentina, 689–691, 800
  as nonbank intermediaries, 133, 136–137, 144–150
    assets of, 138t–139t
    investment composition of, 142t–143t
Insurance Investigation Committee, 286
Inter Colonial Railway, 348–349
Interest rates
  of British commercial banks, 114–115
  of government issues, 212t
    Argentine, 714t
  international convergence of, 754–755
  in United States, decline of, 244
Intermediaries, financial: *see also* Commercial banks
  asset distribution among, 775t
  in Australia, 567–598
    building societies in, 573–575
    depression on, 596–597
    government encouragement of, 597–598
    life insurance companies in, 581–583, 590–591
    life insurance company assets in, in percentages, 587t–589t
    life insurance company assets in, in pounds, 584t–586t
    life insurance company portfolio mix, in percentages, 594t–595t

Intermediaries, financial *(cont.)*
  life insurance company portfolio mix,
      in pounds, 592t–593t
  mortgage banks in, 575–576
  pastoral finance companies in,
      576–578, 580t, 581
  savings banks in, assets and liabilities
      of, 568t
  savings banks in, government-related,
      569–572
  in Canada, 421–470, 424t–425t
      building societies, 433–436
      introduction to, 421–424
      life insurance companies, 430–433
      mortgage and loan companies,
          433–436
      savings banks, 426–430
      securities markets, 436–466, 467t *(see
          also* Securities market)
      summary of, 466–470
  institutional innovation and, 757–759
  on saving and investing decisions, 42–49
  in United Kingdom
      commercial banks in, 93–127, 94t–105t
          (see also under United Kingdom,
          financial sector growth)
      commercial paper markets in,
          127–131
      nonbank, 131–153, 134t, 135t,
          138t–143t
          finance companies, 150–151
          insurance companies, 133, 136–137,
              138t–143t, 144–150
          investment trusts, 151–153
          Post Office Banks, 131–132, 134t–135t
          Stock Departments, 133
          Trustee Savings Banks, 132–133,
              134t–135t
      overview of, 71, 92–93
          by continent, 72t–83t
          by financial institution, 84t–91t
      sterling bill markets in, 127–131
  in United States, non-bank, 278–300,
      424t–425t
      assets of, 280t–281t
      building and loan societies, 298–300
      introduction to, 278
      life insurance companies, 283–291
      savings and time deposits, 291–294
      savings banks, 279–283
      trust companies, 294–298
Intermediation, on savings-investment
      process, 42–49
  in Canada, 469
International Bank of Credit, 3
International Banking Corporation, 296

International finance, British commercial
      banks in, 125–127; *see also*
      United Kingdom
International Harvester, 306, 330, 395
International Investment Trust, 153
International Monetary Fund, in Bretton
      Woods era, 863–864, 869
Interwar period, on frontier economies,
      856–862
Investment Bankers Association, 310
Investment banking, in United States,
      300–312, 793–795
  vs. Britain, 336–337
  British saver and, 795
  commercial banks and, 308–309
  European financial connections and,
      300–301
  evolution of, 301, 828–829
  German-Jewish connection in, 302–304
  life insurance industry and, 309–310, 339
  manufacturing sector and, 306–307
  20th century developments in, 311–312
  underwriting syndicates in, 307–308
  Yankee houses in, 302, 304–306
Investment trusts, as nonbank
      intermediaries, 151–153
Investors, education of, 52, 463–464, 562,
      754, 764
Investor's Monthly Manual, 517
  on British domestic rates of return, 209
Ivanhoe Gold Corporation, 538

J. & W. Seligman, 303
J.B. Were and Son, 607
J.H. Dunn & Company, 458–459
J.H. Sherard Manufacturing, 388
J.P. Morgan, 304, 306, 312, 340, 602, 631,
      788, 814
  British connections of, 334
J.S. Morgan & Co., 304, 331
Jackson, R.V., 481
James, John, 13, 45–46, 272, 276
James Capel & Co., 171
Japan, 877–902
  banks in, 882–896
      government, 890–896
      private, 882–890
  financial infrastructure evolution in,
      880–882
  foreign investment of, 1960s to 1990s,
      38–39, 877–880
  government regulations in, 897–900
  historical lessons from, 900–902
  introduction to, 875–876
  securities exchange in, 896–897
Japan Development Bank Act, 895

Japan Export Finance Bank, 895
Japanese Development Bank, 891, 899, 902
Jarvis Conklin Mortgage Trust Company,
    296
Jay Cooke and Company, 300, 602, 787
    failures of, 301–302
    successes of, 301
Jay's Treaty, 347
Jobbers, 808
John Coates & Company, 543
John E. Thayer and Brother, 300–301
John Lysaght Limited, 543
Johns Manville, 395
Johnson, Joseph F., 399, 404, 417
    on Canadian interest rates, 777
    on mortgage and loan companies, 433
Joint-Stock Bank Act of 1826, 107–109,
    829
Joint-stock structure, of British industrial
    firms, 163
Jones, Charles A., 686
Joseph, L., 112
Josiah Mullens, 600
Joslin, David A., 669
Jusan, 889

Kangarilla Proprietary Silver Mine, 525
Keiretsu, 888
Kelly, Allen, 499
Kendrick, John, 343
Kennedy, William
    on British commercial banks, 106
    on British savers, 209
    on British securities markets, 158, 160,
        161
Keynes, John Maynard, 851–852
Khull, Edward, 611
Kidder, Peabody, 304–305, 334, 814
Kleinwort Bank, in London acceptance
    market, 130
Klondike Gold Reefs, 385
Knox, Frank, 362–363, 364t, 369
Korea, 911–912, 914–915; *see also* Asia,
    NICS in
Korean Development Bank, 899
Kroos, Herman E., 310
Krugman, Paul, 876
Kuhn, Abraham, 303
Kuhn, Loeb, 302, 334
Kuznets, Simon, 342–344, 732

L.P. Morton & Co., 304
La Forestal, 688
Lamoreaux, Naomi, 15
Lanarch, Donald, 631
Land Credit Bank of Australia, 575

Land development, 763–764
Land grants, 483
Land Mortgage Bank of Victoria, 505, 576
Land-related industries, 257–259; *see also*
    Agriculture; Ranching
    in Australia, 539
Land speculation
    in Argentina, 685
    in Australia, 499–500
    in Canada, 408–409, 901
Latin America, 902–910
    financial infrastructure of, 903–904
    introduction to, 902–903
    Mexican case study in, 904–907
    Tequila effect in, 907–910
Lavington, Frederick, 3–4, 925
    on asymmetric information, 756
    on British commercial banks, 112–113
    on British securities markets, 155, 163,
        164–165, 166, 167, 173
Law Number 1130 (Argentina), 789
Lawson, Thomas, 310
Leach's Argentine Estates, 708
Lee, Higginson, and Co., 301, 302, 304–305
Lehman Brothers, 303, 311, 340, 631, 788
Lennon & Cape, 600
Lewis, Cleona, 390
    on United States capital flows, 249–250,
        257
Lewis, Frank, 11
    on United States savings rates, 244–245
Liability, of bank shareholders, 108
Lidderdale, William, 2
Life insurance companies, 144–146
    in Argentina, 690–691
    in Australia, 581–583, 584t–589t,
        590–591, 592t–595t
    portfolio investments of, 799
    in Canada, 403t, 430–433, 797–798
        mortgage market and, 423–426
        new issues market and, 432, 432t
    in United States, 283–291
        assets of, 288t–289t, 292t–293t, 403t
        Canadian investments of, 393
        on capital mobilization, 338–339
        industrial insurance and, 286–287, 338
        investment banks and, 309–310
        mortgage market and, 287–290
        tontine insurance and, 285–286, 338
Life Insurance Companies Act of 1873
    (Australia), 590
Lionel Robinson, Clark & Co., 607
Liquidity
    in Bretton Woods era, 864–865
    British investors and, 198
    financial intermediaries on, 43

Liverpool Mortgage Insurance Company, 563
Lloyds Bank, 111, 374
Loans
  to asset ratio, 113
  collateral-based *vs.* overdrafts, 112–113
Loeb, Kuhn, 19
Loeb, Soloman, 303
London acceptance market, 129–130, 803
London and Australian Agency, 539
London and Brazilian Bank, 667, 670t
London and County Bank, 122
London and Globe Deep Leads Assets, 538
London and River Plate Bank, 665, 666t
  assets and liabilities of, 677t
  branches of, 674
  dividend rate of, 676t
  foreign management of, 667
  loan experience of, 667–670
  reserves of, 673
London and San Francisco Bank, 342
London and Westminster Bank, 177, 178, 179
  as Australian bank agent, 632
  as Australian government's agent, 609, 783
London capital markets: *see also* London Stock Exchange; United Kingdom
  Argentine calls on, in dollars, 700t–701t, 704t–705t
  Argentine calls on, in percentages, 702t–703t, 704t
London Chartered Bank of Australia, 539, 542, 546
London Clearing House, 108
London Discount Market, 337
London Fishmongers and Poulters Company, 55
London Joint Stock Bank, 178
London Stock Exchange, 154–155
  capital created and called on, 837t–838t
  capital transfers and, 25–26
  vs. domestic competitors, 807–809
  foreign issues on, 209, 237, 324t, 341
    Australian, 629t, 639
    Canadian, 467t
  inscribed stock deposits on (Australian), 557
  New York stock exchange and, 323–331, 324t, 331t
  preference shares on, 165–166
  as secondary market, 181–190
  securities quoted on, 156t–157t
  short-term call loans to, 120

Long-Term Capital Management, 876
Los Angeles Times, 875–876
Lough, William, 670, 671, 673
  on Argentine agricultural financing, 707
Lowenfeld, H., 153–154

M. Goldman & Sachs, 303
Macdonald's National Policy, 360, 761
Maddison, Angus, 6, 850, 851
Malaysia, 915; *see also* Asia, NICS in
Manufacturing and commercial capital: *see also* Industrial sector
  in British capital markets, 28t
  in United States, 259–260
Marbury vs. Madison, 267
Marchildon, Gregory, 164
Martinez, Alberto, 735, 737–739, 740
Massel, J.A., 693
Matsuka, Masayoshi, 882–883, 894, 900, 902
McCalmont & Co., 301
McCormick Reaper Company, 330
McFadden Branch Banking Act, 271
McKay, Huntley, 455
Melbourne and Metropolitan Board of Works, 604–605, 607
Melbourne Brewing and Malting Company, 602
Melbourne Hydraulic Power Company, 543
Melbourne Stock Exchange
  dominance of, 612–615
  early development of, 609–612
  government issues and, 601, 605–606
  market value of listings on, 614t
  structure of, 615–620, 624–626
Mercantile Bank of Australia, 505, 507, 557
Mercantile Finance Trustees and Agency Company, 604
Merchant banks
  in Argentina, 686–689
  British
    in Australian market, 630–631
    as underwriters, 167–171
    United States railroad financing by, 302–303, 334, 786–787
  London acceptance market and, 803
  in United States, 787–788
Merchant's Bank, 413, 414, 419
Merchant's Bank of Halifax, 414
Meriwether, John, 876
Merrett, David, 509
  on Australian financial structure, 544, 558–559
  on Australian securities market, 603, 604

Merton, Robert C., 876
Metallgesellschaft A.G., 3
Metropolitan Insurance Company, 286
Mexico, 904–907
  debt crisis of, 35–36
Michie, Ranald, 52, 155
  on Canadian securities market, 451
Midland Bank, 111, 113, 178
  Eurodollar transactions of, 865
Milling, in United States, 335
Mining
  in Argentina, 710
  in Australia, 514, 515, 525, 538–539, 538t
    stock exchange listings and, 611–613,
    637–639
  in Canada, 385, 388, 395
  capital called, in British capital markets,
    31t
  in United States, 258–259, 335
Ministry of Finance (Japan), 897
Mitchell, B.R., 733
Mitsubishi Bank, 884
Mitsubishi Trading Company, 887
Mitsui Bank, 884, 886–887
Mitsui Trading Company, 887
Modigliani, Franco, 11
Molson's Bank, 414
Monetary Times, 435–436
"The Money Trust," 339
Montreal Bank, 405
Montreal Exchange, 443, 444–447
Montreal Power and Water Company,
  388–389
Morgan, J.P., 19, 37, 304, 308–309
Mortgage Bank of the Province of Buenos
  Aires, 684
Mortgage Insurance Company, 563
Mortgages
  in Argentina, 682–686, 683t, 711–712,
    793
    cedulas and, 684–686
    foreign involvement in, 682–684
    insurance companies and, 691
  in Australia, 550–555, 575–576, 636–637,
    781, 784–785
  building and loan societies and, 298–300
  in Canada, 433–436
    chartered banks and, 409–410
    non-bank intermediaries and,
    421–426, 424t–425t, 431–432
    insurance industry and, 146–147, 403t
  in United States, 258
    life insurance companies and, 287–290
    regulation of, 263–264
Morton, Bliss & Co., 304
Morton, Levi P., 304

Morton, Rose & Co., 304
  Canadian underwriting activity of, 419
Mount Catlin Consolidated Copper
  Mining, 538–539
Muhall, E.T., 655–656, 749
Muhall, M.G., 655–656, 749
Municipal Fund Act, 359
Munitions Companies Designated
  Financial Institutions System Act,
  898
Mutual of New York, 145

Nash, R.C., 50–51
The National Bank Decree of 1871
  (Japan), 882–883
National Bank of Australia, 783
National Bank of Australiasia, 632
National Bank of Commerce, 308–309
National Banking Act (U.S.), 249, 263, 267,
  273, 277, 309, 338, 785, 909
  on commercial paper market, 807
National City Bank, 271
National Debt Commissioners, 133
National Discount House, 130
National Financial Control Association,
  899
National General Mobilization Law
  (Japan), 898
National Monetary Commission, 399, 406,
  777
National Mortgage Bank, 684, 686, 793
National product, of United States,
  342–344
National Provincial Bank of England, 110,
  111, 374
National Trust, 440
Naylor, R.T., 419
  on Canadian non-bank intermediaries,
  421–423
Nelles, Henry V., 437, 440
  on bond underwriting, 461
The Netherlands, United States
  investments of, 250–251
Neufield, E.P.
  on bank stability, 418
  on Canadian mortgages and savings
  banks, 426
New Oxley Canada Ranches, 385
New South Wales Liens on Wool and
  Mortgages of Stock Act of 1843,
  548
New York City, as financial center
  post Bretton Woods era on, 873
  World War I on, 854–856
New York Curb Market Association,
  321–322

New York Life, 145, 310
New York Stock Exchange
  evolution of, 315, 318
  formation of, 312–314
  listing requirements of, 237, 328–329,
    341–342, 794
  London Stock Exchange and, 323–331,
    324t, 331t
  membership in, transfer value of,
    319t–320t
  roots of, 442
  signaling policies of, 154
  transaction volume on, 316t–317t
New York World, 420
New Zealand Loan & Mercantile Agency,
    505, 578, 581
Newsweek, 887
Nivison, 632
Non-bank intermediaries
  in Australia, 567–598
    building societies in, 573–575
    depression on, 596–597
    government encouragement of,
      597–598
    life insurance companies in, 581–583,
      590–591
    assets of, in percentages, 587t–589t
    assets of, in pounds, 584t–586t
    portfolio mix of, in percentages,
      594t–595t
    portfolio mix of, in pounds,
      592t–593t
    mortgage banks in, 575–576
    pastoral finance companies in,
      576–578, 580t, 581
    savings banks in
      assets and liabilities of, 568t
      government-related, 569–572
  in Canada, 421–470, 424t–425t
    building societies, 433–436
    introduction to, 421–426
    life insurance companies, 430–433
    mortgage and loan companies,
      433–436
    savings banks, 426–430
    securities markets, 436–466, 467t (*see
      also* Securities market)
    summary of, 466–470
  in United Kingdom, 131–153, 134t, 135t,
      138t–143t
    finance companies, 150–151
    insurance companies, 133, 136–137,
      138t–143t, 144–150
    investment trusts, 151–153
    Post Office Banks, 131–132, 134t–135t
    Stock Departments, 133

Trustee Savings Banks, 132–133,
    134t–135t
  in United States, 278–300, 424t–425t
    assets of, 280t–281t
    building and loan societies, 298–300
    introduction to, 278
    life insurance companies, 283–291
    savings and time deposits, 291–294
    savings banks, 279–283
    trust companies, 294–298
North, Douglas, 753–754, 827–828, 830
North America, British overseas
    investment in, 59, 70t, 72t, 76t,
      80t
North British and Mercantile Assurance
    Company, 147, 636
North British Canadian Investment
    Company Limited, 389–390
North of Scotland Canadian Mortgage
    Company Limited, 389
Northern and Central Bank of England,
    110
Northern Pacific Railway, 302
Northwest Land Company, 394

O'Hagen, H. Osbourne, 173–174
Oil, in United States, 259
OPEC, 873–874
Open Board, 314
Oriental Banking Corporation, 546
Otis Steel, 260
Otto Bemberg, 688
Ottoman Bank, 178
Output per capita, in frontier economies,
    6–7, 7t
Outside village, 437
Overand-Gurney crisis, 119, 633–634
Overdrafts
  of Argentine banks, 671–673
  vs. collateral-based loans, 112–113
Overseas investments
  from British capital markets, 5–6, 9–10,
    19–25, 34–35, 158
  in frontier economies (*see* specific
    countries, e.g., Argentina)
  insurance industry and, 148–149
Oxford Nickel and Copper Company,
    392

Paish, George, 373
Panic of 1873, 246
  Cooke failure and, 302
  on savings banks, 279
Panmure Gordon and Company, 174
Parana Land Company, 708
Parr's Bank, 178, 374

Pastoral finance companies, in Australia, 576–578, 580t, 581, 636–637, 811–814
Pastoral products, Argentine, 645–646
Paternalism, in Australia, 480
Payne, Peter L., 283
Pennsylvania Railroad, 307
Pension Cash Office, 899
People's Cash Office, 899
Perkins, George W., 310
Petroleum and Mining Board, 314
Philadelphia Savings Fund Society, 283
Philippines, 915–916; *see also* Asia, NICS in
Phoenix Insurance, 144
Pierpont, John, 304
Pillsbury, 260
Platt, D.C.M., 711
Pope, David, 558
Port Sarnia Syndicate, 434
Portalis, 688, 689
Portillo, President, 904–905
Post Office Savings Banks
    in Australia, 475–476
    in Canada, 428
    in Japan, 891
    as nonbank intermediaries, 131–132, 134t–135t
    in United Kingdom, 131–132
    in United States, 882
Postan, M.M., 8, 13, 15
    on Industrial Revolution financing, 50
Preference shares, on London Stock Exchange, 165–166
Premier Permanent Building Association of Melbourne, 504–505
Pressnell, Leonard, 130–131
Prime, Ward and King, 300–301
Proctor and Gamble, 3
Promoters
    in United Kingdom markets, 171–175
    in United States markets, 301–302, 331–332, 339–340
Provident Institution for Savings, 283
Provincial exchanges, in UK securities market, 190–195
Provincial Note Act of 1866, 408
Prudential Insurance Company, 286–287
Public utilities, capital called in British markets, 33t

Quaker Oats, 260
Quebec, bonds of, 394
Quebec Bank, 777
Quebec Timber, 385
Queensland National Bank, 512, 631, 783

R. Goldborough and Company, 577
Railroads
    in Argentina, 720–722, 765
    in Australia
        during boom period, 500–502
        government and, 762, 764–765
        subsidy of, 483–485, 487–488
    British loans to, 121, 302–303, 359, 373
        government involvement and, 759–760
    in Canada
        American investment in, 390–391, 392t
        Bank of Montreal and, 420
        construction of, 352–353
        government role in, 359–361, 764–765
        Great Western railway project, 359
        Inter Colonial Railway, 348–349
    financing of, 54
    rates of return from, 213t, 216–217
    in United States, 306, 333
        foreign investment in, 251–252, 255
        on securities markets, 609–610
Railway Share Investment Trust, 181
Ranching, in Argentina, 698t, 699, 699t–705t, 706–708
Real bills doctrine, 780, 791–792, 828
Real Estate Mortgage and Deposit Bank of Melbourne, 563
Reciprocal Trade Agreement, 349
Reconstruction Finance Bank, 891, 899, 902
Redish, Angela, 116
Reed, Howard, 872
Reputational signals, 755–756
Reserve requirements
    of British commercial banks, 118–120
    of United States Banks, 309
Reserves, self-liquidating bills as, 128
Revolutionary War, debt crisis in, 35–36
Riat Brothers, 707
Richard Goldsborough, 603
Rio de Janerio Tramway, 451
Rio Negro Land Company, 708
Ritchie, Samuel, 392
River Plate Fresh Meat Company, 710
Robinson, L.E., 153
Robinson, Lionel, 607
Rockoff, Hugh, 116
Romer, Christina D., 344
Rosas, Juan Manuel, 644–645
Rose, John, 304
Rotella, E., 299
Rothschild's Bank, 331
    in London acceptance market, 130
    as underwriters, 167–168, 177, 179

Rothschild's Bank *(cont.)*
  United States investment banking and,
    301
Royal Bank of Canada, 414, 415–416
Royal Commission on Life Insurance,
    441
Royal Commission on Victorian Banking,
    554
Royal Dutch Shell, 259
Royal Exchange Assurance Company, 144,
    146
Royal Mail Line, 633
Royal Securities Corporation, 457, 460,
    797
Royal Victoria Insurance Company, 440
Rubenstein, W.D., 602

Sachs, Jeffrey, 875
Sachs, Samuel, 303
Santa Fe Land Company, 708
Santiago Estate and sugar Factories, 708
Sarmiento, Domingo, 644
Savings
  in Argentina, 722, 741t
  in Australia, 522–523
  on British capital markets, 200, 204
  in Canada, 355, 356t, 468–469, 797
  and investing decisions, financial
      intermediaries on, 42–49
  rate of
    in Australia, 522–523, 643
    capital accumulation and mobilization
        in, 8–19
    interest elasticity of, 46–47
    in United Kingdom, 56–71 (*see also*
        under United Kingdom, income,
        savings and investments in)
    in United States, 7–8, 332
  in United States, 243–245, 332, 793–795
    vs. Britain, 340–341
    rate of, 7–8
Savings Bank Act of 1841 (Canada), 428
Savings Bank of Baltimore, 48, 283
Savings banks
  Asian NICS, 921
  in Australia
    assets and liabilities of, 568t
    government-related, 569–572
  in Canada, 426–430
  in United States, 279–283, 284t, 921–922
Sawers, John, 508
Schiff, Jacob, 303, 304, 310
Schroeder Bank
  in London acceptance market, 130
  as underwriters, 167–168
Schuster, Felix, 112

Scotland
  Australian investments of, 628, 634–635
  banking practices of, 828
  capitalization rules in, 109–110
  inland bill market in, 801–802
Scottish American Investment Trust, 389
Scottish Australian Investment Company,
    539
Scottish Provident Institution, 147, 636
Scottish Widows' Fund, 147
Scottish Widows' Society, 636
Seaman's Bank, 282
Sears, Roebuck & Co., 311, 340, 788
Second Bank of the United States, 267
Securities Insurance Company, 563
Securities market(s)
  in Argentina, 692–694, 799–800
  in Australia, 598–626
    primary, 599–609
      brokers for, 603–607
      vs. Canada and America, 598,
          601–602, 608
      government new issues in, 599–601,
          605–606
      private securities on, 606–609
    secondary, 609–626, 620–624
      early development of, 609–612
      liquidity of, 799
      Melbourne Exchange dominance
          in, 612–615, 614t
      structure of, 615–620, 624–626
      Sydney Stock Exchange and,
          620–624
    total issues, 1900–1914, 599t
  in Canada, 436–466
    vs. Australia, 598, 601–602, 608
    bond underwriting and, 454–466,
        469–470
    capital called on British market, 448t
    chartered banks and, 418–421
    corporate directorships and,
        438t–439t, 440
    financial group structure in, 440–442
    formal exchange origins in, 444–449
    industrial securities on, 449–452
    listings by industry, 448t
    London market and, 443, 467t
    trading volume of, 452
    vs. United States, 442, 453–454
  in Japan, 896–897
  private *vs.* government control of,
      922–923
  in Singapore, 916
  in United Kingdom, 153–195
    background of, 153–165, 156t–157t
    introduction to, 165–167

primary market in, 167–181, 169t
provincial exchanges in, 190–195
secondary market in, 181–190
in United States, 312–323, 794–795
  consolidation of, 321–323
  evolution of, 315, 316t–317t, 318,
    319t–320t
  formation of, 312–314
  London Stock Exchange and,
    323–331, 324t, 331t
  sales volume of, in 1910, 323t
Selection Acts (Australia), 495–496
Self-liquidating bills, 128
Seligman Bank, 167–168
Seligman Brothers, 303
Shaw, A.G.L., 480
Shaw, William H., 342
Shell Transport and Trading Company,
  259
Sholes, Myron S., 876
Shunting, 192
Simon, Matthew, 248
Sinclair, Alasdair, 363, 368
Singapore, 912–913, 916; *see also* Asia,
  NICS in
Skinner, James, 13, 45–46
Smelting and Refining Company of
  Australia, 543–544
Smith, Sheppard, 553
Snowden, Kenneth, 290, 299
Sociedad Anonima Mercado Cividad de
  Buenos Ayres, 712
South America, British overseas
  investment in, 59, 65, 70t, 72t–73t,
  76t–77t, 80t–81t
South American Cattle Farms, 708
South Building and Loan Association, 300
South Sea Bubble, 51
Sovereign Bank of Canada, 397
Spanish Bank, 675
Spanish Bank of the River Plate, 679
Special Tax Measures Law, 899
Specie Bank, 893, 894
Spence, Clark, 258–259
Sperling & Company, 170
Speyer, Philip, 303
Speyer & Co., 301
Speyer Brothers, 171
Standard Bank of Australia, 542, 562, 634,
  816
Standard Stock and Mining Exchange,
  447–448
State Bank of Southern Australia, 597
Statist, 373
Sterling bill markets, 127–131
Stiglitz, Joseph, 876

The Stock and Share Journal, 611, 615
Stock-brokers, 185, 186–187
  in Argentina, 692
  in Australia, 603–607
Stock Departments, as nonbank
  intermediaries, 133
Stock Exchange of Singapore, 916
Stock-jobbers, 185, 186–187
Stone, Irving, 738–739
Storrow, James J., 308
Strong, Benjamin, 855
Studies in Income and Wealth, 343
Study of Savings, 11
Sulphide Corporation, 514
Sun Life Insurance, 144, 430, 431, 440, 441
Supple, Barry, 150
Supply schedule, intermediation on, 44–45
Svennilson, I., 851
Swanson Bay Forests, 388
Sydney Stock Exchange, 610–611, 620–624
Sylla, Richard, 15, 713
  on correspondent system, 276

Taiwan, 916–917; *see also* Asia, NICS in
Taylor, Alan, 723, 743
Tecka Argentine Company, 708
Telegraph, 620
Temin, 853
Temporary Capital Adjustment Law,
  897–898
Tequila effect, 907–910
Terry's West End Brewery, 602
Thailand, 917; *see also* Asia, NICS in
"The Money Trust," 339
Thomas, Mark, 517
Thomas Biddle and Company, 300
Thompson, Samuel C., 305
Tilly, Richard, 14
  on foreign investment to United States,
    251
Time deposits, 291, 294
The Times, 760
Tobacco, in Australia, 543
Tokyo Stock Exchange, 896
Toniolo, G., 853
Tonti, Neapolitan L., 285
Tontine insurance
  in Australia, 583
  in United States, 285–286
Tornquist, Carlos A., 689, 739
Tornquist, Ernesto, 686, 687–688, 689, 719
Toronto Stock Exchange, 444–448
  listings by industry, 448t
Transaction costs
  financial intermediaries on, 42–43
  institutional innovation and, 757

Transport capital called, in British capital markets, 32t
Transportation system: *see also* Railroads
  in Argentina, 663–665
Trivet, John B., 501–502
Trust and Loan Company of Upper Canada, 433–434
Trust companies
  in Canada, 389
  in United States, 294–298, 309
Trustee Assets & Investment Insurance Company, 563
Trustee Savings Bank (Australia), 571
Trustee savings banks
  in Australia, 571
  in Canada, 429
  as nonbank intermediaries, 132–133, 134t–135t
Trustees Executive and Agency Company, 602
Tulchin, Joseph S., 679, 707
Turner, H.G., 553

U.S. Rubber, 395
Underwriters
  in Canada
    banks as, 418–421
    of bonds, 454–466
    reputation of, 757–758
  in United Kingdom primary market, 167–181, 169t
    merchant banks in, 167–175
    promoters in, 171–175
    syndicates in, 180
  in United States, 307–308, 311, 763
Union Bank of Australia, 539, 542, 545, 548, 557, 631, 782–783
Union Consolidated Copper, 539
Union Discount Company of London, 130–131
Union Life Assurance, 389
Union Mortgage and Agency of Australia, 539
Union of London and Smith's Bank, 112
Unit banking, 785–786
United Discount Corporation, 131
United Kingdom
  British investors in, 195–233
    Argentine investments of, 679, 682–684, 699t
    Australian investments of, 512–513, 517, 556–557, 578, 581, 633–634
    Canadian investments of, 443
    frontier countries rate of return on, 209–233
      yields and, all issues, 211t

yields and, government issues, 212t
yields and, "other" issues, 214t
yields and, railroad issues, 213t
growing sophistication of, 754
identity of, 195–209
  foreign *vs.* domestic holdings in, 206t, 208t
  geographic distribution in, 201t
  industry relative attractiveness in, 203t, 207t
  occupation in, 205t
  relative holdings by residence in, 202t
  stock companies by industry class and, 199t
  by wealth class, 196t, 197t
overseas investment innovations of, 765–767
United States investments of, 795
financial sector growth and evolution in
  bank and nonbank intermediaries in, overview of, 71, 92–93
    by continent, 72t–83t
    by financial institution, 84t–91t
  commercial banks in, 93–127, 94t–105t
    balance sheets of, in percentage distribution, 104t–105t
    balance sheets of, in pounds, 102t–103t
    Bank of England on, 107
    cartel policies of, 114–115
    vs. developing countries, 116
    and frontier countries, 776–793 (*see also under* Institutional change and development)
    Gershenkron on, 93, 106
    industrial lending by, 122–124
    international banking and, 125–127
    legislative environment on, 107–110
    loan practices of, 112–114
    national integration of, 110–112
    number of persons served by, 96t–97t
    numbers of, 94t–95t
    numbers of, all banks *vs.* joint-stock banks, 100t–101t
    portfolio diversification of, 121–122
    public liabilities of, 98t–99t
    reserve requirements of, 118–120
    stability of, 117–120
  commercial paper markets in, 127–131
  inland bill market in, 801–806
  nonbank intermediaries on, 131–153, 134t, 135t, 138t–143t
    finance companies, 150–151

insurance companies, 133, 136–137, 138t–143t, 144–150
investment trusts, 151–153
Post Office Banks, 131–132, 134t–135t
savings banks, 426
Stock Departments, 133
Trustee Savings Banks, 132–133, 134t–135t
securities market on, formal, 153–195
background of, 153–165, 156t–157t
introduction to, 165–167
primary market in, 167–181, 169t
provincial exchanges in, 190–195
secondary market in, 181–190
sterling bill markets in, 127–131
GDP per capita, 1913–1994, 842t–844t, 847–849
income, savings and investment in, 56–71
annual growth rates in 1870–1914, 56, 58t
British Gross National Product and domestic and foreign investment in, 60t–62t
British Gross National Product per capita in, 56, 57t
capital created and called in, 69t–70t
capital export in, 64t–68t
to United States, 249–250, 253t
formal securities markets on, 159
national wealth in, 63t
overseas investments in, 56, 58t
savings and investment overview of, 50–56
United Provinces of the Rio de la Plata, 714
United River Plate Telephone Company, 712, 713
United States, 234–344
balance of payments in, 245–248, 247t
British insurance premiums in, 144
British overseas investments in, 9, 27t–33t, 35t
British savers' link to domestic institutions in, 793–795
capital market development in, overview of, 331–342
banking system in, 336–338
capital flows to, 835t
domestic capital in, 334–336
foreign capital in, 331–335
nonbank intermediaries in, 338–340
secondary markets in, 340–342
economic growth pattern in, pre World War I, 238–243

capital stock composition in, 242t
by sector, 240t–241t
financial markets in, evolution of, 261–323
commercial banks in, 262–278, 836t
asset growth of, 402t
assets of, 268t–269t
branch banking and, 266–267, 271–272, 785–786
vs. British banks, 262, 266, 786–789
commercial paper market and, 273–276
correspondent system of, 276–278
"crony capitalism" of, 900–901
international opportunities and, 262–263
loan length of, 265–266, 416–418
mortgage lending and, 263–264
numbers of, 268t–269t
by region, 270t
stability of, 418
state banks and, 273–276
introduction to, 261–262, 261t
non-bank intermediaries in, 278–300, 424t–425t, 836t
assets of, 280t–281t
building and loan societies, 298–300
introduction to, 278
life insurance companies, 283–291, 292t–293t, 402t
long-term loans and, 909–910
savings and time deposits, 291–294
savings banks, 279–283, 284t, 402t, 426
trust companies, 294–298
securities market in, formal, 300–323
investment banking, 300–312 (*see also* Investment banking)
securities markets, 312–323, 316t–317t, 318t–319t, 323t (*see also under* Securities markets)
financial markets in, late 19th cent., 323–331
stock listings on, 324t
foreign investment in
industrial disposition of, 251–260, 253t–255t
commerce and manufacturing, 259–260
government securities, 255–256
land-related industries, 257–259
railroads, 251–252, 255
political response to, 825–827
GDP per capita, 1913–1994, 842t–844t, 848–850

United States *(cont.)*
  gross national product of, 342–344
    financial asset ratio to, 668–776, 770t,
      773, 775t
  international financial status of,
    comparative, 236t
  introduction to, 234–238
  London and New York stock exchanges
    in, late 19th cent., 323–331
  net change in, 1869–1914, 235t
  overseas investments by, 38
    in Canada, 390–396, 391t–393t
  population of, native born *vs.* total, 656t
  savings-investment aggregates in,
    243–251
    domestic, 243–245
    foreign, 245–251
      industrial structure of, 248–251,
        250t
      temporal patterns in, 245–248, 247t
  savings rate in, capital accumulation and
    mobilization on, 16–20, 44
United States Steel, 306, 340
Upper Fraser River Lumber Company,
  385–388
Urban growth, in Argentina
  financing of, 711–713
  population and, 663, 665
Urquhart, M.C., 368
Utility companies
  in Argentina, 712–713
  in Canada, 388–389
  capital called in British markets, 33t

Vancouver Power Company, 389
Veenendaal, Augustus, 251
Victorian Credit Foncier, 597
Viner, Jacob, 362–363, 364t, 368, 373, 374,
  375t, 377, 384, 395–396, 397–
  398

War Cash Office, 899
Water transportation system, in Argentina,
  663–665
Watson, Katherine, 163
Weatherley, Edward, 55–56
Welland Canal Company, 390
West Argentine Gold Company, 710
Western Australia Agricultural Bank, 572,
  597
Westinghouse, 395
Westminster Bank, 111
White, Eugene, 312
White, G.H., 179
White, W.H., 457
Wilkins, Mira, 250, 765–766
William Noall and Son, 607
Williams, John H., 735, 739
Williamson, Jeffrey, 245
Winnipeg Paint and Glass, 388
Winslow, Lanier & Co., 301, 602
Wood, E.R., 440, 457
World War I
  Canadian financing of, 465
  on frontier economies, 850–856
World War II, on frontier economies,
  862–869
Wright, J.F., 51
Wright, Whitaker, 639

Yokohama Specie Bank, 883, 893, 894–895,
  899
Yucho, 891

Zaibatsu banks, 884, 885–888
Zinc Corporation, 514